BUILDINGS OF MICHIGAN

SOCIETY OF ARCHITECTURAL HISTORIANS

BUILDINGS OF THE UNITED STATES

Buildings of

MICHIGAN

KATHRYN BISHOP ECKERT

New York   Oxford

OXFORD UNIVERSITY PRESS

1993

Buildings of the United States is a series of books on American
architecture compiled and written on a state-by-state basis. The primary objective
of the series is to identify and celebrate the rich cultural, economic, and geographical diversity
of the United States as it is reflected in the architecture of each state. The series has been commissioned
by the Society of Architectural Historians, an organization devoted to the study, interpretation,
and preservation of the built environment throughout the world. People who share
these interests are invited to join the society.

OXFORD UNIVERSITY PRESS

Oxford   New York   Toronto
Delhi   Bombay   Calcutta   Madras   Karachi
Kuala Lumpur   Singapore   Hong Kong   Tokyo
Nairobi   Dar es Salaam   Cape Town
Melbourne   Auckland   Madrid
and associated companies in
Berlin   Ibadan

Buildings of Michigan has been supported, in part, by grants from
the National Endowment for the Humanities, an independent federal agency;
the Pew Charitable Trusts; the Graham Foundation for Advanced Studies in the Fine Arts;
the Michigan Sesquicentennial Fund; and the National Park Service.

LIBRARY OF CONGRESS CATALOGING-IN-PUBLICATION DATA
Eckert, Kathryn Bishop.
Buildings of Michigan / Kathryn Bishop Eckert.
p.   cm.
Includes bibliographical references and index.
ISBN 0-19-506149-7 :
1. Architecture—Michigan—Guidebooks.   I. Title.
NA730.M5E28   1993
720'.9774—dc20   92-7096

Printing (last digit): 9 8 7 6 5 4 3 2

PRINTED IN THE UNITED STATES OF AMERICA
on acid-free paper

Foreword

It is with pride and pleasure that the Society of Architectural Historians presents this volume to the public. It is among the first in the monumental series, Buildings of the United States, undertaken by the society.

Buildings of the United States is a nationwide effort, indeed a national one. Heretofore, the United States was the only major country of the Western world that had not produced a publication project dealing with its architectural heritage on a national scale. In overall concept, Buildings of the United States is to a degree modeled on and inspired by The Buildings of England, the series of forty-six volumes conceived and carried out on a county-by-county basis by the eminent English architectural historian Nikolaus Pevsner, first published between 1951 and 1974. It was Pevsner himself who—years ago, but again and again—urged his American colleagues in the Society of Architectural Historians to do the same for this country. In method and approach, of course, that challenge was to be as different from The Buildings of England as American architecture is different from English. Here we are dealing with a vast land of immense regional, geographic, climatic, and ethnic diversity, with an architectural history—wide-ranging, exciting, sometimes dramatic, as it is—essentially compressed into three hundred years; Pevsner, on the other hand, was confronted by a coherent culture on a relatively small island with an architectural history that spans over two thousand years. In contrast to the national integrity of English architecture, therefore, American architecture is marked by a dynamic heterogeneity, a heterogeneity woven of a thousand strands of originality, or, actually, a unity woven of a thousand strands of heterogeneity. It is this quality that Buildings of the United States will reflect and record.

Unity born of heterogeneity was a condition of American architecture from the beginning. Not only did the buildings of the English, Spanish, French, and Dutch colonies differ according to national origin, in the transformation process they also assumed a special scale and character, qualities that were largely determined by the aspirations and traditions of a people struggling to fashion a new world in a demanding but abundant land. Diversity even marked the English colonies of the Eastern Seaboard, though they shared a common architectural heritage. The brick mutations of the English prototypes in the Virginia Colony were very different from the wooden architecture of the Massachusetts Bay Colony: they were different because Virginia was a plantation society dominated by the Anglican church, while Massachusetts was a communal society nurtured entirely by Puritanism. As the colonies became a nation and developed westward, similar radical contrasts became the way of America's growth. The infinite variety of physical environment, together with the complex origins and motivations of the settlers, made it inevitable that each new state would have a character uniquely its own.

This dynamic diversity is the foundation of Buildings of the United States. The primary objective of each volume will be to record, to analyze, and to evaluate the architecture of the state. All of the authors are trained architectural historians who are thoroughly informed in the local aspects of their subjects. In developing the narrative, those special conditions that shaped the state, together with the building types necessary to meet those conditions, will be identified and discussed: barns, silos, mining buildings, factories, warehouses, bridges, and transportation buildings will take their place with the familiar building types conventional to the nation as a whole—churches, courthouses, city halls, and the infinite variety of domestic architecture. Although the great national and international masters of American architecture will receive proper attention, especially in those volumes for the states in which they did their greatest work, outstanding local architects, as well as the buildings of skilled but often anonymous carpenter-builders, will also be brought prominently into the picture. Each volume will thus be a detailed and precise portrait of the architecture of the state that it represents. At the same time, however, all of these local issues will be examined as they relate to the architectural developments in the country at large. When completed, therefore, the series will be a comprehensive history of the architecture of the United States.

The series was long in the planning. Indeed, the idea was conceived by Turpin Bannister, the first president of the Society of Architectural Historians (1940–1942). It was thirty years, however, before the society had grown sufficiently in strength to consider such a project. This happened when Alan Gowans, during his presidency (1972–1974), drew up a proposal and made the first of several unsuccessful attempts to raise the funds. The issue was raised again during the presidency of Marian C. Donnelly, when William H. Jordy and William H. Pierson, Jr., suggested to the board of directors that such a project should be the society's contribution to the nation's bicentennial celebration. It was not until 1986, however, after several failed attempts, that a substantial grant from the National Endowment for the Humanities, which was matched by grants from the Pew Charitable Trusts and the Graham Foundation, made the dream a reality. The activities that led to final success took place under the successive presidencies of Adolf K. Placzek (1978–1980), David Gebhard (1980–1982), Damie Stillman (1982–1984), and Carol H. Krinsky (1984–1986). Development and production of the first books has continued under those of Osmund Overby (1986–1988), Richard J. Betts (1988–1990), and Elisabeth Blair MacDougall (1990–1993). And all the while, there was David Bahlman, executive director of the SAH at the headquarters of the society in Philadelphia. In New York was Barbara Chernow of Chernow Editorial Services, Inc., who, with her husband, George Valassi, was a valuable resource during the initial stages of the project. A fine board of editors was established, with representatives from the American Institute of Architects, the Historic American Buildings Survey, and the Library of Congress. These first volumes have now been seen through production thanks to the very able work of the managing editor, Susan M. Denny, who joined the project in 1991. Buildings of the United States is now part of the official mission of the Society of Architectural Historians, incorporated into its bylaws.

In the development of this project, we have incurred a number of obligations. We are deeply indebted, both for financial support and for confidence in our efforts, to the National Endowment for the Humanities, the Pew Charitable Trusts, the Graham Foundation for Advanced Studies in the Fine Arts, and the Yes 150! Foundation of the Michigan Sesquicentennial Commission. We would also like to express our gratitude to a number of individuals. First among these are Dorothy Wartenberg, formerly of the Interpretive Research Program of the NEH, who was particularly helpful at the beginning, and our current program officer, David Wise. For the conceptual and practical development of the project, profound thanks go to the current members of the editorial board, listed earlier in this volume, and the following former members: the late Sally Kress Tompkins, the late Alex Cochran, Catherine W. Bishir, S. Allen Chambers, Jr., John Freeman, Alan Gowans, Robert Kapsch, and Tom Martinson. Next are our present and former project assistants—Preston Thayer, Marc Vincent, and Robert Wojtowicz. And there are the two previous executive directors of the society, the late Rosann Berry and Paulette Olson Jorgensen. Finally, thanks are due to our loyal colleagues in this enterprise at Oxford University Press in New York, especially Ed Barry, Claude Conyers, Marion Osmun, Leslie Phillips, and Stephen Chasteen.

The volumes, state by state, will continue to appear until every state in the Union has its own and the overview and inventory of American architecture is completed. The volumes will vary in length, and some states will require two volumes, but no state will be left out!

It must be said, regretfully, that not every building of merit can be included. Practical considerations have dictated some difficult choices in the buildings that are represented. There had to be some omissions from the abundance of structures built across the land, the thousands of modest but lovely edifices, often rising out of a sea of ugliness, or the vernacular attempts that merit a second look but that by their very multitude cannot be included in even the thickest volume. On the other hand, it must be emphasized that these volumes deal with more than the highlights and the high points. They deal with the very fabric of American architecture, with the context in time and in place of each specific building, with the entirety of urban and rural America, with the whole architectural patrimony. This fabric of course includes modern architecture, as, on the other end of the scale, it includes pre-Columbian and Native American remains.

As to architectural style, it was our most earnest intent to establish as much as possible a consistent terminology of architectural history: the name of J. A. Chewning, mastermind of our glossaries, must be gratefully mentioned here.

The *Art and Architecture Thesaurus,* a comprehensive publication and database compiled by The Getty Art History Information Program and published by Oxford University Press, has also become an invaluable resource.

Finally, it must also be stated in the strongest possible terms that omission of a building from this or any volume of the series does not constitute an invitation to the bulldozers and the wrecking ball. In every community there will be structures not included in Buildings of the United States that are clearly deserving of being preserved. Indeed, it is hoped that the publication of this series will help to stop at least the worst destruction of architecture across the land by fostering a deeper appreciation of its beauty and richness and of its historic and associative importance.

The volumes of Buildings of the United States are intended as guidebooks as well as reference books and are designed to facilitate such use: they can and should be used on the spot, indeed should lead the user to the spot. But they are also meant to be tools of serious research in the study of American architecture. It is our earnest hope that they will not only be on the shelves of every major library under "U.S." but that they will also be in many a glove compartment and perhaps even in many a rucksack.

ADOLF K. PLACZEK
WILLIAM H. PIERSON, JR.
OSMUND OVERBY

Preface

The occasion of the sesquicentennial of Michigan's statehood was celebrated in 1987–1989. It was marked by events and projects of all types—festivals, exhibitions, the writing of local histories. But as plans were made for the celebration, the most fitting and lasting commemoration for the Historic Preservation Section of the Bureau of History and the State Historic Preservation Office seemed obvious to me. At that very moment the Society of Architectural Historians was embarking on its monumental Buildings of the United States series of architectural guidebooks, a series devoted to all fifty states. The fortuitous combination of these two events has provided the opportunity to celebrate Michigan's heritage with this book, the first comprehensive study of Michigan's architectural history to encompass the full range of buildings from early settlement to the present, and the full spectrum of building types from vernacular to high-style designs.

Since 1976 I have overseen the Historical Preservation Section of the Bureau of History as it conducted comprehensive statewide survey fieldwork and analysis. *Buildings of Michigan* has drawn on this experience and on related scholarship. The three-year undertaking to prepare the *Buildings of Michigan* manuscript involved a partnership among the Bureau of History of the Michigan Department of State, the Michigan Sesquicentennial Commission, and the Society of Architectural Historians' Buildings of the United States project. The Society of Architectural Historians offered a national framework, including the scholarly review and guidance of the Buildings of the United States Editorial Board, and the managing editors, Barbara Chernow and Susan M. Denny.

As the State Historic Preservation Office, the Historic Preservation Section of the Bureau of History has collected a wealth of unique information and documentation on buildings and districts throughout Michigan. Our staff of historians and architectural historians has amassed a vast collection of material on architects and builders and on high-style and vernacular buildings at all levels of significance in all regions of the state. In our mission to preserve, protect, chronicle, interpret, and present the history of Michigan to its people and visitors, we have established working relationships with scholars of Michigan and of midwestern architectural history.

Administrative support for *Buildings of Michigan* was given by the Michigan Department of State, and recognition is due many people who helped. Special thanks are owed to Richard H. Austin, secretary of state, and to Dennis Neuner, then deputy secretary of state, who graciously agreed (within minutes after the space shuttle *Challenger* went down) that the project should become part of my work in the Historic Preservation Section. I am most grateful to Martha Mitchell Bigelow, then director of the Bureau of History, for her challenge, encouragement, and unconditional support in making a commitment to this ambitious project. I would also like to thank Phillip T. Frangos, current deputy of state services, Michigan Department of State, and Sandra S. Clark, now director of the Bureau of History, for their continuing support. Kenneth Teter of the Hearings Division drew up the draft contract between the Society of Architectural Historians and the Michigan Department of State. Merri Jo Bayles of the Michigan Sesquicentennial Office, Freda Fenner of the Yes 150! Foundation, and Larry Beckon of the Yes 150! Statehood deserve credit for securing financial support for the project.

Financial support for *Buildings of Michigan* came from contributions to the Yes 150! Foundation of the Michigan Sesquicentennial Commission from the following foundations and corporations: Knight Foundation, Kysor Industrial Corporation, The Steelcase Foundation, Rollin M. Gerstacker Foundation, The Dow Chemical Company, Ludington News Company, Hubbell, Roth and Clark, Inc., Louis Redstone Associates, William Kessler and Associates, Inc., and others. Crucial support came from grants to the Society of Architectural Historians from the National Endowment for the Humanities, the Pew Charitable Trusts, and the Graham Foundation and is greatly appreciated.

This project has also been funded, in part, through a grant from the U.S. Department of the Interior, National Park Service (under provisions of the National Historic Preservation Act of 1966, as amended) through the Michigan Department of State. However, the contents and opinions herein do not necessarily reflect the views or policies of the Department of the Interior.

Visual documentation is essential to any adequate recording of architecture, and the fine photographs of Balthazar Korab, who provided almost all of the pictures, are crucial to this book. Some photographs and line drawings came from the Historic American Building Survey (HABS) and the Historic American Engineering Record (HAER). Most historic photographs came from the collection of the Detroit Publishing Company at the Library of Congress; others are from the State Archives of Michigan.

A large body of existing scholarship and sources of information supported this project: the early studies undertaken by Professor Emil Lorch of the College of Architecture and Design of the University of Michigan, the HABS and the HAER documentation and inventories, the State Register of Historic Sites, the National Register of Historic Places, locally designated individual properties and districts, and the comprehensive statewide survey of historic properties.

Good locator maps are essential to a successful guidebook. Both the geographical arrangement and sketch maps were prepared with discussions with Leroy Barnett, geography specialist and archivist with the State Archives of Michigan. Barbara Harris made the sketch maps for the computer cartographers at the Geographic Resources Center in the Department of Geography at the University of Missouri–Columbia, where Christopher L. Salter, director of GRC, Timothy L. Haithcoat, program director, and Karen Stange Westin, project coordinator, were instrumental in completing the final maps for publication.

This volume is the product, in part, of the cumulative survey and research work of the Historic Preservation Section, and the highest degree of credit is owed to its past and present staff. I want to acknowledge the full participation of everyone in suggesting buildings worthy of inclusion, in sharing documentation and research notes, and, in some cases, in drafting entries. Robert O. Christensen assisted with Coldwater, Battle Creek, and South-Central Michigan; Brian D. Conway in Grand Rapids and the Traverse Bay Region; Charles Cotman in Detroit; Richard Harms in West Michigan; Janet L. Kreger in the Saginaw Bay and Saginaw River valley; and Squire Jaros in Oakland County and with the Walter and May Reuther UAW Family Education Center at Black Lake. With support from the Yes 150! Foundation three people joined the staff of the section for one year to assist with research. The enthusiasm and hard work of Laura R. Ashlee, Russell Henry, and Linda Martin were essential to the completion of the book. Another, Gordon Paul Smyth, offered assistance with the computer and word processing.

The staff of the Publications Section also contributed. Useful were Saralee Howard Filler's fort calendar and Roger Rosentreter's county histories, all published in *Michigan History* magazine.

Student assistants and interns played an important role in conducting research and assembling information for the volume, and the following deserve gratitude: Melanie Meyers, William Rutter, Mary Grace York, Janice Bhavsar, Gary T. Reynolds, and Chris Marzoni of Eastern Michigan University; Scott Erbes, Barbara Harris, Debbie Diesen, and Michael Callahan of Michigan State University; Julie Riemenschneider of Michigan State University and Cornell University; Lisa Lipinski of Michigan State University and the University of Illinois; Eric Macdonald and Carrie Scupholm of the University of Michigan; Ginette Gomez and Michele Koch of the University of Notre Dame and John Barrett of Savannah College of Art and Design.

A project of this magnitude is only possible with the collaboration of many scholars and outside specialists. Adolf K. Placzek and William H. Pierson, Jr., editor in chief and coeditor in chief of the series, offered kindly and thoughtful advice and encouragement throughout this undertaking, as well as comments on the manuscript. Damie Stillman of the editorial board of Buildings of the United States also read and commented on the manuscript. My husband, Sadayoshi Omoto of Michigan State University, read and commented on the manuscript. Leonard K. Eaton of the University of Michigan reviewed and commented on my initial proposal to the Society of Architectural Historians. Several historians, architects, and archaeologists, some of whom have served on the State Historic Preservation Review Board, on the staff of the Historic Preservation Section, or as principal investigators on survey and planning projects funded by the National Register program, offered familiarity and expertise with specific areas of the state's architectural history. They contributed brief essays and entries, suggested buildings for inclusion, and provided documentation. Among those who prepared essays and entries are the following, listed in alphabetical order, together with the topic of his or her contribution: David Armour, Fort Mackinac; Dennis Au, Monroe overview; Thomas Brunk, Indian Village in Detroit; Hemalata Dandekar, the Raab and Crawford farms in Washtenaw and Jackson counties; Elizabeth Dull, Kalamazoo and Niles overviews; Leonard K. Eaton, Italianate houses of Manchester; Rochelle Berger Elstein, synagogues; Scott Erbes, polychrome brick houses of Tuscola County; Louis and Saralee Howard-Filler, First Congregational Church of Ovid; John Halsey, Native American building traditions in the introduction; Donald Heldman, Fort Michilimackinac; Charles K. Hyde, the overview on the industrial character of Detroit and entries for industrial complexes in Detroit; Walter Leedy, architectural character of Detroit in the introduction; Maria Quinlan Leiby, Fayette; Carolyn Loeb, Ford Homes in Dearborn; Eric Macdonald, Liebhauser barn and farm in Barry County; Kingsbury Marzolf, Michigan State Capitol; Sadayoshi Omoto, the houses by George W. Maher at Sault Sainte Marie; Phil Porter, the resort architecture of Mackinac Island; Sidney Robinson, Midland overview and the buildings by Alden B. Dow in Midland; Roger Rosentreter, House of David Commune in Benton Harbor; Christine Ruby, Cedar Street Station of the Lansing Board of Water and Light, Brodhead Naval Armory in Detroit, and Iron Mountain Post Office; Anatole Senkevitch, Cranbrook; Denis Schmiedeke, Ypsilanti overview; Linda O. Stanford, Michigan State University campus, Lafayette Plaza in Detroit, and the W. K. Kellogg Manor House at Gull Lake; Linnie Trettin, Alberta, Painesdale, and Fort Wilkins; Marilyn Tuchow, Belle Isle in Detroit and Hackley Park in Muskegon; and Ellen Weiss, Bay View. Others submitted notes and documentation: Richard Albyn, Lake Shore Road and Grosse Pointe, Center for Creative Studies, Kellogg Company Corporate Headquarters, GM Tech Center, and Northland; Irene Henry, Medbury Grove in Highland Park; Miriam Rutz, designed landscapes, including the Detroit Zoological Park, Holland Centennial Park, Lansing Riverfront Park, Flint Riverbank Park, the Homestead, and Gwen Frostic Studio; Denis Schmiedeke, Ypsilanti entries; Michele Spencer, the buildings of Benton Harbor and Saint Joseph; the late Willard C. Wichers, the buildings of Holland and Zeeland.

Other people suggested buildings worthy of inclusion in the guidebook. Connie and Luther M. Barrett pointed out buildings in Escanaba and John Collins in Marshall. Edward Francis suggested contemporary buildings, and Lynn Francis and the Michigan Society of Architects compiled lists of award-winning buildings. John Halsey called my attention to many vernacular buildings and some examples of roadside architecture. Joan and Jeremy Mattson offered information on the buildings of Harold Childs.

The librarians, archivists, and historians at several institutions were also helpful: Ilene Schechter of the Library of Michigan, Ford Peatross of the Prints and Photographs Division of the Library of Congress, and Paul Dolinsky of the Historic American Buildings Survey / Historic American Engineering Record of the National Park Service. Leroy Barnett of the State Archives of Michigan offered advice in defining the seventeen regional divisions of the state.

As a lifelong resident of Michigan, the rewards of this project have been enormous. The countless buildings that have sheltered or surrounded me all my life are now my intimate friends: each has told me its story and I have pressed close to hear and to learn. I hope I have conveyed to the readers both the excitement and enrichment of this gratifying experience.

KATHRYN BISHOP ECKERT

Contents

List of Maps

Guide for Users of This Volume

This guide is arranged geographically. Within the two major regions—the Upper Peninsula and the Lower Peninsula—the counties are grouped into subregions and, in the case of the mineral ranges and metropolis, into even smaller divisions within each peninsula. Mineral ranges, forests and agriculture, and the watersheds of Lakes Superior, Michigan, and Huron dictate the secondary divisions. River basins and surrounding lands inspired tertiary divisions. Transportation routes carved out by early trails that established the pattern for Michigan's later highways and expressway system further shaped the character of the subregions, as they shaped the economies that grew there.

Entries are arranged by county within a region; the first entry in each county is in the county seat, often the county courthouse. Subsequent entries spiral out, moving first northerly, then clockwise. In most cases, counties are arranged in similar fashion within a region. Notable exceptions to this arrangement are the Thumb, West Michigan Shore, Traverse Bay, and Huron Shore regions. In these cases the first entry is a major city (also the county seat) and the next counties follow the shoreline. The city of Detroit is treated in the same manner as a county.

Each entry begins with an identifying code, which is a two-letter abbreviation of the county name and the number of the property within the county (again, Detroit is treated as a county), followed by the name of the property. Next are listed the date it was built, the architect, and dates of major additions or alterations to the property. The address follows. If the street where a property is located has an alternate name, usually a state or federal highway or a county road, it is listed in parentheses. Interstate highways are abbreviated to appear as, for example, I-95; federal highways are designated with "US," for example, Michigan Ave. (US 12); state highways are designated with "Michigan" and the number, for example, Woodward Ave. (Michigan 1); and county roads are listed by county and road number (Schoolcraft County 432). It is the intention of the editors and authors of this series to include descriptions only of extant buildings. Unfortunately, a few buildings have been destroyed while the editing and production of this book have been in progress. Entries for those buildings have not been deleted, but "(destroyed)" is indicated at the end of the entry heading.

Detailed maps of each region and the major cities are provided so that anyone with this book, a state highway map, and a little patience can locate the properties. The maps identify locations of specific structures by entry number, but without the alphabetic code.

Almost all of the properties described in this book are visible from public roads, or in some cases from the water. If they are not, "not visible" is noted at the end of the heading. Buildings that are open to the public are so noted at the end of the appropriate entries. Of course, we know that the readers of this book will always respect the property rights and privacy of others as they view the buildings.

BUILDINGS OF MICHIGAN

Introduction

THE STATE OF MICHIGAN LIES AT THE VERY HEART OF THE
Great Lakes: Lower Michigan is surrounded by three of the lakes—Erie,
Huron, and Michigan; the Upper Peninsula by three—Michigan, Huron, and Superior. The state has 3,251 miles of shoreline, 36,050 miles of streams
and rivers, and 10,188 lakes.

Glaciation that formed the lakes also gouged and shaped the varied topography of the land—exposing the crystalline rocks of the Laurentian Shield in
the Upper Peninsula, creating the fertile farmlands of southern Michigan, and
leaving behind the relatively infertile soil of the northern Lower Peninsula that
supported vast forests of pine and hardwood.

Rich natural resources abounded throughout the state—the copper and iron
ranges of the western Upper Peninsula; the oil and gas fields of the central
and northwestern Lower Peninsula; the salt mines of Saginaw, Bay, and Wayne
counties; and the limestone quarries of Petoskey, Alpena, Rogers City, Monroe,
and Trenton. There were additional forests on the Upper Peninsula, in the
Saginaw Valley, and along the shores of Lakes Huron and Michigan. The soils
of the region, tempered and enriched by the westerlies and by the moisture of
the "lake effect," encouraged fruit growing and muck land vegetable farming.
Then, too, the crisp northern climate, the countless miles of superb lakeshore,
and the abundance of fish and other wildlife in the lakes, streams, and forests
formed an irresistible magnet for recreation.

The economies supported by this landscape developed a variety of special
building types that formed the basis of an architectural profile of the state of
Michigan. At the same time, the character of its architecture has also been
shaped by the changing attitude of the people themselves toward their rich and
splendid land. In its wilderness phase it was perceived as awesome and terri-

3

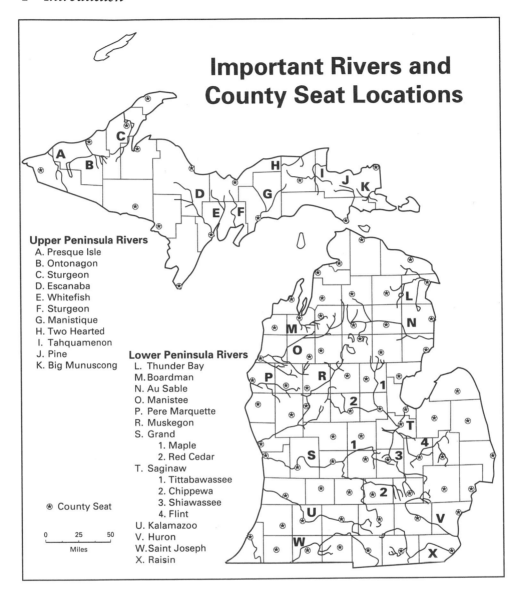

Important Rivers and County Seat Locations

Upper Peninsula Rivers
A. Presque Isle
B. Ontonagon
C. Sturgeon
D. Escanaba
E. Whitefish
F. Sturgeon
G. Manistique
H. Two Hearted
I. Tahquamenon
J. Pine
K. Big Munuscong

Lower Peninsula Rivers
L. Thunder Bay
M. Boardman
N. Au Sable
O. Manistee
P. Pere Marquette
R. Muskegon
S. Grand
    1. Maple
    2. Red Cedar
T. Saginaw
    1. Tittabawassee
    2. Chippewa
    3. Shiawassee
    4. Flint
U. Kalamazoo
V. Huron
W. Saint Joseph
X. Raisin

⊛ County Seat

0   25   50
Miles

fying. Then it came to be viewed as a land of many offerings, a strategically located land that could be conquered to form its own special economy, its own way of life. Finally, in more recent times, this same land has been viewed as worthy of appreciation and conservation. What has emerged architecturally is a special mix of forts and farms, of mines, lumber camps, and mighty factories, of CCC camps and attractive resorts, of small towns, cities, and suburbs, a fascinating mix of buildings that speaks with simple eloquence of the state of Michigan itself.

The Native American Culture

In most areas of Michigan today there are few obvious visible clues to suggest that anyone lived here before the arrival of the Europeans. Nevertheless, forests and woodlots conceal burial mounds and earthworks, while sites of villages and camps still contain certain traces of long-vanished wigwams, lodges, and longhouses. This paucity of visible reminders should not blind us to the accomplishments of our Native American predecessors.

Michigan's first inhabitants arrived over twelve thousand years ago and found a land much different than the one we are familiar with today. Glaciers occupied the northern half of the state while the southern part resembled present-day northern Canada in climate and landscape. Known to us as the Paleo-Indians, these people were hunters of barren ground caribou. Although archaeologists have found no traces of their dwellings in Michigan, analogy with contemporary groups having a similar life-style suggests that they were domed structures erected over shallow depressions scraped in the ground. The dwellings probably consisted of hides stretched over a wooden framework held in place on the ground by stones or clumps of sod. This type of primitive shelter was easily erected and very portable, each an absolute necessity in a migratory pattern of living.

After the glaciers receded to the north, around ten thousand years ago, Michigan's climate moderated. The tundra landscape was replaced by a succession of forest types culminating in the magnificent hardwood and conifer forests encountered by the earliest European explorers. It was from these forests that the Native Americans got the materials they needed to construct the dwellings and other structures necessary for domestic and ritual activities. Michigan Indians never built in stone. It was probably also during the long cultural period archaeologists call the Archaic (8000–1000 B.C.) that certain basic building types were developed and then maintained right on through the historic period by Michigan's primary Native American tribal groups: the Ojibwa, the Potawatomi, and the Ottawa.

The dwellings of the early Native Americans were utilitarian shelters; they were not personal artistic statements or expressions of wealth or achievement. The most basic type was the bark- or mat-covered wigwam. The builder, almost always a woman or group of women, began the construction of a wigwam by thrusting the sharpened butt ends of saplings into the ground (or placing them in dug holes) about two feet apart in an oval or circular pattern. A pole at each end of the arrangement was then bent toward the center with the two tops tied, forming an arc. The remaining poles were then bent toward the center, lashed onto the principal arc, thus forming a domed framework. A space between two of the poles formed a doorway; and a series of mats woven from cattail stalks was placed along the base of the framework, forming the wigwam covering. A hole was left at the top through which smoke could escape. A wigwam typically housed an entire family; one measuring 14 by 20 feet in plan could be built in less than a day and could easily accommodate eight people. Inside the wigwam was a central hearth or fireplace and along the sides were sleeping areas; the rear was used for storage. A deer or bear skin covered the doorway. The use of birchbark for the exterior was restricted to the natural range of the paper birch tree; at the same time, the wigwam-type structure was found all over eastern North America. The bark of elm and other trees served as an adequate, if not as picturesque, substitute.

Another type of dwelling was the so-called summer house. It was constructed by placing a crotched sapling at each corner of a rectangle, which generally measured about 14 by 20 feet. Four poles were bound to the tops of these uprights, creating a rectangular box. At the center of each end, another, taller crotched sapling was erected and a ridgepole secured in the crotches. A series of roof poles was then laid about three feet apart from the ridge pole sloping down to the top of the wall poles on either side. Walls, 6 to 7 feet high, were created by binding poles together vertically and horizontally, spaced again about 3 feet apart. The entire structure, except for the doorway and smoke hole, was then covered with bark sheets tied onto the framework. The door would again have been covered with a skin or woven mat.

The longhouse was an unusual form of dwelling. Huron Indians, fleeing west after being devastated by the Iroquois during warfare in the late 1640s, introduced it into Michigan in a highly developed form. It was a communal dwelling, communally built, about 20 to 30 feet wide, 20 to 30 feet high, and generally 120 to 160 feet long. It sheltered five or six related families. The longhouses were framed with saplings set in the ground in opposing pairs, tied together at the top to form arches, and further supported by horizontal poles. Slabs of chestnut or elm bark formed the walls and roof. There was a smoke hole or vent in the roof. The interior featured a central aisle or passageway with a hearth for each family group. Partitioned sleeping areas, open to the passageway, lay on either side. Above the sleeping platforms were long racks or shelves for storage of clothing and equipment. There were storage areas and small doorways located at each end of the structure. For the Huron and other people who built longhouses, these structures were a physical expression of their way of life—family solidarity, economic cooperation, and consensus rule by adults.

Michigan's Native Americans also had need for several kinds of special purpose buildings. The sweat lodge was a small version of the wigwam with a capacity of one to four people that was used for curative or ritualistic purposes. Heated stones were brought in or a small hearth area was built; steam was created by sprinkling water on the hot stones with grass or cedar branches. Sometimes herbs were placed on the stones or included in the water sprinkled on the stones to heighten or create the curative or desired ritual effect.

The menstrual hut was another variety of small wigwam and was used only by a woman during her menstrual period. Here she lived in isolation from the rest of the group because of the belief that contact with a menstruating woman or anything she touched was harmful and dangerous.

Another specialized structure among the historic tribes was the medicine lodge. This was also a wigwam-type structure, but of much larger size, sometimes 100 feet in length. It was open at the top and had cedar boughs instead of bark for sides. This lodge, the focus of the Medicine Dance or Midewiwin, was used only once or twice a year.

The medicine lodge and the so-called "dance circles" reported by pioneer observers in the early historic period have their roots in sites such as the two-thousand-year-old stockadelike enclosure discovered at the Schultz site, located at the junction of the Tittabawassee and Shiawassee rivers in Saginaw. This structure was almost certainly the locus for important social or religious gatherings.

Of less certain function are the earthworks found in the interior of north-central Michigan. These earthen walls are 1 to 3 feet high and surround a circular or oval area 150 to 300 feet in diameter. They were originally surmounted by a palisade of wooden posts, broken at intervals by "gates," and surrounded by ditches varying in depth from one to five feet. Whether they were "Indian forts" or elaborate ritual structures has not yet been determined.

A final built object type is the burial mound. There were once thousands of them spread primarily across the southern two-thirds of the Lower Peninsula. Varying in height from 1 to 15 feet and from 15 feet to 100 feet in diameter, they were the final resting place for the honored dead of a variety of prehistoric groups between 600 B.C. and A.D. 1000. They are not merely a pile of dirt heaped up carelessly over a body. Preconstruction activities often involved the ritual clearance of the ground surface down to subsoil, the excavation of a burial pit, placement of the bodies or skeletal remains and artifacts in the pit, refilling the burial pit, and then careful construction of the mound, often using specially selected soils.

Today Michigan's residents include some sixty-one thousand Native Americans, a figure that represents only one-half of one percent of the state's population. Some live in tribal communities. Under a 1978 policy directive of the Department of Interior's Bureau of Indian Affairs, seven groups of Chippewa, Ottawa, and Potawatomi are recognized. The tribal communities have built housing funded by the U.S. Department of Housing and Urban Development, and under the American Indian Community Development program, they have constructed other buildings for use as community centers, businesses, and industries, including modern gambling casinos, motels, craft stores, fishing structures, auto parts stores, and structures for wood products industries.

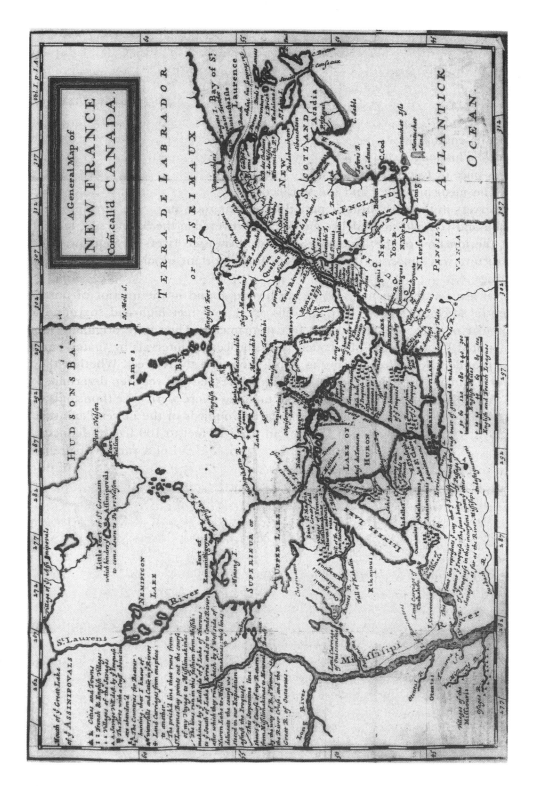

A General Map of NEW FRANCE Com̄, call'd CANADA.

8

French and British Exploration and Early Settlement

Since the easiest access to the area that is now Michigan was the water route up the Saint Lawrence River and across Lakes Ontario and Erie, the first white settlers were from French Canada, and thus the earliest buildings were primitive frontier structures (forts and trading posts) that were French in character. In the seventeenth and eighteenth centuries, French missionaries, fur traders, and soldiers followed the travels of French explorers who had sought a water route to the Pacific. The French and British in the seventeenth and eighteenth centuries and, in the nineteenth century, the Americans organized space and built forts for military defense, trading posts, and missions.

The French attempted to control the hinterland through their Jesuit missions, their military presence, and their licensed traders. Jesuit Father Jacques Marquette established the first mission in present-day Michigan near the foot of the rapids of the Saint Mary's River at Sault Sainte Marie in 1668. Here he directed construction of a fortified enclosure protecting a chapel and a house. Missions at strategically linked waterways such as the Saint Mary's River at Sault Sainte Marie, the Straits of Mackinac, and the Saint Clair and Detroit rivers, which were gateways to Lakes Superior, Michigan, Huron, and Erie, respectively, became central points of contact for Indians, missionaries, fur traders, and officers of French Canada. The missions were located close to Indian villages and were moved to new sites as Indians migrated. Thus, in 1671 Marquette moved to Saint Ignace a mission established in 1670 on Mackinac Island. It was moved again to the south side of the Straits in 1715, and to L'Arbre Croche in 1741.

The major military posts were at the Straits of Detroit and Mackinac. In 1701 Antoine de la Mothe Cadillac established Fort Pontchartrain du Detroit, a fur trading post at the present site of Detroit on the Michigan side of the straits between Lake Saint Clair and Lake Erie. It was the first permanent French settlement on the Lower Peninsula. It had a 200-foot-square enclosure of nearly 20-foot-high log palisades. Within the fortified space were laid narrow streets on which stood the commandant's house, guardhouse and barracks, parish church, priest's house, and other houses. A cemetery and gardens stood outside. Settlers cultivated farms outside the fort on long, narrow lots that ran back from the river. As early as 1708 settlers built simple oak or cedar log-

(Opposite) This French map of new France (now Canada), drawn by Louis Armand de Lom D'Arce after an expedition to Michilimackinac, was published in London in 1735. It shows a view of the area that is now Michigan and the water route up the Saint Lawrence River across Lakes Ontario (then Lake Frontenac) and Erie that gave access to the area. French, English, and Indian villages at Saint Ignace and Sault Sainte Marie, and Fort Saint Joseph at present-day Port Huron, together with hunting grounds, are indicated on the map.

Fort Pontchartrain du Detroit, 1701. The French established a permanent post to control the strait between Lakes Erie and Saint Clair and the fur trade of the Northwest. With its formidable awesome stockade and irregularly shaped bastions at the corners, it stood at the narrowest part of the river between the lakes, on the Michigan side. Partially destroyed by fire in 1703, it was subsequently rebuilt, repaired, and enlarged. The British replaced it with another fort, but Pontchartrain remained the center of Detroit until it burned in 1805.

framed houses sheathed with clapboards. An example is the Moran house built in 1734, once on Woodbridge between Saint Antoine and Hastings but demolished in 1886.

At the conclusion of the French and Indian War in 1763, when France lost nearly all of its North American empire, the area east of the Mississippi River, including what became Michigan, came under British rule. The British replaced Pontchartrain with Fort Lernoult (Fort Shelby), which was built just north of it in 1777–1778. It had a bomb-proof magazine, a storehouse, and barracks. The old French fort on the river remained the center of Detroit until it was destroyed by the 1805 fire.

In 1715 the French had also built Fort Michilimackinac on the Straits of Mackinac at present-day Mackinaw City; and until 1780 it was the center of the Upper Great Lakes fur trade. The fort itself was a palisaded village with houses, gardens, and a church. The British occupied it in 1761. During the American Revolution, the fort's commander, Patrick Sinclair, transported everything portable across the straits and by 1781 he had reestablished the fort at Mackinac Island. Now known as Fort Mackinac, it guarded the straits with three blockhouses and stone ramparts with sally ports; the officers' quarters were stone. Articles of peace signed at Paris in 1783 ceded Michigan to the United States and, in 1796, under the Jay Treaty, the British relinquished their fur trading posts at Detroit and Mackinac.

During the uncertain days of the early territorial period, the U.S. government built forts at the southern tip of Lake Huron and the eastern end of Lake Superior. Among the earliest was Fort Gratiot. Erected in 1814 by the federal government at present-day Port Huron, its purpose was to protect both residents and travelers in the Upper Great Lakes, as well as trade on the Saint Clair River. It also served as a frontier defense post. Further security was added in 1822, when Col. Hugh Brady and two companies of American soldiers began building Fort Brady at the Sault. This new fort was intended first as an impressive show of the military presence, but it also provided defense for the Sault Locks, constructed in 1855. In 1893 the United States moved this fort to New Fort Brady, now the site of Lake Superior State College at Sault Sainte Marie. In 1844, because the federal government anticipated tensions between miners and Indians, the soldiers of the 5th U.S. Infantry erected Fort Wilkins, a cluster of twenty-three buildings within the stockade, to secure the Keweenaw Peninsula. Most were log buildings covered with clapboards and were arranged in a U shape enclosing a parade ground. Verandas fronted both the officers' quarters and the barracks.

During the years of transition from frontier to statehood, the architecture of Michigan was marked by a gradual but accelerating intrusion of established stylistic concepts from the eastern seaboard into the primitive building environment of the hinterland. The building traditions of French Canada, Colonial New England, and New York are evident in the structures those early settlers built. Fur traders and agents, missionaries, and Indian agents constructed trading posts, agency quarters, houses, and missions, while the territorial governor built a territorial courthouse and capitol.

Around 1789 French Canadian fur trader François-Marie Navarre (1759–1836), employing the traditional French technique of *pièce sur pièce*, or log construction, built the Navarre-Anderson Trading Post on the River Raisin. The American Fur Company commissioned Madame Madeline (Magdelaine) Marcotte LaFramboise (1780–1846) to establish a trading post near Grand Rapids. Built in 1806, it was a 30-foot-long hut of logs and bark chinked with clay and was located on the north side of the Grand River, some 2 miles below the mouth of the Flat River, near present-day Lowell. A few years later, in 1817, the American Fur Company erected on Mackinac Island the large symmetrical dormered agency house. This house, however, was in the Federal style, which was then at its height on the East Coast. Its elegance contrasts radically with the more primitive log construction of the French and testifies to the mobility of high-style ideas even on the developing frontier. This interesting house served as the residence of Robert Stuart, the company manager of fur trading operations in the Great Lakes area. The Stuart house was part of a complex that included a warehouse, trading post, and clerk's quarters. Twenty years later, around the time of Michigan's achieved statehood, the fur company reverted to a more primitive form in a group of log buildings and a log house for trader Abraham W. Williams (1792–1873) on the west shore of Murray Bay, Grand Island, near present-day Munising.

In 1827, on the bank of the Grand River, Louis Campau built two block-houses, again constructed of close-fitting logs or blocks and tenons at the corners. One served as a dwelling, the other as a trading post. Just a few years later, however, in 1835, Patrick and Frances Mouton Marantette erected a Greek Revival house on the Saint Joseph River next to their trading post at Not-a-wa-sepe near what is now Mendon. The appearance of the Greek Revival at this early date was another important step in bringing Michigan architecture up to date with the more developed regions of the nation.

Territorial Governor Lewis Cass took up residency in the Colonial French Macomb-Cass house, which was erected by 1819 on the north side of Larned Street between First and Second streets in Detroit. The house exemplified *pièce sur pièce à tenon en coulisse* construction, in which blocks of hewn white cedar timber or logs were closely fitted together and tenoned at the corners into grooved uprights. The one-and-a-half-story, side-gable house was clad in weatherboards and had a steep dormered roof through the center of which rose a massive stone chimney. The interior contained a salon or audience room and dining, drawing, library, and lodging rooms. A house at Sault Sainte Marie, built around 1820 by Obed Wait of Detroit for Indian Agent Henry Rowe Schoolcraft, makes a fascinating contrast. Designed in the Federal style, it had a two-story main block with wings and a door framed with an elliptical fanlight and side lights.

The Mission Church on Mackinac Island also had its roots in New England. Built by William Montague Ferry, a missionary under the sponsorship of the United Foreign Missionary Society, together with Martin Heydenburk, it had a tower and octagonal belfry reminiscent of the early New England church form and Federal antecedents. Not so the church built a few years later by John Sunday (or Shahwundais). A Chippewa from Canada, Sunday was a Methodist missionary who established in 1832 the Kewawenon Indian Mission at Kewawenon, an Indian settlement on Keweenaw Bay north of L'Anse in the Upper Peninsula. The church he built was of simple log and birchbark construction. Later, in 1836–1837, Leonard Slater built at Prairieville in Barry County a log house that served as an Indian mission and school.

Of these early buildings the most ambitious of them all was Obed Wait's Greek Revival territorial courthouse (later the capitol) in Detroit. Built in 1823–1828, this brick structure had an Ionic hexastyle portico. Wait tempered this bold statement, however, with a three-staged steeple, and side lights and an elliptical fanlight around the main entrance, details that added a note of Federal elegance to a basically Greek Revival building.

Frontier Farms and Villages

The migration of more permanent settlers from the established regions of New England and New York, again up the lakes and, in some cases, through the Western Reserve, into southern Michigan resulted in the development of the earliest farms and villages. This migration was enormously facilitated by the opening of the Erie Canal and climaxed at the height of what in architectural terms is called the Neoclassical movement. Architecturally, it flowered in the fine Federal and Greek Revival buildings that characterize the farm country of the southern tiers of counties.

The completion of the Erie Canal in 1825 provided a cheap and safe water route from the East—the Hudson River area of New England and New York—west to Lake Erie and then to Detroit. It became the chief route for emigrants to the Great Lakes country and was instrumental in creating agricultural growth in the West. New Englanders and New Yorkers left worn-out farms for fresh lands in the Michigan Territory and brought their building traditions with them. European immigrants, whose building heritage was even older, also had their way opened into Michigan by the canal. In addition, the canal facilitated the transportation of Michigan products to eastern markets and of supplies to Michigan. By 1836 Michigan used the Erie Canal for shipping grain, and later, for transporting copper and iron to major railroad centers.

In 1805, under the Northwest Ordinance of 1787, Michigan became a territory. The ordinance determined how to govern the lands north of the Ohio River, created the Northwest Territory, and prescribed the conditions by which each territory would become a state. Its provisions aided the western movement into the Michigan Territory by assuring Americans from the northeast a political process to statehood.

The orderly rectilinear grid pattern of north-south and east-west roads, farms, fields, and county lines is the result of the Basic Land Ordinance of 1785. This ordinance provided for the division of western land into townships 6 miles square, each divided into thirty-six numbered sections of 1 square mile or 640 acres, with one section set aside for maintaining public schools. It also established methods of land sale and disposition and required survey prior to settlement. At times, town plans based on this grid system were adjusted to the dominant physical features of the land. As a result, towns like Adrian, Allegan, Grand Ledge, Grayling, and the Monroe Center of Grand Rapids are interesting because of their variation from the monotonous grid pattern. Other exceptions to the rectilinear pattern were found in the earlier claims of French settlers to the narrow ribbon farms extending inland from the water, and in Judge Augustus B. Woodward's partially executed Detroit plan of 1805. The latter called for wide streets radiating from the Detroit River with secondary radials from parks, a scheme that was obviously influenced by L'Enfant's plan for Washington.

Under the Ordinance of 1785 the federal government surveyed the land in advance of sales. Federal surveyors began in 1815 to establish the base line and prime meridian in Michigan Territory. The base line ran east and west at 42 degrees, 26 minutes, 30 seconds north latitude, which is the northern boundary of the state's second tier of counties. The principal meridian was located at 84 degrees, 22 minutes, 24 seconds west longitude, running north from Defiance, Ohio. The principal meridian did not reach the Upper Peninsula until 1840, but in the meantime surveys were pushed forward in southern Michigan.

The first efforts were concentrated on lands likely to attract settlers, and by 1825 most of the southern third of the Lower Peninsula had been surveyed. Progress northward was slow, but between 1835 and 1840 the Lower Peninsula was virtually completed and a beginning had been made in the eastern part of the Upper Peninsula. By 1851 the entire state had been surveyed with the exception of some inland lakes, rivers, and islands. Once surveyed, land was sold at government land offices. The first office opened at Detroit in 1818, and later ones were located at Monroe, White Pigeon, Kalamazoo, Ionia, and Flint.

Aided in the 1820s by the territorial governor's purchase of rights to additional land, by Congress's amendment to land laws that reduced the minimum plot purchasable to eighty acres at a cash price of $1.25 per acre, and by the surveyor general's completion of the land survey, the southern portion of Michigan quickly became a region of frontier farms and villages.

Pioneer families cleared land and built log structures, but these were soon superseded by Greek Revival houses employing New York and New England building methods such as coursed cobblestone and wood. Builder's guides by Asher Benjamin and Minard Lafever, which had helped shape the Greek Revival in the east, also served as sources for Michigan builders in the 1830s and 1840s. Methodists, Baptists, Presbyterians, Congregationalists, Unitarians, and Episcopalians built churches that were derived from eastern Neoclassical examples. The strong Greek Revival interest in southern Michigan was, in part at least, a spillover from the nearby Western Reserve in Ohio, which had so many splendid Greek Revival buildings. At the same time Episcopal churches were affected by Ecclesiology and the Gothic Revival.

The Greek Revival style persisted for better than two decades in Michigan—from the territorial capitol in 1823 to the Caleb Chapel House in Parma in the 1850s—and it embraced all building types. In 1836, for example, C. P. Calkins built a tiny Doric temple-front law office in Grand Rapids. Three years later Alvin Hart, a native of Cornwall, Connecticut, built the Lapeer County Courthouse, an imposing Greek Revival building with a Doric portico and a three-stage tower that still dominates the center of the county seat. In 1853 the graceful, porticoed Greek Congregational Unitarian Church was erected in Detroit. Indeed, the depth to which classical ideas penetrated the American frontier is also manifest in many place names. Just as in New York state, they were classical in origin: Romeo, Adrian, Albion, Ypsilanti, Cassopolis, and Troy.

Sydney T. Smith House, 1840, burned in 1972, Michigan Avenue west of Maute Road, Grass Lake, Jackson County. In 1839 Sidney T. Smith came with his young wife Harriet from Pulaski, New York, to Grass Lake. Soon after their arrival, they built on their farm a beautifully proportioned tetrastyle Doric "temple front" house with balancing wings. The side hall entrance had a fanlight and side lights. The house resembles Minard Lafever's design shown in the frontispiece of his *Modern Builder's Guide* (1833).

Some towns were established in the open country using the grid plan with a village green or courthouse square and streets planted with trees. Marshall is Michigan's best-known and most beautiful example of this concept. Settled in 1831, its wide main street leads to a circular green on which a Doric porticoed courthouse once stood. The street was lined with a tavern, hotel, business blocks, churches, and homes. Elsewhere in the 1830s land speculators platted townsites at locations on ports or on rivers where waterpower could be harnessed. Kalamazoo, Battle Creek, and Grand Rapids are successful examples.

The settlement and development of Grand Rapids followed the typical chronology, with missionary stations and trading posts preceding the opening of the region to settlers. It began in 1825, when the Reverend Slater established a mission on the west bank of the Grand River; at the same time, Rix Robinson and Louis Campau, two traders, set up posts nearby. After treaties were signed and the land was opened for settlement, Campau and Lucius Lyon secured land and platted it and began the settlement that led to the development of Grand Rapids.

The early settlers began to work the land, and in time, growing production created the need both to take crops to market and to get supplies and new settlers into the territory. Roads, canals, and harbors were constructed and natural waterways improved with the aid of federal grants, under the provisions of the General Survey Bill of 1824, which initiated surveys and provided estimates of roads and canals required for national military, commercial, or postal purposes.

By 1837 there were a number of main state roads. These included the Detroit–Fort Meigs (Ohio) from Perrysburg, Ohio, to Detroit; the Chicago Road from Detroit to Chicago; the Saginaw Road from Detroit to Saginaw; the Fort Gratiot Road from Detroit to Fort Gratiot; the Territorial Road; and the Grand River Road from Detroit to Grand Rapids. These roads were built in increments over a period of time. Thus, the Chicago Road was surveyed and started in 1825 and completed to Saint Joseph in 1835. Docks and warehouses for produce and supplies were built at distribution centers such as Detroit, Mackinac, Sault Sainte Marie, and Grand Rapids.

Inns to accommodate travelers were built along the way. Stephen Jennings acquired a Greek Revival house that Allen and Orrin Weston had erected in 1836 on an important intersection of the Grand River Road at Farmington and converted it to an inn. Known as the Botsford Inn, it was purchased, restored, and enlarged by Henry Ford in 1924. Coming in 1843 from Cooperstown, New York, Sylvester and Lucy Walker bought and converted an existing two-story side-gable house with a Federal entrance into an inn for travelers on the Chicago Road. It was located at the well-traveled intersection of the Chicago and La Plaisance roads. On the Chicago Road just east of the Walker Tavern, John Davenport built in the 1850s an inn that is now called Bauer Manor. This side-gable, hipped roof structure has a two-story nearly full-width porch, a form of inn that also appears in the Reuben Bird House erected in 1837 just north of Michigan 34 in Clayton.

The "Toledo War" of 1835–1836 resulted in Michigan's relinquishing to Ohio its claim to the Toledo Strip, a 468-square-mile area stretching from Lake Erie to western Hillsdale County that included Toledo; it received in exchange the western Upper Peninsula. Land sales revenues from this process totaled approximately $500,000. This sequence of events also opened the way for statehood. On January 26, 1837, President Andrew Jackson signed the bill making Michigan the nation's twenty-sixth state.

Lumbering of the Pine Forests

It was no accident that the architecture in the lumbering areas of Lower Michigan should be marked by a predilection for wood. This preference is manifest in a variety of forms ranging from the log structures on the frontier to the fine wooden Queen Anne houses that characterized so many lumbering towns during the late nineteenth century. The sheer abundance of the forest would seem to have mandated that this should be so. Pine forests, dominated by magnificent white pine, the highest quality of which was known as cork pine, ranged through more than two-thirds of the Lower Peninsula. The southern limit of the forest followed a line moving northward from Lake Michigan in the extreme southwest of the Lower Peninsula along the coast of Berrien County through the northern part of Van Buren County and the eastern part of Allegan County and then eastward through the centers of Kent, Ionia, Clinton, and Shiawassee counties before dipping through the southwestern corner of Genesee County and across the middle of Oakland and Macomb counties to the northern tip of Lake Saint Clair. The Upper Peninsula also had pine forests.

Like the other developments in Michigan, lumbering was shaped by the Great Lakes. The geology, topography, climate, soil, and vegetation of the region produced a physical environment favorable to the growth of a great lumber industry. First, encircled by the Great Lakes and the longest shoreline of any area in the nation, Michigan had a ready-made water transportation system with potentially great harbors that connected it to markets in the East and to the Midwest. Second, its network of rivers provided an inner transportation system for moving the logs from the forest; and this same network also served as a reliable source of waterpower for manufacturing the logs into lumber after they arrived at the mills. Third, the Great Lakes exerted an influence on the climate, moderating the temperature but fostering precipitation. Its longer summers and shorter winters and its higher ratio of rain to snow were suited for logging, driving, and manufacturing; and its less extreme temperatures provided an ideal climate for the growth and harvest of pine.

Woodsmen harvested the forests moving in a northward direction up the east and west sides of the state and then into the interior. The course of the frontier was determined by the major drainage basins, harbors, and shoreline. Beginning in 1830, logging and the manufacturing of wood products expanded between 1845 and 1855, and by 1855 had spread up both sides of the Lower Peninsula along its rivers: on the eastern shore there were sawmills from Detroit to Cheboygan, on the western shore, from Allegan to Traverse City. By 1870 commercial lumber manufacturing was well established. The industry reached a peak in the 1890s and was over by 1910. From 1870 to 1900 Michigan led the nation in lumber production.

As Michigan's population grew in the 1830s, there was an increasing need for building materials for dwellings and farm buildings. The early mills on the Saint Clair, Saginaw, Grand, and Muskegon rivers were established to supply this home market. Until 1840 almost all of the lumber produced in Michigan was used for its own domestic, commercial, and agricultural needs. After 1840, however, the urbanizing East, its own supply of lumber nearing depletion, sought

Michigan lumber, which was shipped to Albany and to ports on Lake Erie. The westward migration, especially on the treeless plains, created another outlet; in this case, after 1840, the lumber was shipped to Chicago and Milwaukee and west by way of the Illinois and Michigan Canal. Thus, the Great Lakes connected Michigan to both close and distant potential markets.

Mill sites or lumber manufacturing operations often were located in advance of settlement. The site included plant machinery and dams, docks, housing, and stores. Large mills located along the shore at or near the mouth of rivers became distribution centers.

With the invention of the narrow-gauge logging railroad, the Shay locomotive, and the big logging wheel, and with the arrival in the 1870s of the railroads in general, the forests of the interior of the state were harvested with even greater efficiency and zeal. Although the interior counties supplied logs in ever-increasing abundance, they did not, for the most part, develop as manufacturing centers.

The chartering of over twenty railway corporations in 1837 alone began an extraordinary era of railroading. The completion of the Erie and Kalamazoo and the Adrian and Kalamazoo railroads by the 1840s was followed by the Michigan Southern, Michigan Central, and Michigan Northern railroads in the 1850s and by northern Michigan railroads in the 1860s and 1870s. Lumbering, mining, and tourism all thrived as railroads crisscrossed both peninsulas.

Along with the expansion of the railroads, larger mills with more highly developed technology, together with the transformation from waterpower to steam, made it possible to produce more uniform and finished lumber and more refined and complicated decorative elements, all in sufficient quantity to meet the heavy demands of the ever-growing building trades. It also opened the way for special wood products such as flooring, veneering, and furniture. But the dramatic expansion of the lumbering industry was not without its price. Because of the voracious appetite for lumber that stimulated its growth in the first place, the seemingly inexhaustible forests of the state were suddenly gone, and by the end of the century the industry found itself in a disastrous decline. Indeed, it was not until after reforestation in the twentieth century that a few industries based on lumbering products, such as pulpwood, particle board, woodwork for automobile bodies, and portable and prefabricated housing, became viable.

The architecture that flowered in those parts of Michigan where lumbering was the way of life is a vivid reflection of that dynamic episode in the state's history. It captures with uninhibited delight the special qualities of the people and the place, and does so in forms that exploit to the fullest both the structural and decorative potentials of wood. This is manifest not only in a preponderance of wooden architecture but also, and especially, in the overt enthusiasm with which the craftsmen in these regions handled the material.

This condition was not, of course, unique to Michigan. The seemingly endless tracts of forest that confronted the early settlers and pioneers in this country made it inevitable that from the very beginning the Americans would use wood in abundance and with a special empathy. Indeed, many of the nation's most original and thoroughly national architectural accomplishments were realized in wood. The magnificent forests of Michigan put the state in the mainstream of that development, and the architecture that it produced thus became an effective mirror of what was happening in the nation at large. This same architecture, however, also had a strong regional flavor, evoked in part by the divers components that comprised its base and in part by the individualism of the designers and builders that gave it life. At the very root were the French elements introduced in the early log structures built by the trappers and traders who came down into the region from Canada. These were followed, after the land was opened to settlement, by fresh waves of those later generations of Americans, who came up the Lakes from New York State and western New England, bringing with them long-established methods of designing and building in wood. To add spice to the mix, there were also several small but extremely homogeneous ethnic groups from abroad, each of which had its own ideas about how wood should be used in building.

All of this, together with the growing presence of the professional architect—some emigrants from the eastern establishment, some locally born and trained—made it certain that each episode in American architecture in which wood played a significant role would be received with a ready sympathy: the Greek Revival buildings of Michigan would show the same characteristics of style as those in New York, New England, or the Western Reserve. But they would also speak a language of building that had a strong local accent. The buildings themselves would be conceived and executed by individuals, each conditioned by his own background, each motivated by his personal enthusiasms, each limited by the level of his training and skills. These combinations of circumstances vitalized the established architectural conventions as they permeated the Michigan frontier, and to the degree that they represent conditions and values that were commonly held, it was these same things that gave the architecture of Michigan its regional quality.

The wooden architecture of Michigan captures with uninhibited delight both the dynamics of the lumbering industry and the optimism of the age. The story unfolds quietly in small towns, more urgently in the turbulent cities. Its elements emerge in the crisply cut Greek temple fronts, in the board-and-batten siding and interlocking tracery of the Gothic churches and cottages, in the brackets, corbeling, and open arcading of the Italian villas, all rendered in wood. A special climax was the advent of the Queen Anne in domestic architecture, which flowered in Michigan in the 1880s, when the industry was at its height. A particularly expressive example is the sumptuous house built in Muskegon in 1887–1889 by the city's leading lumberman, Charles H. Hackley. It was designed by Grand Rapids architect David S. Hopkins. In its picturesque towered silhouette, its richly textured and polychrome shingle surfaces, its open lattice and spindle screening, and in its lavishly finished interior, where the tonality and graining of natural wood is evoked in all its splendor, in all these qualities the Hackley house is unsurpassed in Michigan. It sings of wooden architecture and celebrates the forest, it shouts of the ambition of the lumbermen of the Muskegon River valley, and in its expansive exuberance it invites comparison with that triumphant example of building in wood, the spectacular William Carson House in Eureka, California.

As the lumber industry declined and finally closed altogether, many lumbermen left special architectural legacies to the success of the industry itself, and testimonies to their own ambition. The gifts came in the form of civic architecture—libraries, theaters, art museums, and schools. These distinctive buildings often formed a nucleus for the cultural development of the city. Many are fine high-style works designed by recognized Chicago, New York, or Boston architects, or by proficient local architects. Lumberman Charles Hackley was among the most generous, with his gifts to the city of Muskegon. All bearing his name, they include a park in 1890–1891, a granite and sandstone Richardsonian library designed by Patton and Fisher of Chicago and built in 1888–1889, and a Beaux-Arts Classical art gallery planned by Solon S. Beman of Chicago and built in 1911–1912. He also built schools and churches.

The program of reforestation and wildlife protection, promoted by the State Conservation Commission in the 1920s, was continued by the Civilian Conservation Corps and other federal work-relief programs between 1933 and 1942. Trees were planted, trails were cut, and in the Ottawa, Hiawatha, and Huron-Manistee national forests of northern Michigan, rustic structures of native materials were built for administrative, protective, and recreational purposes.

U.S. Forest Service architecture had an intimate relationship with the landscape and was sympathetic to the natural environment. Although it was consistent with contemporary architectural development in the revivalist tradition, the philosophy of nonintrusiveness called for the use of native and natural materials. The designs drew upon traditional models, primarily rural vernacular structures, including design elements found in the Arts and Crafts movement. Its symbols and vocabulary established the agency's strictly pragmatic mission in utilitarian design. The Forest Service used wood and wood products extensively for both economic and associative reasons. The Hiawatha National Forest built its early American Munising Ranger District Administration Site (1937) to fit into its small-town environment, while its Clear Lake Organizational Camp (1938–1939) is rustic. Michigan's Forest Service architecture is more modest than that of the West. Nevertheless, it did influence the construction of hundreds of rustic cabins along the river banks and lakeshores and in the woods.

Copper and Iron Mining

The rich copper and iron deposits in the legendary mineral ranges of the Upper Peninsula were natural resources that would rival the forests in their importance to the state's economy. Mining dominated the rocky spines of the north in the same way that lumbering ruled the forest lands of the Lower Peninsula. But mining and its consequences would also have an impact on architecture. Here, stone would be the common building material; even stone left over from the actual mining process would be used for building purposes. At the same time, a number of specialized building types were created specifically for mining operations. Consequently, there developed a vigorous vernacular mode that added a craggy brow to the architectural profile of the state.

The historical facts that lie behind this development are themselves revealing. In the nineteenth century, scientific surveys sponsored by the federal and state governments provided increasingly accurate and reliable data about mineralogical resources, flora and fauna, and soil conditions. The resulting reports described the physical characteristics of these resources and gave their locations. They also projected their marketability and forecast their importance to the economic development of the state. As early as 1819, exploratory expeditions under the authority of the U.S. Secretary of War, together with the territorial governor of Michigan, were carried out by the scientist and writer, Henry Rowe Schoolcraft (1793–1846). Schoolcraft was also an authority on the North American Indian and was thus a particularly appropriate person to explore the Upper Peninsula. His observations about the various physiographic and geological features along the southern shore of Lake Superior were the first to arouse serious interest in the region's potential. Fully aware of the vast copper deposits, he argued that federally sponsored surveys would "augment our sources of profitable industry" and "promote our commercial independence." It was not until 1841, however, that things began to move. In that year, the report of the state geologist, Douglass Houghton, confirmed the presence of the region's Precambrian iron and copper and attracted the attention of geologists worldwide. It pointed specifically to the rich copper deposits in the western Upper Peninsula and initiated the first copper rush into the area. A decade later, geologists for the federal government, J. W. Foster and J. D. Whitney, studied the Lake Superior region and expanded on the earlier reports, adding further impetus to its development.[1]

This scientific activity was not confined to Michigan. It was but part of a larger exploration of the country as a whole, an exploration made possible by the dramatic advances in the earth sciences that were a mark of nineteenth-century America. At that time, the emerging disciplines of geology and biology represented the cutting edge of knowledge. They held the same fascination for the nation at large as the exploration of space holds for us today, and their revelations were observed with an acute interest that would lead to a dramatic change in the way Americans saw and understood the land in which they lived.

It was not only physical data, however, that the scientific expeditions brought back with them. Their reports also contained vivid descriptions, written with the urgent enthusiasm, of first discovery and permeated with expressions of fascination, awe, and reverence toward a varied and spectacular land. More than that, the veracity of these accounts was confirmed by actual visual images, provided by artists and photographers who had been taken on the expeditions for no other reason than to record what they saw. The reports of Foster and Whitney on Michigan, for example, fully capture this new attitude toward the unbroken wilderness. In part factual, in part intensely romantic, they contain detailed descriptions of the brilliantly colored rocks as they had been shaped by the ceaseless action of the surging lake into striking and beautiful caverns, cornices, grotesque openings and Gothic doorways, arches, and ruinlike shapes reminiscent of antiquity. Equally important, the text is illustrated by lithographs of geological formations that not only have the appearance of architectural forms, but are identified as such—Monument Rock, the Castles, Miner's Castle, the Amphitheater, the Chapel. By thus associating the earth's structure with architectural structure, the imagery of geology has been made to impress the imagery of architecture in such a way as to give wholly new meaning to stone as a building material.

As identified in the various geologic reports, the Copper Range is a narrow spine that runs the entire length of the Keweenaw Peninsula, stretching in a four- to six-mile-wide belt through Ontonagon, Houghton, and Keweenaw counties. Some four hundred copper mining companies operated here between 1872 and 1920. At the center of the range is the Portage Lake Mining District. One of four mining districts in the Copper Range, it held the rich Pewabic amygdaloid and Calumet conglomerate lodes. The earliest discoveries of copper were made at the tip of the Keweenaw Peninsula, in the northern third of the mineral range, and in the Ontonagon vicinity, in the southern third. Later discoveries occurred in the South Range area, just southwest of Houghton.

The Marquette, Menominee, and Gogebic iron ranges are in Marquette, Dickinson, Iron, and Gogebic counties. In 1844 William Burt and Jacob Houghton confirmed Douglass Houghton's reports when they too discovered iron ore at Negaunee. The following year twenty citizens from Jackson opened the Jackson Mine near Teal Lake. By 1875 the mines had shipped over 900,000 tons of iron ore valued at nearly $4 million.

The completion of the Sault Canal (Saint Mary's Falls Ship Canal) around the rapids of the Saint Mary's in 1855 opened shipping between Lake Superior and Lake Huron, and on to the other Great Lakes. To aid navigation, the U.S. Lighthouse Service, established by Congress with the Lighthouse Act of 1789, had already constructed and later improved lighthouses at harbors and river entrances throughout the Lakes. Still later, in the nineteenth century, it went even further to provide markers at islands, points, shoals, and reefs, and built lifesaving stations. The first light on the Michigan coastline was the Fort Gratiot Light, erected at the southern tip of Lake Huron in 1825. Automation of the lights in the twentieth century led to their abandonment, but many more of the lighthouses that remain on the Upper Great Lakes are in Michigan than in any other state. The Bicentennial Lighthouse Fund, appropriated by Congress and administered by the National Park Service, financed their restoration in 1988, 1989, and 1990. Michigan's extensive Great Lakes shoreline is dotted with more lighthouses than any other state in the nation.

With the entire Great Lakes system open to shipping, large-scale mining operations became a reality. Mining structures of all kinds appeared at many locations along the mineral ranges; docks and warehouses were built at transportation and distribution points at Eagle River, Houghton, Marquette, and Escanaba. Some of these specialized buildings were constructed from the dark, gray-black rock discarded from the mines themselves. A significant number, however, were built of a beautiful red sandstone that was indigenous to the Upper Peninsula. Cropping out at various points along the south shore of Lake Superior, this sedimentary rock is made up of sand-sized grains of quartz, bonded together by iron oxide, calcite, authigenic quartz, and silica. It is the iron oxide that gives this lovely material its rich reddish brown color. The most prolific outcropping, the Jacobsville formation, occurs on the Keweenaw Peninsula, southeast of the Keweenaw fault. It extends eastward along the shore of Lake Superior to Sault Sainte Marie and Sugar Island and probably constitutes the bedrock over much of the bottom of Lake Superior in that area. It also crops out from Munising westward to the head of the lake. Until the early twentieth century the Jacobsville sandstone was generally and popularly called Lake Superior sandstone, brownstone, or redstone and prefixed specifically by the name of the place in which it was quarried, such as Portage Entry, Marquette, or L'Anse. Over the years, forty-six companies extracted the famous sandstone from quarries in the Jacobsville formation. Its resonant presence enlivens the streets in the cities and villages throughout the mineral ranges.

From 1870 until 1910, the prosperity of the copper and iron mining, lumbering, and shipping industries of the Lake Superior region created a demand for ever more substantial buildings, and in satisfying this demand, architects, builders, and clients alike preferred the sedimentary rock from the Jacobsville formation. They found the stone suitable because it was beautiful, durable, and carvable. Moreover, because it was extracted easily in large blocks and shipped cheaply by water, it was economical. It was promoted aggressively. The red sandstone city halls and county courthouses, churches, schools and libraries, banks and commercial blocks, and houses they built give the Lake Superior region a distinct identity.

Between 1880 and 1900 the arrival of the Richardsonian Romanesque, which had already permeated most of the upper Middle West, brought exciting new potential to the architecture of Michigan. Not only was it a style of national prominence, but it was one that was particularly suitable to the character of the region. Its dynamic stone masonry, massive forms, and irregular outlines introduced qualities of style that seemed to be almost begging for rendition in Lake Superior sandstone. Indeed, Richardson's own rock-faced style was intentionally geological in some of its imagery and was thus potentially expressive of the physical structure of the Upper Peninsula. But Richardson's intensely poetic style was also responsive to the natural qualities of wood. It therefore had an equally powerful affinity with the forests of Michigan and offered exciting new possibilities for the further enhancement of an already firmly established and joyous commitment to wood.

The Richardsonian mode arrived in Michigan at the height of the lumbering and mining years and was received with flamboyant, if sometimes innocent,

John Munro and Mary Beecher Longyear House, 1890–1892 to 1903–1904, Marquette, Marquette County, (in 1903–1904 it was dismantled, loaded onto railroad cars, and transported and rebuilt in Brookline, Massachusetts); Demetrius Frederick Charlton. The huge scale in the Richardsonian Romanesque style; magnificent view of Presque Isle, Lake Superior, and the city of Marquette; native sandstone and wood building materials; and superb workmanship made the Longyear house the equal of any in the upper Middle West. The house was evidence of the stature of the owners and the city and represents the large houses built by speculators in mineral and timber lands.

The Michigan School of Mines, built 1887–1889 to the plans of John Scott and Company and destroyed in 1968, was located at Houghton in the midst of the Copper Range and the Marquette, Menominee, and Gogebic iron ranges. Built of Jacobsville red sandstone in the geological image of the Lake Superior region, the sturdy Richardsonian building gave credence to the importance of the mineral resources of the Upper Peninsula to the state and the nation. This photograph was taken in 1906.

enthusiasm. It appeared in buildings of all types but was used with the greatest originality in domestic architecture, especially in the towns and cities of the mineral ranges. The best-known example was built in Marquette in 1890–1892 for John M. Longyear, a speculator in mineral and timber lands. The architect was Demetrius Frederick Charlton, the landscape architect the renowned Frederick Law Olmsted. From a spectacular site atop a bluff, this mammoth Richardsonian house overlooked Presque Isle and the rough waters of tumultuous Lake Superior. While open to views of the lake from every direction, it was "presentable" on the west to the town. The house was constructed entirely of Upper Peninsula materials—Lake Superior red and brownstone, Huron Bay slate, and native woods, all handled with robust directness. Richly detailed and finished, the interior was arranged around a great octagonal hall open to the roof. In its bold geological forms and in its sensitive response to the nature of materials, the Longyear house was comparable to the contemporary James J. Hill mansion in Saint Paul, Minnesota. Designed by Peabody, Stearns and Furber of Boston, this huge house is one of the most dynamic examples of

Richardsonian masonry in the upper Middle West. The principal difference between the two is that the Longyear house was more modest, reflecting the less expansive economic situation in Marquette.

A public building in the Richardsonian Romanesque manner that had special meaning for the mineral ranges was the Michigan Mining School. Erected in 1887–1889, two years after the legislature established the school, the building was situated on a slope above Portage Lake at East Houghton, in the very heart of the mining district. It contained all departments of the school—laboratories, classrooms, offices, and library. John Scott designed the symmetrical hipped-roof structure with a dramatic central tower and round-arch windows. The bold exterior walls proclaim their purpose: they are laid in random rock-faced ashlar of Portage Entry sandstone, trimmed with Marquette brownstone. Thus projecting a geological image of the land the building was designed to illuminate, the school not only served but also, through the very nature of its forms, celebrated one of the state's most precious attributes, its rugged spine of mineral resources.

The Richardsonian mode marked the triumphant climax of nineteenth-century romanticism in both American and Michigan architecture. It was also its final affirmation. The World's Columbian Exposition of 1893 in Chicago introduced a wholly different concept of formal relationships, a concept that within a decade would radically alter the direction of architectural design in this country. Its source was the Ecole des Beaux-Arts in Paris. In contrast to the aggressive picturesqueness of the Richardsonian mode, the design principles taught at the Ecole were classical in the highest degree: they espoused symmetry, regularity, harmony, and axial planning; their model was the monumental architecture of ancient Rome. The Ecole began attracting young Americans shortly after mid-century, and by 1890 a sufficient number had been trained there, or had otherwise been influenced by its teachings, to form a mature and outspoken group that was actively practicing its principles. It was these architects, under the leadership of McKim, Mead and White of New York, who were responsible for the design of the Chicago Fair. The grandiose plan that they produced was Beaux-Arts Classicism at its monumental best. It not only rivaled Rome in its colonnaded facades and vaulted interiors, but to create the impression of marble, the preferred material of classicism, the vast majority of the buildings was painted white.

Both the high classicism and the whiteness of the Columbian Exposition would effect the architecture of Michigan as quickly as it would the rest of the nation. Public architecture in particular was conceived in these terms. As a result, the red and brown local sandstone that had so enriched the rough polychrome walls of the Richardsonian era gave way to the smooth surfaces of marble and other whitish limestones that were mandated by classical design. This was especially true on the Upper Peninsula, where the local sandstone had been so conspicuously displayed. Although the vast majority of the Beaux-Arts Classical

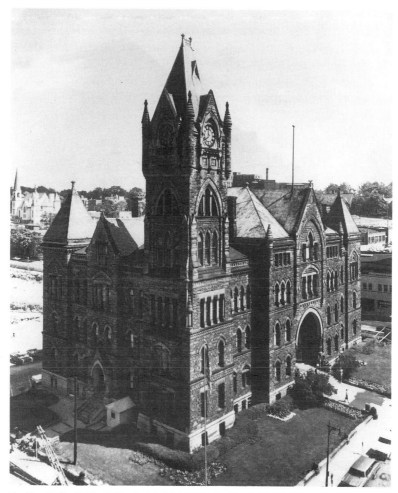

Grand Rapids City Hall, 1885–1888, destroyed 1969, Elijah E. Myers, Grand Rapids, Kent County. One of Michigan's most exuberant High Victorian government buildings, the solid stone Grand Rapids City Hall was destroyed in 1969 to make way for a new governmental center.

designs were by local or midwestern architects, in the larger urban centers of the Lower Peninsula they were occasionally joined by the work of such prominent eastern firms as McKim, Mead and White, Cram and Goodhue, and Shepley, Rutan and Coolidge.

This radical and swift change in architectural direction dealt a fatal blow to the red sandstone quarries of the Upper Peninsula. Indeed, as the twentieth century progressed, stone in general gave way to artificial stone, concrete, and brick. To speed this process, brick manufacturers even mounted a successful campaign against stone. Then, too, the rapid development of steel and reinforced concrete skeletal construction encouraged the use of brick and other synthetic materials, which were lighter and more economical as sheathing for the frame.

The impact of the Columbian Exposition brought to an abrupt end one of the most expressively regional episodes in Michigan's architecture. As the twentieth century progressed, although local architects continued to design with a sensitivity for their time and place and outstanding geniuses continued to make their boldly individual statements, the architecture of the state as a whole became increasingly absorbed into the mainstreams of national development.

Growth of Detroit around the Automobile Industry

Although substantial urban areas developed within all of these economic and geographical nuclei, the principal urban flowering of the state was the growth of Detroit around the automotive industry.

Detroit was founded by the French in 1701 as Fort Pontchartrain du Detroit or Fort Pontchartrain of the Strait. Because of its strategic location on the Detroit River, the city was destined to play a decisive role in the development of the region and the nation. Occupied by the British in 1760 and then by the Americans in 1796, Detroit remained a frontier village into the nineteenth century. While no buildings survive from this earliest period, the city had a gridiron and high earthen ramparts, houses were Quebec types with steeply pitched roofs, sidewalks were of wood, the streets narrow and unpaved, and there were wooden wharfs along the river. Detroit was incorporated in 1805 as the county seat.

After Detroit was destroyed by fire in 1805, the city fathers adopted a visionary plan for a model metropolis that emulates, but does not replicate, L'Enfant's plan for Washington, D.C. Designed by Judge Augustus B. Woodward, it was based on a hexagon, divided into twelve sections that could be added to as the city grew. Principal streets were 200 feet wide, secondary diagonal streets were 120 feet wide, with circles and other open spaces. Although landowners impeded implementation of Woodward's plan and only its vestigial remains can now be seen around Grand Circus Park, the distinctive broad avenues and open spaces still characterize downtown Detroit. Throughout the nineteenth century, too, as a result of Woodward's plan, civic buildings stood in relative isolation, thus never losing visibility—a quality Detroiters found essential; and the Campus Martius, Woodward's city square, provided a long-lasting focal point for government.

During the early decades of the nineteenth century, for political and geographical reasons, river cities such as Cincinnati and Saint Louis grew faster than cities on the Great Lakes. Because of its location on the quiet flowage between the upper and lower lakes, however, Detroit was strategically placed as a transportation center, and by 1818 the first regularly scheduled steamship between there and Buffalo began its service. This was followed in 1825 by the completion of the Erie Canal, and beginning in 1830 radial roads, following old Indian trails, were laid out as military roads extending from Detroit to outstate. All of these transportation advantages contributed to make Detroit the gateway to the Northwest and promoted the settlement of Michigan. In turn, later in the nineteenth century, the extractive industries of Michigan also helped to foster industrial growth in Detroit. More immediately, the resulting need for hotels, warehouses, and other service facilities led to the expansion of Detroit's commercial district.

Most of the settlers in the early nineteenth century were from New England and New York State. These immigrants brought to Detroit the architectural concepts then popular on the East Coast, which led to the creation of a nearly homogenous environment characterized by low wooden buildings painted white and punctuated by tall church steeples. The Federal style dominated the earlier structures, to be followed by the Greek Revival: in general, buildings had low rooflines concealed behind balustrades, an entrance framed with side lights and fanlights, and porches carried on slender columns. Both churches and domestic buildings tended to approximate the historic Greek temple form. By mid-century, some wealthy merchants were seeking countrylike surroundings for their new residences, thus reflecting the growing pressures of the urban scene and the corresponding urge to escape. Increasingly romantic attitudes toward the natural world prompted wholly new relationships between the house and its environment, relationships that owed much to the writings of the Hudson River landscape gardener and architectural critic, Andrew Jackson Downing. Among Downing's many concerns were two that bore directly on these relationships, the house as it appeared when seen in the landscape, and the landscape as it appeared when seen from the house. He urged designs that were responsive to both. To this end he argued against the classical temple and ardently recommended instead houses designed according to picturesque principles. In response to the changes taking place in American society, Downing introduced two new domestic building types: for the middle class, he recommended the cottage with its ornamental bargeboards and Gothic detailing; for those of wealth and discrimination, his choice was the villa, either Gothic or Italian, with its irregular massing, towers, and terraces. It was the latter that attracted those wealthy Detroiters who were seeking the serenity of the countryside. Picturesque buildings also appeared in the city itself, where they created a diversity in the architectural environment. As in most American urban settings, however, a common sense of scale evoked the impression of a consistently designed and uniform city.

Industrial and commercial growth was unprecedented in the second half of the nineteenth century. The population rapidly expanded from 45,619 in 1860 to 205,876 in 1890. No single industry dominated the economy, although at that time Detroit was the leading stove-producing city in the world. In the beginning, Jefferson Avenue was the major retail district, but after the Civil War, the business area began to expand north on Woodward Avenue, following the fashionable residential districts. Jefferson Avenue then became the wholesale warehouse district. Urban sprawl was encouraged by Detroit's level site, which on three sides lacked natural boundaries; and the city was tied together first by a horse-drawn, and later, by an electric streetcar system. These factors affected the building pattern. According to a contemporary commentator, there were many miles of inexpensive but decent houses, each with its little plot of land. This pattern was unlike Eastern cities, where land, labor, and lumber costs were significantly higher.

By the late 1860s, Detroiters, like other Americans, viewed Paris as a model for ideal urban development. Architects in Detroit willingly provided what their clients wanted—buildings in the French Second Empire style, with mansard roofs, projecting center and corner pavilions, and most importantly, architectural sculpture. Julius Theodore Melcher's sculptures of female figures symbolizing Justice, Art, Industry, and Commerce adorned the base of the cupola of the Second Empire Detroit City Hall (1891), and statues of LaSalle, Cadillac, Marquette, and Father Richard occupied niches on its four corner pavilions.

Public sculpture was employed not only to commemorate the past but also to express through visual form the ideals of the period; it could also beautify the city. The first monumental sculpture was a Civil War memorial by Randoph Rogers, the Soldiers' and Sailors' Monument. Erected in the Campus Martius opposite old city hall in 1872, its grouping of statues represents the four branches of the U.S. military service; Victory, Union, Emancipation, and History; and Michigan itself. In the early decades of the twentieth century, public sculpture reflected increased civic pride, as Detroiters erected monuments to honor their heroes. Statues of a governor, a U.S. senator, and a mayor grace Grand Circus Park. By mid-century the public monument came to extol abstract and universal concepts related to people. The huge bronze male figure created by Marshall Fredericks and placed by the city-county building symbolizes "the spirit of Detroit."

Many nineteenth-century buildings were built of Trenton stone, a limestone quarried locally downriver or on Kelley Island in Lake Erie. In response to the increased demand for buildings, Detroit architects were attracted to the latest innovations in building technology. The economic advantage of substituting cast iron for stone was immediately recognized. Iron had long been used for interior columns and beams, but now it was employed for exterior facades. The introduction of new structural materials and of plate glass resulted in stylistic changes as well: facades now could be opened up, creating a feeling of lightness. In some Detroit buildings, brick load-bearing exterior walls were maintained, and decorative cast-iron panels were bolted to them. Cast-iron-fronted buildings continued to be built in Detroit to the end of the nineteenth century.

In the second half of the nineteenth century, Grosse Pointe was transformed

Monroe Block, 1859–1860 and later, demolished 1990, Detroit, Wayne County. Until its demolition in 1990, the Monroe Block was the last collection of pre-Civil War commercial buildings in the city of Detroit. It included the Italianate Williams Block, built for John Constantine Williams in 1859–1860 to the plans of Detroit architect Sheldon Smith and the Second Williams Block designed by Mortimer L. Smith and built in 1872–1873. The block stood opposite the Bagley Fountain on Campus Martius.

into a summer colony, as wealthy businessmen bought up old ribbon farms, first laid out by the French, to realize the recreational advantages of Lake Saint Clair. By 1880 Detroit businessmen began to build year-round houses there. Grosse Pointe was to become a place of escape from the urban scene and a playground for the wealthy. The automobile and the paving of Jefferson Avenue permitted this change. Designers synthesized architecture and landscape into truly magnificent settings for comfortable living. Not wishing to participate in Grosse Pointe's way of life, Henry Ford built Fairlane in Dearborn. In addition, Indian Village, one of several subdivisions to serve as an upper-class residential neighborhood within the city, was platted in the 1890s, but it was not built up until the 1920s. Palmer Park and Palmer Woods were planned in the second decade of this century as ideal residential communities for the upper middle classes, removed from downtown congestion.

The need for openness and for recreational facilities was not limited to the wealthy. In 1879 Belle Isle was purchased by the city and developed into a vast public park. It quickly became popular for boating and picnicking. Soon after, Palmer Park was given to the city. Grand Boulevard was laid out in 1883–1887 as a landscaped residential boulevard, twelve miles long, which extended around the outskirts of the city. It was also intended to serve as a peripheral road, connecting all of the earlier major radial traffic arteries. Thus, by 1890 Detroit had the beginnings of a radial and ring road transportation system that was to be developed in the future.

In the 1820s, Detroit was transformed from a frontier community to a thriving commercial and governmental center, and by the time of the Civil War, it was linked by the railroad to the rest of the nation. Its commercial and industrial buildings slowly expanded into what had previously been residential areas. Prompted in part by Downing, taste had also changed; the Gothic Revival, followed by the Italianate, replaced the earlier Neoclassical buildings. Because of limitations of the local architectural services, Detroiters continued to look to the outside, especially to the East Coast, for architectural ideas and direction. Of the several architectural styles that found their way to Michigan as a result, the one most enthusiastically embraced by Detroiters, was the robust Richardsonian Romanesque. It was used for churches, clubs, houses, and commercial and public buildings.

In the 1890s a radical transformation of the downtown area of Detroit began. Following the example of Chicago, the domes, spires, and cupolas of earlier civic and religious buildings were being overshadowed by a skyline dominated by tall buildings. After several decades of decentralization and urban sprawl, the city turned inward. As density began to increase, expansion was upward into large commercial structures and skyscrapers. By 1894, completely metal frame buildings with terracotta facades began to appear in the city. The earlier homogeneity was shattered by disparities of scale, between low buildings of three to six stories and skyscrapers of up to fourteen stories, disparities that were symptomatic of the rapid growth without planning that was taking place in the city as well as in the nation at large. The need for more office space culminated in the 1920s, when Griswold Street became the heart of the financial district. The result was the erection of a series of monumental skyscrapers. The Penobscot Building of 1928 reached forty-seven stories. Designed by Wirt Rowland of Smith, Hinchman and Grylls, one of Detroit's most productive and significant architectural firms, its simple limestone mass rises dramatically up to the thirtieth floor, when it is topped by a series of cubistic setbacks. The Penobscot Building remained Detroit's tallest structure and a symbol of the city until the completion of the Renaissance Center in 1977. While civic boosters pointed to this downtown growth, new and exciting developments were also taking place in the suburbs.

The first automobiles appeared on the streets of Detroit in 1896, and in a short span of years the city was transformed into the Motor City. Mass production made the automobile accessible to the population at large, and in the resulting economic boom, the city's population grew from 205,876 in 1900 to 993,678 in 1920. This happened where it did, when it did, for a number of reasons. First, the geographical position of Detroit placed it within easy access by water to essential materials, a position, moreover, that had already encouraged the city's development as a center of carriage and wagon manufacturing; it was also a city of diversified, small-scale enterprises with plenty of machine-shop facilities and skilled labor. Most important of all, however, is the fact that the right people, with the right entrepreneurial and technical talent, were there at the right time. By 1900, those Michiganians who had profited from mining, lumbering, supplying coal, and merchandizing had money to invest in the automobile industry. At the same time, those aggressive entrepreneurs and their associates—among them Ransom E. Olds, Henry Ford, and William C. Durant—provided the drive that, between 1900 and 1915, transformed the fledgling auto industry into a world class enterprise. Ford's contribution was technical, the concept of a car for the multitude, a car that was durable, simple, and easy to operate and maintain, a car of standardized design that could be produced on the assembly line—the Model T. Durant was the administrative genius who put together a smoothly functioning industrial organization.

Like many other industrial cities, Detroit was rapidly transformed into a quilt of ethnic neighborhoods; first by immigration from Europe—Germans, Irish, and Poles—and later, by migration from the South of both African-Americans and other Southerners. Evidence of their ethnic and racial traditions is reflected in the large number of religious structures; schools; small, family-run stores; bars; clubs and fraternal organizations; and funeral parlors. Historic black neighborhoods include Paradise Valley, now destroyed, the west side of West Grand Boulevard, and the West Warren and Tireman avenues area.

New manufacturing processes as well as the automobile radically changed Detroit. Since industrial plants required large tracts of land, they tended to be moved to the periphery of the urban core, where they were served by the Michigan Central Belt railroad line. By 1904 congestion was already a problem and an outer belt railroad line was built on the east side. This line opened up a vast corridor for industrial development just outside the city limits. Speculative housing for factory workers was built adjacent to this area. The need for larger and larger sites caused further decentralization of industry. As early as 1906 Henry Ford purchased a 60-acre site in suburban Highland Park for a new factory. Completed in 1914, the moving assembly line was first introduced there. A year later Henry Ford acquired a 2,000-acre site on which to build a super plant, an enterprise that was ultimately conceived as a self-sufficient industrial city. This remote site at River Rouge had not only adequate rail transportation but the potential for a harbor as well. This need for extraordinarily large industrial sites is still present today. In one instance, to attract industry back to Detroit proper, an entire neighborhood, Poletown, was demolished in 1980 so a supercolossal plant could be built for General Motors.

Dodge Main, 1910–1914, demolished 1980–1981, Albert Kahn, Hamtramck, Wayne County. The huge main Dodge automobile plant of the Chrysler Corporation and many wooden gabled workers houses and churches in the surrounding Polish American neighborhood were destroyed in 1981 to clear the site for General Motors' new Cadillac plant, which opened in 1985 employing 6,000 people (now only 3,500) and several hundred robots.

The introduction of reinforced concrete in 1903 opened the way for new methods of plant construction, and owners turned to local architectural firms for innovative solutions. Albert Kahn, one of the foremost industrial architects of the twentieth century, whose long career from 1896 to 1942 coincided with the growth and maturity of heavy industry, was particularly active in Michigan. His designs were motivated more by functional than by philosophical concerns. The Packard Plant (1905), the assembly line at Highland Park (1914), and the consolidation of all aspects of the Ford Motor Company's production in one plant at the River Rouge (1920s) revolutionized industrial construction. In his factory designs Kahn responded to the manufacturing process and programs and to the desire to improve the working conditions.

Just as Henry Ford revolutionized automobile production in his assembly line process, so, too, mass production met the need for workers' housing. Modern Housing Corporation, a subsidiary of General Motors Corporation, built homes in Pontiac and Flint and cities where GMC plants were located. Civic and Chevrolet parks, built quickly between 1919 and 1920 in Flint, are examples.

The automobile changed the man-made landscape of Michigan, as it did that of the rest of the country. Resorts were strung out along highways; people moved out beyond streetcar lines; shopping centers eventually clustered in the suburbs; and new automobile-related building types arose along roadsides, including gas stations, automobile dealerships, drive-in businesses, roadhouses, tourist cabins, motels, and scenic lookout towers. During the 1920s, the great prosperity of the automotive industry built Detroit and brought it to full economic maturity. Quite appropriately in that city, the Fisher brothers and Albert Kahn built a corporate monument to the automotive industry at the New Center (1922, 1928).

Following the philosophy of the Arts and Crafts movement, some Detroit architects and designers believed that the monotonous standardization of industrial methods was detrimental to society, and they sought to remedy the situation through design. Foremost among them was Mary Chase Perry, the driving force behind the Pewabic Pottery Company. She was a woman of considerable talent and was to married architect William Buck Stratton. In the heart of Detroit, the home of mass production, Pewabic was able successfully to establish its handcraft operations and go on to become one of the foremost producers of architectural tiles in the United States. Notable Detroit examples from this operation can be seen in Cram, Goodhue and Ferguson's Saint Paul's Episcopal Cathedral (1911) and in the Church of the Most Holy Redeemer (1920). Newspaper publisher George G. Booth, founder of the Detroit Arts and Crafts Society in 1906, carried on the ideals of the movement when he hired architect Eliel Saarinen, who worked with sculptors and wrought-iron designers for the world-renowned Cranbrook educational complex (1927). Booth's leadership was to have a significant influence on the architecture of the region and beyond.

At the other extreme of architectural activity, catalogs for mass-produced precut portable housing and architectural plan books opened the way for standardized and democratized housing that met the need for affordable homes. Several businessmen in Bay City and Saginaw, where the Michigan lumber industry had left a residue of lumber expertise, capital, and an entrepreneurial spirit, established mail-order, ready-cut house companies. They adapted the technique from the precut designs of Bay City boat builders and advertised the houses nationwide. The North American Construction Company, also known as Aladdin Company, published Aladdin catalogs illustrating bungalows, American foursquare, Queen Anne, Colonial Revival, and Craftsman houses. Also included in the catalog were plans for complete industrial towns with stores, churches, schools, warehouses, hotels, and multifamily dwellings. Between 1906 and 1982 that company alone produced fifty thousand housing units. They ranged in cost from a few hundred to several thousand dollars. The Lewis

Manufacturing Company of Bay City produced and sold through catalogs Lewis homes and Liberty Ready-Cut homes. Others were the Sterling Homes of the International Mill and Timber Company, also of Bay City, M&M Gold Bond Portable Houses and Garages of Mershon and Morley in Saginaw, and Saint Johns Portable Building Company in Saint Johns.

Manufacturers and dealers outside of Michigan produced mail-order catalog houses, many of which were purchased by Detroit and Michigan residents. Sears, Roebuck and Company sold "Modern Homes" beginning in 1908, and Montgomery Ward, its "Wardway Homes." Another was the Gordon–van Tine Company of Davenport, Iowa. The Radford Architectural Company in Chicago sold plans.

Architects and developers within the state made available plans and services that had a major impact on building. Richard B. Pollman drew plans for colonial and modern ranch houses that were published year after year in *Designs for Convenient Living* (Detroit, 1946). In *Gateways to Happiness: A Book of House Plans and a Home-planning Service* (Detroit, 1924), Louise Lathrup published plans and advertised architectural services that were generally available but particularly to purchasers of lots in her new community of Southfield Village, located off Southfield Road between Eleven Mile and Twelve Mile roads. Again, the Miller-Storm Company published *Good Homes: A Book Designed to Help You Plan, Finance and Equip Your Home* (Detroit, 1929) in Detroit.

Development continued in the downtown area of Detroit. Beginning in 1916 the area around Grand Circus Park was radically altered. Washington Boulevard was transformed from a residential street into the city's exclusive shopping district, and by the 1920s the area around Grand Circus Park became Detroit's movie theater district. New hotels and office buildings were continually changing the skyline, as the business core of the city migrated north. Located downtown, the Albert Kahn Associates' Detroit Athletic Club (1915) served as the men's club for automobile industrialists.

With civic improvement in mind and strong political support for planning, an official City Planning and Improvement Commission was established in 1910. At this time, Detroit was one of only five cities in the United States to have such a commission. A preliminary plan by Edward H. Bennett of Chicago was completed in 1915. It was based on Woodward's plan of 1806, on Detroit's existing radial road system, on the French tradition, and on the Chicago Plan of 1909. Bennett envisioned a multi-core metropolis based on function and guided by aesthetic principles of order and hierarchy. While many of the ideas contained in the plan never reached fruition, many did, such as the Cultural Center, Outer Drive, Roosevelt Park, Rouge Park, the Zoo, and the Huron-Clinton Parkway. Largely because of Bennett's plan, voters in 1919 approved funds for the development of a park and playground system. In 1939 the Huron-Clinton Metropolitan Authority was created to develop and maintain recreational facilities in the surrounding five-county area, and to make them accessible by means of parkways and connecting drives.

A Center for Arts and Letters was first proposed by William C. Weber, an art museum trustee. In 1910 the museum purchased an 8.5-acre site on Woodward Avenue, two miles from downtown in a fashionable residential neighborhood. Later it successfully lobbied the Library Commission, with the support of the mayor and City Planning and Improvement Commission, to locate a new library across the street. The monumental grouping of Cass Gilbert's Public Library (1921) and Paul Cret's Detroit Institute of Art (1927) was viewed as offsetting the commercialization of the city's downtown environment. The style chosen for these and other public and commercial buildings at the time was academic classicism, of the Beaux-Arts Classical movement, a style that made its Detroit debut in the late 1880s. While the reasons for choosing this style are complex, appearance alone set these buildings apart and gave them an identity and an associative quality that appealed to Detroiters. A later plan for the area, initiated in 1945, resulted in further clustering of cultural and educational institutions. Adjacent to it is the new campus of Wayne State University, which has important recent buildings by Minoru Yamasaki and Pilafian and Montana.

Consistent with the multi-core concept for a city, General Motors built its headquarters on West Grand Boulevard (1919–1923) The erection of Albert Kahn's Fisher Building and Theater (1927–1929) followed. This project was envisioned as a shopping, office, and entertainment complex, a city within a city, which would be superior to the downtown in its more favorable location and its ability to serve the outward-migrating population. Known as the New Center, it represents the beginning of the concept of satellite town centers, which were to develop in Detroit after the Korean War.

With isolationism, a reaction to growing political tension and the threat of war in Asia and Europe, Detroiters and Michiganians, along with Americans all over the country, reasserted what they considered to be American values. Interest in Americana and the Colonial Revival was heightened in Michigan by Henry Ford's museum at Greenfield Village and by his revival of small mill production and industries everywhere in Michigan in the 1930s. The Colonial American image was also promoted in popular magazines such as *House Beautiful, Ladies Home Journal,* and *Better Homes and Gardens* and in such articles and books as Fiske Kimball's "The Old Houses of Michigan" in *The Architectural Record* (September 1922), and in Rexford Newcomb's *Architecture of the Old Northwest* (Chicago, 1950).

At Greenfield Village in Dearborn, Henry Ford created an idealized early American village. Beginning in 1928–1929, he moved in historic buildings from elsewhere, designed new ones at Dearborn Inn in the colonial image, and constructed replicas of houses of famous Americans. Ford attempted to reconcile rural life and industry by removing his small automobile parts-manufacturing shops from the city and placing them in small hydroelectric-powered mills in the country. Between 1918 and 1944 he developed twenty-four village industries in southeast Michigan.

The trend in building houses and subdivisions of houses in traditional Cape Cod and Dutch Colonial Revival styles, and in the image of the American farmhouse, was followed by a similar trend for resorts, restaurants, churches, schools, banks, post offices, gas stations, city halls, and shopping centers. Blaney Park Resort in the Upper Peninsula to Avenue of Fashions on Livernois Avenue in Detroit, Klinger Lake Country Club near Sturgis, the First Presbyterian Church of Lansing by Munson and Bowd in 1947, the Hillcrest Apartments in East Lansing by Raymond D. Snow in 1939, Bill Knapps restaurants, and Carl Forslund Furniture of Grand Rapids, all are characterized by the traditionalism of the 1930s.

The federal government responded to the Great Depression with government-sponsored New Deal public works projects and emergency relief programs. Through the Public Works Administration (PWA) under the National Industrial Recovery Act of 1933, roads, public buildings, and other projects were built, and through the Civil Works Administration under the same act, local make-work projects were initiated. Later, the Works Progress Administration under the Emergency Relief Appropriation Act of 1935 built or improved roads, bridges, public buildings, aircraft landing fields, and parks. Through these programs, too, artwork of various kinds was installed in post offices, schools, and other public buildings.

The PWA program alone constructed county courthouses, post offices, ice arenas, community buildings, city halls, schools, detention homes, housing projects, and hospitals, as well as utilitarian service-related structures such as highway garages, water purification works, sewage disposal plants, garbage incinerators, bus garages, hydroelectric power plants, municipal power plants, and highway bridges.

Not all the government-sponsored architecture of Michigan was conceived in traditional stylistic terms. When the slums on the east side of Detroit were cleared, for example, they were replaced by the huge, thoroughly modern Brewster and Parkside housing projects (1939) designed by George D. Mason. Outside Detroit there are other fine examples: the Alpena County Courthouse, designed by William H. Kuni and built in 1934–1935, is a bold reinforced concrete building; Carl E. Macomber's Saginaw City Hall (1936–1938) is also reinforced concrete, but its sleek, austere sides are covered with quarry-faced local Bay Port limestone. Other interesting examples are the rustic Pentoga Park Office and Bath House (1936) on Chicagon Lake in Iron County, and the Fancher Elementary School (1937–1938) in Mount Pleasant. The truth is, modern architecture designed for local materials was first introduced into Michigan through government-sponsored projects of the depression era.

In 1940, with the war already raging in Europe, William Knudsen, then president of General Motors, directed the transformation of civilian industrial production to military hardware—tanks, bombers, trucks, aircraft engines. Automobile factories were converted to wartime use and housing for workers constructed at Willow Run, Norwayne, Centerline, and elsewhere.

Albert Kahn Associates, the Ford Motor Company engineers, and the U.S. Department of Defense collaborated in building the mammoth Willow Run Bomber Plant for the manufacture of the B-24 "Liberator" bomber. The plant and a test field were constructed within eighteen months between 1941 and 1942. The complex consisted of the vast steel-frame, brick-faced factory on a concrete slab, with assembly lines and subassembly bays, completely blacked out from daylight. There was also an administration building, a hangar, and a test field.

In Superior and Ypsilanti townships, west of Ypsilanti, the Willow Run Village went up between 1942 and 1943. Designed to accommodate twelve thousand and built under the auspices of the Federal Public Housing Authority, it was intended as temporary housing for these workers at the bomber plant who had come from other parts of the country and were then living in cars, trailers, tents, and shacks. The prefabricated structures were designed by Saarinen, Swanson and Saarinen. The village itself was made up of Willow Lodge, 15 dormitories for 3,000; Willow Court, a park for 960 trailers; the Village, flat-top homes with from four to eight apartments for 2,500 families; West Court, 1,000 gabled roof buildings with apartments; and West Lodge, a large dormitory project of 15 buildings for 3,000 people. There were also a community building, a commercial area, schools, a fire department, and an infirmary.

With growing automobile congestion, the need for an improved road and transit system was apparent. In 1923 a master plan for 205-foot-wide limited-access superhighways with 84-foot-wide median strips was proposed. One interesting result of this innovative plan, which brought Detroit national attention, was the widening of all major highways. Direct road connections were made to Windsor, Ontario, located across the Detroit River, a bridge was built in 1929, and a tunnel in 1930. More radical solutions to congestion were soon needed, however, and following earlier experiments, a comprehensive system of freeways was finally proposed in 1943. Ironically, the building of one of the most efficient freeway systems in the country was to contribute to Detroit's decline; people no longer needed to live close to where they worked.

After World War II city and institutional planners and business people focused attention on slum clearance and urban renewal. Already in 1941 the development of a comprehensive master plan had begun. A year later, in Detroit, Suren Pilafian developed a campus plan for present-day Wayne State University, a plan that aided the transformation from a city-supported teacher and community college to a major state-supported urban university. At the time the school occupied old houses in the Cass Corridor and the former Central High School building, a large late-nineteenth-century Richardsonian Romanesque structure. The new plan called for new buildings arranged around open spaces. Minoru Yamasaki revised Pilafian's plan in 1954 so that it became a compact urban campus with courts linking low-rise buildings; it also had a pedestrian mall. The McGregor Memorial Conference Center, in its delicacy and warmth, is among Yamasaki's finest work in America. It opened in 1958 and was a welcome addition to an otherwise harsh city environment. Leading Detroit architects designed other buildings on the Wayne State University campus in the 1960s and 1970s.

The warehouse district on Jefferson Avenue was leveled and a long-envisioned Civic Center built in its place. The plan opened up downtown to the river front and provided Detroit with governmental, cultural, and major convention facilities, all grouped around the Philip A. Hart Plaza.

Lafayette Park provided new middle-class housing adjacent to downtown. It was initiated by the city planning commission in 1946 to entice suburbanites back to the city. The plan was to redevelop 129 acres east of the center of the city with high- and low-rise apartments and town houses. Carried out in the 1950s and 1960s, it was financed with city, federal, and private funds. While the overall plan for Lafayette Park was a collaborative effort by distinguished architects and planners, specific buildings were individually designed. Among these were Lafayette Park Pavilion Apartments and Courthouses by Mies van der Rohe and Lafayette East by Birkerts and Straub. The initiative to provide new low- and moderate-priced housing, however, did not stop with Lafayette Park. Elmwood Park, designed by Eberle M. Smith Associates, is a subsequent development and further efforts continue today. Together Lafayette Park and Elmwood Park house a downtown residential population of sixteen thousand people, a concentration that has spurred the development of restaurants, bars, and discos. In the 1950s and 1960s, an ethnic neighborhood located just west of downtown was replaced, in part, by an industrial park. Just north of downtown a plan has been implemented to develop a 250-acre medical center that integrates existing medical facilities and provides ready access to the city through its location adjacent to the freeway system.

The suburban exodus from downtown Detroit to the suburbs had resulted in an urban form characterized by a series of multifunction town centers—Fairlane, Southfield, and Troy—located in a broad circle around the city. Detroit had become a polycentric city. By 1967 it was clear that the downtown area needed revitalization. Shortly after the riots of that year, New Detroit, Incorporated, a group of the city's business people led by Henry Ford II, made plans to reconstruct the downtown river front. The result was the development of the Renaissance Center, a hotel, office, and retail megastructure. Designed by John Portman, and located downtown on the Detroit River, this ambitious project has become the symbol of Detroit's revitalization efforts. Since the Renaissance Center, there have been other successful initiatives, both public and private, to develop the downtown area into an attractive residential, commercial, and entertainment area. A powerful unifying factor has been the People Mover, a nearly three-mile elevated and automated transit system that opened in 1987. City government anticipates that the stations along its path will stimulate new development.

The city's desire to redevelop the site of the former J. L. Hudson Company Department Store and its surroundings into the Cadillac Square Mall did not get past the planning stage. In another project, however, city planners succeeded in clearing the site of the Dodge Main and the Poletown neighborhood, to enable General Motors to rebuild a state-of-the-art plant for the manufacture of Cadillac automobiles. Although it displaced hundreds of families in the process, it also created new jobs for other Detroiters.

Because automobile companies preferred to have their corporate headquarters near their plants, downtown Detroit never attained the high density of commercial centers reached in such cities as New York and Chicago. Even in the 1950s the Ford Motor Company chose to build its new world headquarters by Skidmore, Owings and Merrill in suburban Dearborn, and General Motors located its new technical center in Warren, where Eero Saarinen created a new architectural complex to serve and celebrate the automotive age. Banks and other companies, however, remained downtown, some out of necessity. While efforts have been made to revitalize retail shopping in the downtown area, the closure of the J. L. Hudson Company in 1982 left Detroit with no major downtown department store.

The city of Detroit has acquired substantial real estate between the Renaissance Center and the Belle Isle Bridge, 3.5 miles to the east. Here, to keep redevelopment of the river front in balance, the city is creating a system of parks. These green spaces have not only beautified the area but have also encouraged similar private development. Among the successful undertakings is the new Stroh River Place, formerly the Parke-Davis Pharmaceutical Company's industrial complex, which is a model of adaptive reuse that mixes residential, retail, and office functions. By contrast, Harbortown, which is located next door, is a totally new, self-contained development, complete with security gate. Its architecture does not allude to the area's industrial past. In other, more recent developments, however, there are efforts to incorporate new structures with the old, thus bonding the present to the past, as the city looks forward to the future. There is no doubt that the lure of the river, in combination with commitment and investment, make certain that downtown Detroit will remain a vital part of the larger metropolitan area.

Efforts to restore and rehabilitate other sections of the city have resulted in the creation of historic districts such as West Canfield, Indian Village, and Woodbridge. Other initiatives include General Motors Corporation's successful attempt to rehabilitate a midtown neighborhood, known as New Commons. Eastern Market, Detroit's only surviving public market, continues to serve the community. In light of Detroit's declining population, there is some question as to whether the city will be able to acquire the necessary resources to develop and rehabilitate the vast uncared-for areas that remain. Hope remains high, nevertheless, because civic pride is strong, because Detroit remains the center of one of the nation's major industries, and because its location on the Detroit River between the Lower and Upper Great Lakes is unbeatable.

Resorts

The hundreds of miles of wild shoreline, rivers, and inland lakes in Michigan became the setting for some truly exciting resort architecture that in many ways is unique to the state. At the same time, however, it is symptomatic of a growing trend in late nineteenth-century America to seek out and enjoy the natural wonders of this rich and varied land.

Resort life required special architectural forms, and resort architecture became a distinctive building type in vacation communities. The type included hotels and boardinghouses, cottages, villas, boat houses, clubhouses, and casinos. Most had large verandas for people to enjoy the outdoors without exposure to the elements and combined the rusticity suitable to informal vacation life with the comfort required by those accustomed to the conveniences of city life. It reached its heyday between 1890 and 1910 when the summer cottage, hotel, and clubhouse took the form of an open, spacious, and comfortable domestic building, frequently designed by an architect and built of indigenous materials in the Queen Anne, Shingle, or Colonial Revival style.

Because of Detroit's location on a strait between the upper and lower lakes, the area around the city, from the outset, became a delightful recreational center for Detroiters. Early residents of the city enjoyed the opportunity to experience the beautiful, broad Detroit River for boating, rowing, steam excursions, fishing, duck hunting, skating, and picnicking. These recreational pursuits in this natural environment led to the development of splendid resort architecture, with many excellent examples of Queen Anne and Shingle style boat clubs, fishing and shooting clubs, summer houses, hotels, park pavilions, and casinos. Unfortunately, for the most part these buildings are no longer standing. They were erected up the river at Belle Isle, Lake Saint Clair, the Saint Clair Flats, the village of Saint Clair, and Port Huron; and downriver at Grosse Ile and Wyandotte and at Amherstburg and Put-in-Bay, Ontario. They were later, and even simultaneously, duplicated at other lakeside locations reached by steamers and trains throughout Michigan.

A boat club, country club, summer house, and hunting and shooting club exemplify the many superb early resort buildings in the Detroit area. The Detroit Boat Club, organized by Edmund A. Brush in 1839, for example, was the first of its kind in America. Its original boat house was located in a slip on the river front near the foot of Brush Street. The building burned in 1848, but it was replaced with a series of others, increasingly larger in size; in 1891, the club erected another on Belle Isle. When it burned in 1893, it was replaced with a large festive Shingle style structure. Designed by Donaldson and Meier, the huge rectangular hipped-roof boat club displayed an impressive assemblage of verandas, dormers, gables, and conical towers. It stood on a dock, and boats were stored in the lower level with social rooms above. From its sheltered but open verandas and balconies, spectators could observe in comfort the regattas on the river. The present Neo-Spanish boat house, built in 1902 to the plans of Alpheus Chittenden, replaces the 1894 structure.

Up the river at Belle Isle, the city constructed casinos, pavilions, and park buildings on grounds landscaped by Frederick Law Olmsted. On the western end of the island was the shingle-clad casino designed by Donaldson and Meier. It was built in 1884. On all three stories, spacious, covered verandas faced the water and an observation tower rose from the center of the structure giving visitors broad views of the river. Mason and Rice designed a Richardsonian police station for the park. Built in 1894, its indigenous wood and fieldstone exterior walls were appropriate to its natural surroundings. Detroiters enjoyed the park year around. These recreational buildings are evidence of the flowering of resort architecture in the hands of Detroit architects.

Washed by the clear blue waters of Lake Saint Clair, Grosse Pointe became a summer colony known for its Queen Anne and Shingle style cottages and for its distinguished wooden clubhouse. The Grosse Pointe Club, later reorganized as the Country Club of Detroit, was founded in 1884. Two years later it erected a clubhouse on a seven-acre site on the point where the lake and the river meet. It was a large, gabled Shingle style building designed by William E. Brown. At the northeast corner a huge round tower rose to an open 30-foot circular belvedere; from beneath its conical, umbrella-like roof, members could see as far as 15 miles across Lake Saint Clair. A veranda 16 feet wide extended around the north, east, and south sides, forming both a lounge and a promenade. Not far from this expansive clubhouse were a number of summer cottages. One of the most elegant was the John S. Newberry House, a Queen Anne house with Eastlake decoration. Erected at Lake Terrace in 1875, it was later transformed by the addition of a square tower and porte-cochère; it was also covered with shingles.

One of the finest examples of the Shingle style in the Detroit area was the Lake Saint Clair Fishing and Shooting Club. Although organized in 1872, it was not until the mid-1880s, at the north end of Saint Clair Flats Canal, that the club constructed a clubhouse. The large wooden building had a twelve-sided tower at one corner. Resting on pilings at the very edge of the river's main channel, it had a broad porch, banks of windows, and sloping roofs. The body of the clubhouse was smoothly clad in shingles. The designer was the firm of Rogers and MacFarlane. It burned in 1924. Many resort buildings on the

Saint Clair Shooting and Fishing Club, 1886, destroyed 1924, Rogers and MacFarlane, Saint Clair Flats Canal, St. Clair County, historic photo between 1900 and 1920. A piazza wrapped around three sides of the L-shaped Shingle style clubhouse. This was linked by bridges to the boat houses and to the steamboat dock. A belvedere sheltered by a conical roof offered views of the water. The twelve-sided tower room beneath had a huge open fireplace.

Detroit River and the Great Lakes shoreline resembled those built in the mountains and on the seashore in New England and New York State.

The Great Lakes provided a ready-made transportation system for ferry trips and excursions that linked Detroit with other shoreline communities and islands. Detroit also became a gathering center for vacationers from the East and the South. It was a point of embarkation for daily and even longer lake and river trips on excursion steamers. At the same time, many popular, healthful, and beautiful resorts were within easy reach of the city by boat or by train. In the 1870s, steam navigation and railroad companies took full advantage of this lucrative tourist potential. They speculated in resort hotels, provided transportation for city dwellers to remote resort centers, and advertised in published travel guides both their accommodations and passenger service. Typically, resort centers thrived where scenic beauty, a pleasant climate, and a historical past conjoined. They were often at those small lumbering, fishing, and shipping communities that had developed around natural harbors where streams ran into the big lakes. The supreme achievement of these resort establishments

Log cottage near Hotel Lake Gogebic, Gogebic County, historic photo between 1900 and 1910. The walls of the gabled cottage on the shore of Lake Gogebic are log, laid horizontally with interlocking joints in the lower half and vertically above. Log vacation cottages like this one are found in the woods and along the lakeshores and riverbanks of northern Michigan.

remains without contest the fantastic Grand Hotel on Mackinac Island. Designed by Mason and Rice, it was built in 1886 by three transportation companies. Its commodious veranda, which extends the entire length of the building, takes full advantage of its unrivaled location above the Straits of Mackinac.

Government, transportation companies, chambers of commerce, and newspapers promoted these resort centers. Railroad commissioners and the State Board of Health offered information on the summer resorts around the shores of both the Great Lakes and the inland lakes. The board of health published a directory of some 125 summer and health resorts, mineral springs, and sanitaria, giving railroad and steamboat connections and hotels at each. In *A Guide to the Health, Pleasure and Fishing Resorts of Northern Michigan, Reached by the Grand Rapids and Indiana Railroad* (1879, 1882), the Grand Rapids and Indiana

Railroad (dubbing itself the "Fishing Line"), outlined the resorts of the Traverse Region—both the Grand Traverse Bay area including Omena, Northport, Old Mission, and Elk Rapids; and Little Traverse Bay mentioning Charlevoix, Bay View, and Harbor Springs. In *The City of Detroit and Resorts of Northern Michigan* (1883) the Detroit, Lansing and Northern Railroad presented a guide to the city and to resorts reached by the railroad. It told of the resorts of nearby interior lakes—Lake Orion and Orchard and Walled lakes; the inland waterway—Conway Springs, Crooked Lake, Burt Lake, Indian River, Mullet Lake, Cheboygan; Mackinac Island; Marquette. James Gale Inglis's *Northern Michigan Handbook for Travelers including the Northern Part of Lower Michigan, Mackinac Island and the Sault Ste. Marie River, with Maps and Illustrations* (Petoskey, 1898) listed routes north by rail and steamer, giving the names, locations, and characteristics of the resorts. These promotional publications contributed to the settlement and popularity of resort centers and were also a factor in the development of resort architecture itself.

At many charming and pleasant lakeshore fishing, lumbering, and shipping villages, corporations established resort associations and plotted subdivision-like resort communities. Sometimes people from the same town or church established resort associations, using land either purchased cheaply, donated by the adjacent town, or financed by the railroad. Cottages built on this land made it possible for people with common interests to live in a homogeneous community. The Harbor Point Resort, for example, originally named the Lansing Resort, was organized in 1878 by a group from Lansing. These people had at first camped out at the site but later formed a stock company, sold shares to nineteen members, and then purchased the point of land from Father Weicamp of Cross Village. By 1910 there were eight such resort associations in the Harbor Springs vicinity of the Little Traverse Region alone, some divided into as many as two hundred lots.

The number and variety of these associations was considerable: there were the Methodist Episcopal Camp Meeting Ground at Bay View and the Chicago Club at Charlevoix; others were formed at Pointe Aux Barques, Northport Point, Epworth Heights, Les Cheneaux Islands, and Macatawa Park. Even the Northern Hay Fever Association established a resort. It was built between 1883 and 1884 at Topinabee on the Michigan Central Railroad line.

Once the grounds had been cleared, lots plotted, and roads laid, the association usually built a hotel or assembly hall. Then individual members, sometimes after living in tents at the outset, erected picturesque wooden cottages. Frequently they resembled a version of the Queen Anne with Stick style and Eastlake decoration and had dormers, towers, belvederes, and verandas. By the late 1880s large elaborate wooden and shingled cottages appeared on Mackinac Island and at Harbor Springs and Charlevoix. Some were brand new constructions; others had been transformed from earlier simpler cottages. Many were designed by architects.

Architects and builders gravitated to the resort communities to participate in the building rush that took place between 1880 and 1910. Earl H. Mead, for example, after working for three years in Lansing, followed those of his clients who summered at the Lansing Resort (now Harbor Point), and in 1898 opened a permanent office there, all within two years after he first designed a cottage at the Lansing Resort. Over the next thirty years Mead planned hundreds of summer cottages, clubhouses, and other resort buildings in the Little Traverse Bay region. In some of his commissions he remodeled simple first-generation wooden structures into Shingle style and Colonial Revival buildings. His designs were generally rectangular in shape with mountainous roofs and were wooden frames sheathed with clapboard and shingles. Another architect who came to Harbor Springs was Charles Caskey. He made his move after designing cottages at the Presbyterian Resort, present-day Wequetonsing, which was founded in 1877 by people from Allegan. Steeped in the rich wood building tradition of Allegan, a lumbering center on the Kalamazoo River, Caskey created dozens of wooden cottages with large porches at Wequetonsing and on Mackinac Island. Other architects were Darius Moon, a Lansing architect-builder who planned cottages at Bay View and Harbor Springs, and Asbury W. Buckley of Kalamazoo and later Chicago who designed many of the cottages on Mackinac Island. The work of these men, and others like them, contributed substantially to a lively regional resort architecture.

The cottages and summer houses that made up the organized resort centers were not the only residential architecture that would characterize recreational Michigan. There were also the hotels. Indeed, boardinghouses were the first to make their appearance, to be followed quickly by hotels. Many who later built cottages and summer houses stayed at these facilities on their early trips into the recreational areas. As early as 1842 families from southern Michigan and states lying to the south began making their way to Mackinac Island. Each succeeding year more tourists came, and old buildings were remodeled to accommodate them. One of the first to do this was E. A. Franks, who purchased a house formerly used as a home for Indian children and, in 1850, converted it to a hotel; two years later, Charles O. Malley opened the Island House. By the early 1860s the island became even more accessible when the railroads extended their lines to both sides of the Straits and the steamship companies increased the number of steamer arrivals. To meet the increasing influx of vacationers, new hotels, boardinghouses, and cottages went up until, finally, with the construction of the Grand Hotel in 1886, Mackinac Island became one of the most famous resorts in America. Westward through the Straits, and to the south on the west arm of Grand Traverse Bay at Traverse City, the Park Place Hotel was built in 1873. Owned by Hannah, Lay and Company, it was a large, three-story, towered Italianate structure with two-story veranda and connected by a bridge to an earlier structure. A contemporary account describes it as having "large, airy, well-lighted rooms, well-furnished and supplied with all

the necessary conveniences, very broad corridors furnishing splendid prome-
nades." In Petoskey, on the northwest coast, between Traverse City and the
Straits, there were several hotels: the Arlington Hotel was a large frame building with a mansard roof and a two-story wrap-around veranda; the comfortable Clifton House, situated near the railroad depot; and the towered Cush-
man House to which was later added a giant rounded and balustraded Ionic
portico. At Harbor Point the Harbor Point Association erected a "commodious
and elegant" hotel in 1896. Again, a contemporary description tells us what
was expected of a resort hotel at that time:

> The architecture . . . is suggestive of comfort and luxury rather than any
> attempt at vain display. Wide verandas unite with the virgin forest trees in
> sheltering guests from anything like the direct rays of the summer sun. The
> offices, reception room, ladies parlors, dining rooms, and halls are all large,
> airy, well-lighted and beautifully finished in native woods. The great stone
> fireplace in the general reception room and the grates in the ladies parlor
> and offices are all suggestive of delightful evenings when the crisp air of
> Lake Michigan shall assemble the guests around the crackling wood fires.
> . . . Being provided with telegraph and telephone service the club house
> offers every facility for guests who wish to communicate with the outside
> world. Billiard rooms, bowling alleys, and ball rooms furnish facilities for
> the lovers of amusement with the means of diversion. The entire building
> is lighted by gas and furnished with everything which can add to the com-
> fort and convenience of its guests.[2]

Resort centers also developed around the sources of mineral waters that were
alleged to have medicinal curing powers. In Saint Louis, at the very center of
Lower Michigan, magnetic springs of this kind were discovered in 1869. A park
was landscaped, a bathhouse was erected, and the "world-renowned St. Louis
Magnetic Mineral Water" was piped in. Invalids and summer visitors, solicited
largely through advertisements, arrived by railroad and filled the limited accommodations to overflowing. Private houses were quickly turned into boardinghouses, and new boardinghouses and hotels were built. The largest and
most famous was the Park House Hotel and Sanitarium, built in 1881. Located
adjacent to the park and bathhouse, it was a three-story structure with a large
wrap-around veranda supported by bracketed and clustered piers.

The mineral springs at Grand Haven were sufficiently promising to encourage the hope that the site could become the "Saratoga of the West," and in
1872, to capitalize on the floods of visitors, Dwight C. Cutler opened the palatial mansard-roofed Cutler House. At about the same time, first-class hotels for
invalids and resorters were built at nearby Fruitport and Spring Lake.

Michigan's most famous mineral springs resort was Mount Clemens, just north
of Detroit. It had ten bathhouses, each with its own wells, and, by 1915,
seventy-two hotels and boardinghouses had been built there. Among the most
elaborate was the Park Hotel and Baths. This large Beaux-Arts Classical struc-

ture with a two-story Ionic porch was surrounded with private gardens. Important also was the large Medea Hotel and Bath House, a brick and sandstone Richardsonian structure erected in 1882 on Gratiot Avenue. Altered in 1891, added to in 1904, it was demolished in 1990. The designer for the original structure was N. J. Gibbs; for the remodeling and additions, Theophilus Van Damme. An arcaded piazza of Lake Superior red sandstone ran the length of the front of the four-story building.

While all this was going on in Lower Michigan, an undertaking of a different kind was attempted in Marquette, on the northern shores of the Upper Peninsula. In 1892, a group of Detroit area physicians and prominent Marquette citizens organized the Marquette Lake Superior Hotel-Sanitarium Association. Together they financed the construction of a sprawling 325–room resort hotel and sanitarium, designed by Elijah E. Myers, and built in Mountain Park in Marquette. The serene setting provided a sweeping view of the lake and was steeped in the sharp pure air of the north country. This, together with the walking trails and the many modern facilities provided by the hotel and sanitarium, encouraged its promoters to hope that it would become a major retreat for invalids and resorters alike. But such was not to be. The location was too remote and the summer season too short to make the project feasible, and before long it failed. The hotel itself, however, survived until 1929, when it was demolished. It was an impressive sight. Constructed of variegated Marquette brown sandstone on the lower stories and shingles above, its picturesque assortment of wings, towers, and piazzas animated the surrounding countryside at the same time that its naturally textured walls united building and landscape in harmonious accord.

While lakeshore communities and islands proved to be a natural setting for some vigorous high-style resort buildings, Michigan's back woods, with their inland lakes and riverbanks, offered an equally suitable location for several wilderness camps and hundreds of examples of rustic log architecture. Though on a smaller scale, many of the camps and hunting and fishing lodges were conceived in terms similar to Camp Uncas and Sagamore Lodge in the Adirondacks.

Among the early efforts was that of Gilbert Stark and other Saginaw and Bay City people when in 1877 they established Cottage Grove, one of three private resort associations on Higgins Lake. They chose an old logging site amidst a virgin forest of Norway and white pine spared by the lumber barons, where they built stained wooden cottages and cabins and a common dining hall.

In general, the wilderness camp was an isolated, rustic but comfortable, self-sufficient complex where people of wealth could escape urban life. A prime Michigan example is White Deer Lake Camp, built over a period of time by Cyrus H. McCormick, the founder of International Harvester Corporation and the son of the inventor of the mechanical reaper. His first acquisition of land was in 1904, when he purchased 150 acres of dense forest and rugged rock bluffs on White Deer Lake in the western Upper Peninsula. His first camp building, which he located on an island in the lake, was a small single-room gabled structure (Library Cabin) with a stone fireplace and a porch. It was constructed of horizontal logs. Soon a main lodge for entertaining guests was erected. It was a two-story, hipped-roof structure (Chimney Cabin) with a two-story balcony overlooking the lake. Its walls were of horizontal and vertical logs. A large granite fireplace and chimney rose through the center of the house and opened in the living room. Eventually McCormick acquired 17,000 acres with sixteen lakes, and White Deer Lake Camp, built for the most part between 1904 and 1964, grew to a complex of five cabins on an island and several other buildings, including the boat house, caretaker's cabin, dining hall, and servants' quarters, all on the mainland. In 1969 Gordon McCormick donated the 17,000-acre site to the Ottawa National Forest, and in the mid-1980s the buildings were either disassembled and moved off the site or demolished.

Later, in 1920, a group of Detroit industrialists—Harold H. Emmons, Edwin G. George, Sidney D. Waldon, and Frank F. Beall—established the Black River Ranch, an exclusive hunting and fishing camp on over 6,000 acres southwest of Onaway in Montmorency County. They reforested the land, farmed, raised livestock, and conserved wildlife. In 1922, H. Augustus O'Dell, a member of both the corporation and of the architectural firm O'Dell, Hewlett and Luckenbach, drafted plans for the main lodge. Overlooking Silver Lake, the large, two-story, hipped-roof rustic log structure with shed-roof dormers is clad with shingles on the upper story. A balcony encircles the two-story living room, which is fitted with a large welcoming fieldstone chimney and fireplace. Individual bedrooms for each member flank the living area. The ranch now has its own private jet landing strip.

Many modest rustic log camps and cabins line the Au Sable River and other rivers, Lake Gogebic, and other lakes. On a smaller scale are the tiny cottages and the rustic log and synthetic log houses for permanent and seasonal residents of northern Michigan. In the 1920s Earl Mead designed for the Ottawa Lumber Company at Harbor Springs a series of small summer cottages that could be constructed inexpensively. Otsego Log Homes and Great Lakes Logs are other manufacturers of log homes.

After World War I, the character of resort life changed. Automobile transportation and the construction of good roads opened new areas to development and democratized resorting. Cottages were built along lakeshore highways instead of being confined to areas near boat docks and railroad stations, and tourist cabins were built along the highways themselves. Then, too, changing economic and social conditions would no longer support the expensive and elaborate turn-of-the-century life-style. Even so, in at least one instance the image of the rustic log resort has survived until recently to enhance a modern highway. Frank Johnson's ten-room family home was located on the sandy shore of Houghton Lake, the state's largest inland body of water. But the site is also on Michigan 55, the highway that skirts the southeastern shore of the lake. Johnson transformed the original house into a large resort hotel that had walls of interlocking horizontal logs, a gabled center section supported by fieldstone piers, and a huge fieldstone fireplace. Eventually Johnson's Resort was expanded into a rustic log complex with twelve cabins, a tavern, two-hundred-seat dining room, a dance palace, and a fifty-five-unit motel. Known as Johnson's Rustic Village, its multiservice complex and its rustic structural fabric are clearly a deliberate evocation of an exciting episode in Michigan's architectural past.

As the tourist industry burgeoned in response to the automobile, prefabricated cottages, repetitious campsites, condominiums, and franchised motels outnumbered individually designed resort buildings. There were some isolated exceptions, such as the James Douglas House at Harbor Springs, designed by Richard Meier after Le Corbusier's geometric forms; the Amy Alpaugh House (1947), by Frank Lloyd Wright, on a hilltop overlooking Lake Michigan and Grand Traverse Bay north of Northport, and the playful, one-of-a-kind cottages built by Chicagoans at Lakeside, Union Pier, and New Buffalo. For the most part, however, resort architecture in the postwar period displays a mundane uniformity not found previously. Cottage and home owners continue to group together in subdivisions such as L'Arbre Croche and Birchwood Farm Estates, both in the Harbor Springs vicinity, and in developments such as the Homestead and Grand Traverse Resort in the Grand Traverse Bay area.

One such development near Lewiston began in 1952 with a nine-hole golf course built by Detroit stove manufacturer Herman Otto. Another course, of eighteen holes, was soon added, as was a chalet-style lodge. The latter burned in 1985. Otto's son, Ron, rebuilt Garland (named for the family's Garland Stove Company) of butterscotch spruce and lodge-pole pine. It has cathedral ceilings, Italian marble floors, stained glass windows, hand-carved wood doors, Michigan oak woodwork, soaring fieldstone fireplaces, and mounted wildlife. Recently, Thomas S. Monaghan has built a vacation complex on Drummond Island. Designed by Charles Moore and Gunnar Birkerts, the wooden and corrugated metal-sheathed buildings are inspired in part by Michigan's vernacular wood and resort building traditions, distinctive high points in Michigan's architecture.

Ethnic Groups

Many ethnic groups were attracted to Michigan, and each made its contribution to the architecture of the state. Attracted by fertile land, good transportation systems, and rapidly developing mining, lumbering, and manufacturing, diverse European groups arrived in the state between 1837 and 1914. They came from

Cornwall, Ireland, and Germany, and later from Finland, Poland, Austria, and Italy to furnish the labor force in the mineral ranges. These immigrants lived in simple wood company houses constructed by the mining engineers, but they built their own ethnic churches, social halls, saloons, commercial blocks, and schools, all of which retained the patterns and traditions of their respective homelands. Then there were the Irish, who came to Wayne, Houghton, Marquette, and Kent counties as laborers and farmers; the Dutch settled in Holland, Allegan, Kalamazoo, and elsewhere in western Michigan; the Poles made their way to the sugar beet fields of the Thumb and to the potato fields of Alpena County, and later to the automobile factories of Detroit and Hamtramck. Slovenians, Yugoslavs, and Scandinavians also represented significant immigrant groups.

The immigrant builders brought their own decorative and structural traditions, including *Fachwerk*, patterned brickwork, log, and other building methods. They were also motivated by an urgent desire to create structures that resembled those of their homeland. In fact, so powerful was their nostalgia that foreign-born clients sought out their countrymen to serve as architects for their major works, whether or not the designers resided in the state. Francis G. Himpler of New York, for example, built for German parishioners a Roman Catholic church in Detroit that resembled the *Hallenkirchen* of northern Germany. Gordon W. Lloyd of Windsor, Ontario, a master of the Anglican taste, designed churches for Episcopal congregations throughout the state; and Erhard Breilmeier of Milwaukee designed Roman Catholic churches for German- and Polish-speaking parishes. The rich diversity of ideas introduced by these many ethnic groups not only enlivened the architecture of Michigan but also reinforced the grand diversity of that of the nation as a whole.

The church was the most common type of building to receive the distinct mark of the immigrant groups. The Eglise Saint Joseph in Lake Linden was designed by C. Archibald Pearce for French Canadian millworkers. Begun in 1900, and built of red sandstone, this "Roman Byzantine" church may be the best example in Michigan of that immigrant group's architecture. The Irish, too, made their contribution: in 1866 they built Most Holy Trinity in Detroit; and in Parnell, in 1877, Irish laborers, who came to dig a canal on the Grand River, built Saint Patrick's Catholic Church to the plans of Robinson and Barnaby.

The architectural contribution of the many ethnic groups was not confined to churches. They left their stamp also on such building types as houses, farms, schools, social halls for fraternal societies, cemeteries, even fishing villages.

(Opposite) Michigan State Capitol, 1873–1879, Elijah Myers. Interior, House Chamber. Under the Capitol Oversight Committee of the Michigan governor and legislature, the House Chamber of the Michigan State Capitol has been restored to its High Victorian glory, including the richly colored decorative interior painting and woodgraining.

A German musical association, organized in 1849 and incorporated in 1851, erected in 1874–1875 the large Harmonie Hall at the southwest corner of Lafayette and Beaubien streets in Detroit. The Dutch in Holland left four open squares in the center of the city, all intended for the conduct of the town's business. They also built Voorhees Hall at Hope College, using stepped gables and patterned brickwork. The Suomi Synod of the Finnish Lutheran Church built in 1900 in Hancock the red sandstone Richardsonian college and seminary. It was designed by C. Archibald Pearce. Known today as Suomi College, the building served as the headquarters of an institution established to preserve Finnish religion, heritage, and culture and to minister to the Finnish American congregations across the United States. Finns established a fishing village at Big Traverse and farmsteads in Houghton County, and a sauna was conspicuous behind each house.

The impact of ethnic groups continues to the present, with African-Americans, Hispanics, Arabs, and Asians in the twentieth century establishing their own significant presence on existing buildings by adapting them for their reuse. These groups will no doubt soon have greater representation among professional architects.

Historic Preservation

The historic preservation movement in Michigan has been a positive force in shaping the state's architectural profile. No longer concerned solely with preserving the major landmarks, historic district commissions acting under local historic district ordinances are now reaching out to safeguard historic buildings and districts in cities, townships, and villages throughout the state. Individuals and private corporations, institutions and governments have identified, protected, restored, and rehabilitated a broad range of historic buildings, and their preservation has enhanced the public understanding of both the richness and the diversity of the state's architectural legacy. As of 1991, Michigan has more than 1,300 listings in the National Register of Historic Places, including single properties as well as districts containing hundreds of buildings. Between 1981 and 1991, 377 projects were certified to receive federal tax credits, a private investment of $503 million in historic buildings. Private individuals and corporations using tax credits have undertaken large and small rehabilitation projects. Among the most spectacular is Michael Ilitch's restoration in 1988 of the exotic and sumptuous Fox Theatre in Detroit. Governments at all levels and private nonprofit organizations are also restoring buildings. The most monumental project is the restoration of the Michigan State Capitol, launched in 1990 under the sponsorship of the joint legislative and executive committee, the Michigan Capitol Committee. Equally important to a particular region is the Chippewa County Commissioner's restoration of the Chippewa County Courthouse, completed in 1989.

The architecture of Michigan is an open and profusely illustrated book that tells with simplicity and warmth the compelling story of the state, its land, and its people. Rooted in the wilderness, shaped in the dreams of dauntless men and women on the move, textured by human action, it is a story easily read by anyone who is willing to take the time to visit the buildings themselves and to examine them with unbiased curiosity.

THE LOWER PENINSULA

Metropolis

Opening remarks about Detroit's industrial character are by Charles K. Hyde.

DETROIT BECAME THE PREMIER AMERICAN INDUSTRIAL CITY in the twentieth century, due mainly to its meteoric rise as the center of automobile production. Before it became the Motor City, Detroit had considerable success as a manufacturing center with a diverse industrial base. Population jumped from about forty-six thousand in 1860 to nearly two hundred eighty-six thousand by 1900, with growth based on expanding industrial employment. Around 1880, the most important industries were iron and steel, tobacco products, foundries, machine shops, meat packing, flour milling, boots and shoes, and men's clothing. During the last two decades of the nineteenth century, Detroit became the largest producer of heating and cooking stoves in the United States, as well as a major center for shipbuilding, cigar manufacturing, and the production of pharmaceuticals. Other major manufactured products included railroad cars, paints and varnishes, foundry and machine shop products, and beer.

Detroit industry in the nineteenth century was situated on or near the Detroit River, along a narrow band extending about 3 miles east and west from Woodward Avenue. Few of the industrial buildings of this pre-automotive era remain. The Parke-Davis and Company complex on the Detroit River and the Frederick Stearns and Company buildings survive from the pharmaceutical industry, but almost no manufacturing plants from the stove industry, paint and varnish industries, tobacco products, or shipbuilding industries are extant.

In the early twentieth century, Detroit quickly became the Motor City, and the success of the automobile industry, with its high wages and enormous need for labor, contributed to the departure of other industries from Detroit. Ransom E. Olds opened the first Detroit automobile factory in 1899 on East Jefferson Avenue, near Belle Isle. In a very short time, Detroit became the home

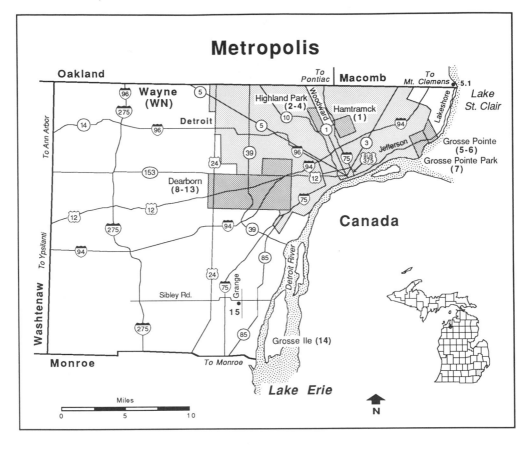

Metropolis

of Cadillac (1902), Ford (1903), Packard (1903), Chalmers (1907), and other automobiles. At the same time, several large independent body manufacturers built factories in Detroit, including the C. R. Wilson Body Company, the Murray Body Company, the Briggs Manufacturing Company, and the Fisher Body Company. Although General Motors has not been Detroit-based, with the exception of its Cadillac Division, the Ford Motor Company and the Chrysler Corporation were Detroit-centered. Throughout the 1910s and the 1920s, Ford was the dominant firm in the industry.

Automobile production in Detroit, well under 20,000 vehicles in 1904, reached one million by 1917, with Ford accounting for 700,000 of these. The explosive growth of the automobile industry during the early twentieth century made Detroit an industrial boomtown. The combined populations of Detroit, Highland Park, and Hamtramck jumped from about 300,000 in 1900 to over one million in 1920 and then to 1.6 million in 1930. The Detroit of 1900 included 23 square miles of territory located along the Detroit River, but extended only about 2 miles inland. The city reached its current boundaries by 1927, with a total area of 139 square miles.

In the late nineteenth century, Detroit was a medium-sized industrial city with a large number of factories, few of them particularly large or architecturally distinctive. The substantial manufacturing complexes such as Parke-Davis and Company or the Michigan Stove Company works consisted of several buildings of standard multistory New England mill design, with masonry bearing walls and extensive use of wooden or cast-iron columns. In the twentieth century, large, integrated automobile manufacturing complexes, with enormous multistory reinforced concrete factory buildings, have dominated Detroit's industrial landscape. Beginning with the Ford Rouge plant, the monumental single-story, steel-framed industrial building encased in glass became the new expression of modern industrial architecture. The new factory designs, while not unique to Detroit, were carried to their logical extreme in the Motor City and had their greatest cumulative impact on the built environment. Detroit produced new industrial architecture as well as automobiles in the twentieth century.

Albert Kahn was both the innovator and advocate of new factory architecture for the automobile industry, and he worked closely with the great automotive innovator, Henry Ford. The peculiar needs of the automobile manufacturers perhaps made innovation inevitable. They required multistory factory buildings that could bear the great weights of machinery and product, could rely heavily on natural lighting, and could be erected quickly and economically. Traditional New England mill designs were simply not adequate. Kahn experimented with reinforced concrete at Packard Building Number 10 (1905), then followed with the Chalmers Plant (1907), the first segments of Dodge Main (1910, demolished 1980–1981), and the stunning success of the Ford Highland Park complex in 1910. The designers of other major automobile plants followed Kahn's lead, readily seen in the later segments of Dodge Main (after 1914), the Uniroyal Plant (1905–1925), the Cadillac Clark Street complex (1921), and dozens of smaller factory complexes and individual buildings.

Remarkably, Kahn and Henry Ford abandoned the new factory design almost as soon as they put it into service. When Ford began to develop his property along the Rouge River in Dearborn, Kahn executed his first sprawling steel and glass industrial building there, the "B" Building, in 1917. Over the next twenty years, Kahn designed more than two dozen major new buildings for the River Rouge complex, all utilizing some variation of the same design. By replacing the multistory plant with single-story steel and glass buildings, Kahn increased the spaces between columns substantially, improved ventilation and lighting enormously, and eliminated all the vertical movements of parts and raw materials, a bane of the multistory factory.

Detroit's architectural landscape clearly reflects its industrial past and present, as well as the impact of the automobile as the primary mode of transportation. A small central business district perched on the Detroit River is flanked by two narrow bands of nineteenth-century industrial growth. Pre-automotive Detroit extended about three miles north, east, and west from the point where Woodward Avenue meets the Detroit River. Beyond those boundaries, the city is a collection of large zones of industrial growth or residential development that mushroomed during the first three decades of this century. Woodward Avenue is Detroit's single unifying spine of retail establishments, commercial buildings, churches, and public institutions.

The river front area extending about 2.5 miles east of Woodward Avenue to Belle Isle was the location of most of Detroit's industry in the nineteenth century. An extensive collection of machine shop and foundry buildings begins just east of the Renaissance Center. The Parke-Davis complex still stands about a mile west of Belle Isle, as does the Stearns pharmaceutical plant at 6533 East Jefferson Avenue, but the industrial character of this district is fast disappearing. All of the industrial buildings between the Parke-Davis complex and Belle Isle have been demolished since 1980, including the Uniroyal complex, metal fabricating plants, and warehouses. This area will soon be primarily commercial and residential in character, a vast change from the past.

Farther east on Jefferson Avenue, close to the riverfront, the next industrial buildings are found about 5 miles from Woodward Avenue. This industrial district extends north for about 3 miles along Conner Avenue. Known as the Conner Industrial Corridor, this conglomeration of factories developed along the line of the Detroit Terminal Railroad, which serves as the spine of this industrial district. The great bulk of the surviving buildings date from the early twentieth century, and most are directly related to the automobile industry. Beginning at the Detroit River and extending northward, this district includes the Detroit Edison Connors Creek Generating Station (1914–1950); the Chrysler Jefferson Avenue complex (1907–1933); the Budd Corporation plant (1919–1937); and the nearby Chrysler Mack Avenue plant (c. 1915). Other significant manufacturers previously located in the corridor include Briggs Manufacturing, Timken Gear and Axle, the Hudson Motor Car Company, and the Chalmers Motor Car Company. This industrial district will soon undergo major changes, with the demolition of the Chrysler Jefferson Avenue plant underway in 1991 and the construction of a new replacement facility.

The greatest concentration of twentieth-century Detroit industry was in the Milwaukee Junction Industrial District, which surrounds the city's major junction of railroad lines. It is called the Milwaukee Junction because it was originally the intersection of the Detroit and Milwaukee Railroad with the Michigan Central Railroad. Broadly defined, the district is bounded by Woodward Avenue on the west, Warren Avenue on the south, Van Dyke on the east, and McNichols on the north. This area contained many of the auto industry's pioneer plants, such as Ford Piquette Avenue (1904), Cadillac Amsterdam Street (1905), and the earliest plants of the Fisher Body Company. Three of the largest integrated plants were erected there, namely Ford Highland Park, Dodge Brothers' "Dodge Main," and Packard Motor Car Company. Other auto manufacturers, including E-M-F, Studebaker, and Hupp located in this area, along with the major automobile body companies, including Briggs, Murray, Fisher, and Wilson. The Chrysler Corporation also built the last major new automobile factory in Detroit, the Plymouth Lynch Road Plant, in this district. The Dodge Main and Hupp plants were demolished in 1980–1981 along with part of the residential area known as "Poletown," to make way for a new General Motors assembly plant, but the rest of the district has maintained its essential industrial character.

Detroit's river frontage extending west of Woodward Avenue has never had the density of industry found east of Woodward. This area is covered extensively with railroad yards, docks, and warehouses. An area of heavy industry, including blast furnaces, chemical plants, refineries, and salt mines, begins at a point about four miles west of downtown and extends downriver to Wyandotte. The Fisher Body Fleetwood plant and related factories on Fort Street and the Ford Rouge complex are the major manufacturing facilities in this area. Detroit's west side has served primarily as a residential area. The sprawling Cadillac Clark Street Plant (1921), the Lincoln Motor Car Company Plant (1917–1939) on Warren Avenue, and the Chrysler DeSoto Division Plant on McGraw Avenue are three notable exceptions to the rule.

New industrial expansion in the late 1930s and after took place at Detroit's outer edges and in the suburbs, in part because the city was largely developed, and large blocks of land were simply not available. The location of new plants was no longer primarily the result of the availability of water transportation or the railroads. Increasingly, surface streets and expressways carried incoming parts and raw materials, as well as the finished products. In the late 1930s and during World War II, the main thrust of industrial expansion was northward into Macomb County along three new industrial corridors: Mound Road, Van Dyke Avenue, and Grossbeck Highway. No complexes of the size of River Rouge were built, but the industrial architecture of the Rouge is endlessly duplicated in the new plants north of Eight Mile Road.

Detroit (DE)

DOWNTOWN (Central Business District)

DE01 Civic Center / Riverfront

Woodward Ave. (Michigan 1) at the Detroit River

In 1890 Mayor Hazen S. Pingree (1840–1901) proposed placing a civic center on the Detroit River at the end of Woodward Avenue. Commissioned by the American Institute of Architects, Eliel Saarinen drew up a design in 1924, but lack of funds prevented its execution. After World War II, Saarinen, Saarinen and Associates developed a new plan that included a city-county building, a circular convention hall, an auditorium and music hall, and four government buildings grouped around a landscaped river front plaza. To-

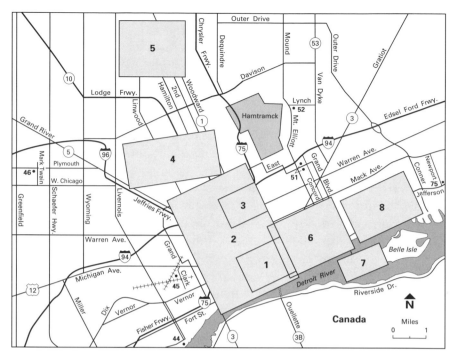

Detroit (DE44–DE46, DE51–DE52, DE75)

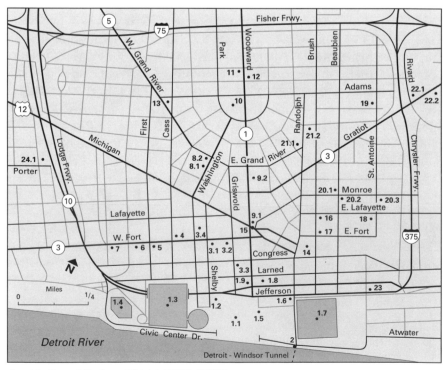

Inset 1. Central Business District (DE01–DE24)

DE01 Civic Center/Riverfront

day, Detroit's Civic Center appears much as Saarinen envisioned, with public buildings arranged around the Philip A. Hart Plaza. It parallels the Detroit River and extends to the Renaissance Center on the east and to the Riverfront Apartments on the west. The plaza is the central point for the even more extensive Riverfront, which links complexes with parks and runs to Belle Isle on the east and to the Ambassador Bridge on the west.

DE01.1 **Philip A. Hart Plaza**

1979, Isamu Noguchi and Smith, Hinchman and Grylls. Woodward Ave. (Michigan 1) at the Detroit River

In the center of the plaza a monumental abstract aluminum and steel sculpture by Isamu Noguchi (1979) rises above a bubbling circular fountain spraying water from its ring in computerized configurations and providing a focus for the pedestrian urban space. A spacious amphitheater near the fountain attracts crowds for summer festivals and winter ice skating. At Woodward and Jefferson avenues a sculpture of a 24-foot-long arm and fist suspended above street level from a pyramid of bronze beams (1986, Robert Graham) honors heavyweight boxing champion of the world from 1937 to 1949, Joe Louis [Barrow] (1914–1981), "the Brown Bomber."

DE01.2 **Veterans' Memorial Hall**

1948–1950, Harley, Ellington and Day. 151 West Jefferson Ave. (on West Jefferson Ave. between Griswold, Shelby, and Atwater streets)

The ten-story, L-shaped International style memorial building is faced with white marble. Above words that convey the building's purpose, "In honored memory of those who gave their lives for their country," the narrow, solid marble northwest wall displays a 30-foot eagle sculpture carved in high relief by Detroit area sculptor Marshall M. Fredericks (b. 1908). Characteristic of the style, the walls and glass surfaces are on the same plane, and the roof is flat. The building holds meeting rooms, lounges, offices, and a ballroom and kitchen.

DE01.3 **Cobo Conference / Exhibition Center**

1960, Giffels and Rosetti. 1985–1989, addition, Sims-Varner and Associates. 1 Washington Blvd. (Washington Blvd. and Jefferson Ave.)

Mayor Albert E. Cobo (1875–1957) supported the construction of this convention and exhibit hall, where Detroit held its first National Automobile Show. Next to Cobo Hall, and connected to it by a three-level glass and steel link, is the circular, green granite-walled Cobo Arena, below which are glass-enclosed offices. An extensive exhibition area is available, and from the lower-level ballroom and cafeteria a panoramic view of the Detroit River and Canada can be seen. The expansion into Cobo Conference/Exhibition Center was planned by Sims-Varner and Associates. The expansion and renovation of light gray granite and green-tinted glass in 1985–1989 doubled the center's size, making it one of the largest convention halls in the country. The facade of the latter structure appears to be built up of modular granite cubes, which are stepped back to reveal glass-walled openings in an otherwise solid mass.

DE01.4 Joe Louis Arena

1979–1980, Smith, Hinchman and Grylls. 600 Civic Center Dr.

This sports arena for basketball and hockey seats twenty thousand. Although Detroit's professional basketball team, the Pistons, elected to move to the Palace in Auburn Hills, the professional hockey team, the Detroit Red Wings, continues to play here.

DE01.5 Henry and Edsel Ford Auditorium (may be demolished)

1955–1956; O'Dell, Hewlet and Luckenbach; Crane, Kiehler and Kellogg. 20 Auditorium Dr.

Home of the Detroit Symphony Orchestra from 1956 to 1989, this wedge-shaped auditorium reflects the 1950s trend in theater design. The mica-flecked blue granite on the curved front wall shimmers at night. Side walls are of white marble. The Ford family, Ford dealers, and the city financed the twenty-nine-hundred-seat auditorium. As of 1991, the building was abandoned.

DE01.6 Mariner's Church

1849, Calvin N. Otis. 1955, remodeled. 170 East Jefferson Ave. (southwest corner of Randolph St. and East Jefferson Ave.)

This sturdy Gothic Revival church was originally built near the Detroit River on the northwest corner of Woodward Avenue and Woodbridge as a sailor's mission. It was founded when Julia Anderson, widow of an early Detroit military commander, bequeathed in 1842 land and money to construct a church for seamen sailing the Great Lakes. It was designed by Calvin N. Otis of Buffalo and constructed of Malden and Trenton gray limestone rubble. To make way for the Civic Center, the church was moved to its current site and remodeled in 1955. Along the way it lost the original wooden pinnacles, battlements, and belfry. The square tower was added and the rose window replaced a large Tudor arch window. Each spring Mariner's Church holds a Great Lakes Memorial Service and a blessing of the fleet. Its trustees want to preserve the church as a bastion of Episcopal values independent of the diocese. The Michigan Episcopal Diocese claims it has legal jurisdiction and ownership of the church.

DE01.7 Renaissance Center

1977, John C. Portman. 1986–1987, remodeled, James P. Ryan. Bounded by East Jefferson Ave., Saint Antoine St., the Detroit River, and Randolph St.

The $350 million hotel, office, and retail megastructure was planned by Henry Ford II, promoted by the Ford Land Development, and financed by five institutions. Designed by noted Atlanta architect John C. Portman, the seventy-three-story cylindrical hotel and four thirty-nine-story octagonal office towers rise from a concrete podium containing shops, theaters, and restaurants. Intended to demonstrate a dramatic renewal for downtown Detroit after the racial disturbances of 1967, to many Detroiters the concrete and tinted glass structure with bridges and atria (a Portman insignia) seems to isolate itself from the city rather than to demonstrate and represent a renaissance of cooperation. James P. Ryan remodeled the Renaissance Center in 1986–1987.

DE01.8 City-County Building

1955, Harley, Ellington and Day. 2 Woodward Ave. (Michigan 1) (northeast corner of East Jefferson and Woodward avenues)

This International style government building houses offices and court and meeting rooms. The thin, vertical white marble strips of the tower section move upward effortlessly for nineteen stories. The tower contrasts sharply with the connected fourteen-story office section, which is more horizontally oriented. Marshall M. Fredericks's 25-foot bronze sculpture *Spirit of Detroit*, which faces Woodward Avenue at the flat end of the tower block, is affectionately called the "Jolly Green Giant." The artist said that the seated male figure with arms outflung symbolizes "the universal spirit of man as an expression of God."[3]

DE01.9 American Natural Resources Company Building (Michigan Consolidated Gas Company Office Building)

1962, Minoru Yamasaki. 1 Woodward Ave. (Michigan 1) (northwest corner of Woodward and West Jefferson avenues)

This graceful, elegant work was designed by Minoru Yamasaki (1912–1985) to house all the administrative offices of the gas company in one location. It creates a strong corporate identity and further affirms the development of the Civic Center area. The thirty-two-story tower on a podium, with reflecting pools and landscaping, employs white marble, precast concrete panels, and lacy vertical grillwork in an otherwise Miesian format.

DE02 Detroit-Windsor Tunnel

1930, Parsons, Klapp, Brinkerhoff and Douglas, supervising engineers. Under the Detroit River between Detroit and Windsor at Randolph St., approximately one block northeast of Woodward Ave. (Michigan 1)

After the Holland Tunnel and the George A. Posey Tube, this is the third major subaqueous vehicular tunnel constructed in the United States. Although a sign with large letters at the entrance announces, "5168 FEET TO CANADA," the tunnel is 5,135 feet long and provides a 22-foot-wide roadway with a 13.5-foot clearance. It cost $23 million to build.

DE03 Financial District

Griswold and Shelby streets between West Larned Ave. on the southeast and West Lafayette and Michigan avenues on the northwest

This center of banking and business activity since the 1870s was converted into a canyon-like setting, not unlike Wall Street, with the erection in the 1920s of the Buhl, Penobscot, and Guardian skyscrapers.

DE03.1 Silvers, Inc. (State Savings Bank / Peoples State Bank)

1900, McKim, Mead and White. 1915 addition, John M. Donaldson of Donaldson and Meier. 151 West Fort St. (Michigan 3) (southeast corner of West Fort and Shelby streets)

This small, refined, white marble Beaux-Arts Classical bank is the only major building in Michigan designed by the great New York firm McKim, Mead and White. (Stanford White drew plans for the Frank J. Hecker Mausoleum at Woodmere Cemetery, Detroit, in 1897, and Charles McKim designed the Saint Mary's Falls Ship Canal Memorial obelisk at Sault Sainte Marie, c. 1907.) The symmetrical massing, white marble material, and classical detail contribute to the formality of the bank. Recessed fluted Ionic columns frame the main entrance off West Fort Street. The entrance composition is flanked by large round-arch windows and is surmounted by two figural sculptures representing industry and commerce. Large round-arch windows pierce the walls of the Shelby Street flank and Congress Street rear. The banking room, which extends the full height of the structure, is surrounded by an arcade of Ionic pilasters with metalwork that screens the offices. A mural of three women, painted by Thomas Dewing, is over the Congress Street exit. The firm of McKim, Mead and White was commissioned to design this little jewel in 1898, when State Savings Bank was the largest bank in Detroit. It was enlarged—doubling its size in 1915—after the Peoples State Bank (the result of the merger in 1907 with the State

Savings Bank) had outgrown this building. The harmonious addition was planned by John M. Donaldson of Donaldson and Meier.

DE03.2 **Penobscot Building**

1928, Wirt C. Rowland of Smith, Hinchman and Grylls. 645 Griswold St. (southwest corner of Griswold and West Fort [Michigan 3] streets)

For a half-century, the Penobscot Building was Detroit's tallest skyscraper—until the completion of the Renaissance Center in 1977. The simple, forty-seven-story, Indiana limestone structure rises unimpeded from a base of Mahogany granite for thirty floors to a series of setbacks that terminate in an apex surmounted by a red neon beacon. Ornamenting the building are American Indian figures and motifs, which are on the grand, four-story entrance archway on Griswold Street, in the carving in travertine and stone, and in the metalwork (in particular, the elevator doors) of the main floor lobby. The H-shaped plan accommodates the lobby and shops on the first floor, banking quarters on the first five floors, and offices above.

DE03.3 **Guardian Building** (Union Trust Company Building)

1927–1929, Wirt C. Rowland of Smith, Hinchman and Grylls. 500 Griswold St. (southeast corner of Griswold and Congress streets)

The Guardian Building is one of the most exuberant Art Deco skyscrapers built in America. Brilliantly colored Arts and Crafts tiles and orange brick, formulated especially for this building and known as Guardian brick, cover the thirty-six-story steel-frame structure. From its location on an entire block in the financial district, the warm and colorful bank building exudes a friendly cordiality.

The bank was built for the Union Trust Company during a period of rapid economic expansion, both for the company and for the city. Founded in 1890, the Union Trust Company joined in 1928 with the National Bank of Commerce and functioned under the direction of the Union Commerce Corporation. This new corporation merged, in turn, with the Guardian Group. When the building opened in 1929, the Guardian Detroit Union Group was Detroit's largest financial institution.

DE03.3 Guardian Building (Union Trust Company Building)

Wirt C. Rowland of Smith, Hinchman and Grylls designed this blazing, bold bank and office building. The taller north tower and the smaller octagonal south tower connected with a navelike block suggest a cathedral. The decorative motifs are made up of interlocking hexagons in terracotta and of stepped arches. The building is profusely ornamented inside and out with geometric designs executed in brilliantly colored terracotta and glazed tile, and gold-stained glass and metal. The architect collaborated with local artists and artisans. Embellishing the building are Mary Chase Stratton's glazed Pewabic tiles and Rookwood tiles; Thomas Di Lorenzo's decorated plaster; New York artist Ezra Winter's (who was born in Manistee, Michigan) huge banking room mural map of Michigan, depicting her industries; Corrado Joseph Parducci's carved stone figures; and Gari Melcher's portraits of the bank's directors. The main floor contains the lobby and banking room; the upper floors, offices. Thus, because of its plan, its lofty banking room with nave and side aisles, and its sumptuous decoration, the bank and office building appropriately was termed a "cathedral of finance." Michigan Consolidated Gas Company (MichCon) currently owns and occupies the building. In 1989 the Secretary of the Interior conferred upon the building a National Historic Landmark designation.

DE03.4 **Detroit Federal Building** (Detroit Post Office, Courthouse, Custom House)

1932–1934, Derrick and Wetmore. Bounded by West Fort St. (Michigan 3), Washington Blvd., West Lafayette Ave., and Shelby St.

The sleekly Moderne federal building stands on the site once occupied by Fort Lernoult, Fort Shelby, and later, in 1897, the U.S. Post Office, Courthouse, and Custom House. This ten-story steel-frame structure with limestone exterior walls has an open center court above the second floor. The building rests on a base of polished black stone. Fluted pilasters mark the recessed entrance. Above the entrance, a relief sculpture of eagles and emblems portrays the building's governmental functions. Of particular interest is the U.S. District Courtroom (Judge John Feikens's Courtroom, Room 733), in which were installed varied polished marble and carved wood trim and furnishings removed from the 1897 U.S. Courthouse that was demolished to make way for this structure.

DE04 **Detroit Club**

1891, Wilson Eyre, Jr. 712 Cass Ave. (northeast corner of Cass Ave. and West Fort St. [Michigan 3])

Founded in 1882 to provide a meeting place and luncheon service for the city's business and professional men, including many of Detroit's political and commercial leaders (such as Russell A. Alger and Charles Lang Freer), the club was originally located in a converted private residence. When this proved inadequate, members purchased this site on Cass Avenue and hired Wilson Eyre, Jr., the Philadelphia architect who had done Freer's house on East Ferry Avenue, to design this new building.
　The Detroit Club is a simplified version of Eyre's C. B. Moore House (1890) in Philadelphia. The symmetrical four-level Richardsonian Romanesque edifice has the medieval turretlike end bays that were a prominent feature of the wooden Queen Anne in America. The walls of the first story are constructed of rough, rock-faced Marquette brownstone and the upper stories, of elongated red Ro-

man brick. The symmetry of the club grows out of its interior use. The interior contains a sitting room, a library, and a grill on the first floor; card rooms on the second; public and private dining rooms on the third; and sleeping rooms on the fourth. The building features finely crafted woodwork, high ceilings, and elegant furnishings. The semioval main dining room occupies both third- and fourth-floor space on the southeast side of the building. Richly paneled in dark wood, it has a small interior balcony and a huge fireplace flanked by wooden Corinthian columns. Game trophies brought back by members from northern Michigan adorn the walls of the first-floor grill.

DE05 **Smith, Hinchman & Grylls Inc. Corporate Headquarters**

1910, 1972, Smith, Hinchman and Grylls. 455 West Fort St. (Michigan 3) (southeast corner West Fort St. and First)

The prolific architectural firm of Smith, Hinchman and Grylls consolidated its scattered operations into this headquarters in downtown Detroit. Originally designed in 1910 by the firm for commercial use, the Cass Building was acquired by the firm, stripped to its reinforced concrete frame, and rebuilt for contemporary use as its own offices for four hundred architects, engineers, and planners. The exterior wall system on the north and west elevations is sheathed in five-foot by three-foot, bronze-tinted glass panes that are seated in aluminum mullions, held in place with silicone sealant, and decorated at each corner by giant, cast aluminum spider clamps that look like jacks.

DE06 **Paul's Automatic Car Wash**

1946. 541 West Fort St. (Michigan 3) (southeast corner of West Fort St. and Second Ave.)

Paul Maraian opened his car wash in 1946 in this straightforward, simple building faced with cream enamel panels banded with red and with its neon sign. He was the first to use the Minit-Man Automatic Car Washer, an endless chain conveyor that pulled the car through a wash provided by overhead sprayers. A blow dryer and six men dried the cars. Appropriately, the Motor City, where Henry Ford introduced assembly-line production methods for the manufacture of automobiles, is the home of the first automated car wash. Still in operation, Paul's Car Wash has attracted the attention of roadside and commercial archaeologists from all over the country.

DE07 **Fort Street Presbyterian Church**

1855, Octavius and Albert H. Jordon. 1876, 1914, rebuilt. West Fort St. (Michigan 3) (southeast corner of West Fort and Third streets [or Third Avenue])

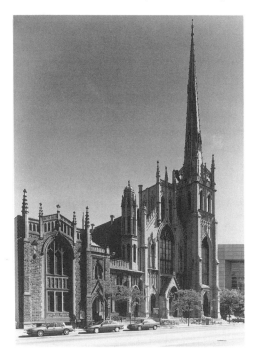

This Gothic Revival church of limestone ashlar was originally designed in 1855 by Octavius and Albert H. Jordon, architects who had migrated three years earlier from Hartford, Connecticut, to Detroit. On the whole, it is late English Gothic. It has a steep gable roof and a large corner tower with a tall, slender, octagonal wood spire utilizing flying buttresses. A smaller tower with an octagonal turret at the northeast corner is modeled after King's College Chapel, in Cambridge, England. Stone tracery, pinnacles, tall windows, and narrow buttresses add to the light, lacy, Perpendicular Gothic quality of the church. Inside, the three-aisled nave and the horseshoe balcony seat about one thousand worshippers beneath a hammer-beam roof. There is also a solid brass lectern and a baptismal font of Caen stone resting on Mexican onyx columns. Two disastrous fires in 1876 and 1914 destroyed the church, but it was rebuilt each time to almost the original plan.

DE08 **Washington Boulevard**

Four blocks on Washington Blvd. between Michigan Ave. and Grand Circus Park

Inspired by the City Beautiful movement and the 1915 plan for Detroit by Edward H. Bennett of Chicago, made after he and Daniel H. Burnham visited the city, this transformation of Washington Boulevard from a deteriorating residential area to an exclusive shopping district occurred between 1916 and 1930. It is equal to the world's loveliest thoroughfares. It was realized by the dreams, plans, and actions of J. Burgess Book, Jr., and his brothers Herbert and Frank Book, real estate speculators, who eventually held 60 percent of the property. Their architect, Louis Kamper (b. 1861), a German-born and -trained Detroit practitioner, had traveled in Europe and worked in the offices of McKim, Mead and White. He designed five of the buildings on the boulevard. Looking up the boulevard, the vista to the north terminates with the Neo-Gothic Fyfe Shoe Store Building (Smith, Hinchman and Grylls, 1919) and the Gothic Revival Central Methodist Episcopal Church (Gordon W. Lloyd, 1866–1867); the vista to the south focuses on the Detroit Free Press Building (Albert Kahn, 1923). Today, the boulevard has been converted, in part, to a pedestrian mall, with an environmental sculpture (1976–1977) by Gino Rossetti.

DE08.1 **Book Building**

1917, Louis Kamper. 1249 Washington Blvd.

Initiating the Washington Boulevard project was the limestone-faced Book Building. It is a thirteen-story office structure with shops on the lower levels. Louis Kamper designed the building in a rather eccentric version of Academic Classicism. The exterior classicistic details include twelve nude caryatid cornice supports. *Buildings and Building Management* for November 9, 1925, regarded the Book Building as one of the most important office buildings in Detroit. It noted that the architectural handling of the front facade and the handsome open lobby that rises three stories and that displays distinctive elevator fronts and cabs was intended "to attract tenants in a high-class shopping and office district."

DE08.2 Book Tower

1926, Louis Kamper. 11265 Washington Blvd. (southwest corner of Washington Blvd. and Grand River Ave. [Michigan 5])

The thirty-six-story Book Tower addition to the Book Building conforms in design and decoration with the original structure. It added more offices and shops. The skyscraper is relieved with horizontal bands of classicistic ornamentation, thus negating Louis Sullivan's ideas about the "proud and soaring" skyscrapers.

DE09 Woodward Avenue Commercial District

Woodward Ave. (Michigan 1) from Jefferson Ave. to Grand Circus Park

Woodward Avenue was Detroit's primary shopping district. Hudson's, Himmelhoch's, Wright Kay, Siegel's, and Grinnell's all survived the movement to the shopping malls in the 1960s but closed by the 1980s.

DE09.1 John J. Bagley Memorial Fountain

1887, Henry Hobson Richardson. 1925, moved to present site, northeast corner of Woodward and Monroe avenues (Campus Martius)

The will of John Judson Bagley (1832–1881) provided for the construction of a fountain on the Campus Martius, the city square that was planned and built after the Detroit fire in 1805. Originally from New York, Bagley was a manufacturer of tobacco products and a prominent businessman who served as governor of Michigan in the 1870s. Bagley intended his bequest to give the people of Detroit a continuous flow of ice water from May through November, on the condition that the city supply the necessary ice. Detroit's first drinking fountain is the only surviving Michigan work of the famed Henry Hobson Richardson (1838–1883). Based on a small ciborium in Saint Mark's Cathedral in Venice, the fountain was carved of unpolished white Worcester granite. It rises more than eighteen feet over a base of four steps. In contrast

DE09.1 John J. Bagley Memorial Fountain

to the smooth surfaces of the Venetian example, the arch spandrels and the column capitals are decorated with intricate foliated vegetal relief work. The base of the fountain was designed to hold "thousands of pounds of ice" to cool the water that was discharged through four lions' heads.

DE09.2 J. L. Hudson Company Department Store

1891, Mortimer L. Smith. 1911–1912, 1925–1928, 1946–1948, additions, Smith, Hinchman and Grylls. Bounded by Woodward Ave. (Michigan 1), East Grand River Ave., Farmer St., and Gratiot Avenue.

In 1891, ten years after Joseph L. Hudson started his mercantile business in rented quarters on the first floor of the Detroit Opera House, the company built an eight-story department store on Farmer Street and Gratiot Avenue. Based on H. H. Richardson's Marshall Field Store in Chicago, the original eight-story commercial building had exceptionally wide round-arch bays, constructed of red brick trimmed with Apostle Island brownstone. With eclectic multistory additions, the store was expanded until it covered an entire city block. A polished pink granite base wraps around the entire building, binding its many additions into a whole. A square tower rises above the Woodward Avenue entrance. For nearly a century, Hudson's was Detroit's premier downtown department store and, for many years, one of the largest in the country. Hudson's merged with Dayton Corporation of Minneapolis in 1974 and closed the doors of its downtown store in 1982.

DE10 Grand Circus Park

Bisected by Woodward Ave. (Michigan 1) and the point of convergence of Washington Blvd., Bagley Ave., Broadway, and Madison Ave.

Grand Circus Park is the northernmost culmination of the city plan devised by Judge Augustus Woodward in 1806. By the 1850s and 1860s the park was surrounded by villas and mansions. Today the spired Central Methodist Episcopal Church, a Gothic Revival limestone structure built to the designs of Gordon W. Lloyd in 1866–1867, remains as evidence of its original noncommercial character. Between 1890 and 1930 the streets surrounding and leading to the park were built up with high-rise, high-quality commercial skyscrapers, hotels, and movie palaces. Among them is the David Whitney Building of 1915 by Daniel H. Burnham of Chicago, at the southwest corner of Woodward and Park avenues. The corridors of the professional office building face an interior court, and the offices have outside windows. Standing in the park are statues depicting and memorializing prominent Detroit and Michigan public figures, including Detroit mayor and Michigan governor Hazen S. Pingree (1840–1901), U.S. senator Russell A. Alger (1836–1907), and Detroit mayor William Maybury (1848–1909). A parking garage was constructed below the park in 1956. Circum-

navigating the park's south side is the People Mover, an elevated and automated transit system nearly three miles long that opened in 1987.

DE11 Fox Theatre

1927–1928, C. Howard Crane. 2111 Woodward Ave. (Michigan 1) (southwest corner Woodward Ave. and Columbia)

Designed for William Fox (1879–1952) and the Fox Theatre chain by local architect C. Howard Crane (see DE32, Orchestra Hall), the Detroit Fox is the largest and most exotic Eclectic Hindu-Siamese-Byzantine theater of the golden age of the movie palace (1925–1930). The Fox stands today, along with its 1929 twin, the Saint Louis Fox Theatre, as one of the relatively few remaining movie palaces in the country. It epitomizes the opulence and grandeur that characterized the era.

The theater is within the core of a ten-story office complex and is constructed of the usual materials employed in motion-picture house construction—steel-frame and reinforced concrete faced with terracotta. On entering the five-story grand lobby of the theater, the visitor's attention is instantly captured by the colossal, unfluted, vermillion Corinthian columns and by the recumbent lions adorning the grand staircase.

The oval-shaped auditorium is surrounded by cusped, Islamic-inspired arches, surmounted by a colonnade of colossal Corinthian columns extending into the balcony. Decorative gilded plaster elephants, griffins, dragons, pagodas, deities, serpents, eagles, and Hindu goddesses cover the base of the columns and virtually every inch of wall space. A 2,000–pound chandelier with twelve hundred pieces of glass hangs from a large dome, outfitted like a tent in the center of the auditorium ceiling. In addition to numerous foyers and lobbies, stage facilities, and an auditorium, balcony, and mezzanine that seat over five thousand, the Detroit Fox has eight dressing rooms, a broadcasting booth, a screening room, an infirmary, and a music library that is valued at over $100,000.

Acquired by Mike Ilitch and Little Caesar's Pizza, the Fox was restored in 1987–1988 to its original exotic splendor. For the restoration, William Kessler and Associates, architects, and Ray Shepardson, restoration consultant, received a 1989 Honor Award from the Michigan Society of Architects. The Fox Theatre is a National Historic Landmark.

DE12 Elwood Bar and Grill

1937. 2100 Woodward Ave. (Michigan 1) (northeast corner of Woodward Ave. and Elizabeth St.)

The tiny, blue and cream-colored bar and grill is one of Detroit's last enameled steel panel Art Deco buildings. A cylindrical tower dramatically anchors the curved southwest corner main entrance. Geometric designs decorate both the tower and the panels on either side of the main entrance. During the restoration in 1988, the interior was redone in three-toned maple, mahogany, and birch woodwork, trimmed with chrome. The Elwood was patronized by office workers during the 1940s to 1960s and by students and the elderly in the 1970s. Today it is used by theatergoers and represents part of the revitalization of buildings in the Grand Circus Park Theater District and on Woodward Avenue.

DE13 Grand Army of the Republic Building

1896–1900, Julius Hess of Hess and Raseman. 1924 Grand River Ave. (Michigan 5) (east side of Grand River Ave. between Cass Ave. and West Adams St.)

At their state encampment held in Detroit in 1891, Michigan Civil War veterans lobbied the city for a memorial meeting building. The result was the largest GAR meeting hall in Michigan. It was financed with $38,000 in city bonds. The designer was well-known Detroit architect Julius Hess (1841–1899), who was born and trained in Zurich. Hess created a massive, fortresslike structure that conforms in plan to its triangular-shaped site. The Richardsonian Romanesque building has two large, crenelated engaged towers flanking the slightly projecting, pedimented main pavilion. The building's exterior walls are beautifully laid with carefully cut, rock-faced, gray limestone and tan sandstone.

DE14 Wayne County Building (Wayne County Courthouse)

1897–1902, John Scott. 1986–1987, restoration and rehabilitation, Quinn-Evans and Smith, Hinchman and Grylls. 600 Randolph St. (at Cadillac Square and bounded by Randolph, East Fort, Brush, and East Congress streets)

This majestic civic building once faced Detroit's second City Hall, which was demolished in 1961. This city hall was a lavish, Second-Empire, cream-colored sandstone structure. Erected in 1868–1871 to the designs of James Anderson at Campus Martius, it stood on the west side of Woodward Avenue. John Scott (1851–1928) designed the Wayne County Building in the Beaux-Arts Classical style. Both the Wayne County Building and the Detroit City Hall had prominent towered centers with balancing end pavilions. The four-story, Berea sandstone courthouse is vigorously English Baroque in character. The main block rests on a raised, rusticated granite basement story and is surmounted by a four-tiered, colonnaded tower that is crowned by a curved hipped roof. A sandstone belt course encircles the building between the first and second stories, and a columned balustrade surrounds the building between the third and fourth stories. A broad flight of stairs fronts the central pavilion and leads to the main entrance, above which is a two-story Corinthian-columned portico. The courthouse is profusely ornamented with sculpture. The pediment of the portico contains a relief by Edward Wagner of Detroit of Gen. "Mad" Anthony Wayne conferring with the Indians; flanking the portico are two bronze groups symbolizing Progress and Victory by John Massey Rhind of New York; and on the four sides of the tower are four female figures of Law, Commerce, Agriculture, and Mechanics.

The structure held the county courts and offices. The interior is finished in a variety of woods, marbles, tiles, and mosaics. The sumptuousness of the building, both inside and out, reflects Detroit's preeminence as the seat of county government—in fact, some thought Detroit the true capital of Michigan.

The last-minute decision of the county commissioners to build with buff Ohio rather than red Lake Superior sandstone disappointed owners of Upper Peninsula quarries, who had counted on John Scott, designer of many red sandstone buildings in the Upper Peninsula, to promote their stone. Unfortunately for them, with the advent of classicism, taste shifted to whiter materials.

The courthouse was sold in 1984 to the Old Wayne County Building Limited Partnership. The partnership invested $25 million in its restoration and rehabilitation in 1986–1987 to the plans of Quinn/Evans and Smith, Hinchman and Grylls Associates. The building was leased back to Wayne County for its use.

DE15 Soldiers and Sailors Monument

1872, Randolph Rogers. Campus Martius

This monumental sculpture, a Civil War memorial, culminates in the personification of Michigan as an Indian queen. She stands atop a four-tiered composition on a granite base with bronze statues representing the Infantry, the Artillery, the Cavalry, and the Marines; allegorical figures of Victory, Union, Emancipation, and History; and medallions of Lincoln, Grant, Farragut, and Sherman.

DE16 Wayne County Morgue and Medical Examiners Office Building

1924–1925, Aaron H. Gould and Son. 400 East Lafayette Ave. (southeast corner of East Lafayette Ave. and Brush St.)

The tomblike morgue is a rare but appropriate use of the Egyptian Revival style in Michigan. A flat roof covers the two-story structure. The exterior walls are gray and white limestone and buff Roman brick. An Egyptian motif of tapered columns topped by cavetto cornices frames the main corner entrance and the first-floor windows. Cubberston and Kelly Company was the contracting firm.

DE17 Globe Tobacco Company Building

1888. A. Chapotin, builder, 407 East Fort St. (northeast corner East Fort and Brush streets)

In 1871 Detroit and Windsor manufacturers, including Hiram A. Walker, who founded the Canadian distillery, established the Globe Tobacco Company. In this six-story, red brick warehouse, the Globe Tobacco Company cured Virginia and Kentucky leaf tobacco and made cigars and pipe and chewing tobacco. The warehouse employs a mill construction technique frequently used from 1880 to 1900 and popular because it spanned large spaces and provided an inexpensive means of fire protection. Masonry load-bearing walls could contain the fire, while heavy timber floor beams supported by massive wooden posts provided a compact, nearly fireproof ceiling. First developed in the factories of New England, this ingenious system was known as "slow-burning construction." The interior of the building followed the open warehouse plan while its exterior mirrors the powerful walls of Richardson's Marshall Field Store in Chicago.

By 1925 the Globe Tobacco Company, no longer in business, abandoned the building but retained its ownership. Subsequently the structure had numerous tenants and became dilapidated. In 1984 the rehabilitation by Louis G. Redstone of this old warehouse into an energy-efficient office building included gutting the entire building to its support beams, wood floors, and brick walls; replacing the original windows with custom-made thermal windows; and cutting a glass atrium through the building's core, to allow a view of its framework and its skylight in this dramatic vertical space.

DE18 Detroit Cornice and Slate Company Building

1897, Harry J. Rill. 733 Saint Antoine St. (southwest corner of Saint Antoine St. and Lafayette)

A sculptured facade of hammered and pressed galvanized steel manufactured to resemble stone by the Detroit Cornice and Slate Company graces the front of the company's own building. Now restored on the exterior and rehabilitated on the interior, the building serves as the architectural offices of William Kessler and Associates.

DE19 606 Horseshoe Lounge

1916, building. 1936, business established. 1907–1913 Saint Antoine St. (northwest corner of Saint Antoine and Beacon streets)

This is the last remnant of Paradise Valley, the major entertainment center of a black neighborhood known as Black Bottom, which flourished between 1910 and 1950 in the area bounded by Brush, Gratiot, Hastings, and Vernor. The business district contained black-owned music stores, groceries, bowling alleys, hotels, restaurants, and seventeen nightclubs. During the 1930s and early 1940s, its nightclubs were true melting pots. Here, blacks and whites drank, danced, and were entertained side by side in a cordial and happy atmosphere, without undue tension or incident. The 606 Horseshoe Lounge, Club Plantation, B&C Club, and Club 666 gave the first big break to many aspiring young singers, dancers, and musicians. Among those who played the Valley were Earl "Fatha" Hines,

the Ink Spots, Ethel Waters, Pearl Bailey, Billie Holiday, Dinah Washington, Ella Fitzgerald, and Bill "Bojangles" Robinson. William T. Johnson, a former waiter at the Detroit Athletic Club, operator of a private club for the city's black bartenders and waiters, and whose personality "just lit up the sky," established the 606 Horseshoe Lounge in 1936. He ran it until his death in 1962. The lounge occupies a commercial building, which was built in 1916. The bricked-up window of the storefront has a large horseshoe outlined in raised brick.

Paradise Valley and Black Bottom survived into the 1950s, until urban renewal and the construction of the Chrysler and Fisher freeways, Stroh's Brewery, and J. L. Hudson's warehouse obliterated them.

DE20 Greektown (Germantown)

1850–1910. On Monroe Ave. from Randolph to the east of Saint Antoine St.

Originally a German neighborhood, Greektown comprises a small enclave of Late Victorian, two-, three-, and four-story red brick commercial buildings with nice Victorian detail and containing stores on the street level and flats above, industrial structures, and churches that date from 1850 to 1910.

DE20.1 Second Baptist Church

1857, 1880, 1917. 1968, addition, Sims-Varner and Associates. 441 Monroe Ave. (northeast corner of Monroe Ave. and Beaubien St.)

Second Baptist Church serves Detroit's oldest black Baptist congregation. It was organized in 1836 by thirteen former slaves who had been members of First Baptist Church. Its members met in various halls and schools until 1857, when the group purchased the Zion Reformed (Evangelical) Church. Here on January 1, 1863, Detroit blacks held the first public celebration of Lincoln's Emancipation Proclamation. An 1880 addition converted the one-story, gable roof limestone church into a two-story building with an auditorium. After a fire partially destroyed the church in 1917, a new structure was built around the shell of the 1880 building. In 1968 a large, four-story office and educational wing with projecting flat roof, asymmetrical composition, and cantilevering was built east of the church to the plans of Howard F. Sims and Harold F. Varner, Detroit's major black architectural firm.

DE20.2 Trapper's Alley (Traugott Schmidt and Sons Furrier and Tannery Buildings)

1853, 1881, 1890, 1912, 1985. 500–558 Monroe Ave. (southeast corner of Monroe Ave. and Beaubien St.)

In 1853 Traugott Schmidt, a young German immigrant, established a furriery and tannery here, where he dealt in and processed wool, fur, and leather acquired through trade with trappers and Indians in the Great Lakes region. As his business expanded, so did the buildings that Traugott Schmidt occupied. All are red brick with stone and brick trim. In 1985 they were converted into Trapper's Alley Market Place, an entertainment, restaurant, and retail center covered by a glass roof.

DE20.3 Saint Mary's Catholic Church

1868–1869, school, Pius Daubner. 1876, rectory. 1884–1885, church, Peter Dederichs. 1035 Saint Antoine St. (southeast and southwest corners of Saint Antoine St. and Monroe Ave.)

In 1833 the Archdiocese of Cincinnati sent Father Martin Kundig to serve German and Irish Catholics who flocked to Detroit in the 1830s. He conducted services in German at a room in Sainte Anne du Detroit Church. Kundig left within a couple of years, but the Reverends Anton Koop and Clemens Hammer continued his work until he returned in 1840. By then the congregation had outgrown the small room at Sainte Anne. Under Kundig's direction, construction of the original steepled brick Saint Mary's Church was begun in 1841 at the southeast corner of Saint Antoine and Croghan (Monroe Avenue) streets. Having organized after the French Sainte Anne du Detroit and the Irish Most Holy Trinity, this parish is the third oldest in Detroit. In 1884 its original building was demolished to make way for the present church.

The present Saint Mary's Catholic Church is the major work of Peter Dederichs (1856–1924), a noted designer of Roman Catholic churches who was born and trained in Germany and who was a lifelong member of this parish. The church shows distinct evidence of its German influence. Twin towers with spires mark the triple-arched portico that is surmounted by a large rose window. Polychromatic red brick and limestone cover the exterior walls. The walls are broken with round-arch windows. The interior, which seats twelve hundred, is a basilica plan with transepts. The towering, double-columned, Corinthian oak altar dates from 1855 and the earlier church. It features a statue of Mary flanked by likenesses of King Wenceslas of Bohemia and Queen Elizabeth of Hungary, a reference to the ethnicity of the first parishioners. Surrounding the main altar is a recessed, seven-sided, domed apse in which paintings depict the seven sacraments. The church's upper clerestory contains paintings of the fifteen mysteries of the rosary. The interior of the church sparkles brightly as a result of the lively refurbishing it underwent in 1986 in celebration of the centennial of the building's construction. Unfortunately, during an earlier restoration in 1969, the brick of the exterior walls was damaged by sandblasting.

In 1868–1869 Saint Mary's Catholic School (now Saint Mary's Community Center) was built at 1035 Saint Antoine Street on the southwest corner of Saint Antoine Street and Monroe Avenue. The large brick Italianate structure with paired, narrow round-arch windows and bracketed hipped roof replaced earlier schools built in 1844, 1848 and 1855. It was designed by Pius Daubner and constructed at a cost of $40,000. In 1876 the Franciscan fathers erected their "elegant" brick residence at 646 Monroe Avenue, just east of the church. It cost $20,000. The Convent of the Sisters of Notre Dame stands at 1032 Saint Antoine Street. This huge German Catholic complex once included as well an orphan asylum for girls.

Saint Mary's was also the home of Detroit's first black and Hispanic missions. On September 11, 1911, Saint Peter Claver Mission, organized for blacks by Father Joseph Wuest, conducted its first services in a second floor classroom in Saint Mary's School. On June 1, 1920, under the direction of J. D. Alanis, Our Lady of Guadeloupe Mission held its first services in the same classroom previously used by the Saint Peter Claver Mission.

This large church says something of the substantial German population in the city of Detroit in the nineteenth century and of the German influence both in this building and in the architecture of the Detroit as a whole.

DE21 Madison-Harmonie

Madison Ave. and Randolph Street vicinity

This intact portion of the original 1805 Woodward plan includes triangular-shaped Harmonie Park and Madison Avenue, a street radiating out from Grand Circus Park. The area was settled by Germans. Recently Harmonie Park was the subject of a study commissioned by Detroit Renaissance. Schervish, Vogel and Merz propose to execute portions of a plan. They would restore and renovate the Harmonie Club and the Madison/Lenox Hotel into a hotel and entertainment facility, create new apartments over commercial buildings fronting on Harmonie Park, and rehabilitate other commercial buildings so that they link this area not only with Grand Circus Park and the Fox Theatre, but also with Monroe Street and Greektown.

DE21.1 Harmonie Club

1894–1895, Richard E. Raseman, 267 East Grand River Ave. (northwest corner of East Grand River Ave. and Center St.)

In 1849 four German immigrants formed the Gesang-Verein Harmonie to meet and sing German Lieder. The club was chartered in 1852. In 1875 the organization incorporated and built a clubhouse at Beaubien and Lafayette. This structure burned in 1893. The present club was designed by Richard E. Raseman (b. 1855), who was one of several German-American Detroit architects to whom the design competition for the building was open. Raseman began his architectural practice in 1883 and worked in partnership with Julius Hess from 1885 to 1891. The Harmonie Club is a monumental four-story Beaux-Arts Classical design. It faces Harmonie Park, a triangle bounded by Randolph Street, East Grand River Avenue, and Center Street. The buff brick walls of the building rise above a rusticated stone foundation. They are interrupted with belt courses and decorative pilasters. The central Ionic order entrance is beneath a broad arch that extends through the second floor. The club contained dining rooms, lounges, meeting rooms, a bowling alley, and two large auditoriums.

DE21.2 Music Hall (Wilson Theatre)

1928, William Kapp of Smith, Hinchman and Grylls.

350 Madison Ave. (southwest corner of Madison Ave. and Brush St.)

Matilda Wilson (1883–1967), the widow of John F. Dodge who married Alfred Wilson, commissioned William Kapp of Smith, Hinchman and Grylls to design this intimate legitimate theater. Kapp was the architect of the Wilson's country house, Meadow Brook Hall, then under construction near Rochester (OK05, p. 161). The lovely, light exterior of the Art Deco theater is faced with buff-colored Mankato stone and orange-tan brick; trimmed with cream, orange, and green terracotta mosaics; and embellished with masks of Tragedy and Comedy and other drama symbols in terracotta by Corrado Joseph Parducci. From the ticket lobby the visitor enters the main lobby and proceeds either down a short flight of stairs to the lounge or up one of two flanking staircases to the main floor of the theater. The auditorium is richly decorated in a Spanish Renaissance theme. Inside the building the colors of the exterior intensify into aquas, rusts, and golds. The walls are paneled in dark wood and travertine. Thomas Di Lorenzo's colorful decorative painting on plastered beams that pose as wood gives focus to the stage. The main floor, mezzanine, and balcony of the auditorium seat nearly eighteen hundred. Six floors of offices are over the ticket lobby. The Wilson Theatre was built at a cost of $1.5 million. It was renamed Music Hall in 1946, after the Wilsons sold it to Henry Reichhald and it became the home of the Detroit Symphony Orchestra. In 1951 Music Hall was sold to Mervin Gaskin who converted it to Cinerama. Plans call for the linkage of Music Hall with Harmonie Park/Madison Avenue and Grand Circus Park and the Fox Theatre into a historic theater district.

DE22 Gratiot Avenue

Gratiot Ave. (Michigan 3) between Broadway and Riopelle Ave. at the Grand Trunk railroad tracks

German migration to Detroit increased dramatically after 1830. The new arrivals settled on the lower east and northeast sides of Detroit, finding work as merchants, brewers, laborers, and tanners. By 1850 the area north of Jefferson Avenue and along Gratiot Avenue was widely known as Germantown. By 1870 the Germans were Detroit's largest single ethnic group.

DE22.1 Trinity Evangelical Lutheran Church and Parish House

1929–1931, church, William E. N. Hunter. 1927, parish house, Bernard C. Wetzel. 1345 Gratiot Ave. (Michigan 3) (northeast corner of Gratiot Ave. and Rivard St.)

Trinity Evangelical Lutheran Church serves one of Detroit's oldest German Lutheran congregations and is the "Mother church" of Missouri-Synod Lutheranism in the city. The congregation began in 1850, the result of a doctrinal dispute with Saint Matthew's Evangelical Church. Until 1866 it occupied a frame chapel on Larned Street near Rivard Street. Then a steepled brick Gothic Revival structure was built on the site of the present church. Services were held here until the present church was constructed between 1929 and 1931.

The church was the gift of Charles Gauss (1875–1937), a Detroit wholesale tobacconist and real estate investor, and his wife, Margaret Strehler Gauss (1875–1939). The Gausses had recently profited from the sale of land on the River Rouge to the Ford Motor Company. Their gift to the church stipulated that the new building be lively and colorful in praise and honor to God. The church was designed by noted Detroit church architect William E. N. Hunter in consultation with the Reverend F. R. Webber, secretary of the Lutheran Missouri Synod's Committee on Architecture. Trinity's own minister, the Reverend Gilbert T. Otte, inspected new churches in New York, Cleveland, and Chicago in search of inspiration for Trinity.

Located on a cramped, triangular lot at a crossroads on the edge of downtown Detroit, Trinity Evangelical Lutheran Church is a large Late Gothic Revival building with a prominent asymmetrical belfry tower. The tower itself soared higher than the Stroh Brewery, then just to the southwest of the church. The church was called a modern adaptation of sixteenth-century English Gothic Pier and Clerestory Church Architecture. The church has a nave and side aisles. The choir and organ are situated in the gallery above the narthex. A triforum provides a passageway over each side aisle. The church is constructed of vari-colored granite and Indiana limestone and has elaborately carved and painted interior decoration and stained glass. The carved stonework of the church's interior and exterior is the work of two important early twentieth-century Michigan sculptors, Corrado Joseph Parducci and Joseph Jungwirth, and executed by Bernasconi for the Batchelder-Wasmund Company of Detroit. Other fittings in the church, which are works of art in themselves, include the stained-glass windows designed and made by Henry Lee Willet of the Willet Studios of Philadelphia; the intricate wood narthex and organ screen by William Ross Company of East Cambridge, Massachusetts; the reredos designed and built by the Rambusch Company of New York; and the lower-story stained glass designed by the Detroit Stained Glass Company. To the east of the church is a three-story, red brick Jacobethan Revival parish house trimmed with gray limestone.

Unlike many urban churches, Trinity Church is financially solvent. This may be attributed, in large part, to its current minister, David Eberhard. Eberhard established the Historic Trinity Foundation and operates historic and cultural programs and activities for senior citizens at the church. In the last eight years membership has increased from 40 to 450 people.

DE 22.2 Saint Joseph Roman Catholic Church

1870–1873, Francis G. Himpler. 1883, tower addition. 1892, spire added. 1907 (1911?), pinnacles added. 1800–1828 Jay St. (southwest corner of Jay and Orleans streets)

Saint Joseph Roman Catholic Church is the German "daughter parish" of Saint Mary's Church. As German immigrants, fueled by the Austrian and Hungarian Revolutions of 1848, poured into the lower east side and along the Gratiot Avenue corridor, the need arose for another parish. A small frame church was constructed in 1856 between Riopelle and Orleans streets. But the continued increased migration of Germans out to East Grand Boulevard and northward in the 1860s brought about the decision to build a larger church. This ample, steeply gabled and pinnacled Gothic Revival church was designed by Francis G. Himpler (1833–1916), a German-born architect who studied at the Royal Academy in Berlin and practiced in New York. He modeled it after the German hall church, in which the nave and aisles are approximately the same height. A 300-foot-tall single tower and spire dominates the neighborhood.

The building is clad in rough-faced, gray Trenton limestone trimmed with brown sandstone. The interior is richly decorated with wood carvings imported from Germany and stained glass either imported from Franz Mayer of Munich and the Tyrolese Art Glass Company of Innsbruck or manufactured by Friederichs and Staffin in Detroit.

DE23 Saints Peter and Paul Church

1844–1848, Francis Letourneau and Peter Kindenkens. 1857, 1877, 1879, 1882, 1892, 1908, additions and alterations. 629 East Jefferson Ave. (northeast corner of East Jefferson Ave. and Saint Antoine St.)

Saints Peter and Paul Church is a fine example of Catholic religious architecture. It is Neoclassical and is closer to English Regency than any other style. It was designed by Francis Letourneau (d. 1860) and Peter Kindenkins supervised construction. The former was a native of Mount Clemens and, when he went to Detroit in the 1830s, was one of the first architect-builders to arrive there. Paired Ionic pilasters frame the modest, slightly projecting, pedimented, central bay of the large, Flemish bond, orange brick structure. A low, triangular pediment surmounts the arched central entry. The square squat tower, which was designed to include a steeple that resembles those created by James Gibbs but which was never built, dominates the street facade. The church follows the three-aisled basilica plan, has a barrel-vaulted ceiling, and seats one thousand. Marble wainscoting lines the interior. The apse has a high, Carrara marble altar of ornate Renaissance design by Gustave Adolph Mueller of Detroit, decorated with sculpture by Joseph Gibbel of New York. Having served its parishioners for more than 130 years, Saints Peter and Paul Church is the oldest extant church in Detroit. Through the years, as the surrounding neighborhood changed from residential to commercial, the congregation, mainly Irish at the outset, decreased; but the church remains as a symbol of Catholicism in Detroit.

INNER CITY

DE24 Corktown

1849–1920. bounded by Michigan (US 12) and Bagley avenues, the John C. Lodge Freeway (US 10), and Fourteenth St.

Corktown is the last remnant of Detroit's Irish immigrant neighborhood that once stretched from Third to Sixteenth Street and from Michigan Avenue to the Detroit River. It contains some of the oldest extant structures in the city of Detroit. Its working-class housing dates from the late 1840s to the early 1900s and ranges from frame cottages on cedar posts to Federal town houses, frame Queen Anne houses (1610–1662 Church Street), and brick structures (1627–1645 Leverette Street and Beyster Terrace at the northwest corner of Bagley and Tenth Street).

Irish immigration to Detroit began in the early 1830s, shortly after the opening of the Erie Canal in 1825 spurred migration westward from New York and Boston. In 1834, the first English-speaking Roman Catholic congregation, Most Holy Trinity, was established for the immigrant Irish. By 1850 one in seven foreign-born residents of Detroit was Irish. Corktown was always an immigrant neighborhood; the Maltese took up residency here in 1900 and Mexicans, in the 1920s. Clearance for the John Lodge Freeway, however, and urban renewal for development of the West Side Industrial Park in the 1950s and 1960s, took their toll on the neighborhood.

DE24.1 Most Holy Trinity Roman Catholic Church and Rectory

1855–1866, church, Patrick C. Keeley. 1886, rectory, Mason and Rice. 1062 Porter St. (northeast corner of Porter and Sixth streets)

As a signal of the heavy concentration of Irish moving to the area west of Woodward Avenue the first Most Holy Trinity Church, a frame structure built originally for the First Protestant Church Society in 1819, was moved in 1849 from its location at Cadillac Square and Bates Street westward to the corner of Porter and Sixth streets. This was replaced in 1855–1866 by the current austere, but imposing Gothic Revival church. It was designed by the prolific Patrick C. Keeley (1816–1896), an Irish-born New York architect who designed many Catholic churches in New York, New England, and Canada; it was built by Stephen Martin. The gable-roofed structure is topped by a 170-foot spire and is built of orange brick with limestone trim. Three recessed entrances give access to the interior, with its nave, side aisles, and organ and choir

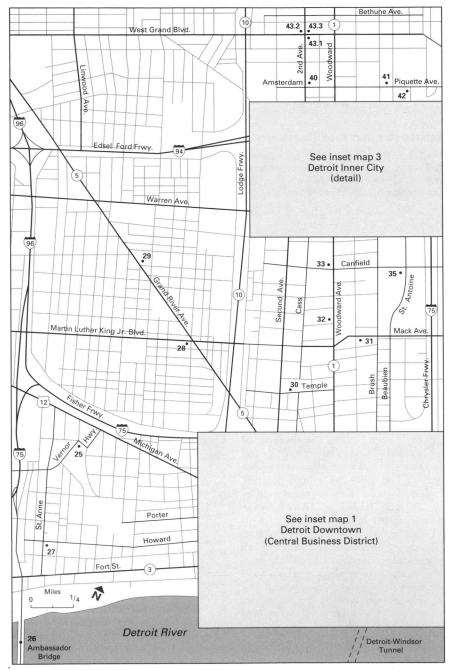

Inset 2. Inner City (DE25–DE33, DE35, DE40–DE43; see Inset 3, p. 81, for DE34 and DE36–DE39)

80

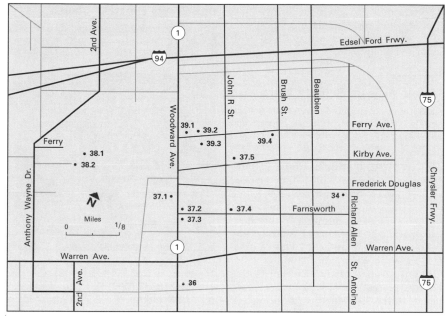

Inset 3. Inner City, detail (DE34, DE36–DE39)

loft. Immediately east of the church is the Richardsonian Romanesque red brick and sandstone rectory.

DE25 **Michigan Central Railroad Station**

1913, Warren and Wetmore, Reed and Stem. 2405 West Vernor (overlooks Roosevelt Park on West Vernor Highway at Michigan Ave.) (US 12)

In 1913 two New York architectural firms noted for their design of railroad stations and hotels, in particular Grand Central Station and the Biltmore Hotel, collaborated to create the Michigan Central Railroad Station. The Beaux-Arts Classical public building adorns Roosevelt Park, a plaza planned by Edward H. Bennett in 1915 after Judge Augustus Woodward's vision of Detroit. The structure possesses paired Composite order columns, arches, and pediments in its symmetrical stone facade, and a grand Roman interior waiting room. Directly but incongruously attached at the rear is a sixteen-story, yellow brick office building that dominates the front structure.

DE26 **Ambassador Bridge**

1927–1929, Jonathan Jones, chief engineer for McClintic-Marshall Company. Across the Detroit River to Windsor, Ontario

Although never as famous as the Niagara suspension bridge, the Brooklyn Bridge, or the Golden Gate Bridge, the Ambassador is Michigan's second-most spectacular bridge, after the Mackinac Bridge. When completed in 1929 to the designs of Jonathan Jones of the McClintic-Marshall Company of Pittsburgh, the Ambassador Bridge was the longest suspension bridge in the world. It extends

9,602 feet, with approaches. The bridge links the United States and Canada and is best seen at night, when its cables are outlined with strings of twinkling lights.

DE27 Sainte Anne du Detroit Church

1886–1887, church, chapel, rectory. 1888, school. Early 1900s, convent and parish hall, French and Coquard. 1000 Sainte Anne St. (bounded by Howard, Eighteenth, Lafayette West, and Sainte Anne streets)

Founded by M. Antoine de la Mothe Cadillac in 1701 and later served by Father Gabriel Richard, who was named pastor in 1802, Sainte Anne's parish is the oldest parish in Detroit and the second-oldest continuously operating Catholic parish in the United States. Only Saint Augustine in Florida is older. Visible from the Detroit River, this grandly elaborate, fully developed High Victorian Gothic church was preceded by seven others. Twin pinnacled towers terminating in octagonal drums and surmounted, in turn, with spires, flying buttresses, and a large rose window in its full glory mark the main portico of the cruciform-plan church. The material is orangish red brick on a limestone foundation. Moving from the narthex into the nave, the visitor is struck by the splendid stained-glass windows of the apse and by the ornate altar. A Gothic arcade with clustered columns separates the nave and side aisles. The pointed-arch windows of the side walls depict saints and memorialize French-speaking families: Medard Beauvais and Anable Brossard, Aldezure Rousseau, Monsier et Madame Isidore Carre, Famille Richard Beaubien, Madame Columbus Campau, Famille Guillaume Groesbeck, and Famille Francois Monnier. A. E. French and Leon Coquard of Detroit were the designers of the church and rectory. Patrick Dee built the church and residence at a cost of $110,000. At the time of its dedication the *Michigan Catholic* called Sainte Anne Church, "one of the grandest Christian temples in the West and . . . *the* grandest Catholic church within the State of Michigan."[4] A school, a convent and a parish hall, dating from 1887 to the 1900s, are part of the complex. The painting of Our Lady of Guadalupe on the north side altar is the only concession to the church's current largely Hispanic congregation.

DE28 Trinity Episcopal Church

1890–1892, church, Mason and Rice. 1925, parish house. 1519 Martin Luther King Blvd. (northwest corner of Martin Luther King Blvd. and Trumbull Ave.)

James E. Scripps (1835–1906) and his wife Harriet (1838–1933) were the benefactors of the Late Gothic Revival Trinity Episcopal Church. Scripps, publisher of the *Detroit News*, was regarded as a connoisseur of art and architecture. The Scrippses' purpose in rejecting Victorian romanticism in favor of a return to historic accuracy was "to give Detroit an example of the old-time church, at once so picturesque and impressive . . . to simulate, if possible, in church architecture a return to the older and more truly artistic forms."[5] The Scrippses engaged an English architect to supply Mason and Rice with archaeological evidence and drawings of details from late fourteenth- to early fifteenth-century southern English churches, namely Holy Cross Church, Canterbury; All Saints, Maidstone (1395); the Chapter House of Canterbury Cathedral (1391–1411); Etchingham Church, Sussex (1386); and others. They commissioned the Detroit firm to incorporate them in this Gothic Revival design that follows the ecclesiological doctrine.

Executed in rock-faced limestone trimmed with buff sandstone, the church has a cruciform plan with a massive square tower at the crossing. Prominent battlements (also present in the Scripps's own home by the same architectural firm that once stood on Trumbull Avenue across Grand River Avenue, 1891), buttresses, tracery, gargoyles, and other-carved stone ornaments contribute to the church's medieval character.

Entrance to the church is through a side porch. In Scripps's own words, "The interior of the church is undoubtedly much more perfect and beautiful than the exterior."[6] The pulpit and reading desk are properly located and the choir is in the chancel. The interior combined the massive pillars of Norman churches with Gothic arcades throughout. Ten stone angels carved in Bedford limestone spring from sidewalls to support the nave beams beneath the wooden ceiling. The stained-glass chancel window showing the baptism of Christ is by Mayer and Company of Munich. The stained-glass window in the west aisle representing Christ as the Good Shepherd and the memorial window to William Scott in the east aisle were manufactured by the Tiffany Glass Company of New York.

A Late Gothic Revival parish house of buff sandstone ashlar was erected in 1925 and is adjacent to the church. The present church replaced a board-and-batten Gothic Revival church that was erected on the site of the parish house in 1880 and named Epiphany Reformed Episcopal Church. The congregation of Trinity (and Epiphany Reformed) was organized as Emmanuel Reformed Episcopal Church in 1879 and was renamed several times.

DE29 Eighth Precinct Police Station

1900–1901, Louis Kamper. 4150 Grand River Ave. (Michigan 5) (northwest corner of Grand River Ave. and Rosa Parks Blvd.)

In 1865 the state legislature created the Detroit Metropolitan Police Department, providing for a permanent force under the control of a four-man commission appointed by the governor. Originally, the department operated out of rented quarters, but the growth of Detroit necessitated the construction of several precinct stations and substations in the 1870s. The substation at Grand River Avenue and Rosa Parks Boulevard, established in 1879, was used until 1900. It was then demolished to make way for this structure, which served as a precinct station for over fifty years.

The Eighth Precinct Station, designed by Louis Kamper in the Châteauesque style, rarely used in Michigan government buildings, today is abandoned and is in badly deteriorating condition. A two-and-one-half-story structure built on an irregular plan, the station combines limestone on its ground floor with brick banded with limestone on its upper stories. A deeply recessed portico, with triple

arches springing from clustered piers, provides a grand entry. The capitals of the columns feature carved likenesses of Governor Hazen Pingree, Detroit Mayor William Maybury, and the first four police commissioners to work in the station. A stone passageway connects the main structure to the garage. Towers with conical roofs and elaborate stone dentils give the impression of battlements. This marvelous building desperately needs rescue or at least recording before it is lost altogether.

DE30 Detroit Masonic Temple

1920–1926, George D. Mason. 500 Temple Ave. (northeast corner of Temple and Second avenues)

The Detroit Masonic Temple is the largest and most beautiful Masonic temple in the world. It was built overlooking Cass Park in 1920–1926 by the Masonic Temple Association. This group of fraternal organizations was formed in 1894 after the leaders of various lodges, chapters, councils, commanderies, and the coordinate Scottish Rite bodies created a joint committee to plan for the erection of a Masonic temple. The association occupied the Lafayette Temple, a Richardsonian structure erected at the northeast corner of Lafayette and First streets in 1893–1895. It was quickly outgrown and replaced by this huge gray Indiana limestone structure. The current temple was designed by George D. Mason, who together with Zacharias Rice, planned the earlier temple. It is unique because it holds all the fraternal branches.

The Masonic temple is used as a lodge hall for forty-seven fraternal orders and as an entertainment center for Detroit social and cultural events. It is appropriately styled in a modernized form of the Gothic, which was thought to best capture the spirit and tradition of the Knights Templar and Scottish Rite. The design borrows medieval castellated towers and Tudor arch motifs such as those found in Hampton Court and in the old "Gothic" library at Yale. The building is skillfully composed of three distinct elements: the Ritual Building, a fourteen-story tower; the Shrine Club (Shrine Mosque), a ten-story tower; and the Auditorium Building, a long, low, seven-story connector that joins the two towers. Within the ritualistic area, the lodge rooms are distinctively decorated with Egyptian, Greek Doric, Ionic, Corinthian, Tudor, and Romanesque motifs. Here also is the oak-paneled Tudor Knights Templar quarters and wood and stone Gothic cathedral and the beautiful sixteen-hundred-seat Scottish Rite cathedral. In the center section of the building is the forty-six-hundred-seat auditorium with its immense stage. Above the auditorium is a huge drill hall; below the auditorium are two large ballrooms. The Shrine Club has offices, guest rooms, billiard rooms, and gymnasiums. On the exterior, sculptured figures represent guards and knights in armor, and forty motifs symbolize the orders.

DE31 Detroit Urban League (Albert and Ernestine Krolik Kahn House)

1906, Albert Kahn. 1928, gallery and garage addition. 208 Mack Ave. (southeast corner of Mack Ave. and John R. Street)

The famous Detroit architect Albert Kahn (1869–1942) designed this house of simple elegance for himself and his family. Termed English Renaissance by Albert Kahn Associates, the house is Kahn's version of the Prairie style. There are also Arts and Crafts elements. The two-story house is constructed with Truscon reinforced concrete floors. Named for the Trussed Concrete Steel Company (formed by Kahn's brother, Julius Kahn), the reinforced concrete and tile formed a flat ceiling over each floor and wood sleepers provided above permitted the nailing of finished wood floors. Red brick laid in English bond and trimmed with stone rises in the exterior walls through the first story; the second story is finished in stucco. Slate covers the hipped roof. A wooden door bordered with beautifully carved rosettes is recessed beneath an arched hood in the center of the front. The stair hall and the reception, dining, and living rooms are lined with wood paneling. In 1928 a large gallery was added at the southwest to accommodate the Kahns' social and business activities and their library and art collection. This room is paneled with wood and decorated with an ornamental plaster ceiling. After Kahn's death the house was acquired by the Detroit Urban League.

DE32 Orchestra Hall

1919, C. Howard Crane. 3711 Woodward Ave. (Michigan 1) (northwest corner of Woodward Ave. and Parsons St.)

The first true concert hall built in Detroit, Orchestra Hall is famous for its marvelous acoustics and its Beaux-Arts Classical design. It was planned by C. Howard Crane, a nationally recognized Detroit specialist in theater design, together with his associates Elmer George Kiehler and Cyril E. Schley. Born in Hartford, Connecticut, in 1885, and a protégé of Albert Kahn, Crane eventually designed some two hundred theaters in the United States, fifty of them in Detroit. According to Kiehler, when Crane simply built a building that pleased the eye, it was found pleasing to the ear as well.[7] It was largely through the design of this acoustically superior auditorium, with its rich gold, silver, and ivory interior trimmings, that music patrons were able to persuade Ossip Gabrilowitsch, a Russian-born pianist and composer who had studied with Rimsky-Korsakov in Vienna, to accept the conductorship of the Detroit Symphony. The completion of the hall, together with the Detroit Public Library (then under construction) and the Detroit Institute of Arts (then being designed), marked a cultural awakening in Detroit.

Orchestra Hall is a splendid piece of academic designing. The large rectangular block is backed at the west by the upward projection of the stage loft's skylight. The exterior material of the building is limestone and creamy yellow brick. Above the limestone base containing storefronts and the lobby entrance, the principal facade displays an ornamental unit made up of colossal pilasters that separate two levels of office windows and of a wide entablature embellished with leafy swags and candelabra. Crowning the front of the hall is a broad entablature with an elaborate frieze ornamented by triads of leafy swags, ribbons, and rosettes separated by cartouches and a cornice with Greek fretwork. A large elliptical cartouche topped by a carved female head with manteling projects through the entablature at the center of the building. The main entrance opens into a shallow vestibule and, in turn, the main ellipitical-shaped lobby. The auditorium is nearly rectangular, with a horseshoe-shaped mezzanine of boxes and a balcony.

For twenty years hundreds of concerts were performed within this great hall, some featuring such famous guest artists as Mischa Elman, Pablo Casals, Arthur Rubinstein, Sergei Rachmaninoff, and Vladimir Horowitz. Plagued by financial problems, the symphony moved in 1939 from Orchestra Hall to the larger Masonic temple (DE30), and in 1956 to the Ford Auditorium (DE01.5). The hall then became a theater and later, a church. In the 1970s and 1980s a citizens' committee to save Orchestra Hall won enough support to acquire and to restore this concert hall. The beautiful restoration was planned and supervised by Richard C. Frank. Once again performances are held here. Recently, the Detroit Symphony Orchestra moved back to Orchestra Hall, and Detroiters say that once again the hall looks as good as it sounds.

DE33 The Whitney (David and Sarah Whitney, Jr., House)

1890–1894, Gordon W. Lloyd. 4421 Woodward Ave. (Michigan 1) (northwest corner of Woodward and West Canfield avenues)

The David and Sarah Whitney, Jr., House is a huge "American Palace" on a scale as elaborate, substantial, and opulent as the James J. Hill House. The latter was built in 1887 of East Longmeadow sandstone to the Richardsonian Romanesque design of Peabody and Stearns, on Summit Avenue in Saint Paul. The architect of the Whitney house was Gordon W. Lloyd (1832–1905), considered the dean of Michigan architects at the time. When the Whitney house was finished, the *Detroit Free Press* said it had the distinction of being "the most pretentious modern home in the state and one of the most elaborate houses in the west," and would vie with the Potter Palmer House in Chicago. The huge, gabled, turreted, and round-arched Richardsonian Romanesque house effects a somewhat uneasy compromise between the picturesqueness of the Gothic and the solidity of the Romanesque. The exterior rock face walls of the house are of purplish pink Jasper, quarried in South Dakota and carved at the building site. The interior construction is metal beams and brick interior walls and partitions. This fireproof technique was common in public buildings at this time but rare in domestic architecture, and the Whitney house represents a very special case. The house contains 42 rooms, 218 stained-glass windows, and 20 fireplaces of different marbles or onyx. The grand hall and staircase are the most impressive spaces in the house.

Originally from Watertown, Massachusetts, David Whitney (1830–1900) arrived in Detroit in 1857. He became one of the most influential businessmen in the Midwest, operating two large wholesale lumber and industrial corporations.

The Whitney house is an architectural treasure rich in materials and with beautiful luxurious interiors—a testament to the position and values of a wealthy lumberman and industrialist in the late nineteenth century. The house is exquisitely and appropriately adapted to new use as a restaurant.

DE34 Dunbar Hospital (Detroit Medical Society, Black Nurses Association, Health Care Network)

1892, Guy W. Vinton Company, builder. 580 Frederick Douglass St. (southwest corner Frederick Douglass and Saint Antoine [Richard Allen Blvd.])

Dunbar Hospital was the first black hospital in Detroit. Showing obvious elements of the Queen Anne style, this narrow brick house has a prominent gable roof supported by paired brackets and a second-floor loggia over an open, round-arch porch.

In response to the growth of Detroit's black community after World War I and to the need for better health care for blacks created by the racial segregation of hospitals, Detroit's thirty black physicians founded the Allied Medical Society, a predecessor of the present Detroit Medical Society. Its main objective was to raise money for a black hospital, and it achieved this goal in 1919, when Dunbar Hospital opened. The hospital eventually outgrew the house, which was sold to black businessman Charles C. Diggs in 1928. Diggs went on to become Michigan's first black Democratic state senator in 1937, after he had moved out of the house. The structure was also the childhood home of Charles C. Diggs, Jr., who became Michigan's first African-American member of the U.S. House of Representatives, in 1954. Today, Dunbar Hospital is owned by the Detroit Medical Society, which uses it as a museum and an office.

DE35 Detroit Receiving Hospital / Wayne State University Health Center

1979; William Kessler and Associates; Zeidler Partnership, Inc., Giffels Associates, Inc. 4201 Saint Antoine St. (southwest corner of Saint Antoine St. and West Canfield Ave.)

This high-tech medical building sparkles with new life and hope in the otherwise drab area southeast of Wayne State University. The building is made up of two parts: Detroit Receiving Hospital, an in-patient emergency trauma center, occupies the five-story structure; the Wayne State University Health Care Center, an out-patient center, is housed in the nine-story structure. Each is part of the Detroit Medical Center, which comprises seven health-care institutions. Each structure contains three interconnecting modules. The modules are cruciform plans with pods arranged around all four sides of a 48-foot-square light well. In the two nursing floors of the hospital, the modules are organized into nursing pods of twenty beds each. In the clinic the modules contain specialty clinic pods with examination and consultation rooms arranged around support facilities. The hospital and the clinic are linked by common food service, clinical laboratories, and other shared services. The entire structure is sheathed in a skin of shiny five-foot-wide aluminum panels and of ribbon windows. It is punctuated by bright, orangish-red porcelain enamel, black air intake cylinders, and bright yellow vaults containing shops. An underground concourse with mirrored periscopes connects the two elements.

DE36 Cathedral Church of Saint Paul
(Saint Paul's Protestant Episcopal Cathedral)

1908–1911, Ralph Adams Cram. 4800 Woodward Ave. (Michigan 1) (northeast corner of Woodward Ave. and East Hancock)

In 1906 Saint Paul's Church officially became the Bishop's Church and was offered the opportunity to establish a cathedral. Within two years Ralph Adams Cram (1863–1942) of Cram, Goodhue and Ferguson of Boston and New York was called on to design a building suitable and appropriate as a cathedral for the diocese. The limestone Gothic Revival cathedral has a narrow-gabled and buttressed nave with side aisles, clerestory, and transepts. A rose window is positioned over the pointed-arch entry portal between projecting buttresses that support pinnacles. A large square tower designed to rise over the crossing was never built.

The nave of the grand interior has a pointed-arch arcade resting on smooth columns. Four huge cylindrical piers at the crossing of the nave and transepts were intended to carry the tower. In the south transept a spiral staircase rises to a minstrel gallery faced with carvings of musicians. The woodwork was made by William F. Ross and Company of Cambridge, Massachusetts, although Joseph Kirchmayer of Oberammergau carved the reredos of the sanctuary, the bishop's seat, and the dean's stall, with their pinnacled canopies and the lectern in dark oak. Designed by Mary Chase Stratton and manufactured at her Pewabic Pottery, the tile floor shows brown glazes in the narthex and nave, tan in the chancel and choir, and blue in the sanctuary. Here a pelican feeding drops of her own blood to her young symbolizes the mother church sustaining young churches. Designed and executed by Heaton, Butler and Bayne of London and Charles J. Connick of Boston, stained glass in brilliant colors fills the windows.

Cram explained, "In St. Paul's Cathedral an attempt has been made to adapt to modern ideals, conditions, and environment that style of architecture which Christian civilization developed for its own self-expression, the so-called Gothic of the middle ages."[8] The architect expressed through modern forms the spirit of the Gothic.

Albert A. Albrecht Company and the Vinton Company constructed the cathedral under supervision of George D. Mason, who was a member of the parish.

DE37 Cultural Center

Bounded approximately by Warren, Cass, and Kirby avenues and Brush St. (two miles north of the downtown business district opposite each other on Woodward Ave. [Michigan 1]) .

In 1910 the Detroit City Planning Commission, under the administration of Mayor Philip Breitmeyer, asked Edward II. Bennett, the well-known urban planner, to prepare suggestions for the orderly development of the fast-growing city, including a center of arts and letters. In this 1915 study Bennett proposed the Cultural Center, comprised first of a new public library and art museum. In the 1940s a later master plan for Detroit expanded the Cultural Center to include other museums, a medical center, and an expanded campus for Wayne State University. The 1965 version of the comprehensive city master plan divided the Cultural Center into three zones: Wayne State University, the Detroit Library, and the Cultural Center Park.

DE37.1 Detroit Public Library

1915–1921, Cass Gilbert. 1960–1963?, additions, Cass Gilbert, Jr., and Francis J. Keally. 5201 Woodward Ave. (Michigan 1) (bounded by Woodward, Putnam, Cass, and Kirby avenues)

The Detroit Public Library is a symbol of cultural life in Detroit. The majestic, white Vermont marble building is surrounded on three sides by terraces. Cass Gilbert (1859–1934), one of America's most prominent architects, designed it in the classical mode of the early twentieth century. In scale and wall treatment the building is more French than Italian. The library's restrained symmetrical facade is broken on the first story by molded openings and flat-headed windows. There is an arched loggia with fluted Ionic pilasters on the second floor, while small squared windows and bas-relief panels adorn the frieze. Inside, a double row of Doric columns lines the central east-west hall. Off the hall staircases on the north and south rise to the second floor. Each begins as a single flight but splits at a landing and ascends to a lofty barrel-vaulted hall. Here the rich golds, reds, greens, and blues of the ceiling explode into view in stunning contrast with the white mar-

ble. The colorful ceiling, together with the series of wall murals painted by Edwin H. Blashfield to depict great artists, musicians, and writers, anticipate the murals and stained-glass windows of Adam Strohm Hall, formerly the main delivery room. Three arches in the east wall of this huge room contain murals by native Detroit artist Gari Melchers (1860–1932) showing historical events and allegorical subjects in the early settling of Detroit: *The Landing of Cadillac's Wife, The Conspiracy of Pontiac,* and *The Spirit of the Northwest.* The two groups of three painted glass windows in this room were designed by Frederick J. Wiley. The fireplace of the original children's reading room is adorned with some of the city's most cherished Pewabic tiles illustrating storybook characters.

The Cass Avenue entrance, with Millard Sheets's brilliantly colored mosaic allegorically depicting knowledge and library services, was added in 1963. At the same time the north and south white marble wings were built to provide space for the browsing and children's libraries and the Burton Historical Collection.

DE37.2 Detroit Institute of Arts

1927, Paul Philippe Cret and Zantzinger, Borie and Medary. 1963–1966, Eleanor and Edsel Ford [South] Wing. 1970–1971, Jerome P. Cavanaugh [North] Wing, Gunner Birkerts and Associates, and Harley, Ellington, Cowin and Stirton. 1981, Main Entrance, Kiley-Walker Designs of Vermont. 5200 Woodward Ave. (Michigan 1) (bounded by Woodward and East Kirby avenues and John R. and Farnsworth streets)

The Detroit Institute of Arts is a civic monument in white Vermont marble that relates to the library across Woodward Avenue and fulfills a portion of the City Beautiful program. It was designed by the Philadelphia architect Paul Philippe Cret (1876–1945). Born in France, Cret was trained at the Ecole des Beaux-Arts, and his work is both rational and urbanely French. In this building the triple-arched entrance, the rhythmic windows, the low profile, and the curved entrance drive all signify his controlled approach. The galleries were arranged so that paintings could be displayed with sculpture and furniture in architectural settings that gave each room the same style as the art it contained. Elizabeth Grossman notes that this resulted from the "heterogeneity of intention" of Cret, the French émigré architect, of Wilhelm Valentiner, the German émigré director, and of the city of Detroit's Arts Commission.[9] Dark gray, polished granite recent additions, which add gallery, research, and administrative space, contrast with and respect the dignified Cret Beaux-Arts Classical design by connecting themselves to the original building with bridges through existing window openings. Noted Postmodern architect Michael Graves was selected in March 1989 to design the master plan for a renovation and addition that integrates the overall composition. The *Detroit Industry* mural devoted to the auto industry and painted by Diego Rivera in 1932–1933 is in Rivera Court.

DE37.3 **Horace H. Rackham Educational Memorial Building**

1940–1941, Harley, Ellington and Day. 106 Farnsworth St. (bounded by Farnsworth and John R. streets and Warren and Woodward avenues [Michigan 1])

This classical building reduced to simple terms formed the third unit of "an architecturally harmonious group" designed for the city's beautiful civic and cultural center. It was built for the Engineering Society of Detroit and the University of Michigan Extension Service with a contribution from Horace H. Rackham (1858–1933) and Mary A. Rackham. The designer was Harley, Ellington and Day of Detroit. The firm created a building with classical simplicity but contemporary influences. The reinforced concrete structure is faced with smooth-cut white Georgia marble. Contrasting dark granite is used for the spandrels between windows. Cast bronze ornaments enrich the granite spandrels enframed by the bronze windows. In its center section, bronze

doors lead to the vestibule, and, in turn, the main foyer of the building. Off the foyer is the large auditorium boldly colored in blue with molded bands of gold and red. Above the auditorium is a banquet hall. The center section connects the two wings of the building. On the east, the wing containing the engineering society holds lounges and meeting, game, and dining rooms; on the west, the wing containing the university has class and lecture rooms.

Marshall M. Fredericks sculpted groups of figures depicting education, sciences, engineering, and structural steel workers. These bas-relief white marble works are placed at the termini of four piers separating the five bronze double doors of the main entrance to the building.

This Rackham memorial building is reminiscent of the Horace H. Rackham Building in Ann Arbor (WA09.3, p. 145).

DE37.4 **Scarab Club**

1928–1929, Lancelot Sukert, 217 Farnsworth St. (northeast corner Farnsworth and John R. streets)

The Scarab Club was established in 1916. Its purpose was "to promote the mutual acquaintance of art lovers and art workers, to stimulate and guide toward practical expression the artistic sense of the people of Detroit, and to advance the knowledge and love of the Fine Arts in every possible manner." Its members included painters, sculptors, architects, engravers, illustrators, musicians, and writers. The club's precursor was the Hopkin Club, which was founded in 1907 and named in honor of Detroit artist Robert Hopkin. Initially the Scarab Club occupied temporary quarters. In 1922, under the club president, Henry G. Stevens, the members selected a site adjacent to the art institute and began plans to build the present clubhouse. It is used for entertainment and social purposes and to provide studio and exhibition facilities for its artist members.

The plain brick building blends the Moderne with the Arts and Crafts. In the facade three groups of windows are recessed between flat piers over a band of zigzag brick and another row of terracotta grilles. High above the entrance a medallion manufactured by the Pewabic Pottery, on which is represented the figure of a scarab in turquoise, green, and gold, distinctly marks the brick wall. The first-floor gallery opens to a courtyard on the north. Over the fireplace on the wooden beamed and paneled second-floor lounge, a mural painted by Paul Honoré depicts the Scarab "family tree." Six well-lighted studios with galleries occupy the third floor. The club was designed by Lancelot Sukert (1888–1966), a Detroit architect who belonged to the Scarab Club. Sukert studied architecture at the Universities of California and Pennsylvania. Before starting his own office in 1921, he worked briefly in New York and in the office of Albert Kahn. Sukert explained that the Scarab Club building is "a composite of ideas contributed by many members." The clubhouse is important to the cultural life of Detroit.

DE37.5 Center for Creative Studies

1972–1975, William Kessler and Associates. 245 East Kirby Ave. (between John R. and Brush streets)

This 32-by-32-foot modular structural system of precast concrete components, with enlarged cylindrical columns designed to distribute mechanical and electrical utilities vertically, resembles a Tinker Toy construction. It was built as art and music schools for the Society of Arts and Crafts and the Detroit Community Music School, the present-day Center for Creative Studies.

Founded in 1906 and incorporated in 1915,

the society patterned itself after the tradition of William Morris for the purposes of reinstituting a standard of beauty in articles of everyday, practical use. The society sought to stimulate an interest in design and handicrafts and to provide a market for the crafts. Its early members included George Gough Booth, Albert Kahn, H. J. Maxwell Grylls, Frank Baldwin, William Buck Stratton, Mary Chase Perry Stratton, Hiram Walker, and William D. Laurie.

The society's School Art Guild occupied rented and remodeled quarters until 1916, when it moved into a stuccoed Early English Cottage building on Watson Street. Designed by Stratton and Grylls, it had salesrooms, galleries, workshops, and a theater. This building was replaced in 1958 with a glass-walled building surrounded by a brick screen wall that created a courtyard. It was designed by Yamasaki, Leinweber and Associates and erected at 245 East Kirby Avenue. The present Center for Creative Studies was designed by Kessler and relates to the Brutalist architecture of Paul Rudolph's Endo Laboratories (1962–1964) in Garden City, New York. The Center for Creative Studies, and the complex as a whole, is an indication of the importance of design in the Motor City.

DE38 Wayne State University Mall

Bounded by Cass, Warren, Third (Anthony Wayne Dr.), and Palmer avenues

DE38.1 McGregor Memorial Conference Center

1958, Minoru Yamasaki. Northwest section of the Wayne State University Mall, which is bounded by Cass, Warren, Third (Anthony Wayne Dr.), and Palmer avenues

In 1954, Minoru Yamasaki, then a staff architect with Smith, Hinchman and Grylls, completed a density study of the Wayne State University campus. He planned a compact urban campus consisting of a series of courts linking low buildings no more than four stories in height. After completing his plans, Yamasaki was asked to design the McGregor Memorial Conference Center. A two-story, steel-framed and concrete building faced in travertine marble and aluminum trim, the conference center overlooks a sunken garden and a reflecting pool. The triangular ends of

DE38.1 McGregor Memorial Conference Center

the V-shaped ceiling beams, which are exposed inside and out, form the basis of a decorative pattern that is repeated with variations throughout the building. End walls are faced with white travertine marble, except for their centers, which feature glass pavilions beneath V-shaped projections. On the inside of the conference center, there are rows of single-story conference rooms on each side of a two-story lounge and reception area. A skylight in the lounge is composed of glass pyramids, ending in the glass pavilions. Everywhere the richness of materials is apparent—in the white marble columns and floors, the teakwood doors, the black leather Barcelona chairs, and the turkey red carpet. While the McGregor Memorial Conference Center is modern in concept, the building draws inspiration from the pointed verticality of Gothic cathedrals, the beauty of the Taj Mahal, and the quiet serenity of the sand gardens of a Japanese Zen Buddhist temple.

DE38.2 College of Education Building

1958–1960, Minoru Yamasaki of Yamasaki, Leinweber and Associates. Northeast section of Wayne State University Mall, which is bounded by Cass, Warren, Third (Anthony Wayne Dr.), and Palmer avenues

Yamasaki is known for his proposal of the "space-use concept," his notion of an urban

university free from abstractions. The Board of Governors of Wayne State University, at the suggestion of Provost Neef, decided to appoint him as architect of the College of Education Building so that the first building of the main campus area designed with those tenets in mind would be worked out specifically by him. In accordance with this approach, Yamasaki designed a structure with windowless classrooms in an inner core, along with elevators, stairs, rest rooms, and other service facilities. The classrooms were air conditioned and well-suited for audio-visual presentations. Glass-enclosed passageways and offices surround the classroom block on the upper three levels. The exterior wall of the building consists of structural precast concrete "trees," 40 feet high and 5 feet wide, and made up of columns and spandrels. One hundred twenty gleaming white sections run around the perimeter of the building. Anodized aluminum sash form narrow, pointed windows that contain gray sheet glass. The building rests on a platform. The exterior wall of the lower level is set back ten feet, and a loggia or arcade encircles it. The top level is recessed and has four roof gardens.

DE39 East Ferry Avenue

1887– . East Ferry Ave. between Woodward Ave. (Michigan 1) and Brush St.

East Ferry Avenue was laid out in 1887 when Woodward Avenue was Detroit's most splendid residential street. Dexter M. Ferry platted lots on both sides of East Ferry Avenue and planted rows of shade trees on both sides of the sidewalk. The lots were sold with building restrictions that required the houses to be set back 40 feet from the sidewalk and to cost no less than $7,000. Some of Detroit's wealthy industrialists as well as middle-class Jewish and African-American families came to live on East Ferry Avenue. One hundred years after it was platted, Preservation Wayne began promoting and sponsoring the stabilization and improvement of East Ferry Avenue. In 1990, in cooperation with the Founders Society of the Detroit Institute of Arts, owner of five properties along the avenue, Preservation Wayne studied alternatives for the future of the area and now recommends the development of an East Ferry Arts and Heritage District. It is hoped that a mix of art galleries; offices for arts, cultural, and community organizations; and restaurants or bed-and-breakfast inns will revitalize the area.

DE39.1 **Frank J. Hecker House**

1888–1891, Louis Kamper. 5510 Woodward Ave. (Michigan 1) (northeast corner of Woodward and East Ferry avenues)

With a fortune amassed from manufacturing railroad cars, Col. Frank J. Hecker (1846–1927), a sometime partner of Charles L. Freer (see DE39.2), built and furnished this magnificent stone residence. Louis Kamper designed it in the Châteauesque manner, inspired perhaps by such examples as the original part of the sixteenth-century French Château de Chenonceaux and the Château d'Azay-le-Rideau. This was done presumably to satisfy Hecker's fantasy of himself as nobility. The interior decoration of the forty-nine-room turreted mansion is sumptuous, with Italian Siena marble floors and walls, English oak paneling, Egyptian Nubian marble fireplaces, and Roman tile. More recently, the Smiley Brothers Music Company reused the mansion as a showroom for its pianos and organs, with the carriage house serving as a two-hundred-seat recital hall and music classroom. Smiley Brothers is no longer in business, and today Preservation Wayne is promoting the marketing of the house for adaptive reuse as professional offices.

DE39.2 **Merrill-Palmer Institute of Human Development and Family Life Offices** (Charles Lang Freer House)

1890–1893, Wilson Eyre, Jr. 71 East Ferry Ave.

The Freer house is a major Detroit monument and one of the finest works of Phila-delphia architect Wilson Eyre, Jr. Freer, Eyre, and artists and craftsmen collaborated to produce this Shingle-style house with a Queen Anne vocabulary. It is a product of both the Philadelphia and Detroit Arts and Crafts traditions.

Charles Lang Freer (1856–1919) founded, with Frank J. Hecker, the Peninsular Car Company, a railroad freight car manufacturing company. Both men prospered from it and related enterprises, enabling Freer to retire in 1900 from active business to pursue his interest in collecting art. He collected American and Oriental art, bequeathing his oriental collection to the Smithsonian Institution, which opened the Freer Gallery in Washington, D.C., in 1923.

The house was designed for Freer's collections. Eyre planned a broadly massed house with strong horizontal lines, a steep roof, and subtle asymmetry within an essentially symmetrical facade. Hard bluestone from Ulster, New York, and wood shingles make up the rich textural surfaces of the exterior walls. The flexible interior plan pivots around a double-story central hall containing a staircase framed by round arches supported by posts and uses basket-weave screens, instead of balusters, to support the stair rail. Built-in furniture and decorative details are very con-

DE39.2 Merrill-Palmer Institute of Human Development and Family Life Offices (Charles Lang Freer House)

spicuous. Thomas W. Dewing and Dwight Tryon assisted with the interior decoration. Scott, Kamper and Scott supervised the construction of the house for Henry Carew and Company. In 1904–1906 an art gallery was added to the space above the stable. Then, in 1909, James Abbott McNeill Whistler's famous Peacock Room, originally commissioned by Frederick Leyland of London and now in the Freer Gallery in Washington, was installed in an addition to the stable and gallery, at the rear of the house.

In its sensitive use of surface textural richness and in its picturesque interplay of projections and recessions, the Freer house epitomizes the visual delights of the Shingle style. It stands as a testament to Freer's aesthetic sensibility at a time when less sensitive industrialists were pursuing grand and often opulent mansions. Open to public.

DE39.3 John and Emma Woodward Scott House

1886–1887, John Scott. 84 East Ferry Ave.

This is the house of noted Michigan architect John Scott. It was built in the picturesque asymmetrical mix of medieval and classical motifs associated with the Queen Anne style at its best. The red brick, Portage Entry sandstone, and shingle structure has a rich assortment of dormers, bays, a tower, and decorative chimneys. Half-timbering and plasterwork finish the front and side gables, and decoratively carved shield motifs surrounded by foliation adorn the pediments of several gables.

DE39.4 Detroit Association of Women's Clubs Clubhouse (William Lennane House)

1913, Smith, Hinchman and Grylls. 5461 Brush St. (southwest corner of Brush St. and East Ferry Ave.)

Built for William Lennane (1872–1941), a building contractor, this house was acquired in 1941, during the presidency of Rosa Gragg, by the Detroit Association of Colored Women's Clubs to serve as a clubhouse. The association, founded in 1922, consisted of ten women's clubs devoted to charitable uplift, scholarship procurement for deserving black youngsters, and the educational and spiritual improvement of its members. The two-and-a-half-story, symmetrical, red brick house is

classically inspired. Block modillions support the corona beneath the flank gable roof. The roof is pierced with prominent gable dormers. Windows are topped with brick headers.

DE40 Cadillac Motor Car Company Amsterdam Street Plant

1905, George D. Mason. 450 Amsterdam St.

Henry M. Leland founded the Cadillac Motor Car Company in 1902, and this building was the main assembly plant until 1920, when Cadillac moved to its Clark Street facility. This three-story, reinforced concrete structure was built in only sixty-seven days and was finished several weeks after Kahn's Packard Building Number 10. It was a pioneer in the use of reinforced concrete for industrial building.

DE41 Ford Motor Company Piquette Avenue Plant

1904, Field, Hinchman and Smith. Northwest corner of Piquette Ave. and Beaubien St.

After quickly outgrowing its first factory on Mack Avenue, the Ford Motor Company built this well-lighted, three-story, rectangular, brick industrial building that exemplifies the standard mill design developed in New England. Provisions were also made for adequate protection against fires through fire walls and an automatic sprinkler system. Repeated arcades containing windows grouped within segmental arches march along the sides of the building and a battlemented cornice runs along the front. Ford first built the Model T here in 1908 and struggled to increase production, before finally moving to the Highland Park Plant (WN03, p. 114) in 1910.

DE42 Fisher Body Plant Number 21

1919, Albert Kahn. Hastings St. at Piquette Ave. (south side of Piquette Ave. between Hastings and Saint Antoine streets)

As opposed to the preceding masonry factory (DE41), this six-story reinforced concrete building exemplifies Albert Kahn's open skeletal structure. One of the four Fisher Body plants located in or near Detroit's Milwaukee Junction Industrial District in the late 1920s, it has served as a body manufacturing plant, an engineering design facility, and, until recently, as a Cadillac limousine plant. It is an outstanding example of the reinforced concrete frame and glass wall construction that marked industrial building during the first decades of the twentieth century.

DE43 New Center

Area around West Grand Blvd. and Second and Lothrop avenues, three miles north of downtown

The New Center area consists of four primary structures linked by skywalks: the General Motors, Fisher, New Center, and New Center One buildings. The baseline for the New Center development of the 1920s was West Grand Boulevard, a broad street surrounding the city, envisioned in the 1870s as a "gravel road where gentlemen with fast horses could let out the reins," though the street was not actually begun until 1891. Growth and movement toward the boulevard on the north was hastened by the coming of the electric railway in the 1890s, which made possible rapid transit out Woodward Avenue. By the 1920s the intersection of West Grand Boulevard and Woodward Avenue was the geographic center of the city, easily reached from anywhere in the city by main avenues for automobiles and by transit lines within walking distance of residential neighborhoods. This new city center was removed from the congestion of downtown Detroit at the river's edge. Here General Motors built its world headquarters, and the Fisher brothers planned and built a new center of commerce for Detroit.

DE43.1 General Motors Building

1919–1921, Albert Kahn. 3044 West Grand Blvd. (southeast corner of West Grand Blvd. and Second Ave. Occupies an entire block bounded by West Grand Blvd. and Cass, Milwaukee, and Second avenues.)

The mammoth General Motors Building, with its eighteen hundred offices, symbolizes the power, prestige, and scale of the largest manufacturing corporation in the world. The fifteen-story building consists of an elongated central block with four projecting wings on the front and four in back, which allow ample natural light and greater air circulation for the employees. A five-story annex is at the

DE43.1 General Motors Building

rear. Created to house a wide scope of activities under one roof, the building contains an auditorium and exposition halls, as well as auto display rooms, shops, a gymnasium, a cafeteria, and lounges. The limestone-faced, steel-frame structure vividly exemplifies Louis Sullivan's tripartite concept of the tall building: an open, arcaded basement element carries unbroken vertical piers through ten stories to a colonnaded crown. Kahn's treatment differs from Sullivan, however, in that he concedes to the prevailing taste of the period by making his ornament classical. The classical motifs seemed appropriate for a headquarters office, in contrast to Kahn's contemporary functional Fisher Body Plant Number 21 (DE42) a few blocks away. William C. Durant, founder of the General Motors Corporation and its president in 1919, commissioned Albert Kahn for this project, which was his largest commission to date. The General Motors Building is a National Historic Landmark.

DE43.2 Fisher Building

1927–1929, Albert Kahn. 3011 West Grand Blvd. (northwest corner of West Grand Blvd. and Second Ave.)

Meant to be a city within a city, the massive, soaring Fisher Building with its vertical emphasis throughout is a structure where one can park, conduct one's business, bank, shop, dine, and be entertained without having to leave the building. It is Albert Kahn's most important nonindustrial building from the 1920s. The seven Fisher brothers—Fred, Alfred, Lawrence, Charles, William, Howard, and Edward—ostensibly built the building as

DE43.2 Fisher Building

a home for Fisher and Company, which had pioneered in making the closed automobile body. In reality they may have intended it as a monument to themselves. The Fisher brothers chose the best materials, the best location, and the best architect, who, in turn, engaged the most talented sculptors, modelers, decorators, and craftsmen as collaborators.

The Fisher Building is a twenty-eight-story tower with two eleven-story wings spanning to the north along Second, and to the west along Grand Boulevard. The exterior bears a striking resemblance to Eliel Saarinen's Chicago Tribune Tower design of 1922. Kahn begins with an arcaded basement unit similar to the one he used in the earlier General Motors Building (DE43.1). Above that, however, the vertical piers rise unbroken to a tapered top, reflecting in dramatic terms the change in attitude toward high-rise design that was signalled by Saarinen's Tribune Tower. The first three floors of the Fisher Building are faced with Minnesota granite; the upper floors, with Maryland marble. A sloped roof originally covered with gold-leafed tile, but now with green tile, tops the structure. Inside, the 44-foot-high, barrel-vaulted arcade is ornamented with paintings, marble, mosaic, and bronze. Blues, peacock greens, gold, and deep orange predominate in the decorative artwork of the arcade. On the rotunda near the main entrance there is a circular design of cherubs and eagles, and elsewhere in the arcade are symbolic muses and

nude figures, flora and fauna, folk art motifs, and eagles. Much decoration is the work of Geza Maroti of Budapest, a proponent of the European Arts and Crafts movement. The Fisher Theater, originally designed as a movie palace by A. S. Graven and A. G. Mayger in a Central American motif, was renovated in 1961. Of three towers intended for the site, only this one was built. In April 1929, the Fisher Building won the Silver Medal Award of the Architectural League of New York as the most beautiful commercial building erected that year. In 1989 it was designated a National Historic Landmark.

DE43.3 New Center One Building

1980–1982, Bruce Graham of Skidmore, Owings and Merrill. 3031 West Grand Blvd. (northeast corner of West Grand Blvd. and Second Ave.)

In 1980 Trizek Corporation of Toronto, which currently owns the Fisher Building, collaborated with General Motors in the construction of the New Center One Building. The project was intended to augment and enhance the existing investments of the two corporations at the New Center. "Any new investment perks up the old," claimed Brent W. Blitz, who was the vice-president for Trizec's eastern U.S. operations. New Center One was the first new office building in the New Center area in fifty years. Sensitive to the high architectural significance of the General Motors and Fisher buildings, the organizations sought a design for the new building that would complement the two National Historic landmarks.

New Center One was designed by Bruce Graham of Skidmore, Owings and Merrill. The eight-story Postmodern office and retail complex is built around a large, naturally lighted atrium. Its simple tripartite division, the round arches, the light color of the precast concrete exterior, and the placement of the building on the site capture the spirit of the historic structures of the New Center. Inside two levels of shops and six floors of offices are arranged around two atriums. In a gesture of concession to historic preservationists, the clear glass tube skywalks that link the new structure to the older buildings at New Center connect through existing window openings.

SOUTHWEST DETROIT

DE44 Fort Wayne

1845–1850, Lt. Montgomery C. Meigs. 6053 West Jefferson Ave.

After border tensions developed between the United States and Canada in 1837, Congress appropriated funds to build Fort Wayne at a major bend in the Detroit River, 3.5 miles south of the intersection of Jefferson and Woodward avenues. The square stronghold is surrounded by a massive masonry wall with triangular corner redoubts and is reached through a tunnel. It contains a barracks, parade grounds, and a powder magazine. Outside the fort are the brick administrative buildings constructed after 1870. Fort Wayne served as a troop training center in the Civil War and as an induction center in World Wars I and II. Today the city of Detroit operates a military museum here.

DE45 Cadillac Motor Car Company Clark Street Plant

1921, Dupont Engineering Company. 2680 Clark St.

This large, integrated manufacturing and assembly plant consists mainly of four-story reinforced concrete buildings of the type commonly built by Detroit auto makers in the 1910s and early 1920s. Unlike the one-story sprawling plants conducive to mass production, Cadillac chose to return to the more traditional multi-level buildings in order to sustain the image of quality not quantity in the production of its cars. Cadillac's manufacturing operations, previously scattered around Detroit, were now consolidated in one location.

WEST SIDE

DE46 Mark Twain Development

1927–1931, Miller-Storm Company. 11310–11344 Mark Twain Ave. (south of Plymouth Rd.)

These sturdy, compact, and unpretentious but charming Tudor Revival bungalows exemplify the many houses designed and built throughout the city by the Miller-Storm Company with the prices ranging from $5,000 to $15,000 for people of moderate means. The dwellings at 11310 through 11344 Mark Twain Avenue are illustrated on page 69 of the company's booklet, *Good Homes: A Book Designed to Help You Plan, Finance and Equip Your Home* (1929). The owners of these homes worked for the nearby Electric Refrigeration Plant (later, in 1937, Nash-Kelvinator, and currently American Motors). On Plymouth Road at the head of Mark Twain, a towered administration building that was built to "enhance the beauty of the whole neighborhood" fronts the plant.[10] The local newspaper account praised the plant for its utility and beauty, "The lines of the buildings are wholly honest and structural." The administration building was designed by Amedeo Leoni, the industrial layout by Wallace McKenzie, and the tower enclosure and industrial units by William E. Kapp—all of Smith, Hinchman and Grylls. The date is 1927.

NORTH AND NORTHWEST DETROIT

DE47 Grand Riviera Theater

1925, John Eberson. 9222 Grand River Ave. (Michigan 5) (northwest corner of Grand River Ave. and Joy Rd.)

A unique, broad, 80-foot-high octagonal tower with three large, arched windows in an eclectic Renaissance Revival, Spanish Revival style designates the entrance to the Grand Riviera Theater. Inside the tower, Eberson created a two-story rotunda with a shallow dome. Elaborately painted decoration between gilded ribs along with light bulbs encircling the oculus in the center of the dome create a fanciful interior. Tall arched windows, terracotta reliefs of vases and flowers, and a plaster bal-

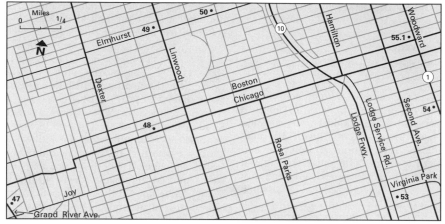

Inset 4. Northwest 1 (DE47–DE50, DE53–DE55; see Detroit map, p. 64; DE44–DE46, DE51–DE52)

Inset 5. Northwest 2 (DE56–DE58)

96

ustrade comprise the second-story decoration of the rotunda. Terracotta was used extensively in the theater facade and lobby of the reinforced concrete structure because it met fire code requirements.

The Grand Riviera Theater was Detroit's first atmospheric theater and is the oldest extant Michigan example of the popular invention of John Eberson. This Viennese-born-and-trained architect introduced the concept in 1923 in the Houston Majestic. The aim of the atmospheric theater was to create an opulent garden setting indoors. When the lights were dimmed, birds, clouds, stars, and mythical creatures were projected onto the plain blue ceiling or sky, allowing for a change in atmosphere without any structural or decorative alterations. False fronts of Mediterranean villas capped with parapets frame the base of the auditorium and balcony walls, simulating an exotic palace garden.

The Grand Riviera was near the junction of three major streetcar lines and was located beyond the downtown theater district in a residential area of smaller, ordinary, second-run movie houses.

DE48 Clinton Street Greater Bethlehem Temple (Shaarey Zedek Synagogue)

1932, Albert Kahn. 2900 West Chicago Blvd. (northwest corner of West Chicago Blvd. and Lawton Ave.)

For its sixth home, the members of the Conservative congregation Shaarey Zedek turned to Detroit's premier industrial architect, Albert Kahn, who had already produced a monumental temple building for their Reform coreligionists at Temple Beth El (DE54, Lighthouse Cathedral). Kahn was influenced by Cleveland's and Chicago's up-to-date Romanesque Revival synagogues and used that style for this polychrome, round-arched edifice; the triple entry is through a colonetted arcade. Inside the sanctuary, which has been sensitively altered, are impressive wooden trusses, twin colonnades, and an elaborately decorated ark wall. Completed despite lawsuits and the depression, the building is a testimony to the success and religious commitment of Jews, and later, of African Americans in Detroit.

DE49 Miller-Storm Company Office

1927, Charles Noble. 12001 Linwood Ave. (northwest corner of Linwood and Elmhurst avenues)

The "Home of Homes" of the Miller-Storm Company is a classy, Tudor Revival structure, posing as a residential complex, that responds to its corner location with gable dormers, half-timbering, and display windows on both Linwood and Elmhurst avenues. The office was an advertisement for the homes sold by the company and may even be classified as a duck, as Robert Venturi developed the term. It was a veritable showroom for the company's houses. It offered customers home plans, a library, and displays of building materials, appliances, and construction methods. George W. Miller and Arthur S. Storm organized the company in 1921. Their objective was to address the problem of home shortages in the city with "sturdy, attractive, modern homes."[11] Miller-Storm Company built all types of single and multiple dwellings at reasonable prices (DE46, Mark Twain Development). The office had land contract, financing, planning, designing, and construction departments, and the company had branch offices throughout the city and suburbs.

DE50 New Mount Zion Missionary Baptist Church (Beth David Synagogue)

1928, John L. Popkin. 2201 Elmhurst Ave. (northwest corner of Elmhurst Ave. and Fourteenth St.)

Described in the 1920s as "early Romanesque with a decided Byzantine feeling," little has been done to alter this synagogue building in spite of its current Christian use.[12] It is a brick and stone building with a projecting central bay; a large, two-story arch frames a triple entrance. The tablets of the law still pierce the roofline at the center of an elaborate arcuated frieze. Solomonic columns and winged lions, reminiscent of San Marco in Venice, lend an exotic eastern air. Financial problems in the depression led the congregation to reconstitute itself as B'nai David, and in the 1950s it followed its members to the northwest suburbs (see OK18, B'nai David Synagogue, p. 173).

DE51 Packard Motor Car Company Plant

1903–1911, Albert Kahn and others. 1580 East Grand Blvd. (both sides of East Grand Blvd., between Mount Elliot and Concord Ave.)

The earlier nine buildings of this complex are of standard mill construction, but Albert Kahn and his brother Julius, an engineer, designed Building Number Ten (1905) using reinforced concrete. This was the first factory building in Detroit to utilize a reinforced concrete frame and interior columns. Kahn's construction permitted larger floor space without the interruption of supporting members—a definite advantage in the automobile manufacturing process. The later Packard Forge Shop (1911) anticipated Kahn's later single-story manufacturing buildings of steel and glass. This complex was the major Packard manufacturing facility from 1903 until 1956, when Studebaker bought Packard and ultimately closed the plant.

DE52 Plymouth Motor Corporation Lynch Road Assembly Plant

1928, Albert Kahn. 6334 Lynch Rd.

Walter Chrysler introduced the Plymouth automobile in 1928 to compete with Ford and Chevrolet in the low-price field and commissioned Albert Kahn to design this assembly complex. The main assembly building, a steel and glass structure, 375 feet wide and 2,490 feet long, was at that time the largest automobile assembly building in the world. The Lynch Road plant was the last major new automobile plant built in Detroit until 1984, when the General Motors Hamtramck Assembly Plant opened.

DE53 New Center Commons

1900–1925. On Bethune, Pallister, and Seward avenues and Virginia Park between Woodward Ave. (Michigan 1) and Seville Row and Lodge Service Drive

The neighborhood has solidly crafted houses dating from the arrival of the streetcar out Woodward Avenue. Laid out in 1893, Virginia Park contains architect-designed houses for upper-middle-class business people and professionals and their families. Building materials were restricted to brick and stone, the homes had a 25-foot common setback, only one house could be built on each 50-foot lot, and homes had to cost at least $5,000. Fearing commercial growth on nearby Woodward Avenue would lower their property values, homeowners started in 1910 the Virginia Avenue Improvement Association and landscaped the entrances in a parklike manner to separate the neighborhood from Woodward Avenue.

Dividing houses into apartments for rentals began in the 1940s and continued through the 1980s. Then, General Motors announced its New Center Commons plan, sponsored six rehabilitations on Virginia Park, and urged other Virginia Park property owners to undertake similar projects. Since then, nearly 150 houses and 50 apartments have been acquired, rehabilitated, and marketed by the New Center Development Partnership, a subsidiary of the General Motors Corporation. For costs ranging from $32,000 to $135,000, people can enjoy in-city living at midtown. Streets have been realigned and landscaped with Urban Development Action Grant funds and made secure by police patrols.

DE54 Lighthouse Cathedral (Temple Beth El)

1922, Albert Kahn. 8801 Woodward Ave. (Michigan 1) (northwest corner of Woodward and Gladstone avenues)

Established in 1850, Beth El was the first Jewish congregation to be organized in Michigan. In 1860 it adopted Reform practices and grew into one of the largest temples in the Midwest. The congregation built some of the most impressive, well-publicized, and influential religious buildings by leading architects. Their earlier home at 3424 Woodward Avenue, by Mason and Kahn, is now the Bonstelle Theater with virtually no resemblance to its original usage. It was noteworthy not only for its classical architecture—the exterior was modeled on the Pantheon, the interior was rich with Louis XVI detailing—but for its flexible plan with movable partitions for overflow seating. Seating is arranged in a semicircle beneath a dome resting on squinches and, in turn, piers. In contrast to the Bonstelle, the facade of the Lighthouse Cathedral retains much of the temple's character. It is an octastyle temple, the Ionic order of which is repeated in the interior. With its attic story and classical portico, it recalls the Lincoln Memorial in Washington and anticipates Angell Hall (WA09, p. 144) on the University of Michigan campus. Albert Kahn, whose reputation in the 1920s was based upon his functional automobile factories, showed himself here to be the master of historical forms as well. The building is monumental in every sense: grand, imposing, dignified, and derived from a monumental classical concept.

The congregation's intent to express patriotism, as well as religious values, is obvious.

DE55 Boston-Edison Neighborhood

1900–1930. On Edison and Longfellow avenues and Chicago and Boston boulevards between Woodward (Michigan 1) and Linwood avenues

Boston-Edison was the premier early twentieth-century residential neighborhood on the north side of Detroit. It is comprised of approximately nine hundred grand period revival residences—mostly Neo-Tudor, Renaissance Revival, and Colonial Revival—within a forty-block, tree-lined area. They were built during the first quarter of the twentieth century for influential and wealthy Detroit families, including the families of Henry Ford, Horace Rackham, the Fisher brothers, the Kern brothers, W. O. Briggs, Rabbi Leo Franklin, the Wagners, the Siegels (150 West Boston Boulevard), the Kresges (70 West Boston Boulevard), and the Grinnells. In the 1950s and 1960s the construction of the John Lodge Freeway bisected the neighborhood, and many changes took place. Although many houses are maintained in their original condition, some were acquired by such institutions as the Catholic Foreign Mission Society of America and the Archdiocese of Detroit, while others became rooming houses.

DE55.1 Sebastian S. and Anna Harvey Kresge House

1914, Meade and Hamilton. 70 West Boston Blvd. (northwest corner of West Boston Blvd. and Woodward Ave. [Michigan 1])

This palatial stuccoed brick Renaissance Revival house was built for Sebastian S. Kresge (1867–1966), and his wife, Anna. Kresge was the founder of the five-and-ten-cent store empire. Once surrounded by beautifully tended landscaped grounds, the house shares a full block with the Benjamin Siegel House, their carriage houses, and servants quarters. The Siegel house is a gray stone Neo-Renaissance structure built about a year later. The entire block is ringed with a black iron fence. The Kresge house is essentially a three-story rectangular mass with a low-pitched hipped roof. Paired, hipped-roof pavilions project on either side of the center section. Faced with wood that rises to a cornice supported by block modillions, it contains the triple-arched and metal-gated openings of the main entrance. The sun room on the southwest and the porte-cochère on the southeast balance the symmetrical composition. Some Craftsmanlike details are evident. The designers were Frank B. Meade (1867–1947) and James M. Hamilton (1873–1941) of Cleveland.

DE56 Palmer Park

Bounded by Pontchartrain Dr., Seven Mile Rd., Woodward Ave. (Michigan 1), and McNichols Rd.

The park consists of nearly 300 acres of the original 725-acre Palmer estate laid out on a gently rolling wooded tract with two small lakes. Half was given to the city in 1893 by Thomas W. Palmer (1830–1913), a speculator in real estate and lumber; the other half was purchased by the city in 1920. A log house that had been the Palmer's summer house and country retreat (1885, Mason and Rice) is within the park.

Across Pontchartrain Drive off Hamilton Drive is the Detroit Golf Club (1917, Albert Kahn), a low rambling clubhouse reminiscent of the cottages of the English countryside. The two eighteen-hole golf courses are surrounded by large, period revival houses.

DE57 Palmer Park Apartments

1925–1964. Bounded by Covington Ave., Pontchartrain Blvd., and McNichols Rd.

Palmer Park is a planned community containing some of the most exuberant apartment buildings in Michigan. The campuslike park, with spacious, landscaped grounds and curving streets, was once part of the country estate of Thomas W. Palmer. Log Cabin Farms was subdivided in 1923 by the Merrill Palmer Institute, according to plans the Palmers had made ten years earlier. Building along the winding streets began in 1925 with the intent of producing luxurious upper-middle-class apartments away from downtown congestion. Within four years, twenty-seven buildings were completed. Included are fine and varied examples of Egyptian, Venetian, Tudor, Moorish, Spanish, Mediterranean, and Beaux-Arts Classical buildings bearing equally prestigious-sounding names, such as El Dorado, Florentine, and La Vogue. In the 1930s Palmer Park's development continued in the Streamline Moderne mode. Soon thereafter, churches, rows of townhouses, and lavish apartments appeared.

DE57.1 Whitmore Plaza

1928, Weidimaier and Gay. 300 Whitmore Rd.

The Whitmore Plaza mingles Moorish accents in an Art Deco design, in a unique and exotic creation with Moorish arches, geometric yellow brick patterns, and decorative elements. The building is arranged in a U shape. Square, towerlike elements terminating in simple battlements and gables rise at the corners of both wings and the center pavilion and are connected to one another by red tile-clad pent roofs.

DE57.2 Saint Paul Temple of the Apostolic Faith (Temple Israel)

1951, 1956, 1960, William E. Kapp. 17400 Manderson

After meeting for several years in the auditorium of the Detroit Institute of Arts, the members of Temple Israel commissioned William E. Kapp, the architect of Meadow Brook Hall (OK05, p. 161) and the Horace H. Rackham Building (WA09.3, p. 145) at the University of Michigan, to design a large and costly temple complex. Drawing upon his Ann Arbor building and influenced by the

apartment buildings of Palmer Park, he produced an Art Deco design. First to be finished was the circular sanctuary of limestone crowned with a classical frieze and a copper cornice with palmettes. An allusion to the Middle East is found in the lotus columns flanking the Egyptoid entrance—perhaps they refer to the statues of Boaz and Jachin that stood before the temple in Jerusalem. The social hall was the second phase of construction and the school wing was finished in 1960. Few alterations to the building were made thereafter. The sanctuary is 40 feet high and 120 feet in diameter, seating twelve hundred beneath a beveled ceiling supported by overly slender Ionic columns. At the center of the room is a large Star of David, but the most noteworthy object, the ark, has been removed. The congregation sold the temple to Word of Faith, and moved in 1980 to a new temple in West Bloomfield.

DE58 Palmer Woods

1915–1970s, Ossian Cole Simonds, landscape architect. Bounded by West Seven Mile Rd., Sherwood Forest Subdivision, Evergreen Cemetery and Woodward Ave. (Michigan 1)

This exclusive residential neighborhood consists of nearly three hundred large houses constructed mostly between 1915 and 1940 after plans by such well-known architects as Minoru Yamasaki, Frank Lloyd Wright, Maginnis and Walsh, Richard Marr, Alvin E. Harley, and J. F. Ivan Dise for leading Detroit industrialists, merchants, corporate officers, doctors, and lawyers. Charles W. Burton (1848–1945), real estate developer and president of the Burton Abstract and Title Company, acquired the acreage from the heirs of Thomas Palmer in 1915 and platted and developed Palmer Woods. The subdivision was landscaped by Ossian Cole Simonds (1855–1931), a civil engineer with Holabird, Simonds and Roche, to retain natural beauty and to add winding drives, wooded vistas, and artistically grouped shrubbery. Architecturally, the Neo-Tudor style dominates the homes of the chief executives of the automobile industry—Fisher Body, General Motors, Chrysler, Chevrolet—and the S. S. Kresge Company. Palmer Woods received the Michigan Horticultural Society's Award of Merit in 1938 for being the finest platted subdivision in Michigan.

DE58.1 **John A. Kunsky House**

1924, C. Howard Crane. 1630 Wellesley Dr.

The large half-timber Neo-Tudor Kunsky house is a rare example of a residence designed by the noted theater designer C. Howard Crane. Crane received many commissions from John A. Kunsky for designs for theaters in his Detroit empire: the Madison (1917), the Capitol (1922), the Palms (1925), and the Michigan (1926). The house is a theatrical rendition of the Neo-Tudor.

DE58.2 **John Salley House** (residence of the Cardinal of the Archdiocese of Detroit / Reverend M. J. Gallagher House)

1924–1926, Maginnis and Walsh. 19366 Lucerne Dr. (corner of Lucerne and Wellesley drives)

The largest house in Palmer Woods was built as the austere and solemn residence of the Cardinal of the Archdiocese of Detroit. It was erected to replace the red brick Bishop's house erected in 1876 on Washington Boulevard. This street had been transformed by real estate developers during 1916–1930 from a quiet residential street into a thoroughfare of public and commercial buildings and was no longer suitable for the residence of the highest ranking member of the Catholic church in Detroit (see DE08). Although the Palmer Woods house was built for the Bishop, it was designed in the anticipation that Detroit would achieve the status of an archdiocese. Boston architects Maginnis and Walsh were the designers of the Neo-Tudor house. The exterior was intended to convey "dignity, without any suggestion of extravagance" or sumptuousness.[13] It was planned to be large enough to accommodate the actual and symbolic needs of the anticipated archdiocese. The house is 40,000 square feet in size and contains more than seventy rooms. The material is variously colored brick trimmed with Briar Hill stone. The symmetrical U-shaped structure faces the apex of the angle created by the intersection of Lucerne and Wellesley drives, and the wings on either side of the center section run parallel to these two streets. Bishop Michael J. Gallagher occupied the house from 1926 to 1937. From 1937 to 1958 Cardinal Edward Mooney lived here, and from 1959 until his death in 1988, Cardinal John Francis Dearden resided here. Then, in 1989, the archdiocese sold the house (Dearden's successor occupied the former John Dodge House at 75 East Boston Boulevard, located conveniently next to Most Blessed Sacrament Cathedral). Currently the house is owned and thoroughly enjoyed by John Salley of the Detroit Pistons basketball team. Salley has taken his stewardship of the house seriously. Except for minor changes—the altar of the now profane chapel adjoining the Cardinal's second-floor living suite serves a different god (there is now a wide-screen television and video), the Cardinal's throne has been removed from the reception room, and reproduction Renaissance paintings replaced with African-American art—the house and its original furnishings are intact.

DE58.3 **William A. and Lura Fisher House**

1925, Richard H. Marr, Bryant Fleming, landscape architect. 1791 Wellesley Dr.

The brick, stone, and slate Neo-Tudor house of the president of the Fisher Body Corporation and vice-president of General Motors and his wife, Lura, is a massive structure with a Tudor-arch limestone entrance. Lavish interior finishings include Waterford crystal chandeliers, European stained glass, and Pewabic tile. Recently, many of the valuable interior fixtures were stripped for sale as salvage. Landscaped by Bryant Fleming, the grounds contain a conservatory and an indoor swimming pool and are connected to the Alfred Fisher House, erected in 1925 at 1791 Balmoral Drive, to the designs of Richard H. Marr.

DE58.4 **Turkel-Benbow House**

1956, Frank Lloyd Wright. 2760 West Seven Mile Rd.

The Turkel-Benbow house is a low, horizontal, L-shaped, Usonian Automatic house built of precast concrete blocks fitted together and joined with steel reinforcing rods and concrete. Wright, in offering the Usonian Automatic houses, hoped that the owners would be able to build the homes themselves using concrete blocks, such as those at Parkwyn Village in Kalamazoo (1948) (KZ14, p. 227). The Turkel-Benbow house is considerably larger than the Wright Usonian concept. Pierced concrete blocks admit ample light into this home, which is absent any large windows. The strong horizontal emphasis is accentuated by the prominent decorated cornice and the trademark flat roof. The Turkel-Benbow work lacks the simplicity of Wright's Goetsch-Winckler house in Okemos (1939) (IN13, p. 301) and other Wright houses in Michigan. Nevertheless, this house is reminiscent of the use of the twentieth-century technology of concrete blocks that Wright experimented with at the Millard house (1923).

EAST SIDE

DE59 **Lafayette Park**

1955–1963; Ludwig Mies van der Rohe; Ludwig Hilberseimer, urban planner; Herbert Greenwald and Samuel Katzin, developers; Alfred Caldwell, landscape architect. One mile east of Woodward Ave.

(Michigan 1); east side of Chrysler Freeway (I-375); .25 mile north of Jefferson Ave.

This 78-acre urban redevelopment project, originally known as the Gratiot Park Development, was planned by Mies and Hilberseimer. A 19-acre park runs north-south through the center of the site and is interspersed with extensive landscaping, planned by Caldwell, to assure privacy and a decidedly suburban environment with no through traffic. The International style high- and low-rise buildings complement one another, delineate space, frame the exterior of the site, and link with access streets via cul-de-sacs and localized parking areas.

The precise proportions and simplicity of these skeletal constructions, which exemplify the Miesian International style, are reaffirmed in the aluminum and tinted glass sheathing of the twenty-one-story Pavilion Apartments (1958) and the twenty-one-story Lafayette Towers (1963). The low-rise, one-story row houses, with their private, brick-walled garden courts (1958), and the two-story townhouses (1958) also reveal the skeletal structuring in their black steel trim, aluminum glazing frames, clear plate glass, and buff brick terminating walls.

In the areas of the low-rise buildings, the parking spaces are approximately four feet below grade. This feature, when combined with the reflection of trees and shrubs in the glass facades, understates the presence of the automobile and accentuates the parklike quality that has rendered this site a highly successful example of urban redevelopment.

Subsequent to 1963, buildings designed by other architects have been erected in Lafayette Park generally following the original plan.

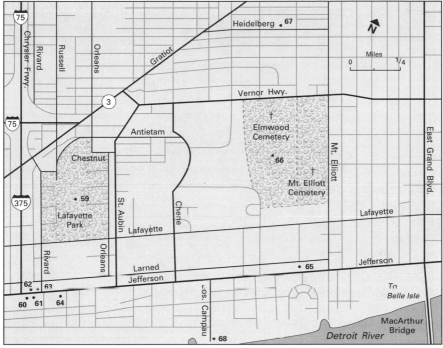

Inset 6. East Side 1 (DE59–DE68)

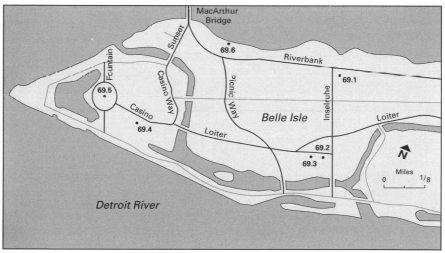

Inset 7. East Side 2, Belle Isle (DE69)

103

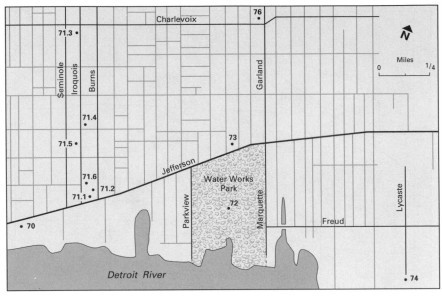

Inset 8. East Side 3 (DE70–DE74, DE76; see Detroit map, p. 64, for DE75)

DE60 **Christ Church**

1861–1863, Gordon W. Lloyd. 1902, chancel lengthened. 960 East Jefferson Ave.

Christ Church is Detroit's oldest Protestant church remaining on its original site. The church was founded in 1845, when Detroit's existing Episcopal church proved too small to house its congregation. In 1846 a wooden church, reportedly designed by Montgomery C. Meigs (1816–1892), was consecrated on this site. Reverend William N. Lyster, one of Michigan's most prominent early clergymen, served as its first rector. In 1860 a stone chapel with bellcote, which still stands at the rear of the present structure facing Woodbridge Street, was erected, and the wooden church torn down. Work then began on the present building. It was completed in 1863.

Christ Church is the supreme expression of the Ecclesiology doctrine. This doctrine affected the form and character of the church. The doctrine was disseminated in the Camden Society's *The Ecclesiologist,* first published in 1841. It spelled out specific liturgical and symbolic reasons for the manner in which the church was conceived and offered advice to builders. Well-known Detroit church architect Gordon W. Lloyd—the architect of the famous Whitney house (DE33)—designed

Christ Church. This Gothic Revival structure uses the Latin cross-plan with rock-faced limestone ashlar trimmed with buff sandstone. At the northeast corner, flanking the front of the building and surmounting the buttresses, are paired crocketed pinnacles. At the northwest corner the four-stage tower with an arcaded belfry, a wedge-shaped gable roof and pinnacles serves as a beacon to direct the faithful to worship. The chancel is on the same axis as the nave but separated from it in definition of its purpose as the principal ceremonial place and of the hierarchy of the laity and clergy. The lofty roof of the single-aisle nave is supported by hammer-beam trusses. The chancel has a simple ribbed vault. Using rich woods, primarily butternut, the interior is the most elaborately finished of the city's nineteenth-century Gothic Revival churches. Two of its many stained-glass windows, *Resurrection Angel* (1915) and *St. Elizabeth of Hungary* (c. 1910), are by Tiffany Studio.

DE61 **Solomon and Sarah Sproat Sibley House**

1848. 976 East Jefferson Ave.

The Sibley house is one of the few surviving mid-nineteenth-century houses in Detroit. The five-bay, two-story, wood-frame, Greek Revival house employs some delicate Federal features as well. The modest entrance porch is flanked by Greek Doric columns supporting a denticulated entablature and pediment. The house is arranged around a central hall. A delicate stairway, with a "switchback," suspended from the second floor climbs spritely to the upper level.

After her husband's death, Sarah Sproat Sibley (1820–1918) built this house next to the original Christ Church for herself and her two daughters. Judge Solomon Sibley was an active member of Christ Church. The Sibley family lived here for almost eighty years; daughter Sarah lived in the house until her death in 1917. In 1925 Christ Church bought the Sibley house for a rectory and church guest house. The Junior League of Detroit is now restoring the house.

DE62 Law Offices (Thomas A. and Elizabeth Jane Maxwell Parker House)

1868, Gordon W. Lloyd. 975 East Jefferson Ave.

Thomas A. Parker (d. 1901), a wholesale grocer and real estate developer who was a vestryman at Christ Church, reportedly built this house to the plans that Gordon W. Lloyd had designed for the rectory of Christ Church, across the street, but that had not been executed. One of many Gothic Revival houses produced by Lloyd between his arrival in Detroit in 1858 and the panic of 1873, this Kelley Island gray limestone and sandstone structure demonstrates the architect's interest in English medieval architecture. Above the Tudor arch doorway, double French doors open onto a balcony. A bay window with parapet to the right of the entrance on the first story is the only departure from the symmetry of this front facade. The interior has been rehabilitated for offices, retaining the decorative woodwork, floors, and staircases.

DE63 Palms Apartment House

1903, Albert Kahn and George D. Mason. 1001 East Jefferson Ave. (northwest corner of East Jefferson Ave. and Rivard St.)

In the Palms Apartment House for the Palms and Book families, Albert Kahn first experimented with the use of reinforced concrete.

His design employs steel-reinforced concrete floors with load-bearing limestone walls. Kahn's brother Julius, who was his chief construction engineer, perfected a precise scientific system for reinforcing concrete. Soon after the Palms was completed, he formed the Trussed Concrete Steel Company and created the famous "Kahn System." The U-shaped Palms Apartment House has polygonal turretlike end bays, bays, and balustrades. Originally it contained eleven luxury apartments.

DE64 Christopher Moross House

c. 1843–1848. 1460 East Jefferson Ave.

The Moross house is the oldest extant brick house in Detroit. It is two stories tall, has three bays, and uses a side-hall plan. Stone lintels adorn the six-over-six windows. The slender proportions, vertical orientation, and paired end chimneys show Federal influence, but the house lacks the delicate curvilinear motifs. Christopher Moross (1822–1901), a Detroiter of French descent, erected this and another dwelling with brick and with profits from his brickyard at Chene Street and East Canfield Avenue. The Detroit Garden Center now occupies the house. Open to public.

DE65 Players

1924–1925, William Kapp of Smith, Hinchman and Grylls. 3321 East Jefferson Ave.

In 1910–1911 Guy Cady, Walter Boynton, Leonard R. Carley, H. J. Maxwell Grylls, Charles P. Larned, Frederick Sweet Stearns, Alexander K. Gage, and Kirkland B. Alexander established the Players Club. For over ten years this exclusive amateur male theater group met and staged performances at various locations in the city. In 1924–1925 the Players built this playhouse. It is a rough-finished brick structure with a tile roof. Three dramatic arched windows are on the second floor. The exterior of the building is decorated with sculpted masks. The interior is Elizabethan in character. From the northeast corner of the lobby a double archway leads to the 180-seat theater. The theater displays colorful murals showing scenes from Shakespeare. At the northwest corner of the lobby a spiral staircase winds up to a large meeting room with fireplace and down to dressing rooms. William Kapp, architect, Corrado Joseph Parducci, sculptor, and Paul Honoré, muralist, collaborated on the building's design. All belonged to the club.

DE66 Elmwood Cemetery

1846. 1891, management plan, Frederick Law Olmsted. Bounded by Walter Bradley Dr., Waterloo Ave., Mount Elliott Ave., and East Lafayette St. (Elmwood Cemetery, 1200 Elmwood Ave.; Mount Elliott Cemetery, 1701 Mount Elliott Ave.; Lafayette St. Cemetery, 3371 East Lafayette St. [southeast corner of Elmwood Cemetery])

In 1846 a group of Detroit gentlemen—Alexander Frazer, John Owen, Charles C. Trowbridge, Henry Ledyard, Israel Coe, John S. Jenness, and others—established Elmwood Cemetery and selected a tract of some 42 acres on the George Hunt Farm, then in Hamtramck Township, in the suburbs of Detroit. Additional acquisitions of land doubled by the early 1890s the size of the cemetery grounds. Then, in 1891, because of the need to adopt some general management principles, the cemetery's board of trustees called on Frederick Law Olmsted to visit Elmwood and to make suggestions. Olmsted noted that Elmwood would soon be in the heart of the haste, bustle, impatience, and disquiet of a great town and that its soothing natural, rural scenery would be a welcoming retreat. He recommended restoring and maintaining its original character with "umbrageous trees and screening thickets." [14]

Today the Protestant Elmwood Cemetery, together with two other cemeteries dating from the nineteenth century—the Catholic Mount Elliott Cemetery and the Jewish Lafayette Street Cemetery—is encircled by an iron fence, within which fully mature trees, meandering roads, and formal medieval style gateways enhance their rural character. The east-side cemeteries are the oldest in Detroit (Lafayette Street Cemetery is the oldest Jewish cemetery in Michigan) and a final resting place for prominent citizens of Michigan.

The stone entrance gate that adjoins the small gable roof Elmwood Cemetery office, designed by Gordon W. Lloyd in 1882, has a large Gothic-arch portal. Originally designed by Albert H. Jordan in 1850–1857, the stone Gothic chapel was rebuilt after a fire. Of particular interest at Elmwood is the Caulkins memorial monument with its inlaid blue and yellow Pewabic tiles and turquoise vase. It was Mary Chase Stratton's memorial to Horace J.

Caulkins (1850–1923), the dental products manufacturer who was her sponsor.

DE67 Heidelburg Project

1987–present, Tyree Guyton, artist. 3600 block of Heidelburg St. (Heidelburg St. between Gratiot and Mount Elliott avenues and Elba) (1991, demolished)

To abandoned city-owned houses and in weedy vacant lots Tyree Guyton applies and installs discarded urban junk—a Superman shirt, a casket, a telephone booth, car parts, baby dolls, and the like. The results are bright assemblages known as The Heidelburg Project. They include *Fun House* at 3670 Heidelburg Street, *Your World* at 3674 Heidelburg Street, *Lost and Found*, and *Baby Doll* (now destroyed). The works seem to transform the hopeless crime- and drug-infested neighborhood into a work of art. They attract so many people to the area that the street is safe again. Tyree Guyton was born in 1955 in Detroit and raised on Heidelburg Street. He studied at the Center for Creative Studies and taught at Northern High School. He works with his grandfather, Sam Mackey, and his wife, Karen.

DE68 Stroh River Place (Parke-Davis Pharmaceutical Company)

1902–present; Albert Kahn; Smith, Hinchman and Grylls; Donaldson and Meier. Foot of Joseph Campau at Detroit River

Located on 14.5 acres on the east river front, northeast of downtown Detroit, River Place is the rehabilitated complex of late nineteenth- and early twentieth-century industrial structures that comprised the Parke-Davis Pharmaceutical Company. Parke-Davis played a key role in early drug research and production. The twenty-one buildings within the complex date from 1891 to 1948. Parke-Davis was a major employer in Detroit before the automobile industry dominated the city's economic life in the twentieth century. Warner Lambert acquired the company in 1970, retaining the Parke-Davis name but sold this plant in 1982, one year after moving out. Other industries on the east riverfront included the Peninsula Car Works, the Michigan Stove Company, and American Eagle Tobacco Company.

Stroh Properties, Inc. (now River Place Properties), purchased the site in 1918 with bold plans to invest $240 million of private and public funds to rehabilitate to the master plans of James Stuart Polshek the extensive space within the old industrial buildings for offices, shops, and residential properties. Most of the buildings are built of brick with light stone decoration and were used for offices, laboratories, and drug production.

Facing the river, the Administration Building (100 River Place, 1927, Smith, Hinchman and Grylls) is the most architecturally distinctive. Pedimented end pavilions flank its central bay, and its windows are grouped within narrow three-story arcades. The reinforced concrete structure is clad with decorative brickwork. Stroh Brewery initially moved its corporate headquarters to the administration building, but now it serves as corporate headquarters for the Talon Group. Detroit Research (Building 55, 1902, Donaldson and Meier), also located on the river, was the first industrial laboratory in the United States built for commercial pharmaceutical research. Its brick form is topped by a large hipped roof with shed dormers and a cupola, and the central entrance portal is richly decorated with classical details. Together with Building 54, a laboratory designed by Kahn in 1942, it is now the River Place Inn, a 109–room luxury hotel rehabilitated to plans by Tomlinson and Harburn of Flint. The Drug Productions Building (300 River Place, 1921, 1926, Albert Kahn), a large brick factory structure with industrial sash, has been rehabilitated into office and retail space, complete with

atriums and modern amenities. The earlier laboratories, warehouses, and production facilities (400 and 500 River Place, 1908) were rehabilitated to the plans of Louis Redstone for use as 247 apartment units. Six Hundred River Place is a new parking garage designed to replicate the appearance of the 1910s and 1920s structures in the complex. On its roof are fifty-four townhouses planned by Redstone. The Personnel Building (1920–1921) will become the River Place Athletic and Croquet Club (1400 River Place) as Tomlinson and Harburn's plans for rehabilitation and new construction are completed. As individual phases of the project are committed to, River Place Properties, Inc., takes on partners. River Place is an excellent example of historic preservation in Detroit.

DE69 Belle Isle Park

1882–1884, Frederick Law Olmsted. In the narrows of the Detroit River, midway between the Canadian and American shores

Situated in the narrows of the Detroit River, midway between the Canadian and American shores and within sight of the Renaissance Center and the Central Business District, lies Detroit's island park, Belle Isle. A glory of idyllic scenery and meandering canals, this park in its setting is one the most unusual of all urban parks to be found anywhere in the United States.

Accessible by auto over the Art Deco MacArthur Bridge, the park is an island, 2.5 miles long and .5 mile wide. It lies a scant two feet above river level in the middle of an international shipping channel, making the viewing of the busy river traffic one of the delights of this maritime setting. This is the kind of activity that Frederick Law Olmsted (1822–1903)—America's greatest landscape architect—had in mind, when in 1882 he submitted his plan for Belle Isle Park. The primary intent of his design was the highlighting of this extraordinary setting and scenery to take full advantage of the abundant woods and water. Some of Olmsted's original plan may still be seen today on the island, although obscured by age, misunderstanding, and poor maintenance. Olmsted's early concept of a canal system for Belle Isle was later altered into another configuration, but the essential Olmsted element, that is, the enjoyment of the various "passages of scenery" from a slowly moving canoe, remains as one of the most delightful experiences to be enjoyed on Belle Isle.

Although Olmsted's philosophy was not to have buildings and monuments intrude into a park setting, Belle Isle has become the repository of many of Detroit's architecturally significant nineteenth- and early twentieth-century buildings and sculpture. Of particular importance is the striking architectural influence that the World's Columbian Exposition of 1893 in Chicago had on the pre-World War II buildings erected on Belle Isle.

Noteworthy buildings on the island include: the Athletic Shelter, an exuberant vernacular example with bold turrets and a sweeping bracketed veranda; the Service Yard, a marvelous small-scaled interpretation of an English nineteenth-century gatehouse; the Horse Stables, with an intricately carved, cut-work pedimented roof, which was originally the shed roof for the Farmer's Market in Campus Martius in downtown Detroit before being reinstalled on Belle Isle in 1879. Of note also are the various other remnants of Detroit's architectural past that dot the island.

Originally designed for pedestrian and carriage traffic only, the island has been invaded by the automobile, and the resultant roads now crisscross the once-bucolic scenery. Poor to nonexistent forestry management, drainage problems, and ill-conceived placement of trendy new park structures mar the park's overall ambiance. Despite these problems, Belle Isle remains the place that Olmsted envisioned, a peaceful green oasis within the harsh city context.

DE69.1 Police Station

1893, Mason and Rice

This imposing structure of rough-dressed fieldstone in the Richardsonian Romanesque manner evokes the feeling of a miniature Norman château with its use of twin shingled turrets massed on either side of the central round arch.

DE69.2 Conservatory

1900–1904, Albert Kahn of Nettleton and Kahn and Mason and Kahn

With its huge central glass dome and symmetrical glazed wings, the Conservatory is an almost unbelievable replication of its predecessor from the World's Columbian Exposition in Chicago. The original elaborate cast-iron cresting disappeared in a later remodeling, but the Conservatory still houses a large botanical collection of plants from the world over.

DE69.3 Aquarium

1900–1904, Albert Kahn of Nettleton and Kahn and Mason and Kahn

The subdued red-brick Aquarium, the companion building to the Conservatory, is to the side and a little behind it. Access is gained through an exuberant Baroque doorway surmounted by a pediment of carved dolphins. A marvel in its time, housing both salt-water and fresh-water fish and a variety of marine life, the Aquarium is still remarkably intact.

DE69.2 Conservatory

Though the exhibits have been brought up to date, the original green-glazed tile interior still exists.

DE69.4 Casino

1904–1908, Albert Kahn

The casino was sited to take advantage of the views of the international shipping channel and the cooling breezes blowing across the head of the island. It was built to replace the original 1887 casino building, which, with its sweeping verandas, gables, and open porches, was a sophisticated use of Queen Anne in the best casino tradition. Designed in the Renaissance Revival style and constructed of buff brick with a terracotta tile roof, it bears a striking resemblance to the Women's Pavilion at the World's Columbia Exposition in Chicago, with its open-air arcade and squared towers. When viewed from the south elevation, the lagoon setting completes the comparison.

DE69.5 Scott Fountain

1914–1928, Cass Gilbert

At the western end of the park, and built on landfill to support it, stands Cass Gilbert's architectural tour de force, the Scott Fountain. This fountain of gleaming white marble with its series of terraced steps and smaller collecting pools recalls, once again, an image of the "White City" of 1893 in Chicago. Originally only part of an even more grandiose plan, the complementing scheme for this site was ultimately rejected as not being suited to the park's natural setting.

DE69.6 Detroit Boat Club

1902, Alpheus W. Chittenden. North of the intersection of Riverbank and Picnic Way

The Detroit Boat Club overlooks the city from its location on the Detroit River just north of the Belle Isle Bridge. The large Spanish Colonial Revival building has plain white stucco walls, arched openings, and a low-pitch red tile roof topped with a squat tower. The interior is arranged around a central wood-paneled reception hall that rises two stories beneath the lighted tower. The open corridor that runs around the hall at the second floor is supported by twisted columns and encircled by a decorative wooden balustrade carved with seahorses and fish. Surrounding the reception hall are a balconied ballroom and dining rooms. These open onto verandas. In addition the club contains dens, smoking rooms, reading rooms, a boat room, and crew quarters. The architect was Detroiter Alpheus William Chittenden (b. 1869), who was educated at Massachusetts Institute of Technology and who specialized in residential architecture. Chittenden belonged to the Detroit Boat Club. The club was organized in 1839. The present clubhouse replaced one destroyed by fire.

DE70 R. Thornton Brodhead Naval Armory (Marine Corps Reserve Center)

1930, Stratton and Hyde. 7600 East Jefferson Ave.

The Brodhead Naval Armory contains perhaps the richest trove of 1930s Works Progress Administration Federal Arts Project (WPA/FAP) murals and other art on building interiors in Michigan. Captain Richard Thornton Brodhead, after whom the armory was named in 1927, convinced the state legislature to build a naval armory in Detroit. Stratton and Hyde designed a large PWA Moderne structure. The building stands on the Detroit River just east of the Belle Isle Bridge. It is classical and formal in proportion and sheathed in smooth limestone. The entrance pavilion is adorned with four sea service emblems manufactured by the Pewabic Pottery. Since the building was operated by the state, it qualified for WPA/FAP art funding, and in 1936 Brodhead was instrumental in the sponsorship of FAP artists for decorating the armory. He also became personally involved—in selecting the artists and checking on their work, and in providing accurate technical information on ships.

The armory contains large-scale murals, plaster wall carvings, and a multitude of wood carvings on doorways, staircases, fireplaces, and benches. The high quality of the artwork is especially evident in the wood carvings. All of the art is devoted to an aquatic theme. This ranged from naval vessels painted by Edgar Yaeger for the dining room and sailors relaxing on deck in a 60-foot mural by David Fredenthal to representations of fish, mermaids, and water plants carved into wood staircases by John Tabaczuk. Even the many wooden doors in the armory have carvings on them, including one with the seal of the State of Michigan. Gustave Hildebrand designed the plaster wall carvings of officers and sailors at work that are on the first floor. The scope and scale of the armory art projects was unusually large; three rooms had murals (a fourth mural was destroyed), and it was claimed at the time that they were second in size only to the Diego Rivera murals at the Detroit Institute of Arts (1933). For this reason, teams of WPA and FAP artists who assisted master artists were employed at the armory. In the Brodhead Armory, alterations were made to harmonize all the artwork with the interior. For example, an entire hall was remade, with additions of book cases and a fireplace, to complement the large mural painted by Fredenthal, and the artists worked together to create a coordinated effect between the murals, wood carvings, and building structure.

DE71 Indian Village

1890s–1920. Bounded by East Jefferson, Seminole, Mack, and Burns avenues

Indian Village is comprised of the eighteenth-century French strip farms of François Rivard and Jacques St. Aubin. These farms and others were acquired by Abraham Cook between 1811 and 1815. Known as the Cook farms, the parcel was nearly 1,200 feet wide and ran north from the Detroit River three miles to what is now Harper Avenue.

Between 1836 and 1893, the land was used primarily as a racetrack for trotters, under the auspices of various groups, the last being the Detroit Driving Club. When the club moved to Grosse Pointe Township in 1893, the Detroit Driving Park closed.

Abraham Cook's heirs formed the Cook Farm Company in December 1893 to "buy, sell, lease, improve, and subdivide real estate." The area bounded by the Detroit River and Seminole, Burns, and Mack avenues was developed as a "first class residential district on a generous scale."[15] Building code, construction cost, and placement of structures on the lots were strictly controlled by the Cook Farm Company to create a dignified and highly desirable subdivision. The romantic name "Indian Village" was selected, although there

was no evidence that Indians had ever lived on the land.

Building begun in 1894 continued at a rapid pace into the late 1920s, when the exodus to the quieter surrounding suburbs began, leaving these large, single-family homes threatened with division into multiple units. Those residents who chose to remain in the area organized to enforce the single-family zoning and in 1937 formed the Indian Village Association, which actively pursues that objective today. Among the prominent Detroiters who lived here were Edsel B. Ford, Robert Craig Hupp, Fritz Govel, Hugh Chalmers, Warren S. Booth, Griffith Ogden Ellis, Robert B. Tannahill, Arthur M. Buhl, Joseph Muer, Ernest Kanzler, and Bernard Stroh.

Styles for Indian Village homes are derived from the full spectrum of architectural tradition, including Colonial Revival, Neo-Tudor, Craftsman, Prairie, Mission, Beaux-Arts Classical, French Eclectic, and Renaissance Revival, all of which were built during the first two decades of this century. Nearly all major Detroit architects designed homes here, including George D. Mason; Louis Kamper; James S. Rogers; Marcus R. Burrowes; Smith, Hinchman and Grylls; Albert Kahn; Leonard B. Willeke; Chittenden and Kotting; Wallace Frost; William B. Stratton; C. Howard Crane; Robert O. Derrick; John Scott; Malcomson and Higginbotham; George V. Pottle; and Leon Coquard. Of the 367 original residences, 349 remain.

DE71.1 Jefferson Avenue Presbyterian Church

1925, Wirt Rowland of Smith, Hinchman and Grylls. 8525 East Jefferson Ave. (northwest corner of East Jefferson and Burns avenues)

Built for a fashionable congregation, this church uses ornamentation sparingly but achieves the architect's desire for combining the Gothic spirit with contemporary needs. It uses stepped buttresses along the nave, the Tudor arch, and the prominent tower at the angle of the L-shaped structure, and has a gymnasium, a billiard room, a Sunday school room, and a dining room. The sanctuary is oriented north-south and is joined to the church school and offices by the lofty bell tower.

DE71.2 Walter S. and Mary Rumney Russel House

1890, Walter S. Russel, designer. 1921, moved. 1075 Burns Ave.

An interesting essay in Richardsonian Romanesque is this rough-cut fieldstone house, originally built in 1890 at 2763 East Jefferson Avenue near downtown, but moved to the present location in 1920–1921. When he re-erected the house, the owner reversed the plan to achieve a mirrored image of itself.

DE71.3 Roscoe B. and Louise Webber Jackson House

1917, Leonard B. Willeke. 2505 Iroquois Ave.

Leonard B. Willeke designed the total environment—house, furniture, hardware, lighting fixtures, tilework, carving, and landscaping. Alfred F. Nygard executed the wood carving. Willeke designed the adjacent Ernest Kanzler Residence at 2501 Iroquois in 1917, with a garden by Jens Jensen, and the Joseph T. Webber Residence, 2475 Iroquois, 1917. Each elevation is carefully studied in the relationship of solid to void and rhythm to detail.

DE71.4 Louis and Emily Kling Kamper House

1915, Louis Kamper. 2150 Iroquois Ave.

Architect Louis Kamper chose to design his own residence, borrowing from the Beaux-Arts Classical tradition in its formal horizontality and extensive use of pilasters and the classical round arch. Kamper was trained in the New York office of McKim, Mead and White before coming to Detroit in 1889, and the influence of that New York firm is evident here.

DE71.5 Robert Craig Hupp House

1909, George Valentine Pottle. 1517 Iroquois Ave.

This is a marvelous Prairie style composition with Oriental influences. Hupp was the founder of the Hupp Motor Car Company, which manufactured the famous Hupmobile.

DE71.6 Arthur H. and Clara May Buhl House

1909, John Scott. 1116 Iroquois Ave.

This steeply gabled brick and stucco Neo-Tudor house was built for a wholesale hardware merchant and his wife. Within the asymmetrical composition is a central projecting entry portal containing a Tudor-arched opening, from which there originally extended a protective wooden gable canopy.

DE72 Waterworks Park

1910 1931, Field, Hinchman and Smith. 10100 East Jefferson Ave. (bounded by East Jefferson Ave., Marquette Drive, the Detroit River, and Parkview Drive)

Detroit's main waterworks have been located on this site since 1878, but none of the original buildings or equipment are extant. Two major sets of pumping equipment are situated in the High Lift Building (1910) and the Low Lift Building (1924). On East Jefferson Avenue at Cadillac Avenue the ornate Beaux-

Arts Classical Hurlburt Memorial Gate (1894) marks the entrance to the park. It was designed by Herman A. Brede and Gustave Mueller and erected in memory of Chauncey Hurlbut (1803–1885), president of the Board of Water Commissioners, who left his estate for the beautification of the park. The fantastic 185-foot brick and sandstone water tower no longer stands. This and the main pumping station and filtration plant of the municipal water system originally were surrounded by a beautifully landscaped park.

DE73 Pewabic Pottery

1907, William B. Stratton. 10125 East Jefferson Ave.

Mary Chase Perry (1867–1961) founded the Pewabic Pottery Company in 1904 and named it after the Pewabic Copper Mine near her hometown of Hancock in the Upper Peninsula. In 1908 she moved her ceramic operation to its permanent studio, this English half-timber cottage designed by a prominent Detroit architect, William B. Stratton, whom she later married. The structure harkens back to the English cottage both in its design, with the steep medieval roof, and in its function as a house for the small industry that became a central part of the Arts and Crafts movement in Detroit. In collaboration with Horace James Caulkins, a Detroit manufacturer of dental products, Perry systematically experimented with new firing techniques and chemical glazes in a revolutionary oil-burning kiln, which led her to the discovery of unique iridescent glazes. Architectural tiles fired by Mary Chase Stratton in the kilns of the Pewabic Pottery can be found in distinguished buildings throughout Michigan and the entire United States. The Pewabic Society of Detroit now offers classes here.

DE74 Connors Creek Generating Station

1914–1951. 200 Lycaste St.

One of the first large-scale fossil fuel plants of the Detroit Edison Company, this massive, sleek, steel and brick powerhouse is a Detroit landmark on the river. The seven large smokestacks, each 227 feet tall, are commonly known by Detroiters as "the Seven Sisters."

Another powerhouse with two stacks, "the Two Brothers," was added in 1951.

DE75 Vanity Ballroom

1929, Charles N. Agree. 1024 Newport Ave. (northwest corner of East Jefferson and Newport avenues)

Terracotta and orange brick, chevron motifs, and Art Deco pilasters make the three-sided entrance pavilion to the Vanity Ballroom a colorful and outstanding example of the Aztec-Art Deco style. The ballroom, which hosted Benny Goodman, Duke Ellington, Jimmy and Tommy Dorsey in its heyday, features a floating maple dance floor set on springs and plaster walls scored like cut stone. Arches that resemble Toltec and Aztec pyramids separate the promenade from the ballroom.

Designed by local architect and philanthropist Charles N. Agree for the Metropolitan Holding Company as part of a commercial block, the Vanity Ballroom was Detroit's last public ballroom. Original furnishings and fixtures, such as a soda fountain, lights, booths, and a jukebox, remain. Attempts to retain and restore the Vanity Ballroom are tentative at best.

DE76 Ossian Sweet House

1919, Maurice Finkel. 2905 Garland St. (northwest corner of Garland St. and Charlevoix Ave.)

In 1925 the move of Dr. Ossian H. Sweet (1895–1960), a black gynecologist, and his family into this modest bungalow in a previously all-white neighborhood provoked violence from his neighbors. Whites stoned the house, and shots fired from within it killed one white and wounded another. Detroit police charged all eleven people in the house with first-degree murder, but only Sweet and his brother Henry were tried. The NAACP hired Clarence Darrow to defend them. Ossian's trial resulted in a hung jury; Henry was acquitted. The defense argued that the Sweets had the right to defend their home against attack. The side-gable bungalow with a central-gable dormer containing a string of three windows is fronted across its entire width by a shed-roof porch supported by four square piers.

Wayne County (WN)

HAMTRAMCK

WN01 **Saint Florian Church**

1925–1928, Ralph Adams Cram of Cram and Ferguson. 2626 Poland Ave. (northwest corner of Florian Ave. and Latham; bounded by Florian and Poland avenues, and Brombach and Latham)

Saint Florian Church towers majestically over a Polish-Catholic, working-class neighborhood of densely packed, modest, early twentieth-century homes. The parish was formed in 1907 in response to Detroit's growing Polish community, which resulted in crowding at the other nearby Polish-American churches, Saint Albertus, Saint Stanislaus, and Saint Hyacinth. As waves of immigrants from eastern Europe flooded the United States, many Poles came to Detroit, where the Packard, Ford, and Dodge automotive companies were building plants in and near the Polish enclave of Hamtramck. By 1920 its population had reached forty-five thousand. A larger, more permanent church was needed, so the present Saint Florian Church was constructed in 1925.

Saint Florian was planned by Ralph Adams Cram (1863–1942) of Cram and Ferguson, a nationally known Boston firm of church architects. Cram was famous for his command of the Gothic, and this church is based on the English Gothic style. The building is impos-

ing; a tall, delicate tower and spire with crockets rises at the crossing. The large, broad, recessed Gothic arch flanked by twin spires enframes both the main entrance and its circular window. Reddish brown brick laid with string courses and bands of diaper work covers the steel-framed structure. The interior is arranged with a nave and side aisles beneath Gothic ribbed vaulting. Its decoration is notable for its use of marble and wood, murals, and stained-glass artistry. The church was built by Joseph Nowakowski and Sons and cost $500,000. J. M. Kase Company of Reading, Pennsylvania, manufactured the stained glass in its New York studio. It won an *American Architect* award for 1929.

The return to Gothicism in Saint Florian Church contrasts with the modern industrialism and technology of the factories, where most parishioners worked. The church was not a return to medievalism for sentimental reasons; built in the grand Gothic tradition of the Catholic faith, this new church was also an expression of the pride and achievement of this new immigrant group.

HIGHLAND PARK

Highland Park, formerly called Whitewood, straddles Woodward Avenue about ten miles northwest of downtown Detroit. It is a part of the 10,000 acres northwest of the city that were opened after Detroit's fire of 1805. Highland Park remained rural until about 1904, when the first waves of outward migration from industrializing Detroit reached its southern boundaries. In 1908, Henry Ford selected Highland Park as the site for an automotive plant that became the largest in the world at the time. Within twenty years the tremendous growth obliterated all traces of previous rural settlement.

The small city is about 3 square miles in size. It follows the spine of Woodward Avenue, along which are located its large church, commercial, and institutional buildings. Most of Highland Park's buildings, including several notable period revival apartment buildings, were built between 1900 and 1930. The Chrysler and Ford plants occupy the central section of the city and divide it into a north and south side.

WN02 McGregor Library

1926, Tilton and Githens, Burrowes and Eurich. 12244 Woodward Ave. (Michigan 1) (northeast corner of Woodward and Rhode Island avenues)

The sedate Beaux-Arts Classical library occupies an entire city block on the site of the residence of Capt. William Stevens, a former miner, who in the 1880s owned about half the land in Highland Park. After his death, his property was acquired by Tracy W. and Katherine Whitney McGregor, philanthropists who used it as an orphans' home and, later, in 1918, gave it to the city for use as the site of a library. The terms of the gift required the newly established McGregor Library Commission to organize and maintain the library and to build within five years a new building "not inferior to the Henry M. Utley Branch Library in the City of Detroit." In 1924 a $500,000–bond issue was approved overwhelmingly. Seeking a building "worthy of the modern city of Highland Park and its progressive citizens," the librarian and the commission visited and studied libraries in eastern and midwestern cities.[16] They selected as their model the library at Wilmington, Delaware, which was designed by noted New York City library architects Tilton and Githens.

The commission for the McGregor Library at Highland Park was given to Edward L. Tilton and Alfred M. Githens, who created what was termed a quiet and dignified "Roman Classic" design. The flat-roofed rectangular building stands on a base of Sauk Rapids, Minnesota, granite and has exterior walls of Indiana limestone. A polychrome terracotta frieze and a full molded stone cornice are derived from the temple of Antoninus and Faustina in the Roman Forum. The main entrance is placed in an ornamented, coffered niche between two engaged, full-height, fluted Ionic columns and flanking pilasters. The bronze doors are ornamented with allegorical figures of knowledge and with others holding winged cars and airplanes.

The interior arrangement is two floors and a basement, with a balcony that encircles the book delivery room. The stacks are located in the basement, allowing the entire first floor to be open to the public. The first floor holds reading, reference, and book delivery rooms and offices; the second floor, a four-hundred-seat auditorium and fine arts, staff, and club rooms. The Greco-Roman inspiration of the interior is best seen in the book delivery room atrium. Here Doric columns support an entablature and a frieze, which features a relief panel cast with figures that reproduce those on the metopes and interior frieze of the Parthenon.

Eurich and Burrowes supervised the construction of the library; Martin-Krausman Company built the structure. The McGregor Library was awarded the distinction of an American Institute of Architects gold medal for design in 1925. This dignified library built in the midst of the burgeoning automobile center, which followed the opening of the Ford Motor Company Plant at Highland Park, helped to reaffirm the importance of culture and learning during the industrialization of the twentieth century.

WN03 Highland Park Plant of the Ford Motor Company

1909–1920, Albert Kahn. 15050 Woodward Ave. (Michigan 1) (northeast corner of Woodward and Manchester avenues; bounded by Woodward Ave., the Conrail tracks, Oakland, and Manchester avenues)

The Ford Highland Park Plant was the first large automobile manufacturing complex in Detroit, the birthplace of mass production, and Albert Kahn's first monumental factory complex. The 30-acre site contained two office buildings and a powerhouse fronting on

Woodward Avenue; several large, four-story, reinforced concrete assembly buildings running parallel with Woodward Avenue; two six-story buildings of similar design extending along Manchester Avenue; and sprawling, one-story, steel-framed shops in the rear of the complex. About two-thirds of the original buildings are extant. It is of special interest that in his design of the administration building Kahn used the same reinforced concrete technique that he used in the design of the utilitarian buildings.

WN04 Medbury–Grove Lawn Residential Area

1914–1924. Eason, Moss, and Puritan avenues, from Hamilton to Woodward Ave. (Michigan 1)

This charming residential district of some 270 homes was built as Highland Park expanded between 1914 and 1924. Many of the houses are among the state's finest examples

of the small Craftsman bungalow, inspired by the Arts and Crafts movement. Others are fine examples of period revivals. Generally, in a pattern found throughout Highland Park, larger more expensive houses are closer to Woodward Avenue. Notable examples include architect Henry Kohner's own house at 179 Eason Avenue, a bungalow built in 1919; the Fremont Barrett House, built in 1915 at 55 Puritan Avenue, an excellent example of the Craftsman style; and the Leonard B. Willeke House, erected in 1920 as his own house and architectural studio, at 39 Moss Avenue.

GROSSE POINTE VICINITY

WN05 **Lake Shore Drive** (Lake Shore Rd.)

Lake Shore Dr. (Lake Shore Rd.) from Fisher Rd. to Vernier Rd. (Eight Mile Rd. [Michigan 102])

In the mid-1880s, wealthy Detroiters purchased French *roture,* or ribbon farms, stretching away from the west shore of Lake Saint Clair, in rural Grosse Pointe. Here they erected summer homes. After a trolley line was extended out East Jefferson Avenue in 1880 and after the road was paved in the early 1900s, these vacation retreats were adapted for year-round use. The advent of the automobile soon thereafter and the economic prosperity of the twenties were the forces that quickly transformed the vacation area into a thriving suburb.

Grosse Pointe is filled with fine, gracious houses. Many were built for engineers, sales executives, and their families, successors to Detroit's auto industry pioneers.

WN05.1 Edsel and Eleanor Ford House

Those along Lake Shore Drive (Lake Shore Road), which is an extension of East Jefferson Avenue, north of Fisher Road, are particularly expressive of the economic and social status of some of Michigan's wealthiest residents.

Some of the finest mansions erected in the early decades regrettably were demolished. These large estates have been subdivided for resale and the mansions razed because of taxes and development pressures. The Joseph B. Schlotman House by Albert Spahr (1915); the partially completed Neo-Tudor John F. Dodge Mansion by Smith, Hinchman and Grylls (1920); the Standish Backus Home (1934) by R. O. Derrick; and Rose Terrace, Anna Dodge's (Mrs. Horace E. Dodge) Louis XV chateau by Horace Trumbauer (1934) are among those lost.

GROSSE POINTE SHORES

WN05.1 Edsel and Eleanor Ford House

1927–1929; Albert Kahn; Jens Jensen, landscape architect. 1100 Lake Shore Rd. (Macomb County)

The Ford estate occupies the largest and most beautifully situated homesite in this exclusive section of Grosse Pointe that stretches along the shore of Lake Saint Clair. Surrounded by an expansive meadow and tall trees, the sixty-room, stately mansion of Briar Hill sandstone has a split-stone roof. It sprawls at the end of a long, curving driveway and has a splendid view of the lake at Gaukler Point. The house is a superb example of the predilection of the automotive tycoons for English architecture; it reflects the cultural aspirations of Edsel Bryant Ford (1893–1943) and Eleanor Clay Ford (1896–1976) and their taste for great art and high-style architecture. In a departure from the elaborate palaces and fortresses favored by many of their contemporaries, the Fords engaged Albert Kahn to reproduce the comfortable Cotswold architecture of Worcestershire, England, but on a grand scale. Based upon their visits abroad and Kahn's research, a rambling structure was developed, characteristic of the picturesque Cotswold homes with their additions over many generations, but much larger. An oak staircase, wood paneling, and a number of large fireplaces were purchased in England and reassembled in the house. The interior was designed by Irving Casson and Company of New York. In 1935 the house was remodeled to include an Art Deco bedroom suite and a first-floor music room planned by Walter Dorwin Teague, a pioneer in industrial design. Formal terraced gardens, a cascading swimming pool, a deep lagoon extending from house to boat house, and a profusion of trees and shrubs, including an "avenue of trees" leading into the estate, complete the setting landscaped by Jens Jensen (1860–1951), one of America's most important landscape architects. The Ford estate is a monument to private wealth, educated taste, and a sense of public responsibility. Open to public.

GROSSE POINTE FARMS

WN05.2 Grosse Pointe War Memorial Association Building (Russell A. and Marion Jarves Alger, Jr., House [The Moorings])

1910–1912; Charles A. Platt; Ellen Shipman, landscape architect. 32 Lake Shore Dr.

The Alger house is a stone-trimmed, stuccoed, Georgian Revival mansion on 4.5 acres of landscaped grounds, on one of the highest elevations along the Michigan shoreline of Lake Saint Clair. The house is one of a handful of houses in Michigan documented as designed by the nationally prominent New York architect Charles A. Platt (1861–1933). It is one of several Platt designed in the early twentieth century on Lakes Erie, Saint Clair, Superior, and Michigan that incorporate the lake frontage as part of the design. In planning the Alger house, Platt took full advantage of the beautiful site. A rectangular bowling green stood between the house and the water, and an elm-lined driveway led to the main entrance off Lake Shore Drive. The main section of the house is a rectangular block with symmetrically designed street- and lake-side facades. It is topped with a low-pitched, red-tiled hipped roof. The pedimented and heavily ornamented central entrance pavilion faces Lake Shore Drive. The entrance itself is surrounded by penciled stone and is topped by voussoirs and a broken pediment supported by a single, elaborately scrolled bracket. This fronts a balconied window enframed with rich carving. The lake facade has loggias and a pergola. The major rooms respond to the lake, gardens, and landscaping. A large central hall is flanked by the dining room and the library, all of which overlook the lake.

Russell A. Alger, Jr. (1873–1930), was the son of Russell A. Alger (1836–1907), a Detroit lumberman who was a Michigan governor, a United States senator, and President McKinley's secretary of war. Alger, Jr., was one of the founders of the Packard Motor Company in 1903 and served as its vice-president for many years. In 1949 the Alger family donated the house to the Grosse Pointe War Memorial Association for use as a community cultural center.

GROSSE POINTE

WN06 Grosse Pointe Public Library

1951–1953, Marcel Breuer. 10 Kercheval Ave. (southeast corner of Kercheval and Fisher avenues)

One of the most notable suburban libraries of the post-World War II era, the Grosse Pointe Public Library was possible because of the availability of a suitable site and the generosity of Grosse Pointe resident Dexter M. Ferry, Jr. The school system transferred to the library an ideal downtown site at Kercheval and Fisher with open ball fields behind it. In 1951 Ferry gave funds to pay for almost the entire cost of the building. The proceeds of the sale of the Murray W. Sales House went toward furnishing and equipping the library, and the Friends of the Grosse Pointe

Public Library raised additional money for equipping the building. At Ferry's suggestion, internationally known Bauhaus-trained architect Marcel Breuer (1902–1981) of New York was chosen to design the building. It was Breuer's first library.

The functional rectangular International style structure is 157 feet by 70 feet in plan. Its brick exterior walls trimmed with sandstone harmonize with the nearby high school. A large glass wall, broken by wood muntins, extends the length of the two-story main reading room, making visible to the public on Kercheval the readers within. A narrow balcony inset within the wall plane runs the entire length of the second floor of the Fisher Avenue facade. In keeping with his vision of the library "as a social, cultural and civic crystalization point [where] literature and art were to be made more accessible in an inviting homelike atmosphere," Breuer furnished it and embellished it with art.[17] A tapestry based on a painting entitled *Sur Fond Noir* by Wassily Kandinsky hangs on the teakwood wall at the east end of the main reading room; a Calder mobile hangs at the west end of the main reading room; and a photo mural designed by Herbert Matter is displayed in the adult reading room.

GROSSE POINTE PARK

WN07 William B. and Mary Chase Stratton House

1927, William B. Stratton. 938 Three Mile Dr.

The talents of William B. Stratton (1867–1938) and his wife, Mary Chase Perry (1867–1961), the Pewabic ceramist, combined to create their personal expression of casual romanticism. In a departure from the antiquarianism demanded by many of his clients, Stratton and his wife returned to the tenets of the Arts and Crafts movement and used their inspiration from Mexican and Spanish architecture to develop a multi-level structure with numerous bays, balconies, and windows. Low, heavily beamed ceilings and weathered oak floors combined with warm, earth-toned brick laid in Flemish bond and Pewabic tile lend an atmosphere of informal, cozy, charming warmth. Of particular interest is the tile, for it was manufactured at Mrs. Stratton's

WN07 William B. and Mary Chase Stratton House

Pewabic Pottery (DE73, p. 112) and covers floors, stairs, window sills, bathroom walls, tub and shower enclosures, basins and water fountains, and fireplaces and hearths. The house incorporates some parts from the Stratton's former house, which was located on East Grand Boulevard in Detroit. The middle terrace running back from the living room ties together the house and garden.

DEARBORN

WN08 Ford Motor Company River Rouge Plant

1917–1938, Albert Kahn. 3001 Miller Rd.

Shortly before 1920, Henry Ford (1863–1947) began to shift his production from the Highland Park location to this 2,000-acre site on the Rouge River. By the late 1930s, Ford had built more than two dozen steel-and-glass, single-story buildings, all designed by Albert Kahn. This was the largest single manufacturing complex in the United States, with peak employment of about 120,000 during World War II. Here, Henry Ford achieved self-sufficiency and vertical integration in automobile production. The complex included dock facilities, blast furnaces, open-hearth steel mills, foundries, a rolling mill, metal stamp-ing facilities, an engine plant, a glass manufacturing building, a tire plant, and its own power house supplying steam and electricity.

WN09 Henry Ford Museum and Greenfield Village (The Edison Institute)

1928–1929, 1930s, 1940s, Robert O. Derrick. 2900 Oakwood Blvd. (bounded by Oakwood Blvd., Michigan Ave. [US 12], Southfield Freeway [Michigan 39], and Village Rd.)

The Henry Ford Museum and Greenfield Village is an ideal American village of historic structures moved in from elsewhere and new buildings designed in this image. The complex is an indoor and outdoor museum built by Henry Ford as a place in which to exhibit his collection of Americana, which contains artifacts and architecture—some dating to colonial times. The Henry Ford Museum is housed in a large brick building, the facades of which, designed by Robert O. Derrick, are replicas of Independence Hall, Congress Hall, the Old City Hall of Philadelphia, and other structures. The collections and exhibits were originally arranged in assembly-line fashion on the ground floor. The museum has exhibits on autos and industry.

At Greenfield Village, more than eighty historic homes, shops, stores, mills, and laboratories stand on 81 acres. Altogether, they are reminders of the development of agriculture, manufacturing and transportation. There is village of shops and mills, including the Wright Brothers Cycle Shop, moved from Dayton, Ohio. Around the green are centered public buildings. The large wooden Greek Revival Eagle Tavern (c.1850), an endgable tavern with a two-story porch supported by piers, was moved here from its original location on the Chicago Road at Clinton. In the residential section are the 1823 house Noah Webster occupied at New Haven, Connecticut and the Greek Revival house that Robert Frost lived in while a fellow at the University of Michigan in Ann Arbor and, moved from Vienna in Western Ontario, the house of Thomas A. Edison's parents and grandparents. Most unusual is the Cotswold cottage from England.

Greenfield Village was a national model in the development of outdoor village museums such as Old Sturbridge Village, Old Deerfield, and the Shaker Museum. It influenced the historic preservation movement.

WN10 Dearborn Inn and Historic Homes

1931, Albert Kahn, architect of inn. 1937, Charles T. Hart of Hart and Shape, architect of homes. Marshall L. Johnson, landscape architect. 20301 Oakwood Blvd.

Like the Henry Ford Museum and Greenfield Village, the Dearborn Inn and Historic Homes were designed as a small American village. They accommodate visitors to the Edison Institute and the Ford Motor Company, some of whom once arrived by air at the Henry Ford Airport. The red brick Adamesque inn was erected in 1931 to the plans of Albert Kahn. In 1937–1938 additional rooms were needed. Charles T. Hart of New York, architect for the L. G. Treadway Service Corporation of New York who managed the inn, convinced the Ford family, the owners, to build reproduction historical houses behind the inn rather than an addition to the inn. Plans called for a "colonial village development" of eighteen historic guest houses in keeping with Greenfield Village, which would be arranged around a swimming pool, tennis courts, and manager's house. Only five of the houses were built. They are the shingled Walt Whitman Farmhouse of Mellville, Long Island; the simple white clapboarded Edgar Allen Poe House of Fordham, New York City; the large Oliver Wolcott House of Litchfield, Connecticut; the rosy-colored brick Barbara Fritchie House of Frederick, Maryland; and the large Patrick Henry House of Red Hill, Campbell County, Virginia. Hart reproduced the Henry house from *Lost Examples of Colonial Architecture*. He replicated the other four based on information in old records and from measured drawings of the houses that still stood. The exteriors are true to the original houses, but the interiors are arranged to accommodate bedrooms, bathrooms, kitchenettes, and parlors. The houses are furnished with reproductions of Windsor and wing chairs, pie-crust and butterfly tables, brass bound desks, and other early American pieces manufactured by Virginia Craftsmen of Harrisonburg. There were large additions to the inn in the 1989.

WN11 Fairlane (Henry and Clara Bryant Ford House)

1913–1915; William H. Van Tine; Jens Jensen, landscape architect. 4901 Evergreen Rd. (University of Michigan-Dearborn; west side of Evergreen Rd., between Ford Rd. [Michigan 153] and Michigan Ave. [US 12])

Originally encompassing over 2,000 acres on the Rouge River, Fairlane was the residential estate of Henry Ford (1863–1947) and his wife Clara Bryant Ford (1866–1950). Marion Mahoney Griffin, a close adherent of Frank Lloyd Wright and wife of the famous Walter Burley Griffin, and then connected with the Chicago firm of von Holst and Fyfe, prepared plans in 1912 for a Prairie style house for the Fords. But a disagreement over contractors and suppliers arose as construction was underway, and the Fords dismissed the firm. William H. Van Tine of Pittsburgh was called in. He altered Marion Mahoney Griffin's plans. The large, Marblehead limestone house resembles the early English or Scottish Baronial style of architecture, but in fact is a blend of the Late English Gothic with the Prairie style. On the river side, a round, medieval, castellated corner tower and a stepped, parapeted gable are applied to the low, horizontal house. The entry side has a porte-cochère. Jens Jensen did the landscaping from 1914 to 1920; the gardens are now being restored. On the grounds are servants' cottages, a pony barn, and a powerhouse that is connected to the house by a 300-foot-long tunnel. Today Fairlane is used by the University of Michigan-Dearborn Campus as a conference center.

WN12 Ford Homes

1919–1921, Albert Wood. Ten blocks bounded by Monroe and Nowlin streets, Conrail (formerly Michigan Central Railroad) tracks and Military St.

This neighborhood represents Henry Ford's brief foray into planned residential construction. The Dearborn Realty and Construction Company, run by Ford's personal secretary, his wife, his son Edsel, and another close associate, bought the already-platted land and began construction in 1919. Located near the Henry Ford and Son tractor plant, these houses were built to enable workers to avoid the long and costly streetcar ride from Detroit. Characteristic of Ford's method of organizing industrial work processes, the construction was carried out by Ford employees using assembly-line production methods. Factory workers were able to work in the fresh air—a balance Ford thought beneficial—in crews responsible for single operations that were carried out in sequence. Materials were bought in quantity, and standard parts were cut and assembled in shops set up on the site. The cost savings achieved in this way allowed the company to meet Ford's goal of using quality materials to construct comfortable and affordable homes.

The designer, Albert Wood, who was a Ford architect, drew up seven models of a standardized house plan. Each model was distributed throughout the subdivision. The original purchaser selected a brick or wood exterior and the color of the roofing shingles. Houses were grouped at staggered setbacks in an attempt to create a sense of variety within the constraints of standardization and the grid of the street plan.

Wood added an occasional colonial detail to what were otherwise mass-produced, early twentieth-century cottages. Their simple lines are characterized by steeply pitched roofs, short central chimney stacks, relatively few dormers, and the grouping of windows as horizontal accents. Carved hoods over some of the entrances provide the only decorative embellishment of their plain facades. By shifting the positions of the entrance and the porch and by varying the alignment of the gable, as well as using hipped-roofed models, Wood achieved unity without uniformity.

Most of the houses have three bedrooms and a bathroom upstairs; the living room, porch, dining room, and kitchen on the first floor are generally arranged around the central core of fireplace and stairs. The simplicity and economy of this plan was matched by a spare interior, with the only decorative details provided by wood trim. This allowed the builders to furnish high-quality bathroom and kitchen fixtures, telephones, and electricity while remaining within the price range of working people. Garages were optional.

This project was not conceived as company housing, since purchase of the houses was not restricted to Ford employees. Yet the Dear-

born Realty and Construction Company maintained control over each house for seven years after it was bought. During this time, the owner agreed not to resell the house, and the company retained the right to buy it back if the owner was thought to be undesirable.

By 1921, 250 houses and the DuVall Elementary School were built. After construction began in 1919, however, a depression in agriculture led to the closing of the tractor plant and to the transfer of its machinery and workers to the new River Rouge auto plant. Less accessible to this factory, the last houses to be finished were slow to sell. Further development of the subdivision, including a planned park along a belt at the north end of the site to act as a buffer between the houses and the railroad tracks, never materialized. The Dearborn Realty and Construction Company, daunted by the vagaries of the construction industry, never built another house.

Changes have been made to many of these houses in the intervening years, including the closing in of porches, the building of additions, and resurfacing. The houses remain immediately recognizable, however, due to the strong lines of the original designs and their curved entrance hoods, which seem to have served successfully as symbols of place.

WN13 Fordson High School

1926–1928, H. J. Keough. 13800 Ford Rd. (Michigan 153), one block west of Schaefer Rd.

In 1928, Webster H. Pearce, who was Michigan State Superintendent of Public Instruction, proclaimed Fordson High School "the most beautiful [school] in Michigan." Designed by H. J. Keough of Detroit, the building set a new standard for academic structures. The design for the school was organized by a 442-foot-long central spine to which wings representing various educational functions were connected.

Inspiration for the building was derived from the Lawyers' Club at the University of Michigan and from the Memorial Quadrangle at Yale University, as well as Rushton and Apethorpe halls in Northamptonshire, England. Clad in seam-faced granite with Briar Hill sandstone trim, the school features a central crowned tower, stone-mullioned windows, hand-carved oak paneling and fireplace, painted wall murals by Zoltan Sepeschy, tapestries, and Jacobean fumed-oak furnishings. With a swimming pool, a greenhouse, laboratories, and an auditorium, a complete educational environment was put into place.

GROSSE ILE

WN14 East River Road

1840s–1870s, Gordon W. Lloyd and others. East River Rd. at Grosse Ile Parkway

East River Road contains a fine collection of Gothic Revival houses built from the 1840s to 1870s for wealthy Detroiters seeking rustic, unspoiled beauty. They were strongly influenced by Andrew Jackson Downing's publications *Cottage Residences* (1842) and *The Architecture of Country Houses* (1850). Overlooking the Detroit River and the marshes and islands of the Ontario shore, the island, an almost perfect rural setting for Downing villas and cottages, was purchased by William and Alexander Macomb from the Potowatomi Indians in 1776. By 1860 fifty people owned property on Grosse Ile. As fish and farm products and crops from the area were being shipped off the island to Detroit, weekend commuters and summer vacationers flowed to the island by boat and rail. East River Road is notable for its houses designed by Gordon W. Lloyd, a prominent English-born Detroit and Windsor, Ontario, architect.

WN14.1 Judge Samuel Townsend and Elizabeth Campbell Douglass House (Littlecote)

1859–1860, Gordon W. Lloyd. 24532 East River Rd.

This little gray stone Gothic Revival cottage was built for a family with "a strong taste for rural life and scenery." Its owner, Samuel Douglass (1814–1898), was a lawyer (and an amateur scientist, who accompanied his cousin Douglass Houghton on expeditions) who commuted to Detroit. The house has intersecting gables with lacy bargeboards, finials, an assortment of porches, an oriel window, and ornamental brick chimneys typical of the style.

WN14.2 Samuel Lewis House (The Wedding Cake)

1860. 24808 East River Rd.

The Wedding Cake, or the Samuel Lewis House, is one of Michigan's finest examples of the rural Gothic Revival villa conforming to the tenets of Andrew J. Downing. In his *The Architecture of Country Houses,* Downing stated that the villa was "the most refined home of America—the home of its most leisurely and educated class of citizens." The towered and gabled asymmetrical Lewis house has pointed arch windows, striking undulating decorative bargeboards, board-and-batten siding, and ornamental brick chimneys, together with a generous veranda. The structure embodies the taste and picturesqueness of Downing-inspired homes. It fulfills Downing's definition of the villa as "a private house, where beauty, taste, and moral culture are at home." Lewis (b. 1878), prominent in Detroit commerce and banking, was "a person of competence or wealth sufficient to build and maintain it with some taste and elegance."[18]

WN14.3 Saint James Episcopal Chapel

1867–1868, Gordon W. Lloyd. 1958, addition. 25150 East River Rd.

Saint James Chapel is an exquisite example of the important early Gothic rural technique of board and batten advocated by Downing. Elizabeth (Lisette) Denison Forth, a former slave and longtime household servant of the John Biddle family, willed her life savings of about $3,000 to build a chapel. With additional contributions from sons William and James Biddle, this chapel was erected in 1867–1868 to the plans of the Biddles' friend, Gordon W. Lloyd. The steeply gabled little building has scalloped bargeboards pierced with quatrefoils, pointed arched windows with tracery, a gable entrance vestibule, and a wooden bell cote. Buttresses support its board-and-batten walls. The interior is best seen in the afternoon, when the sun lights the *Angel of Praise* stained-glass window, which was manufactured by Tiffany and installed in 1898 in the west wall. The chapel is one of Lloyd's finest works and is comparable to the works of Richard Upjohn. This is a supreme example of a small Ecclesiological church.

RIVERVIEW

WN15 **WJR Radio Transmitting Building**

1934, Cyril Edward Schley. Southwest corner of Sibley and Grange roads

WN15 WJR Radio Transmitting Building

The WJR Radio Transmitting Building is an unexpected jewel in a rural, open setting. It was built in 1934, when the radio station moved its transmitting facility from its original location at Sylvan Lake. The Riverview location was considered a great improvement because its flat terrain would be ideal for radio wave propagation. It was also eight miles closer to Detroit and even closer to Toledo, which gave it improved transmission in both directions.

The design by a Detroit architect exhibits all the hallmarks of the zigzag Art Deco style. Its jagged silhouette is stepped back to a central tower. Large rectangular brick piers create a symmetrical and balanced composition on all sides. Bays between the piers are filled with glass blocks. The most striking feature, however, is the lavish use of colorful ceramic tile on the facade. Geometric patterns in red, yellow, green, and black surround the doors and windows. The words "WJR" were written in metal and neon down the single-mast antenna tower, which rose 733 feet—higher than any structure in the state at the time. The ornamentation and the Art Deco style turned a small utilitarian structure into a flamboyant image for the modern age of radio. The building was thought to embody "every new idea in radio science and engineering."[19]

Suburban Satellite Region

THE COUNTIES OF THE SUBURBAN SATELLITE REGION LIE IN a crescent around the south, west, and north of Detroit and Wayne County. With Detroit and Wayne County, they constitute Michigan's only metropolis. The land is undulating, often hilly terrain, dotted with many lakes, streams, and marshes. The River Raisin and the Huron, Rouge, and Clinton rivers run through the region, draining into Lakes Erie and Saint Clair. Near the lakes, the land is flat and marshy. A blend of urban, industrial, and suburban with small-town and rural settlement characterizes the area. The suburban satellites, together with metropolis, contain Michigan's largest concentration of architectural masterpieces.

Monroe County was laid off by a territorial executive act of Lewis Cass, governor of the Territory of Michigan, in 1817. Macomb County was established in 1818, Oakland County in 1819, Washtenaw County in 1822, and Livingston County in 1833. Monroe County was organized in 1822, Oakland County in 1820, Washtenaw County in 1826, and Livingston County in 1836. The settlement in these counties began along rivers. Moravian missionaries, for example, who had lived in the Ohio River valley, settled in 1782 with some of their Indian converts on the Clinton River at New Gnadenhutten, near present-day Mount Clemens, and lived there for three years. But it was not until the 1820s and 1830s, after the territorial roads were constructed, that settlement began in earnest.

The early development of the Suburban Satellite Region radiated out from Wayne County like the spokes of a wheel, in a pattern that has as its apex the center of Detroit, at what is now the intersection of Woodward and Jefferson avenues and Hart Plaza, on the Detroit River. Radial arteries that followed Indian trails precipitated the star-shaped pattern of Detroit's early suburban

123

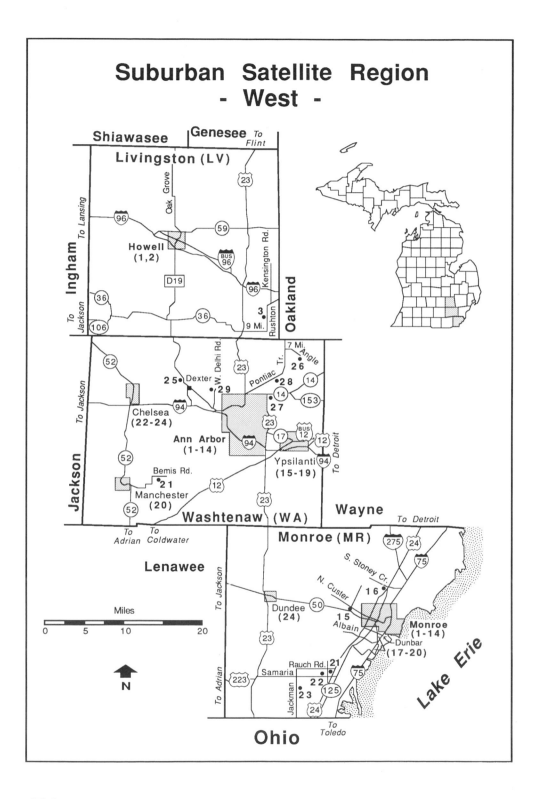

Suburban Satellite Region
- West -

Shiawasee Genesee To Flint
Livingston (LV)
Ingham
To Lansing
Oak Grove
96
59
23
Howell (1,2)
BUS 96
Kensington Rd.
D19
96
Oakland
36
To Jackson
36
106
3
9 Mi.
Rushton

52
7 Mi. Angle
To Jackson
W. Delhi Rd.
23
Pontiac Tr.
26
25 Dexter
29
28
14
14
153
Chelsea (22-24)
94
27
23
Ann Arbor (1-14)
17
BUS 12
12
94
To Detroit
Jackson
52
Ypsilanti (15-19)
94
Bemis Rd.
21
12
Manchester (20)
52
23
Washtenaw (WA)
Wayne
To Adrian To Coldwater
Monroe (MR)
To Detroit
Lenawee
275
24
S. Stoney Cr.
75
N. Custer
16
To Jackson
Miles
0 5 10 20
Dundee (24)
50
15
Albain
Monroe (1-14)
Dunbar (17-20)
N
23
Rauch Rd.
21
223
Samaria
22
75
To Adrian
Jackman
23
125
24
To Toledo
Ohio

Lake Erie

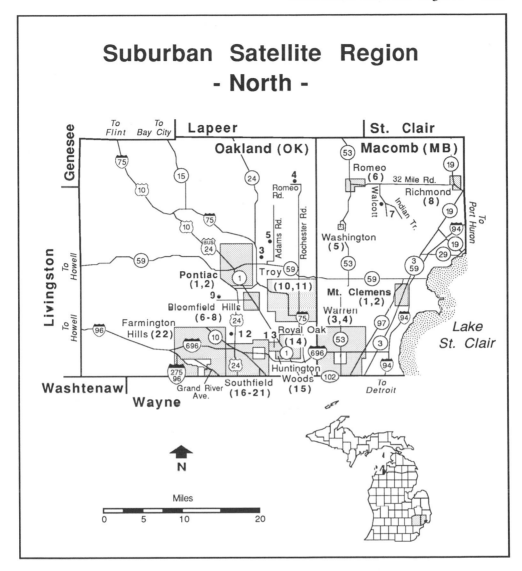

Suburban Satellite Region
- North -

growth. A network of highways was constructed along these early pathways during Michigan's territorial period. Overlying the radial arteries is the rectilinear pattern delineated by the land survey. The French long lots on the River Raisin (some originally from 400 to 900 feet in width by 3 miles in length) deviate from the radial and rectilinear division of land.

A system of roads that, to this day, follows the network of trails used by the earliest settlers was essential to the immigration that began in the late 1820s. Gov. Lewis Cass ordered the construction of a military road northwest from Detroit to Saginaw along the Saginaw Trail, later Woodward Avenue (Michigan

1), US 10, and I-75, bringing settlement to Oakland County; and the Grand River Road from Detroit to Muskegon, present-day US 16 and Interstate 96, encouraging settlement to Oakland and Livingston counties in the 1830s. Development of other overland roadways soon followed. By the late 1830s, 1840s, and 1850s, state and plank roads crisscrossed the region. Villages, cities, and suburbs grew along these trails and roads, evidenced by early farms, houses, taverns, stores, mills, and factories. Greek Revival farmhouses such as the Alonzo Olds House, erected in the 1840s on Rushton Road, remain as vestiges of the territorial and early statehood era.

In the 1840s, 1850s, and 1860s railroads linked the region. The most important was the Michigan Central Railroad, which ran from Detroit through Ann Arbor, and eventually to the Saint Joseph River. Towns developed as the result of the railroad. Chelsea, for example, was founded at the intersection of the Michigan Central Railroad and the Detroit, Jackson and Chicago Railway lines and flourished as a shipping center for wool and as a manufacturing center.

Manufacturing grew in the 1880s and new immigrants met the demand for labor. During the 1900s the automobile, shipbuilding, marine engine, railroad car, and metalworking industries added to that need. The first interurban railroads arrived in the late 1890s, allowing workers access to factories from their residences in the suburbs. The oldest suburbs in the region are Farmington, Royal Oak, and Saint Clair Shores, each of which stands astride a territorial or military road.

The settlement of Royal Oak and the area north followed the construction of the military road from Detroit to Saginaw. In 1838 the tracks of the Detroit and Pontiac Railroad reached Royal Oak, and by 1895 demand for regular transportation to Detroit had grown to the extent that the Oakland Railway electric interurban began regular service in southeastern Oakland County. This line was consolidated with others in the metropolitan area in 1901, forming the Detroit United Railway System. A second interurban, the Highland Park and Royal Oak Railway, initiated service along Stephenson Highway through Madison Heights and Hazel Park in 1917.

Meanwhile, the increasing availability of the automobile by the turn of the century caused further changes in living patterns. By 1934, the interurbans had been replaced by automobile traffic, and in that year those trains ceased operation.

Three of five major industrial corridors in the metropolitan Detroit area run through the Suburban Satellite Region. This industrial decentralization and other factors, namely the Federal Housing Administration (FHA) and the Veteran's Administration (VA) mortgage programs, sewer, and water systems, and the interstate highway network, encouraged outward migration to adjacent suburbs, newer suburbs, and exurbs, in the 1950s, 1960s, and 1970s.

New residential neighborhoods naturally followed the development of industrial corridors. An example is the Central Wayne Industrial Corridor through

Pontiac. Emerging in conjunction with the Ford Motor Company's industrial development in Highland Park during the first two decades of the twentieth century was a building boom throughout the southeastern Oakland County area. As a result, many towns were incorporated during the late teens and twenties. New subdivisions were platted in record numbers, and utilities, churches, schools, stores, and post offices were built to service the growing population. The Modern Housing Neighborhood in Pontiac and Westacres in Oakland County are examples of such planned neighborhoods.

In the meantime, industrialists seeking summer retreats migrated to the small towns, lakes, and farms of the out-county areas. Thus the Buhls, the Scrippses, the Dodges, and other wealthy families spent vacation hours at farms, and, later, at period revival estates in Oakland County, several of which have been turned over to public use as parks and cultural centers. Out Woodward Avenue, Detroiters built in the early twentieth century a colony to rival Grosse Pointe, at Bloomfield Hills.

Today's urban and suburban sprawl occurs along county roads, state highways, and the interstate highways, becoming progressively newer and more rural as it reaches the outer limits of the region. Those major corridors extend from Detroit and for the most part follow the routes of earlier territorial and state roads. The developmental linkage continues by and along concentric rings of roads and connectors such as the Walter P. Reuther Freeway (I-696) in Oakland and Macomb counties. Thus, this horizontal development of space is linked to the automobile, around which Detroit built the largest industrial complex in the world. At the intersections of interstate highways and local expressways are clustered regional shopping centers and town centers of high-rise and horizontal offices, apartments, hotels, and shopping areas that are the focuses of whole corridors of similar development.

Middle-sized cities are represented by Monroe, Ann Arbor, Ypsilanti, Mount Clemens, and Pontiac and small towns, by Dexter, Chelsea, Dundee, Romeo, Howell, and Manchester. Rural areas and pastoral farmland are in all of the counties.

The buildings and historic landscapes of the Suburban Satellite Region are currently subject to development pressures, the same pressures that strain schools and public utilities. Many small exurban villages and cities are havens for commuters to Detroit, Southfield, Troy, Warren, and the like. Their residents have brought with them an interest in preserving the architectural character that attracted them to these communities in the first place. Historic district commissions, working under local historic preservation ordinances, actively review building activity in many of the cities, villages, and counties of the suburban satellite region. Particularly active are the commissions in Ann Arbor, Franklin Village, Romeo, Ypsilanti, and Birmingham.

The scenic beauty of the area and its recreational resources are preserved in the Huron-Clinton Metropolitan Park System. Act 147 of the Michigan Public

Acts of 1939 sanctioned the Huron-Clinton Metropolitan Park. Approved in 1940 and organized in 1942, it was named for the two longest rivers in the metropolitan area. Large public parks were created with the Delhi, Dexter-Huron, Hudson Mills, Kensington, and Stony Creek metropolitan parks and at Metropolitan Beach on Lake Saint Clair.

Selfridge Field, created in 1917 to train pilots and mechanics for the U.S. Army Air Corps, was expanded between 1939 and 1942 to five times its original size. Occupying more than 3,600 acres during the war, it was a hub of military activity. It became a Michigan Air National Guard facility in 1971 and was used by reserve and regular military units. It will be closed in 1993.

Some of Michigan's major educational and cultural institutions located in the area are Cranbrook, the University of Michigan, Eastern Michigan University, Oakland University, and Meadow Brook Hall.

The architecture is representative of the full spectrum of styles and buildings. On the one hand, the many hearty structures that form the backbone of the collections of historic buildings were designed and constructed by local carpenter-builders and stonemasons such as Manases Kinsey, C. L. Gee, and many anonymous craftsmen. To the present day, local architects have designed many of the fine buildings in the area. On the other hand, such internationally known architects as Minoru Yamasaki, Eero and Eliel Saarinen, Albert Kahn, and Gunnar Birkerts did, and are doing, most of their Michigan work in the Suburban Satellite Region and in Detroit. The major Detroit architectural firms of Smith, Hinchman and Grylls, Mason and Rice, William and John Scott, Spier and Rohns created many of the region's high-style buildings in the nineteenth and early twentieth centuries, and architects Albert Kahn, William Kessler, Louis Redstone, and others have been equally active in the twentieth century.

Monroe County   (MR)

MONROE

Settlement began in Monroe County in about 1785, when large numbers of French-Canadians from Detroit carved out homesteads on the *Rivière Aux Raisins* (River Raisin) and the adjoining creeks. This settlement represents one of the first major satellite communities to branch off from Detroit. It grew quickly, but soon Detroit's rapid growth eclipsed Monroe. From this time well into the twentieth century, Monroe's development diverged significantly from Detroit's. Monroe became decidedly rural in the remainder of the nineteenth century and has kept some of that character, in spite of the introduction of the paper, furniture, and automobile industries to the region.

Monroe did not experience the same pressures of the urban sprawl that obliterated so much of Detroit's early architecture. As a result, the effects of the old French long-lot system can still be seen in the farms along the River Raisin, and a handful of homes built in the French mode are still standing. The earliest and most significant of these, the Navarre-Anderson Trading Post, built in 1789, reflects the region's strong ties to Canada in the eighteenth century and to Michigan's first industry, the fur trade.

Also preserved in Monroe are fine ex-

Monroe

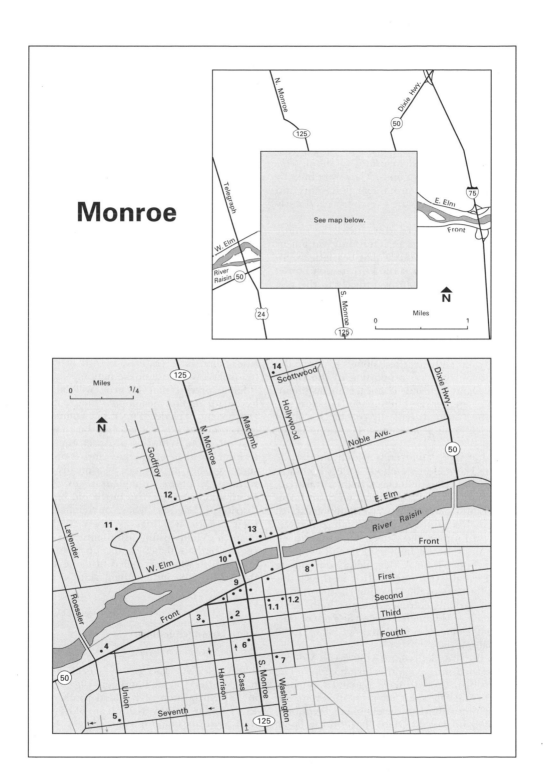

See map below.

Miles
0   1

Miles
0   1/4

amples of the classical traditions brought to the region by the New Englanders and New Yorkers who flocked to the area after the opening of the Erie Canal. These Yankees were attracted to Monroe by the port facilities developed on Lake Erie and the river and by the early roads and rail lines that headed west toward Chicago. The buildings range from elegantly porticoed mansions to simple cottages and utilitarian mills. They were built by some of the most prominent politicians and merchants in the state's territorial and early statehood years.

The New Yorkers who settled the county brought with them an interesting variant of the Greek Revival style that has left an enduring legacy. It was the L-formation house, in which a smaller wing projects to the side of a large front gable end. From the 1840s to the 1890s, New England Yankees, the French, and Germans all eventually employed this vernacular type, so it was the typical farmhouse of nineteenth-century southeastern Michigan. In form, these homes preserve the shape and general proportion of the Greek Revival but have little classical embellishment. Some New Yorkers built them in cobblestone, but the Germans typically constructed them of brick, with a prominent date stone in the gable.

Other styles and trends evident in Monroe in the years after statehood reflect both academic and ethnic influences. In the rural areas, there are a few Pennsylvania German farmsteads and a scattering of German log cabins; the city has a fine representation of Italianate, Second Empire, and Queen Anne structures. The Mann house, built in 1848 and designed by architect John Addey, stands out among the formal-styled homes. It is in the Gothic style but retains the lingering classicism in its use of flanking entrance columns, in the same manner as Maximilian Godefroy's use of classicizing elements in Saint Mary's Chapel (1806) in Baltimore.

In the twentieth century the city of Monroe developed into a manufacturing center. The townships, though, have remained remarkably rural, in spite of pressure from encroaching suburban development from both Detroit and Toledo, Ohio. The industrial boom of the city of Monroe began in earnest in the first decade of this century. In 1906 the Weis Manufacturing Company started producing office furniture and became a leader in its market before it was bought out and moved

in 1963. The founding of the River Raisin Paper Company in 1911 heralded the beginning of the modern paper industry here. In 1917 the Monroe Auto Equipment Company—producer of Monroe Shock Absorbers—started there, and in 1923 the La-Z-Boy Chair Company began in the garage of one of its founders. Most of the manufacturing operations of these industries have moved out, in some cases leaving abandoned factory buildings.

Monroe's industrial growth had a profound effect on residential growth. Since the 1930s the city has experienced unprecedented expansion. Subdivisions have sprung up both within the city and on its borders. The homes built there largely reflected the popular trends in the country. In one instance, though, a Monroe developer was a trend setter. In the 1930s David E. Winkworth designed and built a split-level house. Entering the plans in a contest, it won a prize and was featured in an architectural magazine. Some have credited it with being the first split-level house in the nation.

Some predict that Monroe will be swallowed up in the megalopolis that will link Detroit and Toledo. The rapid commercial growth of the 1980s is moving the county in that direction. With this prospect, the architectural heritage of the city and county assumes greater importance as a means of asserting Monroe's uniqueness of place. Restoration is under way in the old business district of Monroe, where merchants view their historic buildings as assets. With this element to help distinguish themselves in the region, perhaps the city and county can again lay claim to what was called in its heyday in the 1830s, "the independent state of Monroe."

MR01 Loranger Square

First and Washington streets

The square was laid out in a gridiron and named after Joseph Loranger, who offered, in 1817, a portion of his land south of the River Raisin and upstream from old Frenchtown as the location for a new village. Monroe was established as the seat of the government of Monroe County, which was itself created by Territorial Governor Lewis Cass and named after President James Monroe. After the massacre of the River Raisin during the War of

1812, families who had fled the settlement on the north bank of the river at the edge of the Great Marsh returned and new settlers arrived.

MR01.1 **Monroe County Courthouse**

1880–1881, Edward O. Fallis. 1952, additions. 1985–1986 addition, TMP Associates. 1106 East First St. (southeast corner of Loranger Square)

The courthouse was designed by Fallis (1851–1927), a Toledo architect, who had apprenticed with Charles C. Miller, had traveled in Europe, and developed a reputation for his courthouse plans. This two-story, smooth-faced limestone, "single facade" structure has a pedimented central three-bay loggia, a modillioned cornice and an elaborate, mansard-roofed corner tower. It stands on the foundation of an earlier courthouse, built in 1836–1837 and destroyed by fire in 1879. Two undistinguished additions were constructed to the south and west in 1952. An atrium connects the old structure to a glossy, new, tan-with-red-trim south addition by TMP Associates of Bloomfield Hills.

MR01.2 **Monroe City Hall**

1977, Rossetti Associates. 120 East First St.

The modern red brick city hall meets the courthouse on the bias.

MR02 **Oliver and Eliza Disbrow Johnson–Rufus E. Phinney House**

1830s?, 1896. 22 West Second St.

The clapboarded, wood frame, symmetrical Federal structure was updated with Gothic Revival bargeboards, pointed dormers, and a front gable, also with a bargeboard. It was built for Oliver Johnson (1784–1868), an early settler on the River Raisin who arrived from Connecticut no later than 1818. Johnson served as Monroe County judge, having been appointed by the governor of the Michigan Territory, and as a ruling elder in the First Presbyterian Church. The house later was occupied by the Johnson's granddaughter, Mrs. Rufus E. Phinney. Federal features include the window heads, elliptical patterns in the side and transom lights of the front entry, paneled doors, carved pinwheels at the junction of the door trim, and three exquisitely detailed fireplace mantels. The house originally stood on the east side of the public square. Open to public.

MR03 **Oliver House**

1827. 1930s, additions. 204 West Second St. (northwest corner of Second and Harrison streets)

The symmetrical, five-bay, eave-to-the-street house with Neoclassical wooden dentils was originally Federal. It is constructed of limestone quarried on Kelley Island, transported by barge to Monroe, and laid evenly in blocks on the south and east facades and in rubble on the north and west. The house acquired its front porch and its east and west additions, all on concrete block foundations, in the 1930s.

MR04 Amendt Milling Company

1840s. 1895, 1905, remodeled. 317 West Front St.

Formerly the Monroe City Mills, established in 1840, this milling complex was purchased by the Amendt Milling Company in 1895 and converted from water to electrical power. By 1912 the mill was supplied with wheat, corn, and oats stored at company-owned elevators in Ida, Petersburg, Newport, and Monroe, as well as in Ohio. Flour milled here was shipped east to Buffalo and New York City first by boat and Erie Canal barge and later by rail; now it is transported by truck. Sheaves of wheat carved in stone surmount the entry of the Beaux-Arts Classical-style office and revere the raw material processed here. The words "Lotus Flour" (after the flower that blooms in the Monroe marshes in August) executed in red brick on the gray brick walls of the plant advertise the product of the mill.

MR05 WoodCraft Square (Weis Manufacturing Company Plant)

1905–1917. 1982–1983, Gelardin/Bruner/Cott, Inc., rehabilitation architects. 800 West Seventh St. (Union St. at West Seventh St.)

Built by the Weis Manufacturing Company at the beginning of this century and purchased by the La-Z-Boy Chair Company in 1963, this industrial complex has been beautifully rehabilitated as housing for the elderly. The red brick complex of five buildings, three of which are unified into a single long building that extends for 480 feet along Union Street, is distinguished by segmental arched windows and corbeled brick. It represents a fascinating survival into the early twentieth century of the late nineteenth-century factory, many of which were very handsome indeed. The segmental windows, the corbeling, and the fine brickwork were the hallmarks of industrial building from the mid-nineteenth century on. A Postmodern entry porch to a one-story central building invites access to a well-lighted lobby. High ceilings, large windows, and open spaces where workers once planed, lathed, and finished office furniture have become spacious living quarters. The funds for the rehabilitation were provided by the Michigan State Housing Development Authority (MSHDA) financing, HUD Section 8 rental subsidies, Community Development Block Grant (CBDG), and private funds.

MR06 Trinity Episcopal Church

1868–1869, John Addey. 1895, chapel addition. 1898, rectory. 1957, parish hall addition. 304 South Monroe St. (southwest corner of South Monroe and East Third streets)

The small, single-gabled, Gothic Revival parish church is an archetypical Ecclesiological church. The Ecclesiological movement in the Anglican church, which called for a return to traditional medieval forms in ritual and in church building, was a factor in Michigan as well as elsewhere in the country. Trinity Episcopal Church has a corner entry and bell tower, pointed arch windows, wall buttresses, and a polygonal apse. It was designed by Addey (1803–1879), an Irish-born carpenter-joiner who resided in Monroe, and executed in local limestone rubble. Connected by means of a one-story passageway to the west is the rectory, also of local limestone. To the south is a new parish hall.

MR07 Henry V. Mann House (William H. Boyd House)

1848, John Addey. 405 Washington St. (southeast corner Washington and Fourth streets)

Gothic details—window bays, an entry porch, pointed arch windows decorated with tracery, and ornate roof cresting—seemingly are pasted on this crisp and clean, two-story, stucco cube with side wings. The low, hipped-roof house was built for Henry V. Mann, a promoter and stockholder of the Michigan and Southern Railroad, a promoter of the Monroe harbor and canal, a lawyer, and Monroe County treasurer.

MR08 Alfred Isaac and Sarah Toll Sawyer House

1872–1873. 320 East Front St.

The large, symmetrical, brick Italian Villa befitted "one of the most eminent physicians

MR07 Henry V. Mann House (William H. Boyd House)

and surgeons in Southern Michigan [with] an extensive and lucrative practice."[20] It was built for Alfred Isaac Sawyer, M.D. (b. 1828), and his wife, Sarah. Sawyer, who secured the establishment of the homeopathy department at the University of Michigan, served as mayor of Monroe in 1869–1870 and in 1878. Bracketed eaves, corbeled chimneys, an unusual round-arched central wall dormer, corner quoins, and cresting enliven the two-and-a-half-story house. A glazed belvedere crowns its hipped roof. A one-story porch with paired columns, a balustrade, and brackets extends

MR08 Alfred Isaac and Sarah Toll Sawyer House

nearly the full width of the front facade. Open to public.

MR09 **Front Street Commercial District** (River Raisin Esplanade)

South of the River Raisin along Front St. from Smith to Scott streets in the River Raisin Esplanade redevelopment area and South Monroe St. to East Second St.

Most of the buildings are three-story brick Italianate storefronts with round-arched windows, hood molding, and corbeled cornices. Of especial note are the commercial building at 82 West Front Street, the August and Clark Building (12–14 West Front Street), Haeger's (33 West Front Street), built in the 1870s. The Monroe Bank and Trust Building (102 East Front Street), the Reaper Building (123–125 East Front Street), and the Monroe Theater (112 South Monroe Street) are notable twentieth-century structures.

MR10 **Equestrian Statue of George Armstrong Custer**

1910, Edward Clark Potter, sculptor. Southwest corner of West Elm and North Monroe streets

Commissioned in 1909 by the state of Michigan, sculpted by Edward Clark Potter, and erected originally in Loranger Square, the stately equestrian statue of George A. Custer portrays the leader of the Michigan Calvary Brigade during the Civil War, who is even more famous for his involvement in the Indian wars. Custer grew up in Monroe. During the late nineteenth century, the monumental sculpture of heroes and leaders for erection in parks was the primary source of commissions for many sculptors.

MR11 Saint Mary Academy or Monroe Academy (Immaculate Heart of Mary)

800-acre site extending one mile north of the River Raisin to Reinhardt Rd. between Lavender Blvd. and Godfroy.

The Saint Mary complex consists of four major structures on spacious grounds shared with a cemetery, rustic retreats, and cultivated farmland. Three of the buildings stand linked together in a crescent-shaped megastructure. In 1929, after fire destroyed the earlier Saint Mary Academy (which was built across from Saint Mary's Church [1834–1839], at the intersection of West Elm and North Monroe streets), the order of the Servants of the Immaculate Heart of Mary commissioned D. A. Bohlen and Son of Indianapolis to design the new academy and motherhouse in the Art Deco style. They built the structures in one year, on grounds occupied by the fourth major structure, the Hall of the Divine Child. The religious order is derived from the Oblate Sisters of Providence, founded in Monroe in 1846, and associated with the Saint Antoine de la Rivière aux Raisins Church, established here in 1788 and renamed Saint Mary in 1845.

MR11.1 Norman Towers (The Hall of the Divine Child)

1916–1918, Henry J. Rills. 1982–1984, remodeled and rehabilitated, Boston Architectural Team. 810 West Elm St.

A central castellated tower with battlements and buttressed with turrets dominates this four-and-a-half-story, red brick, institutional building lavishly trimmed with limestone. The building's Jacobean elements include symmetry, quoins, oriel windows, parapets, pointed Tudor arches, and tracery. Built as the boarding school for boys, the hall was converted to luxury apartments for senior citizens.

MR11.2 Motherhouse of the Immaculate Heart of Mary Sisters

1931–1932, D. A. Bohlen and Son. 1940, chapel addition. 610 West Elm St.

The huge, three-and-a-half-story, E-shaped motherhouse was built for the novices and professed sisters of the Servants of the Immaculate Heart of Mary, a religious order that numbered over one thousand sisters who taught in ninety-eight parochial schools. It contains the novitiate, the chapel, the professed sisters' quarters, and the infirmary. The building was designed by D. A. Bohlen and Son of Indianapolis, a firm known for its commissions for midwestern Catholic institutions. They worked largely in the Art Deco style, with stepped massing, verticality, and geometric decoration. Extending to the north at the center is the gem of the interior, the IHM Chapel of 1939–1940. At the apex of the motherhouse and the academy, and connecting the two, is the dining hall and kitchen, fronted by a shed-roof passageway. A marble sculpture of Mary, displayed in a limestone statuary niche, stands at the juncture of the two buildings and acts as a catalyst to unify the whole.

MR11.3 Saint Mary Academy

1931–1932, D. A. Bohlen and Son. 502 West Elm St.

Vertical brick ribbons, limestone fluting, and dramatic setbacks seem to heighten this very large, six-story Art Deco girls' school with a central tower and end pavilions. The interior is arranged around a central lobby axis and a marble-and-wrought-metal staircase. Since the mid-1980s, when the boarding school was closed due to lack of enrollment, the religious order of three hundred has gradually converted its dormitories, lounges, classrooms, reception rooms, administration offices, and chapels into a center for lifelong learning.

MR12 Rudolphus Nims House

1836–1837?. 1846–1847?. 1850, 1863, 1911, 1914, additions. 206 West Noble Ave. (northwest corner of Noble Ave. and Borgess)

This four-columned, temple-front house with wings stands as testimony to the idealization of classicism shared by its builders, James Jacques Godfroy, Rudolphus Nims, and John Birch (1790–1870), three men who served both as partners in a land speculation company and as Monroe city officials. When built, the house commanded a view of the River Raisin and of a racetrack below. The clapboard-covered, hewn-oak-frame structure stands on a fieldstone foundation. Its accurate Greek detail, fluted Doric columns, and its large scale are noted by Talbot Hamlin in his book *Greek Revival Architecture in America* (London, 1944).[21] Additions included a dining room, a summer kitchen, and a porch.

MR13 East Elm and North Macomb Streets Residential Area

North Macomb St., from West Elm St. to Vine; and West Elm St., from North Macomb St. to Lincoln

For much of its history, East Elm Street has been Monroe's finest residential street. Its upper-class dwellings, the homes of many of the city's most important business and civic leaders, span over one hundred years. It first developed in the 1820s and 1830s near the Monroe Street bridge over the River Raisin, as scattered houses were constructed along the river road, which is now Elm Street. Later, suburban villas began to appear on the rural landscape north of Elm Street. Because of its attractive topography and easy access to downtown, this area was platted into house lots and built up gradually over the succeeding century as an exclusively residential zone. Elm Street became Monroe's most prestigious address and represents residential building into the 1920s, with almost an entire range of nineteenth- and early-twentieth-century architectural styles.

MR13.1 Joseph Dansard House

1870s. 25 East Elm St.

This was the home of Joseph Dansard (d. 1879), who, with his prosperous father, Benjamin, an early French-born settler of Monroe, established the Dansard Bank. The two-and-a-half-story, Second Empire brick house has two-story bays, a mansard roof with dormer windows, molded cornices and cresting, a dramatic projecting bracketed hood at the central second-floor window, and decorative paired brackets below the eaves.

MR13.2 Governor Robert and Elizabeth Sabin McClelland House

c. 1835, John Anderson, builder. 1840, 1854, 1918, additions. 47 East Elm St.

The two-story, gable-front Greek Revival house possesses a pediment with a full deep entablature and is sheathed by horizontal matched boarding. Its three-bay facade is divided by four full-height pilasters. A rope pattern decorates the piers that support the symmetrical entry porch roof. The west and rear wings are later additions. Apparently the house was built for Ebenezer A. Howes (Howe?) and was acquired in 1840 by Robert McClelland (1807–1880). McClelland was a Michigan legislator, governor from 1851 to 1852, U.S. congressman, and the secretary of the interior under President Franklin Pierce.

MR13.3 Israel Epley and Mary Fishburn Ilgenfritz House

c. 1835?. 1874, enlarged. 62 East Elm St.

This two-story, gable-front, clapboarded Greek Revival house with wing and side entry was built in the 1830s to satisfy the classical taste of its first owners, Henry Smith (1798–1847) and his wife, Elvira. Its portico consists of four boxed piers. Smith was a U.S. Army engineer, who came to Monroe from New York to oversee the construction of the harbor of La Plaisance Bay and other government harbors on Lake Erie. In 1874, nearly thirty years after arriving in Monroe and establishing the nursery business that earned the city the title of the "Flower City," Strasburg-born Israel Epley Ilgenfritz (b. 1824) acquired the house. He and his wife enlarged it to accommodate their twelve children and planted on its grounds many decorative trees and plants.

MR13.4 Boyez and Sarah McLean Dansard House

1898–1900. 157 East Elm St.

This shingle-clad house with a broad overhanging gambrel roof, cross-gable Queen Anne dormer in front, columned fieldstone porch, and tripartite oriel and Palladian windows is a quintessential provincial example of the Shingle style. It belonged to the president of the family-owned B. Dansard and Sons State Bank of Monroe, later the Monroe State Bank and Trust.

MR14   House

c. 1930. 704 Hollywood (northeast corner of Hollywood and Scottwood)

The parade of twentieth-century period revival houses on Hollywood Drive is enlivened with this Spanish Colonial Revival in white stucco with a red tile roof, a patio, and a round-arched entry.

FRENCHTOWN TOWNSHIP

MR15 Navarre-Anderson Trading Post

1789. South side of North Custer Rd. at Raisinville Rd.

The Navarre-Anderson Trading Post survives from the territorial period. The simple one-and-a-half-story log structure utilizes the traditional French construction technique of *pièce-sur-pièce*. Hewn timber is mortised, tenoned, and pegged to form a sturdy framework. The door has a simple but delightful Greek Revival surround. The structure is associated with two early Monroe settlers and traders—French-Canadian   François-Marie Navarre (known as Heutreau, 1759–1836) and Scottish-born John Anderson. It has been moved and restored several times; today it

stands on the River Raisin, in an outdoor park where the Monroe County Historical Museum interprets it as the single dwelling of a fur trader in 1799. Next door is a kitchen building; at the corner is a country store.

MR16 Edward and Marianne Navarre Loranger House

Post-1825, Edward Loranger. 1861, brick lean-to added. 1945, dormers added. 7211 South Stony Creek Rd. (approximately 600 feet northwest of Telegraph Rd. [US 24])

Surviving from the territorial period is this prototype of French-Canadian construction. Facing Stony Creek, this one-and-a-half-story, symmetrical, brick house has gable-end chimneys, a *brique-entre-poteaux* wall dividing the two rooms of the main floor, and a basement kitchen. The exterior walls are laid in common or American bond in which every sixth course consists of headers, the other courses being stretchers. It was built by Edward Loranger (1796–1887), a brick mason who moved in 1816 from Three Rivers, Quebec, to Monroe, where he took occasional contracts in Detroit, Malden, Frenchtown, and Monroe. The brick lean-to was added in 1861. The dormers added in 1945 follow the French-Canadian tradition.

MONROE TOWNSHIP

MR17 Benjamin J. and Helen L. Bronson Greening House

c. 1900. 7305 Dunbar Rd., .4 mile east of La Plaisance Rd.

Surrounded by a nursery grown wild is the large and unhappily altered Colonial Revival house of Benjamin J. Greening, one of the Greening brothers, who owned and operated the Greening Brothers Nursery Company. Founded by their father, J. C. W. Greening, in 1857, it, along with two other nurseries—the Monroe (Ilgenfritz) and the Michigan—gave Monroe the name of "the floral city." Benjamin J. Greening (b. 1882) studied botany and landscape gardening at Harvard University before assuming management of the nursery in 1907. He married Helen L. Bronson in 1911. The *Catalogue of the Greening Bros. Nursery Company* called the house the latest in modern architecture, "a structure of elegance and convenience," and "in keeping with the rest of the beautiful things, buildings and grounds" at the nursery. Composed asymmetrically, the large, solid clapboarded house had a balustraded front porch and porte-cochère. The pediments of its many gables contain fanlights. To the east of the house, a beautiful park once displayed the pleasing effects of landscape improvement. A 1.5-mile-long bicycle path of ground limestone, built by the Greenings, connected the city of Monroe with the nursery. To the southwest, where Dunbar, La Plaisance, and the Detroit and Toledo Shoreline Railroad converge, are the Greening Brothers Nursery storage and packing cellars (now Snow Nursery), a large utilitarian brick-and-tile structure from which nursery stock was loaded onto railroad cars and shipped out. The nursery was in the business of planning and executing landscape designs. It was noted for its winter banana-apple tree.

MR18 R. C. Labadie House (Menard Labadie House)

c. 1818. 6823 La Plaisance Rd., east of Albain

Underneath a house made comfortable and livable with a layer of aluminum siding exists one built with French-Canadian *maison colombage* construction techniques. The clues are the orientation to La Plaisance Creek, the story-and-a-half massing, the symmetry with a slightly off-center door and the steeply pitched roof. At La Plaisance Bay, there once stood a settlement of these simple, log houses, some clapboarded and whitewashed, built by the French, the area's first settlers. Two others examples may be seen at 7044 and 7050 Dunbar Road (.2 mile east of La Plaisance Road).

MR19 Monroe Inn

1928. 14493 Telegraph Rd. (US 24), .25 mile south of Albain Rd.

This inn or roadhouse, with thirteen cabins that are no longer standing, gave lodging to travelers on the main route between Toledo and Detroit before the opening of Interstate 75. The inn is one and a half stories high and has a side-gable jerkinhead roof and shed dormers; there is a rear addition. Covered

with wood siding, grooved to imitate brick, and painted in pale yellowish green, it is marked with a neon sign in the same color. The interior has a 1930s decor. George Pollimac, a Yugoslavian immigrant who had worked as a railroad builder after arriving in America, and his wife, Anna, who had worked as a camp cook, built the inn and cabins. They were inspired by the tourist cabins they stayed in en route to California in 1927.

LaSALLE TOWNSHIP

MR20 Farmhouse

1840s?, Manases Kinsey (Kinzie?), stonemason. Northeast corner of Rauch and Strasburg roads

The two-story, side-gable, symmetrical, classical box-type house was built of local limestone by Manases Kinsey, who was a local stonemason. It is arranged with a center entrance flanked by two windows on the first story. On the second story are four windows across the front. The rusticated cement block front porch and chimney were added later.

ERIE TOWNSHIP

MR21 Rauch Farm

1840s?, Manases Kinsey (Kinzie?), builder. South side of Rauch Rd. between Suder and Strasburg roads, just west of Telegraph Rd. (US 24)

This farm and others on both sides of Rauch Road were settled by members of the Rauch family, made up of Pennsylvania Germans. The symmetrical, side-gabled, classical box-type house is arranged with a center hall and stairs flanked by rooms two deep. It is built of coursed limestone blocks on the front and coursed limestone rubble on the side and rear walls, with corner quoins and window headers. The central entry has top and side lights and a protective gabled porch. The gable-roofed cattle barn rests on a limestone foundation, its hay loft overhanging on the south. Manases Kinsey, a local stonemason, reportedly laid the stone in the walls of this house and in the smaller, but similar stone farmhouse at the northeast corner of Rauch and Strasburg roads.

BEDFORD TOWNSHIP

MR22 Theophilus and Roxanna Osgood House

1846. 744 Samaria Rd. (Michigan 151) (two doors from the northeast corner of Samaria and Minx roads)

Built on 160 acres of land acquired in 1835 from the U.S. government by settlers from western New York State, this provincial Greek Revival house exemplifies the cobblestone masonry wall-building tradition popular there from 1825 to 1865, a tradition that was transplanted across western Ontario, southern Michigan, and Wisconsin, with the opening of the Erie Canal. In this case, Theophilus and Roxanna Osgood gathered cobblestones, three to four inches in size, from nearby Stony Ridge and had a local mechanic lay them in regular horizontal courses in the walls of their one-and-a-half-story, side-gable-and-wing house. A deep plain entablature, stone window lintels and sills, and corner pilaster boards are Greek Revival stylistic elements that hint at their New York State origins. The porch and the dormers are later additions.

MR23 William and Mercy Aldrich Dunbar House

1852, C. L. Gee, master builder. On east side of Jackman Rd., .2 mile north of Erie Rd.

A colorful contrast of coursed, but random fieldstones, with limestone corner quoins dress the front and side walls of this one-and-a-half-story Greek Revival farmhouse. The form is a temple front with a single wing and the entrance on the side. The rear walls are rubble limestone. After arriving here from Massachusetts in 1832, William and Mercy A. Dunbar "reclaimed from the wilderness a productive farm."[22] The house, although clearly vernacular, is ambitious for its time and place. It was later occupied by their son, Addison E. Dunbar.

DUNDEE

MR24 Wolverine Building (Alfred Wilkerson Grist Mill)

1866. 1935, restoration and additions. 242 Toledo St., on the River Raisin

Dundee was one of some twenty "village industry" plants that Henry Ford developed in southeastern Michigan with encouragement from Thomas Edison. Already existing on this site was this clapboarded, wood-frame, Greek Revival gristmill, erected at the dam on the River Raisin by Alfred Wilkerson in 1866 and operated by him until 1880. Operated by R. B. Davis until 1910, it was acquired and converted into a hydroelectric generating plant by the Dundee Hydraulic Power Company. In 1931–1935 Henry Ford bought, restored and added to the mill for the purpose of housing one of his village industries. It was one of many small, water-powered factories along the nation's rivers acquired by Ford and intended to decentralize industry and offer employment to farmers during the winter. In 1938 the Dundee Mill employed eighty workers making copper welding tips, electric welding electrodes, and foundry castings. The addition of the limestone wing and stack enabled Ford to produce the copper tips at this location. The mill was acquired by the Wolverine Manufacturing Company in 1954, and it has been used for township offices since 1970.

Washtenaw County (WA)

ANN ARBOR

Ann Arbor is located in the Huron River valley, and the buildings of the city rise up into the embracing hills. It is the seat of the Washtenaw County government and the home of the University of Michigan. Two commercial districts have developed here, one downtown and the other along State Street, west of the university's central campus. The city is the hub for an agricultural county and a major research center revolving around the university and companies attracted to this environment. In a very real sense it is also a suburb of Detroit, with many employees of the Ford Motor Company residing here. It possesses a large collection of contemporary architecture and maintains its historic buildings with local historic district ordinances and reviews by a historic district commission.

WA01 **Ann Arbor Hands-On Museum** (Ann Arbor Central Fire Station)

1882–1883, William Scott and Company. 219 East Huron St. (northwest corner of East Huron St. and North Fifth Ave.)

In the early 1880s, when the citizens of Ann Arbor decided to replace their wood-frame firehouse with a utilitarian, fireproof, and inexpensive structure, consciously or subconsciously they were seeking an expression of civic pride as well. In May 1882, the city aldermen selected the plans of William Scott and Company of Detroit and completed the Richardsonian building the following year at the modest cost of $10,000. It is boldly polychrome with brick walls and corbeling and stone trim. Decorative gabled wall dormers project from the truncated hipped roof, and windows on the front facade are grouped in threes beneath round and segmental arches above the three pedimented engine portals. An Italianate hose and bell tower rises confidently at the southeast corner of the structure, as if to signal the city's attainment of civic maturity.

WA02 **Ann Arbor Bus Depot** (Eastern Michigan Motorbus Terminal)

1940; Bonfield and Cumming, Cleveland; Douglas Loree, Ann Arbor, associate architect. 116 West Huron St.

Built by Eastern Michigan Motorbus Coaches to serve the Blue Goose, Short Way, and Greyhound lines, the Streamline Moderne bus terminal is an architectural equivalent of the 1940 Greyhound Silversides. The sleek front facade of the steel-frame and concrete depot uses a polished geometry and integrated materials evocative of the speed of modern transportation. The smooth-sawed Indiana limestone exterior wall above a polished black granite base enframes a curved wall of glass sweeping the visitor to the double entrance doors. The aluminum-enframed glass doors with their tubular stainless steel full-width handles add to the horizontality of the exterior. The eye-catching porcelain enamel sign is trimmed with stainless steel and lettered with neon. Its vertical thrust contrasts with the sleek horizontality of the sweeping wall of glass. The plan of the depot is an elongated rectangular interior with a porte-cochère concourse. A ticket counter, a baggage room, and an enclosed loading platform that protected passengers were on the east; a lunch counter, newsstand, telephones, and lockers on the west; and rest rooms on the mezzanine. The interior was finished with smooth plaster, terrazzo flooring, and maple and birch cabinetry. This depot cost $45,000 to build. It met what C. E. Wickman, then the president of the Greyhound Corporation, noted as the bus operator's requirements of adequately providing "for the comfort of the patrons and the efficient movement of his vehicles," while at the same time avoiding "burdening his company with unnecessary fixed charges."[23]

WA03 **Robert S. Wilson House**

1843. 126 North Division St. (southeast corner of East Huron and North Division streets)

The temple-form Wilson house with its tetrastyle Ionic portico is frequently compared with the exquisite Greek temple of Nike Apteros on the Acropolis. One of Michigan's finest examples of the Greek Revival, its proportions and details were probably copied from architectural handbooks. The house is built of brick covered with stucco scored to simulate stone. Located at the left side of the main facade, the entrance has flanking pilasters, side lights, and a rectangular fanlight.

Ann Arbor

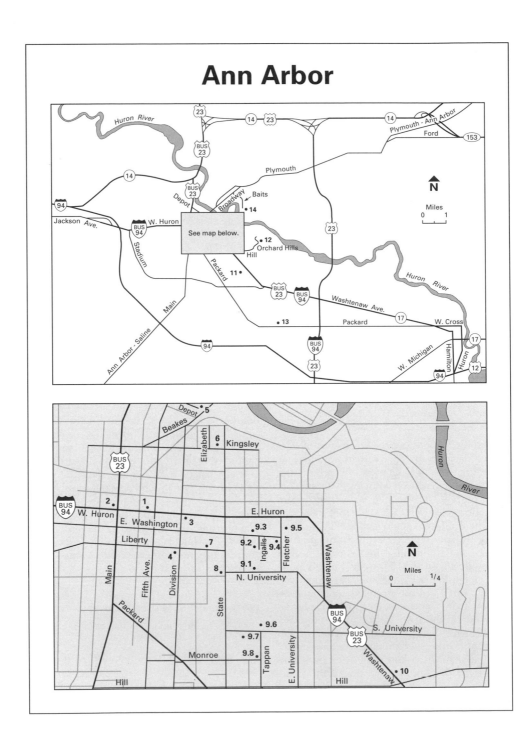

Judge Robert S. Wilson, who came from New York State to Ann Arbor in 1835, had the temple portion added in 1843. The house was probably built in three stages—the middle section in 1835, the temple portion in 1843, and the kitchen and servants' quarters at the rear in 1850.

WA04 **Reuben and Pauline Widenmann Kempf House** (Henry DeWitt Bennett House)

1853. 312 South Division St.

The diminutive one-and-a-half-story wood temple-form house is the embodiment of the simplicity of the Greek Revival style. The four sturdy rectangular piers are a radical distillation of the supremely sophisticated Doric column; three large, cast-iron grilles with an anthemion motif pose as metopes in the frieze but actually screen the windows of the upper story, which is tucked beneath the gable roof. Henry DeWitt Bennett, who was secretary and steward of the University of Michigan from 1869 to 1883, built the house. It was purchased in 1890 by Reuben H. and Pauline Widenmann Kempf, two classically trained music instructors. Reuben Kempf (1859–1945) organized and directed concert series to attract talented artists to the university; his wife, Pauline Widenmann Kempf (1860–1953), taught voice. Open to public.

WA05 **Gandy Dancer** (Ann Arbor Depot of the Michigan Central Railroad)

1886, Frederick H. Spier of Spier and Rohns. 1969–1970, 1975, rehabilitations. 401 Depot St.

This railroad complex by Detroit architects Spier and Rohns, who were noted for their designs for depots on the Michigan Central and Grand Trunk railroad lines, was acclaimed by the *Ann Arbor Courier* upon its completion in 1886 as the finest station between Buffalo and Chicago. Designed in the Romanesque Revival style popularized by Henry Hobson Richardson, this depot's Richardsonian character is powerfully expressed by the native granite fieldstone; by the deep-set round-arched openings on the lower level with groupings of smaller windows above the Syrian-Early Christian entrance arch and the eyelid windows; and by the bold massing of the squat tower, turret,

WA03 Robert S. Wilson House

WA04 Reuben and Pauline Widenmann Kempf House (Henry DeWitt Bennett House)

and gables. The energetic patterns of the arches, the large scale of the rock-faced masonry, and the weight of the massing all tell of the prestige of the Michigan Central Railroad Company. Donald E. Van Curler and

Jack Gree Associates planned the rehabilitation of the depot for use as a restaurant.

WA06 Saint Thomas the Apostle Church

1896–1899, Spier and Rohns. 1902, rectory. 1911, convent. 1929, school. 1964, interior remodeling. 520 Elizabeth St. (northwest corner of North State and Kingsley streets)

Saint Thomas the Apostle Church is one of several fine native granite fieldstone churches in Ann Arbor. Reverend Edward Dionysius Kelley (1861–1919), later Bishop of Detroit and Grand Rapids, began plans for the church in 1896: by then the Irish-Catholic parish had outgrown its earlier wood-frame structure. Since the University of Michigan was included in the parish, Kelley solicited funds for the project among Roman Catholic parishes statewide. The distinguished Detroit architectural firm of Spier and Rohns designed the church. It is a broad and low Richardsonian structure that stands on a bluff. The exterior walls are randomly coursed cut granite fieldstone above a base of fieldstone boulders, and the roof is red tile. A tall pyramidal-roofed campanile rises from the southeast corner of the church, and two shorter ones, from the northern corners. Two still shorter, round, conical-roofed towers are at the southwest and northeast corners. Squat colonnettes with foliated capitals carry the three round-arch openings of the entry on the main south facade, above which is centered a large rose window. Resting in a niche above the window is a statue of Saint Thomas the Apostle. The interior is arranged in a cruciform plan, with a nave and side aisles. It seats one thousand beneath a barrel vault. A plaster ceiling spans the nave. It is inscribed with transverse ribs, diagonal ribs, and bosses. Rose windows are in the transepts. The rectory was built in 1902, the convent in 1911, and the school in 1929.

WA07 Michigan Theatre Building

1927–1928, Maurice H. Finkel. 521–609 East Liberty St.

The Michigan Theatre was the largest movie palace built in Ann Arbor. Constructed for local merchant Angelos Poulos, the Michigan Theatre Building was leased to W. S. Butterfield, Incorporated, noted manager of theaters across the state. The auditorium seats one thousand. Maurice H. Finkel, formerly with Albert Kahn, designed the theater "to harmonize with the cultural atmosphere of the university," using what he called a Romanesque motif.[24] The Otto Misch Company of Detroit built the structure at a cost of $750,000; the Tuttle and Clark Studio of Detroit did the interior. The exterior of the reinforced concrete and brick structure is clad with buff tapestry brick, ornately trimmed with terracotta arches, roped columns, and polychrome tiles. A grand staircase sweeps through the great barrel-vaulted lobby. The coffered ceiling and the walls of the lobby are profusely decorated with rosette ornaments. Besides the theater, the building housed stores, offices, and bowling alleys. Recently, the city of Ann Arbor restored and renovated the theater to the plans of Osler-Milling Architects with Quinn-Evans as a functional and exciting facility in which to stage the performing arts. The original features and surface details of the foyer and the auditorium, now magnificently gold-leafed, recapture the theater's flamboyant expression of the attitudes and aspirations of the age in which it was built. The architects received a 1987 Honor Award from the Michigan Society of Architects for the restoration of the theater.

WA08 Nickels Arcade

1915–1918, Herman Pipp. 326–330 South State St. (faces northwest corner of the University of Michigan Central Campus)

The Nickels Arcade is unique in Michigan; it acts as an important extension of Ann Arbor's commercial development adjacent to the University of Michigan campus. Recognizing that the campus commercial area would flourish, Tom E. Nickels, the son of a meat market proprietor, began this market arcade. He commissioned Herman Pipp (b. 1872) of Ann Arbor, who was the designer of several local commercial and residential buildings, to draft the plans. A. R. Cole and Company of Ann Arbor executed them in 1915–1918. Two levels of shops and offices extend along a 265-foot-long skylighted passageway between South State and Maynard streets. The steel, brick, and concrete structure is clad and detailed with glazed terracotta. In its whiteness and basic design, the arcade is Beaux-Arts Classical, in decorative treatment it is Art Deco. A giant, three-story, three-bay open

WA08 Nickels Arcade

portico, flanked by stores and a bank, fronts the South State Street facade, while brick faces the austere Maynard Street rear. The Farmers and Mechanics Bank originally occupied the prime space on the southeast corner of the building. There are a number of precedents for the market arcade, stretching back to the early nineteenth century in London, Paris, and even Providence, Rhode Island. A notable forerunner was the Halles Centrales, built in Paris in 1853–1858 after the plans of Victor Baltard. The Nickels Arcade is smaller than most other similar projects under one glass roof, such as the Market Arcade erected in Buffalo in 1892. Ideally located facing onto South State Street and the campus pedestrian diagonal, Nickels Arcade is perfectly scaled to its small city environs.

WA09 University of Michigan Central Campus

1837-present. Bounded approximately by South State St., East Huron St., Monroe Ave., and East University Ave.

The University of Michigan at Ann Arbor was inaugurated as part of Michigan's Comprehensive State Education Plan of 1837. At that time, the university moved from Detroit to Ann Arbor. Confident of state support, the regents accepted the Ann Arbor Land Com-

pany's gift of 40 acres on which to develop the school, and they enlisted the services of New York architect Alexander Jackson Davis (1803–1892). Davis produced two elaborate U-shaped building designs, one Gothic Revival and one Greek Revival, but the proposals were too expensive for the fledgling university to execute. By September 1841, however, five simpler Greek Revival buildings—four professor's houses and a main classroom and dormitory building—were erected. These original buildings were the focus of the campus throughout the nineteenth century and into the early decades of the twentieth.

In the latter half of the nineteenth century the campus developed irregularly, with the principal buildings facing upon the major boundary streets. Of the original buildings, only the southwest residence, or the president's house, survives. The university's first permanent president, Henry Philip Tappan (1805–1881), nurtured its early development. The university organized a distinguished faculty, greatly expanded its research facilities, and established a science-oriented curriculum as an alternative to a classical education. The combination Greek Revival and Italianate Detroit Observatory, erected in 1854 at 1308 East Ann Street, contained the first large telescope constructed in the United States, and the first chemical laboratory building at a state university was erected in 1856 (no longer standing). Together they illustrate the university's progress.

By the 1870s the university had attained a national reputation for academic excellence. Skilled at obtaining legislative appropriations, President James Burrill Angell (1829–1916) guided the university and established separate schools of engineering, pharmacy, and dentistry. In 1894, Detroit architects Spier and Rohns designed Tappan Hall, 519 South State Street, a simplified Romanesque Revival classroom structure that was constructed of rust brick. Ten years later they added the West Medical Building (now the Natural Resources Building), a large dignified collegiate building in the Renaissance Revival mode located at 430 East University Avenue. Albert Kahn designed the West Engineering Building at 550 East University Avenue, which was constructed in 1910. Kahn's L-shape plan for the building features a vaulted central archway that serves as the southeast entrance into the diagonal and preserves the diagonal pathway that students had always trekked, criss-crossing the original plot.

The eclecticism continued in 1910, when the Chemistry Building (930 North University Avenue), with buff brick and Indiana limestone trim, was completed to the designs of the Detroit firm of Smith, Hinchman and Grylls, and the Beaux-Arts Classical Alumni Memorial Hall (now the Museum of Art) completed to those of Donaldson and Meier. The latter is at the northeast corner of South State Street and South University Avenue.

With the appointment in 1909 of William L. Clements (1861–1934) of Bay City as regent of the university and as chairman of the Building and Grounds Committee, Kahn assumed a more important role in the university's architectural development. His commissions included Hill Auditorium in 1915; the Natural Science Building, a variant of his industrial designs that was remarkable for its structural efficiency and subtle ornamentation, in 1915; and the General Library, 920 North University, in 1920.

In 1920 a comprehensive plan for campus development was first implemented. Clements organized a Committee of Five to oversee building location and design. It included Kahn, as the university's supervising architect, and Marion Leroy Burton (1874–1925), whose fund-raising abilities helped to spur the largest building expansion in the university's history. Until this time, primarily due to a constant shortage of building funds, the university's architectural development lacked unity.

The central space of the pedestrian diagonal had been haphazardly preserved until the completion of the General Library, which occupied a pivotal area from which all paths diverged. Kahn and the Cleveland landscape firm of Pitkin and Mott developed a plan with a central open space surrounded by a complex of new buildings, designed to accommodate the large growth in student enrollment that had been occurring following World War I. Kahn implemented the plan with his designs for the Clements Library of 1923 and Angell Hall of 1924 (435 State Street), a great classical revival building with a giant Doric portico that unified the university symbolically and housed the expanding College of Literature, Science, and the Arts.

In 1923, Smith, Hinchman and Grylls designed the East Engineering Building (525 East University Avenue), and York and Saw-yer of New York worked on the largest project begun during the Burton era, the $8.5 million Collegiate Gothic Law School Quadrangle, located next to their Martha Cook Building (1915). The Law School was also funded by alumnus William W. Cook. These two projects noticeably extended the campus area to the south and east beyond the limits of the original 40 acres. A few years later, the central campus area began to expand northward beyond the original site; this pattern of expansion continued into the 1930s.

A 1927 site plan developed by Pitkin and Mott created the Campus Mall, a one-quarter-mile-long avenue extending from the Graduate Library north to Washington Street. The mall's development began with the Women's League Building, between North University Avenue and Washington Street. Echoing their 1919 design for the university's Student Union Building, architects Allen B. Pond (1858–1929) and Irving K. Pond (1857–1939) of Chicago developed the league building's five-story plan in a picturesque Collegiate Gothic design. In 1936 the development continued with the Burton Memorial Tower, just north of Hill Auditorium, and in 1938 with the Horace H. Rackham Building (915 East Washington Street). Following World War II, however, the university considerably expanded its facilities, with modernistic structures such as Albert Kahn and Associates' Undergraduate Library (1957), known as "the Ugly," the Harlan Hatcher Graduate Library addition (1967–1970), the Physics and Astronomy Building (1963) at 501 East University Avenue, and Alden B. Dow's cube-shaped Fleming Administration Building (1966–1967).

More recently, historicism and a celebration of the existing architectural heritage is apparent in Hugh Newell Jacobsen's Alumni Center (1982), which responds to its Collegiate Gothic neighbor, the Women's League Building, and in Lukenbach/Ziegelman's addition to Tappan Hall (1984–1985), which complements the Romanesque Revival character of the original building with a large semicircular arch.

Despite this and a few other disappointing intrusions of design and scale, the University of Michigan's central campus still possesses the school's largest concentration of significant structures. Dating from 1840 to 1988, these buildings encompass the diverse architectural and historic development of one of the most distinguished public universities in the world.

WA09.1 Hill Auditorium

1913, Albert Kahn and Ernest Wilby; Hugh Tallant, consulting acoustical engineer. 1921, acoustics improved. 1949, renovations and new seating. 825 North University Ave. (northwest corner of North University Ave. and Ingalls Mall)

In 1910, Arthur Hill (1848–1909), an alumnus and a regent of the University of Michigan, bequeathed $200,000 for an auditorium for university gatherings and musical events. Albert Kahn and associate Ernest Wilby, in consultation with acoustical engineer Hugh Tallant of New York, created a large, distinctive auditorium with superior acoustics. The auditorium was constructed on North University Avenue, facing south toward the university's main pedestrian diagonal. It cost $282,000, and James L. Stuart of Pittsburgh built it. The massive exterior block is broken by an engaged unfluted Doric colonnade in antis, which enframes the stone entrance like a proscenium. The overall surface appearance is, however, Sullivanesque, with decorative red and brown brickwork against brick laid in English bond, terracotta and limestone trim. Anthemion ornamentation runs around the cornice. The 4,200-seat auditorium's unique parabolic shape and double soundproof walls permit every sound from the stage to be heard in all parts of the room.

WA09.2 Burton Memorial Tower (Baird Carillon)

1935–1936, Albert Kahn. 230 South Ingalls St.

The Art Deco carillon tower rises 212 feet over the campus in tribute to Marion Leroy Burton, president of the University of Michigan from 1920 to 1925. An unexecuted design for the tower, with stepped setbacks, submitted at the request of the student body by Eliel Saarinen, who was visiting professor in the university's School of Architecture in 1923–1924, inspired the eventual form planned by Albert Kahn, with its streamlined verticality and setbacks. The fund raising was completed with a gift from Charles M. Baird, a former University of Michigan student who became the university athletic director. Construction began in 1935. A reinforced concrete shell faced with limestone, nearly 42

feet square at the base, carries the large floor area and rigid structural frame necessary to support the 100–ton, 67–bell Baird Carillon. The fountain sculpture in the mall, *Sunday Morning in Deep Waters*, depicts Triton, Greek god of the sea, frolicking in the waves with his piscine children. It was done by Carl Milles in 1940.

WA09.3 Horace H. Rackham Building (Horace H. Rackham School of Graduate Studies)

1936–1938, William Kapp of Smith, Hinchman and Grylls. 915 East Washington St. (bounded by East Washington, Thayer, East Huron, and Fletcher streets)

The Horace H. Rackham Building anchors the north axis of the Ingalls Campus Mall opposite the Harlan Hatcher Graduate Library. Completed in 1938, during a period of increasing demand for graduate study, the austerely modern yet classicistic Rackham Building is a monument to the university's graduate programs, and a memorial to Horace H. Rackham, very characteristic of the 1930s. The building was the gift of the Horace H. Rackham and Mary A. Rackham Fund. Horace H. Rackham (1858–1933) was an alumnus of the university who was a lawyer and an original stockholder in the Ford Motor Company.

The restrained, symmetrical limestone building has a central block with wings and is set back and terraced. A wide staircase leads to the main block, which is punctured by five tall rectangular windows topped by narrow, stylized relief panels and crowned with a copper-clad hipped roof. Three bronze and glass doors open onto a spacious entrance hall richly finished with plastered walls above a black marble base and a green and purple gray slate floor and with a blue green beamed ceiling stenciled in Pompeian red, tan, and gold. Off the entrance hall is a two-story, semicircular lecture hall that seats twelve hundred. The upper floors of the building contain study, music, exhibition, lecture and meeting rooms, and lounges.

WA09.4 Alumni Center

1982; Hugh Newell Jacobsen; Charles Parker, project architect. 200 Fletcher St. (southwest corner of East Washington and Fletcher streets)

In the Alumni Center, Jacobsen of Washington, D.C., created a dramatic, but friendly, building that respects it neighbors. First, a diagonal tunnel pierced through the L-shaped building preserves the footpath trod by students taking a shortcut from Fletcher Street to Burton Tower, across the previously vacant site. Second, the scale of the building and the abstraction of Collegiate Gothic forms, elements, and materials—gables, projecting bays, buttresses, tall chimneys, and brick with limestone banding—respond to its neighbor, the Women's League Building, erected to the plans of Pond and Pond in 1929. This Postmodern design is among the best in Michigan.

WA09.5 Power Center for the Performing Arts

1969–1981, Kevin Roche, John Dinkeloo and Associates. 1980–1981 addition, Jickling, Lyman and Powell. 121 Fletcher St. (adjacent to Felch Park between Huron and Washington streets)

In 1965 the University of Michigan regents commissioned Roche and Dinkeloo of Hamden, Connecticut, to design this elegant performing arts center for contemporary and classic theater. Partially shrouded by trees, the steel-reinforced concrete and reflective glass structure is situated at the edge of Felch Park. Six massive columns firmly balance the front facade, creating the appearance of a magnificent abstracted classical colonnade. The reinforced glass curtain wall of the foyer reflects the trees of the park during the day; but, at night, when the theatergoers gather and the lights come on, the glass becomes transparent from the exterior, allowing glowing views of the interior lobby.

The interior is streamlined. Deeply indented in horizontal frames, the reflecting glass flows around two spiral free-standing staircases that rise to twin 33-foot-long steel-reinforced walkways that arc above the lobby. The walkways lead into the theater where 1,420 seats are arranged in a broad semicircle. The orchestra pit is actually a platform that can be raised to convert the proscenium stage into a thrust stage. A moveable stage lift for the orchestra platform stops on four levels—stage, house, orchestra, and pit.

The Power Center is named for the Eugene B. Power family. Power, a former University of Michigan regent and founder of University Microfilms (now owned by Xerox), contributed $3 million for its construction.

WA09.6 William L. Clements Library of Americana

1922–1923, Albert Kahn and Ernest Wilby. 909 South University Ave.

The William L. Clements Library of Americana is one of the premier buildings on the campus and was Albert Kahn's own favorite among all the buildings he did. It houses the collection of American manuscripts that William Lawrence Clements (1861–1934), an alumnus and regent of the University of Michigan, bequeathed to the university in 1922. Albert Kahn and associate Ernest Wilby of Detroit designed the library to Clements's wishes and employed a late Italian Renaissance variety of Beaux-Arts Classicism. It is a handsome structure that may have been inspired by Vignola's casino for the gardens of the Palazzo Farnese at Caprarola, which Kahn may have photographed on one of his many visits abroad. It may have been even more directly influenced by McKim, Mead and White's Butler Art Institute of 1917 in Youngstown, Ohio.

The Indiana limestone library is approached by a broad-stepped terrace that ascends to a triple arcade supported on two slender Corinthian columns. This forms a screen to a loggia that was originally tiled, with vaulted ceilings in gold and blue mosaic. Three bronze grilled doors provide access to the main room. The interior employs rich materials and colors appropriate to the library's exclusivity.

WA09.7 **Law School Quadrangle**

1923 (1924, Lawyers' Club; 1930, John P. Cook Dormitory Building; 1931, William W. Cook Legal Research Building; 1933, Hutchins Hall), York and Sawyer; Jacob Van Heiningen of Pitkin and Mott, landscape architects. Bounded by South University Ave. and Tappan, Monroe, and South State streets

The Law School Quadrangle is the most beautiful and functional group of educational buildings in Michigan. It is a manifestation of the university's reputation as the Harvard of the Midwest. The Law Quadrangle is made up of four buildings: the Lawyers Club, which has a lounge, a recreation room, guest rooms, a dining hall, a kitchen, and a residence hall; the John P. Cook Dormitory; the Legal Research Building; and Hutchins Hall, which contains administrative and professional offices, lecture, class and seminar rooms, the court room, and the editorial rooms of the law review. The Collegiate Gothic complex faces a central courtyard with an opening at the southeast corner, into which an underground addition to the law library was inserted in 1977–1981, and the buildings are linked by flagstone walks. From the north, one gains formal passage to the inner courtyard through a great central turreted tower. The school recalls the design of the colleges of Oxford and Cambridge and of the Inns of Court in London, but it is adapted to modern academic life. It is inspired by James Gamble Rogers's Harkness Quadrangle at Yale (1916–1919), the finest Collegiate Gothic work in the country. The buildings have gabled dormers, crocketed and pinnacled buttresses, Byzantine-domed towers, arched windows with tracery, oriel bays, and ornamental chimneys. The walls of the buildings are richly finished in rock-faced Weymouth, Massachusetts, granite trimmed with Indiana limestone and covered with ivy; the roofs are clad with slate, the floors, with marble, and the windows, with stained glass.

The Law School was the gift of William Wilson Cook (1858–1930), an alumnus of the university who was general counsel for the Commercial Cable and Postal Telegraph Company in New York City. His will states, "Believing that the character of the law schools determines the character of the legal profession, I wish to aid in enlarging the scope and improving the standards of the law schools by aiding the one from which I graduated." At the University of Michigan, Cook set out to provide the architecture necessary to "place legal education at the university upon the level and with the comprehensiveness of scope to which one of the oldest and most essential professions is entitled."[25]

Edward Palmer York (1865–1928) and Phillip Sawyer (1868–1949), former associates of McKim, Mead and White who were noted designers of public and institutional buildings, planned the large-scale project. Starret Brothers of New York constructed the Lawyers Club in 1923–1924, and James Baird Company built the other structures in 1930–1933. Jacob Van Heiningen of Pitkin and Mott of Cleveland did the landscape plan.

The cathedral-like main reading room of the William W. Cook Legal Research Library, bearing a striking resemblance to King's College Chapel in Cambridge, England, is the Law Quadrangle's most impressive interior space. Large stained-glass windows embraced by Gothic tracery contain the crests of various universities, and the walls are paneled with oak. Similar in its breath-taking lofty beauty is the dining hall of the Lawyers' Club. It has a hammer-beam ceiling, oak paneling, and stone tracery windows with imported English cathedral glass.

Architectural details present some of the most outstanding aspects of the Law Quadrangle. Texts from the will of Cook and the writings of great jurists are carved over entrances and doorways; busts of famous jurists, including Blackstone, Coke, Cooley, Grotius, Justinian, Marshall, Solon, Story, and Webster, peer down from dining hall beams; and carvings, including former presidents of the university, appear in archways on South University Avenue.

The Law School Quadrangle exhibits a rare harmony of architectural style and a concern for the integrity of materials and details. It is a dignified setting for a scholarly discipline founded upon centuries of precedent.

WA09.8 Law Library Addition

1977–1981, Gunnar Birkerts and Associates. Northeast corner of Monroe and Tappan streets

In deference to the Gothic beauty of the Law School Quadrangle and the pedestrian access to it, Michigan architect Gunnar Birkerts, who was born in Finland in 1925 and is a former associate of Eero Saarinen and Alvar Aalto, designed an underground addition to the law library. One does not have the feeling of being in a cave because the structure is lighted with daylight, is decorated in warm greens and yellows, and affords peeks at the York and Sawyer masterpiece. Light moats penetrate the roof, bringing daylight into the building, and mirrors set perpendicular to mullions reflect glimpses of the Gothic details and of the sky. A grand staircase descends three stories to the depths of the building, and balconies off the staircase overlook the light well. The reinforced concrete addition wraps partially around the Cook Legal Research Building and at the top floor connects directly into its main hall. Like the underground additions to Williamson Hall, the campus bookstore for the University of Minnesota, designed by Myers and Bennett/BRW (now BRW Architects) and also erected in 1977, it doesn't disrupt campus pedestrian patterns or block views of historic buildings.

WA10 Henry S. Frieze House

1859–1860, 1870. 1547 Washtenaw Ave. (Business I-94 and US 23)

Born in Boston and a graduate of Brown University, Henry Simmons Frieze (1817–1889) came in 1854 to the University of Michigan to teach Latin. In 1859 he purchased over an acre of land at the outskirts of town and began construction of this Italian Villa home, one of the city's finest residences. Perhaps it was inspired by the many splendid Italian Villas that he may have seen in Providence after his graduation from Brown. The Frieze house is two stories with a hipped roof and intersecting gables, balconies, and porches. A wooden cupola, added in 1870, has a concave hipped roof topped by a finial and a weather vane. Skilled stonemasons from Guelph, Ontario, split, dressed, and laid local fieldstone two feet thick in the exterior walls. The spacious interior has four fireplaces, and the woodwork is oiled walnut and butternut. The fine proportions and skillful construction of the Frieze house make it an important component of Ann Arbor's architectural heritage.

WA11 Beth Israel Synagogue

1978, Hobbs and Black. 2000 Washtenaw Ave. (Business I-94 and US 23) (southwest corner Washtenaw Ave. and Austin)

After sharing space with the Hillel Foundation for many years, Congregation Beth Israel, founded in 1916, commissioned this rambling two-story brick building. Built on a sloping site, the sanctuary has a prominent and handsome ark flanked by full-length windows that open on the rear garden. As the focal point of the prayer hall, the ark is framed within a gently curved arch and features a pair of handsome carved doors. Skylights in the foyer and in the sanctuary admit light into the lively gold-colored and wood-paneled interior.

WA12 William B. and Mary Shuford Palmer House

1952, Frank Lloyd Wright. 227 Orchard Hills Dr.

The Palmer house exemplifies Wright's emphasis on the adaptation of form to nature. The multilevel structure, built of cypress and sand-cast perforated brick, nestles in the hilled site. Wright created this seemingly natural form with the geometric use of a T-shaped plan of equilateral triangles. The three projecting wings shaped by the triangular space give the house a sense of dramatic linear movement. The wings are topped by sloped,

WA12 William B. and Mary Shuford Palmer House

wood-shingled, copper-flashed roofs that form great horizontal planes. The horizontality is emphasized further, and a difficult site rendered uncomplicated, through the careful use of extended retaining walls and a gently rising entrance walk. Through specially created perforated brick a "frieze of light" warms the interior space.[26]

WA13 **Cobblestone Farm** (Benajah and Gessie Ticknor House)

c. 1835–1840. 2781 Packard Rd. (.2 mile east of Eisenhower Parkway)

This two-story, side-gable, Greek Revival residence is one of the finest examples of coursed cobblestone construction in Michigan. It was built for Dr. Benajah Ticknor (1788–1858), a surgeon in the United States Navy who was originally from Connecticut. He purchased nearly 200 acres on the outskirts of Ann Arbor, in Pittsfield Township, in 1835, and built the original portion of the house, now the wooden kitchen wing. The main two-story section of the house was built in 1840, employing the cobblestone building tradition that originated in western New York State. The house was constructed with hand-split laths, hand-hewn timbers, handmade nails, and with stones gathered from the property. The exterior walls of the front are laid with smooth cobblestones arranged in a horizontal herringbone pattern, the side walls with regular courses of cobblestone, and the rear with random rubble fieldstones. Heavy stone quoins reinforce the corners of the structure. Its most conspicuously Greek feature is its in antis Doric entrance motif. The door has side lights. Around 1845 the original wooden ser-

vice wing was enlarged and connected to the main cobblestone building. Today the Cobblestone Farm Association operates a historical museum here.

WA14 **School of Music Building** (Earl V. Moore Building)

1962–1964, Eero Saarinen and Associates. 1100 Baits Ave., North Campus, University of Michigan

In 1947, in anticipation of increased enrollment following World War II and the resultant strains on the Central Campus and Ann Arbor itself, the University of Michigan regents bought 267 acres north of the Huron River for future campus expansion. In 1951 they commissioned Eero Saarinen (1910–1961) to design a master plan to connect the rolling countryside site into a satellite campus and to create a flexible plan that would allow for future construction and expansion. Reflecting the ideals of Cranbrook, Saarinen's plan emphasized a cohesion of buildings with connected pedestrian plazas, highlighted by a square central plaza descending in five terraced planes to a deeply set fountain. Engineering Research, Engineering and the Fine Arts were to share common facilities, such as the food union and a high-rise library. A boulevard and street network would link downtown Ann Arbor and the main campus to this suburban campus.

Saarinen designed the most notable building on North Campus, the School of Music. Surrounded by wooded hills and reflected in its own pond, the building is in perfect harmony with its surroundings. Both exterior and interior walls are brick. Classrooms and sound studios on the main level employ a second-floor slab that appears to float on fiberglass over the structural concrete supporting slab. This isolates these studios and makes them soundproof. To the north is a two-story classroom and practice wing with a low horizontal promenade; to the south are the library, rehearsal, and recital halls. Narrow, full-length windows contrast with the horizontal patterns of brick.

YPSILANTI

Thirty miles west of Detroit, where an Indian trail crossed the Huron River, Ypsilanti was the camping and burial ground for several Indian tribes. In 1809, three French explorers built a log structure on the west bank of the Huron River. It served as an Indian trading post and was one of the earliest structures in the Michigan Territory. In 1823, Benjamin Woodruff acquired the trading post and with several companions established a small settlement on the river a mile south of the post. He named it Woodruff's Grove. It was the first settlement in Washtenaw County.

In 1824, Father Gabriel Richard, representative in Congress for the Michigan Territory, urged the building of a federal highway from Detroit to Chicago, later known as the Chicago Road. Following the Sauk Indian trail, the surveying crew put the crossing of the Huron River nearly a mile north of Woodruff's Grove. In 1825 Judge Augustus Woodward, John Stewart, and William Harwood, combined portions of their own land to form the original plat for a new settlement at the crossing. It was named for Demetrius Ypsilanti, a hero of the Greek War for Independence, who was much admired by Americans for his part in a struggle for freedom so like their own. When fire destroyed the school at Woodruff's Grove, that small settlement was abandoned in favor of Ypsilanti.

Travel from Detroit by stagecoach became possible in 1830, and by 1832 three stage lines served Ypsilanti. In 1835, the military road to Chicago was officially opened. Three years later the railroad from Detroit reached Ypsilanti. The depot was located east of the river, near a sawmill that supplied fuel for the wood-burning locomotives and ties for railroad construction. Two decades later, a spectacular brick masonry station, three stories high with a tower extending to six stories, was constructed.

Adjacent to the depot arose a small commercial district known as Depot Town. It boasted a flour mill, a large farmer's store, an iron foundry, the first fire department in the city, the first clothing store, and the first street with a paved gutter. Throughout its history, the fortunes of Depot Town echoed those of the railroad. Both reached their height in the second half of the nineteenth century and the early years of the twentieth. Most of the structures still standing in Depot Town were built in the 1850s, 1860s, and 1870s. Their concentration at the depot end of Cross Street, thinning out toward the river, reflects the central role played by the railroad and the depot.

A second business district developed on the west side of the river along the Chicago Road, what is now Michigan Avenue. The businesses outfitted travelers and settlers migrating in Michigan. Both business districts were also commercial centers for the agricultural development of the surrounding rural areas.

In 1845 the State Legislature established Ypsilanti Seminary, one of Michigan's first publicly supported secondary schools, and in 1849 a teachers' training school, Michigan Normal School (now Eastern Michigan University). Cleary College was founded in Ypsilanti in 1883 as a school of penmanship. Thus, Ypsilanti became a college town.

Disaster struck the community in 1851, when a great fire swept the downtown, destroying fourteen stores, a lumberyard, and a wagon shop. Several years later, in 1859, fire destroyed the seminary and the original normal school building.

The early development of Ypsilanti was influenced by the river and its abundant waterpower. Mills sprang up along its banks to supply lumber, flour, wool, and machinery parts. Substantial commercial buildings and brick mansions were built. Business enterprises included manufacturers of threshing machines, windows and doors, cabinets, and whip sockets for carriages, breweries, and a health spa.

Citizens expressed their new prosperity in the structures they built for their families, churches, and businesses. From them the community has inherited a rich array of historic architecture and a challenge to preserve its heritage.

On April 12, 1893, occurred the second-greatest disaster to hit Ypsilanti in the nineteenth century—a tornado that destroyed

Cleary College, many homes, and downtown places of business.

As the years progressed, the river industries of the mid-to-late-nineteenth century yielded to manufacturing, and mills gave way to auto-related commerce, which became a major economic force in the community. In 1941 the Ford Motor Company erected a new auto plant in the meadows east of the city at Willow Run. When the United States entered World War II, that plant was quickly converted to wartime production. B-24 bombers rolled off the Willow Run assembly line at the rate of one every 55 minutes. The war years, and those which followed, brought drastic changes to Ypsilanti. Today's community is one of striking diversity. Ypsilanti has awakened to its history and its wealth of historic architecture. A National Trust Main Street Program was instituted in 1984 that encourages improvement in the downtown area. Homeowners are complying with historic district ordinance guidelines, as they rehabilitate their properties. With growing pride, Ypsilanti works to protect and enjoy its heritage.

WA15 **Ypsilanti Water Tower**

1889–1890, W. R. Coats, engineer, Seirn B. Cole. Bounded by North Summit St., Washtenaw Ave., and West Cross St. (Michigan 17)

The 147-foot-high water tower is a landmark in Ypsilanti and was nationally recognized in 1975 as an American Water Works Associa-

tion Landmark. Appropriately, the tower shares the triangular site with the bust of Demetrius Ypsilanti. The enormous weight of water held in the 225,000-gallon steel tank is borne by the rock-faced, squared Ionia stone cylinder, the walls of which are 40 inches thick at the base and which decrease in thickness to 24 inches at the top. Resting on the rim of this stone cylinder is a steel-beam floor carrying the tank and the timber shell of the dome. Originally, the dome was topped with an octagonal cupola. The exterior walls of the tower are clad with Joliet stone. The water tower remains a part of the city's water system. It underwent a $140,000 renovation in the early 1980s.

WA16 **Starkweather Hall**

1896–1897, Malcolmson and Higginbotham. 901 West Forest St. (north of West Cross St. [Michigan 17] and Washtenaw Ave. on the southern edge of Eastern Michigan University Campus)

Starkweather Hall was designed by the Detroit firm of Malcolmson and Higginbotham as a religious center for Michigan State Normal School, present-day Eastern Michigan University. The building was a gift of Mary Starkweather (1819–1897), a local philanthropist. Its exuberant, rusticated granite fieldstone walls, squat bulging Ionia sandstone corner tower with bell-shaped roof, massive arched entries, grouped windows, and decorative reddish orange clay tile sides and roof clearly indicate its Richardsonian character. The asymmetrical massing is also reminiscent of the various Richardson libraries.

WA17 **Daniel and Priscilla Frain Quirk, Sr., House** (Ypsilanti City Hall)

c. 1860. 300 North Huron St. (three blocks north of East Michigan [Business US 12])

This fine Second Empire-style house was built by prominent businessman Daniel L. Quirk, Sr. (1818–1911), founder of the Peninsular Paper Company, the First National Bank of Ypsilanti and other enterprises, and his wife, Priscilla Frain. It is basically an Italianate building with a mansard roof, which is characteristic of much of American Second Empire work. A dormered, mansard-roofed central tower projects from the symmetrically arranged brick residence. Hexagonal slate shingles hung in patterns of gray, red, and tan cover the tower and the main roof. Italianate features include the carved stone window hoods decorated with floral designs, which cap the tall round and segmentally arched windows, and the slender paired columns with Corinthian capitals that flank the elliptical arch entry porch. On the property is a matching carriage house. About 1911 the Quirk family gave the house to the city of Ypsilanti, and it served as city hall from 1914 to 1974. Today it is used for commercial offices. Open to public.

WA17 Daniel and Priscilla Frain Quirk, Sr., House

WA18 **Presbyterian Church** (First Presbyterian Church)

1857; George S. Green, architect; John Femis, builder. 1898–1899, Julius Hess, reconstruction architect. 300 North Washington St. (northeast corner of North Washington and Emmet streets, 1 block south of West Cross St. [Michigan 17] and 1 block west of Huron St. [Business US 12])

This Renaissance Revival Presbyterian Church assumed its present appearance when it was remodeled and enlarged to accommodate the size of the congregation. The red brick church was originally built in 1857 by the Congregationalists and the Presbyterians. It had a single tall steeple and Romanesque appearance. The instability of the steeple and the need for meeting space for its new organizations, societies, and educational programs prompted the congregation, then the First Presbyterian Society of Ypsilanti, to rebuild and refashion the front facade in 1898–1899. This proved more productive than to repair the steeple and reconstruct the rest of the building. Swiss-born Detroit architect Julius Hess (1841–1899) designed the all-new front in the Renaissance Revival style. It has spectacular multistaged twin stair and bell towers crowned with cupolas, between which is placed a recessed entrance supported by one-story polished Doric stone columns under a flat lintel with a Doric frieze. Above the entry in the gabled center section is a round stained-glass window attributed to Tiffany. Hess retained the brick side walls of the building, but embellished their pilasters with Ionic capitals, enlarged the round-arched windows, and installed a new dentiled entablature. From the main entrance, stairs rise to the auditorium, in which three banks of oak pews are arranged around a pulpit. The sanctuary is fitted with beautiful oak woodwork crafted in the Renaissance Revival style. Class and meeting rooms are located underneath the auditorium. (WA19 is located directly across Emmet Street to the south.)

WA19 **Ladies Literary Club Building** (William H. Davis? House)

c. 1842. 218 North Washington St. (southeast corner North Washington and Emmet streets)

The brick tetrastyle temple-front house with wing is another delightful example of the Greek Revival in southern Michigan. Grilles run along the frieze above a row of dentils. Molding outlines the Doric piers and lacy cutwork runs beneath the entablature in the pediment and serves as brackets on the porch of the south wing. The latter decoration probably was applied later in the nineteenth century. Although local tradition and the Historic American Buildings Survey report of 1936 hold that Arden H. Ballard, a speculator in Ypsilanti real estate, built the house, it is more likely that it was constructed for William M. Davis. Recent research indicates that Ballard owned the lot on which the house

stands from 1836 to 1842; then he sold the property to William M. Davis. Davis, in turn, sold the lot for $3,000 in 1845. The rise in property value suggests that the house was built while Davis owned the property.

MANCHESTER

WA20 **Manchester Italianate Houses**

c. 1853–1857, unknown. 206, 214, 220, 224 Ann Arbor Rd. (Michigan 52)

In southeastern Michigan the Italianate style is well represented by six houses on Ann Arbor Road as it enters Manchester from the west. Built between 1853 and 1857, they were dwellings for prosperous townspeople in this thriving agricultural village established two decades earlier. All are brick with wooden trim, and several have limestone window lintels. The buildings rest on rubble foundations. All are basically cubical in form with strongly detailed brackets at the eaves, and some have porches with classical details. The brick, produced locally, is a warm orange red in color and is remarkably consistent in size and texture. It can also be found in the commercial buildings on the main street of Manchester. Like the houses, these are exceptionally well preserved.

Manchester's houses derive from several sources. They certainly owe something to Andrew Jackson Downing's *The Architecture of Country Houses* (1850). Other important pattern books for Manchester's builders were Henry Cleaveland's *Villages and Farm Cottages* (New York, 1856), which shows two house plans similar to those in Manchester, and John Ritch's *The American Architect* (New York, 1849), which contains instructions for masonry, bracket details, and window designs. Downing stated that the villa style symbolized a tranquil domestic life and the good moral character of its owners, a contention that certainly contributed greatly to its widespread popularity in pre-Civil War America. Given the building technology of the time, the villa was reasonably simple to construct, and with a few appropriate details, could provide a note of sophistication in a country that was still largely rural. Good examples of the Italianate houses can be found throughout southeastern Michigan, but those in Manchester are particularly fine. They were, in fact, the ubiquitous American house of the 1850s.

BRIDGEWATER TOWNSHIP

WA21 **Raab Farmstead**

1858 and later, unknown. 11665 Bemis Rd.

The Raab land and farmstead have been in the family since 1850. Like many of the families in this area, the Raab family is of German origin. The farmland includes part of a small lake, Lake Columbia. The farm buildings are sited to take best advantage of the scenic location.

The farmhouse, built in 1858, is set back from and faces Bemis Road. The portion visible from the road is constructed of dressed stone collected on the site. As is typical of many farmhouses, various additions were made. Sometime before 1890, the first addition of a brick masonry chimney and kitchen was built. It was followed by the addition of a wood-frame porch and storerooms.

In its prime, the farm complex included the farmhouse, big barn, horse barn and carriage house, windmill, smokehouse, granary, ice house, corn crib, tool shed, and privy. Most of these structures remain on the site today. Together, they exemplify all the buildings needed to run a sufficiently viable farm to satisfy a regional or national market.

The farm layout is linear, a configuration more efficient for greater mechanization in farm operations following the Civil War and into the turn of the century. The buildings are aligned along an axis road that jogs around the big barn. Its northern elevation faces Bemis Road. The inscription under the gambrel roof, "1913, Lake View Farm, T. A. Raab," identifies the modifications to the barn on this date. Its southern and smaller half, which consists of a barn constructed before 1900 that was moved to the site in 1913, is older. The northern half was then added to create what now stands. The structural beams and columns of the older half are of hand-hewn white oak obtained from land that the Raabs owned in nearby Freedom Township, and the flooring is wide planking. The tongue-and-grooved vertical white pine siding was sent by railroad from Northern Michigan to nearby Manchester. The barn is a three-level bank barn in the German tradition. The lower level was for housing animals; the middle level,

made accessible by the earth ramp to threshers and other machinery, for winnowing and storing grain; and the upper level for storing hay and straw.

CHELSEA

WA22 **Glazier Stove Works**

1903, Claire Allen?. 310 North Main St. (Michigan 52) (northeast corner of North Main and Railroad streets)

In Chelsea, the prominent crossroads of a road linking Flint and Jackson and the Michigan Central Railroad connecting Detroit and Chicago, Frank P. Glazier (1862–1922) founded in 1891 the Glazier Stove Works. The firm manufactured oil-burning heaters and cooking stoves under the brand name B & B, for "Brightest and Best." After fire destroyed the company's first buildings on the east side of Main Street, between Middle Street and the railroad, Glazier purchased the present site, cleared it of houses and buildings, and eventually began construction on a new factory, including the Tower and Welfare buildings and the Spring Plant. It is likely that Claire Allen of Jackson, who had just completed plans for the family's bank at 122 South Main Street, was the architect. The complex includes the prominent local landmark, the corner octagonal brick clock and water tower integrated into the three-story pentagonal building, along with numerous simple brick structures and a recreational building for the employees. Known as the Welfare Building and erected in 1906, the recreational building originally held a swimming pool, a billiard hall, a basketball court, and a theater. The Flemish curvilinear gables, the two-story bay windows, and the ornamental brick chimneys illustrate the Jacobethan Revival style. After the stove works went bankrupt in 1907, the buildings were occupied by the Lewis Spring and Axle Company, manufacturer of the Hollier Eight automobile; they are now occupied by the *Chelsea Standard*.

WA23 **Fourteenth District Court** (George P. Glazier Bank Building)

1901–1902, Claire Allen. 1987–1988, rehabilitated. 122 South Main St. (Michigan 52) (northwest corner of South Main and Park streets)

George P. Glazier (1841–1901) with Michael J. Noyes established the first bank in Chelsea. Upon Glazier's death, his son Frank, who founded the stove works, hired Claire Allen, a capable and respected architect from nearby Jackson, to design this building as a memorial to his father. *The Chelsea Standard* for April 4, 1901, called the Beaux-Arts Classical bank "the finest bank building between Chicago and Detroit." Fronting the trapezoidal plan is a giant in antis Ionic portico, which frames the monumental two-story arched entry. The fieldstone was laid in the walls by George Hindelang. Carved Bedford limestone festoons and shells contrast in color and texture with the rough-hewn blocks of pink and gray granite fieldstone. A massive cornice rests on heavy fieldstone piers with Ionic capitals. Rehabilitated in 1987–1988 to the plans of Lincoln Poley, the building now houses the Fourteenth District Court, and much of the elaborate interior marble and woodwork remains intact. The courtroom occupies the main banking room beneath a skylighted dome.

WA24 **Chelsea Depot of the Michigan Central Railroad**

1880, Mason and Rice. 150 Jackson St. (1 block west of the intersection of Michigan 52)

The Michigan Central Railroad, the first major line in the state, reached Chelsea in 1841 and Chicago in 1852. The railroad line established Chelsea as a shipping point for agricultural and manufactured products. Whereas other towns in the area were built upon rivers as mill towns, Chelsea became the major railroad town in Washtenaw County. This depot is the only one in Michigan known to have been designed by the leading Detroit firm of Mason and Rice. Exquisitely detailed with stickwork, this little wooden depot exemplifies Chelsea's role in the heyday of rail transportation.

DEXTER

WA25 **Gordon Hall** (Judge Samuel W. Dexter House)

1841–1843, Calvin T. Fillmore and Sylvester Newkirk, builders. 8347 Island Lake Rd. (at intersection of Island Lake And Dexter-Pinckney roads)

Gordon Hall is one of the most imposing wooden Greek Revival houses in Michigan. From its hilltop site above the Huron River, the house literally presides over the steepled village of Dexter, to the east. It was built for Samuel W. Dexter (1792–1863), a Boston-born and Harvard-educated politician and newspaperman who was Chief Justice of Washtenaw County from 1826 to 1833, having been appointed by Michigan Territorial Governor Lewis Cass. Named for Dexter's mother, Catherine Gordon Dexter, Gordon Hall has a massive hexastyle Greek Doric portico with somewhat attenuated columns across its pedimented facade. The plan consists of an almost-square central two-story section with two flanking one-and-a-half-story wings. Flanking long side porches have similar but shorter Doric columns. In spite of the recent application of aluminum siding and the division of the interior into apartments, Gordon Hall is important because it shows the context and environment within which such grand temple-front houses were built. Howell Taylor compared it to Monticello. The University of Michigan currently uses the house for faculty housing.

ANN ARBOR TOWNSHIP

WA26 **Salem-Walker Church**

1864. Southeast corner of Angle and Tower roads

The Salem-Walker Church remains as one of the few Greek Revival churches in Michigan still intact. Constructed at a time when the popularity of Greek Revival architecture was on the wane in the state, the church is a simple white clapboard box. Windows flank the transomed, double-doored entrance of the symmetrical end-gable front, the pediment of which has a hexagonal decorative motif. A square tower, each stage with a frieze and corner pilasters, tops the front center of the roof. Pilasters decorate the corners and the entrance. The church began in about 1841 as part of a Methodist circuit consisting of Lapham's Corners (present-day Brookville), the Leland Church, and Salem. The Salem church is the only one of these still standing. It is named after E. T. Walker of the Walker-Hamm family, who donated the land.

buildings were designed by Gunnar Birkerts. Phases one, two, and three include a 220,000-square-foot, four-story office structure with physical fitness activity centers, a conference center, cafeterias, and executive offices; a 235,000-square-foot warehouse and operations plant; and a low-rise office building that begins to complete the desired illusion of a half-mile-long prairie house. In a future phase, the "Golden Beacon," a 1956 design by Wright that was never executed for a tower on a Chicago lakefront site, may be constructed to modified plans by Birkerts. Phase four is the Domino Center for Architectural Design, a museum that houses the extensive Monaghan collections of Frank Lloyd Wright artifacts. The complex is intended to invoke a "friendly campus" atmosphere for the benefit of the employees.

WA27 **Domino's Farms** (Domino's Pizza World Headquarters)

1985–1989, Gunnar Birkerts. Plymouth Rd. (southeast corner of US 23 and Michigan 14)

Situated on a 300-acre rolling pastoral farmland, the Domino's Pizza World Headquarters covers over 1.2 million square feet. Thomas S. Monaghan, long an admirer of Frank Lloyd Wright and a collector of Wright furniture and architectural fragments, had many Wrightian Prairie house features incorporated here, among them the sweeping horizontal lines, the long, low-pitched, copper-clad roofs, natural materials, ribbon windows, and berming. Monaghan, owner of Domino's Pizza and the Detroit Tigers baseball team, has expressed freely his passion for Wright and has satisfied his own architectural imagination in this architectural complex. The

WA28 **The Settlement**

1990, Johnson, Johnson and Roy, landscape architects; Robert Trent Jones, Sr., golf course architect. West of Dixboro Rd., north of Joy Road, approximately 3 miles east of overpass at intersection with US 23

The Settlement is an exclusive residential project and golf course on 635 acres of woodland, water, and gently rolling hills northeast of Domino's Farms. Conceived by Thomas S. Monaghan and the Domino's Farms Development Corporation, it will be a neighborhood of 136 one-million-dollar houses designed by any one of "the Domino thirty of the world's top architects." The initial list of approved architects for the Settlement was drawn up in 1988 by a committee of Ted Pappas, president of the American Institute of Architects; Mildred Schmertz, editor of *Architectural Record;* Aarno Ruusuvuori, director of the Museum of Finnish Architecture, and Toshio Nakamura, editor of *Architecture and Urbanism.* Among the American architects listed are Frank Gehry, Michael Graves, Gwathmey Siegel and Associates, Philip Johnson, Richard Meier, and Charles Moore. Today the list of approved architects has expanded beyond the original professionals to include Hugh Jacobsen, Cesar Pelli, Robert A. M. Stern, and others. Two major hurdles remain before the project can move forward to full development—the issuance of a Michigan Department of Natural Resources permit to fill in and disturb some 7 to 15 acres of wetlands to build the golf course and the rezoning of the use from agricultural to planned-unit development. Under construction today (1990), at a projected cost of $5 million, is the extraordinary Thomas S. and Marge Monaghan House. Designed by E. Fay Jones for a 27-acre wooded site, the large angular house will be built of brown and beige Arkansas ledge rock. Within the 22,000 square feet of space is a master bedroom suite with kitchen, bath, living space, office, and chapel. The house also will have a "fantasy kingdom" for grandchildren. Designs by Mockbee-Cocker-Howorth for a second house for an anonymous client are under preparation. Lots cost between $350,000 and $1.5 million.

SCIO TOWNSHIP

WA29 **William Burnett House**

Pre-1856. 3555 West Delhi Rd.

The William Burnett House is a small cobblestone house commonly known as a "hen-and-chicks" type, derived from its reference to a larger central two-story unit flanked by two smaller one-story wings. The central "hen" is gabled, while the "chicks" present half-gable roofs. It is also known as a basilica type, because of its similarity to Early Christian basilica churches. William Burnett migrated to Michigan in the early 1800s from upstate New York, where cobblestone houses were popular. The Burnett house is unique to Michigan in its cobblestone basilica form. There are quite a few specific details that associate the house with the Classical Revival, including the wide entablature and cornice returns and the strict symmetrical simplicity of form. Fieldstone quoins replace the corner pilasters of other Classical Revival homes. The front entry has a pediment and surrounding pilasters, and the window hoods repeat the pediment motif. The house was acquired by Abram Davis in the 1870s and by Henry Ford in 1940. It is now privately owned.

Livingston County (LV)

HOWELL

Howell is a picture-perfect example of a small Michigan town that serves as the seat of its county's government. The courthouse rests atop a grassy rise, with its clock tower visible from a considerable distance, and stores flank each side of the Grand River Road. Originally called Livingston Centre, the village was settled in 1834 by former residents of Dutchess County, New York, who migrated here along the Grand River Trail. The community was platted in 1835 and was chosen as the county seat in 1836 because of its central location and its cohesive settlement. By 1838 Howell had a flouring mill and a sawmill, and soon after, a hotel. Howell's economy was strengthened by the McPherson family, headed by Scottish immigrant William McPherson, who settled in Howell in 1836. The family amassed its fortunes in the 1860s from lumbering and dairying. William McPherson was a blacksmith, a merchant, and an entrepreneur who founded the McPherson bank in 1865.

LV01 **Livingston County Courthouse**

1889–1890, Albert E. French. 1975–1978, restored and rehabilitated. 200 East Grand River Ave. (Michigan 43 and Business I-96) (bounded by East Grand River Ave. and State, Clinton, and East Barnard streets)

The Livingston County Courthouse occupies a square surrounded by the central business district, and in turn, by avenues of neatly kept late-nineteenth-century homes. It is a handsome Richardsonian Romanesque red brick building trimmed with Ohio bluestone and topped with a multigabled hipped roof crowned by a clock tower. In the interior, highly skilled workmanship is found in the exuberant stenciling and painting and in the decorative ironwork, hardware, and carved woodwork of oak and maple.

In the 1880s county officials realized that the first courthouse, a simple Greek Revival structure with a cupola, which was erected in 1847, was inadequate to the county's needs. The Livingston County Board of Commissioners established a building committee to consider the deficiencies of the existing building. The committee traveled to Mount Pleasant, Ionia, and Mount Clemens to inspect the courthouses there, reviewed plans for the courthouses at Big Rapids and Allegan, and considered sketches that Elijah E. Myers had drawn for the Livingston courthouse. Voters approved in 1889 the committee's recommendation to follow the plans already drawn by Alfred E. French (d. 1927) for the Allegan County Courthouse (now demolished). French was a native of Prince Edward Island, Canada, who went to Detroit around 1877. Waterbury and Wright of Ionia constructed the courthouse between 1889 and 1890. Subsequently, in 1892–1893, the same architectural plans were used for the Barry County Courthouse at Hastings (see BA01, p. 272).

Between 1975 and 1978, sparked by the efforts of the Friends of the Livingston County Courthouse and with advice from William Kessler and Associates, the residents of the county restored and rehabilitated their sturdy government building. The result has served as an inspiration for residents of other Michigan counties contemplating the future of their courthouses.

LV01 Livingston County Courthouse

LV02 **John I. and Charlotte Edwards Van Deusen House**

c. 1858, John I. Van Deusen, carpenter builder. 219 South Walnut St. (2 blocks north of West Grand River Ave. [Michigan 43 Business I 96] and 1 block east of Michigan Ave. [D 19])

The John I. and Charlotte Edwards Van Deusen House is one of Michigan's loveliest Carpenter's Gothic versions of the Gothic Revival style. According to local tradition, John I. Van Deusen (1815–1905) designed and built it himself. Trained as a carpenter in New York, he came to Howell in 1854 with his wife, Charlotte (1828–1905). He owned the Howell Steam Saw Mill, which furnished the planks for the Detroit-Howell-Lansing plank roads and lumber and shingles to builders in Howell. Within two years of his arrival in Howell, Van Deusen purchased the lot for his house, and by 1859 he had completed building his home. To the little house with the steeply pitched, cross-gable roof are applied playful, jigsawn, lathe-turned, and molded wooden details in Gothic motifs. The board-and-batten siding, the lacy barge- boards, the gable finials, the carved hood

LV02 John I. and Charlotte Edwards Van Deusen House

molding, and window bracketing express this carpenter's fascination and delight with the pliability of wood.

In 1918 Harry G. and Mary Caroline Hyde Huntington purchased the house from the Van Deusens' daughter Lela, and until 1989, when they sold it, they proudly continued to give the house the care the Van Deusens had.

GREEN OAK TOWNSHIP

LV03 **Alonzo Whitney and Janet Warden Olds House**

c. 1845. 10084 Rushton Rd. (southwest corner of Rushton and Ten Mile roads)

An interpretation of the simplicity of the classic Greek architecture can be seen in this two-story, wooden, Greek Revival, basilica-type house with an Ionic tetrastyle portico and one-story wings. It has boards laid with flush joints on the front, a dentiled cornice, and graceful, fluted Ionic columns. Coming from New York State in 1832, Alonzo Olds (1810–1898) purchased in 1835 the land on which he later built his house. He raised sheep, built a sawmill, and had increased by nearly eightfold his initial purchase of 80 acres when he sold the house and farm in 1851. The Olds house illustrates the plight of many buildings

LV03 Alonzo Whitney and Janet Warden Olds House

recorded by the Historic American Buildings Survey in the 1930s. It is threatened today by development on all sides, particularly by a housing project to the north that takes its name from this centennial farm.

Oakland County (OK)

PONTIAC

OK01 **Pontiac Silverdome**

1975, O'Dell, Hewlett and Luckenbach. 1200 Featherstone (northwest corner of Michigan 59 and Opdyke Rd.)

The Pontiac Stadium Building Authority was created by the city of Pontiac in 1971 to plan, construct, and maintain a large stadium for major sporting events. Designed by the Birmingham firm of O'Dell, Hewlett and Luckenbach and built by the Barton-Malow Company, the PonMet Stadium (as it was first known) was completed in twenty-three months at a cost of $55.7 million. It currently serves as the home stadium for the Detroit Lions professional football team.

The 770-foot-long and 600-foot-wide Silverdome covers ten acres and has a seating capacity of 80,638. The center of the roof, when fully inflated, is 202 feet above the playing field. The roofing fabric, originally created as a space-suit material for lunar astronauts in the Apollo program, consists of Teflon-coated fiberglass yarn and is held in place by a subsurface webbing of eighteen three-inch-diameter steel cables, anchored at the ends in a reinforced, continuously poured, concrete ring beam. This also serves as a walkway along the perimeter of the building. The dome rises fifty feet above this outer wall; the upper half of the wall is sheathed with sheet-metal siding, while the lower half is faced with painted concrete blocks. A ventilation system incorporating twenty-nine 75-horsepower fans provides the interior air pressure that keeps the roof inflated during sporting events. Only three blowers are needed when the stadium is unoccupied and all doors are closed.

Recognized by the Michigan Society of Professional Engineers as one of ten outstanding examples of engineering in Michigan, the Pontiac Silverdome stands as a monument to innovations in design, construction and cost control for a major domed stadium. "It remains the world's largest air-supported dome-roofed structure."

OK02 **Pine Grove** (Governor Moses and Angeolina Hascall Wisner House)

c. 1845. 405 Oakland Ave. (Business US 24)

Pine Grove is a two-story, brick, Greek Revival house with a large, three-bay, front-gable main section. It was built in accordance with the standard side-hall plan, with a small Doric-columned porch at the entrance on the left. The remainder of the house consists of two wings. One, to the left of the main portico, has a hipped roof in front and a parapeted gable in the rear and is faced on two sides by a colonnade consisting of fourteen one-story fluted Doric columns. A parapet, or panelled balustrade, once masked the roof of this wing, but it has been removed. The other wing, a gable-roofed, one-and-a-half-story, brick ell, extends from the back of the first wing; this latter section may have been constructed before the main portion of the house.

Pine Grove's interior trim includes a walnut newel and stair balustrade; the interior doors are surrounded by architrave moldings; and

the elaborate foyer contains a large entrance doorway with an emblem of the State of Michigan in the transom, all of which is enclosed by a wide elliptical arch molding.

Born in Auburn, New York, Moses Wisner (1815–1863) emigrated to Michigan with other members of his family in 1837. After an early attempt at farming in Lapeer County, he moved to Pontiac in 1844, where he began reading law in his brother's law office and where he also became involved in politics. He was at the Republican party's first national convention at Jackson in 1854 and served as Michigan's governor in 1859–1860. Open to public.

AUBURN HILLS

OK03 **Chrysler Technology Center**

1986–present, CRSS Inc.; HEPY/PHH; Giffels Associates. Bounded by the Chrysler Freeway (I-75), Galloway Creek, Squirrel and Featherstone roads

This mammoth Postmodern megastructure—bigger than the Empire State Building—is Chrysler's high technology center for automotive research and development. Its four-story, 3.3 million-square-foot structure sprawls over 40 acres of its 500-acre site. A 1.8-mile evaluation road is on the eastern portion of the site. It cost nearly $1 billion to build. The building's rounded corners and its sleek and shiny tinted glass and polished brownish red granite exterior skin are intended to evoke the imagery of the automobile.

Under one roof 7,000 employees engaged in all elements of design, engineering, manufacturing, procurement, and supply necessary for the development of new car and truck models will be accommodated in four office/laboratory wings. Each is bisected by a skylit concourse or atrium, punctuated, in turn, with pyramidal domes that connect the whole. The four quadrants pivot around the technology plaza at the crossing, above which rises a huge pyramidal dome. Lee Iacocca, chairman of Chrysler, stated at the dedication in October 1991, "Anyone who sees the place gets a strong message about Chrysler's long-term future." The stately, self-contained, well-digested Postmodern technology center invites comparison with the campus-style General Motors Technical Center (see MB04, p. 176), designed by the Saarinens and

OK03 Chrysler Technology Center

built 40 years ago during the height of the International style.

LAKE ORION AND OXFORD VICINITIES, ORION TOWNSHIP

OK04 **Lawrence D. and Cora Peck Buhl House**

1927, Robert O. Derrick. 1480 West Romeo Rd. (.5 mile west of Walker,in Addison Oaks Park)

Constructed in 1927 as the summer residence and country estate of Lawrence D. Buhl, a successful Detroit hardware merchant, this mansion was the centerpiece of a 700-acre wooded estate containing two small lakes. Architect Robert O. Derrick of Detroit employed variously positioned chimneys, projecting gables, dormers, and two-story bays to relieve what would otherwise be monotonous exterior walls of plain white stucco. The result is a varied and picturesque composition. Subsequently, an addition was attached to the main house and used for large banquets and parties. Also on the property, the Buhls built stables, barns, servants' quarters, a guest house, a greenhouse, and tennis courts. Nearby, other wealthy Detroit families—among them, the Scrippses, Fruehoffs, Ferrys, Hiram Walkers, Arthur Buhls, John Newberrys—built similar country retreats. The entire estate was purchased by the Oakland County Parks and Recreation Commission in 1969, and the mansion now serves as the Recreation Service Center for the Addison-Oaks County Park.

ROCHESTER HILLS

OK05 **Meadow Brook Hall** (Alfred G. and Mathilda Dodge Wilson Estate)

1926–1929, William Kapp of Smith, Hinchman and Grylls. Oakland University (entrance is off the east side of Adams Rd. .25 mile south of the intersection of Adams Rd. and Walton Blvd., just over 3 miles east and north of intersection of Adams with Michigan 59)

Meadow Brook Hall is one of the last and one of the best of the great mansions built by industrialists around Detroit during the first third of the twentieth century. Others are the George Booth House (Cranbrook House, see OK08.1), the Edsel and Eleanor Ford House (see WN05.1, p. 116), and Fairlane (Henry

OK05b Meadow Brook Hall (Alfred G. and Mathilda Dodge Wilson Estate) (staircase)

and Clara Bryant Ford House, see WN11, p. 119). Mathilda Dodge Wilson (1883–1967), widow of John Dodge, and her second husband Alfred G. Wilson had the 110-room Neo-Tudor house erected in 1926–1929 on the site of the former John Dodge farm, a 123-acre tract that was the site of Dodge's vacation house until 1920. Meadow Brook Hall is a stately manor house of stone, brick, and half-timber exterior walls. Individual elements include stone-mullioned windows, oriels, bays, hand-carved gargoyles, battlements, brick diaper work, and decorated clustered chimneys of the revived English Tudor, Elizabethan, and Jacobean styles of the sixteenth and seventeenth centuries.

Inspiration for Meadow Brook Hall came from "ancient manor houses" in England—in particular, Compton Wynyates and Hampton Court. On their honeymoon trip to England in 1925, the Wilsons, accompanied by William Kapp of Smith, Hinchman and Grylls, visited these and other country houses and obtained measured drawings from the Royal Institute of British Architects and the Victoria and Albert Museum. In a later trip to England in 1927, they selected English prototypes for interiors of the hall and purchased antique furnishings.

"To me Meadow Brook Hall is really Amer-

ican, but adapted from the English style of Architecture," said Mrs. Wilson.[27] The house is a product of American materials and American craftsmanship.

Bryant and Detwiler of Detroit were the general contractors. The cabinet work was done by Hayden of New York City and Irving and Casson-A. H. Davenport of New York. Corrado J. Parducci did the ornamental plaster ceilings of the dining hall, which were inspired by Belton house in Lincolnshire, England (1688). The stone sculptures on the portal, the porch, the loggia, and the sun porch were also by Parducci.

When the house was completed in 1929, Mrs. Wilson turned her attention to the gardens, the farms, and the barns. During the depression the Wilsons lived in the farmhouse. Later, fuel restrictions during World War II, staff shortages, and a diminished family size made the hall impractical to operate. Between 1952 and 1953, the Wilsons built Sunset Terrace, a more modest contemporary house also on the grounds, and moved there in 1953. In 1957 they donated the 1,400-acre estate, Meadow Brook Hall, and $2 million to Michigan State University for the creation of a new college, now Oakland University. Meadow Brook Hall remains intact as a conference and cultural center.

BLOOMFIELD HILLS

OK06 Gregor S. and Elizabeth B. Affleck House

1941, Frank Lloyd Wright. 1925 North Woodward Ave. (Michigan 1)

Gregor S. Affleck, a chemical engineer who invented a quick-drying automobile paint and established a manufacturing facility for it in Hamtramck, was quite familiar with Frank Lloyd Wright and his architecture. Originally from Chicago, Affleck had spent his youth near Spring Green, Wisconsin, and had actually known the architect. In 1940, when he and his wife, Elizabeth, commissioned Wright to design their home, they were uninterested in traditional house styles and particularly fond of Falling Water (1935), the residence Wright designed for Edgar Kaufmann at Bear Run, Pennsylvania. Wright first instructed the Afflecks to "find a site that no one else can build anything on," so they selected some acreage in Bloomfield Hills containing a wooded ravine with a small stream leading to a pond.[28]

For this "home for sloping ground," Wright created a house in the Usonian mode, as he had developed the solution in response to his clients' needs for low-cost, but aesthetically pleasing dwellings. He had first enunciated this in his plan for an ideal American city, the Broadacre City design of 1934 (exhibited 1935). A model of the Affleck house was first exhibited at the Museum of Modern Art in November of 1940; the actual house was built by contractor Harold Turner in 1941. The Affleck house represents Wright's continually developing philosophical concern for the self sufficiency of the individual, the decentralization of society, and reverence for nature, as well as the utilization of technology and novel building techniques.

The house is built of pinkish brick masonry and chamfered, lapped horizontal cypress boards over inclined plywood cores. These techniques form both exterior and interior walls. The bedroom and bathroom doors are similarly constructed (with mitered joints and two-way slopes), contributing to the complexity of the design. Although the facade facing Woodward Avenue has only a narrow line of windows under the eaves, the opposite ravine-facing walls feature full-length windows. The centrally placed loggia, where both the pool below and the sky above are visible through horizontal panes, serves as a transitional space between the bedroom and living areas. The elongated living-dining room, with its massive brick fireplace, is enclosed along its exterior by a large cantilevered east balcony and a south terrace. Now owned by Lawrence Technological University, the house is open to the public by appointment.

OK07 Roeper City and Country School
(Martin Luther King Domes)

1969–1970, Glen Paulsen of TMP Associates, Inc. 2190 South Woodward Ave. (Michigan 1) (east side of Woodward Ave., .75 mile north of Long Lake Rd.)

In 1946 George and Annemarie Roeper converted the former Hill estate mansion for use as a private school for gifted children from pre-school age through the twelfth grade. By the mid-1960s the building was no longer adequate to meet the space requirements of their City and County School. The Glen Paulsen architectural firm, which subsequently merged with Tarapata and MacMahon to form Tarapata, MacMahon and Paulsen (currently known as TMP Associates), designed additional instructional and assembly accommodations for the pre-school and primary grades.

The architects devised a complex of eight Styrofoam thermo-plastic domes produced by the Dow Chemical Company's spiral generation method. Two large domes are joined by a large triangular entryway, while three short cylindrical structures connect the six smaller ones to them and function as entry and service units. The domes house classrooms, library, music, research, and general assembly facilities in an environment appropriate to the special character and scale requirements of their 120 three- to eight-year-old pupils. Among the most innovative structures in the Detroit metropolitan area, these domes were built in 1969 and were formally dedicated to the memory of the late Martin Luther King on May 24, 1970.

OK08 Cranbrook

1907–present, Eliel Saarinen, Albert Kahn, George Booth, Bertram G. Goodhue Associates. 1221 Woodward Ave. (Michigan 1), .25 mile south of Long Lake Rd.

Cranbrook had its beginnings in 1904, when George Gough Booth, publisher of the *Detroit News*, and his wife, Ellen Warren Scripps Booth, bought a large farm in the rolling countryside of Bloomfield Hills and named it after the English village of Cranbrook, the Booth family ancestral home. Taking up residence in 1908, the Booths gradually transformed their farm estate into a remarkable cultural and educational complex consisting of their home, Cranbrook House; the Meeting House, which was expanded into the elementary Brookside School; Christ Church, Cranbrook; Cranbrook School for boys; Cranbrook Academy of Art; Kingswood School for girls; and Cranbrook Institute of Science. A superb integration of architectural and landscape design elements, the Cranbrook complex represents a unique masterpiece in the history of American architecture. It embodies the belief shared by its founder, George G. Booth, and its principal architect, Eliel Saarinen, that art should permeate every aspect of life.

Founder of the Detroit Society of Arts and Crafts and the Cranbrook Press (modeled after William Morris's Kelmscott Press), Booth was driven by a lifelong interest and involvement in architecture and the crafts. Avidly pursuing his vision of Cranbrook as a total work of Arts and Crafts design, he planned the new facilities and supervised the creation of an integral complex of buildings and gardens. Booth's conception of Cranbrook, inspired by the American Academy in Rome, projected an art academy where students would pursue independent study under the guidance of masters established in specific fields of art. He also envisioned Cranbrook as a workshop that would produce objects to embellish and improve the American environment and as a community where art would be integrated with daily life.

Eliel Saarinen (1873–1950), who in 1922 had won second prize in the *Chicago Tribune* Tower competition, settled in America and was appointed Visiting Professor of Architecture at the University of Michigan in 1923. One of his students at Michigan was George Booth's son, Henry Scripps Booth, who introduced Saarinen to his father. The elder Booth subsequently commissioned the Finnish architect to help plan the academy and design its buildings.

As president of the Cranbrook Academy of Art from 1932 until 1946, Eliel Saarinen shared Booth's vision of Cranbrook as a working place devoted more to the creation of art than to theoretical teachings. He transformed the school into an institution where all the design arts were integrated and taught together. Although his philosophy of design was informed by a profound Arts and Crafts sensibility, it fostered a breadth of stylistic possibilities. Indeed, the stylistic variety evident in both the Cranbrook buildings and the work of Cranbrook artists epitomizes Saarinen's sense of individuality, which also was reflected in his educational philosophy.

Work on creating the new art community began in 1907 with the building of Cranbrook House, the Booth family residence, by Detroit architect Albert Kahn. Affirming his strong personal support for the Arts and Crafts movement, Booth commissioned the finest artisans to decorate the house and its grounds. The Meeting House, designed and built by George Booth in 1918 as the initial center for religious and instructional gatherings in the community, became the Brookside School in 1922. A few years later the Booths commissioned the firm of Bertram Goodhue Associates to design Christ Church, Cranbrook, so that it might serve as a prominent religious center for the emerging Cranbrook institutions as well as for the surrounding community of Bloomfield Hills. Here, too, as at Cranbrook House, the work of renowned contemporary artists was harmoniously integrated with art treasures from Europe to embellish the graceful Late Gothic Revival stone structure.

The educational buildings that followed were designed by Eliel Saarinen. Saarinen produced several master plans for the Cranbrook complex, but Booth thought them all too pretentious. Although his basic scheme is retained in the organization of Cranbrook School and the Academy of Art, Saarinen gradually modified the more elaborate aspects of his plan.

The first of the educational buildings was the Cranbrook School for boys, a preparatory school conceived to attract young men to sing in the choir of the just-completed Christ Church, Cranbrook. Booth at first intended that Saarinen convert the farm buildings designed in 1911–1912 by Marcus R. Burrowes (1874–1953) into the boys' school, but agreed to build a new complex when renovation proved more costly. Upon Mrs. Booth's insistence that Cranbrook also include a school for girls, Saarinen designed Kingswood School, which opened four years later.

During this active period, Saarinen also planned the Cranbrook Academy of Art as a complex of administrative offices, studios, and living quarters for faculty, artists, and students. Booth and Saarinen gathered a group of artists and craftsmen, many from Europe, to establish a series of studios within the academy. These included weaving studios under Saarinen's wife, Loja, and Marianne Stengell; a department of painting under Zoltan Sepeschy and Wallace Mitchell; and a ceramics department headed by Maija Grotell. A design shop was set up under Charles Eames and Eero Saarinen, and a metalsmith department was established under Harry Bertoia. A department of sculpture was subsequently organized by the Swedish sculptor Carl Milles. Saarinen also founded a post-graduate department of architecture and city-planning, over which he himself presided.

The remaining Cranbrook institution, the

Institute of Science, was also established in the 1930s. Inspired by a rare gem collection purchased by the Booths, the institute was intended initially to enhance the scientific studies of Cranbrook students. Over the years, it has become the largest science museum in the Detroit metropolitan area.

Several more buildings were added to the Cranbrook complex in the period immediately preceding and following World War II. They included a women's dormitory, studios for the department of painting, and additional housing for faculty and students at the Academy of Art. More recent additions have been the Wenger Gymnasium at the Kingswood School and the Gordon Hall of Science and the Ice Arena at the Cranbrook School.

Guided by a new physical master plan, a massive effort to repair and restore the Cranbrook complex is now underway. Plans also call for a major renovation and expansion of the Institute of Science and the construction of new Academy of Art studios and of a performing arts center.

OK08.1 **Cranbrook House**

1907–1908, 1918, 1919–1920, Albert Kahn. 500 Lone Pine Rd.

Situated on the crown of a hill overlooking the estate, Cranbrook House was conceived by George Booth as an Arts and Crafts variant of a traditional half-timbered English manor house. It was designed by Albert Kahn, then a rising young architect in Detroit who had previously built a barn at the Booth home in the city. Works by many artists were an integral part of the house. Sculptors Paul Manship and Mario Korbell; silversmiths Arthur J. Stone, Elizabeth Copeland, and Omar Ramsden; Mary Chase Stratton of Pewabic Pottery and Dr. Henry Mercer of the Moravian Pottery; the Edward J. Caldwell Studio of New York; ironsmiths Samuel Yellin and Frank Koralewski; and the woodcarver Johann Kirschmayer of Cambridge, Massachusetts, all enhanced Cranbrook House through their art.

The central portion was the original house, which on the ground level contains a living room, a dining room, and an office, all reached from a great central hall. In 1918 the library wing by Kahn replaced what had been a pergola to the west. The library, which takes up most of the wing, features a remarkable carved overmantel developed by Kirschmayer from Booth's sketches and ideas. In addition to housing Booth's growing collection of books, the library wing also includes his drafting room, his office, and the "Still" room where he rested. Another wing by Kahn was built in 1919–1920 on the east, to house the Commons (now Oak) Room, scene of many Booth family festivities. Some of these are memorialized in the striking cartouches placed above the room's high linenfold panels. The west, north, and east arcades of the house front on a series of terraces and loggias, commanding splendid vistas of the cascades, lakes, walks, and fountains that embellish the Cranbrook Gardens.

Near the house stands a cluster of distinctive service buildings reminiscent of a hillside hamlet. These include the much-modified Tower Cottage (1908), originally designed by Albert Kahn, and the Garage (1908), Twin Cottage (1910), and Greenhouse (1910). The last three structures were designed by Marcus R. Burrowes, a Detroit architect recommended to Booth by Kahn, who was then too busy designing Henry Ford's auto plants to do the work. Burrowes also designed the south entrance to the Cranbrook Estate (1917), for which Samuel Yellin produced exquisite wrought-iron gates.

From the entrance court on the north, a path leads to the handsome open-air Greek Theater, designed by Burrowes and built in 1915. This pristine classical structure, articulated with the Ionic order, was the first facility at Cranbrook intended for public use.

OK08.2 **Brookside School** (The Meeting House)

1918, George G. Booth. 1928–1930, additions, Henry S. Booth. 550 Cranbrook Rd.

Brookside School originated as The Meeting House. Located at the southern end of the since-enlarged complex, the rustic Arts and Crafts pavilion was designed by Booth himself and asymmetrically conceived in powerful stone rubble. It has a steep roof and oriel casement windows and an irregular roofline. Detroit artist Katherine McEwen decorated the interior of the auditorium, and the furnishings came from the workshops of the Detroit Society of Arts and Crafts. In 1929, George Booth's son Henry served as the architect for additions to the original structure, as well as for the adjoining Headmaster's Residence (1929–1930). The younger Booth's additions enhanced the Arts and Crafts flavor of the original in their massing and lively combination of stucco walls, brick trim, and slate roofs.

OK08.3 Christ Church, Cranbrook

1925–1928, Oscar H. Murray of Bertram G. Goodhue Associates. 1937–1938. 470 Church Rd.

The firm of Bertram G. Goodhue Associates was commissioned by George Booth in 1924 to design the church, with Oscar H. Murray as the chief architect and designer. (Bertram G. Goodhue himself died in 1924.) The church and rectory were erected in 1925–1928; the educational and administrative wing of the parish house was built in 1937–1938. The graceful stone structure, representing Murray's masterful adaptation of English Gothic parish churches, favored by Booth, was the last major collaborative work in this country of leading Arts and Crafts artists and craftsmen.

The exterior is embellished by the exquisite stone figures atop the buttresses, carved by famed architectural sculptor Lee Lawrie, and the magnificent stained-glass windows are by Niccola D'Ascenzo and James H. Hogan.

The soaring, majestic interiors abound in examples of consummate craftsmanship. The open timber work hammer-beam over the nave, decorated by Alfred E. Floegel, is softly lit by the diffused light from the grisaille-glass clerestory windows by G. Owen Bonawit. The frescoes on the three walls of the sanctuary are by Katherine McEwen, a founding member of the Detroit Society of Arts and Crafts; the handsome reredos and the carved narthex screen are by the firm of Irving and Casson of New York. The vaulted ceiling of Pewabic mosaics in the octagonal baptistery is by Mary Chase Stratton; the enameled silver cross on the altar is by Arthur Neville Kirk, a silversmith at the Cranbrook Academy of Art; and candlesticks were crafted by Frank L. Koralewsky of Krasser and Company, Boston.

OK08.4 Cranbrook School

1925–1928, Eliel Saarinen. 520 Lone Pine Rd.

Opened in 1927, Cranbrook School was Saarinen's first executed building in this country. Saarinen's complex consists of handsomely articulated brick buildings (academic building, dining hall, and dormitories) topped with steep red-tile roofs and grouped around courts in the manner of English collegiate quadrangles. Although the general character of this ensemble recalls medieval collegiate complexes, the stylistic character is the result of a creative synthesis using abstract medieval motifs and contemporary Scandinavian work in the spirit of Ostberg and Nyrop.

Cranbrook School, which was awarded the Gold Medal of the Architectural League of New York in 1934, represents Saarinen's finest work in America. The buildings are enhanced with wrought-iron work by Oscar Bach and sculptural ornamentation by Geza Maroti. The quadrangle features bronze sculptures by Paul Manship and Carl Milles.

OK08.5 Cranbrook Academy of Art

1925–1926, 1928–1929, Eliel Saarinen. 500 Lone Pine Rd.

Saarinen extended the contemporized medieval vocabulary of Cranbrook School to the first buildings of the Academy. These included the Architectural Office (1925–1926) and studios (1927–1929); the Arts and Crafts Building and its addition, housing dormitory and studios (1928–1929); and his own and Carl Milles's houses in the ensemble (1928–1930). Inside the Saarinen House, the spatial flow along connecting interior axes, the dramatic studio space, and the integration of specially designed ornamentation all recall his earlier home at Hvittrask, outside Helsinki; at the same time, its streamlined articulations and decorative designs already speak of the more contemporary Art Moderne idiom.

OK08.6 Kingswood School

1929–1931, Eliel Saarinen. 885 Cranbrook Rd.

The Kingswood School for girls, completed in 1931, represents one of Saarinen's more evocative buildings in America. The warm tan brick and copper roofs contrast with the dark red brick and slate roofs of the earlier Cranbrook buildings. The massing of the building is simpler and conforms to the sweep

OK08.6 Kingswood School

OK08.8 **Cranbrook Museum and Library**

1938–1942, Eliel Saarinen. 500 Lone Pine Rd.

of the lakeshore. Dormitory and work areas are skillfully clustered around intimate courtyards. The ensemble, with its broadly overhanging eaves and horizontal bands of windows, bears a certain affinity to Frank Lloyd Wright's Prairie architecture. Its rich array of pronounced Art Deco ornamental details is among the most expressive employed by Saarinen. In the end, Kingswood School bears the unmistakable stamp of Saarinen's innately Nordic creative impulses. It also represents a brilliant product of the architect's close collaboration with his family: Saarinen designed the building; his wife, Loja, designed the rugs, draperies, and fabrics, aided by a corps of weavers; his daughter Pipsan designed the auditorium and dining hall interiors; and his son Eero designed the furniture.

OK08.7 **Cranbrook Institute of Science**

1935–1938, Eliel Saarinen. Institute Way

Saarinen's Cranbrook Institute of Science, which was revised from the original building of 1930 by George Booth, was completed in 1937. Simpler in detail than Kingswood, it relies more upon the sweep of line and mass for its effect. Its horizontal masses with flat roofs and horizontal bands of simply cut window openings with stone trim are suggestive of a classic Nordic mutation of the International style. Its simple lines are reflected in a pool animated by the playful Mermaid and Triton figures executed by Carl Milles. A

Completion of the Cranbrook Museum and Library in late 1942 rounded out Saarinen's earlier master plan for the Academy of Art. Its stark expression, contrasting sharply with earlier Cranbrook buildings, indicates Saarinen's acceptance of the more monumentally abstracted modern classicism advanced by the 1937 international exposition in Paris (the Museum of Modern Art, by J. C. Dondel, et al., together with the German and Soviet pavilions); the stark, monumental propylaeum connecting the museum and library also recalls Asplund's contemporary Woodland Crematorium in Stockholm, as well as Josef Hoffmann's design for the Austrian pavilion at the 1925 Paris exposition. The severely plain walls and monumental propylaeum serve as a background for the cross-axial ensemble of the Triton Pool court and the Orpheus Fountain by Carl Milles.

In 1986 the two hundred-seat Albert and Peggy deSalle Auditorium was built as an underground wing of the museum, located beneath the propylaeum. The deSalle Auditorium was designed by Robert Swanson, grandson of Eliel Saarinen, in collaboration with Jickling, Lyman and Powell of Birmingham and with George Zonars, an interior architect who is an academy graduate and a member of its board of governors.

OK09 Sidney and Madeline Forbes House

BLOOMFIELD TOWNSHIP

OK09 Sidney and Madeline Forbes House

1989, Hugh Newell Jacobson. 1350 Kirkway (west of US 24 on Long Lake Rd. and just west of Franklin Rd., north of Long Lake Rd.)

Hugh Newell Jacobson, one of America's most important contemporary residential architects, drew inspiration from the French chateau for this design. It combines Postmodern freedom with the discipline of the modernists. The central side-gable block is linked by connectors to paired hipped-roof dependencies. Prominent chimneys and large multipaned windows mark the large brick house.

TROY, BLOOMFIELD TOWNSHIP

OK10 K-Mart Corporation International Headquarters

1970–1972, 1977–1978 addition, Smith, Hinchman and Grylls; Johnson, Johnson and Roy, landscape architects. 3100 West Big Beaver Rd. (southwest corner of West Big Beaver and Coolidge roads, 1.5 miles west of intersection of West Big Beaver Rd. and I-75 and nearly 2 miles east of its intersection with Woodward Ave. [Michigan 1])

Early in 1969, Harry Cunningham, president and chairman of the S. S. Kresge Company (now the K-Mart Corporation), planned to move the corporate headquarters from its Art Deco building at 2727 Second Avenue, in the Cass Park area of Detroit, to a new location in Troy to replace the existing overcrowded offices and also to consolidate the scattered company operations.

Smith, Hinchman and Grylls designed a modular scheme that would provide a headquarters complex of several units, each with a floor space of over 10,000 square feet, for a total area of 520,000 square feet. The units are two to four stories tall. For every building unit, an attached core tower contains service facilities, such as lavatories and stairways for each floor and space for mechanical equipment above the roof level.

Several of the units are combined, and courtyards are created between the units, thereby maximizing the window area for offices. Additional elevator core towers and "street" corridors run diagonally across the complex, thus reducing the walking distance between remote sectors. This scheme met the various space needs of different offices, as well as facilitating future building expansion in modular increments.

Cor-ten steel sheathing with a brown patina provides a maintenance-free exterior. Windows of bronze-tinted glass and mahogany-colored silo tile on the exterior of the corner towers adds to the weathered effect.

Johnson, Johnson and Roy, of Ann Arbor, designed the landscaping of the 30-acre site, which includes strategically placed berms and valleys. Sculpture and plantings in the courtyards create a pleasant environment for the employees.

When construction was completed in 1972, this complex was one of the largest corporate headquarters in the nation. One courtyard was roofed over with a skylight to serve as the main lobby. At first, thirteen modules were constructed, oriented diagonally to Big Beaver Road, which runs parallel and perpendicular to the glass-enclosed passageways crossing the landscaped courtyards. The complex contains meeting rooms, employee lounges, a printing plant, specially detailed executive offices, and a cafeteria for six hundred people. Synchronized with the architecture are the interior furnishings and a large selection of works of art, including some large sculptures by British artist Michael Ayrton on commission for this building. In 1977 the plans to accommodate expansion were justified when the K-Mart Corporation (the successor to Kresge) requested that Smith, Hinchman and Grylls design additional modules to nearly double the existing space. (OK10

is very close, on the south side of West Big Beaver Road.)

OK11 **Kresge Foundation Office and Conference Center** (Washington and Catharine Barringer Stanley House, formerly Brooks Farm)

1852. 1982, restoration and rebuilding, William Kessler and Associates. 3215 West Big Beaver Rd.

Washington Stanley, born in 1807 in Shaftsbury, Vermont, emigrated in 1826 with his first wife from Castile, New York, to Troy Township, present-day Troy. They purchased a 160-acre farm on which stood a rustic log cabin covered with basswood slabs. In 1852 Stanley and his second wife, Catharine, built this two-story, side-gable, Greek Revival farmhouse of roughly coursed, split-faced fieldstone. Five bays wide and three deep, the house has shuttered six over six windows with sandstone lintels and sills. Trim consists of dentils along the cornice and fretwork balustrades above the elaborate bracketed wooden Italianate porches at the front (north) and side (east) entrances. These porches were added at a later date.

In 1873 Stanley sold the farm to his daughter Elizabeth and her husband, Frank Ford, whose daughter, Alta Peabody, sold it to Wil-

OK11 Kresge Foundation Office and Conference Center (Washington and Catharine Barringer Stanley House, formerly Brooks Farm)

liam Brooks in 1911. The Brooks family operated a thriving dairy farm here until the 1960s, when all but three acres were sold to commercial developers. In 1982 the Kresge Foundation, an independent philanthropic organization created in 1924, acquired the remaining farmstead from the estate of William Brooks's daughter, Bertha Brooks Parks.

The foundation commissioned the architectural firm of William Kessler and Associates of Detroit to design functional office space that would incorporate the farmstead. Several outbuildings were restored, and a large barn, a replica of one that had stood on the property until its collapse in 1975, was donated by the city of Troy and moved to the back of the lot, where it now serves as a caretaker's dwelling. Two windmills on the property were restored, and a silo and a fieldstone and wooden shed were rebuilt. A 10,000-square-foot semihexagonal addition was also constructed at the rear of the farmhouse, but its low profile and ingenious landscaping allow the earlier structure to remain the primary focus of the site. The Brooks Farm is a triumph in historic preservation.

BIRMINGHAM, BLOOMFIELD TOWNSHIP

Birmingham was a predominantly agricultural community during the nineteenth century, although it was situated along the Saginaw Trail (now Woodward Avenue), a main traffic corridor. The advent of the railroad in 1839 and the electric interurban in 1896 brought Birmingham closer to Detroit than to other communities. The name Birmingham was first applied to the town in 1832 by Roswell T. Merrill, the foundry owner, in the hope it would thrive as a place of industry. Platted in 1836, its post office was named Birmingham in 1838, and it became incorporated as a village in 1864 and as a city in 1933.

The shift to a suburban community began in the early twentieth century. Birmingham grew rapidly in the 1920s. The 1920 population was 3,690, and this more than doubled by 1930. During this decade Woodward Avenue was widened, and Hunter Boulevard was developed into an eight-lane bypass around downtown. The Birmingham Community House was available for meetings in 1923, and in 1928 a new Neo-Tudor municipal building and library opened their doors as part of an ambitious civic center plan. In 1939, six years after achieving city status, Birmingham acquired a new post office. Residential development increased after World War II, along with religious, civic, and commercial construction. Fashionable shops and galleries are found in the vicinity of Maple Road and Woodward Avenue, a Midwest version of Rodeo Drive. Birmingham's population today (1991) is over 21,000, and the city has recently experienced an upsurge in the construction of apartments and offices.

BLOOMFIELD TOWNSHIP

OK12 Temple Beth El

1973, Minoru Yamasaki. 7400 Telegraph Rd. (US 24) (northwest corner of Telegraph and Fourteen Mile roads)

Completed in 1973 at a cost of $7 million, this building is a worthy successor to the congregation's earlier home on Woodward Avenue (see DE54, Lighthouse Cathedral, p. 98). The campus plan consists of a school wing skillfully done in the ubiquitous International style; but it is the sanctuary that is riveting, modeled on the biblical Tent of Meeting, a great tapering concrete frame with aluminum panels whose joints emphasize the vertical thrust of the design. On the interior, windows around the base of the vault not only admit sunlight, they provide views of the landscaping, but make the wall/ceiling appear to float, suspended from an invisible central support. The ark wall, an arresting interplay of gilded metal and warm wood, also draws the eye upward. The drama of the space is itself a presence, dwarfing the eighteen hundred worshippers even when the prayer hall is full. In the foyer is a sculpture commemorating the victims of the Holocaust; in the adjacent space, a museum of Judaica and the stained-glass windows from the earlier temple on Woodward. Several large meeting rooms, combinable social halls, and an office wing complete the building complex by Yamasaki, who had earlier done a similar, and yet quite different, "Jewish cathedral" for a Reform temple in north suburban Chicago. A major influence on the Detroit design was Eric Mendelsohn's unexecuted design for Emanu-El in Dallas (1951).

BERKLEY

OK13 Roseland Park Cemetery

1906, Emile Pielke, landscape designer. Northwest corner at Woodward Ave. (Michigan 1) and Twelve Mile Rd.

The gateway's five 22-foot-high, light gray, Barre granite pillars each depict a pair of caryatids in relief supporting a stone urn. This entrance was originally farther west, facing Woodward, until relocated for the widening of the avenue. The cemetery itself was planned by Emil Pielke, a German-trained landscape designer who also served as Roseland Park's first superintendent.

OK13.1 Roseland Park Mausoleum

1914, Louis Kamper.

When it was dedicated in 1914, the Roseland Park Mausoleum was the largest public mausoleum in the United States. This classically inspired, two-story, reinforced concrete building contains thirteen hundred crypts. The exterior is a regular mass with tall, evenly spaced, round-arched windows and a pedimented and columned entrance porch on the main facade. Three clerestories, partially hidden by a parapet wall, indicate the locations of the white marble-faced interior halls, which are lined with crypts. The classically detailed, two-story central hall also serves as a chapel; both it and the entrance lobby are flanked by double tiers of fluted Doric columns.

ROYAL OAK

OK14 Shrine of the Little Flower

1929–1931, tower; 1933–1936, church; Henry J. McGill. Northeast corner Woodward Ave. (Michigan 1) and Twelve Mile Rd.

The Shrine of the Little Flower is an extravagant Art Deco tower and church built with contributions from radio listeners in much the same manner as Jim Bakker, Oral Roberts, Pat Robertson, and other televangelists have built their empires in recent times. In 1926, Bishop Gallagher commissioned the Reverend Charles E. Coughlin (1891–1979) to establish a parish in Royal Oak, and a tiny shingle church dedicated to Saint Theresa of

OK14 Shrine of the Little Flower

Lisieux was built for twenty-eight families. Coughlin soon purchased radio broadcast time and produced the Radio Shrine of the Little Flower, later the National Radio League of the Shrine of the Little Flower. With donations from a national audience of listeners of his political broadcasts, in which he advocated social reform and opposed international bankers, Communists, labor unions, and the Roosevelt administration, Father Coughlin accumulated enough money to pay for the construction of this church and tower.

Henry J. McGill of New York City designed the complex, with a tower, narthex, and eight-sided church proper to fit on an unusual wedge-shaped lot. The exterior walls of the church are of rough-cut granite from East Weymouth, Massachusetts, trimmed with smooth-cut Indiana limestone. The tower is of limestone and is covered with carvings and relief sculpture depicting church figures and symbolism. The walls are inlaid with stones carved with the flowers of all forty-eight states, whose citizens contributed funds. The windows are recessed within geometric openings covered with bronze grillwork.

The square Charity Crucifixion Tower has a monumental relief of the crucified Christ on the Cross. Behind Christ's head, near the top of the tower and reached by spiral stairs, is the room from which Coughlin broadcast his radio programs. The church is octagonal, with a center altar. Wings containing chapels project from the north and the south, and galleries encircle the entire sanctuary, so that it seats three thousand beneath its tentlike, copper- and nickel-steel-clad dome. The interior is lavishly finished in buff sandstone, travertine, imported marbles, white oak woodwork, and bronze and is embellished with carvings and paintings. Corrado Joseph Parducci did much of the bronze and stone sculpture. Beatrice Wilczynski (1913–1984) of Chicago did the paintings, and Rene P. Chamberllan carved many of the stone reliefs.

HUNTINGTON WOODS AND ROYAL OAK TOWNSHIP

OK15 Detroit Zoological Park

1924–present; Arthur A. Shurtleff, landscape architect; Heinrich Hagenbeck, exhibits. 8450 West Ten Mile Rd. (I-696) (northwest corner of West Ten Mile Rd. and Woodward Ave. [Michigan 1])

The Detroit Zoological Park is a designed landscape planned by Arthur A. Shurtleff (1870–1957), a nationally known Boston landscape architect who had worked in the office of Frederick Law Olmsted. It is the only zoo in America whose exhibits were directly designed by and built under the supervision of Heinrich Hagenbeck, of Hamburg, Germany, who, with his father Carl Hagenbeck (d. 1913), was a world-famous zoo designer. The Detroit Zoo was the first American zoo that was entirely without bars and moated, with panoramic views that included several exhibits in one scene.

The Detroit Zoological Society was established in 1911, and in 1916 a 100-acre site in Royal Oak was purchased. Accepted in 1925, Shurtleff's plan is arranged with a formal central mall that is lined with animal exhibits. The mall connects the birdhouse, a domed Beaux-Arts Classical structure erected in 1926 to the designs of William H. Creaser of Donaldson and Meier, with the bear den. Contrasting with the symmetry of the formal mall are the free-flowing lines of the naturalistic landscape, including two lakes that follow the existing forms of the tree patterns and the topography. The Detroit plan resembles Shurtleff's plan for the Boston Zoological Park at Franklin Park and the Chicago Zoological Park. A miniature railroad runs from the entrance of the zoo at the south border to the northwest corner of the site.

The Detroit Zoo was one of the first zoos in America to utilize for its animal exhibits simulated rockwork enclosures made from gunite, a product used to simulate natural environments. By 1933 the various exhibits—wolverine and raccoon, elephant and rhinoceros, and others—were completed. Additional construction was financed in 1933–1934 under the Civil Works Administration of the Federal Emergency Relief Administration and in 1935 under the Works Progress Administration. The chimpanzee exhibit is the most recent, created in 1989 by Schervish, Vogel and Mers of Detroit, in consultation with Jon Coe, landscape architect and zoo design specialist of Philadelphia.

The Horace H. Rackham Memorial Fountain was presented in 1939 to the zoo by Rackham's widow, Mary, to commemorate his role as first president of the zoological commission. Created by sculptor Corrado Joseph Parducci and designer Frederick A. Schnaple, the work consists of two 10-foot-high bronze bears playfully dancing around a central column, with frogs and turtles at their feet. All this is contained within a large reflected pool lined with blue Pewabic tile and flanked by two subsidiary seal fountains. Together they form an arresting focal point for the zoo's central mall.

Today (1991) the park is an extensive and well-maintained complex of winding pathways and varied structures.

SOUTHFIELD

OK16 Northland Regional Shopping Center

1954, Victor Gruen Associates. Northeast corner of Northwestern Highway (Lodge Freeway or Michigan 10) and Eight Mile Rd.

With the advent of the metropolitan Detroit area freeway system following World War II and the directly related suburban growth, the regional shopping center was born. Northland Center is the first large, regional shopping center built in America. It was designed in 1952 by Victor Gruen Associates of Los Angeles, New York, and Detroit. The infrastructure was a compact cluster plan concept of a city within a city and embraced every aspect of modern-day urban design. It opened for business in 1954, with more than one hundred tenant stores clustered around the J. L. Hudson Company department store, located in the then rapidly developing area northwest of the city. The center has since tripled in size. Its conveniently assembled shops, stores, restaurants, and markets were arranged with pedestrians safely separated from traffic and service vehicles and with parking for almost ten thousand automobiles. Still near the main entrance to Hudson's is Marshall Fredericks's delightful 8.5-foot-tall limestone and bronze *Boy and Bear* sculpture (1954).

In 1957, Hudson's repeated the Northland formula at Eastland. But using Gruen's innovations for Southdale in Minneapolis, the company enclosed the malls and courts and added a second anchor store when it built shopping centers at Westland in 1956 and Southland in Taylor in 1970. Subsequently, Northland and Eastland were remodeled to enclose their malls and courts and were expanded to include additional major department stores and many more shops. Gruen's concept for Northland was adopted by shopping center developers nationwide.

OK17 Vic Tanny International Health Club (Reynolds Metals Regional Sales Office Building)

1955–1959, Minoru Yamasaki. 16000 Northland Dr. (northwest corner of Northwestern Highway [Lodge Freeway or Michigan 10] and Eight Mile Rd.)

Constructed for a leading aluminum producer, this building was intended to highlight the industrial and technological uses of aluminum, particularly for the automobile manufacturers in the Detroit area. As well as displaying aluminum products dramatically, the building held offices for the regional sales staff.

Here Yamasaki (1912–1986) created an artistic three-story, concrete-framed structure upon a white terrazzo podium, surrounded by a pool of water lilies. Interior spaces are created around a central, building-high atrium. This lofty three-story display and lobby space is bathed with daylight filtered through an aluminum space frame with pyramidal skylight elements. Air conditioning, lighting, and acoustical elements are completely integrated with a concrete waffle-slab structural system.

The specially designed gold-anodized aluminum grille wraps around the perimeter of the building. The grille functions as decora-

tion and as a sun screen. Its rich texture contrasts with the relatively clean window walls that it shades.

The Reynolds Metals Building is representative of Yamasaki's work. The famed architect, whose office was located in Birmingham, Michigan, was highly respected for his ability to work with various building materials and to create rich textural compositions using modern architectural forms.

OK18 B'nai David Synagogue

1956, social hall, office, chapel, Louis G. Redstone. 1965, sanctuary, Sidney Eisenshtat. 1967, school wing, Havis and Glovinsky. 24350 Southfield Rd. (1 mile east of Ten Mile Rd. intersection with Northwestern Hwy [Michigan 10] to Southfield and .5 mile south)

Like many rapidly growing suburban religious institutions, B'nai David was built in stages, beginning with Louis Redstone's 1958 Zack building, a long, low, brick structure that resembles public school architecture of the 1950s, and ending with Havis and Glovinsky's 1967 Bauhaus-inspired school wing. For the sanctuary, the congregation chose a California architect, Sidney Eisenshtat of Beverly Hills. The prayer hall, according to Eisenshtat, is an allusion to the altar of the Temple in Jerusalem. A striking edifice, each side of which is a segmental arch with the inverted arch forming the roofline, the structure seems to be poised on the ground like some great winged creature. Between the lower arches of the exterior, one can see the curving stained-glass windows of the circular sanctuary. Just as the building seems to float, the suspended ceiling hovers over the prayer hall; at its center a mesh screen with a circle of lights floats over the worshippers. The circle is the dominant motif in the one-thousand-seat sanctuary: the room is round, the central *bimah* round, and the pews follow the curve of the space. The stained-glass windows are graded in tones from blue at the ark to gold and earth tones at the lobby exit, again drawing the viewer's eyes around the space.

OK19 Prudential Town Center

1973–1989; Sikes, Jennings, Kelly, and Brewer (1000 Town Center, 2000 Town Center, Radisson Plaza Hotel); Solomon, Cordell, Buenz, and Associates (5000 Town Center); 3D/Neuhaus and Taylor (3000 Town

Center, 4000 Town Center). Southfield (bounded by Northwestern Highway [Lodge Freeway or Michigan 10], Civic Center Dr., and Evergreen Rd.)

Prudential Town Center is significant from a city planning perspective. Similar developments in other major United States metropolitan centers are considered by some planners to represent the latest stage in the development of the American suburb, which has historically been viewed as largely residential outgrowths of specific urban centers.

Prudential Town Center is a 69-acre suburban development of gleaming glass and steel commercial towers located approximately twelve miles from central Detroit. The complex is composed of four office towers, a luxury residential tower, and a hotel. Ranging in scale from twelve to thirty-three stories, each building represents the latest, if not the most innovative trends in modern commercial high-rise design. The four office towers and the Radisson Plaza are variations on a theme of steel framing and bronze-gold-tinted wall panels. Two Thousand Town Center is a twenty-eight-story polygonal tower with the top third of one corner stepped back. Crosses brace the narrow ends of the 3000 Town Center tower. Four Thousand Town Center has rounded corners and horizontal banding. The broad convex glass wall of the front of the Radisson Plaza rests on columns. Five Thousand Town Center is undulating, rather like a figure eight.

Critics have often claimed that suburbs are vast wastelands with no definable centers, identities, or sense of community. Over the years, however, many suburban areas have become increasingly independent of their parent cities and, as a result, have evolved definite urban commercial centers. These centers, or pseudo-cities, have manifested themselves in the form of large commercial developments, like Prudential Town Center, rising in the midst of expansive parking facilities, surrounded by quiet residential districts, and served by efficient transportation networks.

The organizational patterns of developments of this nature may appear to be in direct contrast to those of the traditional American city. These new cities seem to lack the integrated social and economic qualities of their models. Nevertheless, it is important to recognize that the manner in which land or space is utilized at any particular time is a reflection of popular societal values. In this respect, Prudential Town Center, in its planning and architecture, is a significant product of twentieth-century American society.

OK20 Shaarey Zedek

1962, Albert Kahn Associates and Percival Goodman (New York). 27237 Bell Rd. (northwest corner of Bell and Eleven Mile roads, on the east side of intersection of Northwestern Hwy. [Michigan 10] and Eleven Mile Rd.)

Sited prominently adjacent to the major expressway into Detroit from the northwest, Shaarey Zedek looms dramatically against the horizon line and recalls Frank Lloyd Wright's Unitarian Meeting House in Madison, Wisconsin. This $3.4 million complex on a 40-acre site contains an education building with twenty classrooms and a library, an office wing, and numerous chapels. The focus of the plan is the sharply peaked sanctuary, with two flanking social halls, whose form has been variously interpreted as the tabernacle in the desert or a holy mountain. The great, jutting, concrete pylon is enhanced by Jan Peter Stern's sculpture, *Mount Sinai*. Even more dramatic than the exterior is the interior of the prayer hall, where Robert Pinart's stained-glass window, depicting the Burning Bush, echoes the thrust of the roof. At the front is a 40-foot-tall marble ark with a Tree of Life at its core. The sanctuary seats twelve hundred people; with the side partitions opened, the combined sanctuary-social halls have a seating capacity of thirty-six hundred.

OK21 Young Israel of Southfield Synagogue

1978, Rossen-Neumann Associates. 27705 Lahser Rd.

(second door south of southwest corner of Lahser Rd. and Winchester, .4 mi north of Eleven Mile Rd.)

Established in 1971, this congregation first met in school buildings and later bought a house, which was demolished to make way for this striking brick fortresslike structure with an austere interior and unusual plan. A ramp leads along the side of the sanctuary so that the worshippers double back to face the entrance wall of the building and are oriented to the east, the traditional direction for Jewish prayer. The interior is of exposed brick, with a unique multi-chambered ark. The slightly elevated women's section runs along the north side of the prayer hall and is separated by a clear partition.

FARMINGTON HILLS

OK22 **Michigan National Corporate Headquarters**

1987–1989; Luckenbach/Ziegelman and Partners; Johnson, Johnson and Roy, landscape architects. 27777 Inkster Rd. (2.25 miles northwest of intersection with I-696)

One of the finest examples of corporate Post modern architecture in Michigan is the Michigan National Corporation Headquarters Building in Farmington Hills. Postmodern buildings such as this one borrow from historic architecture by adapting architectural materials, forms, and ornament to modern building contexts.

In an effort to consolidate administrative activities, Michigan National Corporation initiated the construction of a new headquarters in Farmington Hills. Robert J. Mylod, the company's chairman, along with architects from the firm Luckenbach/Ziegelman and Partners, toured Georgian and Colonial buildings of Harvard University; Historic Williamsburg, Virginia; Thomas Jefferson's Monticello; and the University of Virginia campus. Stylistic influences from these sources manifest themselves in the Postmodern architecture of the headquarters building. It exhibits warm brick exterior walls, arched walkways, inner courtyards, steeply sloped roofs, a cupola, and dormerlike windows. The plan of the building has been organized to produce an intimate campuslike environment.

In its stylistic adaptations and campuslike spatial organization, the Michigan National headquarters building reflects a growing trend in American corporate office design. Moreover, its historicism of traditional eighteenth-century early American architecture exudes a friendly, human, trustworthy, and stable image that this banking institution wishes to project.

Macomb County (MB)

MOUNT CLEMENS

MB01 **Macomb County Building**

1931–1933, George J. Haas. 10 North Gratiot Ave. (Michigan 3) (bounded by North Gratiot Ave., Market St., Broadway St., and Cass Ave.)

The Macomb County Building is a twelve-story Art Deco skyscraper in the heart of Mount Clemens. The exterior walls of the steel-frame structure are clad in gray limestone. The upper stories are stepped back from the main wall plane, and two-story entry pavilions project from the center of three sides. Strong continuous piers and recessed windows grouped in vertical bands seem to thrust the building skyward. Terminating the piers are attached granite sculpture of busts

of military figures—a soldier, a sailor, a marine, and an airman (selected in deference to nearby Selfridge Air Base)—and of a Native American and a Revolutionary War soldier, all carved in granite. Spandrels carved with zigzags flank the sculptures. Bronze plaques at the entrances depicting a sower, a surveyor, a seaman, and a farmer commemorate the early industries and occupations of Macomb County.

In 1929 the Macomb County Board of Supervisors voted to abandon the overcrowded red brick courthouse erected in 1880. George J. Haas (d. 1956) of Saint Clair Shores drafted plans for the new county building. Taxes levied during the previous two years generated $395,000 of the anticipated cost of $662,000 for the new county building. Because construction costs were low, and the project would relieve unemployment, funds were earmarked to carry out this project. The supervisors let the contract to Otto Misch, a general contractor, and construction began in spite of the depression. Federal relief through the WPA, PWA, and CWA, and the refinancing of the county's indebtedness aided its completion. Although skeptics said the "county silo" would never be half-filled, the county building was completed and occupied in 1933.

MB02 Mount Clemens Savings and Loan

1960–1961, Meathe, Kessler and Associates. Northeast corner of South Gratiot Ave. (Michigan 3), and Terry St.

The floating spatial quality of the Mount Clemens Savings and Loan Building and its formalism owes something to Minoru Yamasaki and Eliel Saarinen. A thin, undulating reinforced concrete shell of a roof is supported on four corner columns. From this is suspended a glass curtain wall. The banking room is on the first floor; offices and a community room are on a lower floor that opens onto a sunken garden, over which a bridge connects the building to the parking lot.

GROSSE POINTE SHORES

See WN05.1 (p. 116), Edsel and Eleanor Ford House

WARREN

MB03 Chrysler Corporation Dodge Half-Ton Truck Plant

1937, Albert Kahn. Northeast corner of Eight Mile (Michigan 102) and Mound roads

Perhaps Kahn's most famous plant, this building has two major steel and glass structures: the Assembly Building, 402 by 2,262 feet in plan, and the Export Building, 122 by 242 feet in plan. Kahn utilized cantilevered bent steel beams, allowing the monitors to hang below the roof level and thus improving the lighting.

MB04 General Motors Technical Center

1949–1958, Eliel and Eero Saarinen. Mound Rd., between Twelve Mile and Thirteen Mile roads (bounded

MB03 Chrysler Corporation Dodge Half-Ton Truck Plant

by Mound Rd., Thirteen Mile Rd., Van Dyke [Michigan 53], and Twelve Mile Rd.)

The GM Technical Center is a research center for the technical staff of the General Motors Company. Planned to foster creativity in an idyllic campus setting, it was cast by Eliel and Eero Saarinen, on the pattern of Cranbrook, but with totally different exterior designs. General Motors conceived of the idea in the 1930s, fenced in the newly acquired 900-acre site in 1942, and commissioned the Saarinens to plan its design and development in the 1940s. But the war, postwar strikes, and the postwar concentration of efforts on the conversion to peacetime automobile production delayed construction. The center was built in the late 1950s. It was occupied in 1956–1958.

In the 1940s and 1950s the one-square-mile campus site on which the GM Tech Center stands was in the country and suburbs north of Detroit. The research center planned by the Saarinens (father and son) occupies the western half of this large site, which is divided in half by railroad tracks and the test-driving track. To the east is a separate campuslike area containing the division headquarters of Buick, Oldsmobile, and Cadillac; Chevrolet/Pontiac Canada; and Fisher Guide.

The technical center consists of research laboratories and of engineering, environmental, manufacturing, and design areas. The buildings housing these activities are arranged around a rectangular 22-acre lake. The buildings themselves are long, low, Miesian structures of metal and glass with mass-produced, glazed, modular curtain-wall units. The leak-proof, neoprene-gasketed windows in insulated, enameled, metal sandwich panels were developed by GM engineers. But the

MB04 General Motors Technical Center

special visual strength of these buildings comes from the ceramic brick glazed in brilliant reds, ultramarine, and burnt oranges laid with grout of matching colors on the end walls of most buildings. The gleaming stainless steel water tower rises 138 feet from the north end of the lake, casting a reflection of itself; through this image shoot sprays of water. The round aluminum dome of the Styling Building Auditorium is at the lake's southwest corner. The whole is placed on a ground of grass through which a roadway circumnavigates the campus and is surrounded by thousands of trees.

A spectacular staircase is the focus of the lobby of each of the four major buildings. The Research Staff Administration Building lobby has a spiral floating stair. Spiraling treads of green Norwegian granite are suspended from one point by stainless steel suspension rods. Paintings by Charles Sheeler and Jimmy Ernst, sculptures by Antoine Pevsner, Alexander Calder, and Harry Bertoia, and other works of art are found throughout.

The site plan, the positioning of the elements at the center, the distances between them, and the vistas were planned by Eliel Saarinen. Eero Saarinen, who took over the project for his aging father in 1949, designed the buildings. They are sleek, like cars.

The GM Tech Center initiated the idea of the corporate showcase in the garden. Later, the Ford Motor Company built its world headquarters, designed by Skidmore, Owings and Merrill, known as The Glass House, in Dearborn; Upjohn built its headquarters at Portage (KZ17, p. 228); and Herman Miller, its headquarters in Zeeland (OT12, p. 283). Today, the center is as fresh, pristine, and immaculate as it was on the day it opened.

WASHINGTON TOWNSHIP

MB05 Loren Andrus House

1859–1860, David Stewart, builder. 57500 Van Dyke Rd. (Earl Memorial Highway or Michigan 53)

This large, red brick, octagonal house is a landmark in a fruit-growing and agriculture center along Van Dyke Road. The two-story house is topped by a roof supported by large, ornately carved, Italianate brackets and surmounted by a cupola. A one-story, Corinthian-columned porch surrounds seven sides of the house; a one-story kitchen wing addition extends from the eighth side. On each floor there are four rooms separated by large triangular alcoves. A spiral staircase rises through the center, from the first floor to the cupola. Loren Andrus (1816–1901), son of Michigan pioneers from Genesee County, New York, and assistant surveyor of the Clinton-Kalamazoo Canal in Macomb County, engaged his brother-in-law, David Stewart, who was a local carpenter-builder, to construct the octagonal house.

ROMEO

Romeo is situated among rolling, orchard-covered hills now encroached upon by development, as urbanism creeps in from the south. Originally known as Indian Village for the Chippewa who wintered here, and renamed Hoxies' Settlement, Romeo was settled in the 1820s by New Englanders and upstate New Yorkers drawn to the rich soil of the area. The village was platted in 1830 by Nathaniel T. Taylor, Ashail Bailey, and Major Larned and given what Mrs. Taylor called "a short, musical, classical and uncommon name."

Farming, lumbering, and land speculation formed the economic base at the outset. By the 1850s Romeo became a leading merchandising center, rivaling nearby Mount Clemens. Its hoopskirt, broom, chair, cigar, sash and blind, and carriage factories and its iron foundry contributed to Romeo's prosperity. The Romeo Academy opened in 1836, and a branch of the University of Michigan was located here from the 1840s to 1851, attracting doctors, lawyers, ministers, and teachers. Many participated in the suffrage, prohibition, and abolition reform movements of the period. The Air Line Railroad reached Romeo in 1869 and opened it to broader horizons.

The buildings of Romeo reveal the Eastern origins of its settlers, their intellect and prosperity. Romeo's nineteenth-century houses, churches, and business blocks, and its citizens' efforts to maintain and preserve them approach those of Marshall. The entire village deserves viewing as an authentic picture of a small midwestern community.

MB06.1 Nathan and Mary Ann Dickinson House

c. 1840. 1872, remodeled. 277 North Main St. (Michigan 53)

A symmetrical, two-story, side-gable, frame Greek Revival structure, this was built for Nathan Dickinson (1799–1861), a Massachusetts-born silversmith, dry goods merchant, and timber speculator, and remodeled in 1872 for its next owner. It has a single-story, one-bay porch with columns.

MB06.2 Watson Loud House

c. 1849. 264 North Main St. (Michigan 53) (southeast corner of North Main and Dickinson streets)

The charming Carpenter's Gothic dwelling of Watson Loud features board-and-batten siding, intersecting gables, bays, a plethora of narrow pointed arches, bracketed eaves, and verandas. Loud (1806–1895), a Massachusetts native, practiced medicine and operated a dry goods business in Romeo. A. J. Downing advocated vertical board for country houses because of its durability and expression of strength, truthfulness (it signifies to the eye a wooden house), and the picturesque.

MB06.3 Houses

1840s. 221, 241 North Main St. (Michigan 53) and southeast corner of North Main St. and Bradley St.

Set well back of West Saint Clair Street, on the south side at 221, 241, and at the southeast corner of the street's intersection with Bradley Street, are three end-gable Greek Revival houses that owe something to the New York and New England origins of their builders.

MB06.4 John Thorington House

c. 1860. 117 Bradley St. (southeast corner of West Saint Clair and Bradley streets)

Perhaps the grandest structure in Romeo is the John Thorington House, a two-story, end-gable Greek Revival structure with wings embellished with an ample entablature, anthemion-like gable decoration, and corner pilasters. A single-story columned porch shelters the asymmetrically placed main entrance. John Thorington (1804–1877), a wealthy Vermont-born Washington Township landowner and sheep farmer, retired to Romeo and purchased it as construction was completed.

MB06.5 Rufus Nutting House

c. 1844. 247 North Fremont St. (southwest corner of North Fremont and Church streets)

The Nutting house is a modest, one-story Greek Revival structure with entrance loggia. It was built for the director of the Romeo Academy and headmaster of the Romeo branch of the University of Michigan.

MB06.6 David Rowley House

1871. 307 Chandler St.

Perhaps the best Gothic Revival structure and the source of inspiration for others in Romeo is the David Rowley House. Its steeply pitched gables are decorated with elaborate bargeboards and its one-story porch, with equally ornate pointed arches. The basic form is after Andrew J. Downing's Gothic cottage, but the ornamentation is more elaborate.

MB06.7 Orrin Sisson House

1877. 240 Sisson St.

Built for a prosperous farmer, this tall Second Empire house exhibits a colorfully patterned mansard roof, bay, porch, and dormers. The Rowley (MB06.6), the Rowley-Gray, and the Sisson houses are at the same level of social distinction, and all built in the 1870s, but all differ in style.

RAY TOWNSHIP

MB07 Wolcott's Mill

1845–1847, Arad Freeman/Frederick Beech Wolcott. 1878, rebuilt. 63841 Wolcott Rd. (.5 mile south of 30 Mile Rd., on the west side of Wolcott Rd., southwest of its junction with Indian Trail Rd.)

The Wolcott Mill is a three-story grist or grain mill in the Greek Revival style. It is built of hand-hewn oak timbers clad with clapboard. A wide cornice with ample returns runs beneath the low-pitched gable roof. The mill originally had a high breast water wheel that measured 14 by 16 feet. It was probably housed next to the main structure and used the waters of the north branch of the Clinton River. Now, two Leffel turbines are contained in a turbine pit under the basement of the mill. The mill was completely electrified by the Detroit Edison Company in 1948 and today can run by water or by electric motor power. Arad Freeman, who came in the 1820s from New York State to Macomb County with his father, Benjamin, a miller, built this mill in 1845–1847. It is on the site of one of three mills set up by Benjamin Freeman in Ray Township in 1824. The Freeman family operated the mill until 1864. Eventually, in 1878, the mill was acquired by Frederick Beech Wolcott. He, and later his sons, altered and added to the mill, and between them they ran it for nearly ninety years, until 1967. Today, the Huron-Clinton Metroparks interprets early milling and farm life at Wolcott Mill.

RICHMOND

MB08 Saint Augustine Church

1913, Peter Dederichs. (northwest corner of Main and Howard streets)

Settled by German-Catholic families, Lenox and present-day Richmond remained until the 1930s one town named Lenox. Here Saint Augustine was established as a mission in 1880, and a timber-frame church was built in 1888. The growing number of Catholics in the area necessitated a larger church, and in 1913, under the leadership of the Reverend Edward Schrauder, pastor of Saint Augustine's from 1905 until his death in 1934, the parish began a twenty-nine-year building campaign. Peter Dederichs (1856–1941) of Detroit, a German-born and -trained architect noted for his designs of Catholic churches, schools, convents, and monasteries in Michigan, designed the stone church. The cross-shaped church, with its three-staged twin tow-ers and triple entry, recalls his Saint Mary's Roman Catholic Church, erected in 1885 in Detroit. The low, pointed arch windows resemble the northern Italian Gothic mode. Although Dederichs specified that the buttressed walls of Saint Augustine Church be constructed of the best quality cut stone, instead, they were constructed of cobblestones and fieldstones gathered by the parishioners from their fields. The execution of this high-style design in the locally available material resulted in a delightful vernacular work of architecture that sings native Michigan. A cobblestone rectory of the bungalow type and a school were built adjacent to the church in 1926 and 1930, respectively.

South-Central Border Region

WITH THE OPENING OF THE ERIE CANAL IN 1825, NEW Yorkers and New Englanders migrated westward into Michigan following the early Indian trails. Later, roads and railroads replaced the trails as the migration routes. Settlers took up claims, cleared land, and cultivated it into some of the state's best farms. They transformed the wilderness of the hardwood forests and grassland prairies into replicas of the communities they had known in the East. The gently rolling hills and dales of the south-central border counties became a region of frontier farms and villages.

The architectural character of the countryside of south-central Michigan reflects the background and traditions of these eastern settlers. Settlers came from New York State and New England, sometimes by way of the Western Reserve. As soon as the settlers had raised crops for cash and improved the transportation and communication systems to the East, they began to involve themselves in local government and started in the 1830s and continued into the 1850s to build plain, Greek-inspired homes and churches. The Greek Revival style served equally well for inns, mills, and public and government buildings. The examples range from simple expressions of the temple front with side wings, known as the basilica and seen in the James McAllaster House at Tecumseh, to the coursed cobblestone upright with side wing evidenced in the Nathaniel Wheeler House near Onsted, to the stately temple-front mansion of Jabez Fitch with its giant Ionic portico in Marshall. A remembrance of the eastern prototype and the illustrated builders' guides, especially by Minard Lafever and Asher Benjamin, inspired Michigan builders. After the Greek Revival, Andrew Jackson Downing championed the Gothic and Italian Villa. Those styles, together with the Gothic Revival, the Italianate, the Round Arch mode (or *Rundbogenstil),* and other architectural styles came into favor, and fine examples are found in the South-Central Border Region.

After the cessation of Indian titles, the Legislative Council of the Territory of Michigan set off Lenawee County in 1822, and, in 1829, another group of counties that make up both the first and second tiers, including Jackson, Hillsdale, Branch, and Calhoun. Lenawee County was organized in 1826, Jackson County in 1832, Branch and Calhoun counties in 1833, and Hillsdale County in 1835. Village greens with courthouse squares re-created the physical ambience that the settlers had known in the East: evidence of the New England square remains at Jonesville, although the seat of county government was moved to Hillsdale. At Hillsdale, standing in place of the early Greek Revival courthouse is the grand Renaissance Revival Hillsdale County Courthouse built of local light yellowish brown sandstone.

Early Michigan residents sought to establish commercial ties with the East, and transportation routes were essential to their success in that endeavor. In 1825 they won the authorization of the federal government for the survey for a road from Detroit to Chicago. In 1827 an appropriation of federal funds made construction possible. The development of other corridors followed, many of which are still in use as interstate highways. Three of the six important railroad lines that traversed the Lower Peninsula crossed the counties of the South-Central Border Region, and they connected the area to the Eastern markets. Branches, or feeders, spread over and interlaced the area. First, in 1836, the Erie and Kalamazoo Railroad was built from Toledo to the Kalamazoo River, through Blissfield and Adrian; later, the Lake Shore and Southern Michigan; and still later, in the early 1840s, the Michigan Central Railroad, reached from Monroe to Adrian, Hillsdale, Jonesville, and Jackson. Numerous branches operated as feeders to the main trunk.

Towns developed at crossroads, at points where trails crossed rivers, and where inns and taverns served and sheltered travelers. Jonesville, for example, grew up where the Saint Joseph River and the Chicago Road meet. Later towns, such as Hillsdale, Jackson, Adrian, and Battle Creek, flourished at shipping points for grain, livestock, and produce. Towns were also settled and flourished where waterpower was available. On the River Raisin, power mills were located at Blissfield, Adrian, Tecumseh, and other sites; in the Saint Joseph Valley, they were located at Jonesville, Litchfield, Hillsdale, Union City, and Coldwater; on the Kalamazoo River, mills could be found at Homer, Albion, Marshall, and Battle Creek.

The New England Yankees brought with them the Puritan reformist spirit and expressed it in such movements as the abolition of slavery, temperance, women's rights, dietary reform, utopian socialism, and new schemes of education: they built churches, colleges, sanitariums, and institutes. Baptists founded Hillsdale College in 1855, previously Michigan Central College at Spring Arbor in 1844. Methodists established Adrian College in 1859. Methodist Episcopali-

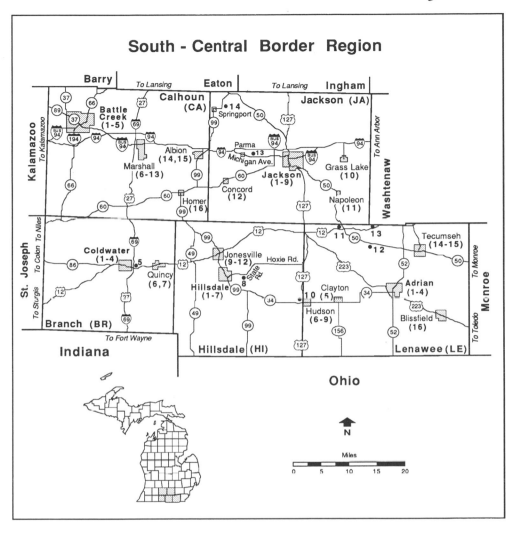

ans planned Albion College in 1833. It was chartered in 1835 as Spring Arbor
Seminary and was moved to Albion in 1839. Seventh-Day Adventists established the Western Health Reform Institute, a hydropathic and dietary cure
institute, in 1866 at Battle Creek (and in 1876, under John Harvey Kellogg, it
became Battle Creek Sanitarium). Quaker and abolitionist Laura Haviland (b.
1806), with her brother Harvey, founded Raisin Institute (1837), Michigan's
first college to admit blacks and women.

Architects with national reputations—Clas and Ferry, Weary and Alford, Albert Kahn, and Hellmuth, Obata and Kassabaum, Inc.—worked in the South-
Central Border Region. While most of the major works of architecture were
designed by architects from Detroit and Toledo, or from the cities of the region, the majority of residential and commercial buildings was designed and

executed by carpenter-builders like C. F. Matthes of Adrian and Marcellus H. Parker, Ebenezer Saxton, and Asbury W. Buckley of Coldwater.

Today, Marshall is a textbook example of historic preservation and civic pride. Battle Creek and Jackson are midsized cities, but the small-town, rural character of the region is retained in Grass Lake, Napoleon, Parma, Hudson, Quincy, Jonesville, and elsewhere.

Jackson County   (JA)

JACKSON

Jackson was settled at the intersection of the Grand River and an Indian trail. People built gristmills on the river, the state opened a prison in 1838, and the Michigan Central Railroad arrived in 1841. By 1871 Jackson was a major railroad junction, with shops and yards and a manufacturing center. Offices and stores are located along Michigan Avenue downtown, and residential areas of large houses are northwest and south of the center of the city.

JA01 **Jackson District Library** (Jackson Public Library)

1903–1906, Ferry and Clas. 244 West Michigan Ave.

Ferry and Clas, creators of the grand, classical Milwaukee Public Library and Museum (1895–1899), won the design competition for the Jackson Public Library, and Andrew Carnegie funded its construction with a gift of $70,000. The result is one of Michigan's most impressive Beaux-Arts Classical libraries. A broad central staircase leads to an elaborate front entrance located in the slightly recessed central part of the symmetrical limestone facade. Six engaged Ionic columns in antis, the central two pairs coupled, screen the recess and support the modillioned cornice that encircles the structure's front and sides. The entry, with its console-supported crown, opens into a central lobby finished with a terrazzo floor inlaid with a grapevine border. Marble wainscoting defines the space, and the open staircase has marble treads. Other interior finishings include hardwood floors, and in the main reading room, a glazed brick fireplace with a Georgian-inspired, pedimented mantlepiece. Here, too, is a metal staircase that leads to the mezzanine stacks.

JA02 **Michigan Theatre**

1929–1930, Maurice H. Finkel. 124 North Mechanic St.

On its opening on April 30, 1930, "This new Spanish Palace of delicate beauty" was heralded by the *Jackson Citizen Patriot* as bringing to Jackson a "new Temple of entertainment." An outstanding feature of Jackson's Michigan Theatre is its terracotta-clad facade, which is one of the finest examples of a movie theater facade in Michigan. Over three stories high, it consists of a balustrade above the entrance, four arches springing from Churrigueresque columns, corbel tables, and arcading. Gold, green, and blue terracotta shields, diamonds, and swags add dynamism to the cream-colored Art Deco exterior. A hexagonal tower literally crowns the building.

The floor plan of the Michigan Theatre is L-shaped, a common space-saving design that allowed the auditorium to be sited on a different axis from the lobby and entrance, an accommodation to its shallow downtown lot.

The Michigan Theatre is a monument to the indecision that gripped the movie industry and theater design at the end of the golden age of the movie palace. Because sound had been installed in almost every motion picture theater by 1930, theater design changed. After 1930, even smaller theaters were built with the capactiy to carry sound. In the *Architectural Forum* for November 1929, Clifford Swann advocated the elimination of curved surfaces and protruding plaster because they interfered with the speakers. Sparse, low-relief plaster ornamentation in Art Deco style, or no ornamental plaster at all, was the common decorative practice. Perhaps silent movies had robbed the patrons of their aural senses, and to compensate, the visual senses had been overburdened with decoration.

In 1930 motion picture exhibitors were un-

Jackson

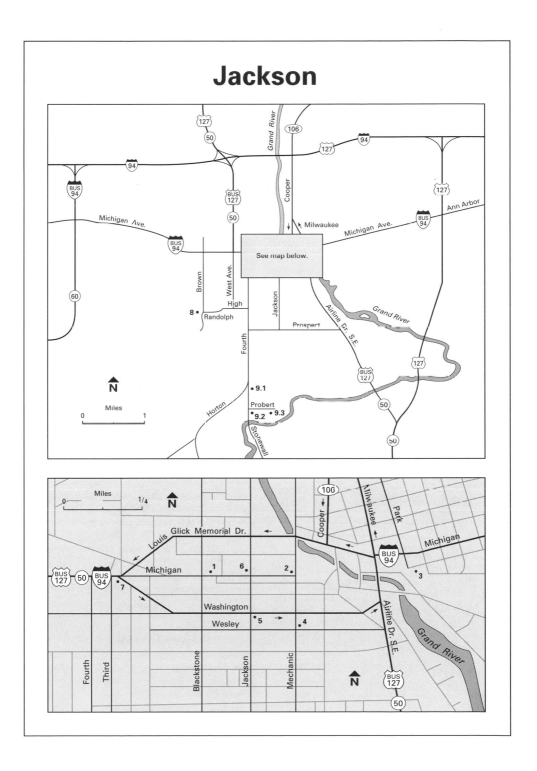

certain if sound motion pictures would last, if vaudeville would revive, or if legitimate theater would become popular again. The low-relief, Art Deco interpretation of Spanish Renaissance plaster ornamentation on the interior of the Michigan Theatre conformed to Clifford Swann's guidelines; the size of the auditorium, with its seating capacity of over two thousand patrons, was consistent with the standards of the golden age of the movie palace, and the stage facilities were large enough to accommodate the rebirth of vaudeville and legitimate theater. The Michigan Theatre stood at the crossroads of technological and design changes. Significantly unaltered but not fully restored, the Michigan still embodies the uncertainties of the movie and entertainment industry.

JA03 **Jackson Amtrak Station** (Jackson Depot of the Michigan Central Railroad / Jackson Union Depot)

1873–1874, H. P. Gardner. 501 East Michigan Ave.

In 1841 the railroad reached Jackson. In the early 1870s, when Jackson was Michigan's third largest city, the Michigan Central locomotive car and repair shops were moved here. In 1874 the outmoded frame passenger depot was replaced by this brick edifice, designed by a Michigan Central master builder. When the depot opened, it was the largest and the finest on the road between Detroit and Chicago, and it visually proclaimed Jackson's role as the rail center for southern Michigan.

The elongated, single-story, red-brick Italianate structure on a cut stone foundation held men's and ladies' waiting rooms and a restaurant trimmed with black walnut, ash, and oak. Two-story, hipped-roof blocks at the ends of the structure contained offices and baggage rooms. Shed roofs supported by cast-iron pillars sheltered passengers at the street and track sides of the depot. Amtrak restored and rehabilitated the depot in 1978 and 1984–1985 for use as a station and offices.

JA04 **Saint Mary Star of the Sea Church**

1923–1926, Frederick Spier. Northeast corner East Wesley and South Mechanic streets

This hammer-dressed limestone, Romanesque Revival church with campanile towers and transepts is a monumental, somewhat classicized rendering of the Romanesque that is reminiscent of the earlier German *Rundbogenstil*. Stained-glass windows manufactured by the Tyrolese Art Glass Company, Innsbruck, Austria; mosaic stations of the cross; mosaics on the apse illustrating Saint Mary Star of the Sea; Carrara marble altars and communion rail; and ornamental wall painting all combine to decorate the rich interior. The church, which cost $375,000, was designed by Frederick Spier of Detroit, once partner in the firm of Spier and Rohns, whose reputation throughout southern Michigan was based on the fine churches and railroad stations it designed in the 1880s and 1890s.

JA05 **Saint Paul's Episcopal Church**

1850–1852, Calvin N. Otis. 1865, 1888, additions. 1898, parish house. 1965, Sunday school. 309 South Jackson St. (southeast corner South Jackson St. and West Washington)

In a manner contrary to the Ecclesiological doctrine, which governed the design of most Episcopal churches in the second half of the nineteenth century, Saint Paul's Episcopal church is Romanesque rather than Gothic. In fact, it is one of Michigan's earliest churches in that mode. In 1851, Saint Paul's sold its old, forty-pew church built by Lemuel S. House to the Free Will Baptist Society. The vestry adopted plans for a new church prepared by Calvin N. Otis of Buffalo, New York. The church is a major work of Otis, who seems to have been a pioneer architect in the Midwest. It is an orangish tan brick structure on a native sandstone foundation, with helmeted square towers at the corners of the west-facing facade. Round-arch windows set within corbeled panels pierce the walls. Hubbell and Langdon built the church in 1850–1852 for a cost of $6,100. There were later additions.

JA06 United Church of Christ (First Congregational Church)

1859–1860, Horatio N. White. 1870, 1871, additions. 120 North Jackson St. (northwest corner West Michigan Ave. and North Jackson St.)

Founded as a Presbyterian congregation in 1841 by thirteen members under the Reverend Marcus Harrison of New York, the church was almost immediately reorganized as a Congregational Church and Society. This followed difficulties arising from the administration of discipline and the passage of a pro-slavery resolution by the Presbyterian Assembly at Philadelphia in 1840. The congregation's second house of worship is another early church in the Round Arch mode, or, as it was then called, the "Norman Gothic." The plans for the First Congregational Church were created by Horatio N. White of Syracuse, New York. Built in 1860 by James Morwick, also of Syracuse, the brick church with asymmetrical towers is located on the only surviving quadrant of the old Jackson town square. Its exterior walls are corbeled and buttressed. In a typical Congregational manner, the austere interior is arranged with three aisles before a central pulpit. There were additions in 1870, and in 1871 the church was raised 8 feet to accommodate parlors, classrooms, and a kitchen.

JA07 The Ionia

by 1915, Claire Allen?. 509–519 West Michigan Ave. (southeast corner West Michigan Ave. and Third St.)

Alternating pedimented half-timbered and shaped Flemish gables adorn the fronts of this row of five attached dwellings, giving

JA07 The Ionia

individuality to each. The row houses are constructed of variegated Ionia sandstone, after which the group of residences was probably named. Jackson architect Claire Allen, who resided at No. 515 at the time of his death in 1942, probably designed the structure. The variation in individual units interestingly resembles that of Summit Terrace (1889) at 587–601 Summit Avenue in Saint Paul, Minnesota.

JA08 The Cascades (Cascades Fountain and Sparks Foundation County Park)

1931–1932, Ronald E. Sargent, engineer. Southwest corner of Brown Rd. and Randolph St.

The Cascades is a spectacular hillside display of sixteen artificial waterfalls and of paired fountains in three oval reflecting pools. These are bathed with changing, multicolored lights synchronized to music and are flanked by three sets of wide steps. Inspired by the water fountains of Barcelona, Spain, William Sparks, industrialist and Jackson mayor, created them with the help of engineers from the Sparks-Withington Company. Mr. and Mrs. Sparks formed the William and Matilda Sparks Foundation, Inc., to develop the swampy bog land west of their home into a recreation spot. They hired the American Park Builders of Chicago to build a golf course, the Cascades, and a Neo-Tudor clubhouse. The county acquired the entire 465-acre park in 1943, and it is Jackson's most famous popular cultural attraction.

JA09 **Stonewall Road**

Between Horton and Probert roads

The road is named for the half-mile-long stone wall that George Brown, a freed black from Vermont, skillfully laid without mortar for Dwight Merriman in 1863. (It won a Michigan Agricultural Society award in 1869.) The road runs along the spine of Jackson's most prestigious twentieth-century residential section. Many of its huge period revival houses, which rival the earlier houses on West Michigan Avenue, were built to the plans of Jackson architect Forrest A. Gildersleeve (d. 1977) for Jackson's prosperous industrialists and businessmen.

JA09.1 **Ella Sharp Museum** (Hillside Farm)

1840s, 1857. 1967–1968, Peter F. Hurst Planetarium. 1968, Exhibition Gallery. 1987, Mildred I. Hadwin Center, Dabbert and Fleming. 3225 Fourth St.

This community cultural complex is made up of a nineteenth-century farmhouse, historic buildings moved onto the grounds, and an art center (Mildred I. Hadwin Center), a planetarium (Peter F. Hurst Planetarium), and a gallery (Exhibition Gallery) that date from the twentieth century. They stand in a park setting on the Hillside Farm site. The site was acquired by Abraham Wing of Glens Falls, New York, in 1855, and passed through the Dwight Merriman Family to their daughter Ella Sharp (1857–1912). Within a short time the Merrimans and Sharps expanded the farm to over 600 acres of pastures and meadows and developed its reputation for its dairy and livestock herds and its orchards. Additions were wrapped around the north and west sides of the farmhouse. The house was then crowned with a three-story, Italianate tower topped with a belvedere, to form the appearance of the present-day museum.

JA09.2 **M. P. Patton House**

1938, Forrest A. Gildersleeve. 3801 Stonewall Rd. (southeast corner of Probert and Stonewall roads)

Striving for historical accuracy, Jackson architect Forrest A. Gildersleeve familiarized himself with the architecture of Colonial Williamsburg and created this Colonial Revival design. The symmetrical two-stage hipped-roof main building is at right angles to the one-and-a-half-story connected dependency.

The chimneys, the nine-over-nine windows, the pedimented door with a surround of fluted Ionic pilasters, and the dormers reveal attention to correctness and add to the authenticity of the design. The red brick walls are laid in Flemish bond.

JA09.3 **Stone Village**

1881–c. 1900. 1701 Probert Rd.

This complex has twelve interrelated, towered, and turreted farm buildings, the largest being a mammoth, 18,000-square-foot barn. It includes a main house, a tenant house, a creamery, a swine barn, and other buildings. Immigrant English stonemasons, under the supervision of Frank Haehnle, built the structures of cut fieldstone. The farm was established in 1881 by Theodore G. Bennett, operator of Jackson's first foundry; it was acquired in 1896 by Herbert Probert, who completed and operated it until 1942 as a dairy farm; and it was converted to an art and theatrical center by the Townsend Beaman family some time in the 1960s. Open to public.

GRASS LAKE

JA10 **Warren Buckland? House**

1836–1838. 423 East Michigan Ave. (3 miles south of I-94)

This four-columned, temple house with a wing is one of several good examples of Greek Revival houses found in Grass Lake. The community was settled on the south shore of Grass Lake in 1829–1830 by people from New York State and New England. They probably borrowed plans from house pattern books such as Minard Lafever's *Modern Builder's Guide* (New York, 1833), which enjoyed widespread circulation in the nineteenth century. Local Michigan builders freely modified the printed source. The Buckland house has a two-story, tetrastyle, Ionic pedimented portico, is flanked by a single, one-story, west wing with square piers and by an east porch, also with square piers. Restrained Greek architectural details are employed in the window surrounds and are more pronounced on the door trim framing a transom light over the doorway. The wood-frame house has a flush-board front facade (in which boards are laid with flush joints), with clapboard on the sides and rear.

NAPOLEON

JA11 Jude's Quarry

1830s to present.

On the south side of Austin Road at the east edge of Napoleon is a sandstone quarry, known today as Jude's quarry, opened in the Marshall sandstone formation and operated by pioneer settlers. William S. Blackmar (b. 1814), a pioneer from Wales, Erie County, New York, together with Abram F. Bolton and a Mr. Goodwin, located, opened, and began operating the Napoleon quarry about the time this agricultural community was set tled, in 1832. Later the quarry was owned and operated by Morgan Case and William Allen. The durable greenish yellow sandstone furnished the building material for many of Napoleon's own structures and was shipped as far as Monroe.

JA11.1 William? Allen House

c. 1845. 325 Nottawasepee St.

At the quarry's edge, the Allen house is a vernacular, symmetrical, two-story cottage built of coursed Napoleon sandstone blocks on the two primary walls and of uncoursed sandstone rubble on the remaining walls.

CONCORD

JA12 William F. and Mary Granger Goodwin House

1850s, James W. and Russell H. Hungerford, builders. 214 Homer St.

Born at Canandaigua, New York, William Goodwin (1812–1896) immigrated to this general farming community on the Kalamazoo River in 1845. Here he operated a mill and mercantile business. He served several terms in the state legislature and senate. In the 1850s distinguished Jackson County builders built this diminutive wooden Greek Revival house for Goodwin and his first wife,

JA12 William F. and Mary Granger Goodwin House

Mary Granger, on the south bank of the river near his mill. The hipped roof of the single-story, cube-shaped house is topped with a square belvedere that contains a single room with windows on all four sides. The main entrance to the house is recessed behind the flush-boarded front wall and is surrounded with side and transom lights. It is sheltered by a porch that runs across the front and that is supported by square Doric piers. Only a handful of little Greek Revival houses with a room at the top were built in south-central Michigan. They are unique to the region. Another is the Alfred and Ruth Eames Paddock House (1843) at 317 Hanover Street.

PARMA VICINITY, SANDSTONE TOWNSHIP

JA13 Caleb M. and Mary S. Chapel House

1845–1850. 8340 East Michigan Ave. (2.25 miles east of Parma)

This house illustrates the National phase of Neoclassicism, a term developed by William Pierson, Jr., and the spread of the Greek Revival style to the Midwest and its adaptation there. The upright and double-wing house was constructed of grayish greenish yellow Parma sandstone quarried on the property by New England Yankees, thirteen years after they had arrived in the Michigan Territory. Coursed, 18-inch-thick, hammer-dressed, and tooled ashlar blocks for the front facade, irregular coursed rubble for the side walls, and uncoursed rubble for the rear wall exemplify the concern for the appearance of the facade. The formality of that facade, however, is modified by the asymmetrical placement of the door and by different treatments for the two flanking wings.

Classical architectural details include side lights flanking the main entrance, which has fluted pilasters supporting an entablature, fluted Doric porch columns, and interior trim. In the pediment formed by the central gable and returns is another classical reference, albeit Roman, in a hand-carved relief of Diana, the Roman goddess of the hunt, identified by the incised letters "Diana." "Caleb M. Chapel June 1850" and in smaller letters, the name of Chapel's wife, "Mary S. Chapel," are also inscribed above the main entrance. The first occupants migrated from Genesee County, New York, in 1832.

SPRINGPORT TOWNSHIP

JA14 Stephen Crawford Farm

1837 and later. 12351 Crawford Rd. (1.5 miles east and 2.5 miles north of Springport, southwest of intersection of Michigan 99 and Michigan 50, on northwest corner of Eaton Rapids [Michigan 99] and Crawford roads)

The Crawford farm has been in the family since 1837, the year of Michigan's statehood, when the 80 acres on which the Crawford farm buildings are now sited were granted by the federal government to Stephen Crawford of Coos County, New Hampshire. Crawford consolidated his claim to the property by constructing a log house. Family records note that it burned and was replaced by another log house. The remains of this second structure may be the ruins to the north of the farmhouse.

As the farm prospered, Crawford was granted an adjacent 40 acres to the south, in 1848. A farmhouse of wood-frame construction replaced the log house. It, in turn, was replaced in 1883 by the present Victorian farmhouse that was constructed of brick manufactured locally in Brooklyn by Crawford's son Allen. The older frame house was moved across Crawford Road, became the property of Allen Crawford's eldest son Orion, and has been modified substantially.

A story in the *Jackson Citizen Patriot* of May 29, 1924, states that since the death of her husband Stephen (the youngest son of Allen Crawford), Mrs. Flossie Crawford had operated the now 170-acre farm "with more than ordinary success." It goes on to note, "Approved modern methods are in use, and the surroundings are kept in shipshape condition. No specialization is engaged in on her farm, Mrs. Crawford says, general farming being the rule. A registered Holstein bull heads a fine herd and there is good average production of grains and fruits."

The barn located to the southwest of the house is a three-level bank barn that was converted to a carriage house at the turn of the century, when the big barn to the south was built. The earth berm on the north side insulated the lower level against the chilling north winds. Doors open out at this lower level to the animal yard on the south, placed to capture the sun's warmth during the long, cold winters. The second level was used for threshing, winnowing, and tool storage, and as a granary. On the third level were mows for storing hay and hay chutes to the lower levels. The foundation is of random rubble stone from the land; the structure is timber-framed, doweled, and mortise-and-tenon joined; and the gable roof is shingled.

The big red barn south of the farmhouse was built at the turn of the century. It has the billowing gambrel roof so familiar to Michigan barn observers and in size and configuration is an excellent example of the typical Michigan big barn. Its gambrel roof increases its volume appreciably and provides more storage for hay and straw in the loft than a gable roof.

Several of the ancillary structures associated with Michigan family farming for local and regional markets, such as the chicken coop, the pig pen, the windmill, and the water pump, still exist on the Crawford farmstead and are visible from Crawford Road. The old sheep barn, the pump room, the corn cribs, and the original fencing of the animal yards unfortunately have not survived the ravages of time and have disappeared from the farmstead.

Lenawee County (LE)

ADRIAN

Adrian was founded on the River Raisin in 1826 by Addison J. Comstock, who, with his father, Darius, projected the construction of the Erie and Kalamazoo Railroad from Toledo to Adrian. The county seat was moved from Tecumseh to Adrian in 1838. All of the buildings listed for this town are on or on streets intersecting Main Street (Michigan 52).

LE01 Lenawee County Courthouse

1884–1886, E. O. Fallis and Company. 1973 to present, restoration. 309 North Main St. (Michigan 52) (bounded by North Main, West Front, North Winter and East Maple streets)

After the old county courthouse burned in 1852, the county government operated out of temporary quarters. In 1884 voters approved the expenditure of $50,000 for the present building, located on a city block at the edge of the downtown business district. Edward O. Fallis (1851–1927) of Toledo, Ohio, prepared plans for the Romanesque Revival structure. Fallis had apprenticed and worked

with Charles C. Miller in that city, had traveled to Spain and Italy, and enjoyed a reputation as a specialist in courthouse design. A heavy central tower with Baroque details over the crossing of the roof dominates this building in a manner similar to the Romanesque churches of Europe. Gable-roofed pavilions project from all four sides of the large, hipped-roof courthouse built of orangish red Zanesville, Ohio, brick, light yellowish tan Stony Point sandstone, and Monclova sandstone. The pedimented and arched entrance pavilion has a large fanlight on the second floor. The building is richly encrusted with red terracotta fascia and panels, some of which are sculptural reliefs of Law, Liberty, Justice, the Goddess of Agriculture, and the celebrated local Indian chief, Tecumseh. There are also brick corbeling, blue and green tile work, and polished granite columns. The interior is finished with carved pine, mosaic floors, and lively ironwork. Allen and Van Tassel of Ionia constructed the building. As outstate Michigan's most opulent nineteenth-century courthouse, the Lenawee County Courthouse says something about the prosperity of this southern agricultural county.

LE02 Clark Memorial Hall (Adrian Independent Order of Odd Fellows Hall)

1887–1888, Beck and Vogt, builders. 120–124 South Winter St. (northwest corner of South Winter and Pearl streets)

In 1845 the Independent Order of Odd Fellows Lodge No. 8 was established by nine Adrian men. Among them was Elihu L. Clark (1811–1880), who had come to Adrian from New York State in 1836 to open a dry goods business. Eventually he became president of the Lenawee County Savings Bank. On his death Clark left $10,000 to the Adrian Lodge, half of which was to be used for the construction of a building for a meeting hall, lodge, and community rooms. In 1888 the building committee authorized the local firm of Beck

LE02 Clark Memorial Hall (Adrian Independent Order of Odd Fellows Hall)

ence for Beaux-Arts Classical architecture then in vogue in Eastern cities. Theirs was designed by Paul O. Moratz of Bloomington, Illinois, and was built by C. Fred Matthes of Adrian at a cost of $45,000. The mass of tan brick trimmed with red sandstone juxtaposes a semicircular medieval chevet and an octagonal conical-roofed tower, intersecting shaped gables, and round-arch recessed entrances. The first floor, Ionic-columned, semicircular rotunda contains the book delivery area and connects the east and north entrances to a semicircular reading room. A spacious, 125-seat auditorium is on the second floor. An oak leaf and acorn motif is carved in the sandstone of the entrance surround, the capitals of the piers supporting the entrance arch, and the oak newel post of the main interior staircase.

LE04 Burnham Historical Building
(George L. Bidwell House)

1860s. 204 East Church St. (southeast corner East Church and State streets)

Overlooking Broad Street, once Adrian's premier residential thoroughfare, and fronting the pleasant Dennis and State streets residential district is the largest, finest, and most exuberant Italianate house in town. The large brick cube is topped with an ornately bracketed, low-pitched, hipped roof and culminates in a belvedere. A scalloped cornice echoes the round-arch motif of the single and triple windows and of the balustraded bay windows and balcony. A one-bay, fluted, Corinthian-columned front porch adds to the Italianate splendor. George Bidwell (1819–1889), a hardware and dry goods merchant who came from Colbrook, Connecticut, and Livingston County, New York, arrived in Michigan in 1836 and had the house built in the 1860s. The house speaks the boisterous language of a self-confident and ambitious client at a dynamic moment in time. Open to public.

and Vogt to erect Clark Memorial Hall. The two-and-a-half-story, reddish orange brick building, now painted white and gray, is distinguished by its fancy Italianate front and a mansard roof. The tripartite front facade is notable at the second story, with a center triple round-arch window flanked by double round-arch windows. Galvanized and cast-iron columns, cornices, a balcony, and a pediment manufactured locally by the Adrian Brick and Tile Machine Company adorn the front. Two stores still occupy the street level; the main lodge hall, with a 16-foot ceiling, stained-glass windows, and original furniture, occupies the second floor.

LE03 Lenawee County Historical Society
(Adrian Public Library)

1907–1909, Paul O. Moratz. 110 East Church St. (corner of Dennis and East Church streets)

The Adrian Public Library was established in 1888 by the combined Ladies' Library Association and Central School and was housed in the city hall. When it owned over twenty thousand volumes, the library won a $27,000 Andrew Carnegie grant and a $5,000 appropriation from the city of Adrian that led to the construction of this Richardsonian Romanesque building. The Adrian Public Library board apparently ignored the prefer-

CLAYTON

LE05 Reuben Bird House

1837, Robb Brothers, builders. 3624 State St.

This inn has the center entrance, two stories, and one-room depth typical of the I-house.

A two-story porch runs along its entire length, articulated by six piers on each floor. This feature is characteristic of a building type that Talbot Hamlin notes in *Greek Revival Architecture in America* (1944) was built in southern Michigan, where few survive, after prototypes found occasionally in New England, Pennsylvania, Ohio, and Tennessee. Reuben Bird (1811–1885) reportedly came from Connecticut to the Michigan Territory and bought the inn while it was under construction by the Robb Brothers.

HUDSON

LE06 West Main Street

1854–1891. West Main St. (Michigan 34), between Howard and Market streets

Hudson's location on the Tiffin River and the subsequent arrival of the railroad assured the town's growth, and the stores along West Main Street became the trading center for the surrounding farms. The architecture of the stores and the business blocks, built between 1854 and 1891, is visually linked by the dominance of round-arch windows, bracketed cornices, and reddish orange brick building material. Much of the brick was produced at a local brick and tile manufacturing company, where, according to the 1869 *Hudson City Directory,* Joseph McKenzie employed a patented brick machine.

LE06.1 Meyer's Department Store

1880s. 304 West Main St. (Michigan 34) (northwest corner of West Main and North Church streets)

In Hudson the stores were designed with as much care as the houses. The architects and craftsmen who erected the town's buildings often used designs and details from architectural pattern books. The design for the arcuated brick cornices in this block and those in the Arcade Block at 215–217 West Main Street were from M. F. Cummings and C. C. Miller's *Architecture. Designs for Storefronts, Suburban Houses, and Cottages . . .* (1865), published in Troy, New York, the town from which several of Hudson's early settlers came. The eight-light, sashed windows with circular architraves are the most intricate in the downtown area. The round-arch form of brick commercial building was found throughout

the country during the second half of the nineteenth century.

LE06.2 Hudson Masonic Temple

1891. 314–316 West Main St. (Michigan 34)

An exuberant and unaltered galvanized and cast-iron facade purchased from a manufacturer of storefronts distinguishes this two-and-a-half-story brick building. Manufacturers of metal fronts advertised them as being more elaborate than masonry fronts and at a fraction of their cost. Pedimented paired oriel windows ornamented with diamond-pressed panels, swags, medallions, and roping are separated by engaged pilasters in the pressed metal design of the upper story. Cast-iron pilasters, dentils, and sills were installed in the first-floor front. The style of this front is Queen Anne, which has classical elements, and is also called Eastlake. It is one that abounds in California, where it is always painted.

LE06.3 B. F. Steiger–N. J. Holmes Building

1891. 305–307 West Main St. (Michigan 34)

A galvanized iron front, related to, but even more elaborate than that of the Masonic temple, graces the B. F. Steiger–N. J. Holmes

Building. It probably was purchased from George L. Mesker and Company of Evansville, Indiana. Mesker's 1904 catalog of iron storefronts boasted, "With our system of marking each piece, our details and descriptions, any carpenter can set our fronts and make a first class job, at a cost of one-half the cost of setting the front of any other manufacturer." In this case, finials and parapets with an inscription identifying the two owners top the cornice of the paired oriel-windowed facade. The largest galvanized front in Michigan is on the Chippewa Hotel on Mackinac Island, installed around 1904 by George L. Mesker and Company for George T. Arnold. Note the round-arch commercial buildings on either side of the Steiger-Holmes building.

LE07 Sacred Heart Roman Catholic Church

1905–1906, Harry J. Rill. 207 South Market St. (northeast corner of South Market and Mechanic streets; South Market St. intersects West Main St. [Michigan 34] 2 block south of Main St.)

Sacred Heart Roman Catholic Church was founded by the Redemptorist Fathers in the 1850s to serve the more than one hundred Catholic families in the area south of the rolling green Irish Hills. Many were Irish immigrants who arrived as early as 1846 to hack out grain fields from the surrounding timberland. In 1866 they built a Gothic Revival brick church on School Street. Under the energetic leadership of the Reverend Joseph F. Hallissey, and despite opposition from some parishioners, that church was replaced in 1905 with the present church; the cost was $60,000. Harry J. Rill, a recognized church architect of Detroit, designed it. The powerful exterior walls of the large, twin-towered, Romanesque Revival edifice were constructed of fieldstone gathered by parishioners from local farms. Between the towers is a cut-stone triple entry with ringed columns and a central segmental pediment. A conspicuous feature is the impressive three-door classical or Renaissance Revival portal in the center. The single-aisled, barrel-vaulted, 500-seat nave has a basilica plan. Stained-glass memorial windows imported from Munich, Germany, fill its round-arch windows, and a Carrara marble altar is in the sanctuary. (LE08 is just north.)

LE08 Hudson Public Library

1903–1904, Claire Allen. 205 South Market St. (southeast corner of South Market and Fayette streets)

Another of the Carnegie-funded libraries, this small city library was designed in a modified Beaux-Arts Classical style by Claire Allen of Jackson and was constructed of local fieldstone by Koch Brothers of Ann Arbor. The public building in a recognized high style scaled to the size of this city's population delighted the people of Hudson. A parapet and flanking Ionic columns in antis lend focus and a degree of formality to the center entrance with a doorway marked by a Gibbs surround. Two years later, 1905–1906, the brick look-alike Mendon library at 314 West Main Street follows Allen's plans. (LE09 is two and a half blocks south.)

LE09 Gamaliel I. Thompson House

1890–1891, C. Fred Matthes (Christian Frederick Matthes), builder?; John L. Matthes and Company, builder?. 101 Summit St. (southwest corner of Summit and South Market streets)

This exquisite Queen Anne house is one of southern Michigan's finest intact examples of this picturesque style. It stands on a prominent hilltop corner site with an expansive lawn that extends for nearly one block. Pushing out from the core of the wooden structure are a profusion of bay windows, dormers, porches, and balconies, as well as a turret—

all richly decorated with carved and turned posts and with scrolled and sawn trim work, half-timbered panels, and cap board. The interior contains a cherry-paneled library, bronze and glass light fixtures purchased from the Bradley and Hubbard Manufacturing Company of Meriden, Connecticut, and oriental rugs from Hudson and Symington of Detroit. The house was designed and built by the Mattheses of Adrian for Gamaliel Ingham Thompson (1843–1926), who came in 1861 from Fort Anne, Washington County, New York, to Hudson, where he became a banker. The house cost $6,700.

HUDSON VICINITY
(Pittsford Township, Hillsdale County)

LE10 William Treadwell House

c. 1863. 446 North Meridian Rd. (US 127) (.5 mile north of Michigan 34), Pittsford Township, Hillsdale County

Mingling urban and rural life on a 9-acre site on the outskirts of Hudson is the William Treadwell House, one of southern Michigan's finest Italian Villas. In his publications on rural architecture, Andrew J. Downing advocated this style for expressing "the elegant culture and variety of accomplishment of the retired citizen or man of the world."[29] Downing also saw the Italian Villa as the most appropriate form for suburban life. Samuel Sloan's design for an Italian Villa called for a location not "in the depths of the forest, but near some frequented highway within a few miles of the city."[30] A tall campanile

tower gives a powerful accent to the house's composition, which includes hooded round-arch windows, prominent paired brackets throughout, balconies, and bays. Living in this extravagant house remained only a wish for its owner. Before it was finished, William Treadwell, owner of the People's Bank in Hudson, was accused of embezzlement and was later tried and convicted. Although he escaped imprisonment, he never occupied the house and was subsequently murdered by his accomplice.

CAMBRIDGE JUNCTION,
CAMBRIDGE TOWNSHIP

LE11 Walker Tavern

c. 1832. 1978, restoration complete. 13220 Michigan 50 (northeast corner of US 12 and Michigan 50)

Located at the intersection of the Detroit-Chicago Road and the La Plaisance Bay Turnpike, the Walker Tavern was constructed as a farmhouse but evolved into an inn to service travelers journeying along the two roads. In the early nineteenth century, a stagecoach trip from Detroit to Chicago took five days. Other hostelries along the route included Ten Eyck's Tavern in Dearborn and the Eagle Tavern in Clinton. In 1843, five years after they came from Cooperstown, New York, to Lenawee County, inn keepers Sylvester and Lucy Walker purchased the tavern. Under their direction, business prospered, and it became necessary to expand both the tavern and the barns.

The Walker Tavern is a clapboarded, two-story frame building on a cut fieldstone foundation. Built circa 1832, the structure is side gabled with a Federal entrance in the center of the symmetrical facade. The roof is low-pitched. The structure has undergone several enlargements and modifications.

According to evidence yielded in archaeological excavations, it is probable that a large Greek Revival porch was added to the front of the structure by the Walkers. (In 1967 it was removed to accommodate the widening of US 12.) The Walker Tavern soon earned the reputation as "the best west of Detroit." The tavern was more than a stopping place for travelers; it was the social and civic center of the community. Its popularity convinced the Walkers to build a larger brick tavern directly across the road, in 1854.

In 1921, Frederic Hewitt, an Episcopal minister, purchased the Walker Tavern and opened it as a tourist attraction. The state of Michigan acquired the property in 1965 and restored the building to its 1840s condition (but without the porch). In 1978 it opened as a museum at the Cambridge State Historical Park.

ONSTED VICINITY

LE12 Nathaniel S. and Nancy Russ Wheeler House

1840s. 7050 Michigan 50 (3 miles east of Onsted Rd.)

The Wheeler house exemplifies Greek Revival coursed cobblestone architecture transplanted to Michigan by New York settlers. Nathaniel S. Wheeler (1808–1885) came in 1833 from Seneca County, New York, to Cambridge Township, where he cleared and fenced this beautiful, but rocky and hilly, site in Section 24 and where he built barns and sheds and "a very commodious and elegantly finished stone house."[31] The sixteen-inch-thick walls of the end-gable-and-side-wing house are constructed of multicolored stones of assorted sizes, gathered locally, and laid neatly

on the front walls. The other walls are rubble, however, thus acknowledging the importance of the front facade. An inner wall of rubble fieldstone was used for greater stability. Border-etched stone quoins, stone lintels, a recessed front entry with fluted Doric columns in antis (similar to plate no. 80 of Minard Lafever's *The Modern Builder's Guide* of 1833), and an ample cornice and returns finish the house.

TIPTON VICINITY, FRANKLIN TOWNSHIP

LE13 Bauer Manor (Davenport House)

1850s. 1280 US 12 (1.25 miles east of Walter J. Hayes State Park and Michigan 124)

Overlooking Evans Lake in the Irish Hills, Bauer Manor is a rare surviving inn that sheltered travelers on the Chicago Road. Its two-story porch is characteristic of the inns of southern Michigan referred to by Hamlin (see LE05). The inn stands on the site of a log tavern built in the 1830s by Henry W. Sisson. The present building was constructed for John Davenport, probably in the 1850s, and operated as an inn until 1864, when Davenport sold it to Henry Lancaster. The hipped-roof, two-story, wood-frame inn is fronted with a full-height double porch articulated by Doric piers. Although the exterior now has aluminum siding, the interior remains intact. Open to public.

TECUMSEH

LE14 Elijah Anderson House

1832, Elijah and Elisha Anderson, carpenter builders. 1851 and later additions. 401 West Chicago Blvd. (Michigan 50) (northwest corner of West Chicago Blvd. and North Union St.)

This carpenter's interpretation of the Greek Revival is a one-story, wood-frame, clapboard-sheathed house with a balustraded, low-pitched roof topped by a square central belvedere (probably added in 1851). A four-columned, Doric porch with a balustrade shelters the central entrance, which is flanked by side lights and surmounted by a segmental transom. With its balustrade and Doric porch, this house is an elegant example of the one-

LE14 Elijah Anderson House

LE15 James McAllaster House

story Greek Revival house with a one-room attic that is unique in southern Michigan (see JA12, p. 189). This house and the Increase S. Hamilton House (1840), across the street at 402 West Chicago Boulevard, were built by the twin brothers Elijah and Elisha Anderson.

LE15 **James McAllaster House**

1839. 1849, wings added, Horatio Keyser. 501 West Chicago Blvd. (Michigan 50) (northwest corner of West Chicago Blvd. and Van Buren St.)

This house is an example of a variation of the temple front with wings also noted as unique to southern Michigan by Talbot Hamlin in *Greek Revival Architecture in America* (1944). In this characteristic house type of Michigan, Hamlin explains, "The depth of the wings in relation to their width is much increased, and the roofs—either hipped or forming half gables at the junction of the main portion of the house—have the same slope as the main roof, frequently rising to a point just under the main cornice."[32] In the case of the James McAllaster House, Horatio

Keyser, a Tecumseh builder, added in 1849 one-story wings to the one-and-a-half-story, temple-form house. The roofline of the wings has the same slope as that of the main structure and continues unbroken. The projecting wings result in a recessed main entrance that creates an "in antis" plan.

BLISSFIELD

LE16 **Hathaway House** (David Carpenter House)

c. 1851. 424 West Adrian St. (US 223)

This large, two-story house with a tetrastyle, fluted Doric portico stands as testimony to the prosperity of David Carpenter (1815–1891), an upstate New York native who became a Blissfield merchant, land speculator, and money lender, and who shared with his time an interest in the Greek Revival style. Flanking the temple front are the original lower wings, which were later raised to their full, two-story height. Open to public.

Hillsdale County (HI)

HILLSDALE

Settled on the Saint Joseph River in 1832, Hillsdale was incorporated as a city in 1855. It was at the junction of the Ypsilanti, Lansing, and Fort Wayne branch and the Lake Shore and Michigan Southern railroads. Like many southern Michigan villages, Hillsdale grew in the 1840s when the railroad built a station here, when the Baptists established a college in the town, and when the legislature made it the seat of county government. Except where noted, all properties are on streets that intersect Michigan 99.

HI01 Hillsdale County Courthouse

1898–1899, Claire Allen. Bounded by Howell, McCollum, Broad (Michigan 99), and Bacon streets

By 1890 the forty-year-old Greek Revival Hillsdale County Courthouse was aged and cramped for space. So, in 1898 the voters of the county approved the expenditure of $45,000 for a new courthouse. This Georgian Revival design by Claire Allen of Jackson was erected using locally quarried, light yellow brown sandstone from the Marshall formation. The style of the building actually derives from William Chamber Somerset House in England. With its arcaded porch supporting a balustraded, Composite portico; a tall three-stage, domed central clock tower with a cupola; a copper-tiled roof and an interior rotunda finished in paneled oak, it seemed everything a courthouse should be. The plan followed the cross-axis model, in which each of the four county offices occupies space off a rotunda in one of the four corners of the building. David Gibbs established the model for this plan in Ohio and in courthouses for Eaton and Ionia counties in Michigan in the 1880s. As supervisor of construction for the Ionia County Courthouse in 1884–1885, Allen was intimately familiar with this arrangement. In 1903–1904, two years after the Hillsdale County Courthouse was completed, he virtually duplicated it in the Van Buren County Courthouse at Paw Paw. Note the human and lion faces carved in the foliated capitals of the square piers of the arcade.

HI02 Hillsdale City Hall

1911–1913, Edwin A. Bowd. Bounded by North Howell, Broad (Michigan 99), Hillsdale and Carleton streets

After a five-year struggle, Hillsdale city officials succeeded in winning approval for the bonding for this $45,000 building. It is a pentagonal building that conforms to its site. Huge Ionic stone columns front the gray canyon-cut stone and orange Puritan pressed-brick building, which is impressive in its restrained dignity. The scagliola wainscoting and Tennessee marble that line the halls of the interior are still visible, despite a remodeling in 1966; the rotunda was closed off to permit installation of first-floor offices and a second-floor conference room.

HI03 Keefer House Hotel

1885, W. H. Myers and Son, builders. 102–106 North Howell St. (southwest corner of North Howell and North streets, just west of Michigan 99)

H. M. Keefer and Charles E. Keefer (1856–1899) built this three-story brick hotel in a central location and within a minute's walk from the railroad depot. The location was especially attractive for traveling salesmen; fifty-four sleeping rooms and sample rooms were contained above and behind the street-level hotel lobby and commercial space. The fancy, red and yellow, polychromatic brickwork seen in the wall panels, the window hoods, and the corbeled cornice are noteworthy.

HI04 Oscar Hancock House

1880. 5 Reading Ave. (which intersects South St. 4 blocks west of Broad St. [Michigan 99])

This house may be Hillsdale's best example of the "Second Empire" style in residential architecture. The three-story, irregularly massed Italianate house has numerous bay windows and elaborate wood trim, and it is capped by a mansard roof broken by dormers. Elaborate plaster ceiling medallions, butternut floors, and a grand open staircase of walnut decorate the interior. The house was built for Oscar Hancock, a leading Hillsdale grocer.

HI05 Frederick W. Stock House

1905. 3 South Broad St. (Michigan 99) (southeast corner of South Broad and Bacon streets)

Stately with its two-story, semicircular entrance portico supported by giant Ionic columns, this Georgian Revival house, complete with a variant of the Palladian window, belonged to one of Hillsdale's most successful business families. Frederick W. Stock (b. 1825) came to Hillsdale in 1869 and bought a flour mill from Henry Waldron and John P. Cook. In succeeding years, Stock developed his mill at 101 East Bacon Street into the largest soft-wheat flour mill in the city. He also built in 1883 the Litchfield Roller Mills, a huge, rambling, Second Empire structure. By 1900, Frederick Stock and Sons Flouring Mill, known as the Hillsdale City Flour Mills, was the largest flour mill in south-central Michigan. The firm remodeled the mill buildings as needed and supplied them with steam power, improved machinery, a roller system (1882), electricity, and added a grain elevator (1887). The house is adjacent to the mill and was built by Stock's oldest son, August.

HI06 **Hillsdale Grange Hall, Hillsdale County Fairgrounds**

1879. 115 South Broad St. (Michigan 99) (southeast corner of South Broad and South streets)

Grange Hall is the architectural pivot of the Hillsdale County Fairgrounds. The Hillsdale Fair has been held on these grounds on the banks of the Saint Joseph River since 1860. Four trapezoidal cross gables with oculi and elaborate carved bargeboards project from the Second Empire building, and a bracketed and braced cupola tops its mansard roof with a festive air. In this hall, county grange organizations display farm and kitchen products. The building is covered with board-and-batten siding frequently used in the Gothic Revival domestic architecture popularized by Andrew Jackson Downing.

HI07 **Central Hall, Hillsdale College**

1874, Brush and Smith (Henry I. Brush and [Hugh? or Mortimer L.?] Smith). College Ave., between West and Hillsdale streets

Established in Spring Arbor in 1844 by a group of Free Will Baptists as Michigan Central College, the school was moved to Hillsdale in 1853. Hillsdale was more attractive, because it was on the line of the Lake Shore and Michigan Southern Railroad and because its citizens raised $30,000 for buildings. On a hill north of town with a full view of the city and the surrounding countryside five adjoining buildings were erected for Hillsdale College between 1853 and 1854, but most were destroyed by fire in 1874. The trustees then adopted a plan to rebuild five disconnected buildings on the center of the 25-acre, tree-shaded park known as College Hill. Brush and Smith, architects of Detroit, with F. M. Hollowell as the superintending architect, designed Central Hall as the centerpiece of a group of brick buildings that is arranged on three sides of a quadrangle, with the principal front to the south. Central Hall is one of three that remain. (The others are the Fine Arts Hall, on the east and Knowlton Hall on the west.) This glorious Second Empire administration building followed closely the popular style of the time and has a central, attenuated, convex-roofed clock tower, with matching towers at the front corners, that is seen from all directions. Except for its mansard roofs, the main part of the building is Italianate and matches the other surviving buildings that form the group. Slender columns support the porch and also seem to support the colossal pilasters of the central pavilion. H. Richard and G. W. Mickle Builders of Jackson constructed Central Hall.

ADAMS TOWNSHIP

HI08 **William R. and Hannah Sykes Kirby House**

1840s. 377 North State Rd. (2.75 miles east of Hillsdale)

From upstate New York, the Kirbys brought a taste for and knowledge of the coursed cobblestone construction technique and applied it in their Greek Revival farmstead at Hillsdale. Born in Yorkshire, England, William R. Kirby (1805–1888) and his wife, Hannah (1801–1876), came to America in 1827. They settled first in Ogdensburg, New York, but in 1831 moved to Lake County, Ohio.

In 1835, after William Kirby made a land-hunting trip to the area and purchased his lands at the federal land office in Monroe, the Kirbys became the first white settlers in the wilderness near Hillsdale. They put up a small log structure in which they lived until the cobblestone house was built. One of the little more than two dozen remaining from many cobblestone structures that were built in the southern three tiers of counties east of Battle Creek, this house rests on a fieldstone foundation and is constructed of cut field-stone walls faced with a veneer of rounded cobblestones laid in horizontal courses. The quoins and the window and doorway lintels and sills are fashioned of cut yellow sandstone from the Stony Point quarries near Mosher-ville, twelve miles away. The house has a two-story, end-gable main section joined by a one-story wing and rear ell. Greek Revival elements are the ample entablature and returns and the frieze-band windows.

Grace Episcopal Church was constructed by a parish organized by Rev. Darius Barker, formerly of Vermont and New Hampshire. It is a joyous hybrid in style, and as such is typical of numerous rural New England churches of the 1840s: the main body of the church, with its deep entablature, corner pi-lasters, and rectilinear tower, is Greek Re-vival; the large double-lancet windows and pointed-arch entrance, however, are Gothic. These two most unlike styles in western his-tory are thus combined with shameless de-light. Other, grander, examples of this com-bination of Classical and Gothic can be found in the Federated Church of Castleton, Ver-mont, and the Congregational Presbyterian Church in Kinsman, Ohio. Also reminiscent of New England is the fact that the church faces a village park, a park that was the site of the Hillsdale County Courthouse, later de-molished, before the seat of county govern-ment was moved to Hillsdale.

JONESVILLE

Settled around 1830 at a ford in the Saint Joseph River and at its juncture with the Chicago Road, Jonesville was incorporated as a village in 1855.

HI09 Grace Episcopal Church

1844–1848. 360 East Chicago St. (US 12)

HI10 Ebenezer Oliver and Sally Ann Grosvenor House

1874, attributed to Elijah E. Myers. 211 Maumee St. (northeast corner of Maumee and Liberty streets, 3 blocks south of US 12)

This handsome Italianate house is attributed to Elijah E. Myers (1832–1909), architect of the Michigan State Capitol; both structures were completed between 1873 and 1878. The house was constructed for Ebenezer O. Gros-venor and his wife, Sally Ann. Grosvenor was a Jonesville banker who served as a state senator, lieutenant governor, state treasurer, and as a member of the state building com-mission that was responsible for the construc-tion of the new Michigan State Capitol. It is rumored that Grosvenor employed in this residential project some of the workmen and used some of the same suppliers involved in the construction of the capitol. Befitting the stature of its original owners, the house stands on a prominent site. Full-height bays project from three sides of the house in an irregular fashion. The reddish orange brick house is richly trimmed with yellow sandstone window hoods and a wide entablature with brackets and molding. It was equipped with all the latest household conveniences—a furnace, gaslights, large closets, built-in cupboards, and, through the use of an innovative gravity-operated water system, running water and flush toilets. It cost $37,000. Open to public.

HI11 **Munro House** (George C. Munro House)

1842. 202 Maumee St. (southwest corner of Maumee and South streets, 1 block south of US 12)

This chaste Greek Revival house is the oldest brick building in Hillsdale County. The two-story gable front is flanked by two shorter wings with fluted Doric-columned porches. In spite of its rigidly symmetrical massing, however, the entrance is off center to the right of the main pedimented block. A one-story pedimented porch occupies the second floor of the end bay, and an elliptical fanlight pierces the pediment of the central section. The house was built by George C. Munro (b. 1814), operator of a gristmill and general store. Open to public.

HI12 **William Walton Murphy House**

1845–1850, Jonathan B. Graham, construction supervisor. 1911, porch added. 305 West Chicago St. (US 12) (northwest corner of West Chicago and Jermaine streets)

In 1837, the year Michigan achieved statehood, William Murphy came to Jonesville. Migrating from Seneca County, New York, he had spent two years working as the land agent for the federal government in Monroe. In Jonesville he opened a law office and a land agency and within a few years began

HI12 William Walton Murphy House

construction of this symmetrical, two-story, five-bay Greek Revival house with a rear wing. Brick manufactured in nearby Moscow probably furnished the building material. A restrained, fluted Ionic-columned porch adds dignity and formality to this house. The interior contains a ballroom and was fitted with marble fireplaces and fancy plasterwork. The house was the scene of many social events connected with Murphy's career as lawyer, publisher, and statesman. Daniel Webster, Horace Greeley, Theodore Parker, and other notable people visited here.

PITTSFORD TOWNSHIP
(Hudson vicinity)
See LE10, p. 195, William Treadwell House

Branch County (BR)

COLDWATER

The improvement of the Chicago Turnpike between Detroit and Chicago (present-day US 12) from a mere trail to "an overland extension of the Erie Canal" precipitated the platting of Coldwater in 1832 and its incorporation as a village in 1837. Coldwater became the seat of Branch County government in 1842. Growth of the town was stimulated by the opening of the Michigan Southern Railroad in 1850, and it became a city in 1861. Coldwater's prosperity in the nineteenth century was based on agriculture, cigar manu-

facturing, cart and carriage building, the breeding, raising, and sale of fine horses, and the presence, after 1874, of the Michigan State School for Dependent Children. The prosperity of Coldwater is expressed, for example, in the exuberant Italianate Tibbits Opera House, with its convex mansard tower, erected in 1882, but now altered on the exterior beyond recognition.

The city today is noteworthy for its exceptional collection of buildings from the second half of the nineteenth century. The overall excellence of the architecture owes much to local architects and carpenter builders Marcellus H. Parker (1821–1902), Ebenezer Saxton (1833–1907), and Asbury W. Buckley (1846–1924). Parker settled here in 1851 and produced during the 1860s, 1870s, and 1880s many of the city's most important buildings, such as the towered brick Branch County Courthouse, now demolished, and the Italianate Lewis Art Gallery. Saxton and Buckley both worked here later in the 1880s and 1890s. Buckley, who is best known in Michigan for his summer cottages at Mackinac Island, continued to work in Coldwater into the twentieth century, even though he moved to Kalamazoo in 1893 and to Chicago by 1901.

BR01 **Branch County Library** (Edwin R. Clarke Library)

1886, Marcellus H. Parker. 1978–1979, addition and renovation, Graheck, Bell, Kline, and Brown. 12 East Chicago St. (US 12) (southeast corner of East Chicago and Division streets)

Edwin R. Clarke (1828–1900), a prosperous druggist and grocer, immortalized himself in Coldwater with the gift of this library to the city. Marcellus H. Parker of Coldwater designed the cross-gable-roof, corner-towered, brick Queen Anne structure, following the plan by W. F. Poole, librarian of the Chicago Public Library, which was published in the *Library Journal.* Large arched windows allow ample light into the reading rooms. The building was fireproof and well ventilated. In 1979, a large addition planned by Graheck, Bell, Kline, and Brown to complement the original building was completed, and the building was renovated.

BR02 **First Presbyterian Church**

1866–1869, John C. Bennett, contractor. 1958–1959, Calvin Hall Educational Building, Harold Fisher and Associates. 52 Marshall St. (northeast corner of Marshall and Church streets, 1 block north of East Chicago St. [US 12])

The lofty 185-foot-high spired central tower of this large church in the Round Arch mode looms over the city and makes this work the most dominant landmark in Coldwater. The corner piers of the tower and of the prominent building itself were originally marked with pinnacles. Round-arch openings pierce the red brick exterior walls that rise to a corbeled cornice that supports the gabled roof. From the center entrance paired stairs lead up to a plain auditorium trimmed in white oak. It seats 650. Originally three banks of pews were arranged before a raised platform with a centrally placed pulpit and the organ. A curved balcony reached by paired staircases is at the rear. The auditorium was once decorated with frescoes by Anton Mahler of Cincinnati. The windows are of the original stained and painted glass made by George A. Misch and Brothers of Chicago. The First Presbyterian Society built the church in 1866–1869 at a cost of $32,000. The First Presbyterian Church was founded in 1837. It held services in schools and in the county courtroom before completing a wood frame church in 1844. This building was replaced by the present church. At its dedication, *The Coldwater Republican* for October 16, 1869, called the new church "a perfect model of elaborate and substantial workmanship."

BR03 **Frank L. and Ella Van Volkenburg Skeels House**

c. 1886, Ebenezer Saxton. 199 West Pearl St. (southwest corner of West Pearl and Walnut streets, 1 block south of West Chicago St. [US 12])

This large, handsome, wood-frame Queen Anne house, with irregular massing and three levels of Eastlake spindlework porches, was built for Frank D. Skeels (1846–1891), an attorney, and his wife, Ella. It demonstrates the tendency toward greater elaboration in decorative work possible with the availability of machine tools.

BR04 **East Chicago Street Residential Area**

1860–1910. East Chicago (US 12) and East Pearl streets between South Hudson and North Sprague

BR03 Frank L. and Ella Van Volkenburg Skeels House

East Chicago Street was the site of one of Coldwater's early Chicago Road taverns, a stop for travelers, immigrants, and land hunters. The street began to acquire an elegant character even before the Civil War, and it is now one of southern Michigan's best streetscapes of 1860–1910 residential architecture.

BR04.1 John T. and Belle Woodward Starr House

1887, Asbury W. Buckley. 161 East Chicago St. (US 12)

Clapboarding, patterned shingling, half-timbering, pebble dash, and panel brickwork finish the highly textured exterior of this Queen Anne house with its complex composition and unusual corner windows. Despite its modest size, the local newspaper in that year commented that it was surpassed by none in Coldwater "in solidity, in warmth, in convenience or in substantial elegance." John T. Starr (1861–1908), a hardware merchant and real estate speculator, built the house at a cost of $9,000.

BR04.2 Jay Millard Chandler–Lucius Wing House

1875. 27 South Jefferson St. (northeast corner of South Jefferson and East Pearl streets, 1 block south of East Chicago St. [US 12])

Jay Millard Chandler built this Second Empire house for the comfort of his new bride, Frances Campbell Chandler, in the frontier of Michigan in the 1870s. Her childhood home in Montour Falls, New York, reportedly inspired the design. The one-and-a-half-story house stands on a full raised basement, with rusticated brick walls simulating stone. Originally, the basement held the kitchen and dining room. The house is enlivened with porches and is topped with a convex mansard roof sheathed in tin. Open to public.

BR05 Abram C. and Catherine Smith Fisk House

c. 1863. 867 East Chicago St. (US 12) (northwest corner of East Chicago St. and Fiske Rd.; .3 mile east of I-69)

Originally encircled by a trotting track and surrounded by fenced pastures, this belvedere-crowned, cubical brick Italianate house was the centerpiece of Branch County's leading horse farm. (The glass walls and door that enclose the porch are a later modification.) Abram C. Fisk (1815–1897) came to Coldwater from Monroe County, New York, in 1835 and settled this farm in 1840. He brought the celebrated Morgan stallion, Green Mountain Black Hawk, to the county in 1851 and pioneered horse breeding in Branch County. Soon the county's horse breeding was compared to that of Orange County, New York (the county provided three thousand horses to the Union army during the Civil War), and the Fisk farm was regarded as one of the finest homes and barns in the county. The Victorian iron gateway was made by the

E. T. Barnum Ironworks of Detroit. The Chicago Road passed through the center of the property, and Fisk owned 40 acres on either side of it. Fisk's early house, a five-bay, center entrance, Greek Revival building erected around 1840, survives across US 12, at 892 East Chicago Street. It is a simplified vernacular type, once common along the Chicago Road.

QUINCY

When the Chicago Road opened in 1833, Quincy was settled. With the completion of the Lake Shore and Southern Railroad in 1852, the town grew as a shipping point and a service center for the surrounding country.

BR06 Star of the West Milling Company

c. 1915–1925, with later additions. Corner of Church St. and the Hillsdale County Railroad trackage, 1 block north of West Chicago St. (US 12)

Rock-faced concrete block and poured concrete elevators, two- and three-story frame

warehouses, and a crisp, orange brick, International style office building comprise this milling company's complex of buildings. Milling and a portland cement plant formed the economic base of Quincy, a shipping point and service center for the surrounding country.

BR07 Charles Crawford House

1910. 41 North Main St. (northwest corner of North Main and Cole streets, 2 blocks north of Chicago St. [US 12])

Primarily a one-story, vernacular interpretation of the Craftsman style, this hipped-roof fieldstone bungalow was the first of its kind erected in Quincy. The multicolored fieldstones were carefully gathered by the owner and beautifully laid in the walls by Cook and Blair of Hillsdale and Charles McCarthy of Quincy. The living room, dining room, and kitchen are on the south, and two bedrooms and a bath on the north. The *Coldwater Courier* for October 2, 1911, deemed it "one of the coziest and prettiest little homes" in the county, thus fulfilling the expectations of numerous bungalow pattern books of that time.

Calhoun County (CA)

BATTLE CREEK

Settled in 1831, Battle Creek began to develop after 1835, when entrepreneur Sands McCamly built a dam, a power canal, and a sawmill on the Kalamazoo River. The village was platted in 1836 and incorporated as a village in 1850. It became a city in 1859, following the completion of the Michigan Central Railroad (later the Grand Trunk) through town in 1845. The opening in 1873 of a second, competing line, the Chicago and Lake Huron, led to lower freight rates, which, along with other factors, contributed to an industrial boom in Battle Creek.

The Seventh-Day Adventist Church established its national headquarters there in the late 1850s, after residents offered the denomination's founders, James and Ellen White, assistance in setting up their newspaper. The Adventist headquarters and its substantial publishing business remained in the city until around 1902–1903. In 1866 the Adventists

founded the Western Health Reform Institute, a hydropathic and dietary cure institution. Dr. John Harvey Kellogg (1852–1943) took it over in 1876 and reorganized it as the Battle Creek Sanitarium. By 1900 the institution was caring for over one thousand patients and remained in operation into the 1940s.

Battle Creek's reputation as the Cereal City began in 1894 with John H. and W. K. Kellogg's invention of Granose, the first flaked breakfast cereal, and Charles W. Post's development of Postum, a cereal coffee. By 1906, Post was marketing his Grape Nuts and Post Toasties, and W. K. Kellogg's Battle Creek Toasted Corn Flake Company (now simply Kellogg's), its Toasted Corn Flakes. Today, Kellogg's, the Post Division of General Foods, and Ralston Purina all have large plants and grain elevators on Battle Creek's southeast side. Kellogg's is the city's largest employer.

The architectural character of Battle Creek

derives in large part from the presence and benevolence of the Kellogg family, who saw to it that the city was blessed with significant civic buildings. Railroad depots and industrial buildings appeared in response to the needs of the cereal manufacturers, and the sanitariums promoted the cereal products. A fine residential section is in the northeast part of the city.

CA01 Battle Creek City Hall Area

Michigan Ave. (Business I-94) and Division St.

CA01.1 Battle Creek City Hall

1913–1914, Ernest W. Arnold. 103 East Michigan Ave. (Business I-94) (northeast corner of East Michigan Ave. and Division St.)

As Battle Creek grew in response to the expansion of the cereal food industry, the first city hall, a Second Empire structure built in 1867–1868 on the site of the present-day Comerica Tower, seemed inadequate. In 1907, Mayor Charles C. Green appointed a committee to study the matter. A site was chosen by public referendum, and in 1912 the city council selected Ernest W. Arnold as architect for the city hall. Arnold created this large, ponderous, Beaux-Arts Classical monument that harmonizes with the nearby Battle Creek Post Office. The red brick with white limestone and terracotta facade has a five-part composition of a central Ionic portico balanced by two blocklike wings with intermediate recessed connectors. A rusticated ground floor, prominent angle quoins, and a heavy

CA01.1 Battle Creek City Hall; and CA01.2 First United Methodist Church (First Methodist Episcopal Church)

parapet add to the Beaux-Arts image. Heavily enriched Neoclassical plasterwork and stained glass highlight the interior of this newly refurbished structure. The building is a major work for Arnold, designer of numerous Michigan school and institutional buildings.

CA01.2 First United Methodist Church
(First Methodist Episcopal Church)

1907–1908, Wilbur Thoburn Mills. 114 East Michigan Ave. (Business I-94) (at the convergence of East Michigan Ave., Main, and Division streets)

Situated on and conforming to a triangular site once thought to be one of the most beautiful and strategic points in the city, the First United Methodist Church seemed to combine sunny lightness and grace with substantial presence. The building fund campaign for the church began with a $10,000 gift from I. W. Robinson. A steepled brick church erected here in 1858 was moved off the site. Wilbur Thoburn Mills of Columbus, Ohio, created an interesting and original building that uses "style" in a free way. At the time it was planned, it seemed to the *Battle Creek Daily Journal*, "a modification of the old Spanish missions of California and Mexico, adapted to the conditions and uses of a modern church."[33] The church actually has many Romanesque elements. The red tile roof was used frequently by H. H. Richardson. Although the wide overhang suggests Spanish origins, the campanile tower with corner turrets and a balcony is equally Italian. The church contrasts sharply with the Beaux-Arts Classical city hall across the street, especially in its red tile roof, the campanile tower (with a balcony) at the front corner, and the shaped parapet over the entrance. The design borrows its Italian and Spanish theme from the Battle Creek Depot of the Grand Trunk Railroad (1905), designed by Spier and Rohns. On the inside, beneath a lighted dome, the galleried auditorium radiates out from the pulpit; parlors stand beyond the auditorium and the Sunday school classrooms are along the east wall.

CA02 McCamly and Jackson Streets

The focus of today's Battle Creek is the McCamly and Jackson streets intersection, flanked by the Kellogg Company Headquarters on the west and McCamly Place on the east.

CA02.1 Kellogg Company Corporate Headquarters

1983–1986, Hellmuth, Obata and Kassabaum, Inc. 1 Kellogg Square (bounded by South McCamby St., Hamblin, South Washington Ave. [Michigan 37], and West Jackson St.)

The Kellogg Company Corporate Headquarters, established in Battle Creek since 1906, contemplated a move out to Battle Creek Township because it perceived that conflicting tiers of local government were inhibiting growth and that this was in the best interest neither of the city nor of Kellogg's employees. Battle Creek and the township resolved the conflict through the annexation of the township and through grants to Kellogg, which, in turn, agreed to build the $70 million headquarters on an 18-acre downtown redevelopment site.

Kellogg Square, an integral part of the Central Business District master plan adopted by the city, is composed of two mirror-image, orange red, office buildings linked by a glass-sheathed atrium. The five-story mass of the 300,000-square-foot corporate headquarters is broken with setbacks and terraces, producing a personal scale and a strikingly distinctive image. Exterior materials are red brick, cream yellow stone, and pale green glass.

Rows of shade trees line the entry plaza walkway between the headquarters and McCamly Square, a retail-hotel complex. The large, skylit atrium flanked by the brick office blocks is the focal point. In a dramatic cascade of escalators and bridges, the atrium organizes the complex and provides a transition from the urban entry plaza to the more pastoral setting of the building. Large trees, floral plants, sculpture, and fountains fill the soaring, sunlit space.

More public spaces, used for dining, con-ference centers, health management, employment, purchasing, and management development, are assembled at the first level. Upper floors, ranging in size from 25,000 to 30,000 square feet, are assigned to management groups, many of which have access to the dozens of private indoor and outdoor terraces adjacent to office and conference areas. Office floors surrounding the atrium are large and flexible, accommodating today's needs and tomorrow's changes, as well as every aspect of the electronic office.

The comfortable, informal interiors reflect Kellogg's corporate philosophy of emphasizing a strong commitment to people and public health. For example, materials were selected for their ability to contribute a light, warm atmosphere; and panel heights were kept low in order to allow natural light to enter, to provide exterior views, and to maintain an open feeling. Wheat and other grain patterns, emblematic of the corporation and its cereal products, are repeated throughout the building in window treatments, the carpeting, the atrium bridges, and other featured areas. A moving bronze "wheat field" sculpture, designed by the architects, graces the reception area. A mobile sculpture, *Triple 'Excetric Gyratory,* by well-known George Rickey, stands on the rear terrace, overlooking the manmade lake.

CA02.2 McCamly Place

1984–1986, The Collaborative, Inc., Toledo, Ohio. 35 West Jackson St. (Michigan 37) (southeast corner of McCamly and West Jackson streets)

McCamly Place is a bilevel, festival marketplace developed by James Rouse's Enterprise Development Company of Columbia, Maryland. Postmodern, like other Rouse developments, such as the Waterstreet Pavilion in Flint (GS01.5, p. 336) and Portside in Toledo, McCamly Place has a light and airy exterior and a cross-axial interior, focusing on a central atrium space dressed up with Prairie-style motifs. The central space contains a seven-foot-high *Wheat Lady* sculpture, created by Don Brown of Renaissance Design, Birmingham, Michigan.

CA02.3 Battle Creek Intermodal Passenger Facility

1982, William Kessler and Associates. 119 South McCamly (north of the Conrail tracks between Liberty, Hamblin, and McCamly)

This sharply dramatic Post-Wrightian train, bus, and taxi terminal uses contrasts in colors (red, turquoise, white, silver, and black) and shapes (triangles, columns, half circles, and rectangles). It is a low, horizontal gable-on-hip-roof structure of black glazed concrete block, with covered concourses on all sides. Gable-roof canopies, each with a semicircular recess underneath undercoated in Chinese red, shelter the train and bus platforms. Heavy, round, glass block columns lit from within support the canopies and extend around the building at the roof's edge. The waiting room seats are grouped in a circle that is veneered in silver transportation sheet metal.

CA03 **Comerica Tower** (Old Merchants National Bank and Trust Company Tower)

1930–1931, Weary and Alford. 25 West Michigan Mall (just northwest of Michigan 66)

The nineteen-story, 239-foot-high Comerica Tower was designed by Weary and Alford of Chicago, specialists in bank design. Of structural steel and reinforced concrete construction, the Bedford limestone-faced structure has a broad-fronted, four-story base topped by a blocky, stepped tower reminiscent of Eliel Saarinen's rejected Chicago Tribune Tower competition entry. In the tower, panels of low-relief natural and floral (wheat and sunflower) forms, a Weary and Alford trade-

mark, line up with the vertical window bands and further accentuate the verticality of the "pier and grille" system in the design of office towers of the 1920s and 1930s. Inside, on the second floor, the vaulted and domed banking room, 71 by 126 feet in plan, is one of Battle Creek's grandest public spaces. Its travertine walls and floors; its grilles and rails of gray iron and white metal alloys; its ceiling and mural decorations designed by Alexander Rindskopf of Chicago in peach, turquoise, and gold lend a sense of soaring elegance to the room.

CA04 **Capital Avenue northeast (Michigan 66) and Van Buren Street, north of Battle Creek River**

This area is on the edge of the downtown, given over largely to churches and cultural and educational buildings. Five late nineteenth- and early twentieth-century churches cluster along Capital Avenue northeast, between Van Buren and Penn streets.

CA04.1 **Battle Creek Amtrak Station** (Battle Creek Depot of the Michigan Central Railroad / Penn Central Railroad Station)

1887–1888, Rogers and MacFarlane (Gregory? and MacFarland). 55 West Van Buren St. (Michigan 37) (Conrail tracks between Capital Ave. and McCamly)

The solid, low-lying Richardsonian Romanesque Michigan Central Railroad Depot exudes the confidence of a city that had recently achieved a population of nine thousand. Then, in 1887, the Michigan Central Railroad Company discarded its depot on North Monroe Street for this structure of red brick and red Lake Superior sandstone. The Battle Creek depot recalls the H. H. Richardson depots at Auburndale, Massachusetts (now demolished), and at North Easton, Massachusetts. Reminiscent of the Richardsonian works is the simple, dramatic, broad roof with a generous overhang. In this example, the heavy, yet upward-thrusting tapering clock tower (a feature not favored by Richardson) lends a dramatic vertical accent to the dominant horizontal of the main rectangular mass. The roof affords shelter, and the powerful broadly arched entry on the off-track side beckons travelers. The depot with its simple geometric shape and its absence of decoration rests firmly alongside the railroad tracks.

CA04.2 **W. K. Kellogg Auditorium**

1934–1936, Albert Kahn. 60 West Van Buren St. (Michigan 37)

The brick and limestone W. K. Kellogg Auditorium is Battle Creek's most important Art Moderne institutional building. It has bold, straight lines and is devoid of overt historicism. Rather it relies for interest "on the interplay of flat surfaces and on variation in material."[34] The building was intended as part of a civic center complex, which also included the Beaux-Arts Classical Battle Creek Central High School (1908–1909) at 100 West Van Buren Street. This building has a five-part facade with an Ionic portico above an arcade as the central element. The three-story, brick auditorium seats 2,700 and cost $750,000.

CA05 **Battle Creek Federal Center Main Building** (Battle Creek Sanitarium)

1902–1903, Frank M. Andrews. 1907–1908, Merritt J. Moorehouse, tower addition. 74 North Washington Ave. (northeast corner of Washington Ave. and Champion St., 1 block north of Michigan 37)

In 1866 the Seventh-Day Adventists founded the Western Health Reform Institute. Under the direction of Dr. John Harvey Kellogg (1852–1943), it became, in 1876, the Battle Creek Sanitarium. A "sanitary retreat for the restoration of bodily health and for training in the right and healthy way to live," the sanitarium served a predominantly wealthy clientele, eventually numbering nearly ten thousand a year. Experiments conducted at the sanitarium by Dr. Kellogg and his younger brother, Will Keith Kellogg (1860–1951), led to the development of new grain and nut products, including dry flake cereal. (In 1906, W. K. Kellogg withdrew to what now has become Kellogg's.)

The first sanitarium main building, a Second Empire structure erected in 1878, burned in 1902. In 1902–1903 the Michigan Sanitarium and Benevolent Association constructed the lower, main part of the present structure. Designed by Frank M. Andrews of Dayton, the five- and six-story, 580-foot-long "Temple of Health," as the local newspaper referred to it, is Beaux-Arts Classical in design.[35] It has a reinforced concrete frame and floors and a buff and grayish buff brick exterior. Its formal exterior centers around a projecting pedimented central pavilion of Ionic columns and is balanced by pedimented end pavilions. Three wings at the rear, containing the women's baths, a gymnasium, and the men's baths, radiate from a rotunda that originally held a palm garden.

The fifteen-story Towers addition, at the south end facing the North Washington Avenue and Champion Street intersection, was built in 1927–1928 to the plans of Merritt J. Morehouse of Chicago at a cost of $3 million. Also in the Beaux-Arts Classical style, the symmetrical, yellow brick masonry structure has a dramatic two-story-high Ionic colonnaded loggia across the primary facade and copper copings, cornices, and roofing. It contains 265 guest rooms, now converted into offices. A luxurious two-story lobby, with fluted marble Corinthian columns, a coffered ceiling, and a mezzanine gave access to men's and women's parlors. Connected to the Towers at the rear is the grand dining room, now the federal center cafeteria, which had a seating capacity of between 750 and 1,000. Standing on one of Battle Creek's highest points, the Tower, with its massive, anthemion-decorated copper cornices, is a landmark from every part of town.

East of the Towers, at the northwest corner of Champion and Brook streets, is the former sanitarium gymnasium (late 1920s), now the

Battle Creek Central High School Field House. Its arched form and massive masonry construction are strongly reminiscent of George Maher's demolished Northwestern University field house in Evanston, Illinois.

The grounds originally were fully landscaped with gardens, walks, and fountains. The sanitarium was self-sufficient; it operated its own farms, greenhouses, dairy, creamery, orchards, power plant, water, and water-softening plants.

Hard pressed by the depression, the Battle Creek Sanitarium declared bankruptcy and went into receivership in 1933, and in 1942 the buildings were purchased by the U.S. Army for use as the Percy Jones Army Hospital from 1942–1953. When the hospital closed, the building complex became the Battle Creek Federal Center.

MARSHALL

Marshall was founded in 1831, one year after Sidney Ketchum, a land speculator from Peru, New York, had staked out his claim at the fork of Rice Creek and the Kalamazoo River. Its convenient location in the south-central region of the territory and on the river and the Territorial Road aided settlement. Moreover, the available water supply for power for mills helped it further. It was named in honor of John Marshall, then the chief justice of the United States. Between 1835 and 1847, the citizens of Marshall hoped that it would be designated as the state capital, but Lansing was selected instead. In the 1850s and 1860s the Michigan Central rail depot and machine shops ensured Marshall's growth. In 1859 Marshall became a city, but the removal of the railroad repair shops in 1874 caused an economic decline.

Marshall owes its unique character as a showplace of Greek Revival, Gothic Revival, and Italianate architecture largely to the preservation efforts of Harold C. Brooks (1885–1978). Brooks began to purchase and restore many of Marshall's finest buildings—his own house, Honolulu House, and at least twelve of Marshall's key buildings. Brooks drew upon the talents of Kalamazoo architect, Howard F. Young (1889–1934), and the noted Danish-American landscape architect, Jens Jensen. With Young's assistance in the late 1920s, he pioneered in the field of adaptive reuse by converting an old stone livery into

a town hall, fire station, and police station. A large portion of the city, roughly bounded by East Drive and Plum, Forest, and Hanover streets, is a National Historic Landmark.

CA06 **Fountain Circle** (Courthouse Square)

1930, Howard F. Young. West Michigan Ave. and Kalamazoo St. (Business I-94)

The centerpiece of fountain circle is a circular Doric colonnade on a raised and stepped circular base containing a fountain. It was given in 1933 as a memorial to Charles Esselstyn Brooks by his son Harold Craig Brooks. The designer was Howard F. Young. The circle was the site of the first courthouse, a brick Greek Revival structure on a Marshall sandstone foundation erected in 1838.

CA06.1 **Marshall Town Hall** (William Prindle Livery Stable)

1857–1858. 1929–1930, renovations, Howard F. Young. 323 West Michigan Ave. (Business I-94) (southwest corner of West Michigan and Park Ave.)

Located on the southeast side of Marshall's fountain circle, the Marshall Town Hall is an excellent and early example of adaptive reuse in architecture. It is one of Marshall's oldest commercial buildings, having served as a livery, a wagon and carriage building shop, an auto garage, and a service station before becoming the town hall. In 1929–1930, Mayor Harold C. Brooks and architect Howard F. Young transformed the broad, two-story livery stable into a Colonial Revival town hall. The front facade of the basic utilitarian structure is rough-cut, light yellowish brown Marshall sandstone, which was taken from the banks of the Kalamazoo River, while the side walls are of fieldstone. The livery had ample segmentally arched entrances on the first floor. Brooks placed a tower, surmounted by a cupola that holds a Seth Thomas clock with four faces on top of the structure's hipped roof, added a wide classical entablature and a central pedimented pavilion, and installed multipaned, double-hung windows all around and a Palladian window in the west wall to admit light to the council chamber. Perhaps Brooks was aware of the preservation and restoration work at Colonial Williamsburg and Greenfield Village at the time and was inspired to do the same for Marshall.

CA06.2 Honolulu House (Abner and Eliza Pratt House)

c. 1860, attributed to William L. Buck. 107 North Kalamazoo St. (southwest corner of North Kalamazoo and Mansion streets, half a block north of West Michigan Ave. [Business I-94])

Based on Hawaiian prototypes, with Italianate stylistic elements, the fanciful Honolulu House is Marshall's most famous structure. The board-and-batten building rests upon a 5-foot Marshall sandstone foundation and has an almost pagoda-roofed central tower. A veranda, with an ornamental railing, triple supports with large triple convoluted brackets projecting from the pier capitals to the eaves, and wooden ogee arches, runs the length of the building. Inside the house, a wide stairway sweeps upward from the main hall to the observation deck in the tower. Large parlors with 15-foot ceilings open off the hall. The walls were covered with decorative paintings by itinerant artist F. A. Grace, depicting tropical vegetation. Abner Pratt (1804–1866) served as the U.S. Consul to the Sandwich (Hawaiian) Islands in 1857–1859. On returning to Marshall because of his wife Eliza's poor health, he built this exotic residence and filled it with tropical decoration, as a remembrance of his consular service. Beautifully restored inside and out, the Honolulu House currently serves as the Marshall Historical Museum.

CA06.3 National House Inn

1835, George Bentley and Nathan Benedict, builders. 315 West Green St. (southwest corner of West Michigan Ave. [Business I-94] and Parkview)

Standing on the southwest side of the fountain circle (originally the public square) is Calhoun County's first brick building and one of Michigan's oldest inns. The National House was a major stagecoach stop along the Territorial Road. After 1879, the building served as a farm wagon and windmill factory, and just after the turn of the century, it was converted to apartments. The plain structure exhibits the simplest elements of the Federal style. The entrance has a segmental transom and side lights, and the windows have stone lintels and sills. Just four years after the founding of Marshall, it was built by local builders George Bentley (1842–1922) and Nathan Benedict for Andrew Mann (1784–1872). The National House Inn reopened for business in 1976.

CA07 Pendleton-Alexander House (Increase Pendleton–Morgan J. and Sarah J. Alexander House)

1856. 281 South Eagle St. (northwest corner of South Eagle and West Hanover streets, 2 blocks south of East Michigan Ave. [Business I-94])

Inspired, no doubt, by phrenologist-architect-author Orson S. Fowler, who lectured in Marshall in 1850 on the economy and simplicity of the octagon mode, Increase Pendleton, a local cabinetmaker, built this octagon house. Fowler's book, *A Home for All or The Gravel Wall and Octagon Mode of Building,* was first published in 1848. In 1875, when he purchased the home, lumber dealer Morgan J. Alexander made extensive repairs. The exterior walls of Marshall sandstone are stuccoed, and Italianate decorative trim has been added. These changes, along with a finial (now removed) are contrary to Fowler's advocacy of simplicity in design.

CA08 Governor's Mansion (James Wright Gordon House)

1839. 612 South Marshall Ave. (nearly 6 blocks south of East Michigan Ave. [Business I-94])

The small Federal house that was intended as the chief executive's official residence stands at the foot of "Capitol Hill," a site designated for the statehouse. It was built by James Wright Gordon (1809–1853), an attorney and a state senator who promoted the designation of Marshall as the state capital in the first decade of statehood. Despite the lost hopes and optimism, the "Governor's Mansion" retains the simple dignity of a house in a frontier city that once aspired to greatness. The two-story white frame structure has a side-hall plan. An overscaled one-story Doric porch and a one-story rear wing were added. The house is Federal in proportion and scale, including the cornice. The latter was made Greek by the addition of the deep entablature, which is not supported by corner pilasters. The house was given to the Daughters of the American Revolution, who restored it in 1966. Open to public.

CA09 **Capitol Hill School**

1860, Sheldon Smith. 603 Washington St. (southeast corner of Washington and Maple streets, 6 blocks south of East Michigan Ave. [Business I-94])

In 1860, when the educators of Marshall decided to build three primary schools, they chose for the Fourth Ward School a site on Capitol Hill facing the vacant statehouse square. All three schools were designed in the Gothic Revival style by Sheldon Smith of Detroit, the first in the dynasty of architects that became the present-day firm of Smith, Hinchman and Grylls Associates. Of the three schools, only this one survives. The two-room, red brick school is cruciform in plan. A hipped roof covers the central portion; pierced, decorative bargeboards in the projecting gables and gable wings and pointed-arch windows provide the Gothic decorative features; the paired brackets and the wide eaves are the Italianate elements.

CA10 **Wagner's Block**

1870–1871, John Mills Van Osdel. 143 West Michigan Ave. (Business I-94)

The sculpturesque stone and iron commercial block was built for Martin V. Wagner (1845–1891), one of Marshall's leading politicians, who served as mayor for four terms. Wagner built the block at age twenty-five, less than ten years after he arrived from Wheeler, Steuben County, New York, and began the study of law. The block was designed by self-taught noted pioneer Chicago architect John

Mills Van Osdel (1811–1892). The front is encrusted with ornamental columns, pilasters, sills, and lintels that surround the flat-arch and keystoned windows of all the floors. A mansard roof caps the three-story structure. It is pierced by a paired central dormer flanked by arched dormers with oval glass. The local newspaper for August 4, 1870, was fully justified in calling this building "an ornament to the city." The first floor held stores, the second floor, offices, and the third floor, a ballroom.

CA11 **Prospect Street Area**

East and West Prospect streets from Brewer St. (Old US 27) to High St.

CA11.1 **Stonehall** (Andrew L. Hayes House)

1837–1838. 1877, porch added to eastern front. 1927, restoration, Howard F. Young. 303 North Kalamazoo Ave. (northwest corner of West Prospect St. and North Kalamazoo Ave.)

Stonehall is one of Michigan's finest examples of the Greek Revival style in combination with the vernacular tradition. The latter is especially evident in the "pentastyle" Doric portico, for an odd number of columns is not at all characteristic of the architecture of ancient Greece. The only entrance to the home, on the east side, has a transom and side lights and is set off by a small extended porch with a pair of Doric pilasters and columns. The house is built of locally quarried, yellowish Marshall sandstone. In 1837–1838, six years after he came here from New Hampshire, Dr. Andrew L. Hayes (1801–1864) built the house. Marshall's first physician, Hayes was also a planter and a land speculator. With advice from Howard F. Young, Lewis E. Brooks (1880–1958), brother of Harold C. Brooks, restored it in 1927.

CA11.2 **Fitch-Gorham-Brooks House** (Jabez Fitch–Charles Gorham–Harold C. Brooks House)

c. 1840. 1921, Jens Jensen, landscape architect. 310 North Kalamazoo Ave. (northeast corner of West Prospect St. and North Kalamazoo Ave.)

Regarded as an outstanding example of the Greek Revival style, the Fitch-Gorham-Brooks House is a two-story, "pentastyle," temple-

CA11.2 Fitch-Gorham-Brooks House (Jabez Fitch–Charles Gorham–Harold C. Brooks House)

form brick building, painted white, with a giant Ionic portico. Ornamenting the pediment on the portico is a half-moon window, with two side lights decorated with wrought-iron grilles, imitating traditional Greek Revival doorways. Although the portico appears symmetrical, the five fluted columns are spaced unevenly to accommodate the window arrangement. The use of five columns in the portico in this work and in Stonehall (CA11.1) is unusual, since the Greek preference was for an even number of columns.

Jabez Fitch (1795–1843), a prominent merchant, temperance advocate, and Presbyterian, built the house in about 1840. Charles Gorham (1812–1901), a mercantile partner of Chauncey Brewer, banker and politician, bought it in 1851. His wife, Charlotte Eaton Hart Gorham, presided "with gracious dignity over the beautiful home, which, as it occupies an elevation, and is of imposing architecture, is one of the notable residences of Marshall."[36] Harold C. Brooks (1885–1978) acquired the house in the twentieth century.

The historical information furnished to the Historic American Buildings Survey of 1934 by Brooks noted the architect as "Richard Upjohn (?)." In fact, there is not the remotest chance this house was designed by him. (There are only two known works by Upjohn in the Greek Revival style, both in Bangor, Maine, and both designed in the mid-1830s. After he moved to New York in 1839 to begin work on Trinity Church, he never again designed a classical building.) The Jens Jenson-designed landscape lies to the north of the house.

CA11.3 **Chastian Mann House**

1861. 219 High St.

Chastian Mann, editor of the *Calhoun County Patriot and Democratic Expounder*, built this T-shape brick Gothic Revival house. The steeply pitched side-gable roof has a prominent center gable containing a double lancet window. Decorative lacy bargeboards and finials ornament all the gables. Side and transom lights surround the center entrance. The entrance is sheltered with a flat-roofed porch supported by open posts with curving supports and paired brackets.

CA12 **Oakhill** (Chauncy M. and Emily L. Brewer House)

1859. 410 North Eagle St. (approximately 3 blocks north of East Michigan Ave. [Business I-94])

Magnificent Oakhill stands atop a steep hill overlooking the town on the northern edge of Marshall and open fields to the northeast. This Italianate example once dominated some 64 acres of farmland. Chauncy M. Brewer (1814–1889), a pioneer who came from Oneonta, New York, to Marshall in 1835 and who achieved prominence in merchandising, banking, and local politics, built it in 1859. The eighteen-room, red brick house is a two-and-a-half-story cube with a square belvedere on top of the roof and with a wide, columned veranda that sweeps from the front around to the side of the structure. Paired brackets support the roof. A two-story, rectangular addition is on the west. The interior is profusely decorated with marble fireplaces, wrought-metal chandeliers, and stained-glass window panels.

CA13 Thomas L. Cronin House

1886, Frederick H. Spier and William C. Rohns. 314 Division St. (approximately 2.5 blocks north of East Michigan Ave. [Business I-94])

Spier and Rohns, known for their depots on the Michigan Central and the Grand Trunk railroad lines, designed this elaborate brick Queen Anne house for merchant Thomas L. Cronin. It has a tall, square, pyramidal-roofed tower on the front, a shorter conical-roofed tower on the rear, projecting gables, decorative brickwork and woodwork, ornate chimneys, and a delicate entrance porch.

ALBION

CA14 Albion City Hall

1933–1936, Frank E. Dean. 112 West Cass St. (between South Superior [Michigan 99] and Clinton streets)

On his inauguration as mayor of Albion in 1931, Norman H. Wiener, together with city councilmen and interested citizens, initiated plans for a new city hall. Dreams for this building were realized within two years, when Harry B. Parker donated the building site, and the Civil Works Administration (CWA), the Works Progress Administration (WPA), and the Emergency Relief Appropriation Act (ERA), in an emergency effort to relieve unemployment, put federal monies into this public works project. Frank E. Dean of Albion, brother of a councilman, designed the city hall in a symmetrical and bland rendition of the Colonial Revival style prevalent during the depression era. The central section of the rough-cut limestone building is flanked by two wings; the fire department is housed in one, and the police department in the other.

A broken segmental pediment with pineapple finial surmounts the central entrance. On the eve of its dedication in 1936, the *Albion Evening Recorder* called the Albion City Hall "one of Southern Michigan's most pretentious municipal buildings." It cost $225,000.

CA15 Albion College Astronomical Observatory

1883–1884. South side of Cass St. between Huron and Hannah streets, 3 blocks east of South Superior St. (Michigan 99)

One of two astronomical observatories erected in Michigan in the nineteenth century, this one was built at Albion College in 1883–1884. (Thirty years earlier the Detroit Observatory was built at the University of Michigan in Ann Arbor.) Samuel Dickie, a mathematics professor who later became the president of the college, led a drive that raised $10,000 to construct and equip the observatory. From the rectangular, two-story, hipped-roof, red brick structure projects a round corner tower topped by the observatory dome. The observatory was equipped with an equatorial telescope manufactured and mounted by Alvan Clark and Sons of Cambridge, Massachusetts, with a transit circle, a sidereal clock, and a chronograph. Slender observation windows pierce the opposite walls of an extended wing. The structure has dentil-trimmed cornices and console-supported window caps. The observatory houses a lecture room.

HOMER

CA16 Tidd-Williams Funeral Chapels, Inc. (Milton and Sophie Dorsey Barney House)

c. 1838–1839. 303 South Hillsdale St. (southwest corner South Hillsdale St. and Everett St.)

Milton Barney (1796–1879) came in 1832 from New Marlborough, Massachusetts, and Lyons, New York, to the site of present-day Homer. After acquiring a large parcel of land on the Kalamazoo River, which would be a source of waterpower for later mills, he plotted the village and named it Barneyville. Barney prospered as an owner of the Homer Mills, and, later, as a merchant and president of the Farmer's Bank of Homer. His side-gable, symmetrical Greek Revival house was built soon after he established the town. Using the cobblestone building technique of Upstate New York, builders laid cobblestones in courses in the walls. Angle quoins mark the corners of the house and simple lintels surmount the windows. The face of the house was lifted with the addition of the arched lined intersecting central gable and the Prairie-style front porch.

Michiana and the Southwestern Lower Peninsula

MICHIANA AND THE SOUTHWESTERN LOWER PENINSULA is a region of woodlands, oak openings, small fertile prairies and grasslands, river bluffs and marshes, sand dunes and lakeshore. It is bounded on the west by the restless expanse of Lake Michigan, which is the terminal pool for the Saint Joseph, Black, and Kalamazoo river watersheds. The Saint Joseph River winds through the southern tiers of counties from its rise in Hillsdale County halfway across the Lower Peninsula. The Kalamazoo River crosses Kalamazoo County on its northwesterly course to its mouth at Saugatuck on the western shore of the state. Both are part of the Saint Lawrence River system.

Attracted first to the small fertile prairies of Saint Joseph and Cass counties, settlers from New England, New York, Ohio, Indiana, Pennsylvania, and Virginia established farms. Later, on the sandy soil of Berrien and Van Buren counties, in a climate tempered by the waters of Lake Michigan, other settlers cultivated orchards, berries, and vineyards and built canneries and wineries. In the muck land along the Kalamazoo River valley, farmers grew celery, vegetables, and mint. In the southern portion of the region, they raised pigs. To support this agricultural region, towns and cities sprang up along the waterways, highways, and railroad lines.

Today three main roads—U.S. Route 12 (US 12), Michigan 60, and Interstate 94 (I-94)—traverse Michiana and the Southwestern Lower Peninsula. U.S. Route 12, or the Chicago Road, is the major route through the southernmost portion of the southern counties and follows the old Great Sauk Trail west from Detroit and Monroe through Tecumseh, Coldwater, Sturgis, and Niles to Chicago. During the early history of the road, where it crosses the Saint Joseph River at Mottville, a "strong and well built timber [bridge] structure" was built

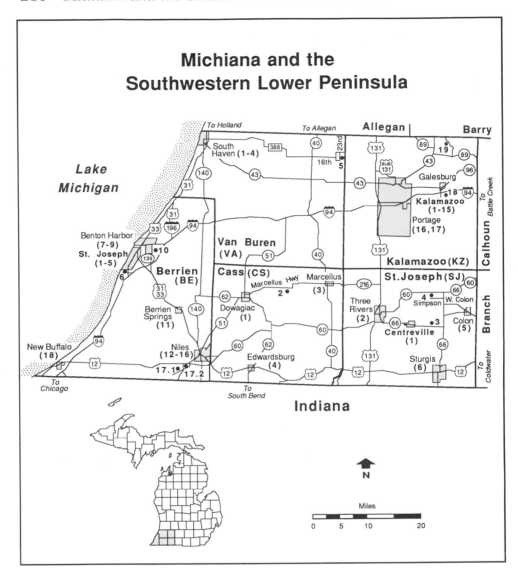

in 1833, and bridges have been at that site ever since.[37] Mottville became a center of river traffic with wharves and warehouses. The Chicago Road is dotted with examples of architecture derived from practices on the Eastern Seaboard, such as the Greek Revival Ezra Miller House at Edwardsburg.

The Saint Joseph River served as a major transportation route for Indians, explorers, missionaries, and fur traders. Prehistoric Indians lived in the Saint Joseph River valley, and French explorers and missionaries, such as Claude Allouez, Claude Dablon, and Jacques Marquette, also came here to build forts and missions on the river's banks. Later, in 1679, René Robert Cavelier, Sieur de la Salle, built Fort Miami, a stockaded camp, at the mouth of the Saint

Joseph River at the present site of the city of Saint Joseph. At first it served as a base for explorations southward into the Mississippi River valley, but it was soon abandoned.

In 1691 other French explorers, seeking to establish authority over the Miami and Potawatomi and to control the fur trade, journeyed 25 miles up the Saint Joseph River and built Fort Saint Joseph near the site of present-day Niles. A Jesuit mission had already been established in the same vicinity in the 1680s. Following the French departure in 1763, the British held the fort until it was captured by the Spanish in 1781. The Spanish only remained a few days, but their stay gave Niles the name "city of four flags."

If people and supplies bound for the interior of Michiana and the Southwestern Lower Peninsula Region traveled up the Saint Joseph River, the river was a means of export as well. Reversing the usual eastward to westward migration pattern into the state, some early settlers in this region came from the south and the west. Others used Niles as a stepping-off point. Located at the juncture of major east-west and north-south land and water routes, Niles was also at the point where the Sauk Trail crossed the Saint Joseph River. From Niles the Kankakee Trail led south to a portage between the Saint Joseph and Kankakee rivers, connecting the Saint Joseph River with the Mississippi by way of the Kankakee and the Illinois rivers.

On the banks of the Saint Joseph River at the site of present-day Niles, Isaac McCoy, a Baptist, established in 1822–1823 the Carey Indian Mission to the Potawatomi. By 1825 more settlers had arrived from Indiana to push farther upriver to Pokagon Prairie in Cass County, and in the 1830s settlers poured into southwestern Michigan. A surprising architectural achievement of this early migration is Woodlawn, the Greek Revival Marantette house. Built next to the trading post in the late 1830s, it remains today. Cass County's early settlers were varied, some were New Englanders, others were from the South; there were also unusually large communities of Potawatomi Indians and blacks. Freed slaves aided by the Quakers settled in Cass County in the 1830s and 1840s. Quakers helped escaped slaves along two different routes of the Underground Railroad that converged just east of Cassopolis. By the 1860s the largest number of blacks in Michigan outside of Wayne County resided in Cass County, where they founded schools and churches, resorts, and farms. The Chain Lake Missionary Baptist Church north of Calvin Center, organized in 1848, is one example.

The region's rivers also served as a means of transporting logs to sawmills and shipping ports. Logs were floated down the Black River to South Haven to be sawed at mills and loaded onto ships. Lumber mills flourished along the Lake Michigan shoreline from the 1850s to 1870. Large companies operated mills at Bridgman, Union Pier, and Lakeside.

Commercial fishing, shipbuilding, and tourism were also important to the region's economy. Resort hotels at South Haven, Saint Joseph, and other coastline communities and inland lakes served vacationers, many of whom arrived by lake steamers from Chicago.

In 1827, after the Indian titles had been terminated by the Treaty of Chicago, the Michigan Territorial Legislature approved the organization of all the territory lying west of Lenawee County into one county—Saint Joseph County. The boundaries of all five counties within Michiana and the Southwestern Lower Peninsula were defined, and they were given names in 1829. They organized their governments, however, at different times: Saint Joseph and Cass counties in 1829, Kalamazoo County in 1830, Berrien in 1831, and Van Buren in 1837.

The establishment of the counties encouraged land sales and land speculation, and in 1831 a land office opened in White Pigeon. One speculator was Lucius Lyon, who had already surveyed land in the Old Northwest Territory from 1823 to 1832. Lyon speculated in land in Kalamazoo County. In 1831 he platted the village of Schoolcraft, which served the Prairie Ronde.

Internal improvements also furthered the settlement and economic development of the region. In 1836 the federal government began dredging and improving the port facilities at Saint Joseph Harbor. From its docks, lumber, flour, wheat, pork, and fruit were taken off river barges, loaded on lake vessels, and shipped out; at the same time, supplies for Kalamazoo, Niles, and South Bend, Indiana, were transported in. In 1863, twenty-seven years after the first improvements were made, the harbor was constructed. Saw milling, flour milling, and boat building developed at Saint Joseph and at South Haven.

Railroads were as important to the growth of this region as they were throughout the nation. Financed with private funds, the Erie and Kalamazoo Railroad was completed in the 1840s. At the same time, the state legislature planned three other railroads, two of which ran across Michiana and the Southwestern Lower Peninsula—the Michigan Southern from Monroe on Lake Erie to New Buffalo on Lake Michigan and the Michigan Central Railroad from Detroit to Saint Joseph, which arrived in Niles in 1848.

Before the Civil War, Kalamazoo County established itself as a leader in Michigan education. In 1833 the Michigan Territorial Legislature chartered the Baptist-sponsored Michigan and Huron Institute (1836) in Kalamazoo to promote education through the establishment of academies and colleges. It opened in Kalamazoo in 1836. The following year the University of Michigan opened a branch there. They merged as the Kalamazoo Literary Institute, and in 1855 it became Kalamazoo College. In 1850 the Michigan Asylum for the Insane was also established in Kalamazoo.

The region has a wide range of industries based on agriculture and other pursuits. Its factories produced washing machines, bicycles, pharmaceuticals, fishing tackle, wood and paper products, stoves and furnaces, featherbones, and carriages.

Today small towns like Constantine, Marcellus, and Schoolcraft dot the rural landscape. Just northeast of the region's center is its largest city, Kalamazoo, the location of some of the state's most interesting buildings. The region's other large communities are Niles and the twin cities of Benton Harbor and Saint Joseph. Also important are Sturgis, Three Rivers, and Dowagiac.

The architecture of the region was influenced not only by the East but also by Chicago. Well-known Chicago architects such as Adler and Sullivan, Frank Lloyd Wright, and William A. Otis designed buildings in Kalamazoo and Saint Joseph. Henry Lord Gay designed the Ladies Library Association in Kalamazoo. Tallmadge and Watson and Wheelock and Clay worked in Niles; F. S. Allen of Indiana designed the Indiana School in South Haven; and C. A. Fairchilds of Kalamazoo designed the Prairie style library in Colon.

Kalamazoo County (KZ)

KALAMAZOO

Kalamazoo is a name familiar to many Americans. Known affectionately as "the Celery City," "the Paper City," and "the Mall City," Kalamazoo has supplied the world with products as diverse as peppermint, corsets manufactured in the world's largest corset factory, reams of fine paper, "hip-zip" knickers, Shakespeare rods and reels, Checker cabs, Gibson musical instruments, Unicap vitamins from Upjohn, and stoves shipped from "Kalamazoo direct to you." The city was immortalized by Carl Sandburg in his poem "The Sins of Kalamazoo" and popularized by the World War II-era song "I've Got a Gal in Kalamazoo." Few cities of similar size are better known.

Beginning around the 1840s, Kalamazoo residents built fashionable homes and commercial buildings following contemporary architectural trends. Many of the city's early neighborhoods and a portion of its late nineteenth-century commercial district have survived relatively intact. The earliest homes and commercial structures were built following the restraint and formality of the Greek Revival. However, by the 1850s the more elaborate and informal Italianate styles and the romantic Gothic Revival rapidly succeeded the symmetry and order of the Greek style. Still following national tastes and trends, Kalamazoo residents embraced the Second Empire, the picturesque Queen Anne, and the Romanesque Revival styles in the prosperous years following the Civil War. Building in the twentieth century continued to reflect national trends, and within the city one can find examples of all those major movements and some works by major midwestern architects. The city has an Adler and Sullivan commercial building and, in its suburbs, two developments by Frank Lloyd Wright. With all this adherence to fashion, one could possibly say that Kalamazoo architecture is not especially innovative; yet Kalamazoo's architecture is a midwestern microcosm of American architecture. Revival and contemporary, conservative and flamboyant, Kalamazoo architecture is alive and working; and much of the historic architecture of Kalamazoo is preserved as an integral part of the community.

KZ01 Bronson Park

1876. 1930s, sculpture, Alfonso Iannelli. 1976, sculpture, Kirk Newman. Bounded by South, Park, Academy, and Rose streets

Michigan's finest civic square and a welcome oasis in downtown Kalamazoo is Bronson Park. It is named for Kalamazoo's founder Titus Bronson, who donated land for this purpose. The first plat map of the town shows "academy square" and "courthouse square" to the east of the park and "jail house square" and "church square" to the west. In 1876 the undeveloped center space, which held an Indian mound, was improved with plantings and a fountain. In 1939 the concrete fountain sculpture, *The Fountain of the Pioneers*, designed by designer and sculptor, Alfonso Iannelli (1888–1965), who created the sprites for Wright's Midway Gardens project, was installed. In 1976, the bronze statue group *Children May Safely Play*, designed by local artist Kirk Newman, was placed in the long reflect-

Kalamazoo

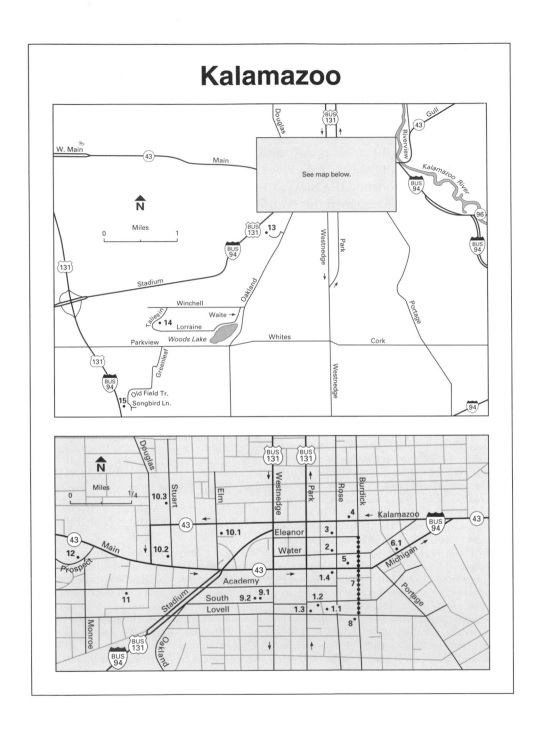

ing pool included in the original design by Ianelli. Fronting the park are churches, government buildings, and clubs.

KZ01.1 Kalamazoo City Hall

1931, Weary and Alford. 241 West South St.

City Hall is Kalamazoo's finest example of Art Deco architecture. Its plan and simplicity reflect its Classical Grecian origins, but its ornament and details are twentieth century. The reinforced concrete structure is faced with limestone. Bold flutings are carved in the giant pilasters, floral and geometric designs along with local historical scenes are in relief panels on the frieze. The frames and spandrels of the recessed window are of dark cast aluminum. The interior of the building is arranged around a three-story, skylighted atrium lobby and is finished with black and gold marble and polished siena travertine. Fountains, stair rails and grilles, lanterns, and a letter box cast in aluminum with stylized carp, birds, pond lilies, and other plants add to the Art Deco imagery. The walls and ceiling of the commission chambers were painted in peach, aqua, and gold geometric designs by German-born artist Otto Stauffenberg. Weary and Alford of Chicago, noted for its designs of banks and public buildings, designed the city hall. The firm also designed the American National Bank (now Old Kent Bank), at 136 East Michigan Avenue, in 1929–1930, in the same Art Deco motif. City Hall

was built by O. F. Miller Company at a cost of $524,000.

KZ01.2 First Presbyterian Church

1928–1930, Charles Z. Klauder. 321 West South St. (southwest corner West South St. and Saint Johns Place)

The First Presbyterian Church is the most splendid church on Bronson Park. The "Gothic Church" replaced the 1885 "Brick Church" that burned in 1926, leaving only a shell, and hastening the building of this new structure. The church was designed by Charles Z. Klauder (1872–1938) of Philadelphia, an architect known for Gothic adaptations—in particular, the Cathedral of Learning (1926–1937) at the University of Pittsburgh. A father and son firm, Moore McQuigg and Son, members of the congregation, built the church as "a labor of love as well as business." It cost $375,000. The flamelike tracery in the prominent stained-glass rose window high above the single, recessed, arched entry is French Flamboyant Gothic. The brilliant blues, purples, and reds of this window and the chancel window contribute to the magnificence of the lofty English open-truss nave. The windows were manufactured by Willett Studios of Philadelphia. The church has low Gothic arcaded side aisles. This Late Gothic Revival steel, concrete, and cut limestone structure is a twentieth-century response to the religious needs of this congregation and yet retains the medieval religious imagery.

KZ01.3 Ladies Library Association Building

1878–1879, Henry Lord Gay. 1913, kitchen wing. 333 South Park St. (northeast corner of South Park and West Lovell streets)

Organized in 1852 as the outgrowth of a reading circle of three women, the Ladies Library Association sought to stimulate learning and culture in Kalamazoo. Designed by Chicago architect Henry Lord Gay, the Ladies Library Association building resembles the works of Frank Furness, best exemplified in the Pennsylvania Academy of the Fine Arts, erected in Philadelphia in 1871–1876. The building was constructed by Bush and Patterson of Kalamazoo in 1878–1879. It is two stories in height and is 30 by 60 feet in plan.

KZ01.3 Ladies Library Association Building

A steeply pitched, slate-covered, hipped roof echoes the Furness character. A stair tower, which is fronted by an entrance porch, rises on the north. This picturesque structure, with its orange red brick walls with lighter limestone trim, and with its decorative tiles and rich corbeling, is a superb example of the High Victorian Gothic. The unusual shed-dormered tower has the appearance of that on a Norwegian stave church. The first floor holds a library, a meeting room, and a museum; the second, an auditorium or lecture hall with a stage. Stained glass depicting literary scenes from Milton, Shakespeare, Burns, and Hawthorne, made by W. H. Wells and Brother, is installed throughout. A gargoyle spout also adds to its medieval appearance.

KZ01.4 **Kalamazoo County Building**

1936–1937, M. J. C. Billingham with Smith, Hinchman and Grylls. 227 West Michigan Ave. (Business I-94/Michigan 43) (southwest corner of West Michigan Ave. and Rose St.)

Seven years after the city built its modernistic city hall, Kalamazoo County erected the Kalamazoo County Building on the north side of Bronson Park. The PWA Moderne government building was designed by Kalamazoo architect M. J. C. Billingham (1885–1959), with Smith, Hinchman and Grylls of Detroit as associate architects. Its modernistic character is well expressed in the smooth ashlar limestone walls and granite basement of the south-facing front facade of the fireproof steel and reinforced concrete structure. Allegorical figures of Justice, Law, and Vigilance, carved in relief by Corrado Joseph Parducci, decorate the north and south facades. Stylized lion's masks and swags ornament the cornice line. The six-story structure was planned to hold county offices, courtrooms, and the jail and sheriff's residence. The building cost $742,590 to build and was paid for with funds from the Public Works Administration. The present county building is the third since the county was organized: the first was a two-story, wooden temple of justice, 42 by 55 feet in plan, erected in 1835 reportedly to the plans of Ammi B. Young, and added to in 1866; the second, built in 1882, was an ornate, three-story, brick and stone building with a central tower and four mosquelike corner towers.

KZ02 **Vermeulen Furniture Company Building** (Lawrence and Chapin Iron Works)

1870–1872, Lemuel Dwight Grosvenor. 1881. 201 North Rose St. (northwest corner of North Rose and Water streets)

This rare, Second Empire style survivor from Kalamazoo's days as a major iron-producing center for the region originally housed the iron foundry of William S. Lawrence and L. C. Chapin. A slate-covered mansard roof tops the three-story structure, and a convex-roofed central pavilion fronts it. Two rows of hooded windows, arranged in groups of three and separated by giant pilasters that are topped by paired brackets, create a pleasing rhythmical movement. The lower two floors, altered in the 1960s, appear incongruous with the late nineteenth-century facade. The building was designed by Lemuel Dwight Grosvenor (b. 1830), who came west in the early 1850s from Worcester County, Massachusetts, to Chicago, to supervise the construction of a section of the Galena and Western Union Railroad. In 1857, Grosvenor returned to New England, where he learned the trade of carpentry and joinery while working in Gardner and Athol, Massachusetts, and in Brattleboro, Vermont. He also studied architectural drawing. In 1860, he went back to southern Michigan, working as a carpenter and as a builder in Kalamazoo before opening an architectural office in Jackson in 1871, at the time he designed this building; it was constructed by Bush and Patterson.

KZ03 **Rose Street Market** (Kalamazoo Masonic Temple)

1913–1915, Spier and Rohns. 1987–1988, rehabilitated. 309 North Rose St. (northwest corner of North Rose and Eleanor streets)

The large, ornamented cube is a testimony to the strength of Freemasonry in Kalamazoo. Eleven local Masonic affiliates formed the Clark Memorial Masonic Association to construct, own, and operate the Masonic temple. The building has a decorative cornice and three-story, tripartite windows in round-arch units. The south and east exterior walls are clad in brown, Greendale Rug Face Brick and are trimmed in white terracotta and metal. The highly eclectic building shows something of H. H. Richardson, something of Louis Sullivan, and something of Spier and Rohns themselves. The interior was arranged with three stacked auditoriums to house the ceremonies of local Masonic lodges and public events. Through the concentrated efforts of preservationists and the Kalamazoo Heritage Committee, the temple was spared demolition and was rehabilitated by Mark Doonan and Emile Mortier of Eugene, Oregon, into commercial space for offices and shops.

KZ04 **Kalamazoo Metro Transit Center** (Kalamazoo Station of the Michigan Central Railroad)

1887, Cyrus L. W. Eidlitz. 459 North Burdick St. (southwest corner of the Conrail tracks and North Burdick St.)

The Michigan Central Railroad Station is clear evidence of the centrality of Michigan's railroad system to the state's predominantly urban and industrial economy. Architecturally, it tells of the widespread use and popularity of the Richardsonian Romanesque. The station utilizes massive round arches, a conical turret, rusticated red Lake Superior sandstone, and a heavy red tile roof with generous overhanging eaves to serve its well-proportioned monumentality. It is a counterpart in a medium-size midwestern city to H. H. Richardson's railroad depots of the early 1880s in small towns in Massachusetts—South Framingham, North Easton, Auburndale. The Kalamazoo depot was designed to meet the practical need for waiting rooms, office functions, and baggage storage. As such, the work is the result of the same no-nonsense attitude that Richardson assumed with his historic Marshall Field Wholesale Warehouse, 1885–1887, in Chicago—to accommodate traveling salesmen who were visiting to examine wares and place orders for shipment. Extravagant and ostentatious display was unnecessary.

The Kalamazoo station was designed by New York architect Cyrus L. W. Eidlitz (1853–1921), who was the son of architect Leopold Eidlitz. The younger Eidlitz also designed the Detroit Railway Station (1883) and the Dearborn Station (c. 1881) in Chicago. The Kalamazoo station now serves as an intermodal transportation center for the city.

KZ05 **Kalamazoo Center**

1972, Elbasani, Logan and Severin. East Michigan Ave. (Business I-94/Michigan 43) between Rose and North Burdick streets

The multi-use office, retail, hotel, conference, and convention center is placed on a diagonal in order to link, in accordance with the city's earlier plans, Bronson Park with the Kalamazoo Mall. Inland Steel Development Corporation and the city collaborated in its development, which was intended to promote downtown redevelopment. A bronze-colored steel and glass skin covers the three-, six-, and ten-story concrete frames. It was designed by a group of architects who had met each other at Harvard's Graduate School of Design and who had worked for Victor Gruen or The Architects Collaborative. The center was scaled appropriately to the conditions of a small city. The Upjohn Company, its present owner, is refurbishing it to serve as an important neighbor to the Arcadia Creek redevelopment project.

KZ06 The Haymarket

Late nineteenth to early twentieth century. East Michigan Ave. (Business I-94/Michigan 43) between Portage and the Conrail tracks

The Haymarket contains a splendid collection of nineteenth-century commercial structures in a rich array of Romanesque Revival, Beaux-Arts Classical, and Chicago Commercial styles that echo the tendencies of commercial districts elsewhere in the Midwest. Uniform in height, these buildings constitute the heart of this late nineteenth-century Kalamazoo business district. In the period between the Civil War and World War II, this was commonly known as the "German district," and the buildings bear names such as Ihling, Rosenbaum, and Desenberg. The structures on the north side of the 200 block of East Michigan are especially well scaled and visually cohesive. They have been newly rehabilitated.

KZ06.1 Arcadia Bank (Desenberg Block)

1885–1887, Adler and Sullivan. 251 East Michigan Ave. (Business I-94/Michigan 43)

The Desenberg Block is one of the few extant Adler and Sullivan buildings outside of Chicago. It contains much of the organic and geometric ornamentation from a critical stage in the development of Louis Sullivan's mature style. In 1882, five years before designing this commercial building, the firm had built the Academy of Music in Kalamazoo, an acoustically and visually successful building that has been demolished. The academy preceded the construction of one of the firm's best-known buildings, the Auditorium Theater and Hotel (1885–1887) in Chicago. Thus, Adler and Sullivan's reputation was solidly established when Bernhard Desenberg approached them to build offices for his wholesale grocery business on the main commercial street of Kalamazoo. The ornament of the three-story block echoes Byzantine and Russian ornament. The cornice, the slender piers terminating in turretlike pinnacles, and the decorative bands between the third-floor windows are reminiscent, too, of Burnham and Root's Rookery Building, erected in Chicago in 1886, and the ornaments resemble those in Sullivan's other buildings of the early and mid 1880s. The influence of Sullivan and the Chicago school was felt in this small midwestern city.

KZ07 Kalamazoo Mall

1959, Victor Gruen Associates. Burdick St. between Eleanor and Lovell streets

On August 19, 1959, more than fifty thousand shoppers helped dedicate the nation's first permanent outdoor pedestrian downtown mall, known simply as Kalamazoo Mall. Responding to traffic snarls, lack of parking, and competing strip development along highways on the outskirts of the city, the downtown merchants assessed themselves $40,000 to hire Victor Gruen Associates to draw a plan to revitalize the city. Gruen proposed a one-way peripheral auto loop around the downtown, strategically spotted parking lots, and the conversion of streets inside the loop into pedestrian malls. The plan was partially executed. Two blocks of Burdick Street, between Water and South streets, were closed to traffic and replaced by pedestrian malls in the first stage of the plan. The city and the merchants shared the cost of the mall. Each merchant refurbished his own storefront to create the architectural look of the 1960s. In 1960 the mall was extended one block north, and in 1973, it was extended one block south. Today, Gruen's vision of a solution for the problem of urban centers stands as proof of his creative imagination: the city has been restored to the people.

KZ08 State Theatre

1926–1927, John Eberson. 1964, facade remodeled. 404 South Burdick St. (southwest corner of South Burdick and Lovell streets)

The fanciful windows and the Renaissance-inspired terracotta exterior trim of the State Theatre merely hint at its elaborate atmospheric interior. Arcades, balconies, castle towers, and a Spanish cathedral window create the illusion of an outdoor Spanish courtyard. It was designed for the Butterfield-Publix-Paramount chain of theaters by John Eberson (1875–1954), one of America's foremost designers of movie palaces. John Eberson pioneered the atmospheric theater, a type of theater in which an elaborate lighting system reproduced on a blue-painted ceiling the effect of the sky—with moving clouds, twinkling stars, and the like—portraying, in turn, daylight, dusk, night, and dawn. His own Michel Angelo Studios produced the ornamental plaster in the State Theatre, including gilded plaster replicas of Donatello's *David* and the *Medici Venus*, which were set in niches flanking the screen. Churrigueresque columns painted blue and gold, arches and false facades completed the decoration of the eclectic Moorish-Italian Renaissance design. Eberson designed two other atmospheric theaters in Michigan: the Capitol (see GS01.2, p. 335) in Flint and the Grand Riviera (see DE47, p. 95) in Detroit. The marquee and the original entrance of the State were modified in 1964.

KZ09 South Street Neighborhood

1840s through early twentieth century. West South St. between Westnedge and Stadium (Business I-94/Business 131) avenues

Within several blocks, South Street affords a virtual catalog of architectural styles from the 1840s to the early twentieth century. The area developed a short distance from the village center as Kalamazoo's first suburb. The comfortable homes built by locally prominent residents reflect the steady economic growth of the town.

KZ09.1 American Red Cross Building
(William A. and Sarah Wood House)

1877–1878, Bush and Patterson, contractors. 530 West South St.

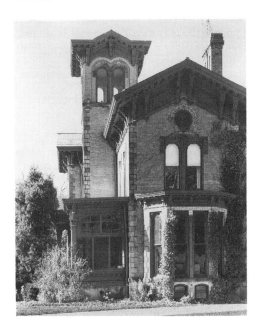

This Italian Villa, complete with a prominent square tower pierced with narrow, round-arch, paired windows, a deep bracketed cornice, and an asymmetrically placed veranda, was built by a local banker and businessman, William A. Wood, and his wife, Sarah. The exterior walls are orange brick with sandstone trim. The nineteen-room house was constructed with imported French windows, a central furnace, and hot and cold running water. The interior has exquisite ornamental plasterwork, carved marble and wood fireplaces, a carved wooden staircase, and other rich woodwork. It was built by Bush and Patterson at a cost of $25,000. The design of the Wood house resembles some of those published in Samuel Sloan's *Homestead Architecture* (1860).

KZ09.2 William H. and Maria DeYoe House

1853. 602 West South St.

The Gothic Revival DeYoe house employs a steeply pitched roof, third-story triple lancet windows with window hoods, label moldings, and diamond-paned oriel and bay windows that evoke the medieval romanticism so popular in mid-nineteenth-century America. The paired, carved decorative brackets along the gables, a feature commonly found in the Italianate style, add to the picturesqueness of this house.

KZ10 Stuart Neighborhood

1850–1900. Stuart, Douglas, West Kalamazoo, and Woodward avenues; Elm and Elmwood streets

The Stuart Neighborhood is named for its most notable resident, Charles A. Stuart, who served as state representative and as U.S. senator. This area prospered following the Civil War and is especially rich in examples of the Queen Anne. The neighborhood is undergoing extensive preservation.

KZ10.1 Amariah T. Prouty House
(Arcadia)

1852. 302 Elm St.

In its steeply pitched and pinnacled gable roof, its elaborate bargeboards, its oriel window, its tracery, and its delicate Tudor-arched veranda, the Prouty house is a rural interpre-

KZ10.1 Amariah T. Prouty House (Arcadia)

tation of the Gothic Revival. The cottage was originally set well back from the road and surrounded by foliage, consistent with advice in the writings of Andrew Jackson Downing.

KZ10.2 Edgar E. Bartlett–James T. Upjohn House

1886. 229 Stuart Ave.

The Bartlett-Upjohn house exudes the picturesque charm of the Queen Anne. The large gabled and clapboarded structure is dominated by a prominent angled, dormered, and spired corner tower and by delightful full-width porches with spindlework.

It was acquired in 1907 by one of the founders of the Upjohn Company.

KZ10.3 Charles E. Stuart House

1854–1858. 427 Stuart Ave.

Also elaborate in detail and imposing in appearance is the Stuart house. This symmetrical, cube-shaped Italianate house has a hipped roof with overhanging eaves, ample entablature, and a large but simple belvedere. The center entrance is crowned with a bracketed and arched hood.

KZ11 Kalamazoo College

Albert Kahn, Aymar Embury II, etc. Bounded by Lovell, Monroe, West Main (Michigan 43), and Catherine streets

Kalamazoo College is a small, liberal arts college that was founded in 1833 as the Michigan and Huron Institute and was renamed Kalamazoo College in 1840. Many of the structures date from the 1920s and the 1930s, when the college underwent a vigorous centennial building campaign. Detroiter Albert Kahn designed Mary Trowbridge Hall and New Yorker Aymar Embury II designed the present Administration Building, Old Welles Hall, Hoben (1937) and Harmen halls, and Stetson Chapel—all within the Georgian Revival style. In the tradition of the nineteenth-century New England meetinghouse, Stetson Chapel (1932) features a colossal Ionic portico and a 109-foot tower topped with a tall, slim, cupola covered with gold leaf.

KZ12 Henderson Castle (Frank Henderson House)

1890–1895, Charles A. Gombert. 100 Monroe St.

Henderson Castle presides over West Main Hill of Henderson Park, a garden suburb platted in the 1880s. The monumental Queen Anne home of Frank Henderson (d. 1899), a manufacturer of fraternal regalia, has an irregular silhouette of gables, turrets, dormers, and a dominant circular tower. The equally extraordinary interior employs stained glass and mahogany, bird's-eye maple, quartered oak, birch, sycamore, and other woods. It was designed by Charles A. Gombert of Milwaukee, who was one of that city's top-ranking architects in the late nineteenth century and the designer of wine and liquor merchant Victor Schlitz's large brick Queen Anne house, erected in 1890 on West Highland Avenue, in Milwaukee.

KZ13 Water Tower, Kalamazoo Regional Psychiatric Hospital (Kalamazoo Asylum for the Insane)

1895, William B. Stratton. Oakland Dr. between Wheaton Ave. and Howard St.

The water tower resembles the keep, or donjon of a medieval castle—in this case, the castle was the insane asylum. Water tanks were enclosed at the top of the 175-foot tower, behind a crenellated yellow brick curtain wall that projects from the red brick cylinder and whose overhang is supported by brackets. The room at the top is reached by a spiral staircase and ladder, and it affords a spectacular view of the hospital and the city. The first buildings at the Michigan Asylum for the Insane at Kalamazoo were erected in 1854–1859 to designs prepared by A. H. Jordon of Detroit, after the embodied experience of the Association of Medical Superintendents, as expressed in a series of Propositions on Construction of Asylums, adopted at a convention in Philadelphia in 1851. Later additions were planned by the prominent Chicago architects, Holabird and Roche. The early buildings no longer stand.

KZ14 Parkwyn Village

1947, Frank Lloyd Wright. 2662, 2801, 2816, and 2822 Taliesin Dr.

In early 1947 a group of young Kalamazoo residents asked Frank Lloyd Wright to design a cooperative subdivision. Wright submitted preliminary drawings for two subdivisions, one facing Woods Lake (then south of the city) and the other south of the village of Galesburg. The former, Parkwyn Village, was originally laid out as forty lots on 47 acres. The ideal lot had a radius of 100 feet. Spaces between the lots and a large central park were designated as park land; however, in order to obtain Federal Housing Authority financing, the lots were squared off so that all boundary lines were contiguous. The houses designed for Parkwyn Village exemplify what Wright called the Usonian Automatic, a small house designed according to the principles of organic architecture. Four houses were built following Wright's designs. The Robert D. Winn House, 2822 Taliesin Drive, features a sweeping semicircular porch facing the lake and is carefully screened from the road. The living room of the Robert Levin House (1948), at 2816 Taliesin Drive, flares dramatically from the fireplace core to the top of the two-story windows. Long and low, the Eric V. Brown

KZ14 Parkwyn Village, Ward McCartney House

House (1949), at 2801 Taliesin Drive, is based on a hexagon and was built in stages, illustrating Wright's philosophy that the Usonian Automatic could be expanded as needed. The Ward McCartney House (1949), at 2662 Taliesin Drive, was built on a diamond module.

KZ15 James and Mary Thorne House

1987, Norman F. Carver, Jr. 4210 Old Field Trail

The James and Mary Thorne House is influenced by the purity of Japanese architecture. It is typical of the architecture of Norman F. Carver, Jr., who is known throughout the Midwest and the United States for his residential designs. Educated at Yale, Carver studied Japanese architecture under two Fulbright scholarships. The Thorne house emphasizes structure and modular organization, and it uses factory-built, stressed-skin panels.

PORTAGE

KZ16 Cathedral Church of Christ the King

1967–1969, Irving W. Colburn. 2600 Vincent Dr. (I-94 near intersection with US 131)

The Cathedral Church of Christ the King, the seat of the Bishop of the Diocese of Western Michigan, commands notice from its high position on a 30-acre park off Interstate 94 (I-94). Sixteen brick piers, or spiky towers, project upward from the red brick cube. The cube contains a central plan, organized around a circular altar on a raised dais of poured concrete. The exterior walls of the steel-frame

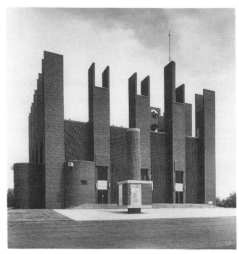

KZ16 Cathedral Church of Christ the King

and poured concrete structure are of red brick and colored glass. The church complex consists of the main church and balcony, a 300-seat undercroft, administrative offices, classrooms, a library, and conference rooms. The building cost $2 million. The influence of Louis Kahn is especially striking, recalling, for example, his Richards Medical Research Building at the University of Pennsylvania.

KZ17 Building 88—Headquarters Building, The Upjohn Company

1961, Skidmore, Owings and Merrill. 7000 Portage Rd. (southwest corner of Portage Rd. and Bishop, 3 miles south of I-94)

The Headquarters Building of the Upjohn Company employs an early use of a ceiling space grid planning system. The structure contains 300,000 square feet of office space and was designed with numerous interior courts to provide all private offices with an exterior view. The integration of a landscaped, parklike setting and a modern office building exemplifies the corporate architecture of the 1960s.

GALESBURG VICINITY, CHARLESTON TOWNSHIP

KZ18 Galesburg Country Homes Acres

1947, Frank Lloyd Wright. 11036, 11098, 11108, 11185 Hawthorne Dr. (south of I-94 on 35th St., 1.5

miles, then east on ML Ave. about .75 mile to 36th St., then south .5 mile to Hawthorne Dr.)

The original 1947 plan for the Galesburg Country Home Acres contained twenty-two circular homesites, each with a radius of 114 feet. Of the four Wright homes built in the area, three follow the Usonian Automatic concept. The Eric Pratt House (1948), at 11036 Hawthorne Drive, is long and low and opens to the south, away from the road. The Samuel Eppstein House, at 11098 Hawthorne Drive, has a dramatic two-story living area shielded from the road by a semicircular retaining wall. The David I. Weisblat House (1948), at 11185 Hawthorne Drive, is protected from the road by a berm but opens onto the rolling park land to the north and west through French doors in the living room. The home owners worked closely with those building houses at Parkwyn Village, even sharing the molds for concrete blocks. The remaining house, designed for Curtis Meyer and built in 1948 at 11108 Hawthorne Drive, is dramatically semicircular in plan, and was built separately.

HICKORY CORNERS VICINITY, ROSS TOWNSHIP

KZ19 **W. K. Kellogg Manor House** (W. K. Kellogg Biological Station)

1925–1927; Benjamin and Benjamin; Edward H. Freyling, landscape architect. W. K. Kellogg Biological Station, 3700 East Gull Lake Dr. (from Michigan 89

north on 40th St., 2 miles to B Ave, then west almost 1.5 miles on B. Ave. to East Gull Lake Dr.)

W. K. Kellogg, the "Corn Flakes King," cereal magnate, and owner of the Kellogg Company, commissioned this Neo-Tudor mansion as part of a 30-acre country estate, with 20 acres of lawns and shrubs and 1,600 feet of Gull Lake shoreline just 15 miles from company headquarters in Battle Creek.

Exterior Tudor characteristics include half-timbering, roughened random brickwork, multiple chimneys with terracotta finials, four-centered pointed arches, casement windows, heraldic shields in leaded glass, and variants of quatrefoil and dogtooth detailing. The gabled roof is of Ludowici Imperial closed shingle tile.

The eighteen-room house, with its asymmetrical open plan reminiscent of the American domestic revival, features a large entry hall with an English Gothic-inspired carved staircase and newel and with Rookwood floor tile that complements the battlemented medieval design of the Rookwood tile fireplace in the living room. It was built by Theodore J. Beyne and G. J. Heckman.

Using an extensive underground sprinkling system, the site was transformed from an eroded cornfield into a picturesque arboretum, with a thatched windmill imported from Holland, a lagoon, and a boat dock.

In 1952 the W. K. Kellogg Foundation gave the estate to Michigan State College (now Michigan State University) as part of the Kellogg Gull Lake Biological Station (now the W. K. Kellogg Biological Station).

Saint Joseph County (SJ)

CENTREVILLE

SJ01 **Harvey and Susan Emily Fenn Cady House**

c. 1867. 135 West Burr Oak St. (southeast corner of West Burr Oak and Clark streets)

Opposite the southwest corner of the courthouse square in this town on the Prairie River stands this delightful example of Italianate domestic architecture so prominent in southwestern Michigan. It is a two-story, red brick cube with a hipped roof and a pinnacled

belvedere. Every seventh course of the common brick bond of the exterior walls consists of alternating headers and stretchers. Prominent paired scrolled brackets support the roof of both the house and the belvedere. The frosting on the cake, however, is the two-story recessed porch. Like the French colonial *galerie*, it runs across one-half of the north-facing facade. Its paneled piers are braced with decorative lacy sawed and scrolled wooden brackets. Harvey and Susan Emily Fenn Cady came to Saint Joseph County in 1835 from Glenville, Schenectady County, New York. Cady (1890–1897) established, in 1873, a

SJ01 Harvey and Susan Emily Fenn Cady House

knitting mill that became the Dr. Denton's Sleeping Garment Mills. All his life Cady promoted the beautification of Centreville. Along its streets he planted hundreds of trees, and across from the courthouse he erected this house.

THREE RIVERS

SJ02 **Carnegie Center for the Arts** (Three Rivers Public Library)

1904–1905, A. W. Rush and Sons. 107 North Main St. (Business US 131)

On a triangular block bounded by Portage, North Main, and Prutzman streets is the trapezoidal Three Rivers Public Library. The footprint of the building conforms to a site shaped by the diagonal section of the grid pattern of the city's streets made by Portage Street as it follows the path of the Portage River. The Portage River and the Saint Joseph and Rocky rivers converge at Three Rivers, dividing the city into several distinct districts. The two-story Shingle style library was built alongside commercial buildings in the business district of the city. It is the ingenious design of A. W. Rush and Sons of Grand Rapids and Kalamazoo.

The asymmetrical main west-facing facade has a gabled block. The exterior walls of both the North Front Street (front) facade and the Portage Street (rear) facade are laid with carefully selected and broken pink granite fieldstones; the walls of the flank are brick. The front windows are trimmed with red Lake Superior sandstone. Lilac slate clads the walls of the front gable and curves into the recessed paired windows of the second story. In the peak are three tiny round-arch win-

dows. Piers support the ample entablature and full-arch crown of the distinctive recessed entrance portal. From the foyer a long hall leads into the heart of the building—the book delivery and reading room on the first floor and to a wooden spindlework staircase that rises to the second floor. The second floor contains an assembly room with a stage and a director's room. Light filtered through a skylight of glass stained aqua, yellow, rose, ocher, and light green and centered on a rosette illuminates a second-floor rotunda and the book delivery room below. In the book delivery room, marbleized Doric columns support broad archways and a fireplace is on the north wall. The main rooms were originally richly decorated in eclectic interpretations of historic period and styles, Louis XIV, Louis XV, and Moorish.

The Carnegie Foundation funded the library's construction with a $12,000 grant; Warren J. Willets (1853–1904), a local banker who was the former president of the Sheffield Car Company, donated the lot. Unlike other Carnegie libraries in the expected Beaux-Arts Classical style, the Three Rivers library is designed in a manner reminiscent of H. H. Richardson's late domestic work. Today the Three Rivers Public Library is adaptively reused as the Carnegie Center for the Arts. Its interior is totally intact and its oak floors still shine "like Cinderella's glass slipper."

NOTTAWA VICINITY, NOTTAWA TOWNSHIP

SJ03 **Nottawa Stone School** (District No. 3 Nottawa Township School)

1870, John W. Schermerhorn, builder. 1880s, addition. Northeast corner of Michigan 86 and Filmore roads (1.5 miles west of North Sturgis Rd. [Michigan 66])

In 1870, the County Superintendent of Public Instruction recorded that this district, which was "considerably below the average wealth of rural districts," erected this one-story fieldstone school with a belfry to replace a wood-frame structure. Probably designed by John W. Schermerhorn, a farmer who was the director of the district and the builder of the structure, it has round-arch windows topped by incipient hood moldings and a center double-door entrance with a fanlight. The noble character of the little school derives from the skillful manner in which the fieldstones are laid in the exterior walls. The stones are regularly coursed in the foundation and randomly coursed in the walls. In the gable, cobblestones are laid in even courses. Poorly conceived tuck pointing has somewhat reduced the exquisite quality of the masonry. At its completion, the school seemed to the same superintendent, "in architectural appearance seldom equaled in the most wealthy rural districts, and in solid convenience and finish . . . a model." It cost $3,000.

MENDON VICINITY

SJ04 **Woodlawn** (Patrick and Frances Mouton Marantette House)

1835 (1840?). 601 Simpson Rd. (north side of Simpson Rd. .5 mile east of Nottawa Rd.)

In a maple grove atop the high south bank of the Saint Joseph River as it bends to the west south of Mendon is situated Woodlawn. This remarkable Greek Revival house was built on this important water route into the state's interior by Patrick Marantette (1807–1878), a Detroiter who in 1833 began operating an Indian trading post established at this site in 1829 by the Godfroy brothers. (The Godfroys, Marantettes, and Moutons were French-Canadian families.) Paneled pilasters mark the corners of the two-story, side-hall-plan, wood-frame house. In the gabled main (south) facade, side and transom lights surround the ceremonial front entrance of the house. The entrance is protected by a porch. The house was obviously approached most frequently from the west, however. A two-story porch runs across two-thirds of the west flank. Square, paneled piers support the balustraded porch at each level. The house resembles examples of Greek Revival domestic architecture that sometimes employed the French *galerie*.

In its isolated surroundings, one can almost experience the ambiance of the setting as it was in the late nineteenth and early twentieth centuries. Looking upstream, the spire of the fieldstone Gothic Revival Saint Edward's Catholic Church, built in 1908 at the northeast corner of State and Lake streets in Mendon to replace the first church of 1872, is visible. Just downstream is the single-span, Pratt through-truss Marantette Bridge. The steel bridge was erected by the Massillon Bridge Company in 1873 to carry Buckner Road (Railroad Street) over the Saint Joseph River. To the south are thousands of acres of prairie originally owned by Marantette.

COLON

SJ05 **Colon Public Library**

1914–1915, C. A. Fairchild and Son. 128 South Blackstone Ave. (northwest corner of South Blackstone Ave. and Canal Street)

The Prairie-style design of this privately funded public library contrasts with the Beaux-Arts Classical designs frequently employed in Carnegie libraries. Oliver B. Culver (1840–1913), a strawberry and melon farmer, bequeathed $15,000 to Colon Township for the construction of a free library and auditorium to honor his late wife, Mary E. Sharer Culver (1844–1912), with the proviso that the local citizens subscribe an additional $3,000 for the purchase of land and for future maintenance. Three days after his will was read, sixty Colon taxpayers signed a petition that met Culver's conditions. The will stipulated that the library should have two stories and a basement, that it contain on the first floor a suitable and convenient ladies' waiting room with a toilet, and that it conform as closely as possible to the Branch County Library (Edwin R. Clarke Library, BR01, p. 202) or the Eckhart Public Library at Auburn, Indiana. C. A. Fairchilds and Son, a Kalamazoo architectural firm, designed the library. Its exterior is identical to the Eckhart Public Library.

The building is a broad-fronted, two-story (plus basement) structure of orange glazed brick. The dramatically projecting gable roof is supported by open brackets and was covered originally with green tile. The highly decorative exterior has broad Richardsonian arched windows in the second story, plaster panels in the gable ends, and skirtlike buttresses above the water table. Green glass windows with a lily motif decorate the main entrance and foyer. Red oak trims the interior. On the first floor is the library room with a fireplace and women's rest room, an auditorium and committee room is on the second, and a museum in the basement.

STURGIS

SJ06 Sturges-Young Civic Center and Auditorium (Sturges-Young Civic Auditorium and Community Center)

1955, A. M. Strauss, Inc. 201 North Nottawa St. (Michigan 66) (northeast corner of North Nottawa and East West streets)

Built in the post-World War II period of a growing economy and swelling American pride and patriotism, this modern civic center was intended as a "facility to advance the American way of life." Gifts from the estates of two families in the names of Stella M. Sturges Taylor, Clara M. Sturges, and Emma D. Young funded the project. The grounds, the building, and the furnishings cost nearly $750,000. A. M. Strauss of Fort Wayne, Indiana, designed the structure in what he called "conservative contemporary." It has three main interior areas: a nearly 1,000-seat main auditorium-theater; a conference room and main dining room that seats 300; and a youth center and a smaller meeting area with a stage, a main floor, and a mezzanine. Red birch and cypress line the walls of the main lobby; slate covers the floor. A large relief sculpture in concrete on the exterior of the auditorium by Ivan Adams of Bloomington, Indiana, depicts symbols of classical and modern entertainment—a lyre, a lute, Greek comic and tragic masks, and a microphone encircled with a segment of motion picture film.

Cass County (CS)

DOWAGIAC

CS01 The Maples (Archie B. Gardner House)

1895–1897, William K. Johnston. 1910, additions. 511 Green St. (which intersects West Division 1 block east of West Main St. [Michigan 62 and 61]

Described by the *Dowagiac Republican* for May 28, 1896, as "overlooking to the northwest a large sweep of vale and verdure," The Maples was one of the rural homes that formed a part of this superb rural landscape. The massive Romanesque Revival stone house was designed for entertaining. It was built for Archie B. Gardner (1870–1944), the grandson of Philo D. Beckwith, who in 1871 founded the Round Oak Stove Company and who was a manufacturer and an international distributor of wood- and coal-burning stoves. Gardner also served as the company's cashier, treasurer, and director. The house was designed by William K. Johnston of Chicago, formerly of Sault Sainte Marie and Muskegon, who in 1890 had just completed the huge, marble Richardsonian Romanesque house at Muskegon for lumber baron John Torrent (see MU01.3, p. 387).

More flamboyant than the Torrent house, the Gardner house seemed at the time to be rustic on the exterior and Colonial Revival on the interior, but it has more Romanesque Revival features. The house, in many ways, owes much to H. H. Richardson's Ames Gate Lodge (North Easton, Massachusetts, 1880–1881): the boulder construction, the sweeping red-tiled roofs, and the massive entrance arch. Its massive shape is walled with huge rough boulders, trimmed with Jacobsville (Lake Superior) red sandstone and Waverly (Holland) gray sandstone, and covered with a red Conesara clay-tiled multiple-hipped roof with flared eaves. A centrally positioned round tower, with a bell-cast roof, and a Richardsonian entry porch dominate the front. A huge stone carriage house is at the rear of the house.

The inside was made for social gatherings, although Gardner spent part of his summers on Maple Island, a retreat for managers of the Round Oak Stove Company, and he wintered at Coconut Grove, Florida. The entrance hall extends the full depth of the building and gives access to the reception hall, a wood-paneled chamber, the library, and, in turn, the dining room and the conservatory. A billiard room is in the basement. The reception room, a full two stories in height, contains a balcony reached by a staircase of bird's-eye maple, an alcove for a band that is backed with stained-glass windows depicting musical instruments and by a 7-foot-broad fireplace. The rooms are finished with mahogany, oak, black walnut, white maple, red birch, ash, and other woods; they are hung with tapestries, hand-painted canvases, and silks; and they are installed with a running fountain, a green onyx mantel, and with silver and gold hardware. A built-in refrigerator and range, electricity, steam heat, and hot and cold running water were some of the house's unexpected modern conveniences.

The Maples is more skillfully designed by far than the eclectic Rockery, the home that Gardner's aunt and uncle, Fred E. and Kate Beckwith Lee, built in 1898, at 407 High Street, with Round Oak Stove Company money.

Standing at the edge of a densely wooded 576-acre forest preserve known as Newton Woods is this two story, wooden, Italianate cube with a square, bracketed, belvedere-topped, hip-roofed main section and an attached two-story wing. A veranda with chamfered square posts spans the entire front of the house. A touch of classicism is evident in the prominent dentil frieze that extends all around the house. George P. Newton (1810–1883), a prominent farmer and civic leader who was the son of a Cass County pioneer, and his wife, Esther (1819–1893), commissioned local builder Christian G. Haefner to erect the house. Haefner was also responsible for the two-story west wing addition in 1868. The house echoes the prosperity of Volinia's largest landholders and projects their "taste and cultivation." Today Michigan State University manages the timber preserve and leases the house to the Cass County Historical Commission, which operates it as a county museum. Open to public.

MARCELLUS

CS03 **Carroll Sherman and Bessie E. Jones House**

1898–1900, Almon C. Varney. 170 West Main St. (Michigan 216)

This well-proportioned house is a good example of a building combining elements of the Dutch Colonial Revival with the sensitive use of richly textured materials. Designed by

VOLINIA TOWNSHIP

CS02 **George P. and Esther Green Newton House**

1865, 1868, addition, Christian G. Haefner. 20689 Marcellus Highway (7 miles west of Michigan 40)

Detroit architect Almon C. Varney (1849–1930), the house was built for Carroll Sherman Jones (1857–1921), the younger son of George Washington Jones, who was one of the cofounders of the village of Marcellus, a livestock-raising center in the prairie land of Cass County. Carroll Sherman Jones served as cashier in the G. W. Jones Exchange Bank, which opened in 1877 in a two-story frame building, but moved into the stone-fronted building erected in 1890 and added to in 1912, at 123 West Main Street. In 1898, Jones commissioned Varney, author of the popular architecture book, *Our Homes and Their Adornments* (1884), to draw up plans for an elaborate shingle and fieldstone house just east of his late father's wooden Queen Anne house at 170 West Main Street. The result is this gambrel-roof structure of rock-faced stone with slate-clad gables and a slate-clad cone-roof round tower. The house's fine classical details include a round porch with Tuscan columns, multilight windows, and dentil-trimmed cornices.

EDWARDSBURG

CS04 Ezra Miller House

c. 1840. 26624 Main St. (US 12)

This small Greek Revival house was built by a pioneer settler, Ezra Miller (1808–1879), who came in 1835 from Onondaga, New York, to this area of the Michigan Territory. Miller acquired 80 acres of land in Edwardsburg, on which he built the house. A one-and-a-half-story, side-gable, symmetrical structure of locally fired red brick with cornice and side returns, it is considered to be the oldest house in Edwardsburg.

Berrien County   (BE)

SAINT JOSEPH–BENTON HARBOR

The twin cities of Benton Harbor–Saint Joseph straddle the mouth of the Saint Joseph River on the sandy southeastern shore of Lake Michigan. This location greatly influenced the early development of both cities. So did economic and cultural ties to Chicago and to South Bend, Indiana, located farther upstream on the Saint Joseph River. Sometimes the two cities worked in concert, but often they worked as rivals. Today, they are separated by racial unrest. The rivalry predates the racial differences, however, and influenced the growth of the cities and their buildings.

Saint Joseph was platted in 1831 on the high southwest bank of the river. It was the early business and shipping center. At first, Benton Harbor had only a few scattered homesteads on three bluffs surrounding the lowlands that merged into marshes on the northeast side of the river. The opening, in 1836, of the territorial road from Detroit to Benton Harbor and the federal dredging of the river sparked the growth of shipping and brought travelers from the east. Plans to build a railroad terminating in the west at Saint Joseph encouraged land speculation and further growth until 1843, when it bypassed the two cities and was routed farther south, through Niles to Chicago. From 1843 until 1869, when a railroad did reach the twin cities, the economy slumped. The area was rural, agricultural, and conservative. Early modest Greek Revival houses exist, but there are few Gothic Revival, Second Empire, and Italianate buildings. The area's economy flourished sufficiently in the 1880s and the 1890s to support a middle-class standard of living. The result was an abundance of Queen Anne houses, most often vernacular in nature.

Among the earliest points of dissension between the two cities were the refusal of Saint Joseph to help rebuild a bridge linking the cities that had been washed out in 1858 and a dispute over docking privileges in Saint Joseph. In 1860 Benton Harbor started building a road across the marsh, a new bridge to Saint Joseph, and a shipping canal. Benton Harbor grew. Its business district developed on the large central lowland, and the residences, on the bluffs that surround the city in three directions. But Saint Joseph was surrounded on three sides by the lake and the river, and it could only grow to the south. As its business district expanded, early homes and buildings were either torn down or moved south.

In the 1890s the two cities united in an effort to acquire the county seat for Saint Joseph. The cities became more industrial and less agricultural. Tourism became an important industry, as Chicagoans escaped on large excursion boats and trains to Michigan beaches, dance halls, river resorts, hotels, and cottages.

By 1950, Benton Harbor had eclipsed Saint Joseph. It had the largest open-air noncitrus fruit market in the world. The House of David, a religious colony founded in 1905, attracted international attention.

The need, in the 1930s and the 1940s, for cheap labor in the foundries of the twin cities and on nearby fruit farms encouraged black migration from the South. Today, Benton Harbor is largely an Afro-American city, and Saint Joseph is mostly Euro-American. The business district of Benton Harbor was nearly deserted in the late 1970s and early 1980s, as merchants left for Saint Joseph and the mall. In 1988 Whirlpool Corporation, which has manufactured home appliances here for eighty years, offered a five-year, $5 million challenge grant to Benton Harbor to resurrect the city. This and the creation of an enterprise zone may help improve the physical appearance and the business climate. New building is occurring in Saint Joseph and in the suburbs of Benton Harbor. There are beautiful old houses in the Pipestone-Colfax area of Benton Harbor.

SAINT JOSEPH

BE01 Whitcomb Tower Retirement Center (Whitcomb Hotel)

1927–1928, Pond, Pond, Martin, and Lloyd. 509 Ship St. (just west of US 33)

The Whitcomb Tower exemplifies the successful adaptation of an older hotel for reuse as a retirement center. The Whitcomb stands on a bluff above the Saint Joseph Harbor, where the Saint Joseph River flows into Lake Michigan. The original Whitcomb Hotel, known as the Whitcomb Sulphur Springs Hotel after being remodeled in 1875 from the still earlier Saint Charles Hotel erected in 1868, was demolished to make way for this

BE01 Whitcomb Tower Retirement Center (Whitcomb Hotel)

structure. Irving K. Pond (1857–1939) and Allen B. Pond (1858–1929) and their associates Edgar Martin and Alfred L. Lloyd drafted plans for the Hotel Whitcomb. The Ponds had studied architecture and engineering at the University of Michigan and had associated in a partnership in Chicago that won acclaim for its designs of hotels, apartments, offices, and college buildings. The seven-and-a-half-story, highly stylized, and modernized Neo-Tudor hotel has a square tower topped with a bell-cast, copper-domed cupola. The brick exterior walls are trimmed with bands and stringcourses of white stone. On the west side are a stone colonnade, stylized stone relief carvings suggestive of the Streamline Moderne style, copper-topped oriels and bays, and a sunken court that once held an enclosed garden lounge and a dance floor. The hotel accommodated resorters and tourists who visited the nearby mineral springs, enjoyed the excellent view of Lake Michigan, and bathed at the beaches of this resort community. In the 1960s Michigan Baptist Homes Inc. purchased the hotel and renovated it to serve as a retirement center.

BE02 Allegretti Architects, Inc., Office Building (Saint Joseph Carnegie Library)

1903–1904, William Augustus Otis. 1982, rehabilitated, Allegretti Architects, Inc. 500 Main St. (US 33)

This delicate red brick Neoclassical Carnegie library is the only known Michigan example of the work of William Augustus Otis (1855–1929), once a student of civil engineering at the University of Michigan and of architecture at the Ecole des Beaux-Arts. Otis executed plans for this library during the period of his independent practice, between 1889 and 1914. A few examples of Otis's work during his association with William Le Baron Jenney, between 1882 and 1889, have been identified in Manistee.

Like other designs by Otis, this library exhibits a scholarly historic treatment suited to modern requirements, beautifully proportioned and lightly detailed. The composition focuses on the corner entrance, which is like a simplified version of Sir John Soane's (1788–1834) Bank of England. Fan-shaped steps lead up to a concave entryway recessed beneath a denticulated and balustraded balcony, supported by fluted Ionic columns and Doric pilasters. The columns have a noticeable entasis, which adds a degree of elegance to the building. The central doorway is flanked by side lights and is capped by a broken segmentally arched pediment. Pedimented pavilions, with brick quoins and recessed round arches, flank the entrance. The interior is distinguished by mahogany casement work, denticulated cove moldings, pilastered archways, and a central skylight. The library was built on a city-donated lot by Max W. Stock, a Saint Joseph contractor, with a grant of $13,500 from Andrew Carnegie. Allegretti Architects, Inc., rehabilitated the building for its own offices in 1982.

BE03 Ina Moriss Harper House

1950–1951, Frank Lloyd Wright. 2571 Old Lake Shore Dr. (east of Lake Shore Dr. (Business I 94)

Situated on a bluff overlooking Lake Michigan along Lake Shore Drive, the Harper house exemplifies Wright's characteristics in the use of broad, sweeping, horizontal roof lines; the richness of the textural interplay of brick, cypress wood, and glass; the placement of the prominent chimney so that it acts as the hub around which the rooms are distributed, and the abundant use of glass to effect a welcome relationship between the exterior and the interior.

BE04 Jack D. Sparks KitchenAid Administrative Center (Washington School)

1937, Warren S. Holmes Company. 1986, rehabilitation and addition, AKA. 701 Main St. (US 33)

In a $3.6 million renovation by AKA, rehabilitation architects, this school was adapted for reuse as a corporate headquarters for KitchenAid Inc., a subsidiary of Whirlpool. The school replaced two earlier school buildings—one built in 1872 and the other in 1889. It was built in 1937 as a Public Works Administration project. It cost $142,661. Critics considered the building among the most innovative, best-designed, and well-constructed schools in Michigan, one that provided functional solutions to the educational needs of the times. The two-story school of yellowish tan and red brick has a center-recessed, arched entry beneath an oriel window bay and has a cupola atop the roof. Its formality is echoed in the balancing projecting end bays. The kindergarten room, retaining the knotty pine wall paneling, the artificial fireplace, the goldfish pond, and the fountain, was converted into a reception area and products display room; classrooms with large bay windows were made into conference rooms and executive offices. The 1986 addition uses brick that is visually harmonious with the older structure. Interior wall tiles and exterior wall copper light fixtures were cleaned, repaired, and replaced.

BE05 The Harbor and Edgewater

The North Pier has a variety of buildings: the Coast Guard facilities, a lighthouse, modern beach houses, and industrial structures. Ridgeway Drive is west of US 33 and runs parallel to the shore of Lake Michigan.

BE05.1 William Verscolani House

1982, Allegretti Architects, Inc. 4 Ridgeway Dr.

From small balconies, large sweeping decks, portholes, and ribbons of windows, this dunes beach house offers views of Lake Michigan and the Saint Joseph River Yacht Basin. A grain silolike stairwell connects all four stories of the core of the structure. In its stratification and in its provision for the uninterrupted view, the Verscolani house is like a 1982 version of Schindler's Lovell Beach House of fifty years earlier. There is also the influence of Le Corbusier here, especially in the rear views.

BE05.2 David Upton House

1956, George, Fred and William Keck. 200 Ridgeway Dr.

George, Fred and William Keck of Chicago designed this International-style beach house for the son of the founders of Whirlpool and Tabor Hill Winery. The rectangle with a flat roof and a large expanse of glass encompasses an inner courtyard.

LINCOLN TOWNSHIP

BE06 Snow Flake Motel

1962, William Wesley Peters of the Frank Lloyd Wright Foundation; Taliesin Associated Architects. 3822 Red Arrow Highway (Business I-94) (northwest corner of Red Arrow Highway [Business I-94] and Glenlord)

Designed in 1960 by William Wesley Peters of the Frank Lloyd Wright Foundation for Sahag Sarkisian and constructed in 1962 at a cost of $1 million, this motel of concrete blocks and steel is unique in its design, landscaping, and plan. By using the crystalline design of a sliding snowflake, reminiscent of the glacial movement of Michigan's Ice Age and the snowy winters of the present, Peters explained his attempt to tie the motel and its interior "garden court" into the surrounding landscape. The path of the sliding snowflake is defined by a rectangular pond with jet fountains that connects two hexagonal swimming pools in the courtyard with the extended entryway of the motel, thus providing access between the courtyard, the motel office, the lounge, and the conference room. The nearly sixty motel units that comprise the six-pointed star design of the structure are reached from the motel's circular drive and from sliding glass doors on the courtyard side. These glass doors open on the courtyard and permit views of both the courtyard and the surrounding hillside. Triangular plantings of flowers and shrubs within the circular drive and the ripple-cut edge of the roof paneling further accent the snowflake plan.

BENTON HARBOR

BE07 Colfax Inn–Landmark Hotel (Mary's City of David Hotel)

1922–1923. 163 Colfax Ave. (northeast corner of Colfax Ave. and Wall St., 1 block east of Main [I-94])

The House of David religious colony, a cooperative utopian community, built this eccentric four-story, ninety-room hotel as one of its largest income-producing properties. After the death of Benjamin (King Ben) Purnell (1861–1927), the commune's leader, it was operated by Mary (Queen Mary) Purnell (1862–1953), Purnell's estranged widow, and the City of David religious sect that splintered off from the main colony in 1930.

The hotel is built of glistening gray rock-faced concrete blocks, which were manufactured by the House of David colony. This highly romantic surface treatment animates the bizarre fluted and festooned colossal columns that mark the rounded corner entrance. Similar columns divide the block into four bays on one side and five bays on the other, each containing triplet windows: they also appear to support the roofline cornice and the wooden balustrade. Bracket-supported, rounded-corner sills project in a shelflike manner under the paired windows of each floor, and a balcony shelters the corner entryway on the first floor. This pattern is echoed on the adjacent bays of single windows that flank the corner bay, further emphasizing the importance of the building's corner. This structure is one of the largest structures built by the House of David commune and is an impressive downtown landmark.

BE08 House of David Commune, Shiloh House

1908. On East Britain Ave. between Eureka and Blaine avenues (just east of intersection with Michigan 139)

The House of David religious commune was founded in 1903 on 130 acres adjacent to Benton Harbor by Benjamin Franklin Purnell, who proclaimed himself King Benjamin, King of the Israelite House of David.

Purnell came to Detroit from Kentucky, then moved to Ohio, where he established a House of David commune in Fostoria, but he left for Benton Harbor because the townspeople were hostile toward his actions. The House of David was a continuation of a new millennium religious sect, which began in eighteenth-century England with Joanna Southcott's vision that she had been chosen to start preparing the world for the second coming of Christ. The sect was spread by the "Israelites" to the United States in 1844. At Benton Harbor, the House of David practiced traditional Christian communitarian life. Its members surrendered their possessions to the group; abstained from meat, tobacco, and alcohol; practiced celibacy; and devoted their personal service to the work of the commune—all in return for daily sustenance, lodging, and the promise of heaven on earth when the time came. The colony was self-sufficient. It owned farmland, grew food, produced electricity, printed a newspaper, and made its own clothing and building materials. Its members were religious converts and former residents of Illinois, Ohio, Indiana, Kentucky, and Michigan. The House of David peaked at one thousand members in the early 1920s.

On the site, colonists built houses, cottages, and a tabernacle. Two dormitories named Bethlehem and Jerusalem, built in 1904 and 1905–1906, respectively, are annexes to Shiloh House, the residence of King Ben, and they stand side by side on the north side of East Britain Avenue, just west of Shiloh and connected by an arcade to it. One architecturally notable extant structure is a three-story residential building called the Ark, built in 1903. It is located on East Britain Avenue between Fair Avenue and Michigan 139.

Shiloh is a large vernacular Queen Anne residence, built in 1908 by the colonists of the House of David commune. The walls are made of large sparkling concrete blocks manufactured of a patented recipe including hematite in a mold at the site by commune members; the wood used for the wooden members was logged from one of the islands owned by the commune in the Beaver Island Archipelago. Reminiscent of the resort architecture that was built at the turn of the century along Michigan's shorelines, the structure exhibits a veranda that sweeps across its symmetrical facade and wraps around the side elevations, seemingly cinching the three-story corner towers to the square core of the building. The central main entrance is surmounted by a triplet recessed porch at the second level and by a single ceremonial porch at the third, which, in turn, is capped by an eight-sided, bell-cast turret with a finial.

Catering to the thousands of tourists, many from Chicago, who traveled to southwestern Michigan by boat, the colony opened a Coney Island-style amusement park adjacent to the commune. It expanded restaurant facilities and built an amphitheater, where the House of David orchestra played for dances. A small train station, located across from the Jerusalem dormitory on the south side of East Britain Avenue, once served as a passenger station for tourists wishing to ride on the miniature trains that traversed the House of David Amusement Park.

The House of David received international attention for its traveling baseball team and its women's jazz band during the 1920s, as well as for its amusement park.

Scandals, a lawsuit, internal dissension, and the death of King Ben Purnell split the commune and its assets into two sects— the House of David led by Thomas Dewhirst and the City of David led by Mary Stollard Purnell, Purnell's widow.[38] (Continue west on Britain Avenue to south on Spring, then two blocks to Miami to reach BE10, Howard Anthony House.)

STONEVILLE VICINITY, TUSCOLA TOWNSHIP

BE09 Grande Vista Gardens

1933–1937. Red Arrow Highway, just southwest of Ridge and just southeast of Business I-94

BE09 Grande Vista Gardens

BE10 Howard Anthony House

The newly regrouped House of David expanded its real estate holdings between 1933 and 1937. It developed the Grande Vista Gardens, a Mission Revival $150,000 tourist court and casino complex located 6 miles southwest of Saint Joseph, along Red Arrow Highway (Business I-94), just northwest of Stevensville. Once rated by the Automobile Association of America as the finest deluxe tourist court in the Midwest, the complex had seventy-two apartments, a gas station, a museum, a café, a nightclub with a ballroom, and a dance floor, and an outdoor electric-lighted flowing waterfall fountain. Only remnants survive of the structures that show "the most conspicuous symbol of the cult's wealth" and of the garden fountains.

Many of the buildings at the colony have been lost to fire and have been vandalized. The House of David was one of the most successful communitarian societies in Michigan, if not in American history.

House, 1908, in Grand Rapids (KT14.7, p. 261).

The Anthony house is the first of three Wright homes built in the twin cities of Benton Harbor–Saint Joseph within a period of five years or so. All three take advantages of the view and surroundings afforded by the Saint Joseph River or Lake Michigan. This house was built for Howard Anthony, the inventor and developer of the Heathkit, which later became the nationwide Heath Company. The low, hovering, cypress and sandstone house nestles at the head of a wooded ravine on a bluff overlooking the Saint Joseph River. The plan of the house is based on diamond-patterned modules. The prominent chimney anchors the building to its site, and the low roof with generous overhanging eaves contributes to its levitation quality. Since Anthony was an avid bird watcher, Wright provided a balcony and windows overlooking the ravine.

SAINT JOSEPH TOWNSHIP

BE10 **Howard Anthony House**

1951, Frank Lloyd Wright. 1150 Miami Rd. (from exit 30 off I-94–US 31, east on Napier Ave. almost 3.25 miles [just west of Saint Joseph River] to Miami Rd., then north on Miami Rd.)

The second wave of Frank Lloyd Wright's influence in Michigan occurred for slightly more than a decade from the mid-1940s to the mid-1950s. This onslaught was exemplified in some two dozen homes designed by Wright in the latter years of this master's career. The first wave took place early in the century and resulted in a handful of homes, most notably the recently restored Meyer May

BERRIEN SPRINGS

BE11 **Berrien County Courthouse**

1838–1839, Gilbert Avery. 313 North Cass St. (US 31) (southwest corner of North Cass and Union streets)

In 1838–1839, one year after Berrien Springs became the seat of the Berrien County government, this wooden temple-front Greek Revival courthouse was built. Four fluted Doric columns support the entrance portico, and pilasters ornament the corners of all four walls. A square, two-stage tower with louvered openings surmounts the gable roof. The courthouse rests on a raised brick foundation. It is one of the two oldest extant courthouses in Michigan. A treasury building,

BE11a Berrien County Courthouse (exterior)

BE11b Berrien County Courthouse (interior)

a sheriff's house, a second courthouse, and a jail, now demolished, were added to the courthouse square complex in the 1860s and 1870s. This group exemplifies the small county courthouse square that gave dignity to the government of the emerging counties of the Great Lakes region in the mid-nineteenth century.

NILES

Located along a principal ford in the Saint Joseph River, Niles was the site of major Miami and Potawatomi Indian encampments, an early Jesuit mission, a French fort, an Indian uprising and treaty, a very short Spanish occupation (enabling present-day Niles to proclaim itself the "town of four flags"), and a Baptist Indian school—all before the first permanent settler arrived with his family in 1823. The first apple and peach orchards in the state, the first horse-powered flour mill in the county, the first water-powered flour mill in southwest Michigan were all located here before the village was platted in 1829. That action even preceded the establishment of the county in 1831. The 1830s marked a major transition in the development of the area: the French were gone, the Baptist school closed, and the Indians had deeded their lands to the United States. Overlapping these changes were the opening of the Chicago Road, the establishment of a stage line in 1831, and the linking of Niles to Saint Joseph and to the territorial road to the north. With the coming of the Michigan Central Railroad in 1848, the pattern of change was complete.

Niles prospered in the decades before the Civil War, and its architecture includes examples of Greek Revival, Gothic Revival, and Italianate styles that reflect the popularity of national trends. The Henry Chapin House and the Michigan Central Railroad Station, the two most prominent structures built before 1900, exemplify adherence to prevailing tastes.

By the early twentieth century the area was a major paper-producing center, the home of the Whirlpool Corporation, and of Simplicity Patterns. Yet little building appears to have taken place between 1900 and World War I, and the construction that followed the war tended to be simple. Reflecting the area's industrial base, neighborhoods in Niles represented much of small-town, working-class America in the period between World War I and the 1950s. Only in the postwar period, with the development of new materials and technologies by the Kawneer Corporation, was local architecture affected by local industry. Because of their long-term durability and maintenance-free exteriors, downtown merchants refronted older buildings with Kawneer-produced aluminum panels, altering the face of Main Street for the next three decades.

BE12 Niles City Hall (Henry Austin Chapin House)

1882–1884, Wheelock and Clay. 508 East Main St. (US 12) (southeast corner of East Main and Fifth [Michigan 51] streets)

BE13 First Presbyterian Church (Chapin Memorial Presbyterian Church)

1915, Tallmadge and Watson. 1927, fellowship hall addition. 13 South Fourth St. (2.5 blocks south of Main St. [US 12])

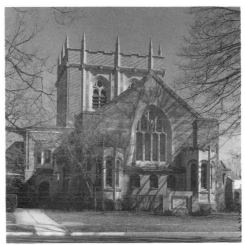

The Henry Austin Chapin House, now the Niles City Hall, is an extraordinary example of the picturesque possibilities of the Queen Anne style. Chapin (1813–1898), a general store operator in Niles, invested in 1865 in Upper Peninsula mineral lands on which an immense deposit of iron ore was discovered in 1878. The Chapin Mine at Iron Mountain paid royalties that Chapin used in constructing this house and in acquiring other real estate in Niles and Chicago. Otis Leonard Wheelock (1816–1886) and William Wilson Clay (1849–1926), specialists in residential work in Chicago, created this one-of-a-kind house in Michigan.

The pressed-red-brick house stands on a foundation of Bedford blue stone, finished with a granite water table. A turreted, round corner tower and a profusion of gables, bays, and projecting and receding porches all but conceal the house's two-and-a-half-story, hipped-roof mass. Panels of herringbone, checkerwork, and lozenge-pattern brickwork, lathe-turned and chamfer-edged posts and beams, metal crestings, sunbursts, and rosette insets lavishly decorate the exterior.

The plan includes a central hall that runs along the main axis of the building, from which open the parlor, the library, the sitting room, and the dining room on the first floor, and the bedrooms on the second. The interior is finished in fine oak, cherry, walnut, and bird's-eye maple, and it is installed with stained glass and fancy fireplaces.

The original First Presbyterian Church, erected soon after the church was founded in 1835, was a small meetinghouse with a seating capacity of 250. It cost $800. It was replaced in 1850 by a larger Greek Revival wooden church with enclosed pews, which cost $10,000. The estate of Charles A. Chapin provided a gift for the present church, which cost $75,000. Chicago school architects Tallmadge and Watson, noted for their ecclesiastic buildings, designed it, and it is a good example of their work. Both men frequented southwest Michigan. Thomas E. Tallmadge (1876–1940), perhaps best known as the author of *The Story of Architecture in America* (1926) and *Architecture in Old Chicago* (1941), was also president of the Summer School of Painting at Saugatuck; Vernon S. Watson (1878–1950) eventually retired in nearby Berrien Springs. The church is a Late Gothic Revival building, constructed of warm gray brick trimmed with buff Bedford stone. A large, squat, square central tower topped by slender pinnacles and encircled with a relief of angels rises over the crossing. Stained-glass windows and stone tracery contribute to the Gothic character. The church is linked by a cloister to the Sunday School and the manse. The auditorium seats 600 before a central pulpit and organ wall. The interior is trimmed in dark red oak.

BE14 Niles Amtrak Station (Niles Station of the Michigan Central Railroad)

1890–1892, Spier and Rohns. 598 Dey St. (just east of Fifth St. [Michigan 51] 6 blocks north of Main St. [Business US 12])

This fine Richardsonian Romanesque station still serves as the last major stop on the old Michigan Central Railroad line (now Conrail) between Detroit and Chicago. It replaced a passenger station that the railroad built as a temporary shelter in 1873, which had in turn replaced an earlier station that had burned, but which served for eighteen years. The Niles depot was intended as the showpiece of the Michigan Central, and it was completed in time to impress travelers to the 1893 Chicago World's Columbian Exposition. German-born architects Frederick H. Spier (b. 1855) and William C. Rohns (1856–1951), whose association in Detroit between 1884 and 1913 resulted in designs for all of the principal depots on the Michigan Central and Grand Trunk Railroad lines, drafted plans for the Niles depot. J. D. Hawks, chief engineer for the Michigan Central, and his assistant, C. W. Hotchkiss, supervised the construction.

The rock-faced Carroll, Ohio, brown sandstone structure is massed in three sections under a substantial hipped and gabled roof. A square, pyramid-roofed stair tower rises to a height of 68 feet on the south and is punctuated by an illuminated clock face that is 5

feet in diameter. Round-arch entries give access and light to the interior, and broad overhangs and shed roofs shelter passengers. The semicircular apselike west section holds waiting rooms and the ticket office; the central section, the kitchen and the dining room; and the eastern section, baggage storage. Above the main floor are offices and apartments.

To beautify the surroundings, John Gipner constructed an elaborate park, with gardens, fountains, and greenhouses like those that Frederick Law Olmsted created for H. H. Richardson's depots on the Boston and Albany railroad. This gave to Niles the nickname "the Garden City." Today, the gardens are gone, but Amtrak has restored the station.

BE15 Paine Bank

1843. 1008 Oak St. (southwest corner of Oak and Eleventh [US 33] streets)

Rodney C. Paine (1806–1875), formerly of New York State, moved in 1842 to Niles after a six-year stay in Saint Joseph. Here, he established an agency of the Farmers and Mechanics Bank of Michigan, which later, in 1848, became his own private business. He erected in 1843 this small, one-story, Greek Revival building on the northwest corner of Main and Third streets. It is a wood-frame, pedimented, templelike, tetrastyle building with fluted Doric portico and pilasters at the corners. Emil Lorch hailed this work as "Niles's most formal classical composition with proportions which are those of masonry rather than of wood."[39] Built in an unstable era of wildcat banking practices and of the panic of 1837, the Greek Revival architectural style symbolized a sense of stability and reason. Originally it stood at 212 Third Street.

BE16 Ring Lardner House (Rodney C. Paine House)

late 1850s. 519 Bond St. (off of Third St., 4 blocks south of Main St. [Business US 12])

On a bluff wooded with maple and cedar trees overlooking the Saint Joseph River is this picturesque, one-and-a-half-story Gothic Revival house. Built for Rodney C. Paine, an early Niles banker, the house echoes Andrew Jackson Downing's advocacy of the picturesque possibilities achieved through the use of sunlight and shadows and in the irregularity of massing in the Gothic Revival style, expressed in *Cottage Residences* (1847) and in *The Architecture of Country Houses* (1858). This effect is especially evident in the scrollwork bargeboards with fleur-de-lis accents at the gable peaks, in the clustered chimneys, and in the wall dormers. Upon Paine's death, Henry and Lena Phillips Lardner bought the house. It was the birthplace of humorist and author Ring Lardner in 1885 and the source of many boyhood memories that appeared in his writings. Lardner (d. 1933) was probably best known as a sportswriter in the 1920s for the *Chicago Examiner*.

PORTAGE PRAIRIE, BERTRAND TOWNSHIP

BE17 Old Chicago Road

Old Chicago Rd. between Orange and Portage roads, but separated by US 31

On the Old Chicago Road in the Saint Joseph River valley on the Portage Prairie just west of the river are two farmsteads, the Peter Womer and the George Rough farms. They were built by Pennsylvania German families, two of several who immigrated into the southwest region of Michigan in the mid-1880s. These Protestant Germans moved west from the fertile Susquehanna River valley in central Pennsylvania, near Selinsgrove, in search of good land and good timber. Prairies, with their fertile grasslands, adjacent woodlots, and water sources, were important settlement destinations in southern Lower Michigan.

BE17.1 Peter and Sarah Rough Womer Farm (Brayton E. Yaw Farm)

1885. 3245 Chicago Rd. (west of US 31, 1 mile southwest of Mayflower Rd.)

Peter Womer (1838–1911), a carpenter and a farmer, purchased his 83 acres of land in Bertrand Township in 1883. He built his house and barn in 1885, with lumber, shingles, and brick picked up at the railroad depots in Niles and in South Bend, Indiana, but presumably milled and made elsewhere. Carpenters from Niles stayed at the farm during the construction but returned to their families on weekends. Unlike the farmsteads of the Pennsylvania Germans, where "barns as big as palaces" overshadowed the house, on

the Womer farm the house is the prominent feature. An 1893 account describes it as a "valuable country estate, second to none in Berrien County." The handsome and commodious house cost $6,000 to build, whereas the "finely finished and capacious barn" cost $2,000.[40]

The two-story house with projecting gables stands on a raised stone foundation, and its red brick walls are trimmed in stone and wood.

The seven-bay, gable-end barn is built in the traditional Pennsylvania or German bank barn form. Womer raised grain, cattle, and hogs. The upper level of the barn contains a hay mow, a hay bale track, and space for grain storage; the middle level houses the threshing floor and the adjacent horse stables; the lowest level contains stalls for farm animals. The barn's exterior is decorated with wide frieze boards, pediment-hooded louvered windows, and oval windows.

Womer succeeded in farming and eventually, by 1893, acquired 1,232 acres of land in southwest Michigan and northwest Indiana. He served as township supervisor, and he held stock in the First National Bank of Niles. The Womer farmstead is evidence of the early success of the Womer family.

BE17.2 George H. Rough Farm (Richard Bassler Farm)

1870s. 2685 Old Chicago Rd. (east of US 31, .75 mile southwest of Portage Rd.)

Built by Sarah Rough Womer's brother, the George H. Rough Farm also has a large brick Italianate house. It has paired brackets and a central cupola.

NEW BUFFALO

BE18 South Cove

1980–present. Harry Weese and Associates. 2 Harbor Isle Dr. (Harbor Isle Dr. between Whittaker and Willard, some 5 blocks west of Buffalo [US 12])

Inspired by the seaside cottage communities of Cape Cod, South Cove is a unique coastal development on the shores of Lake Michigan. The resort complex was designed by Harry Weese and Associates of Chicago in such a manner as to allow residents direct access to

BE18 South Cove

their boats without the usual interference caused by roads, structures, or other obstacles. Boaters at South Cove may literally "park their crafts next to their kitchens."

Individual units feature gable- and shed-roof forms, glazed window walls facing Lake Michigan, wood shingles, and weathered clapboard siding. Through the repetition of popular architectural forms, a variety of living spaces has been provided, ranging from efficiency apartments to three-bedroom, multiple-level homes. Like most Harry Weese designs, South Cove seems harmonious with its waterfront setting, and it reflects the architect's personal belief that good designs must respect their architectural and natural contexts.

Born in Evanston, Illinois, in 1915, Harry Weese has become one of the most prominent Chicago architects of the later half of the twentieth century. Weese studied architecture at the Massachusetts Institute of Technology and Yale University, as well as planning and architecture under Eliel Saarinen at Cranbrook Academy. He has designed college campuses, urban transportation systems, and has dealt with urban revitalization and historic preservation. Other Michigan projects by Harry Weese include Lake Michigan College (1970) at Benton Harbor and the Grand Rapids Convention Center (1980).

Van Buren County (VA)

SOUTH HAVEN

VA01 South Haven South Pier Light

1903. South Pier at the mouth of the Black River outlet to Lake Michigan

From the outer end of the South Haven south pier head, this telescoping, cylindrical, riveted, steel-plate structure has aided navigation at the harbor at the Black River outlet to Lake Michigan since 1903. In 1902 the federal Lighthouse Board replaced the old 1872 wooden structure with a metal pier-head beacon. A Milwaukee firm fabricated the cast-metal work for the tower's modular sections, and the U.S. Lighthouse tender *Hyacinth* shipped the steel and plate metalwork from Milwaukee across the lake, where it was assembled on the pier.

The tapered, 36-foot red stack measures 11 feet 6 inches in diameter at the base. It is capped by an observation deck that is encircled by a wrought-iron railing decorated with latticework. On the deck rests a lantern with a Sixth Order Fresnel glass lens, the smallest in magnitude and the lowest in intensity of the lenses invented by French physicist Augustin Fresnel in 1822. The roof is topped with a ventilator pommel and a lightning rod. A catwalk supported on H-shaped trusses extends the full length of the pier, from the lighthouse to the shore.

The South Haven South Pier Light represents the group of harbor lights built after the Civil War on newly constructed piers. Unlike those on the mainland, pier lights had no residences for keepers. This pier light is one of the smaller steel-frame skeletal lights erected on Lake Michigan. The catwalk is one of four remaining; others are at Saint Joseph, Grand Haven, and Manistee.

VA02 First Hebrew Congregation

1928. 249 Broadway St. (northeast corner of Broadway and Church streets)

With a small permanent Jewish population, South Haven's synagogue was most crowded on summer Sabbaths, when Chicago Jews flocked to the Michigan shore for vacations in the 1920s and 1930s. Before the depression, the First Hebrew Congregation built this eclectic little brick synagogue, marked by a prominent decorative gable end reminiscent of the Flemish gables, or even of the then-fashionable Mission-style gables, and also marked by a similarly fashioned entryway and a large round Star of David window above an arched triple window. This building strikes an exotic foreign note in an otherwise unremarkable streetscape.

VA03 Scott Club

1892–1894, John C. Randall. 652 Phoenix St. (Business I-96) (southeast corner of Phoenix [Business I-96 and Pearl streets)

The Scott Club, a stately Queen Anne structure of rough-cut tan sandstone, tells of the role of women in the late 1800s. In 1883–1884, eight South Haven women organized the social and literary club to foster their intellectual, cultural, and social interests. The membership grew to over one hundred wives and daughters of fruit farmers, tradespeople, and professionals. The members were prominent in the South Haven community and active in other socially important organizations such as the board of education and Woman's Christian Temperance Union. By 1890 the club had outgrown even the sitting rooms of the local churches. Through the joint efforts and resources of the literary club, the antiquarian society, and the reading circle (the predecessor of the Scott Club), the women orchestrated the construction of a building that would serve to promote intellectual, scientific, and cultural enlightenment in addition to providing a reference library for the South Haven community. The women purchased the land on the southeast corner of Phoenix and Pearl streets with the notion that the three groups would share the resulting structure; the first two groups dissolved before construction began. The building was realized through donations of money, materials, and labor from the community and local business people.

Designed and built by John C. Randall, a local architect-builder and planing mill owner, the hipped- and gable-roofed building has a tower in the angle with an open belfry and bell-cast roof. In its clear domesticity and with its bulky tower, it serves as an intermediary between the residential section of South Haven and the east side of the downtown business district. The building displays the decorative wooden brackets, finials, pendants, posts, bargeboards, and spandrels characteristic of

this picturesque style. The main reading room has dual fireplaces with ceramic hearths and golden oak mantlepieces. It is bathed by sunlight filtering through two large stained-glass windows depicting Henry Wadsworth Longfellow and Sir Walter Scott (in whose name the club was incorporated in April 1894), crafted in Innsbruck, Austria, by the Tyrolese Art Glass Institute. The basement holds a kitchen and banquet hall. The interior displays splendid woodworking; the staircase is carved of golden oak with elaborate turnings of the newel post and balustrade. The double entrance doors are heavy carved panels.

VA04 Arundel House (Sara Steuben Summer House)

1890s. 56 North Shore Dr. (northeast corner North Shore Dr. and South St.)

The large, wood and shingled, Colonial Revival summer house overlooks Lake Michigan north of the Black River. It was built by the Steuben family in this resort center only 67 miles by lake ferry from their winter home in Chicago. The cottage resembles the splendid residences designed by Asbury W. Buckley, then of Chicago, but formerly of Kalamazoo and Coldwater, for summer cottagers on Mackinac Island and in the Little Traverse Bay region. The Steuben house is rectangular with a hipped roof. A broad, circular second-story bay and a full-length arcaded first-story

VA05 Mentha Plantation

porch, both with balustrades, permit ample views of the lake. The house also accommodated guests from the adjacent resort, at one time operated by the Steuben family. Open to public.

MENTHA, PINE GROVE TOWNSHIP

VA05 Mentha Plantation

1900–1954. 23rd St. and 18th Ave. (23rd St. from D Ave. [Van Buren County 388/Kal-Haven Trail] to a point 1 mile south of 18th Ave.)

Albert M. Todd (1850–1931), a Kalamazoo mint grower and a mint oil and crystals distiller and dealer, established in the 1890s an experimental commercial mint farm in an extensive black ash and tamarack swamp in the Pine Grove Township of eastern Van Buren County. The purpose of the farm was to promote research to develop hybrid mint plants and to improve agricultural techniques. Todd, also a chemist, had grown mint at his family farm in Nottawa, Saint Joseph County, to which settlers from the Finger Lakes Region of New York State had brought mint-growing skills. One of two such farms developed by the A. M. Todd Company (the other at Campania in central Allegan County),

Mentha and the company town that grew to three hundred people became the operational headquarters for the surrounding 2,200-acre peppermint plantation. Ditches dug to drain the land were developed into a system of drains, dikes, and floodgates to control the water table of the mint fields. Golden willows, as well as maple, cedar, and pine, were planted along roadways as windbreaks. Straddling Todd Avenue (now 23rd Street), which bisects Section 25, the settlement follows a long, narrow plan. Still standing on the east side of the street are the cross-gabled house of the superintendent and several of a row of fifteen to twenty gabled and clapboarded dwellings, originally built for foremen from ready-cut assemblies ordered from catalogs. On the west is the large Colonial Revival company office— the store and the social hall building with its rounded Ionic portico and sunburst-filled pediment. Here also are a boarding house and a big barn, which were among the many agricultural buildings and shops. To the south are the distillery, barns, and other dwellings. Having succumbed to verticillium wilt, the fields were sold to other growers and now yield onions and radishes. Once the producer of 50 percent of the mint grown in the United States, Mentha represents a late nineteenth-century corporate agricultural community devoted to scientific farming.

Grand River Valley Region

RIVERS PLAYED AN IMPORTANT ROLE IN THE DEVELOPMENT of the Grand River valley. The region was organized in the late 1830s. The Grand and the Kalamazoo rivers and their tributaries provided the early means of access and transportation into the region from the Lake Michigan shore. Grand Haven, Singapore, and Saugatuck, at the mouths of these two rivers, became ports of entry for commercial goods and ports of exit for timber products.

Stands of hardwood dominated this region. Since hardwood was more dense and sank at a faster rate than softwood, water transportation of cut logs ended in the Grand River valley long before it did in the Softwood Pine Belt to the north. Consequently, secondary processing, that is, manufacturing, was added to primary processing, which is logging, lumber milling, and flour milling. The ready access to waterpower at the fall of the river at Grand Rapids aided early industrial growth.

During the 1840s and the 1850s, the region experienced a significant influx of Dutch immigrants. Under the leadership of Albertus C. Van Raalte, these immigrants and others, primarily German, came to the area seeking religious freedom and an opportunity for economic improvement. They settled in Ottawa County near the Black River. But the economic vicissitudes of pioneer life caused many of the immigrants, particularly those single and of working age, to leave the Holland area for Grand Rapids. Consequently, immigration spread throughout Ottawa, Kent, and even Allegan counties. These immigrants provided the skilled labor necessary to the various industries of the region, particularly furniture making.

In the western portion of the region, the Dutch influence is reflected in the architecture, as well as in the building material. In 1848, Jan Hendrick Venek-

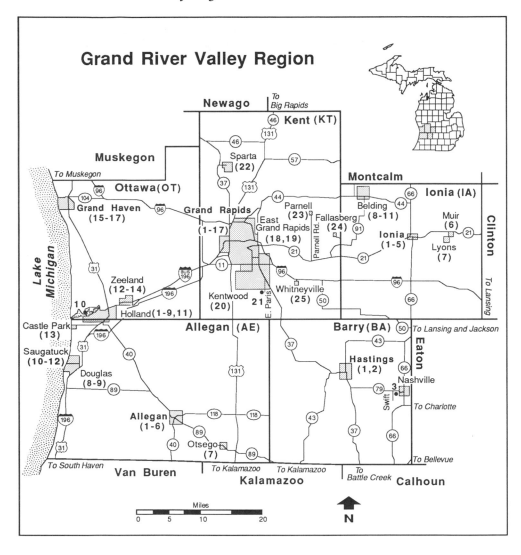

lasen (1800–1877), a recent immigrant from the Netherlands, opened a brick-yard in Zeeland, later adding yards in Hamilton, Cloverdale, Kalamazoo, and Grand Rapids. The firm used locally available clay and produced red and buff bricks, depending on the iron or lime content of the clay. These bricks were used for houses, schools, and municipal buildings during the last half of the nineteenth century and employed patterns of contrasting colors similar to designs in the Netherlands. These designs were also provided by the Veneklasen brickyard as part of the sale of the brick.

But Veneklasen's was not the only brickyard in the region. Other Grand Rapids brick makers produced red brick, as well as a buff brick. Because of the mineral composition of most of the locally available clay, predominantly pale yellowish brick, known as Cream City or Milwaukee brick, was produced during the late nineteenth and early twentieth centuries. Churches, commercial buildings, and many factories, particularly on the north side of Grand Rapids, used this buff brick.

Another local building material was a light yellowish brown sandstone from the Marshall formation, know locally as Waverly sandstone. This sandstone from the Holland area, and from the banks of the Grand River itself, was used throughout the city of Holland, as well as elsewhere in the region. Wood, of course, was the most abundant building material, and wood-frame, clapboard-sheathed structures with decorative carved, turned, and sawn trim abound.

The limited stands of pine in the region, however, resulted in the early shift of the economic base to other industries. Hardwood such as maple and walnut was used for furniture in Grand Rapids, as well as in Holland. The rapids of the Grand River (with a fall of from 15 to 20 feet) were the power force for a series of flouring mills. To service these mills as well as the lumber mills, a machine tool and metal working industry developed. Belding, on the Flat River in Ionia County, was the site of a large silk mill.

As the region grew in population and wealth, Grand Rapids became the home for a number of architects who designed for local, as well as distant, clients. Among these were the father and son, Sidney J. and Eugene Osgood, who did many Masonic temples and county courthouses throughout the state; William G. and Frederick S. Robinson, another father and son, who worked with commercial buildings and churches; David S. Hopkins, who specialized in house plans, which he sold through publications; the firms of J. H. Daverman and Son and later J. and G. Daverman (both founded by Dutch immigrants), who designed pattern-book houses and churches. Churches were their specialty, and dozens of churches designed by Daverman are found throughout the region.

Kent County (KT)

GRAND RAPIDS

Grand Rapids, with a population of nearly 182,000, is Michigan's second-largest city. It is nestled in the Grand River valley 40 miles inland from Lake Michigan. Indians recognized the advantages of the site and used it as a meeting and trading center. "Owashtanong River" ("faraway waters"), so-called by the Indians and translated by the early French traders to "Grand River," flowed south at that point, then turned west and flowed to Lake Michigan. Rapids stretched about 4,000 feet before the turn and quickly dropped 16 feet in elevation. On the east side of the river, a dry, flat plain stretched about 1,000 feet to a steep sand bluff. A broad, swampy plain extended about a mile to the west to the foot of 60-foot-high hills.

French fur trader Louis Campau established a trading post and home at the Indian campsite on the east bank in 1826. He was the first permanent settler of Grand Rapids. A post office was opened in 1832, and the name Grand Rapids was given to the rapidly growing settlement. Incorporated as a village in 1838 and then as city in 1850, with a population of 2,700, the city grew steadily. By the end of the Civil War, it had several railroads and a thriving industrial economy based largely on lumbering.

Grand Rapids

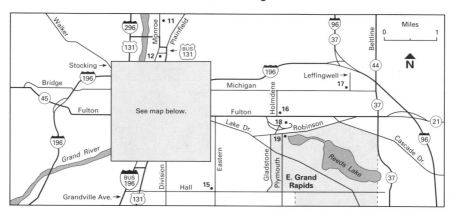

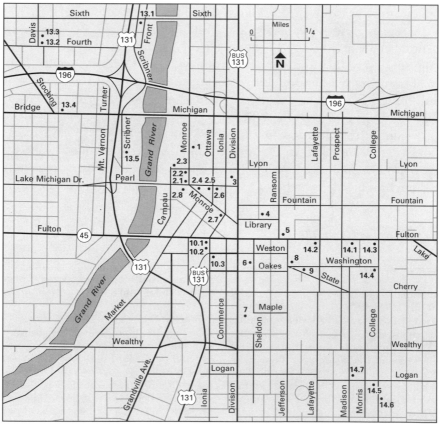

During a period of accelerated growth between 1870 and 1900, as Grand Rapids became the West Michigan center of trade and commerce, there was a great deal of building in the central business district, now called Monroe Center. Grand Rapids has a significant number of fine high-style, late-nineteenth-century buildings that were designed by well-known architects from Chicago and elsewhere, as well as those designed by skilled local architects such as David S. Hopkins, William G. Robinson, and Sidney G. Osgood. In the 1920s some fine skyscrapers were built in Monroe Center. The downtown area remained relatively unchanged until the late 1960s and early 1970s, when urban renewal resulted in the demolition in 1969 of such landmarks as the Grand Rapids City Hall, built in 1885–1888 to the plans of Elijah E. Myers, and the Kent County Courthouse, erected in 1884–1890 to the plans of Sidney J. Osgood. At the same time, it created new landmarks, such as the Vandenburg Center. In recent years, a number of architecturally significant works have been built, or older buildings have been renovated in the lower Monroe area along the river as growth continues.

The west side of the river developed around the industrial base. Homes were built for the working class near factories, and grand churches were built to provide for spiritual needs. The availability of fine craftsmen, an abundance of lumber, and an excellent transportation network led to the success of the furniture industry in Grand Rapids. The display of four Grand Rapids furniture companies at the 1876 Centennial Exposition in Philadelphia called attention to Grand Rapids, and the nation came to regard Grand Rapids as the "furniture capital." Many of these early furniture factories still stand, mostly on the west side, and some are still in operation.

As the city prospered, so did its citizens. Residential construction continued unabated until the 1930s. The area on the bluffs on the east side of the river became the fashionable place to live, with many magnificent houses built in the area known today as Heritage Hill. Upper-middle-class professionals continued to move here as that area developed, with the expansion of streetcar lines. Most who grew wealthy in the early part of this century chose the far eastern edge of the city or East Grand Rapids in which to build their stately grand homes and estates.

KT01 **Vandenberg Center** (City-County Administration Buildings)

1966–1968. Skidmore, Owings and Merrill and O'Bryon and Nachtegall, Inc. 300 Monroe NW (center of block bounded by Ottawa Ave. NW, Lyon NW, Monroe NW, and Michigan NW)

Standing on a raised, monumental plaza over a subgrade parking structure, this International-style government complex consists of the ten-story City of Grand Rapids Administration Building and the low, broad, three-story County of Kent Administration Building. Although considerably different in mass and proportion, they are unified by the overall symmetry, rectangular massing, and rectangular patterns of their Miesian design. The first floor of the city building is recessed behind the outer piers of the structure; the whole glass wall of the county building is recessed behind the structural system. The steel frames are clothed in brown Canadian granite and bronze-tinted glass. The centerpiece of the plaza—indeed, the logo of the city—is Alexander Calder's bright orange red steel stabile, *La Grande Vitesse*, installed in 1969. A Calder-created design was painted on the rooftop of the county building in 1974. Under an extensive, but ill-advised urban renewal plan for the city center, and over the protests of many citizens, the solid, stone High Victorian Gothic Grand Rapids City Hall, erected to the plans of Elijah E. Myers in 1885–1888, was demolished in 1969 and replaced by the Vandenberg Center.

KT02 **Monroe Center**

Bounded approximately by Lyon St., Bostwick Ave., Fulton St., Louis St., the Grand River, the north side of the Civic Auditorium, and Monroe Ave.

The Monroe Center area is the historic core of Grand Rapids's central business district. It is the heart of Grand Rapids today, as it has been since early in the city's history. The distinctive angling street plan of the Monroe Center area resulted from separate developments carried out by two of Grand Rapids's earliest settlers and landowners. Fur trader Louis Campau, Grand Rapids's first permanent settler, established a trading post and built a log home at an Indian campsite on the east bank of the Grand River in 1827. In 1831 he acquired 72 acres of land in the area bounded by present-day Michigan Street on the north, Fulton Street on the south, Division Avenue on the east, and the river on the west. Meanwhile, Lucius Lyon had purchased land surrounding Campau's in 1832 and then acquired the land owned by Campau north of the line between present-day Lyon and Pearl streets. Lyon oriented his streets north of this line to the compass point, while Campau laid his streets out at a 45-degree angle.

The two units remained unconnected except at Division Avenue until the 1870s, when Monroe Avenue was extended to Canal Street. The misalignment of Monroe and Canal (now Monroe) was corrected in 1873 with the creation of Campau Square in front of the later McKay Tower.

The early generations of frame buildings were destroyed by fire or demolished to make way for more substantial brick structures. The 1860s and 1870s were decades of substantial growth, evidenced in the Aldrich and Ledyard buildings near the intersection of Monroe and Ottawa avenues. Growth continued into the early twentieth century. New skyscraper office buildings (the McKay Tower, the Peoples Building, the Michigan National Bank) were built in the 1920s. Monroe Avenue was converted to a pedestrian mall in 1970. Now called Monroe Center, the mall boasts a multilevel plaza and a waterfall sculpture at the foot of Monroe, and it is still considered the heart of the city. Redevelopment in the early 1980s in the riverfront area south of Pearl Street has resulted in some interesting Postmodern architecture.

KT02.1 Amway Grand Plaza Hotel (Pantlind Hotel)

1913–1915, Warren and Wetmore. 1979, rehabilitation. 1981–1983, tower, Marvin DeWinter and Associates. Bounded by Monroe Ave. NW, Pearl St. NW, Campau, and Lyon St. NW

Richard M. DeVos and Jay Van Andel of the Amway Corporation in nearby Ada, together with the city of Grand Rapids, collaborated in making Grand Rapids a remarkable contemporary convention center. In developing the Amway Grand Plaza, De Vos and Van Andel acquired, remodeled, and redecorated the Pantlind Hotel in the late 1970s, to the

plans of Carleton Varney of Dorothy Draper and Company of New York. Originally, in 1913–1915, the Pantlind Hotel Company built the hotel with over 500 hundred rooms on the site of the old Pantlind Hotel (1902), with the assurance that J. Boyd Pantlind (1851–1922), a member of a family of reputable Grand Rapids and Michigan innkeepers, would assume its management, and with the awareness of the demand for hotel accommodations by furniture buyers. The restrained Renaissance Revival structure reflects the Ecole des Beaux-Arts training of Warren and Wetmore of New York, a firm best known for its hotel designs, for Grand Central Station in New York, and for the Michigan Central Station in Detroit (DE25, p. 81). Then the Amway Corporation in 1981–1983 built the sleek, twenty-five-story connecting tower with reflective-glass sheathing, which added 250 more rooms. Marvin DeWinter Associates, Inc., of Grand Rapids was the architect. The Amway Grand Plaza Tower is the tallest building in Grand Rapids; the angular-sloped terminus to its shaft is a landmark on the skyline. The city improved the riverfront and built skyways, bridges, and pedestrian walkways to connect the hotel, the Civic Auditorium, and the Gerald Ford Museum.

KT02.2 Grand Plaza Place (Fine Arts Building [Exhibitors' Building])

c. 1905, Benjamin Hertel. 1925, remodeled. 220 Lyon St. NW

Only the shell remains of what was once a major exhibition building for local manufacturers, as well as out-of-state vendors. Soon after the 1925 remodeling, the showrooms were used extensively by the rapidly growing furniture industry. Colonnades of twisted columns and pilasters, griffins, draftsmen's tools, and urns cast in gold, blue, rose, and green-glazed terracotta lend an Italian Renaissance character to this cream-colored, brick-clad building. Owen-Ames-Kimball of Grand Rapids built it.

KT02.3 George W. Welsh Civic Auditorium (Civic Auditorium)

1932–1933, Robinson and Campau with Smith, Hinchman and Grylls. 1985, restoration and rehabilitation. 227 Lyon St. NW

With the citizens' approval of a $1.5 million bond issue in the midst of the depression, this local relief project was funded. The monumental PWA Moderne civic auditorium is among the state's most impressive buildings in this style. The large, horizontal, smooth-stone building has simplified giant piers to support the entablature of the portico. Low-relief carvings of the shell and wave motif by sculptor Corrado Joseph Parducci; signs of the zodiac; city and state seals; and allegorical figures of sports, industry, the arts, science, and commerce make up the decoration. This 500-seat building has always been a source of local pride. When presented with the alternative of building a new facility in 1983, voters again expressed their commitment to the Civic Auditorium by supporting a $6 million restoration and rehabilitation of the building. It was completed in 1985.

KT02.4 McKay Tower (Grand Rapids National Bank Building)

1915–1916, Williamson, Crowe and Proctor. 1927, eleven-story addition. 146 Monroe Center NW (southeast corner Monroe Center NW and Pearl St. NW)

The triangular site created by the street layout dictated the unusual plan of this Beaux-Arts Classical bank. In 1921–1927 eleven stories were added to the then four-story structure, which was built as the two-story Wonderly Building in 1890 and improved in 1915–1916. Paired, fluted Roman Doric columns starting at the second level support a prominent entablature and enframe the pedimented street-level entrances on three sides of the bank. White terracotta above a granite base clads the steel-frame building. Anthemion antefixes ornament the metopes in the frieze of this "temple of finance." After the bank closed during the depression, it was purchased by politician Frank D. McKay and renamed the McKay Tower.

KT02.5 Ledyard Building (Ledyard Block)

1874, William G. Robinson. 123–145 Ottawa Ave. NW (southwest corner of Ottawa Ave. NW and Pearl St. NW)

With its massive cream brick exterior heavily articulated with elaborate Ionia sandstone window enframements, and with its magnificent florid metal-covered entablature, the Ledyard Block is one of the outstanding

KT02.5 Ledyard Building (Ledyard Block)

Italianate commercial blocks remaining in Michigan. It was designed by William G. Robinson (1895–1907), a pioneer Grand Rapids architect who came from Niagara Falls, New York, in 1865, two years after he established his own firm. Topping the cornice are triangular and broken segmental pediments. Originally serving as stores, offices, and a hotel, the building was constructed for William B. Ledyard (1811–1890), banker and businessman, as one of several investments downtown. The Ledyard Block is part of the remarkable streetscape of splendid Round Arch mode and Italianate commercial buildings at 109–125 Ottawa Avenue NW and at 102–124 Monroe Center, built to replace the frame buildings destroyed by fire in September 1857. Twenty-five buildings along both sides of Monroe, between Market Street and Ottawa Avenue, were destroyed at that time. Today the Ledyard Block has been rehabilitated with a concourse and atrium that link it with commercial buildings to the south.

KT02.6 Trust Building (Michigan Trust Company Building)

1891–1892, Solon S. Beman. 1913, 1920s, additions, Henry Crowe. 1940s, additions. 40 Pearl St. NW (southeast corner of Pearl St. NW and Ottawa St. NW)

This early office skyscraper marked Grand Rapids as the financial center of outstate Michigan. Anton G. Hodenpyl, Lewis H. Withey, Willard Barnhart, Darwin D. Cody, and other Grand Rapids and western Michigan businessmen organized the Michigan

Trust Company in 1889 and built the bank and office building two years later. The building is a major Michigan work of Chicago architect Solon S. Beman (1853–1914). The Richardsonian Romanesque structure rises in four stages to a flat roof, its windows decreasing in size within their round-arch groupings as they progress upward from the huge round-arch openings in the walls of the rusticated coursed sandstone base. To protect against fire, its steel and iron frame is sheathed with fire tiles, its floors are constructed of hollow tile and concrete, and its exterior walls are clad in red sandstone, brick, and terracotta. In 1913 two ten-story sections were added to the rear, and in the 1920s, the eleventh floor was added.

KT02.7 **Michigan National Bank Building** (Grand Rapids Trust Building)

1926, Wirt Rowland of Smith, Hinchman and Grylls. 77 Monroe Center NW (northwest corner of Monroe Center NW and Ionia Ave. NE)

The strong, continuous piers terminating in pinnacles and the dominant three-story arches on the lower levels, with narrower arched forms repeated in the upper portions, give this building a vigorous vertical thrust. In fact, it seems almost a provocative transformation of Richardson's Marshall Field Store into a vertical building. The exterior is sheathed in terracotta with reliefs by Corrado Joseph Parducci. Depicting the early history of the city, they include Indian tomahawks, canoes, pine trees, wolverines, and other native animals. The second-floor banking room and safe deposit vaults still retain the original colonnade, coffered ceiling, marble, terrazzo, and metalwork.

KT02.8 **Campau Square Plaza Building**

1985, WBDC, Inc. 99 Monroe Ave. NW

Situated at an angle to the street, the rectangular-plan office building faces Campau Square to the east. Its deep plum brick and its rose-tinted glass contrasts with the adjacent concrete and reflective glass buildings. The glass facade is broken by vertical bands of fluted brick. Polished granite buttons set in stone surrounds that connect the brick banding distinctively mark the building at the cornice line and above the first-floor level. The main entrance has a large Post-modern semicircular arch.

KT03 **Grand Rapids Art Museum** (Grand Rapids Post Office and Federal Building)

1908–1911, James K. Taylor, Supervising Architect for the U.S. Treasury Department. 135–137 Ionia Ave. NW (bounded by Ionia Ave. NW, Lyon St. NE, Division St. NE [Business 131], and Pearl St. NW)

This monumental federal government building of rusticated gray Vermont granite is an outstanding example in western Michigan of the Beaux-Arts Classical style popularized by McKim, Mead and White. The building replaced a Renaissance Revival federal government building erected in 1879. The two-story, half-columned colonnade at the second level of the original main (west) facade is balanced by two pedimented entry pavilions, and the distinctive tripartite horizontal division is suggestive of the east facade of the Louvre (without its central pavilion) or, even more, the individual blocks of the Place de la Concorde. In its grand and noble character it symbolized the federal presence in Grand Rapids. A congressional appropriation of $500,000 won by Sen. Alden Smith in 1906 assured its construction. When it was declared surplus by the General Services Administration in 1975, the city acquired the building. Under the direction of Steenwyk-Thrall Architects, it was rehabilitated in 1980, without the loss of the elegant interior plasterwork, woodwork, and mosaic flooring, to house the Grand Rapids Art Museum.

KT04 **Grand Rapids Public Library** (Ryerson Library)

1903–1904, Shepley, Rutan and Coolidge. 1965–1967, addition, Ralph R. Calder and Associates in association with Robinson, Campau and Crowe, Inc. 111 Library St. SE (northeast corner of Library St. SE and Bostwick)

The Beaux-Arts Classical library in rusticated Bedford limestone presides over Veterans Memorial Park. The formal, symmetrically massed structure rests on a raised foundation. The central entrance pavilion contains a round-arch window with Ionic columns in antis, which in turn are flanked by round-arch windows. Classical ornamentation—a festooned entablature, a modillioned cornice with anthemions—adds to the library's formal

KT05 Saint Cecilia Music Hall

KT04 Grand Rapids Public Library (Ryerson Library)

dignity. The library was the gift of Martin A. Ryerson (1856–1932), a prominent Chicago industrialist who was a Grand Rapids native and the grandson of Antoine Campau, one of the city's earliest pioneer settlers. Ryerson also donated funds to establish the (Chicago) Art History Library at the Art Institute of Chicago. Aware of Shepley, Rutan, and Coolidge's distinguished library designs in Eastern cities and in Chicago, Ryerson himself probably selected the Boston firm to create his library for Grand Rapids. The 1966 addition wraps around and connects to the rear of the 1903 building but disregards its design. Instead, it presents an arcaded first floor, vertical panels and window strips, and an undulating cornice.

KT05 **Saint Cecilia Music Hall**

1893–1894, Henry Ives Cobb. 1926, remodeling, Rindge and Rindge. 24 Ransom Ave. NE

Nine women led by Ella Matthews Peirce founded in 1883 the Saint Cecilia Society for the purpose of advancing the musical arts in Grand Rapids. Named after the patron saint of music and musicians, the society claims to be the first women's music club in the country to erect and maintain its own recital hall. The hall was designed by Henry Ives Cobb (1859–

1931) of Chicago in the formal and dignified Beaux-Arts Classical style. It differs considerably from Cobb's Fisheries Building for the World's Columbian Exposition, which received praise from European critics. The front facade of the brick-clad music hall has a penciled masonry base, with an arched entryway with heavy voussoirs. Five round-arch windows repeat the entrance motif, and a balustraded cornice completes its formalism. The terracotta cartouches in the spandrels contain a horn, a cello, a triangle, and pipes. A large foyer opens to the 695-seat auditorium originally lit with a golden glow from skylights, and a grand staircase leads to the second-floor dancing hall. A memorial window at the staircase landing was designed by New York artist Frederick Stuart Church, who was a native of Grand Rapids, and was executed by Tiffany Studios. It shows Saint Cecilia seated at the organ. The interior of the auditorium was remodeled and its acoustics improved in 1926 by Rindge and Rindge, architects of Grand Rapids. Its uninterrupted use has added significantly to the cultural life of the city. The building was restored in the 1970s and the 1980s.

KT06 **Ladies Literary Club**

1887, William G. Robinson. 1931, addition and remodeling, Rindge and Rindge. 61 Sheldon Blvd. SE

In 1870 six women who had met for a year to study history organized the Ladies Literary

Association. Incorporated in 1882 as the Ladies Literary Club, its purpose was for "promoting literary, educational and scientific pursuits and to establish and maintain a library." The club built this comfortable, residential-scale meeting house in 1887 to the designs of William G. Robinson, who was obviously influenced by the Richardsonian Romanesque style. A two-story hipped-roof portion with characteristic round-arch openings fronts the one-story rear portion. The former contains the foyer and the library, with meeting rooms above; the latter, the four-hundred-seat auditorium. The south window of the library, illustrating the Casket Story in Shakespeare's *Merchant of Venice,* was designed and executed by Tiffany Studios in 1915. The original building uses Amherst, Ohio, blue stone trim and Grand Rapids pressed brick with terracotta trim. In 1931, Rindge and Rindge of Grand Rapids added the south entrance wing, which contains a new stage.

KT07 **Saint Andrew's Catholic Cathedral**

1874–1876, John Grady. 1901, rebuilding, Ernest Brielmaier and Sons. 1938, chapel addition, Harry L. Mead. 267 Sheldon Ave. SE (southwest corner Sheldon Ave. SE and Maple SE)

This 1903 Gothic Revival cathedral partially replaced the original church, which was designed by parishioner John Grady in 1874–1876 but burned in 1901. The 192-foot-high north tower and spire loom prominently above Grand Rapids in the same manner as the cathedrals of the Middle Ages. Ernest Brielmaier and Sons of Milwaukee, noted specialists in midwestern Catholic church architecture, prepared plans for rebuilding the church, adding transepts, a sanctuary, and sacristies. The reconstruction cost $80,000. Spired towers of unequal height flank the pointed-arch recessed entry. This pale yellowish white Milwaukee brick cruciform-plan cathedral has a nave and side aisles, a gallery over the narthex, and space for some 1,300 worshipers. Slender colonnettes, broad-pointed arches, and ribbed vaulting contribute to the Old World look. In 1915, stained-glass windows from F. X. Zettler of Munich were installed. Among them are the large depictions of the Nativity and the Ascension in the transepts. The Blessed Sacrament Chapel on the north side, designed by Grand Rapids architect Harry L.

Mead, was constructed in 1938. The gymnasium (northeast corner of Sheldon Avenue SE and Goodrich), designed by Colton and Knecht of Grand Rapids, was erected in 1925.

KT08 **Grand Rapids Public Museum**

1940, Roger Allen. 54 Jefferson Ave. SE (northeast corner Jefferson Ave. SE and State St.)

The Grand Rapids Public Museum was constructed with the aid of Public Works Administration funds from the federal government, to the PWA Moderne designs of local architect Roger Allen. The building's broad, smooth surfaces are faced on the south and west sides with buff limestone above a base of polished black granite. The main pavilion entrance flanked by paired projecting bays emphasizes the museum's straightforward formality. The simplified angular detailing and the sparing use of glass-block windows seems to declare the museum function within. The interior was equipped with air conditioning and with artificial lighting to protect the collections. The museum was founded in 1855 as the Grand Rapids Lyceum of Natural History.

KT09 **Calkins Law Office**

1835–1837. 235 State St. SE (east of Jefferson Ave. SE at the apex of State St. SE and Washington Ave.)

Believed to be the oldest extant building in Grand Rapids, this ideal Greek Revival building in miniature was built for attorney Charles P. Calkins (1803–1890), who came to Michigan from Hinesburgh, Vermont. The one-room building is the classic prostyle tetrastyle Greek temple type. The building was moved in 1974 from its original location at Monroe and Ottawa to a triangular-shaped park across from the Grand Rapids Public Museum and has been restored as a pre-Civil War law office. Open to public.

KT10 **Heartside**

1870–1920. Bounded by Fulton St., Division Ave., Wealthy St., and Ionia Ave. SW

Heartside encompasses one of the largest and finest groupings of late nineteenth- and early twentieth-century warehouses and wholesale business blocks in Michigan. The completion, in 1870, of the Grand Rapids and Indiana Railroad, with a station at the western edge of the area, at what is now Oakes Street, sparked the development of Heartside. By 1900, scores of large brick buildings, many with decorative stone or terracotta trim, representing a broad range of late nineteenth-century architectural styles, including commercial Italianate and Richardsonian Romanesque, stood shoulder to shoulder, as if to announce the maturity of commerce in West Michigan.

KT10.1 Blodgett Building

c. 1886. 13–23 Ionia Ave. SW

Built as an investment by Delos A. Blodgett, a West Michigan lumber baron and capitalist, the wholesale mercantile and office building is a broad, six-story, cream brick structure with round, segmental, and square head windows trimmed with terracotta and stone. It is noteworthy for its rich, exuberant detailing and for its original cast-iron storefront columns.

KT10.2 Lemon and Wheeler Company Building

Late 1880s. 27–29 Ionia Ave. SW (northwest corner Ionia Ave. SW and Weston SW)

This five-story building with an angled corner bay is a characteristic example of a commercial Italianate block. The stone lintels of the segmental-arch windows are incised with decorative vines. The building retains its metal storefront and its prominent cornice. It originally served the Lemon and Wheeler Company, which was established as a wholesale grocery company in 1872.

KT10.3 Downtown Senior Neighbors Center and Weston Apartments (Clark Building)

1890s, William A. Chappel?. 32–44 Ionia Ave. SW (southeast corner of Ionia Ave. SW and Weston SW)

This red brick Richardsonian Romanesque building encompasses one of the city's most imposing blocks. This building originally housed the Clark Jewell-Wells Company, wholesale grocers; Melvin Clark later became one of the city's wealthy citizens. Above the

red sandstone first story, the windows of the building are paired to the fourth story (and to the fifth, at the corner bay) under heavy round arches, then they diminish to triple groups at the top within the same bay—a scheme first used effectively by Henry Hobson Richardson in his Marshall Field Wholesale Store in Chicago (1885–1887), except that Richardson used four rather than three. Foliated patterns and human faces carved in sandstone ornament the capitals of piers and pilasters.

KT11 Grand Rapids Water Filtration Plant (City Waterworks)

1910–1912, Herring and Fuller. 1923–1924, 1935, 1938, additions. 1430 Monroe St. NE

This two-story red brick structure with a green-tiled hipped roof tells of the city's growth, which created a demand for a clean water supply. It symbolized faith in city government, which had recently been embroiled in corruption and mismanagement of public funds. The main towered structure in the complex is flanked by twin brick cylindrical tanks housed in low towers with conical tile-covered roofs. Strict symmetry, expressive of the city's renewed dignity as a result of the passage in 1910 of the bond issue in the amount of $395,000, dominates the front facade of the plant. The round-arch central entry is decorated with a filigree like metal faced canopy incorporating the city seal flanked by medallions depicting Aquarius and the city seal. The designers were Herring and Fuller, engineers in New York City. The modern filtration plant treated water taken from the Grand River. Begun in 1910, the filtration plant was completed in October 1912, and water was released into the city pipelines on December 31, 1912. That day the *Grand Rapids Evening Press* suggested that the people of Grand Rapids "toast the New Year with a glass of city water."

An addition in 1923–1924 increased the capacity of the plant. In 1935 the tall chemical tower was doubled in size, and in 1938 WPA funds enabled the city to construct a pipeline to Lake Michigan. Concerned for the health of its citizens, Grand Rapids introduced sodium fluoride into the water supply at this plant in January 1945, becoming the first city in the United States to fluoridate its water. In 1955 the plant was modernized.

KT12 **Berkey and Gay Furniture Company**

by 1888, later additions. 920–964 Monroe St. NW (southeast corner Monroe St. NW and Walbridge)

Two longtime furniture manufacturers, William A. Berkey and George W. Gay, formed in 1873 the Berkey and Gay Furniture Company and built this fully equipped and modern factory between the East Canal and a railroad spur. Using the slogan "for your children's heirlooms," the company produced furniture and established the prominence of Grand Rapids as the "Furniture Capital."

The sprawling, five-story, cream brick structure is extraordinary, for it was contemporary with Richardson's Marshall Field Wholesale Store, 1885–1887. Its superb woodworking facilities and concern for the workers' welfare had few equals at this time. The structure is arranged around two open interior courtyards that provided ample light and ventilation. Groups of three large, two-story round-arch openings at the street level surmounted by paired windows on the upper four levels relieve the long horizontal rows of windows. A parapet caps the building. Interestingly, the Adler and Sullivan Auditorium Building in Chicago, 1886–1890, employs the prominent large arched opening at the street level, a series of windows to effect a vertical movement, and terminates the whole with a parapet. Whereas the Adler and Sullivan work is refined and elegant, the Berkey and Gay factory is direct and robust.

Berkey and Gay Furniture Company, then the largest furniture manufacturer in the city, and three other Grand Rapids furniture manufacturers exhibited at the 1876 Centennial in Philadelphia and established Grand Rapids as the capital of fine furniture.

KT13 **West Side**

West of the Grand River and north and south of Bridge Street

Unskilled factory jobs lured German, Polish, and Irish immigrants to the west side of Grand Rapids in the mid-nineteenth century. By the 1850s Germans had settled the Bridge Street area in significant numbers.

The west side is characterized by the close proximity of housing and factories. Industrial buildings are interspersed among the modest residential surroundings. The opening of the west side power canal in 1866 aided the development of mills and factories along Front Street. The Lake Shore and Michigan Southern Railroad, completed in 1869, and the Grand Rapids and Indiana Railroad, completed in 1870, provided further impetus for growth. Grand Rapids expanded its furniture market to become a major furniture producer by the 1890s. Many of the furniture factories that contributed to the national reputation of the industry in Grand Rapids were located on the west side. Among them were such large and long-surviving furniture manufacturers as Widdicomb, Stowe-Davis, and American Seating.

Most of the employees lived in the surrounding neighborhood predominantly made up of modest wood-frame, single or double houses and in multiple structures, often with Italianate, Queen Anne, and Colonial Revival detailing.

Churches, schools, parish halls, rectories, convents, and the fraternal and social halls with strong ethnic derivations attest to the European ties of many of the residents of the west side.

KT13.1 **Eliphalet Turner House**

1846. 731 Front St. NW (southwest corner Front St. NW and Sixth St. NW)

This Greek Revival house was the home of one of the area's earliest settlers, Eliphalet Haskius Turner (1795–1870), who acted as clerk of the first town meeting, held in 1834. The two-story, front-gable house with the discontinuous cornice has an Ionic column distyle in antis side entry flanked by windows. Built of locally quarried Grand River limestone shortly after the first bridge was constructed across the Grand River, it was the first stone structure built on the west side of the river. Open to public.

KT13.1 Eliphalet Turner House

KT13.2 **Basilica of Saint Adalbert**

1907–1913, Henry J. Harks. 1950, altars remodeled. 650 Davis NW (northeast corner of Davis NW and Fourth NW)

German-speaking Catholic Poles in Grand Rapids originally worshipped with Germans, first at Saint Andrew's, and then at Saint Mary Church. In 1872 they formed the Saint Adalbert's Society to keep together the Polish community in the city. This Romanesque Revival, domed basilica church, built in 1907–1913, replaced their earlier frame church erected in 1881–1882. Twin 134-foot-tall corner towers with domed cupolas flank the triple round-arch entry, above which is a circular stained-glass window. An imposing, copper-clad central dome rises over the crossing. The octagonal cylindrical dome rises from a square base, and on the four corners are sculpted angels facing the cardinal points of the compass. These were carved by the Gondola Brothers of Cleveland. The exterior walls are of evenly coursed, rock-faced Sandusky limestone with Bedford limestone trim, and the roof is covered with red tile. The church is cruciform in plan with a narthex, a nave, side aisles, transepts, and an apse. Henry J. Harks of Cleveland drafted plans for the church; Chris Vierheilig of Grand Rapids supervised construction; Andrew Brothers of Cleveland built it; and A. Artmaier of Chi-

cago designed the stained-glass windows, some depicting Polish saints. The church cost $150,000. This grand and magnificent basilica tells of the importance of Catholicism in western Michigan.

KT13.3 **Saint Adalbert Parish House**

1922, Harry L. Mead. 654 Davis NW

The large red brick and stone-trimmed Jacobethan Parish House cost $65,000 to build.

KT13.4 **Ammerman Building**

c. 1920. 617 and 619 Bridge St. NW (northeast corner of Bridge St. NW and Lexington Ave. NW)

The decorative brickwork, the crow-stepped edge of the tiled gables, and steeply pitched gabled wall dormers and flanking chimneys are characteristic of northern European domestic and commercial architecture.

KT13.5 **Gerald R. Ford Museum**

1981, Marvin DeWinter and Associates. 303 Pearl St. NW (bounded by the Grand River and Pearl, Scribner, and Bridge streets)

The two-story, triangular-plan building constructed of steel and concrete has a 300-foot-

KT13.3 Saint Adalbert Parish House and KT13.2 Basilica of Saint Adalbert

long east wall of glass, mirroring a panorama of the river and the city. The building turns its back on the sight and sound of the expressway immediately to the west and, instead, faces the river and the downtown skyline to the east. A 40-foot-long reflecting pool with a fountain and a water cascade graces the site. The interior contains open gallery areas, a 270-seat auditorium, and a full-size replica of the White House Oval Office. The National Archives and Records Service of the General Services Administration administers the presidential museum. (The Ford presidential archives and library are in Ann Arbor.)

KT14 Heritage Hill

1840–1920. Bounded by Michigan and Union avenues, Pleasant St. and Clarendon Place, and Jefferson and Lafayette avenues

West Michigan's largest and finest concentration of late-nineteenth-century and early-twentieth-century houses lies in this residential district. It is located on the rise of ground on the east side of the Grand River valley overlooking and adjacent to the city's downtown area. The first houses were built here in the 1840s by people who wanted to avoid the recurring floods of the river. Those who prospered as the city grew selected this area in which to build their grand houses, and, by the 1870s, the neighborhood was firmly established as the most prestigious residential section in Grand Rapids. Virtually every style of American domestic architecture, from Greek Revival to Prairie style, is represented in this six-hundred-building district. Precipitated by the demolition of their splendid Victorian-era city hall in 1969, citizens formed the Heritage Hill Association and initiated plans to preserve these fine houses and their surroundings through the creation of the Heritage Hill Historic District, home-improvement citizen's action programs, and revolving fund programs. Their success is evident.

KT14.1 George W. Gay House

c. 1883. 426 Fulton St. E (southwest corner of Fulton St. E and Gay SE)

The gambrel-roof wooden Queen Anne house with its asymmetrical massing, well-pitched gables, angular projections, and tall molded chimneys resembles some of the houses designed by David S. Hopkins (1834–1918). The noted Grand Rapids supplier of mail-order house plans published his drawings in *Houses and Cottages* (1889, 1890) and *Cottage Portfolio* (1886). This house is larger than most and was elaborately finished for the owner of the Berkey and Gay Furniture Company.

KT14.2 J. T. French Company (Abram W. and Elnoa Prior Pike House)

1844–1845. 230 Fulton St. E (second door west of southwest corner of Fulton St. E and Lafayette)

The wooden Greek Revival house has a giant pedimented Doric portico and two colonnaded one-story wings. It was built for Abram W. Pike (1814–1906), a merchant who came from Cincinnati to Michigan Territory in 1827 and to Grand Rapids in 1844, and for his wife Elnoa Prior (d. 1853).

KT14.3 Frederick P. and Caroline Hill Wilcox House

1904, Vierheilig and Clark. 15 College Ave. SE (southwest corner of College Ave. SE and Fulton E)

This massive Dutch Colonial Revival brick house has prominent crow-stepped gables. Its red brick is laid in English bond. The foyer contains murals depicting Robin Hood and Ivanhoe painted by Grand Rapids artist Mathias Alten. Frederick P. Wilcox (1857–1912) moved from New York State and practiced law in Grand Rapids.

KT14.4 Carl Gustav Adolph and Elizabeth S. W. Voigt House

1895, William G. Robinson. 115 College Ave. SE (2 doors south of southwest corner of College Ave. SE and Washington E)

This Queen Anne house, a late work by Grand Rapids architect William G. Robinson, is one of the finest in Heritage Hill. The two-and-a-half-story red brick structure has a steeply pitched hipped roof, projecting bays, a conical-roofed round corner tower, gabled and pinnacled dormers, and a wrap-around balustraded porch, the roof of which is supported by paired fluted Composite columns.

KT14.4 Carl Gustav Adolph and Elizabeth S. W. Voigt House

The interior is richly finished with carved woodwork, parquet floors, stained-glass windows, and tapestry and silk wall coverings. Voight (1833–1908) started a mercantile business with W. G. Herpolsheimer and later owned and operated the Voight Milling Works, selling flour throughout the United States. The Grand Rapids Public Museum operates the Voigt house as a museum. It is filled with Voigt family furnishings.

KT14.5 David M. Amberg House

1910, Frank Lloyd Wright. 505 College Ave., SE

This house was constructed under the direction of Herman Von Holst and Marion Mahony for David M. Amberg, a wholesale liquor dealer, while Wright was in Europe. Late in October 1909, Wright had abruptly turned over to Von Holst the total operation of the studio, including the completion of Wright's commissions at the preliminary stage, among them the Amberg house. The design is no doubt Wright's, with Von Holst and Mahony contributing to the final touches, as was the case of the E. P. Irving residence in Decatur, Illinois, in 1909. The two-story brick house has a low gable roof with wide overhangs, porch, and strip windows. The interior is arranged with an extended L-plan and has notable detailing.

KT14.6 James P. and Emma Sanford Brayton House

c. 1889. 516 College Ave. SE (3rd door south of southeast corner of College Ave. SE and Logan SE)

This monumental wooden Classical Revival house resembles some built from the architectural drawings of David S. Hopkins. A center gambreled gable containing a Palladian window projects from the side-gable structure. This is fronted by a giant balustraded portico with paired colossal Ionic columns. On either side of the portico are one-story, flat-roofed porches supported by paired Doric columns and piers. Ionic pilasters mark the corners of the house. Dentils run along the ample cornice beneath projecting eaves supported by block modillions. The center entrance is surmounted by a shell ornament and flanked with decorative side lights.

KT14.7 Meyer and Sophie Amberg May House

1909, Frank Lloyd Wright. 450 Madison Ave. SE (northeast corner of Madison Ave. S.E and Logan)

The May house was Wright's first large commission in Michigan and one of only two residential structures (other than summer houses) in Michigan from Wright's Prairie style period. The two-story, T-plan residence is situated on the northern edge of the corner lot to take full advantage of the southern light. The shallowly hipped roof covered with red tiles slopes to broad overhangs, emphasizing the horizontality and hovering quality

KT14.7a Meyer and Sophie Amberg May House (exterior)

KT14.7b Meyer and Sophie Amberg May House (interior)

of the house as shelter. Leaded- and colored-glass-accented casement windows and doors open out to terraces and gardens with garden walls and planters, all incorporated in the design to intermingle the interior and the exterior. Burgstaller was the contractor. Wright hired George M. Niedecken of the Milwaukee firm of Niedecken-Walbridge Company to supervise and execute the interior decorative details. May (1873–1936) was a prominent merchant who became the president of A. May and Sons, a men's clothing store chain, in 1906. The Mays influenced the decision of the David Ambergs, Sophie's par-

ents, to build a Wright house a few blocks away at 505 College Avenue SE (KT14.5). Steelcase, Inc., acquired the May house and accurately and fully restored it and the existing original furnishings. It won the distinction of a President's Historic Preservation Award for corporate-sponsored preservation in 1988, sponsored by the Advisory Council on Historic Preservation and the Department of the Interior, in celebration of two decades of achievement under the National Historic Preservation Act of 1966. Open to public by appointment.

KT15 A. B. Watson Mausoleum, Oak Hill Cemetery

1914. Section 5 of Oak Hill Cemetery (northwest corner of Hall SE and Eastern SE)

This tomb is an excellent, albeit late, example of the Egyptian Revival. Papyrus columns with bell-shaped capitals support an entablature surmounted with a concave cornice decorated with the winged-sun disc. Paired sphinxes guard the mausoleum holding the remains of Amasa Brown Watson (1826–1888), a west Michigan lumberman and industrialist, and his wife, Martha.

KT16 Temple Emanuel

1952, Erich Mendelsohn. 1715 Fulton Ave. (north side of Fulton Ave. between Holmdene NE and Lawndale NE)

One of the pioneer Reform congregations in the Midwest, the temple had occupied a churchlike structure built for it by David Sprague Hopkins in 1882, at the corner of Fountain and Ransom (now in a much altered form). German-born Erich Mendelsohn, one of the great figures of modern architecture who built synagogues in Cleveland, Saint Paul, and Saint Louis, designed this low, wide, brick and glass building with butterfly-wing roofs and an unusual sanctuary-social hall plan. Twin rooms, side by side, are separated by an electronically retractable wall, thereby doubling the space for holiday worshipers. The focal wall features a mural by Lucienne Bloch Dimitroff reflecting the festivals of the Jewish year. An inviting foyer contains a beautiful Tiffany window that graced the earlier building, and there is a well-designed school wing and gymnasium in the east half of the building.

KT17 Ahavas Israel Synagogue

1970, Van Biene and Postma. 2727 Michigan SE (.5 mile west of East Beltline [Michigan 44/37] and .5 mile east of Maryland)

The dramatic brick and glass building has an arresting sanctuary facade punctuated by a bronze menorah, a row of arched clerestory windows, and a sweeping roofline. The large prayer hall has an oval wood and concrete ark, with doors that feature a broochlike tree of life in enameled metal. The bare brick ark wall provides a backdrop for further sculpture, and the space is flooded with natural light, which is enhanced by the warm, rich oranges and reds of the interior. The architects were influenced by a design by the New York synagogue architect, Percival Goodman.

EAST GRAND RAPIDS

KT18 Holmdene (Edward and Susan R. Blodgett Lowe, Jr., Estate)

1905–1908; Winslow and Bigelow, architects, with revisions by Frank L. Proctor; Ossian C. Simonds Company and Ellen Shipman, landscape architects. 1607 Robinson Rd. SE (Robinson Rd. runs southwest from intersection with Fulton; Holmdene is 4 blocks west of East Beltline Ave. [Michigan 37])

Holmdene is the country estate of Edward and Susan R. Blodgett Lowe, Jr. The beautiful, large, Neo-Tudor house stands superbly on a rise of ground on 69 rolling and wooded acres of land through which runs a stream. The symmetrically arranged U-shaped house is clad in patterned red brick with limestone trim. The center entrance is flanked by fluted Doric columns and set within a projecting bay that rises to a balconet. The larger of its twenty-two rooms are paneled in dark oak and walnut. There are sixteen fireplaces. Subsidiary buildings are the stables, the garage, the caretaker's house, and storage buildings.

The Lowes commissioned Winslow and Bigelow of Boston, designers of several large city houses and country estates in the East, to plan the house. The style may reflect a remembrance of the English ancestry of Edward Lowe (1860–1938), who came from Ashton-under-Lyne. The landscape design preserves the exquisite natural beauty of the site. It was by Ossian C. Simonds Company of Chicago; the gardens were done by Ellen Shipman of New York. Writing in *Country Life* in April 1928, Mrs. Francis King saw Holmdene as an isolated indication of the progress even smaller midwestern cities were making in building and gardening.

Edward Lowe was an executive with the Grand Rapids Iron Works Company, later renamed Butterworth and Lowe, a company owned by his father and grandfather. Lowe joined the lumbering interests of Delos A. Blodgett, after marrying his daughter, Susan Blodgett, in 1888.

Holmdene was purchased in 1945 by Aquinas College. The house now serves as the residence of the Dominican Sisters associated with the college. Although college buildings have been erected on sections of the grounds, the house, its associated buildings, and its landscape features remain unaltered.

KT19 **Brookby** (John W. and Minnie Cumnock Blodgett Estate)

1928; A. Stewart Walker of Walker and Gillette; Gallagher?, landscape architects. 250 Plymouth Rd. SE (southeast corner of Plymouth Rd. SE and Robinson Rd. SE)

Brookby contains a broad-fronted and winged, red brick, Georgian Revival country house and other subsidiary buildings set on 8 acres of beautifully landscaped grounds with formal gardens, terraces, and manicured lawns overlooking Fisk Lake. The quiet symmetrical house has a low-pitched hipped roof beneath which runs a corbeled brick belt course. The central entrance is flanked by Corinthian pilasters and topped by a segmental arch. The house was built for John W. Blodgett (1860–1951), financier, lumberman, and philanthropist who was the son of pioneer lumberman Delos A. Blodgett, and for his wife, Minnie Cumnock Blodgett, who was nationally known for her work in public health and welfare. The house is an important work of A. Stewart Walker of Walker and Gillette, a prominent New York architectural firm best known for its large revival-style country and suburban houses designed in the 1910s and 1920s.

KENTWOOD

KT20 **Steelcase Corporate Headquarters**

1981–1983, WBDC, Inc., Architects, Planners, Engineers. 901 44th St. (about 1.75 miles east of US 131 on 44th St. and Eastern Ave, on the northwest corner)

The huge corporate headquarters of the furniture maker is located on a 22.5-acre site adjoining the 292-acre main manufacturing complex and is fully landscaped with pond and plantings. WBDC, Inc., Grand Rapids architects, planners, and engineers, designed it as a living laboratory and a working showroom for Steelcase office systems. The building consists of two wings branching at a 120-degree angle from a central atrium. The alternating horizontal bands of red Carnelian granite panels and bronze-tinted glass give a low, ground-hugging appearance to this large structure. It is five levels, with the first floor partially below grade and with successive walls cantilevered to create a sunscreen. The stainless steel sculpture *Two For One*, made by Dennis Jones in 1985, stands before a second-level entrance that leads into the four-story, skylight-topped atrium lobby.

The granite and glass of the exterior continue into the atrium, which is open on all sides, providing views into functioning office areas. Here *Ode IV*, a 22-foot-high stainless steel sculpture created in 1982 by James Rosati to symbolize the "energy and dynamism" of the corporation, rests in a reflecting pool against the backdrop of a water plane. The standard work stations of the offices are based on a modular plan and are, needless to say, outfitted with Steelcase furniture.

The building houses the executive, marketing, finance, and administrative offices of Steelcase. Planned for continued growth, the building was designed to accommodate a third wing.

KENTWOOD AND GAINES TOWNSHIP

KT21 **Steelcase Corporate Development Center**

1986–1989, WBDC, Inc., Architects, Planners, Engineers. 6100 East Paris Ave. (about 2 miles south of intersection of Michigan 37 on East Paris, southeast corner of 60th St. and East Paris)

The Steelcase Corporate Development Center is a seven-story ultramodern pyramid that rises to a height of 128 feet above its prairie-like surroundings in western Michigan. The exterior walls are polished red Carnelian granite and aluminum sandwich panels. The building was designed by WBDC Design Group, Inc., of Grand Rapids to spur creativity and to foster formal and informal interaction among employees of various departments. Openness and privacy accomplish this. Arranged around an atrium are open offices, private "caves" for research and writing, con-

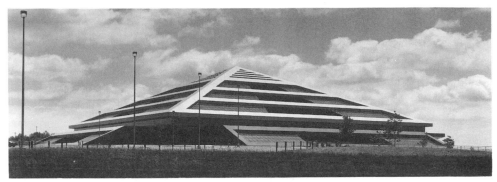

KT21 Steelcase Corporate Development Center

versation areas, and executive and production areas. The building has a health club and cafeteria. Balconies and windows afford scenic views of farm and grassland to the south. Steelcase bought miles of such scenic surroundings to ensure that development would not encroach on this environment. To the north, openings overlook Steelcase's Kentwood manufacturing site. *Synergy*, a 71-foot-tall stainless steel kinetic sculpture created by Dennis Jones of Tucson, Arizona, hangs from the center of the pyramid and is the focus of the atrium. Known as the "town square," this is the building's primary gathering place. This marvelous corporate center shows lessons learned from the Japanese—respect for the environment and for all workers as members of the corporate team.

SPARTA

KT22 Sparta Masonic Temple

1926, Pierre Lindhout. East side of North Union (1 block north of East Division, .75 mile east of Michigan 37)

This three-story, yellow tan brick Masonic temple is one of the most attractive structures in Sparta. It was designed by Belgian-born, Grand Rapids architect Pierre Lindhout, who was formerly with the architectural firm of Osgood and Osgood, specialists in the design of Masonic temples. The symmetry and formality of the Sparta Masonic Temple reflect the classicism of the early twentieth century, though the two sturdy piers flanking the entrance show echoes of Frank Lloyd Wright's Larkin Building (1903). The angular parapet, the overhanging eaves, and the brick orna-

mentation are other elements common to the Prairie style.

PARNELL

KT23 Saint Patrick Catholic Church

1877, Robinson and Barnaby. 4385 Parnell Ave. (southwest corner of Parnell Ave. and Five Mile Rd.)

The steeple of Saint Patrick Catholic Church soars 168 feet above the quiet crossroads of an agricultural community surrounded by land cultivated first by Irish immigrants and by pioneers from New York State and Canada. It marks one of the state's most exquisite rural wooden Gothic Revival churches. The church was designed by William G. Robinson and Frank B. Barnaby of Grand Rapids and was constructed by P. W. Griswold and T. P.

Fitzgerald. It is the fourth church of the second parish established in the Grand River valley region. The parish outgrew the first church, and the second and third churches burned. Paired, slender stained-glass lancet windows with hood moldings, placed between fluted and paneled incipient buttresses, flank the entryway of the central projecting tower of this white clapboard church. Gothic trefoils along with triple-grouped windows under a hooded arch in the second story of the tower add decorative touches. The interior is arranged with a nave and side aisles and with a choir and organ loft above the narthex facing the altar end.

FALLASBURG

KT24 Fallasburg Bridge

1871, Jared N. Brezee, builder. Covered Bridge Rd. over the Flat River (.5 miles southwest of intersection of Covered Bridge Rd. and McPherson St. and just east of intersection of Beckwith and Covered Bridge Rd.)

One of only three covered bridges still open to traffic in Michigan, the Fallasburg Bridge was constructed in 1871 by bridge builder Jared N. Brezee of Ada. It replaced four earlier bridges destroyed by ice jams in 1839, 1844, 1849, and 1860. A bridge was first built here in 1839, two years after the brothers Silas S. and John Wesley Fallass came from Dryden County, New York. The Fallasses platted the village of Fallasburg and built a

sawmill and gristmill on the Flat River. The bridge is made of white pine, with vertical plank on the side walls and a gable roof. It employed the Brown Truss design, which was patterned after the invention of Joseph Brown of Buffalo, New York, in 1857.

WHITNEYVILLE

KT25 Whitneyville Tavern

1853. 5283 Whitneyville Rd. (on south side of river across from mill pond and dam, .35 miles north of the church and cemetery)

This former tavern was once the social center of Whitneyville, a stagecoach stop on the Gull Trail. Along the Gull Trail, later Whitneyville Road, between Battle Creek, Kalamazoo, and Grand Rapids, the Good Intent Line ran coaches three times a week. Whitneyville became a ghost town when the railroad station and siding, along with the post office, the grain mill and stores, moved to nearby McCord. The Neoclassical tavern exemplifies a hybrid of Federal and Greek. The tavern's style is sometimes referred to as "Federal Survival," to the extent that Greek elements, such as the entry, are becoming more prominent. Built in 1853, the structure has an end gable construction and corner pilasters almost standard in Greek Revival houses, popular between 1825 and 1860. The large inn is only half of its original size. Since 1905 it has been a private residence.

Ionia County   (IA)

IONIA

Samuel Dexter of Herkimer County, New York, led settlers to present-day Ionia along the banks of the winding Grand River in 1833. The town's commercial area first grew around Dexter's sawmill and other industries powered by the waters of West Creek. With its establishment as the county seat and as the site of a federal land office in the 1830s, Ionia grew quickly. Its buildings rose to the hills. Ionia was officially incorporated as a village in 1837 (and as a city in 1873). The coming of the railroad in 1859 spurred additional growth. Silos mark the railroad tracks that

run south of Main Street. Local businessmen John C. Blanchard and Osmond Tower formed the Lansing, Ionia and Pentwater Railroad and facilitated shipment of Ionia's pink sandstone to other areas.

The buff brick walls and the lower portion of the rotunda of the original prison buildings of Michigan State House of Correction and Reformatory remain on West Main Street. Today Ionia has three prisons. The red brick Ypsilanti Reed Furniture Company factory has been converted to manufacture automobile parts. At Riverside Park on South Dexter Street are the festive buildings of the Ionia

County Fairgrounds, including grandstands with twin cupolas and stuccoed Beaux-Arts Classical exhibition buildings with Mission Revival motifs erected in 1915–1929.

The architecture of Ionia is best characterized by its numerous Italianate and Round Arch mode structures. Many were built of light yellowish brick manufactured at the West Main Street brickyards of Fred H. Vander Heyden and of yellowish gray to reddish brown sandstone extracted locally at the W. K. Woodward and Company quarries, on the south side of the Grand River 1.5 miles east of Ionia.

All of the buildings listed in Ionia are on Main Street, which intersects Michigan 66, 3 blocks south of Michigan 21, or streets that intersect it or in the nearby north side residential area.

IA01 Ionia County Courthouse

1883–1886; David W. Gibbs and Co. Bounded by Main, Kidd, Washington, and Library streets

The Ionia County Courthouse is one of a number of government buildings that takes its theme from Somerset House in London. The large Georgian Revival structure has a prominent two-tier portico and an elaborate four-stage domed cupola crowned with a statue of Justice. The central pavilion has a triple-arch loggia of Ionia sandstone resting on four rusticated Ohio sandstone piers decorated with capitals, each containing a woman's head carved in deep relief flanked by Ionic volutes and leaves. The upper tier consists of four white wooden Ionic columns on Ionia sandstone bases topped by an entablature and a denticulated pediment containing the state seal surrounded by flags, cannon, and an eagle. The exterior walls of the lowest story are rock-faced, light yellowish brown Ohio sandstone; the remaining upper walls are light reddish brown Ionia sandstone (rock-faced at the second level and smooth-cut above), extracted locally at the W. K. Woodward Quarry.

The interior is arranged in the form of a hollow square with courtrooms and offices around the periphery. The floor is laid with black and white marble, the walls are finished with red oak wainscoting, and the staircase is walnut and butternut.

Concerned with "safety, economy and durability," the building committee obtained plans from David W. Gibbs, an Ohio architect who had designed the Eaton County Courthouse, then under construction. Claire Allen was the contractor for the Ionia project. It cost $57,000, considerably more than the estimated $40,000–45,000. This courthouse replaced a simple, one-story building erected on the public square in 1843, added to and repaired in 1874, and removed in 1883. Like the ancient namesake of the county seat, the classical details of this courthouse reflect the persistence of classical taste in American governmental architecture.

Regrettably, the original windows have been replaced.

IA02 Saint John's Episcopal Church

1882, Orry Waterbury, architect builder. 120 North Kidd St. (southeast corner of Washington and North Kidd streets)

This delightful little gabled High Victorian Gothic church is a visual landmark in Ionia. A square tower with a jerkinhead roof rises at the northwest corner of the structure. Ruskinian polychromy richly ornaments the exterior. Red brick corbeling and checker work and other architectural elements decorate the yellow Vander Heyden brick walls. The church has a cruciform plan. Hammer beams support the roof. The church was designed and built by Orry Waterbury (1839–1929), an Ionia architect and builder, who came as a young man from New York State to Ionia. Here and in the surrounding villages and towns, he spent his life building houses, churches, public buildings, mills, and commercial buildings.

IA02 Saint John's Episcopal Church

IA03 **East Main Street**

Between Library and Rich streets

The spacious houses lining the once red-brick street recall the early years of Ionia, when new fortunes grew and were quickly spent on elegant houses in the fashionable Italianate or Queen Anne styles.

IA03.1 **Hall-Fowler Memorial Library** (Frederick and Ann Eager Hall House)

1869–1870, Lucius Mills, builder. 126 East Main St. (northeast corner of East Main and Library streets)

Considered at the time of its construction "one of the most elegant houses in Western Michigan," the Hall house is, indeed, one of Michigan's finest Italianate residences. An octagonal bracketed belvedere caps the low-pitched hipped roof of the nearly square house. Especially noteworthy are the elaborately carved paired and single brackets supporting the dramatically projecting eaves. Smooth-cut variegated light reddish and yellowish brown Ionia sandstone blocks are laid in the exterior walls in even courses with quoins, and yellow brick is used for the rear wall. The elaborateness of the eave brackets is repeated in the porches. Equally impressive is the rich walnut, oak, and decorative plasterwork of the interior. Frederick Hall (1816–1883) left Vermont and came to Michigan in 1836 and to Ionia in 1841. Here, Hall speculated in land and timber and became a banker. He was considered the county's wealthiest man and was elected Ionia's first mayor in 1873. Hall had local contractor Lucius Mills build this spectacular house. Donated to the city in 1903, it currently houses the public library.

IA03.2 **John C. and Harriet Brewster Blanchard House** (Palestina)

1879–1881. George Badger, builder. 253 East Main St.

This sturdy, generous Italianate house is L-shaped, with full-height polygonal bays on the front and sides. An extension to the rear was added later. The smooth-sawn and polished variegated pink Ionia sandstone from Blanchard's own quarry at Ionia create a richness in its pink, red, and light yellowish brown colors. Quoins define the corners of the house, carved stone hoods crown its windows, and wrought-iron roof cresting tops the low-pitched, bracketed hipped roof. The experiences of John C. Blanchard (1822–1905), once a migrant laborer who rose to become a lawyer, a politician, and the owner of the Ionia Stone Quarry, demonstrate the unlimited opportunities available to some of those willing to take risks in seeking their fame and fortune in this expanding frontier. Born in Cayuga County, New York, Blanchard came west to Michigan in 1836. As final plans for construction of the house were made, the *Ionia Sentinel* for November 12, 1879, predicted that it would be "one of the most commodious of the many elegant dwellings in the city." The Blanchard house today is used by the Ionia County Historical Society Museum.

IA04 Union and High streets (North Side)

On the hill overlooking Ionia's business district, houses stand terraced along the face of the slopes and hillsides. They are set high on lots along High and Union streets that afford sweeping views of the entire city.

IA04.1 Governor Fred W. and Helen Kelly Green House

1923–1924, Harry Mead. 320 North Union St.

An unexpected work in mid-Michigan is this elegant but simple Mediterranean Revival house. The two-story symmetrical steel frame and concrete stuccoed structure is crowned by a broad, overhanging, low-pitched hipped roof covered with green tiles. Round arches supported by paired columns enframe the recessed central north entrance. The interior is arranged with living areas off a central hall. Fred W. Green (1872–1936), a lawyer and a manufacturer of reed furniture who served as mayor of Ionia and as governor of Michigan, engaged Harry Mead of Grand Rapids to design the house. The house is an appropriate backdrop for reed furniture. It was built by Banhagel Brothers. According to the *Ionia Sentinel-Standard* for May 8, 1924, it contained "all the charming simplicity of a modern home." In keeping with Green's interest in the north woods, Mead lined the walls of the basement recreation room with logs and built a fieldstone fireplace, creating the likeness of a rustic lodge.

IA04.2 Isaac H. and Eliza Cooper Thayer House

1870. 114–116 High St. (northwest corner of High and Pleasant streets)

A campanile-like tower with paired windows dominates the front facade of this Italian Villa. The house is built of light yellowish brown brick probably manufactured in Ionia by the Vander Heyden Company. The Thayer house has a low-pitched hipped roof with wide, paired, bracketed eaves. A wooden balcony is over the entryway and a single-story partial-width porch with balustrade runs across the east side of the front. Isaac H. Thayer (b. 1823) and his wife, Eliza (b. 1826), moved from New England westward to Wisconsin and eventually, in 1860, back to Ionia, where Thayer operated a dry goods store.

IA04.3 Saints Peter and Paul Roman Catholic Church

1880–1883, Peter Dederichs. 434 High St.

Saints Peter and Paul Church is a brick Romanesque Revival building with onion domes atop the square towers. These towers flank a triple, round-arch, recessed entrance portico supported by rather spindly sandstone columns with ornate cushion capitals. The exterior walls are Vander Heyden brick, now painted mustard. The interior plan has the traditional barrel-vaulted nave and a wide transept. Light filtered through brilliant stained-glass windows depicting biblical scenes illuminates the interior. It was beautifully redecorated in 1983–1984. The designer was Peter Dederichs of Detroit, a specialist in Catholic church designs. The church was first organized in 1863.

IA05 West Main Street Commercial District

West Main St. between Dexter and Kidd streets

Commercial Italianate features, such as pressed metal cornices and elaborate window hoods, give downtown Ionia an authentic High Victorian charm. Although some of its distinctive structures date from the early twentieth century, many of the two- and three-story buildings date from the late 1800s and are constructed of locally produced light yellowish brown brick or pink sandstone.

IA05.1 Ionia Theatre

1931. 205–211 West Main St. (southwest corner of West Main and Kidd streets)

Marked by its towering Art Deco neon sign, stepped parapet, and marquee, the Ionia Theatre is reached through its single-story lobby which, in turn, is flanked by one-story storefronts.

IA05.2 Silver-Graff Building

1894. 313–317 West Main St.

The two-story, two-unit commercial building—one side for Silver, the other for Graff—is clad in randomly coursed pink and gray rock-faced granite fieldstone. Second-story bay windows near the ends of the facade rise to form octagonal bell-roofed towers. The bays, towers, cornices, and parapets are of richly impressed galvanized metal.

IA05.3 Ionia Armory

1908–1909, Edwin A. Bowd. 439 West Main St. (southeast corner West Main and Dexter [Michigan 66] streets)

A two-story, fortresslike rectangular block fronts the large drill hall of the brick Romanesque Revival Ionia Armory. A heavy corbeled cornice and a corbeled turret, its uppermost portion now gone, project from the structure, which definitely makes a patriotic statement. The center entrance and upper windows are recessed within segmental arches.

MUIR

IA06 Muir Church of Christ

1861, Ambrose L. Soule, builder. 138 Garden St. (northwest corner of Garden and Liberty streets)

This wooden Gothic Revival church was the first house of worship built for the Disciples of Christ in the Grand River valley. The church

was organized in 1856 with twenty-four members. Its first preacher was the Reverend Isaac Errett (1820–1888), a native of New York, who was a member of Soule, Robinson and Company, which founded the village of Muir the same year. A square entry tower with double doors fronts the gable-roof board-and-batten church, and slender pointed-arch windows punctuate the sides. The nave-and-side-aisled interior is fitted with scroll-arm "sofa" pews and with a Gothic-detailed pulpit and lamp stands. The church cost $3,215 to build.

LYONS

IA07 Samuel W. Webber House

1879, John Ashley, builder. 644 Bridge St. (northwest corner of Bridge St. and Tabor)

Samuel W. Webber (1823–1902), an early banker in Ionia County who came west from New England and New York State, built this yellow brick Italianate house for himself and his family. Sited among a stand of mature oak trees and surrounded by a wrought-iron fence, the asymmetrically arranged structure has a low-pitched hipped roof supported by elaborate paired brackets. It has tall, segmental arched windows with stone brackets and window hoods and is crowned with cresting.

BELDING

IA08 **Richardson Mill Apartments**
(Richardson Silk Mill, Mill Number Four)

1886–1887, Frederick A. Washburn, construction supervisor. 1898, 1910, additions. 1986, renovated for apartments. 101 Front St. (on the Flat River and bounded by Front and Main streets)

For nearly fifty years the people of Belding walked down to the Flat River to work in the Richardson Silk Mill. Before the advent of rayon, nylon, and other synthetic products in the 1930s, the mills in Belding employed some 1,200 silk workers, more than a quarter of the town's population. This mill was the first of four mills owned by the Belding Brothers and Company in Belding. In 1855, after locating in Patterson's Mill, which was renamed Belding in 1891, the Belding brothers, David (1832–1907), Milo (1833–1917), Alvah N. (1838–1925), and Hiram H. (1835–1890), sold silk thread from their home; they expanded and ultimately organized the company in 1863. The mill was built by George P. Richardson, formerly manager of the Belding Brothers' Cincinnati office. On its completion it was sold to Belding Brothers and Company. The mill housed the manufacturing of silk thread, including all the equipment necessary to transform bulk baled silk into dyed and spooled sewing thread.

The Richardson Silk Mill is a fine example of late-nineteenth-century industrial architecture in the Round Arch mode, comparable to the best in Lowell and Lawrence, Massachusetts. The mill is a rectangular, flat-roofed factory with load-bearing exterior walls of yellow brick. It has an internal support system

of metal posts and heavy wooden beams. The masonry walls give vertical stability. The double floors are 4 inches of solid oak. This construction technique, with its heavy beams, was known as "slow burning construction" and was standard in industrial building until the advent of reinforced concrete. Two pinnacled and pyramidal-roofed square towers containing stairwells, an elevator, and water towers rise over the mill as symbols of corporate power. The towers were not only used for water tanks but also kept the vertical circulation outside the main body of the mill, thus reducing the danger of fire spreading from floor to floor. Installed within the mill were banks of spinning and winding machines powered by a suspended drive that extended the length of the structure. Frederick A. Washburn of Rockville, Connecticut, supervised construction and installed the machinery. The use of whitish yellow brick together with bands of red brick, as evidenced in the brickwork in the Holland–Grand Rapids area, lends a distinct regional character to this industrial example. In 1986 the mill was renovated into more than seventy apartment units and still serves proudly as the symbol of "Michigan's Silk Mill City."

IA09 **Alvah N. Belding Library**

1917–1918, Frank P. Allen and Sons. 302 East Main St.

Not unlike a mausoleum is this ponderous Beaux-Arts Classical library. It was Alvah N. Belding's gift to the city in memory of his parents, Hiram and Mary Wilson Belding. Above a raised penciled foundation, large, multi-paned round-arch windows are arranged symmetrically around a projecting pedimented entry portico supported by heavy square piers and two Ionic columns in antis. The smooth, white Indiana limestone exterior adds to its memorial character. A modillioned cornice reinforces the dominant horizontality. Green tile covers the roof. The interior is rich and profuse—Georgia marble lines the lobby, Vermont Verde Antique marble trim is used in the rooms, and the woodwork is of oak and cypress. The library was designed by Frank P. Allen (1856–1933) of Grand Rapids, publisher of the architectural book, *Artistic Dwellings* (1891, 1892, 1893).

IA10 **Belding Post Office**

1940–1941, Louis A. Simon, Supervising Architect, U.S. Treasury Department. 201 East Main St.

Constructed by the Federal Works Agency Public Building Administration in the restrained stripped formal classicism of 1940, the post office has a Doric tetrastyle in antis. The brick walls are laid in common bond and the roof is hipped. The post office contains a New Deal-sponsored mural, *Belding Brothers and Their Silk Industry*, by Marvin Beerbohm. The scene in the naturalistic muted work depicts the four well-dressed Belding brothers inspecting lengths of silk produced by workers straining over their machines. A world map in the center background may allude to the prominence of the company, which had a total of eight mills in Belding and New England.

IA11 **Belrockton Dormitory**

1905. Southeast corner of East Main and Hanover streets

Constructed by the Belding Brothers and Company, the Belrockton is the only one remaining of three dormitories for young women recruited as laborers from outlying farms. It housed 125 women who lived under the supervision of matrons in a manner similar to the paternalistic practice at Lowell, Massachusetts, and contained sleeping rooms above the first-floor dining and sitting rooms. The name Belrockton is a combination of Belding, Rockville (Connecticut), and Northampton (Massachusetts). The large, L-shaped, three-story brick structure with classical detailing was fronted with broad wooden porches on all floors.

Barry County (BA)

Barry County was organized in 1839 and was named for Postmaster General William Barry, who served under President Andrew Jackson. Pioneers first settled the county's less densely timbered western areas and took up farming. Today, the county continues to rely on agriculture, which is now supplemented by light industry. Its judicial seat of government is located on the Thornapple River, a tributary of the Grand River.

HASTINGS

BA01 **Barry County Courthouse**

1892–1894, Albert E. French. 220 West State St. (bounded by West State, South Church, and East Court streets, and Broadway [Michigan 37/43])

On a tree-shaded square, the site of three earlier county courthouses since 1842, stands the Barry County Courthouse. The massive red brick and ashlar structure is symmetrical in design and is marked by a complex roofline of dormers and gable peaks topped by a central clock and bell tower. In its Queen Anne Palladian window, its Richardsonian Romanesque window arches, and the Romanesque Revival portal, the courthouse echoes the late nineteenth century's stylistic eclecticism. The second-floor courtroom is an expansive space with a typical balustered railing and a broad judge's dais. The courthouse is a carbon copy of the Livingston County Courthouse (LV01, p. 157). A large, simple Queen Anne house shares the courthouse square. Currently used as the courthouse annex, it previously contained the sheriff's home and the jail.

BA02 **First Methodist Church**

1910–1911, William E. N. Hunter. 1949. 1961, educational unit, Christopher King. 209 West Green St. (northwest corner of West Green and South Church streets)

A 40-foot-high, Roman-inspired dome on an octagonal drum marks the red brick First Methodist Church as one of Michigan's most unusual churches, made even more distinctive by its small-town location. The church was also remarkable for its association with

BA01 Barry County Courthouse

The Sunday school department could be opened by folding doors to make an auditorium seating 1,000.

Spence Brothers of Saginaw constructed the church. It cost $43,177 to build. The church is the third home of a congregation established in 1841 as a class belonging to the Kalamazoo district. In 1845 a log church was built. The current structure's predecessor, a small Greek Revival building erected in 1859–1860 and now lacking its original steeple, still stands at 322 West Jefferson Street.

NASHVILLE VICINITY, CASTLETOWN TOWNSHIP

BA03 Liebhauser Twelve-sided Barn
(Round Barn)

1916–1917. 7004 Scott Rd. (Michigan 79) (southwest corner of Scott and Swift roads)

prolific Detroit-based architect William E. N. Hunter (1858–1947). Hunter's numerous church designs for Methodist congregations were usually in the Neo-Gothic mode, but here he created an unusual individualistic departure into the Beaux-Arts Classical vocabulary. Drawing on the style's predilection for freer interpretation of the classical forms, Hunter began with a strictly symmetrical design of alternating recessed and projecting bays. Decoration is fairly limited, restrained by rigid symmetry and, no doubt, by a modest budget. The recessed bays are quite simple, marked only by two large round-arch windows. The gabled projecting bays, however, are more complex. In each, paired windows are topped by a limestone cornice. Above the cornice is an awkward festoon supporting a single round window; the festoon and circle forms are echoed in the pediment above. A continuous cornice with massive dentils is an attempt to tie the whole design together.

The interior exemplifies the "Akron-plan" church, which was common from the 1880s to the 1910s. The auditorium is shaped as a quarter circle with semicircular seating for 350, which stands on a floor that slopes downward toward a pulpit backed by an organ case. Two side balconies seat 200 more. A semicircular Sunday school department area behind the sanctuary has two tiers of rooms (now partitioned off) against its rear wall.

This unusual polygonal barn was built in 1916–1917 by Ed Liebhauser, a druggist in nearby Nashville who owned the farm. Liebhauser contracted with a local carpenter to have two smaller barns removed from the site and the lumber reused to construct an immense twelve-sided barn in their place. Heavy timbers from these two barns, along with the standard dimensional lumber and metal cladding, were used to erect the structure, which is approximately 85 feet in diameter and 65 feet in height, from the basement to the rooftop.

Although unusual in size and shape, the barn was in many respects designed as a common northern bank barn, with the basement level exposed to the south providing grade level access to a barnyard and insulated by earth to the north, providing direct access to the main floor, which was used as a haymow.

One of the major advantages of circular barns, as touted by their proponents, was increased storage capacity and more efficient use of space, since there were no odd corners. A team of horses with a wagon rig could enter the Liebhauser barn, turn around completely inside, and exit through the same doorway. Hay could be stacked to near-ceiling level by lifting it to an iron track circling the interior heights of the building. The main floor haymow easily stored all of the hay from the 412-acre farm, as well as every piece of equipment used on the farm at that time, and the basement level accommodated over two hundred ewes and their lambs. Although not currently used for agricultural purposes, the Liebhauser barn remains in good condition, continues to serve as a landmark for the Nashville community, and is symbolic of the importance of traditional and innovative agricultural practices to the community's evolution.

Allegan County (AE)

ALLEGAN

Settled in 1835, incorporated as a village three years later, and reincorporated in 1858, Allegan is located on horseshoe bend in the Kalamazoo River. The river afforded waterpower for sawmills, paper mills, and other industries. Allegan serves as a center for the surrounding fruit and dairy farms.

AE01 **Winchester Inn** (Alby and Electa Hooker Dickenson Rossman House)

1869. 524 Marshall St. (Michigan 89) (southeast corner of the park at Fifth and Marshall streets)

This fine yellow brick Italianate house was built in 1869 by Alby Rossman (1812–1893), an Allegan pioneer. Originally from eastern New York, Rossman came to Allegan in 1836 and opened a foundry and a machine shop on the millrace. High on the plateau above the river, he platted the 15-acre Rossman Addition to the village, and here he built his house, surrounded by the park. Prominent ornamental paired brackets support the eaves of the low-pitched hipped roof. The house has columned and bracketed porches and decorative bay windows. There are stone hood moldings above the windows, some of which retain the original working shutters. A fanlight is above the main entrance. Made in Rossman's own foundry, the hand-puddled cast-iron fence has a pattern of interlocking circles that is echoed in the roof cresting of the house.

AE02 **Oscar T. Booth House**

1868–1871. 107 Delano St. (southwest corner Delano and Cedar streets)

Built for lumberman Oscar T. Booth, the L-shaped Italian Villa has a balcony in the square tower, a finial atop a flared pyramid roof, and a decorative entablature. The house has paired windows and a large porch on the

AE02 Oscar T. Booth House

south side with carved posts and a cast-iron balustrade; it is clad in tongue-and-groove boards. The carriage house on the grounds dates from the same period. Local tradition attributes the design to the same architect-builder as the Italianate David Doane and Hannah Davis House at 302 Cutler Street (see AE04).

AE03 **Gen. Benjamin D. Pritchard House**

1866–1867. 330 Davis St.

On a wooded ridge in the western part of Allegan overlooking the city, this Gothic Revival house was built in 1866–1867 by one of Allegan's most noted citizens. Gen. Benjamin D. Pritchard (1835–1907) was a lawyer and a banker, who became a Civil War hero because of his part in the capture of Jefferson Davis. Pritchard came to Allegan from Ohio in 1856. The house has steeply pitched cross gables over an H-shaped plan. Twin gables in the front have paired, pointed-arch windows on the second story. A large veranda, added later, wraps around one corner of the house. The elegant hanging oval staircase in the entryway was built to Pritchard's own design.

This structure owes much to a plan in Andrew Jackson Downing's *Cottage Residences* (1842). Like the River Cottage example, the Pritchard house is built on a hill to take advantage of the fine view and shows cross gables, peaked dormers, bay windows, and porches.

AE04 **DeLano Inn** (David Doane and Hannah Davis House)

1869, David Doane Davis, builder. 302 Cutler St. (northwest corner of Cutler and Walnut streets)

This large, cubical Italianate house was built in 1869 by David Doane Davis (1814–1871) and his wife, Hannah. Davis came to Allegan in 1834–1835 from Hartford, Washington County, New York. Trained as a carpenter and joiner, Davis built many of the town's early buildings and invested his profits in real estate. The *Allegan Journal* for September 1877 described the Davis house as "one of the most elegant structures in our village." The building has an octagonal cupola, prominent paired ornamental brackets, and a large wrap-around porch. Small oval windows pierce the ample entablature, and straight bracketed hood moldings ornament the two-over-two windows below. Davis also built a carriage house and surrounded the lot with a splendid ornate hand-puddled, cast-iron fence that was made by the A. Rossman and J. Hoxie foundry.

AE05 **Seventh-Day Adventist Church**

1863. 229 Cutler St. (3rd door east of southeast corner of Cutler St. and Walnut)

The Seventh-Day Adventists built in 1863 this "plain but neat house of worship."[41] Organized in 1861, it was one of the first churches established by the Adventist Society in Michigan, after it moved its headquarters in 1855 from New England to Battle Creek by way of Rochester, New York. John Andrews, cofounder of the sect, reportedly presided at the dedication services in 1864. Today this church is the oldest Adventist church still in use in Michigan. The simple, front-gabled Greek Revival church is eccentric in that it has a prominent octagonal Italianate belfry. In contrast, a heavy classical cornice over a plain frieze crowns the exterior clapboarded walls. The walls are pierced by square-headed twelve-over-twelve windows. Beneath a shuttered window with fanlights, the central main entry double door is framed by fluted Doric pilasters. The octagonal belfry rests on a square base and is topped with a cross-gabled roof supported by brackets, the latter is terminated with a finial. It contains four round-arch louvered openings, each flanked at its base with ornate scroll brackets. The center-aisled sanctuary seats 300, which is quite surprising since in 1861 the initial membership in the church was only nine people. The pulpit was designed by Ellen G. White, a prolific author and one of the founders of the Seventh-Day Adventist Movement in Michigan.

AE06 **Second Street Bridge**

1886, King Iron Bridge and Manufacturing Company. Second St. over the Kalamazoo River

The Second Street Bridge over the Kalamazoo River was built in 1886 by the King Iron Bridge and Manufacturing Company of Cleveland, Ohio, one of the nineteenth century's most important bridge-building firms. Zenas King, founder of the company, designed and patented in 1861 a much-improved bowstring truss, which first met with skepticism because it used less iron than earlier metal trusses. His design proved to be strong as well as inexpensive, and his company became one of the largest iron bridge companies in the nation. For the Allegan bridge, the builder chose to use a double-intersection Pratt truss structure of wrought iron and structural steel; the bridge is 18 feet wide and 225 feet long. There are eighteen wrought-iron truss verticals with diagonal bracing, wood beams and planking, iron finials on the end posts, latticed metal handrails, and a wood-floored pedestrian walkway. It is one of the largest King double-intersecting Pratt through-trusses remaining in the United States. Following a local effort to save the structure from demolition, the bridge was restored in 1983 with monies from the U.S. Department of Transportation's secondary road funds administered by the Michigan Department of Transportation. It won a National Historic Preservation Presidential Award through the Advisory Council on Historic Preservation for bridge preservation in 1988.

OTSEGO

Otsego was a paper-manufacturing center on the Kalamazoo River. The river generated power for the paper mills. Otsego was settled in 1832 and incorporated in 1865.

AE07 Richard Thompson House

1880s. 319 East Allegan (Michigan 89)

This little house on the main street of this small paper-manufacturing city on the Kalamazoo River resembles a prototype of the design that Charles W. Caskey developed in the Allegan vicinity and later employed for cottages on Mackinac Island. It has a Latin cross-plan and a three-sided porch that wraps in a U-shape around the front wing. The rooms flow together and the porches merge the inside with the out-of-doors. In particular, it is like the William Gilbert Cottage (MK 15, p. 552) constructed on the West Bluff of Mackinac Island in 1889. A native of Allegan, Caskey first went to northern Michigan in the 1880s to build cottages at the Presbyterian Resort, what is now Wequetonsing (EM09, p. 412), and established himself as a builder in Harbor Springs. This plan was ideally suited for the cottages he built in the Little Traverse Region and on Mackinac Island. It is a fascinating and truly regional invention.

DOUGLAS

Douglas is located on the Kalamazoo River, a short distance from its outlet into Lake Michigan. The village was laid out in 1861 and incorporated in 1870.

AE08 Dutcher Lodge No. 193 Masonic Hall

1875. 1902, east addition. 86 Center St. (northwest corner of Center and Union streets)

The Dutcher Lodge is the oldest public building in Douglas and the oldest Masonic lodge still in use in Allegan County. The building is a plain, two-story wood-frame structure with a shed roof sloping to the rear. The east half addition, constructed in 1902 to provide space for a village hall on the ground level, doubled the size of the original structure. A modestly bracketed cornice is also ornamented by dentils. The two-over-two windows are shuttered. Both front entrances are treated with classical pilasters and entablatures. The building contains a large hall downstairs and the Masonic temple and other rooms upstairs. The first meeting of Dutcher Lodge occurred in 1866, presided over by its First Worshipful Master, Thomas Benton Dutcher (1836–1903), for whom the lodge was named. A native of Pennsylvania, Dutcher helped plat the village of Douglas in 1854 and was a lumberman and gristmill operator.

AE09 Union School

1866–1867. 138 West Center St.

The school is one of the first union schools in the Douglas area. It resulted from the consolidation of several village schools into a centralized school where all grades were taught. The large, two-story wood-frame structure has classical proportions with Italianate decorative features. A bracketed bell tower rises from the large, bracketed cross-gable roof, as if to announce its educational purpose. Paired pilasters and a low-pitched, bracketed pediment frame the double-door entrance. All grades were taught here until the 1920s, when the high school students began to go to Saugatuck. The building was in continuous use as a school until 1957, when a new school was completed. It was converted in 1963 into four apartments.

SAUGATUCK

This picturesque resort community and art colony is on the Kalamazoo River near its mouth in the sand dunes along Lake Michigan. The river widens into a small lake that forms a harbor. Saugatuck developed in the

1860s and 1870s as a sawmill and tannery town. Nearby peach orchards, boat building, and commercial fishing have been important industries.

AE10 All Saints Episcopal Church

1872–1874, Gordon W. Lloyd. 252 Grand St. (southwest corner of Hoffman and Grand streets)

All Saints Episcopal Church is one of the finest and best-preserved board-and-batten Gothic Revival churches in Michigan. Four years after the congregation was admitted to the Michigan Diocese in 1869, it selected Detroit architect Gordon W. Lloyd to design the church. Born and trained in England, Lloyd had Anglican connections that won him favor among those seeking designs for Episcopalian churches loosely based on the English parish church model. Lloyd knew the requirements of the Ecclesiology movement. Ecclesiology was an important factor in the spread of the Gothic Revival in nineteenth-century America. All Saints is an Ecclesiological church. Of all Lloyd's other Michigan churches, All Saints is most closely related to Saint James Episcopal Chapel (WN14.3, p. 121), also an Ecclesiological church, built on Grosse Ile in 1867. Lloyd's plans for All Saints were executed by George Harnes, George E. Dunn, and William Dunning, highly skilled local carpenters who were part of the wood building tradition of ship carpenters present in Saugatuck. Their crisp and expressive interpretation of the

"woodiness" of the building material is noteworthy.

All Saints is a simple, steeply pitched gable-roofed structure with a spired open belfry that towers over the vestibule at the northeast corner. Two-stage buttresses support the north and south walls. The walls are pierced with pointed Gothic windows and a rose window, all with foiled mullions. The church is embellished with scalloped bargeboards, trefoil and quatrefoil patterns, cross-timbering, and ornamental hood moldings. The nave has a hammer-beam roof and vertical board-beaded wainscot. The connecting parish hall and rectory were added in 1945–1946.

AE11 Oxbow Summer School of Painting

1873 to present. North end of Park (west off Blue Star Highway on Center St. in Douglas .3 mile, then north on Ferry St. 1.3 miles and north on Park .6 mile)

Established in this idyllic location in 1910, the Oxbow Summer School of Painting is one of the oldest summer art programs in the country. It was founded by John C. Johanson of the Chicago Art Institute, along with Frederick F. Fursman and Walter M. Clute. Later, in 1915, Thomas Eddy Tallmadge (1876–1940) assisted in the school's development. They bought the Riverside Hotel at Oxbow Lagoon to be used for classes. The inn was built in late 1873 by Charles Schriver (1842–1905), who had come to Saugatuck from Buffalo, New York, with his brother Henry to operate a commercial fishing business. At that time, before a cut was made to aid navigation, the Oxbow Lagoon was a bend in the Kalamazoo River, and the site served as a landing for river shipping. Summer boarders stayed at the Schrivers' home, and eventually it became one of the early resort hotels patronized by Chicagoans, who arrived by boat. The original part of the inn, known today as the Oxbow Inn, is a plain symmetrical Italianate structure with a belvedere. Long verandas tie together and unify this early portion and a later 1880s addition. The school also has three small gable-roofed outbuildings, which were built by the Schrivers in the 1890s as the caretaker's cottage, stable, and shed. They were adapted in the 1920s for use as student quarters. Several artists in residence and prominent Chicagoans, including distinguished Prairie school architect and author Tallmadge, built cottages on the grounds of the school. The Tallmadge cottage, erected in 1923, is a simple, green-stained, clapboarded structure trimmed with red. With its wood footings, screened windows with awning drops, fireplace, and decorative carving on the exposed interior studs, it is the epitome of the simple Michigan summer cottage. Newer structures house glassblowing, papermaking, and print-making studios. Many of its students have attained national recognition: Peter Agostini, Richard Artschwager, Janet Fish, Leon Golub, Joan Mitchell, Claes Oldenburg, Richard Hunt, and Peter Saul.

AE12 Kemah Cottage (William and Alys Springer Cottage)

1906, Thomas E. Tallmadge. 1926, remodeling, Carl Hoerman. 633 Pleasant St. (southwest corner Pleasant and Allegan streets)

Kemah Cottage was built in 1906, reportedly to the designs of Tallmadge, for Fred S. Thompson (1854–1932), a Chicagoan who had summered at Saugatuck since 1896. *Kemah*, an Indian word for "in the teeth of the winds," is an appropriate name for this breezy spot on Allegan Hill above the lake, which was also the site of an Indian burial. The house was sold in 1926 to William Springer (1884–1941), also from Chicago, who was a member of the Chicago Board of Trade. A few months later, Kemah was damaged by fire, and Springer and his wife, Alys, hired Carl Hoerman to remodel the house. Hoerman, a Bavarian-born architect and artist well-known for his landscape paintings, was then artist-in-residence at the Oxbow Summer School of Painting. A friend of the Springers, he designed for them a very personal and inspired reflection of their interests.

The Saugatuck *Commercial Record* for 1932 described the transformed Kemah Cottage as "a delight to the eye because of its charming roof line, quiet dignity, and artistic landscaping," and as "a distinguished example of the 'House Beautiful,' " in which every detail accounts for itself in artistic terms.

The house is a modified English Cottage design with a false thatched roof. It has a varied roofline with many gables, clapboard siding, and a large columned porch, as well as a porte-cochère. In the garden, Hoerman built a concrete and limestone cavern, where one can find a fountain, stalactites and stalagmites, and Indian wall paintings. Every aspect of the interior was created by Hoerman as well—Art Nouveau and Wrightian stained-glass windows, hand-carved wood panels and doors, light fixtures, and wrought-iron grilles. The solarium features a fountain whose base was comprised of rocks gathered on a western trip taken by Mrs. Springer and Hoerman and a massive stone fireplace. A verse over the window reads, "In rain and shine, my port divine, A world my own, Kemah my home." The basement has a rathskeller with its original fittings. Open to public.

LAKE TOWN TOWNSHIP

AE13 The Castle

1889–1890. 6700 Bryant Ave., Castle Park (off southwest corner of 146th Ave. and 66th St.)

The Castle is the architectural centerpiece of a summer cottage resort colony in the wooded dunes along Lake Michigan. Michael Schwarz, a retired real estate promoter from nearby Holland, built it in 1890 as his home. It was used as a summer camp from 1893 to 1895. The following year the site was opened as a summer resort. John H. Parr converted the house into a hotel. The brooding castellated Romanesque Revival structure has a round tower, a square turret, and a battlement. From a battered rusticated Waverly sandstone foundation, pale yellowish tan Veneklassen (Zeeland) brick rises in the exterior walls. Round-headed windows are surrounded by brick arches. Later additions complement the main building. A marbleized slate fireplace is in the living room. Today the Castle Park Association uses the Castle for a library and community building.

Ottawa County (OT)

HOLLAND

In 1847 a group of Dutch immigrants under the leadership of Reverend Albertus C. Van Raalte, a secessionist pastor from Rotterdam, selected a 1,000-acre site at the mouth of the Black River and established a town. They built homes, farms, and businesses. In 1851 a pioneer school was founded. It became Hope College in 1866. As other Dutch immigrants arrived, they established nearby separate communities—Overisel, Zeeland, Vriesland, Drenthe, and Graafschap.

A sawmill, a gristmill, a brickyard, a shingle mill, and a stave factory were developed in Holland. The harbor was improved so that ships could pass from Lake Michigan into the Black River and Black Lake (Lake Macatawa). In 1867 the village incorporated as a city.

A fire in 1871 destroyed most of Holland, but the Dutch-American city was rebuilt using, among other materials locally quarried sandstone from the Marshall sandstone formation, once called Waverly stone. Mature factories were added. Tourists from Chicago and Grand Rapids vacationed at Ottawa Beach and Macatawa Park on Lake Michigan.

The architecture of Holland shows some Dutch influence.

OT01 **Centennial Park**

1876. Bounded by West 10th St., Central Ave., West 12th St., and River Ave.

Acting on Governor Bagley's suggestion to the state's citizenry to plant trees to celebrate the nation's centennial in 1876, the city of Holland transformed Market Square, platted in 1847 but deserted for a number of years, into a Victorian design called Centennial Park. Later, community public buildings were built facing this park. Initially the park contained gravel paths and newly transplanted trees. Other improvements soon followed—lighting was added in 1894; oak benches installed in 1896; the central 20-foot-high fountain of tufa rock was built and donated in 1902 by Tenius Ten Houten, and rest rooms were completed in 1904 and refurbished in 1989.

OT02 **Netherlands Museum** (Henry Kremers House)

1889, George Dalman. Southeast corner of East 12th St. and Central Ave.

Built for Henry Kremers (d. 1911), a local physician who also served as mayor, this picturesque two-and-a-half-story Queen Anne house stands on a cut fieldstone foundation with exterior first-story walls of split fieldstone. The second story is clad in brick with decorative wood shingles on the gable ends. The house was a family residence until 1914, a city hospital until 1929, and a Hope College fraternity house until 1939, when, with the aid of Works Progress Administration funds, it was renovated for use as the Netherlands Museum.

OT03 **Michigan Bell Telephone Building**

1929–1930, Smith, Hynchman and Grylls Associates, Inc. 13 West 10th St.

The Dutch heritage of the people of Holland is reaffirmed in the stepped gable of the Michigan Bell Building. The steel-frame reinforced concrete building is built on a granite base and faced with brick trimmed with Bedford limestone. The use of Flemish bond in the brickwork adds to the greater decorative effect. A frieze of carved stone and brick laid in intricate patterns divides the first and second stories, and the colorful spandrel panels of yellow, green, red, and blue tiles divide the second and third. The windows and the doors are topped or surrounded by radiating lighter-colored stone. Crow-stepped gables present a stark silhouette against the lighter sky, and the authentic Flemish baked red clay tile adds to the building's colorfulness.

The relationship of the architectural firm of Smith, Hinchman and Grylls with the telephone utility company began in Detroit in the late nineteenth century. The firm's ability to provide both architectural and engineering services enabled it to modernize buildings in such a way as to serve a growing technology. In cities throughout Michigan, SH&G created a corporate identity for Michigan Bell. This modern building demonstrated Holland's progressiveness as much as its banks and public buildings did. It is a meld of modernism and traditional Netherlandish architecture in a city heavily populated by the Dutch. A. J. DeKonig built the structure at a cost of $16,000.

OT04 **Third Reformed Church**

1874, John R. Kleyn, builder. 1891, belfry added. 1952, parish hall and educational wing. 110 West 12th St. (southwest corner of West 12th St. and Pine Ave.)

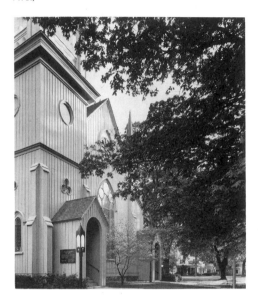

The Gothic Revival Third Reformed Church bears a striking similarity to Richard Upjohn's wooden churches. The Reverend Albertus C. Van Raalte, founder of the Holland Colony, first organized the church in 1867 and donated the land for the first house of worship. This church burned in the 1871 fire that destroyed two-thirds of the city. The present church is of a balloon-frame construction, with board-and-batten siding. It has pointed-arch windows, wall buttresses, and pinnacles, and rests on a foundation of locally quarried sandstone from the Marshall sandstone formation. The spired square corner tower with an open belfry was added in 1891. The auditorium-plan interior is adapted to the needs of the Reformed service, with the congregation arranged around the central pulpit to enable the members to see the preacher and to hear the spoken Word. Architecturally, the grouping of the pews in front of the pulpit eliminated the center aisle. Clustered col-

umns support the Gothic arches of the interior. The platform furniture, originally made for Saint Nicholas Collegiate Church of New York, was installed in 1952. The parish hall and educational facilities are more recent—both were built in 1952. The church was restored in 1967–1968.

OT05 **Isaac Cappon House**

1872–1873, John R. Kleyn, builder. 228 West 9th St. (southeast corner of West 9th St. and Washington Ave.)

This mildly Italianate wooden house was built by local builder, John R. Kleyn (b. 1841) for Isaac Cappon (1830–1902), a Dutch native who ran the Cappon and Bertsch Leather Company Tannery. Cappon, a leading industrialist and civic leader, was Holland's first mayor. The two-story, T-shaped house has decorative brackets, polygonal bays, and rounded decorative window hoods. One of the best-preserved houses built soon after the fire of 1871, it retains many of its original furnishings and its decorative detailing. The house remained in the Cappon family until the late 1970s. It is now a part of the Netherlands Museum.

OT06 **Tower Clock Building** (Holland City State Bank Building)

1892. 190 River Ave. (northwest corner of River Ave. and West 8th St.)

Looming impressively in its ruggedness over River Avenue is this three-story commercial block in a vernacular interpretation of the Richardsonian Romanesque. When built at the main intersection of downtown Holland in 1892, the Holland City State Bank Building was the largest and most substantial structure in the commercial district. Its exterior walls are of locally quarried Waverly sandstone. A solid, truncated square clock tower anchors the southeast corner of the building. The street facade was historicised during rehabilitation efforts motivated by the National Trust Main Street program.

OT07 **Peoples State Bank**

1928, Donald J. Lackie. 36 East 8th St.

In keeping with the intent of the officials of the Peoples State Bank, this colorful bank building projects an "atmosphere of friend-liness and trust." Showing "traces of the Italian influence in its conception," the exterior design of the bank is predominantly vertical.[42] In each of three bays, slender, two-story paired windows are grouped beneath larger round-arch windows of the third level. The center entry is positioned beneath a balconet. The entire front of the building is clad in variegated ivory terracotta highlighted with blues and greens. The interior is warm and open, and conducive to easy conversation between teller and patron. The colonnaded banking room is two stories high with a mezzanine extending around the lobby on three sides. The walls are clad in ivory, cream, and gold terracotta, the floor is covered with hand-colored faience tiles in blues, greens, gold, and black, and the ceiling is coffered with panels originally decorated in ivory, blues, lavenders, and rose. Bolhuis Company was the builder.

OT08 Pillar Christian Reformed Church
(Old First Reformed Church / Ninth Street Christian Reformed Church)

1856, Jacobus Schrader. Southwest corner of East 9th St. and College Ave.

One of few buildings to survive the fire of 1871 that destroyed most of Holland, the wooden temple-front hexastyle prostyle clapboarded Neoclassical church is Holland's oldest church building. The frame and columns are constructed of hand-hewn oak timbers. The Doric order, however, is Palladian, not Greek. The church is thus typical of many provincial temple-form buildings of the Greek Revival era in which a Palladian or Roman order was used, instead of the Greek. Also not Greek is the three-stage octagonal arched bell tower with a cupola, surmounted by a copper cock, symbolic of Peter's denial, which tops the square tower. The church stands on land given to the congregation of the Reformed Church in America by the Reverend Albertus C. Van Raalte, founder and first pastor of the Holland colony. It was built to the designs of Jacobus Schrader (1812–1899) of Holland by local builders Verbeek, Venema, Zalsman, and Slenk, with the assistance of volunteers from the congregation. The present church replaced a log church that was located on the site of Pilgrim Rest Cemetery. In 1884 the majority of the congrega-tion seceded as part of a larger religious movement in the community to the Christian Reformed denomination.

OT09 Voorhees Hall (Elizabeth R. Voorhees Women's Dormitory)

1907, Samuel Mast. 72 East 10th St.

The construction in 1907 of this women's dormitory hall marked the admission of women to the formerly all-male liberal arts Hope College. The college was chartered in 1866 under the auspices of the Dutch Reformed Church. The marked Dutch flavor of Voorhees Hall is an outward and visible sign of the cultural ties of the people of Holland and Hope College to the Netherlands. The two-and-a-half-story building rests on a raised foundation. It has crow-stepped gables both in roof and dormers. Its orangish red brick walls, which are laid in a diamond pattern in the upper story, are in strong contrast with the Bedford limestone in the foundation, quoins, voussoirs, and window sills. The hall currently holds faculty offices. The Gordon and Margaret Van Wylen Library to the west is a Postmodern visual companion piece designed by Shepley, Bullfinch, Richardson, and Abbott of Boston and built in 1989 by Pioneer Construction.

OT10 Marigold Lodge (Egbert H. and Margaret J. Gold Summer House)

1913, Thomas Eddy Tallmadge, of Tallmadge and Watson. 1922, sun porch. 1116 Hazel Ave. (off Waukazoo Dr., on the north shore of Lake Macatawa)

Situated on Superior Point on the north shore of Lake Macatawa, a favorite summer resort of Hollanders and Chicagoans, Marigold Lodge is one of Michigan's outstanding Prairie style landmarks. This extended two-story but formally elegant house, with its rambling rear wing, is arranged to offer views of the lake from all rooms. Its sweeping horizontality, the prominent piers, a low-pitched hipped roof, and the stucco and wood trim exterior are hallmarks of Tallmadge and Watson's Prairie architecture. Thomas Eddy Tallmadge (1876–1940) of Tallmadge and Watson of Chicago, a noted member of the Prairie school, designed the summer lodge for Egbert H. Gold (1868–1928), and his wife, Margaret. Gold was a manufacturer of radiators and heating systems. In 1977, Herman Miller, Inc., an office design systems concern, rehabilitated the complex for use as an educational and visitor's center. Open to public.

HOLLAND (Graafschap Vicinity)
[Allegan County]

OT11   Herman Miller Design Yard

1988–1989, Jeffrey A. Scherer of Meyer, Scherer and Rockcastle, Ltd. 375 West 48th St. (146th Ave./Matt Urban Dr.) (.5 mile west of intersection of US 31 and Washington [Business I-196/Business US 31])

Herman Miller Design Yard is a building complex that was conceived as a means of assembling and consolidating the various stages of the furniture manufacturing design process on one site. Located in a rural setting between the communities of Graafschap and Holland, the building forms, materials, and organization are borrowed from nearby agricultural structures. The vernacular forms include connected corrugated silver metal buildings—with ventilators and clerestories, white houses with porches and bright red silos, many placed on fieldstone foundations, and all arranged to resemble a farm. The campuslike placement of individual buildings on the site, as well as the melding of traditional agrarian elements, puts this corporate complex magnificently in tune with its pastoral setting. The Design Yard won a citation from *Progressive Architecture* magazine as one of the top fifteen designs of 1988.

ZEELAND

One of the early Dutch settlements in the Black River valley near Holland, Zeeland grew

OT11 Herman Miller Design Yard

from a farming village to an industrial center. It was incorporated as a city in 1905.

OT12 Herman Miller Headquarters Building

1958, George Nelson and Gordon Chadwick. 1969. 1970, addition, A. Quincy Jones. 8500 Byron Rd. (northwest corner of Byron Rd. and Michigan 21)

The corporate headquarters for this manufacturer of office systems is a campus plan modeled after a European village square. It stands at the northeast edge of Zeeland on a 100-acre site that was acquired in the 1950s by the DePree family. Max DePree, whose father D. J. DePree founded the Herman Miller company in 1905, sought to build an indeterminate ("non-precious, non-monumental") building, which people can own and in which people are empowered to effect changes with grace, that is, a building that truly acknowledges the way people work and behave in the work place. The DePrees called on noted industrial designer George Nelson (1908–1988) of New York, who had designed many pieces of furniture for the company, to plan the five-building campus plan with the possibility of interrelated modular expansion. In 1970 Max DePree had A. Quincy Jones (1913–1979) of California add a 40-foot-wide skylighted "spine" expressway connecting all of the buildings for people, materials, and

equipment. The space is based on the vernacular concepts of village, path, and landmark developed by Frank Gehry, Charles Moore, and others. The city-plan interior design uses tower clocks, graphics, artwork, color, and office systems to subdivide the space into neighborhoods. The brick exterior walls of the International-style steel-frame structures are broken by grids or slots of windows; the interior has exposed truss work. The buildings contain offices, manufacturing operations, warehousing, health care facilities, and a cafeteria. The site is landscaped with ponds, trees, and sculpture.

OT13 Max DePree House

1954, Charles Eames. Northeast corner of Division St. and Rich Ave.

Charles Eames, who was employed by Herman Miller, Inc., as a furniture designer, created this International-style house for Max DePree, the current chairman of the board of Herman Miller and the son of D. J. DePree, founder and former president of the company. The rectangular, two-story, all-timber structure is fronted with a modular grid with repeated vertical elements. An open balcony and railing, covered by the flat overhanging roof, extends across the back of the second story overlooking a garden and woods. The house was built by local craftsmen. Several additions planned for in the original design were executed subsequently.

OT14 Poest-Leeuw House

1887. 376 Franklin Rd. (100th Ave.) (southwest corner of Franklin Ave. [100th Ave.] and Felch St.)

The unique polychrome brickwork of this cross-shaped house on the flat farmlands of

OT14 Poest-Leeuw House

Zeeland reflects a patterning technique that pervaded western Michigan's "Dutch Kolonies," particularly southern Ottawa and northern Allegan counties. The orange, red, and pale yellowish white brick was manufactured in Zeeland by H. J. Veneklasen and Sons, later the Zeeland Brick Company. The company operated yards for red brick at Kalamazoo and in Hamilton (Allegan County) and for pale yellow brick at Zeeland (Ottawa County) and Cloverdale (Barry County). Decorative patterns in bricks of a color different from the walls are found along the gable, cornice, windows, doors, and base of the structure. Their six varieties of window hoods and nine cornice and gable patterns were used interchangeably by builders, some of them appearing in this house. Skilled Dutch brick masons probably brought the building techniques from their homeland and built homes for their countrymen reminiscent of those in the Netherlands. Although the technique is most prevalent in farmhouses, it was also used in churches, schools, factories, and fire halls. Some 120 examples remain in the two-county region. The arrival of the Pere Marquette Railroad in 1872 permitted easy shipment of the brick to Chicago, Traverse City, Battle Creek, and elsewhere, and it contributed to the spread of polychrome brickwork.

GRAND HAVEN

Grand Haven is located where the Grand River flows into Lake Michigan. In 1834 settlers arrived, in 1835 the town was platted, and in 1836 a sawmill was built. The economy developed around sawmills and shingle mills,

ship building, commercial fishing, tourism, and resorts. During the 1950s and 1960s, in response to a perceived urban decay, local citizens rallied for construction in 1963 of a huge musical fountain on the Grand River. In 1990 a Postmodern multimission Coast Guard Station by Progressive Architects Engineers opened on the harbor.

OT15 Edward P. and Clara Virginia White Ferry House

1871–1872, Phillip Wooley. 514 Lafayette St. (second house from southeast corner of Lafayette and Fifth streets)

The extravagantly elegant clapboarded wooden Italianate house richly encrusted with carving is associated with the pioneer family of Ottawa County. Its first occupants were Edward P. Ferry (1837–1917) and his wife, Clara Virginia White. The son of William M. and Amanda Ferry, who landed at the site of present-day Grand Haven in 1834, Ferry was a local lumberman and entrepreneur. Elaborately carved and molded surrounds crowned with round hoods capped, in turn, with small pediments ornament the tall, narrow windows and doors. An intricately carved entablature, the frieze of which is pierced by hexagonal windows, encircles the house below a low-pitched hipped roof supported by paired brackets. Through the front double doors within the recessed entrance are a pair of etched, frosted-glass doors leading to the hallway. The interior has two marble mantels and extensive wood trim. The fancy wood trim was probably installed to the Ferrys' orders in 1874, when they acquired the house. The current owners have demonstrated their love for the woodwork in the application of yellow and blue paint.

OT16 Arend and Kate Howard Vander Veen House

1870–1872. 508 Washington Ave. (one door east of southeast corner of Washington and Fifth streets)

The large, asymmetrical, towered Italianate house was built on a bluff overlooking the harbor and business district of Grand Haven for local physician Arend Vander Veen (d. 1930) and his wife, Kate. Vander Veen was born in Amsterdam but left the Netherlands with his parents to join the Van Raalte Colony that founded Holland. Single and paired round-arch windows with carved hoods pierce the exterior brick walls. Brackets support the straight low-pitched mansard roof, which was originally decorated with iron cresting. Black walnut woodwork and plasterwork highlight the interior. The front porch was probably enclosed later. The house was built by local masons Hartger Jonker and John Van Dougen and carpenter Charlie Ball.

OT17 **First Reformed Church**

1913–1914, Daverman and Associates. 301 Washington St. (northeast corner of Washington and Third streets)

This rectangular church with a corner bell and clock tower topped, not with the expected spire, but with a bell-shaped roof clad with green oxidized copper, is easily recognized as another work of the west Michigan specialists in the design of Dutch Reformed churches, Daverman and Associates of Grand Rapids. Segmental pediments mark the tower and the main facades of the building. Its tan brick exterior walls trimmed with white painted wood are broken by large stained-glass windows. Access to the church is gained through the pedimented entrance in the tower. Stairs lead down to the social hall and up to the worship space. The sanctuary is arranged in what its architects called "the Dayton plan." The auditorium is above a social hall. Its four banks of pews rest on a downward sloping floor and form a semicircle before the off-center pulpit, the choir, and the organ case. The church cost $26,000 to build. The First Reformed Church organized in 1850 and incorporated in 1865. The present building replaced earlier churches burned in 1889, 1907, and 1913.

Capital Region

THE CAPITAL REGION IS IN THE MIDDLE OF THE LOWER PENIN-
sula's gently rolling agricultural plains. At its very center, at the juncture
of the Grand and Red Cedar rivers at Lansing, is the state capital. Highways radiate out in all directions from the capital linking it not only with the
seats of county government within the tri-county area but also with the major
population centers of the state. Most of the latter are within two hours driving
time from Lansing.

The earliest building erected in the Capital Region may have been a log
trading post near present-day Maple Rapids that was opened by George Campau in 1835 before he moved to Grand Rapids in 1842. An influx of New
Yorkers and New Englanders followed in the 1830s, settling in all three counties. They migrated from the South and the East into the region, first along
rivers and then along the Grand River and Territorial roads, to build houses,
farms, churches, civic buildings, and schools.

The three counties of the region were organized in the late 1830s: Eaton in
1837, Ingham in 1838, and Clinton County in 1839, and with them came the
need for courthouses. The substantial late nineteenth-century courthouses that
replaced earlier wooden ones remain in the center of a square surrounded by
commercial and religious buildings in all three seats of county government—
Charlotte, Mason, and Saint Johns. Lansing and rural Stockbridge are also arranged around a public square.

Lansing is the largest city in the Capital Region and is the state capital. Promoted by land speculators, it was founded as the capital city in 1837, but the
state government remained in Detroit for another ten years.

Land speculation was also the motivation for the founding of Saint Johns.
The present-day seat of Clinton County was established in the 1850s by inves-

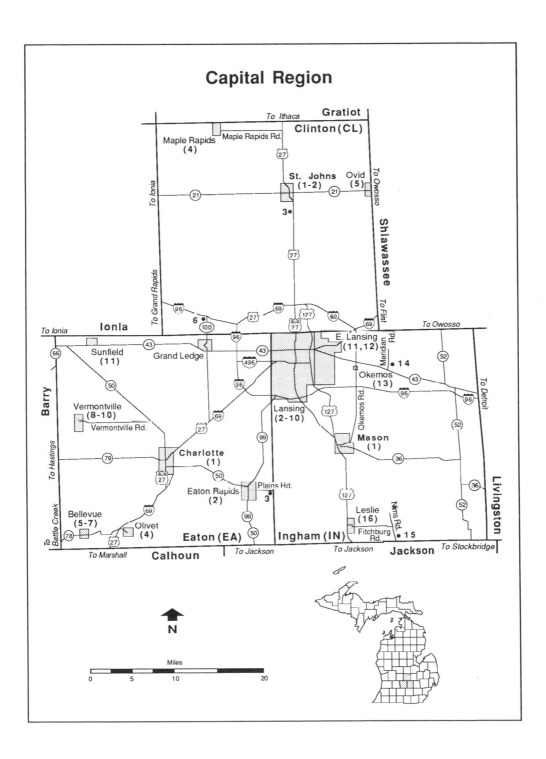

Capital Region

tors who anticipated Saint Johns's position as a major stop on the railroad that linked Owosso and Ionia.

Other communities in the Capital Region were founded with more lofty purposes. Vermontville was established in 1836 by the Reverend Sylvester Cochrane of East Poultney, Vermont, and known as the Union Colony. The town is based on a New England model. Olivet was founded eight years later, in 1843, by the Reverend John J. Shipherd, who established Oberlin College in Ohio. He came to what is now Olivet, purchased the land on a hill among tall oaks and maples, and the following year opened Olivet College. Its old buildings are arranged around a campus green.

The Michigan legislature selected Lansing Township as the site for the state capital in 1847 because of its central location in the state. The choice was made over Detroit, Marshall, Ann Arbor, Battle Creek, Albion, and Jackson, which also vied for this designation. The original capitol was a modest, two-story, wood-frame Greek Revival building with a cupola that was built in 1847–1848. The present Neoclassical stone building that replaced it in 1873–1879 is currently under restoration.

In 1850, in an effort to improve transportation to the capital city, the legislature offered charters to build plank roads. Thus, the Lansing and Howell Plank Road Company was formed, and by 1853 the road between Lansing and Detroit was complete. The old Lansing and Howell Plank road was the precursor of Michigan 43. The road to Mason was also turned over to a turnpike company in the 1850s and rebuilt as a plank road.

To provide for practical farming and agricultural instruction, the Michigan state legislature chartered in 1850 an agricultural college to be built ten miles west of Lansing in Meridian Township. Seven years later, in 1857, a building was completed and Michigan Agricultural College opened to students. The college was selected as one of the nation's first two state agricultural colleges eligible for a federal grant under the 1862 Land Grant Bill. The campus is an arboretum park and one of the most beautiful in the nation, enhanced in no small measure by the expansive college farms that still sprawl south of the main Michigan State University campus.

Backed by Lansing investors, Ransom E. Olds started the Olds Motor Vehicle Company in 1897, which was acquired by General Motors Company in 1908. Olds directed his attention to his newly established REO Car Company and built a factory in Lansing. Olds introduced the "curved dash" Oldsmobile, which sold for around $650 and began the trend toward building inexpensive automobiles that eventually culminated with the Model T Ford in Detroit. In 1900 fourteen hundred cars were sold, and four years later, in 1904, production reached four thousand cars. In another four years, production reached 65,000 cars selling at the much higher average price of about $2,000 each. Other automotive manufacturers followed the lead of Ransom Olds and built plants in Detroit; more expensive cars were being built by many more companies. (This trend toward more expensive cars was reversed with the appearance of the Model T first produced at the Ford Highland Park plant in 1908. It sold for $850, but the price continued to drop as a result of the moving assembly line production introduced at the Highland Park plant.)

Today Lansing remains the focus of the Capital Region. In addition to the plants of GMC's Oldsmobile Division, Lansing has the buildings of state government. Clustered around the historic capitol is a complex of modern office buildings housing government services. To the east, in neighboring East Lansing, more than forty thousand students attend Michigan State University. Historic neighborhoods of period revival houses north of Grand River Avenue are within walking distance of the campus. Metropolitan Lansing is anchored at the east and west by the Meridian and Lansing regional shopping malls. It is surrounded by the small towns of Saint Johns, Mason, Eaton Rapids, and Charlotte, and, in turn, by the even smaller hamlets of Williamston, Stockbridge, Leslie, Olivet, Bellevue, Grand Ledge, and Ovid.

Ingham County   (IN)

MASON

Mason was settled in 1838 at the juncture of two Indian trails In 1840, two years after Ingham County was established, it was designated the county seat.

IN01 Ingham County Courthouse

1902–1905, Edwin A. Bowd. Bounded by Jefferson Ave. and Maple, Barnes, and Ash (Michigan 36) streets

Marking the seat of Ingham County government with a tall, square, domed clock tower visible for miles from the surrounding farmlands, the courthouse is sited in the center of a square in Mason. Around three sides of the square are arranged the storefronts of the village. With its symmetrical massing, dramatic central tower, mansard roof, squat corner pavilions, columned portico, and rusticated light grayish yellowish brown sandstone, the Ingham County Courthouse is a noteworthy example of Beaux-Arts Classical courthouse design. It was one of the first major commissions of Edwin A. Bowd (1865–1940), who later designed numerous distinguished public and academic buildings in southern Michigan. The Lansing architect was born and trained in England and began his career in 1883 in the offices of Gordon W. Lloyd in Detroit. The interior of the court-

house is arranged around a rotunda beneath the central tower. This circular hall gives access to county offices in each corner of the building. The south portion of the second floor holds the courtroom. Its seats form a semicircle around the raised platform containing the judge's bench. The interior of the entire building is finished with oak woodwork and ornamental plasterwork. The present courthouse replaced a gabled brick structure with a cupola erected in 1848.

LANSING

Situated in thick woods and swamp lands at the confluence of the Grand and Red Cedar rivers, Lansing grew and developed as the commercial center for the central Michigan farming area, an automobile manufacturing center and the state capital. Neighboring East Lansing became the home of a major state university.

In 1835 two timber cruisers in Ingham County created Biddle City, a 65–block plat, and sold lots to sixteen farmers in Lansing, New York. After struggling with their heavily wooded and flood-stricken new land, only two remained.

In 1847, when the Michigan State Legislature selected Lansing as the site of the state capital, Lansing achieved stature and devel-

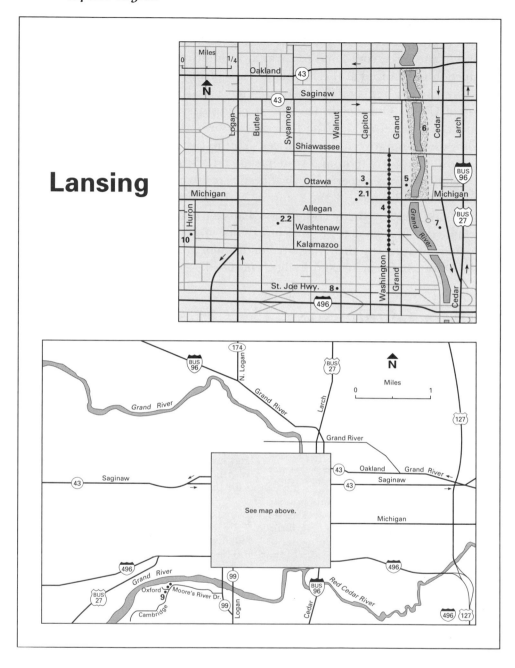

opment ensued. This growth was aided by the completion of the Lansing and Howell Plank Road, which connected the capital with Detroit. The founding of Michigan Agricultural College (now Michigan State University) in 1855 at East Lansing and its support under the 1862 Morrill Act facilitated growth in the Lansing area. Between 1863 and 1873, five railroads reached Lansing. The population doubled and industries appeared. In 1878 the present Michigan State Capitol building was dedicated.

Ransom E. Olds began the Olds Motor Vehicle Company in 1897, and within seven years it was the largest producer of automobiles. Then, in 1904, Olds began the REO Car Company, and in 1908 Willie Durant and General Motors acquired the Olds Company.

Although Lansing has benefitted from the diversity of its three primary employers, the absence of a major philanthropist, to some degree, accounts for the city's relatively small number of architectural monuments.

IN02 **Michigan State Capitol Complex**

1921, 1938, 1947, Harland Bartholomew, city planner and landscape architect; Smith, Hinchman and Grylls. 1963–1968, office buildings, Smith, Hinchman and Grylls. 1986–1988, Michigan Library and Historical Center, William Kessler and Associates, Inc. Bounded by Capitol Ave. and West Allegan, Butler, and West Ottawa streets

The ten-block capitol complex crossed by two depressed streets, Walnut and Pine, includes a landscaped mall-plaza over two levels of parking, with the focus on the monumental site sculpture, *This Equals That*, by Michael Heiser, 1980. Flanking the mall to the west of the capitol are four "calm and dignified" office buildings typical of the architecture of the 1960s· the Treasury Building (1968), the Stevens T. Mason Building (1953), the G. Mennen Williams Law Building (1968), and the Transportation Building (1967). To the far west are the undistinguished twin South and North Ottawa Towers buildings (1983).

Harland Bartholomew encouraged a wider appreciation of the value of Lansing's dignified and impressive public buildings in his *Comprehensive City Plan Report* of 1921. He condemned the practice of haphazardly spotting magnificent buildings. In particular, he cited the State Office Building (now the Lewis Cass Building) by Munson and Bowd with Albert Kahn, 1919–1922, and located several blocks southwest of the capitol. He suggested that a new capitol, when needed, be placed on the site west of Pine Street between Ottawa and Allegan streets and that the intervening blocks between the present capitol grounds and the new site be developed as a mall, with subsidiary state buildings arranged on either side. Seventeen years later, in 1938, Bartholomew advocated a capitol complex that would be expressive of the dignity and importance of the state of Michigan, yet in harmony with the scale of Lansing.

After revising a similar 1947 plan, Smith, Hinchman and Grylls executed it in the 1960s.

Until then only three state government buildings existed, the Michigan State Capitol, the Lewis Cass Building, and the Stevens T. Mason Buildings. Many state workers housed in rented quarters throughout Lansing and the Capital Region moved into the office buildings next to the domed capitol. The Michigan Library and Historical Center, proposed in the Bartholomew and the Smith, Hinchman and Grylls plans, became a reality in 1986–1989. The restoration of the Michigan State Capitol, promoted intially by the Friends of the Capitol and spearheaded by the Capitol Oversight Committee, was executed under the direction of Richard C. Frank.

IN02.1 **Michigan State Capitol**

1872–1878, Elijah E. Myers. 1989–present, restoration, Richard C. Frank. On the square bounded by Capitol Ave. and West Allegan, West Ottawa, and Walnut streets

Prominently located on a rise at the end of a grand approach along Michigan Avenue from the east is Michigan's third statehouse, a domed Neoclassical structure of light grayish yellowish brown Berea sandstone. During the first ten years of statehood, from 1837 to 1847, Detroit was Michigan's capital, and the legislature was housed in a small Greek Revival courthouse and capitol building with an Ionic portico and three-staged steeple erected in 1823–1828 to the plans of Obed Wait. In 1847 the capital was moved to Lansing, and a small two-story wooden capitol with a cupola was constructed. It soon proved inadequate. In June 1871 the State Board of Building Commissioners appointed by Gov. Henry Baldwin held a competition for the design of the new capitol. Early in 1872 the commission unanimously selected from among twenty entries the plans of Elijah E. Myers (1832–1909), a native of Philadelphia, who was then living in Springfield, Illinois. Myers had designed numerous county courthouses, including a huge structure in Carlinville, Illinois, that was more costly than the Michigan State Capitol building. The Michigan capitol came in under cost, which pleased the Michigan legislators. The cost of the Michigan capitol was often compared in the Lansing press with the new New York State Capitol, then under construction in Albany and so in excess of its budget that it was destined to become the most expensive state capitol to date.

The restrained Myers plan is essentially a

IN02.1a Michigan State Capitol (exterior)

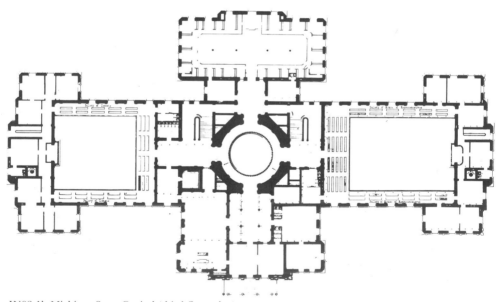

IN02.1b Michigan State Capitol (third-floor plan)

Renaissance design with little of the Baroque scale seen in the national capitol in Washington, D.C. Although many of the individual features are quite similar to the Capitol in Washington—and no doubt derived from similar sources—the scale is more domestic than monumental. The Lansing capitol is, nevertheless, a very large building, measuring 420 feet in length and 267 feet in height, especially when compared with the smaller statehouses built elsewhere in the preceding decades.

It has been suggested that Myers was influenced by Joseph Mangin and John McComb's

New York City Hall (1803–1812). The rusticated base, found prominently in the Italian Renaissance palazzi and a common feature in Renaissance Europe and in Georgian England, is prominent in Myers's work as well as in the Mangin design. On some corners this rough texture is evident in the stones of the corners as well. Smooth stone is used on the upper levels; the stones of the first level are outlined by exposed joints, while those above have flush joints.

The front entrance is quite reserved, emphasized only by a two-story colonnade that creates a porch at the first-floor level, a covered balcony at the second, and an open balcony at the third. On the rear elevation this is reduced to a narrower colonnade only one story high.

A restrained elegance is seen in the window heads and in the pilasters. The Tuscan, Ionic, and Corinthian orders are used in the first, second, and third stories, respectively, in single and coupled columns and pilasters, and even the short top floor has highly decorated pilasters, in this case Ionic.

The slender attenuated dome resting on a peristyle is divided by ribs into sixteen sections, each with an oval window. The dome is capped by an octagonal lantern with alternating windows and columns, all topped with marvelous two-layered sets of bracketed cornices.

The building's exterior becomes more decorative as it rises, a feature echoed in the interior, becoming both more elegant and more Baroque, as well as grander in scale, with richer and more profuse decoration of marbles, slates, woods, and paintings. The two main legislative chambers and the monumental halls and entryways leading into them make generous use of classical elements and details. These impressive spaces are focused on a central rotunda ringed with columns and balconies rising from the first-floor level with its glass floor, to the inner dome with its eight painted, classically attired female figures representing Arts, Sciences, Education, Law and Justice, Commerce, Labor and Industry, Agriculture, and Communication, and with its oculus, revealing a painted starlit sky.

The Michigan State Capitol was completed late in 1878 and dedicated on the first of January of the following year. Myers went on to design state capitols in Texas (Austin) and Colorado (Denver) but kept his base of operations in Michigan.

New statehouses constructed after the Michigan capitol tended to resemble Myers's design in size and mass. They were larger, longer and higher than those of the pre-Civil War period, usually with a central portion well emphasized and with elements brought forward to represent wings. Charles Bulfinch's Massachusetts State House in Boston, 1795–1798, ushered in the era of the strong English Neoclassic influence. His nearly two years stay in Europe, and especially his admiration for William Chambers's Somerset House, 1776–1786, the river front in particular, was incorporated into his Boston work. Unlike Somerset House, however, the Massachusetts State House reveals more of Bulfinch's own predilection for the local tradition of building in wood. As a result the Boston work is simpler and sharply delineated, whereas the Somerset House is more severe and heavy. This same sense of domestic scale and refined elegance is present in the capitol at Lansing. Myers brought a new sense of scale, refinement, and elegance to state capitol designs.

Michigan's capitol ranks as one of the nation's best surviving examples of civic architecture displaying the decorative painted arts of the Victorian period. Woodgraining, stenciling, striping, glazing, gilding, freehand painting, and the use of metallic paints were employed to provide rich embellishment. The work of the Friends of the Capitol sparked the initiation of restoration during the celebration of the sesquicentennial of statehood. In 1991, under the Capitol Oversight Committee of the Michigan governor and legislature and with the supervision of Richard C. Frank, restoration is in full progress. The restoration of the richly colored High Victorian decorative interior painting is truly remarkable.

IN02.2 Michigan Library and Historical Center

1985–1988, William Kessler and Associates, Inc.
Bounded by West Washtenaw, Butler, West Allegan, and Sycamore streets

In celebration of Michigan's sesquicentennial anniversary of statehood, the state of Michigan, the Michigan legislature, and the secretary of state opened the Michigan Library and Historical Center. This five-story, 250,000-square-foot Postmodern structure is the home

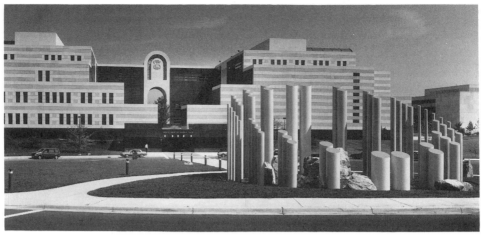

IN02.2 Michigan Library and Historical Center

for the interpretation and conservation of the state's history. The building is everything a government building should be. The distinctive stepped design is faced with alternating horizontal strips of light and dark limestone above a base of polished black granite. It features full-height glass arches and atriums at the ends of the east and west wings. A courtyard with the white pine, Michigan's state tree, in the center and surrounded at the base by a fountain sculpture depicting the Great Lakes in intense blues, violets, and greens by Glen Michaels is the light and airy focus of the building. Copper covers the walls of the building enclosing the courtyard. The lofty main reading room of the library is breathtaking. The archives reading room, forum, and board room are spectacular. The interior color scheme is blue, green, and brown to match the state's lakes, woodlands, and beaches. A conceptual story line of Michigan's history in the museum flows through enlarged displays and dioramas of prehistoric times, mining, lumbering, farming, and industry, designed in concept by Jean André of British Columbia. A sculpture, *Polaris Ring*, by David Barr (1988) is before the main (south) entrance and is reminiscent of Stonehenge.

IN03 **Central United Methodist Church** (Central Methodist Episcopal Church)

1889–1890, church, Elijah E. Myers. 1922–1923, temple house, 1942, Mary-Sabina Chapel, Lee and Kenneth Black. 215 North Capitol Ave. (northwest corner West Ottawa St. and North Capitol Ave.)

One of four churches once facing the great capitol square, Central United Methodist Church is among the finest Richardsonian Romanesque churches in Michigan. A massive, buttressed square tower rises 85 feet at the southeast corner and a squat, conical roofed, round tower at the southwest corner of the gabled and buttressed compact mass. The finest solid grayish red and yellowish brown variegated Ionia sandstone, rock-faced and randomly coursed, forms its exterior walls. Double round-arch entrances within the south gabled facade give access to the vestibule, and in turn, paired staircases to the auditorium. The auditorium seats nearly 700 worshippers in four banks of pews arranged in a semicircle and sloping downward before a raised platform holding a central pulpit and huge round-arch loft that originally held the organ case. A gallery over the vestibule is reached by stairs in the square and round towers. The bright, cheerful, and warm interior is finished in red oak and has beautiful carved hammer beams. Magnificent glass windows, colored in yellows, roses, and blues, are dedicated to the memory of James Turner (1820–1869), Mary Horner Sanford (1838–1887), and others. The Temple House and chapel additions carefully defer to the original plans of Elijah E. Myers. The four-story Temple House was erected for the purpose of assisting in the "physical, intellectual, social and spiritual life." It contains a banquet hall, auditorium surrounded by two floors of Sunday School rooms, offices, public lounges, recreation hall, gymnasium, and bowling alleys. Richard H. and Gertrude E. Scott dedicated the chapel to their mothers, Mary and Sabina, for "rest, meditation and prayer." The artistry of the decorative work of the Mary-Sabina Chapel, some of which was executed by Corrado Joseph Parducci, is notable.

Central Methodist Episcopal Church was organized in 1861. The congregation built a brick church in 1863 and occupied it until the present church was erected. Construction cost $50,000.

IN04 Washington Mall

1970s, Johnson, Johnson and Roy. Washington St. from Shiawassee to Kalamazoo St.

The North Washington Square Mall is an urban renewal project. It features a fountain and wall reliefs of cast concrete forms and voids containing stained-glass panels by W. Robert Youngman (b. 1927) and *Construction #150*, a curvilinear highly polished stainless steel mechanized sculpture, by José de Rivera, 1972.

IN04.1 Knapp's Office Center (J. W. Knapp Company Department Store)

1937–1939, Orlie A. Munson of Bowd-Munson. 1940, west addition. 300 South Washington Ave. (southwest corner of South Washington Ave. and West Washtenaw St.)

With its sleek lines and rounded corner, this five-story former department store is one of Michigan's finest Streamline Moderne commercial structures. It is remarkable for the machinelike clarity of its horizontal design and its brilliant colors. The striking facade is finished with alternating bands of yellow maul

macotta (concrete blocks veneered with enameled metal panels) wall surfaces and glass block windows interrupted by vertical window-pierced, blue maul macotta pylons that rise from the store's four principal entrances. Founded by Joseph W. Knapp and others as the Jewett and Knapp Dry Goods Store in 1896, and reorganized as J. W. Knapp Company in 1908, the retailers had their department store designed by important Lansing architects in a fashionable style and built by the Christman Construction Company, which was noted for its skill and knowledge of concrete building technology.

IN05 Lansing Board of Water and Light, Ottawa Street Power Station

1937–1940, Bowd-Munson Company. Northeast corner of North Grand Ave. and East Ottawa St.

The Ottawa Street Power Station is an architectural surprise in the Art Deco style. It was designed by Bowd-Munson Company of Lansing for the Lansing Board of Water and Light. The work approaches the PWA Moderne style in its definite classical and formal character, combined with the angularity of the Art Deco style. Symbolizing the combustion of coal, the polished black granite base of the sixteen-story, set-back brick structure changes to purple gray and progressively lighter shades of red, orange, yellow, and yellowish gray brick toward the top. Doors of polished metal and glass highlight the main entrance. The $4 million plant generates electricity and steam. It is located on the west bank of the Grand River on the site of the earlier downtown steam and electric plant, which was built in 1908 by the Michigan Power Company.

IN06 **Lansing Riverfront Park**

1975–1976, Robert L. O'Boyle of O'Boyle, Cowell, Rohrer and Associates, Inc., landscape architects. Both sides of the Grand River from about Michigan Ave. to Oakland Ave.

Although much smaller in scale and less grand than San Antonio's Paseo del Rio, this urban park along the Grand River was also designed for spontaneous and planned individual and group activities. The first phase was completed for the national bicentennial in July 1976. The park and the river walk extend to the north and the south, and, like San Antonio's, allow direct contact with the Grand River for several miles. Visual and performing arts events, exhibitions, and special festivals occur in the park. The land along the river was reclaimed, and most structures were removed. The salt storage shed was transformed into a natural amphitheater, and the railroad bridge was turned into a pedestrian walkway that links the east and west sides of the river. Berms and plantings add a three-dimensional quality to the area. The river walk is a biking, jogging, and walking trail that connects museums and other cultural and civic centers: the Lansing Center (TMP Associates, 1986–1987), the Lansing Municipal Market (C. E. Thornton, City Engineer, 1938), and the William A. Brenke Sculpture-Fish Ladder (Joseph E. Kinnebrew, sculptor, and Robert O'Boyle, landscape architect, 1980–1981).

IN07 **Lansing Board of Water and Light Dye Conditioning Plant** (Cedar Water Conditioning Plant)

1938–1939, Black and Black. 148 South Cedar St.

The Board of Water and Light Conditioning Plant building is a reinforced concrete building with glass block windows and a formality achieved by the balancing wings around a central vertical entrance. The facade, in fact the entire exterior, is designed along severe geometric lines. Over the vertical entrance are stylized sculptural reliefs, found frequently on buildings of this time. Inside the conditioning plant are murals and a ceramic sculpture created under the WPA Federal Art Project and devoted to the water theme.

The exterior sculpture, a large, stylized female figure of *Aquarius the Water Bearer*, pours water from an urn to two small infants lo-

IN07 Lansing Board of Water and Light Dye Conditioning Plant (Cedar Water Conditioning Plant)

cated beneath her who symbolize the city of Lansing. It was done by Samuel A. Cashwan, in 1938–1939. On the second-floor lobby there are three large murals by Frank Cassara showing the effects of water and the activities of building employees. In *Water as a Destructive Element,* people struggle against ravaging flood waters, but in *Water as a Positive Force,* on the opposite wall, people harvest crops and a bountiful life. Painter Charles Pollock, brother of the leading Abstract Expressionist Jackson Pollock, covered one wall with images of figures doing scientific research and work corresponding with activities behind the doorway marked "lab."

Other interior features of the building are in the Streamline Moderne style. The water filtration gallery contains aluminum railings with the curved simplified lines that echo the design of automobiles and trains. Such modernist designs executed in industrial materials add to the contemporary appearance that exemplified progress.

IN08 **Michigan Chamber of Commerce Building**

1986–1987; Smith, Hinchman and Grylls; Johnson, Johnson and Roy, landscape architects. 600 South Walnut St. (northwest corner of South Walnut and West Saint Joseph streets)

Combining ample use of glass with older Collegiate Gothic stylistic references in the traditional gable forms, the Chamber of Com-

IN08 Michigan Chamber of Commerce Building

merce Building is Lansing's boldest Postmodern structure. Its multiple gabled and parapeted bays, clock tower, and reddish brown brick and bands of whitish gray cast stone abstract and recall architecture of the 1920s, predating the smooth, monolithic glassed office building of the 1950s and 1960s. The glass clock tower and eastern facade, however, are strictly contemporary, creating a striking, yet integrated, contrast of old and new.

IN09 J. H. Moores and Riverside Homes Subdivisions

1920–1930. South of the Grand River along Moores River, Cambridge, and Nottingham drives

Twenty-two members of the Lansing Country Club conceived of and developed this exclusive 1920s subdivision as Riverside Homes Association. It is located east of Francis Park on the south bank at a bend in the Grand River, the northwest fairways of the country club, and upwind of the Oldsmobile plant. This association reserved the right to approve purchasers of lots and to set costs for houses at the minimum of $7,500 to $12,000. The scheme for the subdivision was planned by the American Park Builders of Chicago in the image of the "ideal home environment—a country place close to the world of outdoors, yet near to the pulse of business affairs."[43] Set on large wooded lots along winding streets are the large, secluded, period revival, as well as contemporary houses, for automotive in-

dustrialists, leading merchants, and professionals. The subdivision resembles Palmer Woods in Detroit (see DE58, p. 100) but is scaled to the economy of a midsize Michigan city.

IN09.1 Harold F. and Ragna Mickelson Harper House

1927–1929; Harold C. Beckett of Akitt and Beckett, Detroit; Clarence Whybrow, interior designer. 1408 Cambridge Dr. (southwest corner of Cambridge Dr. and Oxford Rd.)

The largest and most lavish Neo-Tudor house in the subdivision is the 35-room Harper house. The turreted and gabled light yellowish and grayish brown Indiana sandstone house has a slate roof and ornamental clustered chimneys. Marble, woodcarving, mosaics, and frescoes decorate the interior. The site is landscaped with pools, a fountain, gazebo, and sunken garden. It was built for Harold F. Harper (1881–1949), the president and general manager of the Motor Wheel Company, and his wife, Ragna Mickelson (1880–1953).

IN09.2 Wingspan (Talbert and Leota Fry Abrams House)

1950–1951; William H. Baugh, architect; Grover M. Pratt, architect. 1310 Cambridge Dr. (southwest corner of Cambridge and Moores River drives)

The contemporary light yellowish brown and gray sandstone ranch house, essentially a long rectangular form with rounded corners bisected by a shorter, similarly round-cornered rectangle, is appropriate for its original owner, aerial photography pioneer, Talbert Abrams (b. 1896). Abrams founded the Abrams Instrument Corporation and Abrams Aerial Survey Corporation. He explained that the shape of an airplane's shadow on the upper surface of a cloud bank as he and his wife, Leota, were flying at 15,000 feet inspired the plan of this house.

IN09.3 Governor's Mansion (Howard and Letha Sober House)

1959, Wallace Frost. 2520 Oxford Rd.

The Sober house expresses the values of upper-middle-class Americans in the 1950s.[44] Its large living room, bar, and dining room, separated from a kitchen concealed from the public eye, were designed for a particular sort of entertaining, the cocktail party; the basement bomb shelter expresses the wish that technology could solve the problems it created; and the bringing of the indoors out through the patio and glass walls, and the outdoors in through plants, garden courts, and atriums convey a relationship of man and nature as coequals. Rochelle Elstein calls the house a "conservative fusion of modernity and traditionalism." The house was designed by Wallace Frost of Birmingham. Frost studied with Paul Cret and worked with Albert Kahn. The clients were Howard and Letha Sober. Sober (1895–1986) was a pioneer in the auto transport, or haul-away, business. From the exterior the low, horizontal, L-shaped gray limestone house is deceptively compact; it has 10,300 square feet. Ten years after it was built, Sober donated it to the state of Michigan to serve as the governor's mansion, and it functions as such today.

IN10 Darius B. and Ellen Sprague Moon House

1894, Darius B. Moon. 214 Huron St.

The Moon house is an exuberant two-and-a-half-story Queen Anne structure with a prominent three-story square tower that adds to the picturesqueness of its silhouette. The house's richly sculptural Eastlake exterior detailing includes chamfered and turned woodwork, paneled and patterned shingle gable trim, bracketing of various types, and galvanized tin roof crestings. The house was probably designed and perhaps even built by Darius B. Moon (1851–1939). Moon was a New York-born, self-taught architect-builder. His "List of Buildings I Have Designed" includes 150 entries for houses (including the towered brick Ransom E. and Metta Olds House, built in 1903 at 720 South Washington Avenue, but now demolished), schools, and commercial buildings in the Capital Region, most of which were probably executed.

EAST LANSING

IN11 Michigan State University

Bounded approximately by Grand River Ave. and Hagadorn, Mount Hope, and Harrison roads, with farms south of Mount Hope Rd. and north of I-96

Founded in 1855, Michigan State University became a pioneer land-grant institution whose campus of 5,263 acres is an arboretum-park, including thousands of species and varieties of trees and shrubs intermingled with over four hundred buildings assigned to academic programs and research, housing and related services, and agriculture.

The Red Cedar River divides the campus into its northern and southern components and distinguishes many of the pre-1945 buildings from recent designs. The initial buildings were erected on the north side in an "oak opening" or grassy knoll surrounded by large oak trees. According to old board minutes, even in its earliest days, there was sentiment expressed that "the premises shall be properly laid out and tastefully arranged."

Aesthetically, the influence of the English picturesque landscape tradition and of Andrew Jackson Downing prevailed as random accents for such buildings as College Hall (1857–1919), an unadorned, classically inspired brick classroom facility known as the first to be erected in the United States solely for the purpose of scientific agricultural education.

By the turn of the century, in anticipation of growing needs, Ossian C. Simonds, a Grand Rapids landscape architect, was hired to assess the campus park development. In 1906, he informed the board that the area of the oak opening should be designated "as a sacred space from which all building must forever be excluded. This area contains beautifully rolling land with a pleasing arrangement of groups of trees, many of which have developed into fine specimens."[45] With this advice, in 1913, a committee of faculty and board members employed Frederick Law Olmsted, Jr., of Boston, one of the foremost landscape architects in the United States. On May 15, 1915, the Olmsted brothers submitted their report to the board. They noted that "while the architecture was not good, it was not aggressively bad; and it so happened that a fortunate combination of a pleasing topography, a soil and climate favorable to the growth of trees, a fair sprinkling of fine native trees to start with, and a long period of generally judicious planting and care, created what is undoubtedly one of the most beautiful examples, in some respects probably the very best example, of the type of landscape characteristic of the American college campus of the 19th century."[46]

For future building, they proposed the broad use of the college quadrangle as a spatial delineator that would be halfway between the "broad," rolling picturesque campus of the small nineteenth-century college and the precisely defined courts and streets of urban campuses. Their proposal was accepted, although their subsequent specific recommendations met with resistance. In 1920 there was even an alumni campaign to "save our circle" to assure that the sacred space and the surrounding circular drive were preserved.

From 1923 to 1945, T. Glen Phillips, a Detroit planner and landscape architect, served as a consultant who affirmed the spirit of the early campus with sensitivity to the picturesque intermingling of the terrain, extant buildings, and vegetation. After 1945, Harold Lautner, professor and landscape architect, served as planning director and worked closely with President John Hannah during a period of vast expansion of the south campus. In the Campus Development Plan (1960), strategies for establishing "a functional framework of varied land uses," determining "systems of vehicular and pedestrian circulation," and formulating "general guidelines for the preservation of open space" were established.[47] In 1968 the Board of Trustees approved a zoning ordinance "to preserve the campus

environment of spaciousness and landscape beauty, promote order and unity, and minimize congestion."[48]

The winding streets and sidewalks of the north campus were not manifested in these new developments. The topography did not suggest meandering passageways, and the large-scaled academic buildings, dormitories, and parking ramps required blocks of land for pedestrians and automobiles. What does remain constant is the ongoing reassessment of walking and driving distances and their relationship to the siting of campus plantings and architecture.

Today, the entire campus reflects the mainstream developments in American architecture of the last one hundred years. Circle Drive is slightly larger than it was in the late nineteenth century, but its randomly arranged trees and shrubs still acknowledge the "sacred space."

Cowles house (1857) is the oldest building on campus. More interesting is the group of buildings that stands along the intersection of East and West Circle drives and constitutes the old Laboratory Row and the Library-Museum (1881–1909). Stylistically, elements from the High Victorian Gothic, the Richardsonian Romanesque, and the Beaux-Arts Classical, respectively, permeate these buildings: Eustace Hall (Honors College), 1888; Bacteriological Laboratory (Marshall Hall), 1902; Old Botany, 1892, 1908; Dairy Laboratory (Chittenden Hall), 1901; Entomology Laboratory (Cook Hall), 1889; Agriculture Hall, 1909; and the Library-Museum (Linton Hall), 1881.

In the 1920s and 1930s, like many other colleges and universities, Michigan State favored the Gothic. Beaumont Memorial Tower (1928) and the MSU Memorial Union (1924) are prime examples of the scholastic spirit.

Between the wars, numerous Public Works Administration (PWA) buildings were erected, and after World War II temporary quonset huts were installed for classroom and residential use to meet pressing enrollment demand. In these postwar years, the International style predominated. The Clark L. Brody Hall complex (1954–1955) is an accomplished example of the volumetric spaces and steel-skeletal construction that form the vocabulary for this style. More modest, but equally successful, is University Village Apartments arranged in relation to cul-de-sac parking.

The more expressionist aspects of 1960s and 1970s architecture are reflected in the Clarence L. Munn Ice Arena (1974) situated next to a stand of tall evergreens. The Clifton and Dolores Wharton Center for the Performing Arts (1982) is clearly visible from numerous streets and traffic circles and impressively asserts its presence as a Postmodernist form in dark-brown brick. The Breslin Center (1988–1989) is the most recent Postmodern example.

For the Office of Campus Parks and Planning, which oversees all development of the campus park, the basis upon which Michigan State won the Architectural League of New York award in 1954 is still an essential ideal: strive toward "excellence in handling mass and space with relation to site and function and the integration of planting as part of the over-all composition."[49]

IN11.1 Linton Hall (Library-Museum)

1881, Charles A. Marsh, Mr. Appleyard (W. P. Appleyard?), supervising architect. 1947, addition, Bowd-Munson. West Circle Dr.

This High Victorian Romanesque symmetrical brick, limestone, and fieldstone building served as the Library and Museum and then as the president's office. It was renamed Linton Hall after Robert S. Linton who, as registrar, introduced the innovative perforated IBM class enrollment card in 1939.

IN11.2 Beaumont Memorial Tower

1928, Donaldson and Meier. South side West Circle Dr.

John W. Beaumont (class of 1882) and his wife donated the funds to erect this Collegiate Gothic memorial, which stands on the site of College Hall (1857–1919). The exterior relief, *The Sower*, is a stylized Art Deco panel carved by Fred Pfeiffer and Son, on the basis of a design by Lee Lawrie, an outstanding sculptor of the day.

IN11.3 Michigan State University Memorial Union

1924, Irving K. Pond and Allen B. Pond. 1936, addition, Bowd-Munson. 1949, addition, Ralph Calder. 1980, addition, Mayotte, Crouse Dhaen. Southeast corner of Abbott Rd. and Grand River Ave. (north side of West Circle Dr.)

IN11.2 Beaumont Memorial Tower

This scholastic Gothic multipurpose building was erected as a memorial to those graduates and former students who gave their lives in World War I. Students and faculty as well as alumni and governing board members assisted with the digging of the basement. In 1935, with Public Works Administration funds, the ownership was transferred from the alumni association to Michigan State.

IN11.4 Clark L. Brody Complex

1954–1955, Ralph L. Calder. Southwest corner Michigan Ave. and Harrison Rd.

Clark L. Brody Hall is the dormitory-classroom building for this residence hall complex. Purportedly, at the time of its completion it contained the largest kitchen-dining hall facility of a nonmilitary installation.

IN11.5 University Village

1953–1955, Manson and Carver. South of Kalamazoo St., west of Harrison Rd.

This complex won the 1955 Honor Award from the Western Michigan Chapter of the American Institute of Architects for its simple solution to the need for highly functional two-story, one- and two-bedroom brick apartments for students and faculty.

IN11.6 **Clarence L. Munn Ice Arena**

1974, Daverman Associates. West side of Chestnut Rd., south of Demonstration Hall

This reinforced concrete structure with its steel-framed sloping roof and berms was named for "Biggie" Munn, a former athletic director.

IN11.7 **Clifton and Dolores Wharton Center for the Performing Arts**

1982, Caudill, Rowlett and Scott, original architects. Bogue St. between East Shaw Lane and Wilson Rd.

The monumentality and the precise unadorned outlines of this asymmetrical performance center include a 2,500-seat Great Hall and some dramatically dynamic internal spaces. The exterior landscaping features a large nonobjective sculpture, *Orpheus*, by Melvin Leiscrowitz. In 1986 the center's landscaping and beautification were honored with a National Landscape Award from the American Association of Nurserymen.

IN11.8 **College of Engineering Academic Buildings Addition**

1988–1989, Albert Kahn Associates. Northeast corner Wilson and Red Cedar roads

Colossal brick piers support the pedimented portico, and a large oculus in the pediment marks the front entrance of the three-story Postmodern addition to the College of Engineering Building. The addition is linked to earlier structures on the north and east so that the whole encloses a quadrangle. Aluminum windows in strings are recessed within bays of orange red brick. This contrasts subtly with the light orangish brown brick walls punctuated with royal blue ceramic tile and trimmed with paint of the same color that are the primary exterior material of the structure.

IN12 **Islamic Center of East Lansing**

1979, Freeman, Smith and Associates. 920 South Harrison Rd.

The Islamic Center reflects the multicultural character of the university-oriented East Lansing community. Muslims among the student body created the demand for their own house of worship. The modern mosque fits easily and compatibly with its neighbors—the University Lutheran Church and the University United Methodist Church. The prominent, stylized, onion-shaped dome on the three-sided tower clearly defines and expresses the historic origins of the religious group it serves. The minaret, the mihrab, the mimbar, and a tank for the ritual ablution identify the simpler liturgy of this faith. There is no added decoration on the exterior to detract from the simple function prayers required five times a day. With the increasing diversity of the American population, Buddhist and Hindu temples will probably also become a part of the religious architectural scene.

OKEMOS

IN13 **Goetsch-Winckler House**

1939, Frank Lloyd Wright. 2410 Hulett Rd. (approximately 1 mile south of the intersection of Okemos Rd. with Michigan 43)

The Goetsch-Winckler house represents Frank Lloyd Wright's venture of the 1930s and later into the house affordable for people of moderate means. The Usonian house shows the usual Wrightian concern for the house as shelter in harmony with nature. It was constructed for $9,500 in 1939 for Alma Goetsch (1901–1968) and Kathrine Winckler (1898–1976), faculty members of the Art Department at Michigan State University. Originally designed to be one of seven homes for the university faculty clustered around a communal farm on property to the southeast of the campus, the Goetsch-Winckler house was the only one executed (although on a different site than the proposed cluster location). Funding fell through for the others.

Constructing a house of moderate cost was solved here by convincing the occupants to see life in simplified terms. The house rests on a concrete slab that incorporates radiant heating and eliminates the need for a basement. The kitchen or "workspace" is partially incorporated with the living-dining room and adapted to the contemporary condition of declining domestic service. The substitution of the carport for a garage acknowledged that the car does not require stabling. Costs were minimized by eliminating a visible roof, trim, and painting, and by constructing the walls

IN13 Goetsch-Winckler House

to include the furniture. Any ornamentation is integral and comes from the natural pattern of construction as exemplified in the windows.

Interpreting the house as a shelter, Wright designed his domestic architecture with a hovering, protective quality. He scaled the Goetsch-Winckler house to the human being and kept it in a low, quiet relationship to the ground.

Through the placement of the structure on the site, the low horizontal design, the use of natural materials, and the expanses of glass doors in the living area, Wright related the Goetsch-Winckler house to nature.

WILLIAMSTON VICINITY, MERIDIAN TOWNSHIP

IN14　Saint Katherine's Chapel

1887. 4650 North Meridian Rd. (.5 miles north of Grand River Rd. [Michigan 43])

The wood-frame, board-and-batten country chapel with four cusped windows and ornamental gable is an excellent example of rural vernacular church architecture in the High Victorian Gothic Revival style. It was built on his Springbrook Farm for John Harris Forster (1822–1894) and his wife, Martha Mullett. Forster, pioneer surveyor, miner, and engineer, later served in the Michigan Senate. Their large, towered brick house, erected in 1874, stood south of the chapel until 1961, when it was demolished to make way for the A-frame church. The Forsters selected the site for their home because it was a beautiful spot near the state capitol, just off the Lan-

IN14 Saint Katherine's Chapel

sing-Detroit Plank Road. Forster presented the chapel to the Protestant Episcopal Diocese of Michigan in 1888 in memory of his daughter, Kitty (Katherine Fell), who died at age six.

BUNKERHILL TOWNSHIP

IN15　Burning Tree Farm (Henry B. Hawley House)

c. 1860. 5333 Nims Rd. (1.2 miles north of North Territorial Rd.)

This residence is a variant of the double-wing, temple-type late Greek Revival style that appeared in south-central Lower Michigan in the mid-nineteenth century. It was probably built by Henry B. Hawley, a New Yorker who settled first in Henrietta Township, Jackson County, prior to settling on this farm in 1850. The farm was improved by Aaron Brower in the 1830s and 1840s before Hawley acquired it. The Hawley house may have been based on one of Minard Lefever's designs in *The Modern Builder's Guide* (1833 plus later editions) and on a double-wing temple type that is found in western New York State. This stylistic variant portrays an apparent symmetry with the superimposed two-story central gabled front and two lateral one-story attached wings. The porch balustrade extends along the eaves of the wings, creating an open deck at the second-story level. The three-bay recessed entrance is identically fenestrated on the first and second floors around a centrally located door.

LESLIE

IN16 **Leslie City Hall** (GAR Memorial Hall)

1903, Joy and Barcroft. 107 East Bellevue St. (southwest corner of East Bellevue St. and Commercial Dr.)

C. W. Tufts, a former Leslie man, commissioned Joy and Barcroft of Detroit to design this memorial hall for the Grand Army of the Republic and the Woman's Relief Corps. The hall was built in the spirit of community cooperation: farmers hauled in fieldstones for the front wall; men volunteered their labor; townspeople fed the workers; and literary society and church women sponsored fundraising events. When completed in 1903, the GAR's Dewey Post #60 deeded the hall to the village of Leslie. Large, round-arch and segmental-arch openings with stone headers pierce the cut fieldstone walls of the front (north) facade, which are skillfully laid in random courses. The east and south walls are composed of hollow concrete block formed at the site in molds and are pierced by tall, narrow rectangular windows with plain stone lintels and sills. Altogether, this building illustrates the merging of a strong vernacular tradition with a strong civic pride.

Eaton County (EA)

CHARLOTTE

Settled in 1839, incorporated as a village in 1863 and as a city in 1871, Charlotte is surrounded by fertile farmland. It is the judicial seat of Eaton County, once a leading producer of maple syrup.

EA01 **Second Eaton County Courthouse**

1883–1885, David W. Gibbs and Company. Bounded by West Lawrence (Michigan 79) and Bostwick avenues, West Harris St., and North Cochran Ave.

Situated one block north of the central business district in the center of the public square on the site of the first courthouse, the brick and stone Renaissance Revival structure gives prominence to Charlotte as the seat of government for an agrarian county. The rectangular, two-and-a-half-story structure on a raised foundation has pedimented tetrastyle pavilions and brick pilasters. It is topped by a three-staged cupola with a square base, columned open belfry, and octagonal domed

EA01 Second Eaton County Courthouse

clock tower surmounted by a pressed zinc statue of the *Goddess of Justice*. Inside, beneath the dome, is a lofty rotunda with colored glass skylight. The basement held the public library and vaults, the first-story offices, and the second the courtroom.

This is the first of two mid-Michigan court-houses designed by D. W. Gibbs and Company of Toledo, Ohio. In the 1880s as many Michigan counties were replacing their wooden frontier courthouses with more substantial masonry ones the architectural firm specialized in courthouses.

Originally from Massachusetts, Gibbs worked as a builder and draftsman before opening an architectural office in Toledo in 1874. In the Eaton County Courthouse, Gibbs repeated his successful classical cube formula with pedimented pavilions and the whole crowned by an elegant cupola—a formula that met the expectations of the 1880s for courthouse design. Without doubt Gibbs was aware of Bulfinch's masterpiece, the Massachusetts State House in Boston, of nearly a century earlier. Both the Boston work and the Charlotte work employ rustication on the elevated basement and red brick for the main stories. The spacing of the flat brick piers on the first level corresponds to the columns of the pavilions so that the vertical supporting function continues in an uninterrupted manner. This sensitivity to design is evident more markedly in the Boston example.

The genesis for the cubical form with pedimented pavilions is seen in the Henry County (Ohio) Courthouse (1880–1882), which retains the popular mansard roof. Gibbs elaborated on the formula further in the Fayette County (Ohio) Courthouse (1882–1884). While the Charlotte courthouse was underway, he repeated it again in Michigan, a mere 35 miles northwest of Charlotte, in the Ionia County Courthouse (1883–1886, see IA01, p. 267), and again, in 1884–1886, in Ohio in the Marion County Courthouse. The scheme used at Charlotte and in Ionia was attempted by Claire Allen of Jackson in his designs around the turn of the century for the Hillsdale, Van Buren, and Shiawassee County courthouses (see HI01, p. 198, and SE01, p. 339).

EATON RAPIDS

Located on the Grand River, Eaton Rapids was once the center of Michigan's largest sheep-raising area. The rapids of the river furnished the power for woolen mills that now stand vacant.

EA02 **Eaton Rapids Camp Ground** (Michigan State Holiness Camp Meeting Ground)

1885. Along the east bank of the Grand River at the end of McArthur Dr. (just east of Michigan 99)

In 1885 Methodists established this religious summer camp meeting ground for church members from Michigan, Ohio, and Indiana. It is located on a 32-acre woodlot along the winding banks of the Grand River in the extreme southeast portion of Eaton Rapids. The focus of this camp is the 1,000-seat, white-painted wooden polygonal tabernacle (Callen Memorial Auditorium) with sides that swing up and out; when propped up, they afford worshippers a view of the green space and shelter from rain. Over seventy little gabled cottages occupy the grounds. Conceived in a variety of picturesque styles, most of these fascinating vernacular houses have porches, some with modest, decorative, machine-turned wood trim. The roads were carefully routed so that their alignment spelled the word "Holiness." The Michigan State Holiness Camp Meeting Association built a two-story clap-boarded frame hotel (Grace Hotel) and a dining hall in 1900.

HAMLIN TOWNSHIP

EA03 **John and Amanda Rorabeck Montgomery House**

1848, John E. Clark. 1960s, 1970s, additions. 11900 Plains Rd. (southwest corner of Plains and Waverly roads)

Built as designed by John E. Clark for John and Amanda Montgomery, who were pioneer Yankee settlers in Hamlin Township, this squat one-and-a-half-story, gable-front-and-side-wing house was constructed of sandstone taken from the banks of the Grand River. The stone was sized and squared into blocks, hammer-dressed and chiseled, and hauled by oxcart to this site at the corner of Plains and Waverly roads. The first-floor six-over-six windows of the house are symmetrically placed on each elevation. The gable front is capped by a simple entablature with a denticulated frieze and slight cornice returns. An inscription carved in stone over the central entrance notes the architect, the owner, and building date.

Brought from Ireland to upstate New York as an infant, John Montgomery (1804–1891) moved with his wife, Amanda, west to the Michigan Territory in 1831. They lived in Dexter, Washtenaw County, for five years before purchasing 500 acres of U.S. Government land in Eaton County. A log shanty served as their home in the wilderness until a more substantial house was built. It is possible that Montgomery took his preference for a stone house, as well as for the Greek Revival style, from his acquaintance with Caleb M. Chapel, who was living in a Greek Revival sandstone house near Parma (see JA13, p. 189).

OLIVET

EA04 **Olivet College**

1858

The Reverend John J. Shipherd arrived here in 1844 with thirty-nine followers from Oberlin College in Ohio and founded Olivet Institute. The campus surrounds a green and stands on an oak- and maple-covered hill above the village of Olivet. Olivet became a college in 1858.

EA04.1 **Burrage Library**

1889–1890, Arthur Bates Jennings. South Main St. (Old US 27) (northeast corner of South Main and College streets)

Promoted by Joseph L. Daniels, librarian of Olivet College, and funded with gifts of $35,000 from Leonard Burrage and Lucy E. Tuttle, the Burrage Library was designed in the Richardsonian Romanesque style by Arthur Bates Jennings (1849–1927). Jennings was an Eastern architect noted for his church designs, and his work at the Burrage Library testifies to the Richardsonian presence in the Midwest. The library is a solid and substantial building of rock-faced, mottled grayish red and yellowish brown Ionia sandstone on a granite foundation. In typical Richardsonian manner, it is also a massive asymmetrical structure with two octagonal towers, the tallest of which is 85 feet; the building measures 110 feet by 52 feet in plan. Clearly apparent from the exterior are the reading room with its many windows and the stacks with fewer windows. Critics admired the fireproof building for its economy, convenience, and utility, its well-furnished and well-lighted interior, and its adaptability for future changes.

EA04.1 Burrage Library

EA04.2 **Lester K. Kirk Collegiate Center**

1962, Meathe, Kessler and Associates, Inc. West of Campus Square in the block bounded by South Main (Old US 27), Cottage, College, and Shipherd streets

The delicate precast reinforced concrete and glass student activities center nestles in a clearing on the otherwise wooded campus. Imitative form and innovative technology are its hallmarks. The building's slender vertical support columns rise out of the ground and branch out to support the roof slabs in a cantilevered manner. Expansive curtain walls of plate glass and aluminum framing make the natural and historic beauty of the surrounding campus easily visible. And, yet, the building in its white classical formality is elevated slightly and is set apart from its surroundings. In 1989 the American Institute of Architects–Detroit Chapter gave its 25 Year Award to the Olivet Student Center. The award acknowledges that this outstanding design has retained its originality and relevance over time.

BELLEVUE

EA05 **Bellevue Municipal Building**
(Citizens Bank)

1908, Leonard H. Field. 201 North Main St.

Leonard H. Field (1873–c. 1944) of Jackson designed this bank building in a vernacular

EA04.2 Lester K. Kirk Collegiate Center

picturesque mode with a touch of classicism in the entry motif. Charles G. Secore, a Bellevue stonemason, laid the exterior walls with rock-faced fieldstone trimmed with red sandstone. The various geometric shapes (circles, triangles, hearts, spear points, and diamonds) and colors of stone inlaid in the local fieldstone exterior lend a playful vernacular quality to an otherwise solid, regular building. This rough masonry, together with the low-pitched roof of red Spanish tile and broad overhanging eaves, are reminders of Richardson; the pedimented modillioned entrance on the short end, flanked by a pair of Doric columns, represent the classical touch. The interior is finished in oak and floored with tile mosaics in aqua and salmon. On the building's completion, a local reviewer in the *Bellevue Gazette* for January 14, 1909, rather shrewdly and accurately observed that the entry resembled "the finest modern office buildings . . . in Washington," and the interior seemed "beautiful and homelike." The building served as a bank from 1909 to 1931, becoming the Bellevue Municipal Building in 1934.

EA06 Bellevue Mill

1852, Horatio Hall, carpenter builder. Northeast corner of Mill and Riverside streets

Standing on the west bank of the Battle Creek River, this water-powered gristmill is evidence in the village of Bellevue of the importance of the grain-processing industry in the well-being and economic growth of all fron-

tier communities. Firmly built on a rubble stone foundation, the tall, rectangular three-and-a-half-story structure is composed of an interlocking frame of massive 12-by-12-inch walnut timbers and 3-by-12-inch floor joists and covered with board-and-batten and tongue-and-groove siding. Pulleys, drive shafts, and chutes used in the milling process remain intact inside. Built for Manlius Mann of Marshall by Horatio Hall, a Bellevue carpenter-builder, the mill operated from 1852 to 1958. In 1888 a Smith Roller Process was installed. In 1928, when A. G. Butler acquired the mill, turbines were added, and flour was milled under the trade name, Bellevue Blue Bird Flour. In its plainness and concern for utility, it exemplifies the strong vernacular tradition in much the same way as did the early textile mills in New England. Current owners are in the process of rehabilitating the mill for use as a summer house.

BELLEVUE TOWNSHIP

EA07 Dyer Lime Kiln

1875–1899. Sand Rd. (.75 mi south of Michigan 78 and adjacent to 8710 Sand Rd.)

Only ruins remain of one of three perpetual limekilns that operated in the Bellevue area until 1899. The Dyer Lime Kiln is a chimney kiln fitted with cast-iron damper and draft controls that regulated more efficiently the lime burn and, in turn, yielded a more consistent product than that produced by cruder earlier methods. Thomas Roberts and Charles Dyer built the Dyer Lime Kiln.

VERMONTVILLE

Settlers came from East Poultney, Vermont, in 1836 to establish at Vermontville the "Union Colony." The colony was devoted to the preaching and teaching of Congregationalist ideals. The former Vermonters who settled this area invoked New England methods of land distribution in their new Vermontville. Land was purchased in the name of the colony and distributed under a township proprietor system reminiscent of the seventeenth-century New England land distribution system. After the village was platted, every colonist received a 10-acre rectangular house lot oriented along the major east-west road that linked Charlotte to Hastings. At the intersection of this road with the north-south road that linked Marshall and Ionia and bisected the village, one-acre lots were set aside from the four corners for the establishment of a village commons. Farm lots of 160 acres located outside of the village were distributed to each colonist.

EA08 Vermontville First Congregational Chapel and Academy

1843–1844. Northwest corner of North Main and West Main streets

This meetinghouse was built by the original settlers of Vermontville. The first story of the meetinghouse served as the church until the First Congregational Church (EA09) opened in 1864; the second floor was used as a school. Clapboarding clads the exterior walls of the two-story, gabled, wood-frame structure. These are pierced by twelve-over-twelve windows.

EA09 First Congregational Church

1862–1864. 341 South Main St. (southwest corner of South Main and West Main streets)

Reminiscent of Congregational meetinghouses of New England, the simple, vernacular, wood structure was built in 1862–1864 on the village square by the congregation founded by Vermont settlers. The gable-front rectangular structure has a projecting single square entry tower and steeple terminating

EA09 First Congregational Church

in an octagonal spire. A whisper of medieval verticality is exhibited in the attenuated windows and in the buttresses that are placed at the front corners. The round-arch windows also hint at the Romanesque. These features reflect the trend in the Congregational Church during the 1850s and 1860s to favor the Romanesque.

EA10 Vermontville Opera House

1896–1898. 120 South Main St. (on west side of South Main St. between First and Second streets)

This wonderful little vernacular opera house expresses the spirit of community cooperation in which the commercial district of Vermontville was rebuilt after a fire at the turn of the century. The village and township of Vermontville collaborated in the construction of the civic building. The one-story rectangular building rests on a raised basement. It has masonry walls, a mansard roof, and a truncated corner tower with bell-cast roof. Village funds built the brick lower portion, which serves as a library, and township monies funded the red-brick upper portion, which contained the opera house and multipurpose community room. Three local businessmen paid for the opera stage on which hung an oleographic curtain manufactured in Battle Creek that depicted a scene in Venice.

SUNFIELD

EA11 Sunfield Grand Army of the Republic Post #283 Hall

1899. 115 Main St.

This false-fronted, gable-roofed, clapboarded meeting hall stands as a monument to soldiers and sailors who served in the Civil War. It was built in 1899 by local members of the Samuel W. Grinnell Post #283 of the Grand Army of the Republic from wood cut from the site and adjacent lands. This is one of ten such halls established in Eaton County. It represents the small, modest halls, in contrast to the most elaborate one in Detroit (DE13, p. 73). Chartered in 1884, the Grinnell Post was disbanded in 1934, but descendants of these soldiers and sailors organized their own groups, the Sons of the Veterans and the Daughters of Union Veterans. The building is a single-story "one part commercial block," as Richard Longstreth uses the term.[50] Four carved brackets support the simple cornice. Three trees planted in a row in front of the structure are memorials to three Union heroes: Gen. Ulysses Simpson Grant (1822–1885), Gen. William Tecumseh Sherman (1820–1891), and Gen. Philip Henry Sheridan (1831–1888).

Clinton County (CL)

SAINT JOHNS

Located on the Detroit, Grand Haven and Michigan Railroad and on US 27, the city produced farm implements. Saint Johns is the judicial seat of Clinton County.

CL01 Saint Johns Municipal Building and Bement Library

1938–1940, R. V. Gay. Northwest corner of East Walker and Spring streets (4 blocks west of US 27 intersection with Walker)

A Public Works Administration grant of $22,500 and a bequest of $20,000 from the estate of Louisa J. Bement in memory of her daughter, Jennie Louise (1868–1893), enabled the city of Saint Johns to build this civic structure for city offices and the public library. R. V. Gay (1895–1943), who worked for Warren S. Holmes Company, architects of Lansing, but who was born and raised in Saint Johns and educated at the University of Michigan, drafted plans for the building. The ordinary little two-story rectangular structure is in the flat and stylized mode of the PWA Moderne style. Its buff-colored brick walls are decorated with fluted stone piers and panels and pierced with steel-frame windows. The building holds an auditorium and dining hall with stage and kitchen, public toilets, the commission chamber and city offices, in addition to the library. The interior has the expected glass block wall to conceal electric lights, a terrazzo floor, and birch woodwork. Hudson and Howe, general contractors of Owosso, built the structure. The building is typical of the many PWA projects found in the state.

CL02 Saint Johns Central Elementary School (Saint Johns Union School)

1885–1886, Oliver M. Hidden of Watkins and Arnold. 205 West Baldwin St. (bounded by Baldwin, Church, Park, and Ottawa streets)

After the twenty-year-old Union School was destroyed by fire in March 1885, this "$30,000 temple of learning" (*Clinton Independent*, January 4, 1886) was built to designs of a firm specializing in public buildings. It was for Saint Johns' 625 primary, elementary, and high school students. The huge, two-and-one-half-story, reddish orange brick structure rests on a raised fieldstone basement and is accented with stone trim and capped with a slate roof topped by a bell cupola. From the central block project links and end pavilions in an overall five-part plan. The plan was arranged with classrooms in the central block and dependencies and with stairways, a library, and administrative offices in the hyphens. Acting on advice from the state superintendent of public instruction for all Michigan school districts, the Saint Johns building committee paid special attention to convenience, lighting, heating, ventilation, and fireproofing for this then modern school building.

BINGHAM TOWNSHIP

CL03 **Crosby Mint Still**

1918. 2588 South US 27 (west side of South US 27, .1 mile north of Parks Rd.)

This mint still on the Crosby farm south of Saint Johns is one of the few reminders in the Capital Region of the major role that central Michigan played in the 1920s through the 1940s in the production of the nation's peppermint and spearmint. Most of this simple one-story, three-crib, wood-frame barn is covered by shiplap siding; the southern side is an open pass-through for the unloading of the mint crop from the field wagons for distillation in the still. A tall, square tapered brick chimney stack towers over the north end of the structure. J. E. Crosby established his mint operation in about 1918. Oils produced in early mint distillation were first used medicinally. Now they are used as flavorings for chewing gum, toothpaste, and mouthwash. A verticillium wilt, which precipitated the movement of mint growing from the southwest Michigan region into the fertile muck lands of central Michigan, also infected the croplands here and hastened its decline in the late 1940s. Certain strains of spearmint, less susceptible to the wilt fungus, are still grown today. The historical importance of mint production for the region is celebrated in a festival during the mint harvesting season in August in Saint Johns.

MAPLE RAPIDS

CL04 **Creasinger and Hewitt Block**

1874. Southwest corner of Main and Maple (Clinton County 490) (6.5 miles west of US 27)

This exuberant High Victorian Gothic commercial block was built by pioneer Maple Rapids businessmen Isaac Hewitt (1839–1920)

and Solomon P. Creasinger (b. 1844) and, thus, is associated with the village's first settlers. Hewitt's father, William, came from Steuben County, New York, by way of Dewitt to present-day Maple Rapids. He platted the village in 1852 and built a dam and sawmill on the Maple River. The younger Hewitt operated a sawmill and gristmill, store and bank. Creasinger was a banker. (In 1835, George Campau had established a trading post at the site.) The two-story square brick block is encrusted with corbeling, finials, and iron cresting and trim and is decorated with rich polychrome. The structure is divided into two identical parts, each marked by a pedimented entablature; the tympanum of each is inscribed with the name of its owner. Beneath these, the upper windows are paired within pointed-arch panels and, like all windows on the building, are crowned with carved hoods. An elaborate cornice separates the upper from the lower story. The lower story has two storefronts. The structure is a two-part commercial building, as Richard Longstreth developed the term. The first floor contained commercial space and second story contained offices or apartments. The second story is reached through a center door at the street level. Residents of Clinton County regarded the bank as "handsomely furnished throughout, and the most commodious for such purposes in the county."[51]

OVID

CL05 **The Belfry** (First Congregational Church of Ovid)

1872, George Fox, master carpenter. 1899, moved. 1900, additions. 222 North Main St. (southeast corner of Main and Pearl streets)

The eight pewter-colored finials tipped with gold leaf atop the tower of the former First Congregational Church serve as a shining crown for the rural community of Ovid. The First Congregational Church was organized in 1871; the following year this white clapboard frame building was built at High and Park streets by master carpenter George Fox. This original structure was 34 feet by 58 feet in plan. The long, narrow pointed-arch windows are evidence of the Gothic Revival style. The square tower is topped by an octagonal belfry and is surmounted by the eight aforementioned tall graceful octagonal finials. The

CL05 The Belfry (First Congregational Church of Ovid)

First Congregational Church, soaring to 75 feet in height, is the tallest church in the village. Light streams into the open-beamed sanctuary filtered through many colored windows adding to the effect of medieval Gothic.

In 1899 oxen pulled the structure to the more central location of Main and Pearl streets. The move to the Main Street and the expansion of the building reflected the congregation's position as "one of the great social forces in the county," according to the local county history.

After more than a century of providing for worship, in 1978, the First Congregational Church of Ovid moved into private hands. Its new owners, both historians, restored the exterior and have kept much of the interior intact, including the pews, the stained glass and the bell.

EAGLE TOWNSHIP

CL06 Adam and Zanah Keebler House

1912. 11945 West Grand River Highway (1.5 mile east of Eagle and just west of Michigan 100)

This rectangular, two-story, cross-gabled farmhouse, built by Adam Keebler and his son, Will, for their son and brother, Charles, and his new wife Zanah, embodies the persistence of the vernacular tradition of building with the materials most readily available and least expensive. In this case, ordinary conduit tiles were used for building material. The house is among the largest of several other utilitarian structures in the area—sheds, barns, garages—built of local clay conduit tile. The nearby Grand Ledge Clay Products Company, which began operations in 1906, had available many "seconds" or rejects of the tile conduits. Glazed clay hollow conduit tiles were laid up in courses in much the same as bricks. Here the walls are horizontal stretcher bond courses mortared, and the ends of the hollow tiles sealed with mortar. At the building's corners, the tile ends from each wall overlap in a manner reminiscent of the square notching technique used in log construction. When laid in double thickness as in the Keebler house, the tiles provided superb insulation against the severe cold Michigan winters and hot humid summers.

Saginaw Bay
and River Valley Region

ONCE DENSELY FORESTED WITH STANDS OF TOWERING white pine and some hardwood, the Saginaw Bay and River Valley Region is immediately accessible to the water transportation of the Great Lakes. The gently flowing Saginaw River, with its tributaries the Cass, Shiawassee, Tittabawassee, and other rivers, empties into the waters of Saginaw Bay, a thumblike projection of Lake Huron.

Those rivers were the transportation network that attracted traders, the first Euro-Americans to establish themselves in the Saginaw Bay and River Valley Region. Traveling up the Saint Lawrence River and into the Great Lakes, they arrived in the early nineteenth century and built primitive log trading posts along the riverbanks. In 1816 Henry Bolieu, a French trapper, canoed from the headwaters of the Saginaw River down the Shiawassee River and built a log trading post at its intersection with the East Branch River near present-day Byron. That same year French Canadian fur trader Louis Campau built a two-story log building on the Saginaw River at what is now Saginaw. Two years later, at the request of Michigan Territorial Governor Lewis Cass, he built a council house. One year later, in 1819, Jacob Smith (1780–1825) came from Quebec, French Canada, and erected at a ford on the Flint River, later known as the Grand Traverse, a log house that served as a trading post as well as his dwelling. It was the site of present-day Flint.

These early trading posts were also the sites of later settlement. Near Bolieu's trading post on the Shiawassee River, Samuel Dexter founded Byron in the mid-1820s. Near Leon Tromble's trading post established about 1792 at the mouth of the Saginaw River, Joseph Tromble (1809–1882), an employee of the American Fur Company, and his brother Mader bought land some three miles upstream from the point where the river enters Saginaw Bay and built a

two-story wood-frame house in 1836–1837, the site of Bay City. They speculated in land and built houses, and eventually, in 1872, Joseph Tromble constructed his own large brick house. In 1837 Benjamin O. and Alfred L. Williams erected a log trading post, also on the Shiawassee River, at the site of
present-day Owosso.

Michigan Territorial Governor Lewis Cass and Ottawa and Chippewa Indian
leaders signed the Treaty of Saginaw in 1819. The treaty gave hunting rights
to the Indians provided the lands were owned by the federal government. But,
even so, the federal government feared that relations between the Euro- and
Native Americans would remain unsettled. So in 1822 it built a military garrison on the west side of the river on the site of the Hotel Fordney at Saginaw
to protect settlers from any unrest. Soon, however, in 1823 Fort Saginaw was
ordered evacuated.

Within six years, in 1829, the federal government began work on a military
road from Detroit through Pontiac to Saginaw. At the wooden bridge at the
Grand Traverse John and Polly Todd, who came from Pontiac, opened an inn
in 1830, forming the nucleus for a settlement by 1833. After these settlers and
others from New York and New England took care of their most immediate
needs and built dwellings, they erected single-room log schools, churches, and
county buildings—a courthouse and jail, and a poorhouse and farm.

Settlement was often aided and advanced when easterners speculated in
townsites and even platted towns. In the late 1830s Andrew Mack established
the Shiawassee County Seat Company and platted the town of Corunna; Norman Little of New York platted an extensive town that became Saginaw on the
east side of the Saginaw River; and Albert Miller platted Portsmouth, now a
part of Bay City, and established a steam sawmill operation. Plank roads, railroads, and the dredging of rivers into navigable waterways further encouraged
growth and settlement.

The counties of the Saginaw Bay and River Valley were set off in the 1820s
and 1830s. The organization of three followed in the 1830s: Saginaw County
in 1835, Genesee County in 1836, Shiawassee in 1837. Midland County was
organized in 1850 and Bay County in 1857. With county organization came the
construction of the region's first government buildings—county courthouses.
Genesee County, for example, erected in Flint in the late 1830s a solid rectangular building of oak logs to serve as a courthouse and jail. In 1851 it was
replaced by a fireproof brick structure planned by Pierce F. Cleveland and
David Schram and built on courthouse square. The grand High Victorian Saginaw County Courthouse erected to the plans of Frederick Hollister in the late
1880s represents the high level of architectural achievement during the lumbering era.

The Saginaw Bay and River Valley Region was the first region in Michigan
to experience large-scale lumbering. Pine from the dense forests was easily
transported down the Saginaw River and its tributaries to mills on the river

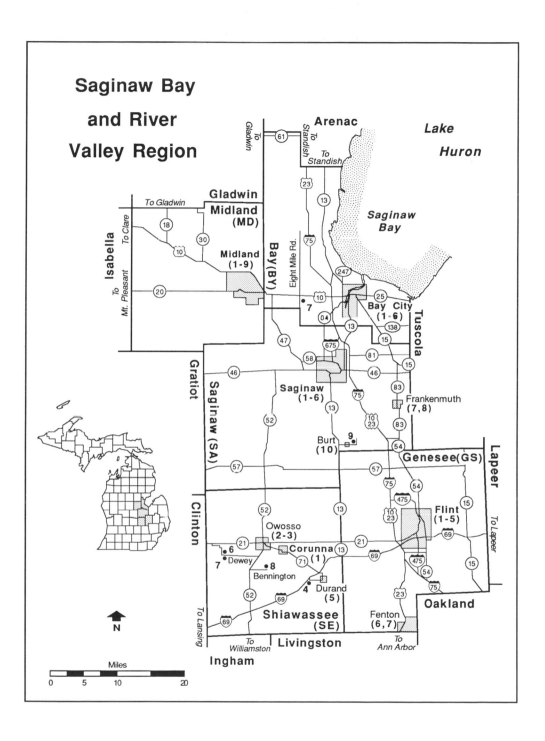

Saginaw Bay and River Valley Region

Lake Huron

Saginaw Bay

Arenac

Gladwin

Midland (MD)

To Gladwin

Isabella

Midland (1-9)

Bay (BY)

Eight Mile Rd.

Bay City (1-6)

Tuscola

Gratiot

Saginaw (SA)

Saginaw (1-6)

Frankenmuth (7,8)

Burt (10)

Genesee (GS)

Lapeer

Owosso (2-3)

Corunna (1)

Dewey

Bennington

Durand (5)

Flint (1-5)

Shiawassee (SE)

Fenton (6,7)

Oakland

Clinton

To Lansing

To Williamston

Livingston

To Ann Arbor

Ingham

N

Miles
0   5   10   20

and on to Saginaw Bay and Lake Huron. Lumber supplied much more than a local market; it was shipped down the lakes to Detroit, Toledo, Cleveland, and Buffalo. Lumbering in the region began soon after timber cruisers and lookers searched the Saginaw Valley and acquired land in the 1830s and 1840s. Sawmills were operating on the Thread River south of Flint in the 1830s. By 1854 nearly thirty sawmills operated on the Saginaw River and its tributaries. By 1872 thirty-six mills operated between Portsmouth (now Bay City) and the mouth of the river, some of the largest in the country. In the 1870s and 1880s, as logging companies cleared the pine forests of the Saginaw Valley and operated mills on the river, there was even more activity. In 1880 there were thirty-two sawmills on the Saginaw River near Bay City.

The considerable number of wood and masonry houses built with profits of the lumbering industry that remain in Saginaw and in Bay City are reminders of the lumbering era. And many prosperous lumbermen are remembered in their public architectural legacies. Jesse Hoyt and Henry W. Sage left funds for libraries in Saginaw and Bay City, respectively. Lumberman Ezra Rust provided Saginaw with a beautifully landscaped park that stretches for more than a mile along the Saginaw River.

Because of the phenomenal scope of the lumbering industry in the Saginaw Bay and River Valley Region, it was only natural that industries related to wood would emerge here. Shipbuilding began in the 1850s, and the Defoe Shipbuilding Company was established in 1905. The wagon and carriage industry, promoted, in part, by the region's farming, also used wood. Ready-cut and portable houses were manufactured at the Aladdin plant in Bay City and at the Mershon and Morley factory in Saginaw. Another by-product of the lumbering industry was salt production. Wood scraps from the mills were burned to evaporate the water from brine which was pumped from subterranean aquifers. In the 1890s Herbert H. Dow extracted bromine and other products in Midland and founded Dow Chemical Company in 1897.

Durand became a major railroad center for the region and the state. The first railroad passed through in 1856. But by the early twentieth century the city was the largest railroad center outside Detroit. Near its large Richardsonian depot once stood a forty-two-stall roundhouse.

As the supply of lumber was exhausted, agriculture, notably the cultivation of sugar beets, replaced it. German farmers experimented with sugar beet production in 1895 in Frankenlust and Monitor townships. Here remain their polychrome yellow and red brick farmhouses and Gothic Revival Trinity Lutheran Church. Sugar refineries were constructed in the area around Bay City and Saginaw. The Michigan Sugar Company built a beet sugar factory at Essexville in 1898. The Monitor Sugar Refinery was at Bay City. Surrounding fields were also cultivated with beans, and numerous grain elevators rise beside the railroad tracks in the communities of the region.

The urbanization and industrialization of the region is centered in the tri-cities area of Saginaw, Bay City, and Midland, and in Flint. Their importance as the focuses of the region during the lumbering era of the late nineteenth century and other activities in the early twentieth century is recognized in their monumental post offices and federal building, their city halls, waterworks, schools, libraries and churches, as well as in their houses. Midland is famous for its twentieth-century residences and churches designed by Alden B. Dow.

Located on the Flint River, Flint became the center of carriage manufacturing at Flint. The great success of that industry was a logical precursor of the factories today that produce Buicks and Chevrolet trucks for General Motors. The substantial neighborhoods of workers' housing are evidence of the character of the city.

Saginaw County (SA)

SAGINAW

The site of Saginaw presented a ridge of dry land unusual along the otherwise swampy course of the Saginaw River. It first grew in economic importance in the 1820s, when the American Fur Company and other fur buyers established trading posts. When the transfer of Indian lands was completed by treaty in 1819, settlement of tradesmen and farmers followed. Military protection at Fort Saginaw was provided starting in 1822, and the first land was platted on the west side of the river in 1830. Many of the new residents came from New York State or Canada and were of German, Scottish, or English descent. To Alexis de Tocqueville, who visited the community in 1831, Saginaw was "the farthest point inhabited by Europeans to the northwest of a vast peninsula of Michigan. It may be considered an advance post, a sort of watchtower, placed by the whites in the midst of the Indian nations." [52]

Lumbering and the closely linked industries for salt production, machinery manufacture, and shipbuilding began in the 1850s. Growth soon overflowed the west side of the river, and two separate and competing communities were established: Saginaw City, incorporated on the west side in 1857; and East Saginaw, incorporated in 1859. The development of the west side seemed marked by a conservatism that allowed East Saginaw to sprint ahead. East siders created by 1900 a larger commercial district, a more diverse industrial base, and neighborhoods of grander homes. Fortunately, the two towns were

amalgamated by state law in 1889, and during the lumber boom's peak years from 1875 to 1900, residents were forced to work together. This cooperation, along with economic diversification, softened the blow from lumbering's demise at the turn of the century. Lumbermen shifted their emphasis to the manufacture of wood products. As a lake port that rivaled Bay City in importance and as the hub of five railroads by 1881, Saginaw became a transportation and distribution center. Between 1900 and the Great Depression, the city promoted the development of agriculture, sugar manufacture, and, most importantly, heavy-metal-based industries linked to the automobile industry that continue today.

WEST SIDE (Saginaw City)

SA01 Michigan Avenue

1870–1910. Michigan Ave. between Remington and Lee streets (Michigan Ave. runs perpendicular to Michigan 58 and Michigan 46)

Fort Saginaw, the military garrison established in 1822, which was located near the present-day intersection of Court and Hamilton streets, was the original nucleus of the Saginaw City business district. The two small residential districts along North and South Michigan Avenue were the west side's grandest. Located a respectable distance from the Saginaw City business district and along the main north-south thoroughfare, the two

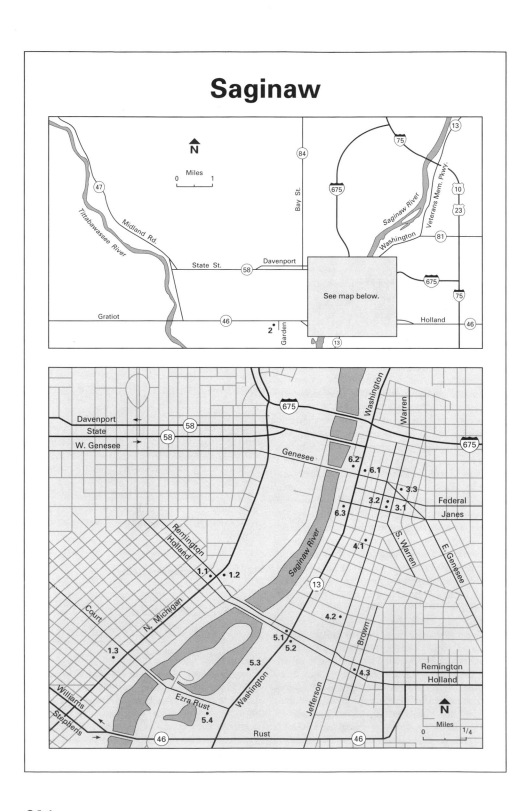

Saginaw

neighborhoods became the sites of new "up-scale" houses. These were neither the residences of Saginaw City's earliest settlers nor of its middle-class workers and professionals. Rather, second generation businessmen, lumbermen, and investors chose to live here and build Carpenter's Gothic, Italianate, Queen Anne, and, later, Georgian Revival houses that more closely paralleled the residential developments of the east side.

SA01.1 Gilbert Stark House

1885. 1027 North Michigan Ave. (southwest corner of North Michigan Ave. and West Remington St.)

A dormered corner tower marks the stark asymmetry of this wooden Queen Anne house. It is richly decorated with scroll saw work. The house was built for Gilbert Stark, an attorney and the son of George Stark.

SA01.2 Saginaw Art Museum (Clark L. and Lizzie Merrill Ring House)

1904, Charles A. Platt. 1926, garage. 1970, classroom connector. 1126 North Michigan Ave. (northeast corner North Michigan Ave. and West Remington St.)

In 1904 lumber baron Clark L. Ring (1861–1933) and his wife, Lizzie Merrill Ring (1862–1912), contracted Charles A. Platt of New York to design their house and gardens. This nationally recognized specialist in domestic architecture (in particular, large homes and country estates) was a logical choice for the Rings. Their daughter married William Gwinn Mather, for whom Platt had designed a home in Cleveland, Ohio. Platt created for the Rings a symmetrical three-story, red-brick Georgian Revival house with rich classical ornamenta-

tion. Gable dormers and end chimneys project from the hipped roof. A central pedimented pavilion contains the front entrance, which is flanked by two free-standing Doric columns. An entablature with a denticulated molding frames the entire structure and the cornice of the front pediment. An elliptical window in the tympanum of the pediment is ornamented with four white brick keystones similar to the keystones in each of the window caps at the first- and second-story levels. Quoins are found on all corners of the house.

In 1946 the Rings' daughters, Mrs. Edward Isaiah Garrett and Mrs. William G. Mather, gave the residence and gardens to the city. It now houses the Saginaw Art Museum. The museum constructed an annex on the northern end of the house, which connects the house and garage.

SA01.3 Saginaw County Government Center

1972; Wigen, Tinknell and Associates, architects; Giffels and Rosetti, engineers. 111 South Michigan Ave. (southwest corner of South Michigan Ave. and Court St.)

In 1972 the second Saginaw County Courthouse, a towered High Victorian red brick structure with a mansard roof erected in 1884–1885 to the plans of noted Saginaw architect Frederick W. Hollister (1847–1923), was demolished to make way for this county governmental complex. The Government Center is a strikingly simple bulky cube. Sheathed in bone-colored stucco panels, it is marked by a strict delineation of horizontal, louvered windows and narrow piers; the use of wide spandrels between floors and the wide cornice-line fascia gives the building horizontality. It seems to hover on a pedestal. A bridge connects the first story to a landscaped plaza. A matching jail is to the southwest.

SA02 Ammi and William Wright House

1854. 207 Garden Lane (just south of Michigan 46)

Ammi Wright (1822–1912) came to Saginaw in 1851 and became a leading member of the group of businessmen who made fortunes in Saginaw. First, in 1859 he bought into the established Miller and Paine Sawmill, and by 1865 he bought out his partners' shares. He used this mill and three additional mills to generate the capital that he then invested in a retail lumber business, the First National Bank of Saginaw, two railroad companies, and the Saginaw-Saint Louis Plank Road. Wright lived in this wood-framed and clapboard-sheathed Italianate home, then down a garden lane of elms on the outskirts of town, until he left Saginaw in 1878; at that time he deeded the house to his brother William. It may have been then that the brothers updated and enlarged the rather typical Michigan farmhouse with the square three-story tower and other Italianate detailing to reflect current fashions and their affluence. The house has intersecting gables with the tower in the ell and a porch along the front.

EAST SAGINAW

SA03 Central City

1860–1920. Bounded by Genesee, Hoyt, and Jefferson Ave., just east of Franklin (Michigan 13)

James M. Hoyt of Eli Hoyt and Company in New York City invested in Saginaw timberlands during the 1850s and purchased lands on the east side of the river. Bolstered by this early infusion of Eastern capital, East Saginaw quickly matched, and then surpassed, the development of the west side.

SA03.1 Hoyt Public Library

1887–1890, Van Brunt and Howe. 1920–1921, porch and reference room addition, Edward L. Tilton. 1959, light tan brick addition, Frederick Wigen. 1979, exterior restoration. 505 Janes St. (northeast corner of South Jefferson Ave. and Janes St.)

Jesse Hoyt (1815–1882), a New York investor in Saginaw timberlands, left to East Saginaw the gift of a site and $100,000 with which to build and operate this library and to purchase books. In preparing and choosing plans for the building, the library trustees visited several midwestern libraries and enlisted the advice of Frederick Poole (1821–1894), who was the head of the Chicago Public Library and who later was elected president of the American Library Association. Poole felt that a librarian should plan the utilitarian and departmentalized interior of the building and that an architect should design the exterior. Elijah E. Meyers of Detroit; Van Brunt and Howe of Boston; McKim, Mead and White of New York; and H. H. Richardson of Bos-

SA03.1 Hoyt Public Library

ton responded to a competition for its design and submitted plans. In 1886 the trustees rejected those plans prepared by Richardson, America's leading architect and a foremost designer of small libraries, in favor of those drawn by Van Brunt and Howe, presumably because they followed Poole's instructions. According to Poole's plan, the library was to be cruciform in plan, utilitarian, and with side rather than sky light, and the reading room lighted from the north. (Richardson's design for the Hoyt Library was executed in 1887–1888 as the Howard Library in New Orleans).

Although not by Richardson, the building with its round corner tower, arches, intersecting gables, and rough stone exterior clearly reflects his influence. The exterior walls are constructed of randomly coursed grayish white limestone, quarried locally at Bay Port, and are trimmed with red Portage Entry sandstone. The interior is finished in oak. From the vestibule and hall, off the original round-arch entrance portico on Jefferson Avenue, which is now closed, a stairway ascended to the original book delivery room and the main portion of the building. The original reading room fronts on Jefferson Avenue, and the original book room to the east. The second floor contains the upper portion of the book room and a lecture room, stage, trustee's room, and room for special collections. The Norman porch decorated with arches and columns of carved red sandstone was modeled after Canterbury Cathedral in England and added in 1920–1921 on the Janes Street side of the building. It became the main entrance. This addition includes a large reference room and stacks and the conversion of the main reading room to a children's room.

SA03.2 Saginaw County Castle Building
(Saginaw Post Office [Castle Station])

1897–1898, William M. Aiken. 1937, remodeling and addition, Carl E. Macomber. 500 Federal St. (southeast corner of Federal St. and South Jefferson Ave.)

Castle Station is a fashionable civic building and one of the fanciest post offices every built in the country. Through the efforts of Aaron T. Bliss (b. 1837), Congress appropriated $100,000 in 1889 for the construction of the Saginaw Post Office. Civic leaders and the residents of East Saginaw rejected the first plans of the federal architects as unacceptably plain. Their demands for a new proposal yielded plans for this French Châteauesque building. The grayish white Bedford limestone mass is accented with rounded towers and finials on every peak of its steeply pitched, red slate roof. Its architect, William M. Aiken (1885–1908), who was supervising architect of the U.S. Treasury Department, explained that the French medieval chateau style commemorates the early French settlers in Saginaw. The corner towers suggest the defensive feature of frontier life, while the carving of the pinnacles and finials draws its imagery from the fauna and flora of the area. Because of its "exclusive design, its rich trimmings, its imposing style," the *Saginaw Courier Herald*

for July 3, 1898, thought the government building the "handsomest in the United States." Together with the Hoyt Library, the two formed a block that would serve forever "as an emblem of nineteenth century grandeur." Charles W. Gindele of Chicago, under the supervision of George H. Miller, built the structure.

In 1937 the building was remodeled and enlarged. A rear tower was demolished to make room for the expansion of the workroom and lobby. The building currently houses the Historical Society of the Saginaw County Museum. The lobby remains intact, and exhibits occupy the workroom space.

SA03.3 Saginaw Federal Building

1976, Smith, Hinchman and Grylls. 100 South Warren St. (northeast corner of South Warren and Genesee streets)

The General Services Administration built the federal office building as an environmental demonstration project during the nation's bicentennial celebration. Energy-saving features of the poured concrete, stucco-sheathed building are a partially below-ground main-floor level, earth berms on the north and south facades, limited window glazing, and a huge water-paneled solar heat collector that is both functional and ornamental. Office and public spaces are simply detailed with exposed brick walls, low ceilings with recessed lighting, and carpeted or rubber-padded floors.

SA04 South Jefferson Avenue

1885–1930. South Jefferson Ave. from Millard to Atwater St.

By the last quarter of the nineteenth century, many of Saginaw's wealthy lumber barons and industrialists lived on the east side, particularly on or near South Jefferson Avenue. In May 1893 the worst fire ever to strike Saginaw began around the sawmills, near the site of the present city hall. It consumed hundreds of buildings in a one-mile-long and four-block-wide swath. The buildings on South Jefferson Avenue were destroyed by the blaze because the avenue's dry ridge-top location and dense settlement of wood homes fueled the fire. While the fire was a major catastrophe for the community, the reconstruction of South Jefferson transformed the avenue into a unique chronicle of the architectural styles that prevailed as Saginaw left its lumber era and adjusted to a new economic order. Queen Anne and Eastlake styles predominate from the years immediately following the conflagration; period revival and Prairie styles and Craftsman houses take the upper-middle-class neighborhood through the first three decades of the twentieth century.

SA04.1 Clarence Hill House

1886, Frederick W. Hollister. 523 South Jefferson Ave. (northwest corner of South Jefferson Ave. and Thompson St.)

This house was built for Clarence Hill (1855–1901), a lumberman who compounded the fortune he made in the Thumb with profits from lumber operations in Gladwin County and the Wiaska Bay area of Lake Superior and with iron ore profits from the Mesabi Range of Minnesota. Local architect Frederick W. Hollister designed the house, and Steve Winkler built it. It is another elaborate Queen Anne structure of stone, brick, and wood, with a heavy overlay of carved and cut wood detailing and a corner tower with a bell-cast roof and fish-scale-shingled skin. The horseshoe screened porch is a prominent feature of the wooden version of the Queen Anne.

SA04.2 Henry and Catherine Preuszol Passolt House

1868, Ludwig E. V. Bude. 1105 South Jefferson Ave. (southwest corner of South Jefferson Ave. and McCoskry St.)

The brick Italianate Passolt house is one of the few that survived the 1893 fire. Passolt (1836–1914) was a wealthy and outspoken Saginaw soap manufacturer who believed the carelessness of the lumbermen at their mills would some day destroy the city. Accordingly,

he built his own home of masonry and incorporated every fireproofing technique available in its construction. It was designed by Ludwig Ernest Volusin Bude (1827–1910), a German-born engineer who arrived in Saginaw in 1855 and earned a reputation as a drainage expert, bridge engineer, architect, wood carver, cabinet maker, and teacher. Before the ready availability of architects in Michigan, Bude and other engineers, who had gone to Saginaw to work on internal improvement projects, prepared the architectural plans for major projects. From the front of the symmetrical hipped-roof house projects a full-height gabled portion containing the entrance. It is sheltered with a columned and classically detailed porch. The richly corbeled and paneled exterior walls rise to dramatically projecting eaves supported by paired scrolled brackets.

SA04.3 Martin P. Gale House

1912, J. Frederick Beckbissinger. 1415 Brown St.

Built for Saginaw businessman Martin Gale, this house is a square symmetrical Prairie style building in brown brick and shingles. It was designed by Saginaw architect J. Frederick Beckbissinger (1871–1963), who developed proficiency in the Prairie style. Horizontally and symmetrically massed with an ample roof overhang, the house is a fine example of the twentieth-century architecture found in this still attractive post-fire neighborhood. Nearby on Holland Court are several additional Beckbissinger Prairie style houses.

SA05 The Grove

1870–1936. South Washington Ave. (Michigan 13) between Holland and Ezra Rust Dr.

The Grove is unique among Saginaw's neighborhoods because of its parklike setting. Surrounded by Hoyt and Ezra Rust parks, Lake Linton, and Ojibway Island in the Saginaw River, the ample lots with deep setbacks and mature trees seem to be a park within a park. The Grove is also a special blend of residential and nonresidential uses.

SA05.1 Saginaw City Hall

1936–1937, Carl E. Macomber. 1315 South Washington Ave. (Michigan 13) (northwest corner of South Washington Ave. and Holland)

This sleek but somewhat austere depression-era city hall was built on the site of the old city hall that was designed in 1890 but that burned on April 9, 1935. A Public Works Administration (PWA) grant of $114,000 and Saginaw money furnished the $312,526 for the new building. The city hall was designed by Carl F. Macomber (1889–1964) of Saginaw. It seemed to combine beauty with utility. The rectangular, flat-roofed structure measures 140 feet by 120 feet in plan and has two stories and a basement. The construction is reinforced concrete and solid masonry. The exterior walls of the building are covered with quarry-faced Bay Port limestone trimmed with sawed Indiana stone. The full-height rounded entrance pavilion is adorned with pilasters and capitals simplified and shorn of all ornamentation. Between them are spandrels faced with marble. Decorative aluminum trims the exterior. The arc of the entrance accommodates an interior curved staircase. The council chamber and courtroom are paneled in oak. The basement provides space for the Public Welfare Department and a small courtroom; the first floor, city offices and records storage; the second floor, the council chamber, mayor's office, and department of public works.

SA05.2 **B'nai Israel Synagogue**

1953, social hall, Frantz and Spence. 1964, sanctuary, Deming, Beach and Waters. 1424 South Washington Ave. (Michigan 13) (southeast corner of South Washington Ave. and Holland)

In the postwar move to suburbia, B'nai Israel, founded in 1876, sold its tile-trimmed, faintly Byzantine building at 216 South Second Street (now Spiritual Israel and Its Army Church, the facade is still recognizably that of a synagogue). On extensive acreage south of the city center, donated by a member, it erected an all-purpose brick and glass auditorium with meeting space and classrooms. A decade later Glenn Beach built a dramatic, biblically inspired sanctuary based upon the Tent of Meeting in the desert, as described in the book of Exodus. A huge concrete and stone "Mount Sinai" thrusts up from the roof, and its base in the sanctuary provides a spectacular backdrop for a portable ark resting on curved staves. Like a canvas tent, the ceiling of the prayer hall seems to sag slightly between the beams, and the canopies that surmount the entrances look like raised tent flaps. The sanctuary and social hall are separated by a wall of richly colored stained-glass windows depicting the Twelve Tribes of Israel.

SA05.3 **Montague Inn** (Robert and Edwina Montague House)

1929–1933, Frantz and Spence. 1581 South Washington Ave. (Michigan 13) (across from Hoyt Park)

Designed by Robert B. Frantz and James A. Spence of Saginaw, this Georgian Revival house was built for residents prominent in Saginaw for their successful investments in the sugar beet processing industry. The huge, completely modern, red brick house is on a spacious site that runs back to Lake Linton. It has a carefully balanced facade, asymmetrical fenestration with bays at the rear, dormers in the gabled and hipped roof, and square chimneys. Poured concrete walls are veneered with brick. The sunny interior rooms are arranged around a large central hall with an open staircase. They are exquisitely finished with fireplaces and painted wood paneling. Servants' quarters stand in a separate wing that projects to the rear of the house. A five-car garage is behind the house. Open to public.

SA05.4 **Saginaw Water Works**

1926–1929; Victor André Matteson, architect; Hoad, Decker, Shoecraft and Drury, engineers. late 1960s, addition, McNamee, Porter and Seeley. 522 Ezra Rust Dr. (northwest corner of Ezra Rust Dr. and South Washington Ave.)

The surprising Collegiate Gothic styling makes this waterworks look more like a stone-clad university building than a water treatment facility. The waterworks purifies and pumps

SA05.4 Saginaw Water Works

cold water taken originally from the Saginaw River but, since 1949, from an intake at Whitestone Point on Lake Huron to the city and surrounding communities. Victor André Matteson, a Chicago architect noted for water plant designs, created the beautiful and functional architecture for the Saginaw Water Works. The three interconnected structures, clothed and arranged inside and out in the Collegiate Gothic motif, stand in the center of Ezra Rust Park, near a small lake.

The buttressed central tower contains a 125,000-gallon steel water tank that stores water used to backwash the filters. Beneath the tower is the vestibule and cross-vaulted lobby, and to the rear are the administrative offices and laboratories. The east wing houses the gallery of eighteen filters, whose operating tables are made of Italian green serpentine marble topped with polished Belgian black marble. The west wing holds the pumping station. The treatment section is at the rear.

Matteson subsequently designed waterworks modeled after the Saginaw plant in Cedar Rapids, Iowa, in 1926–1929 and in Fort Wayne, Indiana, in 1931–1935.

SA06 East Saginaw Commercial District

North Washington St. between Johnson and Federal

SA06.1 Bancroft-Eddy Building (Hoyt Block)

1870–1871, John Wrege, builder. 1894, upper addition, Cooper and Beckbissinger. 100 North Washing-

ton St. (Michigan 13) (northeast corner of North Washington and Genesee streets)

The impressive, six-story, limestone commercial building designed and built by John Wrege, of Saginaw, provided choice locations for shops at the first-floor level and for professional offices above. The building is ornamented by quoins, delicate stringcourses that link the windows horizontally, and a crowning bracketed cornice. As the windows rise in the walls they change from rectangular to segmental to round arched—all with ornamental surrounds and hoods. The Brancroft-Eddy Building is a fine example of the use of the Round Arch mode for commercial and industrial building during the second half of the nineteenth century. Today it is adaptively reused for apartments.

SA06.2 Second National Bank

1925, Smith, Hinchman and Grylls. Northwest corner of North Washington (Michigan 13) and Genesee streets

Modeled after the Buhl Building in Detroit, the bank indicates Saginaw's position as the center of trade and commerce for the Saginaw Valley. It is a typical early skyscraper with an eclectic application of historical detail. Large, arched windows admit light to the banking room in the three-story base of the building that occupies the lower portion of the building. The nine-story tower above holds offices. The arcaded upper stories have three floors of windows behind a row of columns. A cornice projects at the roof. The top arcade and corbeled cornice are Romanesque.

SA06.3 Michigan Bell Building (Michigan Bell Telephone Company Office Building)

1929–1930, Smith, Hinchman and Grylls. 309 South Washington Ave. (Michigan 13) (southwest corner of South Washington Ave. and Janes St.)

The Michigan Bell Telephone Company's Saginaw office building was erected in 1930 to serve as headquarters for the northern part of the Lower Peninsula and to house new automatic dial telephone equipment for this central mid-Michigan district. Michigan Bell prided itself on it construction of fine buildings to enhance the communities that it served. Between 1925 and 1930 it erected forty-five new, practical, and attractive buildings. The Saginaw office was among the largest and most imposing. Termed "a modern American style of architecture," the squat, eight-story building is one of the few Art Deco structures in Saginaw.[53] It was constructed to be fireproof; gray limestone clads its concrete and brick skeleton with steel reinforcement. Its sturdy construction, reinforced by seventy-four cement footings buried 18 to 22 feet underground and by seventy-four reinforced steel columns, supported the installation of heavy machinery and could accommodate the addition of three more stories. The top two stories are set back and crested—almost crenelated—with low-relief chevrons. This building and a 1974 addition still house all of Michigan Bell's equipment for the Saginaw Valley Region.

FRANKENMUTH

Fifteen immigrants from Neuendettelsau, Germany, arrived in the Saginaw area in July 1845. They acquired land for a mission on the Cass River in present-day Frankenmuth and established a settlement. During 1846 eighty more settlers arrived, and in less than a decade more than a hundred cabins, homes, shops, and farmhouses had been built. With the abundant pine forests in the area, logging became the community's first major industry at the time of the Civil War. The forest areas were exhausted in fifteen years, however, and the village, whose population included builders, farmers, millers, blacksmiths, brewers, and butchers, began to develop in new ways. By 1900, eight cheese factories, the area's first woolen mill, several sausage factories, a brewery, mills such as the Star of the West Milling Company, an insurance company, a bank,

and four hotels that by 1895 already were serving the town's famous chicken dinners, could be found in this German community. Frankenmuth has remained an agricultural center, a popular tourist destination, and the residence of people working in Saginaw and Flint. Although many buildings have been hidden by fantasy Bavarian ornamentation that has come to be a Frankenmuth trademark, other buildings remain intact and reflect the community's past.

SA07 Frankenmuth Bavarian Inn

1888. 1957, renovations, Mr. Leder of Chicago. 1969, Glenn M. Beach and Doc Waters (Clarence L. Waters ?). 1970–1987, interior renovations, Glenn Beach. 1978, bridge addition, Milton S. Graton of Ashland, New Hampshire. 713 South Main St. (northeast corner of River and South Main streets)

Theodore Fischer, a former bartender at the Exchange Hotel (now Zehnder's Restaurant), established the Union House Hotel in 1888. The William Zehnder, Sr., family, distant relatives of Fischer and descendants of nineteenth-century German immigrants, purchased the restaurant in 1950 and continued serving chicken dinners. Inspired by a family trip back to Bavaria in the 1950s, the Zehnders extensively renovated, enlarged, and redecorated the restaurant in 1959 in a fantasy Bavarian theme. In 1971 William ("Tiny") Zehnder even sent Glenn M. Beach to Bavaria to inspect its architecture with an eye toward reproducing it in Frankenmuth. The Bavarian Inn's motif, accented by a 50-foot-high glockenspiel, echoes Frankenmuth's German heritage. Behind the inn a replica of a nineteenth-century wooden covered bridge known as the Holz-Brücke spans the Cass River.

SA08 Saint Lorenz Lutheran Church

1879–1880, C. W. Griese. 1965–1967, addition and remodeling, Merritt Cole and McCallum. 10145 West Tuscola (northwest corner of Mayer and West Tuscola streets)

The broached spired tower of this rose brick Gothic Revival German Lutheran church rises 163 feet over the flat farmland and is visible for miles. The church has a nave, transepts, and an apse. Pointed arches mark all three original portals of the south facade. The buttressed and corbeled brick exterior walls are pierced with Gothic windows. A double arcaded balcony sweeps around three sides of the nave, and huge stained-glass windows line the chancel and transepts. In 1965–1967 the nave was extended to accommodate 1,400 worshippers, east and west porches were added, and the church was remodeled and repaired.

TAYMOUTH TOWNSHIP

A watershed for the Birch Run, Pine Run, Silver Creek, and Flint rivers, Taymouth Township began lumbering at the same time as Saginaw to the north. The township was established in 1842.

SA09 Saint Paul's Episcopal Mission

1874. Seymour Rd., south of East Burt Rd.

The little wooden church recalls the lumbering heyday of the nineteenth century. Its charming vernacular interpretation of Gothic-inspired church design, complete with board-and-batten siding, pointed-arch windows, and open bell tower accents a small hill overlooking the Flint River. It is an archetypal example of the small bellcote type church-

recommended by Richard Upjohn for communities on the frontier.

BURT, TAYMOUTH TOWNSHIP

SA10 Burt Opera House

1891. 12888 Nichols Rd.

Wellington R. Burt (b. 1831) was an important figure in the lumber industry of the Saginaw Valley. As a large stockholder in the Cincinnati, Saginaw and Mackinaw Railroad, he made certain that a section of the line passed through Burt, a Taymouth Township settlement named after him. The railroad arrived in 1888. In 1891 Burt directed that construction begin on this small, red brick opera house embellished with brick quoins and topped with a clipped gable roof end. The front porch was added later. By 1892 Burt had requested the support of Taymouth Township voters on his bid for a state senate seat on the Democratic ticket. Although he won this election, he could never parlay this support into countywide backing for higher office; Burt lost his 1900 race for U.S. Representative from the Eighth District.

Midland County (MD)

MIDLAND

Midland is a precious example of a small town, far from major lines of communication, that grew up with a sense of itself in relation to an international perspective. The self-reliance that characterizes a small town struggled with importations from the world at large. Although it began in a traditional way, as traders at mid-century and later lumbermen displaced Chippewa Indians and set up a community at "the forks," where two rivers and several trails converged, by 1900 it was part of a world chemical industry. The building stock before the turn of the century is representative of traditional styles and construction methods of the period. But something in the ground was to produce unexpected changes in the physical appearance of the town.

The presence of brine in wells drilled as early as 1878 drew the young Herbert H. Dow (1866–1930) to set up a process that extracted bromine and chlorine from the brine. A driving commitment to experiment and expansion led Dow to build his own large, picturesque home in 1899 and to take on the German bromine cartel in 1903. (The Herbert H. Dow House at 1038 West Main Street is a National Historic Landmark.) The choice was made early to take the extraordinary resources derived from international business and make the town a beautiful place in which to live and bring up families. Schools, churches, parks, and tree-lined streets are combined according to suburban ideals generated at the same time as the chemical company. The company town, downwind from the ever-enlarging chemical works, developed a "garden city" ambience of distinctive houses set in cultivated nature. The garden-industrial complex brings conflicting forces together in a striking way.[54]

MD01 Midland County Courthouse

1925–1926, Bloodgood Tuttle. 1958, southeast addition, Alden B. Dow. 1979, rear addition, Robert E. Schwartz and Associates. 301 West Main St.

In the 1920s county voters approved three bond issues for a total sum of $180,000 to construct a new courthouse replacing the first, a small, frame structure built in 1856. Herbert H. Dow, founder of Dow Chemical Company, offered to assist in financing the building if he were allowed a free hand in the selection of architect, artist, and design. The result was a county courthouse unique in Michigan, and one described at the time of its opening in January 1926 as reflecting a "modified Tudor" or "Tudor country house" style.

The courthouse is a low, two- and three-story building with stone walls, half-timbered and stuccoed gable ends, hipped roofs sheathed in orange, red, and tan clay tiles, and dormer windows breaking the cornice lines. It is distinctive for the residential appearance that Bloodgood Tuttle of Detroit and Cleveland created and for its softly glistening exterior wall murals painted by Paul Honoré of Detroit. The murals, executed with thick layers of a new material—"Magnesite Stucco," developed in the Dow Company laboratories and applied with a palette knife—depict various human forms, pine trees, and abstracted backgrounds. The key interior public space, the second circuit courtroom, is highlighted by a segmental-arch vaulted ceiling, walnut woodwork and dais screen, and an additional mural by the building's artist. The large, cross-shaped addition to the southeast side of the courthouse and the later, three-story addition to the back both blend well with the original courthouse because of the careful use of sympathetic building materials and designs.

MD02 Alden B. Dow Studio and Home

1934–1941, Alden B. Dow. 315 Post St. (Post St. off of Main St., 6 blocks northwest of the intersection of Main St. and Michigan 20)

Alden Dow's own studio, placed along a stream and a plum grove in the parklike garden of his father's house, opened his career with the most beautiful expression of his picturesque architecture. Asymmetrical forms, richly patterned copper roofs, and one-foot-square concrete blocks wander through carefully selected foliage and along the controlled stream. The lowest room actually sits 18 inches in the water! The residence added in 1940 is elevated to gain privacy. Although Dow (1904–1982) apprenticed with Frank Lloyd Wright in the summer of 1933, the lyrical composition of his studio and home is very much his own.

MD03 Post Street Archives (Post Street School)

1870. 205 Post St. (north side between Main St. and Dow Pond)

The Post Street School is a small, red brick building modernized into a hybrid of late nineteenth- and early twentieth-century architectural features, including a corner tower with a steeply hipped roof and finial and a projecting front bay with pedimented gable end, a denticulated cornice line, and multipaned, leaded glass windows in bow-arch enframements. Once a more typical school building of the day, it was the institution at which Grace A. Ball, later the wife of Herbert H. Dow, taught. Through the generosity of the Dow family, it became Midland's Little Theatre in the 1930s and today is the Post Street Archives, containing the records of the Dow Chemical and Dow Corning companies and the papers of Herbert and Willard Dow.

MD04 John and Ranny Reicker House

1961, Alden B. Dow. 3211 Valley Dr. (Valley Dr. intersects Orchard Dr. north of Main St. and 1 block northwest of Post St.)

The Reicker house testifies to Alden Dow's skill at composing simple surfaces and intriguing detail thirty years after his earliest work. The three-level grid of the ceiling structure makes the ordinary function of roofing a house an ornamental delight. Light poles transform the geometry of woodworking into an organic form. Brick walls topped by wooden structure provide another combination for the architect to compose in balanced contrasts.

MD05 **Benjamin F. Bradley House**

1874. 1969, moved. Upper Emerson Park, southeast of the intersection of West Main St. and Cook Rd.

Benjamin Bradley (1843–1922), who moved to Midland from New York State in 1866, owned both grocery and dry goods stores. The enterprises were prosperous and allowed their owner to engage in other activities. Bradley devoted himself to local political affairs, serving, for example, as postmaster in Midland for fifteen years and at other times as president of the village council, alderman, ward supervisor, and member of the board of education. In business, he became president of the Midland Publishing Company and founder of an insurance company, Bradley and Arbury. Bradley's Gothic Revival cottage is a large, two-story, frame structure measuring 40 feet by 40 feet in plan. It includes such typical design features as ogee-shaped porch friezes, Gothic-arch windows, and multiple gables with fanciful bargeboards. In 1969 a local historical group raised funds to save the home from demolition and move it into Emerson Park, on the Tittabawassee River.

The home is restored and serves as a local museum.

MD06 **John S. Whitman House**

1934, Alden B. Dow. 2407 Manor Dr. (Manor Dr. intersects Helen Dr. on its west end, which intersects Eastman [Business US 10])

The compact intricacy of this seven-level house won it the grand prize for residential architecture in the Paris Exposition of 1936. The concrete blocks, called unit blocks, were manufactured by Whitman's company. The interplay of high and low spaces on the inside is matched by the composition of the block walls, plaster planes, and window bands on the outside. The cubic complement to the free extension of Dow's own studio and house, the Whitman house similarly reflects the architect's adaptation of Wrightian influence.

MD07 **Bertha E. R. Strosaker Memorial Presbyterian Church**

1953, Aymar Embury II. 1310 Ashman St. (southeast corner Ashman and Reardon streets, 6 blocks northeast of Indian/Business US 10)

Although Alden Dow was asked if he would design a "colonial" church, he declined, and a New York architect, who worked with a New York contractor, designed this "American Georgian" church of brick and limestone for 550 worshippers as a memorial to the sister of a member of the Dow Chemical Board. The dominant portico has Corinthian columns of solid Indiana limestone 24 feet high, 3 feet in diameter, and weighing 14

MD02 Alden B. Dow Studio and Home

tons each. The building has a three-stage asymmetrical tower. (Continue southwest on Ashman to reach West Larkin, then northeast to reach MD08, First United Methodist Church.)

MD08 **First United Methodist Church**

1947–1950, Alden B. Dow. 315 West Larkin (northeast corner of West Larkin and Jerome [Michigan 20] streets)

The First Methodist Church, as it was known when it was dedicated in 1950, employs a simplified geometry of brick planes topped by wide copper bands that Alden Dow used extensively after World War II, particularly in public buildings. It was given an Award of Merit by the American Institute of Architects in 1956. High spaces contrasting with low ones continue his earlier expressions of spatial variation, but with a more generalized vocabulary than was used in private residences. Geometric complexity appears in stained-glass windows along the side aisles and with outstanding effect in the chapel to the right of the entrance.

MD09 **Tridge**

1981, Gilbert/Commonwealth Engineers. Confluence of the Chippewa and Tittabawassee rivers

This unique pedestrian bridge connects three major land areas currently divided by the confluence of the Chippewa and Tittabawassee rivers. Radiating from a single center pier, each span is 300 feet from midstream to land. The Tridge is constructed of treated timbers. Uncongested access to a variety of activities previously inconvenient to reach is gained by the Tridge. It was the inspiration of Carl and Esther Gerstacker.

Bay County (BY)

BAY CITY

Before 1830, Bay City suffered a bad reputation. Settlers avoided the area because they had heard of its impenetrable forests and insect-infested river swamps. Timber speculators did not need astute business sense, however, to see that these same dense forests and watery surroundings made Bay City a prime target for lumbering. Bay City stands on both sides of the Saginaw River, a naturally wide, deep, navigable river, which drained over 8,000 square miles of, at the time of settlement, timberland. Starting in 1837, sawmills proliferated and workers arrived. By 1859 Bay City had growing salt and shipbuilding industries to complement its lumbering, was formally established as a village, and had the homes, shops, schools, churches, and roads that attracted settlers. By 1870 more than 7,000 people lived in the city, and

the area's lumber boom began in earnest. Fortunes were made and reflected in the fine homes, business blocks, and civic improvements of the community. Unfortunately, at the turn of the century, Bay City's 30,000 residents suddenly faced a declining lumber industry. However, businessmen and financiers exercised the same speculative skills that had carved the city from the swamps in the 1840s. They developed sugar beets as the new basis for the area's economy, and factories were retooled to produce sugar, animal feed, and high-proof spirits. Lumbermen turned their stripped acreage into farmland; coal was discovered; iron foundries, knitting mills, gristmills, canning factories, brickyards, and woodenware manufacturers sprang up. Compared to many other Michigan communities, Bay City's transition into the twentieth century was a success.

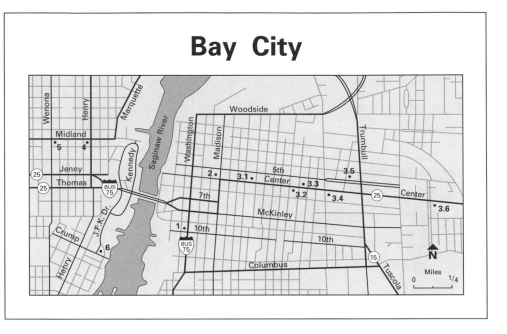

Bay City

BY01 Bay City Hall

1894–1897, Leverett A. Pratt and Walter Koeppe. 301 Washington St. (Business I-75) (northwest corner of Washington [Business I-75] and 10th streets)

Led by Alderman Kroeneke, voters approved in 1889 a bond issue to erect a modern new building to satisfy the needs of a growing and

prosperous city. They conceived of an office for all time, "a building whose capacity and convenience could never be overtaxed and which would be both a credit and an ornament to the city."[55] The Bay City Hall is a massive and magnificent public monument designed in the Richardsonian Romanesque style made famous by H. H. Richardson. It has wide rounded arches, deeply recessed windows, and a multigabled red-tiled roof. Its corner clock and bell tower soars 180 feet

BY01b Bay City Hall (stairs)

above the east bank of the Saginaw River in a gesture of civic spirit and pride. The city hall is constructed of granite and of light grayish yellowish brown Berea sandstone quarried at Amherst, Ohio. Inside, a grand atrium extends from the ground floor some 65 feet to a huge skylight. A grand staircase with an elaborately scrolled cast-iron banister rises through all four floors of the building. The interior offers a rich display of ornamental metal and woodwork.

Designed by Leverett A. Pratt (b. 1849) and Walter Koeppe (d. 1912) of Bay City, the city hall cost $164,000 to build. On March 22, 1897, the mayor described the new building as, "Beautiful in conception, artistic and finished to its smallest detail, convenient in arrangement, and admirably adapted to every need of the public service, it leaves nothing to be desired." The building was restored during the late 1970s and remains today one of the last grand old city halls in the state still serving as the seat of city government.

BY02 Bay County Building

1931–1934, Joseph C. Goddeyne. 515 Center Ave. (Michigan 25) (northwest corner of Center and Madison avenues)

The Bay County Building was the special project of Samuel G. Houghton, a popular county circuit court judge. It was developed during the depression as a county-funded

project meant to relieve local unemployment problems. In 1931 voters authorized the Bay County Board of Supervisors to raise $375,000 for a county courthouse. The new building replaced a sixty-eight-year-old brick Italianate structure created by C. K. Porter of Buffalo, New York. This one was designed by Joseph C. Goddeyne (1889–1964), a prominent Bay City architect.

The county building is a massive, eight-story, sharply rectilinear structure on a weighted base. Piers rise up the entire face, creating a strong vertical emphasis, and the upper stories are stepped back. Its steel frame is sheathed in limestone and granite. Its Art Deco styling is a clean and functional departure from the revival styles popularly used at the time for governmental structures in Michigan and elsewhere. The building's interior is intact, maintaining its original Art Deco detailing and many of its furnishings. Of special interest is the entry foyer, with its painted ceiling fascia and engraved brass elevator doors and the fourth-floor circuit courtroom, with its original oak wainscoting, balcony, and relief plaster wall sculptures.

BY03 Center Avenue (Michigan 25)

1870–1929. Center Ave. (Michigan 25) between Madison and Green streets

Bay City in the 1870s was a lumber boom town with a citywide housing shortage. Wealthy businessmen needing housing for their families and an opportunity to display their fortunes sought a new area of town in which to build. Platted as a broad east-west thoroughfare linked with the commercial district along the east side of the Saginaw River, Center Avenue proved to be the most appealing. The avenue's history is associated closely to the families who pioneered the area's lumber, salt, coal, and sugar beet industries. Its sixty-year continuum of fine architecture includes examples of all the major Victorian and revival styles and illustrates that Bay City weathered the turn-of-the-century economic upheaval, when virtually all lumber-based industries foundered and a new economy based on sugar beets and coal was born.

BY03.1 Trinity Episcopal Church

1885–1887, Philip C. Floeter. 1896, rectory. 1924, parish house, Smith, Hinchman and Grylls. 911 Center Ave. (Michigan 25)

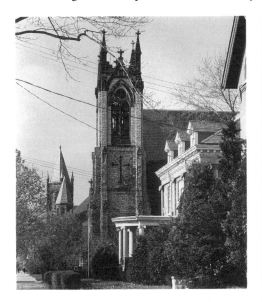

The Gothic Revival Trinity Episcopal Church displays typical asymmetrical massing, window tracery, and a square, buttressed and pinnacled corner tower. Rough-faced Bay Port limestone is laid in the exterior walls. The cruciform-plan interior has reredoses carved in 1923 by Alois Lang, a Grand Rapids craftsman and artist born in Oberammergau, Germany. The church building proper was designed by Philip C. Floeter (b. 1849) of Bay City. From Chatham, Ontario, he came to the United States in 1863 and to Bay City in 1881 to work in the office of E. W. Arnold. In 1886 Floeter designed the Madison Avenue Methodist Church, also Gothic Revival, but built of the locally manufactured yellow brick commonly used in this area. In 1924, a small chapel on the north of Trinity Episcopal Church was connected to the church and adapted for use as a parish house designed by Smith, Hinchman and Grylls. It includes an auditorium and guild room.

BY03.2 Frederick Bradley House? Selwyn Eddy House?

1887–1889. 1400 Center Ave. (Michigan 25) (southeast corner Center and Lincoln avenues)

The house and carriage house epitomized the wooden Queen Anne lumber baron's house. It approaches in size and detail, though not in design, the Charles Hackley and Perry Hannah houses in Muskegon and Traverse City.

BY03.2 Frederick Bradley House? Selwyn Eddy House?

BY03.3 Fremont B. and Addie McCormick Chesbrough House

1890–1891. 1515 Center Ave. (Michigan 25) (northwest corner of Center Ave. and McLellan St.)

This heavily massed picturesque house was built for Fremont B. Chesbrough, another Bay City lumberman. One of the largest and most unusual houses on Center Avenue, the exterior walls are brick and stone; each room of the interior, however, displays different woods. The house epitomizes the late nineteenth-century interest in the natural qualities of materials: rough stone, brick, slate, terracotta, and various unpainted woods.

BY03.4 William Sharp, Jr., House

1918, Aladdin Company. 2130 Center Ave. (Michigan 25)

This "readi-cut" mail-order home was manufactured by the Aladdin Company, the Bay City brainchild of William J. and Otto Sovereign. William Sharp, Jr., a sales manager for Aladdin, selected this stately and strong country house design called "The Villa" from the company catalog. It was one of the most elaborate houses available. The center en-

BY03.4 William Sharp, Jr., House

trance of the symmetrical hipped-roof house has dignified columns. Pergola-like wings flank the main block. Windows of the lower level are grouped in twos and threes beneath broad arcades.

BY03.5 Otto Sovereign House

c. 1912–1914, Aladdin Company. 2157 Fifth St.

The general manager of North American Construction Company, later the Aladdin Company, built for himself this "readi-cut" home called "The Brentwood." The gabled house is marked by diamond-paned casement windows, a second-story balcony, a hooded entrance, and pergola porte-cochère. Other examples of Aladdin Homes are "The Winthrop" at 1414 Fifth Street and "The Lamberton" at 2138 Fifth Street. The former is characterized by its low, one-story gabled form with bracketed eave supports and shingles; the latter, by its steep gabled roof with exposed rafters, stucco walls, hooded front entrance, and pergola side porch.

BY03.6 Temple Israel

1961, Alden B. Dow. 2300 Center Ave. (Michigan 25) (southeast corner of Center Ave. and Green St.)

A long, low, Frank Lloyd Wright-inspired design was executed by Alden Dow for Temple Israel, a product of the merger of several Bay City Jewish congregations. The school and office wing is a sweep of brick wall set under wide eaves; the sanctuary is at the rear. The sanctuary and social hall, both rhomboidal in plan, are separated by movable partitions. The prayer hall features a large ark and platform set into one corner of the room—the corner of which is fashioned of a concrete grid into which colored glass blocks are set. The blues and purples of the windows complement the soft greens of the interior.

BY04 Midland Street Commercial District

1860s–1929. Midland St. between Catharine and Litchfield

From the very start, the Midland Street Commercial District, on the west side of the Saginaw River, was in competition with Bay City's central business district on the east bank. The original settlement here, begun in the 1860s and known first as Wenona and later as West Bay City, boasted such prominent citizens as Henry W. Sage and John McGraw, whose west-side lumber mill became one of the world's largest by the end of the century. For a while its population growth kept pace with Bay City's. Its street system, many of its shops and homes, its schools, churches, and civic amenities compared favorably with those across the river. But in spite of its healthy growth, West Bay City was outstripped in the 1880s and 1890s, and in 1903 was consolidated with its rival across the Saginaw River into one municipal unit. A compact area, four blocks long, on Midland Street, was West Bay City's commercial showpiece. Its small two- and three-story commercial blocks, capped with heavy cornices and frequently embellished with awnings and flags, displayed good, though basic, examples of Queen Anne, Italianate, Romanesque, and later, Georgian Revival, Chicago School, and Art Deco styling. Today, private and public investments along Midland Street are creating a preservation success story; while the district's individual buildings are modest, its newly revitalized reflection of nineteenth- and early twentieth-century commercial life is worth seeing.

BY05 Sage Library (Bay County Library System—Sage Branch)

1882–1884, Leverett A. Pratt and Walter Koeppe. 1983–1984, restoration, John T. Meyer of Wigen, Tinknell, Meyer and Associates. 100 East Midland St. (southeast corner of East Midland St. and Wenona)

In the early 1860s Henry W. Sage (1814–1897) came to Bay City from Connecticut by way of Ithaca, New York. With his business partner, John McGraw, he established what would become the city's largest lumber mill. Sage lived and worked in West Bay City and was known for his financial and business acumen, as well as his generous philanthropic pursuits, the most lasting of which was the construction of a library (free public library, reading room, and debating room) and a collection of 10,000 books. (As Alexander Agassiz returned copper profits to Harvard and the city of Boston, Sage's success in the lumber business benefitted Cornell). Sage wanted the library to play a role in producing "a higher intellectual and richer and truer social development in the community." The library was designed by Pratt and Koeppe, Bay City's best-known architectural firm. At the time of its dedication, on January 16, 1884, the building was called "a bewildering mixture of styles termed modern architecture." Its Ruskinian appearance makes it High Victorian, but some of its major features, such as the round arches and the corbeling, are Romanesque. Its polychromatic exterior walls are of red brick, with buff brick and Amherst blue stone trim. They display reverse corbeling, a quatrefoil, a sculpture niche, a polygonal bay, and dormers. The first floor holds classrooms; the second, the reading room with an octagonal bay window and fireplace enframed in ceramic tile. The library cost $50,000. The elegant grounds contain a beautiful Victorian fountain depicting Leda and the Swan cast by Mott Foundry of New York. The library remains in full use today as a branch of the Bay County Library System.

BY06 Mader and Joseph Tromble House (Center House)

1835–1837, Nathan C. Case, builder. Veterans' Park (off Michigan 25, west of Saginaw River)

The Tromble house was a wayside stop for the traders and land speculators who ventured into the Bay City area and surrounding wilderness before its settlement. Mader and Joseph Tromble, French-Canadian fur traders, arrived here in the early 1830s. They built this two-story, wood-frame and clapboard-sheathed structure on the east side of the river; it contained their living quarters, trading post, and inn. With the exception of the addition of a lean-to kitchen, the building retains its original form. Threatened by redevelopment, the house was moved from its original site to Veterans' Park, on the west side of the river. It is undergoing restoration.

MONITOR TOWNSHIP

BY07 Trinity Lutheran Church

1897. 20 East Salzburg Rd. (southeast corner of Eight Mile and Salzburg roads)

Descendants and members of the German colony that established Frankenlust settled Monitor Township. They cleared their lands of timber, and with their profits established sugar beet farms. They built this rural yellow brick Gothic Revival church. The Trinity Lutheran Church bears the inscription: EV LUTH DREIEINIGKEITS KIRCHE V.A.C. AD 1897. It has pointed-arch windows, buttresses, and stone finials at every outcropping. The entry and bell tower terminate in an open octagonal drum and, in turn, a huge steeple visible for miles around. The entry porch is a recent addition. The interior features vertical board wainscoting and an apse flanked by paired pilasters with Corinthian capitals. The semicircular dome above the altar is blue-green with gold leaf, with stained-glass windows below.

The fine brick houses in the township, such as those at 517 Salzburg, 4117 Mackinaw, 3565 Seven Mile, and 1907 Midland roads, reflect the prosperity of this German-settled area, established in 1869. They exhibit a sturdy Queen Anne-inspired design highlighted by red or yellow brick construction with contrasting brick quoins and band courses.

Flint

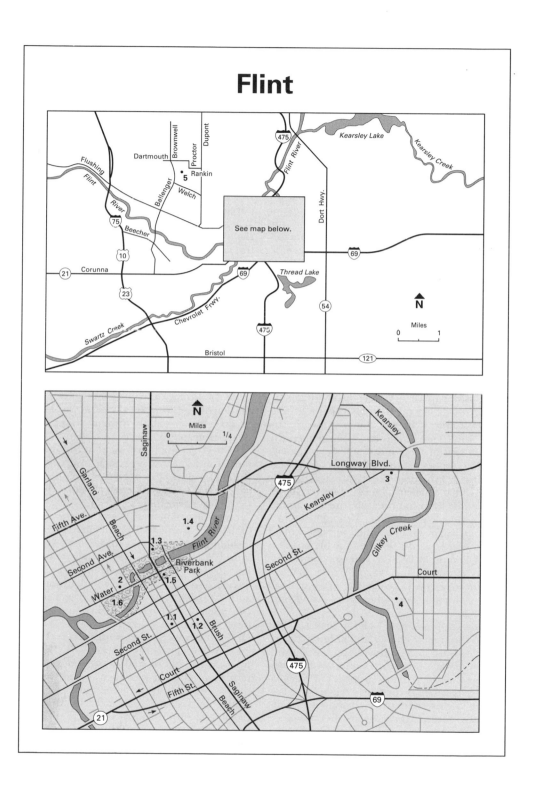

Genesee County   (GS)

FLINT

Jacob Smith was the first Euro-American to venture into the Flint area, establishing a trading post in 1811. After the peaceful signing of the 1819 Saginaw Treaty that transferred Chippewa lands to the United States government, he built a permanent cabin on the north bank of the Flint River near a crossing that the Indians had traversed for centuries. Around this key crossing Flint began to grow. By 1830 the first tavern, sawmill, gristmill, and several houses were built. When the Saginaw Turnpike between Detroit and Saginaw opened in 1833, crossing the Flint River at the "Grand Traverse," early settlers from New York State, New England, and Oakland County began to arrive in greater numbers. During the decades of the 1830s, 1840s, and 1850s, a blacksmith shop, a brick school, a post office, hotels, churches, additional grist and sawmills, a woolen mill, and a potash soap factory were established and built. A stage line ran to Pontiac; even a circus was hosted in 1846.

By 1860 Flint, which had been named the county seat in 1838 and established as a city in 1855, was well into its short-lived lumbering era, which lasted only from 1850 to the early 1880s. Lumbering seemed merely a prelude to the more important business of horse-drawn vehicle production. Although the first carriage works was established in Flint around 1850, vehicle production became big business only when the William A. Paterson Company, James Whiting's Flint Wagon Works, William C. Durant's and J. Dallas Dort's Flint Road Cart Company, and other firms came onto the scene.

Flint was proclaimed "The Vehicle City" by 1905, when more than 150,000 horse-drawn vehicles were made annually by the Durant-Dort Carriage Company alone. With skilled workers, physical plant, suppliers of raw materials, distributors for finished products, and plenty of investment capital available, Flint made a natural transition to motor vehicle production in the early twentieth century. This transition also caused Flint's population to explode from 13,000 in 1900 to 157,000 in 1930 and changed its physical appearance from that of a small nineteenth-century town

to that of a wealthy twentieth-century industrial center. Two, or perhaps three model automobiles had already been assembled in Flint before A. B. C. Hardy began production of the Flint Roadster at his Flint Automobile Company facility in 1902.

Flint's most famous car, however, was the Buick. Although David Dunbar Buick had developed his car in Detroit, in 1903 James Whiting, of the Flint Wagon Works, bought the Buick Motor Car Company and moved it to Flint. By early July of 1904 a new model was finished, and on August 13 of that year the first production vehicle was completed. The company suffered financial troubles until William C. (Billy) Durant assumed control, made the Buick one of the nation's best-selling cars, and used it as the foundation for the establishment of the General Motors Company in 1908.

The Chevrolet car also achieved its first real production success in Flint. Buick race driver Louis Chevrolet developed and started production of his Chevrolet Classic Six in Detroit. In 1911, however, Billy Durant became Chevrolet's principle financial backer and moved the Chevrolet operation to Flint. Production started in 1912 and was such a success that Durant used the company to regain the control he had lost over General Motors during expansion difficulties.

Eventually, more than twenty different kinds of motorized vehicles were made in Flint, not including the military vehicles used during World Wars I and II. Many other industries manufactured products related to the automobile, and these firms clustered around the auto factories. Thus, in addition to Durant, Dort, Buick, and Chevrolet, Flint's auto-based history soon included such men as William C. Orwell, Charles Stewart Mott, Albert Champion, Walter P. Chrysler, Harry H. Bassett, Enos A. DeWaters, and many more. While the image of Flint has been tarnished over the past decades, it is a community that once battled Detroit for supremacy in the automobile industry. Its attractive areas of workers' housing, fine neighborhoods of management's homes, high-style downtown buildings, public and cultural facilities, and active auto manufacturing complexes speak of how close it came to winning the battle.

GS01 **Flint Central Business District**

1870–present. Roughly bounded by the Flint River, Harrison St., Temporary I-69, and Church St. on the south side of the Flint River, and by East Second Ave., the Flint River, and North Saginaw St. on the north side of the river

After Jacob Smith built his cabin on the north side of the Flint River around 1820, John and Polly Todd opened a tavern on the south side, in what soon grew to be the first portion of Flint's central business district. Commercial growth centered on the south side not because it was a more attractive area, but because the land deeded to Jacob Smith and his heirs in the Saginaw Treaty of 1819 remained unsalable due to title problems. Thus, sawmills, gristmills, and handsome wood-frame buildings sprang up to house new commercial and retail activities. By the time the carriage era began in 1880, however, this first generation of buildings had already been lost to fire and redevelopment, being replaced with two- and three-story brick Italianate commercial buildings. Some of these remain today, but they have been modernized beyond recognition. Fortunately, several noncommercial remnants from the two early eras still stand. To the north of the Flint River, buildings from the late nineteenth and early twentieth centuries reflect construction undertaken only after the title problems with the Smith land had been unraveled.

Today Flint's downtown presents an early twentieth-century streetscape. While marred by recent low-quality rehabilitation efforts and urban blight that have left almost no retail commercial facade intact, a heritage made possible by the wealth generated through the automobile industry is still reflected in its banks, theaters, fraternal halls, and governmental buildings.

GS01.1 **Flint Elks Lodge Building**

1913–1914, Malcolmson and Higginbotham. 142 West Second St. (northeast corner of West Second and Beach streets)

The Lodge Number 222 of the Benevolent and Protective Order of Elks was organized in Flint in 1891. It occupied temporary rented quarters until 1914, when its membership reached one thousand and it built this temple. Malcolmson and Higginbotham of Detroit designed the two-and-a-half-story, symmetrical, red brick club building in a simplified version of the Renaissance Revival style. A decorative frieze runs beneath the truncated and tiled hipped roof. The lodge hall contained game rooms, lodge rooms, and offices on the main floor; an assembly room and banquet hall on the top floor; and bowling alleys, handball courts, and dining rooms on the ground floor. H. V. Snyder and Son Company of Battle Creek built it. The structure cost $84,000. At its dedication on December 18, 1914, the *Flint Daily Journal* reported that visiting Elks proclaimed the building the finest Elks clubhouse in Michigan.

GS01.2 **Capitol Theater Building**

1927–1928, John Eberson. 140 East Second St. (southwest corner of East Second and Harrison streets)

The Capitol Theater and its arcade of offices and stores is designed in a fantasy of the "Hispano-Italian style of the 15th century."[56] The Flint Building Corporation and Walter S. Butterfield, owner and developer of a string of what were by then seventy-five Michigan theaters, organized as the Capitol Building Company. Their purpose was to erect cooperatively this block-long structure. Noted theater designer John Eberson of Chicago, who originated the "atmospheric" theater, drafted plans for the building. (See DE47, Grand Riviera Theater, p. 95.) The interior of the Capitol Theater was created to give the audience the impression of being seated in an Italian patio. It contains facades of palaces, towers of castles, and a facsimile of an old Italian cathedral window. Beneath its domed sky-blue ceiling twinkling with stars and vibrant with moving fleecy white clouds, the theater seats 2,000. In this luxurious setting Flint theatergoers enjoyed stage and screen entertainment. The exterior of the two- and three-story theater block is clad with buff-colored brick and encrusted with terracotta piers, colonnettes, and roofline crestings. Henry L. VanDerHorst of Kalamazoo was the general contractor for the building. It cost $425,000 to build.

GS01.3 **Northbank Center** (Industrial Savings Bank)

1922–1923, Davis, McGrath and Kiesling. 1986, rehabilitated. 432 Saginaw St. (southeast corner of North Saginaw St. and East Second Ave.)

The Industrial Savings Bank was founded in 1909 as a financial institution to serve north-side merchants and factory workers, but it was later expanded to serve the entire city. Its founders and early officers were a group of automobile magnates, including Walter P. Chrysler, Charles W. Nash, A. B. C. Hardy, and Charles Stewart Mott. According to the *Flint Daily Journal* for December 13, 1923, Davis, McGrath and Kiesling of New York designed this bank after "the ancient Temple of the Winds at Athens." The first four floors and the two upper floors carry Grecian motifs. The twelve-story, steel-frame, reinforced concrete modern eclectic building is sheathed in variegated Indiana limestone and light-colored pressed brick. Its three-story base is delineated by fluted pilasters with foliated capitals. It is crowned with a wide copper cornice, punctuated with anthemions and lions' heads, that projects from the eleventh floor and forms a railing for a promenade that encircles the structure. The lower floors held the bank; the middle floors, offices; and the upper five floors, the club facilities of the Industrial Mutual Association, a benefit society that provided carriage and auto workers with the equivalent of health and life insurance. The Realty Construction Company of Flint built the bank at a cost of nearly $1.5 million. In 1986 it was rehabilitated for offices and retail use.

GS01.4. Industrial Mutual Association Auditorium

1929, Juan de Leonardi Hargrove of Smith, Hinchman and Grylls. 815 East Second Ave.

The large, brown brick stylized Romanesque Revival hall was built by the Industrial Mutual Association, an association of factory workers that provides health and life insurance benefits, educational and recreational opportunities. It seated over 6,200 and cost $1.25 million. Its most distinctive features are the twin round-headed arches under relieving arches and the large band of diamonds beneath the corbeled cornice. In the early 1980s it was adapted for use as Autoworld, a theme park, but that enterprise has closed.

GS01.5 University Pavilion (Waterstreet Pavilion)

1984, The Collaborative, Inc. South Saginaw St. at the Flint River

University Pavilion was a festival marketplace created by James Rouse's Enterprise Development Company. The fanciful metal-and-glass structure marked by a riverfront rotunda filled with shops and restaurants was created to revitalize downtown Flint. Today the University of Michigan–Flint has adaptively reused it for administrative offices, the bookstore, and a food court.

GS01.6 Riverbank Park

late 1970s. Lawrence Halprin and Associates, landscape architects. On the banks of the Flint River between Grand Traverse and Beach streets

The Riverbank Park began with the formation of a small citizens' committee concerned with the U.S. Army Corps of Engineers' plans for flood control on a downtown section of the Flint River. The committee sought a more natural method of flood control and wanted to promote the decaying metropolitan area. Halprin and Associates, an internationally known landscape architecture firm in San Francisco, was hired and citywide citizen workshops were held. Through these "collective creativity" workshops, the community guided the future of Riverbank Park. The park utilizes concrete and plant material in angular and geometric forms. Interest points along the river include the *Archimedes Screw*, a sculptural device that is propelled by water at the falls; two islands; an amphitheater; water walls; a play area; a fish ladder; picnic sites; and sculptures. The park draws hundreds of residents downtown from spring through fall.

GS02 Flint Chamber of Commerce (Durant-Dort Carriage Company Office)

1895–1896. 316 Water St. (northeast corner of Water and Mason streets)

On the north side of the Flint River, once the site of early sawmills, soap works, sash and door factories, textile mills, and carriage works, is the Durant-Dort Carriage Company Office. It is considered to be the 1908 birthplace of General Motors. William Crapo Durant (1861–1949) and J. Dallas Dort (1861–1925) erected the building in 1895, enlarged the roof in 1900, and increased it from two to three stories in 1906, as they transformed the Durant-Dort Carriage Company into one of the nation's largest manufacturers of horse-drawn vehicles and directed the early destiny of Buick.

GS02 Flint Chamber of Commerce (Durant-Dort Carriage Company Office)

The two-and-a-half-story, red brick structure has a hipped roof pierced by pedimented dormers and supported by consoles. It is restored with its early twentieth-century offices and serves as the focal point of what is today called Carriage Town.

GS03 **Applewood** (Charles Stewart Mott Estate)

1916, Herbert E. Davis of Davis, McGrath and Kiesling, architects; William Pitkin, Jr., landscape architect. 1400 East Kearsley St. (southwest corner of East Kearsley St. and Longway Blvd.)

The Charles Stewart Mott House is one of the few auto leaders' houses in Flint that survived the construction of Interstate 475, the development of the Flint Cultural Center along East Kearsley Street between Avon and Walnut, and the urban renewal of the East Street residential area. Located east of the blocks where the other homes once stood, Applewood is a two-and-a-half-story, light brown brick, slate-roofed Neo-Tudor country house. A reflection pool, formal gardens, and a greenhouse; a garage, caretaker's cottage, and a gatehouse; and several low, brick farm buildings complement the house. The twenty-one-room main house reflects the relatively modest, yet comfortable life-style of Mott and his family. The main gallery has marble floors, marble door enframements with broken cornices and decorative finials, and a vaulted ceiling; the living room has full-height wood paneling and a decorative pressed-plaster ceiling. The house was designed by Mott's brother-in-law, Herbert E. Davis of Davis, McGrath and Kiesling of New York City.

Charles Stewart Mott (1875–1973) directed General Motors for sixty years and engaged in local governmental, military, and philanthropic activities. Restoration of the house and garden is under way, with advice from Johnson, Johnson and Roy, Inc. Open on occasion to public, for educational purposes.

GS04 **Woodlawn Park Residential Area**

1920 to present. Roughly bounded by East Court and Beard streets, Linwood Ave., and Woodlawn and Burroughs parks

In the 1920s the automobile industry's explosive growth placed intense pressure on housing. Woodlawn Park was promoted by private developers to house the managers, as well as other Flint professionals. Platted as early as 1911, but not developed until further platted in 1923, the neighborhood was touted as an "exclusive development" of custom-built, brick and half-timbered homes. Two parks also added to the area's appeal. Woodlawn Park, donated to the city by J. Dallas and Marcia Webb Dort, and Burroughs Park, donated by J. Edington and Louise H. Burroughs, are still attractions today in the 50-acre, 115-home neighborhood and help maintain its status as an attractive place to live.

GS05 **Civic Park**

1919–1920; Davis, McGrath and Kiesling, architects; William Pitkin, Jr., landscape architect. Bounded by Welch Blvd., Dartmouth, and DuPont streets, Third Ave., and Brownell Blvd.

Civic Park is a planned neighborhood of automobile workers' houses built almost overnight by the Modern Housing Corporation. This subsidiary of the General Motors Company was incorporated in 1919, during the postwar boom in the auto industry, to build homes in cities where GM had plants. Its

purpose was to house properly workers at Buick, Chevrolet, and Oakland, the present-day Pontiac plants, who had been forced by housing shortages to live in squalid tent colonies and shack towns. The Civic Park neighborhood, together with Chevrolet Park, a similar development of six hundred mass-produced houses erected between 1919 and 1930 just to the south, and other GM facilities is platted on 1,000 acres. The neighborhoods are linked by Chevrolet Avenue to the Chevrolet plants to the south.

Modern Housing Corporation had the DuPont Engineering Company lay out the gently winding streets, wide boulevards, and broad public spaces of Civic Park. It followed plans prepared by William Pitkin, Jr., of Boston. Modern Housing Corporation also built the first one thousand homes here and at Chevrolet Park. To do so, it created under Allan J. Saville, chief engineer, a work camp of bunkhouses, mess halls, commissaries, a narrow-gauge railroad, and sawmills; and it employed forty-six hundred construction workers. Streets, sidewalks, and sewers were laid; and 950 houses were put up in just nine and one-half months. Houses could be purchased for $3,500 to $8,500 with a 5 percent down payment. A worker could choose from twenty-eight one- and two-story, wood or brick models drafted by Davis, McGrath and Kiesling. The most common was a two-bay, two-story Colonial Revival home with stuccoed first-story exterior walls, wood-shingled second-story walls, gambrel roof with gable end to the street, and a wide dormer above each eaves line. The neighborhood has a school, park, and community center. Civic Park is a well-planned community that reflects the economic, political, and social power of a burgeoning automobile company in a post-World War I industrial town. It remains a vital, middle-class neighborhood today, with an active interest in preservation.

FENTON

Although Clark Dibble from New York State was the first to settle along the Shiawassee River at the site of present-day Fenton, Robert Leroy and William Fenton, partners in a Pontiac mercantile business, developed the town site after buying out Dibble in 1836. As the partnership opened the village's first store and spurred other entrepreneurs to build

mills, stores, and hotels in the commercial area and residences nearby, the mill-town period of Fenton's early development was well under way. The arrival of the Detroit and Milwaukee Railroad in 1856 spurred a second period of growth; a fruit-preserving operation, a woolen mill, a tannery, a brewery, a whip-socket factory, and other manufacturing enterprises were added. More plats were opened; two-story brick stores replaced the earlier wood ones downtown, and more elaborate homes sprang up as Fentonville prospered during the last quarter of the nineteenth century. Fenton's third period of growth reflects the overshadowing economic influence of Flint. Fortunately, the city was able to develop new industrial activities, the most important of which was the production of cement, following the discovery of marl deposits in nearby Ponemah and Silver lakes. After coming to a standstill in development during the depression, Fenton introduced many new light industrial activities and actually promoted its role as a "bedroom community" for Flint. It remains a prosperous city with plenty of small-town character, in spite of the loss of its downtown to urban renewal in the 1970s.

GS06 Fenton Community Center

1937–1938, Eliel Saarinen. 150 Leroy St. (northwest corner of Leroy and Ellen streets)

In the heart of this small agricultural and manufacturing village is this gathering place for citizens. The Fenton Community Center came about through the fondness of Mary A. Horton Rackham for Fenton. In December 1936 the Horace H. Rackham and Mary A. Rackham Fund appropriated to the village $200,000 for the construction of a modern structure for recreational, civic, and educational enterprises. The gift included a perpetual endowment of $145,000 for the maintenance and operation of the structure. Horace Rackham (1858–1933) was one of the twelve original stockholders in the Ford Motor Company, and Fenton was the childhood home of his widow, Mary. Internationally known architect Eliel Saarinen of Bloomfield Hills, noted for his design of Cranbrook, with his son Eero as consultant, designed the community center. The tan brick structure is a crisp and clean design that stands on the banks of the Shiawassee River. The plan measures 60 feet

GS06 Fenton Community Center

served as landscape architect for the 3-acre site.

GS07 **Fenton Seminary**

1868. 1900, rebuilt. 309 High St. (southeast corner of High and State streets)

From atop a hill, appropriate to the lofty status of a school for young women but within walking distance of the business center of the village, the Fenton Seminary overlooks the village of Fenton. Rosina L. Dayfoot (1824–1869), a graduate of Mount Holyoke College, founded the institution under the auspices of the Baptist church as a preparatory school for Kalamazoo College. It offered young women a literary, musical, art, or business education until it closed in 1886. Then the school was acquired by the Baptist Ministers Aid Society, which operated it as a home for aged and destitute ministers from five midwestern states. In 1899 fire destroyed the roof, porch, and interior of the original four-story Second Empire fieldstone school, built in 1868. The Baptist Ministers Aid Society rebuilt it in 1900 with a hipped roof, stepped central gable, and fanciful pinnacled dormers. A central flight of stairs leads to the main entrance. A porch extends across the front, with a balcony loggia above it on the central pavilion. The two-and-a-half-story boxy structure is on a fully raised foundation.

by 100 feet and has two levels, with the rear open to a view of the river. The building has low, horizontal massing and flat roofs with extended eaves that seem to float one above the other. The vertical motif of the large chimney is echoed in the regularly spaced windows. Open brickwork gives textural interest to the front. The building contains an auditorium, banquet hall, recreation hall, and meeting rooms. The interior is beautifully finished in every detail. Mrs. F. W. Whittlesey

Shiawassee County   (SE)

CORUNNA

Andrew Mack, a prominent Michigan citizen and a friend of both Territorial Gov. Lewis Cass and Gov. Stevens T. Mason, owned over 150 acres of land at the site of what would become the village of Corunna. As a respected ship's captain, a colonel in the War of 1812, and as mayor of Detroit in 1834, Mack was in a strong social and economic position to influence the development of the town. After Shiawassee County was established in 1835, he used his influence to have Corunna named the county seat. Mack established the Shiawassee County Seat Company to manage the development of the town site. What ensued was a no-nonsense settlement period during which all energies focused on

keeping the community alive. By the early 1860s, Corunna was an established village and in direct competition with the thriving community of Owosso, located less than three miles to the west. Over the next four decades, this competition continued. Corunna's population doubled by 1880, then tripled. Detroit and Grand Rapids were markets for its shipments of lumber, broom handles, spokes, animal yokes, and other wood products; flour and wool; and agricultural implements and wagons.

SE01 **Shiawassee County Courthouse**

1903–1906, Claire Allen. 200 North Shiawassee St. (between MacArthur and Corunna streets)

After Corunna was proclaimed the county seat in 1836, the Shiawassee County Seat Company platted the town, promoted its financial and commercial success, and in 1839 donated a public square and county office site. The county board of supervisors built a small wooden courthouse in 1842 and a larger brick one in 1854. Voters elected in 1903 to erect a new courthouse incorporating elegance and the latest in fireproofing techniques. The well-executed Beaux-Arts Classical building that is the result was termed by the *Owosso Evening Argus* for May 4, 1905, "French renaissance design, somewhat Americanized." Pedimented pavilions project from the center of each side of the symmetrical building, and a three-tiered Baroque cupola with a tiled dome tops its hipped roof. Giant Composite columns support the entry portico. Light grayish yellowish brown Berea sandstone sheathes the exterior walls, which are penciled through the first-floor level and marked with Composite pilasters. Oculi, cartouches, and voussoirs punctuate the upper portions of the building. Above the main entrance is a balcony supported by consoles. Beneath the eaves the cornice is supported with consoles and the frieze is decorated with dentils. The grand public structure was fitted with an elegant interior. A center full-height open rotunda is circumscribed by an elaborate metalwork railing. A similar metalwork staircase, together with rich decorative paint-

ing, accents the main corridors. The large courtroom occupies the north portion of the building. The room is paneled in oak and has a carved wooden judge's dais and backdrop. The seats are arranged beneath a dome lighted with glass stained green, gold, and purple. Twelve winged female figures, each holding a sign of the Zodiac, are painted in the Art Nouveau decorative style in the dome encircling the stained glass. The colors of the decoratively painted frieze and ceiling follow those of the stained glass. The courthouse was designed by Claire Allen of Jackson, noted for his courthouses in Hillsdale, Gratiot, and Van Buren counties. In fact, the Shiawassee County Courthouse nearly duplicates the Gratiot County Courthouse. Rickman and Sons of Kalamazoo constructed the new building at a cost of $140,000. The courthouse proclaimed Corunna's position as Shiawassee County's unchallenged political center, if not its commercial hub.

OWOSSO

The earliest settlers in the Owosso area were drawn by the sharp bends and white-water rapids of the Shiawassee River that promised an easily tapped and ample source of waterpower. Alfred L. and Benjamin O. Williams arrived first. They were followed by Elias Comstock, who brought a family and built a permanent home; Daniel Ball, a friend of the Williams brothers, who brought other settlers from New York State; Dr. John Barnes, a graduate of Amherst College and the town's first physician; and the Gould Brothers—Daniel, Amos, Ebenezer, and David—who arrived between 1837 and 1843 and became the town's first lawyers, bankers, and entrepreneurs. By 1837 Daniel Ball had completed a dam and millrace that supplied power to the town's infant timber- and crop-processing industries. The first modest wooden Greek Revival homes and commercial buildings were built. In the late 1850s and 1860s the Detroit and Milwaukee, the Ramshorn, and the Jackson, Lansing, and Saginaw railroads reached Owosso, and the town developed as a regional marketing center. The rail lines attracted an unusual number of fine furniture manufacturers. First, Lyman Woodard established the Woodard Furniture and Casket Company; during the 1870s, the Estey Furniture Factory and the Robbins Table Company selected

Owosso as their home. The craftsmen, artisans, and designers in the city displayed their prosperity and good taste through the construction of residences and commercial, public, and religious buildings in a full range of Italianate, Carpenter Gothic, Queen Anne, Romanesque Revival, and Eastlake styles. During the last two decades of the nineteenth century and the first years of the twentieth, Owosso witnessed the establishment of additional industries based on steel, such as the 1891 Owosso Manufacturing Company that grew into the General Motors-affiliated Mitchell-Bentley Corporation; iron, such as the 1908 Independent Stove Company, maker of the "Renown Stove"; and agricultural products, such as the 1903 Owosso Sugar Company. Continued prosperity allowed residents to continue building, now in a full vocabulary of popular revival styles. Overall, the economic picture remained bright for Owosso until the beginning of the depression. After the 1930s, the community was revitalized as a railroad shipping center for its still-agricultural county, as a business and shopping center, as an area of light industrial and furniture manufacturing, and as a bedroom community for Flint, Lansing, and Saginaw.

SE02 Oliver Street Residential District

1850–1930. Roughly including Oliver St. to the North, Hickory St. on the east, Williams St. on the south, and Third St. on the west. (The neighborhood is 4 blocks north of Michigan 21 and is bisected by Michigan 52.)

From the very beginning, Oliver Street was the residential area chosen by Owosso's leaders. After the Williams brothers built here in 1838 and 1840, industrialists, merchants, bankers, professionals, and entrepreneurs followed men who made their fortunes during Owosso's different stages of development and invested some of their wealth in grand residences and churches.

SE02.1 Amos and Louisa Peck Gould House

c. 1860. 1873, remodeled. 515 North Washington St. (northwest corner of North Washington and West Oliver streets)

Amos (b. 1808) and his wife, Louisa Peck, built this large yellow brick house with exquisite sawed wooden trim. The house took its present appearance in 1873, when the

SE02.1 Amos and Louisa Peck Gould House

Goulds remodeled their earlier house into this elaborate structure. The corbeled brick exterior walls are broken by round-arch and segmental-arch windows and two-story bays. A mansard roof with dramatic paired scrolled brackets under its highly projecting eaves and with pedimented dormers with round-arch windows tops the Italianate house. Delightful scrolled and cut woodwork is lavishly applied to the porches. Gould was Owosso's first mayor and banker, a district judge, a state senator, and a land and timber speculator. The Owosso Historical Commission is restoring the house for use as a museum.

SE03 Curwood Castle (James Oliver Curwood Studio)

1922, Harold A. Childs. 224 Curwood Castle Dr. (Curwood Castle Dr. intersects West Alison St. 4 blocks west of Michigan 52)

Curwood Castle is a small French Norman fantasy created by Lansing architect Harold A. Childs to serve as the writing studio of adventure author and conservationist James Oliver Curwood (1878–1927). The asymmetrical picturesque castle is marked with conically roofed towers. Decorative boulders project at widely spaced intervals from the stucco exterior walls. A spiral staircase winds up the tallest tower to a tiny round room lighted with eleven long, narrow, round-arch windows. Here, during the last four years of his life, Curwood continued writing his popular novels about the Northwest and Canadian north that drew on his boyhood interest in the great forests of Michigan. Curwood met movie directors and publishers in the castle's beamed hall with stage and fireplace.

DURAND VICINITY, VERNON TOWNSHIP

SE04 Williams-Cole House

c. 1854. 6810 Newburg Rd. (southwest corner of Newburg and Vernon roads)

A lively overlay of wooden Carpenter's Gothic board-and-batten siding, decorative barge-boards, and molding tracery window caps lend a pretend Gothic appearance to this originally T-shaped Greek Revival farm-house. Greek Revival elements include the wide entablature with windows in the me-topes of the frieze and the entry surrounded with ample boards and side and transom lights. Believed to have been built by Daniel Williams, the son of Benjamin Williams, who was one of the two brothers who settled Owosso in the early 1830s, the house and 240 acres in Vernon Township were purchased by agriculturalist William N. Cole in 1876 and was held in the Cole family for thirty-two years.

DURAND

SE05 Durand Depot of the Grand Trunk Western Railroad

1905, Spier and Rohns. 200 Railroad St. (south of the intersection Main and Marquette streets)

The Grand Trunk Railway Company of Canada built this large Richardsonian depot to serve one of the state's busiest railroad centers at the turn of the century. Fire destroyed it the same year it opened, but it was rebuilt immediately. The two-and-a-half-story building measures 49 feet in width and 244 feet in length. Tan Missouri granitory brick covers the exterior walls above a flared base of Bedford stone. The depot is topped with a gigantic hipped roof. A canopy, which encircles the station above the first story, shelters three sides of the depot. On the northwest side two symmetrical rounded bays with conical roofs flank a center pedimented gabled dormer. During its heyday in the 1910s and 1920s, the depot became the daily stop for thirty-five passenger, nine local, and one hundred freight trains. The general offices of the Grand Trunk Railroad and the freight and ticket offices of the Ann Arbor Railroad occupied the upper floor; large waiting and dining rooms, the lower floor. Once surrounded with a park and flower beds, the depot, somewhat reminiscent of H. H. Richardson's railroad stations, was considered the finest in the state, outside of the big cities.

MIDDLEBURY TOWNSHIP

SE06 James Rogers and Anna Herrick Van Dyne Farm

1880. 1960 South Austin Rd. (northwest corner of South Austin and Dewey roads)

James Rogers Van Dyne (b. 1836), the son of New Yorkers, came to this area from Oakland County with his brother Charles in 1862. James established a farm in Section 26, while Charles settled on an adjacent farm in Section 35; Charles built the first house, in which the brothers lived for several years. In 1867, however, James married Anna Herrick and in 1868 built his own house. This first wood house served the family until the early 1880s when a new house was constructed on the site; the old house was moved to the west and used as a chicken coop. The new home, though built later and more simply, looked much like brother Charles's: a two-story, L-shaped, clapboard-sheathed building with bow-arch windows and decorative porches. The farmstead, which includes several other nineteenth- and early twentieth-century barns and

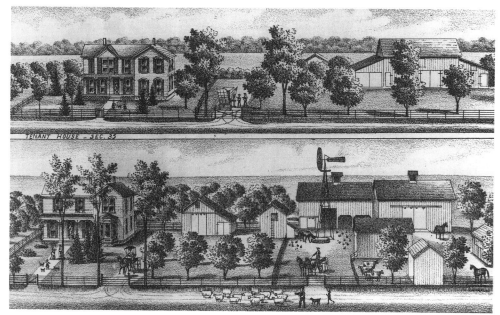

TENANT HOUSE - SEC. 35

SE06 James Rogers and Anna Herrick Van Dyne Farm; and SE07 Charles Van Dyne Farm

sheds, as well as contemporary structures, remains active and in Van Dyne family hands. The "elegant" James R. Van Dyne House and nine large barns on Section 26, together with his tenant house (formerly Charles Van Dyne's house [SE07]) on Section 35, were illustrated in *Portrait and Biographical Album of Clinton and Shiawassee Counties, Michigan.*[57] Together they are representative examples of nineteenth-century Michigan farmhouses.

SE07 Charles Van Dyne Farm

c. 1865. 7625 Dewey Rd. (southwest corner of Dewey and Austin roads)

Charles Van Dyne, who came from New York to Michigan with his brother James, settled his Middlebury Township land in 1862. Soon after he built his residence, a two-story, Gothic Revival-inspired, L-shaped, upright-and-wing, wood-framed and -sheathed building. Within a gabled peak that projects from cornice line in the center of the ell, paired round-arch windows are set beneath a pediment. A porch with decorative supports runs the full width of the ell at the first story. The house has round- and segmental-arch and trabeated window enframements. The brothers both lived here until James built his own home

across the road. Charles only stayed in the area until 1885, when he sold the farm to James and moved farther west; the home remained in Van Dyne family hands until 1983. A vertical-wood-sided, gable-roofed milk barn built during the 1880s; a slope-roofed chicken coop; and a gambrel-roofed hay barn from the early 1900s remain on the farmstead.

SHIAWASSEE TOWNSHIP

SE08 Maple River Church

1868, Reverend George M. Reynolds. Around the intersection of Colby and Bennington roads and then west along Bennington Rd., approximately one mile

In 1837 four young couples settled in the rich farmland of the Maple River area. Under the spiritual and aesthetic guidance of the Reverend George M. Reynolds, a preacher and a talented, self-trained architect, the settlers established a small rural community. They included a cemetery and, using designs prepared by Reynolds, built a church, octagon schoolhouse, and several fine Greek Revival farmhouses. The centerpiece of the rural community is the elegantly proportioned and finely detailed Maple River Church, organized by Baptists, but now handed down to the Reorganized Church of Jesus Christ of Latter Day Saints. It was built in 1868. A three-tiered bell tower rests atop its gabled roof. The board-and-batten-sided structure has corner pilasters, a full entablature, sixteen-over-sixteen windows, and a double-door central entry with transom. Above the vestibule, and overlooking the two-aisled sanctuary, is a choir loft.

The Thumb

THE THUMB OF THE MITTEN-SHAPED LOWER PENINSULA IS itself a peninsula surrounded by the waters of Lake Huron, the Saint Clair River, and Lake Saint Clair. The land juts out into Lake Huron with Saginaw Bay on its west. On the east, the waters of Lake Huron and the Saint Clair River form the international boundary between the United States and Canada.

The basis of the economy of the Thumb has been lumbering, commercial fishing, grindstones and salt, maritime commerce, shipbuilding, farming, and tourism.

State highway Michigan 25 follows the coastline of Lake Huron from the base of the Thumb at Port Huron to the tip at Port Austin and then along Saginaw Bay to Bay City. The Thumb is bisected by Michigan 53 on its route from Port Austin on the north through Imlay City to Detroit. This road traverses both flat and rolling fertile agricultural and small-game hunting lands. The northern cities of the Thumb are marketing centers for grains, vegetables, and beans; the southern portion lies in a fruit-growing belt and livestock area. Michigan 46 runs east-west from Port Sanilac to Saginaw. Interstate 69 (I-69) cuts across the state from Flint to Port Huron, where it connects with the Blue Water Bridge that spans the Saint Clair River and joins the Canadian highway system.

The Grand Trunk Railroad, from Chicago to Port Huron, takes a nearly parallel course to Interstate 69 (I-69) through the southern portion of the Thumb and follows the Saint Clair Tunnel beneath the Saint Clair River to connect with the Canadian Via Rail System.

Port Huron is the largest city in the Thumb and one of the oldest cities in Michigan. The territory at the outlet of Lake Huron and at the source of the

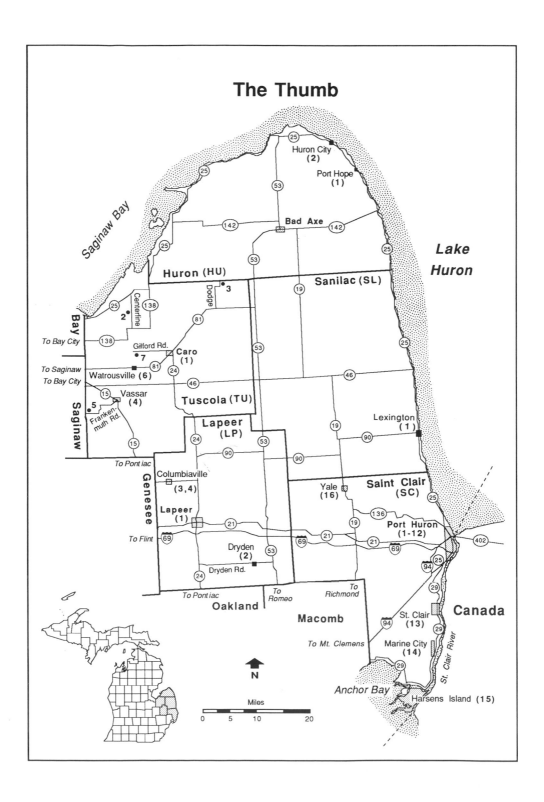

The Thumb

Huron City (2)

Port Hope (1)

Bad Axe

Saginaw Bay

Lake Huron

Huron (HU)

Centerline

Dodge

• 3

2•

Bay

To Bay City

Gilford Rd.

Caro (1)

• 7

Sanilac (SL)

Saginaw

To Saginaw
To Bay City

Watrousville (6)

Vassar (4)

Franken-
muth Rd.

• 5

Tuscola (TU)

Lexington (1)

Lapeer (LP)

To Pontiac

Genesee

Columbiaville
(3,4)

Lapeer (1)

To Flint

Yale (16)

Saint Clair (SC)

Dryden (2)

Dryden Rd.

To Pontiac

To
Romeo

To
Richmond

Port Huron
(1-12)

Oakland

Macomb

To Mt. Clemens

St. Clair (13)

Canada

Marine City (14)

St. Clair River

Anchor Bay

Harsens Island (15)

N

Miles

0   5   10   20

Saint Clair River was noted by French missionaries and explorers in the seventeenth century. The French recognized the importance of its strategic location for the domination of Lake Huron and the Saint Clair River. Here French trader and explorer Daniel Greysolon, Sieur du Luth, built in 1686 Fort Saint Joseph to keep English fur traders from traveling up the Great Lakes. The French abandoned the fort in 1688. On the same site Americans built Fort Gratiot in 1814 to protect residents of the Upper Great Lakes from the British and to control trade and travel on the river. Fort Gratiot was abandoned in 1879 and dismantled in 1882.

French settlers from Detroit drifted into the Port Huron area in 1782. Anselm Petit, together with seven others, moved up from Detroit in 1790 to settle at the mouth of the Black River. They speculated in land, fished, and trapped beaver.

Settlement at Port Huron and along the Saint Clair River in Saint Clair County began in earnest in the 1820s and 1830s. Sparked by the construction of the federal turnpike from Fort Gratiot to Detroit, which was under construction in 1826, and completed to Mount Clemens by 1831, people rushed to acquire land in the Port Huron area. John Thorn laid out land on the north bank of the Black River, Daniel B. Harrington and F. C. White of Whitesboro, New York, on the south bank. In 1832 the Black River Mill Company erected a large steam-driven mill. In 1837 the four settlements at the confluence of the Black and Saint Clair rivers merged to form Port Huron.

Soon other communities along the Saint Clair River were settled. The village of Saint Clair was settled in 1828 by Thomas Palmer. Three years later, in 1831, Samuel Ward laid out the village of present-day Marine City. In 1836 Algonac was established.

Growth of the interior of the Thumb lagged, due to the absence of major roads and to reports of hostile Indians, and an unhealthy climate. In 1828, James Deneen and his family moved from Trumbull County, Ohio, to Lapeer County. In 1831 A. N. Hart of Cornwall, Connecticut, settled at the junction of the Flint River and Farmer's Creek in west central Lapeer County at present-day Lapeer, and Jonathan R. White of South Hadley, Massachusetts, settled along Flint River opposite Hart. The stately Greek Revival courthouse at Lapeer solidified the location of the county seat and also represented the penetration of the frontier by eastern architectural values.

In 1829 Edward Petit established a trading post at the mouth of Shebeon Creek in the southwestern part of Huron County. Five years later, in 1834, Aaron G. Peer discovered sandstone deposits at the northernmost point of Huron County. He and a relative purchased land and developed the grindstone industry. In 1839 Jeduthan Byrd built a water-powered sawmill on Bird Creek at present-day Port Austin. By the mid-1850s a steam-powered sawmill operated at the settlement. Lumbering flourished. In 1860 Huron County had sixteen sawmills.

In 1835–1836 Ebenezer Davis (1797–1880) settled in Tuscola Township and become its first white settler. Others trickled to this area in small numbers until 1850. Then, after receiving a land grant of 3,000 acres to build a bridge over the Cass River at Bridgeport, Townsend North and James M. Edmunds, built a sawmill and dam on the river at present-day Vassar. Then they opened a store, sought public improvements and promoted settlement. Settlers flocked here after the Civil War.

Lumbering was the first major economic activity in the Thumb. The Black, Pine, Clinton, and Belle river systems furnished a means of transporting the logs to mills and a source of power for operating the mills. The docks at such harbors on Lake Huron as Huron City and Port Hope hummed with the arrival of people and supplies and the export of lumber and millwork. Logs from the pine forests of Lapeer County were floated down the Flint River to sawmills at Flint or on to Saginaw and Bay City.

As early as 1780, a sawmill operated at Marysville. After fire destroyed the village of Detroit in 1805, four other sawmills were built to supply the lumber needed to rebuild the town. In 1837 there were thirty sawmills in Saint Clair County. The lumber industry expanded further in the 1840s, to peak in the early 1870s.

In the fall of 1871, fire raced across the central Lower Peninsula, burning large areas of the Thumb. An even worse fire, the Great Forest Fire of 1881, fueled by extensive piles of slashing on its cutover lands, spread across the Thumb, destroying some thirty-four thousand buildings. These two fires caused severe damage, but they cleared cutover lands for farming.

After the fire of 1881 agriculture really developed in the Thumb. Corn, dry beans, oats, wheat, corn, barley, and potatoes were cultivated, and cattle and dairy cows were raised. In the 1890s sugar beets were introduced and, beginning in 1898, sugar beet factories and refineries were opened. In the twentieth century, navy beans became the leading farm product.

Commercial fishing began in the Bay Port area on the islands in Saginaw Bay around 1850. The Gillingham family settled on North Island and took up fishing. Bay Port was established in 1885, when the railroad was extended to this point to pick up limestone and sandstone at the nearby quarry and to transport tourists to a newly built hotel. Then the Gillinghams moved their operations to Bay Port and built necessary fish shanties. Saginaw investors formed the Bay Port Fish Company in 1895. This company and the Gillingham Fish Company operated a fleet of forty-two fishing tugs and made Bay Port the largest freshwater fishing port in the world during the 1930s and 1940s. Herring and walleyes were shipped out by boxcar to eastern markets. Buildings for making nets, building boats, processing fish, and storing ice and twine lined the point of land.

The Thumb developed new industries as lumbering waned. Port Huron became a center for shipbuilding, maritime commerce, and a center for rail transportation. The resort industry grew as Detroiters and other city dwellers built cottages and hotels along the Lake Huron shore—at Gratiot Beach, Harbor Beach, Port Hope, Huron City, and Pointe Aux Barques—and along Lake Saint Clair and the Saint Clair River, at Harsens Island, and the Saint Clair Flats. Others came to fish and hunt duck and small game.

Saint Clair County was set off in 1820 and organized in 1822. Lapeer and Sanilac counties were established in 1822 and organized in 1833 and 1848 respectively. Tuscola and Huron counties were established in 1840 and organized in 1850 and 1859.

German and Polish, French Canadian, Irish, and other groups are represented in the population of the Thumb.

Saint Clair County (SC)

PORT HURON

Port Huron lies at the foot of Lake Huron and the head of the Saint Clair River. Though incorporated in 1857, the city of Port Huron began its actual commercial growth in the 1820s, as people spilled out from the Fort Gratiot Military Reservation along the Black River. Aided by the construction of a military road from Fort Gratiot to Fort Wayne, Port Huron's economy began to flourish, driven by the lumber and related shipbuilding industries. Ironically, the fires of 1871 and 1881 that ravaged the Thumb's timber supply benefitted Port Huron by forcing economic diversification.

Thus came the development of a commercial district concentrated along Military Street and Huron Avenue, starting in the 1870s. Of its diverse architecture, the most notable structures date from the late 1870s through the 1920s. Particularly impressive are the unusual designs by local architect George L. Harvey (1870–1942) of Butterfield and Harvey (a fine remaining example is the polychrome High Victorian Romanesque White's Art Hall, c. 1888, 1102 Military Street), as well as several outstanding examples of classical styles. Though much of Port Huron's commercial architecture has been hidden by incongruous alterations, numerous significant buildings remain, recalling the image of a young, energetic city.

SC01 **Federal Building** (Port Huron Post Office and Customhouse)

1874–1876, Alfred B. Mullett, Supervising Architect, United States Treasury Department. 526 Water St. (southeast corner of Water and Sixth streets)

In 1872 Congress authorized the Department of the Treasury to purchase a suitable site in Port Huron and to erect on it a building to accommodate the customhouse, bonded warehouse, and other government offices. Port Huron was the port of entry for the Customs District of Huron, which had been created by Congress in 1865. Comprised of twenty-two counties and extending the length of Lake Huron, from Lake Saint Clair to the Straits of Mackinac, it was one of four such districts in Michigan.

The site selected overlooked the Saint Clair and Black rivers. Plans for the government building were prepared under the supervision of Alfred B. Mullett (1834–1890), then supervising architect of the Treasury Department. The building seemed to be a composite of styles, "the Italianate predominating."[58] Begun just after the Second Empire State, War and Navy Building in Washington, D.C., also by Mullett, it reverts to a kind of Italianate classicism that marked a number of federal government buildings during these years. It is a plain Neoclassical structure, three stories in height with a bracketed hipped roof surmounted by an octagonal cupola topped by a curved mansard roof. Pedimented entrance pavilions mark the front and rear facades. The exterior walls are rusticated Sandusky, Ohio, limestone on the base, and smooth-cut light yellowish brown Berea, Ohio, sandstone on the upper stories. Pilasters with modified Corinthian capitals extend the full height of the upper two stories. A carved stone cornice encircles the building. Much of the original black walnut and butternut woodwork, black and white marble flooring, and iron staircase remain intact inside, await-

Port Huron

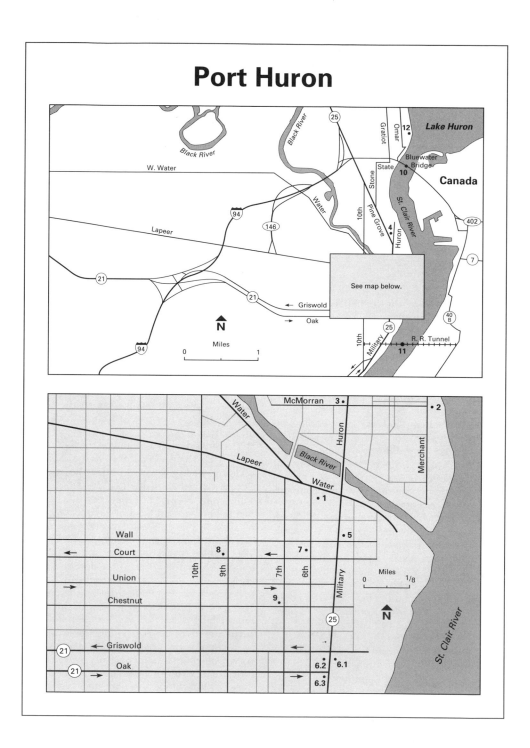

ing restoration. The building served as a facility to promote and foster the commerce and navigation of the country, receive and distribute mail, and administer justice. The people of Port Huron anticipated that the customhouse would further Port Huron's importance as a business center on what was then the Northwestern frontier. It cost $200,000 to build.

SC02 **Port Huron Municipal Office Center**

1975–1978, Richard Cogley. 100 McMorran Blvd. (at the terminus of McMorran Blvd., Merchant St., and the Saint Clair River)

The city of Port Huron sold its existing space in a thirty-year-old building it occupied jointly with the county and commissioned local architect Richard Cogley to design this monumental office center on a large site on the reclaimed river bed. Known locally as the "Taj Mahal," it is in the New Brutalism style. An entrance plaza with fountain is positioned at the terminus of McMorran Boulevard, before the main building. The structure consists of a cube-shaped administration building and a low circular structure containing a public meeting room connected by an entrance lobby. It is placed over a parking garage. Smooth, hammer-finished, white Georgia marble and reflective glass sheath the cast-concrete structure of the administration building and the lobby, and broken-faced, textured white marble masonry units and the same glass serve as the skin of the building that contains the public meeting room. The complex cost $7.5 million to build. It is somewhat reminiscent of the Boston City Hall, erected in 1962–

1969 to the plans of Kallmann, McKinnell and Knowles.

SC03 **McMorran Place**

1959–1960, Alden B. Dow. 1964, junior arena addition. 1965, arena tower. 701 McMorran Blvd. (northwest corner of McMorran Blvd. and Huron Ave.)

In 1955 Clara E. McKenzie, Emma McMorran Murphy, and Andrew J. Murphy announced plans to build, equip, and donate a combined auditorium and sports arena in memory of their father, Henry McMorran. The huge complex is made up of a broad 1,169-seat auditorium and meeting rooms and two arenas—the pavilion and the main arena. Fronting the Huron Avenue facade of the large, rectilinear, light orangish brick complex is a limestone "memorial" wall, on which is centered a giant sunburst clock cast in anodized aluminum finished in gold. Before this backdrop, two large scuptures, a male and a female personifying Night and Day, rise above a pool. The wall and pool sculptures are the work of noted Michigan sculptor Marshall M. Fredericks. A slender 150-foot-tall octagonal tower marks the entrance to the pavilion and the arena.

SC04 **Davidson, Staiger, Adair, Hill Law Offices** (Modern Maccabees Temple / Ladies of the Modern Maccabees Temple)

1904–1906, George I. Harvey. 901 Huron Ave. (at the apex of Pine Grove [Michigan 25] and Huron Ave.)

Prominently located on a triangular site at the convergence of Huron Avenue and Pine Grove in a residential section of the city is the headquarters of the Ladies of the Modern Maccabees, a beneficiary society for women. The temple is an imposing but feminine Beaux-Arts Classical design created by a local architect, George L. Harvey. The two-story limestone structure stands on a raised penciled foundation of the same material. A giant pedimented portico supported by Composite columns and reached by a monumental staircase fronts the cube. An entablature with a block modillion-supported cornice supports a parapet wall that fronts a low-pitched roof, which is topped by a shallow dome clad with red tile. The interior is arranged around a central grand staircase underneath the lighted dome. The staircase leads upward, splitting at a landing and culminating in a tower room underneath the dome. The fabulous Composite-columned lobby has golden scagliola wainscoting. The floral-motif of the mosaic floor, in blues, roses, and golds, swirls around an insignia of the Modern Maccabees original order.

In 1902 the Ladies of the Modern Maccabees severed its ties with the Knights of the Modern Maccabees, with which it had organized as an auxiliary in 1886. In 1904–1906, as the membership to whom it offered "Industry, Fraternity and Protection" approached fifty thousand in Michigan alone, the organization built this building. In 1926 the women and men merged into one organization, known as the Maccabees, and moved in 1928 to their headquarters in Detroit.

SC05 **Harrington Inn** (Harrington Hotel)

1896. 1026 Military St. (Michigan 25) (northeast corner Military and Wall streets)

This large and luxurious hotel was once the center of Port Huron's tourist trade. The red brick and basically Romanesque structure has a rounded towerlike corner on its southwest side, bays, and balconies; in contrast, a piazza and balustraded porches are aggressively classical and are supported by paired Ionic columns. Although the *Port Huron Daily Times* for February 27, 1896, called the building "colonial" in style, it is really a bizarre mixture of high classicism with Romanesque/Queen Anne. The two porches have paired Ionic columns and are topped by a balustrade. The building is arranged in a U shape, which permits the placement of its 128 rooms around a light well. The grand columned lobby has a fireplace and is richly paneled in wood. Originally it was furnished with "quaint, colonial furniture." Charles F. Harrington (b. 1842), a Port Huron financier, established the Harrington Hotel Company and had this structure built. When it opened in 1896 the chamber of commerce hoped it would induce further investment in Port Huron. The hotel resembles those found at the turn of the century in Mount Clemens, Petoskey, and other resort cities of Michigan. The Westin Financial Group recently rehabilitated the hotel into ninety assisted-living units for older people.

SC06 **Military Street Residential Area**

Military St. (Michigan 25) from Jenkinson St. to Chestnut St.

Formerly the military road built between Detroit and Fort Gratiot, Military Street became the most prominent promenade leading into downtown, and the residential enclave of both the rich and the middle-class, white-collar people.

SC06.1 **John J. Jenkinson House**

1887. 1820 Military St. (Michigan 25)

This beautifully painted and restored house is Military Street's largest and most ornate Queen Anne structure. The asymmetrically massed house is a picturesque assemblage of shapes and textures. Gables, porches, bays, a porte-cochère, a turret and a tall, round, conical-roofed corner tower project from the house. It is clad with clapboards and shingles, and trimmed with carved and turned posts and brackets. The house was built for John J. Jenkinson, a lumberman and real estate speculator.

SC06.2 **The Castle** (John W. Thomson House)

early 1890s. 1719 Military St. (Michigan 25)

Known as The Castle, this Richardsonian house was built for John W. Thomson (b. 1817), an agent for the Lake Superior Transit Company and numerous other steamboat lines and Port Huron's Deputy Collector of Customs during the Lincoln administration. The house is constructed of randomly coursed, rough-faced, yellowish brown Berea sandstone. It has a massive, three-story, conical-roofed corner tower with an open third-floor porch that affords a view of the busy ship traffic on the Saint Clair River.

SC06.3 Wilbur F. and Margaretta Turner Davidson House

1890. 1707 Military St. (Michigan 25) (southwest corner of Military and Oak [Michigan 21] streets)

This richly textured Queen Anne house with an irregular cross-gable, tall chimneys, a one-story Ionic porch, and a hipped-roof design has been handsomely restored. The interior is resplendent with leaded and stained-glass windows, fireplaces, and black oak, maple, butternut, cherry, and pine finishes. The house was built for Wilbur F. Davidson (1852–1913) and his wife, Margaretta Turner. Davidson was a dry goods merchant who became a local utilities magnate.

SC07 Port Huron Museum of Arts and History (Port Huron Public Library)

1903–1904; Patten and Miller, architects; George L. Harvey, superintendent of construction. 1115 Sixth St. (southwest corner Sixth and Wall streets)

In 1902 steel entrepreneur and America's premier philanthropist Andrew Carnegie gave the city of Port Huron $45,000 for the construction of a library. The grant was awarded with the stipulation that the city provide the site and $4,000 a year for maintenance. Normand S. Patten (1852–1915) and Grant Miller (1872–1956), Chicago architects, recognized for their designs for over one hundred Car-

negie libraries throughout the Midwest, created plans for a two-story, Indiana limestone structure in the Beaux-Arts Classical style. The main focus of the formal and ponderous building is a projecting pedimented entrance pavilion approached by a monumental staircase. Colossal fluted pilasters with capitals in a variation of the Ionic order are paired with cartouches and flank the entrance. This is surmounted by a half-circle light, and above, an antefix marks the ridge of the pediment. Block modillions support the corona under the cornice and parapet. The interior was arranged with reading rooms (now galleries and lecture room) to the north and south off a circular book delivery room encircled with Doric columns on the first floor and a lecture room, museum, and stacks off a circular art gallery on the second floor. William H. Maxwell of Angola, Indiana, built the library at a cost of $39,000.

SC08 Mount Sinai Congregation

1924, George L. Harvey. 903 Court St. (northwest corner of Court and Ninth streets)

One of the few outstate Michigan synagogues to remain Orthodox, Mount Sinai was founded as a cemetery association in 1885 and reorganized as a congregation in 1895. Now serving a diminishing Jewish population, the building has been little changed in sixty years. It is a brick and wood Greek cross-plan quasi-Georgian building with twin Ionic columns and paneled corner piers flanking the entrance and narrow round-headed windows in the side walls. White stone sills and water table and a Star of David in the pediment provide decorative accents. The *bimah* is defined by a proscenium arch within which a discordant 1970s ark rises behind a similarly nonconforming wrought-iron balustrade. The reader's desk, consonant with Orthodox usage, is separated from the ark. The small balcony at the rear of the prayer hall was originally the women's gallery.

SC09 Saint Joseph Catholic Church

1922–1923, Donaldson and Meier. Northwest corner Seventh and Chestnut streets

In 1889 the Most Reverend John S. Foley, bishop of the Diocese of Detroit, denied the request of the German Catholic Saint Joseph's Society, which had formed the previous year, to establish a distinctly German parish, but permitted the founding of a new Catholic church without ethnic restriction. The present Saint Joseph Catholic Church replaced the church that was erected for the congregation in 1890. The new one was designed by Donaldson and Meier, a Detroit architectural firm responsible for many Catholic churches, including Holy Redeemer at 1721 Junction in Detroit, which was built at the same time and in the same style but is much larger. The Romanesque Revival Saint Joseph Church is fronted with a richly textured and patterned gabled front. Twin square towers with open belfries, balconets, and octagonal tiled roofs flank a recessed, arcaded entrance. Six polygonal-shafted columns with floriated Romanesque capitals and decorated bases support the recessed entrance porch. A rose window enframed with rectangular panels of decorative brickwork is over the entrance, and there are rose windows in the transepts as well. Dark red brick laid in English bond and trimmed with limestone is resplendent with corbeling and checker work inlaid with relief sculptures. This is punctuated by Pewabic tiles molded with various cross motifs and fired with iridescent glazes in blues, greens, and golds in the panel over the east portal. Red tiles cover the roof. The Latin cross-plan church has a nave with side aisles, as well as transepts. It has a barrel-roof ceiling.

SC10 Blue Water Bridge

1937–1938; Modjeski and Masters, consulting engineers; Monsarrat and Pratly, Canadian associates; George L. Harvey, architect. I-94 across the Saint Clair River between Port Huron and Sarnia

This sweeping steel cantilever highway bridge links Port Huron and Sarnia, Ontario. Ferries operated by the Port Huron Sarnia Ferry Company, established in 1881, transported people, cars, and goods across the river before the Blue Water Bridge was built. Plans made in 1927 to span the swiftly moving Saint Clair River with a bridge languished during the depression. In 1937 the Michigan Highway Commission and the Minister of Highways for Canada hired Ralph Modjeski and Frank H. Masters and their Canadian associates, Monsarrat and Pratley, to design the bridge. It has an overall length of 6,463 feet; the main span is 871 feet in length; the anchor arms are 326 feet long each; and approaches consisting of deck girder and deck

truss spans are 2,283 feet long on the American side and 2,657 feet long on the Canadian side. Caissons sunk to rock 95 feet below water level make up the two main piers. The bridge's main span clears the heavily navigated Saint Clair River by 150 feet. The Missouri Valley Bridge and Iron Works and the Kansas City Bridge Company built the piers for the main span. E. C. Nolan and Son of Detroit built the American approach piers. Russell Construction Company of Toronto built the Canadian approach piers. (Charles K. Hyde says that the American Bridge Company fabricated and erected the main span, the Wisconsin Bridge and Iron Company erected the American approaches, and the Sarnia Bridge Company built the superstructure for the Canadian approach span.) A Streamline Moderne plaza, designed by Norman B. Forbes and by George L. Harvey of Port Huron graced the American side until the bridge was rehabilitated in 1987.

SC11 Saint Clair Tunnel

1889–1891, Joseph Hobson, chief engineer. Canadian National Railroad under the Saint Clair River, between Port Huron and Sarnia, Ontario

The Saint Clair Tunnel is the first international submarine railway tunnel in the world. It is 6,025 feet long and with its approaches is 11,553 feet long. It cost nearly $3 million to construct. At the urging of Henry Tyler, president of the Grand Trunk Railway, the directors of the Grand Trunk organized the Saint Clair Tunnel Company in 1886 to build a tunnel between Port Huron and Sarnia. The Grand Trunk had been completed to Chicago six years earlier, and ferries had carried railroad cars across the swiftly moving, frequently ice-jammed, and heavily navigated river. Joseph Hobson (b. 1834) of Guelph, Ontario, designed and built the tunnel. To accomplish this he constructed, set in place, and successfully operated two gigantic tunneling shields based on the tunneling method invented by Alfred E. Beach of New York City and patented in 1868. Beach designed the shield for the tunnel under Broadway, New York, and the design was used in Buffalo, Chicago, under the Hudson River, and in London. Made of 1-inch-thick plate steel, the shields were 21 feet 7 inches in diameter and 16 feet long. Twenty-four hydraulic rams located around the rear of the shield forced the sharpened leading edge of the shield into the clay. Men in the front of the shield removed and carried back the soil through the shield. An air pressure system aided in upholding the soft earth of the tunnel heading. As the shield progressed, the iron tube was constructed. The walls of the tunnel are composed of segmental flanged iron plates connected by bolts. One ring is composed of thirteen of these iron plates and a key. The lower half is lined with brickwork. The round-arch portals of the tunnel are within rusticated limestone walls surrounded by voussoirs. Over them is a small pediment containing the inscription "Saint Clair, 1890." Westinghouse Company installed electricity to haul the trains in 1907, making the tunnel both well-lighted and clean.

SC12 Fort Gratiot Lighthouse

1029, Lucius Lyon. 1861, light raised. 1875, light keeper's house. Garfield and Omar streets

Located at the confluence of Lake Huron and the Saint Clair River, the Fort Gratiot Lighthouse was the first lighthouse built on Lake Huron. The present light replaces one erected in 1825, but destroyed by a storm in 1828. It is a white-painted, conical, brick tower, built in 1829 by Lucius Lyon (1800–1851), an engineer and land surveyor who worked for the United States Surveyor General. It cost $4,445. In 1861 the light was raised 20 feet to its present height of 86 feet. The double light keeper's house was built in 1874–1875. It is

a plain red brick house capped by a jerkin-head roof.

SAINT CLAIR

In 1765 British officer Patrick Sinclair established a military and trading post at the confluence of the Pine with the Saint Clair River to control the transportation of supplies from Detroit to Michilimackinac. It was closed twenty years later. The village was laid out in 1818 but replatted in 1828 by Thomas Palmer, who came to establish a lumber camp and sawmill to process pine timber cut in surrounding forests. The railroad and river navigation assured Saint Clair's growth. In 1881, huge, towered Oakland House opened, and its mineral springs and bathhouse were considered "next to the celebrated houses at Baden Baden."[59] Today the resort tradition of this river region is carried on by the well-known Neo-Tudor Saint Clair Inn, erected in 1925–1926 to the plans of Walter H. Wyeth. Lovely large houses line North Riverside Avenue (Michigan 29).

SC13 William and Mark Hopkins Houses

c. 1876–1880, Charles Marsh?. 613 and 615 North Riverside Ave. (Michigan 29) (west side of North Riverside Ave., south of Brown St.)

The pair of elaborate, towered, orangish red brick Italianate and Second Empire houses with mansard roofs stand side by side on the crest of a hilltop overlooking the Saint Clair River. The spectacular site originally extended to the river. The houses have ornate bracketed window hoods and cornices. The brothers Mark (1832–1914) and William S. Hopkins probably built them with a portion of the proceeds of the $20 million estate their son and nephew, Mark Hopkins, left to his heirs in Saint Clair. The younger Hopkins made a fortune from a tool business he established in the goldfields of California and in his interest in the Union Pacific Railroad Company. The William Hopkins House on the south reportedly is a copy in miniature of his uncle's house in Menlo Park, California. Distinguished University of Michigan architecture professor Emil Lorch and local historians attributed the design of the Mark Hopkins House to Charles Marsh, a skillful southeastern Michigan architect, who came from Rochester, New York, to Detroit, probably by 1875.

MARINE CITY

Located at the confluence of the Belle with the Saint Clair River and surrounded by agricultural land, Marine City prospered from its lumber mills and shipbuilding industry. It was incorporated in 1865. The city has many fine buildings and beautiful old houses of retired ship captains, summer resorters, and others that run along Main Street (Michigan 29) and closely overlook the shipping channel on the north end of town, among them two very extraordinary works of architecture: Holy Cross Church, a pinnacled twin-towered Late Gothic Revival limestone structure designed by Harry J. Rill and built in 1903–1904, and the orangish red brick Richardsonian Marine City Hall designed by Mason and Rice and built in 1884–1885.

SC14 Main Street Residential District

1830s-1890s. South and North Main St. (Michigan 29) between Jefferson St. and a point just north of Woodworth St.

Marine City's most prominent historical thoroughfare, Main Street was home to major figures in the city's early shipbuilding and shipping industries. The fine houses of shipyard owners, shipbuilders, and Great Lakes captains date from the 1830s to the 1890s and display the various styles fashionable over the years.

SC14.1 Ward-Holland House

c. 1832. c. 1950s. 433 North Main St. (Michigan 29)

One of Michigan's oldest brick houses, the orangish red brick Ward-Holland house follows a symmetrical, side-gabled design. Its most dominant Greek Revival features are its doorway side lights and transom light and its raking cornice with returns (its pedimented front porch is not original). An interesting period element is the house's devil trap, below the south gable. This device consists of a small, blind, wall opening that tricks the devil into believing it is an entry. Elliptical fanlights are in the gable ends. The structure's first occupant, Capt. Samuel Ward (1784–1854), otherwise known as "Uncle Sam the Steamboat King," was one of Marine City's founders. He settled here in 1819 and soon turned to shipbuilding. Under his dominant presence, Marine City and his holdings in various businesses grew rapidly; when Ward's son Eber died in 1875, estimates of his personal value ranged from $10 to $30 million. In 1876 Robert Holland (b. 1831) purchased the Ward shipyards, docks, and the house, which is still occupied by the Holland family. Holland added to the house a full-width one-story front porch with turned posts and decorative bracing.

SC14.2 Ebenezer Westbrook House

c. 1840–1845. 613 North Main St. (Michigan 29)

This wooden, temple-front Greek Revival house has a double front porch supported by full-height piers. Its simple stylistic detailing includes a broad cornice band and dentils. Horizontal boards are laid flush on the front. Clapboards cover the other walls. The house is believed to have been built by Ebenezer Westbrook.

HARSENS ISLAND

To reach Harsens Island, take the automobile ferry at the landing at 3647 Pointe Tremble Rd. (Michigan 29), .5 miles west of Algonac city limits and Chris Craft Boat Works.

SC15 South Channel Drive

South Channel Dr., from Grand Pointe Subdivision to Maple Leaf Subdivison on the south

SC15 South Channel Drive

Harsens Island was developed beginning in the 1870s, as a resort area within easy reach of the Detroit docks by steamship. Private clubhouses, resort hotels, and grand summer houses went up all along the "Flats," as the banks of the Saint Clair River delta are called. During the 1890s, five private clubhouses and seven public resort areas lined the channel. All of the big hotels are gone, but many turn-of-the-century houses along South Channel Drive survive as reminders of the days when the Saint Clair Flats was an acclaimed luxury resort community.

SC15.1 Aaron A. and Mary Dennis Parker House

1896. 1250 Circuit Dr. (fourth house northeast of Orchid Blvd. and South Channel Dr.), Grand Pointe Subdivision

The elegant Georgian Revival Parker house, with its wide double verandas and graceful Ionic portico, has an identical twin, the Chester and Fannie Ruehle Haberkorn House, three houses farther up the channel. Occupying extensive frontage along the channel, the two houses were located on either side of the Grand Pointe Hotel, which opened in 1890, and by 1906 had been expanded to 150 rooms. The hotel was destroyed by fire in 1909, but the five homes built around it in the Grand Pointe subdivison remain. The subdivision was developed by the Grande Pointe Improvement Company. Organized in 1888, the company acquired the northeastern point of Harsens Island, platted streets, and sold lots.

Aaron A. Parker (b. 1844) was president of the White Star Line, the steamship company that brought Detroiters to the resorts on Harsens Island aboard the big side-wheeler *Tashmoo*, and manager of the Buffalo and Detroit Transportation Company. Parker also developed Tashmoo Park.

SC15.2 Tashmoo Marina (Tashmoo Park)

1899. 3280 South Channel Dr.

Founded in 1896, Tashmoo Park was developed by the White Star Lines in 1899 on 60 acres as an amusement park and picnic ground. Located just below Sans Souci, it attracted parties of conventioneers, factory picnic groups, Sunday schools, and other day excursionists, most of whom arrived on the excursion steamers of the White Star Lines.

In 1899 a large casino was built. Open on all sides, its huge, low-sweeping hipped roof, topped by festive cupolas crowned with flags, sheltered visitors. In 1912 a dance pavilion was constructed. Also open on all sides, its huge roof, supported by steel trusses, covered a 10,400 square foot hardwood dance floor. The park had a large dock, bathhouse, and bathing grounds. In the 1920s amusement rides were added. The old Tashmoo casino and dance pavilion have been adaptively re-used as boat storage sheds for the marina occupying the park grounds today. From 1897 until 1936 it was served by the side-wheeler *Tashmoo*.

SC15.3 Gray Gables (John A. or William A. Gray House?)

c. 1890. 3556 South Channel Dr. (northwest corner South Channel Dr. and Saint Clair Ave.), Maple Leaf Subdivision

The Maple Leaf Subdivision was platted in 1889 and developed by Detroiters along broad grounds that sweep back from the river as an exclusive summer resort. The area was named for the many maples that grew along the riverbank. Gray Gables is a beautifully restored Shingle style house. Its broad but steep gabled roof is broken by a central gabled dormer and sweeps down to shelter the full-width front porch, now enclosed by glass for year-round use. The prominent octagonal corner tower with a Palladian motif affords an excellent view of Saint Clair River traffic.

YALE

SC16 James and Louise Livingston McColl House

1899, Isaac Erb. 205 South Main St. (Michigan 19)

This substantial clapboard Queen Anne house is a landmark in this agricultural center. It was designed by Port Huron architect Isaac Erb for Yale industrialist and banker, James McColl. The house is a complex variety of shapes: bays project from the walls, shingled gables intersect the hip roof, and a bell-roofed turret perches on the northeast corner. A large distinctive porch with balustraded railings runs across the front. One Richardsonian feature is the eyebrow dormer piercing the south roof. Originally the roof was covered with slate. Extensive leaded art-glass windows and original scroll and spindle woodwork highlight the spacious interior.

James McColl was a partner in the flax industry with fellow native Scotsman James Livingston, whose daughter, Louise, he married in 1889. Though the pair was also involved with banking, McColl's passion was to create a powerful linen industry in the United States, based in Saginaw. His flax factories would then provide the needed, partially processed flax; in the end, however, the more efficient cotton fiber was king. His house, now completely restored, is a monument to his otherwise successful life.

Sanilac County   (SL)

LEXINGTON HEIGHTS

SL01 Valentine Falzon Cottage (Stone Castle)

c. 1929–1939, Valentine Falzon. 7345 Elm St. (northeast corner Elm and Byron streets)

This unique whimsical beach-stone cottage tells of the persistent creativity and energy of Valentine Falzon. An Italian immigrant skilled in stone cutting, Falzon imaginatively and painstakingly built this cobblestone cottage during the depression while unemployed. He used found materials like Lake Huron beach stone, cast-iron radiator sections, and wooden produce crates. A pentagonal porch with pointed-arch windows projects from the front of the one-story, square building. A two-story, pentagonal wing with a balustrade roof and castellated tower extends from the side. A cobblestone fence marked with gateposts topped with miniature replicas of the Eiffel Tower and the Leaning Tower of Pisa, surrounds the house. A three-tier planter and a wishing well of cobblestones ornament the yard of this delightful personal fantasy.

Huron County   (HU)

PORT HOPE

HU01 William R. and Mary Leuty Stafford House

1866. 4467 Main St.

From its elevated site, Port Hope's finest house overlooks the remains of its owner's sawmill, planing mill, salt works, and docks and commands "an extended and magnificent view of Lake Huron." William R. Stafford (1828–1916), an enterprising man who exploited the resources of Huron County and built up the town of Port Hope, in the 1850s secured needed capital from friends back east in New Hampshire for investments in the pine lands of Huron County. The lumber was hauled to Port Hope. Here it was sawed and planed, some of it manufactured into sashes and doors, and loaded onto ships bound for lumberyards owned by Stafford and his partners at Cleveland. When the forests were depleted, Stafford sold or farmed the cutover lands and milled flour. In 1866 he and his wife, Mary Leuty (1841–1926), erected this wooden Italian villa. A tower with a flared and pinnacled roof rises from the embrace of the wings of the house with a front gable and wing plan. The house has paired brackets, a balustraded porch, front bay window, and oculi. Adjacent to the Stafford house is the Isaac Leuty House, a Gothic Revival structure erected in the 1870s at 7955 School Street for Stafford's father-in-law; and the Frederick and Elizabeth Stafford House, a Queen Anne house built in the late 1880s for their daughter is at 4489 Main Street.

HURON CITY

HU02 Pioneer Huron City Museum

1881–1882. Pioneer Huron City, on Pioneer Rd., just north of Michigan 25

The saga of Huron City began in 1853 with the arrival of Langdon Hubbard (1816–1892), a partner in the firm of R. B. Hubbard and Company. Although a sawmill had existed in Huron City since about 1845, the efforts of Hubbard were responsible for its growth. Under his guidance, lumber and flouring mills, shingle production, and shipping facilities were developed. The Great Fires of 1871 and 1881 destroyed the town, but it was rebuilt after each. Hubbard's perseverance paid him well; by the mid-1880s he owned 30,000 acres of land, as well as a large Huron City farm. The timber destruction from the 1881 fire and the depletion of the town's water wells soon after transformed Huron City from a lumbering center to a mere summer retreat for the Hubbards. Through the initial efforts of Langdon Hubbard's granddaughter, Carolyn Hubbard Lucas, and later her descendants, Huron City is today Pioneer Huron City, a museum complex containing a number of both original and relocated structures, including an inn, a general store, a church, and houses.

HU02.1 **The Inn**

1882

The clapboard inn is a simple structure with thin pilasters and a wide cornice trim band. Its full-length porch has a denticulated cornice and plain posts, brackets, and roof deck balustrade. As with all of the remaining original structures, the inn was part of the rebuilding after the 1881 fire. Its use as an inn ended with the decline of Huron City, after which it served as a community center.

HU02.2 **Hubbard-Phelps Church**

1885. 1925

Towered entry bays with belfries flank the main facade of the clapboard Gothic Revival chapel. Simple decorative boards pierced with quatrefoils and trefoils ornament its numerous gables, whose wall surfaces are punctured by round windows with quatrefoil tracery. Two-over-two stained-glass windows with triangular surrounds complete the structure's fenestration. During the 1920s the church was enlarged to accommodate the crowds attracted to Yale English professor William Lyon Phelps's (1865–1943) sermons, the first of which were in the 1880s. After Phelps's marriage to Hubbard's daughter, Annabel (1863–1939) in 1892, Huron City became their summer home, so that by 1922 he preached almost every summer Sunday. Known throughout the nation as a critic for *Scribner's Magazine* and as a syndicated columnist, his services drew around one thousand people.

HU02.3 **Lakeside (Langdon and Amanda J. Lester Hubbard House) / Seven Gables (William Lyon and Annabel Hubbard Phelps House)**

1882

This large clapboard house is the third Hubbard residence to occupy the site; the first two were destroyed in the Great Fires of 1871 and 1881. The present picturesque structure has a steeply pitched roof, bargeboards, and pointed-arch gable windows. Paired cornice brackets support the roof of the Italianate porch and first-floor bay window. As the house of Langdon Hubbard and his wife Amanda (1842–1869), the structure was known as Lakeside; William Lyon Phelps later changed the name to the literature-inspired Seven Gables. The house's romantic decoration makes it a centerpiece of the complex.

HU02.4 **Langdon Hubbard General Store**

c. 1882

This simple, utilitarian general store was operated for Langdon Hubbard by various men who were also winter caretakers for Seven Gables. While it ceased to function in 1953, it remains as a typical example of a Michigan country store.

Tuscola County (TU)

CARO

Caro is the center of sugar beet growing and refining.

TU01 **Tuscola County Courthouse**

1932–1933, William H. Kuni. 440 North State St. (Michigan 81)

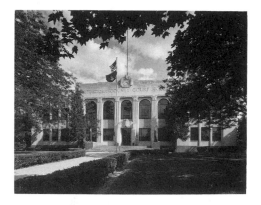

An Italianate brick courthouse built in 1873 to the designs of Porter and Watkins of Bay City had served the community until it emerged from the pioneer stage of development. As the thriving agricultural county needed more space for business and for the safeguarding of valuable records, in 1926 the electors of Tuscola County voted to assess a special tax of one mill for seven years to create a special fund for a new courthouse. In 1931 the building committee reviewed plans submitted by more than two dozen architects and selected the proposal of William H. Kuni of Detroit. Final plans and specifications for a modernistic government building were approved that year. In 1931 Cecil M. Kelly of Flint, formerly of Caro, got the contract to build the structure and began work by removing the old brick Italianate courthouse from the large well-manicured site donated by Caro pioneer Peter DeWitt Bush (1818–1913).

The present two-story courthouse was thought to have "balance, grace and dignity."[60] The main facade of its central portion contains windows recessed in five vertical bays beneath round arches separated by fluted pilasters with capitals carved in unique relief. In the cornice above the main entrance is a round clock. Balancing wings are marked by slender piers that separate windows and by square piers that rise at each corner and project above the cornice line. The structure rests on a foundation of Minnesota granite and is faced with smooth Indiana limestone decorated with patterned banding and relief sculpture.

Equally grand is the interior, whose lobby leads to a sweeping staircase lit by a large artglass window. On the stair landing between the first and second floors, the stained-glass window depicts Lewis Cass signing a treaty with the Indians on the banks of the Cass River as it flows through Tuscola County. It was manufactured by the Detroit Stained Glass Works Company. Both the lobby and the barrel-vaulted second-floor ceilings display beautiful moldings carrying various geometric patterns. Wood paneling is used extensively in the circuit courtroom on the second floor.

The new courthouse seemed modern in every respect. The local newspaper said it possessed "extraordinarily beautiful lines, a harmonious balance, good detail, and a plainness that gives it stateliness and character."[61] Moreover, depression prices had reduced its estimated cost of $300,000 to $180,000.

AKRON TOWNSHIP

TU02 Nelson Harrington House

1903. 4811 Centerline Rd.

Displaying a flamboyant taste for texture and color, the patterned and polychromatic brick houses of Michigan's Thumb rank among the state's finest examples of vernacular architecture. The unique houses, which were built on the lonely rural plains of the region primarily from 1900 to 1920, rely for decorative effect solely on the use of brick, instead of more typical turned wood or wrought-iron ornamentation. The Nelson Harrington House displays a number of features typical of polychromatic houses, such as the diamond-shaped panel below the front gable and the sawtooth-like quoining. Both devices are constructed of bricks whose color contrasts with those used in the rest of the house.

The source of the Thumb's unusual mode of building may be found across Lake Huron in the farmhouses and small towns of southern Ontario, where polychromatic and patterned brick architecture had been used since the early nineteenth century. The intricate diamond-shaped, sawtooth, and rectilinear patterns found in the Thumb, however, were a later variation that became popular in Ontario roughly from 1860 to 1890. This mid-century popularity of polychromatic and patterned brick in Ontario was most likely promoted by John Ruskin's popular *The Stones of Venice* (1851–1853) but more specifically by the widely circulated magazine *The Canada*

Farmer, which showed the fanciful decorative possibilities of brick. *The Canada Farmer,* in particular, stressed the need for "proper" rural houses, illustrating various plans, including some executed with polychromatic and patterned brickwork.

If the way in which brick was used for decoration changed during the period from 1860 to 1890, the fundamental building style to which it was applied did not. In the Province of Ontario, an irregular T- or L-plan with simple Gothic Revival elements, such as sharply peaked, one-bay-wide gables, was the canvas for the vernacular brick palette. The long-lived popularity of the Gothic Revival in rural Ontario was the product of several factors—its nationalistic associations with Britain, its emphasis in publications like *The Canada Farmer* as being fashionably picturesque, and the relative ease with which it could be applied to a simple house.

The transplantation of rural Ontario's patterned and polychromatic brick building traditions to Michigan came through migration. From the 1830s to 1900, large numbers of Ontario natives, as well as immigrants passing through Ontario, flooded into Michigan's Thumb. They were driven to the state primarily by economic factors, the most prevalent being a scarcity of arable land in southern Ontario. Other motivations included the attraction of Michigan's booming lumber industry, followed by the availability of cheap land in Michigan during the Civil War, and later an agricultural depression in Ontario caused by the flood of crops from Canada's western provinces. Throughout the nineteenth century, Michigan offered a fresh start to these farmers, who possessed a building vocabulary grounded in the Gothic Revival and the use of brick for ornamental effects.

Beyond the use of polychromatic and patterned brick, the Harrington house, by an Ontario immigrant, reflects the Ontario influence through the use of the steeply pitched, one-bay-wide gable typical of the rural Ontario Gothic Revival. Additionally the Harrington house's irregular T-plan is identical to that found on many of its Ontario predecessors.

The popularity of patterned and polychromatic brick also passed into the non-Canadian immigrant community.

GAGETOWN VICINITY, ELKLAND TOWNSHIP

TU03 Octagon Barn of the James L. and Cora Warner Purdy Farm

1922–1924; James Purdy; John and George Munro, carpenters. 6948 Richie Rd.

In 1922–1924, two years after putting up their eighteen-room house on 500 acres two miles southeast of Gagetown, James Purdy (1869?-1950), a Gagetown banker, and his wife Cora, built this huge timber-frame octagonal barn. It was designed in a circular plan to permit the efficient and economic raising of Black Angus cattle. The octagon barn measures some 100 feet in diameter. Above 48-foot-high walls a two-stage roof is pierced with shed dormers that project from a clerestory and is topped by a cupola. Multiple windows admit light into the interior in a way uncommon in round barns. Feed was dropped from the mow down the center. An overhead tramway that encircles the second floor was used to load and unload hay from the upper loft. Tradition has it that Purdy and his carpenter-builder sketched the design for the barn from their observations of circular barns in California.

VASSAR

TU04 Townsend and Celia Gibson North House

1865. 1880, remodeling and addition. 325 North Main St.

Commanding a high bluff on the Cass River, the Townsend North House overlooks Vassar. The Queen Anne house took its present appearance in 1880 as the reworking and addition to an earlier house built by the Norths in 1865. A massive, square, pyramid-roofed tower rises from the angle of the structure's L-shaped plan and dominates the asymmetrically gabled mass. Unlike many Queen Anne houses, the North house has extensive unadorned clapboarded wall surfaces, although the gables do have simple vertical boards. Eastlake decoration includes turned spindlework in the porch friezes and turned trusses in the gables. Behind the beautiful etched-glass front door is a modern nineteenth-century home; it was the first in town with central heating and a hot and cold water system. It is finished with cherry, walnut, and oak. Born in Ulster, New York, Townsend North (1814–1889) came to Washtenaw County in 1836 and to Vassar in the late 1840s. North was granted 3,000 acres of land for participating in building the first bridge over the Cass River at Bridgeport. He founded the town of Vassar and established its first sawmill in 1849, as well as a bank, and a woolen mill. North also served as state senator from 1874 to 1875. On the centennial of the founding of Vassar, the *Tuscola County Pioneer Times* for July 29, 1949, articulated the community's affection for the North house. "Standing proud and tall on a bluff it is reminiscent of the majestic forest which was felled to bring commerce and civilization to a community."

TUSCOLA TOWNSHIP

TU05 John Stern House

c. 1880. 9906 Frankenmuth Rd.

Built by the Bavarian native John Stern, the end-gabled house uses projecting sawtooth

TU05 John Stern House

quoins like the William Kirk and William Ellison houses, and it also incorporates a rounded, two-story, recessed archway with a second-story balcony in the middle of the front facade. Taken with the more typical examples from the early twentieth century, the nineteenth-century examples of patterned and polychromatic brickwork demonstrate the distinctive influence that rural Ontario building traditions had on Michigan's Thumb.

WATROUSVILLE, JUNIATA TOWNSHIP

TU06 Richard C. and Flora Chubb Burtis House

1879–1880. 2163 South Ringle Rd.

This small, but exquisitely detailed Second Empire brick house was built on a 40-acre plot of land for Richard C. Burtis (b. 1824), a local dry goods merchant, and his family. Burtis came here from Troy, New York, in 1857. The front bay window of the one-and-a-half-story asymmetrical house terminates in a tower that rises above the multicolored slate-clad, straight mansard roof. The mansard tower itself is pierced by dormers and crowned with a finial. The house has porches, bays, and dormers and is richly trimmed with decorative brackets and lacy carvings.

TU06 Richard C. and Flora Chubb Burtis House

FAIRGROVE TOWNSHIP

TU07 **William Kirk House**

1880. 5509 Gilford Rd.

Built in 1880 for a prominent Tuscola County citizen who became its state representative in 1890, this house is notable for its Ontario-influenced decorative brickwork. Projecting sawtooth quoins, piers, window hoods, and friezelike bands executed in two colors of brick create an unusual mix of three-dimensional and chromatic effects on an Italianate cube with gabled ell. Two miles away at 5821 Dixon Road in Denmark Township is an identical house built for William Ellison, who came from Ontario in 1872.

Lapeer County (LP)

LAPEER

Lapeer was established in 1831. Encouraged to explore the area by Judge Daniel LeRoy of Pontiac, who had speculated in land here, three men from New York State, Alvin N. Hart, Oliver B. Hart, and Joseph Morse, selected the site for settlement. Before Alvin Hart (1804–1874) returned from New York to Lapeer to begin settlement, the Pontiac Mill Company constructed a sawmill on Farmers Creek at the eastern edge of the current city. In November of 1831, Hart arrived with his family and additional settlers, only to find that Jonathan R. White of the Pontiac Mill Company already was there. Neither Hart nor White was willing to retreat from his settlement plan, so the townsite developed as two separate and fiercely competitive communities. The rivalry of these early years culminated with a courthouse war. It began when both families had courthouses constructed in the neighboring plots and promoted their use for county functions. The county finally purchased Hart's courthouse in the eastern plot, in 1858, the year after the village was incorporated, insuring the rancorous but inevitable union of the two competitive settlements.

In 1869 Lapeer was incorporated as a city, and within three years, boasted 3,000 resi-

dents and a prosperous downtown shopping area along Nepassing Street. Growth was steady, because Lapeer served a richly forested hinterland supporting in the county thirty-four manufacturers of wood products and seventy sawmills; within the town, several flour mills and foundries were active. With the arrival of the Port Huron and Lake Michigan Railroad in 1871 and the Detroit and Bay City Railroad in 1872, expanded markets were opened to farmers purchasing the cleared timberlands. By 1880 the town's business district had expanded substantially; new residents had built homes, as well as churches, schools, and a variety of community buildings; the town had erected additional bridges and roads; and in 1895, the state opened the Lapeer Home for Feeble-Minded and Epileptics. Agriculture dominated the local economy after the turn of the century; one of the major crops during the first half of the twentieth century was potatoes, but increasingly land was devoted to dairy farming. The Michigan Central Railroad arrived in 1904 and further spurred development. Automobile parts manufacturers were established to serve the automobile industry in Flint and Detroit; tools and aircraft specialty parts also were produced by local industries. Today, in addition to maintaining this industrial base and serving the county's farmers, Lapeer functions as a bedroom community for Flint and Port Huron and for Detroit's northern suburbs.

LP01 **Lapeer County Historical Society Museum** (Lapeer County Courthouse)

1845–1846, Alvin N. Hart?. Nepassing St. (southwest corner of Nepassing and Court streets; bounded by Nepassing, Court, Clay, and Cedar streets)

The Lapeer County Courthouse tells of the rivalry between the two families who settled Lapeer, the Harts and the Whites. The twin settlements of Hart and White were designated as the seat of Lapeer County government in 1835. The first board of supervisors met in the winter of 1835–1836 but gave no indication as to which town would actually be the seat of government. So the Whites completed a modest frame structure in 1840, and it was accepted by the board of supervisors on July 4 of that year. Apparently this small building was chosen over an equally modest one begun earlier by the Harts. Undaunted, the Harts began construction of a new, bigger, and much more elaborate courthouse that was completed before 1846. The board purchased it from Hart in 1853 for $4,500.

This is the present two-story Greek Revival Lapeer County Historical Society Museum. It rests on a raised foundation and has a giant pedimented portico supported by four colossal fluted Doric columns. A three-tier square tower that contains the entry and staircase and diminishes to a polygonal tier then a dome rises from the rear portion of the roof. The building is constructed of native pine on a brick foundation and sheathed with boards and battens. Horizontal boards laid with flush joints cover the exterior walls of the tower, and quoins in imitation of stone define its corners. Divided circular staircases in the tower lead to the second-floor courtroom. The heavily molded wood door and window enframements, wainscoting, and floors of the second-floor courtroom and other interior spaces are intact, but the interior detail is not as elaborate as the exterior. The Lapeer County Courthouse remains a fine provincial example of the dignified Greek Revival style.

DRYDEN

LP02 **John W. and Polly Parkhurst Day House**

1856. 4985 Dryden Rd. (northeast corner of Dryden Rd. and Rochester St.)

Unusual ornamentation decorates this wooden Greek Revival house in the agricultural center of Dryden. It is a two-story, three-bay main temple-front structure with a single-story ell. Four attenuated full-height Ionic columns support the pedimented portico. Their extremely attenuated proportions, however, and the delicate scale of the round-arch brackets and finials that link them, are Federal, and not Greek. Wide entablatures, flush-board siding, and a center door with elaborately molded enframement detail the two-story portion of the main facade. Additional brackets and finials, also delicate in scale, ornament the recessed porch of the ell that includes an eavesline and wide entablature facing the street. The innocent mixture of Federal elements with a basically Greek Revival format makes the Day house typical of many untutored hybrids that marked the American frontier. John W. Day (1810–1881), a farmer who moved from Macomb County in 1836, built this home on 160 acres in Dryden Township in 1856 for himself and his wife Polly, who was a native of Lima, New York, and their family.

The Heartland

ONCE HEAVILY TIMBERED WITH HARDWOODS IN THE SOUTH and pine in the north, dotted with lakes, swamps, and bogs, and laced with rivers and streams, the Heartland of Michigan today is a region of open fields and woods. Well-established farms in the south and oil wells and refineries in the central and northern portions now replace the forests. North of Clare the hilly and wooded land is sparsely populated, for the land is poorly suited for farming and the growing season is short. Eight miles north of Clare, where elm and oak abruptly give way to jack pine and bush, the glacial moraine marks the beginning of northern Michigan—the land known to Michiganians as "Up North." US Route 27 bisects the region. The rivers and streams in the east drain into Lake Huron, those on the west flow into Lake Michigan.

Hunters, trappers, and settlers arrived in the counties of the Heartland in the 1840s, 1850s, and 1860s, making their way up the rivers and streams. In the 1840s settlers arrived in Montcalm County. Some time before 1843 Nathan Hersey, a trapper, traveled into Osceola County. In 1846 Arnold Payne and his family moved from Ingham County to what became Fulton Township in Gratiot County, began clearing land, and built a log house. They became that county's first settlers; others slowly followed.

In the 1850s the first permanent settlers arrived in Mecosta County. John Parish, a hunter and a trapper, built in 1851 a cabin one mile north of present-day Big Rapids, at what is now Paris. But in the 1850s and 1860s, Mecosta remained an isolated county. In 1854 pioneer families founded the settlement of Salt River, now Shepherd, in Isabella County. In 1861 Marvel Secord and his family traveled from Midland up the Tittabawassee River by canoe and built a log house at Dick's Forks. They were the first permanent Euro-American settlers in Gladwin County.

365

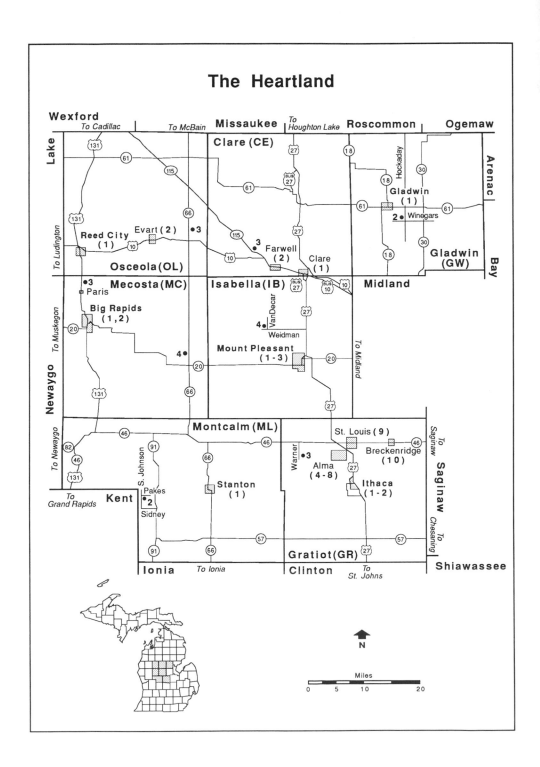

The Heartland

Lumbering was the first industrial activity vital to the economic development of the Heartland. It began here in the 1850s, later than it did along the coast-lines and near the mouths of the major rivers. In 1850 Delos A. Blodgett formed a lumbering partnership in Muskegon with Thomas D. Stimson and James Kennedy, headed up the Muskegon River in a canoe to a point above any other lumbering camp, and established a camp at the junction of the Hersey and Muskegon rivers, near present-day Hersey in Osceola County. They claimed land, cut timber, and in 1858 built a sawmill and gristmill at Hersey. This sawmill and others became the foci for settlement and later towns. In 1851 Blodgett and Stimson continued even farther up the Muskegon River and cut the first pine in Clare County. Lumbering boomed in the region after the Civil War, and Blodgett and Stimson's operation grew accordingly. Eventually they logged in several adjacent counties, shipping large quantities of timber to saw-mills in Muskegon.

The rivers and streams of the region furnished a ready-made system for transporting logs to mills at shipping harbors on or near Lakes Huron and Michigan. To float their logs downstream, loggers built dams that flooded large areas of land. The Muskegon and Tittabawassee rivers and their tributaries, together with the Flat and Chippewa rivers, all carried logs to processing mills downstream. Even so, it was only after the Flint and Pere Marquette Railroad was built in the 1870s to Clare, Farwell, and Reed City, and narrow-gage log-ging railroads were run into Clare, Osceola, and Gladwin counties that a trans-portation system was developed that permitted the full harvest of the forests of the Heartland. The result was the establishment of such lumber and mill towns as Big Rapids, Howard City, Greenville, Stanton, and Evart. These mill towns in the forests all possess excellent examples of Michigan's lively wood building tradition. At Farwell, for example, the Detroit firm of Mason and Rice designed the Queen Anne Hitchcock house.

With the exhaustion of forests in the 1890s, the economy of the southern portion of the region shifted to agriculture. The farms of the Heartland pro-duced oats, grains, clover, potatoes, sugar beets, dry beans, soybeans, and live-stock. Herdsmen and dairymen developed large ranches in the vicinity of Clare. Their billowing barns, capable of storing huge quantities of hay and sheltering livestock, and their tall silos are visible as one travels along U.S. Route 27. Large grain elevators stand along the railroad tracks at Breckenridge, Clare, and other towns.

Some of the region's rivers provided the waterpower for mills, factories, and industries. In the 1880s William Horner's maple flooring company and the Reed City Woolen Mills were important manufactories on the Muskegon River in Reed City. In 1908 Frank S. Gibson began making wooden refrigerators and agricultural implements in factories and foundries on the Flat River in Green-ville, and in 1931 the company made modern refrigerators.

The arrival of the Grand Rapids and Indiana Railroad on its route north in the 1870s ensured the growth of Howard City, Reed City, and Big Rapids. It brought large numbers of fishermen and hunters to the lakes, streams, and woods of the region and aided the growth of outdoor recreation. Many log and wood hunting and fishing cabins were constructed. Later, in the first decades of the twentieth century, the network of good improved roads crisscrossed the Heartland. At Clare, automobile travelers were served by the Doherty Hotel.

Natural gas and oil deposits were discovered near Mount Pleasant in 1927, in Gladwin County in 1934, and in northern Montcalm in the 1920s and 1930s. The oil industry helped to ease the strain of the Great Depression on the people of the Heartland. The profits of the oil industry went into some of the region's buildings, and the growth of three of its principal cities, Mount Pleasant, Alma, and Gladwin, was the direct result of this newly discovered resource. The Moderne Gladwin County Courthouse erected in 1939 to the plans of Frederick D. Madison exemplifies the architecture built with oil profits.

Numerous institutions have established schools in the Heartland. In 1884 Woodbridge Ferris founded Ferris Industrial School, the precursor of Ferris Institute and present-day Ferris State University; the first campus building was erected in 1893. In 1885 the Presbyterian Synod of Michigan established Alma College in Alma. The Dunning Memorial Chapel with its tall steeple and columned semicircular portico (1940–1941) is a landmark. In 1891 the Mount Pleasant Improvement Company was formed; it acquired 60 acres of land and sold lots. In 1893 Mount Pleasant was selected as the site of Central Normal School and Business Institute at Mount Pleasant. Two years later this institution was given to the state and became the Central Michigan Normal School, now Central Michigan University. In 1893 the United States Indian Industrial School opened at Mount Pleasant as part of a cultural assimilation program for Chippewa Indians. It was taken over by the state in 1927 but virtually closed in 1933. A small Indian reservation is on 1,220 acres near Mount Pleasant.

The lumbermen of the region also nurtured new industries and institutions. Ammi Wright, the Saginaw and Alma lumberman, promoted the establishment of the Alma Sanitarium, the precursor of the Masonic Home, and of Alma College. He inaugurated Michigan's sugar beet industry. In 1906 the Alma Sugar Company and others formed the Michigan Sugar Company. The factory complex, now empty, remains in Alma.

The region's ethnic groups are represented by Danes, who came to Montcalm County in large numbers in the 1850s, blacks, who came to Mecosta County after the Civil War, and Germans, who arrived in Reed City.

Isabella County (IB)

MOUNT PLEASANT

Situated on the Chippewa River, Mount Pleasant originated as a trading post and was settled in 1861. It is at the juncture of U.S. Route 27 and Michigan 20. The community was incorporated as a village in 1875 and as a city in 1889. After the close of the lumbering era, the surrounding rolling farmland produced grain, potatoes, and grass, and a condensed milk factory was opened. The river supplied waterpower for sawmills and the manufacture of sashes, doors, staves, flour, and castings. In the late nineteenth century, a U.S. government Indian school and a state-supported college were established at Mount Pleasant. In the twentieth century, oil refineries of the central Michigan gas and oil fields, as well as education, became the basis of Mount Pleasant's economy.

IB01 Michigan Condensed Milk Factory (Borden Creamery)

1908, Henry Herring. 320 West Broadway (west of Mosher, east of the Chippewa River)

The Michigan Condensed Milk Factory, designed by Henry Herring, a Borden Company engineer from New York, is a large two-story red brick structure with a gabled roof topped by eight cupolas that may have served as ventilators. On behalf of local farmers, local attorney Samuel W. Hopkins contracted with the Borden Company to build a subsidiary milk condensing plant in Mount Pleasant. The plant greatly improved agriculture and the economy in the Mount Pleasant vicinity. Prices of cattle and pastureland increased, and the efficiency resulting from the process led many crop farmers to change to dairy farming.

IB02 Fancher Elementary School (Fancher School)

1936–1937, G. M. Merritt and Lyle S. Cole. 801 South Kinney (southeast corner South Kinney and East High streets)

The Public Works Administration touted the Fancher School as one of the two most exemplary PWA projects in Michigan and illustrated it, together with the Saginaw City Hall (SA05.1, p. 320), in its report on the accomplishments of the program in the state. Detroit architects designed the school in the Collegiate Gothic style favored for educational buildings in the 1920s and 1930s. The rather formidable and highbrow style and the friendly scale of the little school make it a welcome neighbor on Mount Pleasant's premier residential street, which links Central Michigan University on the south with the commercial district on the north. The exterior walls of the school are of light yellowish brown Briar Hill sandstone trimmed with limestone. The northern gabled wing contains a specially designed kindergarten finished with a fireplace and a drinking fountain alcove surrounded with colorful Pewabic tile, a metal light fixture with circus animal cutouts, and a wooden ceiling supported with oak timbers. The school had nine other classrooms, three work areas, and two rooms for a cafeteria and play area. Pewabic tile decorates the water fountains and other areas of the interior. The south gymnasium wing is a later addition. Vollmer Construction of Saginaw built the school at a cost of $110,000. The monies for the project were a match of federal and local funding. Critics called the school "the most beautiful and practical of its kind" and indicative of the progress the city had made with the development of the oil industry.[62] It was named for early local lawyer and school board member Isaac A. Fancher.

IB03 A. J. Smith House

c. 1930, A. J. Smith. 205 North Kinney (northwest corner of North Kinney and Mosher streets)

Although this rambling Spanish Colonial Revival house, with its red clay tile roof and stucco exterior, looks indigenous to California, it was actually designed by architect A. J. Smith of Mount Pleasant as his own home. The center portion is two stories with an extended portico. A cross-gable addition is attached to the north side, and an octagonal tower is on the south. While the rear of the building is free of ornamentation, the front and side facades are elaborately embellished with frieze boards carrying applied decorative motifs. The unusual stained-glass windows emphasize the Mediterranean flavor of the structure. Smith may have substituted them for iron grilles, which are prevalent in Spanish Colonial Revival buildings. The Smith house is an exceptional example of a style that was rarely seen in Michigan.

WEIDMAN VICINITY, NOTTAWA TOWNSHIP

IB04 **Woodyvale Round Barn** (Richard Stevens and Sons Round Barn–Tom Mills Round Barn)

1908, Tom Mills. 3159 North Vandecar Rd. (northwest corner of Weidman and North Vandecar roads, 4 miles east of Weidman)

After the opening of the Michigan Condensed Milk Factory in Mount Pleasant in 1908, dairy farming increased rapidly in the surrounding farmlands. Tom Mills, a pro-

gressive and innovative farmer who wanted to design "the perfect dairy barn," built this horizontally sided, two-level circular barn. The barn is 60 feet in diameter and 50 feet in height. Thirty milking stanchions radiated from a centrally positioned silo to permit the convenient feeding of livestock. Hay is stored on the second floor, beneath the trusses of an immense domed roof, unobstructed by vertical support posts. In the 1960s two rectangular pitched-roof pole barns were added to accommodate two hundred cows and calves in all.

The usefulness of the round barn for dairy farming was recognized throughout the Midwest. Between the 1880s and the 1910s agricultural experiment stations and agricultural colleges published and widely distributed articles, circulars, and bulletins on the economy of the construction of the round barn, its labor efficiency and ventilation. The round barn may be linked to the technological advances of the Industrial Revolution, as seen in the railroad locomotive roundhouses, and to the octagon mode advocated by Orson Squire Fowler in his publication, *The Octagon Home* (1853). The popularity of these utilitarian structures declined after World War I for several reasons. They were difficult to light, their self-supporting roofs often failed and were expensive to repair, and they did not make good wind breaks for the livestock when turned out in the barnyard. The Stevens barn is one of less than thirty polygonal and round barns that survive in the state.

Gratiot County (GR)

ITHACA

GR01 **Gratiot County Courthouse**

1900–1902, Claire Allen. East Center St. (bounded by East Center, South Jeffrey Ave., East Newark, and South Main)

In 1899 the people of Gratiot County elected to bond the county in the amount of $34,000 for a courthouse "for safe and careful preservation of the public records of the county, and for the proper and commodious transaction of its business."[63] The citizens of Ithaca donated $4,000 to ensure its construction on courthouse square in the county seat of

Ithaca, rather than in Alma. The plans and specifications of the distinguished architect Claire Allen (1853–1942) of Jackson for a Beaux-Arts Classical creation were selected from those of more than a dozen architects. The result is a fine courthouse design.

The rectangular structure measures 76 feet by 112 feet in plan. Its smooth-cut light yellowish brown sandstone exterior walls are penciled to the second story. Pedimented pavilions, three of which contain round-arch entrances, project slightly from the center of all four sides of the building. The one-story main entrance portico is arcaded and topped by a balustrade. The arches are carried on

GR01 Gratiot County Courthouse

heavy Composite columns with spiral fluting and on corner piers with panels containing figurative relief carving. All four pediments are carved with floral motifs. A cornice supported by consoles encircles the building. A powerful three-stage clock and bell tower with balustrades, oculi, and an octagonal-sided domed roof supported by fluted Composite columns rises 120 feet from the ground and tops the courthouse. The hipped roof is covered with slate. A. W. Mohnke of Grand Rapids was the builder, and Jere. Marks of Saint Louis supervised its construction.

The interior of the courthouse pivots around a rotunda in the same manner as does the Shiawassee County Courthouse (SE01, p. 339). It is finished in oak and marble. A clock made in 1905 by N. Johnson of Manistee is on the second floor. The courtroom occupies the east end of the upper stories of the building. The seats slope toward the classically detailed judge's bench and ornamental wall beyond. The courthouse was heated with steam. The building cost $74,103 to build. The present courthouse replaced a wooden Italianate structure with an open cupola erected by William C. Beckwith in 1871–1872. The new courthouse was regarded by the *Gratiot County News* in 1902 as the "best outside of Detroit and Grand Rapids."

GR02 Elmer and Jenny Heath House

1892. 310 South Jeffrey Ave. (second door south of the southwest corner of South Jeffrey Ave. and South St.)

The varied gabled roofline, the conical tower, and the rich texture of the clapboard and shingle siding of the Heath house demonstrate the persistence of the Queen Anne style throughout Michigan. This house is a showplace of decorative techniques. The gables are stuccoed with pebble dash, including broken china crockery and glass, and the wood decorations in the peaks, which depict cherubs and foliation, were carved by Jenny Heath herself. Her husband, Elmer, was a hardware merchant.

RIVERDALE, SUMNER TOWNSHIP

GR03 Solomon LaPaugh House

c. 1879–1880. 5833 Warner Rd. (Gratiot County 549) (between Lincoln and Van Buren roads, approximately 6 miles west of Alma and just over 2 miles south of Michigan 46)

Solomon LaPaugh (1830–1893), whose ancestors emigrated to Philadelphia from Germany in 1764, built this house shortly after his first home burned in 1879. The steeply pitched paired front gables and the ornately carved second-story porch demonstrate a modest Gothic influence, but there is also evidence of the Italianate style in the stacked bay windows, paired side windows, and central tower. In fact, it is a splendid vernacular house, trying a bit of everything. The house now has a central entrance with an eyebrow transom and side lights and remains relatively unchanged, except for the entrance and rear addition built in 1984.

ALMA

Alma is located on the Pine River, the Pere Marquette and Ann Arbor railroads (now the Mid-Michigan Railroad), U.S. Route 27, and Michigan 46. Once in the midst of an extensive lumbering region, the surrounding land was transformed into farms. The river afforded a source of waterpower for the early establishment of mills, a foundry and machine shop, and a farm implement factory. Artesian wells and mineral springs suited the town for development as a sanitarium. Alma citizen and lumberman Ammi W. Wright promoted the founding of a college, a sugar factory, and the Masonic Home. Presbyterians founded Alma College here in 1885. Today Alma is a center of oil and sugar beet districts.

GR04 **Alma's Public Building** (Alma City Hall)

1902, Haug and Schuermann. 1935, late 1930s, additions. 225 East Superior St. (Business US 27) (northwest corner of East Superior and Gratiot streets)

In 1902 the citizens of Alma voted to bond the city for $12,000 for the site and construction of a city hall. Haug and Schuermann of Saginaw designed the structure in quasi-Romanesque terms. A medieval clock tower, rather German in character, rises from the southeast corner of the two-story, hipped-roof, red brick building. Police and fire department additions were put on in the 1930s. A gabled and columned dormer and small cupola were removed.

GR05 **Alma Sugar Company**

1898–1899. 200 and 217 North Court (bounded by North Court, the C&O railroad tracks, and Ely St.)

All that remains of the Alma Sugar Company plant are the office, seed house, and a warehouse. In the late nineteenth century, researchers at Michigan Agricultural College, now Michigan State University, determined that the Saginaw Valley had the proper soil for raising sugar beets. Ammi W. Wright and other entrepreneurs inaugurated the state's sugar beet industry. In 1898–1899 an immense refining plant was built on this site. It was erected by the Kelby Manufacturing Company, under the supervision of H. N. Kilby (Kelby?), construction engineer. The main building stood five stories in height and was 300 by 90 feet in plan. The complex

GR05 Alma Sugar Company

included a boiler house, a lime kiln, beet sheds constructed of wood, a sugar storehouse, a cooper shop, a pulp dryer, and other sheds and barns. The office is a two-story white brick gable-roof structure, 30 by 55 feet in plan. A crow-step parapeted intersecting gable is in the front. A panel recessed in an arch above the window bay is inscribed "Alma Sugar Co. 1899." The seed store, also parapeted, is a one-story gabled brick structure. A flat-roofed, one-story extension has been removed. Consolidated into the Michigan Sugar Company in 1906, the plant operated until 1956.

GR06 **Ammi Willard and Anna Case Wright House**

1886–1887, Spier and Rohns. 503 North State St. (northwest corner of North State and East Downie streets)

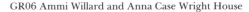

GR06 Ammi Willard and Anna Case Wright House

Having amassed a fortune in the Ammi Wright Lumber Company, which held 30,000 acres of timberland in Gladwin, Clare, and Roscommon counties and was one of the largest to operate in the Saginaw Valley, Ammi Willard Wright (1822–1912) came to Alma in 1884. Two years later he built for himself and his second wife, Anna Case, this large stone house, designed by Detroit architects Spier and Rohns, noted for their designs for railroad depots. The boxy Richardsonian building of randomly coursed rock-faced Ionia sandstone rests on a Vermont granite foundation. From it project gables, bays, and porches ornamented with balustrades, columns, and carved and checkerworked sandstone. The hipped roof is covered with clay tile. The house had the modern conveniences of hot and cold running water, gas lighting, and was wired for the future use of electricity. The chimneys and the porte-cochère have been removed. G. S. Young of Alma supervised its construction. Wright helped the burgeoning city of Alma in the 1880s by building a hotel, an opera house, and a sanitarium. He also invested in the sugar refinery, other manufacturing companies, banks, and railroads, and contributed to Alma College, the Masons, and the city. The handsome stone house says something about the strength of the character of this mid-Michigan capitalist.

GR07 **Dewey Funeral Home** (Francis and Louisa Yeomans King House / "The Orchard House")

1904, Arthur Heun. 1928, 1967, additions. 731 North State St. (northwest corner of North State and Orchard streets)

Located on Alma's finest residential street and surrounded by lovely gardens is this large eclectic house, designed by Arthur Heun, a member of the Steinway Group of Prairie school architects in Chicago. Heun (1866–1946) was born in Saginaw and studied architecture with his uncle, Ludwig Ernest Volusin Bude of Saginaw and later of Grand Rapids, before working at 812 Steinway Hall in Chicago and earning a reputation for his domestic designs. The large red brick house has intersecting gables and battered piers on its protected entryways, all of which suggest medieval origins. The ribbon band windows, on the other hand, hint at the architect's Prairie school background. The house was added to in 1928 and 1967, and a central entrance was removed. Francis and Louisa Yeomans King had, indeed, come from Chicago to live in Alma in 1902, after a stay at the Alma Sanitarium. Francis King (b. 1863) was a banker and manufacturer who served as president of the Alma Board of Trade, as well as mayor of Alma in 1907–1908 and state senator in 1913. Louisa Yeomans King (b. 1864) was a horticulturist who was a founder of the Michigan Federation of Garden Clubs and an author of several horticulture books.

GR08 **Michigan Masonic Home**

1930–1931 to present, Osgood and Osgood. 1200 Wright Ave. (Business US 27)

This group of residential, hospital, and nursing care structures stands on an open tract of land on the outskirts of Alma. It is operated by the Grand Lodge of Free and Accepted Masons of Michigan. Seven original buildings erected between 1930 and 1931 are included in this complex of Colonial Revival structures. The two-and-a-half-story brick buildings have gable and gambrel roofs with flat-roof and gable dormers. Buildings "B" and "H" each have extended full-width square-piered porticos and shed dormers. In 1910 fire destroyed the first Masonic Home (erected in 1891), on Reed's Lake near Grand Rapids. Ammi W. Wright donated to the Masons the former Alma Sanitarium (1885), a white brick four-story structure on State Street that accommodated two hundred guests. In 1929 the sanitarium was considered outdated and the present site was purchased. The Grand Rapids architectural firm of Osgood and Osgood, specialists in designs for Masonic temples, designed the home.

SAINT LOUIS

GR09 **John A. and Catherine Jenkins Elwell House**

1880–1885, John Elwell and an unknown Swedish architect?. 103 Delaware St. (northwest corner of West Washington Ave. [Michigan 46] and North Delaware St.)

This splendid house stands on the most prominent site in this quarter of Saint Louis as a stunning climax of the Queen Anne style

GR09 John A. and Catherine Jenkins Elwell House

in the lumbering regions of Michigan. John A. Elwell (1832–1910) came to this town on the Pine River in 1875 from New York City to lease, extend, improve, and operate the Chicago, Saginaw and Canada Railroad (later part of the Pere Marquette system). He brought with him needed capital and business expertise. Local tradition has it that Elwell wanted to create for himself and his wife, Catherine, a house similar to one he remembered in his Swedish homeland; he may even have imported the services of a Swedish architect. Most likely Elwell himself, with perhaps a Saginaw architect, and a Mr. Leach, who was a carpenter and "the best contractor/builder available," collaborated in its design, drawing for inspiration on an architectural book.[64] Together they hand-picked the lumber—all of it native to Michigan—and built this magnificent dwelling.

The rambling house is a picturesque assemblage of gables, porches, bays, a balcony, and a conical-roofed polygonal corner turret. Stickwork outlines the bays and stories of the exterior clapboarded wall plane, and decorative king-post trusses span the paneled and shingled gables. The whole is ornamented in the Eastlake decorative manner, with carved, chiseled, gouged, and scrolled posts, brackets, friezes, and panels. Cresting and finials frost the ridge of the shingled roof once clad with green slate. A matching carriage house is on the ample grounds. Unequaled by any resi-

dence in the area, the Elwell house stands as testimony of this wealthy pioneer's importance to Saint Louis.

GR10 Breckenridge

East Saginaw (Michigan 46) and Arnold Rd.

Elevators of the B&W Co-op along the south side of the Mid-Michigan Railroad (formerly Pere Marquette Railroad) tracks mark Breckenridge as a farming center. The old Farmers State Bank building of Breckenridge, formerly the First State Savings Bank, 1913, Joseph Rosatti of Cowles and Mitscheller, 228 East Saginaw, exemplifies the influence of Louis Sullivan in Michigan. Here, removed from the influence of Eastern Beaux-Arts Classicism, one banker retained the powers of independent thinking.[65] The solid rectangular bank shows the solidity and stability expected of such a building. The support piers of the front and side elevations, however, are encrusted with lively Sullivanesque terracotta ornament. Broad leaded-glass windows ensured good lighting for the banking room, which was one large space. Although not as prevalent in Michigan as in Iowa, Wisconsin, Minnesota, and elsewhere, the evidence of Louis Henry Sullivan and his disciples William Gray Purcell and George Grant Elmslie did appear in the state from time to time, as is richly illustrated here. Now covered with a synthetic sheet material and cedar shake front, the building still displays some of its original detailing.

Montcalm County (ML)

STANTON

Settled in 1862 and incorporated as a village in 1869, Stanton became a city in 1881. Its location on the Pere Marquette Railroad ensured its development as a shipping center for lumber and shingles cut at local mills. After the lumbering era Stanton continued as the seat of county government, the shipping center for surrounding potato farms that were sustained by the sandy loam soil, and as a center for resort lakes.

ML01 Montcalm County Courthouse

1910, Edwyn A. Bowd. 211 West Main St. (Michigan 66) (bounded by West Main, South Court, Walnut, and Vine streets)

The Montcalm County Courthouse was built high in the center of courthouse square as the pine forests dwindled and the economy of the county shifted to agriculture. In 1860, fifty years earlier, the Montcalm County seat was moved from its temporary location in Greenville to a site in the forest in the northeast quarter of Section 1, Township 10 North of Range 7 West. Land was acquired for the county courthouse grounds and village, and lots were platted for churches and houses. In 1870 Seth Sprague built the first courthouse for $1500. The present courthouse replaced the second courthouse, a brick and stone structure with a mansard roof and cresting. It was erected in 1879–1880 by Jacob V. Consaul of Grand Haven at a cost of $23,000.

After five years of failed attempts, proponents for a new courthouse succeeded in winning over the voters. In April 1910 a bond issue for $58,280 was passed for the construction of a new courthouse, jail, and sheriff's residence. Edwin A. Bowd of Lansing came up with the design for a simple Beaux-Arts Classical structure with Georgian overtones

that met the requirements of a modest budget but conveyed the dignity of county government. This scheme resembles his designs for the Wexford County Courthouse (1910–1911) and the Holland City Hall (1909–1911). The flat-roofed rectangular light orangish brown brick building stands on a raised smooth sandstone foundation. Paired giant Ionic columns support a center-pedimented entrance portico. An entablature, the cornice of which is supported by block modillions, encircles the building beneath the parapet. Wright and Prall of Ionia built the courthouse.

MONTCALM TOWNSHIP

ML02 Little Denmark Evangelical Lutheran Church

1877–1879, Nels Christensen, Carl Jensen, Christian J. Nielson, and Matias Bossen, builders. 1958, parish house and narthex addition. 1031 South Johnson Rd. (southeast corner South Johnson and Pakes roads, 2 miles north of Sidney Rd.)

A large number of Danish immigrants settled in Gowen in the late 1850s. Originally from Soby, Denmark, most were attracted to Michigan by reports from friends of good wages, an abundance of jobs, and cheap land. Danish-born local men, Nels Christensen, Carl Jensen, Christian Nielsen, and Matias Bossen built a clapboarded structure with a steeply pitched gable roof and round-head windows. Early interior fittings, including the white oak Gothic altarpiece, with its painting of the Ascension of Christ done in 1909 by Christian Rydahl of nearby Sidney, remain intact. Pressed metal wall paneling, fabricated by the Berger Manufacturing Company of Canton, Ohio, and installed in 1905, also remains in place. The narthex and parish house were added in 1958.

Mecosta County (MC)

BIG RAPIDS

Big Rapids is situated on the big rapids of the Muskegon River at the site of a dam that

raised the water level high enough to float logs downstream. Because of the dam, several sawmills were built here. Lumbermen financed the construction of the Muskegon and Big Rapids Railroad. This railroad provided an easy means to transport logging supplies past the dam, where they could be loaded on rafts for movement farther upriver. This activity caused Big Rapids to grow as a commercial center. With the arrival of the Grand Rapids and Indiana and the Pere Marquette railroads it became a railroad center. The discovery of mineral water brought tourists to the area in the late nineteenth century. Then Woodridge N. Ferris established a school at Big Rapids, later known as Ferris Institute, to teach industrial and commercial arts. It was incorporated in 1923, became a state-supported college in 1949, and was renamed Ferris State College in 1963.

hotel in a large portion of the building on the Maple Street side.

The rest of the building contained stores, offices, a lodge, and an armory space. The weighty first story is faced with granite and distinguished by polished columns that vaguely resemble the Composite order that support the main entrance portico. The red brick exterior walls of the upper stories are broken by bays that are delineated by pilasters and that contain segmental-arch windows. The decorative cornice line is punctuated by parapets that marked the main entrances below. The building certainly was one of the largest and most ornate in Mecosta County at the turn of the century and was considered "the finest in Northern Michigan."

MC01 Nisbett Building

1888–1902, J. H. Fisher (1900 hotel completion). 101 South Michigan Ave. (southeast corner of South Michigan Ave. and Maple St. [Michigan 20])

This ambitious Neo-Romanesque commercial block, built intermittently over a fourteen-year period, presides over the main intersection of the business district. Daniel Comstock, president of the Mecosta County Savings Bank, began construction on the portion of the building that fronts South Michigan Avenue in 1885, and when this phase was completed, the bank moved into the corner rooms. With the onset of the panic of 1893 the bank closed, and construction abruptly was halted. The building went into the receivership of the Michigan Trust Company of Grand Rapids with an appraised value of $150,000. In 1900 local publisher William Nisbett (1846–1923) purchased the building for $20,000. He completed much of the construction, hiring J. H. Fisher, a Grand Rapids builder, to create a

MC02 Old Mecosta County Jail

1893, N. J. Gibbs?. 220 South Stewart St. (west side of South Stewart St., between Elm and Linden streets)

The pretentious posture of this plump Queen Anne brick government building belies its original use as the Mecosta County Sheriff's residence and jail. Beneath a slate-clad hipped roof with intersecting gables, the two-story symmetrical brick structure rests on a rusticated fieldstone foundation, opposite the present county courthouse and jail, in a square reserved for public buildings. Corner oriel turrets on bases embossed with rinceaux and topped with bell-cast roofs surmounted with finials balance the center gable of the main facade. A pedimented wooden porch, whose tympanum is decorated with a floral pattern, protects the main entrance. This is surrounded by three segmental-arch tripartite windows with voussoirs, the center one—on the second floor—topped, in turn, by an oculus. The sheriff's residence fronts a rear wing containing the jail. The structure was probably designed by N. J. Gibbs of Mount Clemens, who did the courthouse that no longer stands. Open to public.

PARIS, GREEN TOWNSHIP

MC03 **Paris Park** (Paris Fish Hatchery)

1881, A. B. Cram. 1887, second hatchery building. 1937, renovation and expansion. 22412 Northland Dr. (Business US 131) (.1 to .2 mile north of 22 Mile Rd.)

In 1881 the State Board of Fish Commissioners established the Paris Fish Hatchery at the site of Cheney Creek, a tributary to the Muskegon River, and alongside the Grand Rapids and Indiana Railroad tracks. This was Michigan's second fish hatchery (the first was established in 1873 at Crystal Springs, near Pokagon, in Cass County), in which salmon and trout fingerlings were artificially propagated and reared for transportation in specially equipped railroad cars to other hatcheries for implantation in streams. A hatchery, ponds, and overseer's residence were constructed on the west side of the highway. In 1887 a second hatchery building, 40 by 80 feet in plan, was built on the east side of the highway. A. B. Cram of Detroit designed both hatcheries. The design of the board-and-batten structures, featuring steeply pitched, gabled roofs, was duplicated later in the hatchery built at Sault Sainte Marie in

1894. In 1937, as the fish hatchery program reached its peak in Michigan, and under the auspices of the Works Progress Administration, the hatch house of 1887 was expanded, renovated, and given its present Colonial Revival appearance. The white-painted clapboarded building has arched dormers in its steeply pitched intersecting gable roof, a cupola, and green-painted shutters.

One-half mile south, on Paris Creek at Paris (on the west side of Northland Drive, .1 mile north of Water Street), is a cobblestone hatch house, well house, and retaining wall erected in 1933 to the plans of Ernest Batterson of Kalamazoo, under the sponsorship of the federal government (WPA or CCC). It was closed shortly after opening because the water supply was insufficient.

The fish-rearing ponds have always been the pride of the local citizenry. Since 1976 the Mecosta County Park Commission has operated the hatchery as a county park.

REMUS VICINITY, WHEATLAND TOWNSHIP

MC04 **Wheatland Church of Christ**

1883. 25 Eleven Mile Rd. (southwest corner of Eleven Mile Rd. and 30th Ave. [Michigan 66])

This simple clapboarded frame structure (now covered with aluminum siding) has served continuously for the same congregation for over one hundred years. Following the Civil War, blacks from Ontario, southwest Michigan, and Ohio migrated to the Remus area, obtaining employment in both agriculture and in the burgeoning lumber industry. Deacon Thomas Cross (1826–1897) of Virginia established the congregation in 1869, when he moved his family of twelve with two other black families to Michigan's heartland. The church was built on Cross's own land, with local materials, by local builders and is a good example of functional vernacular architecture. At a time when segregation was the norm in Michigan, the Wheatland Church of Christ opened its doors to blacks, whites, and Indians.

Osceola County   (OL)

REED CITY

In 1927 the county seat was moved from Hersey to Reed City, named after J. M. Reed and Company, which had platted the town in 1870.

OL01 Livingston House

c. 1890, George F. Barber; Henry Marzolf, carpenter-builder. 343 West Upton

An architectural pattern book must have been the source of the design for this intricate and fanciful Queen Anne house embellished by Henry Marzolf as he built it. Marzolf was a local carpenter builder who came to Reed City from Listowel, Ontario. This and the delightful wooden houses to the east and west (Luin K. Parkhurst House, 1891, 335 West Upton Street and Fred Atherton House, 1891–1896, 349 West Upton Street) are evidence of the lively wood building tradition of Michigan's former lumbering regions.

EVART

Where the Pere Marquette Railroad crossed the Muskegon River, Evart also became the center for logging supplies, transshipment, and river driving on the upper Muskegon.

OL02 John and Elizabeth Downing Wilkinson House

1884. 408 Main St. (northeast corner of North Main and East Fourth streets)

This picturesque wooden house exemplifies the excellent wood craftsmanship found in even the smaller sawmill towns of Michigan. It was called by the *Evart Review* for March 28, 1884, "a fine new house of Maltese cross Gothic architecture," but it is really Queen Anne in style. The gable-front-and-wing plan of the house embraces a mansard-roofed tower. The house was finished with "the best pine siding without knots." Horseshoe decorative trusses in the shingle-clad gables are reminiscent of the Stick style. Carved panels, friezes, and running boards on the porches, bays, window enframements, and gables embellish the exterior of the house in a manner common to the Eastlake decorative mode. The Evart Planing Mill crafted the railing and newel post of the central hall staircase. A steeply gabled board-and-batten carriage house stands at the rear of the lot. The house was built for Dr. John H. Wilkinson (1845–1918) and his wife, Elizabeth. From Oxford County, Ontario, with a degree from the University of Medicine and Surgery of Philadelphia, Wilkinson came to Evart in 1873. He practiced medicine in Evart for forty-five years.

SYLVAN TOWNSHIP

OL03 Fred and Ferne Feikema Round Barn (Charles Warden Round Barn)

1907. 5660 Michigan 66 (on east side of South Michigan 66, .5 miles north of Grand Rd. and 1.5 miles north of US 10)

Built in 1907 for a retired railroad man by the name of Warden, this round barn exemplifies the experimentation, innovation, and technological change that was occurring in agriculture in the late 1800s and early 1900s. A mortared rubble-stone foundation supports the circular structure. A board-and-batten exterior sheaths a wood frame made up of interlocking joints and joists. The interlocking frame and conical roof are designed to be self-supporting and require few vertical support posts. As a result, the interior space was utilized to the fullest on both the working dairy floor and in the loft and haymow. A cobblestone milk-cooling shed is attached to the southeast side of the barn. A silo constructed in the center of this barn, which once provided ventilation and a central food and bedding distribution point for the dairy cows, has been removed. The barn and farm have ceased their dairy function but are used for beef cattle. The cupola projection that protrudes from the center of the conical roof is a remnant of that silo.

Clare County (CE)

CLARE

Clare is a crossroads at the intersection of U.S. Route 27 and U.S. Route 10 and at the gateway to northern Michigan. Its most prominent building is the Doherty Hotel (1922–1924). The hotel served as a convenient stopping place for motorists. The community was platted on the Flint and Pere Marquette Railroad, and it became a shipping center for sheep, cattle, and hogs. Grain elevators stand as evidence of the importance of agriculture and shipping to Clare. The community was incorporated as a village in 1879 and as a city in 1891.

CE01 **Clare Middle School** (Clare Public School)

1922. 1950. 1963. Bounded by State and Pine streets, Wheaton Ave., and East Hemlock St.

The projecting center section of the school lies between balancing two-story wings of classrooms. Square stair towers define the corners of the center section. Between them is a row of two-story round-arch windows that is shielded by a pent roof clad with tiles. The exterior walls are faced with decorative brickwork. Hanging in the auditorium are four murals painted in 1938 by Gerald Mast of Detroit. They depict the gas, oil, and agriculture industries of the community and the academic and recreational activities of the school. They were sponsored by the Federal Art Project of the Works Progress Administration. A sculpture, *The Pioneer Mother,* created by Samuel Cashwan (b. 1900), is in front of the building. The art work is rumored to have been the first sponsored by the WPA for an outstate Michigan school.

FARWELL

CE02 **George and Martha Hitchcock House**

1885, George DeWitt Mason and Zacharias Rice. 205 East Michigan St. (northeast corner of East Michigan and Superior streets)

George Hitchcock (d. 1889), the leader of the Farwell City Company, was Clare County's first postmaster and treasurer. His prosperity came from investments in the county's valuable stands of pine, harvested after the Pere Marquette and the Toledo and Ann Arbor railroads arrived in the 1870s, and from the operation of a sawmill. His wife, Martha, founded the Ladies Library Association in Farwell. Their house stands on the site of the old courthouse, which Hitchcock acquired after the structure burned in 1877 and the county seat was moved to Harrison. Hitchcock commissioned Mason and Rice, renowned Detroit architects who had offices in the same building as Hitchcock's brother-in-law and partner, Edmund Hall, to design the Queen Anne house. The two-and-a-half-story, wood-frame, clapboarded house with an angled gable and a steeply pitched hipped roof supported by consoles was built of timber chosen from Hitchcock's own forests and milled in Saginaw. It has gables, dormers, bays, and porches with turned posts and balusters. Basswood, golden oak, tiger-eye maple, cherry, birch, ash, and pine finish the interior.

FARWELL VICINITY, SURREY TOWNSHIP

CE03 Beechwood Farm

1900. 3690 Michigan 115 (1 mile northwest of US 10 on north side of Michigan 115)

The house at Beechwood Farm is clad in the fieldstones found in abundance in the vicinity of the glacial moraine north of Clair. Pioneer lumberman and conservationist Josiah L. Littlefield built this house in 1900 in the center of a lumbering camp. Today Concordia Lutheran College owns the structure as part of a conservation camp. The farm buildings stand in a beech woodlot. The house is a two-story, end-gable structure with a shed wing to the northwest and a rear single-story wing. The main entrance is placed on the side of the house in response to the barnyard. The exterior walls are veneered with large fieldstone boulders, each of which is surrounded by a band of cobblestones, like a string of pearls.

Gladwin County (GW)

GLADWIN

Gladwin was established by lumbermen and settled in 1876; it was incorporated as a village in 1885 and as a city in 1893. It is located on the Cedar River, the Michigan Central Railroad and Michigan 61. Today Gladwin is a center for hunting and fishing.

GW01 Gladwin County Building

1939, Frederick D. Madison. 1980, addition, Irvin Hacker. 401 West Cedar (Michigan 61) (southwest corner of West Cedar and North Bowery avenues)

In 1939 an oil boom brought an influx of people to Gladwin County and eased the economic burdens of the Great Depression in central Michigan. At the same time, the state removed a severance tax on crude oil and returned it to the county for a municipal purpose. These economic developments prompted all sixteen supervisors of Gladwin County to agree that they should build a new courthouse. The reinforced-concrete building was designed in the Moderne style by a Royal Oak architect. The rectangular, flat-roofed, light yellowish brown brick structure

has a heavy and monumental balanced symmetry. The exterior is ornamented with cut stone panels set beneath the upper windows. They are carved in intaglio and contain local scenes of lumbering, farming, dairying, oil production, hunting, and skiing. The scenes are simplified and stylized, with the major forms carved most broadly. Township names are incised in stones that run along a water table above the structure's foundation. Stylized plant motifs are carved in other stone panels. The Art Deco lobby is finished with a chamfered ceiling painted with zigzags and a floor inlaid with an Indian head. Charles C. Englehardt constructed the courthouse, which cost $82,000 to build.

GW02 Buckeye Township Hall

1939. 1498 South Hockaday Rd. (northwest corner of South Hockaday and Winegars roads, 7 miles southeast of Gladwin; Hockaday Rd. intersects Michigan 61 2.5 miles east of Gladwin; Winegars Rd. is 2.5 miles south of Michigan 61 and 3 miles west of Michigan 60)

Organized in 1882, Buckeye Township held its first meeting on April 3 at the Smallwood

Settlement schoolhouse. Nearly sixty years later, with profits from the oil fields in the township, the township built this simple Colonial Revival fieldstone hall for meetings and elections. The modest T-plan building is dignified with a two-stage tower with a balustrade on the lower level that rises at the crossing of the T and a bracketed round-arch hood filled with a sunburst that crowns its asymmetrical, slightly recessed entrance. Brick chimneys are at both ends of the structure's side-gable front portion. Characteristic of the style, the interior is paneled with knotty pine.

West Michigan Shore Region

PRIOR TO THE TREATY OF WASHINGTON IN 1836, LAND THAT includes the West Michigan Shore Region belonged to the Indians. White settlers came in 1836–1837 to harvest the forests. Much of Michigan was in the North American White Pine Belt that stretched from the Atlantic Ocean to Mississippi River. In Michigan, interspersed through the hard and softwood forests, stood an average of 5,000 board feet of pine lumber per acre of land. Because of its cell structure, pine was an ideal building material, and it floated well, so lumbermen could take advantage of the river systems in the region. The Muskegon, White, Pentwater, Pere Marquette, Big Sable, and Big and Little Manistee rivers flow into smaller lakes before emptying into Lake Michigan. These smaller lakes provided a ready means for sorting logs and served as well as protected harbors for the vessels that carried lumber to market. Lumbermen such as Charles Mears, Martin Ryerson, and Henry Pennoyer came to the region during the late 1830s and early 1840s.

Mills were built of logs along the smaller lakes; log structures also served for housing. By the late 1840s, these original groups of mills and houses would be augmented by a store, a meeting place, and perhaps even a school that might also function as a church. To facilitate transportation, docks and wharves were built. At the same time, channels from the smaller lakes into Lake Michigan were opened to permit ships direct access to the mill docks. During the late 1850s Chicago, immediately across the big lake, began a period of economic growth that would make it the leading entrepôt in the Midwest; and growth required lumber—West Michigan lumber. Meanwhile, on the western shore itself, small communities became villages; some became cities. Because of its ready availability, the primary building material was wood. In the process of building, however, nothing was wasted: scrap wood was used for fuel, sawdust

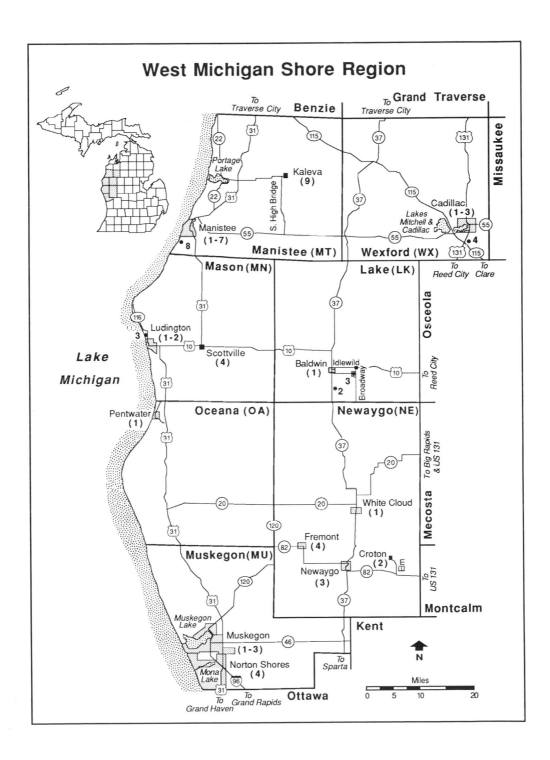

West Michigan Shore Region

Benzie

To Traverse City

To Traverse City

Grand Traverse

Missaukee

Kaleva (9)

Portage Lake

Cadillac (1-3)

Lakes Mitchell & Cadillac

Manistee (1-7)

8

Manistee (MT)

Wexford (WX)

To Reed City   To Clare

Mason (MN)

Lake (LK)

Osceola

Ludington (1-2)

3

Scottville (4)

Baldwin (1)   Idlewild

3

2

Broadway

To Reed City

Lake Michigan

Oceana (OA)

Newaygo (NE)

Pentwater (1)

To Big Rapids & US 131

Mecosta

White Cloud (1)

Fremont (4)

Croton (2)   Elm

To US 131

Muskegon (MU)

Newaygo (3)

Montcalm

Muskegon Lake

Kent

Muskegon (1-3)

Norton Shores (4)

To Sparta

N

Mona Lake

To Grand Rapids

Ottawa

Miles

0   5   10   20

To Grand Haven

was used as landfill, even for street paving. Consequently fire was a constant problem. So much so, in fact, that during the 1870s and 1880s, parts of entire towns burned, and many structures were lost. It was not until communities accumulated wealth that brick and stone buildings were erected and fire departments established. Those buildings that do remain, therefore, date to the 1870s and 1880s, during the heyday of lumbering.

As early as the 1880s, some residents realized that the lumbering boom would not last, so they set about attracting new industry to the region. Tourism was promoted, taking advantage of the lakes and rivers. Fruit farming was introduced into the land formerly used for growing pine and other trees; dairy farming was proposed for other areas. During the 1890s these transitions were in progress, and in the end new industry replaced lumbering. Some lumbermen participated in this process, others moved on to lumber elsewhere.

Muskegon County (MU)

MUSKEGON

Muskegon is situated on the south shore of Muskegon Lake, in the seven-mile-long area from Lake Michigan to the mouth of the Muskegon River.

The "Lumber Queen of the World," as Muskegon was called during the 1880s when it was the largest lumber-producing city in the world, began in 1836 as a single mill site where the Muskegon River flows into Lake Michigan. By 1854 a population of 339 lived in the area, 252 of whom were employed in one of ten mills. The population increased to 1,700 by 1860 and to 2,700 by 1864. The village was incorporated in 1861. The extensive pine land up the Muskegon River continued to feed the mills that ringed Muskegon Lake until, in 1867, forty-six mills cut a record 665,344,000 board feet. It seemed to one chronicler of the time that prosperity "would not soon end."

But end it did. By 1894 most of the available timber was cut, and the onset of a severe national economic depression caused forty-one of the forty-six mills to close. Several lumbermen remained after their mills closed and set about bringing alternative industry to the Muskegon area. Lumberman Newcomb McGraft sold the city 80 acres of land for $100,000 in a transaction overwhelmingly approved by a public vote. The land was developed into McGraft Park, and the proceeds from the sale were turned over for adminis-

tration to the city's leading lumberman, Charles H. Hackley (1837–1918). Hackley administered the subsidies from the $100,000 and interest accrued on the unspent balance to attract new industry. Among the fourteen firms drawn by the Muskegon bonus plan, as it was known locally, were the Shaw-Walker Company and Central Paper Company, as well as the Amazon Knitting Company, which employed as many as six hundred people.

A second such plan led to the creation of the city of Muskegon Heights. A group of leading businessmen bought land and platted it in 1890. Residential lots were sold for $130 or $160, depending on their location. The purchase price was payable in installments, an important feature since banks of the time were not allowed by law to use land as loan collateral. The proceeds from the sale were used as subsidies.

The new industry that came to Muskegon provided employment for former mill hands. This industry was predominantly in secondary wood processing, such as manufacturing sawed wood into products such as washing machines, refrigerators, and the like. But other industry during the 1920s was quickly tied to automobile production. Tourism was touted to take advantage of the many beaches. Although the extreme wealth of some of the lumbermen was not repeated in later years, Muskegon did not become a ghost town and obtained a longer-lasting economic base.

Muskegon

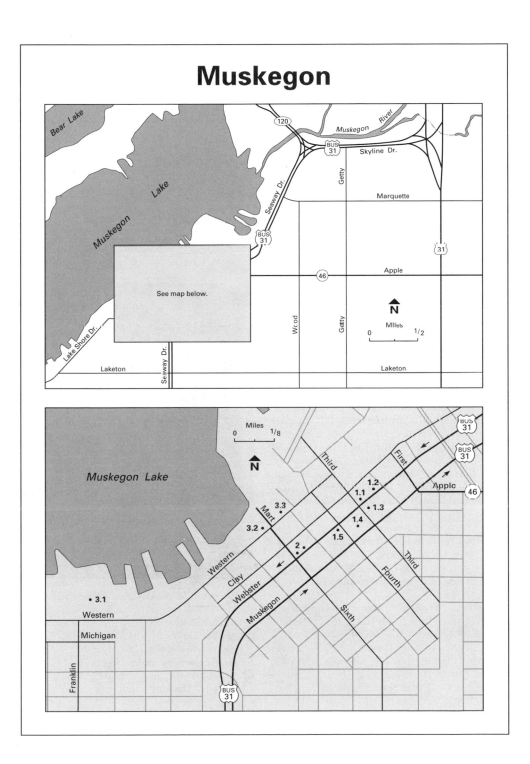

Hackley's donations to the city and its monuments include a library, a park, a hospital, a soldiers and sailors' monument, a manual training school, and a gymnasium.

MU01 **Hackley Park**

1890–1891, Olaf Benson. Bounded by Webster (Business US 31) and Clay avenues and Third and Fourth streets

Lumber baron Charles Hackley is known for his many philanthropies to the citizens of Muskegon, but none is more appreciated than Hackley Park. Hackley announced his gift in 1890; it was his second to the city. Hackley purchased the block, had the buildings razed, the ground landscaped, and erected the statue in the center at a cost of almost $51,000. This small, flat oasis of trees and greenery within the surrounding residential historic district has become a symbol of the past and oftentimes functions as the very heart of the city.

Chicago landscape gardener and designer Olaf Benson was summoned to Muskegon to draw up a plan highlighting and enhancing another of Hackley's philanthropies, the Civil War commemorative Soldiers and Sailors Monument, by Joseph B. Carabelli. The park was to be, in essence, the frame for this memorial, and to this end it functions very well.

The monument is a huge Corinthian column that rises 82 feet from its granite base. Topping it, a bronze female figure of Victory wields her banner aloft. On the four corners of the column's pedestal are four 7-foot-high bronze statues representing each of the four different branches of service during the Civil War. It is surrounded by an ornate and intricate cast-iron fence whose design incorporates symbols significant to the cessation of the war.

Radiating from the central monument out to the park's four corners are four diagonal walkways. A secondary ovoid walkway encircles the park halfway between the monument and the framing outside sidewalk. On each of the four outside corners are large bronze statues of Civil War heroes: Lincoln and Farragut by C. H. Niehaus and Grant and Sherman by J. Massey Rhind.

Of note is the unusual use of a granite and concrete aggregate formed into octagonal and square blocks. The basic design and texture that these buff-colored blocks impart to the park's walkways are more representative of

twentieth-century taste than of that of the nineteenth.

Within the park are the four antique lamp standards that encircle the central monument. Later gifts of Hackley, they were an early attempt to illuminate the monument at night.

Bordering other Muskegon architectural treasures (Hackley School, Hackley Public Library, Saint Paul's Episcopal Church), the park was restored in 1987.

MU01.1 **Hackley Public Library**

1888–1889, Normand S. Patton of Patton and Fisher. 1899, addition. 316 West Webster Ave. (Business US 31) (north corner of Third St. and West Webster Ave.)

Constructed of pink syenite granite with purplish reddish brown "raindrop" Lake Superior sandstone trim, this Richardsonian Romanesque building was solidly built during the years when the supply of timber, essential to Muskegon's economy, began to fail. The library building and contents, which were Charles H. Hackley's first gift to the people of Muskegon, cost over $100,000. Hackley originally planned to spend $1,000 and donate the necessary lumber for a library, but the threats of fire convinced him that a fireproof stone building was needed. Later, in 1899, Hackley made available $75,000 more for an addition.

The building committee selected in 1888 Patton and Fisher of Chicago, famed for their schools and libraries. This design was chosen over designs submitted by five other firms, including Van Brunt and Howe, Whitney and Mundy, D. S. Hopkins, S. J. Osgood, and E. E. Myers. The library is composed of gabled facades, a massive octagonal tower, and small turret bound together in an asymmetrical but coherent mass. A wide, semicircular arch spans the main recessed entrance. The spandrels that embrace it on either side and the archivolt that defines its lower profile are all richly carved with floral motifs. Normand S. Patton (1852–1915) called the style of the building "American Romanesque," which clearly signifies that the Richardsonian Romanesque was already regarded as a national style. The Hackley library owes something to Richardson's Oliver Ames Free Library (1877–1879) and Memorial Hall (1879–1881) in North Easton, Massachusetts. The interior plan is based on a plan suggested by William F. Poole, director of the Newberry Library in Chicago and spokesman for the American Library Association movement that advocated economy and practical utility in library construction. The solidity and strength of this weighty granite structure, built when it was, convey in eloquent terms the perseverance of its advocates in the face of crisis.

MU01.2 **Hackley Art Gallery**

1911–1912, Solon S. Beman, later addition. 296 West Webster Ave. (Business US 31) (north side of West Webster between Second and Third streets)

The Hackley Art Gallery is one of the few galleries in western Michigan designed specifically to house works of art. It was built with funds in the amount of $43,500 from a $150,000 bequest from Charles H. Hackley in 1905 that called for the purchase of pictures to be placed in the Hackley Public Library. Solon S. Beman of Chicago designed this building with yellowish white brick trimmed with limestone in the Beaux-Arts Classical style. The formal and balanced facade is without windows above the raised foundation but is decorated with pilaster-enframed tablets bearing the names of painters, sculptors, and architects. Greek Doric columns of Vermont marble support the festooned projecting entrance portico; other details are also Greek. Carved lions' heads project from the cornice. Originally, the hipped roof had skylights over the galleries. The main stairs lead from a spacious vestibule up to the art gallery and down to a 200-seat auditorium. The main stair hall is clad in Vermont marble; other floors, in gray Tennessee marble.

MU01.3 **John and Caroline Honner Torrent House**

1891–1892, W. K. Johnston of Johnston and Johnston. 315 West Webster Ave. (Business US 31) (east corner of West Webster Ave. and Third St.)

This huge, towered Richardsonian extravaganza is the only stone residence of its size in Muskegon. The structure is random rock-faced gray granite set on a foundation of Joliet, Illinois, limestone. The hipped and gabled roof is covered with red tile. The house measures 94 feet by 60 feet in plan, is 62 feet high, and contains 31 rooms, each trimmed with a different wood—mahogany, cherry, rosewood, bird's-eye maple, California redwood, sycamore, red birch, oak, and pine. W. K. Johnston of Muskegon designed it for John Torrent (1833–1915) and his wife, Caroline. One of the leading lumbermen of the city, Torrent came to western Michigan from Watertown, New York, by way of Ontario, Canada. Torrent and Charles Hackley were rivals in business and in public life. Thus, when Torrent decided to build his home, he was determined that it would be grander than Hackley's wooden Queen Anne house. Indeed, the Torrent house cost $250,000 to build, as compared to the expenditure of little more than $50,000 required for the Hackley house. Moreover, the Torrent house stands prominently on the public square fronting the Hackley Public Library and the school grounds. It is a monument in stone, but, in expression of the owner's love of the forest, it is finished inside with every kind of wood imaginable. In its size and costliness, and in its extraordinary design, the house is nearly comparable to the stone house erected for lumber baron David Whitney (DE33, p. 85) to the designs of Gordon W. Lloyd in 1890 in Detroit.

MU01.4 **Hackley School Administration Building** (Hackley School)

1891–1892, F. S. Allen. 349 West Webster Ave. (Business US 31) (south side of West Webster Avenue between Third and Fourth streets)

This stone Richardsonian Romanesque school is based on Henry Hobson Richardson's Allegheny County Courthouse, erected in Pittsburgh, Pennsylvania, in 1884–1888, and resembles the Old Duluth Central High School by Palmer and Hall, also built in 1891–1892. From the center front of the structure, a square tower soars to extreme heights over Hackley Park and the city. The building combines in a bulky asymmetrical mass every other Richardsonian ingredient—gables, towers, turrets, round arches, and rock-faced masonry. After the Muskegon High School, which preceded this building, burned in 1891, the school board was unable to secure the funds needed for its reconstruction. Many of the lumber mills had closed or were closing, and the citizenry was unable to pay the increased tax. After several futile months of trying to raise the $40,000 needed, Charles H. Hackley offered the city a $75,000 bond at 5 percent for twenty years to rebuild the school. If the 5 percent annual interest payments would be applied toward maintenance of the library, he further proposed to give the principal to the city. F. S. Allen of Illinois, architect for many schools in that state, designed the school. It was built at a cost of $91,000. The school currently serves as the administration building for the Muskegon Public Schools.

MU01.5 Temple B'nai Israel

1948, Ernest Grunsfeld, Jr. 391 West Webster (Business US 31) (south corner of West Webster Ave. and Fourth St.)

Intended as a community center for the religious and social needs of all "hues of Jews," the 135 Jewish families of Muskegon engaged Ernest Grunsfeld, Jr., a Chicago architect famed for his museum and institutional buildings, to provide a blocky two-story stone and concrete building with notched corners and broad fenestration. Unlike the ubiquitous sanctuary-social hall plan, this building has a sanctuary with balcony for overflow seating; the social hall is in the basement. The prayer hall is unusual in that it has an open organ and choir balcony above the deeply recessed ark, an arrangement more often found in Christian churches than in synagogue design.

MU02 Webster Avenue

Webster Ave. (Business US 31), between Sixth and Fifth streets

MU02.1 Charles H. and Julia E. Moore Hackley House

1887–1889, David S. Hopkins. 484 West Webster Ave. (Business US 31) (north corner of West Webster and Sixth St.)

The sumptuous Queen Anne house of lumberman Charles H. Hackley is unexcelled in Michigan. Its irregular silhouette is composed of assorted gables, clustered chimneys, bays and porches, and an octagonal corner tower, all of which either project from or recede into a basically square mass. The rich textures of latticework and shingles and the skillfully carved, turned and molded spindles, posts and horseshoe Oriental-like openings, and rich polychrome enliven the surface of the pine-clapboarded wood-frame structure to the very heights of picturesqueness. The house was richly polychrome. The interior is even more lavishly ornamented with cherry, oak, and butternut woodwork, fireplaces, stained glass, fabric wall covers, ceramic tile, and metals. The Kelly Brothers Manufacturing Company, highly skilled Muskegon woodworkers, did the exquisite interior carving. The reception hall gives the first and most opulent impression of the grandeur of the house.

Hackley came to Muskegon in 1857, reportedly with seven dollars in his pocket. When he died in 1905 his estate was worth more than $12 million. He gave over $6 million to the city during his life and through his will. This home is eloquent testimony to both his personal flamboyance and his success. It cost more than $50,000 to build. It was located just up the hill and three blocks away from the Hackley and Hume offices on Western Avenue and Eighth Street. The house was designed by David S. Hopkins, the Argyle, New York-born architect who came to Grand Rapids in 1864 and who originated a mail-order system of selling house plans.

MU02.2 Thomas and Margaret Ann Banks Hume House

1889, David S. Hopkins. 472 West Webster Ave. (Business US 31)

Like the Hackley house next door, the Thomas Hume House was designed by David S. Hopkins and built at the same time by the same carpenters and workmen. It is a larger Queen Anne residence with a profusion of porches, bays, tower, and gables to accommodate the Humes' large family of seven children. But it is also less ostentatious than the Hackley house and is a gentle, but clear reminder that Hackley, who owned three-fourths of Hackley and Hume, was the senior partner of the firm. The carriage house behind and between the two houses was held in common, each half reflecting the style of its respective home. Hume (1848–1937) came to Muskegon in 1872 and worked his way up to the position of bookkeeper for Hackley and McGordon. Later Hackley made Hume a partner, and Hume carried on many of the day-to-day details of running Hackley and Hume.

MU03 West Western Avenue

Stretches along the shoreline of Muskegon Lake from west of Franklin St. to Third St.

MU03.1 Lumbertown (Hartshorn Curtain Roller Company)

c. 1885, power house. 1893, east building. 1903, west building. 1908, center building. 1150 West Western Ave. (north side of West Western Ave., west of Franklin St.)

This two-story concrete and brick manufacturing plant complex is typical of industrial structures from the late nineteenth century. The west building, erected in 1903, was one of the earliest in the region to use reinforced concrete. In this building the Temple Manufacturing Company, begun in Muskegon in 1872, utilized lumber mill waste for fuel and processed unmarketable lumber into curtain rollers. The rollers were shipped to the Hartshorn Curtain Roller Company in New Jersey for the installation of a patented spring fixture. In 1893 Hartshorn bought the Temple Company and moved the entire operation to Muskegon. The building has been converted into a mall of shops known as Lumbertown.

MU03.2 Union Depot

1893–1895, A. W. Rush. 586 West Western Ave.

On the main thoroughfare of the city, within view from the front doors of the businessmen who promoted it, is the Union Depot. The Richardsonian Romanesque structure of red brick and reddish brown variegated raindrop Jacobville sandstone stands on the former site of the Blodgett and Pryne sawmill, near the Central Wharf. A network of tracks was laid on the north, and walks once connected it to the docks that stretched into Muskegon Lake. Spacious walks led from the streets to the depot. The depot has a steeply pitched hipped

MU03.2 Union Depot

roof with wide projecting eaves, which originally was covered with slate. Rising through it, on the main facade, is a great squat square central tower with battered walls; cut into it, through a massive Richardsonian arch, is a cavelike recessed entry. A short corner turret and a gable flank the tower and help to give the depot a picturesque silhouette. The interior was finished in oak and black ash woodwork, bronze and steel grillwork, paneled and tinted steel ceilings, and massive ornamental fireplaces.

Muskegon businessmen worked eagerly for the construction of the Union Depot and offered various railroads—the Chicago and West Michigan, the Muskegon, the Grand Rapids and Indiana, and the Toledo, Saginaw and Muskegon—a financial incentive to build it where they did. Previously the city had been served by a small frame structure with a waiting room, by then so dilapidated and flimsy it was called locally a "rattle and bang" depot. The original design, prepared in 1893 by Sidney J. Osgood of Grand Rapids for a larger, more ornate pinnacled and dormered stone structure with a tall tower, languished during the panic of 1893. Work resumed in 1894, at which time the architect scaled the plans to a more modest size. It cost between $15,000 and $16,000 to build. The depot served as the main railroad terminal for the city during the years when lumbering was declining.

MU03.3 Amazon Knitting Mill (Amazon Hosiery Mill)

1895. 1899, addition. 530–550 West Western Ave. (north side of West Western Ave., between Mart and Fifth streets)

The Amazon Hosiery Company was one of several businesses enticed to Muskegon between 1895 and 1905 by the Muskegon Chamber of Commerce's cash incentive program. The Amazon Hosiery Mill, under the presidency of George W. Powell, was brought in 1895 to Muskegon from Michigan City, Indiana, with a $5,000 subsidy and a free building site from the Muskegon Chamber of Commerce. In exchange, Powell agreed to employ from five to six hundred local workers. During the economic downturn in 1897, the firm was caught short in liquid assets and was on the verge of bankruptcy. To provide ready cash, Charles H. Hackley and his partner, Thomas Hume, bought the firm, changing its name from Amazon Hosiery to Amazon Knitting Company. By 1899 the company's condition improved, and the addition to the structure was made. Hackley and Hume also sold their interest back to the previous owners, once those owners were able to reacquire it.

The mill is made up of two sections: the one-story brick building erected in 1895, which has a two-story hipped-roof tower at the juncture of two one-story wings; and the larger, four-story, U-shaped building with corner towers, added in 1899. The twin towers resembling Italian Romanesque or Lombard campaniles rise over the northeast and southeast corners of the building in a signal of corporate power. Both hold water tanks that fed the building's fire sprinkler system; the southernmost tower has a clock.

NORTON SHORES

MU04 Saint Francis de Sales Church

1964–1967, Marcel Breuer and Herbert Beckhard. 2929 McCracken (McCracken is 1.75 miles west of the intersection of Norton and Seaway Dr. [US 31] and 1.75 miles west of the intersection of Sherman Blvd. and Seaway Dr.)

Saint Francis de Sales Church by world famous architect Marcel Breuer soars dramatically and simply over its working-class neighborhood. This church was designed in

MU04 Saint Francis de Sales Church

response to the Catholic church's spirit of reform and represents a new approach to religious architecture. A 75-foot-high, ban- ner-shaped concrete trapezoid topped by a concrete trough that houses the suspended bells creates a unique skyline. Twelve angular concrete arches span the interior space, connecting the trapezoidal planes of the front and rear walls. The inner space is wide at the rear and narrows to the bell-shaped sanctuary in a way that focuses the worshipper's attention upon the altar. Hyperbolic paraboloid side walls of unadorned reinforced concrete that do not support the roof enclose the large space. For this work Breuer and Beckhard were awarded a Silver Medal from the American Institute of Architects. The AIA jury said of Saint Francis de Sales Church, "The inner space conveys a powerful religious experience; the whole concept has great dignity."

Oceana County (OA)

The first white settlers in Oceana County came during the early 1840s and were lumbermen. One of the most notable of these was Charles Mears. Mears (1814–1896) built lumber mills along the county's Lake Michigan shoreline, platted towns, began commercial enterprises, and established several farms to supply the workers at his mills. During the 1880s Mears was also instrumental in establishing a brickyard in Claybanks Township, where large deposits of yellow clay were found. In 1884 F. O. Gardner purchased the operation and renamed it the Pentwater Brick Company. As a result many structures were built with this yellowish white brick. With the end of lumbering, the economy of the county fell sharply. An agricultural boom begun prior to World War I was cut short by the postwar agricultural depression. Since then, fruit farming and tourism have become the bulwarks of the county's economy.

PENTWATER

OA01 **Brass Anchor** (Pentwater News Buildling)

1884. 500 South Hancock St. (southeast corner of South Hancock and Fifth streets)

This modest Italianate Pentwater brick commercial structure stands independently, rather than in a row of storefronts. The interior is remarkably intact and serves today as a marine supply store.

OA01 Brass Anchor

Mason County   (MN)

LUDINGTON

Founded near the site of the Baird and Bean lumber mill, Ludington became the largest town in Mason County. The Pere Marquette River watershed, which empties into Lake Michigan at Ludington, provided the sources of power and transportation for pine logs from a three-county area that were to be sawed at, and shipped from Ludington. Ludington took its name from James Ludington, a mill owner who moved from Milwaukee to this site in 1859. In 1864 the community was named the Ludington Post Office. Three years later Ludington platted the town. It was incorporated in 1873. Like other communities, Ludington was almost completely destroyed by fire in 1872 and again in 1881. Lumbering brought growth and wealth to the community. The largest lumber firm was the Pere Marquette Lumber Company, owned by James Ludington after 1869. Following lumbering came a successful transition to industry, agriculture, and tourism. Since 1942 Dow Chemical Company has pumped brine from salt wells and extracted magnesium on the site of the former Morton Salt Company.

MN01 **Mason County Courthouse**

1893–1894, Sidney J. Osgood. 300 East Ludington Ave. (US 10) (bounded by East Ludington Ave., Loomis, Delia, and Rowe streets)

Sited on the center of a grassy square at the east end of the commercial district is the Richardsonian Romanesque courthouse. The square, dark red brick structure rests on a raised reddish brown Jacobsville sandstone foundation and displays beltcourses, window sills, and lintels of the same sandstone. It has a complex combination hipped and gabled roof crowned by a central, pyramidal roofed clock tower. The main entrance is recessed within a round Richardsonian arch. Intersecting broad corridors divide the main floor into quarters, each occupied by one of the four principal county offices—clerk, register of deeds, probate, and treasurer. The courtroom is on the third floor. Original decorative plaster wainscoting, wood chimney pieces, ceramic tile floors, pressed metal ceilings, and staircases are found within. In 1892 voters of

Mason County elected to bond the county for the sum of $50,000 to purchase property and build this new courthouse. After advertising for plans for a structure to cost not more than $40,000, the building committee selected the plans prepared by Sidney J. Osgood, one of the leading architects in Grand Rapids and western Michigan, who did four Lower Peninsula courthouses between 1887 and 1900. Charles T. Gatke built the courthouse. It was furnished by Grand Rapids School Furniture Company. The courthouse is notable for its high-quality design.

MN02 **Ludington Post Office**

1932–1933, James A. Wetmore. 1956–1957, modernized. 202 East Ludington Ave. (US 10) (northeast corner of East Ludington Ave. and North Harrison St.)

Standing south of a residential area containing Ludington's grandest late nineteenth- and early twentieth-century homes and west of the public library is the Ludington Post Office. The high-style classical building is an elegant monument that speaks of the federal presence in Ludington. Its construction was sponsored by the federal government during the depression era, under the auspices of the Public Works Administration. The structure has a formal and balanced facade. The main entrance is placed in the center bay of a five-bay central pavilion and is topped with a

MN03 Epworth Heights

broken pediment. The other four bays are filled by round-headed double windows, each of which is surmounted by an arched fanlight. The brick building has a balustraded mansard roof pierced by dormers; the short corner wings are quoined, an engaged Ionic order defines the bays of the central pavilion.

LUDINGTON VICINITY

MN03 **Epworth Heights**

1890s. North of Ludington

North of Ludington near Lincoln Lake is the Epworth Heights summer resort. The Epworth Assembly of Methodists established the association in the 1890s for church members. It was developed on land donated by the Citizens Development Company. The resort was promoted by the Pere Marquette Railroad and the First National Bank of Ludington, who hoped it would become a Chautauqua. In 1894 roads were cut through the hills,

stairways to the lake shore were installed, and the Epworth Hotel was erected. The unique cottages are built on lots laid out to take advantage of the hilly topography. Although it began as a Methodist camp meeting ground similar to Bay View, north of Petoskey, Epworth Heights never added a Chautauqua program, as Bay View did.

SCOTTVILLE

MN04 **Mason County Road Commission Office and Garage**

1940, R. V. Gay. 510 East State St. (US 10)

Built as a Works Progress Administration project, this reinforced concrete structure holds the offices and garage of the county road commission. It was designed by R. V. Gay of Saint Johns. Trusses support the bowed roof of the garage. The front facade is marked with rounded corners and glass blocks.

Manistee County (MT)

MANISTEE

The city began with the Stronach Brothers mill site in 1840. When Manistee County was organized in 1855, the city of Manistee became the seat of county government. By 1867 twenty-one sawmills were operating around Manistee Lake. The city harbor was improved for lake vessel travel, a light station was built, and later a lifesaving station was added to

further aid navigation. In 1871, a particularly dry year, fires occurred throughout the Midwest, most notably in Chicago and Peshtigo, Wisconsin. Most of the buildings in Manistee also burned that summer. Consequently, the city was rebuilt with more durable materials, and the city's existing downtown buildings date to 1871–1910. The lumbermen of Manistee regularly transacted business in Chicago.

As a result of this connection, Chicago architects received commissions to design churches, houses, and civic buildings in Manistee. All of the buildings listed for Manistee are within a few blocks of the south bank of the Manistee River. First through Eighth streets intersect US 31.

MT01 Ramsdell Theatre and Hall

1903, Solon Spencer Beman. 101 Maple St. (southeast corner of First and Maple streets)

The Ramsdell Theatre and Hall is the finest of several opera houses built in small Michigan cities at the turn of the century, including the Calumet Theater (HO14.3, p. 475) and the Kerridge Theater in Hancock (now demolished). The Ramsdell was substantially built, beautifully decorated, and possessed the latest electrical devices, heating, ventilation, and fire protection.

Thomas Jefferson Ramsdell (1833–1917), Manistee's first lawyer and a civic leader, brought art and culture to the wealthy lumbering town of Manistee with this gift to the city. In planning this gift, he set out to build a modern theater of "Grecian architecture" capable of accommodating any troupe; he also included an assembly hall. Like others in Manistee, he turned to a Chicago architect—in this case, Solon S. Beman (1853–1914)—for the ambitious design of this Neoclassical monument.

The theater is flanked on the north by the assembly hall; the juncture of their distinct masses is marked by a square campanile tower.

The stage house and scene loft rises 75 feet at the rear. The facade of the theater is accented by a pedimented central pavilion. The entrance is in the center, fronted by a flat-topped portico of coupled Doric columns. A denticulated and modillioned cornice beneath the hipped roofs and brick quoins at the corners detail the red brick building.

The seating of the auditorium is arranged in a horseshoe shape beneath a domed ceiling with a graded first floor and two tiers of boxes and galleries. It holds 1,200. It is elegantly decorated in light green and gold. Scenic artist Walter Wilcox Burridge painted on the drop curtain a scene entitled *A Grove Near Athens;* Frederic Winthrop Ramsdell, the Beaux-Arts-trained son of the theater's donor, painted murals of Arcady in the lobby and of Venus in the dome of the auditorium. The social hall holds a huge oak wood-paneled dance hall around which chairs are placed on a slightly raised dais; it also has an orchestra balcony. The dance hall is above the lobby, parlors, dressing rooms, and kitchen of the first floor.

Manistee was already recognized as a theater town because it was easily accessible by lake ferry from Wisconsin, was close to Cadillac and Traverse City for troupes on a circuit, and enjoyed a cool climate—thereby permitting a summer show season—so the completion of the Ramsdell Theatre assured its position as the premier theater town in the area. The theater opened with a production of *A Chinese Honeymoon.* Planned as a legitimate theater, the Ramsdell was purchased by Butterfield Theatres in the 1920s but was never converted to sound. The Ramsdell Theatre has been owned by the city since 1943 and is still used for legitimate theater productions.

MT02 River Street Commercial District

River St.

Manistee's principal commercial district was developed along River Street, which curves along the south bank of the Manistee River. The buildings are primarily, but not exclusively, Victorian Italianate designs constructed of brick, with rounded arches, heavy cornice lines, and brackets under the eaves.

MT02.1 Vogue Theatre

1938, Pereira and Pereira. 385 River St. (southwest corner of Poplar and River streets)

MT02 River Street Commercial District

Pereira and Pereira, well-known theater architects of Chicago, built this ultramodern streamlined feature film theater for the Butterfield Theatres. The reinforced concrete structure is faced with cement plaster and two-tone brick veneer. The entrance is deeply recessed within a half-circle and leads to a modernistic lobby originally decorated with indirect lighting, a mirrored ceiling, and walls of figured wood depicting historic scenes of Manistee.

MT02.2 Ramsdell Building

1891, Frederick W. Hollister. 399 River St. (southeast corner of River and Maple streets)

Thomas J. Ramsdell invested in this distinguished Richardsonian Romanesque bank and office building. In quality of design, workmanship, and materials, it is comparable to the Marquette County Savings Bank (MQ03.1, p. 491) but scaled to the economy of Manistee. Frederick W. Hollister of Saginaw designed it. A round tower, its conical roof now gone, rises at the corner of the structure, curiously supported by a squat, polished granite Romanesque column. A broad Richardsonian arch and a pedimented square opening supported by polished granite Romanesque piers give access to the building from Maple and River streets, respectively. The exterior walls are randomly coursed, rock-faced gray granite for the ground floor and brick trimmed with red sandstone and terracotta above. The building held the Manistee County Savings Bank (organized in 1891), law offices, and a drugstore.

MT02.3 Haley Block

1883. 419–423 River St. (south side, between Oak and Maple streets)

This elegantly embellished Italianate commercial block was built by the Haley sisters, Ellen, Eliza, and Kate, milliners to Manistee's ladies. Having lost five shops to fires between 1871 and 1883, they rebuilt the present block in brick. Next door to their shop, they put up an elaborate three-bay, two part brick business block and crowned the entire grouping of three storefronts with a single ornamental galvanized iron cornice. This lacy decorative motif along the cornice, the equally delicate treatment of the wood spandrels beneath, and the carved stone window hood moldings add a touch of femininity appropriate to its enterprising owners.

MT03 Manistee Fire Hall

1888, Frederick W. Hollister. 280 First St. (southwest corner of First and Hancock streets)

This robust gabled and towered Richardsonian Romanesque fire hall was designed by Frederick W. Hollister of Saginaw in what was called "a modern classic style of architecture."[66] The building has a square corbeled watch and hose-drying tower originally surmounted with a flagstaff and a copper-covered round corner tower. The exterior walls are red pressed brick, now painted bright cherry red, trimmed with buff cut sandstone and green painted wood. They are broken by round-arch and rectangular windows. A large horseshoe window adorns the front gable. The building is covered with a steep roof originally clad in slate. The interior is paneled with red pine "beaded ceiling." The first floor held the chief's office, hose carts, engines, trucks, and stalls for six horses. The second floor held a reading room and dormitory for firefighters, and a hay loft. As plans for the building were completed, the *Manistee Democrat* for October 25, 1888, predicted that the fire hall would be "one of the finest buildings in northern Michigan, and a credit to the city." Brownrigg and Reynolds built the structure. Today, the fire hall has been adapted to house mechanized fire-fighting equipment, but it remains the oldest fire station in continuous use in Michigan.

MT04 **Danish Lutheran Church** (Our Savior's Evangelical Lutheran Church)

1868–1870, Christian Peterson, builder. 1888, tower addition. 1898, interior renovated. 300 Walnut

One of the few Manistee buildings to survive the 1871 fire, this church is also one of the oldest extant Danish Lutheran churches in the United States. An entry and bell tower with an octagonal spire surmounted by a weather vane fronts the gable-roofed, wood-framed and clapboarded church. All openings are round-arch, in keeping with the mid-century trend among nonconformist denominations. It has a simple center aisle interior. Scandinavian Lutherans built the church, but in the mid-1870s the Swedes and Norwegians formed their own congregation, and the church was dedicated as the Danish Lutheran Church.

MT05 **First Congregational United Church of Christ**

1888–1892, William Le Baron Jenney and William Otis. 412 Fourth St. (northeast corner of Oak and Fourth St.)

The First Congregational Church is one of a few churches by William Le Baron Jenney (1837–1907), the Chicago architect noted for his role in the development of the modern steel-frame skyscraper, from the period of his short partnership with William Otis. For eight years after it was established, and before building the present church, the First Congregation Society met in a brick structure erected in 1870. John Canfield (1830–1899), pioneer Manistee lumberman and its weal-

MT05 First Congregational United Church of Christ

thiest citizen, who served as chairman of the building committee and who donated most of the funds for the church, selected the architect. Like Canfield, Jenney was from Massachusetts. In 1876 he designed Canfield's High Victorian Gothic house, and in the 1880s, four other residences in Manistee.

The Richardsonian Romanesque church is built of pressed red brick, ornamental terracotta, and limestone. It measures 128 feet in length and 75 feet in width. A huge entry and bell and clock tower rise mightily at the southwest corner of the edifice over what was a frontier town of lumberjacks, in a stance of moral authority, temperance, and missionary zeal. The tower of this church, together with the steeple of the Guardian Angels Church, 1888–1890, mark the harbor from the lake.

The first story contains the vestibule, lecture room, parlors, library, classrooms, and kitchen, which could be combined into larger spaces needed for social gatherings by opening wide sliding doors. The worship space rests on the first story. It is cruciform, or nearly T-shaped in plan, with stubby transept arms and a broad central nave. It is, in fact, and in keeping with Congregational doctrine, an auditorium-type space, with the pews arranged in a semicircle around the central pulpit. It seats 610. The ceiling, faced with plain wooden boards, is supported by wooden roof trusses and laminated wooden arches.

Originally a gallery suspended by iron rods from the trusses swept around three sides of the nave and transepts, holding 390 additional seats. An organ and choir loft stood above and behind the pulpit. Memorial windows crafted by Louis Comfort Tiffany and installed in 1901 grace two windows.

MT06 E. P. and Belle Randall Case House

1880, William Le Baron Jenney. 467 Fourth St.

The only survivor, and the most modest of five houses designed by William Le Baron Jenney in Manistee, this one was for E. P. Case (1845–1886), John Canfield's bookkeeper. The L-shaped, clapboarded wooden house rests on a limestone foundation. Its intersecting gabled roof with wide overhang is supported by open brackets and decorative king-post trusses and crowned with finials. A picket fence pattern trims the peak of the front gabled dormer.

MT07 Patrick and Susan Agnes McCurdy Noud House

1894–1895, Holabird and Roche. 202 Maple St. (southwest corner of Maple and Second streets)

This handsome red brick Neo-Georgian house with exquisite interior woodwork was built to the plans of noted Chicago architects Holabird and Roche for a Manistee lumberman and his wife. Patrick Noud (1845–1925) came up the Great Lakes to the northwestern Lower Peninsula, where he worked as a log driver, foreman, and superintendent and eventually acquired a sawmill and lumber company in Manistee. In 1891–1892 Noud served as mayor of Manistee. The huge house is massed with intersecting pedimented gables. A full-height round bay projects from the Second Street facade. The windows have large single panes below six-over-six upper sections and are topped with splayed caps containing keystones. Modillions support a denticulated cornice that crowns the entablature. Porches with classical detailing front both the north and east facades. The interior of the house conveys the delight of its owners in the products of northern Michigan's forests. It is richly and elegantly finished in quarter-sawed oak with birch, ash, and other woods. The *Manistee Daily News* for October 30, 1895, said, "Various costly woods have been used in the different rooms and they all harmonize perfectly." In particular, it likened the large reception room to "a dream." Here the piano-polished antique oak woodwork blends with a ceiling finished in richly modeled plaster relief work of "Empire design" colored cream and gold and tan brown walls inlaid with scrolled plaster molding, colored terracotta, and gold.

FILER TOWNSHIP

MT08 John and Alice Swainson–George and Caroll Whitehead Vacation House

1965, Meathe, Kessler and Associates. Professional Dr., Professional Club, Lakeland Subdivision (from US 31 take Manistee-Mason County Line Rd. west 3 miles, then north on Red Apple Rd. .75 mile, then west and south on Professional Dr.). Visible from the water

This fantastical wood-shingled vacation house was built for the Swainson and Whitehead families in a woods on the eastern shore of Lake Michigan near Manistee. Its unusual amorphic massing with walls that seem to rise to become the shed roof is clad with irregular courses of randomly cut shingles. Entrances and windows, three of which are large pointed openings, their sides splayed outward, are recessed into the body of the structure, offering protection, and balconies project from it, affording access to the out-of-doors. A deck surrounds the entire house. The chimney is fieldstone. The interior is arranged with four bedrooms and informal living, dining, and kitchen spaces, all of which open directly outside. The house exists in harmony with its surroundings and invites the occupants to mingle with nature. It illustrates the

1960s concern and appreciation for the natural environment. Like the Queen Anne houses of the lumber era, this vacation house expresses a love for wood. Its design won an award from the Michigan Society of Architects in 1966.

KALEVA

MT09 John J. Makinen House

1939–1942. 14551 Wuoksi Ave. (southwest corner of Wuoksi and Kauko avenues)

Sixty thousand glass bottles sparkle in the exterior walls of the Makinen bottle house, a unique example of vernacular architecture. John J. Makinen (1871–1942) designed and built the house to utilize surplus and obsolete bottles from his Northwestern Bottling Works.

He used a technique that he developed in 1932, which was based on an attempt in 1909 to course bottles with mortar, bases pointing out, which were held in place by the studding. Makinen felt the sealed airspace in the bottles would be a natural insulator. Printed in bottle bottoms across the front of the house are the words "Happy Home." The Makinen house exemplifies an early twentieth-century architectural fad for using unusual, eye-catching, often scavenged, materials, such as bottles, petrified wood, corn cobs, and coal for building purposes. The heyday for these exhibitionist structures came in the 1920s and 1930s, when rapidly increasing auto travel and tourism and the growing use of cameras by the general public encouraged both the construction of highly visible tourist-attracting landmarks and the widespread dissemination of information about them.

Wexford County   (WX)

CADILLAC

At the intersection of three major highways and on the shores of Lake Mitchell, Cadillac is the principal community of Wexford County. It was named for Antoine de la Mothe Cadillac, founder of Detroit, by the lumbermen who founded it. Unique to the region, Cadillac became a railroad lumbering town, shipping sawed lumber by rail, rather than by lake vessel. Rail transport cost more than lake vessel, but the rail facilities allowed Cadillac sawmills to mill and ship hardwoods, which, because of their density, could not be economically floated downriver to lake ports for sawing.

The building of the Grand Rapids and Indiana Railroad in the 1870s and the proximity of Lakes Mitchell and Cadillac soon made Clam Lake, what is now Cadillac, the focus of the county's commercial activity. Platted in 1872 by William Mitchell, a director of the Grand Rapids and Indiana Railroad, Cadillac became the county seat in 1882. Cadillac was a leading source of hardwood products, specifically flooring, at the turn of the century. Cadillac maple flooring was used in the White House renovations of the 1920s. Other industry was established in Cadillac, and tourism now is part of the county's econ-

omy. The city displays an unusual collection of splendid public buildings.

WX01 201 North Place (Cadillac City Hall and Fire Station)

1900–1901, William W. Williamson. 201 North Mitchell St. (US 131) (northwest corner of North Mitchell and West Mason streets)

The large but restrained Richardsonian Romanesque municipal building was constructed during a period of optimistic city growth. In 1899 voters elected to bond the city for $10,000 for a city hall. Previously the city owned only a firehouse on Cass Street, and its offices were scattered throughout town in rented quarters. The city council wanted to consolidate all city offices and its own chambers under one roof. William W. Williamson (1865–1927) of Grand Rapids drew plans for a building that would "meet the public needs of an enterprising Michigan municipality." The broad-fronted rectangular structure has a round-arch entrance set in a gabled pavilion flanked by pyramidal-roofed piers. Round-arch doors on the east facade mark the entrances to the fire station. Rows of arched windows pierce the upper stories. The building is clad is smooth-faced gray stone above a foundation of rock-faced stone. An ornamental wood staircase connects the first, second, and third floors. The building has been rehabilitated for commercial use.

WX02 Michigan Department of Transportation District 3 Headquarters Building (Cobbs and Mitchell, Inc., and Mitchell Brothers Company Building)

1905–1907, George D. Mason. 100 East Chapin St. (southeast corner East Chapin and South Mitchell [US 131] streets)

In an effort to maintain Cadillac's economy during the waning of lumbering, Cobbs and Mitchell, Inc., which was the largest lumber firm in Cadillac, built this office. It intended the building to serve as its business office and as a showplace in which to advertise the company's products. George D. Mason of Detroit designed the structure. The single-story Beaux-Arts Classical building has a main central portion with balancing wings. It stands on a three-quarter smooth-faced gray granite and sandstone foundation and is covered with a hipped roof above a frieze ornamented with fretwork. The exterior walls are clad with English bond brick. The grand center entryway is festooned and pedimented. Cobbs and Mitchell explained that the interior was planned to demonstrate "the finer possibilities of Michigan hardwoods" for interior finish, flooring, and furniture. Accordingly, it was finished throughout with the nine various woods obtained from the forests of the Cobbs and Mitchell and the Mitchell Brothers companies: Cadillac gray elm, white maple, bird's-eye maple, sap birch, red birch, curly red birch, red beech, red oak, and clear hemlock. Paneling, flooring, wall covering, draperies, and furniture were united in "a general scheme of harmonious construction and decoration adapted to the practical requirements of business" and to "a dignified and permanent exhibit of the finer uses of Michigan woods."[67]

WX03 Frank J. and Maude Belcher Cobbs House

1898, James R. Fletcher, contractor. 1906, east addition. 1987, restored. 407 East Chapin St. (3 blocks northeast corner of US 31)

This large, clapboarded, gambrel-roofed house is Cadillac's most full-blown example of Colonial Revival architecture and the equal of

WX03 Frank J. and Maude Belcher Cobbs House

any of the mansions built by lumbermen in this region of Michigan. A Palladian window decorates the front-facing gambrel gable, and beneath it the front entrance has side lights and a fanlight. Fluted Scamozzi Ionic pilasters outline the building's corners, while in the front veranda fluted Doric columns support a frieze with dentils. Many windows have architrave trim with molded caps, and round-headed dormers project from the roof. The house was the home of Frank J. Cobbs (1872–1912) and his wife, Maude. Cobbs was one of the principals in the firm of Cobbs and Mitchell, whose lumbering and wood products operations were a major part of Cadillac's economy in the late nineteenth and early twentieth centuries. It was built by James R. Fletcher of Cadillac.

CADILLAC VICINITY, CLAM LAKE TOWNSHIP

WX04 Kysor Industrial Corporation World Headquarters

1981–1982, Dallas B. Peacock. 1 Madison Ave. (just north of the northeast corner of Michigan 115 and US 131)

The headquarters of Kysor Industrial Corporation is a startling white presence among the forests of northern Michigan. In the New Formalism style of architecture, it is a self-contained, free-standing block with symmetrical elevations, a projecting roof slab above columnar supports and glass and marble materials. A design in the classical tradition,

"something along the lines of the ancient Parthenon in Athens, Greece," was what Ray Weigel, chairman of the board and chief executive officer, ordered of the architect. Kysor Industrial Corporation manufactures heating and air-conditioning systems and systems for commercial vehicles and refrigeration.

Lake County (LK)

BALDWIN

LK01 Lake County Courthouse

1926–1927, Frank P. Allen and Son. 800 Tenth St. (northwest corner of Tenth St. and Michigan [Michigan 37])

From its location at the head of Michigan Avenue (Michigan 37), the main street of the village of Baldwin, the Lake County Courthouse faces south and presides over the community. This red brick Neo-Georgian courthouse is the finest public building in Lake County. The boxlike structure has flanking one-story wings and an elaborate pedimented portico supported by pilasters and paired colossal Corinthian columns. A decorative cornice with dentil blocks encircles the building. The interior is trimmed extensively with oak woodwork. Frank P. Allen and Son of Grand Rapids, authors of *Artistic Dwellings from $700*

Upwards (Grand Rapids: 1891, 1892, 1893), designed the structure; Cadillac Cabinet and Construction built it. Baldwin was designated the seat of Lake County government in 1887, sixteen years after the county was set off from Mason County in 1871 and at the outset of its twenty-year logging period. Long before the present courthouse was built, the county's economy had turned to recreation in the form of hunting, fishing, boating, and camping.

PLEASANT PLAINS TOWNSHIP

LK02 **Shrine of the Pines** (Raymond W. Overholzer House)

1939, Raymond W. Overholzer. East side of Michigan 37, two miles south of Baldwin

Desirous of paying tribute in his own special way to the beauty and grandeur of Michigan's white pine forests, Raymond W. Overholzer (1892–1952) built a unique house and its furniture of pine. On the wooded banks of the Pere Marquette River he had Louis Merrill of Merrill Brothers Loggers construct a large L-shaped cabin of pine logs hauled from the forests around Bitely and Baldwin. Overholzer spent the rest of his life painstakingly handcrafting over two hundred pieces of furniture, furnishings, and utensils from pine wood and stumps, fully exploiting the claylike carvability of the sensuous natural forms. All were hand rubbed with resin and pitch to a high-luster finish. The building was Overholzer's home but is now a museum featuring his handiwork. Open to public, May to November.

LK03 **Idlewild**

1915–1935. South of US 10, east of Baldwin

LK03 Idlewild Clubhouse, Idlewild

Located on 1,300 acres of lightly rolling hills punctuated by intermittent low-lying swampy zones and four lakes in the Pere Marquette River watershed, Idlewild was one of America's most popular black resorts. It was developed in 1915 in an effort to utilize cutover timberland for a black resort. It was intended for a small but distinguishable black middle class, largely composed of professionals and small businessmen established in urban centers, who were barred from white resorts by segregation laws or unofficial practices. Erastus and Adelbert Branch, white land speculators from White Cloud, Michigan, organized the Idlewild Resort Company and marketed 25-by-100-foot lots for $35 each in the company's platted tracts adjacent to Idlewild Lake. On an island in the lake, connected with the mainland by footbridges and an automobile bridge, they also built a large clubhouse, which no longer stands. Black realtors in Chicago supervised well-organized sales campaigns and sponsored excursion tours for prospective buyers from that city and others. Testimonials of respected professional men appeared in promotional literature. For example, Dr. Thomas W. Burton, an Ohio physician, conveyed Idlewild's appeal to middle-class blacks, "When you stand in Idlewild and look around at Nature's beauty, breathe the fresh air and note the freedom from prejudice, ostracism and hatred, you can feel yourself truly an American citizen."

At first, tents were pitched, but later, unpretentious cottages were built. Eventually, five hundred structures stood here. Constructed between 1919 and 1935, most were small, gable-roofed vacation cottages, simple bungalows, and occasional multifamily dwellings. In addition, a hotel and grocery stores were put up between 1925 and 1940 so that the community was totally self-sustaining. In 1921 Herman Wilson, a black businessman, developed the Paradise Garden subdivision west of the initial settlement, including Harmony, Unity, Joy, Miracle, Creation, and Grandeur streets. In 1923 he built the Paradise Club. From its inception through the rhythm-and-blues era, the club was the scene of performances by well-known artists. Louis Armstrong performed at the resort prior to World War II, and Joe Louis trained there on occasion. Following the war the area's popularity increased as society in general became more mobile and such entertainers as Billy Eckstine, Della Reese, and T-Bone Walker all performed at Idlewild. The resort flourished as segregation persisted. Attendance of property owners, resorters, and guests peaked at twenty-five thousand on July 4, 1959.

The resort declined during the late 1960s, when federal and state civil rights statutes allowed blacks to patronize formerly all-white resorts in most parts of the country. Many longtime lot owners abandoned their allegiance to the community because of the inroads of what were perceived as commercialistic, "honky-tonk" postwar developments. Although showing physical signs of decline, today Idlewild is a retirement and vacation community.

Newaygo County (NE)

WHITE CLOUD

NE01 Newaygo County Road Commission Garage

1925. Northwest corner of Gibbs and Court

The huge utilitarian building held the equipment necessary to repair and maintain the roads of Newaygo County. The front (east) facade of the barrel-roof garage is faced with orange brown brick laid in common bond and trimmed with cream terracotta. The serious treatment given to the front marks the structure as a government building. Wide openings and the broad interior expanse permit easy access and easy maneuverability for large trucks and equipment. The prominence of the county road commission garage says something about the importance of the development and maintenance of good county roads to the economic well-being of most Michigan counties.

CROTON

NE02 Croton Dam

1906–1908. 1915, addition. Croton Dam Rd. at the Muskegon River

Croton Dam was one of Michigan's first large-scale electrical generating plants and the site of innovations in construction engineering and in the transmission of electrical power. It consists of an earth embankment, a concrete and brick powerhouse, and a concrete spillway. The powerhouse for the turbines and generators is a brick L-shaped building resting on a reinforced concrete foundation, which in turn rests on about three thousand round oak piles. Steel trusses support the gabled roofs. The dam is 670 feet long. During its construction and after, engineers from all over the world visited Croton Dam. The lake behind the dam provides recreational facilities. The powerhouse is still extant and produces electricity for Consumers Power Company. William Augustus Foote of Adrian, entrepreneur and financier, his brother James Berry Foote, an electrical engineer, and William G. Fargo, a civil engineer from Jackson, collaborated to build the dam for the Grand Rapids-Muskegon Power Company.

NEWAYGO

Located in a valley of the Muskegon River, Newaygo was settled in 1836 and incorporated as a village in 1867.

NE03 Saint Mark's Episcopal Church

1883. 1891, tower addition. 1921, altar enlarged. 30 Justice St. (east side of Brooks Park between Wood and Quarterline streets)

The Episcopal Church Society of Newaygo was organized in October 1872 by the friends and families of William and Elijah Bennett. The Bennett brothers came from New York State in the late 1850s to work for the Newaygo Lumber Company. Originally planned as a frame building, Saint Mark's Episcopal Church was built of yellow brick after fire destroyed Newaygo in 1883. Will Courtright donated a 700-pound bell to the congregation, and in 1891, the red brick tower was added. The church is a rather fine classicized distillation of the Gothic. The corbeling in the stout corner tower, the wide-arched wooden belfry, the flat hood moldings over the pointed windows are interesting features. The interior has wide pine floorboards, wood trim around the windows, and wood wainscoting. Windows dedicated to the memory of James McKee, James Harold McKee, and C. Irving are stained red, green, yellow, purple, and blue and painted with fleur-de-lis in black on a stenciled cross-hatched background of the same color.

NE02 Croton Dam

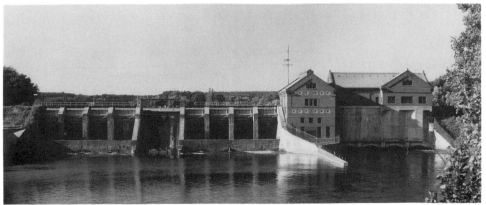

FREMONT

NE04 **Fremont Community Building**
(Community Memorial City Hall /
Soldiers Memorial Community Building)

1920, Mann and MacNeille. 101 East Main St. (Michigan 82) (northeast corner of East Main St. and Merchant Ave.)

The citizens of Fremont built this community building "as a fitting memorial to commemorate the brave deeds and heroic sacrifices" of the city's World War I servicemen. They thought the community building to be a more appropriate means for a memorial to the democratic ideals the men had fought for than a monument of bronze or stone. Freemont had no auditorium, recreational center, or library. At a special election in 1919, voters elected to bond the city for $60,000 to build the memorial building. Mann and MacNeille of New York, specialists in schools, churches, and houses, designed the building in the long-enduring Colonial American architectural style.

The restrained Colonial Revival structure has a giant Doric pedimented portico with a semicircular tympanum window. It is reached by a flight of stairs and balanced by single-story wings that extend to the east and west. Within the portico are set three entrances surmounted by elliptical fanlights. The chocolate-colored Pennsylvania-faced brick exterior walls are laid with mortar of the same color. The building contains an auditorium, kitchen, dressing and cloak rooms, and library; as well as the city offices, gymnasium, bowling alleys, and billiard rooms. It was built by Thomas Mullins of Fremont.

Traverse Bay Region

WHEN THE GRAND RAPIDS AND INDIANA AND THE CHIcago and West Michigan railroads reached northwestern Michigan in the 1870s, they opened this picturesque area to large numbers of summer vacationers. Earlier, steamers sailing the Great Lakes had carried visitors from more southerly cities to the small lumbering, fishing, and shipping communities that had developed by natural harbors, where rivers and streams ran into Lake Michigan along the shores of Little Traverse and Grand Traverse bays. The reports of the ideal climate, the scenic beauty, and the rich heritage of Indian history that marked the area encouraged those who longed to escape from the increasingly industrialized cities of the Midwest to visit northern Michigan. Railroads, attempting to recover from the decline of the lumbering industry, and steamship companies built hotels and promoted the tourist trade by circulating handbooks with train and boat schedules and with descriptions of resort life and of accommodations.

Resort centers in the Traverse Bay Region emerged between 1870 and 1900 as "religious associations, pleasure seekers, and invalids came to enjoy the charming scenery and the health giving atmosphere." By the summer of 1893 the *Petoskey Daily Resorter* (July 22, 1893) claimed:

> It is no exaggeration to say that . . . the summer resorts of Northern Michigan . . . comparatively unknown a dozen years ago . . . are now the most popular in America. Every resort has the clear air of Colorado, and the fishing and boating advantages of the Thousand Islands. Petoskey with its artesian mineral well and baths, is a Saratoga . . . Bay View, a Chautauqua . . . Harbor Point, a young Nahant . . . Mackinac, a Newport . . . Grand Traverse Bay excels Champlain . . . every inland sheet of water is a Lake George . . . the Upper Peninsula . . . includes the beauties of the Palisades, the Saint Lawrence and the White Mountains.

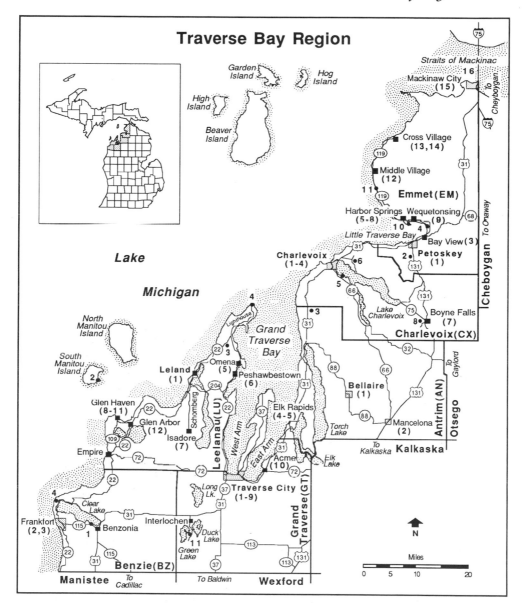

Traverse Bay Region

A wave of cottage building followed the construction of hotels. As the *Daily Resorter* observed, many families who enjoyed a summer in northern Michigan were filled with the desire to own a cottage or summer home, which was more comfortable than a hotel. Property owners grouped together in resort associations to "enjoy the society of all their friends and have those advantages which can only be secured by a community." Distinctive white frame hotels and boardinghouses, cottages, villas, clubhouses, and casinos were built so that "those fond of a summer's outing could rest from the whirl of business and society."

Typical of resort architecture at its peak in the 1890s was the cottage of Professor Jean Charlouis at Bay View. Built in 1895, it was designed for comfort and followed no special style of architecture. "Elaborate scenic effects" greeted the eye on every side, while "verandas, balconies, dormers put out from the house unexpectedly in all directions."

Structures in communities adjacent to resort associations reflected the resort business. Railroad depots and dockage facilities served vacationers who arrived by train and boat. Hotels and boardinghouses rented rooms. "Thoroughly metropolitan" stores supplied patrons accustomed to a "fine line of goods."

Emmet County   (EM)

PETOSKEY

Petoskey hugs the shore of Little Traverse Bay and is bisected on the north-south axis by Bear River. The central business district and neighborhoods in the western portion of the city lie on the lowlands that border the bay, the neighborhoods to the east and south climb up hillsides that rise to "graceful heights."

Petoskey was named for Ignatius Pe-to-se-ga, a Chippewa and early landowner in the area in 1852, when Euro-American settlers arrived. The economy depended at first on lumbering, the manufacturing of wood products, and limestone quarrying. With the arrival of the Grand Rapids and Indiana Railroad in 1873 and the Chicago and West Michigan Railroad in the 1880s, however, the city became the center of resort traffic for northwestern Lower Michigan, as trains as well as steamers delivered city dwellers. Stafford's Perry Hotel, with its large veranda, and the towered and shingled Little Traverse Regional Historical Society Museum, the former railroad depot, are the most notable reminders of the late nineteenth and early twentieth century resort industry. The exclusive shops in the Gaslight District, which winter in Palm Springs, Scottsdale, and Delray Beach, and the large marina tell of the continued importance of tourism to Petoskey.

EM01 **Little Traverse Regional Historical Society Museum** (Petoskey Depot of the Chicago and West Michigan Railroad)

1891–1892. Pioneer Park on West Lake St.

Having completed its line from Elk Rapids to Petoskey in 1892 and wanting to lure tourists

EM01 Little Traverse Regional Historical Society Museum (Petoskey Depot of the Chicago and West Michigan Railroad)

on its passenger trains to this point, the Chicago and West Michigan Railroad Company built this grand depot as a festive gateway to the resorts of the Little Traverse Region. The park surrounding it was laid out in May 1893. (The Grand Rapids and Indiana Railroad began service to Petoskey in 1874, when the place was just a "backwoods settlement.") This substantial train depot reflects the railroad stations of H. H. Richardson. From its dominant, shingled, conical-roofed square central section stretch one-story flanking hipped-roof wings with broad, sheltering overhangs. A porte-cochère and entrance porch with rounded, shingle-covered columns on heavy stone bases and supporting segmental arches define the main entrance from the street. The depot now houses a local history museum.

PETOSKEY VICINITY, BEAR CREEK TOWNSHIP

EM02 Town and Country Log Homes

1980s. 4772 US 131 South (northwest corner of US 131 and Gruler Rd.)

This house is a model for precut natural wood homes manufactured, packaged in any style, and sold by Town and Country Log Homes and its thirty-eight-year-old collaborator, Boyne Falls Log Homes, to those who seek "a unique and individual lifestyle." The cedar log walls, available in hand peeled, rough-sawn, or smooth finish, provoke associations with a building type that "dates back to the early French trappers," while the cathedral-like great rooms, greenhouses, master suites, lofts, and decks satisfy present-day tastes for gracious living. Full, enclosed-shell, and structural-shell packages as well as customized designs are assembled with the aid of computer programs. The cedar log wall system, which the company calls a "post and sill thermoloc system," sandwiches polyurethane sealant between longitudinal sections of logs and mill-finished interior. Named Elk River, Bayview, Heritage, Woodbine, Centennial, and Cedarbrook, they sell for from $18,000 to $130,000. They are advertised to look as appropriate at the end of a manicured cul-de-sac as they do tucked in a wooded setting, although they seem best suited to rustic surroundings. Numerous companies manufacture precut log homes and sell many in northern Michigan for vacation homes.

BAY VIEW

EM03 Bay View

1876 to present

Founded in 1876 as a Methodist camp meeting and resort, Bay View is a religiously oriented summer community of 437 privately owned cottages, 2 hotels, and 29 additional structures, all belonging to the Bay View Association, which also owns the land and governs life in the enclave. Sinuous curving streets line natural terraces on the northern half of its 338-acre tract, terraces that cascade from a 200-foot elevation down to Little Traverse Bay. Cottages are mostly Victorian—420 were in place by 1900—and are beautifully maintained, with much historic fabric intact. They sit with even setbacks on narrow lots, without fencing and immersed in greenery, a clear evocation of the enterprise's communal purpose.

Camp meetings, including this one, were founded in wilderness areas to benefit both religious and physical health. The first seekers slept in tents edging the preaching space, remote from civilization and its cares. Like the Kentucky frontier revivals of the early nineteenth century, Bay View's first meeting was a charged, emotional affair in which participants bathed in nature and powerful religious feelings, interlocking body and spirit in an ambience of refreshing green. Today the original preaching space, a bookstore, the speakers' stand, many cottages, and, most important, the remarkable romantic community plan remain intact.

Bay View is the only camp meeting in the country with a romantic plan. Most revivals were laid out with a simple geometric enclosure about the preaching space, a grid, or, in a few ambitious examples, to a radial concentric scheme, with lanes as "spokes" in the "wheel." Bay View's design counters the ordinariness of the common urban grid by exaggerating the site's rugged topography to get a sense of otherworldliness—all to aid relaxation and religious feeling. The community's founders were familiar with such landscaping from the new Jackson cemetery and from the "mazy" camp meeting at Martha's Vineyard, Massachusetts, which Bay View set out to imitate, and its professionally planned neighbor, Oak Bluffs. The Bay View exercise in sinuously curved streets to intensify nature may have been important for subdivision planning in the twentieth century, when Bay View became famous and much visited.

Unlike most camp meetings, Bay View's goals from the start included intellectual and scientific development, along with religious work and healthful rest. In 1885, inspired by the programs at Chautauqua (Fair Point Camp Meeting), New York, Bay View hired John M. Hall to build a summer assembly, or

"Chautauqua," around the revival. Hall began with a Michigan Department for the two thousand state members of the New York Chautauqua Literary and Scientific Circle, a four-year home study program for adults who had not had a college education. The Bay View summer assemblies eventually included a variety of programs: specialized Bible and music studies (the latter still operating), summer homes for the Epworth League of young Methodists, the Woman's Christian Temperance Union, and after 1893, John Hall's own Bay View Reading Circles, in direct competition with the mother Chautauqua in New York. Summer residents were now coming from a wide geographic range—the upper Midwest and points beyond, from New York to Alabama to California. As an independent Chautauqua, Bay View hosted national platform stars: William Jennings Bryan, Frances Willard, Booker T. Washington, Jane Addams, Carl Sandburg, Bruce Catton, Lillian Hellman, and many others. All of these activities took place in The Campus, the Tabernacle Park of the camp meeting area renamed and improved by a series of grand Queen Anne structures overlooking the preaching space with its two ancillary structures. The Chautauqua functions embraced and preserved those of the camp meeting, just as continuing governance by the Bay View Association, with its institutional memory and supportive residents, has preserved it all.

EM03.1 **The Campus**

Bounded by Park, Fairview, and Encampment avenues

A line of grand Queen Anne buildings looks down on the broad, flat terrace of the former Tabernacle Park with its camp meeting preaching space and two board-and-batten structures. The Chautauqua-era institutional buildings create a mood of comfort and security, but also festivity, with their sheltering verandas, varied silhouettes of gables, dormers, and turrets: visually involving skylines poised over horizontal masses of embracing security. An intriguing variety of patterned shingles and shiplap boarding along with the rich array of sunburst gables, bargeboard, jigsaw work, and brackets add to the cheer.

The delicate scale of the Speakers' Stand and Bookstore (1877 and 1880, Campus 18) is in tune with the cottages built by B. F. Darling of Jackson for the meeting's founders. Its elegant bell-cast roofs and the gracefully countercurving brackets are exemplary of the features that give these buildings their own, distinctive character.

The Queen Anne Chautauqua Cottage (1887, P. L. and D. Siebert, Campus 1) was the "home away from home" of the Michigan correspondence students of the Chautauqua Literary and Scientific Reading Circles, a place to gather in the summer for directed discussions of winter reading matter. From its gabled clapboarded mass project a square tower with a pyramidal roof, a shed roof dormer, and an ample porch with turned posts.

Evelyn Hall (1890, F. X. Oliver, Campus 5) is the largest of the Queen Anne structures for the summer assembly program. It is joyous with its herringbone shiplap, shaped shingles, decorative bargeboards, and balustrades. A veritable scaffold of porches and a two-story gazebo meld the three-story turreted pile into the air and verdure, all for the Women's Christian Temperance Union, which built it as a summer headquarters.

John M. Hall Auditorium (1914, W. E. N. Hunter, Campus 4) is a solid exception to the later Victorian charter of The Campus. Hunter employed an Ionic portico in a classical facade for a dignity in keeping with national trends and with John M. Hall's ambition to develop the assembly into a summer university. The auditorium behind this academic facade is surprisingly light and airy, seating seventeen hundred under four steel trusses spanning 102 feet.

Bay View Library (1923, Earl H. Mead, Campus 10) is finely crafted in orange brick with stepped vertical bands welding the chimney to its wall and reflects lessons learned from Cranbrook (OK08, p. 163).

EM03.2 **Residential Area**

Bay View's 1876 plan set off residential lots—to be leased from the landowning association—in sinuous curving lines along the contours and terraced ridges overlooking Little Traverse Bay. As an alternative, lots also lined inward-looking crescents bordering the parks. The curving roads exaggerate the naturally rugged site. Sidewalks, set away from roads in varying distances, leave shifting widths of grass border. Often, as in Evergreen Park, one of the several small wooded places laced through the residential zones, the sidewalk parts from the road completely, enhancing the mood of tranquility and ease.

The earliest cottages, from the late 1870s and probably designed by B. F. Darling of Jackson, were built to a variety of plans reflecting various rural house types of the middle of the century. Probably slightly later are cottages that are Bay View variations of a specialized building type, the camp meeting cottage, invented on Martha's Vineyard, Massachusetts, about 1860. The camp meeting cottage is a two-story, symmetrically massed, end-gable building with a central entrance. For the Bay View version, a two-story porch under a projecting gable has been added to enliven the facade, while on at least the ground floor, the corners of the main block are cut on the diagonal, leaving an angled wall wide enough for a window. Other cottages combine the rural house and camp meeting cottage types in an exuberant display of patterned shiplap boarding and other woodworking devices of marvelous originality.

The following cottages, mostly from the 1880s, have been selected for their closeness to The Campus. Many other original variants can be found all over the community.

The Louise A. Shier Cottage (1877, B. F. Darling, 318 Woodland [Block 2, Lot 8]) is one of the first three cottages at Bay View and was occupied by Rev. Dr. W. H. Shier, a trustee for thirty-eight years. This flank gable structure with inserted front gable and porch on delicate supports has board-and-batten siding on the ground floor.

Moon Cottage (George Osburn Cutter Cottage) (c. 1877, 322 Woodland [Block 2, Lot 10]) is in the row of cottages facing the bay,

a site favored by the founders. It is an extravaganza of shiplap boarding, distinguished by the varied profiles of the molded board itself as well as by the patterns in which the boards are laid.

James Kirk Perrin Cottage (1877, 409 Fairview [Block 2 Lot 12]) is a typical Bay View camp meeting cottage with canted corner and a two-story porch, which is fronted by the encircling veranda and the octagonal turret suspended over the porch void.

Pink Cottage (David J. and Caroline Dow Dykhouse Cottage) (1881, 321 Park [Block 2, Lot 13]) is in superb historical condition. With its flush boarding and pattern-book window surrounds intact, this cross-gable cottage has a wealth of bargeboard plus an octagonal cupola.

The turn of the century was marked by a number of distinctive Shingle style houses in an insistent variety of shapes, rooflines, and "colonial" detailing, all possibly designed by Earl H. Mead of Harbor Springs and Lansing. One example is the Edward J. and Elizabeth Neithercut Cottage (c. 1900, 223 Park [Block 1, Lot 11C]), a cross-gable shingle and shiplap bungalow with sensitively curved corners to the gable window and Tuscan columns bordering the recessed porch.

The Sidney and Ruth L. Butterfield Cottage (c. 1879, B. F. Darling, 201 Park Avenue [Block 1, Lot 21]) is a superbly preserved hipped-roof house, which is almost square in plan, has board and batten siding, and a bracketed porch wrapping it on four sides. It was associated with Rev. William H. Brockway of Albion College, a member of the committee that laid out the grounds.

The Ruth Gentry Cottage (c. 1879, 207 Fairview [Block 20, Lot 3,4]) is very similar to the camp meeting type invented at Martha's Vineyard, Massachusetts.

Several Bay View themes are exemplified in the Parsons Cottage (Jeanne F. Pentler Cottage) (c. 1889, 226 Knapp [Block 26, Lot 3]): canted corners on the first floor, herringbone shiplap, a two-story scaffold of porches with brackets and fretwork, a special cross-gabled pavilion on the second-story porch, and elaborate lattice and spindlework.

Octagon Cottage (Robert and Joanne F. Bartholomew Cottage) (1880s, A. M. Apted, 431 Moss Avenue [Block 19, Lot 10]) is the only Bay View cottage with this unusual shape. A distinctive feature of the Waites Cottage (Esther W. Brightmans Cottage) (1887, 604

Springside [Block 18, Lot 8]) is the Moorish detail of the series of arches on the lattice porch. The Elizabeth Maxon Shier Cottage (1900, 410 Beech [Block 16, Lot 6]) is one of the many cottages probably designed by Earl H. Mead. The shingle and shiplap suburban houses carry on the theme of Victorian recessed porches—semipublic areas that reinforced the sense of community. This elegant gambrel has paired Tuscan columns and other fetching classical details. Alridon Cottage (Thomas A. Hunter Cottage) (c. 1889, 714 Woodland [Block 32, Lot 9]) has canted corners with windows, a two-story porch, and a rich display of carpentry in the gable peaks.

HARBOR SPRINGS VICINITY

EM04 **Harbor Inn on the Bay** (Ramona Park Hotel)

1910. 1929. 200 Beach Rd. (south of Michigan 119, along Little Traverse Bay)

This large white resort hotel with its dominant red metal roof is visible from across Little Traverse Bay. The original building, erected in 1910, consisted of the octagonal tower, lobby, dining area, and about thirty guest rooms. The large east wing was added in 1929. The building echoes the growth of the Little Traverse Bay region as a popular resort area. The hotel flourished during the first quarter of the twentieth century as summer vacationers were attracted to the clean air, clear bay, scenic woods, and mineral waters. An artesian well still flows behind the hotel. The hotel was winterized in 1964.

HARBOR SPRINGS

Surrounded by wooded hillsides, Harbor Springs overlooks a beautiful natural harbor formed by the projection of Harbor Point across the northern part of Little Traverse Bay. The area was a summer village for Ottawa and Chippewa. Here, in 1827, Father Pierre D' Jean founded the Mission of the Holy Childhood of Jesus. The village was incorporated in 1881, the city in 1932. Its early economy depended on lumbering, but tourism rapidly developed in the 1870s with the arrival of trains and steamers. City dwell-

ers were attracted to the exquisite scenery, crisp northern climate, and cold-water springs.

Superb examples of Shingle style resort architecture—hotels, summer houses, and clubhouses—remain in the Harbor Point, Wequetonsing, and Roaring Brook resort associations in the Harbor Springs vicinity. Much of it was designed by Earl H. Mead, who moved here from Lansing in 1898 and practiced throughout the early twentieth century. But many other buildings, including the village hall, the high school, Methodist church, and commercial buildings, were also planned by Mead.

Today, the Little Traverse Conservancy is actively protecting the landscape of the area.

EM05 **Ephraim Shay House**

1892, Ephraim Shay. 396 East Main St. (Michigan 119) (southwest corner of East Main and Judd streets)

The creative mind of Ephraim Shay (1839–1916), inventor of a maneuverable logging locomotive that permitted large-scale, year-round logging operations, even in the most inaccessible timberlands, produced this multiple hexagon house. The house is composed of a two-story octagonal central section, from which extend six semioctagonal wings, each a single room with five windows, so that from the center one can see in any direction. The first floor of the octagon is a sitting room, the second an observatory. Except for the stone foundation, all surfaces, both inside and out, are sheathed in embossed metal. The exterior walls are metal pressed to imitate brick; the interior walls are metal pressed in various motifs. The original metal roof has been replaced with a similar red metal one. To one local writer in the *Petoskey Daily Resorter* for

September 5, 1894, the house seemed "as great a novelty as his (Shay's) locomotive."

EM06 Holy Childhood of Jesus Church and School

1892, church. 1913, 1926, school, Indian School Brother Hilarion Held. 150 West Main St.

The Holy Childhood of Jesus Church stands in a commanding location at the head of Main Street, visible to all who enter Harbor Springs from the east. It is a simple, Neo-Romanesque white-painted wooden gable structure with a center-steepled entry and bell tower and an apse. The spire is broached. A fanlight is over the door and a small rose window is in the tower above the entrance. An arched appliqué of wood runs along the entablature beneath the cornices. Just northeast of the church is the three-story brick school. Both the school and the church replace earlier structures associated with the Indian mission.

In the eighteenth century, Jesuit missionaries from the Saint Joseph Mission for the Potawatomi and Miami, located over two hundred miles to the south, and from the Marquette Mission at Saint Ignace, visited the Ottawa, who had moved to L'Arbre Croche, the shore area between Harbor Springs and Cross Village. In 1823 the Ottawa of L'Arbre Croche petitioned President James Monroe and Congress for a Christian minister. So as to separate Christian from non-Christian Ottawa, Father Pierre D'Jean transferred in 1829 a mission he had established two years earlier at Middle Village, L'Arbre Croche, to a new village at this site, present-day Harbor Springs.

Father D'Jean and the Indians built a log church and a rectory and school. The school was both a boarding and day school, with 23 boarders in its initial enrollment of 63, who were taught in French reading, writing, arithmetic, and vocational skills. D'Jean was followed by Father Frederick Baraga. Under the Franciscan Fathers, who arrived in 1884, and the School Sisters of Notre Dame, who came in 1886, the school served L'Arbre Croche and missions in the northern portion of the Lower Peninsula until it closed in 1983.

Between 1885 and 1907, as the numbers of boarders and day students increased to more than 200, three-story frame structures were constructed and added to for classrooms, dormitories, workshops, an infirmary, a chapel, and a convent. Eventually all wooden buildings were replaced by the brick structures that remain today. The original log building stood until the clapboard school was finished in 1892–1893.

Little Childhood of Jesus Church remained essentially an Indian mission until the early 1900s. As the Euro-American population increased with the rise of logging camps and sawmills and with the seasonal arrival of resorters, it began to serve these members of the parish as well.

Enrollment at the Indian school declined as other welfare programs assisted families who kept children at home and sent them to public schools. Then, in 1974, living quarters were confined to the first floor because of state safety requirements.

EM07 Earl H. Mead House

c. 1910, Earl H. Mead. 151 East Bluff Dr.

Earl H. Mead (1871–1936) was an architect whose own house exhibits in miniature many of the earmarks of his hand—a steeply pitched complex hip roof with flaring eaves and hip roof dormers, a classically detailed porch, in this case, with square piers, grouped windows with diamond-shaped panes above rectangular-shaped panes. Moreover, the one-and-a-half-story clapboarded structure lacks reference to historic styles. It is positioned on the bluff with a spectacular view of the village, the bay, and Petoskey beyond.

EM08 Marina Village

1968–1971, H. Jack Begrow. On Little Traverse Bay and Bay St. (southwest corner of East Bay and Zoll St.)

Looking toward the harbor from Little Traverse Bay, the white triangular planes created by the walls cut by the shed roofs of this group of condominiums resemble the lines and masses of boats in a regatta tied at slips in the marina. The tall chimneys mimic the masts. Ward and Roma Walstrom commissioned H. Jack Begrow of Charlevoix to design the project at the yacht basin and Walstrom's marina, overlooking the bay and Harbor Point, for well-to-do, year-round vacationers. The units are clustered into three groups of from nine to twelve units each. The exteriors are off-white vertically grooved plywood siding with charcoal shingles and

EM08 Marina Village

black-anodized window and door frames. The condominiums are among the first erected in northern Michigan.

WEQUETONSING

EM09 Wequetonsing, East Wequetonsing and West Wequetonsing

1877 and later. Wequetonsing is bounded on the south by Beach Dr. and the shore of Little Traverse Bay (Lake Michigan) from a point just west of First Avenue to a point just east of Fifth Avenue, and on the north by Michigan 119. West Wequetonsing is bounded on the west by approximately Zoll St. and on the east by the western boundary of Wequetonsing. East Wequetonsing is bounded on the west by Wequetonsing and on the east by Ramona Park.

The Wequetonsing Association, formerly the Presbyterian Summer Resort, was established in 1877 on the harbor adjoining the eastern boundary of Harbor Springs. People from Allegan, Michigan, and Elkhart, Indiana, platted the resort on 8 acres of land given to them by the citizens of Harbor Springs so that "worn-out and sweltering humanity could repair to recover health and enjoy rational recreations."[68] The grounds were cleared, lots sold and leased, and a boardinghouse built. By 1880 the association had a hotel. By 1899 the resort had an assembly hall for religious and social purposes. The most elaborate cottages, many of which have been winterized, face Little Traverse Bay. Smaller cottages stand on terraced lots facing streets that lead up from the harbor. North of Michigan 119 is the Wequetonsing Golf Club.

After building a cottage for E. H. Pope at Wequetonsing, Charles W. Caskey established a construction business in Harbor Springs in 1880. This Allegan native subsequently built many cottages at Wequetonsing, Harbor Point, Bay View, and Mackinac Island. Earl H. Mead, a Lansing and Harbor Springs architect, who in the late 1890s worked in partnership with Thomas White of Lansing, designed more than twenty cottages at Wequetonsing. Darius Moon, also a Lansing architect, designed houses for Wequetonsing, Roaring Brook, and Bay View.

EM09.1 Marwood (George B. and Jennie E. Crank [Mary Cluff?] Spear Summer Cottage)

1900, Mead and White. 49 Beach Dr. (northeast corner of Beach Dr. and Fifth Avenue), Wequetonsing

Central bay windows that are pulled up into terminal conical-shaped towers with flaring eaves distinguish this hipped-roof clapboarded and shingled summer cottage and offer a view of the harbor. The curvature of the overhanging roof and the verandas that wrap around the front of the structure emphasize the building's sheltering and hovering qualities. It recalls Bruce Price's umbrella motif in designs at Bar Harbor in Maine. Inside, space flows in a circular manner around the living and dining room fireplaces and the stairway. A den in the projecting wing gives privacy. George B. Spear (b. 1858), president of the Saint Louis, Missouri, Edible Nut Company, built the cottage on the occasion of his second marriage in 1900.

EM09.2 **The Archway** (William M. Parker House)

c. 1900. 61 East Beach Dr., East Wequetonsing

The Archway typifies the large, comfortable summer house found at Wequetonsing, Harbor Point, and Mackinac Island at the end of the century. Bays and porches project from this gambrel-roof cottage, and other porches recede, so that it offers opportunities to mingle with nature in all kinds of weather. It was constructed of indigenous materials—stone, wood, and shingles—and the exterior originally was stained brown or green or weathered to blend with its natural surroundings.

EM09.3 **R. A. Files Cottage** (The Barr Cottage)

c. 1900. 63 Beach Dr. (3 doors west of Beach Dr. and Pennsylvania, East Wequetonsing)

The boldly arched and towered stone and shingle cottage is Wequetonsing's finest example of the Shingle style, especially as it is found in the superb stone and shingle houses that marked the New England coast during this creative period in American domestic architecture.

HARBOR SPRINGS

EM10 **Harbor Point** (Harbor Point Resort)

1878 and later, Earl H. Mead et al. Entrance is off southeast corner of Glen Dr. and Traverse St. Visible from the water

Harbor Point is the most exclusive of the eight summer resorts, some divided into as many as 200 lots, which were established in the Harbor Springs vicinity by 1910. It was organized in 1878 by a group of Lansing, Michigan, businessmen who had camped out at Harbor Point. They formed a stock company, sold shares to 19 members, and purchased the 52-acre point of land from Father Wiecamp, a Franciscan monk of Cross Village. The grounds were laid out "for the leasing and occupancy of lots by members, together with the use of the surrounding grounds by them, under regulations of the association, and without streets, alleys, or other grounds usually open to the public."[69] To maintain control over the resort's future, the association's board of directors retained title to the land. After receiving approval from the board, a member could purchase a $100 share of stock, which entitled him or her to select a lot on which to build a house costing not less than $100.

Initially the underbrush was cleared, walks

and drives were built, and a hotel, dock, boat and bathhouse were built. Five years later, in 1883, some 30 new cottages were built. The earliest of these were modest Stick style wooden structures built by local craftsmen for as little as $250. The cottages of the 1890s, however, were more "hospitable homes" and offered more extensive, modern, and convenient accommodations. In 1900 at Harbor Point, a "splendid cottage" with 14 rooms and modern conveniences could be built for $4,000. Some were designed by architects from the home cities of the summer visitors. Thirty were designed or altered by Earl H. Mead, who came to Harbor Springs from Lansing in 1898 and established a practice there. Mead generally designed rectangular-shaped structures with steeply pitched roofs with generous overhangs. He covered wooden frames with clapboard and shingle siding, applied classical details, and planned open interior spaces.

By 1899 Harbor Point had turned into an exclusive upper-class resort, with families from all over the Midwest occupying its 80 cottages and casino. Residents of Harbor Point have included bankers, railroad employees, justices, manufacturers, Detroit lumberman David Whitney, Chicago chewing gum magnate William Wrigley, Jr., Cincinnati soap manufacturer David Gamble, and Chicago Great Lakes transit company owner Albert W. Goodrich. Harbor Point is a midwestern variant of Newport.

Access to Harbor Point is restricted to members and guests, and no cars are allowed. Most cottages on the point may be viewed by boat, however.

EM10.1 Telgham and Anna W. Pickering Summer House

1898–1902, Mead and White. Lot 27. Visible from the water

One of the more fanciful and ornate cottages designed by Mead and White, this was built for Telgham Pickering and his wife, Anna (1888–1906). Pickering was a Cincinnati hardware merchant. A picturesque assortment of shapes flows around the mass. Interior and exterior spaces merge by means of towers, dormers, covered porches, balconies, stairways, and large windows. Shingle roofing and shingle and clapboard siding integrate the composition. Originally they were painted a dark color such as olive to blend with "Dame Nature, herself."

EM10.2 Albert W. and Carrie Lois Stafft (Elizabeth McKay?) Goodrich Summer Cottage

1900, Mead and White. Lot 2. Visible from the water

Albert W. Goodrich (1869–1938), owner of the Goodrich Transit Company, the largest of the Great Lakes steamship lines, built this cottage. It is designed for its site near the tip of the point: the rectangular-shaped mass fills up the lot; and the verandas, which sweep around the structure, give access to the breezes and views of both the bay and the harbor. The two-and-a-half-story wooden building rests on a stone foundation. Shingles, probably once stained brown or green, cover the exterior walls of the second story, which curve out above a beltcourse repeating the curvature of the roof. Clapboarding sides the lower walls. The placement of the recessed main entry on the side of the cottage is a distance from the road and walk but gives privacy to the verandas, the centers of resort life. The interior is organized along a single axis extended by verandas at the first floor. The open living area flows from hall to sitting room and from hall to dining room, each connected to an outdoor sitting area in a manner suited to informal vacation life. The kitchen, pantry, and service entry, distinctly separated from the living area, were convenient and well equipped for a household with servants. The upper floors, enlarged by the space above the verandas and under the mountainous shingled roof, provide generous bedroom space for large families of several generations on vacation. The interior is finished throughout in beaded ceiling laid vertically below a wainscoting and horizontally above. Ornamental latticework decorates openings around the stairway. It is fitted with inglenooks near fireplaces.

L'ARBRE CROCHE, FRIENDSHIP TOWNSHIP

EM11 James Douglas House

1971–1973, Richard Meier and Associates. 3490 Lake Shore Dr. (Michigan 119) (on Lake Shore Dr., .4 mi south of Stutsmanville Rd.)

This International style house resides among a collection of log and contemporary vacation homes that line beautiful Lake Shore Drive north of Harbor Springs. It was designed by

EM11 James Douglas House

the famous American architect Richard Meier and owes something to Le Corbusier. The Douglas house is dramatically situated overlooking Lake Michigan on a steep, densely wooded slope that drops down to the lake at a 45-degree angle. When viewed from the lake, the static machined quality and stark whiteness of the house contrast with the rustling evergreens and water. At the same time the horizontal layers of the house punctuated by the dramatic verticals of the chimneys, mullions, and overall massing mimic the horizontal planes of the road, beach, and water overlapped by the tall vertical pines.

Only the roof and entry level are visible from the roadway, but the house drops to four levels below. As in other Meier houses from this period, the entry extends beyond the limits of the building. Approached by the flying bridge, the volume of the house below is suddenly and surprisingly revealed. The vertical arrangement of the house is emphasized in the entry vestibule, which overlooks the living and dining areas below. The entry vestibule also opens to a large roof deck, which, like other elements in the house, suggests the metaphor of a land-based ship. Decks on all levels of the house provide magnificent breath-taking views and a sense of being thrust out to soar above the water and trees. This feeling is emphasized again in the freely suspended and projecting exterior stairway connecting the decks. And yet within the house one feels confined to a treetop glass box.

MIDDLE VILLAGE, FRIENDSHIP TOWNSHIP

EM12 Saint Ignatius Church

1889. Lower Shore Rd.

Tucked behind a dune on the lakeshore, this clapboarded wood-frame church with a one-

story wing addition is picturesque in its simplicity and isolation. It is the third structure to serve the Indian settlement on the site of a Jesuit Mission established near here by the French in 1741. A central entry tower with open belfry and spire project from the simple Gothic Revival building. Pointed-arch windows with double-hung sash pierce the walls. Tongue-and-groove wainscoting and pressed-metal ceiling and walls adorn the interior of the church. In the cemetery adjoining the church on the south, wooden crosses mark the graves of the Ottawa.

CROSS VILLAGE

EM13 Legs Inn

c. 1921, Stanislaw Smolak. 1930–1966, additions. 6425 Lake Shore Dr. (Michigan 119) (northeast corner of Lake Shore Dr. and First St. [Levering Rd.])

Over a lifetime, Stanislaw Smolak (1887–1968) built his tavern, curio shop, and living quarters of local fieldstone and natural and man-made found objects. From Kamionka, Poland, Smolak went to Detroit in 1912. He worked in the auto factories before moving in 1921 to northern Michigan. Here his friendship with the Ottawa earned him the name Chief White Cloud. The enterprise earned the name Legs Inn for the rows of inverted cast-iron stove legs that form the roofline parapet on the exterior of the building, only one distinctive feature of one of Michigan's most noteworthy examples of local individualistic architecture. The entire building and furnishings carry out Smolak's desire to fill his time making use of discarded stuff. Tree limbs, logs, roots, stumps, and driftwood are hand carved and crafted into the most fantastical animals and grotesques, birds and snake sculptures, and furniture borrowed from native Woodland Indian and European tradition. They lend a mood of terror, even the sublime, to this structure at a remote outpost in northwestern Lower Michigan. The place abounds with flags, totem poles, and stuffed moose, deer heads, and other wildlife.

EM14 Redpath Memorial Presbyterian Church

1921, Earl H. Mead. 6532 Lake Shore Dr. (Michigan 119) (southwest corner of Lake Shore Dr. and Third St.)

This sturdy little end-gable church constructed of local heavy fieldstones and cobblestones shows Earl H. Mead's ability to pay attention to detail. The structure has slightly battered walls, flared eaves, broad Gothic pointed-arch windows, an entry porch, and a cupola with bell. After the earlier Presbyterian church was ruined in the fire of 1918 that destroyed most of Cross Village, the Reverend John Redpath led the effort to build this church.

MACKINAW CITY

EM15 Colonial Michilimackinac

1715–1781. West of I-75 on the south shore of the Straits of Mackinac (entrance is under the Mackinac Bridge, on Straits Avenue, east of I-75)

At the northernmost point of Michigan's Lower Peninsula, on the south shore of the Straits of Mackinac, lies the archaeological site

of Michilimackinac. For the most part it is overlain by the modern town of Mackinaw City, although all of Fort Michilimackinac and at least portions of an adjacent contemporary fur-trading village survive within Michilimackinac State Park. First established around 1715 by French-Canadians as a mission and small fur-trading compound, this post aided in a successful attempt to deter attack from the feared Iroquois Indians. Some time during the 1730s the settlement was completely rebuilt and greatly enlarged by the French, and its function became one of the fur trade exclusively. The 1730s town was designed in the style of Sebastien le Prestre Marquis de Vauban, military and architectural genius of the Court of Louis XIV. It prospered until 1744, when with the outbreak of hostilities with Great Britain, additional fortifications were built. Included was a triangular Vauban-style defensive earthwork on the west side of the palisaded town, which is still visible. Most French buildings enclosed within the 1730s palisade were of unhewn post-in-the-ground (*poteaux en terre*) construction. Wood was the only readily available building material in the area.

With the close of the French and Indian War in 1761, British forces arrived and occupied Michilimackinac. Nevertheless, for the next two decades Michilimackinac retained its French provincial architectural character, in large part because the peace treaty allowed French-Canadians to keep their real and improved properties, including their parish church and its attached rectory. While attempting to convert the old palisaded town to a military fort, British authorities actually encouraged the fur trade through trading policies more liberal than those of the French. The fur trade continued to grow. By 1765 many fur-trading activities were, by order, moved outside of the palisade, and thus a new village grew up around the fort. By the late 1770s this new settlement contained over one hundred houses.

Two types of vernacular architecture are present at Michilimackinac. First, and by far the most common, is the unhewn upright post-in-the-ground construction of the French. Less evident are buildings in piece-on-piece (*pièce sur pièce*) method, constructed during both the French and British periods. Ecclesiastical buildings of the French inside the fort and all British buildings there are built in this manner. Data from archaeological and historical research provide architectural information used in the reconstruction of buildings dating to the time of the American War of Independence (1770s).

During the French period, all fur traders and soldiers lived in long multidwelling row houses that have their origins in medieval Brittany and Normandy. At Michilimackinac these lengthy structures, up to 130 feet long, contained from four to six dwellings each, with a total of seven row houses inside the fort and an unknown number that date to the British period in the village outside. Row houses are distinguished by unhewn upright logs set into a ditch to anchor the building to the ground. Heavy uprights were placed at 6-foot intervals in the walls and at the corners, with the interstices between them filled with less substantial logs. Some of the row house ruins, particularly those dating from the 1730s French town, such as the powder magazine, have wattle-and-daub wall construction. Later French upright log buildings have daub only between the uprights. Windows and doors were generally placed in the outside walls only. Occasionally the small dwellings (about 23 feet square) contained two rooms, one for storing trade goods and the other for living quarters, the latter of which always possessed a stone fireplace and a stick-and-clay chimney. Roofs were steep and often contained dormers, the only source of light in the garret above the first floor. A simple interior staircase connected the first floor with the garret. Shingles for the roof, and frequently for the unhewn upright log walls as well, were made of cedar bark, an architectural trait the French borrowed from local Native Americans. Of the 34 houses inside the fort in 1766, 31 were of unhewn post-in-the-ground French row house type.

Piece-on-piece log construction is rare at Michilimackinac during the French period. The Church of Sainte Anne and the adjoining Jesuit rectory are the only French examples of this building method known before British occupation. Both consisted of hewn logs placed horizontally one on top of the other, and both buildings are reconstructed on the site. British construction at Michilimackinac in general is typical of British military architecture of the eighteenth century in North America. Because the French were able to retain their property, the British had little space inside the fort in which to build. British authorities enlarged the old French

palisade in 1765 by expanding outward the north and south curtain walls. All the same, there was only enough space inside to build five new buildings. One of them, the soldiers' barracks (1769), has been reconstructed and is an excellent example of British military architecture at the site. It consists of unhewn horizontal piece-on-piece walls placed on a foundation of limestone flagstones. It possesses a relatively low-pitched roof covered with cedar shakes. It is presumed that this method of building and variations thereof were used in the village surrounding the fort. Archaeological excavation, however, has thus far revealed only three buildings in the village, and all three are of the unhewn French post-in-the-ground construction.

As archaeological excavation and reconstruction continue, the overwhelming French-Canadian architectural character of colonial Michilimackinac becomes more evident. Obvious French resistance to changing architectural types of the eighteenth century is clear evidence of overall French opposition to British military occupation of Michilimackinac. French persistence in the old ways is also a monument to their ethnocentrism, which survives into our own time.

EM16 Mackinac Straits Bridge

1954–1957, David B. Steinman. Interstate Highway 75 (I-75) across the Straits of Mackinac

The Mackinac Bridge spans the 5-mile-wide Straits of Mackinac and links the Upper and Lower peninsulas of Michigan. This engineering marvel is the longest suspension bridge in the world.

Since the achievement of statehood in 1837, Michigan citizens struggled with the question of how to join the two peninsulas. People suggested a series of bridges, causeways, or tunnels between islands but had to use ferries or travel around through Chicago and Wisconsin to reach the other peninsula until the Mackinac Bridge opened. Plans to construct a bridge were drawn up in 1934–1935 but languished during the depression and World War II. In 1950 the legislature established the Mackinac Bridge Authority, which selected three of the most prominent bridge engineers in the world to study the problem of bridging the straits: David B. Steinman (1887–1961), consulting or designing engineer for some four hundred bridges all over the world; Othmar H. Ammann, formerly chief engineer for the New York Port Authority; and Glen B. Woodruff, chief engineer of design for the San Francisco-Oakland Bay Bridge and chief engineer on the rebuilt Tacoma Narrows Bridge. In 1951, when the results of their study reported that the building of a bridge across the straits would be physically and economically feasible, the authority sought the financing.

The authority retained David B. Steinman to design the Mackinac Bridge. The bridge was built in two years and cost nearly $100 million. The four-lane structure is 26,195 feet long. Each of two ivory-colored towers rises to over 552 feet above the water and each rests on a base of masonry sheathed in steel that reaches down to bedrock 206 feet below water. Each tower measures 116 feet in diameter. The bridge's main span measures 8,614 feet from anchorage to anchorage and crosses the 280-foot gorge that slices east and west across the bottom of the Straits. In the center, the bridge clears the water by more than 150 feet, thereby permitting the safe passage of all ships that sail the Great Lakes. The coming of the bridge eliminated lines of cars at the ferries that sometimes (during deer-hunting season) stretched for as long as seventeen miles and produced a waiting period of up to nineteen hours.

Charlevoix County (CX)

CHARLEVOIX

Named in honor of the early French explorer Pierre-François-Xavier de Charlevoix, the city fronts on Lake Michigan, Round Lake, and Lake Charlevoix. A navigable channel connects the big lake to Round Lake, which serves as an inland harbor for pleasure boats. After the Pine River was dredged in 1876 to form the channel, Charlevoix's economy developed around the land-locked port. Lumber sawed at mills on the shore of Lake Charlevoix, pig iron, fish, and cordwood for fueling lake steamers were shipped from docks at Charlevoix. The resort industry flowered in the 1870s as resort associations were established on terraces above the lake. Their picturesque cottages, clubhouses, and boat houses remain. Today condominiums occupy choice frontage on Lake Michigan and line Round Lake.

CX01 "Dwarf" or "Mushroom Houses"

1902–1950s, Earl A. Young. Bounded by Park, Grant, and Clinton streets, 2 blocks east of Park St., which intersects US 31 south of the bridge

The playful expressionistic or organic dwellings known locally as "dwarf," "mushroom," or "Hansel and Gretel" houses were designed and built by a visionary and self-trained local builder for sale or rent to romantics and dreamers on vacation. In addition to the houses in this block, the same local builder, Earl A. Young (1889–1975), built houses in his Boulder Park Subdivision, an office at 224 Bridge Street (US 31), three houses on Round Lake, and the Weathervane Inn overlooking the harbor north of the bridge. Typical of his works, the houses on Park and Grant streets are diminutive, imaginative and fantastic structures built of local limestone, fieldstone, and shipwrecked timber. They have undulating wood shingle roofs and large fireplaces. Young's favorites were his own house at 306 Park Street and the Weathervane Inn.

Born in Mancelona, a major railroad junction 27 miles south of Charlevoix in Antrim County, Young studied business at the University of Michigan. He read architectural journals, attended building shows, and constructed buildings intuitively from his own charcoal-drawn sketches. Owners of Young houses have included a college professor, a lawyer, a factory manager, an interior decorator, and a lieutenant governor of Illinois.

CX02 Lincoln Logs Motel

late 1930s. 820 Petoskey (US 31) (on US 31, 1 mile northeast of US 31 [Bridge Street] bridge over channel between Lake Michigan and Round Lake, just before Mercer Avenue)

These cozy, rustic, log tourist cabins fitted with fireplaces and furnished with log furniture were designed to meet the romantic expectations of the automobile traveler for overnight accommodations in northern Michigan.

CX03 **Chicago Club** (Chicago Summer Resort)

1880. From the intersection of Prospect and East Dixon avenues northeast to Cherry Street and southeast to Round Lake

Members of the First Congregational Church of Chicago established in 1880 the Chicago Summer Resort, the present-day Chicago Club, on the north side of the Pine River Channel overlooking Lake Charlevoix. A stock company was organized and incorporated in June 1881. Shares sold at $100 each. To accommodate the stockholders and their families, a large Stick style clubhouse containing twenty-seven bedrooms, sitting rooms, and a large dining room was built in 1881 in the center of the newly cleared grounds. Although it has lost its landmark belvedere, the building still has its broad two-story wrap-around veranda and stick ornamentation and is well maintained. Large summer homes were built on the 40-acre terraced and wooded site around the hotel overlooking Round Lake, the channel, and Lake Charlevoix. Roads through the grounds are private, but a drive to the end of East Dixon Avenue affords a good view of some of the summer homes in the Chicago Club. At the end of East Dixon Avenue, at 325 Cherry, is the Pere Marquette Depot. This frame depot was the stopping point for Charlevoix summer resorters. A similar depot, now gone, on the other side of the channel serviced the Belvedere Club.

CX04 **Belvedere Club** (Charlevoix Summer Resort)

1878. From the intersection of Belvedere and Ferry avenues southwest and north to Round Lake and east to Lake Charlevoix

The present-day Belvedere Club is a summer resort of 86 summer houses in a 50-acre parklike setting on two terraces overlooking Round Lake and Lake Charlevoix. It was established in 1878 as the Charlevoix Summer Resort Association. Aware of the successful promotion of land at Bay View for use as a camp meeting ground by the Methodist Episcopalians (see EM03, p. 407), several Charlevoix businessmen sought similar land development for this area. In 1877 they offered 25 acres fronting on Round Lake to a Kalamazoo-centered Baptist group for $625, provided improvements were made within a specified time. The following spring a committee from Kalamazoo visited this site, along with other sites offered in northwestern Michigan. They liked the location and accepted the offer.

The Charlevoix Summer Resort Association was formed, and its first meeting was held in Kalamazoo on June 21, 1878. By the end of that year, a pier, bathhouse, and six cottages on the upper terraces had been built. The association bought 25 additional acres in 1880. By 1900 the majority of the cottages were constructed. Most cottages originally lacked kitchens, and the resorters took their meals at a large frame hotel that once was located at the intersection of Belvedere and Ferry avenues. For the most part, the cottages are of wood-frame construction and range from simple vernacular to elaborate and commodious high-style structures. All were built for summer use only. The frame boat houses that follow the curved shoreline are unique. While roadways through the Belvedere Club are private, a drive to the end of Belvedere Avenue and along Ferry Avenue presents a view of some of the houses.

EVELINE TOWNSHIP

CX05 **Albert H. and Anna Loeb Summer House**

1917, Arthur Heun. East side of Michigan 66, 2.5 to 3 three miles southeast of US 31. Visible from the water

The Albert H. Loeb Summer House is a great Neo-Norman house designed by Prairie school architect Arthur Heun (1866–1946) that sprawls high above Lake Charlevoix. Built of rough, uncut native fieldstone, it is the centerpiece of a complex that originally included a farm, caretaker's houses, and the Ernest Loeb House (1922) on 2,200 acres of land.

In 1916 Albert H. Loeb, vice-president of Sears, Roebuck and Company in Chicago, decided to build a summer house and farm in northern Michigan. He secured the advice of Arthur Heun and the famous landscape architect Jens Jensen, who recently had collaborated in designing and landscaping his spacious, red brick Neo-Tudor house on Ellis Avenue in the fashionable Kenwood neighborhood of Chicago's South Side. Together they sought a site for a house in which Albert and Anna Loeb and their family could summer and entertain guests, and for a scientific experimental farm on which they could test implements and equipment sold by Sears. Jensen suggested a site at Ludington, Michigan, but the Loebs chose instead this site at Charlevoix overlooking the lake. Here the Loeb family had spent vacations for several years. The Loebs drained and reclaimed much of the land. They incorporated into the landscaping Jensen's plans for planting a natural woods, groves of sugar maple, cherry and plum orchards, and a kitchen garden, although they dismissed him after a disagreement over the selection of the site.

The Loeb house follows a U-shaped plan. The living and dining rooms flank a center foyer, which is reached from a long covered entranceway. Through the entrance to the foyer and patio beyond unfolds a view of Lake Charlevoix. Upstairs are twelve bedrooms, some with adjacent sleeping porches.

The Loeb farm, now an outdoor rock concert site, stands next to Michigan 66. It was planned as a model modern scientific farm.

The cow barn, diary buildings, stables, and gatekeeper's house were built of rough native fieldstone in a style compatible with the house. At the farm the Loebs raised champion Holstein-Friesian cattle, Belgian horses, and Duroc-Jersey hogs. Towers, turrets, archways, stone walls, and tile roofs give the buildings a castlelike appearance, inspiring the local nickname Castle Farms.

Born in Saginaw, Heun studied architecture under his uncle Volusin Bude of Grand Rapids and went in 1887 to Chicago, where he worked for Francis M. Whitehouse. Heun associated with Frank Lloyd Wright and with the Steinway Group of architects who occupied the Steinway building, which became a center of architectural activity from its opening in 1896. Heun developed a reputation for domestic designs, in particular, country houses. He counted as his clients the Meekers, Armours, and Loebs. The Loebs commissioned him to design their Ellis Avenue house on the advice of Jensen, whose landscape work they had admired. Heun also designed a rustic log house for the Armours, at Long Lake, near Traverse City.

The Loeb house and farm and Granot Loma and Loma Farms, the Louis Kaufman house and farms on Lake Superior near Big Bay in Marquette County (MQ18, p. 499), are among Michigan's great summer estates.

HAYES TOWNSHIP

CX06 Greensky Hill Mission Church (Pine River Indian Mission)

1864–1865. Greensky Hill Rd., off Old US 31 (US 31, 1 mile northeast of Charlevoix, then east 2 miles on Charlevoix-Boyne City Rd. [Charlevoix County 56], then north .4 mile on Old US 31, then east on Greensky Hill Rd.)

Methodist Episcopalians, one of four denominations that, in the 1860s, established missions in this region with a significant Indian population, founded the Pine River Mission. Until this larger one-room log meetinghouse was built in 1864–1866, the members of the mission worshipped in a small schoolhouse. The present church was built under the direction Peter Greensky (1807–1866). Greensky was the mission's preacher and a Chippewa who had ministered to Methodist Indian missions throughout northern Michigan; he had also served as an interpreter of the Indian language to Peter Daugherty. The Missionary Society of the Methodist Episcopal Church called the building a "block-house" because it is built of hewn timbers neatly dovetailed at the corners.

BOYNE FALLS

CX07 **Wolverine Hotel**

1911. 300 Water St.

The Wolverine Hotel was the product of the growth and optimism that Boyne City experienced as the lumbering boom peaked in the area, around 1910. Although Boyne City had half a dozen hotels at the time, the Wolverine Hotel was a community showplace. It is a simple, three-story building with a flat roof and wrap-around porches. The first-floor lobby has tile mosaic floors and oak woodwork. In 1985 it was restored to the plans of Richard Neumann of Petoskey.

BOYNE FALLS VICINITY, BOYNE VALLEY TOWNSHIP

CX08 **Boyne Mountain Lodge**

1950s-1970s. Off Boyne Mountain Rd., off US 131, .5 mile south of Boyne Falls

Boyne Mountain is the first of two summer and winter resorts developed by Everett F. Kirsher (b. 1915). (The other is Boyne Highlands in Emmet County.) The complex has ski slopes and lifts, eighteen- and nine-hole golf courses, tennis courts, swimming pools, an airport, and convention facilities. For his concept for Boyne Mountain, Kirsher drew on childhood memories of rough-hewn oak log and stone buildings in his native Tennessee—in particular, Gatlinburg, but fantasy Bavarian prevails. Local builders executed it in local limestone, hand-hewn oak beams, and stucco. The Boyne Hof, an A-frame building containing a lobby and lounge with a fieldstone fireplace, is the oldest building. The A-shaped central portion is flanked by two-story hotel wings. Flowers painted on the stucco give the "impression of Bavaria." After salmon fishing in Scotland, Kirsher returned to Boyne Mountain to refine the scheme in the Civic Area. In the Civic Area, buildings are delineated into smaller units to give the impression of a medieval village. Kirsher states that his scheme finally comes together in his own house, which is a sprawling baronial manor house, complete with playhouse, in the spirit of Meadow Brook Hall, but it is assembled with ready-made windows, doors, and other elements.

Antrim County (AN)

BELLAIRE

AN01 **Henry Richardi House**

1895. 402 Bridge St.

In 1895, when Henry Richardi (b. 1863) bought out the Bellaire Wooden Ware Company (Richardi and Bechtold), which was his father's business and Bellaire's primary employer, he erected across Antrim Street from the factory one of northern Michigan's finest wooden Queen Anne houses. Gables, overhangs, bays, and a square corner tower with bell-cast roof project from the boxy wooden mass of the house. A hand-carved lion's head in the pediment over the entrance and lathe-turned beaded latticework in arched silhouette front the two-tiered porches. Exquisite hand carving and expert carpentry abound throughout the house—in the carved capitals

AN01 Henry Richardi House

of the porch columns, in rows of square panels enframed by windows, in the staircase, and on and on. Bird's-eye maple finishes the living room and a different wood trims every other room. The fine craftsmanship is the product of the German woodworkers employed in the Richardi factory, who assisted in the construction of the house.

MANCELONA

AN02 **Mancelona Municipal Building** (Mancelona Fire Hall)

1933, Arvid Johnson, stonemason. 1975, front doors. 1980, rear addition. 120 West State St. (near the northeast corner of West State and Monroe streets)

In 1933 the Mancelona Fire Hall was built with funds from the Civil Works Administration (CWA) in the center of the business district of the village of Mancelona. The practical-minded village firemen proudly modeled it after the neighboring filling station and machine shop and used local materials in its construction. The square building measures 60 feet by 60 feet in plan. It has a barrel-vaulted roof "like that on A. J. Robb's building."[70] The exterior front walls are laid with cut fieldstone; the other walls are rock-faced cement block. Rounded stone pillars with dome-shaped caps mark the corners of the ornamental facade and stone pillars, 2 feet in diameter, separate the four 10-foot-wide doors.

The fire hall was one of four projects funded by the CWA in Mancelona in 1933. Besides the construction of the fire hall, they included a new pump house for the fire booster pump, an addition to the basement of the school, and grading and drainage gutters on eight streets. Together they cost $17,480 and put fifty men to work. In 1980, an addition doubled the size of the building so that the village also could use it for municipal offices.

ATWOOD VICINITY, BANKS TOWNSHIP

AN03 **Wayside Chapel**

1968. East side of US 31, .2 miles north of Atwood

The diminutive, four-pewed roadside chapel, not much larger than a two-door four-

passenger car, serves as a wayside chapel for travelers along US 31 and, as the Atwood Christian Reformed Church (which manages the chapel) explains, is a symbol of "our travels along life's highways."

ELK RAPIDS

AN04 **Elk Rapids Township Hall**

1882–1883, Charles Peale. Southwest corner of River and Spruce streets

With the prosperity of the Elk Rapids Iron Company, originally known as Dexter and Noble, the growth of Elk Rapids created a need for a permanent meeting place and governmental center. The township board voted to construct a town hall in 1882, authorized the expenditure of $3,000 for the venture, and commissioned a local designer, Charles Peale, to plan the building.

The Elk Rapids Township Hall is a long narrow building with a mansard roof. It is built of locally fired, yellowish white brick. The building has round-arch windows, false buttressing, and three triangular designs in the brick on the front facade. The entry vestibule on the front of the building is an unfortunate recent addition. The hall seats 600 before an ornately enframed stage and a stage curtain painted with advertisements. It has been the scene of plays, dances, patriotic celebrations, and political meetings.

AN05 **Hughes House** (John and Martha Hughes House)

Late 1860s. 109 Elm St. (northeast corner of Elm and Traverse streets)

This large, simple, rectangular, two-and-a-half-story, gable-roofed, wood building was built as an inn. Located on the stagecoach road that ran between Traverse City and Petoskey, the Hughes house bustled with daily and overnight business and tourist trade. Then Elk Rapids established itself as one of the nation's leading producers and exporters of charcoal. It was also popular as a resort area. Stagecoaches traveled daily to Traverse City, making connections with the Grand Rapids and Indiana Railroad and several trips each week were made to Charlevoix and Petoskey. The inn was converted to a residence in 1898, and the porch that runs along the south and west sides of the large frame building was added and the interior altered. A large sunburst design radiates from a semicircular window in the north gable end of the otherwise simple rectangular structure.

Grand Traverse County (GT)

TRAVERSE CITY

Traverse City is located on the West Arm of Grand Traverse Bay, where the Boardman River enters the bay. In 1847 William Boardman bought pine lands on the Boardman River, and, together with his son, began logging and milling operations. In 1851, Hannah Lay and Company acquired the Boardman operations, and the development of the town followed. As the lumbering and wood products industries came to a close, cutover lands in the surrounding area were cultivated with cherry orchards. The city became the center of cherry growing and processing and hosts an annual cherry festival in July. Meanwhile, the resort industry developed, and the towered wooden Park Place Hotel, with its full-width veranda, as well as other resort hotels that no longer stand attracted tourists. Today Traverse City is the largest city in northern Lower Michigan. The interesting historic commercial district runs along Front Street. Many of the neighborhoods contain splendid examples of wooden architecture that date from the lumbering era. Some curious early twentieth-century motels and tourists' cabins remain on the sandy beach of Miracle Mile and are visible from Munson Avenue (US 31).

GT01 Grand Traverse County Courthouse

1898–1899, Rush, Bowman and Rush. 1979–1981, renovation, Architects International. Southwest corner of Boardman and Washington streets

The red brick and sandstone Richardsonian Romanesque courthouse stands conspicuously in courthouse square on the highest ground in the city. A clock tower rises majestically from its roof. Next to the courthouse once stood the county jail and sheriff's residence, erected in 1882–1883.

The first county buildings in Grand Traverse County were built on land donated by Hannah, Lay and Company, three years after the county was organized in 1851. A fire destroyed them in 1862, and the county offices were housed in temporary quarters until this courthouse was constructed in 1898–1899. The Grand Traverse County Board of Supervisors chose the plans drafted by Rush, Bowman and Rush of Grand Rapids, who designed at the same time a nearly identical stone courthouse for Cass County in Cassopolis, in southwestern Michigan. A disagreement between the board of supervisors and the architect and contractor over costs delayed construction for one year. The board dismissed the Grand Rapids firm and called in Cassius M. Prall of Pontiac and Traverse City, an architect who then was working on the construction of buildings at Northern Michigan Asylum, what is now Traverse City State Hospital, to supervise construction.

In 1979–1981, after a new city and county governmental center was built nearby, the courthouse was renovated by Architects International of Chicago for use as district and circuit courts.

GT02 Traverse City Opera House

1891, E. R. (E. H.?) Prall. 106–112 Front St.

Situated on the main street in the heart of the active central business district, the three-story, red brick and sandstone, Richardsonian City Opera House is the pride and joy of Traverse City. The building is a two-part commercial block, in which it is divided horizontally into two distinct zones; the street level contains three or four stores, and the second and third floors hold the opera house. The front facade is divided into three bays. On the second story, square-headed windows separated by engaged clustered colonnettes are grouped in fours within each bay; on the third level a group of five round-arch windows is positioned beneath a central pediment and flanked by strings of three smaller similar windows. Clustered colonnettes, stringcourses, and spandrels richly decorate the front. From the street a single flight of stairs rises to the lobby of the theater. Beneath eight barrel vaults and a dome, the theater seats 1,200 in the moveable chairs of the main floor and in a balcony that sweeps

Traverse City

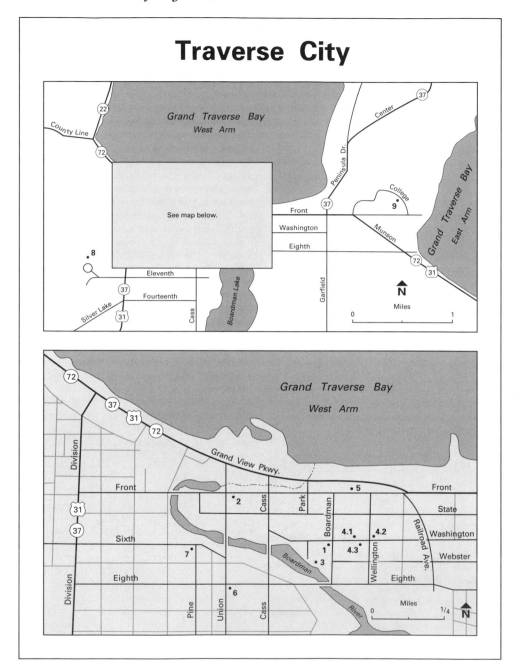

See map below.

around above. The interior of the theater is richly colored with decorative painting.

In 1890 three Traverse City merchants—Charles Wilhelm, Anton Bartak, and Frank Vortruba—purchased from Perry Hannah a site next to the Masonic temple. They com-missioned E. R. Prall of Pontiac, then working on buildings at Northern Michigan Asylum, to draft plans for a commercial building for their individual stores and for an opera house. The opera house is equipped with removable seating so that it can be used as a social and banquet hall. For fifty years after its opening in 1891 until its closing in the 1940s, the City Opera House was a center of cultural and social activity. Here, the people of Traverse City attended the performances of local amateurs, traveling companies, high school students, minstrels, and magicians; listened to sermons of evangelist preachers; saw movies; and held dances, box lunches, and banquets.

In 1978–1979 the City Opera House Heritage Committee hired William Kessler and Associates of Detroit to study the feasibility of restoring the opera house, and in the 1980s the committee began its restoration in phases for use as a performing arts center.

GT03 Temple Beth El

1886, J. G. Holliday. 311 South Park St. (east side of South Park St., between Washington St. and the Boardman River)

The distinction of being the oldest Michigan synagogue building in continuous use for Jewish worship belongs to Beth El of Traverse City, founded in 1882 as an Orthodox congregation by Polish and Lithuanian immigrant peddlers who would become prosperous merchants in Traverse City. Four years later they spent $1,000 to erect a two-story clapboard and shingle building, on land donated by a leading lumber merchant. A simple gable-end structure with spindlework and a Star of David at the gable peak, it was remodeled in 1971, converting the upper story, once the women's section, into an apartment for visiting rabbinical students.

GT04 Boardman Neighborhood

1870–1910. Bounded by State St., Railroad Avenue, Webster St., and Boardman Avenue

The pleasant, tree-shaded streets of this neighborhood near downtown afford vistas of Grand Traverse Bay to the north and Boardman Lake to the south. Boardman Neighborhood stands on some of the oldest continuously occupied plats in the city. Well-maintained, predominantly clapboard houses that reflect a cross section of the architectural styles prevalent in northern Michigan during the late nineteenth and early twentieth centuries are concentrated here. They were built by people connected with the region's lumber-based economy and show it in their finely finished woodwork. The area was named for Henry Boardman, an early Traverse City

lumberman who later sold his holdings to three Chicago entrepreneurs, Perry Hannah, Tracy Lay, and William Morgan. With the reorganization of the firm of Hannah, Lay and Company, Traverse City's development began in earnest.

GT04.1 William Cary and Lola Peckham Hull House

1905. 230 Wellington St. (northwest corner of Wellington and Washington streets)

An imposing pedimented portico with paired giant Ionic columns pretentiously flanking the entrance of this house adheres to the tenets of Academic Classicism. The square-bodied house has a hipped roof pierced by gabled dormers. Ionic corner pilasters, an entablature ornamented with swags and a modillioned cornice, and a carved swag over the entrance further embellish the neighborhood's most imposing house. It was built for the son of the president of the Oval Wood Dish Company.

GT04.2 Henry S. and Kate Pfeiffer Hull House

1894. 229 Wellington St. (northeast corner of Wellington and Washington streets)

A wrap-around porch with triplet clustered ornamental columns and railing, an octagonal corner tower with bell-cast roof, a decorative brick chimney, and a pyramidal-roofed porte-cochère picturesquely adorn this Queen Anne structure that rivals in opulence the remarkable Perry Hannah House, now the Reynolds Funeral Home (GT07). A half shell carved in wood is in the tympanum of the pediment above the porch entrance. Like the Hannah house, it is exquisitely finished in ornately carved native woods. It was built for Henry S. Hull, the president and founder of the Oval Wood Dish Company and also the president of the First National Bank, and his wife, Kate Pfeiffer. A. W. Wait built it for the Hulls at a cost of about $10,000.

GT04.3 Houses

1927, Claun Fisk, builder. 440, 444, 448 East State St. and 212 and 214–216 Wellington St.

According to local historians, these five cozy little quasi-English cottages at the southwest corner of East State and Wellington streets probably were built for speculation or rental by Claun Fisk to plans prepared by his father. The backyards adjoin one another, and a community garage serves all five. The gabled roof of the house at 448 East State Street swoops nearly to the ground, giving it the appearance of having an A-shaped frame. Its exterior walls are covered with stucco and half-timbering. The structure with the jerkin-head gables at 214–216 Wellington is a double house.

GT05 Traverse City Main Sewage Pumping Station

1932; Fry and Kasurin, Inc., architects; Hoad, Decker, Shoecraft and Drury, engineers. 435 East Front St.

Because of its conspicuous location on East Front Street just three blocks from the center of the commercial district, the city officials of Traverse City paid special attention to the design of this little sewage pumping station. Fry and Kasurin planned it in the PWA Moderne style, and H. G. Christman Company of Lansing built it in 1932. Fluted pilasters of cast stone give a sense of strength to the symmetrical structure with a shallowly pitched hipped roof. Medallions containing Indian heads punctuate the light yellowish brown brick exterior walls beneath the modillioned cornice line with an official-looking mark that labels it a local governmental structure. The interior has tile walls and ornamental railings and stairs. It is arranged with gallery, motor, and pump floors.

GT06 Crandall's Service Station (Mac's Super Service Station)

1935. 501 South Union St. (southeast corner South Union and Eighth streets)

Sheathed in gold, white, green, and yellow terracotta tiles, this Art Deco neighborhood gas and service station remains sleek and shiny after fifty years. Its parapeted entry is placed at a 45-degree angle to the rectangular structure and is accented by chevrons and topped by an anthemion. The words *washing, greasing, batteries,* and *tires,* displayed on a light-colored band of tile above individual service bays advertise the goods and services available here.

GT07 Reynolds Funeral Home (Perry and Anna Amelia Flint Hannah House)

1891, William G. Robinson. 305 Sixth St. (southwest corner of Sixth and Pine streets)

Perry Hannah (1824–1892), a lumberman who was one of Traverse City's earliest settlers and most noted citizens, built for himself and his wife, Anna, this majestic Queen Anne house in 1891. Forty years earlier, together with A. Tracy Lay and James Morgan, he organized Hannah, Lay and Company and began logging operations in the Grand Traverse region. The company became one of the largest of its kind in the Midwest, with a steam-powered sawmill in Traverse City and marketing headquarters in Chicago. In the 1880s the firm ceased its lumbering operations, and Hannah invested his holdings in a local bank and a department store.

Noted Grand Rapids architect William G. Robinson (1935–1907) designed the three-story house with more than forty rooms. (The Hannah house precedes the equally opulent and sumptuous brick Queen Anne house that Robinson planned for Carl Gustav Adolph Voight in Grand Rapids in 1895 [KT14.4, p. 260]). The asymmetrical, cross-gabled massing, round corner turrets, ornamental-capped chimneys, and a wide, sweeping porch mark the house at once as part of the larger Queen Anne movement in American domestic architecture. The imaginative use of wood, however, seen especially in the intricately carved and inlaid festoons, crests, and floral and geometric motifs running along barge-boards and window surrounds, panels, and peaks, the clapboard treatment, and the hardwood interior finish in which every room is paneled in a different wood, distinctively imparts the interests of the owner to the structure. Together with the wide curved staircase with a balcony that winds from the lower to the upper hall, it identifies the house equally with the pine and hardwood forests of Michigan, and with Hannah, whose life was shaped and sustained by those forests.

GT08 Traverse City State Hospital
(Northern Michigan Asylum)

1885–1915, Gordon W. Lloyd. Division and Eleventh streets

The Northern Michigan Asylum for the Insane, the third institution in Michigan's initial attempt to care humanely for the "pauper insane," remains as a testament to the Victorian era through its pastoral setting and awesome architectural image. In 1881, to alleviate overcrowding at the existing asylums, the Michigan legislature appropriated $400,000 for the erection of a third hospital.

The board of commissioners selected a 339-acre wooded site with a marshy, treeless plain, near Traverse City. This site offered an abundant supply of water and "a most beautiful outlook commanding the city, Grand Traverse Bay and the hills beyond." Gordon W. Lloyd, a prestigious Detroit architect, designed the original asylum building (Building No. 50) according to the widely accepted "Kirkbride plan," developed by Dr. Thomas Story Kirkbride. Kirkbride (1809–1883), superintendent of the Pennsylvania Hospital for the Insane, was the most notable American psychiatric physician of his time and one of the thirteen founders of the Association of Medical Superintendents of the Insane (presently the American Psychiatric Association). In 1851, the association put forth a set of twenty-six rules, drafted by Kirkbride, as a permanent guide for the construction of institutions for the insane. At least thirty asylums were built using derivations of this plan in the thirty years following. Perhaps the major feature of the plan was the linear projection of two wings, separated by sex and patient classification, from a central administration building. The wings were to have a central corridor, to be used as dayrooms, flanked by private sleeping rooms. Another main feature of the plan was the limiting of patients to 250 to allow for personal supervision by the superintendent. Combined with forced heat and ventilation, a pastoral setting, and fireproof construction, this plan was to provide each patient with fresh air and sunshine in which to recuperate safely and quickly. It was believed that if the insane were allowed to live in sanitary and beautiful conditions, they could be cured at a rate of ninety to one hundred percent. This conviction was known as the "cult of curability," which nobly served, however incorrect, as a catalyst for state-sponsored reform.

The Northern Michigan Asylum was designed in this era of curability according to Kirkbride's tenets. Two patient wings, composed of wide corridors and private sleeping rooms, flank a towered central administration building. The wings run off the center section, following its axis, then each is linked by a connector to yet another wing that extends at a 45 degree angle. Continuous ventilation passages ran through the basement for the supply and distribution of fresh air and forced heat. The exterior walls of the building are laid with yellowish white brick manufactured locally at the Markham brickyards in Greilickville. The exterior features stone sills, metal and wood cornices, and a combination of hipped and gabled roofs. The immense horizontal expanse of the three-story building is broken by pedimented bays and pavilions that project at regular intervals from the main body. Segmental-arch caps in brick relief surmount the windows. The building is encircled by string courses. A classically detailed porch marks the main entrance. Galvanized metal ventilation towers, gabled dormers, and iron cresting, which have been removed, rose above the slate roof. Lloyd agreed with the Kirkbride ideal of a plain exterior to reflect the regimented routine to be carried out within. Lloyd said in the 1884 report of the board of commissioners, "The building front is of Italian character, modified by considerations of expense and climate, avoiding elaborate detail and depending on general grouping, . . . picturesque light and shade effects, . . . a general aspect of suitability to its purpose, and an avoidance of all purely decorative features."

Fourteen cottages (a construction belief that was developed after the "failure" of the Kirkbride plan), infirmaries, and staff residences were added to the Traverse City hospital as the need grew. A farm, greenhouse, and orchards employed patient labor and furnished much of the institution's food. The grounds were beautifully landscaped with trees. The Michigan Department of Mental Health officially closed the hospital in 1989, and today (1991) the citizens of Traverse City are determining the best possible use for the surplus buildings and highly valued site. The original building is important in the birth of reform in American treatment of its insane. It reveals the heritage of the psychiatric movement, the sentiments of the cult of curability, and Thomas S. Kirkbride. It is a remarkable work by one of Michigan's most notable nineteenth-century architects. It remains as a testament to the Victorian era, both in its style and in its use.

GT09 Fine Arts Building, Northwestern Michigan College

1973, The Architects Collaborative (the campus is entered from 1701 East Front St. off College Dr. to parking lot F, the building is opposite parking lot F)

Designed by the well-known firm The Architects Collaborative (TAC) of Cambridge,

Massachusetts, the successor firm of the great Bauhaus master Walter Gropius, the Fine Arts Building is an unexpected but welcome respite from the usual college building. Northwestern Michigan College, the state's first community college, serves a five-county area and has experienced increasing enrollment since its founding in 1951. This building's abundant use of glass and wood, a nearly A-frame roof, and a functional interior arrangement work easily for its location on this wooded campus and for its utility as a community arts center.

TAC designed the interior so that two dissimilar wings radiate from a central hub, the lecture hall. The shorter wing contains the traditional walled rectangular classrooms and a music room. The longer wing contains ample open space for studio classes in graphic design, printmaking, painting, drawing, sculpture, and ceramics and is divided only by movable walls and storage cabinets. The structure is marked by floor-to-ceiling, inward-slanting glass window walls combined with laminated wooden beams, mullions, and steel trussing. In its uniqueness, the Fine Arts Building stands out among the other yellow brick rectilinear campus buildings and is the focus of the eastern portion of the campus. Yet with its human scale and its roughly textured, unpainted vertical exterior boards, it nestles comfortably and harmoniously amid northern Michigan pine and oak.

ACME

GT10 Grand Traverse Resort Village

1983-present; Greyheck, Bell and Kline; Community Design, Louis Redstone, Jack Nicklaus. 6300 North US 31

The Grand Traverse Resort Village is a "total destination" mega-resort and conference center that runs all day, all night, all year. On 850 acres of rolling orchard land atop a 180-foot-high bluff overlooking the east arm of Grand Traverse Bay, it conspicuously intrudes on the landscape. Paul and Sue Nine of Bloomfield Hills, Michigan, acquired a 179-acre parcel of land with a golf course here in 1973 with the intent of developing a resort equivalent to Hilton Head on the South Carolina coast and the Greenbrier in West Virginia. Within five years they increased their land holdings to 439 acres and built a golf course. In 1978–1980, with a nearly $14 million loan from the Farmers Home Administration, they built a 245-room hotel, convention center, and indoor sports complex to the designs of Greyheck, Bell and Kline of Traverse City. Travel promoters call the resort "a jewel that can become the largest single resort in the entire country if all goes as planned." Locally, the project has been controversial at best. Many local people would have preferred no growth here at all. Many others fought against nearby strip development.

In 1982–1984 additional investors spent $3.5 million on the construction of a Jack Nicklaus-designed eighteen-hole golf course. A 8,000-square-foot outdoor pavilion with a year-round, yellow tentlike roof manufactured by Owens-Corning Fiberglass Corporation covers a landscaped patio for parties and concerts. Condominiums and "condovillas" created by Community Design and costing from $75,000 to $360,000 are clustered along fairways. The Tower is a 15-story, 186-room, hotel with a tinted-glass skin over a steel frame, designed by Louis Redstone and built for $27 million. On the grounds are tennis courts, a swimming pool, and jogging and ski trails. The architecture is ordinary; the setting is sublime.

INTERLOCHEN VICINITY, GREEN LAKE TOWNSHIP

GT11 Interlochen Center for the Arts

1928–1981, Alden B. Dow, et al. Michigan 137, 1.5 miles south of US 31

Interlochen Center for the Arts is a summer music camp and a college preparatory creative arts academy. It is situated on a narrow, 1,200-acre wooded campus between Green and Duck lakes, 14 miles southwest of Traverse City. From the National Music Camp founded in 1928 by Joseph E. Maddy (1891–1966), a music teacher at the University of Michigan, Interlochen grew and expanded. The Interlochen Arts Academy was established in 1962. As the Interlochen Center for the Arts evolved, Alden B. Dow (1904–1983), a major Michigan architect who was a Taliesin Fellow with Frank Lloyd Wright in 1933, planned the campus expansion from a summer camp built in the vernacular tradition to include a year-round school. To the original wooden and cobblestone cabins, practice buildings, and concert bowls of the summer camp, and to the Maddy Administration Building erected in 1952, were added the winterized permanent classrooms, library, dormitories, and performing arts building required for an academic institution in this northern climate. Dow subsequently designed many of the arts academy buildings. These include three domed structures for the sciences, language arts, and library, arranged off an enclosed and heated linear concourse that serves both as a passageway and exhibit area: the Dow Science Building (1962), the C. S. Mott Language Arts Building (1963), and the Liberal Arts Building (1967). Other buildings by Dow are the dormitories (1964 and 1965), a store, the enlarged and enclosed Kresge Auditorium (1964), and the Corson Auditorium (1975). The buildings were funded by such Michigan and midwestern foundations as Herbert H. and Grace A. Dow, C. S. Mott, S. S. Kresge, and Eli Lilly.

Leelanau County (LU)

LELAND

LU01 Fishtown

1900–1930s. On the Leland River below the dam and at the harbor

Fishtown is one of the last remaining commercial fishing villages, outside of the Native American fisheries, in Michigan. Originally, in 1853, Antoine Manseau (1810–1856) built

a sawmill at the confluence of the Carp River, now the Leland River, and Lake Michigan. Just upstream he and John I. Miller (b. 1822) built a dam. From 1870 to 1884 the Leland Lake Superior Iron Company smelted iron ore from the Upper Peninsula here. In the 1870s commercial fishermen began using the Carp River, and fishing, pig iron, and lumber became Leland's industries. In 1886 the construction of a breakwater, improved in 1937 and 1966, provided Leland with a good harbor and helped the fishing industry. At its peak, eight full-scale commercial fishing businesses operated here.

From the dam to its mouth, the Leland River is lined with docks, shanties on pilings, and boats. Fishermen built the wood and shingled shanties as places in which to store and repair nets and clean and sell fish. Next to them are net racks, and behind are icehouses, smokehouses, and gas sheds. A network of dirt paths connects the village. After World War II the sea lamprey devastated the Great Lakes whitefish and lake trout industry. Today fish shanties shelter gift shops and art studios patronized by tourists. In 1962–1964 the county transferred the dam to Fred Hollinger, who built the shingled and stuccoed Falling Waters Motel and Fisherman's Cove Restaurant. They were designed by Suttons Bay architects Arai and Hummel, borrowing the form and materials of the old shanties.

SOUTH MANITOU ISLAND, LELAND VICINITY

LU02 **South Manitou Island Light**

1858, lightkeeper's house. 1870, tower. Just south of Sandy Point, the southeast point on the island

The South Manitou Lighthouse marks the Manitou Passage, which runs between the mainland and the Manitou Islands and serves as the major shipping channel between Chicago and the Straits of Mackinac. The harbor on South Manitou Island is one of the few natural deep-water harbors on Lake Michigan between Chicago and the straits, and the island possessed a vast supply of timber. Woodburning steamers frequently stopped at South Manitou Island to take on hardwood for fuel. A light station has aided navigation here since 1839. The yellow brick lightkeeper's dwelling was constructed in 1858, the 104-foot-high conical brick tower, in 1870. The light was abandoned in 1958. The National Park Service at Sleeping Bear Dunes National Lakeshore owns it today.

NORTHPORT VICINITY, LEELANAU TOWNSHIP

LU03 **Northport Indian Mission Church**

1882–188?. 1912, steeple. East side of Michigan 22, just northeast of Swede Rd (Leelanau County 633) and 2 miles southwest of Northport

Methodist missionaries began preaching among the Indians near Northport in the late 1850s. By 1878 the Northport Indian Mission had 42 members. In 1882 Peter Shawandase, Joseph Lightsky, Joseph Redbird, and Peter Yagua-ge-zheek, the trustees of the mission, acquired this one-acre site southwest of Northport and built the church. It cost $600. The small, wooden, gable-roof mission church has a center entry tower with an transom-lighted double door and an open belfry and short steeple. The steeple was built by George Bigelow in 1912 for $265.

LU04 **Grand Traverse (Cathead Point) Lighthouse**

1858. 1899, fog signal building. At the northern terminus of Lighthouse Point Rd. (Leelanau County 629) adjacent to Leelanau State Park

The Grand Traverse Lighthouse marks the tip of the Leelanau Peninsula and the entrance into Grand Traverse Bay. The second structure on the site, it was built in 1853 to guide ships in the Manitou Passage. The light tower, surmounted by a nine-sided, cast-iron lantern, projects from the gable roof of the brick, two-story keeper's dwelling. A climb to the top permits breathtaking views across the bay as far as Charlevoix. The brick fog signal building was built in 1899. The wonderful beach stone sculpture in the yard around the lighthouse says something about the lonely life of a Great Lakes lighthouse keeper. In 1972 the Coast Guard erected a steel skeletal structure with an automatic light and abandoned this lighthouse. Today the Grand Traverse Lighthouse Foundation operates a museum in the lighthouse.

OMENA

LU05 **Omena Presbyterian Church** (Grove Hill New Mission Church)

1858, William Putt, Robert Campbell and Eusebius? Dame, builders. East side of Michigan 22, just north of Leelanau County 626

The steepled white wood-frame church is in the simplified New England tradition. The interior is arranged with two side aisles separating three banks of pews. Twelve-over-twelve windows, four on each side and two on the front, give ample light to the sanctuary. The few alterations include the replacement of two front doors with windows, the insertion of the central entry, and the addition of the steeple to the bell tower. The Reverend Peter Dougherty (1805–1894), a graduate of Princeton Theological Seminary and a Presbyterian missionary, arrived in the Grand Traverse area in 1838. He organized a Protestant mission for the Indians at present-day Old Mission in 1843. He moved the mission across the bay in 1852 and built the New Mission Church on the high bluff east of Omena. The work of the mission continued until about 1870, when the boarding school was abandoned, and the church was placed under the Presbytery. Today the church holds services only during the summer resort season.

PESHAWBESTOWN

LU06 **Super Bingo Palace (and Leelanau Sands Gambling Casino) of the Grand Traverse Band of the Chippewa and Ottawa**

1983–1984, 1987–1988, Charles Eister, Harry Galbraith, Judson Jones. West side of Michigan 22, 4 miles north of Suttons Bay

A cluster of five large, natural-stained, wood-sided, one-story, gable-roofed buildings makes up this complex—a casino where one hundred can play blackjack, poker, and craps, a bingo hall that holds 400, an administration building, a commodity and art store, and a motel. The site plan, administration building, and gambling casino were designed and built by Charles Eister, husband of a Native American and resident of Peshawbestown, in consultation with Harry Galbraith, a retired downstate county building inspector. Judson Jones,

a Grand Rapids architect, did the Bingo Palace. The buildings were designed so they would not detract from the small Indian village, settled in 1852 by a band of Ottawa from Harbor Springs. They were built with funds from the U.S. Departments of Housing and Urban Development, and Health and Human Services, and a loan underwritten by the Bureau of Indian Affairs. Having won the federal government's recognition as the governing body of the tribe and having been given the retention of inherent rights to self-government, the tribal council of the Chippewa and Ottawa Indians operates them for profit.

ISADORE

LU07 **Holy Rosary Church and School**

1921–1923, church, Brielmaier and Sons. Northwest corner of Shomberg Rd. and Leelanau County 645

Rising above farmlands cultivated by generations of Polish Americans and standing hard by the road at the four corners of Isadore in central Leelanau County are the red brick religious buildings (church, convent, and school) and the cemetery of Holy Rosary Polish-Catholic parish. The church was organized in 1888. In the 1920s the building committee selected a proficient Milwaukee architectural firm noted for its church designs to plan what was termed a Roman-style church. The building cost $35,000. The church is entered through a central tower. The central aisle is flanked by rows of pews taken from the earlier church and by six pairs of stained-glass windows executed by the F. X. Zettler Company of Munich. Inscribed in an arch over the altar are the words *"Krolowo Rozania S W. Modl Sie Za Nami."* Like the church, the square-shaped, hipped-roof school stands on a raised, cut fieldstone foundation. Buried in the cemetery are families of the early settlers: Stephen Miemczynski, Adam Popa, George Cichocki, Paul Peplinski, Paul Palusyoski, and others.

GLEN HAVEN

LU08 **Pierce Stocking Scenic Drive**

Approximately 4 miles south of Glen Haven, 1.5 miles north of the southerly intersection of Michigan 22 and Michigan 109

A 7.6-mile-long drive with spectacular panoramic vistas of the Manitou islands, the Lake Michigan shoreline, and the wondrous Sleeping Bear Dunes was opened in 1967 by Pierce Stocking (1908–1976) on his own land. Stocking, a lumberman and native of northern Lower Michigan, wished to share the scenic beauty of the Sleeping Bear region, while protecting the fragile site. Having acquired the site as part of the national lakeshore, the National Park Service improved the drive and added overlooks in 1986.

LU09 Sleeping Bear Inn

1857 (c. 1860?). 1890s, additions. 1928, porch. Southeast corner of Michigan 209 and Sleeping Bear Dr. (Michigan 209 intersects Michigan 22 between Glen Haven and Glen Arbor)

C. C. McCarthy, who ran a sawmill and dock at Glen Haven, probably built this frontier hotel (village inn) to accommodate early settlers arriving by ship at this point of entry into the forested lands of northern Michigan and for cordwood cutters who supplied the lake steamers. The wood-frame inn is a simple, side-gable, two-story structure with back wing additions of the 1890s and a porch addition of 1928. The inn was acquired in 1870 by the Northwestern Transportation Company of Cleveland, which had twenty-four vessels on the lakes, carrying passengers and freight between Chicago and Ogdensburg, New York. Still later, in 1881, it was taken over by D. H. Day, who also took over the lumbering operation.

Across the road is the Glen Haven Store, also known as the D. H. Day Store, where villagers gathered and tourists bought tickets for dunesmobile rides on Sleeping Bear. To the south is the six-car garage built in the 1920s to shelter the dunesmobiles and to serve as annex sleeping space for the inn.

LU10 Sleeping Bear Point Life Saving Station

1901, 1931. Off Sleeping Bear Dr., .75 miles northwest of Michigan 209

This complex of four wood-frame buildings was built as part of a national system of aid to navigation. Under contract to the United States Life Saving Service, now the U.S. Coast Guard, Robert H. B. Newcombe built it after plans prepared in 1890 for the Marquette, Michigan, Life Saving Station. The keeper and crew, generally men familiar with local weather conditions, used the station as a base from which to patrol beaches and to launch small wooden rowboats to rescue shipwreck survivors. They lived in the main building. Beneath a small center gable, a comfortable front porch marks the simple, wooden, side-gabled dwelling. The board-and-batten boat house, through whose large, paired double doors boats were launched, stands nearby. Its hipped roof with flaring eaves is supported by exposed rafters and is topped with a short conical-roofed cupola. Other buildings are a privy; a storage shed for wood, coal, and kerosene; and a larger work shed, originally constructed on pilings 20 feet from shore to accommodate a 34-foot-long lifeboat. A signal tower, built in 1914, also survives. Operations at the station ceased in 1944. The Coast Guard officially closed the station in 1958. It is now operated by the National Park Service as the Sleeping Bear Dunes National Maritime Museum.

LU11 D. H. Day Farmstead (Oswagotchie)

1900s. 6141 Michigan 109

Lying on 400 acres in the midst of an open meadow surrounded by wood lots and orchards and in the shadow of Sleeping Bear Dunes is the Queen Anne farmhouse and the dairy, bull, and pig barns built by D. H. Day (1851–1928). Day acquired the farm from the Northwestern Transportation Company in the 1870s, cleared it, and put it into service employing modern agricultural equipment and methods. Here he grew hay and corn to feed his prize herd of two hundred Holsteins and four hundred hogs. By the 1920s an orchard of five thousand cherry trees grew here. The magnificent 116-foot-long dairy barn, with its poured concrete silo, octagonal cupolas with bell roofs, and a vaulted and ogee roof with slightly flared eaves to permit water drainage,

LU11 D. H. Day Farmstead (Oswagotchie)

is both picturesque and functional. Day's foreman lived in the large Queen Anne farmhouse. Its asymmetrical intersecting gabled mass is covered with clapboard. A large porch wraps around the front and sides of the first story. The gables are clad with shingles and pierced with Palladian windows. Spindlework ornaments some corner windows.

GLEN ARBOR

LU12 The Homestead

1970s, Johnson, Johnson and Roy, landscape architects. West side of Michigan 22, 2 miles north of Glen Arbor

This spectacular site on Sleeping Bear Bay where the Crystal River flows into Lake Michigan was excluded from the Sleeping Bear Dunes National Lakeshore because of the political savvy of its developer, Arthur Huey. Here Huey created a year-round resort, with tennis, hiking, swimming, and skiing. Johnson, Johnson and Roy of Ann Arbor superbly landscaped the 193-acre site that rises 320 feet from the lakefront to a ridge. JJ&R took

advantage of the landform. Steep slopes provide dramatic views for the clusters of condominiums, the units of which step down the slopes. Through the use of careful grading, boardwalks, and decking, the landscape architects preserved the sand dunes, vegetation, and trees. Parking is buffered by berms and vegetation, and a network of trails separates pedestrians from automobiles. The lovely old rustic wooden, rambling Homestead Inn, designed by Earl H. Mead of Harbor Springs, was built against the steep wooded hill in 1929 to accommodate the classroom, dormitory, and dining hall of the Leelanau Schools and remodeled for the 1970s resort. A clay tennis court complex with low fences constructed of timber and wire mesh and a sunken center court with seating is tucked into the setting.

The Homestead resembles the nineteenth-century resort association of the Traverse Bay Region but affords the owner greater anonymity. It is interesting to speculate on the reaction pioneer lumberman D. H. Day might have had to this resort. He had offered a site near here to the federal government for the permanent summer national capitol. In 1927 he announced plans for an exclusive summer community, Day Forest Estates. The development plan of 2,000 acres, prepared by American Park Builders of Chicago, projected a clubhouse, beach and tennis club, polo field, aviation landing field, winter sports area, and 120 sites from 5 to 35 acres in size. It was only partially executed and then abandoned.

LU12 The Homestead

Benzie County (BZ)

BENZONIA VICINITY, BENZONIA TOWNSHIP

BZ01 **Gwen Frostic Studio**

1960s. 5140 River Rd. (Michigan 608), just west of Higgins Rd. and 2 miles west of US 31 in Benzonia

Gwen Frostic, a noted Michigan naturalist and printmaker, carved her rambling cave-like fieldstone and cedar studio and shop into a hill on 285 acres on the Betsie River, molded it around a duck pond, and let the natural flora and fauna take over. From the inside, the structure affords views of the surrounding wetlands. Doorways open onto decks that reach out with even closer views of nature. Poured concrete floors that withstand the great weight of the Frostic printing presses also hold impressions of the leaves, deer tracks, and other natural objects the nature artist loves to draw. In the studio Gwen Frostic prints her sketches of trees, flowers, weeds, birds, frogs, and the like on stationery, greeting cards, calendars, and books. The building houses her studio, printing plant, mail-order operation, and shop.

FRANKFORT

BZ02 **211, 219, and 231 Leelanau Avenue**

c. 1900. 211, 219, and 231 Leelanau Avenue (north side of Leelanau between Second and Third streets)

BZ02 211, 219 and 231 Leelanau Avenue

High on a hill that overlooked Betsie Bay and Lake Michigan before the construction of other houses obstructed the view stands a group of wood-frame, clapboard, and shingle houses of some pretension. Tucked into the corner of a front L of the Queen Anne Edwin and Marguerite Lobb House at 211 Leelanau Avenue, erected in 1900–1903 by B. S. Brumley of Caro, is a three-story pyramidal-roofed tower fronted with a conical-roofed, one-story, wrap-around porch. A profusion of wings, bays, gables, porches, and towers extends from the rectangular James Lockhart House (Morningside Bed and Breakfast), built in 1895 at 219 Leelanau Avenue, and from the Gothic Revival A. G. Butler House, erected in 1869 at 231 Leelanau Avenue. All three were used as summer houses.

BZ03 **Kristin E. Acre House**

c. 1900. 503 Crystal Avenue (Michigan 22) (northwest corner of Crystal and Park avenues)

The castellated Neo-Gothic house executed in concrete block at the northern edge of town must have seemed strange to the people of Frankfort. A crenelated rounded corner tower and crenelated front parapet applied to a flat-roofed box make it a modest example of the style. It is unusual in Michigan. A larger wooden residential example is found in the A. J. Waters House at 201 Duncan in

BZ03 Kristin E. Acre House

Manchester; a high-style stone example is the Ethelbert Crofton and Charles Fox House, known as the Castle, at 455 Cherry Street, Southeast, in Grand Rapids.

LAKE TOWNSHIP

BZ04 **Point Betsie Lighthouse** (Point aux Becs Scies Light)

1858. 1880s, tower replaced. 1895, lightkeeper's house remodeled. Point Betsie Rd. and Lake Michigan at Point Betsie (west off Michigan 22, 4 miles north of Frankfort)

Nestled among the sand dunes of the Lake Michigan shore at Point Betsie is one of Michigan's most beautifully sited and easily accessible lighthouses. A 37-foot-high light was constructed in 1858 at Point Betsie to mark the south end of the Manitou Passage. It was replaced in the 1880s by the present 100-foot-high light tower, which is surmounted by a ten-sided cast-iron lantern. Adjoining the tower is a gambrel-roofed lightkeeper's house, enlarged with six rooms and renovated in 1895 to its present ample double-house appearance. The tower and the house are painted white to increase the daytime visibility of the station to ships. The Coast Guard automated the light in 1983.

North-Central Lakes and Forests Region

THE WHITE PINE FORESTS AND THE LAKES, STREAMS, AND rivers on which the initial economy of the North-Central Lakes and Forests Region was founded in the late nineteenth century, and which wisely were replenished by twentieth-century reforestation and conservation programs, are the basis for the region's outdoor recreation industry today. The logging camps and sawmills from the earlier years and the depression-era Civilian Conservation Corps (CCC) camps are no longer extant. Many camps, mills, and towns were lost to fires that plagued the region. Many rustic hunting and fishing camps, however, along with canoe landings, cottages, and golf and ski lodges—tangible architectural evidence of the pursuit of outdoor activities—do survive and are among the most interesting buildings of the region today. The huge modern but rustic Garland Golf Course erected of precut Montana logs in the Lewiston vicinity in 1986–1987 is a contemporary example. These facilities are easily accessible by automobile and camper to weekend vacationers from the urban centers of southeastern Michigan and northern Ohio. Houghton and Higgins lakes, at the heart of the region, are particularly appealing and easily reached via Interstate 75.

The North-Central Lakes and Forests Region was first settled in the 1870s by the lumbermen who came to harvest the white pine. At first, the logs were floated down the rivers to sawmills. It was not, however, until networks of narrow-gauge logging railroads were opened to the Michigan Central, the Detroit and Mackinac, and the Jackson, Lansing and Saginaw railroads that the full harvest of the forests became possible. Lumbering companies ran huge logging, transporting, and milling operations.

As lumbering waned in the early twentieth century, the people of the North-Central Lakes and Forests Region realized that the region's sandy soil was un-

436

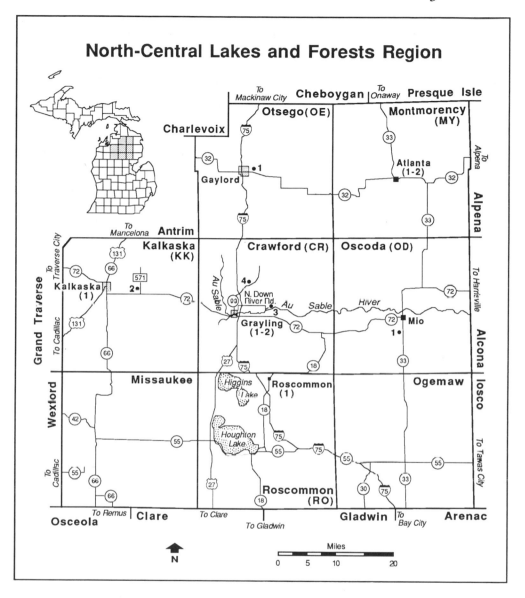

North-Central Lakes and Forests Region

suitable for farming. Nevertheless, a few farms were established on some of the region's cutover lands, most notably in Kalkaska and Missaukee counties. Potatoes, apples, and Christmas trees were cultivated, and livestock and dairy cattle raised. In most of the areas, however, farming is nonexistent. Instead, outdoor recreation became a new segment of the region's economy. The trout streams and natural beauty were advertised, and accommodations and transportation were promoted by railroads; the Grand Rapids and Indiana Railroad's "Fishing Line," which pushed its way north through the northwestern corner of the region, is a good example. Grayling fish attracted fishermen to the Au Sable River, but because of unrestricted overfishing, the species became extinct by the 1930s. Today the region celebrates its outdoor activities with canoe, trout, tip-up town, and maple syrup festivals.

Conservation efforts attracted the formation of sportsmen's hunting and fishing clubs. Reforestation programs initiated in 1903 were carried on by the Michigan Department of Conservation in 1924 and continued by the CCC in the 1930s. The CCC planted seedlings across barren cutover wastelands and built campgrounds.

Large acreage in Oscoda, Iosco, Ogemaw, and Alcona counties is included within the boundaries of the Huron National Forest. The Au Sable, Mackinaw, and Pere Marquette state forests conserve timberlands throughout the region. The Hartwick Pines is in Crawford County.

The discovery of oil and national gas in the Kalkaska area in 1970s was followed by the drilling of oil and gas wells and a petroleum boom.

Crawford County (CR)

GRAYLING

Located on the Middle Branch of the Au Sable River and the Mackinac Divison of the Michigan Central Railroad, Grayling was platted in 1874 by the railroad. It was named for the fish once plentiful in the Au Sable River. The picturesque wooden houses of Peninsular Avenue best express the architecture of this city in the woods. In 1914 the Grayling State Fish Hatchery was established on the East Branch of the Au Sable River.

CR01 **Ray's Canoe Livery**

1941. James St. (Business I-75 and Old US 27) and Au Sable River

Built where the river meets the road, the one-and-a-half-story, gabled, rustic log building serves as a fly-fishing shop, a canoe livery, and a shopkeeper and canoe guide's residence. Ray Snider, the owner and river guide who designed and built the canoe livery, was inspired by the Hartwick Memorial Building (CR05), which contains the logging museum at Hartwick Pines. The site was first occupied by Chief Shoppenagon, a Chippewa trapper, hunter, and guide. Ray's Canoe Livery is among the five finest of some 150 canoe liveries, most in the Roscommon and Grayling areas.

CR02 **Rialto Theater**

1930, R. V. Gay. East side of Michigan, between Peninsular and Spruce

R. V. Gay (1895–1943) of Saint Johns designed this tan brick movie theater. It cost $35,000. It resembles the Eaton Theatre in Charlotte, which Gay designed the same year. The entrance and marquee are centered between piers with recessed brick panels containing in each a small window surrounded by corbels above a billboard. The tan brick Masonic temple (1930) to the north is a congenial neighbor in its scale.

GRAYLING TOWNSHIP

CR03 **Wa Wa Sum** (Michigan State University Research Facility in Fisheries, Wildlife, and Forestry)

1898–1933 (1897, bunkhouse and dining room, Rubin Babbitt, builder. 1921–1922, big camp lodge, Ed Kellogg, builder.) From Michigan Ave. in Grayling 5.5 miles east on North Down River Rd., then south .75 mile on Whirlpool Rd., then east on Wa Wa Sum Dr. to Camp Wa Wa Sum. Visible from the river

Wa Wa Sum is one of the best examples of a summer fishing camp on the Au Sable River, once the state's outstanding trout stream. It was built and added to between 1898 and 1933 for J. Secour and James Brown Bell of the Champion Spark Plug Company and other Toledo industrialists and businessmen, who in 1898 acquired 250 logged-over acres high on the north bank of the Au Sable River. The river was the habitat of brook, brown, and rainbow trout, and grayling. For the fishermen and their families the camp served as a base of their vacation operations. The camp was named Wa Wa Sum, which means "Plain View" in Chippewa and refers to the unobstructed view to the south before reforestation.

The camp consists of six one-story log buildings: a main lodge (1921–1922); a dining room, kitchen, and caretaker's building (1897–1898); a recreation building known as the bullpen, where the men played poker (1907); the river guide's cabin (1933); and a boat house and barn (1933). All are built of red pine logs on a base of tamarack logs. Some have fieldstone foundations and chimneys. The centerpiece of the complex is the main lodge. From each end of the large main room, which is arranged around a huge stone fireplace, extend sleeping areas that were for the Secour-Stranahan families and the Bell family. Each wing has three bedrooms, a kitchen, and bath. A porch runs along the south side of the building, overlooking the river and boat landing below. Riverboats, unique craft indigenous to the Au Sable River, are in the open-sided pole-frame boat shed. The long, narrow, flat-bottom boats were suited for the fast-moving shallow waters of the river. The guide takes the stern, the fisherman the bow. "Live fish wells" located in front of the guide's seat held water in which the catch was stowed. Rubin Babbitt, an Au Sable River guide in the Grayling area, built the earliest structures; Ed Kellogg of nearby Lovell built the later buildings.

The women and children of the Secour-Stranahan and Bell families typically spent the summer at Wa Wa Sum; the men went on the weekends. Leaving Toledo after work on Thursdays, they were greeted at the Grayling railroad depot at 4:30 A.M. by the camp's river guides, who had paddled the riverboats through the night 17 miles upstream from the camp. Then they fished their way downstream to the camp.

Wa Wa Sum is similar to other camps like Camps Gingerquill, Pahwanee, Shoppenagon, and Club Thunderbird on the main stream and the North Branch of the Au Sable River. Today Michigan State University uses the camp for a research facility in fisheries, wildlife, and forestry studies.

CR04 **Hartwick Memorial Building**

1934, R. B. Herrick. Michigan 93, Hartwick Pines State Park (4 miles west of exit 259 of I-75 and 7 miles northeast of Grayling

This rustic log building and the surrounding forest of towering virgin white pine is a memorial to Edward Edgar Hartwick (1871–1918) of Grayling, who died in World War I, given by his wife, Karen B. Hartwick. R. B. Herrick prepared the plans for the building that resembles an early twentieth-century Michigan hunting, fishing, and vacation lodge, and the structure was constructed by workers of the Civil Conservation Corps. A porch runs the full length of the west facade of the gable-roofed building. A huge stone fireplace stands in the open and balconied main room of the building.

Otsego County (OE)

GAYLORD

Plotted in 1873 and incorporated as a village in 1881, Gaylord was incorporated as a city in 1922. It became a warehouse and distribution center for the produce grown in nearby potato fields and a manufacturing center for hardwood products—woodenware, butter bowls, barrel hoops and staves, and shoe last blocks. The wide, well-lighted streets and excellent stores led the Works Progress Administration to conclude in *Michigan: A Guide to the Wolverine State* (1941) that Gaylord was one of the most modern cities in northern Michigan. Today tourism is important to the economy.

GAYLORD VICINITY, LIVINGSTON TOWNSHIP

OE01 **Hidden Valley** (Otsego Ski Club)

1939, Hugh T. Keyes. 1947-present. Off Michigan 32 one mile east of Gaylord

Hidden Valley is Michigan's first and best reflection on Swiss Alpine architecture. Donald B. McLouth (1902–1954), founder and president of McLouth Steel Corporation, together with other Detroit industrialists and ski enthusiasts C. Thorne Murphy, Alvan MacCauley, David Wallace, Gordon Saunders, and Lang Hubbard, established in 1939 the Otsego Ski Club. Seeking snow and hills comparable to New England and Canada, they acquired land hidden in the beautiful valley of the fast-flowing Sturgeon River, where they cut ski trails. In 1947, after World War II, Hugh T. Keyes, a Detroit architect noted for his Georgian Revival houses in Grosse Pointe, who was trained at Harvard and had worked in the office of Albert Kahn, designed lodges and cabins as part of the club's expansion program. They are in a loosely interpreted form of Swiss Alpine models preferred by the club members who had skied in the Alps. The buildings are named the Logmark, Tyrol Lodge, Hilltop Lodge, Forest Lodge, the Loft, and Main Lodge, and serve as dormitories and bedrooms, dining rooms, and recreation hall. The buildings have fieldstone foundations and fireplaces, vertical log exterior walls and knotty pine interior walls. Gables containing scrolled bargeboards, bell towers, balconies, bays, cut woodwork, and gaily painted wood trim abound. McLouth promoted the adoption of the Tyrolean theme by the city of Gaylord, which is evident in every direction from Main Street and even in the Otsego County Courthouse (1968, Frank and Stein). The private ski club has grown into a year-round outdoor recreational facility on 4,300 acres. Open to public.

Montmorency County   (MY)

ATLANTA, BRILEY TOWNSHIP

MY01 **Joey's Shell Station**

1931. 1940s, restaurant. 1950s, garage. 103 State St. (Michigan 32) (southwest corner of State and West streets)

In 1931, when the railroad withdrew from Atlanta and highway transportation increased in importance, the Alpena Oil Company built the two-story, end-gable fieldstone and shin-gle gas station. It is at the crossroads of Michigan 32, which runs between Torch Lake and Alpena, and Michigan 33, which goes from Onaway and Cheboygan to Mio and the Thunder Bay River. The restaurant was added in the 1940s, the garage in the 1950s. At this one-stop shop, gas, food, live bait, and hunting and fishing equipment are sold to tourists and to employees of the county road commission and of the state conservation headquarters, Atlanta's main employers.

MY02 **Log Bungalow**

c. 1920. 120 State St. (Michigan 32)

This small, rustic, temple-front bungalow and garage are interpreted in readily available cobblestones and logs, the building materials favored in the North-Central Lakes and Forests Region because of their association with rugged individualism.

Oscoda County (OD)

MIO, BIG CREEK TOWNSHIP

OD01 **William W. Maier House** (Perma-Log Company)

1940s. 2248 South Mount Tom (on Michigan 33, 2.5 miles south of Mio)

William W. Maier (1899–1966) developed a technique for siding the exterior walls of buildings with concrete shaped in the form of logs. This sheathing is applied to a steel mesh base anchored by nails to the walls. His house and office also display this Perma-Log construction. The exterior walls of the one-story ranch are covered with the ersatz material, and the chimneys are sculpted to resemble tree trunks. Maier came from Ontario to Detroit in the 1920s, where he learned the lathing and plastering business. At 12063 Saint Mary's Street, in the northwest portion of the Motor City, he built for himself his first concrete log house. Maier moved to Mio in 1940 and developed the Perma-Log business. His grandson continues to install Perma-Log throughout the state, especially in the northeastern Lower Peninsula. The distribution of this technique is confined to Michigan.

Roscommon County (RO)

ROSCOMMON

RO01 **First Congregational Church of Roscommon**

1961, Dow-Howell-Gilmore-Associates, Inc. 109 South Main St.

An asymmetrical nearly A-frame fronted by a tall slender symmetrical A-frame gable prolonged as a spire creates a feeling of awe and reverence in the visitor to this modest church. The mass is clad with redwood inside and out. Exposed beams reveal to the worshiper the framework of the structure. A large glass wall runs the full length of one side of the

RO01 First Congregational Church of Roscommon

sanctuary. Slender windows pierce the wall behind the altar, illuminating a transparent cross into the sanctuary.

Kalkaska County   (KK)

KALKASKA

Since the headwaters of the Boardman and Manistee rivers are at Kalkaska and pine forests were abundant, lumbering became the dominant economic activity during the last decades of the nineteenth century. Agriculture was somewhat successful on the cutover land, particularly in growing potatoes. But recreation, especially trout fishing, also became important to the area's economy. In the early 1970s, however, oil and natural gas deposits were discovered, which led to rapid growth.

KK01 Kalkaska County Historical Museum (Kalkaska Depot of the Grand Rapids and Indiana Railroad)

1920. East side of Cedar St. (US 131) between Elm and Oak streets

Standing on the tracks of the Grand Rapids and Indiana Railroad (now the Penn Central), whose arrival in 1873 solidified Kalkaska as the county seat, and opposite the commercial buildings built between 1903 and 1910, is this sturdy red brick depot. Its hipped roof has an ample overhang to shelter passengers. It replaced an earlier wooden depot destroyed by fire. In front is the National Trout Memorial (1966), a 17-foot-high brook trout sculpted in fiberglass by Leo Nelson of South Boardman to celebrate the region's primary source of recreation.

EXCELSIOR TOWNSHIP

KK02 Excelsior Town Hall

1901, Thomas Evans, builder. Southwest corner Kalkaska County 571 and Wagenschutz Rd.

In 1900, twenty-five years after Excelsior Township was founded, its citizens decided to build a town hall. Using plans purchased for $7, they constructed this plain, gable-roof, wood building. It cost only $1,085. From 1907 to 1927, Excelsior High School held classes here. It still serves the township as the public meeting hall.

Huron Shore Region

THE HURON SHORE REGION BORDERS LAKE HURON AT THE northeastern corner of the northern tip of the Lower Peninsula. Through it flow the waterways of the Thunder Bay, Cheboygan, Rifle, Au Sable, and Pine rivers. The abundance of fish, the vast forests and limestone deposits, and those rivers and lakes that afforded both a transportation system and a source of power furnished the basis for the economy of the region.

U.S. Route 23, formerly the shore trail, follows the Lake Huron coastline through the Huron Shore Region from Mackinaw City at the Straits of Mackinac at the north to Standish on the south.

Euro-American settlement in the Huron Shore Region began in the 1820s and 1830s. Sites at the mouths of rivers were selected for trading posts, fishing ports, and sawmills. An early trading post on the Au Sable River was established in the 1820s by a French-Canadian trader named Chevalier. Located on 640 acres granted to him in 1823 by the federal government, it became the center from which he traded goods for fish, furs, and game with Chippewa and white traders, hunters, and fishermen. He left the area in 1833, but his place was taken by George Hulett Duell, Horace D. Stockman, and others, who purchased land at the mouth of the river and founded the community of Au Sable in 1849. The commercial fishing industry that developed here grew rapidly, and thousands of barrels of fish were shipped south to Cleveland and Cincinnati.

Attracted not only by the fine gill-net fishing available in Thunder Bay but also by stands of pine, spruce, fir, and other timber, and by the rivers that could be harnessed to power sawmills, settlers came into Alpena County in the 1830s. In 1859 the first steam sawmill in Alpena County was started at Alpena.

Arenac County was established in 1831 and reorganized in 1883. The other

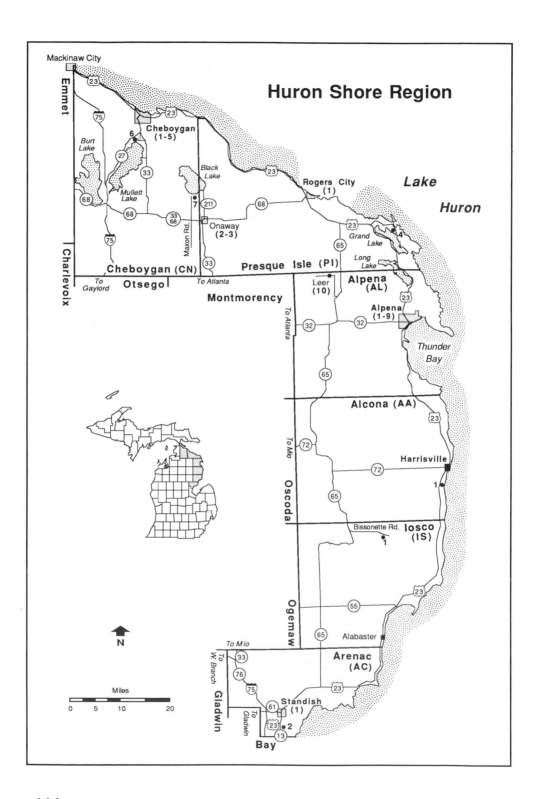

Huron Shore Region

Mackinaw City

Emmet

23

75

Burt
Lake

6

27

Cheboygan
(1-5)

23

33

Mullett
Lake

68

Black
Lake

Rogers City
(1)

68

23

Lake

Huron

68

7 211

Grand
Lake

65

4

75

33
68

Onaway
(2-3)

Long
Lake

Charlevoix

Maxon Rd.

33

To
Gaylord

Cheboygan (CN)

Otsego

To Atlanta

Presque Isle (PI)

Montmorency

Leer
(10)

Alpena
(AL)

Alpena
(1-9)

23

To Atlanta

32

32

Thunder
Bay

65

Alcona (AA)

23

To Mio

72

Harrisville

72

1

65

Oscoda

Bissonette Rd.

Iosco
(IS)

1

23

Ogemaw

55

65

Alabaster

To Mio

Arenac
(AC)

33

To
W. Branch

76

23

75

N

Gladwin

61

Standish
(1)

To
Gladwin

23

2

Miles

13

0   5   10   20

Bay

444

six counties were established in 1840. Cheboygan County was organized in 1853, Iosco and Alpena counties in 1857, and Alcona County in 1869. Presque Isle County was organized in 1871 and reorganized in 1875. County courthouses that were restrained versions of more sophisticated designs in the southern part of the state emerged as evidence of the attainment of political maturity.

Lumbering in the Huron Shore Region peaked in the 1890s. The architectural result of this prosperity is seen in the wooden Queen Anne houses and courthouses of Alpena and Cheboygan, in particular, and in the opera house at Cheboygan, now altered beyond recognition. But some of the region's lumbering-era architecture was lost to forest fires. On July 11, 1911, Michigan's last great forest fire wiped out whole towns in the Huron Shore Region, including Oscoda and Au Sable.

The pine forests of the southern portion of the region have been conserved in the Huron National Forest. Reforestation was undertaken in the 1930s. Other timberlands are preserved in the Au Sable and Mackinaw state forests.

Limestone, gravel, cement, gypsum, and clay shale are mined in the Huron Shore Region. Near Alabaster, Douglass Houghton discovered outcroppings of gypsum in 1837. By 1841 William McDonald and others sought workable deposits, and in 1861 William S. Patrick developed the first gypsum mine. The gypsum quarried at Alabaster and processed in Chicago earned for the 1893 Columbian Exposition in Chicago the title "the White City."

Francis and Cynthia Crawford, the earliest pioneers in Presque Isle County started a stone quarry, then opened a fuel station for wood-burning steamers on Lake Huron. In 1910 the Michigan Limestone and Chemical Company was formed at Calcite, formerly Crawford's Quarry, to extract limestone. In 1920 U.S. Steel acquired the limestone operation. It is still one of Rogers City's major industries and is beautifully illustrated in a mural in the city's post office.

In 1903 limestone quarrying began in Alpena County. The LaFarge Company (formerly the Huron Portland Cement Company) is Alpena's largest employer. The Besser Company, established in 1904 and inventor of a concrete-block-making machine, is Alpena's second-largest employer and the world's largest manufacturer of equipment that produces concrete blocks. Limestone, concrete, and concrete block were employed extensively in the buildings of the region. Alpena, the largest city in the northeastern Lower Peninsula, is noted for its concrete and concrete block buildings.

In the 1870s the inland water route was opened to link Lake Huron with Lake Michigan from the mouth of the Cheboygan River through Mullet and Burt lakes to Crooked Lake, Conway, and Little Traverse Bay, permitting travel through the interior of the northern Lower Peninsula before roads were laid out. It opened Burt and Mullet lakes, two of Michigan's largest inland lakes, to tourism, and cottages were built along the route.

Lighthouses at Presque Isle, Mackinaw City, Thunder Bay Point, Sturgeon

Point, and elsewhere aided navigation on Lake Huron and at the Straits of Mackinac.

Cabins, summer cottages, camps, and motels are strung out along U.S. Route 23 on the Lake Huron shore from the Straits of Mackinac to Saginaw Bay. They also appear along rivers, on the lakeshore, and on inland lakes such as Long, Grand, Black, Mullet, and Burt lakes. Tourism and outdoor recreation—hunting, fishing, boating, camping, snowmobiling, and cross-country skiing—are important to the economy today. In the late nineteenth and early twentieth centuries, industrialists built log wilderness camps and hunting and fishing lodges in the region. Fine rustic log lodges stand at Black River near Onaway and at Grand Lake.

Camp Skeel expanded in 1941–1942 to serve as an auxiliary field for the defense of Sault Sainte Marie and the Straits. It became Oscoda Army Air Field in 1942 and was renamed Wurtsmith in 1953.

Alpena County   (AL)

ALPENA

Attracted by the vast stands of timber, the many rivers that could be harnessed to power sawmills, and the fine gill-net fishing available in Thunder Bay, settlers arrived here in the 1830s. By 1858 the lumber industry was under way, and it continued to dominate Alpena's economy until surpassed by the cement industry in the early twentieth century. Logging peaked in the 1880s, when Alpena's population reached 11,000. The Huron Portland Cement Company began in 1907 as an expansion of a 1903 Thunder Bay limestone quarry operation initiated by the Michigan Alkali Company of Wyandotte. The plant at Alpena became one of the world's largest cement-producing facilities in the twentieth century. In a related industry, Herman and Jesse Besser invented and manufactured a machine for making concrete blocks. The Bessers' philanthropic activities made a deep impact on Alpena in the form of donated and purchased lands for various schools and churches, the creation of the Besser Foundation and of the Jesse Besser Museum. Always the gift carried the stipulation that the building erected on the donated land or with the donated funds be constructed of concrete block. When title to land held by Besser was acquired by private individuals or corporations, it, too, came with a covenant that improvements be made in concrete. Thus, the nineteenth-century architecture of Alpena is limestone and wooden Queen Anne, and the twentieth-century architecture is gray concrete.

AL01 Alpena County Court House

1934–1935, William H. Kuni. 720 Chisholm St. (US 23) (bounded by Chisholm, Eighth, Lockwood, and Ninth streets)

Designed by William H. Kuni of Detroit, financed by loans and grants from the Public Works Administration of the National Industrial Recovery Act of 1933, the Alpena County Courthouse is an example of "pump priming" in the depression period. In addition, the construction of the courthouse used local materials and local labor. The Henry C. We-

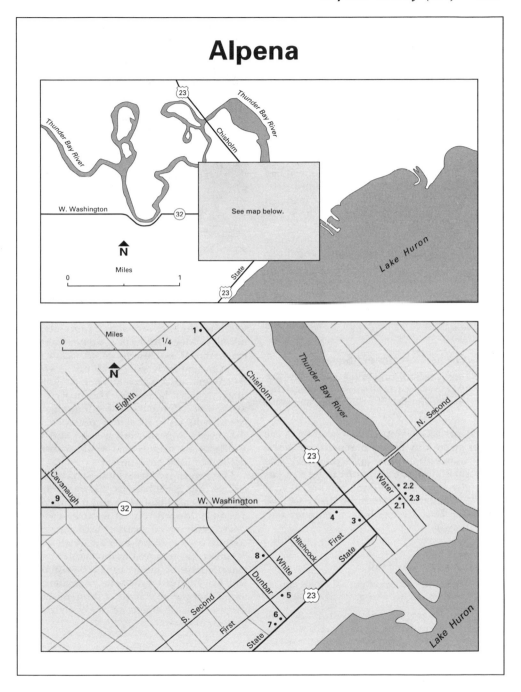

Alpena

ber Construction Company of Detroit, pioneers in the use of reinforced concrete construction technology, poured the concrete made with Huron portland cement for the two-story, fireproof monolithic courthouse during the extremely cold temperatures of Alpena's winter months. The concrete was then sandblasted and treated with "Resto-crete" to enrich its color; a chemical waterproofing agent was also used.

Situated in the center of a grassy terraced square planted with trees, the courthouse is modernistic, with its flat roof, vertical bays, fluted and reeded pilasters, steel-sashed windows, and eagle-topped, parapet-mounted clock. Sculptural decoration depicts the appropriate figures of Law and Justice; and the fascia designs show images of the county's lumbering, shipbuilding, farming, fishing, and recreational industries. The interior vestibule and lobby are decorated with zig-zag and chevron motifs and a terrazzo floor inlaid with geometric patterns; an aluminum stairway with travertine marble treads has an art glass window at the landing; and the courtroom is trimmed in walnut.

One local writer dubbed the courthouse "Fort Alpena," another thought it combined beauty, artistry, dignity, utility, and convenience, and the speaker at the building's dedication suggested that it was a mighty structure worthy of the inscription "give me men to match my pine."

AL02 **Alpena Government Square**

1904–1908, city hall. 1911–1912, federal building. 1919–1922, National Guard Armory. Around a Civic Square bounded by First St., Park Place, and Water St.

The Alpena Government Square follows the tenets of the City Beautiful movement of the early twentieth century and embraces three monumental white masonry Beaux-Arts Classical government buildings around a civic square located on the south bank of the Thunder Bay River, where it empties into Lake Huron.

AL02.1 **Alpena City Hall**

1904–1908, Clark and Munger. 208 North First St. (south corner of First and Water streets)

The first of the twentieth-century government buildings built on the square was the Alpena City Hall, which was designed by Clark and Munger of Bay City and built by Richard Collins of Alpena at a cost of $50,000. This stately structure blends Georgian and other classical elements in a public building design formula established in Michigan by David Gibbs's courthouses and followed by those of Claire Allen. The Alpena work presents an interesting comparison on a national level with Bulfinch's Massachusetts State House,

AL02.1 Alpena City Hall

1795–1798, though on a drastically reduced scale. Each incorporates the arched window openings on the second level—although they are blind arcades in the Michigan work—arched piers marking the projecting entryway, and a columned balcony. Until the late 1950s the Alpena City Hall had a cupola, which would have served as a prominent terminus as does Bulfinch's dome. Contrastingly, the Massachusetts State House used wood prominently along with brick, whereas the Alpena work used the then popular Indiana Bedford limestone. The larger Boston work, with its prominent wooden dome, succeeds in its sense of stately presence, while the smaller Alpena work is solid and heavy and lacks the majesty one would wish for in the seat of local government.

The two-story, steel-frame structure with intersecting gabled wings stands on an elevated rusticated basement and is topped with a red tile, hipped roof. It features a second-story, pedimented portico with single and coupled Ionic columns over an arcaded entry. A cupola was removed in the late 1950s. The exterior is of top-grade, light yellowish brown Indiana Bedford limestone, a material selected over the objections of those promoting the use of local limestone or concrete made from local cement.

AL02.2 **Alpena Federal Building**

1911–1912, James Knox Taylor. 145 Water St.

Promoted in Congress by 10th District Congressman George A. Loud, the Federal Building is evidence of the federal government in Alpena and the city's prominence in northeastern Lower Michigan. Its large, semicircular arched, symmetrically arranged first-story windows with compound arched enframements and keystones set in recessed panels, its modillioned cornice and balustraded roofline, its smooth-coursed limestone over brick masonry, its coupled Doric pilasters, and its five-part composition, all these features mark it as an example of Beaux-Arts Classicism.

AL02.3 National Guard Armory (Memorial Hall)

1919–1922, Aaron H. Gould and Son. 201 Water St. (northeast corner of Water and First streets)

This enormous concrete structure, one of the largest in northern Michigan, was constructed during an era of immense civic optimism, economic prosperity, and concern for the idealized city. Memorial Hall was built by the citizens of Alpena County with funds raised locally as a memorial to World War I veterans. Aaron H. Gould and Son of Detroit planned it with a gymnasium, auditorium, and meeting rooms for use by veterans groups, boys clubs, and other civic organizations. Its seven-part composition with coupled Doric pilasters between the giant arched window openings adheres to a rigid symmetry. The building was constructed completely from concrete, with the cement donated by the Huron Portland Cement Company. The company was founded in Alpena in 1907, and was, by then, the world's largest cement producer. The state of Michigan acquired the hall in 1959 for use by the National Guard.

AL03 IOOF Centennial Building

1876, William Mirre. 150 East Chisholm St. (US 23) at Washington and First streets

The IOOF Centennial Building is a three-story, flatiron-shaped structure located on a triangular site. It was built by Samuel Enoch Hitchcock (1798–1881), New York-born Alpena land and real estate speculator. The designer was William Mirre, a German-born surveyor who arrived in Detroit in 1868 and who worked on the lake survey before going to Alpena in 1871 to serve as Alpena county and city surveyor. Ornamental hood moldings, paneled walls, quoins, cornice bands, the inscription, "Centennial 4 July 1876"—all laboriously laid in brick by Fred Ludwig—articulate the walls of the three-story, decorative structure. The recessed corner entrance, with

its second-floor balcony above, was added in 1910. The people of Alpena expressed their admiration of Hitchcock for investing in the development of the city and in the building, with its substantial and convenient qualities.

AL04 Trinity Episcopal Church

1883–1887, Charles N. Cornell. 120 East Washington Ave. (Michigan 32)

Trinity Episcopal Church is a gable-roofed, Gothic Revival parish church designed by a local architect and built of rusticated rubble limestone, probably from the Alpena Limeworks and Quarry. It has an asymmetrical facade with a segmental-arch entrance and a square corner tower with steeple. Stained glass fills the pointed windows, which are topped with smooth ashlar hood moldings. The interior is virtually intact, with original wood floor, oak pews, wainscoting, and wood truss vaulting.

Before the construction of this $20,000 stone church, Episcopalians met in an 1867 building, built by former easterners prominent in Alpena's early lumbering and commerce.

AL05 Jesse H. and Anna Mulvane Besser House

1938–1939, Joseph C. Goddeyne. 232 First Ave.

This solid concrete masonry house displays inside and out the versatility, durability, and beauty of the concrete blocks made from equipment manufactured by its original occupant, Jesse H. Besser (1882–1970). One of Alpena's leading industrial pioneers, Besser established, along with his father Herman Besser, the Besser Foundry and Machine Shop in 1904. The Bessers invented a machine for making concrete blocks from the cement produced from the area's rich limestone deposits and promoted the use of concrete masonry worldwide. Today the Besser Company is the world's largest manufacturer of equipment that produces concrete blocks.

Besser selected Joseph C. Goddeyne, a Bay City architect, whose plans frequently called for concrete construction, to design his modern house. The rectangular-shaped house topped by a flat copper roof employed reinforced concrete joists throughout. Bands of ribbon windows that wrap around the corners and add to the effect of volume, the unadorned walls of light pink, glazed, and ground concrete blocks made from Wisconsin aggregate, and the characteristic asymmetry echo the influence of Neutra and Schindler. The most modern and efficient equipment was installed throughout the house.

Across the street is the concrete block Thunder Bay Junior High School (Alpena High School, 1941), which also added to this city's experience of modernism in architecture.

AL06 Charles R. and Florence Parshall Henry House

1902–1904, Owen Fox, contractor and mason. 303 State Ave. (US 23) (southwest corner of State and Dunbar streets)

The solid, comfortable, fieldstone Queen Anne Henry house fronts on Thunder Bay. Characteristic of the Queen Anne is the irregular silhouette, intersecting gable, round tower, and the turreted, ample porch. It is reminis-

cent in its rough texture of the domestic work of H. H. Richardson. The fieldstones, from the bottom of Lake Huron at the nearby Cathro area, and from glacial deposits on North Point, were laid by Owen Fox, a local stonemason, using Alpena portland cement for the mortar in the 18-inch-thick walls. The interior features three brick and tile fireplaces, various types of hardwood woodwork, and antique brass fixtures.

Born in Lenawee County, Charles R. Henry (1856–1926) was a lawyer and newspaper publisher who arrived in Alpena to participate in the prosperity of the 1900s. In 1884 he served as state senator.

AL07 Joseph B. and Louise McDonald Comstock House

1892, Fred A. Wilson, contractor. 313 State St. (US 23)

This two-and-a-half-story house is built appropriately of wood for Joseph Comstock (1860–1894), a member of the Comstock lumber and banking family. His forebearer, A. W. Comstock, came to Alpena in 1862 and organized a logging and lumber operation that later became the Bewick, Comstock and Company lumber mill.

With a three-story octagonal tower with a frieze of carved panels, a wrap-around porch featuring a profusion of fine spindlework and elaborately turned posts, the ubiquitous turret, and carved sunburst motifs, the house is an elegant reminder of Alpena's prosperous nineteenth-century lumbering era. Furthermore, the Comstock house illustrates the rage for the picturesque possibilities in the wood version of the Queen Anne, as executed by unidentified local craftsmen in Michigan's lumbering region.

AL08 Herman and Hattie Ely Besser House (Lutes House)

1923. 403 South Second St.

This bungalow was the first home built of Bes-Stone Split Block. The blocks were manufactured by the Besser Manufacturing Company using a formula patented in 1925 that covered aggregate gradation, use of larger stone chips for decorative split face effect, proper use of cement and water and mixing and splitting information. Herman Besser (1853–1926), founder of the Besser Manufacturing Company, built the house in 1923. He and his wife, Hattie Ely (1855–1943), came from Erie County, New York, to northern Michigan in 1882.

AL09 Concrete Block Houses

1923–1924, Elroy C. Bobolts. 707, 711, 715 West Washington Ave. (Michigan 32)

Elroy C. Bobolts of the Besser Company prepared for Herman Besser rough sketches of these multiple houses, and two brothers from Bay City built them of Bes-Stone Split Block made by the Besser Manufacturing Company. The rock-faced concrete blocks were packed by hand, tipped up, cured, and then placed face down in the wall. Brackets supporting the cornices of the flat roofs and the open work pattern in which the blocks of the porches are laid give decoration to the flat-topped boxy bungalows. Windows are arranged in bands.

LEER, LONG RAPIDS TOWNSHIP

The settlement of Long Rapids began in 1885 when George Speeckly built a water-powered saw and gristmill and opened a store here.

AL10 Leer Lutheran Church

1899. 10430 Leer Rd. (southwest corner Leer and Carr roads)

Immigrants from Leer, Norway, who came to Alpena between 1869 and 1872, established in 1874 a colony 25 miles north of the city. Here they found rolling hills and rocky sink holes that reminded them of their native land. The first families moved here in 1879. The Norwegian school located on the Ed Olsen farm served as a church. In 1899, under the leadership of Pastor Lorentz C. Johnson, this small group of dairy farmers and their families built the church on land donated by Keri Burud. A lot in the adjoining cemetery was given to each man who helped clear the land. The names on the headstones remind us of the heritage of the Norwegian settlers and their descendants—the Olsens, Christophersons, Engers, Hansens, Alfsens, Larsons, Jacobsens, and Barsens.

The wood-frame, gable-roof church has a projecting central entry tower with a louvered belfry topped by a spire. Though hardly recalling the Norwegian stave churches, the Leer church employed timber, thus reinforcing the importance of regional materials and the ethnic building tradition. The ethnic identification remained until 1922, when the English language was introduced in religious services. Though the exterior is now sided in aluminum, the interior remains as it was after the 1941 renovation.

Presque Isle County (PI)

ROGERS CITY

PI01 Rogers City Post Office

1940, Louis A. Simon. 188 North Third St. (Business US 23) (northwest corner Third St. and Michigan)

The Rogers City Post Office is a simple, flat-roofed rectangular block of poured concrete in the Moderne style embellished only with a modified Greek fretwork pattern above and below the windows.

The government-sponsored lobby mural, *The Harbor at Rogers City*, was painted in 1941 by Michigan artist James Calder. In a precise and pristine manner it depicts the local industrial scene—the quarrying and shipping

PI01 Rogers City Post Office

of limestone for use in the manufacturing of cement, in blast furnaces, and in road building. The scene shows the docks at the Michigan Limestone and Chemical Company (the Calcite Plant), with tugboats, cranes, the loading of ships, and the huge piles of crushed limestone. The Rogers City quarry is today one of the largest limestone quarries in the world.

ONAWAY

PI02 Presque Isle County Historical Museum (Presque Isle County Courthouse–Onaway City Hall)

1908. Northwest corner of State (Michigan 68) and Maple streets

The county courthouse at Onaway was built by Merritt Chandler (b. 1843), a lumberman who constructed roads and cleared swamps in exchange for grants of public land under the Swamp Lands Act. He speculated in Presque Isle County land and real estate, promoted Onaway, and was also involved in an ill-fated attempt to establish Onaway as the county seat. In 1908 he built this courthouse

and offered it to the county at no cost, but his offer was rejected. He then tried to create a new county, with Onaway as the county seat, a scheme that was declared illegal. After a bitter fight, the county seat remained in Rogers City and Chandler donated his courthouse to the city.

The design combines elements from the monumental work of H. H. Richardson in a two-and-a-half-story structure of rusticated concrete blocks set on a high fieldstone base. It has an asymmetrical facade with a massive tower positioned southwest of the central raised pedimented portico, and a large round arch over the entrance.

PI03 Onaway Masonic Hall (Lobdell and Bailey Company Offices)

1901. North side of Washington Ave. (Michigan 68) between Poplar and Michigan Ave.

A wood products company built this office and residence for its owner in a style reminiscent of the French Colonial houses that stood along the Mississippi River in Missouri in the late eighteenth and early nineteenth centuries. It displays a steeply pitched, ridged and flared pavilion-hipped roof and a two-story wrap-around veranda. The interior is paneled with white birch.

The Lobdell and Bailey Company, later the American Wood Rim Company, manufactured bicycle rims and automobile steering wheels. Employing 750 men by 1902 in the manufacture of a product that used local wood, the company was the chief employer and most important industry in what was then called, "The Town that Steers the World." The plant burned in a disastrous fire in January 1926, and after the fire Onaway's population was reduced by more than half. Today the Onaway Masonic Order uses the structure.

PRESQUE ISLE TOWNSHIP

PI04 Presque Isle Lodge

1922. 8211 Grand Lake Rd. (10 miles north of US 23 and 2.5 miles south of Presque Isle Harbor)

N. A. Eddy, owner of the Habitant Corporation of Bay City, built this large rustic lodge near Grand and Lotus lakes and filled it with rustic furniture manufactured by his company. The lodge is constructed of wooden slabs rounded to resemble logs. It is arranged with a dining room and hall with a huge fieldstone fireplace and twenty-seven bedrooms.

Cheboygan County (CN)

CHEBOYGAN

CN01 Old Cheboygan County Courthouse (Cheboygan County Courthouse)

1869, J. F. Watson, builder. 229 Court St. (southeast corner Court and South Huron streets)

At first glance this courthouse hardly appears to be a public building. Like Richard Munday's Old Colony House (Old State House), 1739–1741, in Newport, Rhode Island, here is an excellent example of the earlier colonial view of the public building as a domestic building, but built slightly larger in size. J. F. Watson, the builder of the Old Cheboygan County Courthouse, probably had no knowledge of the Greek Revival as promulgated in the writings of Benjamin and Lafever. This building is vernacular in its simplicity and in its distilled treatment of Greek details like the deep entablature. Small six-over-six windows suggest the ample space within. It accurately captures the pioneer condition during the county's settlement as a fur trading, lumbering, and sawmilling center. The plain balloon-frame, clapboarded, two-story structure with gable roof and cupola had county offices on the first level and a courtroom on the second. For forty years, this sturdy wooden building served as a courthouse; and later it was used as a fire house, a meeting hall, a church, and law offices.

CN02 Jacob J. and Cornelia McArthur Post House

1886, Frederick W. Hollister. 528 South Huron St. (northwest corner of South Huron and Taylor streets)

Jacob J. Post (1839–1912), a prominent Cheboygan hardware merchant, banker, and city official who came here from New York State,

CN02 Jacob J. and Cornelia McArthur Post House

built this beautiful Queen Anne house to the designs of Frederick W. Hollister, a Saginaw architect whose works can be found in several Michigan lumbering towns. The two-story, clapboarded structure is enhanced by the lively and irregular arrangement of gables, dormers, chimneys, bay windows, and porches embellished with spindlework, latticework, coffering, shingles, and rosettes. The interior features a large two-story foyer and four tiled fireplaces, art glass, and parquet floors.

CN03 Huron Street Tabernacle Assembly of God Church (Saint Paul's United Methodist Church)

1905. Southwest Corner of Huron and Pine streets

Organized in 1868, the Methodist community replaced its frame building erected in 1872 with this auditorium-plan church in the Mission Revival style popular throughout the country between 1905 and 1920. Spanish design elements found in the church include the cream-colored stucco exterior with brown trim over poured concrete walls, the scalloped coping on its gables, and its tall campanile displaying paired columns on all four sides. The Pine Street facade has a quatrefoil window.

At its dedication, the *Cheboygan Democrat* for May 26, 1905, described the church as "a beauty, and . . . perfectly fitted up for a modern, progressive society." Modern and progressive, too, was the selection of the Mission Revival style just emerging in California.

CN04 Swiss Chalet Bungalow

c. 1920. 333 North Huron St. (southwest corner of Huron and Backus streets)

This whimsical, front-gabled Swiss Chalet bungalow is the best of several excellent Craftsman-type houses found in Cheboygan and Rogers City. Inspired by the work of the Greene brothers and the English Arts and Crafts movement and publicized throughout this country by magazines such as *House Beautiful* and *Good Housekeeping*, these modest, low buildings with broad proportions, overhanging eaves, and exposed roof supports were found in the far reaches of Michigan in the first two decades of this century. They display many different secondary influences, as exemplified in the Oriental bungalow nearby at 120 Ball Street.

Alpine details appear in the steep gable roof and dormers and the Swiss bracketed balcony above the entrance. The wide, over-hanging eaves are supported by decorative knee braces and the rafter ends are left exposed. Small square blocks on the bargeboards and the frieze simulate exposed purlins and joists. These are repeated on the porch columns. The gable ends are decorated with false half-timbering while the lower walls are clapboard. The cobblestone steps and the shamrock detailing on the balcony add to its delightful character.

CN05 Archibald P. and Cornelia Newton House

1871. 337 Dresser St.

One of the grandest residences in Cheboygan, the Newton house is a two-story red brick Italianate structure with wrap-around porch, bracketed hipped roof, and narrow windows with elaborate hood moldings. It is topped by a decorative belvedere that affords a view of Lake Huron. It was built by Archibald P. Newton, a prominent merchant, fisherman, and entrepreneur who served as the village's first elected president in 1870. Newton and his brother bought Saint Helena Island in 1853 and developed it as a fuel and supply port for shipping on the Great Lakes. He also established the area's first facility for the extraction of tannia from the bark of hemlock trees, a product used in tanning leather. This industry became important in the development of Cheboygan's economy between the 1870s and the 1920s.

The Italianate style was very popular in Michigan and embodies formal dignity and picturesque elements quite fitting for a family dominant in Cheboygan's business and social life.

BENTON TOWNSHIP

CN06 Hack-Ma-Tack Inn

1894. 8131 Beebe Rd. (south of Michigan 33 on Carter Rd. 1 mile, then west of Hackmatack Rd., .25 mile to east bank of the Cheboygan River)

Chicagoan Watson Beebe built Hack-Ma-Tack Inn as a private fishing and hunting lodge and named it for the tamarack, or larch tree. Later Beebe converted it to a family resort hotel, rebuilding and expanding the facility many times. The inn is a rustic, fortlike log building, 200 feet long, with dining areas and six guest rooms. The main two-story section has a gable roof and is flanked by a four-story log tower, which is not without a relationship to the popular campanile tower of the Italian villa. The interior features a large stone fireplace, log rafters, and Indian motifs. Now it is a restaurant frequented by boaters.

In front of the inn, a 400-foot dock runs along the Cheboygan River, which is one link in the 38-mile-long chain of lakes and rivers connecting Lake Huron with Crooked Lake close to the Lake Michigan shore that is known as the Inland Waterway. Indians and fur traders short-circuited the dangerous trip between the two Great Lakes through the Straits of Mackinac by following this route from Cheboygan River to Mullet Lake, Indian River to Burt Lake, and Crooked River to Crooked Lake, with only a short portage to Little Traverse Bay. Today the Inland Waterway has two locks and can accommodate boats up to 65 feet long.

ONAWAY VICINITY, WAVERLY TOWNSHIP

CN07 The Walter and May Reuther UAW Family Education Center at Black Lake

1967–1970, Oskar Stonorov. Maxon Rd. (Cheboygan County F05) (entrance is approached from a point approximately 4 miles north of the intersection of Maxon Rd. [Cheboygan County F05] and Michigan 68/Michigan 33, 2 miles west of Onaway). Not visible from the road

This complex consists of about twenty buildings on roughly 1,000 acres of land adjoining the south shore of Black Lake. In January 1967, the United Auto Workers international executive board purchased a large parcel of forested land adjacent to Black Lake as the site for the Family Education Center that Walter Reuther (1907–1970) had proposed, upon election to his eleventh term as UAW international president in April 1966. This secluded vacation spot was then owned by the Maxon Advertising Agency. Nearby was the former retreat of Detroit advertising agency owner Louis Maxon. Maxon enjoyed the opportunities for hunting and fishing the area provided and had constructed a number of rustic log buildings for the use of his family and guests, including a large lodge (still in use) with a two-story central hall, a stable (now named The Inn), and a children's playhouse.

Oskar Stonorov, a Philadelphia architect who had previously designed Solidarity House, the UAW's International Headquarters in Detroit, was hired to provide architectural direction for Black Lake. He submitted detailed plans, taking into account Walter Reuther's desire to have the buildings conform to and emerge from the land's contours, not be imposed upon them. Reuther had examined nearly every tree on the property and was determined to preserve the hemlocks, aspens, maples, oaks, and pines for visitors' enjoyment. No tree could be cut without his personal permission; some buildings were altered to accommodate them.

The buildings have been so arranged that they all have views of the streams and ponds; the impression of exterior and interior space blending into a harmonious whole has been reinforced by the use of panoramic glass window walls in combination with wood and stone. The ocher-streaked Wisconsin limestone in the new buildings contrasts with the chalky, but costlier, local stone formerly employed for the hillside terraces above the muskrat ponds. The largest structural wood timbers are laminated beams and columns of Douglas fir from Oregon; the latter were fabricated in Washington State with equipment once used to turn the masts of wooden sailing ships. Exterior surfaces, decks, and smaller structural members are of cedar, while interior doors and trim are red birch and railings and visual highlights are teak.

The major buildings at the center are connected with glass-enclosed passageways so that one may walk from one end of the complex to the other without setting foot outdoors, yet never lose sight of the surrounding scenery. A spacious two-story structure consists of a 300-seat dining room and a lecture room-banquet hall (also 300 seats) above, with a recreation center on the floor below. In the main dining room, circular Swedish wooden lighting fixtures complement the wooden ceiling, which is partially supported by a laminated fir beam 72 feet long (the largest in the complex). A central fireplace provides an interesting focal point to the immense room. It consists of a large tripartite bronze cauldron situated on a black marble base and surmounted by a biconical bronze chimney. Faceted on this is a wide band at eye level with sculptural panels and bearing the raised inscription "HIC DOMUS FACTUS EST A.D. MCMLXIX" and the Michigan motto "SI QUAERIS PENINSULAM AMOENAM CIRCUMSPICE." A circular stair with a teak railing descends to exhibit space and a recreation center, fronted by a garden, where a half-length memorial statue of Walter Reuther is displayed.

The corridor leading from the main dining room connects to two two-story living unit buildings. These are conjoined by an enclosed passageway containing a small lounge area with a panoramic view of the Japanese bridge that leads across the stream to the Reuther memorial grove. Celebrating Reuther's love of trees, it was planted by trade unionists from around the world. After dark, large bronze lighting fixtures by the Florentine sculptor Vivalli illuminate the bridge from either end. (He also created the circular figure group *The Children of the World*, next to the road leading from the front gate.)

The spacious main student lounge, situated behind the entrance lobby, forms a central focus to the complex's residential section, in which space-defining curvilinear interior stone walls are penetrated by linteled archways and a mezzanine suspended from the ceiling. A fireplace in the center of the lounge is surmounted by a two-story bronze chimney sculpture that also echoes the contours of the surrounding walls. A smaller parallelogram-shaped lounge shares with the main lounge a view of the Walter and May Reuther Memorial Sanctuary on the far shore of the main pond. (This sanctuary contains a lantern-shrine donated by Japanese trade union members and two evergreen trees planted by the

Reuthers' daughters *in memoriam*). The main lounge itself is trapezoidal; in fact, there are few right-angled corners in any of the rooms that constitute the residential center.

Also connected by passageways are the day care center; the leadership studies center, containing classrooms, an audio-visual laboratory, a library-bookstore, and offices; and the gymnasium-auditorium-swimming pool building. Each of the two sections of this latter structure is covered by a copper roof in the shape of a parabolic curve and supported by immense laminated fir arches. This roof also acts as a solar collector for hot water. At the center of the three passageways connecting these buildings with the residential complex stands the Hub, a small roughly spiral-shaped structure with a circular masonry fireplace at the center. Around the room's circumference is a sculptural representation of the planets and signs of the zodiac showing their relative positions at the time of Walter Reuther's birth.

Located near the Maxon Lodge is the Youth Center, a building with shiplike projections and curved-glass windows; the exterior is faced with vertical logs. Of similar construction, but situated on a prominent hill affording an excellent view of Black Lake, stands the former summer residence of Louis Maxon. It is a rustic but spacious circular building now used as a guest house for visiting dignitaries. Standing nearby is Hilltop, a summer camp for children eight to fourteen years old.

The Walter and May Reuther UAW Family Education Center at Black Lake is a very special adaptation of a large building complex to a site that thoughtfully keeps man-made structures in harmony with the natural surroundings. In several aspects, Black Lake parallels Cranbrook, where another esthetically concerned patron (George Booth) worked closely with a carefully chosen architect (Eliel Saarinen) to design a series of institutional buildings within a naturally scenic setting. To complete the sense of esthetic harmony, outdoor sculpture by a single sculptor is displayed throughout the grounds (Milles at Cranbrook; Vivalli at Black Lake). The major difference between the two complexes is that Cranbrook evolved over a course of three decades, whereas the Black Lake center was developed by the UAW in a tenth that time.

The Reuthers and Oskar Stonorov saw the fruition of their dream, but, shortly thereafter, on May 9, 1970, all three perished in a plane crash en route to the Pellston airport. Subsequently, the UAW International Executive Board voted to name the center in honor of Walter and May Reuther as a lasting memorial tribute.

Alcona County (AA)

HARRISVILLE TOWNSHIP, SPRINGPORT

AA01 **Springport Inn** (Joseph Van Buskirk House)

1878; N. J. Gibbs; Elias Stockwell, master builder for house and designer for dining room. 659 US 23, 1 mile south of Harrisville

Situated on a rise of ground in the fishing and lumbering town of Springport that as-

cends from the shore and commands a splendid view of Lake Huron, this uninhibited vernacular house was regarded as the county's finest, and a model of beauty and convenience. *The History of the Lake Huron Shore* (Chicago, 1883), termed the house Swiss-Gothic style, but it is really a vernacular mix that defies style in favor of a succulent feast. The house is a two-story, balloon frame, clapboarded structure with intersecting pitched roofs, the gables of which are elaborately ornamented with open woodwork. Its balconies, porches, and bays are frosted with Eastlake spindlework and Italianate detail. The house was built after plans of N. J. Gibbs, who was a Mount Clemens designer, for Joseph Van Buskirk, a lumberman and sawmill and store operator. *The History of the Lake Huron Shore* illustrated it with the sawmill, store, and docks of the farming and lumbering operations. These and residences of Van Buskirk's employees made up the hamlet of Harrisville. The Freethinkers, a German society, purchased the house in 1920 to serve as their clubhouse. In 1924 Carl E. Schmidt acquired and added to the house and converted it to an inn.

Iosco County (IS)

AU SABLE VICINITY, OSCODA TOWNSHIP

IS01 **Cooke Hydroelectric Plant**

1911–1912. On Au Sable River (from Michigan 65 approximately 6 miles east on Bissonette Rd., then 3.25 miles northeast on Cooke Dam Rd. to the plant)

This was the first of six hydroelectric plants constructed on the Au Sable River by the Consumers Power Company between 1911 and 1923. Three horizontal Allis-Chalmers turbines and three General Electric genera-

tors installed here produced the power that was transmitted at the then unprecedented level of 140,000 volts to Bay City, Saginaw, and Flint. J. B. Foote of Consumers Power Company innovated in the use of tapered steel towers and cap and pin insulators, which became standard for most of the electrical industry. The dam is an earth-filled type with a concrete core wall, and it creates a head of 41 feet. The powerhouse is a gable-roof rectangular brick building. The concrete spillway contains three tainter gates that can discharge 15,800 cubic feet per second.

Arenac County   (AC)

STANDISH

AC01 **Arenac County Courthouse**
1964–1965, R. S. Gerganoff. 120 North Grove St.

On April 4, 1892, the voters of Arenac County elected to move the county seat from Omer to Standish. The town already had been a center for the county's lumbering and agricultural industries, but its designation as its new seat of government allowed it to surpass quickly its neighbors in size and importance—and to maintain that lead to the present day. In 1892 the county erected in Standish the county's third courthouse, a large, red brick, Richardsonian Romanesque building. The building was demolished to clear the site for construction of the fourth Arenac county courthouse. Bays of glazing and enameled panels strongly delineate the front facade of the two-story, L-shaped International style structure. R. S. Gergonoff of Ypsilanti, an architect noted for his International style designs for public buildings, was the architect.

STANDISH TOWNSHIP

AC02 **Saganing Indian Mission Church**
1875–1876. 5446 Sturman Rd. (between Worth and White's Beach roads)

The Saganing Indian Mission was established by Joseph Cabay, a Methodist missionary from Boston, and his wife, Mary Henderson Cabay, who came to the area to minister to the Chippewa. After her husband died, Mary Cabay married a Chippewa Indian, Peter Sagatoo. In 1875, after raising funds among influential Michigan and Eastern Methodists, she initiated construction of this mission church. A simple wood-framed structure, with balanced, bow-arch fenestration and a centered front entryway, the church is now sheathed in asbestos siding. It remains in full use today and maintains its nearby Indian cemetery.

THE UPPER PENINSULA

The Copper Country

PROJECTING FOR ONE HUNDRED MILES TO THE NORTHEAST, into the broad waters of Lake Superior, the bold thrust of the Keweenaw Peninsula forms the most northerly reach of the state of Michigan. It is a dramatic climax to a varied and beautiful land. There was a time, however, when this remote region was also the repository of one of the state's most valuable resources: a narrow spine called the Copper Range, which runs the entire length of the peninsula, once held rich deposits of copper. This remarkable geological feature is flanked by sandstone.

About 45 miles from its outer tip, the Keweenaw Peninsula is pierced by Portage Lake and the Lake Superior Ship Canal, forming the Keweenaw waterway, which opened in 1873. This intrusion into the land virtually transforms a major portion of the peninsula into an island. From the southern shores of Portage Lake the land rises abruptly to a gentle incline that forms the site for the business district of Houghton. From the northern shores the land rises more gradually from the village of Hancock to an elevated plateau that extends northeasterly beyond to Keweenaw County. It was this area, known as the Portage Lake Mining District, in particular that at one time contained one of the richest copper fields in the world. At its northern boundary the villages of Laurium and Calumet, once made up of Red Jacket, Blue Jacket, Yellow Jacket, Limerick, Tamarack, and other enclaves named after mine locations, merge together to form one continuous community.

Prehistoric Indians had taken copper from the Lake Superior region, and French explorers had noted the existence of this red metal as early as the seventeenth century. In 1772 Alexander Henry prospected for copper on the Ontonagon River near Victoria. His *Travels*, published in 1809, reported the presence of a large boulder of copper weighing approximately 6,000 pounds near

461

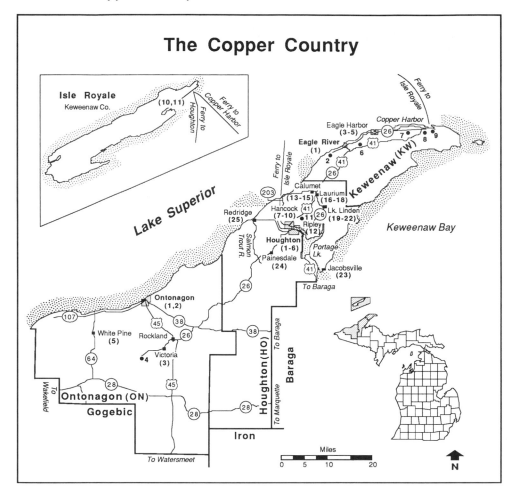

The Copper Country

the mouth of the Ontonagon River. In 1841, Julius Eldred led a well-publicized campaign to remove the Ontonagon boulder from the Ontonagon River and display it in Detroit. Subsequently, it was moved to the Smithsonian Institution in Washington. Further attention was drawn to the area in 1841, when state geologist Douglass Houghton submitted his fourth annual report describing the location and extent of the copper deposits of the Keweenaw Peninsula. Congress purchased the lands from the Chippewa in 1843, and a speculative craze, encouraged by the federal land policy, began and lasted three years. The government abandoned the leasing policy in 1846 because it was difficult to administer. In 1847 it called for an identification of Lake Superior mineral lands and then sold the permits at $2.50 an acre. Later, in 1850, the fee was reduced to $1.25 an acre.

The Copper Country was settled and developed when investors from Boston, New York, Chicago, Marquette, and Lower Michigan speculated in the region's mineral resources and in its rugged land. After prospectors and geologists had identified the location and extent of the mineral resources, Alexander Agassiz, Quincy Adams Shaw, William A. Paine, W. H. Mason, and others established, developed, and finally consolidated the Copper Range, Quincy, and Calumet and Hecla companies into giant mining operations. Towns grew up around the mines and mills and at the transportation centers of Houghton and Hancock. Hordes of Cornish, Irish, German, French-Canadian, and Scandinavian immigrants, followed by Austrians, Hungarians, and Italians, flocked to the region to work as miners, trammers, and laborers. Mining engineers and technicians arrived from the East to supervise and manage them. The rush of industrial, social, commercial, and educational activity created a demand for buildings. Copper Country architecture achieved a special harmony with the land because its architects and builders used, with sensitivity and understanding, the materials of the area—native Jacobsville sandstone, taken from the site or quarried locally at Portage Entry, and poor mine rock discarded from the mines.

The mining industry was aided by the opening of the locks at Sault Sainte Marie in 1855 and the completion of the Lake Superior Ship Canal in 1873. Railroads also aided in this development; the Mineral Range Railroad connected Houghton with Hancock in 1873, the Duluth, South Shore, and Atlantic reached Houghton in 1883; in 1885, a railroad over a drawbridge connected Hancock and Houghton, the major commercial centers of the region.

The architecture that emerged out of the interaction of the land, the resources, and the people in this region ranged from the strictly vernacular for the workers to the fashionable high styles for the owners and managers. Professionally trained architects were virtually unknown in this remote mining region until the 1890s. Clients called upon Henry Ottenheimer, Erhard Brielmaier, John Scott, and other architects from Chicago, Milwaukee, Detroit, and Marquette to design major public buildings. By the late 1890s local governments, businessmen, and religious groups employed Demetrius Frederick Charlton, the first trained architect to reside permanently in the Upper Peninsula, or itinerant architects such as Charles K. Shand, who followed the development westward across the country to design city halls, courthouses, churches, banks, and commercial blocks. Men with little professional training, but experienced as builders, designed and built most of the Copper Country's architecture. The works of these men quickly developed to form a strong vernacular tradition, which is especially distinguished by the character and quality of Jacobsville red sandstone.

The end of mining came in the twentieth century. Deteriorating labor relations led to the Michigan copper district strike of 1913–1914. In 1923 the Calumet and Hecla reincorporated and consolidated its numerous mining properties. The depth of the mines increased and the copper content of the ore diminished. The Calumet and Hecla sought other means of profit making by capturing large quantities of copper lost in the milling process, extraction of ore from amygdaloid rock in new mines, and reclamation of copper from mill sands. Mining was hard hit by the Great Depression. It closed permanently in 1968.

In the middle and late twentieth century, tourism, education; and high technology replaced copper as the basis of this region's economy.

Houghton County   (HO)

HOUGHTON

HO01 **Houghton County Courthouse**

1886–1887, J. B. Sweatt. later additions. 401 East Houghton Ave. (bounded by East Houghton Ave., Huron St., South Ave., and Dodge St.)

Somewhat unexpected in this region is this gaudy, polychromatic, three-story, Venetian Gothic courthouse that brings the vision of John Ruskin to Upper Michigan. This is apparent not only in the detailing but especially in the polychrome mixture of cream-colored Milwaukee brick (manufactured at the Seager and Gunnis brickyard at Lake Linden) walls with Upper Peninsula red sandstone trimmings from quarries at Marquette, L'Anse, and Portage Entry. This polychromy is further enriched by green-oxidized Lake Superior copper roofing and by iron and wood

from Marquette. J. B. Sweatt, an architect and builder in Marquette with fifteen years of experience, some of which was in Chicago, did the plans for the courthouse. Sweatt designed and built many public buildings from Sault Sainte Marie to Houghton in the Lake Superior Region. The courthouse is composed of the original structure, a rectangular block from which project central pavilions with parapeted dormers, a four-story tower, and north and west wing additions. The curbed mansard roof, the grouping of windows beneath red sandstone lintels connected by bands that encircle the structure, and the decorative entablature unite the composition. Porches supported with posts and Gothic-arch brackets and trimmed with quatrefoils enliven the design further. The interior is richly finished with wood; red, rich brown, and light yellowish brown floor tiles; ornamental plaster; an oak staircase; and stone fireplaces.

HO02 **Shelden Avenue**

Both sides of Shelden Ave. (US 41), from Franklin Square to the Houghton-Hancock Lift Bridge

Shelden Avenue served as the commercial center for the Portage Lake Mining District, the most important copper mining and processing area in the Copper Range. The district developed during the boom years of the mining industry in the late nineteenth and early twentieth centuries. After the 1920s the economy dramatically slowed, then began a long, slow decline. The commercial buildings reflect the culmination of Houghton's commercial growth, which was inextricably tied to the mining industry.

Between 1899 and 1901 several Houghton businesspeople who had prospered from investments in mines and land built a group of masonry commercial buildings at the intersection of Shelden Avenue and Isle Royale

Street, the heart of Houghton's commercial district. The Sheldens, Dees, Wrights, Seagers, and Calverlys commissioned Henry Leopold Ottenheimer (1868–1919) of Chicago to design them. Ottenheimer, a student of Adler and Sullivan, was the architect of the Chicago Elks Club and the Chicago Hebrew Institute Gymnasium, among many public buildings, banks, and stores in Chicago. In spite of the association with one of this country's famous architects, however, the influence of Sullivan on Ottenheimer's Houghton works is modulated by the strong regional tradition of building with sandstone and by an apparent local taste for classical detail. The Houghton people contracted with Paul F. P. Mueller (1865–1934) of Chicago, an engineer for Adler and Sullivan and Frank Lloyd Wright, to execute the plans prepared by Ottenheimer. The James Dee Block, the Douglass House Hotel, and the Shelden-Dee Block show the preference for brick and local sandstone. The group of structures complemented the prestigious Richardsonian Romanesque First National Bank, built on the northeast corner of this intersection ten years earlier.

In the 1970s the city of Houghton revitalized its central business district and targeted its marketing at the people who live and visit here—students at Michigan Technological University, longtime residents, and tourists. Leveraging private and local funds with federal and state grants, it has refurbished Shelden Avenue, constructed a parking deck, and connected the stores with a system of interior corridors and skywalks that is appropriate for the severe winters here, just as was done in Minneapolis and Saint Paul.

HO02.1 Shelden-Dee Block

1899–1900, Henry L. Ottenheimer. 512–524 Shelden Ave. (US 41) (northwest corner of Shelden Ave. and Isle Royale St.)

The large three-story Shelden-Dee Block was designed by Henry L. Ottenheimer. It was commissioned by James R. Dee and Mary E. Shelden (1845–1935), members of early pioneer families who speculated in the mineral and timberlands of Michigan's copper frontier. One large block of stores and office suites was divided into identical halves, one for each investor. Brick and smooth-cut and richly carved red Portage Entry sandstone cover a steel frame. There is quite a lot of Louis Sullivan in the building: the tripartite division between base, shaft, and top; the emphasis on the verticals in the engaged pilasters that articulate the frame with recessed spandrels and secondary verticals between; in the clearly articulated door motifs; and in the ornament in the frieze. A rich and ornate copper cornice supports the roof. Paul F. P. Mueller constructed the building. The Shelden-Dee Block is a classical version of Chicago School design.

HO02.2 Douglass House Apartments Saloon and Restaurant (Douglass House)

1899–1900, Henry L. Ottenheimer. 1902, addition. 517 Shelden Ave. (US 41) (southwest corner of Shelden Ave. and Isle Royale St.)

The four-story hotel was financed by the Douglass House Company, a group of stockholders made up of Houghton businessmen intent on promoting the welfare of Houghton by meeting the demand for decent hotel accommodations in the Copper Country. Henry L. Ottenheimer designed the building, and Paul F. P. Mueller and Herman Gundlach built it. The construction of the hotel in pressed light orangish yellow brick ornamented with white-glazed terracotta trimming marked the shift away from the darker sandstone construction. A loggia-embellished primary facade features twin corner towers with cupolas. When the hotel was converted to apartments for older people in 1984, the barroom on the ground floor was left intact.

HO02.3 Houghton National Bank (National Bank of Houghton)

1888–1889, Scott and Company. 1984, rehabilitated. 600 Shelden Ave. (US 41) (northeast corner of Shelden Ave. and Isle Royale St.)

The three-story, red pressed-brick National Bank of Houghton is inspired by the Richardsonian Romanesque in the use of the five prominent round-arch windows and foliated carving in the rusticated red sandstone of the first level and in the doubling of the rhythms of the arches in each of the two arcades above. It reportedly was the first brick commercial building in the Copper Country. The contractors speeded up construction by working into the night under lights. On its completion, the *Portage Lake Mining Gazette* for August 15, 1889, called the building "appropriate in size and construction to its function as a financial institution." It stated that the banking rooms, with "their massive antique oak counter, doors and wood finish, their great floor space and height of ceiling," were superior to any north of Milwaukee and equivalent to many in Chicago. There is, in fact, a definite shadow of Richardson's Marshall Field Store in the building. Unfortunately the interior is no longer intact, and the original windows have been replaced.

HO02.4 Houghton Masonic Temple Building

c. 1905, Charles W. Maass and Fred A. H. Maass. 616–618 Shelden Rd. (US 41) (northwest corner of Shelden Ave. and Portage St.)

The four-story Masonic Temple Building is steel skeleton construction with an exterior skin that combines the textures of coursed rusticated red sandstone with smooth-cut red sandstone pilasters. The pediment of the central entrance is supported by consoles. Its tympanum contains a cartouche with the compass and square, symbolizing the great architect of the universe. Other Masonic imagery appears in the entablature between elaborate brackets that support the dramatically projecting cornice. The Masonic apartments occupy the entire third and fourth floors and are richly ornamented with mahogany and classical detailing. The building was designed by the Maass brothers of Laurium and Houghton and constructed by Herman Gundlach, also of Houghton.

HO03 Saint Ignatius Loyola Church

1889–1902, Erhard Brielmaier. 1928, entrance. 1956, memorial hall and kitchen. 703 East Houghton Ave. (southeast corner of East Houghton Ave. and Portage St.)

This large steepled Catholic church built of solid red Portage Entry sandstone commands

a view of the Portage Canal and Hancock. It has a strong Middle European flavor and is one of the finest works yet identified in the Upper Peninsula of E. Brielmaier and Sons, a Milwaukee firm of noted church architects for German, French, Irish, and Polish parishes. The Reverend Anton Rezek, Jr., led the campaign to build Saint Ignatius Loyola Church. A spired tower rises at the center of the gabled structure's north facade. It contains the belfry with a pointed-arch louvered opening set beneath a pinnacled gable in each face. The tower is positioned between two shorter pyramidal roof towers. The buttressed exterior walls are laid with evenly coursed, rock-faced sandstone that displays some leaching to white commonly found in Jacobsville stone. A corbeled entablature supports the roof. The church has a nave, short transepts, and apse. A plaster ceiling spans the entire church, illuminating the aisles. It is inscribed by a wide system of ribs, made up of liernes and tiercerons, transverse ridge ribs, transverse ribs, modified diagonal ribs, and decorative bosses. Although the rib system is English, the wide open spaces hint at German influence. The triangles between the ribs of the vault over the altar are richly ornamented. A soft yellowish white, pink, rose, and gold coloration adds to the lovely light decoration. The Gothic windows have brilliant stained-glass memorial windows manufactured by the Gavin Art Glass Works of Milwaukee. The grossly inappropriate classical enclosure of the front portico was added around 1928 to adapt the church to the harsh climate.

HO04 College Avenue (US 41)

From the campus of Michigan Technological University on the east, to Franklin Square and Shelden Ave. (US 41) on the west

College Avenue is a residential area of large houses generously set back on spacious lots along a narrow, level brow of land between two slopes. This broad thoroughfare links Houghton and East Houghton, the area once occupied by farms, villas, and mining operations, and, after 1885, by the Michigan School of Mines, now Michigan Technological University. The most prominent early house, but one no longer standing, was that designed in the 1870s by Carl F. Struck of Marquette, for Jay Abel Hubbell (1829–1890), lawyer, judge, and statesman who promoted the establishment of the Michigan Mining School. Remaining homes include splendid variants of the Colonial Revival, constructed mostly in wood for prominent local merchants, lawyers, mining managers, politicians, land speculators, and businessmen. As the twentieth century progressed, the college grew to the east and west, replacing many residences that once graced the avenue. Some of the larger homes were taken over by fraternities. After World War II new buildings replaced some old ones or were built on lots formerly comprising the generous grounds of old homes.

HO04.1 Allen Forsyth and Caroline Willard Reese House

1899–1900, Henry L. Ottenheimer. 918 College Ave. (US 41)

The Reese house is among the most costly, handsome, and substantial houses on College Avenue. The house is sited overlooking Portage Lake Ship Canal and the towns beyond. It was designed in the Colonial Revival style by Henry L. Ottenheimer of Chicago and Houghton and built by H. Ferg. The asymmetrical, two-and-a-half-story wooden house has dormers, fluted Ionic corner pilasters, a two-story polygonal corner tower at the southwest, and a two-story main porch supported by giant fluted Ionic columns. The interior, with its art glass, mahogany, and English oak, equals the stateliness of the exterior. It is arranged with a center hall surrounded by living room, study, and dining room. Allen Forsyth Reese (1858–1944), a descendent of Keweenaw Peninsula pioneers, was a lawyer.

HO05 Michigan Technological University (Michigan School of Mines)

1887 to present. US 41, East Houghton area

Through the efforts of Jay Abel Hubbell of Houghton the school was established in 1885 to train mining engineers, metallurgists, and geologists. Major expansion has occurred since 1965, when Johnson, Johnson and Roy, landscape architects, drew up a modern campus plan and proposed to centralize the campus by using high-rise buildings linked by pedestrian malls. US 41 was rerouted, and the area south of the central campus opened for development. In 1981, on Fairview Street, the Student Development Complex was built on south campus. From the beginning, Herman Gundlach and Company constructed most of the buildings. The most recent addition is the Walker Arts and Humanities Center (1985, Alden B. Dow and Associates), where a portion of an old structure was incorporated into the new building.

HO05.1 ROTC Building (Clubhouse and Gymnasium)

1904–1906, Charlton and Kuenzli, architects. 1416 College Ave. (US 41)

The oldest remaining structure on campus and the fourth building erected is the Clubhouse and Gymnasium. Neo-Tudor in style, it contains a running track suspended from the roof trusses in the western wing. This, together with those other early buildings that comprised the old campus at the completion of the first building campaign in 1908, flanked Hubbell Hall (1887–1889), a Richardsonian Romanesque sandstone building by John Scott and Company of Detroit. Unfortunately, Hubbell Hall was demolished in 1968 and was replaced by the eleven-story Mechanical Building. Overlooking the Portage Canal at East Houghton, the old buildings once lined the 300 block of College Avenue, "a street as beautiful as North Avenue in Cambridge, Mass.," according to the school's Eastern-educated promoters.[71]

HO05.2 Daniell Heights Housing

1960, 1965, Minoru Yamasaki. Woodmar Dr. at Division St. (Division St. intersects US 41 at the east edge of the Michigan Technological University campus)

Daniell Heights Housing, the housing designed by Minoru Yamasaki for married students and built in 1960 and 1965, invokes in its imagery the steeply pitched roofs, the elevated walks known as "Calumet snow walks," and the clustering of company houses found at mining locations. Indeed, when viewed from Hancock and Ripley, the complex resembles these earlier utilitarian clusters. This sensitive regional statement by Yamasaki is in sharp contrast to his more famous towered World Trade Center in New York (1966–1970).

HO06 Houghton-Hancock Bridge

1959; Martin McGrath, chief engineer; George Jacobson, bridge engineer; Al Johnson Construction Company, general contractor; American Bridge Company, superstructure erection. US 41/Michigan 26 over Portage Lake

The twin-towered, vertical lift bridge carries four highway lanes on the upper segment and a railroad track on the lower level across Portage Lake Ship Canal. When fully raised, the lift span provides a clearance of 104 feet for shipping. This bridge serves as a vital link joining the cities of Hancock and Houghton.

HANCOCK

Hancock, named for John Hancock, one of the signers of the Declaration of Independence, was platted on the north shore of Portage Lake in 1858 by Samuel W. Hill, agent of the Quincy Mining Company. This Eastern-based company had opened a mine and office on land on the hill just north of Hancock that it acquired from Columbus Christopher Douglass. Douglass was a geologist who had speculated in mineral lands after assisting Douglass Houghton on the scientific survey of the region in 1844.

Hancock developed after Douglass established a store at the townsite in 1859. By 1865 there were several buildings: a hardware store, an apothecary, banks, churches, saloons, stores, fraternal halls, and boardinghouses. In 1869 a disastrous fire destroyed three-fourths of the settlement. The village was rebuilt with brick and stone structures, wherever possible, as a safeguard against future fires. Hancock incorporated as a village in 1875 and later enacted a fire ordinance. The city grew as a commercial and social center for the neighboring residential enclaves that sprang up at

the Quincy, Pewabic, Franklin, and Hancock mine shafts on the hill. It also served as a waterfront center for copper processing, lumber milling, and shipping. Hancock reached its peak in growth and development with the culmination of productivity at the Quincy Mining Company around 1900.

A strong ethnic identity, especially of the Finnish and Cornish, still characterizes Hancock's population. The first Finns arrived in 1864, after the Quincy Mining Company recruited miners from northern Europe; they were followed by the Cornish and the Italians.

HO07 Hancock City Hall (Hancock Town Hall and Fire Hall)

1898–1899, Charlton, Gilbert and Demar. 399 Quincy St. (US 41), opposite Montezuma Park overlooking the Portage Canal

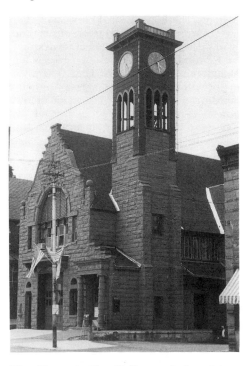

The Hancock City Hall was designed in a vernacular mode that shows the Dutch stepped and Flemish curved gable and was constructed of evenly coursed, rock-faced, clear reddish brown Portage Entry sandstone, in a manner reminiscent of H. H. Richardson. The city hall was built as a stable and ornamental local government building during the years when the local mining industry achieved one of its greatest periods of growth. The two-story, end-gable building has a square clock tower at one side, above which was originally set a tall spire, and a broad-arch front window. It housed the fire department on the first floor and the village offices and council chambers on the second. The solid town hall symbolized the stability, security, and permanence of Hancock in a region of many transitory and impermanent mining towns. The city hall has been restored and rehabilitated under the direction of Francis J. Rutz of Hitch, Incorporated.

HO08 Detroit and Northern Savings and Loan Association Building

1972, Morris Allen of Tarapata, MacMahon, Paulsen Corporation. 400 Quincy St. (US 41) (southwest corner of Quincy St. and Montezuma Park)

Because it restates the spirit of Hancock, this eight-story cylindrical tower and cube, housing the Detroit and Northern's corporate headquarters, blends with its surroundings, despite its large size, but rather delicate scale. Morris Allen borrowed the upright shapes from mine structures and used native copper for the exterior and native wood for the interior. The mirrored glass exterior reflects the buildings and the life of the very city where this institution was founded in 1889. The space inside the tower displays photo-graphic collages of Copper Country lakes, forests, people, and mining by Homer Mitchell, a locally born artist.

HO09 Suomi College (Finnish Lutheran College and Seminary)

1898 to present. Bounded approximately by Quincy (US 41), Scott, Pine, White, and Ryan streets

In 1896 the Suomi Synod of the Finnish Lutheran Church, which had organized in 1890, established this institution to preserve Finnish religion, heritage, and culture, and to minister to the Finnish-American congregations. Juho Kustaa Nikander and the other University of Helsinki-trained theologians who made up the consistory had knowledge of the earlier training of Swedish Americans for church work at Augustana College, Rock Island, Illinois, and at Gustavus Adolphus College, Saint Peter, Minnesota.

After reviewing prospective sites for the college in West Superior, Wisconsin; Saint Paul, Minnesota; and Marquette and Houghton, Michigan, the Suomi College committee selected a site on Quincy Street in Hancock because of the city's large Finnish population. In 1897 the school opened in temporary quarters in Hancock. Three years later, the first building, presently known as Old Main, was completed. Finns in Finnish settlements throughout America, mining companies, and public officials contributed funds for the school.

Suomi expanded and diversified in the twentieth century. In 1904 a seminary was added, and in 1924 the school became a junior college. The seminary was moved to Illinois in 1958, but Suomi remains the only institution of higher education to be established by Finnish Americans in the United States.

Among the interesting buildings on campus are the Vaino and Judith Hoover Center (1895), a Queen Anne house with classical detailing at 525 Quincy Street, and Nikander Hall (1939), a classroom building designed by Eero Saarinen and Robert Swanson.

HO09.1 **Old Main**

1898–1899, C. Archibald Pearce. Quincy St. (US 41) at Dakota St.

This rugged and somewhat crudely Richardsonian building, with its rock-faced reddish brown Portage Entry sandstone walls, is reminiscent of a medieval castle. In its brooding boldness, robustness, and fortresslike appearance, it conveys an appropriate sense of great strength and tenacity. Altogether, it symbolizes the unity of the Suomi Synod, the endurance of Finnish people against displacement by Czarist Russia, and the validity of Finnish culture, tradition, and values in the midst of the American melting pot. The building once housed the president and provided a dining room, classrooms, and assembly rooms. Today it is a women's dormitory.

HO09.2 **Nikander Hall**

1939, Eero Saarinen and Robert Swanson

This modern brick classroom building with steel casement windows seems to climb up the hill north of Old Main.

HO09.3 **Finlandia Hall**

1984, Morris Allen of TMP Associates, Inc. Summit St.

This four-story red brick dormitory, housing 184 students, study and recreation areas, and snack bar, brings Postmodernism to Upper Michigan. The division of the rectangular structure into four staggered sections lends to the structure a domestic character similar to the miner's vernacular houses that surround it. Moreover, the clearly defined entry, paucity of windows, southerly orientation, and steep-pitched roof suit it to its northern climate.

HO10 **East Hancock**

1890–1920. Bounded approximately by Front St., Dunstan St., Mason Ave., and Vivian St.

After the Dakota Heights Land Company filled in the ravines that scarred the site, East Hancock was subdivided into residential lots. Agents of the Quincy Mining Company, local merchants, and professionals built some eighty houses in varied turn-of-the-century designs. The quiet, tree-lined succession of sloping streets, sandstone and cobblestone retaining walls, and elegant houses overlook Portage Lake and Houghton to the west and link Hancock with the Quincy Mine to the east. A public stone staircase built as a WPA project descends from Cooper Avenue to Front Street.

HO10.1 **Andrew Kauth House**

1902–1907. 318 Cooper Ave.

Representative of the more elegant houses is the two-story Colonial Revival Andrew Kauth House, with its giant Doric-columned portico and continuous second-story balcony that extends the full width of the building. Coupled columns flank an inner pair that enframes the central entry with fanlight. It was built for a German-American businessman and saloonkeeper.

HO10.2 **Temple Jacob**

1912, Henry L. Ottenheimer. Front St. (Michigan 26/US 41), just east of Houghton-Hancock Lift Bridge

Temple Jacob, originally Orthodox, but by 1913 a Conservative congregation, serves a small Jewish population in this charming but eccentric building sited below the residential area but atop a sloping site, on the major highway into Hancock-Houghton from the northeast. A low-pitched raking cornice and zipper brickwork adorn the entrance of this copper-domed building. Above the basement social hall-classroom is a sanctuary; the latter has a balcony, originally the women's gallery, now little used. There is a Georgian ark crowned by lions supporting the tablets of the law. Behind the balcony is a tripartite stained-glass window whose pale hues are repeated in the memorial windows around the room. Archie Verville was the builder.

QUINCY AND
FRANKLIN TOWNSHIPS

HO11 **Quincy Mining Company Location**

1846–1931. 1937–1945. Quincy Hill (both sides of US 41/Michigan 26, 1.5 miles northeast of the center of Hancock

Known as "Old Reliable" for the long series of dividend payments to stockholders, the Quincy Mining Company began when investors from Detroit and Marshall, Michigan, established the company in 1846; they incorporated and purchased land here in 1848. Shortly before, in 1845, the Pittsburgh and Boston Mining Company opened the Cliff Mine at the northern tip of fissure veins in the Copper Range, where pure native copper appeared in large masses; in 1847 the Minnesota Mining Company opened a mine at the southwestern tip, near Rockland. The Quincy Mining Company explored the land for copper and, at the same time, reorganized because of the need for capital and management. It moved its offices first to Philadelphia, and then in 1858 to New York, since its primary investors resided there and in Boston. In 1854 Columbus Christopher Douglass discovered the first extensive vein of amygdaloid copper, or the "Quincy Lode," and in 1855 he sank two shafts. In the 1860s the "Quincy" ranked first nationally in copper production, and 3,000 people lived and worked on the hill at the Quincy, Pewabic, and Franklin mine locations. But eventually, the production of the Calumet and Hecla Mining Company superseded the Quincy's production.

The Quincy Mining Company succeeded and grew because it took advantage of technological advances, acquired land to permit the tapping of the Pewabic Lode, and in general because of good management and well-trained workers. By 1905 the Quincy employed 1,850 people in Michigan. On the hill, the company built a machine shop, a roundhouse, a boilerhouse, a blacksmith shop, a warehouse, dry houses, carpenter shops, kiln houses, shaft and rock sorting houses, powder magazines, and other surface structures. For its workers it built\boardinghouses, single-family dwellings, tenement houses, a hospital, and bathhouses. Workers lived in residential enclaves, which were clustered at shafts, known as locations, called Limerick, Swedetown, Frenchtown, and Hardscrabble. The mines were connected by railroad to a stamp mill at Torch Lake and by tramway to a smelter at Ripley.

The Michigan copper strike of 1913–1914 weakened both the labor force and the company. World War I brought a temporary demand for copper, but the depletion of ore, the opening of mines in the West, and the drop in copper prices during the depression brought a gradual end to copper mining. Mining operations ceased in 1957, although the reclamation plant produced copper until 1967. The Quincy Mining Company is a National Historic Landmark.

HO11.1 **Mine Agent or Superintendent's House**

1880–1881. West side of US 41

After losing its mine agent to the Calumet and Hecla Mining Company, the Quincy Mining Company, in an act of paternalism, built this house for its chief administrative officer in Michigan, to make living conditions in this godforsaken wilderness as comfortable as possible. Samuel B. Harris, an experienced Cornish-born miner and manager who had worked in the Wisconsin lead-mining district before coming to the Copper Country, lived in the house while he was the mine agent from 1884 to 1902; but Charles Lawton, who was agent from 1905 to 1946, occupied it longest. The two-and-a-half-story, side-gable, clapboard structure has a three-story central tower, a one-story front porch, and a two-story rear wing. The massing and detailing are Italianate. It has paired round and segmental-arch windows and double brackets supporting the eaves.

HO11.2 **Community Action Agency** (General Office)

1895–1897, Robert C. Walsh. West side of US 41

The General Office is a curious building, conceived as a simple colonial domestic block with a hipped roof and pedimented pavilion. In keeping with this conception, the porch is supported by a classical order. The construction, however, is heavy rock-faced masonry, from the basement through the tall chimneys, and the windows on the first floor are topped by bold Richardsonian arches. In the end, it is the late nineteenth-century tone that prevails. It was designed by Robert C. Walsh, an

HO11.2 Community Action Agency (General Office)

architect from Morristown, New Jersey, where the Quincy's home office was located. The fact that Walsh may never have seen the site or the native sandstone with which the office was constructed may account for some of the contradictions in the building, although the rough texture and large arches must have been specified by him. Local people equated the fine Portage Entry red sandstone office with the abilities of the clerical officers of "the world's richest mine."

HO11.3 **Mine Shaft Number Two** (Headframe)

1907–1908. East side of US 41

The headframe is a steel-framed structure covered with corrugated sheet metal that rises some 148 feet from the ground over the number two shaft, which eventually reached 9,000 inclined feet into the earth. The configuration of the roof, which is pitched in two distinct segments, reveals the accommodation to the inclined shaft that brought the cars up. The base of the erect portion of the headframe contains a round, riveted steel storage bin into which the skips dumped copper ore, and in turn, from which the ore was loaded into railroad cars that were pulled underneath the bin. The two skeletal steel stanchions supported the steel cables leading from the hoist house. The shaft served as "mission control" for the mining operation, carrying men, supplies, and ore in and out of the mine.

HO11.4 **Mine Shaft Number Two Hoist House**

1919–1920. East side of US 41

HO11.3 Mine Shaft Number Two (Headframe); and HO11.4 Mine Shaft Number Two Hoist House

HO11.4 Mineshaft Number Two Hoisthouse (interior)

The hoist house is a reinforced concrete fireproof building with twenty load-bearing columns and a gabled roof. The red brick exterior veneer is broken with huge arched windows. The structure housed the mammoth Nordberg hoist, which was employed to reach the extreme inclined depth to which the number two shaft penetrated the rich Pewabic lode. Measuring 60 by 54 by 60 feet, it is the largest steam-powered mine hoist ever manufactured; it could lift a 10-ton load of copper from a depth of 6,000 feet at the rate of 3,200 feet per minute. The attention paid to the architectural character of this purely utilitarian building says something about the aesthetic awareness, as well as the technical aggressiveness of the company.

RIPLEY

HO12 Ripley Smelter, Quincy Mining Company

1898, 1904, James Cooper. Royce Rd. off Michigan 26

Coursed cut reddish brown sandstone furnace buildings, one with a frame addition (1904), a sandstone mineral warehouse, gable-roofed frame warehouses, smaller warehouses, and miscellaneous shop buildings survive as part of the smelter complex. Here, until 1969, furnaces smelted copper ore and produced refined copper ingots, cakes, wire bars, anodes, and other products. Copper ore was shipped from mines and also from a reclamation plant at Mason, four miles to the east, which processed ore that had been reclaimed by dredge from stamp sands deposited in Torch Lake. Refined copper was loaded onto ships from a wharf at the smelter.

CALUMET

HO13 Calumet and Hecla Mine Location

1860s. 1880–1939. Along Red Jacket Rd. between Sixth St., Calumet Ave. (US 41/Michigan 26), and the Armory

Under the direction of Alexander Agassiz (1835–1910), Swiss-born, Harvard-educated scientist and son of the world-famous geologist, Louis Agassiz, the Calumet and the Hecla mining companies merged in 1871 into the Calumet and Hecla Mining Company. The original companies had organized in 1864 and in 1866, respectively, to work one of the richest copper deposits in the world. Using the financial backing of Quincy Adams Shaw and other Boston investors, along with his own managerial skills and technical knowledge, Agassiz made C&H the dominant mining company in the Copper Range. In the 1870s it mined 50 percent of the nation's

HO13 Calumet and Hecla Mine Location

copper. Calumet became the most civilized community in the Copper Country.

A roundhouse, warehouses, a machine shop, a blacksmith shop, a gear house, pattern shops, and other surface structures now stand idle along either side of a line of mine shafts that once straddled the Hecla and Torch Lake Railroad. They represent the company's period of greatest growth between 1880 and 1910. Most were designed by Erasmus Darwin Leavitt, Jr., a machinery designer, together with other company engineers, and were built of mine waste rock, brick, and red Lake Superior sandstone rubble.

Hoping to stabilize the work force as a group of family men and to improve employee efficiency, health, and morality, C&H provided the largest and most extensive programs for workers of all the companies in the Copper Country. By 1914 the company had invested nearly $1 million in 1,200 houses for miners and their families, built an armory and 10 schools (including Calumet High and Manual Training School on Calumet Avenue), donated land for a YMCA, constructed and equipped a hospital and a 35,000-volume library, built a $50,000 bathhouse for residents, and subsidized 30 local church groups.

At the locations and villages that grew up around C&H mine shafts—Blue Jacket, Yellow Jacket, Raymbaultown, Tamarack, and others—the company built rental houses for its employees. Most common were the single- and double-family houses built between 1870 and 1910. They are end-gable, two-and-a-half-story clapboarded or shingled houses on raised mine waste rock foundations. They were sold in the 1930s and 1940s to private individuals, who adapted them for continued use. In the winter, occupants connect the entries to the street by systems of planks on sawhorses known as "Calumet snow walks." The social and economic differentiation of Calumet residents is best seen by comparing the simple miners' houses near Saint Mary's Italian Church on Portland Street between Ninth and Tenth streets with the more elaborate dwellings of merchants and professionals along Eighth Street, and with those of supervisory personnel along Calumet Avenue. Calumet is a National Historic Landmark.

HO13.1 **Calumet Clinic** (General Office Building of the Calumet and Hecla Mining Company)

early 1890s, Shaw and Hunnewell. 100 Red Jacket Rd. Northwest corner Red Jacket Rd. and Calumet Ave. (US 41/Michigan 26)

HO13.2 **Lake Superior Land Company Office** (Library)

1898, George Russell Shaw and Henry S. Hunnewell. 101 Red Jacket Rd. (southeast corner of Red Jacket Rd. and Mine St.)

The general office building and library are opposite each other on Red Jacket Road. Both were designed by the noted Boston firm of Shaw (George Russell Shaw was related to Quincy Adams Shaw) and Hunnewell. They were conceived in broad Italianate terms, with

traces of the Queen Anne and Richardson in the library, and are built of carefully selected dark- and light-colored mine waste rock with red brick and red sandstone trim laid by Italian stonemasons. The Queen Anne is especially notable in the patterned chimney stack and end gable of the library. The basement contained 21 bathrooms for miners and their families; the first floor held a vestibule, book delivery room, catalog room, librarian's room, and stacks; the second floor contained a children's reading room, an adult reading room, and a hall or smoking room; and the attic held a meeting gallery. Erected, furnished, and equipped with thousands of books shipped from Boston by the Calumet and Hecla Mining Company, the library served the employees of the company and residents of the Calumet Township school district. Thus, with the reading room upstairs and baths downstairs, Alexander Agassiz took care of both mind and body.

HO14 **Fifth and Sixth Streets**

Fifth and Sixth streets between Scott and Pine streets

Settled in the 1860s and incorporated in 1875, the village of Red Jacket, later named Calumet, grew up on the northwest edge of the Calumet and Hecla mine location. The Calumet and Hecla Mining Company did not permit businesses on its property and had no company store, so stores and saloons were built beyond company boundaries, together with social halls and government buildings. From its business district along Fifth and Sixth streets, Red Jacket, with a population of 3,078 at the turn of the century, served a larger mining community of 40,000.

The fifty some commercial structures on Fifth and Sixth streets reflect Red Jacket's commercial development during the boom years, as frame houses and stores were followed by sandstone and brick business blocks. These rectangular-shaped structures with plain side walls define the streetscape, presenting from time to time imposing three-story facades of wood, sandstone, brick, and metal. Most are embellished with stock elements, sometimes in lavish combinations with terracotta trimming, metal cornices, turrets, bays, cast-iron thresholds, and columns.

Buildings for commercial and governmental use were built for the immigrants who either arrived with trade skills or who had worked in the mines and accumulated enough wealth to start their own businesses. These buildings were after plans by itinerant and local architects.

Calumet has been called "an ethnic conglomerate," and this district demonstrates distinct ethnicity. One block away, on Seventh Street between Elm and Pine streets, once stood the Italian Hall, where, on Christmas Eve of 1913, the year of the copper strike, 72 women and children were crushed to death because of a false fire alarm. The event is memorialized in Woody Guthrie's song, "1913 Massacre" (1972).

HO14.1 **Bernard Shute's Bar** (Marco Curto's Saloon)

1893. 1900, additions and improvements. 322 Sixth Street

Shute's Bar is a two-story red brick structure, with a barroom on the first floor, a basement that once held a gambling room, and living quarters on the second floor. Decorative galvanized metal cornices project between the two stories and at the roofline. This and other saloons in Red Jacket served as important social centers for immigrant groups. The barroom retains the original fittings of the 1900 improvements, including the highly varnished oak cabinets and counter with marble bases, beveled glass doors, and a multicolored glass canopy centered over a wide wall mirror. Italian-born Marco Curto established his saloon in 1893, after working for the C&H.

HO14.2 **Edward Ryan Block**

1898, Charles K. Shand. 305–307 Sixth Street

Commissioned by Edward J. Ryan (1842–1900), an Irish-American known as "the merchant prince of the Copper Country," the three-story, Richardsonian Edward Ryan Block is solidly and substantially built of top-grade, red Portage Entry sandstone. It has a galvanized metal cornice and projecting bay with pedimented false front, the latter ornamented with short fluted pilasters and a decorative pediment. Two large stores occupy the first floor, and flats, the upper floors.

HO14.3 **Calumet Village Hall and Calumet Theater** (Red Jacket Town Hall and Opera House)

1885, J. B. Sweatt. 1899–1900, addition and alterations, Charles K. Shand. 340 Sixth St. (southeast corner of Sixth and Elm streets)

In 1898 the common council of the village of Red Jacket launched a campaign to build a new opera house under the guise of building and improving its public buildings. To accomplish this, the fire department was moved from the village hall across Sixth Street to a new structure designed in a vernacular interpretation of the ubiquitous Richardsonian style. Then the council commissioned Charles K. Shand to draft plans to enlarge the village hall with the addition of a 1,200-seat opera house, to convert the former fire department quarters into a kitchen and dining room, and to enlarge the council rooms and village offices.

The light yellowish brown brick town hall and opera house, in what Shand termed the Italian Renaissance style of architecture, rests on a first story of Portage Entry sandstone. The use of triple and paired round-headed openings, blind arcades, and a balustrade suggest Renaissance features. The whole is covered with a copper roof and trimmed with copper cornices. A square clock tower at the northwest corner of the opera house structure originally rose to a square open bell tower, which in turn was surmounted by an octagonal cupola. Proud that "Copper Country products formed a conspicuous part of the building," the *Copper Country Evening News* for October 2, 1899, called the town hall and opera house "the finest north of the Straits of Mackinac." The materials, style, substance, and use of this public building for cultural purposes affirmed Red Jacket's importance in the Upper Peninsula.

A visual high point of the auditorium is a horseshoe-shaped proscenium arch, ornamented above the curve of the arch with plaster relief and murals of the fine arts. Although the Calumet Theater was initially a legitimate theater and burlesque house, it has also served as a motion-picture theater. In the mid-1970s the theater was fully restored and has recently returned to its original use for the performance of legitimate theater.

HO14.4 Red Jacket Fire Station

1898, Charles K. Shand. Just south of the southwest corner of Sixth and Elm streets

The two-story Red Jacket Fire Station has a low, open campanile with a pyramidal roof at the southeast corner, balanced by projecting pedimented parapets at the opposite corner. A prominent arcade at the first level, marked by three large arched openings for the firehouse doors and by flanking smaller entry arches at the corner, dominates the facade. A stepped-gable parapet directly above the middle arched opening attempts to give the work a degree of formality. Evenly colored, reddish brown, top-grade, rock-faced sandstone on the south and east walls and variegated reddish brown and white rubble on the north and west walls add a distinct regional character. Firemen's quarters were on the second level, and the firefighting equipment was housed on the first. The designer, Shand, was an itinerate architect who worked only briefly in the Copper Country.

HO15 Sainte Anne Roman Catholic Church

1899–1901, Charlton, Gilbert and Demar. Southwest corner of Scott and Fifth streets

Built of Portage Entry red sandstone in an early twentieth-century version of the Gothic for a French-Canadian parish, Sainte Anne firmly and visibly separates the residential, civic, and business from the industrial areas of the community. Wall buttresses between the windows are applied to the long side walls of the rectangular church. A triple entrance on a north porch gives access to three small vestibules and to the 400-seat nave. An attached corner tower rises in three stages to an open belfry surmounted by an octagonal spire. Calumet was known as the "city of churches" because nearly each ethnic group

built its own church. Another is the Slovenians' Saint Paul the Apostle Church (Saint Joseph's Austrian Church) of 1902–1904, the double-spired, Richardsonian red sandstone extravaganza at 301 Eighth Street (northwest corner of Eighth and Oak streets) by Erhard Brielmaier and Sons of Milwaukee, which rises authoritatively over the village like a cathedral of medieval Europe.

LAURIUM

Laurium was a residential community for managers of the Calumet and Hecla Mining Company and bankers, professional people, and merchants in Calumet. It has many large late nineteenth- and early twentieth-century houses.

HO16 Paul P. Roehm House

1895–1896, Paul P. Roehm, builder. 101 Willow Ave. (southwest corner of Willow Ave. and First St.)

The region's preeminent stonemason and supplier erected this house for himself. The rock-faced, Portage Entry red sandstone dwelling achieves a vernacular character from its simplification of Richardsonian forms. The unpretentious tower, capped by a sloping conical roof that rises out of the massive picturesque composition, is a case in point. The heaviness also derives, in part, from the stone building material, from the muscular random masonry walls, and from the roughly hewn and tapered stone piers of the porch. The house is thoughtfully adapted to the climate. The entry hall, dining room, drawing room, and library pivot around a central chimney, with fireplaces placed on a diagonal in the core of the building, in a manner not unlike seventeenth-century British Colonial works in New England or even such as the early Frank Lloyd Wright work, the Winslow house (1893). Ample fireplaces provide warmth; sliding doors permit the closing of rooms to contain heat and reduce drafts. South-facing windows in the tower admit light into a reading alcove of the library, and the early morning sunlight enters a sun room at the rear; beyond is a sitting room and kitchen.

HO17 Johnson and Anna Lichty Vivian, Jr., House

1898, Demetrius Frederick Charlton. Northeast corner of Pewabic and Third streets

This large Shingle style house combines Portage Entry red sandstone at the first level with shingles at the upper level. The house was built for a local merchant, banker, and industrialist and was among the finest and most modern in the county when completed. A rounded Ionic porch projects from the rectangular structure, and a conical-roofed open porch is set on top of a rounded full-height bay. The use of shingles to sheathe the structure and the picturesque massing of rectilinear, triangular, and curved shapes recalls that trend in American architecture during the last quarter of the nineteenth century that prompted Vincent Scully's use of the term "Shingle style" to describe one phase of suburban architecture in the northeastern United States.

HO18 Jukuri's Sauna

1950. 600 Lake Linden Ave. (Michigan 26) (northeast corner Lake Linden Ave. and Iroquois St.)

This sauna was built in 1950 by Emil Jukuri, operator of a nearby gas station, to provide a public sauna for the large Finnish population of Laurium and Calumet. The concrete block building is faced with orange brick and glass blocks. The knotty pine paneled interior contains twelve sauna units, each made up of a sauna, shower, and changing room.

LAKE LINDEN

Situated at the head of Torch Lake, Lake Linden developed around the lumber mills and the Calumet and Hecla Mining Company's stamping mills and reclamation plant. The stamping mills opened in 1866 to crush and leach out copper ore, and the reclamation plant was built in 1913 to recover copper from sand or tailings accumulated from the earlier stamping mills.

HO19 Lake Linden Village Hall and Fire Station

1901–1902, Charles K. Shand. 401 Calumet St. (Michigan 26)

The Lake Linden Village Hall and Fire Station is a timid but prominent public building with Richardsonian overtones. It is two and a half stories high and built of light yellowish brown brick trimmed with red sandstone. The round-arch central entrance is within a square tower that rises to a smaller square portion topped by an octagonal cupola. The three-stage tower is flanked by parapeted, pedimented pavilions, each containing arcaded windows beneath an oculus. The first floor holds offices, the second, the council chambers and a ballroom.

HO20 Dad's Home

1939. Northwest corner of Front and Fourth streets

Inspired by the habit of retired lumberjacks and miners to congregate in the back of a grocery store or on the street corners, Joseph L. Brand, Houghton County official, built this social center. The rustic log structure measures 18 by 24 feet in plan and has a large gabled porch across the front and a large stone fireplace inside. The building was equipped with log card tables, lounging benches and chairs, and a radio, running water, newspapers, magazines, and other furnishings of a club. It cost only $3,500 and was paid for with federal funds.

HO21 Saint Joseph Church (Eglise Saint Joseph)

1900, C. Archibald Pearce. 1912, addition, Demetrius Frederick Charlton. A. F. Wasielewski? 701 Calumet St. (Michigan 26)

French-Canadian Catholics built the "Roman Byzantine" Eglise Saint Joseph of alternating courses of rough and smooth-cut Portage Entry red sandstone blocks.[72] Its gabled front (east) facade incorporated a columned porch and twin steeples. Twelve years after it was completed, they moved the main entry from the east facade to Calumet Street. The rich and ornate barrel-vaulted basilica has a nave with side aisles. An organ loft is over the narthex. There are two altars, one on top of the other. The stained-glass windows recall the French-Canadian origins of the church's members. They are memorials to the Prince-Barbeau families and to Patrice Grégoire, Edouard Gerten, Léo Demars, Philibert Lebeau, and L'Union des Sociétés Canadiennes Françaises et des Dames Auxiliaires and others. This church is the most intact example of the large churches remaining in the Copper Country.

HO22 First Congregational Church of Lake Linden

1886–1887, Holabird and Roche. Southeast corner of First and Tunnel streets

The First Congregational Church is a white pine balloon frame structure with Gothic windows and hints of Queen Anne in the deco-

ration. With its asymmetrical tower it stands on a raised mine rock foundation and is sheathed with richly textured shingles and cut-wood patterns in herringbone, squares, pinwheels, and rosettes. From each of two entrances within the front porch, stairs lead up to the auditorium. The pews are arranged in a semicircle around the pulpit and a pipe organ manufactured by G. House of Buffalo, New York. The wainscoting and ceiling are finished in panels of "beaded ceiling" and furnish a warm background for the windows colored in pastels. The basement contains a kitchen and large meeting rooms that can be divided or combined by means of sliding doors. A largely Scottish congregation of copper milling officials and local businessmen were responsible for the building of this church. They called upon the noted Chicago firm of Holabird and Roche to design it. The church is representative of Upper Peninsula buildings designed by architects working in Eastern and Midwestern cities and demonstrates their availability to some of those living here, perhaps due to business connections. Emery and McCurdy constructed the church at a cost of $8,325.

JACOBSVILLE, TORCH LAKE TOWNSHIP

Jacobsville owes its existence to the red sandstone bluff north of the Portage River on Keweenaw Bay. Its quarry industry flourished from 1883 to 1918, involved a dozen companies, and employed scores of immigrant laborers.

HO23 Jacobsville Finnish Evangelical Lutheran Church

1886, Leander Sinko. Not visible from the road (from Lake Linden south on Boatjack Rd. to Dreamland then east on Rabbit Bay Rd. to Jacobsville)

Isolated among pines and underbrush, the lovely, little, white-painted wooden church with a delicate open belfry is a pristine reminder of the Keweenaw's boom years. Leander Sinko, a skilled Finnish-American craftsman, who was noted locally for his ability to make houses, sailboats, skis, and hockey sticks, built it. His Finnish ancestry is clearly evident in the setback form of the tower. The congregation joined the Suomi Synod of the Finnish Lutheran Church soon after it was established in 1889. The church seats approximately 100. It served the Finnish population of Jacobsville for ninety years, as the economy changed from quarrying to strawberry growing and fishing. In 1952 its small congregation deeded the building to the Gloria Dei Church, the Finnish Evangelical Lutheran congregation at Hancock. The church holds Sunday evening vespers in the summer and stands as a sturdy reminder of the hearty souls who lived, worked, and worshiped at this northern outpost.

PAINESDALE, ADAMS TOWNSHIP

HO24 Painesdale

1899–1967. On Michigan 26, 7 miles southwest of Houghton

Painesdale is an early twentieth-century mining community, which was planned, financed, and managed by East Coast developers and inhabited by immigrant miners and their families. Painesdale is named after William A. Paine of Boston, founder of the Paine, Webber and Company brokerage firm, who was a chief investor in the Copper Range Company and its president for thirty years. The Copper Range Company promoted and developed a section of the mineral range southwest of Portage Lake that contains the Atlantic, Baltic, and Isle Royale lodes. The Champion Copper Mine located near Painesdale was an important producer from 1899 to 1916, and, under the direction of its parent corporation, the Copper Range Company, it continued to produce intermittently until 1967. Rows of stock-designed miners' houses with sharp gable roofs and shingled or clapboarded siding form a community image of efficiency and homogeneity in Painesdale, even today. Noticeable remodelings have failed to obscure the strong sense of architectural line, scale, and arrangement of form that remains Painesdale's distinction as a single-industry company town. Moreover, they represent the changing heritage of a community whose legacy of copper mining dependence, though not forgotten, has faded into the past.

Originally, the Champion Copper Company's holdings consisted of approximately forty buildings and structures, including four shaft houses and four hoist houses, a railroad depot, an office, and several boiler houses. A half-dozen major buildings, a scattering of small sheds, and a number of ruins remain today adjacent to mountainous piles of discarded mine rock. They include handsome mine rock and sandstone masonry buildings like the E Shaft hoist house and the nearby machine shop, both rectangular buildings with gabled roofs and cut coursed sandstone walls (1902). The Copper Range Company offices were located in a large, two-and-a-half-story symmetrical structure clad with clapboarding and topped with a steep hipped and dormered roof (1902). Located at the southeast corner of Hubbard Avenue and Third Street, it is positioned between the officials' houses and the mine. The E Shaft house, a functionally designed, steel headframe covering the shaft itself, stands southeast of the office (1906–1908).

North and west of the mine are located four residential enclaves of worker housing, known as locations, and a separate district containing officials' houses. B Location, C Location, E Location, and E Addition, or Seeberville, developed from north to south alongside operations following the course of the Champion copper lode. Rows of vernacular worker housing display elements borrowed from early nineteenth-century New England mill villages. Most frequently the houses were patterned after a shingled saltbox double house with six-over-six sash windows. An example is the B Location double house with paired front entrances sheltered by a nearly full-width porch at 198–200 Evergreen Street. Alternately, they were patterned after a narrow, gable-roofed single-family dwelling clad in either shingles or clapboards such as the C Location house at 162 Iroquois Street. This end-gable dwelling rests on a mine rock foundation, an asymmetrical gabled porch supported with turned posts, is covered with a shingled roof. Some of these houses were updated with leaded-glass windows and modest turned accents such as spindlework on the porches, but these details have disappeared where later remodeling has occurred. The houses in these locations were built, several at a time, between 1904 and 1917.

Mining engineers' and other officials' houses represent more cultivated architectural styles and include motifs from bungalows and from Colonial Revivals. These houses are symmetrical, boxy wooden buildings with gabled roofs and classical details. They stand in a less uniform pattern on spacious lots rather in tight rows. One example is the Goodell house (1904, 32 Hubbard Avenue). Built as a residence, it was later purchased by Copper Range and converted to a company clubhouse. The two-story, shingled bungalow has a front shed dormer and an original double-columned back porch. Another is the Hubbard house (1903, Alexander C. Eschweiler [1865–1940] of Milwaukee, 31 Hubbard Avenue). Built by the Copper Range Company for general manager Lucius L. Hubbard, this large Craftsman-influenced gabled house is the most elaborate house in Painesdale. Bracketed gables accentuate a symmetrical facade and the main entrance, framed by a shed-roofed porch with pediment and brackets. The shingled and clapboarded house rests on a raised cut red sandstone foundation.

East of C Location, the Copper Range Company landscaped a public square and around it built the Sarah Paine Public Library, the Albert Paine Methodist Church, and the Jeffers High School. The library (1902–1903, Alexander C. Eschweiler) and an elementary school no longer stand, but the towered Neo-Gothic church (1907) clad in shingles and clapboards still marks the northwest corner of the green. The huge red sandstone high school (1909–1910, 1935, Alexander C. Eschweiler, Goodell Avenue) is the most elaborate structure in Painesdale. Its rock-faced stone walls, coursed evenly on the raised basement and randomly above, are articulated with smooth-cut window surrounds and quoins. The buttressed projecting entrance pavilion has a richly carved Tudor arch. Other important public buildings, such as the Finnish Athletic Hall, no longer stand. However, the village green atmosphere still exists, and a number of small churches continue to represent the ethnic diversity of Painesdale.

REDRIDGE, STANTON TOWNSHIP

HO25 Redridge Dam

1900–1901; J. F. Jackson, engineer; F. Foster Cromwell, hydraulic engineer. Off S-554, less than .25 mile south of the center of the village of Redridge, about 10 miles west of Houghton.

When the Baltic Mining Company built a stamp mill on Lake Superior, just west of the Salmon Trout River, a log dam, built by the Atlantic Mining Company across the river in 1894, proved inadequate. So the two mining companies decided to build jointly a new dam and to share the larger water supply. Because there was no suitable building stone available in the vicinity, they chose to construct a steel gravity dam. This structure was only the second dam of that design in the United States and the first of significant size. Crews began construction on the new Redridge Dam in May 1900 and completed it in November 1901. The designer was J. F. Jackson, engineer for the Wisconsin Bridge and Iron Company, with F. Foster Cromwell, a hydraulic engineer from New York, serving as the consulting engineer. The entire project cost $150,000, with the foundations accounting for $90,000 of the total. Overall, the Redridge Dam is 1,006 feet long, consisting of a center steel-and-concrete section 464 feet long and two earth embankment wings with concrete core walls. This remarkable structure created a reservoir of 600 million gallons, ample storage for the two mills, which used an average of 25.5 million gallons daily. The Redridge Dam is one of only three steel dams erected in the United States between 1895 and 1910. It is the largest of the two surviving structures and exemplifies a type of dam construction briefly considered as an alternative to more traditional methods.[73]

Keweenaw County (KW)

EAGLE RIVER

Located where the Eagle River flows into Lake Superior, the village of Eagle River was founded in 1843 and platted by the Phoenix Mining Company in 1855. In the 1840s and 1850s, as eastern speculators explored the rich copper deposits in the rugged cliff to the west, this port community served as a shipping and distribution point for the early copper industry. During this period, too, eighteen mines opened nearby. Eagle River is the seat of county government and became a resort center in the twentieth century, when the automobile brought tourists to the peninsula.

Along the northeast bank of the river, on

East Main Street between Third and Second streets, stands a row of hotels, boarding-houses, warehouses, stores, saloons, and houses whose vernacular Greek Revival origins lie concealed under later nineteenth-century additions and twentieth-century sidings.

KW01 Keweenaw County Courthouse and Sheriff's Residence and Jail

1866; courthouse; 1886, sheriff's residence and jail; J. B. Sweatt, Hampson Gregory? 1925, courthouse remodeled. Bounded by Fourth, East Main, Third, and Pine streets

Like a meetinghouse on a New England public square, and enclosed by a 3-foot-high public wall on the east and south sides, stands the Keweenaw County Courthouse and Sheriff's Residence and Jail. It was designed and built originally as a simple frontier building by J. B. Sweatt of Marquette, but transformed in 1925 into its present stark white classical appearance. The courthouse for this sparsely populated remote county is remarkable in its formality and its classically inspired motifs. These include the giant Doric columns with fillets and bases, a pediment forming a projecting portico, a modillioned cornice, and pedimented side dormers. The sheriff's residence and jail is similarly treated in its vernacular interpretation of the classical vocabulary.

EAGLE RIVER VICINITY, ALLOUEZ TOWNSHIP

KW02 Sand Hills Lighthouse

1917–1919. Off Five Mile Point Rd. at Five Mile Point, 3.5 miles southwest of Eagle River. Visible from the water

The Sand Hills Lighthouse and fog signal warned sailors of the shoals off Eagle River. The light yellowish brown brick lighthouse is arranged in a U-shape, with the square light tower in the middle section of the U. Its large size and formality are surprising. Since, at the time of construction, the road from Ahmeek had not yet been opened, and materials had to be brought in by barge, the structure cost $100,000 to build. The light was tended for twenty years, until automated in 1939.

EAGLE HARBOR

First, in the second half of the nineteenth century, Eagle Harbor was a mining port, and later, in the twentieth century, a resort community. A light, built in 1871, marks the south rolling rocky shore of the beautiful harbor.

KW03 Holy Redeemer Church

1854. Northwest corner of South and Fourth streets

Holy Redeemer Church is a small, vernacular Gothic pine frontier church, with tower, steeple, and wrought iron cross. It was built by Reverend Henry L. Thiele, the first priest ordained by Bishop Frederic Baraga in the Catholic dioceses of Marquette and Sault Sainte Marie. Thiele was dispatched to Eagle Harbor to minister to the residents of nearby mining locations on the Keweenaw Peninsula. Unfortunately, aluminum siding has been applied to the exterior walls of the church. The pulpit is unusual in that is placed atop the confessional, which uses the Gothic lancet window motif.

KW04 Eagle Harbor Lighthouse

1871. 1895, fog signal. On east side of promontory at west entrance to Eagle Harbor

Eagle Harbor Lighthouse is a brick gabled-roof keeper's dwelling and octagonal light tower that held a Fourth Order Fresnel lens

KW04 Eagle Harbor Lighthouse

made by Sautter of Paris. It replaced a light built here in 1851. A fog signal was added in 1895.

KW05 **Lake Breeze Hotel**

1880s. 1920s. Off Lighthouse Rd., just south of Eagle Harbor Light

Originally a warehouse for storing supplies for mining companies, this one-and-a-half-story shingled structure with a wrap-around porch now serves as a resort hotel. It overlooks a well-protected harbor on Lake Superior. Eagle Harbor served as an excellent port until the 1880s, when the opening of the Keweenaw waterway offered better shipping facilities. In 1923, Alice Mitchell, daughter of William Pettit Royal (1826–1911), the original owner of the warehouse, opened a tea room and ushered in the resort function of the building. She was aided by the growing automobile travel.

CENTRAL, HOUGHTON TOWNSHIP

KW06 **Central**

1856–1898. Off US 41, 3.75 miles north of Phoenix

From 1856 to 1898 the Central Mining Company extracted and stamped copper taken from the rich vein of pure copper running through the midsection of Keweenaw Point, and it built here a town for the Cornish miners it employed. Indicative of the town that came to be known as Central are orderly rows of over a dozen extant dwellings; the John F. Roberts House (c. 1875); the Central Methodist Church (1869), a simple wooden church

with a vernacular castellated entry tower; and foundations and ruins, rock piles, orchards, and other overgrown vegetation. Central reached a population of 1,200 in 1883, when over 130 boardinghouses and single-family dwellings for miners and mine officials stood here. There were also engine houses, shaft houses, rock houses, a stamp mill, a woodworking and machine shop, captain's and superintendent's offices, and a tramway. Today the few remaining houses serve as primitive hunting lodges and summer camps; the church is the scene of an annual July 21 homecoming of former Central residents and their descendants.

EAGLE HARBOR AND GRANT TOWNSHIP

KW07 **Brockway Mountain Drive**

1930s. Between Eagle Harbor and Copper Harbor

This 10-mile scenic drive with turnouts affords spectacular views of Lake Superior, the passing ships, and the rugged Keweenaw Peninsula. A stone wall broken by piers at lookout points runs parallel to the drive. The parkway was named for Daniel Brockway, an early pioneer and settler who was postmaster at Fort Wilkins in the 1840s and at Copper Harbor in 1866–1868; from 1861 to 1863, he was manager of the Phoenix Hotel in Eagle River and, from 1881–1892, agent of the Cliff Mine.

COPPER HARBOR VICINITY, GRANT TOWNSHIP

KW08 **Keweenaw Mountain Resort** (Keweenaw Mountain Lodge and Golf Course)

1933–1935. 1937. South side US 41, 1.5 miles southwest of Copper Harbor

Promoted by Keweenaw County Road Commissioner Ocha Potter to increase tourism in the Keweenaw Peninsula, this rustic resort was hacked out of 167 acres of rolling timberland. It was funded by the Civil Works Administration (CWA), the Emergency Relief Administration (ERA), and the Works Progress Administration (WPA) to provide work for the unemployed labor force in the peninsula after the mines closed. It is still operated

KW08 Keweenaw Mountain Resort (Keweenaw Mountain Lodge and Golf Course)

today by the county road commission. Logs cut in 1933–1934 to clear land for laying out the nine-hole golf course were crafted into cabins, lodge, and furniture. A row of nearly two dozen log cabins with living rooms and fireplaces flank the driveway leading up to the lodge. The huge log lodge hall with a broadly pitched gable roof has large stone fireplaces, a stone entry hall, and enclosed porches. The buildings of the complex are rustic and resemble those built in the western national parks. The Keweenaw Mountain Lodge and Golf Course was one of the largest public works projects in the Upper Peninsula: the WPA spent $21,480 in the construction of the golf course and club house and $117,440 in the construction of twenty tourist cabins; ERA spent $19,818 to build a power line from Eagle River to serve the resort; and CWA and ERA funded the rest.

KW09 **Fort Wilkins**

1844. US 41 at the northern tip of the Keweenaw Peninsula

Fort Wilkins was built in 1844 to keep law and order in the western Upper Peninsula's booming nineteenth-century copper mining district. This typical frontier army post was garrisoned by small numbers of federal troops from 1844 to 1846, prior to the Mexican War, and from 1867 to 1870, following the Civil War. Between periods of military occupation, and for a half century thereafter, civilians periodically used fort buildings as summer residences and as hunting camps. The property was acquired by the state of Michigan in 1923 as part of a state park.

Since 1923, restoration and reconstruction efforts have transformed Fort Wilkins into a frontier garrison once again. Sixteen of the original twenty-three buildings survive, twelve

of them restored structures dating from the 1840s. The site is an impressive formation of vernacular military architecture, symmetrically arranged to face south across the parade ground toward Lake Fanny Hooe. These rectangular buildings were constructed of hewn timber on stone masonry foundations, with gabled and wood-shingled roofs. Some of the buildings, notably the three containing officers' quarters, are sided with weatherboards and whitewashed. Green shutters frame the windows, and a broad piazza fronts each block of quarters and faces both the parade ground and most other important buildings in the fort. To each side of the officers' quarters stands a mess hall, with kitchen attached, and a company barracks. A bakery, hospital, quartermaster's building, sutler's building, powder magazine, and an ice house also stand inside the reconstructed log palisade. Located outside the stockade to the east are three reconstructed married enlisted men's cabins. Less polished dwellings than the officers' quarters, or even the company barracks, these buildings are reconstructed of unhewn logs, horizontally laid, with sharp-notched corners.

Both individually and as a strategically arranged whole, the buildings of Fort Wilkins tell about military life on the northwest frontier at mid-nineteenth century. Military service at Fort Wilkins, however, was routine and uneventful, and today's visitor to the restored fort is most struck by the isolation and severe climate with which its occupants, housed in simple log structures, had to cope.

HOUGHTON TOWNSHIP

KW10 **Rock Harbor Lighthouse**

1855. Middle Islands Passage (north 1/2 section 26, township 66 north, range 36 west)

Rock Harbor Lighthouse is one of the oldest extant lighthouses on the Great Lakes. It was used less than ten years, however, first from 1855 to 1858, and then from 1874 to 1879. The one-and-a-half-story, gable-roofed, rubble stone and brick light keeper's house is attached to a 50-foot high cylindrical tower of stone and brick surmounted by a beacon. The light marked the rocky Middle Islands Passage for ships supplying copper mines. It was abandoned for much of this century, except for occasional use for summer camping parties and by commercial fishermen. In

1939 it was transferred to the National Park Service.

KW11 **Pete Edison Fishery**

1895–1935, Mattson, Anderson, Mike Johnson. On the south shore of Rock Harbor .25 mile west of Rock Harbor Lighthouse (north 1/2 section 26, township 66 north, range 34 west)

An assemblage of commercial fishing structures and equipment—fish house, net house (1895), house (c. 1900), sleeping cabins, privy, chicken coop (1934), docks, equipment and wooden packing barrels, net dryers and nets, floats, fish cleaning tables, and fishing boats—remain to remind us of the once flourishing fishing industry on Isle Royale. Pete Edison and previous occupants built the structures of logs and materials salvaged from abandoned mining and fishing settlements. From 1916 until the early 1980s, Edison left his winter home in Minnesota each summer between mid-April and early November to bring up catches of lake trout, herring, and siskiwit from nearby shoals off this remote island. The fishing industry first boomed in the 1880s, when railroads connected Lake Superior with markets to the south.

Ontonagon County (ON)

ONTONAGON

The only safe port on Lake Superior between Eagle River and Ashland, Wisconsin, Ontonagon developed as a lumbering and shipping center with saw and paper mills.

ON01 **Ontonagon Lighthouse**

1866–1867. 1890, kitchen addition. On the west bank of the Ontonagon River at Lake Superior off Michigan 64

On the west bank of the Ontonagon River at Lake Superior stands the Ontonagon Lighthouse. It replaced an earlier one built in 1852, as Ontonagon Harbor became a shipping point for copper and lumber and an arrival point for men and supplies bound for nearby mines. The plans for this lighthouse and the lighthouses at Marquette and on South Manitou Island are the same. Within the 9-foot-square tower at the center front of the structure, a cast iron spiral staircase rises to a watchtower and a light. This and the gabled keeper's dwelling are constructed of pale yellowish white brick on a red sandstone foundation and trimmed with gray sandstone. A small kitchen addition of the same material is attached at the rear. Service was discontinued in 1964.

ON02 **Ontonagon Elementary School**
(Ontonagon Township School Addition)

1938, Warren S. Holmes Company. 301 Greenland Rd. (Michigan 38) (southeast corner of Greenland Rd. and Parker Ave.)

Artwork funded by the Federal Emergency Administration of Public Works enhances the two-story red brick Ontonagon Elementary School addition to the Beaux-Arts Classical Ontonagon Township School. Stone panels incised in sunk relief with allegorical figures depicting education—a musician, athlete, scientist, craftsman, artist, and scholar—surround the main center entrance; ceramic tiles decorated with whimsical figures line the hall walls; and a linoleum floor inlaid with storybook characters and a tiled fish fountain enliven the kindergarten room.

ROCKLAND TOWNSHIP

ON03 **Victoria Mine Site**

1850. 1858. 1899. Victoria Rd., 4 miles southwest of Rockland

Once a thriving copper-mining town, Victoria is now reduced to foundations, mine pits, and several log structures. The site was discovered in 1772 by Alexander Henry, an English explorer, but drew national attention through the efforts of Julius Eldred, who removed from the Ontonagon River the famed 6,000-pound Ontonagon copper boulder, now housed in the Smithsonian Institution. The Forest Mining Company of Boston began operating here in 1850. It was reorganized as the Victoria Mining Company in 1858, but a forest fire and spring flood that year destroyed the mill and many of the surface structures, thus closing the mine for half a century. In 1899 the reorganized Victoria Copper Mining Company reopened it and ran it until 1921, when it closed forever.

Of the nearly two hundred structures that stood here during World War I, when the population of the mining town peaked at 1,850, only a handful of the dovetailed log workers' houses remain. Although some may date from the 1850s, they were altered with foundations, new floors, interior plaster, and lean-to additions. The Society for the Restoration of Old Victoria leases the 10 acres on which they stand. Just to the south, the sawmill location shows the foundations of nine structures and of an old road, now used as a snowmobile trail. Adjacent to the mine area was the company boardinghouse, store, hospital, offices, ballroom, warehouses, and other structures. Five company houses now serve as private dwellings. In the mining area are two mine shafts, now sealed in concrete, and the foundations of other mining structures.

ON04 Victoria Dam and Hydroelectric Plant

1929–1931, Holland, Ackerman and Holland. Victoria Dam Rd., 1 mile south of Victoria and 5 miles southwest of Rockland

On Victoria Dam Road is the Victoria Dam and Hydroelectric Plant, built for the Copper Range Company's hydroelectric development and acquired by the Upper Peninsula Power Company in 1947. The four-arch concrete dam extends across a deep gorge. Downstream from the dam is the brick powerhouse with its large windows and vertical piers, which holds the original installation of turbines and generators.

WHITE PINE, CARP LAKE TOWNSHIP

ON05 White Pine Townsite

1953, Pace Associates. 1970–1971, Alden B. Dow Associates Inc. and Land Value Developments, Inc. Michigan 64, 6 miles south of Silver City

White Pine is a post-World War II townsite planned by sociologists, architects, the federal government, and mining company officials. In 1953 the federal government financed the development of White Pine because it was concerned over the vulnerability of the nation's foreign mineral sources. By 1970 the White Pine Division of the Copper Range Company employed 2,600 people.

To "achieve a suitable and dependable employee force," and to encourage skilled mechanics and other mine workers to take up residence at White Pine, rather than to commute 110 miles each way each day, the company commissioned Alden B. Dow and Associates to plan the development, construction and financing of White Pine. The master plan, developed in 1970–1971, conceived of neighborhood units of 200 houses, separated by access streets, natural ravines, wooded areas, and drainage points, and surrounded by a large plot of natural woods; residential areas bordered by a golf course; a mobile home park clustered in circles; scattered apartments; and a separate commercial area. Herman Gundlach of Houghton executed plans for the Mineral River Plaza, a commercial center with a 58,000-square-foot shopping mall; the Konteka Building, a restaurant and bowling alley; and White Pine Housing. Roycraft Industries Incorporated, a Michigan manufacturer of industrialized housing and mobile homes, provided modular housing. But ties to home prevail, and many workers continue to commute daily from Calumet and Ironwood. The plan was only moderately successful, because of the hesitancy to move to a one-industry town and the emphasis on FHA 235 housing, for which miners are ineligible because their wages are too high.

Arnold R. Alanen observes that White Pine is similar to Babbitt, Hoyt Lakes, and Silver Bay, which were developed in the 1950s on the iron range of Minnesota. All four are located on large reserves of land with little competing development. Their residential areas are bypassed by traffic routes to the mine and removed from the extractive and processing activities. Today, like the others, White Pine consists of "relatively barren pocket[s] of open spaces surrounded by magnificent wilderness environments of pines."[74]

The Iron Ranges

The Marquette Iron Range
(Marquette and Baraga Counties)

The substance of the economy of Marquette County is found in the valuable iron in the hills around Marquette. This promising resource was known to the Indians and French missionaries of the early seventeenth century, and to trappers of the early nineteenth century, but it was not until 1844, when William Burt and Jacob Houghton (1827–1903), the brother of Douglass Houghton, discovered iron deposits near Teal Lake, twelve miles west of Marquette, that development of the region began. Their discovery substantiated Douglass Houghton's earlier reports of extensive iron deposits and this, together with subsequent findings, brought an onslaught of entrepreneurs and fortune hunters to recently organized Marquette County.

Following Burt and Houghton, in 1845 Philo M. Everett explored the area and located lands for the newly formed Jackson Mining Company, the first organized mining company in the region. In 1846, after sending one ton of ore to the mouth of the Carp River and then on to Pittsburgh for scientific testing, he opened the Jackson Mine. A year later, three miles east of Negaunee on the Carp River, he built the Jackson Forge for the production of iron.

By 1853 three mining companies—the Jackson, the Lake Superior, and the Cleveland—operated in the Marquette Iron Range, but further development required an effective means of transporting the ore from the mines to the large furnaces that were located near the coal fields of the Lower Lakes. The completion in the 1850s of the first railroad and modern ore docks at Marquette and Escanaba and the opening of the locks at Sault Sainte Marie provided such

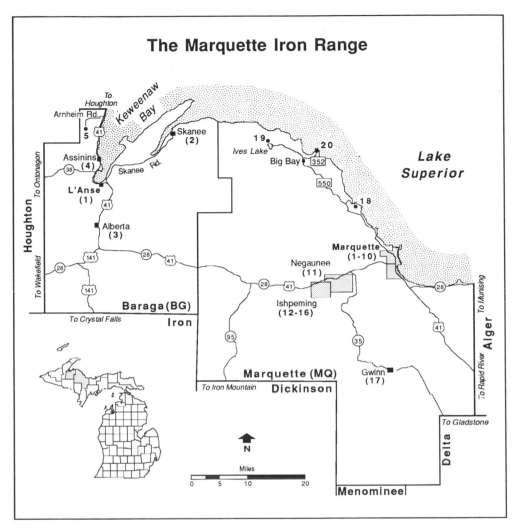

The Marquette Iron Range

facilities. Mines at Ishpeming and Negaunee followed, with others at Gwinn and at Republic, Champion, and Michigamme. A network of railroads connected the mines to the docks at Marquette and Escanaba. The architectural consequences were the workers' and managers' houses, which sprang up at the various mine locations, and the more specialized utilitarian types of structures, such as headframes, shaft houses, warehouses, and machine shops.

Mining on the Marquette Iron Range continued to expand in the early years of the twentieth century. In 1909, Marquette's 48 operating mines employed 6,546 men and shipped 4.2 million tons of ore. The Cleveland-Cliffs Iron (CCI) Company, which had been formed in 1891 by the consolidation of the Cleveland Iron Company, the Jackson Iron Company, the Iron Cliff Company, and the Pioneer Iron Company, operated 10 mines with 1,700 employees. In 1919 iron production peaked with 4.8 million tons. From there it was downhill, and large-scale production ended in 1929. Today the CCI manages the Empire and Tilden mines only, the last of Michigan's great iron ore industry. Since the deposits of high-grade ore have been largely exhausted, the current method is to extract low-grade ore from waste rock by a crushing and grading process that eventually results in pellet-sized ore. Moreover, foreign competition and fluctuations in the North American steel industry have caused large-scale cutbacks in iron mining in general throughout the United States.

Marquette County   (MQ)

MARQUETTE

Marquette is located on Marquette Bay, an inlet of Lake Superior midway between the Saint Mary's and Montreal rivers, which form the eastern and western boundaries of the Upper Peninsula. The city nestles beneath highlands that rise first to a plateau, then to a chain of hills. Belts of geologic formations encircle the community and rocks crop out everywhere. The land all around is covered with heavy forests of pine and hardwood and broken by rivers and valleys.

In 1849 Amos Rogers Harlow, Waterman A. Fisher, and Edward Clark of Worcester, Massachusetts, together with Robert J. Graveraet of Mackinac Island, organized the region's second iron concern, a forge known as the Marquette Iron Company. On learning of the discovery of iron ore on Lake Superior, Harlow consulted with J. W. Whitney of Boston, who with J. D. Foster had conducted the geological survey of the Upper Peninsula. Encouraged by Whitney's report, Harlow and his party moved forward and later that same year reached the present site of Marquette. Attracted by the area's excellent harbor, they cleared ground, erected a few simple wooden buildings, and constructed a forge for the production of iron from ore that could be transported from nearby mines.

As the rail network expanded later in the century, Marquette became the Upper Peninsula's leading shipping center. Prior to the advent of rail transportation, Marquette bore little resemblance to the flourishing "Queen City of the North" characterized by later writers. By 1862, however, the community's population exceeded 1,600, and investment returns on mining and shipping interests sent the local economy soaring. Lumbering, the extraction of sandstone, and tourism followed. The city fast became a regional center of commerce, finance, government, and speculation in land, minerals, and timber.

Building activity created demands for materials and labor that the people of Marquette could not meet, despite the region's vast resources. Aware of the shortages, architects, carpenters, builders, and suppliers in Detroit and Cleveland advertised their goods and services in the Marquette newspapers for the 1860s. In their quest for high-style results, Marquette clients in turn called upon architects from Chicago, Cleveland, Milwaukee, and Detroit to design their increasingly complex buildings. By 1875, however, the city was able to claim its own building suppliers, sandstone quarries, as well as builders, carpenters, and masons; and for three years, even an architect, the Norwegian-born Gothic Revivalist, Carl F. Struck, was in residence. Yet, it was not until nearly 1890, that Demetrius Frederick Charlton, a fully trained architect, opened a practice in Marquette.

From the time of settlement, building stone had been blasted out of quarries and taken from excavations to be used for foundations, mines, and roads. It was not until industry developed a need for substantial and utilitarian structures, however, and brought into the region the engineers, workmen, and masons capable of understanding and handling stone, that it was used for building purposes. Once it became available, however, mining, furnace, railroad companies, and government agencies found the local sandstone ideally suited for varied building needs. Between 1869 and 1900, more than a dozen companies intermittently extracted brown sandstone from quarries in Marquette County. What wasn't used locally was shipped to large midwestern cities.

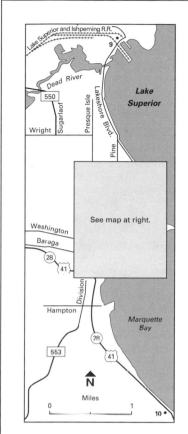

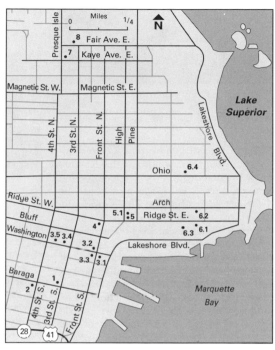

Marquette

By the 1870s the town had progressed socially and economically to the point where the people of Marquette were ready to use the native stone for their own domestic and public buildings. The need for substantial new structures, some to replace primitive wooden ones, and a disastrous fire of June 1868 that destroyed both the business district and much of the residential section, also encouraged the use of stone. At the same time, the rich timber resources of the area provided both the inspiration and the substance for a lively wooden architecture.

Marquette was incorporated as a city in 1871, and during the twenty years following the fire, the population tripled. By 1890 its population had reached 10,000, and despite the panic of 1873, the community experienced one of its biggest building booms. The many fine residences and commercial buildings attested to the city's prosperity. By the turn of the century, writers regarded Marquette as the best built, wealthiest, and most beautiful city on the south shore of Lake Superior, yet despite its highly civilized character, the dense wilderness still was never far away. A handbook to the city claimed that Marquette seemed "a large city in miniature." It combined the vigor and roughness of the West with the polish and sophistication of the East.

Today Marquette remains the Upper Peninsula's largest city. Northern Michigan University, the state prison, and K. I. Sawyer Air Force Base make government the county's largest employer.

MQ01 Marquette County Courthouse

1902–1904; Charlton, Gilbert and Demar; Manning Brothers, landscape architects. 1977, courthouse annex addition. 1984, restoration. 400 South Third St.

MQ01 Marquette County Courthouse

(bounded by Third St., West Baraga Ave., Fourth St., and Spring St.)

In 1902 the voters of Marquette County approved the issuance of bonds worth $120,000 for a new courthouse, and the original wooden courthouse, built in 1857, was moved off the site. In its place, on a hill that slopes gradually toward Marquette Bay, the county commissioners erected the present steel-frame Beaux-Arts Classical courthouse at a cost of $240,000. Its rock-faced masonry walls, so joyously out of character with its classical detailing, are of the red sandstone of the North Country, a material long out of favor elsewhere. The building is domed, with a three-story central mass flanked by two-story wings; a colossal Doric columned portico marks the entrance. A Doric entablature, the cornice of which is copper, encircles the building. The courtroom on the second floor, which is under the dome with stained-glass lights, is finished with mahogany. At a time when half of the forty thousand residents of the county resided in the iron range towns of Ishpeming and Negaunee, the solid dignified courthouse proclaimed Marquette as the seat of county government. Under the supervision of Lincoln A. Poley, it was gloriously restored in 1984.

MQ02 Saint Peter's Roman Catholic Cathedral

1880–1890, Henry G. Koch and Son; Hampson Gregory, master builder and contractor. 1935, rebuilt. 311 West Baraga Ave. (southwest corner of West Baraga Ave. and Fourth St.)

The original Saint Peter's Cathedral, built in 1864 and itself Romanesque, was destroyed by fire in 1879. The Diocese of Marquette replaced the burned-out structure with the present twin-towered Romanesque Revival

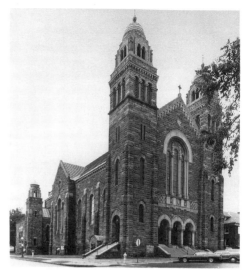

MQ02 Saint Peter's Roman Catholic Cathedral

church. Constructed of variegated Marquette brownstone, it took ten years to complete at a cost of $100,000. Since no architect capable of creating a structure of this magnitude and grandeur resided in the Upper Peninsula in the 1880s, the church was designed by a noted firm in Milwaukee. Although a Wisconsin city, Milwaukee was close to the Upper Peninsula, less than one day away by train on the Chicago and Northwestern Railroad, and had more of a commercial affinity with the towns of that region than Detroit.

Triple arches mark the main entrance of the church. The plan has a single-aisled, barrel-vaulted nave, two small side aisles and short transepts, and measures 100 feet in length by 80 feet in width. The church was profusely decorated with memorial cathedral glass windows from George A. Misch of Chicago and with woodwork from Hager and Johnson of Marquette. The cost and beauty of its material, its large size, and the elegance of its design and finish reflect the struggle of the Catholic church, through the Diocese of Marquette, to establish its identity in a burgeoning youthful city on the American frontier. In 1935, after another fire, the church was rebuilt extensively.

MQ03 Washington and Front Streets

Marquette's commercial district extends north, south, and west from Lake Superior, and from a center point at the intersection of Washington and Front streets.

MQ03.1 Marquette County Savings Bank

1891–1892, Barber and Barber. 107 South Front St. (southeast corner of Front and Washington streets)

The Marquette County Savings Bank was organized in 1890 by Nathan M. Kaufman (1862–1918), a merchant and speculator in mines, and by other Marquette businessmen as a convenience for small depositors and to facilitate real estate loans. Within four months, funds amounting to more than $100,000 were on deposit, and the directors began plans for the present modern bank and office building. Located at the principal intersection of downtown Marquette, it is on a site sloping east toward the lake and south toward the railroad's final approach to the ore docks. The steel-frame, fireproof structure rises five stories at Front Street, six at Washington Street and seven at the rear. The outer walls of the first floor are Rock River brownstone laid in rock-faced ashlar. Above that they are red pressed brick. Semicircular bays, the northwest of which terminates in a three-faced clock tower, rise from the second story to the flat roof and flank the pedimented central entry section. This is decorated by stone spandrel panels carved with stylized foliated designs. The recessed entry is supported by polished granite columns. The elevator and ventilating shafts, staircase, and lavatories are

arranged on the south wall to deaden the noise of the ore cars that once passed through the Jackson cut to the docks. A Duluth firm with no previous connections in Upper Michigan designed the bank. At the time, according to the *Marquette Mining Journal* for April 18, 1891, it was termed "modern American with Gothic feeling," but is, in fact, a fascinating commercialized version of the Queen Anne style.

MQ03.2 Harlow Block

1887, Hampson Gregory. 102 West Washington St. (northwest corner of Washington and Front streets)

The Harlow Block is a straightforward commercial design of the Victorian era by a local stonemason and builder. Constructed of plain variegated Marquette brownstone locally called "raindrop" for its purplish brown iridescence, it is a rather heavy-handed version of the Italianate style that marked Main Street America during the 1860s and 1870s. Amos R. Harlow (1815–1890), a founder of Marquette, was admired for his real estate developments that built up and improved the city and afforded employment. He built the block as speculative office and store space. It gave tenants a good address in a substantial building located in the very heart of the downtown business district.

MQ03.3 First National Bank (First National Bank and Trust Company Building)

1926–1927; Uffinger, Foster and Hookwalter; Mowbray and Uffinger Inc. 101 West Washington St. (southwest corner of Front and Washington streets)

The First National Bank is a monumental banking temple in grayish white Bedford, Indiana, limestone. The *Marquette Daily Mining Journal* for January 20, 1926, reported that the Beaux-Arts Classical design "follows the precedent established by the masters of the classical period modified to meet modern requirements of the banking business and modeled to avoid the commonplace." Engaged Composite columns and piers support the entablature of the entrance pavilion and flank the bronze doors of the main entrance to the main banking room. Between the columns, round-arch windows pierce the stone walls. On the Front Street flank of the building the bronze doors are positioned between bronze lanterns on stands and Composite pilasters. Block modillions support the corona under the cornice. The rich and lavish interior displays marble and bronze, metal grilles, ornamental plaster, and harmonious gold and blue decorations. Louis G. Kaufman (1870–1942), bank president, sought the architectural skills of New York specialists in bank and office design to create an imposing, dignified, and fireproof bank with a big city appearance.

MQ03.4 Marquette Post Office

1936; Le Roy Gardner; Louis A. Simon, supervising architect. 202 West Washington St.

On a site formerly occupied by the huge 1889–1891 brick and sandstone federal customhouse, courthouse, and post office is the modernistic United States Post Office. Fluted pilasters divide the Bedford limestone facade of the monolithic building into seven bays. Approached by a short flight of stairs, the center entrance is surrounded by Kasota stone and surmounted by a carved eagle. The designer was Le Roy Gardner, with Louis A. Simon as supervising architect. The lobby contains a WPA-sponsored mural, *Marquette Exploring Shores of Lake Superior,* painted by Dewey Albinson.

MQ03.5 Old Marquette City Hall

1893–1894, Lovejoy and Demar. 220 Washington St.

This monumental government building is a blend of Second Empire, Renaissance Revival, and Richardsonian Romanesque styles.

Constructed by Emil Bruce in red brick and purplish brown sandstone after designs by a Marquette firm, it must have seemed at the time to deny the pervading economic depression and express a confidence in the future of the iron hills and iron industry. Above a recessed round-arch entrance, a central mansard hipped roof lends civic presence to the three-story, hipped-roof, boxlike structure. During the panic of 1893, Mayor Nathan M. Kaufman, known locally as a "capitalist and progressive," convinced the city council and citizens to issue bonds for $50,000 to build a city hall with local labor and local materials, thereby putting some Marquette men back to work.

MQ04 Peter White Library

1902–1904, Patton and Miller. 1958, west addition. 1982, entrance moved to north. 217 North Front St. (southwest corner Front and Ridge streets)

The Beaux-Arts Classical design of the Peter White Library, constructed of smooth-cut grayish white Bedford, Indiana, limestone, contrasts sharply with the warm reddish brown brick and sandstone structures in the Gothic, Italianate, and Richardsonian Romanesque styles that were built in the preceding thirty years in Marquette. The library board explained that it chose white stone "so as to furnish a variation to the dark stone which is characteristic of the architecture of Marquette." The *Marquette Daily Mining Journal* for September 22, 1904, argued, "It is of a beautiful whiteness, and as it is the only structure of the material in the city it has a distinctive air that would have been hopelessly lost had Lake Superior sandstone been used." Round-arch windows with keystones pierce the walls on the raised first story; on the second story the windows are rectangular. An ornamental cornice encircles the red tile hipped roof. Stairs ascend to the projecting main central entrance portico, which is marked by four giant fluted columns in antis. The building was named for Peter White (1830–1908), founder in 1872 of the public library in Marquette. Together with Nathan M. Kaufman and John M. Longyear, he was also a substantial contributor to the present structure. As a member of the World's Columbian Exposition Commission, White probably admired the white classicism of the exposition buildings in Chicago. A Chicago firm noted for its designs for libraries and college buildings designed the Marquette library.

MQ05 Saint Paul's Episcopal Church

1874–1876; Gordon W. Lloyd; Carl F. Struck, supervising architect. 1989–1990, entrance and offices, Paul Bilgen of Robert Carl Williams Associates. 318 High St. (northeast corner of Ridge and High streets)

This is one of the major ecclesiastical designs of the region. It stands on the site of the parish's first church, a wooden structure built in 1857 and moved in 1874 to make way for this building. The Gothic Revival structure was designed by one of the Midwest's most fashionable church architects for Marquette's wealthiest religious community. Executed in clear brown Marquette sandstone by the most skilled craftsmen, its rich hammer-faced walls and high-style Gothic forms celebrate both the social and economic achievements of the parish and the city. Modeled after Saint Paul's Cathedral at Fond du Lac, Wisconsin, the asymmetrical church was conceived in the strictest ecclesiological terms. It has a steeply pitched roof, two transepts, and a buttressed and crenelated square entry tower placed at a 45-degree angle to the southwest corner. Gothic elements appear in the stained-glass lancet windows and in the authoritative detailing in the stonework and window tracery. The church seats 500 in two banks of butternut pews divided by a center aisle beneath an open wood truss ceiling and is illuminated by light filtered through the brilliant red, blue, and green stained-glass windows. The woodwork was designed and crafted by A. Gustafson of Hager and Wallaster, local furniture manufacturers. Saint Paul's Church is so elegant and splendid inside and out that some regarded it as out of character with this city in the wilderness. The bold but fussy Postmodern addition and porte-cochère testify to the continuing commitment of this congregation to its landmark church.

MQ05.1 Morgan Memorial Chapel

1887–1889, Cobb and Frost. 318 West High St.

Connected to the north of Saint Paul's is the exquisite little 200-seat Morgan Memorial Chapel. It is a single-gabled chapel with a south entrance porch. Buttresses support its beautiful rock-faced variegated Marquette sandstone walls. *The Resurrection Window*, a lovely stained-glass creation manufactured by Tiffany, fills the large Gothic opening in the front (west) gable. Its deep reds and blues fade in the center to pale greens, blues, and browns, and the whole contrasts with the rich wood of the hammer-beam ceiling and paneling. This addition to Saint Paul's Church was commissioned by Peter White in memory of his son, Morgan Lewis White, and was executed by a noted Chicago firm.

MQ06 Ridge, Arch, Michigan, and Ohio Streets Residential District

1860s-present. Ridge, Arch, Michigan, and Ohio streets from Front St. to Cedar St.

High on a ridge with a magnificent view of Marquette Harbor, Lake Superior and Presque Isle, the owners and managers of Marquette iron and shipping industries lived in large houses next to their furnaces, railroad yards, and docks. Here Peter White, Edward Breitung, John Longyear, and others built houses after designs by Detroit and Chicago architects. They are comparable to the houses on Summit Avenue in Saint Paul, Minnesota, but scaled to the economic situation in Marquette.

For ten years, from 1890–1892 to 1903–1904, before it was dismantled, loaded onto railroad cars, and transported and rebuilt in Brookline, Massachusetts, the John and Mary Beecher Longyear House, the largest and most carefully planned house of Lake Superior sandstone ever constructed in the region, overlooked the lake from its one-block site on the high bluff at the corner of Arch and Cedar streets. Built for Longyear (1850–1922), a timber and mineral lands speculator, the Richardsonian Romanesque house was designed by Demetrius Frederick Charlton and landscaped by Frederick Law Olmsted.

MQ06.1 Henry R. and Mary Hewitt Mather House

1867, Carl F. Struck of the Henry Lord Gay Company. 1878, addition. 450 East Ridge St.

This Gothic Revival house with decorated bargeboard, lancet windows extending into gables, hooded windows, and board-and-batten siding exemplifies America's premier wood building tradition. Clearly reflecting the writings of A. J. Downing, it is among the oldest

MQ06.1 Henry R. and Mary Hewitt Mather House

in the neighborhood. The house was designed by Henry Lord Gay, who had studied with Sidney Stone in New Haven and worked with W. W. Boyington in Chicago. At the same time, Gay planned for Mather and Peter White Marquette's first major commercial block, the First National Bank and Superior Building (now destroyed). Mather (1824–1888) came from Cleveland to Marquette to invest in mineral lands and became the first president of the Cleveland Iron Mining Company.

MQ06.2 Andrew A. (and Laura Grenough?) Ripka House

1875, Carl F. Struck. 430 East Arch St.

The Philadelphia-born and -educated manager of the railroad company and dock, who was also a speculator in mines, built this parapeted Gothic Revival house. Its random ashlar walls are of rock-faced, variegated brown sandstone from the quarries of the Marquette Brownstone Company. Carl F. Struck, a Norwegian-born architect who practiced in Marquette from 1872 to 1875, before moving west to Minneapolis and eventually to Tacoma, Washington, demonstrated in the Ripka house his skill in the use of the Gothic Revival style and his knowledge of Andrew Jackson Downing's principles.

MQ06.3 Daniel H. Merritt House

1880, Hampson Gregory. 410 East Ridge St.

The nearly square Italian Villa with Second Empire detailing has a projecting center tower topped by a concave mansard roof. A wrought-iron balconet at the center of the tower is covered by a bracketed hood. A porch, supported by simple columns and ornamental scrolled brackets, wraps around the east and south sides at the ground floor. The house was designed by an English immigrant, Hampson Gregory (1833–1921). Steeped in the stone building tradition of his native Devonshire, Gregory built it of roughly dressed, evenly coursed, variegated reddish brown and white sandstone. The interior is fitted with woodwork finished in Marquette shops. It was built for Daniel Merritt (b. 1833), a pioneer industrialist and employee of the Lake Shore Iron Works (owner of the Iron Bay Foundry and Machine Shops) who was also an investor in mining companies, banks, and land. The house in its solidity seems to demonstrate the financial and social success of its owner and the skill of its builder.

MQ06.4 Julian M. Case House

1886–1887, John Wellborn Root. 425 Ohio St.

A rare surviving example of the domestic architecture of the great Chicago architect, John Wellborn Root (1850–1892), this handsome dwelling brings the sophistication of the Eastern Shingle style to the mineral and timberlands of the Upper Peninsula. Its round tower with octagonal base and its broad asymmetrical massing typically articulate the outward pushing interior spaces. The mass is covered with shingles on the upper level and clapboards on the lower. Inside, the great entry hall features a spindled staircase and leaded-glass windows. Sliding doors permit the opening of the entire first floor into a large space suited for entertaining, or the closing off of cozy rooms in which mirrors and tiles conduct heat generated by the fireplaces. Victorian gadgetry fills the house. Leonard K. Eaton notes that in this small work Root has paid as much attention to technological and environmental considerations as in his large works.[75]

MQ07 **Small Fryes Day Care Center** (John and Vida Gallagher Lautner House)

c. 1915, Joy Wheeler Dow. 109 Presque Isle (northeast corner of Presque Isle and Kaye Ave.)

This American Colonial Revival house is reminiscent of its New England and English origins in its weathered clapboarding, twelve-over-twelve symmetrically arranged windows, a massive central clustered chimney with decorative top, front overhang with pendants, and steeply pitched roof. The interior is finished with open wood beams and oak flooring laid in a herringbone pattern. The living room fireplace is recessed in a cozy inglenook. In its conservatism the Laughton house seems to guard against change and to protect the status quo.

MQ08 **Sports Training Complex (Superior Dome), Northern Michigan University**

1990–1991, TMP Associates, Inc. Northern Michigan University (just north of the Physical Education In-structional Facility and one block east of Presque Isle Ave.)

Situated on the shore of Lake Superior at Northern Michigan University, the 150-foot-tall, 531-foot-diameter, wooden-domed structure is the largest wooden sports dome in the world. It covers over 5 acres and seats 8,000. The dome is sturdy, as well as large, so as to withstand heavy snow and winds. Forty buttresses, each anchored by a 5-foot-wide and 2.5-foot-high concrete tension ring, support the dome. The dome is constructed of Douglas fir beams and Douglas fir tongue-and-groove decking. It contains a turf playing surface, synthetic playing surface for courts, and a building support area.

The state of Michigan constructed the sports training complex as an instructional, training, competition, and multipurpose facility for students, faculty, athletes in training at the U.S. Olympic Education Center and the Great Lakes Sports Training Center, and area citizens. Since the 1970s Northern Michigan University had sought funds for an enclosed sports facility. With the indication that the governor (James J. Blanchard) supported the construction of a sports training complex on the campus at Northern Michigan University, the university won from the United States Olympics Site Selection Committee a designation as an Olympic Training Center. Subsequently, the legislature appropriated $22 million for construction. Later phases of construction to the dome will add sports medicine, media and public areas, offices, and locker rooms and will provide an ice arena for hockey, figure skating, and speed skating.

MQ08 Sports Training Complex (Superior Dome), Northern Michigan University

Now the only U.S. Olympic Education Center in the nation, Northern operates several year-round resident training programs.

MQ09 Lake Superior and Ishpeming Ore Dock and Approach

1911–1912; R. C. Young, chief engineer, Lake Superior and Ishpeming Railroad, designer of reinforced concrete superstructure; J. F. Jackson, vice-president, Wisconsin Bridge and Iron Company of Milwaukee, designer of structure. Lake Shore Blvd. and Lake Superior and Ishpeming Railroad, Upper Harbor (Presque Isle Harbor) south of Presque Isle Park

Jutting out like a leviathan into Lake Superior, the 1,200-foot-long reinforced concrete and steel dock contains 200 ore pockets with a capacity of 250 tons each and a total storage capacity of 50,000 tons. The ore pockets open into tapered chutes that insert into the bulk ore carriers. Rising 75 feet above the water, the dock is approached by a one-mile-long earth embankment with a 1.5 percent grade. A steel trestle, 600 feet in length and 70 feet in height, connects it to the dock. Built by the LS&I Railroad, a subsidiary of CCI, the dock revolutionized the loading of ore vessels. To the northeast is Presque Isle Park, one of Michigan's most beautiful parks. City officials heeded the advice of Frederick Law Olmsted, who visited the park site while planning the grounds for the John Longyear House and did nothing at all to disturb its wild natural character.

MQ10 Marquette Branch Prison (Upper Peninsula Branch Prison and House of Correction)

1887–1889, William Scott and Company. 1960 US 41 South

Established by the Michigan legislature in 1885, the prison stands on a site in Marquette thought "too beautiful for a prison."[76] It was selected competitively, however, because of the city's location, advanced development, and aggressive businessmen. English-born William Scott, who practiced architecture in Detroit in partnership with his sons, Arthur and John, designed the prison after the Ionia House of Correction in Ionia, Michigan, and dispatched Demetrius Frederick Charlton to Marquette to supervise construction. (Charlton remained in Marquette and became the Upper Peninsula's most prominent architect.) The High Victorian Romanesque structure with square central tower and octagonal turrets is constructed of reddish brown Marquette sandstone trimmed with red Portage Entry sandstone and covered with an immense hipped roof of Lake Superior slate. The prison follows the Auburn rather than the Eastern State penal system, which advocated the rehabilitation of criminals through a regime of nighttime sleep in cells and daytime work in common areas. Only the administration building, northwest cell block wing, and rotunda remain of the original complex, but the lovely historic gardens before the administration building have been restored.

NEGAUNEE

MQ11 Negaunee City Hall

1914–1915, John D. Chubb. Bounded by Silver, Case, Kanter, and Jackson streets, approximately 6 blocks south of US 41/Michigan 28

The two-story, highly eclectic city hall and public library building occupies one full city block and overlooks a small park to the west.

MQ11 Negaunee City Hall

A 94-foot-high clock tower rises over the main entrance as an aggressive symbol of its civic authority. Alternate courses of white pressed brick and grayish white limestone with terracotta detailing form the contrasting patterns of its busy walls. It was designed by the same Chicago and Marquette architect who was responsible for the designs of the Negaunee High School of 1908–1909 and the Negaunee National Bank of 1910. This flamboyant government building was planned at the time when the population of Negaunee was on the rise and the production from Negaunee mines was approaching its peak. It makes a statement about the optimism of a small frontier city reaping the fruits of a generous land.

ISHPEMING

MQ12 **Ishpeming City Hall**

1890–1891, Demetrius Frederick Charlton. 100 East Division St. (Michigan 28) (southeast corner of East Division and Main streets)

"Sturdy, commodious and well-crafted," the Ishpeming City Hall occupies a corner of the primary intersection of town. This Richardsonian Romanesque public building of brick and red sandstone is remarkable for its bold asymmetry. The cost was $31,340. Built in 1890, when the Cleveland-Cliffs Iron Mining Company was the region's chief producer of ore, its complex, weighty massing and irregular round-arch and square-headed fenestration are all poised around a distinctive corner

MQ12 Ishpeming City Hall

tower and vigorously articulate its compound internal functions of city hall, library, and jail. The gigantic round-arch entry at the foot of the tower is reminiscent of H. H. Richardson's Allegheny County buildings in Pittsburgh, Pennsylvania.

MQ13 **The Mather Inn**

1931–1932; James S. Ritchie of Ritchie Associates; Warren H. Manning, landscape architect. 107 Canda St. (bounded by Canda, Main, Barnum, and Maple streets; Southeast Lake Shore Dr., which intersects US 41/Michigan 28, to Spruce then northeast on Barnum)

In 1928 fire destroyed the Nelson House, a hotel built on this site in 1880. Recognizing the need for a "modern and distinctive hotel" for travelers (*Ishpeming Iron Ore*, March 14, 1931), mining company visitors, and the community, S. R. Elliott, manager of mines for the Cleveland Cliffs Iron Company, spearheaded the organization of the Ishpeming Hotel Company. Its major shareholders were the Cleveland Cliffs Iron Company and its president, William G. Mather, but over three hundred Ishpeming residents also held shares. The company erected this large, fireproof Colonial Revival inn to the plans of a Boston architect. The four-story inn was built of steel, concrete, and red brick. A two-story balustraded portico runs along the front of the inn. Among its important public rooms are a pine-paneled main lobby with a large open fireplace, a men's clubroom, and a sunken dining room. It has 47 rooms and three apartments. All were furnished with early American furniture from Carson, Pirie Scott of Chicago. Warren H. Manning landscaped the south sloping site with a rock garden wall, terrace, elms, and large spruce.

MQ14 Edward R. and Jennie Bigelow Hall House

1885. 112 Bluff (South of Pine, which is 1 block west of Main St., from its intersection with Division St. [Business Michigan 28] and 3 blocks to Bluff St.)

Inspired by Sunnyside, Washington Irving's house at Tarrytown, New York, this Gothic Revival house with crow-stepped gables stands on a bluff overlooking Ishpeming. A high-rise apartment building now obstructs the view. C. H. (C. F.?) Hall reportedly built the house for his son, Edward, employing Italian stonemasons to lay the walls of native granite trimmed with smooth-cut brownstone. Altogether it is a rather quaint but appealing historical essay.

MQ15 Cliffs Cottage (William G. Mather Chalet)

1891, Charlton and Gilbert. 1902, addition. 282 Jaspar Street (1 block south of intersection with Bluff St.). Not visible from the road

The Swiss-inspired hilltop cottage built of local mine rock, sandstone, and logs for the president of the Cleveland-Cliffs Iron Mining Company is a fanciful contrast to his Beaux-Arts Classical lakeshore country house near Cleveland, Ohio, designed by Charles Platt in 1907–1908. Today the company and its employees entertain guests in the Mather chalet.

MQ16 Cliffs Shaft Mine Headframes

1919, George W. Maher. Lake Shore Dr. on south shore of Lake Bancroft from US 41/Michigan 28 (take Lake Shore Drive south to Lake Bancroft)

In the prominently located headframes for the A and B shafts of the Cliffs Shaft Mine of the Cleveland-Cliffs Iron Company (in 1919 the largest producer of hard hematite ore on the Marquette Iron Range), William G. Mather sought to combine architectural beauty with practicality. He achieved this through the col-

MQ16 Cliffs Shaft Mine Headframes

laboration of the Condron Company, structural engineers in Chicago, with George W. Maher (1864–1926), a Chicago School architect of considerable reputation. Their joint effort resulted in these remarkable reinforced concrete obelisks. Their blunt profiles and austere geometry make it difficult to escape the notion that architect Maher still had fresh in his mind H. H. Richardson's renowned Ames Monument in Sherman, Wyoming. With no interruption in the use of the hoist, they were constructed around existing wooden headframes dating from the sinking of the mines in the 1870s, completely enclosing them. The hoisting ropes were changed over on successive weekends and the old wooden structures dismantled. The operational use of the pair was replaced by the C shaft in 1955.

GWINN, FORSYTHE TOWNSHIP

MQ17 Gwinn

1907–1909, Warren H. Manning, landscape architect. Michigan 35

William Gwinn Mather, president of the CCI from 1890 to 1909, selected Boston landscape architect Warren H. Manning to design this model town in the Swanzy Iron District. Its purpose was to create a "pleasant, wholesome and high environment for future inhabitants." Mather's interest in a planned town was influenced by projects elsewhere—the National Cash Register Company's planned suburb for Dayton, Ohio; Lord Lever's suburb Port Sunlight outside Liverpool, England; and mining towns in Westphalia, Germany. To ensure that the community would never be relocated where the company might open up new deposits beneath it, Mather and Manning selected "a verdant isle among the pines" on the Middle Branch of the Escanaba River and removed from the iron ore deposits. Gwinn was laid out in a free and asymmetrical grid pattern. The business and commercial area was planned around a commons, and the residential area radiated out from this hub and the river. Some trees were planted, some indigenous trees were saved. Provision was made for churches, schools, a clubhouse, hospital, railroad depot; there were fourteen house types and twenty-four double houses. The characteristics of Upper Peninsula architect Demetrius Frederick Charlton, then working in a red brick Classical Revival style, can be seen in the superintendent's wooden house and the brick commercial and public buildings. Though much smaller than the United States Steel Corporation's town of Morgan Park near Duluth (the most important example of corporate town planning in the Lake Superior area), Gwinn, nevertheless, attracts attention for its freshness in the context of northern Michigan and its iron ore industry.

POWELL TOWNSHIP

MQ18 Granot Loma (Louis G. and Marie Young Kaufman Summer Estate)

1919–1923, Marshall and Fox. 1924?, 1927 or 1928, additions. Off Sauk Head Lake Rd., 1 mile northeast of Marquette County 550, 15 miles northeast of Marquette. Visible from Lake Superior

Woodsy, primitive, luxurious, Granot Loma is Michigan's most splendid wilderness camp. The self-sufficient rustic summer estate of Louis G. Kaufman, a Marquette banker and son of a Jewish immigrant, stands in isolation on 10,000 wooded acres and 9.5 miles of Lake Superior shoreline. Granot Loma is almost a textbook example of the Adirondack Rustic style, a style popular and widespread throughout America and used at Glacier and other national parks. It reflects the rejection in certain areas of American architecture of the high styles of the past and the growing interest in the wooden examples found in Japanese and Swiss architecture. Granot Loma surpasses most wilderness camps in its great size, in the substantiality of its construction,

MQ18 Granot Loma (Louis G. and Marie Young Kaufman Summer Estate)

and in its modernness. The monumental main lodge is made of log and fieldstone, is 215 feet by 300 feet in L-shape plan, has fifty rooms and thirty-two fireplaces. The sturdy spruce logs were hand rubbed to the ruddy brown of dried pine needles, and the slate roof is the gray and green of the surrounding trees. Secured to a granite outcrop on the very edge of Lake Superior opposite tiny Garlick Island, it is actually an engineering marvel in steel, concrete, and glass, in spite of its primitive outward appearance. It is as profusely decorated as any stage set imaginable, with wallpaper of birch and cedar barks, handcrafted wood furniture, Indian artifacts, and colorful objects in brilliant oranges, greens, yellows, reds, blacks, and whites. It cost $2 million to build. Guest cabins and other structures stand nearby. Close at hand are the Loma Farms, where the Kaufmans scientifically raised prize cattle. The complex of fourteen "ultramodern" fireproof buildings includes a piggery, slaughter house, horse stable, cattle barn, pheasant house, boardinghouse, manager's house, creamery, and office. It was planned by the Louden Barn Plan Department of the Louden Machinery Company of Fairfield, Iowa. All have walls of rose-colored vitrified clay hollow tile and are roofed in asbestos shingles of a similar hue. The camp was named Granot Loma for the first initials of the Kaufman children: GRaveraet, ANn, OTto, LOuis, MArie. In Granot Loma, Kaufman rivaled the Huron Mountain Club of Marquette's social elite. Granot Loma is a monument to the American dream of combining luxury with the beauty of nature.

BIG BAY VICINITY, POWELL TOWNSHIP

MQ19 John and Mary Beecher Longyear Summer House (The Stone Cottage)

1901–1902, Demetrius Frederick Charlton. On north shore of Ives Lake, 3.5 miles from entrance to Huron Mountain Club, which is off Marquette County 550 approximately 4 miles northwest of Big Bay

Overhanging tranquil Ives Lake against the backdrop of the Huron Mountains is John Longyear's rustic summer house. Like Granot Loma, Longyear's retreat employs the theme of the Adirondack Rustic style to its fullest. Tucked against the rocky shore, the gabled granite cottage exposes its lower story as the site drops down to the water's edge. A wooden porch supported and braced by cedar posts and brackets thrusts itself from the structure over Ives Lake. The rosemaling decoration used in the interior probably derives from Longyear's visits to his mining operations in Spitzbergen, Norway. Adjacent to the summer house was his farm. Nearby, where the Pine River empties into Lake Superior, is the Huron Mountain Club (Huron Mountain Shooting and Fishing Club) that Longyear, Horatio Seymour, Jr., and other Marquette men founded in 1889 as a private natural and wildlife reserve where members could enjoy hunting, fishing, and outdoor life. The club and its members gradually acquired 21,000 acres of land. There, inaccessible to the public but visible from the lake, the rustic but comfortable T-shaped, pine log clubhouse (1892, Demetrius Frederick Charlton) complements its natural surroundings and served as a residence for visitors until the first cabins were erected in 1894. Since then, forty-six wooden and log cabins and camps that harmonize with nature have been built on either side of the Pine River. Members now include affluent Michigan families like the Fords, Algers, Ferrys, Bentleys, and Angells—many of whom exploited the resources of the wilderness but saved this particular wilderness as sanctuary and hideaway for themselves.

The Stone Cottage was built next to the Longyear's Emblagaard Dairy Farm, which he established in 1893 as a model farm. It included a dairy building and cow stable and modern and convenient houses.

MQ20 Big Bay Point Lighthouse Bed and Breakfast (Big Bay Point Lighthouse)

1896, Office of the Lighthouse Engineer, 11th District. End of Lighthouse Rd., 4 miles northeast of Big Bay on Schenk St. and Marquette County 352

The Big Bay Point Lighthouse sturdily stands on a rocky point halfway between Marquette and Portage Entry, which projects from the south shore of Lake Superior halfway between Marquette and Keweenaw Bay. A harborage with certain winds is on either side of the point, and here ships changed their course. The establishment of a light station at Big Bay Point was recommended by the Lighthouse Board in 1892: "[The point] occupies a position midway between Granite Island and Huron Island, the distance in each case being 15 to 18 miles. These two lights are invisible from each other and the intervening stretch is unlighted. A light and fog signal would be a protection to steamers engaged in passing between these points. They include all the Lake Superior passenger steamers running between Duluth, Buffalo, and Chicago which carry freight and stop between all the important points on the south side of Lake Superior, including Marquette and the copper ports on Portage Lake. Quite a number of vessels have in past years been wrecked on Big Bay Point."[77] Congress authorized the establishment of a light station at the point on February 15, 1893, and appropriated $25,000 on August 18, 1894, to execute the work.

A square tower rises from the center of the boxy rectangular keepers' double dwelling to support the round steel watch room and lantern, which is now automated. The structure is clad with smooth red brick trimmed with brown sandstone quoins, stringcourses, and lintels. Nearby is a fog signal station of brick.

Baraga County (BG)

L'ANSE

Located at the southern end of Keweenaw Bay, where the shore is rimmed with great rocky cliffs of red sandstone, L'Anse was a stopping point for French explorers, trappers, and missionaries. Growth as a shipping center for lumber was anticipated when the Marquette, Houghton and Ontonagon Railroad terminated here in 1872. L'Anse Brownstone Company opened a quarry northeast of the village in the Keweenaw Bay area in 1875 and ran it until 1879. Three other quarries operated here in the 1890s.

BG01 United Methodist Church

1879, 1951, church moved to L'Anse and clad in stone. Northwest corner of Main and Bendry streets

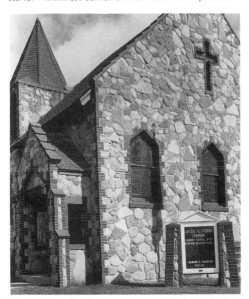

In 1951, after the operations at Henry Ford's (earlier Hebard's) sawmill declined, this Neo-Gothic structure, built originally in pine as the Union Church by Charles Hebard (1831–1902) at Pequaming, was moved from the forest to L'Anse. Here it was given a geological image. It was veneered with water-washed reddish brown Lake Superior beach stone in a manner distinct to this locale and trimmed with red brick. This technique may be attributable in part to the skills of the craftsmen

who resided in this area and who took advantage of the artistic possibilities of the abundant beach stones. Certainly it conveys their interest in the rocky land. The 150-seat, side-and-center aisled interior remains unchanged. A collection of large houses veneered in a similar fashion with smooth water-washed and -polished brownstone stands at 325 Front, 7 North Front, and 206 Broad streets. A motel, gas station and garage, fraternal hall, and the chimneys of many houses are clad with beach stone.

SKANEE, ARVON TOWNSHIP

BG02 Arvon Township Hall

1915, Charles W. Maass. South side of Lower Skanee Rd. and encircled by Park Rd.

The Arvon Township Hall is one of a pair of two-story, wood-frame and shingled hipped-roof buildings with cupola designed by a Hancock architect and used by the people of Skanee for over seventy-five years. The broad-fronted, sunny Colonial Revival building has a central pedimented entry pavilion in which is recessed a porch supported by square piers. Situated on Huron Bay, and named for the Swedish province of Skone, Skanee was a shipping and business center for the Huron Bay Iron and Slate Company in the 1870s and 1880s and for lumber companies. As Scandinavian fishermen and farmers prospered, it grew. The town hall has served township government with offices, kitchen, meeting hall, and assembly room. It is a companion piece to the Arvon Township School, with its cupola, built five years earlier on the south side of Skanee Road (1 mile east of Town Road and .5 mile west of Roland Lake Road). Although now covered with aluminum siding, the school still holds four classrooms.

ALBERTA, L'ANSE TOWNSHIP

BG03 Michigan Technological University's Ford Forestry Center (Alberta)

1936 (1938?). On US 41, 8 miles southwest of L'Anse

The hamlet of Alberta was built in 1936 (1938?) to house workers at one of the Ford Motor Company's early mill operations, which produced lumber for making automobile parts. At its peak of operation, Alberta housed about fifty workers and their families. This self-sustaining sawmill community was both a showplace of modern sawmill technology and an experiment in an industrial community, one of four in Michigan's Upper Peninsula (others are Pequaming, Kingsford, and Big Bay) and one of several others statewide for which Henry Ford was famous.

Alberta was laid out on a north-south axis between the sawmill and school with broad, tree-lined boulevards fed by narrower streets. A water and sewer system, a pair of school-houses, fire house, church, twelve model houses with garages, a pond, and ample garden plots were a part of the plan. Surrounded by forest, the model village with its neat lawns and freshly painted houses had an unreal quality. The houses, all slightly different in design, are one-and-a-half or two-story wood frame structures with gable roofs and enclosed porches. All were equipped to use heat, light, and water furnished by the mill operation. Originally, they had clapboard siding and were painted white, but today several have been resided or painted different colors. The mill, whose smokestack rises above the forest, was kept spotlessly clean during the fourteen-year period when it produced up to 15,000 board feet of lumber per day. Today the mill suffers from neglect. However, the varnished interior, hardwood floors, and steam-driven band saw remain intact.

In 1956, shortly after Ford ceased milling operations at Alberta, Michigan Technological University acquired the sawmill, community, and 4,000-acre Ford Forest for use as a forestry training and conference center.

ASSININS

BG04 Holy Name of Jesus Indian Mission (Assinins)

1843. 1881, convent and orphanage. 1970s-present, chapel and other buildings. US 41, 2 miles north of Baraga

Named for Chief Edward Assinins, the first Chippewa to be baptized by Father Frederick Baraga, and established in 1843, this was the last mission Baraga founded before he was appointed bishop of Upper Michigan. The simple wooden chapel (1970s) with tapered walls and interlocking log corners is in the image of the chapel Baraga constructed at La Pointe on Madeline Island in the Apostle Islands. From here he traveled throughout the region by boat, dog team, and on snowshoes, thus earning the name the "Snowshoe Priest." A cemetery contains graves of Indians, fur traders, and pioneers. The sandstone Convent and Orphanage of the Catholic Mission (1881), now in ruins, resembles in style the French Colonial house type built by French Canadians in Quebec. Some of the activities of the Keweenaw Bay Tribal Center, Head Start Program, Indian Health Services, Home School Coordinator, and Law Enforcement Program and the tribal council chambers and the tribal construction company are contained here today. Nearby the tribal community has built efficient modern housing, community centers, a gambling casino, and campgrounds.

PELKIE, BARAGA TOWNSHIP

BG05 Hanka Finnish Farmstead (Herman and Anna Wilhelmina Hanka Farm)

1896–1924, Askel Hill. Off US 41, 10 miles north of Baraga at Arnheim, take Arnheim Rd. west 4.3 miles, then south on Askel Rd. 1.3 miles, then east .5 mile (northwest 1/4 of northeast 1/4 of section 19, township 51 north, range 33 west)

Tucked deep in the Sturgeon River valley, the Hanka farm is a complex of eleven buildings and related landscape features that represent the establishment of an agricultural way of life in rural Keweenaw Peninsula by Finnish immigrants, and the transfer of Finnish folk architectural tradition to the western Great Lakes Region. Herman and Anna Wilhelmina Hanka came to the Calumet area from Vaasa, Finland, in 1880 and took up an 80-acre homestead claim on Askel Hill in 1896. Members of the Hanka family lived here until 1966. The Hankas were part of a large immigration between 1870 and 1920 of some 10 percent of the Finnish population to the United States, about half of which came to the cities and rural areas of the western Great Lakes Region. Dissatisfied with the hardships and hazards of the mines, the Finns abandoned them in large numbers and participated in a back-to-the-land movement reinforced by the preaching of the Apostolic Lutheran Church.

Previous farm experience in Finland, together with the physical characteristics of this region and economic forces, determined the kinds of buildings constructed on the Hanka farm, their sequence of construction, and the way of life the Hankas established. The largely self-sustaining subsistence farming (dairy farming supplemented by hunting, chicken raising, apple and vegetable growing, and seasonal odd jobs) called for many small specialized buildings. The one-and-a-half story, rectangular, double-pen, horizontal log farmhouse *(tupa)* resembles the *parituba,* or Nordic pair house. It was built in two stages—in 1896, the original homestead cabin, and before 1915, a one-and-a-half story addition to the west and the raising of the height of the cabin. It exhibits horizontal axe-hewn log construction with full dovetail corner notching and wood frame, shed-roof entries, all Scandinavian traditions. A barn complex of connected cattle barn *(navetta,* 1910), hay barn

(lato, 1896), woodshed *(puusuoja,* pre-1924), and outhouse *(kaymala)* extends along the same axis, only 50 feet from the house, in a manner characteristic of Finnish construction. Log hewn and timber and pole construction techniques were used in these buildings and may represent the work of different craftsmen: the Finnish work custom, *talkoo,* calls for a spontaneous cooperation on the part of the people of a rural neighborhood. The only timber-frame building is the field hay barn used for hay storage. A frame grain storehouse *(aitta,* pre-1924) was used for storage of grain, apples, and flour. The loft may have been used as a traditional Finnish sleeping area *(luhti aitta)* for guests or children. The smoke sauna *(savusauna,* c. 1896) contains a bench and a chimneyless stove and was used for bathing, cooking, grain-drying, and storage. Two airvents extend through the roof. Other structures include a stable *(talli),* chicken coop *(kanahakki),* milk house *(maitohuone,* pre-1924), root cellar *(kellari,* 1935), well, and blacksmith shop *(paja).*

The Menominee Iron Range (Iron and Dickinson Counties)

Harvey Mellon, a United States surveyor, reported in 1851 the discovery of iron near present-day Iron River and Stambaugh, a finding that became known as the western deposits of the Menominee Iron Range. Exploration for ore in what are now the towns of Quinnesec and Vulcan, and the city of Iron Mountain in the eastern Menominee Range, took place in the 1860s and 1870s.

Mining on the Menominee Iron Range began at Quinnesec in 1873 and flourished after 1879, when the Chapin Mine at Iron Mountain opened and the Chicago and Northwestern Railway built a line from its ore docks at Escanaba to the eastern deposits. Iron Mountain took the lead with three mines, the Hewitt, the Ludington, and the Chapin, all operating here. From 1880 to 1934 the Chapin Mine alone produced 27 million tons.

The western deposits of the Menominee Range were first exploited in 1880 by the Crystal Falls Iron Company in eastern Iron County. The last mines to be developed were in the vicinity of Iron River. They were aided by the arrival of the Chicago and Northwestern Railway in 1882. Discovery of new deposits of iron ore, coupled with the reopening of mines closed during the economic depression of the 1890s, contributed to the growth of the iron ore industry. The Hiawatha at Stambaugh became a leading producer, and by 1922 the iron

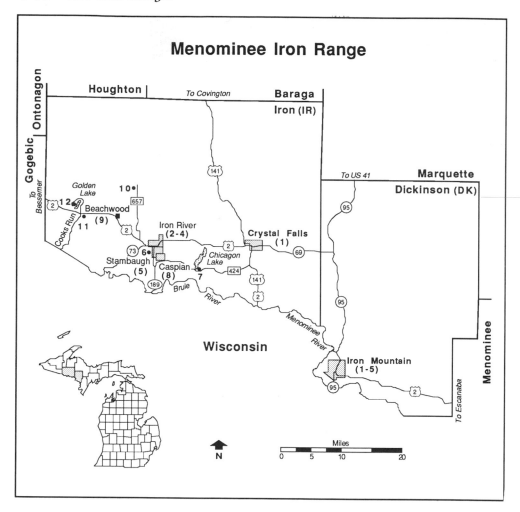

Menominee Iron Range

mining industry employed twenty-six hundred people, 25 percent of Iron County's population.

Iron mining on the Menominee Range peaked in 1920, declined gradually in the 1930s, and eventually closed in the 1970s.

Iron County   (IR)

CRYSTAL FALLS

Located on the Paint River, Crystal Falls is the seat of Iron County government.

IR01 Iron County Courthouse

1890–1891, J. E. Clancy. 2 Sixth St.

In 1885 the state legislature set off Iron County from Marquette County and designated Iron River as the temporary seat of county government. Four years later, county voters elected to move the county seat from its temporary location in Iron River to Crystal Falls, the oldest and largest town in the county.

IR01 Iron County Courthouse

The board of supervisors substantiated this decision by building this towered and turreted reddish brown brick and stone Richardsonian Romanesque courthouse. It is spectacularly positioned on the crest of a high hill at the head of Superior Avenue, the city's principal business street, where it commands a view of the Paint River valley and the countryside beyond. Built in 1888 to the designs of J. E. Clancy, a Wisconsin architect noted regionally for his plans for public buildings, the courthouse solidified the permanent location of the seat of Iron County government in Crystal Falls. Paired polished diorite columns quarried from outcroppings on the Paint River flank the main arched entrance. The proud tower topped by a hexagonal clock-tower-belfry and a statuary group of Law, Mercy, and Justice manufactured in galvanized metal by W. H. Mullins of Salem, Ohio, proclaim the building's function as the courthouse. The polished black oak interior finish confirms the formal nature of the building as a symbolic seat of county government. Louis A. Webber of Menasha, Wisconsin, built the courthouse. It cost $40,000. On its completion the *Crystal Falls Diamond Drill* boasted that the Iron County Courthouse was the finest structure of its type north of Milwaukee or Detroit.

IRON RIVER

The mines in Iron River and Stambaugh were the last to be developed on the Menominee

Range. The city has a fine collection of bungalows.

IR02 Saint Mary's Assumption Catholic Church

1910–1911, Erhard Brielmaier. 1922. 105 Fifth Ave. (south of Adams St. [US 2] on Fifth Ave.)

The Late Gothic Revival red brick church, with a pinnacled central square tower and belfry topped by a truncated turreted steeple, was built for a Polish-speaking parish to the designs of Erhard Brielmaier, a German-born Milwaukee architect noted for his Catholic churches and other ecclesiastical structures. Notable Gothic elements on the exterior are the simple lancet windows, the buttressing, and a polygonal apse. It was constructed on the fieldstone foundation of the previous church, built ten years earlier in Young's subdivision to the city by members of a two-hundred-family congregation, comprised mainly of miners and farmers of Iron River, Stambaugh, Caspian, Gaastra, and neighboring settlements.

IR03 Houses of Seventh and Eighth Avenues

Early twentieth century. Seventh and Eighth avenues, from West Boyington to West Division streets (3 blocks south of Adams St. [US 2] on Seventh and Eighth avenues)

Many comfortable foursquare, homestead temple-form, and bungalow houses were built in Iron River in the early twentieth century during Iron County's period of greatest economic activity. Several of the most noteworthy are on Seventh and Eighth avenues in the southwest quarter of Young's Addition to the city. The Harvey Van Wagner House (c. 1920) at 103 North Seventh Avenue, and the Joseph Joseph House (1925) at 105 North Eighth Ave. are noteworthy, as well as the Wall-Seppanen house.

IR03.1 Wall-Seppanen House

c. 1915. 21 North Seventh Ave.

Craftsman ornamentation is applied to this little stucco bungalow. The concealing of the upper story in the one-and-a-half-story height, the interpenetration of inner and outer space achieved by the roof that sweeps over the

IR03.1 Wall-Seppanen House

veranda, and the hoodlike roof over the bay mark this house as a variation of the bungalow form. Exposed roof rafters, triangular braced supports under the eaves, extended rafter ends, and the cobblestone exterior chimney express the materials and construction in a way characteristic of the Craftsman style. It was built for James S. Wall (b. 1852) and his wife, Britania Nichols. Wall was manager of the Oliver Iron Mining Company and also president of the Miners' State Bank. Later, in 1943, it was occupied by the family of Wayne E. Seppanen, a mining engineer and superintendent of the Caspian Mine.

IR04 Iron County Fair Exhibition Hall

1931, David E. Anderson. Iron County Fairgrounds (gate at intersection of West Franklin St. and north of Adams St. [US 2] on Forest St.)

The polygonal exhibition hall is the architectural centerpiece of the Iron County Fairgrounds. The two-story central octagonal core with three one-story wings radiating from it is made of concrete blocks set in red mortar. It is covered with a low-pitch roof with clerestory windows and has jerkinhead roofs on the wings. The main gabled entrance features a porthole window in the gable, recessed brick concentric wall arches over the triple doors, and a tympanum in the lower arch that identifies the construction date. The Iron County Park Commission and the Iron River School Board selected the site, and the Iron County Board of Commissioners appropriated funds for the construction of the exhibition hall. The Iron County Fair was first held in 1899, an outgrowth of the annual exhibitions of the Iron County Agricultural Society, organized to encourage the production of quality crops and livestock as a basis for a stable agricultural economy.

STAMBAUGH

IR05 Joseph Harris House

c. 1916. 165 Washington Ave. (from US 2 in Iron River, south on Iron County 424 at Stambaugh Hill, then up the hill to Washington Ave.)

This massive stucco foursquare house has a distinctive heavy front porch and porte-cochère of four low segmental arches resting on five heavy square posts and topped with a parapet, the outside bay serving as a porte-cochère. A low gabled dormer is over the center of the entrance. The general horizontality, the generous overhang, the rectangular wall panels, and the low hipped roof characterize the Prairie style. The house possesses all the characteristics of the American Foursquare house form, as Clem Labine and Patricia Poore defined the term in the *Old House Journal* for January 1982, and as Alan Gowans developed it in *The Comfortable House* (1986). It is two stories on a raised basement, has a veranda running the full width of the first story, and is capped by a low pyramidal roof that contains dormers. As well, it probably has an interior plan of four nearly equal size rooms per floor. The owners of the house were members of the Harris Clothing Store family.

STAMBAUGH TOWNSHIP

IR06 Hiawatha Mine Number One Headframe

1926. Hiawatha Mine Location (from Iron River south on Fourth Ave. [Michigan 189] .75 mile, headframe is on west side of Selden Rd. [Michigan 189])

Built by the Munro Mining Company, the steel headframe of Iron County's deepest and most productive mine rises majestically 120 feet from a steel and concrete base. Iron ore was stored in six bins in the lower level and then dumped into ore cars pulled underneath.

Explorations by Richard L. and William H. Selden resulted in the discovery of good ore here in 1882. Its great depth and the lack of rail transportation from the site prevented the development of the mine for nearly ten years. In 1891 William Selden and Findley Morrison formed a partnership to work the Hiawatha Mine Number One site, and ore was first mined in 1893.

The Victor Schlitz Mining Company owned the mine until 1905, and the Thomas Furnace Company of Milwaukee, until 1907. Then the Munro Mining Company of Buffalo, New York, acquired the mine and improved the underground workings, increasing the annual production to a uniformly high level. The M. A. Hanna Mining Company purchased the mine in 1929 and extensively improved its surface structures, including the nearby hoist house and dry house, and continued to extract ore until 1950. Eventually, the site was mined to eighteen levels of 2,100 feet. It shipped over 8.5 million tons of hematite ore between 1893 and 1950.

IR07 Pentoga Park Office and Bathhouse

1936. 1630 Iron County 424, Pentoga Park, south of Chicagoan Lake

The Works Progress Administration (WPA) sponsored the construction of two rustic county park structures of local materials on the wooded shores of Chicagoan Lake. Both the Pentoga Park Office and the Pentoga Park Bathhouse used locally quarried granite for the thick random ashlar walls and cedar for the shingle roofs. The park office is a small, square, hipped-roof structure that houses the Iron County Park Service offices and public rest rooms. The park bathhouse is an L-shaped, gable-roofed building, with an open dressing area protected by a high granite wall extending from its east side.

Efforts to establish the Pentoga County Park began in 1918 with the county-sponsored program to preserve and maintain a Chippewa burial site on the south shore of Chicagoan Lake. Once the location of an extensive Chippewa village, the burial ground, containing five spirit houses, was all that remained of the settlement. The property was purchased by the county in 1922, and the park established in 1923. Named in honor of the wife of Chief Edwards, the last Indian chief to reside at Chicagoan Lake, Pentoga Park became the headquarters of the Iron County Park Service.

CASPIAN

IR08 Italian Society Duke of Abruzzi Hall

1914. 1929, rehabilitated. East side of McGillis Ave., between Morgan and Sawyer streets (2 to 4 blocks east of Brady Ave.)

Dedicated to "the reciprocal solidarity of men through mutual aid and the keeping of the social good," Degli Società Duca D'Abruzzi was organized on September 26, 1909, in response to the many Italian families who settled here. In 1914, the society built this one-story, rectangular, gable roof, red brick structure. In a dim reflection of its Italian origins, it proudly displays a yellow brick false front topped by a segmental arch and centered around a round-arch entrance door and vestibule. The building provides a center for the continuance of Italian traditions, including a large dance hall and a wine-making and sausage-seasoning room. In the yard next to the hall is a grass boccie court.

BEECHWOOD, IRON RIVER TOWNSHIP

IR09 Beechwood Store

1912. 215 Beechwood Rd.

Built along the tracks of the Chicago and Northwestern Railroad, the Beechwood Store is a well-preserved, frame, front-gabled country store and post office. It served as the commercial, social, and civic center of the tiny Swedish settlement of Beechwood. Built for Albert J. Sandgren and Andres J. T. Anderson, brothers-in-law and community leaders, it provided second-floor living quarters for the Anderson family. A garage just west of the store, built in 1920, was used as a gas station and automotive repair shop. The store carried a complete line of groceries and meats, hardware and dry goods. The Beechwood Post Office and the Iron River Creamery Station, for dairy farmers in the area, also were included in this building.

IRON RIVER TOWNSHIP

IR10 **Camp Gibbs**

1935. 129 West Camp Gibbs Rd., west of Iron County 657, Ottawa National Forest

The Civilian Conservation Corps (CCC) reforestation camp is located 2 miles south of the old lumbering town of Gibbs City. From this camp, one of three CCC camps established in Iron County alone, two hundred CCC workers of the 3604th Company constructed miles of truck trails for fire control and for forest development and utilization, installed fire lookout towers and telephone lines, reforested thousands of barren acres, and managed existing forest lands in the Ottawa National Forest. The 3604th Company was established on June 14, 1935, as an offshoot of the 63d Company at the Paint Lake Camp, about 12 miles to the northwest. The company moved to this site two months later. The enrollees lived in tents until they had constructed the camp buildings.

The complex of modest one-story, woodframe structures includes a mess hall and kitchen, an officers' club, a post exchange, a powerhouse, a laundry and clothing supply building, a bath and shower house, a mechanic's shop, a truck garage, four barracks, two officer's quarters, and a recreational hall. Abandoned at the beginning of World War II, the buildings are used only with the permission of the U.S. Forest Service by recreational clubs.

STAMBAUGH TOWNSHIP

IR11 **Cooks Run Trout Feeding Station**

1933–1934. 180 Cooks Run Rd.

The Michigan Conservation Department (now the Department of Natural Resources), with funds from a Civil Works Administration (CWA) grant, constructed this trout-feeding station, with a small hatchery pond and dam, and several small, frame and log structures along Cooks Run Stream. The stream is a tributary of the Paint River, whose waters eventually flow into Lake Michigan's Green Bay. Fingerlings at Cook River were raised and planted in the Great Lakes. A simplified form of the Adirondack Rustic style is evidenced in the one-and-a-half-story, roughly H-plan, log caretaker's cabin. It is a noteworthy example of vernacular wilderness camp architecture, which utilizes local materials and displays outstanding craftsmanship and decorative details. Its light fixtures and stairway were fashioned of mitered tree roots by Frank Rawnick, a local wood carver. The trout-feeding station was promoted as a tourist attraction in the late 1930s and 1940s and was given to Iron County in 1961 for operation as a park.

IR12 **Van Platen–Fox Lumber Camp** (Camp Filbert Roth)

1921. 281 University Rd.

The camp office and store, cook house and mess hall, and two bunkhouses are the only surviving structures of a once large logging camp that the Van Platen–Fox Lumber Company built along the western shore of Golden Lake in 1922. It operated until 1935. The one-story, wood-frame camp buildings rest on concrete blocks and are finished with vertical pine plank siding. Headquartered in Iron Mountain, with extensive lumbering operations in the western Upper Peninsula and northern Wisconsin, the Van Platen–Fox Lumber Company acquired property, put up a camp, and began harvesting hardwoods around Golden Lake in 1921. The Chicago and Northwestern Railroad transported the logs from Basswood, 2.5 miles to the northeast, to lumber mills in Crystal Falls, Menominee, and other points south. Since 1937 the University of Michigan has used the site as a summer training camp for its forestry students, adding classroom buildings and log cabins.

Dickinson County (DK)

IRON MOUNTAIN

Iron Mountain is located in the center of the Menominee Iron Range. The range's most productive mines—the Chapin, the Pewabic, and the Millie—were located here. The Chapin Mine was the largest producer, yielding 27 million tons of iron ore from 1880 until 1934. From the 1870s through World War II, however, lumbering was also an important industry. An interesting outgrowth was Henry Ford's plant in Kingsford, where he manufactured wooden components for his automobiles.

Since Iron Mountain is near the Menominee River and several lakes, the availability of waterpower aided the city's development: it was incorporated as a city in 1890. Also serving the city were two major railroads, the Chicago and Northwestern and the Chicago, Milwaukee and Saint Paul. Iron Mountain became the center of commerce and distribution for the range and possesses the region's largest commercial district.

DK01 Dickinson County Courthouse and Jail

1896–1897, James E. Clancy. 500 South Stephenson Ave. (US 2/US 141) (east side of South Stephenson Ave., between C and D streets)

In 1896, five years after Dickinson County was established by the state legislature by dividing Menominee County, voters elected to borrow $32,000 to acquire a site and build a courthouse and jail. Until then the county leased space in the Wood Building, in the 200 block of East Ludington Street. The selected site occupies a full block on a hillside south of the central business district, where it faces the main thoroughfare and is plainly visible from the trains that ran through the city on either railroad. Here the county built a formal rock-faced red brick Richardsonian courthouse trimmed with Portage Entry red sandstone. An entry, bell, and clock tower rises 88 feet over the city. The round-arch entrance, with prominent voussoirs, is flanked by granite columns. The building was designed by James E. Clancy, a Green Bay, Wisconsin, architect responsible for planning several courthouses in northern Michigan and Wisconsin, including the neighboring Iron County Courthouse (IR01, p. 504). The medieval-looking castellated sheriff's residence and jail stand to the south of the courthouse. E. E. Grip and Company of Ishpeming built the courthouse. The *Iron Mountain Range Tribune* (January 2, 1897) remarked that the "elegant, commodious and complete" county buildings seemed to mark "the progress of Dickinson County" and to place her "in the Front Rank of Progressiveness."

DK02 Commercial National Bank and Trust Company Building (Commercial Bank)

1927, A. Moorman and Company. 500 Stephenson Ave. (US 2/US 141) (west side of Stephenson Ave., between A and B streets)

The Commercial Bank is Iron Mountain's most prestigious commercial and professional building. A Minneapolis architectural firm designed it in the Art Deco style. The six-story, steel and concrete, fireproof bank building held banking rooms on the first and second floors and professional offices above. Faced in light yellowish brown brick, it occupies one full block with the first two stories, while a towerlike center section rises four stories. On the exterior, vertical architectural lines increase the illusion of height, and stylized depictions of fleur-de-lis and rams' heads in yellowish white terracotta strengthen its Art Deco image. The bank's directors were superintendents of the Penn and Oliver mining companies and the Ford Motor Company's Kingsford plant.

DK03 Iron Mountain Post Office

1934–1936, J. Ivan Dise and L. R. Hoffman. 1968, addition, Harry W. Gjelsteen. 101 West Ludington St.

The one-story brick Art Deco Iron Mountain Post Office building contains one of the most outstanding and best-preserved examples of mural art sponsored by the federal government for a building in Michigan.

During the Great Depression in the 1930s, under the auspices of Franklin D. Roosevelt's New Deal administration, the federal government commissioned artwork for many Michigan buildings. There were several projects responsible for the embellishment of public buildings with murals and sculpture, the best known being the Works Progress Administration's Federal Art Project (WPA/FAP). The U.S. Treasury Department also administered several projects, namely the Public Works of Art Project (PWAP), the Treasury Relief Art Project (TRAP), and the Section of Fine Arts. The FAP was a program run by officials in each state that placed artwork in public buildings such as schools, hospitals, armories, and the like, whereas the Treasury Department projects provided artwork in federal buildings.

The most complete representation of New Deal art in Michigan buildings is from the

Treasury Section of Fine Arts program (1934–1943). Almost all the artwork commissioned for Michigan under this section remains in the original buildings for which it was intended, mostly post offices. The Iron Mountain Post Office building is unique, as it contains artwork from TRAP and the Section of Fine Arts. The latter permitted the artist to execute five murals with the subject of pioneering and western expansion. Themes dealing with American history, especially early exploration and settlement, were important during the depression era, when people looked back to a time of strength for guidance through the then current national crisis.

Most of Michigan's post office art consists of works that deal with the individual community. In this case, however, artist Vladimir Rousseff painted scenes that pertain more generally to the western United States, in works titled *Moving West, Washing and Carrying Gold, Watching an Early Train, Stage Coach, Ferry Boat,* and *Fight with Indians.* Under the Treasury Section's program, one percent of the building construction cost was reserved for artistic embellishment, and artists were chosen competitively. Bulgarian-born Rousseff, who lived in Chicago and had a studio in a small town near Iron Mountain, was selected to do the murals based on entry sketches for a major competition for the Post Office Department Building in Washington, D.C. Although many government artists had difficulty relating their murals to the architecture of the building, Rousseff successfully overcame this problem by unifying the separate murals through a common color scheme that was harmonious with the interior tones of the building; he also linked them by an overall theme. The paintings also complemented the building through internal elements of the composition. The federal art projects were successful in that they brought original painting and sculpture to smaller towns such as Iron Mountain in buildings that everyone visited, in this case, the post office.

DK04 Menominee Range Historical Museum (Carnegie Free Public Library)

1901–1902, James E. Clancy. 300 East Ludington St. (northeast corner of East Ludington St. and Iron Mountain Ave.)

James E. Clancy, a locally recognized specialist in public buildings on the Menominee Iron Range, designed the Carnegie library in the Beaux-Arts Classical style. This work is built solidly and substantially of gray Amberg, Wisconsin, stone and rests on a rough-faced rusticated stone basement foundation. A pedimented and balconied entry pavilion with fluted Ionic columns covers one half of the front and is flanked by penciled and arcaded walls. The Carnegie Free Public Library stands prominently on an elevated corner site. W. H. Sweet built the structure at a cost of $17,500.

DK05 Immaculate Conception Church

(Italian Catholic Church of Mary Immaculate of Lourdes / Chiesa Cattolica Italiana Maria Santissima Immacolata di Lourdes)

1902–1903. 500 Blaine St.

Complete with an attached campanile in the rear, this vernacular version of an Italian Renaissance church was built in an Italian enclave in the Gay Subdivision of Iron Mountain, on land purchased from the Houghton Mineral Land and Mining Company. Sandstone quarried locally on Millie Hill was used, and the labor was furnished by volunteers overseen by Rev. Giovanni Pietro Sinopoli. Sinopoli was a native of Catonia, Sicily, and a member of a religious order founded by Bishop Scalebrini to care for Italian immigrants. He arrived in Iron Mountain in April 1902; the church was dedicated nine months later, on January 1, 1903. A false front with connecting volutes over the side aisles makes up the primary facade of the church. The interior is arranged with a nave and side aisles. Large octagonal tracery connected by straight members is applied to the barrel ceiling. The Menominee Stained Glass Works manufactured the stained-glass windows. Anton Rezek, an early twentieth-century historian of the Diocese of Marquette and Sault Sainte Marie, described the red sandstone church as, "in style exclusively Italian so that one cannot mistake the character of the building nor the nationality of its owners."[78]

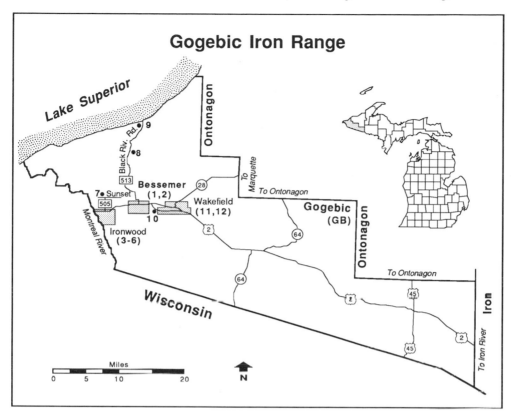

Gogebic Iron Range

The Gogebic Iron Range

Lying south of Lake Superior, in a narrow belt that extends from Lake Gogebic to the Montreal River and on into Wisconsin, the Gogebic Iron Range was the last iron range opened in Michigan. In 1871, after examining William A. Burt's survey notes, Raphael Pumpelly, a Harvard geologist, discovered iron ore here and selected lands for acquisition by Eastern speculators that were to become the Newport and Geneva mine sites. With the arrival of the railroad in 1884, the Colby Mine opened at Bessemer. Subsequently, a chain of mining operations was established on the Gogebic Iron Range at Ironwood, Bessemer, Ramsey, and Wakefield—twelve mines between 1884 and 1887, and at least twenty more by 1925. The ore was transported by rail to the great ore docks at Ashland, Wisconsin, and Escanaba, where it was loaded onto ore boats and shipped down the lakes to steel mills and outside markets. Eventually, however, the mines became too deep, the ores too impure, and the profits dissipated, so that in 1966, the last mine on the Gogebic Range was closed.

Gogebic County   (GB)

BESSEMER

Situated in a valley 7 miles east of Ironwood, Bessemer was incorporated as a village in 1887, and as a city in 1889, when it reached a population of more than 2,500. It developed after the opening of the Colby Mine and the completion in 1884 of the Chicago and Northwestern Railroad through this site to Ironwood. The setting off of Gogebic from Ontonagon County and the selection of Bessemer as the seat of county government in 1887 enhanced growth of the region. Federal relief during the decline of mining and the depression that followed enabled Bessemer to build a city hall, in the same way that federal relief provided other western Upper Peninsula communities with schools and community buildings.

GB01 Bessemer City Hall and Community Building

1934–1936, N. Albert Nelson. 401 South Sophie St. (at end of South Sophie St., which intersects US 2, against Colby Hill)

This craggy stone building was designed by N. Albert Nelson (1893–1949) of Ironwood in a free and fluid vernacular interpretation of the Neo-Tudor style. A broad center gable with half timbering laid vertically and infilled with stucco embraces a smaller battered gable containing the main double door. An oriel window also graces the front. The glass blocks and the windows are modern touches. The Bessemer City Hall and Community Building holds city offices, the fire department, and a public auditorium. The project was paid for with federal CWA and WPA funds and with

city funds. The building demonstrates the artistic ability of this very interesting Ironwood architect, although he studied architecture by correspondence with a technical school in Sweden, from where he emigrated, and learned through on-the-job experience. Nelson was also an artist known for his imaginative pen-and-ink sketches.

GB02 Frick Funeral Home

1934, N. Albert Nelson. 304 South Sophie St. (which intersects US 2)

Tucked among the storefronts of South Sophie Street is this somber and dignified little Neo-Tudor stone building trimmed with red sandstone. It was built as a funeral home to the plans of N. Albert Nelson. The front is boldly faced with rock-faced local stone and half timbering infilled with stucco. A segmental-arch entrance with decorative carving is positioned in a pavilion. The recessed door has a fanlight. Windows are grouped in twos and threes. A pent roof crowns the structure.

IRONWOOD

Founded in 1885, Ironwood rapidly became the leading city on the Gogebic Iron Range. The city was incorporated in 1889. It was named either after James R. Wood, a mining captain on the Gogebic Range whose nickname was Iron, or after its two natural resources, iron and wood.

The arrival of the Milwaukee, Lake Shore and Western Railroad (later the Chicago and Northwestern Railway), at Watersmeet in the southeast corner of the county in 1884, brought a flood of immigration to Ironwood, transforming the wilderness hamlet of trailblazers, attracted by the 1884 report of iron ore by New York speculator J. Lansear Norrie, into a center of activity. Shortly after, the Wisconsin Central Railroad linked Ironwood with ore docks at Ashland, Wisconsin. Then within a few years the Duluth, South Shore and Atlantic Railroad arrived. Ten years later, Ironwood had 10,000 people and had developed as a respectable business and commercial center. By comparison, its twin city, Hurley, Wisconsin, which is nestled among the hills on the west side of the raging Montreal River, had many saloons, was plagued by prostitution and gambling, and was known as the hell-hole of the range.

The Norrie, Aurora, Newport, Pabst, and Ashland mines operated within the city limits; most of them were eventually run by the Oliver Mining Company. Ironwood embraced the suburban towns of Jessieville and Monticello, once locations of mines, miners' houses, and stores.

Railroad tracks divide the city in half, with the residential quarter on the northwest and the commercial, industrial, and an earlier residential area on the south. In 1887, fire destroyed the downtown business section, and it was rebuilt in a more substantial manner. By the 1890s, handsome business blocks, many of Lake Superior sandstone, and comfortable houses replaced wooden stores and shacks. Municipal sewers were installed and the Gogebic Electric Railway and Light Company streetcar connected Ironwood and Hurley.

By the 1960s, the demise of iron mining had resulted in a 30 percent countywide reduction in population from its 1920 high. Residents of Ironwood and Gogebic County have compensated for that loss by developing a year-round outdoor recreation industry. Today, Ironwood is the center of skiing, canoeing, fishing, hunting, and hiking.

GB03 Ironwood Municipal–Memorial Building

1923, Bell and Kinports. Northwest corner of McLeod Ave. (US 2) and Marquette St.

In an expression of civic pride and commemorative spirit, the citizens of Ironwood raised $500,000 through a municipal bond issue to honor local veterans of World War I with this Beaux-Arts Classical community building. Bell and Kinports of Minneapolis prepared the plans and Albinson Company built it. The pentagonal, two-story reinforced concrete and steel structure is clothed in whitish gray terracotta and stone and is embellished inside with marble, decorative plaster, murals depicting mining and logging, and art glass. It contains a swimming pool, a gymnasium, an auditorium, and municipal offices. The building exudes classical refinement and detailing.

GB04 Ironwood Theatre

1924–1925, Seaman Block; 1927–1928, Ironwood Theatre; both by N. Albert Nelson. 109 East Aurora St. (southeast corner of Aurora and Lowell streets; Aurora is parallel to McLeod Ave. [US 2] 1 block northwest)

Built when Ironwood was the hub of Michigan-Wisconsin iron ore mining, the Ironwood Theatre was a regional status symbol. It was also a major achievement for local architect N. Albert Nelson and for his client Charles Seaman, a businessman and civic leader. The Ironwood Theatre sat 1,200 patrons on opening day, June 30, 1928, making it the largest movie palace of the golden age of the movie palace (1925–1930) in the Upper Peninsula.

No architectural or decorative style dominates the eclectic building. Rather, it is modern, with an eclectic blend of historic elements. Unique in Ironwood, the Moorish scheme in the foyer and promenade was a standard stylistic formula for exoticism in national movie palace design. The facade of the Ironwood Theatre is part of the Seaman Building, erected in 1924–1925. It is distinguished from the block by its bronze marquee, a neon sign, and stained-glass windows in the transom behind the marquee. Conservative in comparison with other movie palace facades of the era, the stained-glass window behind the marquee of the Ironwood Theatre alluded to morally respectable institutions such as churches. The proscenium arch took the form of a semidome with pseudotripartite vaulting. Today, the facade of the theater has been restored to its original state and the interior is undergoing restoration.

GB05 **Ironwood Area Historical Museum**
(Chicago and Northwestern Railroad Depot)

1892, Charles W. Grindle. Off Frederick St., between Suffolk and Lowell streets

This red sandstone and brick structure, with its hovering hipped roofs and round-arch openings, is a provincial reflection of the railroad stations of H. H. Richardson. It served as the passenger depot for the Chicago and Northwestern Railroad, the line that connected the mines of the Gogebic Range with the ore docks on Lake Superior at Ashland, Wisconsin, and aided in the development of Ironwood and the Gogebic Iron Range. It separates physically the south commercial district from the north residential area. During the railroad's most active years, twelve trains stopped here daily. To the southeast at 100 East Ayer Street is the Neo-Spanish Ironwood Post Office (1931, James A. Wetmore).

GB06 **Luther L. Wright High School**

1924–1925, Croft and Boerner. 600 Ayer St., between Monroe and Curry streets

The design of the large, earth-colored brick school pays academic attention to classical detail. The three-story structure has a central pedimented entry pavilion with an elaborate Spanish Baroque doorway embellished with intricate designs in yellowish white and blue terracotta. Above the entrance is a triple-arch window. The school was planned by Croft and Boerner of Minneapolis to be of fireproof construction and large enough for 1,400 pupils. Peter J. Nickel constructed it at a cost of $925,000. It was named for the first superintendent of schools in Ironwood.

IRONWOOD TOWNSHIP

GB07 **Ironwood Homesteads**

1937. On Sunset, from .75 mile west to .5 mile east of Lake Superior Rd. (Gogebic County 505)

Ironwood Homesteads is a small, New Deal, garden community project of the United States Resettlement Administration, built on a site "with good agricultural possibilities," less than three miles north of Ironwood. With its garden community projects, the administration

GB07 Ironwood Homesteads

intended to achieve efficiency and conservation in housing and land use, and in the process, to create jobs. At Ironwood Homesteads 132 units costing $10,403 each, for a total of nearly $1.4 million, were initiated. There were one-, two-, and four-family concrete block and brick dwellings, all with gable roofs and shed or gable dormers. The front entries were enclosed against the harsh climate. A community building, a store, and the post office were also part of the project. The houses were touted as practical, modern, and low-cost garden units. According to local rumor, the project may have been built as part of a plan to relocate the city of Ironwood to the north, because it was built over a valuable vein of ore. Ironwood Homesteads is smaller than the New Deal greenbelt town of Greendale near Milwaukee, which was completed in 1938.

GB08 **Copper Peak Ski–Flying Slide**
(Chippewa Hill)

1970, Lauren A. Larsen, engineer. Black River Rd. (Gogebic County 513), 10 miles north of Bessemer, Ottawa National Forest

The Gogebic Range Ski Corporation erected this giant ski slide on Chippewa Hill with federal funds to alleviate economic distress. At construction, it was one of five in the world; the others were in West Germany, Norway, Austria, and Yugoslavia. From this 282-foot-high and 469-foot-long Cor-Ten steel structure, ski fliers (jumpers) achieve speeds of 65 to 75 miles per hour before reaching the takeoff, more than 600 feet above ground. A 810-foot-long chairlift carries them from the base of the hill to the base of the tower, and an elevator in the tower takes them to the top. Chippewa Hill is the site of the discovery of a rich copper vein reported in 1846.

GB09 Black River Harbor Site and Marina

1930s. Black River Parkway (Black River Rd./Gogebic County 513), Ottawa National Forest

This recreational complex was constructed on the rugged Lake Superior shoreline at the mouth of the Black River by the Civilian Conservation Corps (CCC), with technical assistance from the National Park Service and under the direction of Gogebic County. It includes a combination bathhouse and recreation building, an ice house, a custodian's cottage, a Boy Scout building, boat docks, and a suspension bridge for pedestrians. Of particular interest is the T-shaped, gable-roof, native stone, and wood bathhouse and recreation building built by the men of the 3601st Company CCC, Camp Norrie, Ironwood, in 1939. The Black River Parkway developed from a wagon road running from the mouth of the Black River to the village of the Chippewa Mining Company, near what is now Copper Peak. It served as a supply route for early mining activities, fishermen, and sportsmen.

RAMSEY VICINITY, BESSEMER TOWNSHIP

GB10 Keystone Bridge

1891. Chicago and Northwestern Railroad over the Black River (east of Mill St., 100 yards north of Bessemer Township Memorial Park)

The Chicago and Northwestern Railway Company built this stone arch bridge over the Black River with limestone quarried at Kankauna, Wisconsin, and shipped in by rail. It is 44 feet in width and 57 feet in height. Its wing walls measure 50 feet.

WAKEFIELD

Wakefield is situated on the south side of Sunday Lake, a 2-mile-long body of water, and on the Milwaukee, Lake Shore and Western Railroad. It is 6 miles east of Bessemer. It was settled in 1866, incorporated as a village in 1877, and as a city in 1910. The business district is located on Sunday Lake Street. A city park, also used as a tourist camp, is along the lake shore.

GB11 Gogebic Chiefs Hockey Arena (Wakefield Ice Arena)

1939. Michigan 28 (on the shore of Sunday Lake)

The Wakefield Ice Arena was built in 1939 as a WPA project. The building is ten bays in length; each bay is separated by piers. Rock-faced local stone is irregularly laid in the exterior walls. Poured concrete quoins and window surrounds and the entry portal with its horizontal lines and glass bricks give the arena a Streamline Moderne appearance. The public skating rink is surfaced with naturally frozen ice and lies beneath a trussed and barreled ceiling. The Pullar Community Building (John D. Chubb, 1938–1939) at Sault Sainte Marie, the Dee Stadium at Houghton, and the Calumet Armory at Calumet are other public ice arenas in Upper Peninsula cities, where ice skating and hockey are popular winter sports.

Central Upper Peninsula

THE MAJESTIC FORESTED LAND OF THE CENTRAL UPPER Peninsula lies between the rugged shore of Lake Superior on the north and the gentler sandy shore of Lake Michigan on the south. Harbors on both of the big lakes are sheltered by islands and bays. Grand Island protects the harbor at Munising Bay on Lake Superior. On Lake Michigan, Green Bay shelters the harbor at Menominee, and Little and Big Bays De Noc give refuge to harbors at Escanaba, Gladstone, and Fayette.

U.S. Route 2 traverses the southern Upper Peninsula, following first the north shore of Lake Michigan on its long route from Saint Ignace through Escanaba, and then passing inland through Hermansville along the Wisconsin state line to Ironwood. Michigan 28 runs through the heart of the region on its route west through the Upper Peninsula from a point just south of Sault Sainte Marie to Wakefield just east of Ironwood. The nearly straight, 50-mile section of Michigan 28 known as the Seney Stretch extends from Seney through desolate swampland to McMillan on the east and to Shingleton on the west. Among the most scenic drives in the state is the portion of Michigan 28 that follows briefly the south shore of Lake Superior from Munising to Marquette.

The forests of Alger, Luce, Schoolcraft, Delta, and Menominee counties and a system of water transportation supplied the foundation of the economy of the Central Upper Peninsula. Although these vast virgin forests were apparent to the French voyageurs and missionaries and to traders who explored the coastlines of Lake Superior and Lake Michigan in the seventeenth and eighteenth centuries, logging and milling did not begin in earnest until the mid-nineteenth century.

Fur trading and fishing were the earliest economic ventures. In the late 1790s Louis Chappieu built a palisaded log fur-trading post on the south side of the

516

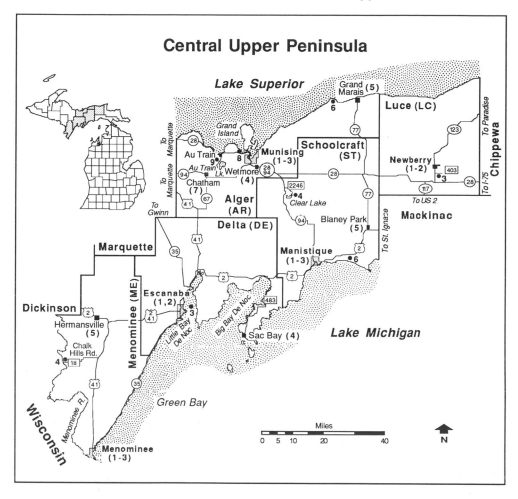

Menominee River at the site of what is now Marinette, Wisconsin. In the 1820s William Farnsworth and Charles Brush, agents of the American Fur Company, established a post on the north side of the Menominee River. Other traders and settlers followed. The American Fur Company built its first structure on Grand Island in the mid-1820s. In the 1830s Indian trader L. A. Roberts and his wife built a cabin on the banks of the Escanaba River. In the 1840s fishermen came from Saginaw to Saint Martin Island and other islands off the Garden Peninsula and engaged in commercial fishing. Fishermen from these islands settled Sac Bay in 1854 and Fairport in 1855.

Lumbermen followed the traders and fishermen. In the 1830s they built sawmills at the mouths of the Menominee, Cedar, Ford, Escanaba, Rapid, Whitefish, Sturgeon, and Manistique rivers on the north shore of Lake Michigan. They also built upstream, and later along the Two Hearted River and at the mouth of the Tahquamenon River on Lake Superior. In the 1850s the N. Ludington Company, the Marinette Lumber Company, and Abner Kirby and Company—organized by New York, Chicago, and Milwaukee investors—all began cutting logs along the Menominee River. In the 1860s and 1870s, the Chicago Lumber Company and eighteen other enterprises operated at Manistique. In the late 1880s logging giants such as Isaac, Robert, and Samuel Stephenson formed lumbering companies to cut forests of soft and hardwoods and to mill the logs into boards near Menominee. The industry peaked between 1889 and 1900, when twenty-three mills operated at the mouth of the Menominee River. The lumbering industry was augmented with wood product and paper manufacturing. Menominee, Escanaba, and Manistique grew and developed around docks and mills. The prosperity of the lumbering and shipping era is best seen in the commercial buildings, banks, public libraries, churches, and houses in Menominee and Escanaba. The character of the architecture is connected to the preoccupation with wood as a dimension of life.

In the 1870s, C. J. L. Meyer of Fond du Lac, Wisconsin, founded Hermansville and built a saw and shingle mill, a hardwood flooring factory, and a company town. This town of wooden buildings stands intact in Menominee County and is one of the state's best examples of a lumbering or wood products company town. The Queen Anne IXL Office Building is, in fact, one of the buildings that speak most eloquently for the Upper Peninsula. Other company towns based on iron processing, charcoal producing, or lumber cutting and milling are at Munising, Fayette, Newberry, and Manistique.

The mines of the Marquette, Menominee, and Gogebic iron ranges contributed to the economy and growth of the Central Upper Peninsula. Railroad companies coveted Escanaba's deep-water harbor on Lake Michigan, which was closer by far than Marquette Harbor to the steel mills at Chicago, Cleveland, and Pittsburgh. The Peninsula Railroad from Negaunee to Escanaba opened in 1864, and docks were built to load and ship iron ore from the Marquette Iron Range to steel mills below. In the late 1870s, a rail line was laid from Escanaba westward to the ore fields of the Menominee Range. Today, pellets of ore from the Marquette Range are shipped from Escanaba.

Smelting furnaces created a need for charcoal, and the hardwood forests of the Central Upper Peninsula furnished the timber that was burned to charcoal in furnaces throughout the region. From the mid-1860s to 1890, using local limestone for flux and local hardwood for charcoal, the Jackson Iron Company smelted iron ore from Negaunee at Fayette on the Garden Peninsula of Delta County. Blast furnaces for smelting iron ore into pig iron were operated by the Bay Furnace Company at Onota and the Schoolcraft Blast Furnace in Munising. The Menominee Furnace Company built charcoal kilns to convert hardwood to charcoal for the manufacture of pig iron. Blast furnaces made pig iron at Menominee. In a related industry, the Vulcan Furnace Company operated charcoal kilns in Luce County and built furnaces and company houses at Newberry in 1882. In yet another example the White Marble Company built kilns near Gulliver in 1889. Lime mortar was produced by roasting limestone or dolomite in the large stone kilns.

Today paper mills are found throughout the Central Upper Peninsula. The Manistique Pulp and Paper Company, organized in 1916, operates today as a division of Field Enterprises, Inc., with mills at Manistique. Mead Paper Company has mills in Escanaba, and Kimberly Clark has mills at Munising. The Louisiana-Pacific Corporation Plant opened in Newberry in 1985 to make particle board.

Excellent fishing, hunting, camping, and winter sports attract tourists to the scenic forests, streams, and lakes of the Central Upper Peninsula. Blaney Park, a resort on cutover land, and tourist cabins and motels along the major highways are among the remnants of the tourist industry that flourished in the 1930s with the widespread increase in automobile transportation.

Dairy and livestock farming has been of some importance in Alger, Menominee, and other counties. Michigan State University, formerly Michigan Agricultural College, built an experiment station with huge barns at Chatham.

Much of the land in the Central Upper Peninsula is under the jurisdiction of the national and state forests and parks, and the U.S. Forest Service has its administrative buildings for the Hiawatha National Forest at Munising and Manistique. Pictured Rocks National Lakeshore stretches along nearly twenty miles of Lake Superior coastline eastward from Munising to Grand Marais and encompasses 29,000 acres. Hiawatha National Forest, Lake Superior and Tahquamenon River state forests, Seney National Wildlife Refuge, and Tahquamenon Falls State Park preserve vast acres of wilderness and forest.

Alger County (AR)

MUNISING

Incorporated as a village in 1897, and as a city in 1919, Munising is sited on Munising Bay, one of the most beautiful natural harbors in Michigan. It is encircled by steeply rising hills and faces Grand Island, to the north. First an Indian encampment, Munising developed with iron furnaces in the 1870s and later with a tannery, sawmills, a paper mill, and tourist attractions. Pictured Rocks National Lakeshore, established by Congress in 1966, features a multicolored sandstone escarpment that rises from 50 to 250 feet and extends for over twenty miles from Munising to Grand Marais to the east. Nineteenth-century explorers, travelers, artists, and scientists admired and, from their different perspectives, described the awesome and fantastical shapes, caves, arches, and promonto-

ries gouged and carved into the stone by the action of waves and ice, naming them Miners' Castle, Lover's Leap, Battleship Rock, Grand Portal, Chapel Rock, and the like.

AR01 Alger County Historical Museum (Elizabeth Lobb House)

1905–1907, Edward DeMar. 203 West Onota St. (southwest corner of West Onota and Lynn streets, 2 blocks southwest of intersection of Lynn St. and Munising Ave. [Michigan 28])

The large, comfortable, wooden house was built for Elizabeth Lobb (1845–1926). Lobb was an English immigrant who owned and operated the Anna River Brick Company near Au Train and who received royalties paid by the Princeton Mine for extracting ore on Lobb land. Her house was designed by Edward

DeMar, a recognized Upper Peninsula architect with offices in Sault Sainte Marie. It is Prairie style with classical details. A large porch supported by single, paired and triple Doric columns wraps around the front and side of the house, projecting in a semicircle in the center, and overlooks Munising Bay. The hipped roof is supported by block modillions and has an ample, sweeping overhang. It is punctuated by hip- and shed-roof dormers with cross-hatch windows. The house's gracious interior is trimmed with oak woodwork and stained glass. Today, the Alger County Historical Society runs a house museum here. (AR02 is less than one block southeast.)

AR02 Saint John's Episcopal Church

1906, Demetrius Frederick Charlton. 127 West Onota St., near Lynn St.

This tiny sandstone and brick church reportedly was modeled by Charlton after an unidentified English country church seen by the Right Reverend G. Mott Williams, bishop of Marquette, during a visit to Great Britain in 1900. George Leiphart of Munising built it. Elizabeth Lobb donated, in memory of her husband, the large stained-glass window, *Jesus Knocking at the Door*. It is set within a Tudor arch.

AR03 Munising Ranger District Administration Site of the Hiawatha National Forest

1937. 601 Cedar St. (Michigan 28)

High on a hill overlooking Munising Bay, enrollees of the 3613th Company, Civil Conservation Corps, Camp Evelyn, under the supervision of Harry Person and Con Liephart, built for the Hiawatha National Forest a ranger station office, dwelling, garage, oil storage house, and warehouse to standard Forest Service plans 68a, B-72, 74, 23, and 14. These plans were intended to create institutional buildings that would fit into their small-town surroundings, in this case Early American, rather than rustic ones. The specifications called for paint colors in "colonial ivory, with silver gray and colonial green trim," and a chimney of local brownstone.

WETMORE, MUNISING TOWNSHIP

AR04 Wetmore Lookout Tower

1930s. 2518 Federal Forest Highway 13 (west side of Federal Forest Highway 13, 1.2 miles south of Michigan 28/Michigan 94) in Hiawatha National Forest

The 100-foot-tall steel tower and stairway were erected on a high point of land for use in detecting forest fires. The vertical members of the structure are braced with horizontal, vertical, and cross members. Nine flights of stairs, each concluding at a landing, rise up through the center of the steel superstructure and lead, eventually, to an enclosed lookout at the top of the tower.

GRAND MARAIS

AR05 Teenie Weenie Pickle Barrel Cottage

1927, Harold S. Cunliff. Southwest corner of Lake Ave. and Veteran St.

Once the summer home of William and Mary Donahey, cartoonists and creators of children's books, the pickle barrel is an interconnected pair of staved orange barrels, one small one and one quite large. It is a giant-size version of the "Teenie Weenie" homes created by the Donaheys "under a rose bush in the woods" in their *Chicago Tribune* cartoon strip. It was built originally by the Monarch Pickle Company of Chicago on the shore of Grand Sable Lake. When the site was acquired by the Pictured Rocks National Lakeshore, the Pickle Barrel Cottage was moved to Grand Marais, a resort center that was formerly a commercial fishing village.

BURT TOWNSHIP

AR06 Au Sable Light Station

1873–1874. 1909, light keeper's house. At Au Sable Point, 1.5 miles northeast off H-58 and 12 miles northwest of Grand Marais in Pictured Rocks National Lakeshore

A light tower, two dwellings, a fog signal house, and a boat house make up the Au

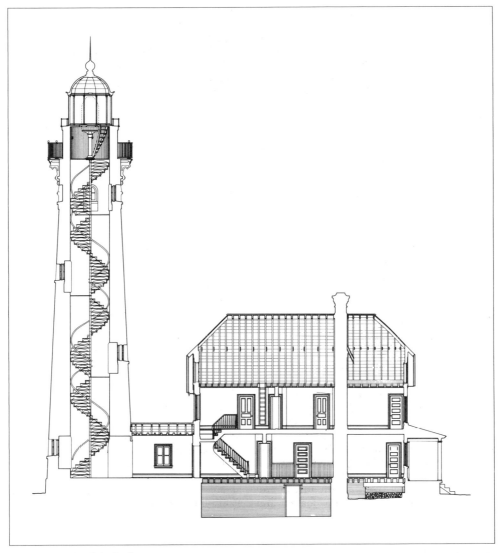

AR06 Au Sable Light Station

Sable Light Station complex. It was built by the U.S. Coast Guard twenty-two years after the opening of the Soo Locks to aid shipping of lumber, coal, grain, copper, and iron. The tower (1873) is linked by a passageway to a red brick double house with a jerkinhead, gabled roof (1873, 1909). The red brick, seven-room keeper's dwelling (1909) stands to the west. The boat house was built by 1910. The National Park Service has restored the light station. Open to public.

CHATHAM

AR07 **Pacific Hotel** (Chatham Hotel)

1904, 100 Rock River Rd. (Michigan 67) (southeast corner of Rock River Rd: and Munising St. [Michigan 94])

In 1904, three years after the Lake Superior Railway reached Chatham, Edward Levy, a grocer and saloon keeper, built this modest vernacular three-story, twenty-room hotel to lodge loggers, prospective real estate buyers, salesmen, and travelers. The gray rock-faced limestone for the walls was quarried south of the town hall in Chatham. It is randomly coursed on the front and laid in rubble on the flanks. The square-headed windows have stone lintels and sills. An inscription stone reads, "The Pacific 1904." Originally the building was fronted by a two-story porch. A bracketed wooden cornice supports the flat roof. The stone hotel was one of the few structures to survive the Chatham fire of 1925. It is among Chatham's most important buildings. (The others are the Michigan State University agricultural experiment station and the railroad depot.)

CHRISTMAS VICINITY, AU TRAIN TOWNSHIP

AR08 Bay Furnace

1869–1870. Just east of Christmas, northeast off Michigan 28 in Hiawatha National Forest

These ruins of this furnace include a 45-foot-high, closed-top stack with 9-foot boshes. It was built of large reddish gray sandstone blocks extracted from Powell's Point by the Bay Furnace Company. The company processed iron here from 1870 to 1879. The hot blast and boilers were located at the top. To convert iron ore taken on the Marquette Iron Range into pig iron, the furnace burned charcoal from hardwood cut from nearby forests and produced in nearby kilns. Ships loaded and

AR08 Bay Furnace

unloaded at a company-owned dock on the lake.

AU TRAIN VICINITY, AU TRAIN TOWNSHIP

Au Train was a fishing village. Its forests and kilns supplied charcoal for the Munising Furnace. Some local residents recall when Au Train was a village of white-washed log houses.

AR09 Charles Paulson House

1883. US Forest Rd. 227B (Au Train Forest Rd.) 2 miles south of Michigan 28 on the western shores of Au Train Lake

According to local tradition, the one-and-a-half-story log house with a dormer and a rear addition was built with dovetailed corners on Au Train Lake by a Swede who had worked as a miner before homesteading here. A similar log house, the Clifford Martin House, is at 505 Woodland in Au Train. Today the Paulson house serves as a museum.

Luce County   (LC)

NEWBERRY

Located in the Tahquamenon River valley, Newberry was a lumbering and woodworking center but is now given over to hunting and fishing. In 1879 Detroit and eastern investors promoted a railroad line through the wilderness to connect the Marquette Iron Range with Saint Ignace. Completed in 1881, the Detroit, Mackinac and Marquette Railroad linked Detroit and Lower Michigan with the rich mineral regions and commercial centers of the western Upper Peninsula. The follow-ing year John S. Newberry and other businessmen created the Vulcan Furnace Company for the manufacture of charcoal iron at a key location along the new railroad. The settlement was located in the center of lush pine and hardwoods. Newberry grew as a center of logging and charcoal. Luce County was set off from Mackinac and Chippewa counties in 1882. Sawmills were established. In 1895 the construction of the red brick Georgian Revival Newberry Hospital for the Insane began.

LC01 Luce County Historical Museum
(Luce County Sheriff's Residence and Jail)

1894, Lovejoy and Demar. 411 West Harris

The lone survivor of Luce County's nineteenth-century courthouse complex is this robust Queen Anne structure built to the plans of a Marquette architectural firm. The building has horseshoe and round arches, recessed entries, a turreted corner tower, and intersecting gables and is clad in a rich texture of Marquette brownstone, pressed brick, and shingles. It cost $10,000 to build.

LC02 Falls Hotel

1914–1915. 301 South Newberry Ave. (Michigan 123) (southeast corner of South Newberry Ave. and John St.)

The three-story brick hotel was built on quicksand at a time when the lumbering industry in the Newberry vicinity was in decline. Herman Gundlach (1887–1945), a Houghton contractor, erected it on footings that rest on railroad ties. This solution recalls the raft, rail, and caisson foundations used in the building of skyscrapers in Chicago in the 1880s to the 1890s. In fact, before coming to Houghton, Gundlach had worked on the construction of the Auditorium Building and others in Chicago. The ample first-floor lobby, reading room, and dining room—well-lighted and finished in oak—and the comfortable guest rooms on the upper floors made the hotel a favorite with travelers. The building replaced the McLeod House, an earlier hotel, that burned in 1914. The hotel reflects Newberry's determination to survive after the white pine was gone. It still serves as the center of community activity.

NEWBERRY VICINITY, McMILLAN TOWNSHIP

LC03 Newberry Regional Mental Health Center (Upper Peninsula Asylum for the Insane and Feeble-Minded)

1898-present; Demetrius Frederick Charlton; Charlton, Gilbert and Demar; Derrick Hubert. Bounded approximately by Michigan 123, Luce County 403 (Michigan 28A), and Luce County 402 (Michigan 28A)

In 1893 the Michigan legislature established the state's fourth psychiatric hospital and selected for its site this 560-acre parcel of land in "a healthful and easily accessible" part of the Upper Peninsula. The first buildings, designed by Charlton and his Marquette firm, consisted of a large U-shaped series of interconnected red brick Georgian Revival buildings. They included an administration building, a hospital, and eleven resident cottages, each with a capacity of from fifty to one hundred patients, arranged in the form of a quadrangle and connected by covered walkways. South of the quadrangle were houses for physicians and other hospital personnel. On a farm on the site, patients grew vegetables and raised cattle and hogs for their own consumption. Also on the grounds were a training school for attendants and nurses and an occupational therapy building. During the depression era, resident cottages and staff housing, an administration building, wards, and a kitchen were built with WPA funds to the designs of Derrick Hubert of Menominee. Since more patients are now treated in the community rather than in institutions, the population of the hospital has declined, and the Michigan Department of Mental Health has declared surplus and demolished many buildings at Newberry State Hospital.

Schoolcraft County (ST)

MANISTIQUE

At the mouth of the Manistique River, on the north shore of Lake Michigan, Manistique grew as a lumbering center with mills and docks after 1860 and flourished until the white pine was exhausted in 1900. It was established as the county seat in 1879.

ST01 Manistique Water Tower
(Manistique Pumping Station)

1921–1922, Fridolf Danielson. In Riverside Park, north side of Deer St. (Michigan 94), west side of the Manistique River and the Riverside Park flume

A prominent landmark in Manistique is the 200-foot-high, metal-domed, red brick, octagonal water tower. Its eight recessed wall panels, each with a single segmental-arch window near the top, stand on a prominent base of cast concrete and buff brick that rises to a height nearly one-third the total height of the structure. Paired triglyphlike ornaments decorate the frieze. A pedimented entrance pavilion projects from the base; over the entrance is a large segmental-arch light. The structure houses a 200,000-gallon steel water tank built by the Chicago Bridge and Iron Works Company. The city of Manistique erected the municipal water tower and a nearby pumping plant.

ST02 Manistique Paper Company Dam and Flume

1918–1920; H. F. Storrer, construction engineer; C. A. P. Turner, consulting engineer. On the Manistique River from a point .25 mile north (approximately the end of Cedar St.) of Deer St. (US 2) to a point .25 mile south (approximately the end of Mackinac Rd.) of Deer St. Visible from the Siphon Bridge

William J. Murphy of the *Minneapolis Tribune* purchased the riparian rights for the river, and the Manistique Pulp and Paper Company constructed this dam and flume. The reinforced concrete flume is 160 feet wide, 28 feet high and 3,300 feet long, and runs parallel to the Manistique River. It has a carrying capacity of 8,000 cubic feet of water per second. Standing at the head of the flume is the concrete dam. Five radial gates control the flow of water into the flume, and six control the flow from the river. It runs from the northeast to the southwest.

ST03 Siphon Bridge

1919. Deer St. (Michigan 94) over the Manistique River

A 300-foot-long reinforced concrete girder bridge is built through the upper part of the Manistique Paper Company's concrete flume. Local residents call the structure the "siphon bridge" because the roadway is four feet below the level of the Manistique River.

HIAWATHA TOWNSHIP, HIAWATHA NATIONAL FOREST

ST04 Clear Lake Organizational Camp

1938–1939. Off Forest Rd. 2246 (Clear Lake Rd.), east of Michigan 94; 4.5 miles off Michigan 94 from the north and 2 miles off Michigan 94 from the south

Standing on 25 acres on the eastern shore of Clear Lake in the Manistique Ranger District of the Hiawatha National Forest is a rustic camp meant to serve "organizations of welfare purposes and low income groups whose financial standing would ordinarily prevent the renting of a camp for meetings and outings." The camp includes an administration building, a mess hall, an infirmary, a custodian's dwelling, a bathhouse, a comfort station, and cabins. All are gable-roofed and wood-framed, with board-and-batten exteriors on concrete foundations or pier foundations; some have rubble stone chimneys. Enrollees of the 3613th Company, Civil Conservation Corps, at Camp Evelyn, built them using the standard plans of the Forest Service Region Nine, United States Department of Agriculture.

BLANEY PARK, MUELLER TOWNSHIP

ST05 Blaney Park

1926–1950. On Michigan 77 one mile north of the intersection of US 2 and Michigan 77

Blaney Park is the remains of a large resort developed on cutover timber lands by Harold and Stewart Earle, owners of the Wisconsin Land and Lumber Company of Hermansville. In 1907 the Wisconsin Land and Lumber Company acquired Blaney, a company town with headquarters, stores, and houses established in 1902 by the William Mueller Lumber Company. The resort grew into a huge operation, with dozens of buildings, a golf course, an airport, and a swimming pool. In 1927, after laying out a golf course and forming Lake Anne Louise, the Earles opened in the center of town a resort tavern called Celibeth. In the 1930s dozens of old and new cottages and a lodge were fitted for resort service. In 1938 a group of Colonial Revival cottages, originally painted white with green shutters, was constructed one mile from the village at the northwest corner of Michigan 77 and US 2. The resort reached its heyday in the 1940s and 1950s, when middle-class vacationers came by automobile from all over the United States and stayed for weeks. It declined in the 1960s and 1970s, as jet travel enabled Americans to seek more exotic vacation destinations, and was sold in the late 1970s.

GULLIVER

ST06 Fisher's Old Deerfield Resort

1926. Gulliver Lake Rd. (Schoolcraft County 436) (500 feet south of US 2 on Schoolcraft County 432, then west off Schoolcraft County 432 on Gulliver Lake Rd.)

Located in the woods on the northwest shore of Gulliver Lake just off US 2, the major road across the Upper Peninsula, the little rustic log inn and tourist cabins served a clientele of automobile tourists who drove to the north woods and lakes to fish for small mouth bass, tiger muskies, and pike, to hunt small game and deer, and to experience camp life. The L-shaped structure is constructed of native logs with lock joints. The cozy interior reveals the log rafters, joists, and tenons and is dignified with two stone chimneys and fireplaces. It possesses another essential element—pine furniture manufactured by the Rittenhouse Furniture Company. Twenty of the original fifty clapboarded cabins remain on the grounds. As William S. Wicks noted, the log dwelling allowed the modern city dweller to return to "forest primeval" for change, recuperation, pleasure, and health with "some traces of his civilization."[79]

Menominee County (ME)

MENOMINEE

Named for the Menominee Indians who inhabited the area along the river, where fish and game were plentiful, Menominee developed at the mouth of the Menominee River, on Green Bay. By 1890, twenty-three steam-powered lumber mills were operating at the twin cities of Menominee, Michigan, and Marinette, Wisconsin. The fishing and the paper- and iron-producing industries broadened Menominee's economic base. These industries were aided by the construction of a harbor in 1874. People of Menominee have always associated closely with Wisconsin, Chicago, and the West. Investors and managers of Menominee lumbering concerns frequently resided in Chicago, where they maintained lumberyards supplied by shiploads from Menominee. Immigrant Norwegians, Danes, Swedes, Poles, and Germans settled in Menominee to work as laborers, but many left for the newly active lumber centers in the Gulf and Pacific regions, when the local stands of pine were depleted during the first decade of this century.

ME01 Menominee County Courthouse

1874–1875, Gurdon P. Randall. 839 Tenth Ave. (south side of Tenth Ave., between Eighth and Tenth streets)

A cupola-topped red brick cube arranged symmetrically with a central pedimented pavilion projecting slightly from each facade and unified with a bracketed wooden cornice, stone stringcourse, and stone quoins gave Menominee County an appropriate image for

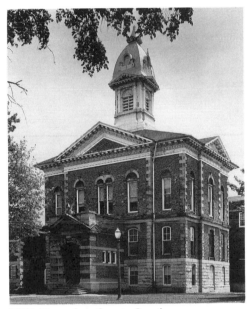

ME01 Menominee County Courthouse

its seat of government. The plans for the courthouse were prepared by Gurdon P. Randall (d. 1884) of Chicago, a specialist in courthouse designs who once worked in Asher Benjamin's office; his scheme was selected over those submitted by seven other designers. The courthouse is arranged with the jail on the first floor, offices on the second, and the courtroom on the third. Cummings and Hagan were the construction contractors. It cost $30,000. The county attached a jail to the south of the courthouse in 1902, and an addition to the rear in the 1930s. In the late

1970s and early 1980s, one hundred years after it was completed, the courthouse was restored under the direction of William Kessler and Associates.

ME02 First Street Central Business District

1880–1910. On Green Bay from Tenth Ave. to Fourth Ave.

The district of commercial and civic buildings stretches north and south of Victory Park, a green space on Green Bay with a bandstand and marina between the Spies Public Library and Eighth Avenue. Once the shoreline of the Menominee Peninsula was lined with lumber mills and yards and piers. The *Birdseye View of the Towns at the Mouth of the Menominee River: Menekkaune, Wisconsin; Menominee, Michigan; Marinette, Wisconsin* (1881) is an good pictorial record of the appearance of the area in its lumbering heyday.

ME02.1 A. D. Paalzow Block

1887. 401 South First St.

The A. D. Paalzow Block is an elegant two-part brick commercial block fitted with windows and fronted with prefabricated cast-iron vertical members and a galvanized iron cornice, entablature, and pediment. Mesker and Brothers of Saint Louis, Missouri, manufactured the iron members for this building. Mesker and other manufacturers of iron architectural elements advertised in their catalogs that a facade assembled from iron parts provided an elaborate front at a fraction of the cost of masonry construction. This building has held a department store, a furrier, and a wholesale grocery.

ME02.2 Shale Building

1895, Charles W. Maass. 601 First St. (northwest corner of First St. and Fifth Ave.)

The Shale Building is a large, rambling, three-story, light yellowish white brick structure trimmed with red Portage Entry sandstone and enlivened with bays, a conical-roofed corner turret, and ornamental brickwork. It held offices and a first-floor saloon. The *Menominee Democrat* for November 1895 called the building "one of the handsomest in the city, occupying as it does, the most prominent corner in the business center." Visible for miles offshore, it is a landmark for ships bound for Menominee harbor.

ME02.3 Spies Public Library

1903–1905. 940 First St.

In 1903 Augustus Spies, a prosperous lumberman, announced he would build and maintain a public library in Menominee as a monument to the Spies family. Soon after, Charles Spies, a member of the family, left for a tour of the Northwest to inspect a number of libraries and to decide on an appropriate style for the building. The architect remains unknown, but the Beaux-Arts Classical library is an impressive family monument. The focus of its balanced one-story facade is a three-bay centerpiece articulated by fluted Ionic columns and arches with a recessed central doorway. A balustraded parapet encircles the roof. The quoins at the corners of the white limestone exterior walls are penciled. On March 31, 1905, Spies presented this gift to the city of Menominee.

ME02.4 Commercial Bank

1905. 1935, A. Moorman and Company, alterations. 949 First St.

The classicism of the Beaux-Arts tradition inspired the scheme of the remodeling of the bank in 1935. A. Moorman and Company, Minneapolis specialists in bank design, drafted the plans. Colossal limestone Ionic columns in antis support the portico, which is filled with large metal-frame windows separated by marble spandrels. A cornice supported with consoles is beneath the paneled parapet. A distinctive black and white neon sign projects from the center.

ME03 John Henes Park

1907, Ossian Cole Simonds. On Green Bay on Henes Park Rd. (off Henes Park Dr. at intersection with North Shore St. [US 35])

Situated on 50 acres at Poplar Point on the shore of Green Bay just north of Menominee, Henes Park is a natural park that maintains the essential qualities of the native landscape. "It is one of the choicest beauty spots of Michigan and the natural grandeur of its scenery has been deftly enhanced by the skillful and subtle efforts of the landscape work of O. C. Simonds of Chicago."[80] Born in Grand Rapids, Simonds (1857–1931) is recognized for his landscape designs for cemeteries, parks, subdivisions, and residences throughout the Midwest. This park was the gift of John Henes to the city of Menominee. An arch marks the entrance to the park. Here a boulevard skirts the lake and circles the virgin forest of oak, maple, beech, ironwood, basswood, hemlock, pine, and balsam. The park has a rustic cedar log shelter house designed by Derrick Hubert, a sandy swimming beach protected by a 500-foot-long concrete breakwater, a well-equipped children's playground, lawn tennis grounds, nine trails (named after the poets Schiller, Goethe, Shakespeare, Milton, Virgil, Longfellow, Whittier, Homer, and Tennyson), groves of

planted trees, and a bog garden. A Menominee citizen observed, "In a spirit of patriotism Mr. Henes has given to the people of Menominee a park which in natural beauty and grandeur cannot be excelled anywhere— a spot so lovely that from the time he first viewed it he fostered the thought that a place so liberally endowed with graces of nature should belong to the people. Acting on this inspiration, he purchased the land and presented to the people the magnificent property."[81]

HOLMES TOWNSHIP

ME04 Chalk Hill Dam and Hydroelectric Plant

1926–1927, Holland, Ackerman and Holland, designers and engineers. Menominee River, Menominee County G18 5 miles west of Banat, and 11 miles northwest of Daggatt

The Northern Electric Company, under the authority of the Railroad Commission of Wisconsin, constructed this dam at Chalk Hill, 58 miles upstream from the point where the Menominee River flows into Green Bay. It is one of twelve hydroelectric plants operated today by the Wisconsin Electric Power Company along the banks of the Menominee or its tributaries. The Menominee forms the border between Michigan and Wisconsin. (Four others on the Menominee River are operated by other electric and paper companies and municipalities.) The Chalk Hill project includes a powerhouse, 133 feet by 36 feet in plan, a 300-foot-long spillway constructed of reinforced concrete on bedrock with eleven tainter gates and a 27.7-foot head of water, and an earth dike. The steel-frame and brick-clad Collegiate Gothic powerhouse rests on a reinforced concrete substructure set into bedrock. Its Craftsmanlike interior resembles "a cathedral of power." Stained glass, tiling, and wrought-iron work furnish the backdrop for the turbines. Identical to it is the White Rapids Hydroelectric Project, also erected by the Northern Electric Company in 1927–1928, about 2 miles downstream in Holmes Township. The Chalk Hill and, presumably, the White Rapids plants were designed by Holland, Ackerman and Holland, engineers of Ann Arbor and Chicago, and constructed by Siems, Helmer, Shaffner, Inc., of Minneapolis.

HERMANSVILLE, MEYER TOWNSHIP

Hermansville is a company town established in 1878 by Charles Julius Ludwig Meyer, of Fond du Lac, Wisconsin, founder of the Wisconsin Land and Lumber Company, a company owned and operated until 1943 by his son-in-law and descendants, George Washington, G. Harold, and Stewart Earle. At Hermansville, Meyer built a sawmill to process pine lumber taken from the surrounding 50,000 acres in what is now Meyer Township. This, in turn, he manufactured into sashes, doors, and blinds at his huge Fond du Lac plant. In 1888 Meyer opened another mill at Hermansville, where he installed modern precision machinery that finished hardwood flooring from kiln-dried rock maple. Wisconsin Land and Lumber Company marked its products with an IXL within a bull's-eye ring and sold them to builders and architects engaged in building up the West.

Hermansville

The population of Hermansville, where the owners and employees of the Wisconsin Land and Lumber Company worked and lived, reached a peak of twelve hundred in 1911. The big mill yard, which lies south and west of the junction of the Chicago and Northwestern and the Minneapolis, Saint Paul and Sault Sainte Marie railroads, contained the company's hardwood mills and concrete boiler house. To the northeast of the mill yard is the two-and-a-half-story, wood-frame clapboard Queen Anne office building. Erected in 1882–1883, its decorative spindlework in the gable and porch, its horizontal and vertical patterns of shiplap and stickwork on the exterior walls, and its interior stencil work (recently restored by Conrad Schmidt Studios of Milwaukee) make it the centerpiece of present-day Hermansville. Finished hardwood covers the floors throughout.

Separated from the mill yard, on the north side of the Chicago and Northwestern Railroad's tracks, is the residential area. Company-built cottages and houses are arranged with a school and churches in a grid of streets north of First Street, which runs parallel to the Chicago and Northwestern Railroad. The Methodist Episcopal Church, erected in 1903 at the northeast corner of Linden and Second streets, blends such Gothic and classical elements as pointed windows, intersecting gables, a corner bell tower, and an entry porch.

Along the north side of First Street and extending for two blocks west of Main Street are the public and commercial structures built by the company during the years of greatest prosperity, from 1910 to 1930. They include the community club (1926), the hotel (1911–1912), the post office (1924), and the IXL General Store and apartments (1924).

Delta County (DT)

ESCANABA

Escanaba developed as an iron shipping port in 1863, when railroad men constructed the first dock in this natural deep-water harbor on Little Bay de Noc. From this dock, ore from the Marquette, Menominee, and Gogebic ranges was shipped to steel centers on the lower lakes more quickly and cheaply than it could be shipped from Marquette. Pine and hardwood products and paper have augmented the economy. Escanaba incorporated as a village in 1866 and as a city in 1883. It reincorporated in 1891.

DT01 **Saint Joseph Catholic Church and William Bonifas Fine Arts Center** (Saint Joseph Church, Memorial Building, and Auditorium)

1937–1939, Foeller, Shoeber and Berners. 709 and 700 First Ave. South (southwest and northwest corners of First Ave. South and South Seventh St.

This sumptuous religious and cultural complex is one of the finest in the Upper Peninsula. Gifts from lumberman William Bonifas (1865–1936) and his wife, Catherine (1868–1948), financed in large part the construction of Saint Joseph Church and the auditorium and gymnasium that is now the William Bonifas Fine Arts Center. The buildings were designed by Foeller, Shoeber and Berners of Green Bay, Wisconsin, in the Neo-Romanesque style. The church is cruciform in plan, with a lofty nave and arcaded side aisles. A campanile rises at the crossing of the nave and the east transept. A rose window pierces the north wall above the triple-arched recessed entry that is supported by Romanesque columns with foliated capitals. Rose windows are also in the transepts. The buttressed exterior walls of the buildings are buff stone from Kasota, Minnesota. The interior of the church is embellished with black, buff, rose, and salmon marbles, as well as mosaics and stained glass. The auditorium and gymnasium is T-shaped, with a tower in the crossing. The present church replaced an earlier red and yellow polychrome brick Gothic Revival structure built in 1873 to the designs of C. F. Struck. Before work on the church began, the Memorial Building and Auditorium was completed. This lavish religious complex is evidence of the importance of Escanaba to the Upper Peninsula. Some call Escanaba Upper Michigan's second capital, after Marquette.

DT02 **Ludington Street**

Ludington St., from Fourth St. to Seventeenth St.

DT02.1 **East Ludington Gallery / Erickson and Godley Block** (Escanaba Masonic Block)

1884 ?, J. B. Sweatt?. 1890, 1905–1918. 617–619 Ludington St.

The four-story red brick and sandstone commercial block and Masonic fraternity has its large plate glass storefront windows, piers, and arcade intact, but the bracket cornice is now gone. The upper story was added later.

DT02.2 **American Dream Realty Company** (First National Bank)

1904, Demetrius Frederick Charlton. 623 Ludington St. (southeast corner of Ludington St. and Seventh St.)

DT02.1 East Ludington Gallery / Erickson and Godley Block (Escanaba Masonic Block); and DT02.2 American Dream Realty Company (First National Bank)

The three-story brick and red sandstone commercial block respectfully relates to its older neighbor, the Masonic Building. This is accomplished by the equal width of the building, the three-bay division, and the steady rhythm of the square and round-arch windows set in recesses separated by piers with foliated capitals and decorated with stone sills and lintels. It was built for the Rathfon Brothers, merchandisers of men's clothing. The bank moved in 1910.

DT02.3 **Delft Theater**

1914, Charlton and Kuenzli. 907–913 Ludington St.

The Semer Land Company built the 1,000-seat theater, originally known as the Delft Opera House, for popular amusement, vaudeville, and motion pictures and leased it to M. W. Jopling, manager of the Marquette Opera House. Jopling booked the same companies in Marquette and Escanaba. The theater adjoins a block of stores and a large hall. The storybook Dutch Renaissance Revival design is similar to a theater that once stood in Iron River. A large, stepped gable projects from the center of the parapeted, tile-clad, side-gable roof. Lively polychrome wall surfaces add to the Dutch image.

DT02.4 Delta Building (Richter Brewing Company)

1901. 1615–1619 Ludington St.

Built for John Richter and a group of stockholders, the brewery could produce 30,000 barrels of beer a year. This symmetrical, twin-towered brew house rises four stories and is 80 feet by 150 feet in ground dimensions. Its brick walls are corbeled and pierced by round-arch windows. It was once equipped with an ammonia-type refrigeration system and drew its water from an artesian well. Richter's Select and Richter's Special Brew were sold locally. After prohibition and until the early 1940s, the Delta Brewing Company brewed Peninsula Pride, Buckingham Ale, Delta Special, and Hiawatha Draught.

DT03 Ice Shanty City

present. Little Bay de Noc

Every year from December to April, sports fishermen in search of perch, walleye, and northern pike haul between fifteen hundred and two thousand shanties on skids onto the ice of Little Bay de Noc and turn the bay into an ice shanty city. All winter long, the men and women of the Escanaba area retreat to their shanties. The shanties have wood-burning and gas stoves. A road across the ice from Gladstone to Stonington cuts 20 miles off the automobile trip to the point.

FAYETTE, GARDEN PENINSULA

The Jackson Iron Company established Fayette as a company town in 1867 to support the operation of a new charcoal iron blast furnace complex on the edge of Snail Shell Harbor. The village grew to about 500 residents in the mid-1870s, then gradually tapered off in population during the 1880s, reflecting the declining fortunes of the charcoal iron industry in general. After the company permanently closed its furnaces in December 1890, most of the remaining residents left to seek work elsewhere. During the next several decades, Fayette was home to a small group of commercial fishermen and several failed summer resorts. The state of Michigan purchased the all-but-vacant townsite and surrounding land in 1959. It has since developed the land as a state park combining unique historical and scenic attractions.

The Jackson Iron Company viewed construction of Fayette as a necessary, but secondary, aspect of its smelting operation at Snail Shell Harbor. It therefore made no particular effort to create a well-built or aesthetically pleasing community. Local woods and limestone from the adjacent bluff, sparingly augmented by imported brick, were used for both the residential and the industrial and commercial structures. The lack of ornamentation further underscores the company's utilitarian perception of Fayette's buildings.

The layout of the village emphasizes the centrality of iron smelting to Fayette's existence. Most visitors arrived in Fayette by boat (or across the ice in winter), and they were

DT03 Ice Shanty City

Fayette

greeted by the sight of two blast furnaces looming up over the water as they entered the inner harbor. The stacks were flanked by charcoal kilns and storage sheds. Barns, workshops, and offices stood behind the furnaces. A hotel, a livery stable, and a very few shops were adjacent to the industrial area. Housing extended to the south and northwest from the economic and geographic center of the village. The company superinten-

dent's house was not only the largest in town, it also had a commanding view of the harbor and stacks. Moreover, it was located safely upwind of the smoke and smells of the furnace complex.

SAC BAY

DT04 Samuel Elliot House

1895. Sac Bay Rd., off Delta County 483

Intricate, lacy, cut-out stars, circles, swirls, and loops frost the gable end, bargeboard, and arcaded front porch of the delightful little wooden house with a steeply pitched gable roof. The house was built by Samuel Elliot in 1895, after fire destroyed his earlier house. Elliot was an early settler, woodworker, sawmill operator, and shipbuilder who had come from Wisconsin by 1861. Unusual in this part of Michigan, the house reveals the pleasure Elliot took in the workability of wood.

The Sault
and Mackinac Region

T HE SAULT AND MACKINAC REGION IS STRATEGICALLY LO-
cated at the Rapids of the Saint Mary's River on the international boundary between the United States and Canada, and at the Straits of Mackinac where Lakes Huron and Michigan converge. Throughout its long history,
Indians, missionaries, explorers, traders, soldiers, fishermen, shippers, manufacturers, and resorters have gathered here. At the Sault and at the Straits they
built missions, forts, and Indian agencies. On the lakeshore they built lighthouses and lifesaving stations, summer cottages, and hotels. Along highways they
built motels and curio shops. They connected both the Upper and Lower peninsulas and the American and Canadian Saults with bridges. They built locks,
a hydroelectric plant, and a canal at Sault Sainte Marie.

Michilimackinac, present-day Mackinac County, was created by the proclamation of Territorial Governor Lewis Cass in 1818, under the provisions of the
Ordinance of 1787. Chippewa County was set off from Mackinac County in
1826 and organized in 1827. Saint Ignace and Sault Sainte Marie, the present
county judicial seats, are located on the Straits and the Saint Mary's River, all
set against a background of sharply rising hills.

To the east of Point la Barbe and the town of Saint Ignace lies Mackinac
Island, the uppermost in a chain of three islands that bounds the Straits of
Mackinac; just off the easterly tip of the Upper Peninsula is Drummond Island.
High rocky bluffs of Niagara dolomite and limestone, so characteristic of the
region, not only surround the whole of Drummond Island but also wall portions of Mackinac Island and the eastern Upper Peninsula itself. The mighty
eroding action of an earlier sea has shaped these great faces of rock into natural wonders with provocative architectural overtones: they are appropriately
called Castle Rock, Arch Rock, Chimney Rock, Sugar Loaf Rock, and Devil's

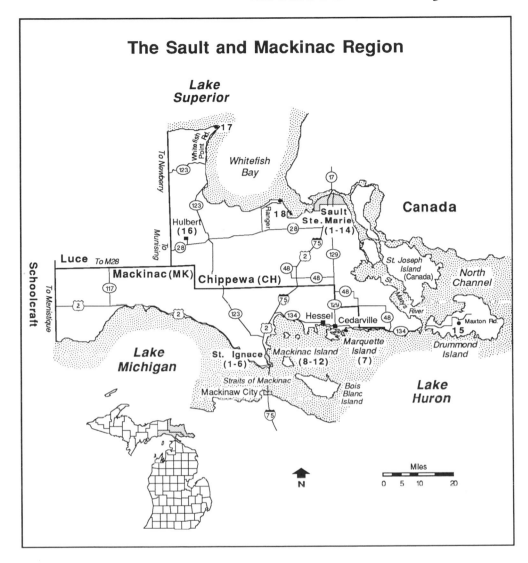

The Sault and Mackinac Region

Kitchen and are clearly visible from Saint Ignace and Mackinac Island. Both physically and visually, this dramatic geological display must surely have been a factor in prompting the sympathetic handling of stone that marks so much of the architecture of the Upper Peninsula.

Euro-Americans settled the Sault, the Straits, and Mackinac Island before they settled any other place in the Upper Peninsula. The region was not only a center of trade and commerce but also served as a control point for the Northwest. Mackinac Island once was the most important military and fur-trading center on the Great Lakes. The struggle to control the Straits led to conflicts between the French and British and later the British and Americans.

(The French built two forts and the British built one at the Straits. The French built one fort and the Americans two at the Sault.)

French Jesuits constructed in 1668 a palisaded log chapel and house at the Sault. It became the center for Father Jacques Marquette's missionary work and the first permanent white settlement in the Upper Midwest. Two years later, in 1671, Marquette established a mission chapel named for Saint Ignatius of Loyola at the site of present-day Saint Ignace. In the 1690s Saint Ignace was a French village of sixty houses and the mission and was the center of French culture in the Great Lakes. The Jesuits continued their work at the mission until 1705, when the mission was abandoned and burned.

To protect Marquette's mission and to control the fur trade with a military presence, the French built in 1690 Fort de Baude on a hill at Saint Ignace. Antoine de la Mothe Cadillac assumed command of Fort de Baude in 1694. Two years later, in 1696, disagreements with the Jesuits over the extent of military strength needed at this post led to Cadillac's departure, to the abandonment of Fort de Baude, and to the establishment of a fort at Detroit.

Around 1715 the French returned to the Straits of Mackinac and constructed a new fort named Michilimackinac at present-day Mackinaw City. The British took over Fort Michilimackinac in 1761. In 1779 American military successes in the Ohio River valley and elsewhere prompted the British to move Fort Michilimackinac to Mackinac Island. The transfer was completed in 1781. The Treaty of Paris in 1783 ended the American Revolution and made the Straits of Mackinac part of the United States, but the British failed to evacuate Fort Mackinac until 1796. Subsequently the Americans expanded the fort. During the War of 1812 the British took Fort Mackinac, but in 1815, under Treaty of Ghent, the Americans reoccupied the fort. In 1875 Congress created the second national park from the 1,000-acre military reservation at Fort Mackinac. In 1895 the army abandoned Fort Mackinac and the park became Michigan's first state park.

In 1750 Louis le Gardeur, Sieur de Repentigny, constructed a fort and attempted to create a military presence and trading post on the Saint Mary's River at Sault Sainte Marie. The French dominated the Sault until the British took possession in 1762. From 1763 to 1812 the Sault was a center for British fur-trading activities.

After the War of 1812, John Jacob Astor established the headquarters of the American Fur Company on Mackinac Island. The height of its operations occurred in the 1820s.

In the 1820s Territorial Governor Lewis Cass led a scientific expedition to the Upper Great Lakes. Setting out from the Sault, the party coasted along the south shore of Lake Superior to determine the extent of mineral resources and to promote settlement. In 1822 Col. Hugh Brady and American soldiers built a stockaded fort called Fort Brady at Sault Sainte Marie, and Henry Rowe Schoolcraft became the U.S. Indian agent at Sault Sainte Marie. New Fort Brady was built in 1892.

The construction of the Michigan Lake Superior Power Company hydroelectric plant and canal at the turn of the century precipitated great optimism at the Sault about its industrial future.

Transportation has been important to the Sault and Mackinac Region, which is evident in many structures in the region. British and French fur traders used a lock and canal on the Canadian side of the Saint Mary's River that was built in 1797, but it was destroyed by Americans in 1814. The difficulty of portaging raw materials and supplies around the rapids in the Saint Mary's River was solved in the 1850s, when Charles T. Harvey, agent of the Saint Mary's Falls Ship Canal Company, broke ground for the Sault Locks. As compensation for construction, Congress awarded to this company of eastern capitalists 750,000 acres of public land. The locks opened in 1855 and permitted the efficient shipping of ore, grain, lumber, and other resources and supplies from Lake Superior to the lakes below. At the turn of the century, a City Beautiful government park known as Canal Park was developed at the locks.

The Marquette, Saint Ignace and Sault Sainte Marie and the Duluth, South Shore and Atlantic railroads connected Saint Ignace with the West. The arrival of the railroads at Saint Ignace increased the importance of the community, and in 1882 the seat of county government was transferred from Mackinac Island to Saint Ignace.

For centuries boats carried people and supplies between Mackinac Island and the Upper and Lower peninsulas. The Mackinac Bridge Authority was established in the 1950s to construct a bridge to span the Straits of Mackinac between Saint Ignace and Mackinaw City. Its opening in the late 1950s linked the two peninsulas.

Mackinac Island has always been an important stopping place for those touring the Great Lakes. With the expansion of rail and steamship travel in the 1880s, trains and boats brought summer visitors from midwestern cities to enjoy the healthy climate, scenic beauty, and recreational opportunities of the Mackinac area. The erection of the Grand Hotel (1887) and the splendid summer cottages on the east and west bluffs of Mackinac Island made it the state's premier resort.

Lumbering flourished in the eastern Upper Peninsula. Sawmills were built at Shelldrake, Emerson, Detour, Bay Mills, Drummond Island, and the Sault. Fishing also played an important role in this region.

Chippewa County   (CH)

SAULT SAINTE MARIE

Once a frontier outpost for Jesuit missionaries, fur traders, and explorers, Sault Sainte Marie, on the international boundary between the United States and Canada, is the vital link between the rich resources of the Lake Superior region and the nation's industrial centers. In 1853, with a population of nearly 2,000, the city's future was transformed by the completion of the $1 million

Sault Sainte Marie

See map below.

Saint Mary's Falls Ship Canal. It had locks that opened the lakes to shipping, ushering in a new age for transportation on the Great Lakes. Growth and prosperity led to the incorporation of the village of Sault Sainte Marie in 1874. Predictions, however, that the Sault would become a national manufacturing center, based on the local optimism in the 1900s, were never fully realized.

Today, as it was at the time of its founding,

the importance of the Saint Mary's River to the welfare of Sault Sainte Marie cannot be overestimated. This river has been an ever-pervasive factor for this border city.

CH01 Chippewa County Courthouse

1877, William Scott. 1904, addition, R. C. Sweatt. 1988–1989, restoration. Bounded by Maple St., Bingham Ave., Spruce St., and Court St.

Designed by William Scott, a trained English-born Detroit architect who resided in Windsor, Ontario, the Chippewa County Courthouse is in the Second Empire style. The two-story courthouse is arranged symmetrically with a pedimented projecting center pavilion containing a two-tiered clock tower with a convex mansard roof. The external walls are limestone from Drummond Island trimmed with Marquette brown sandstone. The mansard roof is covered with slate. The building cost $24,000 to build. This impressive heroic structure speaks to the confidence and optimism of the citizens of the Sault in the late nineteenth century. It was beautifully restored in 1989 under the supervision of Lincoln A. Poley.

CH02 Federal Building

1909–1910, James K. Taylor. 209 East Portage Ave.

The formal white Federal Building rises splendidly in the midst of an open park once occupied by Old Fort Brady. The fort operated until 1893, when its garrison was removed to a newer fort for greater protection of the locks. Erected to the designs of the supervising architect of the United States Treasury, this three-story classical building has a penciled ground floor, engaged Ionic columns and giant piers articulating the central portion of the main facade, and an entablature and balustrade encircling a low-hipped tin roof. The imposed cold formality through the use of Vermont granite and white Bedford limestone contrasts markedly, and

not a little unhappily, with the warm vernacular character of the city that derived from its widespread use of heavy, red canal rock. Appropriately, the Federal Building housed the post office and other governmental offices. In the 1970s, it was declared surplus.

CH03 Saint James Episcopal Church

1902–1903, James Calloway Teague. 533 Bingham Ave. (southeast corner of Bingham Ave. and Carrie St.)

This double-transept Late Gothic Revival church resembles the small parish churches found on the Eastern Seaboard that were influenced by the English Ecclesiological movement. It has prominent buttresses on the corners of the heavy squat square tower with broad, pointed-arch openings and is topped with battlements. Coursed sandstone excavated from the power canal, then under construction, and red sandstone used for the trim add to the look and flavor of the English parish church.

CH04 Eastern Upper Peninsula Intermediate School District Building
(Sault Sainte Marie Carnegie Library)

1903–1904, James Calloway Teague. 1936, addition, Bowd, Munson Company. 315 Armory Place

Similar to many other libraries built through the generosity of Andrew Carnegie is this small but monumental Beaux-Arts Classical structure of smooth ashlar limestone, with later rear additions of brick. The initial cost was $30,000. The entry is flanked by paired Ionic columns (tetrastyle in antis) supporting an unadorned parapet and guarded by a pair of stone lions donated by Chase S. Osborn (1860–1949). Osborn was a Sault resident and an avid outdoorsman, but more importantly he is remembered as a governor of Michigan for a brief period from 1911 to 1912.

CH05 Sault Locks (Saint Mary's Falls Ship Canal)

1855–present. On the Saint Mary's River at Locks Park

Completed in 1855 under the direction of Charles T. Harvey (1826–1912), the Saint Mary's Falls Ship Canal opened shipping

CH01 Sault Locks (St. Mary's Falls Ship Canal)

around the Saint Mary's Rapids between Lake Superior and the lower Great Lakes. Since 1797, there had been at this general location a small, 38-foot navigation lock for canoes and small craft. It was built by the Northwest Fur Company on the Canadian side of the river but was destroyed by American troops during the War of 1812.

In 1855, assisted with a 750,000-acre federal land grant to finance construction, the state of Michigan built the Sault Lock. It measured 350 feet in length, 70 feet in width, and had two lock chambers, each with a lift of 18 feet. In 1881 ownership of the canal was transferred to the U.S. Government under the control of the Army Corps of Engineers, which still administers the canal. A second lock, the Weitzel, 515 feet long and 80 feet wide, was built between 1870 and 1881. Both the State and Weitzel locks have undergone numerous changes to accommodate larger and larger vessels. Between 1887 and 1896 the original State Lock was replaced by the Poe Lock, 800 feet long and 100 feet wide. Two new locks, the Davis (1907–1914) and the Sabin (1911–1919), were added and brought the total number of operating locks to four. The Davis and Sabin locks, the oldest remaining on this site, are identical, each measuring 1,350 feet in length, 80 feet in width, and 23.1 feet in depth. In 1943 the Weitzel Lock was replaced by the MacArthur Lock, 800 feet long, 80 feet wide, and 31 feet deep, and in 1968 the Poe Lock was replaced by the New Poe Lock, measuring 1,200 feet in length, 110 feet in width and 32 feet in depth.

The Administration Building (1896) is an 80-foot square, three-story stone building with a hipped roof and with an observation and control tower on its southwest corner.

An obelisk monument of red Connecticut granite, designed by Charles Follen McKim of the famed New York firm of McKim, Mead and White to commemorate in 1905 the fiftieth anniversary of the opening of the Saint Mary's Falls Canal, is located in Brady Park adjacent to the locks.

CH06 Elmwood (Henry Rowe Schoolcraft House)

1826–1827, Obed Wait. 1880s, remodeled. 1986–1987, moved and stabilized. On the Saint Mary's River and Water St. north of Glenn Ave. along a waterfront parkway at the eastern edge of the Sault Canal

Elmwood was built for Henry Rowe Schoolcraft (1793–1864), noted explorer, ethnologist, geologist, and Indian agent, in the Federal style by Obed Wait, builder of the Old Territorial Capitol and Courthouse in Detroit in 1828. The house was drastically transformed into a Queen Anne structure in the late 1880s, when the gables, bays, dormers, shingles, and spindlework were added.

After accompanying Lewis Cass in 1820 on his expedition through the Great Lakes to seek the source of the Mississippi River, Schoolcraft returned to Sault Sainte Marie, where he was appointed U.S. Indian Agent. Elmwood served as the agent's house and office, a dormitory for Indians visiting on official business, and a storehouse. Elmwood was not only the focal point for Indian affairs in the entire upper Great Lakes but also a social center for the people of Sault Sainte Marie and Fort Brady. The Indian Agency was removed to Mackinac Island in 1833, and Elmwood lost its luster and status. Among those who later lived in Elmwood was Charles T. Harvey in the 1850s, who supervised the construction of the Saint Mary's Falls Canal. Harvey called the house the only mansion of any pretense west of Mackinac.

Elmwood was used for offices during the early part of this century. The Michigan Lake Superior Power Company acquired it, and Elmwood was transferred eventually to the Chippewa County Historical Society. In the late 1970s, the society moved the house to its present location two blocks upstream from where it had stood for 150 years. It was stabilized in 1986–1987 and reopened as a museum.

CH07 **Edison Sault Power Plant** (Michigan Lake Superior Hydroelectric Power Plant)

1896–1902; Hans A. E. von Schon, engineer; James Calloway Teague. Over the Power Canal and on the Saint Mary's River, off Portage Ave. East, Johnston St., and Union

This wonderful building is the very essence of man and nature at work in northern Michigan. People at Sault Sainte Marie long had recognized the importance of the rapids of the Saint Mary's River as a source of power. The rapids drop 20 feet at this point and draw on Lake Superior as a "mill pond," or reservoir. In 1885 prominent area businessmen organized the Saint Mary's Falls Water Power Company, acquired land, and began constructing a power canal on the American side of the rapids. The project ran into financial difficulties and was abandoned in 1887.

In 1894 Francis H. Clergue organized the Michigan Lake Superior Power Company and purchased the unfinished canal from the city of Sault Sainte Marie for $265,000, which was the amount of bonded indebtedness. Between 1898 and 1902 Clergue produced waterpower at the American Sault by constructing a 2-mile power canal and the longest horizontal-shaft hydroelectric powerhouse in the world. The project cost $4 million and was supervised by engineer Hans A. E. von Schon.

The powerhouse superstructure was designed by Teague and built in the geological image of the land. Rough reddish brown sandstone excavated from the earth and discarded as the canal was constructed was laid in the walls of the steel-frame and masonry building. The building measures 1,400 feet in length, 100 feet in width, and 75 feet in height. It rests on a foundation of ten thousand 20-foot piles. There are 81 turbine pit walls of concrete blocks, each 100 feet long, 20 feet high, and 3 feet thick. Above them are 81 penstock partitions. The great length of the building is broken by hipped-roof end pavilions, a hipped-roof center section and connectors. Splayed and corbeled piers divide each connector into bays, within which the windows of the first two stories are grouped beneath segmental arches with voussoirs. Above them march a row of tiny square-headed windows. An entablature with a cornice of block modillions encircles all three pavilions. The powerhouse combined in an unusual design the functions of dam, powerhouse, and factory. Above the combination penstock-generator floor, which also contained a series of steel-plate bulkheads, is a ¼-mile-long factory floor and above it a ⅛-mile-long supplementary floor.

Local businessmen thought the development of waterpower would promote industry at the Sault and transform it into a metropolis rivaling Minneapolis, Detroit, or Chicago. But the hydroelectric plant attracted only one industry, the Union Carbide Company, and the Sault remained, and still remains, a small city of 15,000. Moreover, the plant failed to produce sufficient revenue to cover the interest on bonds used to finance its construction and went into receivership. Defects in the foundation of the powerhouse also limited the operating capacity of the plant. Currently the plant is owned and operated by the Edison Sault Electric Company.

CH08 International Railroad Bridge, American Locks Section

Straus Bascule Bridge Company of Chicago, 1913. 1945. Over the American Locks on the Saint Mary's River

The original International Railroad Bridge opened in 1887 and links the American and Canadian Saults. It has undergone numerous changes. In 1913, when the Davis and Sabin locks were under construction, the two lattice truss spans—each 104 feet long—and one of the ten 239-foot camelback truss spans were removed and replaced with a Straus Trunnion Bascule Bridge, designed by the Straus Bascule Bridge Company of Chicago and built by the Pennsylvania Steel Company. This trunnion bridge, commonly called the "Jackknife Bridge," is 23 feet in width and 336 feet in length. The swing span was replaced in 1945 by a vertical-lift bridge, 21 feet in width, 369 feet in length, and with steel towers each 175 feet high and equipped with 70-ton counterweights.

CH09 International Railroad Bridge, River Section

1887; J. Reid; Dominion Bridge Company of Lachine, Quebec; and Detroit Bridge and Iron Works. Over the Saint Mary's River

Four railroad companies (the Duluth, South Shore, and Atlantic; the Minneapolis, Saint Paul, and Sault Sainte Marie; the Grand Trunk Western; and the Canadian Pacific) collaborated to build the International Railroad Bridge across the Saint Mary's River. The three bridge builders responsible were J. Reid, who built the substructure; the Dominion Bridge Company of Lachine, Quebec, which underbid all of the American companies because it could import cheap duty-free Scottish steel and then could fabricate the structural members in Canada, built the superstructure; and the Detroit Bridge and Iron Works built the rest of the bridge crossing the American Navigational Canal. The river section consisted of ten steel camelback through trusses, each 239 feet long, resting on finished ashlar piers, each anchored in the bedrock of the river bottom. One of these trusses was removed in 1913 to enable construction of a new moveable bridge over the American Locks, but nine of the original spans remain. The International Railroad Bridge was the vital west-east connection for Sault Sainte

Marie. The growing lake and railroad traffic and the immense waterpower potential that could be harnessed for industry at the Sault precipitated grand predictions that manufacturing and commerce would flourish here.

CH10 International Highway Bridge

1962, Steinman, Boynton, Gronquist, and Londson. I-75 over the Saint Mary's River

Until this bridge was opened in 1962, automobile traffic between the American and Canadian Saults was carried by ferry. In 1935 the Michigan and Ontario governments established an International Bridge Authority to plan and finance a highway bridge to replace the ferry for automobile traffic. More than two decades passed before construction began. The bridge was designed by the firm of Steinman, Boynton, Gronquist, and London of New York and cost $20 million. The structure, 2.76 miles long, including approaches, has a two-lane roadway 28 feet wide. The bridge is comprised of a 2,471-foot American approach, a 2,942-foot Canadian approach, and a 9,280-foot river section resting on sixty-two reinforced concrete piers. A four-span, 1,260-foot-long cantilevered truss crosses the American Navigation Canal. In order not to interrupt navigation, it was erected without falsework through the use of balanced additions of steel members in assembling the two main spans of 540 feet each. The Canadian crossing, a single main span of 430 feet and two side spans of 200 feet each, was simpler to construct.

CH11 Lake Superior State University (New Fort Brady)

1892–1893. 1946. 1971. Bounded by Ryan St., Easterday Ave., Meridian St., Fourth Ave. West, I-75, and Sheridan Dr.

A former military post found renewed life as an educational institution after World War II, first for Michigan College of Mining and Technology (what is now Michigan Technological University) and currently for Lake Superior State University. Fort Brady was authorized by Congress in 1886. The secretary of war sold old Fort Brady on the Saint Mary's River, purchased this site on higher ground for better protection of the Soo Locks, and assigned Q.M. George S. Hoyt to build a full four-company post in which to garrison the troops. After the end of World War II, officers' quarters became faculty housing; soldiers' barracks, student housing; and the headquarters buildings, college offices. Today the artillery site is the location of married student housing, and the parade ground the site of a new library (1971).

CH12 Sault Sainte Marie Water Tower

c. 1900. Southeast corner Ryan St. and Easterday Ave.

Used until recently, this 78-foot-tall conical-roofed water tower is 45 feet in diameter and has a 370,000-gallon capacity. The lower portion is built of the ubiquitous coursed canal rock and the upper of brick.

CH13 Robert G. and Christina Bain Ferguson House

1906, George W. Maher. 801 Prospect St.

This large, two-and-a-half-story shingled dwelling on a cobblestone foundation is one of two unexpected examples showing the influence of the Prairie School in the northeasternmost portion of the state. George W. Maher (1864–1926), often identified with the Prairie School, is credited by H. Allen Brooks as "one who developed a consistent and personal style." Brooks compares Maher favorably with Wright: "His influence on the Midwest was profound and prolonged and, in its time, was certainly as great as was Wright's."[82] Nine extant blueprint sheets clearly establish the Ferguson house as an almost exact duplicate of Maher's earlier Edgar G. Barratt (also spelled Barrett) House in Kenilworth, Illinois,

1896. The Barratt house was illustrated in *The Inland Architect and News Record* for February 1897, and it is highly possible that Ferguson, then the prosperous owner of Ferguson Hardware Company, may have seen that illustration, admired it, and wanted the same for himself.

Noticeable changes from the Barratt house are in the use of brick instead of fieldstone for the chimneys and cobblestone instead of fieldstone for the foundation. Just as the Barratt house expressed the character of a fashionable residence in the Chicago suburb, the Ferguson house expressed the essence of the fashionable residence at the Soo.

CH14 William L. and Cecile Wyman Murdock House

1906–1907, George W. Maher. 501 North Ravine Rd.

Only two doors away from the Ferguson house is another George W. Maher design. Although this home is often referred to by local residents as the work of Frank Lloyd Wright, newspaper accounts of the time identify the architect as George W. Maher, with Marshall N. Hunt as his contractor. According to the *Sault Sainte Marie Evening News*, May 12, 1906, for an estimated cost of between $10,000 and $12,000, the house would be "one of the handsomest homes in the city."

Broad projecting eaves, a prominent chimney, and an unusual projecting entrance flanked by two heavy, squat concrete pillars characterize the Prairie School influence in this stuccoed, low-lying house. The unique feature of the entrance is the thin, curved segmented arch motif with two curious projecting elements near the ends, a theme that is also carried out in the interior. Maher used this unusual feature in two earlier examples in Oak Park and Kenilworth in the suburbs of Chicago.

Maher employed an unusual decorative motif, the thistle, in the stained glass on the front door, on the capitals of the squat flanking pillars, and throughout the interior in the tile mosaic over the fireplace, the stenciling over the top corners of the dining and living rooms, and on the leatherlike fabric hanging in the hall and in the living room. In carrying the thistle theme throughout the house, Maher demonstrated his "motif-rhythm theory" or the "floral element of the locality" theory of design, in which a plant indigenous to the area and/or a specific geometric shape was used as the unifying decorative element.

William Murdock was the treasurer and superintendent of the Northwestern Leather Company, a major company in Sault Sainte Marie that shipped one-third of its production to England. Eventually, Murdock moved back to Boston where the headquarters of the tannery were located, but his home retains evidence of his presence in the freely sculptured concrete dog at the base of the entrance pillar, the dog that once pulled the small Murdock children in their wagons.

DRUMMOND ISLAND, DRUMMOND TOWNSHIP

Reached by ferry from the mainland village of De Tour across the De Tour Passage of the Saint Mary's River, Drummond Island is a paradise in Lake Huron for hunters, fishermen, and boaters. The island is rocky, wooded, and isolated.

CH15 The Rock

1989, 1990, Charles W. Moore, Gunnar Birkerts and Associates. Off Maxton Rd., Sections 21 and 16, Township 42 North, Range 6 East

In 1985 Thomas S. Monaghan, founder of Domino's Pizza, acquired the Bayside Lodge, cabins, and boat house in Section 16 on Potagannissing Bay and, soon after, an old sawmill in Section 21 for the purpose of establishing a corporate retreat. First named the Saw Mill Center Complex, the development was recently opened to the public under the name "The Rock."

CH15.1 Resort Hotel (Motel)

1990, Charles W. Moore. Maxton Rd., section 21, township 42 north, range 6 east

Modeled on a traditional nineteenth-century frontier logging community, this coherent complex has a main street, town square, and covered walkways. The resort motel is of log construction. The log walls are laid horizontally with interlocking corners and rise to steeply pitched hipped and gabled roofs clad in corrugated metal. The combination of the log walls, the beach stone chimney, and the Drummond Island limestone (dolomite) walkway places the building in the vernacular wooden building tradition native to northern Michigan. Easily transportable, the corrugated metal material is ideally suited to island building.

CH15.2 Bowling Center

1990, Charles W. Moore. Maxton Rd., section 21, township 42 north, range 6 east

Corrugated metal-clad towers distinguished with ornamental wooden structures inspired by Russian churches mark the entrances to this bowling center building. It is covered with a corrugated metal-clad gabled roof, which is stepped down to form clerestories. The exposed rafters and supports underneath the roof and the posts supporting the porch extending around the building are painted bright colors.

CH15.3 Outdoor Chapel

1989, Gunnar Birkerts and Associates. Section 16, township 42 north, range 6 east. Not visible from the road

Near the Bayside Restaurant and Lodge, the Outdoor Chapel fills a small clearing in the

dense woods and is sheltered by a canopy of trees. The chapel is constructed of 8-inch-by-8-inch stepped oak timbers that culminate in the center behind the altar to form a backdrop. It seats 50.

HULBERT

CH16 **Hulbert Methodist Chapel** (Hulbert Tahquamenon Chapel)

1935, Sundt and Wenner. Northeast corner Maple and Third streets, 1.5 miles north of intersection of Michigan 28 and Hulbert Rd.

At Hulbert, a tiny lumbering town near Tahquamenon Falls, is a rustic log community chapel and hall built in 1935 with funds granted by the Federal Emergency Administration of Public Works and donated from local businesses and outside companies. The simple gable-roof structure is made of native spruce logs, now stained reddish brown, and rests on a beach stone foundation. Its chimney, which serves also as a bellcote, is constructed of Lake Superior beach stones gathered at Bay Mills and laid in even courses with each large stone encircled by a band of small stones. The interior has a chancel at one end and a stage with a fireplace at the other. Reversible seats manufactured by the Manitowoc Church Furniture Company of Waukesha, Wisconsin, orient the audience toward one end when used as a house of worship, or toward the other when used as a lecture hall or theater. The pulpit rests on a log stand. The log exterior walls and knotty pine interior celebrate the forest. Stained-glass memorial windows are green, turquoise, gold, purple, and red. Alvin C. Doten of Newberry, the Methodist minister who then served ten or more churches and missions in the far-flung communities of the Eastern Upper Peninsula, led the campaign to raise funds for the "Little Church in the Big UP." The Methodist Bureau of Church Architecture worked out the plans.

WHITEFISH TOWNSHIP

CH17 **Great Lakes Shipwreck Historical Museum** (Whitefish Point Light Station)

1861. 5 miles northeast of Shelldrake at the end of Whitefish Point Rd.

Since 1849 there has been a lighthouse at Whitefish Point to warn of the dangerous shoals and a narrowed shipping channel at the northern end of Whitefish Bay, an area so dangerous that it is known as the "Graveyard of the Great Lakes." The existing iron pile tower of the Whitefish Point Light was built in 1861 and is supported by an open pyramidal skeleton of horizontal and diagonal bracing built to withstand the severe winter weather on Lake Superior. A round cast-iron stair tower ascends 42 feet to the lantern.

Other structures at the site are the light keeper's dwelling, chief's quarters, crew's quarters, a boat house, pipe shed-wood shed, fog signal building, oil house, and alcohol house. The chief's quarters contain some exhibits and a shipwreck video theater. In 1987 the Great Lakes Shipwreck Museum opened in a new building designed by Truman Cummings, Woodland Builders, of Harbor Springs, Michigan. In 1990 the Whitefish Point complex received 55,000 visitors, despite its isolated location.

BAY MILLS TOWNSHIP

CH18 **Point Iroquois Light Station**

1871. 1905, additions. 1911–1930?, remodeling. Just off Lake Shore Dr., 6 miles northwest of Brimley in the Hiawatha National Forest

This conical brick light tower and attached houses for the keeper and assistant keepers marked Point Iroquois for ships as they passed from Lake Superior into the Saint Mary's Canal. The larger house and tower were built initially in 1871 with a congressional appropriation of $18,000 and replaced an earlier wooden tower and house of 1855 (no longer standing). In 1905 an additional house was attached to the mass, and the 1871 house was enlarged by raising the roof to accommodate a second floor. Some time between 1911 and 1930, the 1871 west house was remodeled to accommodate two families, thus providing housing for three light keepers in all at the complex. The walls of the multigabled house are brick and half-timber infilled with stucco. The tapered tower rises nearly 51 feet to a lantern deck on which rests the light. A cobblestone wall surrounds the complex. In 1962 the Coast Guard decommissioned the light and soon after transferred the property to the United States Forest Service.

Mackinac County (MK)

SAINT IGNACE

MK01 **Mackinac County Courthouse**

1936–1937, G. Harold Thompson. 100 Marley St.
(bounded by Marley, Truckey, and Portage streets)

The handsome reinforced concrete and masonry Art Moderne Mackinac County Courthouse heralds a new age in governmental buildings. It was built in 1936–1937, ostensibly to expand and reface an earlier brick structure erected on the site in 1882. Actually, it gave the county a much-desired brand-new building. The project was financed with funds from the Works Progress Administration (WPA).

In 1936 the WPA awarded Mackinac County a grant of $30,944 to repair the existing county courthouse. The official work as specified on the federal application, now located in the National Archives, called for removing the roof, erecting an additional story, reroofing the building, and recovering the exterior with limestone and pressed brick. According to local tradition and historians, the chairman of the board of supervisors and the building committee wanted an all-new structure and acted accordingly. With the independent and resourceful spirit characteristic of the residents of the Upper Peninsula, they tore down three sides of the existing courthouse and wired the Honorable Prentiss M. Brown (1889–1973), then a U.S. senator, for funds under this federal government-sponsored program to repair the building. Then they tore down the remaining wall, received additional funds, and finished the job that resulted in an all-new structure for Mackinac County.

The architect for the project was G. Harold Thompson (b. 1903), a native of Cheboygan, who was trained at Chicago Technical College and worked in Chicago as a draughtsman and supervising architect. Thompson specialized in residential work around the inland lakes of northern Lower Michigan.

The Mackinac County Courthouse emphasizes the streamlined second phase of the Art Deco style popular in the 1930s. It is a tripartite, three-story, flat-roofed central block on a raised foundation with slightly lower projections to the east and west. Gray Indiana limestone (cast stone?) pilasters rise the full height of the building. Between the pilasters the walls are laid in a zig-zag pattern with coursed smooth-cut Briar Hill sandstone and infilled with brick. An ornamental metal grille over the main entrance depicts scenes recalling frontier Mackinac—a hunter, a trapper with dog sled, an Indian, and the forest. Above, inscribed in stencillike letters characteristic of the time, are the words Mackinac County Courthouse. The third-floor courtroom is a period classic.

This plain geometric design of the building reflects the contemporary movement in the United States to emphasize the future rather than the past and to break with the historicist tradition of the earlier Beaux-Arts or period styles. In his speech at the dedication of the building, Thompson described his attempt to build "the largest and most modern court house possible with the money available, one free from unnecessary architectural detail." His rejection of nonessential decoration and his use of a harmonious balance of volumes makes this structure look forward to the International style in Michigan, albeit about a decade late.

MK02 **Warren and Florence Highstone House**

1949. 100 Truckey St. (southeast corner of Truckey and Dickinson streets)

This little ranch house is one of less than fifty known examples in Michigan manufactured between 1946 and 1950 by the Lustron Homes Company of Columbus, Ohio. The company was established in 1946 by Carl Strandlund of Minnesota, who was a former employee of the Chicago Vitrius Company, which manufactured the building materials for gas stations and hamburger stands. These prefabricated houses attempted to offer a solution to the postwar housing shortage. They illustrate in building construction the application of new materials and new methods of manufacturing and handling. They were low in maintenance.

The exterior and interior surfaces of the house are finished in porcelain-enameled modular steel panels. The house was built on a concrete slab. This house is the standard two-bedroom model known as the Westchester and is finished in desert tan; a steel plate bearing its serial number located in the utility room testifies to its origins. It cost about $8,000.

Warren and Florence Highstone, local merchants, first read about Lustron houses in *Life* magazine. Attracted by their uniqueness and carefree maintenance, they located a Michigan dealer in Sturgis and placed an order. All the parts arrived in one trailer, and the house was assembled over an excavated foundation in two weeks.

Lustron Homes advertised its product and received attention in such national magazines as *Popular Mechanics, Better Homes and Gardens, Life, Look,* and *Collier's.* Just under 2,500 were built nationwide before the company went bankrupt in 1950. (Some say lumbermen, brick manufacturers, and others forced the company out of business.) Most were located in New York City, Long Island, Connecticut, the New Jersey Shore, Ohio, Indiana, Illinois, and Iowa. In Michigan Lustron houses are found in the larger cities of southern Lower Michigan—Ann Arbor, Battle Creek, Benton Harbor, Detroit, Flint, Grand Rapids, Jackson, and Muskegon.

MK03 Saint Ignace Municipal Building

1939–1940, David E. Anderson. 396 North State St. (Business I-75) (southwest corner of North State St. [Business I-75] and Goudreau Ave.)

The plainness and severity of this modest little city hall match the drabness of the depression era in which it was built. It was designed by David E. Anderson, constructed under the supervision of C. A. Minier, and financed with funds from the Works Progress Administration. The classical and formal rectangular two-story brick block is on a raised basement and topped with a flat roof. It has

enough Moderne details to convey a contemporary feeling. Windows are grouped within vertical panels between pierlike members with a hint of a capital. Horizontal cast concrete decorative bands make up the frieze of the entablature and a cornice with a decorative zig-zag-like motif runs above. Stairs rise to the center entrance, which is surrounded by a decorative cast stone enframement.

MK04 Indian Village

1977. 499 North State St. (Business I-75)

Neon and wooden tepees attract motoring tourists to this colossal souvenir warehouse at Saint Ignace on the shore of Lake Huron. The building is a decorated shed, as Robert Venturi developed the term. The long metal building is faced with cedar bark, wallpapered with birch bark decorated with pictographs of arrows, animals, canoes, and headdresses, and is jam packed with curios and articles crafted by Native Americans. Birch logs appear to support the roof. This 1977 version replaced the earlier Indian Village shop and museum erected here by Clarence Eby in 1927 and is still one of several tourist attractions at one of Michigan's spectacular natural landmarks. Others nearby are the souvenir shop at Castle Rock and the Curiosity Shop—Curio Fair overlooking the Straits of Mackinac.

MK05 Marquette Mission Park and Museum of Ojibwa Culture (Saint Ignace Mission)

Nineteenth century. Northwest corner of North State (Business I-75) and Marquette streets

This nineteenth-century wooden chapel with front gable and a series of arched windows was moved from its original location on Moran Bay to this site, now a city park overlooking Lake Huron and the Straits of Mackinac. It stands on the site of the Huron Indian village that was also the location of the Saint Ignace Mission of Father Jacques Marquette (1637–1675) and where he was buried in 1677. The mission was named to honor Saint Ignatius Loyola, founder of the Jesuit order. It was first established by Father Claude Dablon in 1669 on Mackinac Island and moved here in about 1672, where it was maintained until about 1706. Archaeologists have not yet discovered the exact location of the original mission church, although there were extensive excavations conducted in the 1970s and 1980s revealing the extent of the historic Indian village and portions of several Huron longhouses.[83] The chapel has been adapted for use as a museum of Ojibwa culture.

MK06 Ship Cottage

1950s. Mackinac Trail (Business I-75) (opposite North Bay Inn and Trade Winds Motel, south of Evergreen Shores and across from Mackinac County Airport)

A wooden boat resting in a cradle whimsically serves as the entrance to a split-level cottage partially visible from the road and overlooking Lake Huron. To complete the nautical theme, the owner has laid a welcoming gangplank threshold, flanked by heavy anchor chain painters.

MARQUETTE ISLAND, LES CHENEAUX ISLANDS (Hessel and Cedarville Vicinity), CLARK TOWNSHIP

MK07 Les Cheneaux Club Subdivision

1887. Marquette Island, Les Cheneaux Islands. Visible from the water

In 1887 the completion of the railroad to Saint Ignace and Mackinac City, along with the expansion of steamer service to the Upper Great Lakes, opened up the natural beauty and spectacular fishing of the Les Cheneaux area for development as an ideal location for summer resorting. The following year, Bay City railroad executive William L. Benham purchased and subdivided a point of land on Marquette Island, the largest in the Les Cheneaux group. He intended to develop a summer resort similar in plan to Bay View. Accordingly, the original plat of the Les Cheneaux Subdivision featured clusters of small lots outlined by gently curving avenues linked by narrower footpaths; a large central area was reserved for a clubhouse and a dock site was selected. Benham, together with a group of prominent Bay City businessmen, organized the Les Cheneaux Island Resort Association, later named the Les Cheneaux Club, for the purposes of "recreation, rest, amusement . . . improvement of such property as it may from time to time own, and the erection and maintenance there of Residence,

Hotels, Club Houses, etc." The earliest club shelters were canvas tents on wooden platforms or unfinished frame cabins, erected along the shore. The club grew rapidly as well-to-do residents of Chicago, Detroit, and other urban centers built permanent summer dwellings. By 1900 a large clubhouse-hotel and some thirty cottages with boat houses had been built. Each cottage typically occupied several of the 245 original platted lots. A tennis court and playground were on the grounds; a nine-hole golf course was laid out across the channel.

The clubhouse was the center of activity until 1940. Its fully staffed kitchen and dining room served cottagers three meals a day. Ice and groceries were delivered daily to club members by boat from establishments in Cedarville and Hessel. Families enjoyed swimming, hiking, hunting, fishing, and dancing. After World War II, the availability of other vacation options led to a decline in summer resorting at Les Cheneaux Club. The old clubhouse is gone, but many cottages remain, including the gabled Shingle style S. J. McPherson House with its upper story porch, erected in the 1890s on lots 56–58 on the southwest side of Club Point; and the gable-dormered C. G. Waldo House, also built in the 1890s on lots 51–55 on the southwest side of Club Point.

MACKINAC ISLAND

MK08 Fort Mackinac

1780 to 1895. Huron Rd. (on the bluff above Marquette Park, between Fort St. and South Garrison Rd.)

Located on a bluff 150 feet above the harbor on Mackinac Island, Fort Mackinac was a military post from 1780 to 1895. The extant buildings date from 1780 to 1885 and include some of the oldest structures in Michigan. The fort complex includes buildings both within and without the walls. Over the years some structures have been torn down, burned, and rebuilt, but all existing buildings are original.

The British army began the construction of Fort Mackinac in 1780, when it moved its fort from Michilimackinac (present-day Mackinaw City) to a more strategic location on Mackinac Island. Unlike the previous wooden palisaded fort, which was designed only as protection against Indians, the new

MK08 Fort Mackinac

fort was designed to withstand modern cannon fire. Consequently, the thick walls of Fort Mackinac were constructed of limestone quarried from the surrounding bedrock and bonded with lime mortar manufactured in nearby limekilns.

The Mackinac Island fort was separated from the civilian community, but the cannon emplacements were located so they could rake the main street and the palisade of the town. Although the wooden barracks, provisions storehouse, and guardhouse were moved to the new fort, construction of a new massive stone blockhouse, now referred to as the Officers' Stone Quarters, reflected the changing times. This two-story building with 3-foot-thick walls was still unfinished when the British finally relinquished the fort to the Americans in 1796. Eventually the structure was completed and served as a residence for officers at the fort.

Soon after the Americans took control, they constructed three stone blockhouses with hewn-timber overhangs. Pierced both for cannon and muskets, the blockhouses provided better defensive capabilities and also served as living quarters for soldiers. Despite its defenses, Fort Mackinac was captured by the British in the first engagement of the War of 1812, held until 1815, and returned to the Americans after the war. Using horizontal squared timbers mortised into corner uprights, the American army built additional officers' quarters in 1816 and a new guard-

house in 1828. The old provisions storehouse, which was used as a hospital, was so deteriorated that it was replaced by a hipped-roofed building constructed of heavy uprights on approximately 2-foot centers. The spaces between the uprights were filled by chunks of logs, and the exterior was clapboarded. This building marked the return to frame construction in all subsequent structures.

In 1835 a two-family frame officers' quarters was built directly on the north wall line of the fort. Its placement both inside and outside the defensive curtain confirmed that Fort Mackinac was no longer under fear of attack.

During the next thirty years, many of the buildings encircling the parade ground were replaced with frame buildings. The four-room post headquarters was erected in 1853. A new two-story barracks was constructed in 1859 to replace one that had recently burned. That same year a large, two-story hospital with a veranda on both floors was erected immediately east of the fort to which it was joined by a wooden ramp. A shedlike quartermaster's storehouse was constructed in 1867 on earlier foundations and was connected to the post headquarters by a little passageway.

Following the Civil War tourists flocked to Mackinac Island, and in 1875 Congress created Mackinac National Park as the nation's second national park. In order to administer the park, the garrison of the fort was expanded, creating a need for additional buildings. Inside the fort, the 1780 stone powder magazine was demolished and its walls incorporated into the basement of the 1877 commissary building. A post schoolhouse was erected straddling the fort wall in 1879. A few years later, in 1885, reflecting a growing concern for military sanitation and hygiene, a post bathhouse was constructed.

Other new buildings outside the walls were a small morgue and a hospital steward's quarters on the east side of the fort. On the west side of the fort, two large one-and-a-half-story houses were erected for fort officers. One was a two-family unit; the other housed a single family. Reflecting the current attitude and need for good ventilation, they have high ceilings and large verandas on the south side. Additional single-story living quarters for lieutenants and married enlisted men were erected in the open area to the rear of the fort. During this time the rotting palisade was taken down and replaced by a white picket fence.

In 1895 the federal government transferred Fort Mackinac to the Mackinac Island State Park Commission, which continues to oversee the fort. In order to generate revenue, many buildings were remodeled into small apartments. During the 1930s the WPA did some restoration work, including replacing the picket fence with a cedar palisade that still exists.

The current restoration of Fort Mackinac began in 1958 and was financed with the sale of revenue bonds. Since then the fort buildings have been systematically restored to their pre-1895 appearance.

MK09 **Indian Dormitory**

1838, Oliver Newberry?. 1966, restored. Huron St. (next to Marquette Park at northeast corner of Huron and Fort streets)

Built in 1838, this square wooden structure served as the office and living quarters for the U.S. Indian agent, Henry Rowe Schoolcraft, and as a dormitory for Indians visiting the post on business. As a result of the Treaty of Washington (1836) between the Ottawa and Chippewa nations and the United States, the Indians ceded to the United States government two-thirds of the western half of the Lower Peninsula and the eastern half of the Upper Peninsula. The government agreed to provide temporary lodging for Indians who came to Mackinac to conduct business with the agent and to secure trade goods. In 1850 the building became a dormitory for Indian children, and in 1869, a school for island children.

The Indian dormitory is a simple, symmetrically arranged square plan. It has two stories on a full exposed foundation. A single flight of stairs rises to the center entrance, which is surrounded with a transom and side lights and flanked by six-over-six windows.

MK10 **William McGulpin House**

c. 1780. Southwest corner of Fort and Market streets

Constructed around 1780 of logs with dovetailed corners, this little house may have been moved to Mackinac Island from Fort Michilimackinac. Perhaps it was used originally as a summer house for transient fur traders. After 1817 it was made a year-round residence and

the windows were enlarged, the interior walls lathed and plastered, and the exterior covered with beaded clapboarding. In 1982 the Mackinac Island State Park Commission purchased this building. Concealed beneath asbestos shingles and later additions was a good example of eighteenth-century French-Canadian domestic architecture. It was moved, restored, and opened to the public in 1983.

MK11 **Mission Church**

1829–1830, Martin Heydenburk. Huron St. (northeast corner Huron St. and Mission Hill Rd.)

The Mission Church is a simple classical wooden building with a single square tower with entry and a pinnacled and spired octagonal belfry that resembles its New England colonial and Federal antecedents. Built between 1829 and 1830 by Martin Heydenburk, a carpenter and teacher at the Mission School, with funds raised by the villagers and traders of Mackinac Island and a gift from John Jacob Astor, it served the Protestant Indian mission begun here in 1822. The Reverend William Montague Ferry, a Massachusetts-born graduate of Union and Rutgers colleges, established a mission post on Mackinac Island under the auspices of the United Foreign Missionary Society. Its purpose was "to civilize and educate" the Indians and, in exchange for protection from the fort, to exert a moral and religious influence on both the men at the fort and the native inhabitants of the island. The mission closed in 1837 as the island's population declined with the withdrawal of the American Fur Company. After remaining unused for more than fifty years, in the 1890s the church was reopened at irregular intervals for interfaith services for island and summer residents, and in 1955 was acquired by the Mackinac Island State Park Commission.

MACKINAC ISLAND RESORT ARCHITECTURE

The Straits of Mackinac have a long history of French, British, and American presence from the seventeenth-century fur trade to late nineteenth-century tourism. Following the American Civil War, Mackinac Island became a popular summer resort noted for its historic charm, natural beauty, and healthy environment. Many of the structures built during this era remain as well-preserved examples of late nineteenth-century resort architecture.

The federal government created the Mackinac National Park in 1875, in response to the island's growing popularity as a summer resort and in order to preserve its historic and natural wonders. From throughout the Midwest, visitors flocked to the island, coming by train and steamboat. Early visitors here found a few resort hotels, including the Mission House, a converted 1825 Indian mission school first used as a hotel around 1850, the Island House (1852), and the Lake View House (1858). But these few hotels could hardly accommodate the rush of new visitors to the island in the 1870s.

From 1875 through the turn of the century, several hotels expanded their facilities, and new hostelries sprung up. By 1910 visitors could choose from several new hotels, including the Murray (1882), Chippewa (1902), and Iroquois (c. 1902) hotels. But the construction and success of the colossal and classy Grand Hotel (1887) assured Mackinac's reputation as a premier Great Lakes summer resort. One of the largest summer hotels in the world, the Grand boasted a sweeping 627-foot veranda with a spectacular view of the Straits, a palatial dining room with elegant appointments, and accommodations for more than one thousand guests.

Mackinac Island's popularity as a summer resort gave rise to three cottage communities: Hubbard's Annex on private property and

the East and West bluffs in the Mackinac National Park.

In 1882 Gurdon S. Hubbard (1802–1886) developed an 80-acre tract of land on the island's southern bluff into a summer cottage community. Hubbard's Annex was an immediate success, and fifteen cottages were built within the first five years. Harbor Springs contractor Charles W. Caskey designed and built most of the early Annex cottages based on one simple design. These vernacular cottages were small, symmetrical, cross-gable homes decorated with applied Carpenter's Gothic ornamentation. Several of these cottages still stand today with little modification. Among the best examples are the D. C. Holliday (1883, Lot 5, Block 6), William McCourtie (1883, east 1/2 of Lot 2, Block 5), and Hezekiah Wells (1883, west 1/2 of Lot 2, Block 5) cottages.

Cottage construction on the National Park's East and West bluffs began in 1885. Several of the early park cottages were also vernacular homes with Carpenter's Gothic trim. The William D. Gilbert Cottage (1889, Charles W. Caskey), constructed on Lot 21 at the top of the West Bluff, and the Phoebe Gehr Cottage (1885, Charles W. Caskey), on Lot 21 of the East Bluff, are excellent examples of these vernacular homes. Shingle style architecture, popular at Eastern resorts such as Oceanside, was especially popular on the East Bluff, where the John Atkinson (1885, Alfred G. Couchois, Lot 17), and H. L. Jenness (1892, Matt Elliott, Lot 19) cottages were constructed.

When the Grand Hotel established a new image of elegance and fashion on Mackinac Island beginning in 1887, cottage owners responded by constructing larger, more palatial summer homes. Architects designed massive Queen Anne villas that dwarfed their small, vernacular neighbors. Several cottagers tore down their smaller houses and/or remodeled in the Queen Anne style in order to remain fashionable. Three such second-generation cottages, which stand near the top of the West Bluff, were designed by Asbury W. Buckley of Kalamazoo and, later, Chicago. They are the William Amberg (1892, Lot 22), Alexander Hannah (1892, Lot 23), and David Hogg (1893, Lot 24) cottages.

In 1895 the federal government turned the National Park over to the state of Michigan, and the Mackinac Island State Park was created. The state park continued to lease land to prospective cottage owners into the twentieth century. In 1902 Frederick W. Perkins, a Chicago architect who was trained at the Massachusetts Institute of Technology and at the Ecole de Beaux-Arts, designed a massive, shingled cottage for Lawrence Young on the bluff between the Grand Hotel and Fort Mackinac. Since 1945 the Young cottage has been the official summer residence for Michigan's governor.

From 1895 to 1905 period revival styles emerged in the cottage communities. The Henry Davis (1895, Lots 3 and 4, Block 3) and John Weiss (c. 1905, Lot 3, Block 14) cottages in Hubbard's Annex have elements of Colonial Revival styling. In 1903 Michael Cudahy built Stonecliffe, an immense Neo-Tudor summer home on 200 acres of private property in the middle of the island. On the East Bluff the Milton Tootle (c. 1900, Lot 20) and Charles C. Bowen (c. 1895, Lot 22) cottages are stately examples of Beaux-Arts Classical architecture.

Mackinac Island's hotels and cottages chronicle Late Victorian and various revival styles designed for use in a summer resort environment. The overall effect is light, airy, and festive. Interiors are designed for the free flow of fresh lake breezes. Similarly, both hotels and cottages are generously supplied with large windows and sets of double doors, wide verandas and open belvederes—elements designed to integrate Mackinac's pleasant summer climate with the interior of the cottage.

Mackinac Island remains one of Michigan's most popular summer resorts. The historic character of the island today is enriched by the many extant late nineteenth-century resort era structures.

WEST BLUFF

MK12 Grand Hotel

1887; George Mason of Mason and Rice?; Charles W. Caskey, builder. 1918, additions. Northwest corner of West Bluff Rd. and Cadotte Ave.

The Grand Hotel exceeds all superlatives ever written to describe its stately majesty and festive quality. Sited high atop the West Bluff overlooking the Straits of Mackinac and silhouetted against the green woods and blue skies of summer, the grand white hotel is visible for miles from the water and from the Mackinac Bridge, which connects the two peninsulas of Michigan. The Grand Hotel's classical columned facade is one of the most enduring images of Mackinac Island. The Grand is one of the few large wooden resort hotels of the late nineteenth century that still stand today. Constructed of Michigan white pine, it features a three-story veranda that extends the full length of the hotel. Guests of the hotel line the veranda to enjoy beautiful scenic views of the Round Island Lighthouse, ships passing through the Straits, and sparkling blue waters. Additions and enlargements have expanded the hotel to twice its original size.

The slender colossal columns that line the veranda easily and gracefully support a fourth level. The veranda is rounded at each corner and relieves the otherwise harsh straight lines of the rectangular structure. Seven colossal coupled columns support a slightly projecting central entry and emphasize the symmetry of the facade. And, as if to repeat the symmetry of the whole, twin low-lying dormers with

MK12 Grand Hotel

multiple windows enframe a central open belvedere.

In 1882 U.S. Sen. Francis B. Stockbridge of Michigan purchased the site of the hotel and formulated a scheme to finance its construction. He created interest in the building and the oversight of the operation of the hotel among the three major transportation companies that served the island and that wanted to promote the use of their transportation systems. Thus, the Detroit and Cleveland Navigation Company, the Michigan Central Railroad, and the Grand Rapids and Indiana Railroad formed the Mackinac Island Hotel Company, which, in turn, built the hotel in 1887. To build the hotel, the stock company commissioned Charles W. Caskey, an architect-builder who had come north to Harbor Springs from Allegan, Michigan, to take part in the building rush in the resort communities of northwestern Lower Michigan in the 1880s. Caskey executed plans prepared by George Mason of Mason and Rice in Detroit. The company leased the operation of the Grand Hotel to managers and firms experienced in operating hotels in New England and elsewhere. Among the wealthy Midwesterners assembled at the Grand Hotel for its opening in 1887 were the lumber barons the Algers, Newberrys, and Blodgetts; the Potter Palmers and Marshall Fields; and the meat packers, the Armours and Swifts.

Today, the Grand Hotel is probably Michigan's major architectural attraction.

MK13 **John and ? O'Neill Cudahy House**

1888. Lot 25, West Bluff

John Cudahy, the Chicago meat packer, built this huge Shingle style house atop terraces and a foundation of craggy field and limestone boulders on the West Bluff above the Grand Hotel. A round corner tower with a bell-cast roof, a square room with belvedere, hipped-roof dormers, and a classically detailed sweeping porch project from the structure. Diamond, fish-scale, and rectangular shingles cover the exterior walls. *Prominent Citizens and Industries of Chicago* (1901) noted, "In addition to his handsome residence at Thirty-second street and Michigan Avenue, which was built in 1883, Mr. Cudahy has a beautiful summer home at Mackinac."

MK14 **Cairngorn** (William Amberg Cottage)

1892, Asbury W. Buckley. Lot 22 West Bluff Rd.

From this large asymmetrical wooden Queen Anne cottage protrude conical-roofed octagonal and domed round towers, receding porches and sweeping veranda, and shed roof dormers. All was planned so that, whether

MK13 John and ? O'Neill Cudahy House (far right); MK14 Cairngorn (William Amberg Cottage) (far left)

from inside the bank of windows or open balcony of one of the towers or from one of the porches or bays, the residents of this cottage were poised to enjoy the magnificent view of the Straits from the high vantage point on the West Bluff. The generous overhang of the bracketed eaves and the covered porches offer protection against the sun and the weather. The picturesque and irregular mass is covered with a variety of decoratively cut shingles. The swag running along the frieze adds a festive touch. Behind this summer house and others on West Bluff stand necessary carriage houses and stables and paddocks, for no automobiles are allowed on Mackinac Island.

MK15 **William D. and (Mary) Angie Bingham Gilbert Cottage**

1889, Charles W. Caskey. Lot 21 West Bluff Rd.

The Gilbert cottage is an excellent example of the island's early vernacular cottages, which are characterized by cross-gable roofs, railed wrap-around porches, interior chimneys, and horizontal shiplap siding and which are similar to the Richard Thompson house in Otsego (see AE07, p. 276). Turned posts and scrolled and sawed brackets with stars, circles and S curves support the porch. The same wooden cutwork ornaments the gables and eaves. The windows are forty-eight small panes over one large pane. The cottage was built for William D. Gilbert, a Grand Rapids lumberman and banker, and his wife Mary A. Bingham. Mrs. Gilbert was the daughter of Rev. Abel Bingham, a noted missionary among the Ojibwa at the Sault.

HUBBARDS' ANNEX

MK16 **Henry Davis Cottage**

1895, Asbury W. Buckley. Lots 3 and 4, Block 3, Hubbards' Annex

The large, classicized Queen Anne cottage was built for Henry Davis of Springfield, Illinois. A central gable containing a Palladian window projects from the symmetrical mass of the house. A large, classically detailed porch, with a pediment marking the location of the central entrance, sweeps around the structure. The house is crowned with a hipped roof with projecting eaves and with a flat deck

surrounded by an iron cresting. Ornamental shingles decorate the exterior.

EAST BLUFF

MK17 **Donnybrook** (John and Lida Lyons Atkinson Cottage)

1885, Alfred G. Couchois, builder. Lot 17 Huron Rd., East Bluff

This asymmetrical Shingle style cottage was built for John Atkinson (b. 1841), a Detroit lawyer, and his wife Lida Lyons. A large octagonal tower with an open upper level beneath a conical roof rises above an open octagonal porch at the southwest corner of the house. This marvelous breezy lookout was particularly appropriate for lake or seaside cottages. The house is clad in shingles.

MK18 **Charles C. Bowen Cottage**

c. 1895. Lot 22 Huron Rd., East Bluff

Charles C. Bowen remodeled a simple vernacular cottage built by Charles W. Caskey into this elaborate white classical mansion. The impressive two-tiered, balustraded Ionic portico with two dramatic semicircular projections runs the full width of two houses. It connects and conceals a T-shape house on the west with a side gabled house on the east. A denticulated entablature on the first level and block modillions support the eaves of the second level.

WEST FORT LOT

MK19 **Governor's Summer House** (Lawrence Andrew Young Summer House)

1901–1902, Frederick W. Perkins. West Fort Lot (bounded by Fort and Spring streets, west of Huron Rd.)

Built on the second-highest site on the bluff overlooking the Straits for Young (1869–1923), a Chicago lawyer and railroad man, who participated in the development of the Grand Hotel and Mackinac Island as a resort center, the huge Shingle style house was acquired in 1945 by the state of Michigan for use as the governor's official summer house. The rectangular, shingle-clad mass rests on rugged native limestone boulders, which also form the chimneys. From the mammoth hipped roof with dramatic flaring eaves supported by exposed decorative rafters project gabled dormers with similar flaring eaves. These windows and others, as well as the comfortable porch that wraps around three sides of the structure, afford spectacular views of the shipping channel and the Straits. The porch's posts are braced with slightly curving decorative brackets. The main double-door entrance is surmounted by a fanlight. Originally the shingled siding was stained a dark color to blend with nature. Frederick W. Perkins (1866–1928) of Chicago was the designer. Patrick Doud constructed it for $15,000.

Notes

1. H. R. Schoolcraft, *On the Number, Value, and Position of the Copper Mines on the Southern Shore of Lake Superior,* 17th Cong, 2d Sess., S. Doc 5, 1822, pp. 7–28. Douglass Houghton, Fourth Annual Report of the State Geologist, Michigan, House Doc. 27, 1841. J. W. Foster and J. D. Whitney, *Report on the Geology and Topography of a Portion of the Lake Superior Land District, in the State of Michigan* (part 1, Copper Lands, U.S. 31st Cong, 1st sess., House Exec. Doc. 69, 1850; part 2, The Iron Region, Together with the General Geology, U.S. 32d Cong., Spec sess., Senate Exec. Doc. 4, 1851).

2. *Daily Resorter,* June 27, 1896.

3. *Detroit News,* July 12, 1958.

4. *Michigan Catholic,* November 13, 1887.

5. *Trinity Church Detroit* (Detroit: Thomas Smith Press, n.d.), 7.

6. Ibid., 17

7. A. Craig Morrison and Lucy Pope Wheeler, "Historic American Buildings Survey Report: Orchestra Hall," National Park Service, 1972, 1973, 1976, 11.

8. Ralph Adams Cram, "The Cathedral: A Sermon in Stone," *St. Paul's Cathedral, One Hundred Years: 1824–1924* (Saturday Night Press, Detroit, c. 1924), 41.

9. Elizabeth Grossman, "The Detroit Institute of Arts: Heterogeneity of Intention" (Paper delivered at the Forty-second Annual Meeting of the Society of Architectural Historians, Montréal, Canada, April 12–16, 1989), 2.

10. *Detroit News,* February 1, 1931.

11. Miller-Storm Co., Inc., *Good Homes: A Book Designed to Help You Plan, Finance and Equip Your Home* (Detroit: Howe Publishing Co., 1929), 3.

12. *Michigan Jewish Chronicle,* 5 (July 22, 1927): 3–5.

13. *Michigan Catholic,* December 11, 1924.

14. *Elmwood Cemetery, Detroit* (Detroit: John Bowman and Son, 1895), 13.

15. "Thirteenth Annual Historic Indian Village Homes and Garden Tour, June 8, 1985" Pamphlet. See also *Detroit Evening News* June 6, 1985, 6.

16. McGregor Public Library Dedicated March 5, 1926, Program, n.p., 1926, 6, 12.

17. Hawkins Ferry, "Art Objects in the Central Library," (Lecture at the Grosse Pointe Public Library, February 14, 1954, Reference Collection, Grosse Pointe Public Library, Mimeographed), 1.

18. Andrew Jackson Downing, *The Architecture of Country Houses* (New York: D. Appleton and Co., 1850), 258, 259, and 257.

19. *Detroit Times,* September 30, 1934.

20. Talcott E. Wing, *History of Monroe County, Michigan* (New York: Munsell and Company, 1890), 351.

21. Talbot Hamlin, *Greek Revival Architecture in America* (London: Oxford University Press, 1944), 293.

22. John McClelland Bulkley, *History of Monroe County, Michigan* (Chicago and New York: Lewis Publishing Company, 1913), 983.

23. Manferd Burleigh and Charles M. Adams, *Modern Bus Terminals and Post Houses* (Ypsilanti, Michigan: University Lithoprinters, 1941), preface.

24. *Ann Arbor News,* January 5, 1928.

25. *American Architect,* 126:2459 (November 19, 1924): following page 488, after plate 174.

26. "A Brick Triangle for Thinking," *House and Home* (September 1960), 110.

27. John B. Cameron, *Meadow Brook Hall: Tudor Revival Architecture and Decorations* (Rochester: Oakland University, 1979), v. Matilda R. Wilson to Shelby Newhouse, September 17, 1967.

28. Mary Ann Affleck Lutomski to Bruce Annett, Lawrence Technological University Public Relations Archives, February 16, 1978.

29. Downing, *Country Houses,* 286.

30. Samuel Sloan, *The Model Architect* (Philadelphia: E. S. Jones and Company, date?), 12.

31. W. A. Whitney and R. J. Bonner, *History and Biographical Record of Lenawee County, Michigan* (Adrian: W. Stearns and Company, 1879), 260.

32. Hamlin, *Greek Revival Architecture in America,* 294–95.

33. *Battle Creek Daily Journal,* October 22, 1906.

34. "The Skyline of 1936," *Architectural Forum* 65:4 (October 1936), 362.

35. *Battle Creek Daily Moon,* June 1, 1903.

36. *Portrait and Biographical Album of Calhoun County, Michigan* (Chicago: Chapman Brothers, 1891), 192.

37. *History of St. Joseph County, Michigan* (Philadelphia: L. H. Everts and Co., 1877), 23.

38. For more information on the House of David, see Roger L. Rosentreter, "House of David: Hoax or Heaven?" *Michigan History* (July-August): 29–39.

39. *Niles Daily Star,* February 9, 1957.

40. *Portrait and Biographical Record of Berrien and Cass Counties* (Chicago: Biographical Publishing Co., 1893), 561.

41. *History of Allegan and Barry Counties, Michigan* (Philadelphia: D. W. Ensign and Company, 1880), 162.

42. *Grand Rapids Herald,* December 30, 1928.

43. *Riverside Homes,* Lansing: Riverside Homes Company, c. 1921, 3–4.

44. Rochelle Elstein, "The Howard Sober House: Artifact of the 1950s," *Chronicle of the Historical Society of Michigan*, (Winter 1980), 4–7.

45. Harold W. Lautner, "From an Oak Opening: A Record of the Development of the Campus Park of Michigan State University, 1855–1969," (East Lansing: Michigan State University, 1978 v. 1, unpublished), 84.

46. Olmsted Brothers Report to State Board of Agriculture, Lansing, May 10, 1915 (courtesy of the Michigan State University Archives and Historical Collections), 3–4.

47. Michigan State University. *The Campus Development Plan* East Lansing Michigan (October 1966), 5.

48. Michigan State University. Zoning Ordinance Adopted by the Board of Trustees, April 18, 1968, 1.

49. Lantner, v. 2, p. 54.

50. Richard Longstreth, *The Buildings of Main Street: A Guide to American Commercial Architecture* (Washington, D.C.: Preservation Press, 1987), 54.

51. *History of Shiawassee and Clinton Counties, Michigan* (Philadelphia: D. W. Ensign and Company, 1880), 453.

52. James Cook Mills, *History of Saginaw County, Michigan* (Saginaw, Michigan: Seeman and Peters Publishers, 1918), 76.

53. "Equipment Being Manufactured for Saginaw's New Dial Office," *The Michigan Bell* (March 1930), 7.

54. See Sidney K. Robinson, *Architecture of Alden B. Dow* (Detroit: Wayne State University Press, 1983).

55. *The Bay City Tribune*, March 23, 1897, 1.

56. Booklet published by The Capitol Theatre, c. 1928 (Flint Public Library, general reference department, Flint, Michigan), 180.

57. *Portrait and Biographical Album of Clinton and Shiawassee Counties* (Chicago: Chapman Brothers, 1891), 431.

58. William Lee Jenks, *History of St. Clair County* (Chicago: A. T. Andreas and Company, 1912), 512.

59. Ibid.

60. Among collection of editorial clippings from *Pontiac Press* and reprinted in the *Tuscola County Advertiser*, 1932; and *Vassar Pioneer Times* clippings in the scrapbook of Dorr N. Wiltse, Caro, Michigan, 1920s.

61. Ibid.

62. *Isabella County Times News*, August 13, 1936.

63. Willard D. Tucker, *Gratiot County, Michigan* (Saginaw: Seeman and Peters Publisher, 1913), 1238.

64. George Healy, *The Castle on Delaware Hill* (Saint Louis, Michigan: n.p., 1985), 3.

65. Leonard K. Eaton, "The Louis Sullivan Spirit in Michigan," *Quarterly Review of the Michigan Alumnus* 64 (Spring 1958): 215–20.

66. *Manistee Democrat*, October 25, 1888.

67. Cobbs and Mitchell, *Michigan's Woods in Use* (Cadillac: n.p., n.d., c. 1907), 5.

68. *The Traverse Region* (Chicago: H. R. Page and Company, 1884), 139.

69. *Harbor Springs Northern Independent*, July 25, 1882.

70. *Bellaire Record*, December 14, 1933.

71. *Marquette Mining Journal*, February 4, 1888.

72. *Houghton Daily Mining Gazette*, January 1, 1900.

73. See Terry G. Reynolds, "A Narrow Window of Opportunity: The Rise and Fall of the Fixed Steel Dam," *The Journal of the Society for Industrial Archeology*, vol. 15, no. 1, 1989: 1–20.

74. Arnold R. Alanen, "The Planning of Company Communities in the Lake Superior Mining Region," *Journal of the American Planning Association*, vol. 45 (July 1979): 256–78.

75. Leonard K. Eaton, "John Wellborn Root and the Julian M. Case House," *Prairie School Review* 9 (Third Quarter):18–22.

76. *Marquette Mining Journal*, April 28, 1988.

77. U.S. Department of Commerce Light-House Board, "Annual Report of the Light-house Board of the United States to the Secretary of Treasury for 1892," Washington: Government Printing Office, 1867–1910.

78. Antoine Ivan Rezek, *History of the Diocese of Sault Ste. Marie and Marquette*, vol. 2 (Chicago: M. A. Donahue and Co., 1907), 344.

79. William Wicks, *Log Cabins and Cottages: How to Build and Furnish Them* (New York: Forest and Stream Publishing Company, n.d.), 7

80. Alvah L. Sawyer, *A History of the Northern Peninsula of Michigan and Its People*, vol. 1 (Chicago: The Lewis Publishing Company, 1911), 597.

81. Ibid., 600.

82. H. Allen Brooks, *The Prairie School* (Toronto: University of Toronto Press, 1972), 36, 330.

83. Susan Branstner, "Tionontate Huron Indians at Michilimackinac," *Michigan History* (November-December 1989): 24–31.

Suggested Reading

For serious students of Michigan architecture, the index of *Michigan History* (1917 to present) refers to many articles on local buildings, architects, and cultural landscapes. The index of *Michigan Pioneer and Historical Collections* (Lansing, 1874–1912) refers to early accounts of the settlement, development, and growth of the state and its architecture.

The Emil Lorch Papers, Michigan Historical Collections, Bentley Library, University of Michigan, contain the correspondence, fieldnotes, and sketches prepared by the noted dean of the university's College of Architecture as he conducted surveys of buildings throughout the state in the 1930s. This information guided the preparers of the Works Progress Administration's *Michigan: A Guide to the Wolverine State* (New York, 1940s). Lorch himself, in fact, wrote the architectural summary for the guide. The Historic American Buildings Survey teams also selected works from Lorch's survey data for their early inventories of the state. The HABS and HAER (Historic American Engineering Records) data books, representing efforts in the 1930s, 1960s, and 1975 to the present are located in the Prints and Photographs Division of the Library of Congress in Washington, D.C.

The photographs of the Detroit Publishing Company and the Farm Security Administration also at the Library of Congress are invaluable.

The National and State Register historic designation files, state survey data, and survey reports contain documentation and information on thousands of buildings in Michigan. The files are located at the Michigan Bureau of History.

The Albert Kahn Archives in Detroit and the Alden B. Dow Archives in Midland hold architectural records related to the careers and buildings of Kahn and Dow. The Cranbrook Archives of the Cranbrook Educational Community in Bloomfield Hills has the architectural records for Cranbrook and some additional records for other projects by the Saarinens. The State Archives of Michigan has records and drawings of Michigan's lighthouses and the Michigan State Capitol.

The records of building committees and photographs found in many local historical societies, libraries, and regional archives, and local newspapers (most of which are available on microfilm at the Library of Michigan in Lansing) re-create the story of many local public and private buildings.

GENERAL SOURCES

Alanen, Arnold. "The Planning of Company Communities in the Lake Superior Mining Region." *Journal of the American Planning Association* 45 (July 1979): 256–78.

Andrews, Wayne. *Architecture in Michigan.* Revised and enlarged edition. Wayne State University Press, 1982.

Bald, F. Clever. *Michigan in Four Centuries.* New York: Harper and Brothers Publishers, 1954.

Benson, Barbara Ellen. "Logs and Lumber: The Development of the Lumber Industry in Michigan's Lower Peninsula, 1837–1870." Ph.D. diss., Indiana University, 1976.

Bigelow, Martha Mitchell. "Michigan: A State in the Vanguard." In *Heartland: Comparative Histories of the Midwestern States,* edited by James H. Madison and Thomas J. Schlereth, pp. 32–58. Bloomington and Indianapolis: Indiana University Press, 1988.

Brooks, H. Allen. *The Prairie School.* Toronto and Buffalo: University of Toronto Press, 1972.

Brunk, Thomas W. *Leonard B. Willeke. Excellence in Architecture and Design.* Detroit: University of Detroit Press, 1986.

Dunbar, Willis F. *Michigan: A History of the Wolverine State.* Grand Rapids: William B. Eerdmans Publishing Company, 1965.

Eckert, Kathryn B. "The Sandstone Architecture of the Lake Superior Region." Ph.D. diss., Michigan State University, 1982.

Elstein, Rochelle Berger. "Synagogue Architecture and the Midwest: Material Culture and the Dynamics of Jewish Accommodation, 1865–1945." Ph.D. diss., Michigan State University, 1986.

Everett, Franklin. *Memorials of the Grand River Valley.* Chicago: The Chicago Legal News Company, 1878.

Farmer, Silas. *The History of Detroit and Michigan.* Vol. 1, general. Detroit: Silas Farmer & Co., 1889.

Ferry, W. Hawkins. *The Buildings of Detroit.* Rev. ed. Detroit: Wayne State University Press, 1980.

Hamlin, Talbot. *Greek Revival Architecture in America.* New York: Oxford University Press, 1944.

Hildebrand, Grant. *Designing for Industry: The Architecture of Albert Kahn.* Cambridge: MIT Press, 1974.

History of the Lake Huron Shore. Chicago: H. R. Page and Company, 1883.

Holleman, Thomas J., and James P. Gallagher. *Smith, Hinchman & Grylls.* Detroit: Wayne State University Press, 1978.

Hyde, Charles K. *The Northern Lights: Lighthouses of the Upper Great Lakes.* Lansing, Michigan: Two Peninsula Press, 1986.

———. *Historic Bridges of Michigan.* Detroit: Bureau of History and Wayne State University Press, forthcoming.

Kern, John. *A Short History of Michigan.* Lansing, Michigan: Michigan History Division, Michigan Department of State, 1977.

557

Lewis, David L. and Goldstein, Laurence, eds. *The Automobile and American Culture*. Ann Arbor: The University of Michigan Press, 1983.

Macmillan, Margaret Burnham. *The Methodist Church in Michigan: the Nineteenth Century*. Grand Rapids: the Michigan Area Methodist Historical Society, 1967.

McGee, John W. *The Catholic Church in the Grand River Valley 1833–1950*. Grand Rapids: n.p., 1950.

Meier, Richard. *Richard Meier, Architect*. New York: Oxford University Press, 1976.

Newcomb, Rexford. *Architecture of the Old Northwest Territory*. Chicago: University of Chicago Press, 1950.

Page, H. R., ed. *The Traverse Region*. Chicago: H. R. Page & Co., 1884.

Rezek, Rev. Antoine Ivan. *History of the Diocese of Sault Ste. Marie and Marquette*. 2 vols. Chicago: M. A. Donahue and Co., 1906, 1907.

Pear, Lillian Myers. *The Pewabic Pottery*. Des Moines, Iowa: Wallace-Homestead Book Company, 1976.

Robinson, Sidney K. *Architecture of Alden B. Dow*. Detroit: Wayne State University Press, 1983.

Ruby, Christine M. Nelson. "Art for the People: Art in Michigan Sponsored by the Treasury Section of Fine Arts, Michigan, 1934–1943." Ph.D. diss., University of Michigan, 1986.

Sawyer, Alvah. *A History of the Northern Peninsula of Michigan and Its People: Its Mining, Lumber and Agricultural Industries*. 3 vols. Chicago: The Lewis Publishing Company, 1911.

Schwietzer, Robert and Michael W. R. Davis. *America's Favorite Homes*. Detroit: Wayne State University Press, 1990.

U.S. Department of Interior. National Park Service. Historic American Engineering Record. *The Lower Peninsula of Michigan. An Inventory of Historic Engineering and Industrial Sites*. By Charles K. Hyde and Diane B. Abbott. Washington, D.C.: U.S. Department of the Interior, 1976.

U.S. Department of Interior. Heritage Conservation and Recreation Service. Historic American Engineering Record. *The Lower Peninsula of Michigan: An Inventory of Historic Engineering and Industrial Sites*. By Charles K. Hyde and Diane B. Abbott. Washington, D.C.: U.S. Department of the Interior, 1978.

Works Progress Administration. *Michigan: A Guide to the Wolverine State*. New York: Oxford University Press, 1941–1949.

SPECIFIC PLACES

Ann Arbor

Bugbee, Gordon P. *Domino's Mansion*. Louisville, Kentucky: Pinaire Lithographing, 1988.

Benton Harbor

Adkin, Clare. *Brother Benjamin: A History of the Israelite House of David*. Berrien Springs, Michigan: Andrews University Press, 1990.

Fogarty, Robert S. *The Righteous Remnant*. Kent: Kent State University Press, 1981.

Breckenridge

Eaton, Leonard K. "The Louis Sullivan Spirit in Michigan." *Quarterly Review of the Michigan Alumnus* 64 (Spring 1958): 215–20.

Detroit

Bluestone, Daniel M. "Detroit's City Beautiful and the Problem of Commerce." *Journal of the Society of Architectural Historians* 47 (September 1988): 245–62.

Fahlman, Betsy. "Wilson Eyre in Detroit." *Winterthur Portfolio* (Autumn 1980).

Meyer, Katharine Mattingly, and Martin C. P. McElroy, eds. *Detroit Architecture: AIA Guide*. Detroit: Wayne State University Press, 1980.

Miller-Storm Co., Inc. *Good Homes: A Book Designed to Help You Plan, Finance and Equip Your Home*. Detroit: Howe Printing Company, 1929.

Pare, George. *The Catholic Church in Detroit 1701–1888*. Detroit: the Gabriel Richard Press, 1951.

Fayette

Quinlan, Maria. "Charcoal Iron-Making at Fayette, Michigan, 1867–1890." Master's thesis, State University of New York College at Oneonta, 1979.

Grand Rapids

Baxter, Albert. *History of the City of Grand Rapids, Michigan*. New York and Grand Rapids: Munsell & Company, 1891.

Gratiot County

Tucker, Willard D. *Gratiot County, Michigan*. Saginaw: Seemann & Peters, 1913.

Grosse Pointe

Bridenstine, James A. *Edsel & Eleanor Ford House*. Woodland, Maryland: Wolk Press, 1988.

Hancock

Lankton, Larry D., and Charles K. Hyde. *Old Reliable: An Illustrated History of the Quincy Mining Company*. Hancock: The Quincy Mine Hoist Association, Inc., 1982.

Hickory Corners

Stanford, Linda Oliphant. *W. K. Kellogg and His Gull Lake Home: From Eroded Cornfield to Estate to Biological Station*. Hickory Corners, Michigan: W. K. Kellogg Biological Station, Michigan, State University, 1983.

Houghton County

Alanen, Arnold R., and William H. Tishler. "Finnish Farmstead Organization in Old and New World Settings." *Journal of Cultural Geography* 1:1 (Fall/Winter 1980):66–81.

Ironwood

Triponi, Marianne. "The Ironwood Theatre as Symbol." Master's thesis, Michigan State University, 1989.

Ishpeming

Hayden, J. Ellzey, and Lucien Eaton. "Building Reinforced-Concrete Shaft Houses." *Proceedings of the Lake Superior Mining Institute* 22 (1922): 124–33.

Kalamazoo

Schmitt, Peter I., and Balthazar Korab. *Kalamazoo: Nineteenth-Century Houses in a Mid-Western Village.* Kalamazoo: 1970.

Kent

History of Kent County, Michigan. Chicago: Charles C. Chapman and Company, 1881.

Les Cheneaux Islands

Pittman, Philip McM. *The Les Cheneaux Chronicles: Anatomy of a Community.* Charlevoix, Michigan: Peach Mountain Press, Ltd., 1984.

Mackinac Island

Porter, Phil. *View From the Veranda: The History and Architecture of the Summer Cottages on Mackinac Island.* Reports in Mackinac History and Archaeology. Number 8. Mackinac Island State Park Commission, 1981.

Marshall

Skjelver, Mabel Cooper. *Nineteenth-Century Homes of Marshall, Michigan.* Marshall, Michigan: 1971.

Marquette

Eaton, Leonard K. "John Wellborn Root and the Julian M. Case House." *Prairie School Review* 9 (1972): 18–23.

Monroe

Bulkley, John Mc Clelland. *History of Monroe County.* Chicago: Lewis Publishing Company, 1913.

Monroe County

Hogg, Victor, and Balthazar Korab. *Legacy of the River Raisin: The Historic Buildings of Monroe County, Michigan.* Monroe: Monroe County Historical Society, 1976.

Muskegon

Howarth, Shirley Reiff. *Marcel Breuer: Concrete and the Cross.* Muskegon: Hackley Art Museum, 1978.

Breisch, Kenneth A. "The Hackley Public Library." Master's thesis, University of Michigan, 1976.

Rochester

Cameron, John B. *Meadow Brook Hall Tudor Revival Architecture and Decoration.* Catalog to Exhibition October 14–November 11, 1974. Meadow Brook Art Gallery, Oakland University, Rochester, Michigan, 1979.

Sault Sainte Marie

Omoto, Sadayoshi, "Historic Preservation and a Small Michigan Town." *Small Town* 10 (May-June, 1980): 16–19.

U.S. Department of the Interior. National Park Service. Historic American Building Survey/Historic American Engineering Record. *Sault Ste. Marie: A Project Report.* By Terry S. Reynolds et al. Washington, D.C.: U.S. Department of the Interior, 1982.

Glossary

AIA See AMERICAN INSTITUTE OF ARCHITECTS.

abacus The top member of a column capital. In the Doric order, it is a flat block, square in plan, between the echinus of the capital and the architrave of the entablature above.

Adamesque A mode of architectural design, with emphasis on interiors, reminiscent of the work of the Scottish architects Robert Adam (1728–1792) and his brother James (1732–1794). It is characterized by attenuated proportions, bright color, and elegant linear detailing. Adamesque interiors, as one aspect of the broader Neoclassical movement, became popular in the late eighteenth century in Britain, Russia, and elsewhere in northern Europe. Simplified versions of these interiors began to be seen in the United States around the year 1800 in the work of Charles Bulfinch (1763–1844) and Samuel McIntire (1757–1811). Adamesque interiors, often emulating original Adam designs, were again popular in the 1920s. See also the related term FEDERAL.

American Adam style See FEDERAL.

American bond See COMMON BOND.

American Foursquare See FOURSQUARE HOUSE.

American Institute of Architects The national professional organization of architects, established in New York in 1857. The first national convention was held in New York in 1867, and at that meeting, provision was made for the creation of local chapters. In 1889, the American Institute of Architects absorbed the independent Chicago-based Western Association of Architects (established 1884). The headquarters of the national organization moved from New York to Washington in 1898. Abbreviated as AIA.

American Renaissance Ambiguous term. See instead BEAUX-ARTS CLASSICISM, COLONIAL REVIVAL, FEDERAL REVIVAL.

Anglo-Palladianism, Anglo-Palladian An architectural movement in England motivated by a reaction against the English Baroque and by a rediscovery of the work of the English Renaissance architect Inigo Jones (1573–1652) and the Italian Renaissance architect Andrea Palladio (1508–1580). Anglo-Palladianism flourished in England (c. 1710s-1760s) and in the British North American colonies (c. 1740s-1790s). Key figures in the Anglo-Palladian movement were Colen Campbell (1676–1729) and Richard Boyle, Lord Burlington (1694–1753). Sometimes called Burlingtonian, Palladian Revival. See also the more general term PALLADIANISM and the related term GEORGIAN PERIOD.

antefix In classical architecture, a small upright decoration at the eaves of a roof, originally devised to hide the ends of the roof tiles. A similar ornament along the ridge of the roof.

anthemion (plural: anthemions). A Greek ornamental motif based upon the honeysuckle or palmette. It may appear as a single element on an antefix or as a running ornament on a frieze or other banded feature.

antiquity The broad epoch of Western history preceding the Middle Ages and including such ancient civilizations as Egyptian, Greek, and Roman.

apse, apsidal A semicircular or polygonal feature projecting as a major element from an important interior space, especially at the chancel end of a church. Distinguished from an exedra, which is a semicircular or polygonal space, usually containing a bench, in the wall of a garden or nonreligious building. A substantial apse in a church, containing an ambulatory and radiating chapels, is called a chevet. The terms apse and chevet are used to describe the *form* of the end of the church containing the altar, while the terms chancel, choir, and sanctuary are used to describe the liturgical *function* of this end of the church and the spaces within it. Less substantial projections in nonreligious buildings are called bays if polygonal or bowfronts if curved.

arbor 1 An openwork structure covered with climbing plants. Distinguished from a trellis, which is generally a simpler, more two-dimensional structure, often attached to a wall. Distinguished from a pergola, which is an openwork structure supported by a colonnade, creating a shaded walk. **2** A grouping of closely planted trees or shrubs, trained together and self-supporting.

arcade 1 A series of arches, carried on columns or piers or other supports. **2** A covered walkway, one side of which is part of a building, while the other is open, as a series of arches, to the exterior. **3** In the nineteenth and early twentieth centuries, an interior street or other extensive space lined with shops and stores.

arch A curved construction that spans an opening. (Some arches may be flat or triangular, and many have a complex or compound curvature.) A masonry arch consists of a series of wedge-shaped parts (voussoirs) that press together toward the center while being restrained from spreading outward by the surrounding wall or the adjacent arch.

architrave 1 The lowest member of a classical entablature. **2** The moldings on the face of a wall around a doorway or other opening. Sometimes called the casing. Distinguished from the jambs, which are the vertical linings perpendicular to the wall planes at the sides of an opening. Distinguished from surround, a term usually applied to the entire door or window frame considered as a unit.

archivolt The group of moldings following the shape of an arched opening.

arcuation, arcuated Construction using arches.

Art Deco A decorative style stimulated by the 1925 Exposition Internationale des Arts Décoratifs et Industriels Modernes, held in Paris. As the first phase of the Moderne, Art Deco is characterized by sharp angular and curvilinear forms, by a richness of materials (including polished metal, stone, and exotic woods), and by an overall sleekness of design. The style was often used in the commercial and residential architecture of the 1930s (e.g., skyscrapers, hotels, apartment buildings). Sometimes called Art Deco Moderne, Deco, Jazz Moderne, Zigzag Moderne, Zigzag Modernistic. See also the more general term MODERNE and the related terms MAYAN REVIVAL, PWA MODERNE, STREAMLINE MODERNE.

Art Moderne See MODERNE.

Art Nouveau A style in architecture, interior design, and the decorative arts that flourished principally in France and Belgium in the 1890s. The Art Nouveau is characterized by undulating and whiplash lines and by sensuous organic forms. The Art Nouveau in Britain and the United States evolved from and overlapped with the Aesthetic movement.

Arts and Crafts A late nineteenth- and early twentieth-century movement in interior design and the decorative arts, emphasizing the importance of handcrafting for everyday objects. Arts and Crafts works are characterized by rectilinear geometries and high contrasts between figure and ground, and the furniture often features expressed construction. The term originated with the Arts and Crafts Exhibition Society, founded in England in 1888. Designers associated with the movement include C. F. A. Voysey (1857–1941) in England and the brothers Charles S. Greene (1868–1957) and Henry M. Greene (1870–1954) in America. The Arts and Crafts movement evolved from and overlapped with the Aesthetic movement. For a more specific term, used in the United States after 1900, see also CRAFTSMAN.

ashlar Squared blocks of stone that fit tightly against one another.

attic 1 The area beneath the roof and above the main stories (or story) of a building. Sometimes called a garret. **2** A low story above the entablature, often a blocklike mass that caps the building.

axis An imaginary center line to which are referred the parts of a building or the relations of a number of buildings to one another.

balloon frame construction A system of light frame construction in which single studs extend the full height of the frame (commonly two stories), from the foundation to the roof. Floor joists are fastened to the sides of the studs. Structural members are usually sawn lumber, ranging from two-by-fours to two-by-tens, and are fastened with nails. Sometimes called balloon framing. The technique, developed in Chicago and other boomtowns of the 1830s, has been largely replaced in the twentieth century by platform frame construction.

baluster One of a series of short vertical members, often vase-shaped in profile, used to support a handrail for a stair or a railing. Balusters that are thinner and simpler in profile are sometimes called banisters.

balustrade A series of balusters or posts supporting a rail or coping across the top (and sometimes resting on a lower rail). Balustrades are often found on stairs, balconies, parapets, and terraces.

band course Ambiguous term. See instead BAND MOLDING or STRINGCOURSE.

band molding In masonry or frame construction, any horizontal flat member or molding or group of moldings projecting slightly from a wall and marking a division in the wall. Not properly a synonym for band course. Simpler horizontal bands in masonry are generally called stringcourses.

bandstand A small pavilion, usually polygonal or circular in plan, designed to shelter bands during public concerts in a garden, park, green, or square. See also the related terms GAZEBO, KIOSK.

banister 1 Corrupted spelling of baluster, in use since about the seventeenth century. Now occasionally used for balusters that are thinner and simpler in profile than classical vase-shaped balusters. **2** Improperly used to mean the handrail of a stair.

bargeboard An ornate fascia board that is attached to the sloping edges (verges) of a roof, covering the ends of the horizontal roof timbers (purlins). Bargeboards are usually ornamented with carved, turned, or jigsawn forms. Sometimes called gableboards, vergeboards. Less ornate boards along the verges of a roof are simply called fascia boards.

Baroque A style of art and architecture that flourished in Europe and colonial North America during the seventeenth and eighteenth centuries. Although based on the architecture of the Renaissance, Baroque architecture was more dynamic, with circles frequently giving way to ovals, flat walls to curved or undulating ones, and separate elements to interlocking forms. It was a monumental and richly three-dimensional style with elaborate systems of ornamental and figural sculpture. See also the related terms RENAISSANCE, ROCOCO.

Baroque Revival See NEO-BAROQUE.

barrel vault A vaulted roof or ceiling of semicircular or semielliptical cross section, forming a tunnellike enclosure over an apartment, corridor, or similar space.

basement 1 The lowest story of a building, either partly or entirely below grade. **2** The lower part of the walls of any building, usually articulated distinctly from the upper part of the walls.

batten 1 A narrow strip of wood applied to cover a joint along the edges of two parallel boards in the same plane. **2** A strip of wood fastened across two or more parallel boards to hold them together.

Sometimes called a cross batten. See also the related term BOARD-AND-BATTEN SIDING.

battered (adjective). Inclined from the vertical. A wall is said to be battered or to have a batter when it recedes as it rises.

battlement, battlemented See CRENELLATION.

Bauhaus 1 Work in any of the visual arts by the faculty and students of the Bauhaus, the innovative design school founded by Walter Gropius (1883–1969) and an active force in German modernism from 1919 until 1933. **2** Work in any of the visual arts by the former faculty and students of the Bauhaus, or by individuals influenced by them. See also the related terms INTERNATIONAL STYLE, MIESIAN.

bay 1 The interval between two recurring members. A facade is frequently measured by window bays, a skeletal frame by structural bays. **2** A polygonal or curved unit of one or more stories, projecting from the wall and usually containing grouped windows (bay windows) on each story. See also the more specific term BOWFRONT.

bay window The horizontally grouped windows in a projecting bay (definition **2**), or the projecting bay itself, if it is not more than one story. Distinguished from an oriel, which does not rise from the foundation and has a suspended rather than rooted appearance. A semicircular or semielliptical bay window is called a bow window. A bay window with a central section of plate glass in a late nineteenth-century commercial building is called a Chicago window.

beam A structural spanning member of stone, wood, iron, steel, or reinforced concrete. See also the more specific terms GIRDER, I-BEAM, JOIST.

bearing wall A wall that is fully structural, carrying the load of the floors and roof all the way to the foundation. Sometimes called a supporting wall. Distinguished from curtain wall. See also the related term LOAD-BEARING.

Beaux-Arts Historicist design on a monumental scale, as taught at the Ecole des Beaux-Arts in Paris throughout the nineteenth century and early twentieth century. The term Beaux-Arts is generally applied to an eclectic Roman-Renaissance-Baroque architecture of the 1850s through the 1920s, disseminated internationally by students and followers of the Ecole des Beaux-Arts. As a general style term Beaux-Arts connotes an academically grounded discipline for historical eclecticism, rather than one single style, as well as the disciplined development of a *parti* into a fully visualized design. More specific style terms include Neo-Grec (1840s-1870s) and Beaux-Arts Classicism (1870s-1930s). See also the related terms NEOCLASSICISM, for describing Ecole-related work from the 1790s to the 1840s, and SECOND EMPIRE, for describing the work from the 1850s to the 1880s.

Beaux-Arts Classicism, Beaux-Arts Classical Term applied to eclectic Roman-Renaissance-Baroque architecture and urbanism after the Neo-Grec and Second Empire phases, i.e., from the 1870s through the 1930s. Sometimes called Classic Revival, Classical Revival, McKim Classicism, Neoclassical Revival. See also the more general term BEAUX-ARTS and the related terms CITY BEAUTIFUL MOVEMENT, PWA MODERNE.

belfry A cupola, turret, or room in a tower where a bell is housed.

bellcote A small gabled structure astride the ridge of a roof, which shelters a bell. It is usually close to the front wall plane of the building.

belt course See STRINGCOURSE.

belvedere 1 Any building, especially a pavilion or shelter, that is located to take advantage of a view. See also the related term GAZEBO. **2** See CUPOLA (definition **2**).

blind (adjective). Term applied to the surface use of elements that would otherwise articulate an opening but where no opening exists. Used in such combinations as blind arcade, blind arch, blind door, blind window.

board-and-batten siding A type of siding for wood frame buildings, consisting of wide vertical boards with narrow strips of wood (battens) covering the joints. (In rare instances, the battens may be fastened behind the joints. If the gaps between boards are wide and the back battens approach the width of the outer boards, the siding is called board-on-board.) See also the related term BATTEN.

bowfront A semicircular or semielliptical bay (definition **2**).

bow window A semicircular or semielliptical bay window.

brace A single wooden or metal member placed diagonally within a framework or truss or beneath an overhang. Distinguished from a bracket, which is a more substantial triangular feature, and from a strut, which is essentially a post set in a diagonal position.

braced frame construction A combination of heavy and light timber frame construction, in which the principal vertical and horizontal framing members (posts and girts) are fastened by mortise and tenon joints, while the one-story-high studs are nailed to the heavy timber frame. The overall frame is made more rigid by diagonal braces. Sometimes called braced framing.

bracket Any solid, pierced, or built-up triangular feature projecting from the face of a wall to support a projecting element, like the top member of a cornice or the verges or eaves of a roof. Brackets are frequently used for ornamental as well as structural purposes. Distinguished from a brace, which is a simple barlike structural member. Distinguished from the more specific term console, which has a height greater than its projection from the wall. See also the related term CORBEL.

brick bonds, brickwork See the more specific terms COMMON BOND, ENGLISH BOND, FLEMISH BOND, RUNNING BOND.

brique-entre-poteaux In French colonial and post-colonial architecture, a form of half-timber construction in which bricks are used as filler between the vertical posts and the horizontal framing members. Also called *briquette-entre-poteaux*.

British colonial A term applied to buildings, towns, landscapes, and other artifacts from the period of actual British colonial occupation of large parts of eastern North American (c. 1607–1781 for the United States; c. 1750s-1867 for much of Canada). The British colonial period saw the introduction into the New World of various regional strains of English and Scotch-Irish folk culture, as well as high-style Anglo-European Renaissance, Baroque, and Neoclassical design. Sometimes called English colonial. Loosely called colonial or Early American. See also the related term GEORGIAN PERIOD.

Brutalism An architectural style of the 1950s through 1970s, characterized by complex massing and by a frank expression of structural members, elements of building systems, and materials (especially concrete). Some of the work of Paul Rudolph (born 1918) is associated with this style. Sometimes called New Brutalism.

bungalow A low one- or one-and-a-half-story house of modest pretensions with a low-pitched gable or hipped roof, a conspicuous porch, and projecting eaves. This house type was a popular builders' type from around 1900 to 1930. The term bungalow was also loosely applied to any vernacular building of a semirustic nature, including vacation cottages and lodges.

buttress An exterior mass of masonry bonded into a wall that it strengthens or supports. Buttresses often absorb lateral thrusts from roofs or vaults.

Byzantine Term applied to the art and architecture of the Eastern Roman Empire centered at Byzantium (i.e., Constantinople, Istanbul) from the early 500s to the mid-1400s. Byzantine architecture is characterized by massive domes, round arches, richly carved capitals, and the extensive use of mosaic.

Byzantine Revival See NEO-BYZANTINE.

campanile In Italian, a bell tower. While usually freestanding in medieval and Renaissance architecture, it was often incorporated as a prominent unit in the massing of picturesque nineteenth-century buildings.

cantilever A beam, girder, slab, truss, or other structural member that projects beyond its supporting wall or column.

cap A canopy, ledge, molding, or pediment over a window. Sometimes called a window cap. Distinguished from a hood, which is a similar feature over a door. See also the related term HEAD MOLDING.

capital The moldings and carved enrichment at the top of a column, pilaster, pier, or pedestal.

Carpenter's Gothic Term applied to a version of the Gothic Revival (c. 1840s-1870s), in which Gothic motifs are adapted to the kind of wooden details that can be produced by lathes, jigsaws, and molding machines. Sometimes called Gingerbread style, Steamboat Gothic. See also the more general term GOTHIC REVIVAL.

carriage porch See PORTE-COCHÈRE.

casement window A window that opens from the side on hinges, like a door, out from the plane of the wall. Distinguished from a double-hung window.

casing See ARCHITRAVE (definition 2).

cast iron Iron shaped by a molding process, generally strong in compression but brittle in tension. Distinguished from wrought iron, which has been forged to increase its tensile properties.

cast-iron front An architectural facade made of prefabricated molded iron parts, often markedly skeletal in appearance with extensive glass infilling. Prevalent from the late 1840s to the early 1870s.

castellated Having the elements of a medieval castle, such as crenellation and turrets.

cavetto cornice See COVED CORNICE.

cement A mixture of burnt lime and clay with water, which hardens permanently when dry. When a fine aggregate of sand is added, the cement may be used as a mortar for masonry construction or as a plaster or stucco coating. When a coarser aggregate of gravel or crushed stone is added, along with sand, the mixture is called concrete.

chamfer The oblique surface formed by cutting off a square edge at an equal angle to each face.

chancel 1 The end of a Roman Catholic or High Episcopal church containing the altar and set apart for the clergy and choir by a screen, rail, or steps. Usually the entire east end of a church beyond the crossing. In churches that have a long chancel space, the part of the chancel between the crossing and the apse, where the singers participate in the service, is called the choir. The innermost part of the chancel, containing the principal altar, is called the sanctuary. 2 In less extensive Catholic and Episcopal churches, the terms chancel and choir are often used interchangeably to mean the entire eastern arm of the church.

Châteauesque A term applied to masonry buildings from the 1870s through the 1920s in which stylistic references are derived from early French Renaissance châteaux, from the reign of Francis I (1515–1547) or even earlier. Sometimes called Château style, Châteauesque Revival, Francis I style, François Premier.

chevet In large churches, particularly those based upon French Gothic precedents, a substantial apse surrounded by an ambulatory and often containing radiating chapels.

Chicago school A diverse group of architects associated with the development of the tall (i.e., six- to twenty-story), usually metal frame commercial building in Chicago during the 1880s and 1890s. William Le Baron Jenney, Burnham and Root, and Adler and Sullivan are identified with this group. Sometimes called Chicago Commercial style, Commercial style. See also the related term PRAIRIE SCHOOL.

Chicago window A tripartite oblong window in which a large fixed center pane is placed between two narrow sash windows. Popularized in Chicago commercial buildings of the 1880s-1890s. See also BAY WINDOW.

chimney girt In timber frame construction, a major wooden beam that passes across the breast of the central chimney. It is supported at its ends by the longitudinal girts of the building and sometimes carries one end of the summer beam.

choir 1 The part of a Roman Catholic or High Episcopal church where the singers participate in the service. Usually the space within the chancel arm of the church, situated between the crossing to the west and the sanctuary to the east. 2 In less extensive Catholic and Episcopal churches, the terms choir and chancel are often used interchangeably to mean the entire eastern arm of the church.

Churrigueresque Term applied to Spanish and Spanish colonial Baroque architecture resembling the work of the Spanish architect José Benito de Churriguera (1665–1725) and his brothers. The style is characterized by a freely interpreted assemblage of such elements as twisted columns, broken pediments, and scroll brackets. See also the related term SPANISH COLONIAL.

cinquefoil A type of Gothic tracery having five parts (lobes or foils) separated by pointed elements (cusps).

City Beautiful movement A movement in architecture, landscape architecture, and planning in the United States from the 1890s through the 1920s, advocating the beautification of cities in the image of some of the most urbane places of the time: the world's fairs. City Beautiful schemes emphasized civic centers, boulevards, and waterfront improvements, and sometimes included comprehensive metropolitan plans for parks, parkways, and transportation facilities. See also the related term BEAUX-ARTS CLASSICISM.

clapboard A tapered board that is thinner along the top edge and thicker along the bottom edge, applied horizontally with edges overlapping to provide weathertight siding on a building of wood construction. Early clapboards were split (rived, riven) and were used for barrel staves and for wainscoting. The term now applies to any beveled siding board, whether split or sawn, rabbeted or not, regardless of length or width. (The term is sometimes applied only to a form of bevel siding used in New England, about four feet long and quarter-sawn.) Sometimes called weatherboards.

classical orders See ORDER.

Classical Revival Ambiguous term, suggesting 1 Neoclassical design of the late eighteenth and early nineteenth centuries, including the Greek Revival; or 2 Beaux-Arts Classical design of the late nineteenth and early twentieth centuries. Sometimes called Classic Revival. See instead BEAUX-ARTS CLASSICISM, GREEK REVIVAL, NEOCLASSICISM.

classicism, classical, classicizing Terms describing the application of principles or elements derived from the visual arts of the Greco-Roman era

(seventh century B.C.E. through fourth century C.E.) at any subsequent period of Western civilization, but particularly since the Renaissance. More a descriptive term for an approach to design and for a general cultural sensibility than for any particular style. See also the related term NEOCLASSICISM.

clerestory A part of a building that rises above the roof of another part and has windows in its walls.

clipped gable roof See JERKINHEAD ROOF.

coffer A recessed panel, usually square or octagonal, in a ceiling. Such panels are also found on the inner surfaces of domes and vaults.

collar beam A horizontal tension member in a pitched roof connecting opposite rafters, generally halfway up or higher. Its function is to tie the angular members together and prevent them from spreading.

Collegiate Gothic 1 Originally, a secular version of English Gothic architecture, characteristic of the older colleges of Oxford and Cambridge. 2 A secular version of Late Gothic Revival architecture, which became a popular style for North American colleges and universities from the 1890s through the 1920s. Sometimes called Academic Gothic.

colonial 1 Not strictly a style term, but a term for the entire period during which a particular European country held political dominion over a part of the Western Hemisphere, Africa, Asia, Australia, or Oceania. See also the more specific terms BRITISH COLONIAL, DUTCH COLONIAL, FRENCH COLONIAL, SPANISH COLONIAL. 2 Loosely used to mean the British colonial period in North America (c. 1607–1781 for the United States; c. 1750s-1867 for much of Canada).

Colonial Revival Generally understood to mean the revival of forms from British colonial design. The Colonial Revival began in New England in the 1860s and continues nationwide into the present. Sometimes called Neo-Colonial. See also the more specific term GEORGIAN REVIVAL and the related terms FEDERAL REVIVAL, SHINGLE STYLE.

colonnade A series of freestanding or engaged columns supporting an entablature or simple beam.

colonnette A diminutive, often attenuated, column.

colossal order See GIANT ORDER.

column 1 A vertical supporting element, usually cylindrical and slightly tapering, consisting of a base (except in the Greek Doric order), shaft, and capital. See also the related terms ENTABLATURE, ENTASIS, ORDER. 2 Any vertical supporting element in a skeletal frame.

Commercial style See CHICAGO SCHOOL.

common bond A pattern of brickwork in which every fifth or sixth course consists of all headers, the other courses being all stretchers. Sometimes called American bond. Distinguished from running bond, in which no headers appear.

Composite order An ensemble of classical column

and entablature elements, particularly characterized by large Ionic volutes and Corinthian acanthus leaves in the capital of the column. See also the more general term ORDER.

concrete An artificial stone made by mixing cement, water, sand, and a coarse aggregate (such as gravel or crushed stone) in specified proportions. The mix is shaped in molds called forms. Distinguished from cement, which is the binder without the aggregate.

console A type of bracket with a scroll-shaped or S-curve profile and a height greater than its projection from the wall. Distinguished from the more general term bracket, which is usually applied to supports whose projection and height are nearly equal. Distinguished from a modillion, which usually is smaller, has a projection greater than its height (or thickness), and appears in a series, as in a classical cornice.

coping The cap or top course of a wall, parapet, balustrade, or chimney, usually designed to shed water.

corbel A projecting stone that supports a superincumbent weight. In medieval architecture and its derivatives, a support for such major features as vaulting shafts, vaulting ribs, or oriels. See also the related term BRACKET.

corbeled construction Masonry that is built outward beyond the vertical by letting successive courses project beyond those below. Sometimes called corbeling.

corbeled cornice A cornice made up of courses of projecting masonry, each of which extends farther outward than the one below.

Corinthian order An ensemble of classical column and entablature elements, particularly characterized by acanthus leaves and small volutes in the capital of the column. See also the more general term ORDER.

cornice The crowning member of a wall or entablature.

Corporate style An architectural style developed in the early industrial communities of New England during the first half of the nineteenth century. This austere but graceful mode of construction was derived from the red-brick Federal architecture of the early nineteenth century and is characterized by the same elegant proportions, cleanly cut openings, and simple refined detailing. The term was coined by William Pierson in the 1970s.

cottage 1 A relatively modest rural or suburban dwelling. Distinguished from a villa, which is a more substantial and often more elaborate dwelling. **2** A seasonal dwelling, regardless of size, especially one located in a resort community.

cottage orné A rustic building in the romantic, picturesque tradition, noted for such features as bay windows, oriels, ornamented gables, and clustered chimneys.

course A layer of building blocks, such as bricks or stones, extending the full length and thickness of a wall.

coved ceiling A ceiling in which the transition between wall and ceiling is formed by a large concave panel or molding. Sometimes called a cove ceiling.

coved cornice A cornice with a concave profile. Sometimes called a cavetto cornice.

Craftsman A style of furniture and interior design belonging to the Arts and Crafts movement in the United States, and specifically related to *The Craftsman* magazine (1901–1916), published by Gustav Stickley (1858–1942). Some entire houses known to be derived from this publication can be called Craftsman houses. See also the more general term ARTS AND CRAFTS.

crenellation, crenellated A form of embellishment on a parapet consisting of indentations (crenels or embrasures) alternating with solid blocks of wall (merlons). Virtually synonymous with battlement, battlemented; embattlement, embattled.

cresting An ornamental strip or fencelike feature, usually of metal or tile, along the ridgeline or summit of a roof.

crocket In Gothic architecture, a small ornament resembling bunched foliage, placed at intervals on the sloping edges of gables, pinnacles, or spires.

crossing In a church with a cruciform plan, the area where the arms of the cross intersect; specifically, the space where the transept crosses the nave and chancel.

cross rib See LIERNE.

cross section See SECTION.

crown The central, or highest, part of an arch or vault.

crown molding The highest in a series of moldings.

crowstep Any one of the progressions in a gable that ascends in steps rather than in a continuous slope.

cruciform In the shape of a cross. Usually used to describe the ground plans of buildings. See also the more specific terms GREEK CROSS, LATIN CROSS.

cupola 1 A small domed structure on top of a belfry, steeple, or tower. **2** A lantern, square or polygonal in plan, with windows or vents, which is located at the summit of a roof. Sometimes called a belvedere. Distinguished from a skylight, which is a lesser feature located on the slope of a roof. **3** In historic English usage, synonymous with dome. A dome is now understood to be a more substantial feature.

curtain wall In skeleton frame or reinforced concrete construction, a thin nonstructural cladding of stone, brick, terracotta, glass, or metal veneer. Distinguished from bearing wall. See also the related term LOAD-BEARING.

cusp The pointed, roughly triangular intersection of the arcs of lobes or foils in the tracery of windows, screens, or panels.

dado A broad decorative band around the lower portion of an interior wall, between the baseboard and dado rail or cap molding. (The term is often applied to this entire zone, including baseboard and dado rail.) The dado may be painted, papered, or covered with some other material, so as to have a different treatment from the upper zone of the wall. Dado connotes any continuous lower zone in a room, equivalent to a pedestal. A wood-paneled dado is called a wainscot.

Deco See ART DECO.

dentil, denticulated A small ornamental block forming one of a series set in a row. A dentil molding is composed of such a series.

dependency A building, wing, or room, subordinate to, or serving as an adjunct to, a main building. A dependency may be attached to or detached from a main building. Distinguished from an outbuilding, which is always detached.

diaper An overall repetitive pattern on a flat surface, especially a pattern of geometric or representational forms arranged in a diamond-shaped or checkerboard grid. Sometimes called diaper work.

discharging arch See RELIEVING ARCH.

dome A major hemispherical or curved roof feature rising from a circular, polygonal, or square base. Distinguished from a cupola, which is a smaller, usually subordinate, domical element.

Doric order An ensemble of classical column and entablature elements, particularly characterized by the use of triglyphs and metopes in the frieze of the entablature. See also the more general term ORDER.

dormer A roof-sheltered window (or vent), usually with vertical sides and front, set into a sloping roof. Sometimes called a dormer window.

double-hung window A window consisting of a pair of frames, or sashes, one above the other, arranged to slide up and down. Their movement is sometimes stabilized by a system of cords and counterbalancing weights contained in narrow boxing at each side of the window frame. Sometimes called guillotine sash.

double-pen In vernacular architecture, particularly houses, a term applied to a plan consisting of two rooms side by side or separated by a hallway.

double-pile In vernacular architecture, particularly houses, a term applied to a plan that is two rooms deep and any number of rooms wide.

drip molding See HEAD MOLDING.

drum 1 A cylindrical or polygonal wall zone upon which a dome rests. **2** One of the cylinders of stone that form the shaft of a column.

Dutch colonial A term applied to buildings, towns, landscapes, and other artifacts from the period of actual Dutch colonial occupation of the Hudson River valley and adjacent areas (c. 1614–1664). Meaning has been extended to apply to the artifacts of Dutch ethnic groups and their descendants, even into the early nineteenth century.

Dutch Colonial Revival The revival of forms from design in the Dutch tradition.

ear A slight projection just below the upper corners of a door or window architrave or casing. Sometimes called a shouldered architrave.

Early American See BRITISH COLONIAL.

Early Christian A style of art and architecture in the Mediterranean world that was developed by the early Christians before the fall of the Western Roman Empire, derived from late Roman art and architecture and leading to the Romanesque (early fourth to early sixth century).

Early Georgian period Not strictly a style term, but a term for a period in British and British colonial history approximately coinciding with the reigns of George I (1714–1727) and George II (1727–1760). See also the related term LATE GEORGIAN PERIOD.

Early Gothic Revival A term for the Gothic Revival work of the late eighteenth to the mid-nineteenth century. See also the related term LATE GOTHIC REVIVAL.

Eastlake A decorative arts and interior design term of the 1860s and 1880s sometimes applied to architecture. Named after Charles Locke Eastlake (1836–1906), an English advocate of the application of Gothic principles of construction and design, rather than mere Gothic elements. Characterized by simplicity and solidity of forms, which are sometimes embellished with chamfered, turned, or incised details. Sometimes called Eastlake Gothic, Modern Gothic. See also the related term QUEEN ANNE.

eaves The horizontal lower edges of a roof plane, usually projecting beyond the wall below. Distinguished from verges, which are the sloping edges of a roof plane.

echinus A heavy molding with a curved profile placed immediately below the abacus, or top member, of a classical capital. Particularly prominent in the Doric and Tuscan orders.

eclecticism, eclectic A sensibility in design, prevalent since the eighteenth century, involving the selection of elements from a variety of sources, including historical periods of high-style design (Western and non-Western), vernacular design (Western and non-Western), and (in the twentieth century) contemporary industrial design. Distinguished from historicism and revivalism by drawing upon a wider range of sources than the historical periods of high-style design.

Ecole, Ecole des Beaux-Arts See BEAUX-ARTS.

Egyptian Revival Term applied to eclectic works or elements of those works that emulate forms in the visual arts of ancient Egyptian civilization.

elevation A drawing (in orthographic projection) of an upright, planar aspect of an object or building. The vertical complement of a plan. Sometimes loosely used in the sense of a facade view or any frontal representation of a wall, whether photograph or drawing, whether measured to scale or not.

Elizabethan period A term for a period in English history coinciding with the reign of Elizabeth I (1558–1603). See also the more general term TU-

DOR PERIOD and the related term JACOBEAN PERIOD for the succeeding period.

embattlement, embattled See CRENELLATION.

encaustic tile A tile decorated by a polychrome glazed or ceramic inlay pattern.

engaged column A half-round column attached to a wall. Distinguished from a free-standing column by seeming to be built into the wall. Distinguished from a pilaster, which is a flattened column. Distinguished from a recessed column, which is a fully round column set into a nichelike space.

English bond A pattern of brickwork in which the bricks are set in alternating courses of stretchers and headers.

English colonial See BRITISH COLONIAL.

English Half-timber style. See NEO-TUDOR.

entablature. In a classical order, a richly detailed horizontal member resting on columns or pilasters. It is divided horizontally into three main parts. The lowest is the architrave (definition 1), the structural part, and is generally an unornamented continuous beam or series of beams. The middle part is the frieze (definition 1), which is generally the most freely ornamented part. The uppermost is the cornice. Composed of a sequence of moldings, the cornice overhangs the frieze and architrave and serves as a crown to the whole. Each part has the moldings and decorative treatment that are characteristic of the particular order, but modern adaptations often alter canonical details. See also the related terms COLUMN, ORDER.

entablature block A block bearing the canonical elements of a classical entablature on three or all four sides, placed between a column capital and a feature above, such as a balcony or ceiling. Distinguished from an impost block, which has the form of an inverted truncated pyramid and detailing typical of medieval architecture.

entasis The slight convex curving of the vertical profile of a tapered column.

exotic revivals A term occasionally used to suggest a distinction between revivals of European styles (e.g., Greek, Gothic Revivals) and non-European styles (e.g., Egyptian, Moorish Revivals). See also the more specific terms EGYPTIAN REVIVAL, MAYAN REVIVAL, MOORISH REVIVAL.

extrados The outer curve or outside surface of an arch. See also the related term INTRADOS.

eyebrow dormer A low dormer with a small segmental window or vent but no sides. The roofing warps or bows over the window or vent in a wavy line.

facade An exterior face of a building, especially the principal or entrance front. Distinguished from an elevation, which is an orthographic drawing of a building face.

Fachwerk A form of half-timber construction introduced by German-speaking immigrants.

false half-timbering A surface treatment that simulates half-timber construction, consisting of a lattice of broad boards and stucco applied as an exterior veneer on a building of masonry or wood

frame construction. Most commonly seen in domestic architecture from the late nineteenth century onward.

fanlight A semicircular or semielliptical window over a door, with radiating mullions in the form of an open fan. Sometimes called a sunburst light. See also the more general term TRANSOM (definition 1) and the related term SIDELIGHT.

fascia 1 A plain, molded, or ornamented board that covers the horizontal edges (eaves) or sloping edges (verges) of a roof. Distinguished from the more specific term bargeboards, which are ornate fascia boards attached to the sloping edges of a roof. Distinguished from a frieze (definition 2), which is located at the top of a wall. **2** One of the broad continuous bands that make up the architrave of the IONIC, CORINTHIAN, or COMPOSITE ORDER.

Federal A version of Neoclassical architecture in the United States popular from New England to Virginia, and in other regions influenced by the Northeast. It flourished from the 1790s through the 1820s and is found in some regions as late as the 1840s. Sometimes called American Adam style. Not to be confused with FEDERALIST. See also the related term ROMAN REVIVAL.

Federal Revival Term applied to eclectic works (c. 1890s-1930s) or elements of those works that emulate forms in the visual arts of the Federal period. Sometimes called Neo-Federal. See also the related terms COLONIAL REVIVAL, GEORGIAN REVIVAL.

Federalist Name of an American political party and the era it dominated (c. 1787–1820). Not to be confused with FEDERAL.

fenestration Window treatment: arrangement and proportioning.

festoon A motif representing entwined leaves, flowers, or fruits, hung in a catenary curve from two points. Distinguished from a swag, which is a motif representing a fold of drapery hung in a similar curve. See also the more general term GARLAND.

finial A vertical ornament placed upon the apex of an architectural feature, such as a gable, turret, or canopy. Distinguished from a pinnacle, which is a larger feature, usually associated with Gothic architecture.

fireproofing In metal skeletal framing, the wrapping of structural members in terracotta tile or other fire-resistant material.

flashing A strip of metal, plastic, or various flexible compositional materials used at roof valleys and ridges and at chimney corners to keep water out. Any similar material used to protect door and window heads and sills.

Flemish bond A pattern of brickwork in which the stretchers and headers alternate in the same row and are staggered from one row to the next. Because this creates a more animated texture than English bond, Flemish bond was favored for front facades and more elegant buildings.

Flemish gable A gable whose upper slopes ascend

in steps rather than in a straight line. These steps may be rectilinear or curved, or a combination of both.

fluting, fluted A series of parallel grooves or channels (flutes), usually semicircular or semielliptical in plan, that accentuate the verticality of the shaft of a column or pilaster.

flying buttress In Gothic architecture a spanning member, usually in the form of an arch, that reaches across the open space from an exterior buttress pier to that point on the wall of the building where the thrusts of the interior vaults are concentrated. Because of its arched construction, a flying buttress exerts a counterthrust against the pressure of the vaults contained by the vertical strength of the buttress pier.

foliated (adjective). In the form of leaves or leaflike shapes.

folk Not a style term in itself, but a descriptive term, applicable to all the visual arts and all styles and periods. Applied to **1** a regional, often ethnic, tradition in which continuities through the years in the overall appearance of artifacts (including buildings) are more important than changes in stylistic embellishment; **2** the work of individual artists and artisans unexposed to or uninterested in prevailing or avant-garde ideals of form and technique. Approximate synonyms include anonymous, naive, primitive, traditional. For architecture, see also the more general term VERNACULAR and the related term POPULAR.

four-part vault See QUADRIPARTITE VAULT.

foursquare house A hipped-roof, two-story house with four principal rooms on each floor and a symmetrical facade. It usually has a front porch across the full width of the house and one or more large dormers on the roof. A common suburban house type from the 1890s to the 1920s. Sometimes called American Foursquare, Prairie Box.

frame construction, frame Ambiguous terms. See instead BRACED FRAME CONSTRUCTION, LIGHT FRAME CONSTRUCTION (BALLOON FRAME CONSTRUCTION, platform frame construction), SKELETON CONSTRUCTION, TIMBER FRAME CONSTRUCTION. Not properly synonymous with wood construction, wood-clad, or wooden.

French colonial A term applied to buildings, towns, landscapes, and other artifacts from the period of actual French colonial occupation of large parts of eastern North America (c. 1605–1763). The term is extended to apply to the artifacts of French ethnic groups and their descendants, well into the nineteenth century.

fret An ornament, usually in series, as a band or field, consisting of a latticelike interlocking of right-angled linear elements.

frieze 1 The broad horizontal band that forms the central part of a classical entablature. **2** Any long horizontal band or zone, especially one that has a chiefly decorative purpose, located at the top of a wall. Distinguished from a fascia, which is attached to the horizontal edge of a roof.

front gabled Term applied to a building whose principal gable end faces the front of the lot or some feature like a street or open space. Sometimes called gable front. Distinguished from side gabled.

gable The wall area immediately below the end of a gable, gambrel, or jerkinhead roof.

gableboard See BARGEBOARD.

gable front See FRONT GABLED.

gable roof A roof in which the two planes slope equally toward each other to a common ridge. Sometimes called a pitched roof.

galerie In French colonial domestic architecture, a porch or veranda, usually sheltered by an extension of the hip roof of the house.

gambrel roof A roof that has a single ridgepole but a double pitch. The lower plane, which rises from the eaves, is rather steep. The upper plane, which extends from the lower plane to the ridgeline, has a flatter pitch.

garland A motif representing a rope of entwined leaves, flowers, ribbons, or drapery, regardless of its shape or position. It may be formed into a wreath, festoon, or swag, or follow the outline of a rectilinear architectural element.

garret See ATTIC (definition **1**).

gazebo A small pavilion, usually polygonal or circular in plan and serving as a garden or park shelter. Distinguished from a kiosk, which generally has some commercial or public function. See also the related terms BANDSTAND, BELVEDERE (definition **1**).

Georgian period A term for a period in British and British colonial history, and not, in architecture or the other visual arts, a sufficiently specific style term. The Georgian period begins with the coronation of George I in 1714 and extends until about 1781 in the area that became the United States (and in Britain, until the death of George IV in 1830). See also the related terms ANGLO-PALLADIANISM, BRITISH COLONIAL.

Georgian plan See DOUBLE-PILE and DOUBLE-PEN.

Georgian Revival A revival of Georgian period forms—in England, from the 1860s to the present, and in the United States, from the 1880s to the present. Sometimes called Neo-Georgian. See also the more general term COLONIAL REVIVAL and the related term FEDERAL REVIVAL.

giant order A composition involving any one of the five principal classical orders, in which the columns or pilasters are nearly as tall as the height of the entire building. Sometimes called a colossal order. See also the more general term ORDER.

Gingerbread style See CARPENTER'S GOTHIC.

girder A major horizontal spanning member, comparable in function to a beam, but larger and often built up of a number of parts. It usually runs at right angles to the beams and serves as their principal means of support.

glazing bar See MUNTIN.

Gothic An architectural style prevalent in Europe

from the twelfth century into the fifteenth in Italy (and into the sixteenth century in the rest of Europe). It is characterized by pointed arches and ribbed vaults and by the dominance of openings over masonry mass in the wall. The Gothic was preceded by the Romanesque and followed by the Renaissance.

Gothic Revival A movement in Europe and North America devoted to reviving the forms and the spirit of Gothic architecture and the allied arts. It originated in the mid-eighteenth century. Sometimes called the Pointed style in the nineteenth century, and sometimes called Neo-Gothic. See also the more specific terms CARPENTER'S GOTHIC, EARLY GOTHIC REVIVAL, HIGH VICTORIAN GOTHIC, LATE GOTHIC REVIVAL.

Grecian A nineteenth-century term for GREEK REVIVAL.

Greek cross A cross with four equal arms. Usually used to describe the ground plan of a building. See also the more general term CRUCIFORM.

Greek Revival A movement in Europe and North America devoted to reviving the forms and the spirit of Classical Greek architecture, sculpture, and decorative arts. It originated in the mid-eighteenth century, culminated in the 1830s, and continued into the 1850s. Sometimes called Grecian in the nineteenth century. See also the more general term NEOCLASSICAL.

groin The curved edge formed by the intersection of two vaults.

HABS See HISTORIC AMERICAN BUILDINGS SURVEY.

HAER See HISTORIC AMERICAN ENGINEERING RECORD.

half-timber construction A variety of timber frame construction in which the framing members are exposed on the exterior of the wall, with the spaces between timbers being filled with wattle-and-daub (i.e., woven lath and plaster) or masonry materials, such as brick or stone. These masonry materials may also be covered with stucco. Sometimes called half-timbered construction.

hall-and-parlor house, hall-and-parlor plan A double-pen house (i.e., a house that is one room deep and two rooms wide). Usually applied to houses without a central through-passage, to distinguish from hall-passage-parlor houses.

hall-passage-parlor house, hall-passage-parlor plan A two-room house with a central through-passage or hallway.

hammer beam A short horizontal beam projecting inward from the foot of the principal rafter and supported below by a diagonal brace tied into a vertical wall post. The hammer beams carry much of the load of the roof trussing above. Hammer beam trusses, which could be assembled using a series of smaller timbers, were often used in late medieval England instead of conventional trusses, which required long horizontal tie beams extending across an entire interior space.

header A brick laid across the thickness of a wall,

so that the short end of the brick shows on the exterior.

head molding A molding or set of moldings designed to shelter and embellish the top of a door or window. Sometimes called a drip molding. See also the related terms CAP (for windows) and HOOD (for doors).

heavy timber construction See TIMBER FRAME CONSTRUCTION.

high style or high-style (adjective). Not a style term in itself, but a descriptive term, applicable to all the visual arts and all styles and periods. Applied to the works of the masters and their schools and disciples, usually reflecting a cosmopolitan awareness of traditions beyond a particular place or time. Usually contrasted with vernacular (including the folk and popular traditions).

high tech Term applied to architecture in which building materials and elements of building systems are used to celebrate contemporary technology. Elemental geometric forms, primary colors, and metallic finishes are used to heighten the technological imagery.

High Victorian Gothic A version of the Gothic Revival that originated in England in the 1850s and spread to North America in the 1860s. Characterized by polychromatic exteriors inspired by the medieval Gothic architecture of northern Italy. Sometimes called Ruskin Gothic, Ruskinian Gothic, Venetian Gothic, Victorian Gothic. See also the more general term GOTHIC REVIVAL.

hipped gable roof See JERKINHEAD ROOF.

hipped roof A roof that pitches inward from all four sides. The edge where any two planes meet is called the hip.

Historic American Buildings Survey A branch of the National Park Service of the United States Department of the Interior, established in 1933 to produce detailed documentation of American architecture. Such documentation typically includes historical and architectural data, photographs, and measured drawings, and is deposited in the Prints and Photographs Division of the Library of Congress. Abbreviated as HABS. See also the related term HISTORIC AMERICAN ENGINEERING RECORD.

Historic American Engineering Record A branch of the National Park Service of the United States Department of the Interior, established in 1969 to produce detailed documentation of sites and structures associated with industry, transportation, and other areas of technology. Abbreviated as HAER. See also the related term HISTORIC AMERICAN BUILDINGS SURVEY.

historicism, historicist, historicizing A type of eclecticism prevalent since the eighteenth century, involving the use of forms from historical periods of high-style design (usually in the Western tradition) and, occasionally, from favored traditions of vernacular design (such as the various colonial traditions in the United States). Historicist influences are designated by the use of the prefix Neo- with a previous historical style (e.g., Neo-

Baroque). Distinguished from the more general term eclecticism, which draws upon a wider range of sources in addition to the historical. See also the more specific term REVIVALISM.

hollow building tile A hollow terracotta building block used for constructing exterior bearing walls of buildings up to about three stories, as well as interior walls and partitions.

hood A canopy, ledge, molding, or pediment over a door. Distinguished from a cap, which is a similar feature over a window. Sometimes called a hood molding. See also the related term HEAD MOLDING.

horizontal plank frame construction A system of wood construction in which horizontal planks are set or nailed into the corner posts of a timber frame building. There are, however, no studs or intermediate posts connecting the sill and the plate. See also the related term VERTICAL PLANK FRAME CONSTRUCTION.

hung ceiling See SUSPENDED CEILING.

hyphen A subsidiary building unit, often one story, connecting the central block and the wings or dependencies.

I-beam The most common profile in steel structural shapes (although it also appears in cast iron and in reinforced concrete). Used especially for spanning elements, it is shaped like the capital letter "I" to make the most efficient use of the material consistent with a shape that permits easy assemblage. The vertical face of the "I" is the web. The horizontal faces are the flanges. Other standard shapes for steel framing elements are Hs, Ts, Zs, Ls (known as angles), and square-cornered Us (channels).

I-house A two-story house, one room deep and two rooms wide, usually with a central hallway. The I-house is a nineteenth-century descendant of the hall-and-parlor houses of the colonial period. The term is commonly applied to the end-chimney houses of the southern and mid-Atlantic traditions. The term most likely derives from the resemblance between the tall, narrow end walls of these houses and the capital letter "I."

impost The top part of a pier or wall upon which rests the springer or lowest voussoir of an arch.

impost block A block, often in the form of an inverted truncated pyramid, placed between a column capital and the lowest voussoirs of an arch above. Distinguished from an entablature block, which has the details found in a classical entablature. Sometimes called a dosseret or supercapital.

in antis Columns in antis are placed between two projecting sections of wall, in an imaginary plane connecting the ends of the two wall elements.

intermediate rib See TIERCERON.

International style A style that originated in the 1920s and flourished into the 1970s, characterized by the expression of volume and surface and by the suppression of historicist ornament and axial symmetry. The term was originally applied by Henry-Russell Hitchcock and Philip Johnson to the new, nontraditional, mostly European, architecture of the 1920s in their 1932 exhibition at the Museum of Modern Art and in their accompanying book, *The International Style*. Also called International, International Modern. See also the related terms BAUHAUS, MIESIAN, SECOND CHICAGO SCHOOL.

intrados The inner curve or underside (soffit) of an arch. See also the related term EXTRADOS.

Ionic order An ensemble of classical column and entablature elements, particularly characterized by the use of large volutes in the capital of the column. See also the more general term ORDER.

Italianate 1 A general term for an eclectic Neo-Renaissance and Neo-Romanesque style, originating in England and Germany in the early nineteenth century and prevalent in the United States between the 1840s and 1880s, not only in houses but also in Main Street commercial buildings. The Italianate is characterized by prominent window heads and bracketed cornices. Called the Bracketed style in the nineteenth century. See also the more specific term ITALIAN VILLA STYLE and the related terms RENAISSANCE REVIVAL, ROUND ARCH MODE, SECOND EMPIRE. **2** A specific term for Italianate buildings that are predominantly symmetrical in plan and elevation. Distinguished from Barryesque, which is applied to more formal institutional and governmental buildings.

Italian Villa style A subtype of the Italianate style (definition **1**), originating in England and Germany in the early nineteenth century and prevalent in the United States between the 1840s and 1870s, mostly in houses, but also churches and other public buildings. The style is characterized by asymmetrical plans and elevations, irregular blocklike massing, round arch arcades and openings, and northern Italian Romanesque detailing. Larger Italian Villa buildings often had a campanile-like tower. Distinguished from the more symmetrical Italianate style (definition **2**) by having the northern Italian rural vernacular villa as prototype.

Jacobean period A term for a period in British history coinciding with the rule of James I (1603–1625). See also the related term ELIZABETHAN PERIOD for the immediately preceding period, which itself is part of the TUDOR PERIOD.

Jacobethan Revival See NEO-TUDOR.

jamb The vertical side face of a door or window opening, amounting to the full thickness of the wall, and usually enriched with paneling, moldings, or jamb shafts (which are engaged columns set into a splayed, or angled, jamb). In an opening containing a door or window, the jamb is distinguished from the reveal, which is the portion of wall thickness between the door or window frame and the outer surface of the wall. (In an opening without a door or window, the terms jamb and reveal are used interchangeably.) Also distinguished from an architrave (definition 2), which consists of the moldings on the face of a wall around the opening.

jerkinhead roof A gable roof in which the upper portion of the gable end is hipped, or inclined inward along the ridgeline, forming a small triangle of roof surface. Sometimes called a clipped gable roof or hipped gable roof.

joist One of a series of small horizontal beams that support a floor or ceiling.

keystone The central wedge-shaped stone at the crown of an arch.

king post In a truss, the vertical suspension member that connects the tie beam with the apex of opposing principal rafters.

kiosk Originally, a Turkish summer palace. Since the nineteenth century, the term has been applied to any small pavilion or stand, usually found in public gardens, parks, streets, and malls, where it serves some commercial or public function. Distinguished from a gazebo, which may be found in public or private gardens or parks, but which usually serves as a sheltered resting place. See also the related term BANDSTAND.

label 1 A drip molding, over a square-headed door or window, which extends for a short distance down each side of the opening. **2** A similar vertical downward extension of a drip molding over an arch of any form. Sometimes called a label molding.

label stop 1 An L-shaped termination at the lower ends of a label. **2** Any decorative boss or other termination of a label.

lancet arch An arch generally tall and sharply pointed, whose centers are farther apart than the width or span of the arch.

lantern 1 The uppermost stage of a dome, containing windows or arcaded openings. **2** Any feature, square or polygonal in plan and usually containing windows, rising above the roof of a building. The square structures that serve as skylights on the roofs of nineteenth-century buildings—particularly houses—were also called lantern lights, and, in Italianate and Second Empire buildings, came to be called cupolas.

Late Georgian period Not strictly a style term, but a term for a period in British and British colonial history approximately coinciding with the reigns of George III (1760–1820) and George IV (1820–1830). In the United States, the Late Georgian period is now understood to end some time during the Revolutionary War (1775–1781) and to be followed by the Federal period (c. 1787–1820). In Britain, the Late Georgian period includes the Regency period (1811–1820s). See also the related term EARLY GEORGIAN PERIOD.

Late Gothic Revival A term for the Gothic Revival work of the late nineteenth and early twentieth centuries. See also the more specific term COLLEGIATE GOTHIC (definition 2) and the related term EARLY GOTHIC REVIVAL.

lath A latticelike, continuous surface of small wooden strips or metal mesh nailed to walls or partitions to hold plaster.

Latin cross A cross with one long and three short arms. Usually used to describe the ground plans of Roman Catholic and Protestant churches. See also the more general term CRUCIFORM.

leaded glass Panes of glass held in place by lead strips, or cames. The panes, clear or stained, may be of any shape.

lean-to roof See SHED ROOF.

lierne In a Gothic vault, a short ornamental rib connecting the major transverse ribs and the secondary tiercerons. Sometimes called a cross rib or tertiary rib.

light frame construction A type of wood frame construction in which relatively light structural members (usually sawn lumber, ranging from two-by-fours to two-by-tens) are fastened with nails. Distinguished from timber frame construction, in which relatively heavy structural members (hewn or sawn timbers, measuring six-by-six and larger) are fastened with mortise-and-tenon joints. See the more specific term BALLOON FRAME CONSTRUCTION.

lintel A horizontal structural member that supports the wall over an opening or spans between two adjacent piers or columns.

load-bearing Term applied to a wall, column, pier, or any vertical supporting member, constructed so that all loads are carried to the ground through the wall, column, or pier. See also the related terms BEARING WALL, CURTAIN WALL.

loggia 1 A porch or open-air room, particularly one set within the body of a building. **2** An arcaded or colonnaded structure, open on one or more sides, sometimes with an upper story. **3** An eighteenth- and nineteenth-century term for a porch or veranda.

Lombard A style term applied in the United States in the mid-nineteenth century to buildings derived from the Romanesque architecture of northern Italy (especially Lombardy) and the earlier nineteenth-century architecture of southern Germany. Characterized by the use of brick, for both structural and ornamental purposes. Also called Lombardic. See also the related term ROUND ARCH MODE.

lunette 1 A semicircular area, especially one that contains some decorative treatment or a mural painting. **2** A semicircular window in such an area.

Mannerism, Mannerist 1 A phase of Renaissance art and architecture in the mid-sixteenth century, characterized by distortions, contortions, inversions, odd juxtapositions, and other departures from High Renaissance canons of design. **2** (not capitalized) A sensibility in design, regardless of style or period, characterized by a knowledgeable violation of rules and intended as a comment on the very nature of convention.

mansard roof A hipped roof with double pitch. The upper slope may approach flatness, while the lower slope has a very steep pitch, sometimes flaring in a concave curve (or swelling in a convex curve) as it comes to the eaves. This lower slope usually has windows, and the area under the roof often amounts to a full story. The name is a corruption of that of François Mansart (1598–1666), who designed roofs of this type, which was revived in Paris during the Second Empire period.

Mansard style, Mansardic See Second Empire.

masonry Construction using stone, brick, block, or some other hard and durable material laid up in units and usually bonded by mortar.

massing The grouping or arrangement of the primary volumetric components of a building.

McKim Classicism, McKim Classical Architecture of, or in the manner of, the firm of McKim, Mead and White, 1890s-1920s. See Beaux-Arts Classicism.

medieval Term applied to the Middle Ages in European civilization between the age of antiquity and the age of the Renaissance (i.e., mid-400s to mid-1400s in Italy; mid-400s to late 1500s in England). In architecture and the other visual arts, the medieval period included the end of the Early Christian period, then the Byzantine, the Romanesque, and the Gothic styles or periods.

Mediterranean Revival A style generally associated since the early twentieth century with residential architecture based on Italian villas of the sixteenth century. While not a major revival style, it is characterized by symmetrical arrangements, stucco walls, and low-pitch tile roofs. Sometimes called Mediterranean Villa, Neo-Mediterranean. See also the related term Spanish Colonial Revival.

metope In a Doric entablature, that part of the frieze which falls between two triglyphs. In the Greek Doric order the metopes often contain small sculptural reliefs.

Middle Ages See Medieval.

Miesian Term applied to work showing the influence of the German-American architect Ludwig Mies van der Rohe (1886–1969). See also the related terms Bauhaus, International style, Second Chicago school.

Mission Revival A style originating in the 1890s, and making use of forms and materials from the Spanish and Mexican mission architecture of the eighteenth and early nineteenth centuries. Not to be confused with Mission furniture of the Arts and Crafts movement. See also the more general term Spanish Colonial Revival.

modern Ambiguous term, applied in various ways during the past century to the history of the visual arts and world history generally: **1** from the 1910s to the present (see also the more specific terms Bauhaus, International style); **2** from the 1860s, 1870s, 1880s, or 1890s to the present; **3** from the Enlightenment or the advent of Neoclassicism or the industrial revolution, c. 1750, to the present; **4** from the Renaissance in Italy, c. 1450, to the present.

Moderne A term applied to a wide range of design work from the 1920s through the 1940s, in which aspects of traditionalism and modernism coexist and in which eclecticism (from a historical, exotic, or machine aesthetic) is inseparable from the urge for stylization. Sometimes called Art Moderne, Modernistic. See also the more specific terms Art Deco, PWA Moderne, Streamline Moderne.

modillion One of a series of small, thin scroll brackets under the projecting crown molding of a classical cornice. It is found in the Corinthian and Composite orders. Distinguished from a console, which usually is larger and has a height greater than its projection from the wall.

molding A running surface composed of parallel and continuous sections of simple or compound curves and flat areas.

monitor An extensive shed-roofed feature on a roof, containing a band of windows or vents. It may be located along one of the roof slopes (a trapdoor monitor) or along the ridgeline (a clerestory monitor), and it usually runs the entire length of the roof. Distinguished from a skylight, which is a low-profile or flush-mounted feature in the plane of the roof.

Moorish Revival Term applied to eclectic works or elements of those works that emulate forms in the visual arts of those parts of North Africa and Spain under Muslim domination from the seventh through the fifteenth century.

mortar A mixture of cement or lime with water and a fine aggregate of sand used to secure bricks or stones in masonry construction.

mortise-and-tenon joint A timber framing joint that is made by one member having its end shaped into a projecting piece (tenon) that fits exactly into a hole (mortise) in the other member. Once joined, the pieces are held together by a peg that passes through the tenon.

mullion **1** A post or similar vertical member dividing a window into two or more units, or lights, each of which may be further subdivided (by muntins) into panes. **2** A post or similar vertical member dividing a wall opening into two or more contiguous windows.

muntin One of the small vertical or horizontal members that hold panes of glass within a window or glazed door. Distinguished from a mullion, which is a heavier vertical member separating paired or grouped windows. Sometimes called a glazing bar, sash bar, or window bar.

National Register of Historic Places A branch of the National Park Service of the United States Department of the Interior, established by the National Historic Preservation Act of 1966, to maintain files of documentation on districts, sites, buildings, structures, and objects of national, state, or local significance. Properties listed on the National Register are afforded administrative—and, ultimately, judicial—review in instances where projects funded or assisted by federal agencies might have an impact on the historic property. Properties listed on the register may also be eligible for certain tax benefits.

nave 1 The entire body of a church between the entrance and the crossing. **2** The central space of a church, between the side aisles, extending from the entrance end to the crossing.

Neo-Baroque Term applied to eclectic works or elements of those works that emulate forms in the visual arts of the Baroque style or period. Sometimes called Baroque Revival.

Neo-Byzantine Term applied to eclectic works or elements of those works that emulate forms in the visual arts of the Byzantine style or period. Sometimes called Byzantine Revival.

Neoclassical Revival See BEAUX-ARTS CLASSICISM.

Neoclassicism, Neoclassical A broad movement in the visual arts which drew its inspiration from ancient Greece and Rome. It began in the mid-eighteenth century with the advent of the science of archeology and extended into the mid-nineteenth century (in some Beaux-Arts work, into the 1930s; in some Postmodern work, even into the present). See also the related terms BEAUX-ARTS, BEAUX-ARTS CLASSICISM, CLASSICISM, and the more specific terms GREEK REVIVAL, ROMAN REVIVAL.

Neo-Colonial See COLONIAL REVIVAL.

Neo-Federal See FEDERAL REVIVAL.

Neo-Georgian See GEORGIAN REVIVAL.

Neo-Gothic Term applied to eclectic works or elements of those works that emulate forms in the visual arts of the Gothic style or period. The cultural movement that produced so many such works in the eighteenth, nineteenth, and twentieth centuries is called the Gothic Revival, though that term covers a wide range of work.

Neo-Grec An architectural style developed in connection with the Ecole des Beaux-Arts in Paris during the 1840s and characterized by the use of stylized Greek elements, often in conjunction with cast iron or brick construction. See also the more general term BEAUX-ARTS.

Neo-Hispanic See SPANISH COLONIAL REVIVAL.

Neo-Mediterranean See MEDITERRANEAN REVIVAL.

Neo-Norman Term applied to eclectic works or elements of those works that emulate forms in the visual arts of the eleventh- and twelfth-century Romanesque of Norman France and Britain.

Neo-Palladian See PALLADIANISM.

Neo-Renaissance Term applied to eclectic works or elements of those works that emulate forms in the visual arts of the Renaissance style or period. The mid- to late nineteenth-century cultural movement that produced so many such works is called the Renaissance Revival, though that term covers a wide range of work.

Neo-Romanesque Term applied to eclectic works or elements of those works that emulate forms in the visual arts of the Romanesque style or period. The mid-nineteenth-century cultural movement that produced so many such works is called the Romanesque Revival, though that term covers a wide range of work.

Neo-Tudor Term applied to eclectic works or elements of those works that emulate forms in the visual arts of the Tudor period. Sometimes called Elizabethan Manor style, English Half-timber style, Jacobethan Revival, Tudor Revival.

New Brutalism See BRUTALISM.

New Formalism A style prevalent since the 1960s, characterized by symmetrical arrangements, rich materials (marble cadding, metal grillework), and stylized classical (even Gothic) detailing. Architects associated with this style include Philip Johnson (b. 1906), Edward Durell Stone (1902–1978), and Minoru Yamasaki (1912–1985).

newel post A post at the head or foot of a flight of stairs, to which the handrail is fastened. Newel posts occur in a variety of shapes, in profile and cross section, and are generally more substantial elements than the individual balusters that support the handrail.

niche A recess in a wall, usually designed to contain sculpture or an urn. A niche is often semicircular in plan and surmounted by a half dome or shell form. See also the related terms AEDICULE, TABERNACLE (definition **1**).

nogging Brickwork that fills the spaces between members of a timber frame wall or partition.

octagon house A rare house type of the 1850s, based on the ideas of Orson Squire Fowler (1809–1887), who argued for the efficiencies of an octagonal floorplan. Sometimes called octagon mode.

oculus A circular opening in a ceiling or wall or at the top of a dome.

ogee arch A pointed arch formed by a pair of opposing S-shaped curves.

order The most important constituents of classical architecture are the orders, first developed as a structural-aesthetic system by the ancient Greeks. An order has two major components. A column with its capital is the main vertical supporting member. The principal horizontal member is the entablature. The Greeks developed three different types of order, the Doric, Ionic, and Corinthian, each distinguishable by its own decorative system and proportions. All three were taken over and modified by the Romans, who added two orders of their own, the Tuscan, which is a simplified form of the Doric, and the Composite, which is made up of elements of both the Ionic and the Corinthian. The Romans often used the orders as a structural system in the same manner as the Greeks. Unlike the Greeks, however, they also applied them as decoration to the surfaces of walls that were supported by other means. Sometimes called classical orders. See also the related terms COLUMN, ENTABLATURE, GIANT ORDER, SUPERPOSITION (definition **1**).

oriel A projecting polygonal or curved window unit of one or more stories, supported on brackets or corbels. Sometimes called an oriel window. Distinguished from a bay window, which rises from the foundation and has a rooted rather than a suspended appearance. However, a multistory projection in a tall building, whether cantilevered out or built from the foundation, is called a projecting bay or a unit of bay windows.

overhang The projection of part of a structure beyond the portion below.

PWA Moderne A synthesis of the Moderne (i.e., Art Deco or Streamline Moderne) with an austere late type of Beaux-Arts Classicism, often associated with federal government buildings of the 1930s and 1940s during the Public Works Administration. See also the more general term MODERNE and the related terms ART DECO, BEAUX-ARTS CLASSICISM, STREAMLINE MODERNE.

Palladianism, Palladian Work influenced by the Italian Renaissance architect Andrea Palladio (1508–1580), particularly by means of his treatise, *I Quattro Libri dell'Architettura* (*The Four Books of Architecture,* originally published in 1570 and disseminated throughout Europe in numerous translations and editions until the mid-eighteenth century). The most significant flourishing of Palladianism was in England, from the 1710s to the 1760s, and in the British North American colonies, from the 1740s to the 1790s. Sometimes called Neo-Palladian, Palladian classical. See also the more specific term ANGLO-PALLADIANISM.

Palladian motif A three-part composition for a door or window, in which a round-headed opening is flanked by lower flat-headed openings and separated from them by columns, pilasters, or mullions. The flanking sections, and sometimes the entire unit, may be blind (i.e., not open).

Palladian Revival See ANGLO-PALLADIANISM.

Palladian window A window subdivided as in the Palladian motif.

parapet A low wall at the edge of a roof, balcony, or terrace, sometimes formed by the upward extension of the wall below.

parquet Inlaid wood flooring, usually set in simple geometric patterns.

parti The essential solution to an architectural program or problem; the basic concept for the arrangement of spaces, before the development and elaboration of the design.

patera (plural: paterae). A circular or oval panel or plaque decorated with stylized flower petals or radiating linear motifs. Distinguished from a roundel, which is always circular.

pavilion 1 A central or corner unit that projects from a larger architectural mass and is usually accented by a special treatment of the wall or roof. **2** A detached or semidetached structure used for specialized activities, as at a hospital. **3** In a garden or fairground, a temporary structure or tent, usually ornamented.

pediment 1 In classical architecture, the low triangular gable end of the roof, framed by raking cornices along the inclined edges of the roof and by a horizontal cornice below. **2** In Renaissance and Baroque and later clasically derived architecture, the triangular or curvilinear culmination of a prominent part of a facade. **3** A similar but smaller-scale feature over a door or window. It may be triangular or curvilinear.

pendentive A concave surface in the form of a spherical triangle that forms the structural transition from the square plan of a crossing to the circular plan of a dome.

pergola A structure with an open wood framed roof, often latticed, and supported by a colonnade. It is usually covered by climbing plants, such as vines or roses, and provides shade for a garden walk or a passageway to a building. Distinguished from arbors or trellises, which are less extensive accessory structures lacking the colonnade.

period house Term applied to suburban and country houses in which period revival styles are dominant.

period revival Term applied to eclectic works—particularly suburban and country houses—of the first three decades of the twentieth century, in which a particular historical or regional style is dominant. See also the more specific terms CO-LONIAL REVIVAL, DUTCH COLONIAL REVIVAL, GEOR-GIAN REVIVAL, NEO-TUDOR, SPANISH COLONIAL RE-VIVAL.

peripteral (adjective). Surrounded by a single row of columns.

peristyle A range of columns surrounding a building or an open court.

piazza 1 A plaza or square. **2** An eighteenth- and nineteenth-century term for a porch or veranda.

pictorial projection A system of visual representation in which an object, building, or space is projected onto the picture plane in such a way that the illusion of three-dimensional depth is created. Distinguished from orthographic projection, in which the dimension of depth is excluded.

picturesque An aesthetic category in architecture and landscape architecture in the late eighteenth and early nineteenth centuries. It is characterized by relationships among buildings and landscape features that evoke the qualities of landscape paintings, in which the eye is led past a variety of forms and spaces into the distance and the mind is led to contemplate a sense of age (by means of ruins, fallen trees, weathered rocks, and mossy surfaces on all of these). In actual settings, asymmetrical and eclectic buildings, indirect approaches, and contrasting clusters of plantings heighten the experience of the picturesque.

pièce sur pièce In French colonial and post-colonial architecture, a method of stacked log construction utilizing heavy timber corner posts and intermediate posts with slots or mortises into which the tapered or tenoned ends of horizontal logs are fastened. The technique requires no log-to-log corner notching and allows for the use of shorter logs between posts.

pier **1** A freestanding mass, supporting a concentrated load from an arch, a beam, a truss, or a girder. While generally rectilinear in plan, piers in buildings based upon medieval precedents are often curvilinear in plan. **2** An upright portion of a wall that performs a columnar function. The pier may be continuous with the plane of the wall, or it may be distinguished from the plane of the wall to give it a columnlike independence.

pier and spandrel A type of skeletal wall organization in which the vertical metal columns (and their square-cornered cladding) project in front of the plane of windows and their spandrel panels. The spandrel panels may be exposed structural spanning members. More often they provide decorative covering for the structure.

pilaster **1** A flattened column, with or without fluting, that is attached to a wall. It is usually finished with the same capital and base as a freestanding column. **2** Any narrow, vertical strip attached to a wall. Distinguished from an engaged column, which has a convex curvature.

pillar Ambiguous term, often used interchangeably with COLUMN, PIER, or POST; see instead one of those terms. (Although the term pillar is sometimes applied to columns that are square in plan, the term pier is preferable.)

pinnacle In Gothic architecture, a small spirelike element providing an ornamental finish to the highest part of a buttress or roof. It has a slender pyramidal or conical form and is often articulated with crockets or ribs and is topped by a finial. Distinguished from a finial, which is a smaller feature appearing by itself.

pitched roof See GABLE ROOF.

plan A drawing (in orthographic projection) representing all or part of an object, building, or space, as if viewed from directly above. A floor plan is a drawing of a horizontal cut through a building, usually at the level of the windows, showing the configuration of walls and openings. Other types of plans may illustrate ceilings, roofs, structural elements, and mechanical systems.

plank construction General term. See instead the more specific terms HORIZONTAL PLANK FRAME CONSTRUCTION, VERTICAL PLANK CONSTRUCTION.

plate **1** In timber frame construction, the topmost horizontal structural member of a wall, to which the roof rafters are fastened. **2** In platform and balloon frame construction, the horizontal members to which the tops and bottoms of studs are nailed. The bottom plate is sometimes called the sill plate or sole plate.

plinth The base block of a column, pilaster, pedestal, dado, or door architrave.

Pointed style A nineteenth-century term for Gothic Revival.

polychromy, polychromatic, polychrome A many-colored treatment, especially the combination of materials in various colors or the application of

surface color, to articulate wall and roof planes and to highlight structure.

popular A term applied to vernacular architecture influenced by such publications as books of the orders, builders' guides, style books, pattern books, mail-order catalogs, architectural periodicals, and household magazines. Architecture in the popular tradition may be built according to commercially available plans or from widely distributed components; or it may be built by local practitioners (architects, builders, contractors) emulating buildings that are represented in publications. The distinction between popular architecture and high-style architecture by lesser-known architects depends on one's point of view with regard to the division between vernacular and high-style. See also the more general term VERNACULAR and the related term FOLK.

porch A structure attached to a building to shelter an entrance or to serve as a semienclosed sitting, working, or sleeping space. Distinguished from a portico, which is either a pedimented feature at least one story in height supported by classical columns or a more extensive colonnaded feature.

porte-cochère A porch projecting over a driveway and providing shelter to people leaving a vehicle and entering a building or vice versa. Also called a carriage porch.

portico **1** A porch at least one story in height consisting of a low-pitched roof supported on classical columns and finished in front with an entablature and pediment. **2** An extensive porch supported by a colonnade.

post A vertical supporting element, either square or circular in plan. Posts are the integral vertical members of a frame or truss, whether of wood or metal. Posts may also carry fences or gates, or may serve as freestanding markers (e.g., mileposts).

post-and-beam construction A structural system in which the main support is provided by vertical members (posts) carrying horizontal members (beams or lintels). Sometimes called post-and-girt construction, post and lintel construction, trabeation, trabeated construction.

Postmodernism, Postmodern A term applied to work that involves a reaction against the ideas and works of various twentieth-century modern movements, particularly the Bauhaus and the International style. Postmodern work makes use of historicism, yet the traditional elements are often merely applied to buildings that, in every other respect, are products of modern movement design. The term is also applied to works that are attempting to demonstrate an extension of the principles of various modern movements.

poteaux en terre In French colonial and post-colonial architecture, a construction technique in which closely spaced vertical timbers, hewn flat on two or four faces, are set deep in the ground to form the structure of a wall. The spaces between timbers are filled with brick, clay or other soft materials.

Literally translated, the term means "posts in the earth." Distinguished from *poteaux sur sole*, in which the vertical timbers rest on horizontal wooden sills.

poteaux sur sole In French colonial and post-colonial architecture, a construction technique in which closely spaced vertical timbers, hewn flat on two or four faces, rest on a horizontal timber sill to form the structure of a wall. The sill, in turn, rests on a stone foundation. The spaces between the vertical timbers are filled with brick, clay, or other soft materials. Literally translated, the term means "post upon a sill." Distinguished from *poteaux en terre*, in which the vertical timbers are set directly into the ground.

Prairie Box See FOURSQUARE HOUSE.

Prairie school, Prairie style A diverse group of architects working in Chicago and throughout the Midwest from the 1890s to the 1920s, strongly influenced by Frank Lloyd Wright and to a lesser degree by Louis Sullivan. The term is applied mainly to domestic architecture. An architect is said to belong to the Prairie school; a work of architecture is said to be in the Prairie style. Sometimes called Prairie, for short. See also the related terms CHICAGO SCHOOL, WRIGHTIAN.

pre-Columbian Term applied to the major cultures of Latin American (e.g., Aztec, Maya, Inca) that flourished prior to the discovery of the New World by Columbus in 1492 and the Spanish conquests of the sixteenth century. Distinguished from North American Indian, which is generally applied to indigenous cultures within the area that would become the United States and Canada.

pressed metal Thin sheets of metal (usually galvanized or tin-plated iron) stamped into patterned panels for covering ceilings and exterior and interior walls or into molding profiles and other details for assembly into exterior and interior cornices. Loosely called pressed tin or stamped metal. Prevalent from the 1870s through the 1920s.

program The list of functional, spatial, and other requirements that guides an architect in developing a design.

proscenium In a recessed stage, the area between the orchestra and the curtain.

proscenium arch In a recessed stage, the enframement of the opening.

prostyle Having a columnar portico in front, but not on the sides and rear.

provincialism, provincial Term applied to work in an isolated area (such as a province of a cosmopolitan center or a colony of a mother country), where traditional practices persist, with some awareness of what is being done in the cosmopolitan center or the homeland.

purlin In roof construction, a structural member laid across the principal rafters and parallel to the wall plate and the ridge beam. The light common rafters to which the roofing surface is attached are fastened across the purlins. See also the related term RAFTER.

pylon 1 Originally, the gateway facade of an Egyp-

tian temple complex, consisting of a truncated broad pyramidal form with battered (inclined) wall surfaces on all four sides, or two truncated pyramidal towers flanking an entrance portal. 2 Any towerlike structure from which bridge cables or utility lines are suspended.

quadripartite vault A vault divided into four triangular sections by a pair of diagonal ribs. Sometimes called a four-part vault.

quarry-faced See ROCK-FACED.

quatrefoil A type of Gothic tracery having four parts (lobes or foils) separated by pointed elements (cusps).

Queen Anne Ambiguous but widely used term. 1 In architecture, the Queen Anne style is an eclectic style of the 1860s through 1910s in England and the United States, characterized by the incorporation of forms from postmedieval vernacular architecture and the architecture of the Georgian period. Sometimes called Queen Anne Revival. See also the more specific term SHINGLE STYLE and the related terms EASTLAKE, STICK STYLE. 2 In architecture, the original Queen Anne period extends from the late seventeenth into the early eighteenth century. 3 In the decorative arts, the Queen Anne style and period properly refer to work of the early eighteenth century during the reign of Queen Anne (1702–1714, i.e., after William and Mary and before Georgian). 4 In the decorative arts, eclectic work of the 1860s to 1880s is properly referred to as Queen Anne Revival.

quoin One of the bricks or stones laid in alternating directions, which bond and form the exterior corner of a building. Sometimes simulated in wood or stucco.

rafter One of the inclined structural members of a roof. Principal rafters are primary supporting elements spanning between the walls and the apex of the roof and carrying the longitudinal purlins. Common rafters are secondary supporting elements fastened onto purlins to carry the roof surfacing. See also the related term PURLIN.

raking cornice A cornice that finishes the sloping edges of a gable roof, such as the inclined sides of a triangular pediment.

random ashlar A type of masonry in which squared and dressed blocks are laid in a random pattern rather than in straight horizontal courses.

recessed column A fully round column set into a nichelike space only slightly larger than the column. Distinguished from an engaged column, which appears to be built into the wall.

refectory A dining hall, especially in medieval architecture.

regionalism 1 The sum of cultural characteristics (including material culture, language) that define a geographic region, usually extending beyond a single state or province, and coinciding with one or more large physiographic areas. 2 The conscious use, within a region, of forms and materials identified with that region, creating an architecture that is in keeping with the historical architecture of the region, and even a distinctive new regional style.

register A horizontal zone of a wall, altarpiece, or other vertical feature. Usually synonymous with story, but more inclusive, allowing for the description of zones with no corresponding interior spaces.

relieving arch An arch, usually of masonry, built over the lintel of an opening to carry the load of the wall above and relieve the lintel of carrying such load. Sometimes called a discharging arch or safety arch.

Renaissance The period in European civilization identified with a rediscovery or rebirth *(rinascimento)* of classical Roman (and to a lesser extent, Greek) learning, art, and architecture. Renaissance architecture began in Italy in the mid-1400s (Early Renaissance) and reached a peak in the early to mid-1500s (High Renaissance). In England, Renaissance architecture did not begin until the late 1500s or early 1600s. The Renaissance in art and architecture was preceded by the Gothic and followed by the Baroque.

Renaissance Revival 1 In architecture, an ambiguous term, applied to (a) Italianate work of the 1840s through 1880s and (b) Beaux-Arts Classical work of the 1880s through 1920s. **2** In the decorative arts, an eclectic furniture style incorporating a variety of Renaissance, Baroque, and Neo-Grec architectural motifs and utilizing wood marquetry, incised lines (often gilded), and ormolu and porcelain ornaments. Sometimes called Neo-Renaissance.

rendering Any drawing, whether orthographic (plan, elevation, section) or pictorial (perspective), in which shades and shadows are represented.

reredos A screen or wall at the back of an altar, usually with architectural and figural decoration.

return The continuation of a molding, cornice, or other projecting member, in a different direction, as in the horizontal cornice returns at the base of the raking cornices of a triangular pediment.

reveal 1 The portion of wall thickness between a door or window frame and the outer face of the wall. **2** Same as jamb, but only in an opening without a door or window.

revival, revivalism A type of historicism prevalent since the eighteenth century, involving the adaptation of historical forms to contemporary functions. Distinguished from a more pervasive historicism by an ideological conviction that sought to rationalize the choice of a historical style according to the values of the historical period that produced it. (The Gothic Revival, for instance, was associated with the Christianity of the Middle Ages.) Revival works, therefore, tend to invoke a single historical style. More hybrid works are manifestations of a less dogmatic historicism or eclecticism. See also the more general terms HISTORICISM, ECLECTICISM.

rib The projecting linear element that separates the curved planar cells (or webs) of vaulting. Originally these were the supporting members for the vaulting, but they may also be purely decorative.

Richardsonian Term applied to any work showing the influence of the American architect Henry Hobson Richardson (1838–1886). See the note under the more limiting term RICHARDSONIAN ROMANESQUE.

Richardsonian Romanesque Term applied to Neo-Romanesque work showing the influence of the American architect Henry Hobson Richardson (1838–1886). While many of Richardson's works make eclectic use of round arches and Romanesque details, many of his works show a creative eclecticism that transcends any particular historical style. The term Richardsonian, therefore, is a more inclusive term for the work of his followers than Richardsonian Romanesque—a term that continues to be widely used. Sometimes called Richardson Romanesque, Richardsonian Romanesque Revival.

ridgepole The horizontal beam or board at the apex of a roof, to which the upper ends of the rafters are fastened. Sometimes called a ridge beam, ridgeboard, ridge piece.

rinceau An ornamental device consisting of a sinuous and branching scroll elaborated with leaves and other natural forms.

rock-faced Term applied to the rough, unfinished face of a stone used in building. Sometimes called quarry-faced.

Rococo A late phase of the Baroque, marked by elegant reverse-curve ornament, light scale, and delicate color. See also the related term BAROQUE.

Romanesque A medieval architectural style which reached its height in the eleventh and twelfth centuries. It is characterized by round arched construction and massive masonry walls. The Romanesque was preceded by the Early Christian and Byzantine periods in the eastern Mediterranean world and by a variety of localized styles and periods in northern and western Europe; it was followed throughout Europe by the Gothic.

Romanesque Revival Ambiguous term, applied to **1** *Rundbogenstil* and Round Arch work in America as early as the 1840s and **2** Richardsonian Romanesque work into the 1890s. Sometimes called Neo-Romanesque.

Roman Revival A term, not widely accepted, for a version of Neoclassicism involving the use of forms from the visual arts of the Imperial Roman period. Applied to various works in Italy, England, and the United States, where it is most clearly visible in the architecture of Thomas Jefferson. See also the related terms FEDERAL, NEOCLASSICISM.

rood screen An ornamental screen that serves as a partition between the crossing and the chancel or choir of a church.

rosette A circular floral ornament similar to an open rose.

rotunda 1 A circular hall in a large building, especially an area beneath a dome or cupola. **2** A building round both inside and outside, usually domed.

Round Arch mode   The American counterpart of the German *Rundbogenstil*, characterized by the predominance of round arches, whether these are accentuated by Romanesque or Renaissance detailing or left as simple unadorned openings. See also the related terms ITALIANATE, LOMBARD, RUNDBOGENSTIL.

roundel   A circular panel or plaque. Distinguished from a patera, which is oval shaped.

rubble masonry   A type of masonry utilizing uncut or roughly shaped stone, such as fieldstone or boulders.

Rundbogenstil   Literally, "round arch style," a historicist style originating in Germany in the 1820s and spreading to Britain and the United States from the 1840s through the 1860s. It is characterized by an eclectic combination of Romanesque and Renaissance elements. See also the related term ROUND ARCH MODE.

Ruskin Gothic, Ruskinian Gothic   See HIGH VICTORIAN GOTHIC.

rustication, rusticated   Masonry in which the joints are emphasized by narrow recessed channels or grooves outlining each block. Sometimes simulated in wood or stucco.

sacristy   A room in a church where liturgical vessels and vestments are kept.

safety arch   See RELIEVING ARCH.

sanctuary   **1** The part of a church that contains the principal altar. Usually the innermost space within the chancel arm of the church, situated to the east of the choir. **2** Loosely used to mean a place of worship, a sacred place.

sash   Any framework of a window. It may be movable or fixed. It may slide in a vertical plane (as in a double-hung window) or may be pivoted (as in a casement window).

sash bar   See MUNTIN.

Second Chicago school   A term sometimes applied to the International style in Chicago from the 1940s to the 1970s, particularly the work of Mies van der Rohe. See also the related terms INTERNATIONAL STYLE, MIESIAN.

Second Empire   Not strictly a style term but a term for a period in French history coinciding with the rule of Napoleon III (1852–1870). Generally applied in the United States, however, to a phase of Beaux-Arts governmental and institutional architecture (1850s-1880s) as well as to countless hybrids of Beaux-Arts and Italianate forms in residential, commercial, and industrial architecture (1850s-1880s). Sometimes called General Grant style, Mansard style, Mansardic. See also the related terms BEAUX-ARTS, ITALIANATE (definition 1).

section   A drawing (in orthographic projection) representing a vertical cut through an object, building, or space. An architectural section shows interior relationships of space and structure, and may also include mechanical systems. Sometimes called a cross section.

segmental arch   An arch formed on a segmental curve. Its center lies below the springing line.

segmental curve   A curve that is a segment (i.e., less than half the circumference) of a circle or an ellipse. The base line of the curve is a chord measuring less than the diameter of the larger circle from which the segment is taken.

segmental pediment   A pediment whose top is a segmental curve.

segmental vault   A vault whose cross section is a segmental curve. A dome built on segmental curves is called a saucer dome.

setback   **1** In architecture, particularly in the design of tall buildings, a series of upper stories that are stepped back to allow more sunlight to reach the streets. **2** In planning, the amount of space between the lot line and the perimeter of a building.

shaft   The tall part of a column between the base and the capital.

shed roof   A roof having only one sloping plane. Sometimes called a lean-to roof.

Shingle style   A term applied primarily to American domestic architecture of the 1870s through the 1890s, in which broad expanses of wood shingles dominate the exterior roof and wall planes. Rooms open widely into one another and to the outdoors, and the ample living hall or stair hall is often the dominant feature of the interior. The term was coined in the 1940s by Vincent Scully for a series of seaside and suburban houses of the northeastern United States. The Shingle style is a version of the Anglo-American Queen Anne style. See also the related terms COLONIAL REVIVAL, STICK STYLE.

shouldered architrave   See EAR.

side gabled   Term applied to a building whose gable ends face the sides of a lot. Distinguished from front gabled.

side light   A framed area of fixed glass alongside a door or window. See also the related term FANLIGHT.

sill course   In masonry, a stringcourse set at windowsill level, usually differentiated from the wall by its greater projection, its finish, or its thickness. Not applicable to frame construction.

sill plate   See PLATE (definition 2).

skeleton construction, skeleton frame   A system of construction in which all loads are carried to the ground through a rigid framework of iron, steel, or reinforced concrete. The exterior walls are curtain walls (i.e., not load-bearing).

skylight   A window in a roof, specifically one that is flush with the roof plane or only slightly protruding. Distinguished from a cupola (definition 2), which is a major centralized feature at the summit of a roof. Distinguished from a monitor, which is an extensive roof feature containing a band of windows or vents.

soffit   The exposed underside of any overhead component, such as an arch, beam, cornice, or lintel. See also the related term INTRADOS.

sole plate See PLATE (definition **2**).

space frame A series of trusses placed side by side and joined to one another by triangulated rods, tubes, or beams, so that the individual planar trusses are united into a three-dimensional structural framework. Often used in roof structures requiring long spans.

spandrel **1** The quasi-triangular space between two adjoining arches and a line connecting their crowns, or between an arch and the columns and entablature that frame it. **2** In skeletal construction, the wall area between the top of a window and the sill of the window in the story above. Sometimes called a spandrel panel.

Spanish colonial A term applied to buildings, towns, landscapes, and other artifacts from the various periods of actual Spanish colonial occupation in North America (c. 1565–1821 in Florida; c. 1763–1800 in Louisiana and the Lower Mississippi Valley; c. 1590s–1821 in Texas and the southwestern United States; c. 1769–1821 in California). The term is extended to apply to the artifacts of Hispanic ethnic groups (e.g., Mexicans, Puerto Ricans, Cubans) and their descendants, even into the early twentieth century. See also the related term CHURRIGUERESQUE.

Spanish Colonial Revival The revival of forms from Spanish colonial and provincial Mexican design. The Spanish Colonial Revival began in Florida and California in the 1880s and continues nationwide into the present. Sometimes called Neo-Hispanic, Spanish Eclectic, Spanish Revival. See also the more specific term MISSION REVIVAL and the related term MEDITERRANEAN REVIVAL.

spindle A turned wooden element, thicker toward the middle and thinner at either end, found in arch screens, porch trim, and other ornamental assemblages. Banisters (i.e., thin, simple balusters) may be spindle-shaped, but the term spindle, when used alone, usually connotes shorter elements.

spire A slender pointed element surmounting a building. A tall, attenuated pyramidal form with any number of thin triangular faces that are unbroken or articulated only with crockets, pinnacles, or small dormers. Distinguished from a steeple, which is divided into stages and which may be topped with a spire.

splay The slanting surface formed by cutting off a right-angle corner at an oblique angle to one face. A reveal at an oblique angle to the exterior face of the wall.

springing, springing line, springing point The line or point where an arch or vault rises from its supports and begins to curve. Usually the juncture between the impost of the support below and the springer, or first voussoir, of the arch above.

squinch An arch, lintel, or corbeling, built across the interior corner of two walls to form one side of an octagonal base for a dome. This octagonal base serves as the structural transition from a square interior crossing space to an octagonal or round dome.

stair A series of steps, or flights of steps connected by landings, which connects two or more levels or floors.

staircase The ensemble of a stair and its enclosing walls. Sometimes called a stairway.

stair tower A projecting tower or other building block that contains a stair.

stamped metal See PRESSED METAL.

steeple **1** A tall structure rising from a tower, consisting of a series of superimposed stages diminishing in plan, and usually topped by a spire or small cupola. Distinguished from a spire, which is not divided into stages. **2** Less commonly used to mean the whole of the tower, from the ground to the top of the spire or cupola.

stepped gable A gable in which the wall rises in a series of steps above the planes of the roof.

stereotomy The science of cutting three-dimensional shapes from stone, such as the units that make up a carefully fitted masonry vault.

Stick style A term applied primarily to American domestic architecture of the 1850s through the 1870s, in which exterior wall planes are subdivided into bays and stories outlined by narrow boards called "stickwork." The term was coined by Vincent Scully in the 1940s for a series of houses with clearly articulated wall panels and sticklike porch supports and eaves brackets. Sources include the English and German picturesque traditions, as well as the French rationalist tradition. See also the related terms QUEEN ANNE, SHINGLE STYLE.

story (plural: stories). The space in a building between floor levels. British spelling is storey, storeys. Sometimes called a register, a more inclusive term applied to horizontal on a vertical plane zones that do not correspond to actual floor levels.

Streamline Moderne A later phase of the Moderne, popular in the 1930s and 1940s and characterized by stucco surfaces with rounded corners, by horizontal banding, overhangs, and window groupings, and by other details suggestive of modern Machine Age aerodynamic forms. Sometimes called Streamline Modern, Streamline Modernistic. See also the more general term MODERNE and the related terms ART DECO and PWA MODERNE.

stretcher A brick laid the length of a wall, so that the long side of the brick shows on the exterior.

string In a stair, an inclined board that supports the ends of the steps. Sometimes called a stringer.

stringcourse In masonry, a horizontal band, generally narrower than other courses, extending across the facade of a building and in some instances encircling such features as pillars or columns. It may be flush or projecting; of identical or contrasting material; flat, molded, or richly carved. Not applicable to frame construction. Sometimes called a band course or belt course. More elaborate horizontal bands in masonry or frame construction are generally called band moldings.

strut A column, post, or pole that is set in a diagonal position and thus serves as a stiffener by triangulation. Distinguished from a brace, which is usually a shorter bracketlike member.

stucco 1 An exterior plaster finish, usually textured, composed of portland cement, lime, and sand, which are mixed with water. **2** A fine plaster used for decorative work or moldings.

stud One of the vertical supporting elements in a wall, especially in balloon and platform frame construction. Studs are relatively lightweight members (usually two-by-fours).

Sullivanesque Term applied to work showing the influence of the American architect Louis Henry Sullivan (1856–1924).

sunburst light See FANLIGHT.

supercapital See IMPOST BLOCK.

supercolumniation See SUPERPOSITION (definition 1).

superimposition, superimposed See SUPERPOSITION.

superposition, superposed 1 The use of an ensemble of the classical orders, one above the other, as the major elements articulating a facade. When this is done, the Doric, considered the simplest order, is used on or near the ground story. The Ionic, considered more complex, comes next; and the Corinthian, considered the most complex, is used at the top. Sometimes the Tuscan order or rusticated masonry may be used for the ground story beneath the Doric order, and the Composite order may be used above the Corinthian order. Sometimes called supercolumniation, superimposition. See also the related term ORDER. **2** Less commonly, any vertical relationship of architectural elements (e.g., windows, piers, colonnettes) in any style or period.

superstructure A structure raised upon another structure, as a building upon a foundation, basement, or substructure.

Supervising Architect The Supervising Architect of the United States Treasury Department, whose office was responsible for the design and construction of all major federal government buildings (such as courthouses, customhouses, and post offices) from the 1850s through the 1930s. The Office of the Supervising Architect was formally established by Congress in 1864 and lasted until 1939, when its functions were absorbed into the Public Buildings Administration (and in 1949, into the General Services Administration).

supporting wall See BEARING WALL.

surround An encircling border or decorative frame around a door or window. Distinguished from architrave (definition **2**), a term usually applied to the frame around an opening when considered as a series of relatively flat face moldings.

suspended ceiling A ceiling suspended from rodlike hangers below the level of the floor above. The interval between the floor slab above and the suspended ceiling often serves as a space for ducts, utilities, and air circulation. Sometimes called a hung ceiling.

swag A motif representing a suspended fold of drapery hanging in a catenary curve from two points. Distinguished from a festoon, which is a motif representing entwined leaves, flowers, or fruits, hung in a similar curve. See also the more general term GARLAND.

tabernacle 1 A niche or recess, usually on an interior wall, framed by columns or pilasters and topped by an entablature and pediment. Distinguished from an aedicule, which more often occurs on an exterior wall. See also the related term NICHE. **2** In the Jewish religion, a portable sanctuary. **3** In Protestant denominations, a large auditorium church.

terracotta A hard ceramic material used for **1** fireproofing, especially as a fitted cladding around metal skeletal construction; or **2** an exterior or interior wall cladding, which is often glazed and multicolored.

tertiary rib See LIERNE.

thermal window A large lunette window similar to those found in ancient Roman baths (thermae). The window is subdivided into three to five parts by vertical mullions. Sometimes called a thermae window.

three-hinged arch An arch in two major segments anchored with cylindrical "hinge" pins at either end and at the crown. Movement within the arch, caused by temperature changes, the torsion of wind movements, or other forces, can be absorbed by the movement of the arch around the pins, thereby avoiding stresses that would occur in the structural frame if the arches were fixed.

tie beam A horizontal tension member that ties together the opposing angular members of a truss and prevents them from spreading.

tier A group of stories or any zone of architectural elements arranged horizontally.

tierceron In a Gothic vault, a secondary rib that rises from the springing to an intermediate position on either side of the diagonal ribs. Sometimes called an intermediate rib.

tie rod A metal rod that spans the distance between two structural members and, by its tensile strength, restrains them against tendencies to collapse outward.

timber-frame construction, timber framing A type of wood frame construction in which heavy timber posts and beams (six-by-sixes and larger) are fastened using mortise and tenon joints. Sometimes called heavy timber construction. Distinguished from light frame construction, in which relatively light structural members (two-by-fours to two-by-tens) are fastened with nails.

trabeation, trabeated construction See POST-AND-BEAM CONSTRUCTION.

tracery Decoration within an arch or other opening, made up of narrow curvilinear bands or more elaborately molded strips. In Gothic architecture, the curved interlocking stone bars that contain the leaded stained glass.

transept The lateral arm of a cross-shaped church, usually between the nave (the area for the congregation) and the chancel (the area for the altar, clergy, and choir).

transom 1 A narrow horizontal window unit, either fixed or movable, over a door. Sometimes called a transom light. See also the more specific term FANLIGHT. 2 A horizontal bar, as distinguished from a vertical mullion, especially one crossing a door or window opening near the top.

transverse rib In a Gothic vault, a rib at right angles to the ridge rib.

trefoil A type of Gothic tracery having three parts (lobes or foils) separated by pointed elements (cusps).

trellis Any open latticework made of strips of wood or metal crossing one another, usually supporting climbing plants. Distinguished from an arbor, which is generally a more substantial yet compact three-dimensional structure, and from a pergola, which is a more extensive colonnaded structure.

triforium In a Gothic church, an arcade in the wall above the arches of the nave, choir, or transept and below the clerestory window.

triglyph One of the slightly raised blocks in a Doric frieze. It consists of three narrow vertical bands separated by two V-shaped grooves.

triumphal arch 1 A freestanding arch erected for a victory procession. It usually consists of a broad central arched opening, flanked by two smaller bays (usually with open or blind arches). The bays are usually articulated by classical columns, supporting an entablature and a high attic. 2 A similar configuration applied to a facade to denote a monumental entryway.

truss A rigid triangular framework made up of beams, posts, braces, struts, and ties and used for the spanning of large spaces. The major horizontal or inclined members are called chords. The connecting vertical and diagonal elements are called the web members.

Tudor arch A low-profile arch characterized by two pairs of arcs, one pair of tight arcs at the springing, another pair of broad (nearly flat) arcs at the apex or crown.

Tudor period A term for a period in English history coinciding with the rule of monarchs of the house of Tudor (1485–1603). Tudor period architecture is Late Gothic, with only hints of the Renaissance. See also the more specific term ELIZABETHAN PERIOD for the end of this period, and the related term JACOBEAN PERIOD for the succeeding period.

Tudor Revival See NEO-TUDOR.

turret A small towerlike structure, often circular in plan, built against the side or at an exterior or interior corner of a building.

Tuscan order An ensemble of classical column and entablature elements, similar to the Roman Doric order, but without triglyphs in the frieze and without mutules (domino-like blocks) in the cornice of the entablature. See also the more general term ORDER.

tympanum (plural: tympana). 1 The triangular or segmental area enclosed by the cornice moldings of a pediment, frequently ornamented with sculpture. 2 Any space similarly delineated or bounded, as between the lintel of a door or window and the arch above.

umbrage A term used by Alexander Jackson Davis (1803–1892) as a synonym for veranda, the implication being a shadowed area.

vault An arched roof or ceiling, usually constructed in brick or stone, but also in tile, metal or concrete. A nonstructural plaster ceiling that simulates a masonry vault.

Venetian Gothic See HIGH VICTORIAN GOTHIC.

veranda A nineteenth-century term for porch. Sometimes spelled verandah.

vergeboard See BARGEBOARD.

verges The sloping edges of a gable, gambrel, or lean-to roof, usually projecting beyond the wall below. Distinguished from eaves, which are the horizontal lower edges of a roof plane.

vernacular Not a style in itself, but a descriptive term, applicable primarily to architecture, covering the vast range of ordinary buildings that are produced outside the high-style tradition of well-known architects. The vernacular tradition includes the folk tradition of regional and ethnic buildings whose forms (plan and massing) remain relatively constant through the years, in spite of stylistic embellishments. The term vernacular architecture is often used as if it meant only folk architecture. However, the vernacular tradition in architecture also includes the popular tradition of buildings whose design was influenced by such publications as books of the orders, builders' guides, style books, pattern books, mail-order catalogs, architectural periodicals, and household magazines. Usually contrasted with high style. See also the more specific terms FOLK, POPULAR.

vertical plank construction A system of wood construction in which vertical planks are set or nailed into heavy timber horizontal sills and plates. A building so constructed has no corner posts and no studs. Two-story vertical plank buildings have planks extending the full height of the building, with no girt between the two stories. Second-floor joists are merely mortised into the planks. Distinguished from the more specific term vertical plank frame construction, in which there are corner posts.

vertical plank frame construction A type of vertical plank construction, in which heavy timber corner posts are introduced to provide support for the plate, to which the tops of the planks are fastened. See also the related term HORIZONTAL PLANK FRAME CONSTRUCTION.

vestibule A small entry hall between the outer door and the main hallway of a building.

Victorian Gothic See HIGH VICTORIAN GOTHIC.

Victorian period A term for a period in British, British colonial, and Anglo-American history, and not, in architecture or the other visual arts, a sufficiently specific style term. The Victorian period extended across eight decades, from the coronation of Queen Victoria in 1837 to her death in 1901. See instead EASTLAKE, GOTHIC REVIVAL, GREEK REVIVAL, QUEEN ANNE, SHINGLE STYLE, STICK STYLE, and other specific style terms.

Victorian Romanesque Ambiguous term. See instead RICHARDSONIAN ROMANESQUE, ROMANESQUE REVIVAL, ROUND ARCH MODE.

villa 1 In the Roman and Renaissance periods, a suburban or rural residential complex, often quite elaborate, consisting of a house, dependencies, and gardens. 2 Since the eighteenth century, any detached suburban or rural house of picturesque character and some pretension. Distinguished from the more modest house form known as a cottage.

volute 1 A spiral scroll, especially the one that is a distinctive feature of the Ionic capital. 2 A large scroll-shaped buttress on a facade or dome.

voussoir A wedge-shaped stone or brick used in the construction of an arch. Its tapering sides coincide with radii of the arch.

wainscot A decorative or protective facing, usually of wood paneling, applied to the lower portion of an interior partition or wall. Distinguished from a dado, which is the zone at the base of a wall, regardless of the material used to cover it. Wainscot properly connotes woodwork. Sometimes called wainscoting.

water table 1 In masonry, a course of molded bricks or stones set forward several inches near the base of a wall and serving as the cap of the basement courses. 2 In frame construction, a ledge or projecting molding just above the foundation to protect it from rainwater. 3 In masonry or frame construction, any horizontal exterior ledge on a wall, pier, or buttress. Often sloped and provided with a drip molding to prevent water from running down the face of the wall below.

weatherboard See CLAPBOARD.

weathering The inclination given to the upper surface of any element so that it will shed water.

web 1 The relatively thin shell of masonry between the ribs of a ribbed vault. 2 The portion of a truss between the chords, or the portion of a girder or I-beam between the flanges.

western frame, western framing See FRAME CONSTRUCTION.

winder A step, more or less wedge-shaped, with its tread wider at one end than the other.

window bar See MUNTIN.

window cap See CAP.

window head A head molding or pedimented feature over a window.

Wrightian Term applied to work showing the influence of the American architect Frank Lloyd Wright (1867–1959). See also the related term PRAIRIE SCHOOL.

wrought iron Iron shaped by a hammering process, to improve the tensile properties of the metal. Distinguished from cast iron, a brittle material, which is formed in molds.

Zigzag Moderne, Zigzag Modernistic See ART DECO.

Photography Credits

All photographs not specifically listed were taken by Balthazar Korab.

INTRODUCTION

Page 8, Lanhotan, Louis Armand de Lom D'Arce. A General Map of New France, com[monly] call'd Canada. *New Voyages to North America.* London, 1735. Volume 1, opposite page 1. William L. Clements Library; **p. 10,** Fort Pontchartrain du Detroit, 1701. State Archives of Michigan; **p. 15,** Sydney T. Smith House, State Archives of Michigan; **p. 24,** John Munro and Mary Beecher Longyear House, Marquette County Historical Society; **p. 25,** Michigan School of Mines, Library of Congress; **p. 27,** Grand Rapids City Hall, State Archives of Michigan; **p. 31,** Monroe Block, Manning Brothers Historical Collection; **p. 34,** Dodge Main, State Archives of Michigan; **p. 44,** Saint Clair Shooting and Fishing Club, Library of Congress; **p. 45,** Log Cottage near Hotel, Lake Gogebic, Library of Congress; **p. 53,** Michigan State Capitol, Dietrich Floeter

METROPOLIS

DE01 Civic Center, with Penobscot and Guardian buildings and J. L. Hudson Department Store, Library of Congress; **DE03.1** Silvers, Inc. (State Savings Bank/ Peoples State Bank); Library of Congress, Detroit Publishing Company Collection; **DE09.1** John Bagley Memorial Fountain, State Archives of Michigan, Allen Stross; **DE09.2** J. L. Hudson Company Department Store in 1891, Burton Historical Collection of the Detroit Public Library; **DE14** Wayne County Building (Wayne County Courthouse), Library of Congress; **DE47** Grand Riviera Theater, Library of Congress, Historic American Buildings Survey, Drew Eberson; **DE67** Heidelberg Project, Robert Turney; **DE69.2** Conservatory, Belle Isle, Library of Congress, Detroit Publishing Company Collection; **DE71.6** Arthur H. and Clara May Buhl House, Library of Congress, Detroit Publishing Company Collection; **DE72** Waterworks Park, Hurlburt Gate, Library of Congress, Detroit Publishing Company Collection; **WN12** Ford Homes, Park Street, collections of the Henry Ford Museum and Greenfield Village; **WN14.1** Judge Samuel Townsend and Elizabeth Campbell Douglas House (Littlecote), Library of Congress, Detroit Publishing Company Collection

SUBURBAN SATELLITE REGION

WA03 Robert S. Wilson House, Library of Congress, Historic American Buildings Survey, S. Lucas; **WA16** Starkweather Hall, Library of Congress, Detroit Publishing Company Collection; **LV03** Alonzo Whitney and Janet Warden Olds House, Library of Congress, Historic American Buildings Survey

MICHIANA AND THE SOUTHWESTERN LOWER PENINSULA

KZ13 Water Tower, Kalamazoo Regional Psychiatric Hospital (Kalamazoo Asylum for the Insane), Preservation Urban Design, Inc.; **BE18** South Cove, Howard N. Kaplan; **VA05** Mentha Plantation, A. M. Todd Company Archives

GRAND RIVER VALLEY REGION

KT13.1 Eliphalet Turner House, entrance detail, Library of Congress, Historic American Buildings Survey, Allen Stross; **IA03.1** Hall-Fowler Memorial Library (Frederick and Ann Eager Hall House), Library of Congress, Historic American Buildings Survey, Allen Stross; **AE10** All Saints Episcopal Church, Michigan Bureau of History

CAPITAL REGION

IN02.1b Michigan State Capitol, plan of the third floor, State Archives of Michigan; **IN14** Saint Katherine's Chapel, Library of Congress, Historic American Buildings Survey, Marcus G. Trumbo; **EA09** First Congregational Church, Library of Congress, Historic American Buildings Survey; **CL05** The Belfry (First Congregational Church of Ovid), Library of Congress, Historic American Buildings Survey, Allen Stross

SAGINAW BAY AND RIVER VALLEY REGION

SA03.1 Hoyt Public Library, Library of Congress, Detroit Publishing Company Collection; **SA03.2** Saginaw County Castle Building (Saginaw Post Office [Castle Station]), Library of Congress, Detroit Publishing Company Collection; **SE06** James Rogers and Anna Herrick Van Dyne Farm and **SE07** Charles Van Dyne Farm, *Portrait and Biographical Album of Clinton and Shiawassee Counties* (1881)

THE THUMB

SC07 Port Huron Museum of Arts and History (Port Huron Public Library), Library of Congress, Detroit Publishing Company Collection; **SC15** South Channel Drive, Harsens Island, Library of Congress, Detroit Publishing Company Collection

THE HEARTLAND

GR06 Ammi Willard and Anna Case Wright House, Library of Congress, Detroit Publishing Company Collection

WEST MICHIGAN SHORE REGION

LK03 Idlewild, Idlewild Club, State Archives of Michigan

TRAVERSE BAY REGION

EM09.2 The Archway (William M. Parker House), Library of Congress, Detroit Publishing Company Collection; **EM09.3** R. A. Files Cottage (The Barr Cottage), Library of Congress, Detroit Publishing Company Collection; **EM10** Harbor Point, Casino, Library of Congress, Detroit Publishing Company Collection; **EM10.1** Telgham and Anna Pickering Summer House, Michigan Bureau of History; **EM15** Colonial Michilimackinac, Donald Heldman

NORTH-CENTRAL LAKES AND FORESTS REGION

OD01 William W. Maier House (Perma-Log Company), William Maier; **RO01** First Congregational Church of Roscommon, Hedrich Blessing, Alden B. Dow Archives

HURON SHORE REGION

AAO1 Springport Inn, *History of the Lake Huron Shore* (H. R. Page and Co., 1883)

THE COPPER COUNTRY

HO02.1 Sheldon-Dee Block, Kathryn Bishop Eckert; **HO05.2** Daniell Heights Housing, Michigan Technological University Michigan Technological University, Kathryn Bishop Eckert; **HO07** Hancock City Hall (Hancock Town Hall and Fire Hall), Kathryn Bishop Eckert; **HO09** Suomi College (Finnish Lutheran College and Seminary), Library of Congress, Detroit Publishing Company Collection; **HO11.2** General Office, Quincy Mining Company, Michigan Technological University Archives and Copper Country Historical Collections, Roy Drier Collection; **HO11.3** Mine Shaft Number Two (Headframe) and **HO11.4** Mine Shaft Number Two (Hoist House) Quincy Mining Company Location, Kathryn Bishop Eckert; **HO13** Calumet and Hecla Mine Location, Kathryn Bishop Eckert; **HO13.2** Superior Land Company Office (Library), Michigan Technological University Archives and Copper Country Historical Collections; **HO17** Johnson and Anna

Lichty Vivian, Jr., House, Michigan Technological University Archives and Copper Country Historical Collections; **HO19** Lake Linden Village Hall and Fire Station, Michigan Technological University Archives and Copper Country Historical Collections; **HO22** First Congregational Church of Lake Linden, Michigan Technological University Archives and Copper Country Historical Collections; **KW08** Keweenaw Mountain Resort (Keweenaw Mountain Lodge and Golf Course), Tom Buchkoe

THE IRON RANGES REGION

MQ01 Marquette County Courthouse, Library of Congress, Detroit Publishing Company Collection; **MQ06.1** Henry R. and Mary Hewitt Mather House, Tom Buchoe; **MQ08** Sports Training Complex (Yooper Dome), Northern Michigan University; **MQ09** Lake Superior and Ishpeming Ore Dock and Approach, Library of Congress, Detroit Publishing Company Collection; **MQ10** Marquette Branch Prison (Upper Peninsula Branch Prison and House of Correction), Tom Buchcoe; **MQ11** Negaunee City Hall, Tom Buchcoe; **MQ18** Granot Loma (Louis G. and Marie Young Kaufman Summer Estate), Tom Buchcoe; **IR03.1** Wall-Seppanen House, Steve Karpiac, Bureau of History; **IR08** Italian Society Duke of Abruzzi Hall, Steve Karpiac, Bureau of History **GB01** Bessemer City Hall and Community Building, Robert O. Christensen Collection; **GB03** Ironwood Memorial Building (Ironwood Municipal Building), Gerald Kinnunen **GB07** Ironwood Homesteads, Library of Congress, Farm Security Administration Collection; **GB11** Gogebic Chiefs Hockey Arena (Wakefield Ice Arena), Ken Aho

CENTRAL UPPER PENINSULA

AR06 Au Sable Light Station, Library of Congress, Historic American Buildings Survey, Jeff Bostetter and Hugh Hughes; **AR08** Bay Furnace, Kathryn Bishop Eckert; **ME02.2** Shale Building, Kathryn Bishop Eckert; **DT02.3** Delft Theater, John LaPorte; **DT03** Ice Shanty City, John LaPorte

THE SAULT AND MACKINAC REGION

CH05 Saint Mary's Falls Ship Canal (Sault Locks), Library of Congress, Historic American Engineering Record; **CH07** Edison Sault Power Plant (Michigan Lake Superior Hydroelectric Power Plant), Library of Congress, Historic American Engineering Record; **MK11** Mission Church, Historic American Buildings Survey, Library of Congress; **MK12** Grand Hotel, historic photo between 1900 and 1906, Library of Congress

Index

Pages with illustrations are indicated in bold.